P9-EDB-354

The Kingfisher
CHILDREN'S
ENCYCLOPEDIA

The Kingfisher
CHILDREN'S
ENCYCLOPEDIA

Editor: John Paton

Kingfisher Books

NEW YORK

EDITOR
John Paton

PROJECT EDITORS
Jennifer Justice
Maggi McCormick

EDITORIAL CONSULTANT
Brian Williams

DESIGN
Terry Woodley

PICTURE RESEARCH
Elaine Willis

KINGFISHER BOOKS
Grisewood & Dempsey Inc.
95 Madison Avenue
New York, New York 10016

This revised one-volume edition
first published in the United States
in 1992. Originally published in
multiple volumes in 1989.

2 4 6 8 10 9 7 5 3 1

Library of Congress Cataloging-in-Publication Data
The Kingfisher children's encyclopedia / editor, John Paton.
p. cm.
"Revised one-volume edition"——T.p. verso.
Rev. ed. of Children's encyclopedia. 1st ed. in the U.S. 1990.
Includes index.
Summary: Presents facts on more than 1300 subjects from Aardvark
to Zoo.
1. Children's encyclopedias and dictionaries.
[1. Encyclopedias and dictionaries.] I. Paton, John, 1914–
II. Title: Children's encyclopedia.
AG5.D74 1992
031——dc20 92–4785 CIP AC

ISBN 1-85697-800-1

Printed in Italy

FOREWORD

In compiling **The Kingfisher Children's Encyclopedia**, the editorial team had one overriding aim: it must be a work that children will find easy to use and will *enjoy* using. Is an entry likely to be one that a child will look up? Is the text really understandable by someone who knows little or nothing about the subject? Is the writing level too high or too low? Do the illustrations add to the usefulness of the item? These were foremost among the questions we had constantly to bear in mind and impress on the hundreds of individuals who took part in the project.

Ease of use was achieved by employing an alphabetical arrangement, with copious cross-references in SMALL CAPITALS throughout the articles. The use of these cross-references will ensure that the reader is guided to the maximum amount of information on any topic; an item that does not appear alphabetically in the main body of the book will often be found in the index.

An encyclopedia such as this is the result of a process of continuing growth and revision over several years. Many people are involved—writers, editors, consultants, reviewers, authenticators, artists, designers, picture researchers, producers . . . To all of them is due the credit for any success that this encyclopedia brings.

John Paton
Editor
1992

ABOUT *your* ENCYCLOPEDIA

This encyclopedia is very easy to use. All the entries are arranged in alphabetical order. You should find most of the information you want by first looking up the main entry word. If the subject you are looking for does not have its own entry, look in the index at the back. Usually you will find some information about your subject in another article.

•

Throughout the encyclopedia you will find words printed in small capitals, like this: HEALTH. These words are cross-references. When you see one, you will know that there is a separate entry on the subject in your encyclopedia. That entry may have more information about the subject you are looking up.

•

Subject symbols appear next to each heading. These are helpful when you are browsing through the encyclopedia and want to find entries on Transportation, for instance, or History, or Countries and Places—there are 16 symbols in all.

•

Throughout the encyclopedia you will come across "special feature" entries. These can be used to help you with your school projects, or you can look them up in just the same way as the other entries. You will find them listed at the back of the work.

In addition to the main text there are See-it-Yourself panels which show in a practical way how you can find out more about the subject.

•

There are Fact Panels containing at-a-glance information on the biggest, highest, longest, etc. And the outside column has a host of fascinating snippets of additional and often surprising information.

•

The index is comprehensive, with over 4,000 entries. It is followed by a subject index which groups together all entries in a particular subject area. You will find this subject index particularly useful in school project work.

•

The encyclopedia contains more than 2,000 color illustrations—drawings, photographs, diagrams, and maps—all designed to amplify and simplify the main text.

•

By using your encyclopedia you will discover a wealth of information about people, ideas, events, and the world around you.

THE SUBJECT SYMBOLS

Each entry in this encyclopedia has its own easily recognized symbol opposite the heading. This symbol tells you at a glance which area of interest the entry falls into—is it animals, history, or science? Below are the 16 subject areas we have used. At the back of the work there is a list of articles divided into subject areas.

PLANTS AND FOOD From microscopic plants to gigantic trees—what they are, how they grow, the food they provide.

THE ARTS Drawing, painting, sculpture, crafts, ballet, modern dance, drama, theater, TV, motion pictures, etc., plus the great artists.

PEOPLES AND GOVERNMENT Descriptions of peoples of the world, the things they do and the way they govern their countries.

LANGUAGE AND LITERATURE How language is constructed, plus descriptions of great playwrights, novelists, poets, etc.

SPORTS AND PASTIMES Competitive sports, great athletes and sporting stars, plus descriptions of many hobbies.

ASTRONOMY AND SPACE Birth of the universe, the solar system, galaxies, space exploration, etc.

SCIENCE How science is applied in everyday life, the elements, sources of energy, important scientists, etc.

ANIMALS Descriptions of behavior, homes, and individual species; mammals, birds, reptiles, fish, insects, etc.

MACHINES AND MECHANISMS Explanations of everything from simple machines to jet engines, plus descriptions of their inventors.

TRAVEL AND TRANSPORTATION The history and development of aircraft, ships, railroads, cars, motorcycles, etc.

HUMAN BODY How the body works, the process of birth, aging, diseases, immunity, genetics, etc.

BUILDINGS The history and development of architecture, modern construction and design, famous buildings and architects, etc.

OUR EARTH How the Earth was formed, and how it is still changing, its deserts, mountains, oceans, rivers, etc.

HISTORY Great events and great figures from ancient civilizations up to the present.

COUNTRIES AND PLACES Descriptions, flags, maps, essential statistics, etc. for all countries, plus places of interest.

RELIGION, PHILOSOPHY, AND MYTH How these have changed through history and the ones that have survived.

HOW TO GET THE MOST *from your* ENCYCLOPEDIA

***The Kingfisher Children's Encyclopedia* contains many features to help you look things up easily, or simply to have fun just browsing through. Almost every page has several illustrations and there are fact boxes, See-it-Yourself panels, special feature entries, and literally hundreds of cross references to help you find your way around. Some of those features are shown here. We hope you will enjoy exploring your encyclopedia.**

- **Subject symbols**
- **See-it-Yourself panels**
- **Fact boxes**
- **Country boxes**
- **"Nuggets"**
- **Special feature entries**
- **Cross references**

SPECIAL FEATURE entries are longer and more detailed than most entries. They will help you with school projects. You will find a list of these special feature entries at the back of the encyclopedia.

FISH

Fish were the first animals with backbones (vertebrates) to develop on Earth. They are animals best adapted to life in water. They b means of gills, and they swim by using their f tails. Fish are found in salt and fresh water, fr cold polar seas to the warm tropics.

Scientists divide fish into three groups. Th *cartilaginous* fish have gristly, rather than bo skeletons, and leathery skins, not scales. The the sharks and rays. The *bony* fish make up t and largest, group. All these fish have bony s covering their body. The third, and smallest, the *lungfish*, which are unusual in being able out on land and breathe air.

People have eaten fish since earliest times the world's fishing fleets catch millions of to every year.

SUBJECT SYMBOLS allow you to find quickly those entries on a similar theme. They will make browsing more interesting.

MCKINLEY, WILLIAM

WILLIAM MCKINLEY

Twenty-fifth President 1897–1901
Born: Niles, Ohio
Education: Allegheny College, Meadville, Pennsylvania
Occupation: Lawyer
Political Party: Republican
Buried: Canton, Ohio

McKinley, William

William McKinley was the 25th president of the United States. He was elected to serve two terms, but was assassinated six months after the start of the second. During his presidency, the United States became a major industrial power as well as an important world power. Cuba, Puerto Rico, and the Philippines all became American dependencies, and Hawaii became a United States territory. At home, the success of American industry brought problems, too. McKinley believed that U.S. businesses should be protected from foreign competition by high tariffs. Many of his political opponents were against these tariffs. McKinley was a politician all his adult life. Despite his cold and stubborn personality, he was popular with many people.

Madagascar

Madagascar is the fourth largest island in the world. It is in the Indian Ocean, off the east coast of Africa. The country of Madagascar has fertile coastal plains, a rugged central plateau, and a warm, tropical climate. Coffee, rice, sugar, and vanilla are among the leading crops.

Between the 800s and 1300s, Arab colonies were set up in Madagascar. In the 1800s, the island came under French control. It gained independence from France in 1960. The government is socialist.

MADAGASCAR

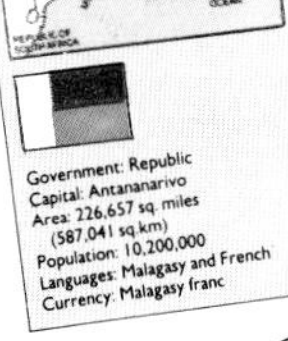

Government: Republic
Capital: Antananarivo
Area: 226,657 sq. miles (587,041 sq.km)
Population: 10,200,000
Languages: Malagasy and French
Currency: Malagasy franc

Madison, James

James Madison (1751–1836) was the 4th president of the United States. As president, his major problem was to keep the United States out of the Napoleonic Wars in Europe. Both Britain and France seized American ships, each believing that U.S. trade was helping the other. Many people in the United States were angry at this, and in 1812 Britain and America did go to war, despite all Madison's efforts to avoid fighting. Earlier, Madison played an important part in writing the U.S. CONSTITUTION. His writings on the nature of federal power influenced many people.

Magellan, Ferdinand

Ferdinand Magellan (1480–1521) was a Portuguese sailor and explorer. In 1519 he sailed west from Spain, around Cape Horn, and into the Pacific Ocean. Magellan was killed by natives in the Philippines. But one of his five ships returned safely to Spain, having completed the first voyage around the world. Of the crew of 265 who set sail with Magellan, only 16 survived the voyage.

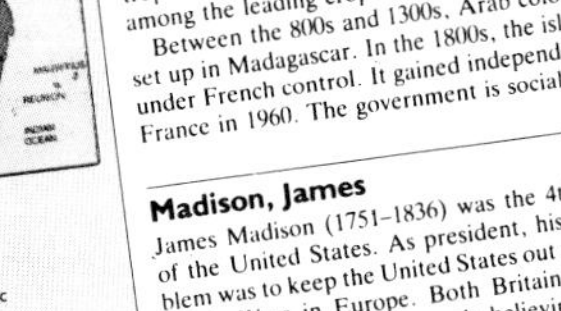

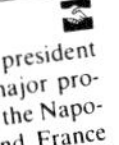

Magic

Many primitive peoples used magic. It was their way of trying to control what happened around them.

FACT PANELS appear throughout the encyclopedia giving you details on historical dates, facts and figures, highest, longest, biggest, etc.

THE TEXT is full of information and yet easy to read. Cross-references appear as SMALL CAPITALS. Turn to these entries for more information on the subject you are looking up.

SEE-IT-YOURSELF panels show you how to do simple experiments and make things. They will help you understand the subject you are looking up.

on a trawler. Trawlers fish in waters as far ...d the Arctic Ocean. Some stay at sea for ...ing their catches in deep freezers on board.

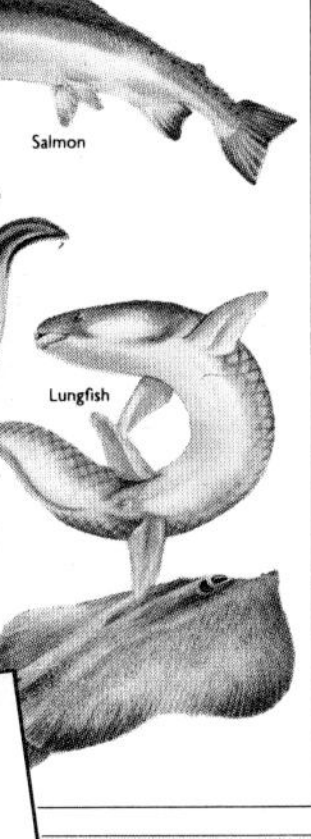

WHAT IS A FISH'S SIXTH SENSE?

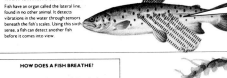

Fish have an organ called the lateral line, found in no other animal. It detects vibrations in the water through sensors beneath the fish's scales. Using this sixth sense, a fish can detect another fish before it comes into view.

HOW DOES A FISH BREATHE?

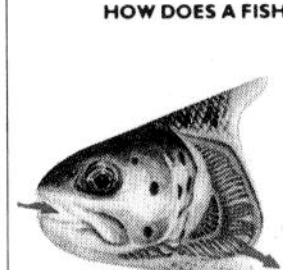

A fish breathes by means of gills on each side of its head. It takes in water through its mouth and, as the water passes over the gills, the gills extract oxygen from the water. The oxygen enters the fish's bloodstream. Fish are cold-blooded.

HOW DOES A FISH SWIM?

Most fish swim by beating their tails from side to side. They use their fins for steering and balance.

WHY CAN'T SEA FISH LIVE IN FRESH WATER?

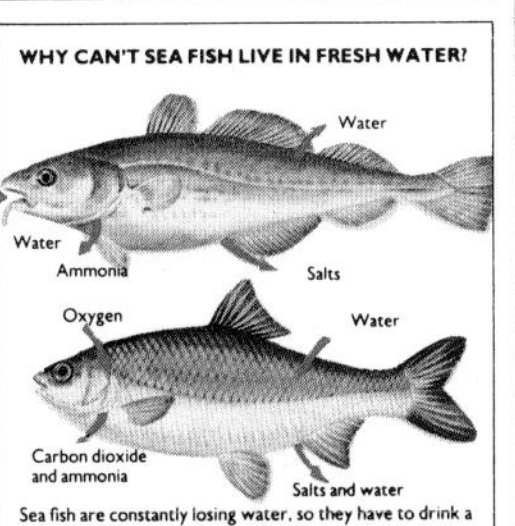

Sea fish are constantly losing water, so they have to drink a lot. Unwanted salt is excreted in their urine. Freshwater fish take in water through their skin. They excrete large volumes of water. Regulation of the amount of salt in a fish's body is also carried out by the gills and the kidneys.

SOME INTERESTING AND UNUSUAL FISH

Archer Fish This river fish catches insects by squirting water at them.
Catfish, like other bottom-dwelling fish, have feelers or "barbels" to help them find food.
Cleaner fish remove parasites and food scraps from the jaws of fierce barracuda.
Eels have an amazing life cycle, migrating from Europe and America to the Sargasso Sea to breed.
Flatfish A baby flounder swims upright. But as it grows, one eye travels across its head, and its body twists until the fish is lying on its side.
Flying Fish glide, using their long stiffened fins as wings. They take to the air to escape pursuing enemies.
Mudskippers use their leg-like fins to crawl over the mud to find food.
Pilot Fish often swim with sharks. They feed on the sharks' leftovers.
Porcupine Fish have prickly skins and blow themselves up like balloons to baffle a hungry enemy.
Salmon swim upriver to breed, often returning to the spot where they were born.
Scorpion Fish This fish is one to keep away from, for it has poisonous spines.
Sea Horse This curious-looking fish carries its ... a pouch.

For more information turn to these articles: EEL FISHING GOLDFISH LAKE OCEAN RIVER SALMON TROPICAL FISH TUNA

261

OVER 2,000 ILLUSTRATIONS and photographs have been used, including hundreds of maps and many cutaway diagrams.

ALL SPECIAL FEATURE entries have a list of other entries you should read for further information.

STRANGE-BUT-TRUE facts and figures appear throughout in "nuggets." Many are amusing — all are fascinating.

FLOWER

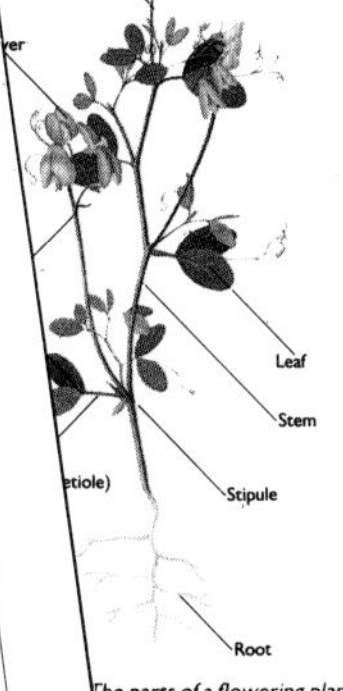

...e loops ... long ...he first ...ther to ...he same ...ive it a ...r and the ends ...strip, ...efore ...ut the ...nter. The separate ...orms two ...hird ...wice the ...! These ...overed by a ...ematician, ...n 1858.

415

The parts of a flowering plant. ... flower cut away to show its ... Fertilization occurs when pollen ... the anther unites with an ovule in ... ovary. The ovule becomes a seed

...useflies lay their eggs in ...ng matter. The life cycle can be ...te in a week in warm weather. The sponge-like mouth is drawn in the circle.

Eggs, Larva, Pupa

266

Flower

There are about 250,000 different kinds of flowering plants in the world. Their flowers come in a dazzling array of colors, sizes, and shapes. Some grow singly. Some grow in tight clusters. Many have showy colors, a strong scent, and produce a sweet nectar. Others are quite drab and unscented.

Whatever they look like, flowers all have the same part to play in the life of the plant. Flowers help plants to reproduce themselves. Inside a flower are male parts, called *stamens*, and female parts

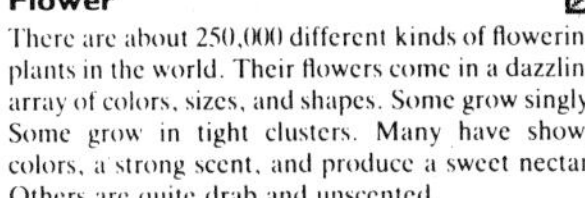

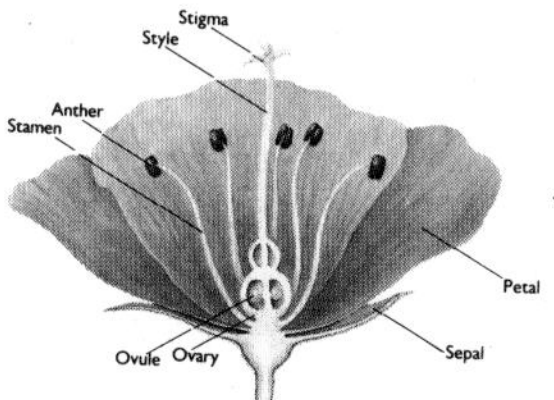

known as *pistils*. The stamens contain hundreds of powdery grains of pollen. These fertilize the pistil. Then a FRUIT begins to form and grow. Inside the fruit are the SEEDS for a new generation of plants. The seeds are scattered in different ways. They may be blown by the wind, or carried off by birds and animals. From them, new plants will grow.

Fly

Flies are winged insects. They are one of the largest groups of insects in the world. There are more than 750,000 different kinds of flies. They have two pairs of wings, one pair for flying and a smaller set behind the main pair to help them to balance in flight.

Many flies are dangerous. They spread deadly diseases such as cholera and dysentery. They pick up germs from manure and rotting food and carry them into homes, where they leave them on our food.

Some flies bite and feed on the blood of animals. Horseflies and gadflies attack cattle and horses in great swarms. Tsetse flies, which live in the tropics, spread sleeping sickness among domestic animals and humans. Blowflies lay their eggs in open wounds on the skin of animals. The maggots that hatch from the eggs eat into the flesh and cause great harm.

Fog

What we call fog is simply a low-lying bank of CLOUD. Fog forms when warm, moist air comes into contact with cold ground. As the air cools, the moisture it contains forms the tiny droplets that make up any cloud.

Fog may form when warm air currents blow across chilled water or land. This kind is common around the coast. Another kind occurs on still, clear winter nights, when the cold ground chills the air above it and there is no wind to blow the resulting fog away.

Food

Anything that people eat can be called food. But it makes more sense to talk of it as being only those plant and animal products people enjoy eating.

Primitive and ancient peoples often ate insects and animals raw, or only very lightly cooked.

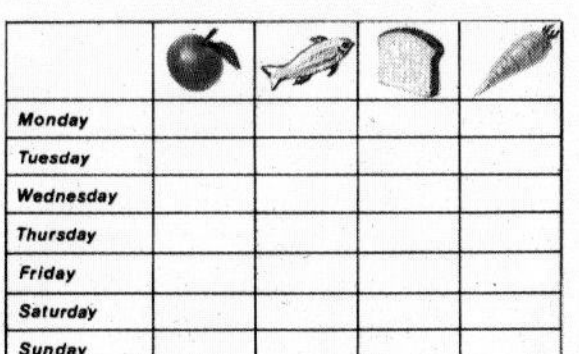

Monday				
Tuesday				
Wednesday				
Thursday				
Friday				
Saturday				
Sunday				

SEE IT YOURSELF

You can find out whether you are eating enough healthy foods by making a chart like the one on the left. Draw pictures at the top to show the four main food groups—fruit, meat or fish, bread or rice, and vegetables. Every day, check the box under each group when you have eaten something in that group. After a few days, look to see how you have done. If you have at least one check in each box, you are probably eating a healthy diet.

FOOD

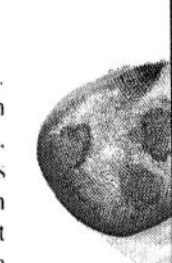

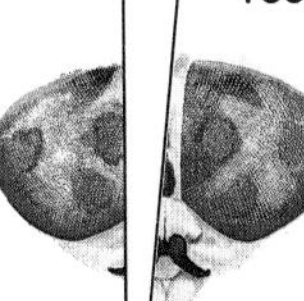

▲ A fly has two huge compound eyes made up of thousands of six-sided lenses.

The famous "London fogs" of Sherlock Holmes's day are now a thing of the past. They were not really fogs, but smogs. Smog is caused by drops of water condensing on smoke particles or the exhaust gases of cars or factories. Air pollution is a serious problem in many large cities.

267

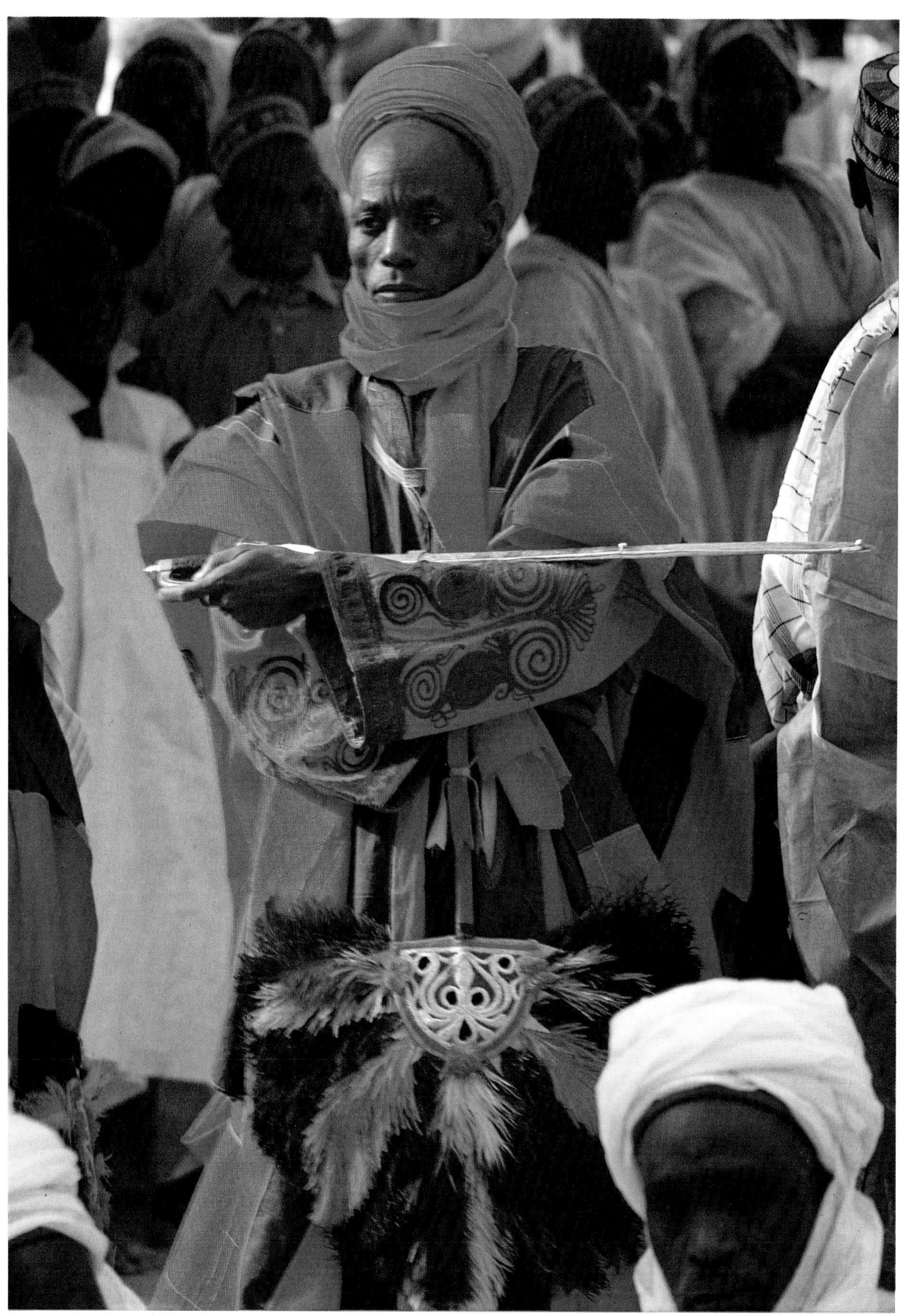

A Nigerian man wearing colorful traditional costume (see AFRICA)

A

Aardvark

The aardvark is an animal that eats TERMITES. When it has broken open a termites' nest with its powerful claws, it pokes in its long, sticky tongue and pulls it out covered with the insects. The aardvark lives in central and southern Africa. It has large ears like a donkey and is an expert burrower. If caught away from its home it can dig a hole for itself at astonishing speed. The word "aardvark" is Dutch for "earth pig." These shy animals can be 6 ft. (2 m) long and nearly 3 ft. (1 m) high.

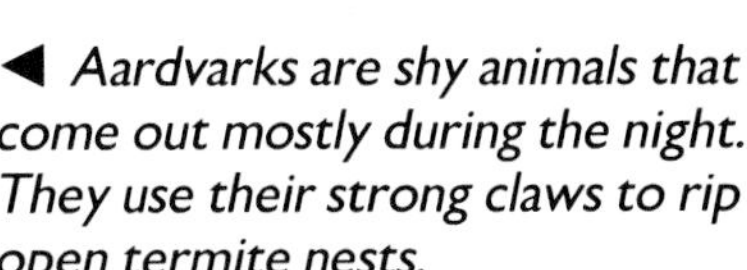

◀ *Aardvarks are shy animals that come out mostly during the night. They use their strong claws to rip open termite nests.*

Abacus

The abacus is a simple counting machine first used by the ancient Greeks and Romans. It consists of rows of beads strung on wires; those on the first wire count as ones, those on the second wire count as tens, on the third wire they count as hundreds, and so on. The abacus is still used in some Eastern countries. The Romans sometimes used small stones as counters. They called these counters *calculi*, and it is from this that we get our word "calculate." The abacus can be used to add, subtract, multiply, and divide.

▼ *The abacus here shows what each bead counts when it is pushed toward the bar. The top abacus reads 7—two 1 beads pushed to the bar and one 5 bead. If we want to add 171 to the 7, we push one more 1 bead to the bar, add a 50 and two 10s for the 70, and one 100 bead—178.*

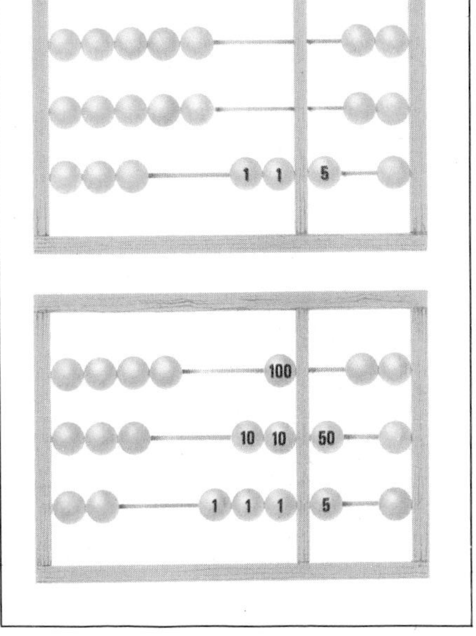

In the past, when all writing had to be done laboriously by hand, abbreviations saved time and space. In ancient Greek and Roman manuscripts, abbreviations were carried so far that special training is now needed to decipher them. We still use some of these ancient Roman abbreviations.

Many of the words we use daily began as abbreviations. We seldom stop to think that "bus" is short for "omnibus," "flu" for "influenza," "zoo" for "zoological gardens," and "cello" for "violoncello."

Abbreviation

An abbreviation is a shortened form of a word or a group of words. Words and phrases are shortened to save space. Sometimes the first and last letters of a word are used, such as *St.* for "Saint" or *Dr.* for "Doctor." Sometimes only the beginning of the word is used, as in *Sept.* for "September." A period is placed after the abbreviation to show that it is a shortened form.

Aborigine

The word "aborigine" really means the first people who lived in any country. But it is now used when we talk about the natives of AUSTRALIA. These are slim black people with broad noses and black wavy hair. They came to Australia thousands of years ago from southeastern Asia. In Australia they had no permanent homes, but wandered about the desert hunting or gathering their food. Their weapons were the boomerang and the throwing spear.

The Aborigines were very badly treated by the white men who came to Australia. Today Aborigines have rights as Australian citizens.

▼ *Aborigines like to keep many of their old traditions. Here a group performs a spear dance to the booming music of a didgeridoo.*

Acceleration

When a car increases speed, it accelerates. If it is traveling at 40 miles an hour and increases speed to 50 miles an hour after 1 minute, it has accelerated at a rate of 10 miles per hour per minute.

If you drop a ball from the top of a tall building it accelerates—goes faster and faster—as it falls. It reaches a velocity of 32 ft. (9.8 m) per second after one second. After two seconds it reaches a velocity of 64 ft. (19.6 m) per second. Every second that it falls, it increases its speed by 32 ft. (9.8 m) per second. The ball accelerates as it falls because it is being pulled down by the force of GRAVITY. The strange thing is that the force of gravity pulls everything down at the same speed. If there was no air and you dropped a feather and a baseball from the top of a building at the same time, they would hit the ground together. Of course, air holds up the feather much more than the ball. The feather's shape makes the difference.

Accounting

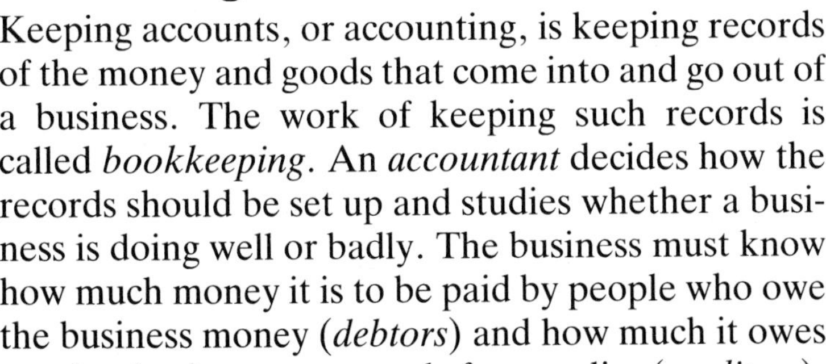

Keeping accounts, or accounting, is keeping records of the money and goods that come into and go out of a business. The work of keeping such records is called *bookkeeping*. An *accountant* decides how the records should be set up and studies whether a business is doing well or badly. The business must know how much money it is to be paid by people who owe the business money (*debtors*) and how much it owes to other businesses or people for supplies (*creditors*).

Today, most accounting records are kept on computers, but people still have to feed the right information to the machines.

Acid

An acid is a liquid chemical COMPOUND that is often poisonous. Some acids, such as sulfuric acid, nitric acid, and hydrochloric acid, are very strong and can *corrode*, or eat away, even the strongest metals. Other acids are harmless. These include the citric acid that gives lemons and oranges their sharp taste, and the acetic acid in vinegar. Lactic acid forms when

▼ *When a ball is dropped, it accelerates—goes faster and faster. It is pulled toward the Earth by the force of gravity. A baseball and a tennis ball would fall at the same speed.*

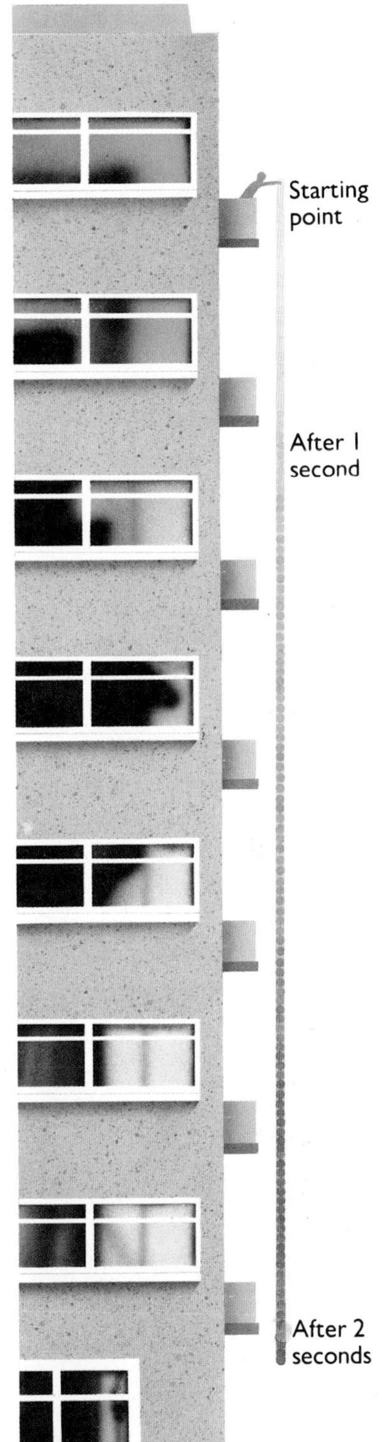

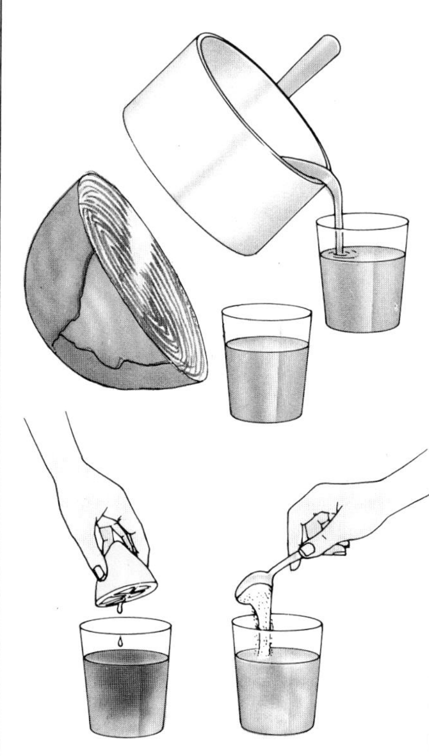

SEE IT YOURSELF

Cut half a red cabbage into strips. Put the strips into a pan of hot water and let the mixture cool. Strain the liquid and pour into clean glasses. Add a few drops of water. This shows the neutral color. Now add a few drops of lemon juice to one glass to show its acid color, and some baking soda to the other glass to show its alkaline color.

milk goes sour. All acids turn a special sort of paper called *litmus* red.

Some substances are the opposite of acids. They are called *alkalis* or *bases* and turn litmus paper blue. Baking soda is an alkali.

Acid Rain

All rain is very slightly ACID. The weak acid in rainwater can eat away the limestone in buildings and statues. Limestone is an alkali.

Rain can also react with the waste gases sent out by power plants, factories, and cars. Such gases can be carried great distances by the wind. Then they fall as weak sulfuric acid and nitric acid, so they are called acid rain. After a time, lakes and streams are slowly poisoned by the acid rain, threatening plants and wildlife. People are trying to reduce the waste gases poured out by industrial nations or to make them less harmful.

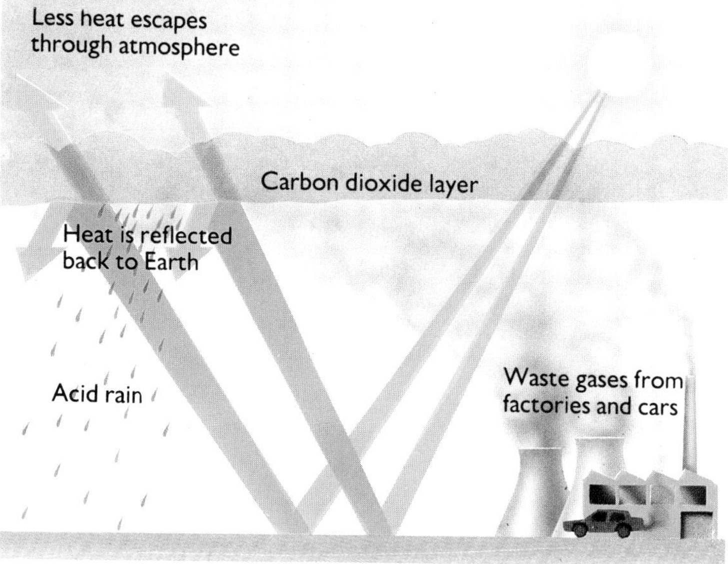

▲ *Two of the main threats to our atmosphere are acid rain and the "greenhouse effect." They are both caused by gases sent out by power plants, factories, and cars. The greenhouse effect is caused by a "blanket" of carbon dioxide gas in the air which traps the Sun's heat and prevents some of it from escaping into space. The Earth can become warmer over the years.*

◀ *Scientists are not in agreement on how much damage is done by acid rain. The trees in this picture have been damaged severely.*

Acoustics

Acoustics is the study of SOUND and how it travels. When an architect designs a concert hall or theater, he or she must carefully consider the sound quality of the building. Will a full range of sound waves from speech and music reach every seat? Will there be disturbing echoes from the walls and ceiling? Or will the sound from the stage be absorbed too much by soft materials such as curtains, causing sound to be muffled?

Sound waves travel in straight lines, and they can be reflected or absorbed by surfaces that they strike. Various reflectors and baffles can be attached to walls and ceilings to turn the sound waves in the best direction.

▲ *A tractor being tested to find out exactly how much sound it gives out. It is in a specially designed room that absorbs all the sound from every part of the vehicle.*

Acropolis

"Acropolis" is a Greek word for the high central part of many ancient Greek cities. The most famous acropolis is in ATHENS, the capital of modern Greece. On top of the Acropolis are the ruins of ancient temples built in the 400s B.C. when Athens

▼ *The Acropolis of Athens as it must have looked about 400 B.C. The Propylaea, with its six rows of pillars, was a magnificent entrance gateway. At the highest point stood the Parthenon.*

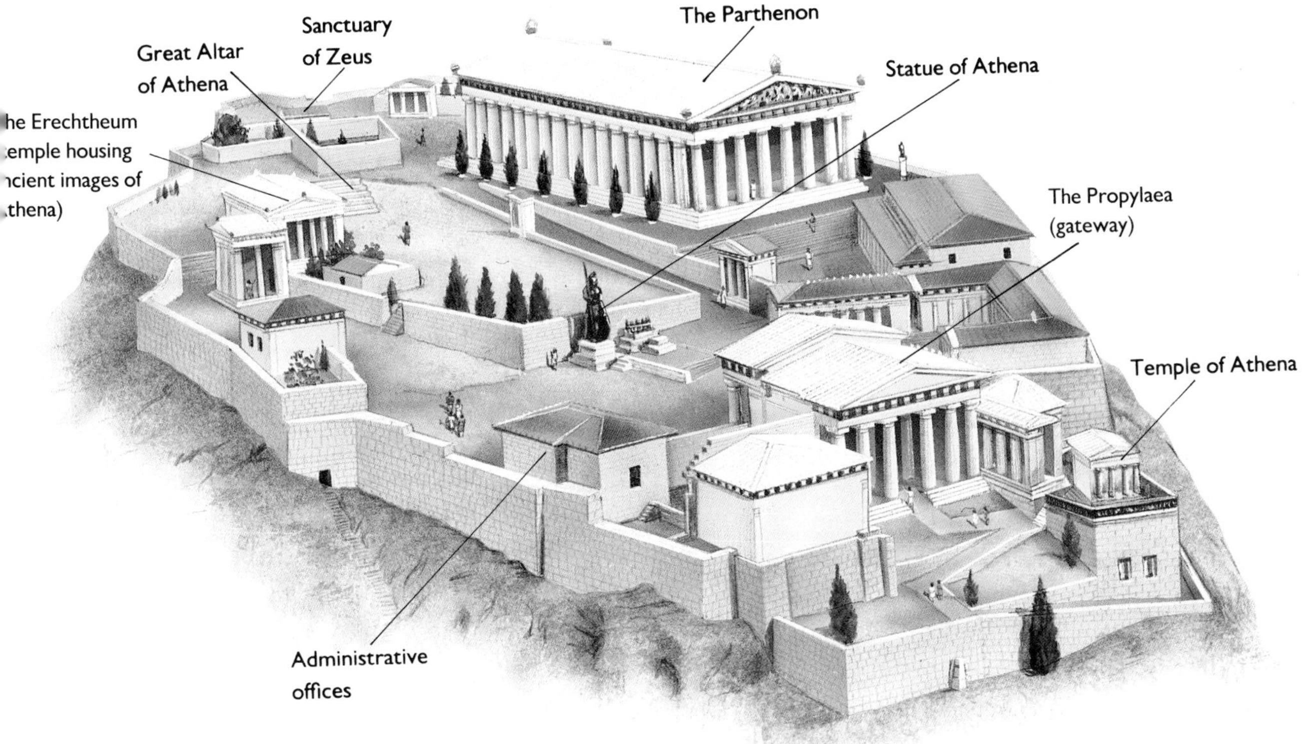

Sanctuary of Zeus
The Parthenon
Great Altar of Athena
Statue of Athena
he Erechtheum
emple housing
ncient images of
thena)
The Propylaea (gateway)
Temple of Athena
Administrative offices

was a rich and powerful city. The Parthenon, the largest and most important of these temples, was built to honor Athena, the patron goddess of Athens.

Many people think that the Parthenon on the Acropolis in Athens is the most perfect building ever built. But we are very lucky that any of the great white marble building is left to admire. Through history it has served as a Byzantine church, a Roman Catholic church, a Turkish harem, and a Turkish powder magazine. In 1687, a direct hit by Venetian artillery caused the gunpowder in the Parthenon to explode, scattering debris all over the Acropolis. Later, many of the Parthenon's sculptures were taken away by Lord Elgin, who was British ambassador to Greece. They are now in the British Museum in London.

Acting *See* Theater

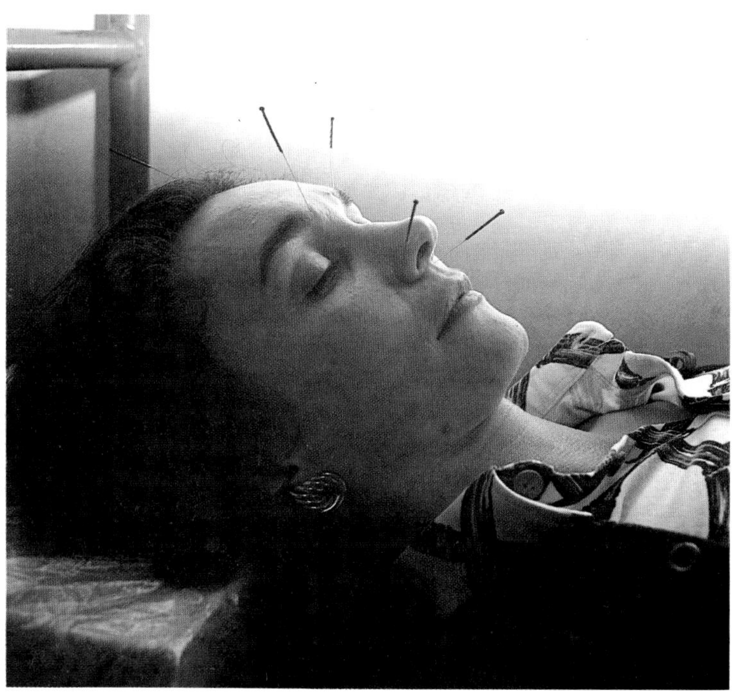

► *In acupuncture, the metal needles are usually inserted only a little way into the patient.*

Acupuncture

Acupuncture is an ancient kind of medical treatment in which thin needles are used to puncture various parts of the body. The treatment was developed by the Chinese about 5,000 years ago, and it is still used today. Chinese doctors have performed surgery with acupuncture as the only anesthetic. In recent years, acupuncture has begun to be accepted in the West as a branch of alternative medicine. It is often used in the treatment of such complaints as headache, asthma, and arthritis.

JOHN ADAMS

Second President 1797–1801
Born: Braintree (Quincy), Mass.
Education: Harvard College
Occupation: Lawyer
Political Party: Federalist
Buried: Quincy, Mass.

Adams, John

John Adams (1735–1836) was the second president of the United States. His family were farmers in MASSACHUSETTS. He studied at Harvard College and became a lawyer. Adams was a leader in the American colonies' fight for independence from Britain, and in 1774 he went to the First Continental Congress. In 1776 he signed the Declaration of Independence. He served under George Washington as the first vice president, and followed him as president in 1797. He was the first president to live in the White House.

John Adams was not a popular president. He fought a split in his own party, the Federalists, over his determination to avoid war with France. He was not re-elected in 1800, when Thomas Jefferson was chosen instead. John Adams was the only president whose son also served in the office.

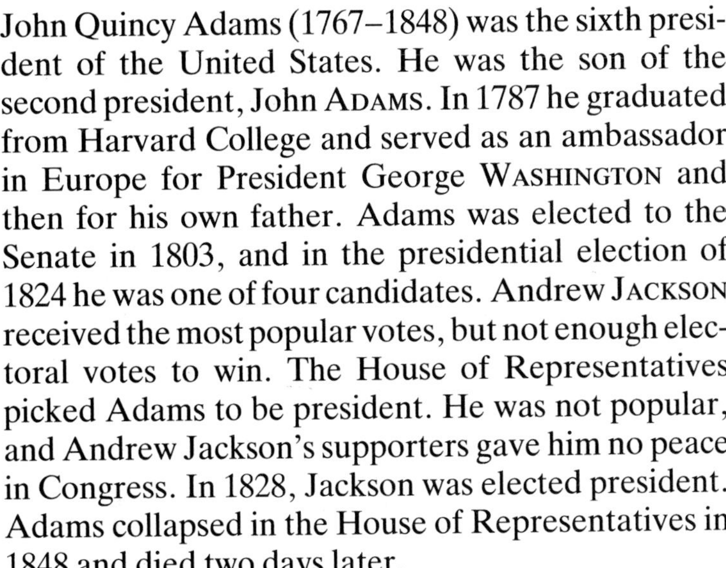

Adams, John Quincy

John Quincy Adams (1767–1848) was the sixth president of the United States. He was the son of the second president, John Adams. In 1787 he graduated from Harvard College and served as an ambassador in Europe for President George Washington and then for his own father. Adams was elected to the Senate in 1803, and in the presidential election of 1824 he was one of four candidates. Andrew Jackson received the most popular votes, but not enough electoral votes to win. The House of Representatives picked Adams to be president. He was not popular, and Andrew Jackson's supporters gave him no peace in Congress. In 1828, Jackson was elected president. Adams collapsed in the House of Representatives in 1848 and died two days later.

JOHN QUINCY ADAMS

Sixth President 1825–1829
Born: Braintree (Quincy), Mass.
Education: University of Leyden, Netherlands; Harvard College
Occupation: Lawyer
Political Party: Federalist, then Republican
Buried: Quincy, Mass.

Addiction

When people take some drugs for a long time they become *addicted*—they need to keep on taking them. Their need for the drug is called *addiction*. There are different kinds of addictive drugs. Some are painkillers such as opium and morphine. Some are *depressants* such as sleeping pills. Others are *stimulants*, which pep up the nervous system. "Speed" is one of these. Marijuana and LSD are *hallucinogens*, which make people see and hear things that are not really there. Addicts hurt themselves and may die because of drugs. *Withdrawing* people from drugs is very difficult and is seldom successful.

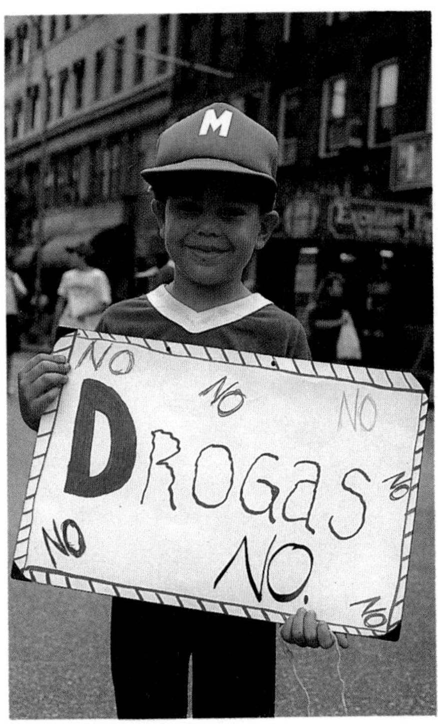

▲ *Drug addiction is a serious problem worldwide. It is easier to prevent addiction than to stop it once it has taken hold.*

For any adhesive to work well, the surfaces to be stuck together must be very clean. Grease, dirt, and water prevent the adhesive from touching the surfaces as closely as it should. Even the grease of a fingerprint or the moisture of your breath can stop proper adhesion.

Adhesive

Adhesives are substances that are used to stick things together. There are many different kinds of adhesive. For centuries, people have used adhesives made from boiling up animal bones, hide, and horn to produce glue. Plants such as corn and potatoes can be made into a starch paste that is good for sticking paper. Natural liquid rubber sticks fast to almost anything.

Modern manmade adhesives are better than natural ones because they are much stronger. Epoxy resins, for example, are very strong. They can be used to stick parts of airplanes together.

Adjective

An adjective is any word that describes or modifies a NOUN. A "gray horse" is more exact than just "a horse." We can make it more exact still by writing "a big, friendly, gray horse." The words *big*, *friendly* and *gray* are adjectives describing the noun *horse*.

Adjectives usually come before the noun, but they can also come after it: "The pie is *delicious*." The word *delicious* describes the pie. It is an adjective.

Adolescence

Adolescence is the time when a child is growing up to become an adult. The changes of adolescence usually begin to take place in girls of 10 to 13 and in boys of 11 to 14. The changes go on for several years, and the adolescent's body changes in many ways. A girl's hips become wider and her breasts start to develop. She has her first menstrual period. This is a sign that she can one day have babies. A boy's voice becomes deeper and his beard starts to grow. Both boys and girls develop hair in their pubic areas and under their arms.

During adolescence, young people often feel awkward and have emotional upsets, but these things pass. Soon boys and girls become young men and women and learn to do more and more for themselves, so that they do not depend so much on their parents.

▼ *A Jewish boy prepares for the bar mitzvah ceremony. This ceremony, which takes place on the Sabbath nearest to his thirteenth birthday, marks his passing from adolescence to adulthood.*

Advertising

Advertising is usually a means of telling people about things they can buy and persuading people to buy them. The most popular *media* (means of advertising) are television, radio, newspapers, magazines, and posters. Governments use advertisements, too. They tell us things like "Smoking is bad for your health."

Today, advertising is a huge industry that employs millions of people, including writers, artists, photographers, actors, and salesmen. Many of the people who work in advertising are employed by advertising agencies—firms that produce advertisements for clients who have goods or services to sell. Each company uses its own special name for a product. That special name is called the company's *brand name*. No other company can use that name. Advertisers try to make the products they are selling appear as desirable and as good value as possible. Many countries have laws that stop advertisers from making false claims about their products.

▼ *City centers are favorite places for advertisements because many people see them. Neon signs flash their message; billboards are all around. Advertising is a multibillion dollar industry.*

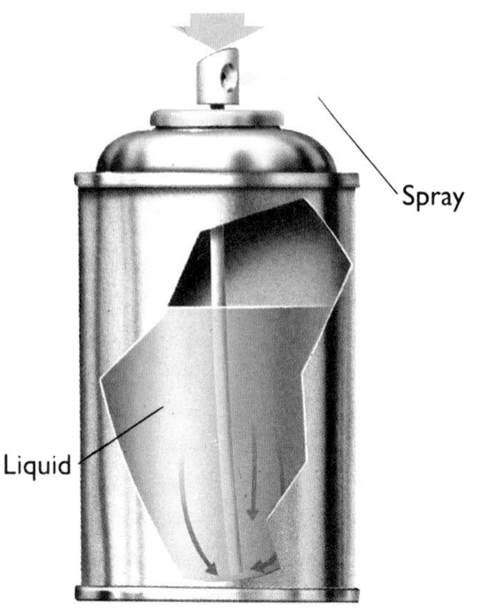

▲ *When you press down the button on an aerosol can, a gas under pressure forces the liquid up a tube to the top and out as a fine spray.*

Aerosol

When scientists talk about an aerosol they mean a cloud of very fine particles floating in air or some other gas. The particles can be liquid, as in a mist, or solid, as in smoke.

When most people speak of an aerosol they mean something that sprays paint, cosmetics, or insecticides. It consists of a can containing a liquefied gas under high pressure. The can also contains the paint or other substance to be sprayed. When a button on the cap is pressed, a fine nozzle opens and the gas forces out the paint in the form of a fine spray.

Scientists are trying to ban the use of harmful chemicals in aerosols. They say that the chemicals in aerosols (chlorofluorocarbons or CFCs) are drifting up in the air and are slowly destroying the OZONE LAYER. The ozone layer is a layer of gas about 12 miles (20 km) above the Earth. It absorbs most of the Sun's dangerous ULTRAVIOLET rays.

Aesop

Aesop (about 620–560 B.C.) was an ancient Greek storyteller. His stories are today known as *Aesop's Fables*. The characters in his stories are usually animals, but they behave like humans, with virtues and weaknesses. One famous story tells of a race between a tortoise and a hare. The hare is so sure of an easy win that he takes a rest during the race. This allows the slow, plodding tortoise to win.

Some historians believe that Aesop was a slave who was freed because he told his stories so well.

AFGHANISTAN

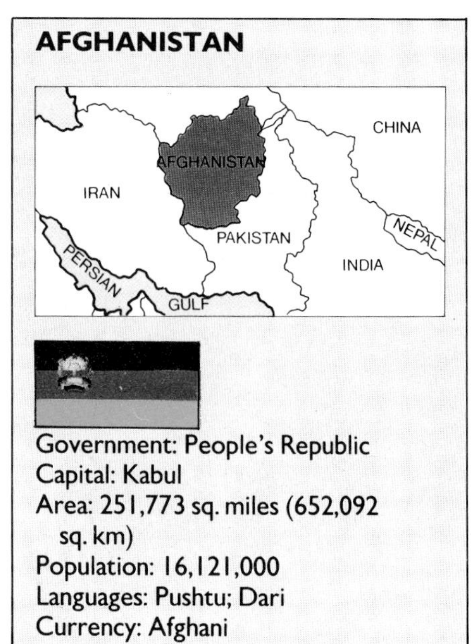

Government: People's Republic
Capital: Kabul
Area: 251,773 sq. miles (652,092 sq. km)
Population: 16,121,000
Languages: Pushtu; Dari
Currency: Afghani

Afghanistan

Afghanistan is a country in ASIA. It is a mountainous land and has no seacoast. It is nearly as big as Texas. The capital and largest city is Kabul. Nearly all the people are Muslims. In 1978 the government was overthrown by rebels friendly to the U.S.S.R., but Muslim bands continued to fight against the new government. In 1979 Russian troops took over the country. This caused worldwide opposition and the Russians had to withdraw their troops in 1988.

Africa

Africa is the world's second largest continent. It covers an area of 11,700,000 sq. miles (30,319,000 sq. km), one-fifth of the world's land. Africa stretches from the Mediterranean Sea in the north to the Cape of Good Hope at its tip in the south. Large parts of Africa are empty wasteland. The scorching SAHARA DESERT spreads over much of the northern part of the continent. Near the EQUATOR, which runs through the center of Africa, are thick rain forests. There the trees grow so close together that their leaves blot out the sunlight.

More than a third of Africa is a high, flat plain, or plateau. Grassland called *savanna* covers much of the plateau region. Great herds of grazing animals roam the savanna. They include zebras, giraffes, wildebeest, and impala. Other animals, such as lions, cheetahs, and hyenas, prey upon the grazing animals. In the past, many animals were killed by hunters, but today special reserves have been set up to protect them.

Mt. Kilimanjaro, the highest mountain in Africa, rises 19,340 ft. (5,895 m) in Tanzania. Africa's largest lake, Lake Victoria, lies between Kenya and Tanzania. The continent's great rivers are the NILE, Zaire (formerly called Congo), Niger, and Zambezi.

▲ *Africa is a huge continent. It is more than three times as big as the United States. The great Sahara Desert covers most of northern Africa. It separates the Arab countries along the Mediterranean from the Negro countries of central Africa. Most of the rest of Africa is grassland, or savanna.*

▼ *Waterholes are very important to the animals of central Africa. Gathered around to drink are zebras, impalas, elands, and guinea fowl. An ostrich and a giraffe wait their turn.*

▲ *This beautifully carved ivory mask was worn as an ornament by the king of the West African kingdom of Benin. Great empires grew up in Africa before the white people came.*

▼ *Africa has many tribal religions. But more and more people are becoming Muslims. Today there are more than 100 million Muslims in Africa. Most of them are in the north of the continent. Here Muslims gather at a mosque in Nairobi, Kenya.*

Many different types of people live in Africa. In North Africa are ARABS and Berbers, who mostly follow the Muslim religion. So-called "black Africa" lies south of the Sahara Desert. The Negroid peoples who live there make up three-fourths of Africa's population. People with European and Asian ancestors make up the rest of the population.

Most Africans are farmers, growing crops such as cocoa, coffee, cotton, sisal, and tea. Africa produces nearly three-fourths of the world's palm oil and palm kernels, which are used to make items like soap and margarine. The continent has valuable mineral resources, too, including gold and diamonds, copper, and tin.

The Dark Continent

For centuries Africa was called the "Dark Continent" because Europeans knew little about it or its people. The Phoenicians and Romans had built trading centers along the north coast and they knew of the great early civilization in Egypt. But the lands to the south remained a mystery.

The first Europeans to learn more about this huge unexplored continent were the Portuguese. They were the first to find a sea route to India by sailing around the southern tip of Africa. They hugged the coast, fearing to sail out of sight of land. Soon the African coastline was charted. But it was still a long time before people became interested in exploring inland. From the 1400s, European sailors began to ship slaves from Africa. About 14 million slaves were taken to the Americas between 1500 and the 1800s. Usually these slaves were bought from tribes that lived along the African coast. So Europeans did not need to travel into the interior of the great continent.

By the 1800s the countries of Europe were becoming interested in setting up colonies in Africa. Brave explorers like David Livingstone, Mungo Park, and Henry Stanley traveled into the interior, and soon the continent had been carved up between the European powers. The Europeans brought new ways of life to Africa. Missionaries brought the Christian religion and set up schools.

After some years many Africans began to resent being ruled by foreigners. During the 1950s and

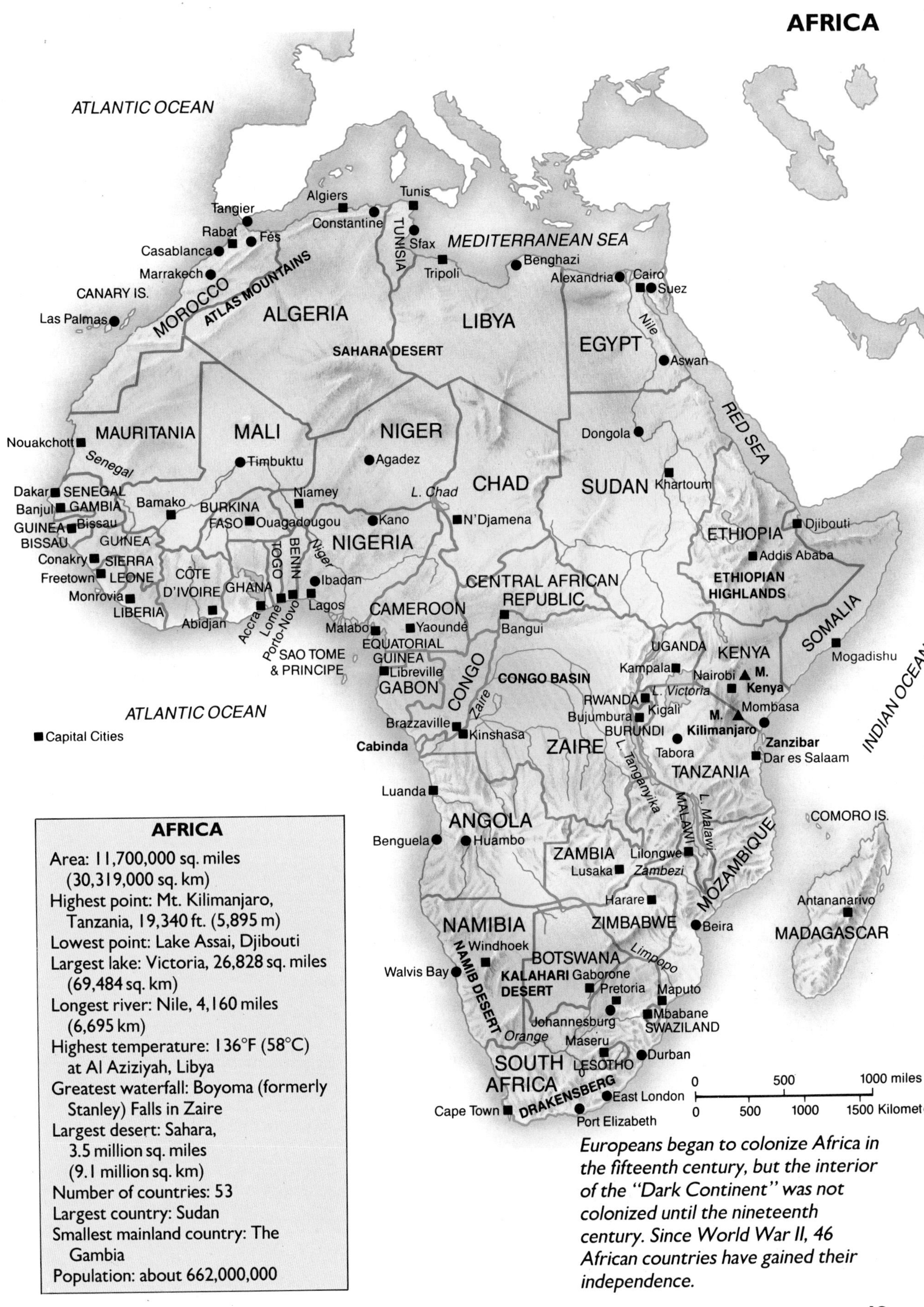

AFRICA

Area: 11,700,000 sq. miles (30,319,000 sq. km)
Highest point: Mt. Kilimanjaro, Tanzania, 19,340 ft. (5,895 m)
Lowest point: Lake Assai, Djibouti
Largest lake: Victoria, 26,828 sq. miles (69,484 sq. km)
Longest river: Nile, 4,160 miles (6,695 km)
Highest temperature: 136°F (58°C) at Al Aziziyah, Libya
Greatest waterfall: Boyoma (formerly Stanley) Falls in Zaire
Largest desert: Sahara, 3.5 million sq. miles (9.1 million sq. km)
Number of countries: 53
Largest country: Sudan
Smallest mainland country: The Gambia
Population: about 662,000,000

Europeans began to colonize Africa in the fifteenth century, but the interior of the "Dark Continent" was not colonized until the nineteenth century. Since World War II, 46 African countries have gained their independence.

Most of Africa is a great plateau or tableland surrounded by a narrow coastal plain. The average height of the African continent is 2,460 ft. (750 m) above sea level—twice the height of the Empire State Building in New York City.

People, on average, live much longer in developed countries than in the underdeveloped world. In Sweden for example, 22 percent of the population is over 65. In Zimbabwe only 3 percent of people reach that age. Women live longer than men. A baby boy born in the United States today can expect to live to about 72, a girl to about 79.

▼ *A rabbit aged 4 years is a "very old" rabbit, but a dog is not "very old" until it is about 15 years. A human being becomes "very old" when he or she is about 80. Some tortoises live to be up to 100 years old.*

1960s most former colonies became independent African countries. Many were poor and some have had bloody civil wars as different rulers fought for power. But today the countries are working together to help one another and to develop industry and their natural resources. Many of the richer nations of the world are helping them in this task.

Aging

How old is "old?" This is a very difficult question to answer. When a mouse is 4 years old it is as old as a dog of 15 or a person of 80. Humans age more slowly than almost any other animal; only some kinds of land tortoise live longer. But our bodies are continuously wearing out. As we grow older our eyesight may weaken, our hearing become less clear; our memory may become poor, our skin wrinkle, and our limbs become stiff. Doctors are not sure why these changes take place—and why they take place at different ages in different people.

AIDS

AIDS (Acquired Immune Deficiency Syndrome) is caused by a virus named HIV. The AIDS virus attacks white blood cells that fight off viruses and bacteria when they enter the body. When these white blood cells are destroyed, the patient can become very ill with a disease that would not be serious to a

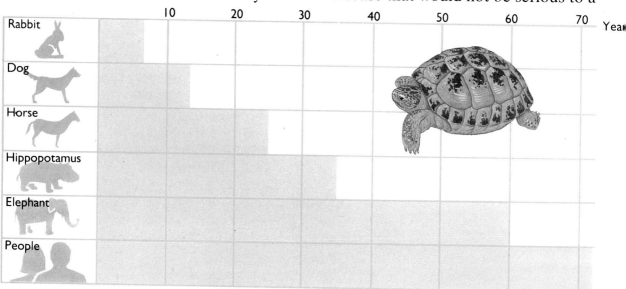

10 20 30 40 50 60 70 Years

Rabbit
Dog
Horse
Hippopotamus
Elephant
People

healthy person. Because the body of a person with AIDS has lost its means of fighting disease, the patient can often die.

AIDS is passed from person to person in three main ways: by intimate sexual contact, by exposure to blood infected with HIV, and by transmission to a baby in an infected mother's womb. People most likely to catch the disease are drug addicts who inject themselves with drugs and share hypodermic needles. However, anyone can catch AIDS through intimate sexual contact with someone who has the HIV virus. People who have been infected with HIV may not become seriously ill until years later. AIDS is a serious world problem.

Air

Air is all around us—it surrounds the Earth in a layer we call the *atmosphere*. All living things must have air in order to live. Air is colorless and has no smell. Yet it is really a mixture of a number of different gases. We can feel air when the wind blows, and we know air has weight. Air carries sound—without it we would not be able to hear, because sounds cannot travel in a VACUUM.

The chief gas in air is nitrogen, which makes up nearly fourth-fifths of the air. About one-fifth of the air is made up of OXYGEN. Air also holds some water in very fine particles called vapor.

The air that surrounds the Earth gets thinner the

Air is heavier than you think. The average roomful of air weighs more than 100 pounds (45 kg)—about as heavy as you are. The air we breathe is about 14 times as heavy as the gas hydrogen.

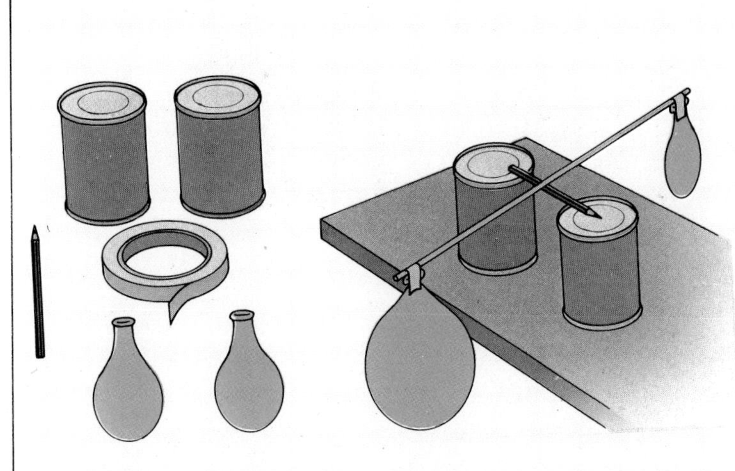

SEE IT YOURSELF

Prove to yourself that air has weight. Make a simple balance using two cans, a pencil, and a long stick marked in the center. Tape two identical balloons to the ends of the stick and see how they balance. Now, remove one of the balloons, blow air into it, and fix it back in place. The balloon full of air makes the balance dip down. Air really does have weight.

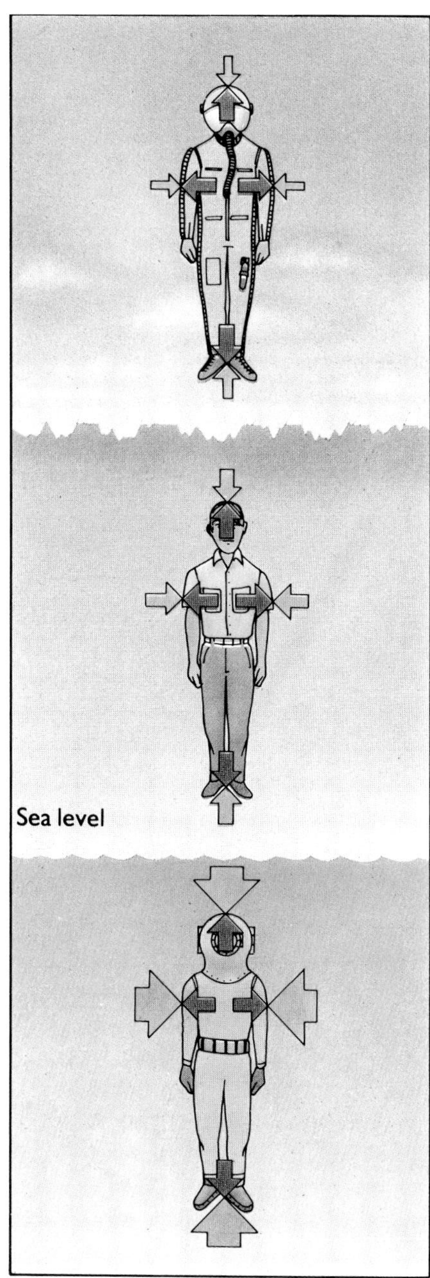

▲ *We live under about a hundred miles of air. Why are we not squashed flat? We are not squashed because everything inside our bodies is at the same pressure as the air around us. But air pressure changes with height. The higher you go, the less air there is above you. This is why the pilots of high-flying aircraft need to wear special suits and take their own oxygen supply with them. Deep-sea divers also need special suits to prevent their bodies from being crushed by the weight of water.*

higher you go. All high-flying aircraft have to keep the air in their cabins at ground level pressure so that passengers can breathe normally. In the same way mountaineers carry their own air supply because the air at the top of high mountains is too thin to breathe properly.

Warm air expands and becomes lighter. The air around a heater becomes lighter and rises. Cool air moves into its place. This too warms and rises, so an entire room can be heated by moving air as it goes around and around.

Aircraft

For thousands of years people dreamed about being able to fly. Myths and legends are filled with tales of supermen who could fly. Yet it was only at the beginning of this century—on December 17, 1903—that the Wright brothers made the first successful airplane flight. Seventy years later, *Concorde* was crossing the Atlantic in three hours. (See pages 18 and 19.)

Air Cushion Vehicle *See* Hovercraft

Air Force

AIRCRAFT were first used as fighting machines during WORLD WAR I. By 1939, most countries had an air force. The Germans had built up a strong Luftwaffe (air force) which they used in their successful "blitzkrieg" attacks at the start of WORLD WAR II. The Germans knew that no land battle could be won without control of the skies above the battle area. When the Luftwaffe failed to knock out the Royal Air Force in the Battle of Britain, HITLER canceled his plans to invade Britain.

As the war progressed, long-range bombers played an increasing part in the tactics of the British, American, German, and Japanese air forces. The war ended when U.S. airplanes dropped two atomic bombs on Japanese cities.

Today, guided missiles have cut down the part played by bombers, but piloted planes are still

◀ *Some fighter aircraft are designed to do several jobs in air warfare. The Tornado can act as a low-level bomber as well as an air defense fighter. Its wings can be swept back for high speed flight or extended to help it travel at lower speeds.*

needed as a defense against fast strike bombers. The modern bomber can fly close to the ground at very high speed, slipping under the enemy's radar screen without being spotted. Transport aircraft can fly troops, complete with tanks and weapons, anywhere in the world in a few hours. The helicopter is now a vital part of any air force. It carries troops and evacuates the wounded. Helicopter "gunships" can attack ground targets.

Airport

An airport is one of the busiest places in the world, as all day and nearly all night jet airliners take off and land—at peak periods at the rate of one a minute.

Airports have three main jobs: they must handle passengers, mail, and freight; they must be sure that all aircraft take off and land safely and on time; and they must provide hangars and workshops so that planes can be checked regularly.

The center of operations at the airport is the air-traffic control tower, where controllers organize the landing and takeoff of each aircraft. With complicated electronic aids, including computers and radar, the ground controller guides the pilot of the aircraft from a height of 4 to 5 miles (6 to 8 km) onto a concrete runway about 2 miles (3 km) long.

There are more than a hundred scheduled airlines in the United States. They are regulated by the Federal Aviation Administration.

▼ *At the beginning of World War I the soldiers in the trenches of the Western Front took potshots at any aircraft that flew overhead, whether it was friend or foe. So warplanes began to be marked with their national flags. However, as these could often be confusing at a distance, the special symbols of the world's air forces were gradually adopted.*

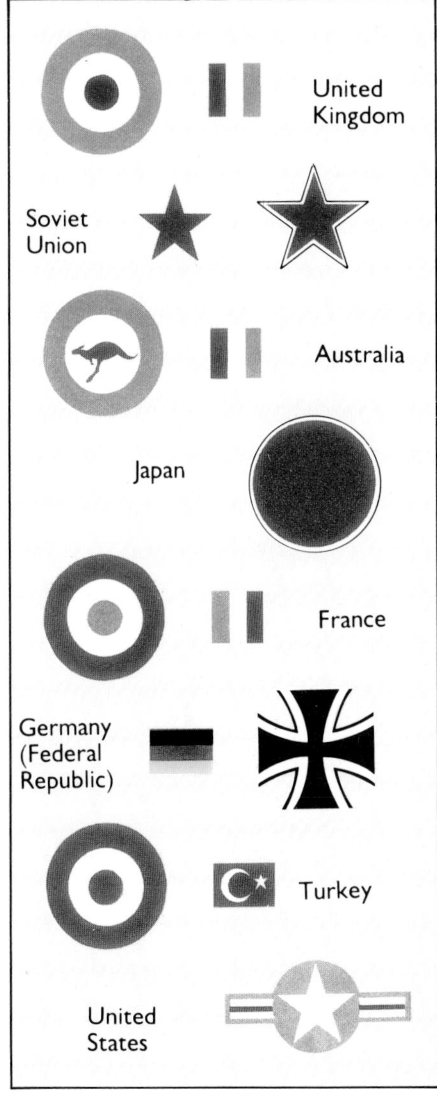

Aircraft

From earliest times people dreamed of being able to fly like the birds. Brave but foolhardy inventors leaped from high towers wearing wings, but all such attempts ended in failure. In the late 1500s Leonardo da Vinci drew plans for a helicopter, but such a machine could never have been built in his day.

The conquest of the air by people began with the first balloon flight in 1783. Later, airships, steerable balloons with engines and propellers, took to the sky. Inventors built gliders, proving that flight was also possible using winged airplanes that were heavier than air.

It was the development of the gasoline engine in the 1880s that made powered airplanes a practical possibility. In 1903 the Wright brothers made the first controlled and powered manned flight in their flimsy airplane, the *Flyer*.

Since that historic flight, progress in aviation has been amazingly rapid. Today we live in a world where people take air travel for granted. Supersonic jet aircraft, such as *Concorde*, can fly the Atlantic Ocean in three hours. Space shuttles can fly into space and return to land on a runway like an airliner.

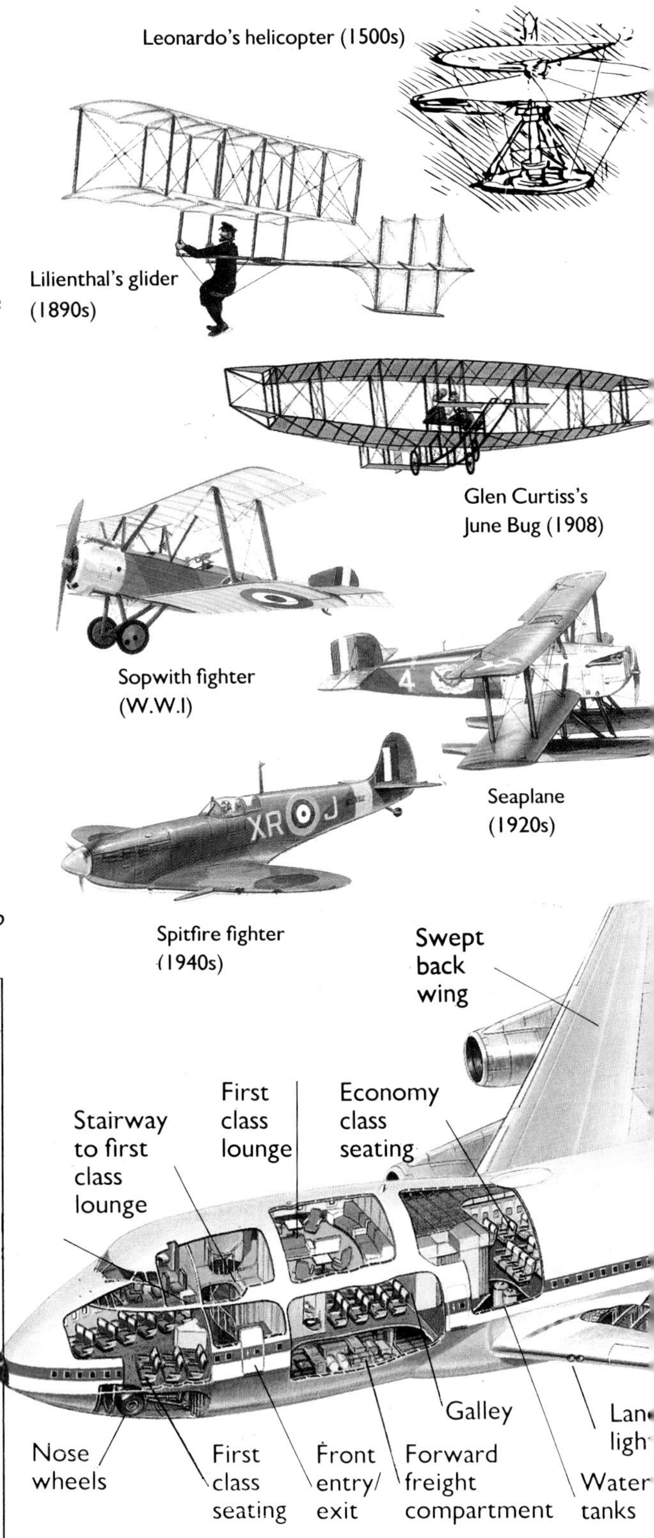

▶ *A selection of aircraft throughout the ages, ranging from Leonardo's 16th century helicopter to the popular and highly efficient Concorde.*

Leonardo's helicopter (1500s)

Lilienthal's glider (1890s)

Glen Curtiss's June Bug (1908)

Sopwith fighter (W.W.I)

Seaplane (1920s)

Spitfire fighter (1940s)

Swept back wing

First class lounge

Economy class seating

Stairway to first class lounge

Galley

Nose wheels

First class seating

Front entry/ exit

Forward freight compartment

Lan ligh

Water tanks

HOW A PLANE FLIES

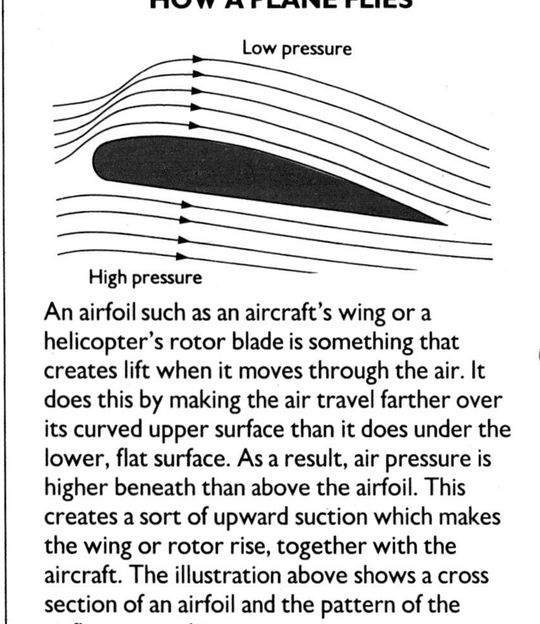

An airfoil such as an aircraft's wing or a helicopter's rotor blade is something that creates lift when it moves through the air. It does this by making the air travel farther over its curved upper surface than it does under the lower, flat surface. As a result, air pressure is higher beneath than above the airfoil. This creates a sort of upward suction which makes the wing or rotor rise, together with the aircraft. The illustration above shows a cross section of an airfoil and the pattern of the airflow around it.

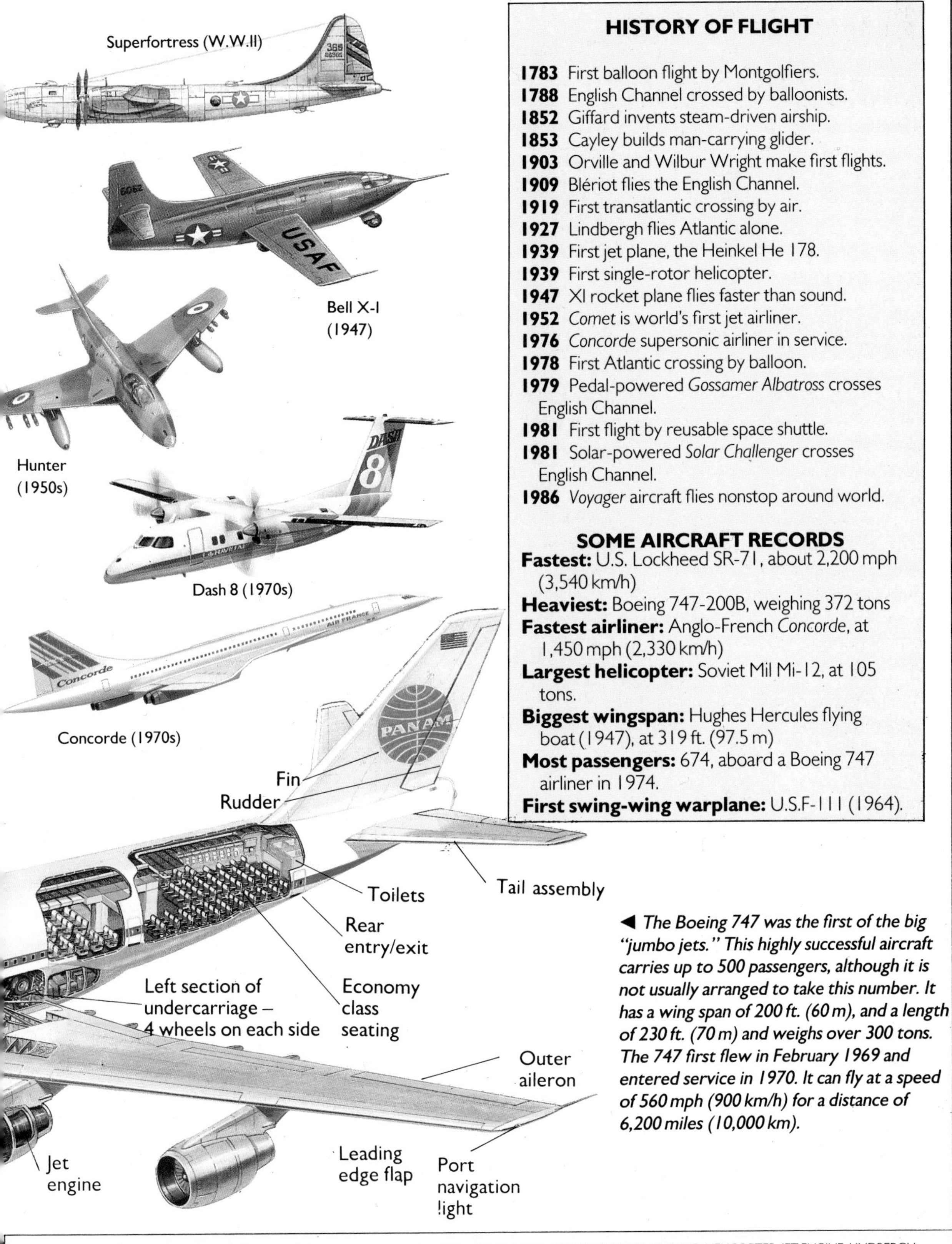

HISTORY OF FLIGHT

1783 First balloon flight by Montgolfiers.
1788 English Channel crossed by balloonists.
1852 Giffard invents steam-driven airship.
1853 Cayley builds man-carrying glider.
1903 Orville and Wilbur Wright make first flights.
1909 Blériot flies the English Channel.
1919 First transatlantic crossing by air.
1927 Lindbergh flies Atlantic alone.
1939 First jet plane, the Heinkel He 178.
1939 First single-rotor helicopter.
1947 XI rocket plane flies faster than sound.
1952 *Comet* is world's first jet airliner.
1976 *Concorde* supersonic airliner in service.
1978 First Atlantic crossing by balloon.
1979 Pedal-powered *Gossamer Albatross* crosses English Channel.
1981 First flight by reusable space shuttle.
1981 Solar-powered *Solar Challenger* crosses English Channel.
1986 *Voyager* aircraft flies nonstop around world.

SOME AIRCRAFT RECORDS

Fastest: U.S. Lockheed SR-71, about 2,200 mph (3,540 km/h)
Heaviest: Boeing 747-200B, weighing 372 tons
Fastest airliner: Anglo-French *Concorde*, at 1,450 mph (2,330 km/h)
Largest helicopter: Soviet Mil Mi-12, at 105 tons.
Biggest wingspan: Hughes Hercules flying boat (1947), at 319 ft. (97.5 m)
Most passengers: 674, aboard a Boeing 747 airliner in 1974.
First swing-wing warplane: U.S.F-111 (1964).

◀ *The Boeing 747 was the first of the big "jumbo jets." This highly successful aircraft carries up to 500 passengers, although it is not usually arranged to take this number. It has a wing span of 200 ft. (60 m), and a length of 230 ft. (70 m) and weighs over 300 tons. The 747 first flew in February 1969 and entered service in 1970. It can fly at a speed of 560 mph (900 km/h) for a distance of 6,200 miles (10,000 km).*

For more information turn to these articles: AIR FORCE; AIRPORT; BALLOON AND AIRSHIP; BLERIOT; GLIDING; HELICOPTER; JET ENGINE; LINDBERGH; PROPELLER; RADAR, and WRIGHT, ORVILLE and WILBUR.

ALABAMA

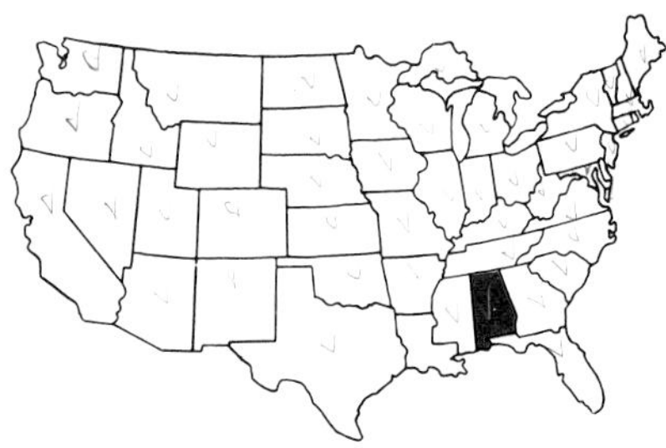

Capital: Montgomery
Population: 4,040,587
Area: 51,705 sq. mi. (133,915 sq. km)
State flower: Camellia
State bird: Yellowhammer
State tree: Southern Pine
Statehood: December 14, 1819, 22nd state

Airship *See* Balloon and Airship

Alabama

Alabama is one of the Southern states. It lies on the Gulf of Mexico between GEORGIA and MISSISSIPPI. It is a major industrial state because of its rich resources of iron ore and coal. Birmingham, the state's largest city, is the iron and steel capital of the South. Mobile, at the mouth of the Mobile River, is a busy seaport.

For a hundred years Alabama depended on cotton. This is still an important crop, but the state's mild climate also produces crops ranging from soybeans to corn and peanuts to peaches. Alabama has long, hot summers, mild winters, and rainfall is usually abundant.

The French made the first settlement on Mobile Bay in 1701. The Confederate States were organized in 1861 in Montgomery, the state's first capital.

Alaska

Alaska is the most northerly state in the United States. It is also the largest, though it has fewer people than any other state. About a third of Alaska lies north of the Arctic Circle. At its westernmost point, the state is only 50 miles (80 km) from the Soviet Union. Most of Alaska's people live in Anchorage, the largest city, Fairbanks, and Juneau, the capital.

Alaska used to rely on a few industries such as fish-

▼ *Rockets on display at the George C. Marshall Space Flight Center in Huntsville, Alabama.*
Below right: Mount McKinley in Alaska rises to 20,320 ft. (6,194 m). It is the highest mountain in the United States.

ing and lumbering, but in 1969 vast deposits of oil were discovered. The oil industry is now the state's largest.

Vitus Bering, a Danish explorer working for Russia, was the first European to land in Alaska, in 1741. In 1867, the United States bought Alaska from the Soviet Union for only $7.2 million—about 2 cents an acre! Alaska's gold rush, from 1899 to 1902, brought thousands of prospectors to Nome and Fairbanks. In 1912, Congress made Alaska a U.S. territory.

ALASKA

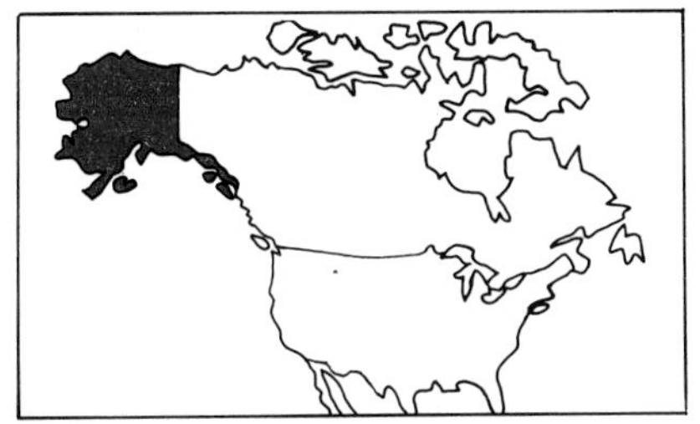

Capital: Juneau
Population: 550,043
Area: 591,004 sq. mi. (1,530,700 sq. km)
State flower: Forget-me-not
State bird: Willow Ptarmigan
State tree: Sitka Spruce
Statehood: January 3, 1959
49th state

Albania

Albania is a small, rugged country that lies between Yugoslavia and Greece on the eastern shore of the Adriatic Sea. Most Albanians live in small, remote mountain villages. Albanian farmers grow wheat, barley, tobacco, and cotton. Beneath the ground there are deposits of chrome, copper, iron, oil, and natural gas. Albania was ruled by Turkey for over 400 years. After World War II it became a communist state, but by 1991 the country was moving away from communism.

ALBANIA

Government: Communist
Capital: Tirana
Area: 11,100 sq. miles (28,748 sq. km)
Population: 3,250,000
Language: Albanian
Currency: Lek

Albatross

The albatross is a large seabird that spends most of its time in the air over the oceans. The wandering albatross can have a wingspan of over 11 ft. (3.5 m), the largest span of any bird. Most albatrosses live in regions south of the equator, where they soar gracefully over the waves. They come ashore only to breed or in stormy weather. Albatrosses will follow ships for hundreds of miles, picking up scraps of food thrown overboard.

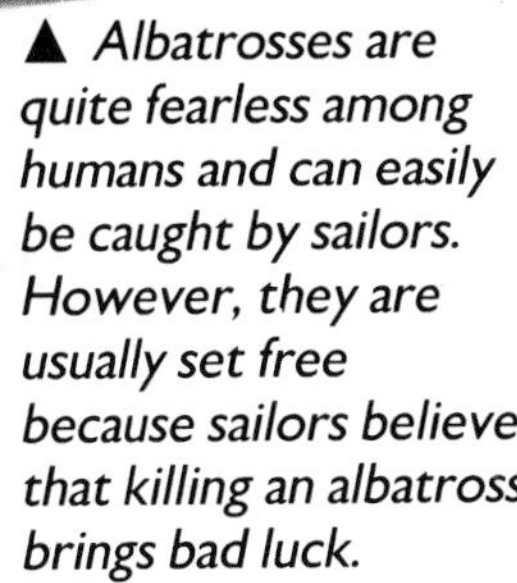

▲ *Albatrosses are quite fearless among humans and can easily be caught by sailors. However, they are usually set free because sailors believe that killing an albatross brings bad luck.*

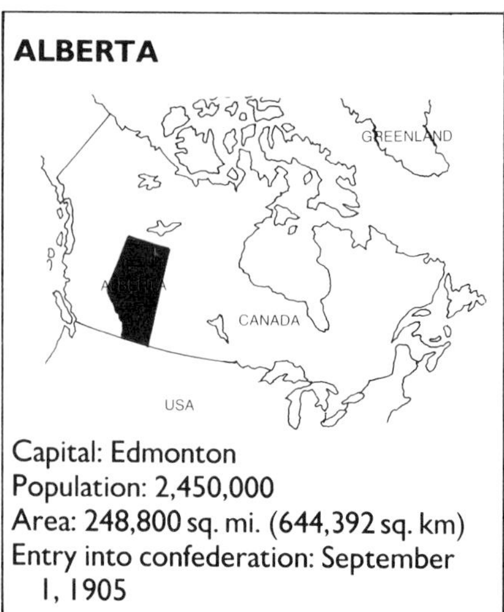

Capital: Edmonton
Population: 2,450,000
Area: 248,800 sq. mi. (644,392 sq. km)
Entry into confederation: September 1, 1905

Alberta

Alberta is the westernmost of Canada's prairie provinces. It has grown quickly in population and industrial production. Just over a century ago, buffalo roamed the wide prairies in the southeast. Today, vast wheatfields and large cattle ranches cover hundreds of square miles. Among the Rocky Mountains in the southwest are national parks, game preserves, and mineral springs. Millions of tourists come to visit Banff National Park. Alberta has coal, oil, and natural gas in abundance. The province's oil resources are vast; a deposit near Lake Athabasca in the north is thought to contain the world's largest single reserve. Most people live in Edmonton or Calgary.

▼ *An alchemist and his assistant. Alchemists experimented with the impossible task of changing cheap metals into gold.*

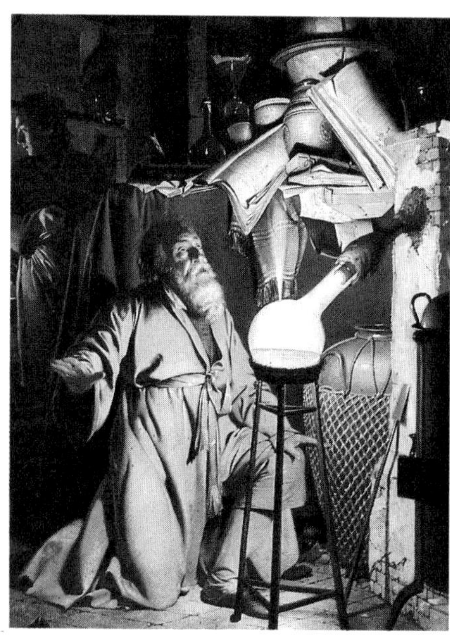

Alchemy

The chemistry of the MIDDLE AGES was called alchemy. It was a strange mixture of magic, science, and religion. The people who practiced alchemy dreamed of producing a magic substance which they called the "philosopher's stone." This substance would be able to change cheap metals such as lead into gold; it would also cure diseases and keep people young. Needless to say, the alchemists never found the philosopher's stone, but in their search they learned a great deal about chemistry and invented apparatus that chemists still use today.

Alcohol

There are many different kinds of alcohol. The kind we know best is the alcohol in wines and spirits such as whiskey and gin which can make people intoxicated.

Alcohol is formed by a process called FERMENTATION. In fermentation, YEASTS act on the sugar in grain and fruit to produce alcohol. If strong alcohol is needed, the liquid has to be DISTILLED.

Alcohols are found in many things. They are used in the making of perfumes, drugs, and antiseptics. They dissolve oils, fats, and plastics. The alcohol called glycol is used as an antifreeze in car radiators because, like all alcohols, it has a low freezing point.

Alcott, Louisa May

Louisa May Alcott (1832–1888) is famous for writing one book—*Little Women*. It tells the story of a New England family during the Civil War and is based on the life of her own family. Louisa herself is the book's heroine, Jo, while her real-life sisters are the other characters in the book. *Little Women* was published in 1869 and was an immediate success.

Alexander the Great

Alexander the Great (356–323B.C.) was a ruler of GREECE and one of the greatest generals who ever lived. The son of Philip of Macedon, the young Alexander was taught by Aristotle, the famous Greek philosopher. His father taught him to win battles.

Alexander conquered the Greek city-states after he became king when Philip died in 336 B.C. He then marched east to conquer Persia, which was at that time the greatest empire in the world. By 327, Alexander's empire stretched from Greece to India. When his armies reached India they were worn out from marching and fighting. Alexander had to turn back. When he reached BABYLON he became ill with a fever and died. He was only 33. Alexander's body was carried back to Alexandria, the great city he had founded in EGYPT. There it was placed in a magnificent tomb.

When Alexander was a boy, he tamed the great and spirited Bucephalus, a horse that no one else dared to ride. The famous horse carried Alexander as far as India, where it died. Alexander built a city over its grave and named the city Bucephala. The city has been lost, but people think it is somewhere in modern Pakistan.

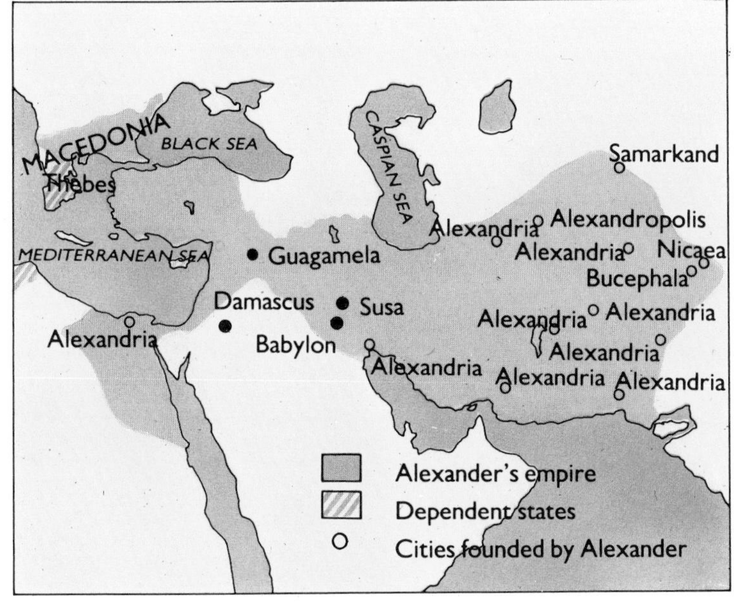

◀ *As can be seen on this map, most of the cities founded by Alexander were named after himself. The above picture of the great general is part of a mosaic found at Pompeii in Italy.*

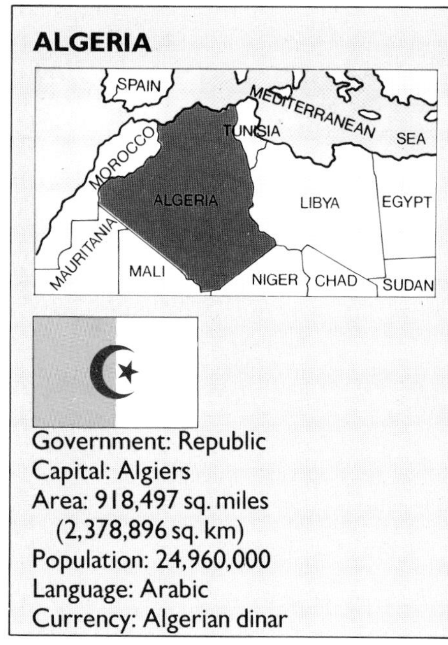

ALGERIA
SPAIN
MEDITERRANEAN
SEA
TUNISIA
MOROCCO
ALGERIA
LIBYA
EGYPT
MAURITANIA
MALI
NIGER
CHAD
SUDAN
Government: Republic
Capital: Algiers
Area: 918,497 sq. miles (2,378,896 sq. km)
Population: 24,960,000
Language: Arabic
Currency: Algerian dinar

Algebra

Algebra is a branch of mathematics in which letters stand for numbers. A letter can represent one number at one time and an entirely different number at another time. Algebra also uses signs to represent connections between letters.

Algeria

The large African country of Algeria covers an area nearly twice the size of Alaska. The great Sahara Desert covers most of Algeria, and few people live there. Most Algerians live in a narrow strip along the Mediterranean. Algiers is the largest city.

Many nations have controlled Algeria. The French captured the country in 1830 and stayed there until the Algerians rebelled in 1954. The country won its independence in 1962 after a war.

Most of Algeria's wealth comes from oil, natural gas, and other minerals.

Alligator and Crocodile

The alligator is a large reptile that belongs to the same family as the crocodile. There are two species: one is the American alligator of the southeastern U.S.; the other is the smaller Chinese alligator that

▼ *Crocodiles are sometimes bred for their skins to make shoes, handbags, and other articles. This is a crocodile farm in Zimbabwe.*

lives in the YANGTZE RIVER. Alligators look very much like crocodiles, but have broader, flatter heads with rounded snouts.

Crocodiles are clumsy on land, but in the water they move swiftly without a sound. They hunt fish, turtles, and water mammals. Crocodiles and alligators lay their eggs in nests or holes in the ground.

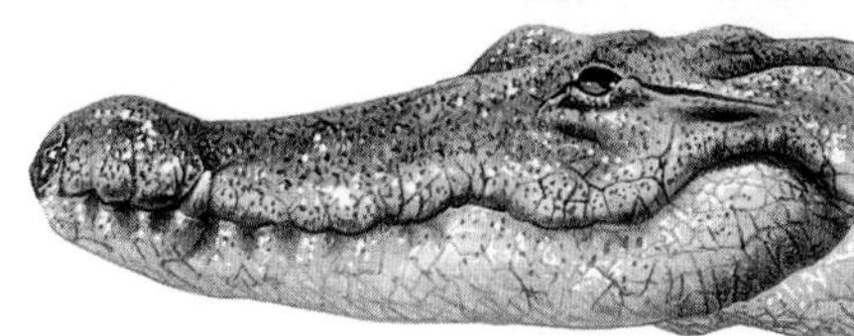

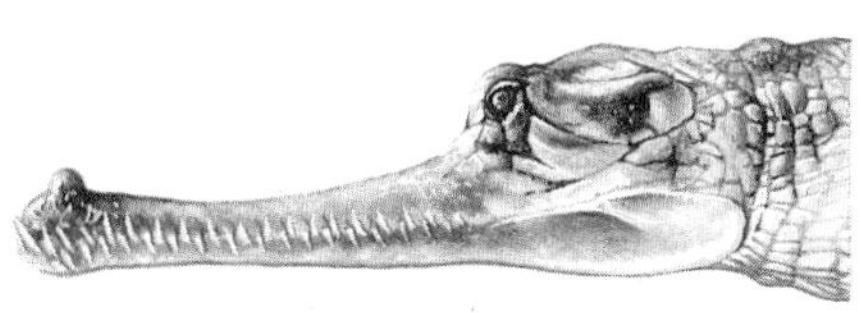

▲ *When the crocodile (top) closes its jaws, the fourth tooth in its lower jaw sticks out. The alligator (center) has heavier jaws than its relative the gharial (bottom).*

Alloy

An alloy is a mixture of two or more METALS. The mixture is usually more useful than each metal by itself. For example, a soft metal such as COPPER can be strengthened by adding ZINC to it to form *brass*, or TIN to form BRONZE, both of which are strong metals.

USEFUL ALLOYS

Alloy	Made mostly of	Some uses
Steel	Iron, carbon and other elements	Cars, girders, tools, etc.
Brass	Copper and zinc	Gears, propellers, scientific instruments, etc.
Bronze	Copper and tin	Scientific instruments, bells, etc.
Pewter	Tin, antimony, lead, and copper	Household utensils
Dentist's amalgam	Mercury and copper	Teeth fillings
Cupronickel	Nickel and copper	"Silver" coins
Invar	Nickel and iron	Precision instruments, watch balance wheels
Sterling silver	Silver and copper	Tableware

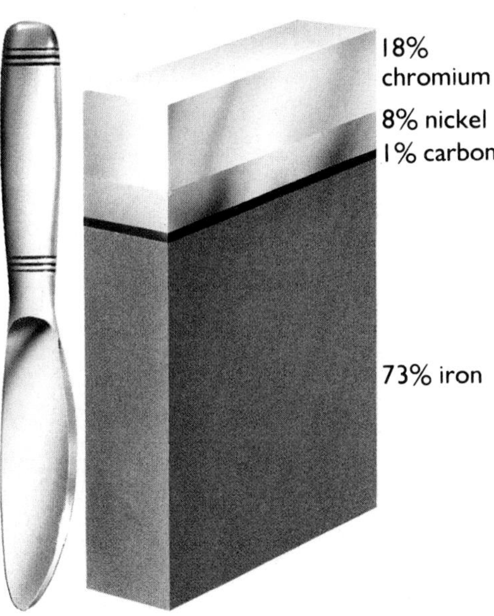

▲ *Pure iron is not very strong and rusts easily. It is mixed with chromium, nickel, and carbon to make stainless steel, the alloy used for eating utensils.*

Alphabet

An alphabet is a group of letters, or symbols, used to write down a language. The word "alphabet" comes from the names of the first two letters in the Greek alphabet: *alpha* and *beta*. The 26 letters in the English alphabet mostly come from the Roman alphabet of 2,500 years ago. Other alphabets in common use today include the Greek, Arabic, Hebrew, and Russian or *Cyrillic* alphabets. Most contain symbols for vowels (soft sounds like "a" and "e") and consonants (hard sounds like "t" and "s"). But the Arabic and Hebrew alphabets have consonants only. Vowels are expressed by marks above and below the consonants.

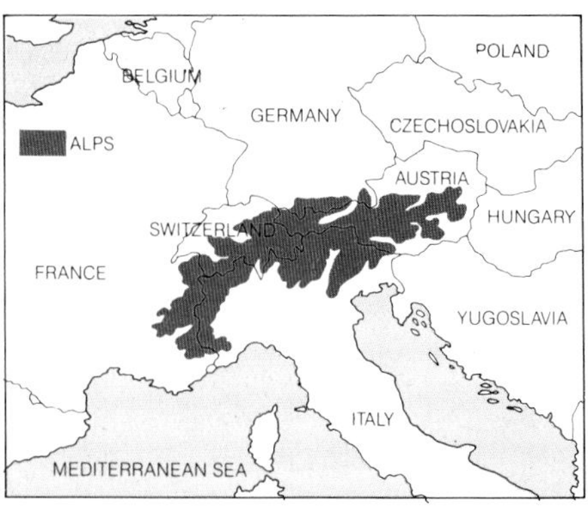

Alps

The Alps are the greatest mountain range in EUROPE. They are centered in SWITZERLAND, but they stretch from France all the way to Yugoslavia. Mont Blanc, 15,770 ft. (4,807 m) high, is the highest peak in the Alps. There are many lakes in the valleys; the largest is Lake Geneva.

The Alps attract many tourists. They go to ski and climb, and to admire the magnificent scenery.

► *The Alpine region is known for its wildlife—rare flowers like the white edelweiss, shown here, and birds such as the golden eagle.*

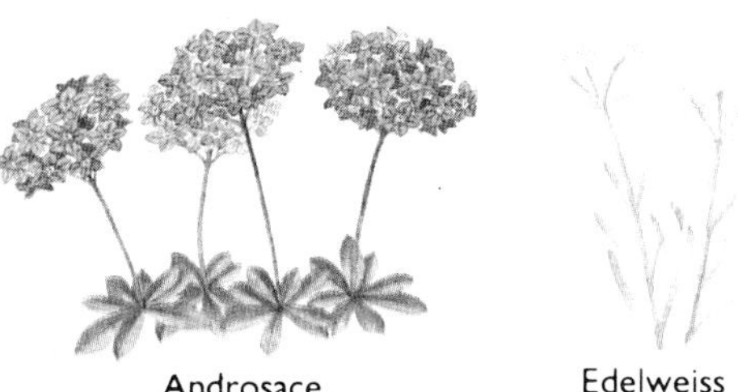

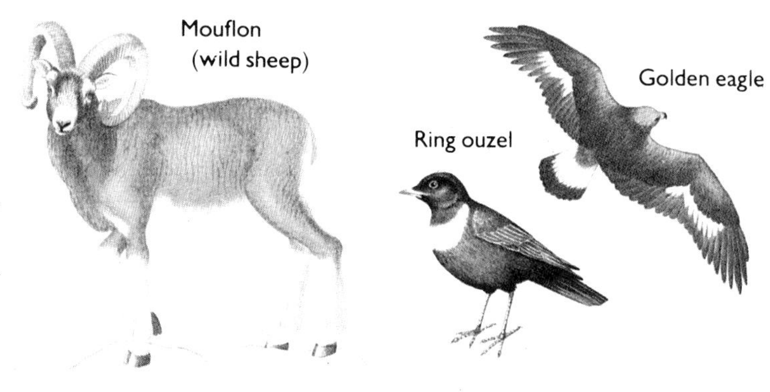

▼ *Because aluminum is a good conductor of electricity and heat, it is used for electric power cables and cooking foil. Its lightness is the reason for its use in aircraft and tennis rackets.*

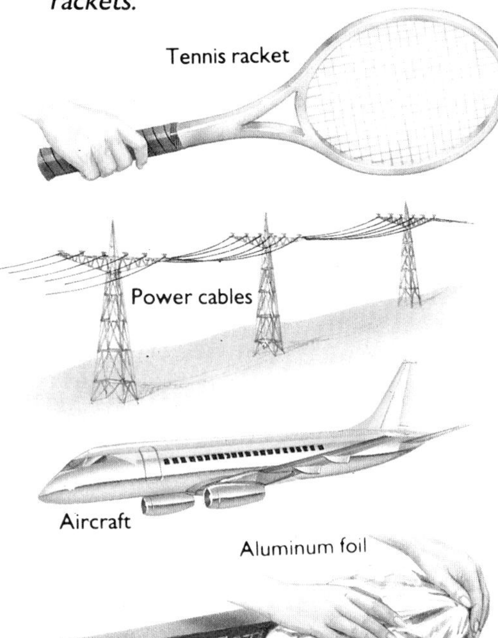

Aluminum

There is more aluminum in the Earth's crust than any other metal. But until less than 200 years ago no one had ever seen this silvery metal. When aluminum was first used it was much more expensive than gold because it was very difficult to separate the metal from the materials it was mixed up with in the earth.

Most aluminum is now produced from an ore called bauxite. The bauxite is treated with chemicals and placed in a big electric furnace. An electric current is passed through and aluminum falls to the bottom of the furnace.

Aluminum is light—it weighs only a third as much as steel. It and its ALLOYS are especially useful where lightness and strength are important. It is also a good conductor of heat and electricity.

Amazon River

The Amazon is the mightiest river in South America, and, at a length of 4,000 miles (6,437 km), is the second longest in the world, after the Nile. It flows from Peru through Brazil to the Atlantic Ocean. Almost the whole of the Amazon basin is dense tropical forest. In the 1540s a Spanish explorer saw female Indian warriors on the Amazon's banks, so the river was named after the Amazons (female warriors) of Greek legends.

The Amazon pours out so much fresh water into the Atlantic that more than 100 miles (160 km) out at sea from the river's mouth the ocean's water is still fresh. The great river is one to six miles ($1\frac{1}{2}$ to 10 km) wide along most of its length. In places it is so wide that a person on one bank cannot see the opposite side of the river. The average depth of the river is about 40 feet (12 m). More than 200 tributaries flow into the Amazon.

America

The word "America" is often used to mean the United States, but it originally described a much larger area which today is more properly called the Americas. The Americas include North America, Central America, and South America, and the islands of the Caribbean.

American Colonies

The Spanish were the first European nation to settle in North America. In 1565 they established a fort at St. Augustine, Florida. It was not until after 1600 that the English came. But the English, unlike the Spanish, French, and Dutch, had really come to stay. They gained control of most of the Atlantic coast from New England to Georgia, an area that was to become the original 13 states.

In 1607, Jamestown Colony was founded. Then, in 1620, the Pilgrims set sail from Plymouth, England, to found Plymouth Colony in Massachusetts. Ten years later, another group of Puritans braved the wild Atlantic to set up colonies in Boston and Salem. By 1700, most of the East Coast was dotted with settlements. The Native Americans often lent a helping hand to the colonists, but some tribes were not so friendly. They were angry because the newcomers had taken their hunting grounds.

Two main ways of life gradually grew up. In the northern colonies, people worked their own small farms and made their own furniture and clothing. They were fishermen, trappers, and traders. Farther south, people owned much larger estates, called plantations. They grew cotton, tobacco, or rice. Plantation owners often lived in great mansions, while the fields were worked by black slaves. Most settlers were English, but some were German, French, Dutch, Swedish, Irish, and Scottish.

▲ *The* Mayflower *brought the first Pilgrims from England. They landed at Plymouth Bay on December 26, 1620.*

American History

Up to 1763, the American colonies had a great deal of independence and were satisfied to be under English rule. In tha year, however, the French and Indian War ended and Englar gained Canada and all the French lands west of the Alleghenies. Because the American colonists had not helped much in the war England decided that they could not settle in the new lands. An England levied a whole new series of taxes that the colonists thought were very unfair. Relations grew worse, and in 1776 th colonists declared their independence. (See Boston, Declaration of Independence, Revolutionary War.)

The Revolutionary War ended after the Battle of Yorktown 1781. The United States was an independent nation. It was not until 1787 that fifty-five of the most important men in the coun met to work out a new constitution. These men included Benjamin Franklin, George Washington, Alexander Hamilton, and James Madison. The Constitution they produced is still the basis of the United States system of governmer George Washington became the first president in 1789.

During the next 20 years Americans pushed westward into t land west of the Appalachians. When Thomas Jefferson bough the Louisiana Territory from France in 1803, he doubled the nation's size in one stroke.

During the 1800s the British navy controlled the seas and beg to interfere with American shipping. This, plus the desire of son congressmen to annex Canada, led to the War of 1812. During the war the British burned much of the new capital, Washingtor but Andrew Jackson decisively defeated them at New Orlear

After the war, the westward expansion speeded up. A new state was admitted almost every year. Then the issue of slavery began to divide the nation. The North wanted to abolish slavery the South needed slave labor on the plantations. The victory of the anti-slavery candidate, Abraham Lincoln, in the presidenti election of 1860 helped to start the Civil War. (See Civil War.

▲ *A medicine man of the Iowa Plains Indians. Next to buffalo hunting, warfare was the chief activity of the Plains Indians.*

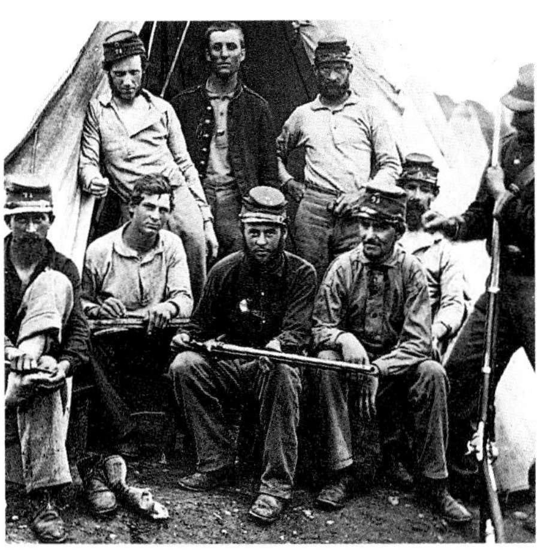

▲ *The Civil War has been called the first modern war. The men who fought in it were the first to use breechloading weapons, which were loaded from behind the barrel instead of at the muzzle. The telegraph and railroads were used for the first time in warfare.*

► *On May 10, 1869, the tracks of the Central Pacific Railroad (left) and the Union Pacific Railroad (right) met at Promontory, Utah. At last, a rail line ran across the United States from coast to coast.*

The years after the Civil War were difficult, but soon the untry began to prosper—especially in the North. Railroads ead west, opening up vast areas for land development, cattle, nbering, and mining. By 1890, the United States stretched from Atlantic to the Pacific.

When World War I broke out in 1914, people in the United ates thought they could avoid becoming involved. But by 1917 ey were drawn in on the side of Britain and France against rmany.

After the defeat of Germany, the United States became more d more prosperous. But in 1929 the stock market crashed and Great Depression began. Millions of people were employed. The government, under Franklin Roosevelt, started ny new projects. Dams, public buildings, and bridges were nstructed to provide jobs, and the country slowly recovered.

World War II broke out in 1939 between Adolf Hitler's rmany and then Italy on one side and France, Britain, and their es on the other. The United States did not want to enter other war, but in 1941 the Japanese, who had become the allies Germany, bombed Pearl Harbor, Hawaii. From that moment, United States was at war.

When the war ended with the dropping of atom bombs on two anese cities, everyone decided that there must never again be a orld war. The United Nations was founded, but U.S. troops re involved in limited wars in Korea and Vietnam. The main reat to world peace was the distrust between the United States d her allies on one side and the U.S.S.R. and the Eastern Bloc es on the other. Each side had built up huge stocks of nuclear naments. Toward the end of the 1980s, however, the Cold ar began to thaw slightly as the United States and the Soviet ion signed agreements to reduce certain types of nuclear apons. In the 1990s, the collapse of communism further eeded the thaw.

The United States is the wealthiest nation on earth, and U.S. chnology advances by leaps and bounds. On July 20, 1969, two nericans became the first men to set foot on the Moon. The essage they left there said: "We came in peace for all mankind."

▲ *A World War I recruiting poster for the U.S. army.*

▼ *General Norman Schwarzkopf led the Allied forces in the Gulf War of 1991.*

▼ *Man in space. An astronaut stands on the space shuttle's remote manipulator arm.*

For more information, turn to these articles: AMERICAN COLONIES; AMERICAN INDIANS; BOSTON; CIVIL RIGHTS; CIVIL WAR; CONGRESS; CONSTITUTION, UNITED STATES; DECLARATION OF INDEPENDENCE; FRENCH AND INDIAN WAR; INDEPENDENCE DAY; LOUISIANA PURCHASE; PILGRIM SETTLERS; PRESIDENTS; REVOLUTIONARY WAR; SPANISH AMERICAN WAR; and UNITED STATES OF AMERICA.

Native Americans were the first people to grow potatoes, corn, cocoa, tomatoes, tobacco, and many kinds of beans.

Some famous American Indians were Sitting Bull, Pocahontas, and Tecumseh.

American Indians

American Indians are the native peoples of the Americas—that is, the first people to live here. When Christopher COLUMBUS reached America in 1492 he thought he had arrived in the "Indies" (Asia), so the Native Americans were mistakenly called "Indians."

The native peoples of the Americas are thought to have crossed to the North American continent from Asia about 20,000 years ago. Very gradually, over the centuries, they spread through North America and down into what is now CENTRAL and SOUTH AMERICA. They developed different ways of life according to where they lived. "Native Americans" now usually refers to the Indians of North America.

There, in the eastern woodlands, the Iroquois and Algonquin tribes hunted deer and built domed wigwams (huts) of wood and bark. On the Great Plains, tribes such as the Sioux and Cheyenne lived off the huge herds of BISON which they hunted. In the deserts of the southwest, the Acoma and Hopi tribes built villages of *adobe* (dried mud bricks). Along the coast of the Pacific northwest, tribes such as the Haida and Kwakiutl built huge totem poles of elaborately carved wood.

When Europeans began to settle in America, conflict broke out as they invaded the tribal hunting grounds. Many Native Americans were killed or forced to move farther west. By the late 1800s almost all the tribes had been given land on special reservations by the U.S. government. Today many Native Americans are working to gain equal opportunities for themselves as American citizens.

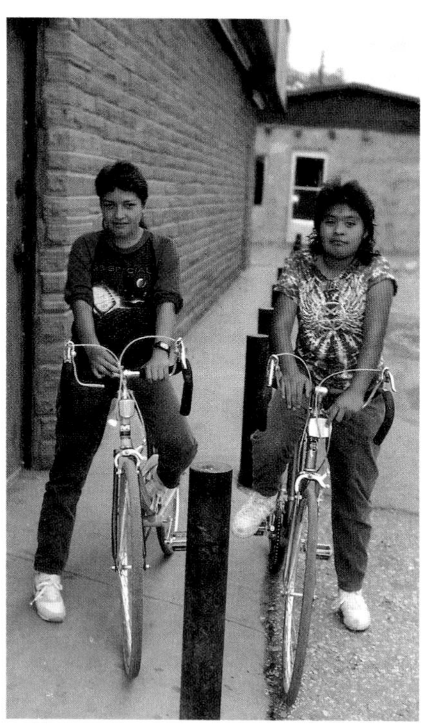

▲ *In the United States today it is often difficult to tell just who is a Native American. These teenagers are Zunis of New Mexico.*

▶ *An old painting of a Sioux village. It shows women working on buffalo skins.*

American Revolution *See* Revolutionary War, American

Amphibian

Amphibians are animals such as FROGS, TOADS, salamanders, and newts. They can live in water or on land, but most of them start their lives in water. Amphibians are cold-blooded creatures. They do not drink like other animals, but absorb water directly through their skins. For this reason they must keep their skins moist. Amphibians were one of the earliest groups of animals on Earth.

All amphibians have backbones. Nearly all of them lay their eggs in water, in a layer of jelly which protects them. When the young amphibians hatch, they feed on algae (tiny water plants). A young frog at this stage is called a tadpole. It breathes the oxygen dissolved in water through gills. After two or three months the tadpole begins to change into an adult. Its tail gradually disappears, and its gills turn into LUNGS. Hind legs and then front legs appear. The little frog leaves the water and spends the rest of its life as an air-breathing adult. But it must return to the water to mate and lay its eggs.

▲ *Amphibians such as the toad and newt are creatures that are at home both on dry land and in the water. All amphibians have tails when they are babies. Some kinds, such as toads, lose their tails as they grow, but others, such as newts, keep them all their lives. The toad has stubbier legs than a frog, and its body is usually wider and flatter. It also has a rougher skin than a frog.*

Andersen, Hans Christian

Hans Christian Andersen (1805–1875) was a Danish storyteller, whose fairy tales, such as *The Little Mermaid* and *The Ugly Duckling*, are still popular all over the world.

Andes

The Andes mountain range is the longest in the world. It stretches for more than 4,350 miles (7,000 km) down the west side of South America, running the whole length of the continent. Several peaks are more than 20,000 ft. (6,000 m) high, and Aconcagua, on the border between Argentina and Chile, is the highest mountain in the Americas at 22,834 ft. (6,960 m). Many of the peaks are active volcanoes. The Andes are rich in minerals such as copper, silver, and gold.

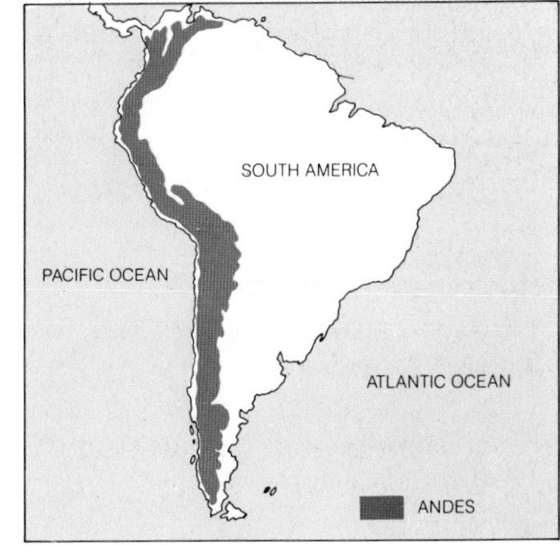

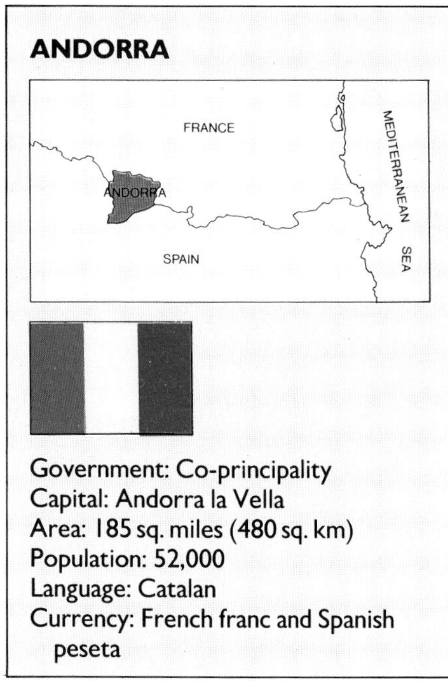

Government: Co-principality
Capital: Andorra la Vella
Area: 185 sq. miles (480 sq. km)
Population: 52,000
Language: Catalan
Currency: French franc and Spanish peseta

Andorra

Andorra is a tiny country on the border between France and Spain. It is so small that you could almost fit two Andorras into New York City. Since 1278 the principality of Andorra has been ruled jointly by the bishop of Urgel in Spain and a French ruler. The main industry is tourism. The capital is Andorra la Vella, and there are only 52,000 people in the country.

Angle

An angle is formed when two straight lines meet. The size of all angles is measured in degrees. The angle that forms the corner of a square is called a *right* angle and has 90 degrees. An *acute* angle is less than 90 degrees; an *obtuse* angle is between 90 and 180 degrees.

Angola

The People's Republic of Angola is a large country facing the Atlantic Ocean in southwestern Africa. Portugal claimed the region in 1482.

Black Angolans rebelled against the Portuguese in 1960 and fighting broke out. In 1975 Portugal granted the Angolans full independence. A fierce struggle then began between rival Angolan factions, some of them aided by Russian, Cuban, South African, and United States arms and troops. The 14-year war ended in 1989 when the government and the rebels agreed to a cease-fire.

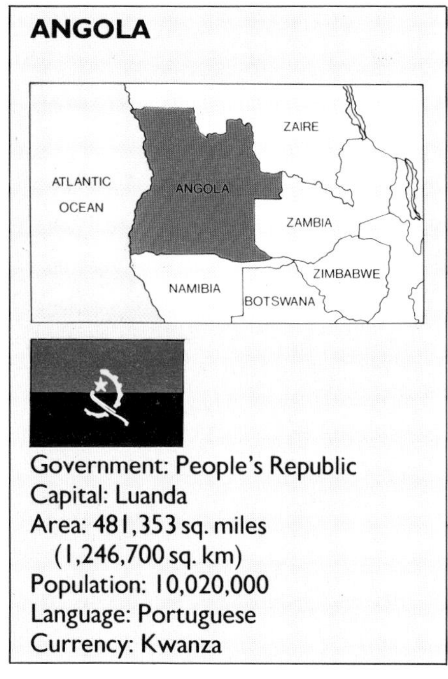

Government: People's Republic
Capital: Luanda
Area: 481,353 sq. miles (1,246,700 sq. km)
Population: 10,020,000
Language: Portuguese
Currency: Kwanza

Animals

An animal is any living thing that is not a PLANT. No one knows how many different kinds of animal there are on Earth; hundreds of new kinds are discovered every year. The biggest difference between animals and plants is in the way they get their food. Animals eat plants or other animals. Plants make their food out of substances taken in through their roots or leaves. Animals can also, unlike plants, move about at some time in their lives.

Some animals such as the tiny amoeba reproduce by just splitting in two. In most other animals the female produces eggs that are fertilized by the male. Creatures such as the cod produce millions of eggs, of which only a very few ever hatch and even fewer reach maturity. These animals never see or care for their young. Other animals such as elephants and human beings develop the fertilized egg inside their bodies, and the mother feeds and cares for her infant for months or years.

▼ *Below are some common vertebrates (animals with backbones) and invertebrates (those without). Since invertebrates have no internal bones, some of them have an outside shell for protection.*

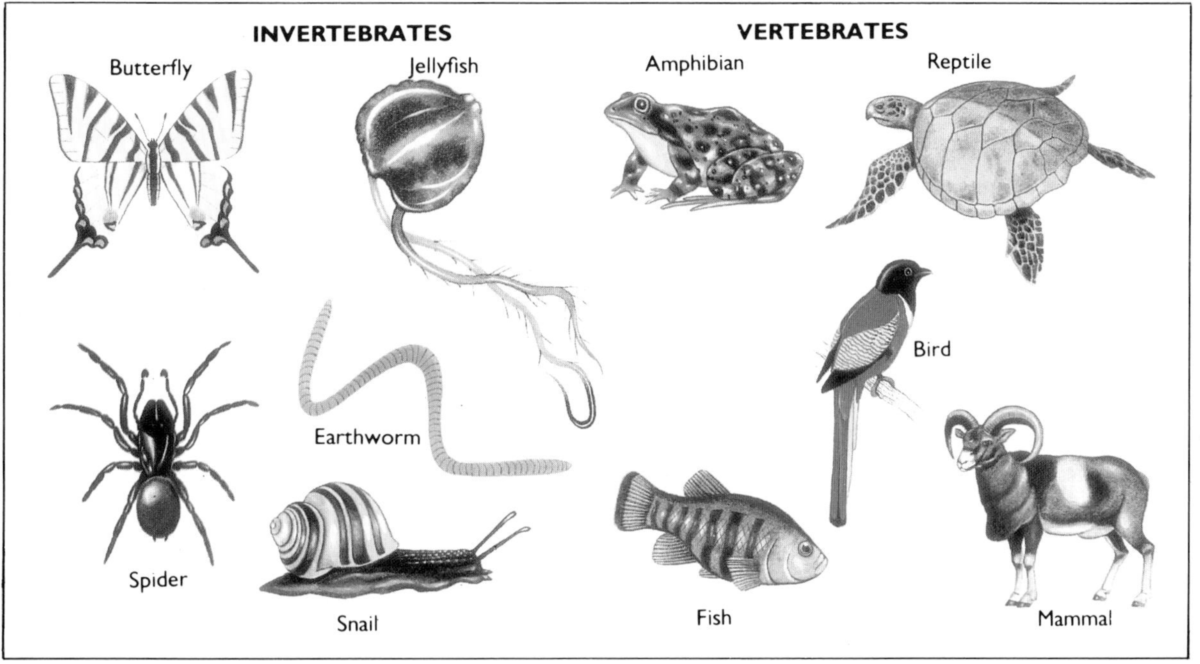

Ant

Ants are "social" insects—they live together in colonies. Some colonies are in heaps of twigs; others are in chambers deep in the ground. Still others are in

▼ *The ant queen lays her eggs (1). Workers take eggs to nursery, where they hatch into larvae (2). Larvae are fed by workers (3). Larvae spin cocoons, in which they become pupae (4). Young ants come out of cocoons (5). Waste is taken away and stored (6).*

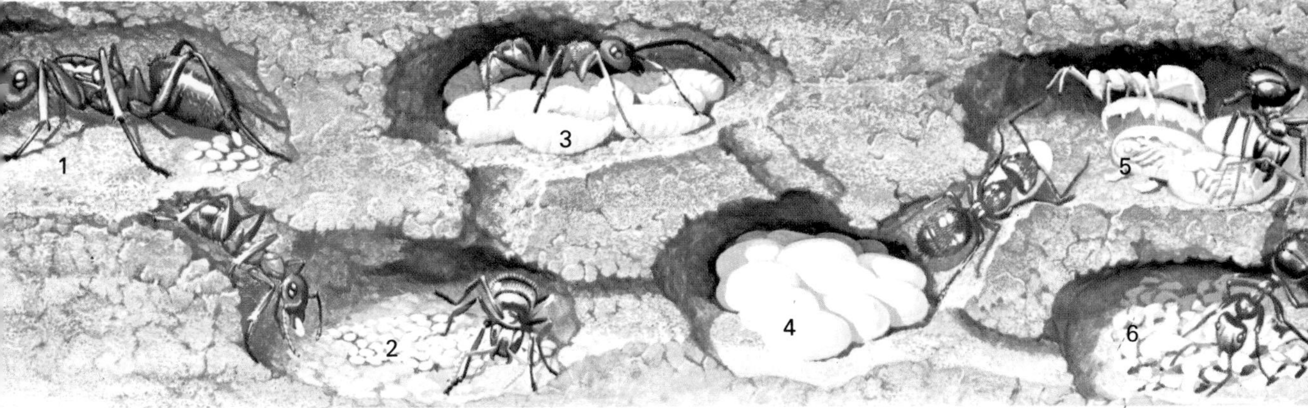

hills of earth or sand. There are three types of ant: males, queens which lay eggs, and workers or females that do not mate or lay eggs.

Fierce army ants march across country in a great horde that may have as many as several million ants. They devour anything in their path.

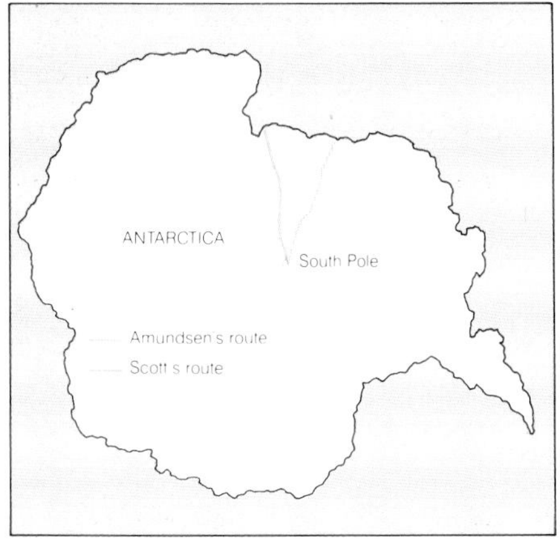

▲ *The Norwegian explorer Roald Amundsen was the first person to reach the South Pole in 1911. He was closely followed by Captain Robert Scott of Britain.*

Antarctic

The Antarctic is the continent that surrounds the SOUTH POLE. It is a vast, cold region, with very little animal or plant life on land. Nearly all of the Antarctic is covered by an ice cap, broken only by a few mountain ranges. This ice cap is as much as 15,000 ft. (4,500 m) thick in places.

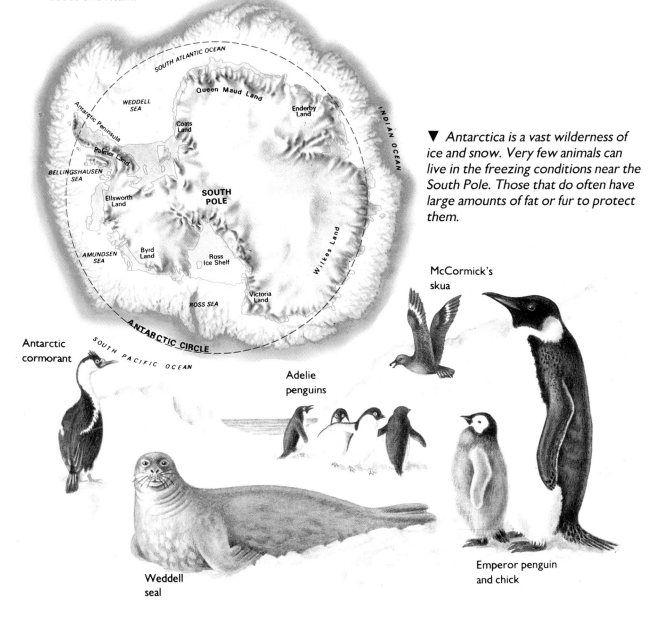

▼ *Antarctica is a vast wilderness of ice and snow. Very few animals can live in the freezing conditions near the South Pole. Those that do often have large amounts of fat or fur to protect them.*

McCormick's skua

Antarctic cormorant

Adelie penguins

Weddell seal

Emperor penguin and chick

Anteater

The anteater of South America is a curious creature with a long, tapering snout. This snout is specially shaped to dig out ants, termites, and grubs from their nests. It catches the insects with its long, whip-like tongue. An anteater may measure over 6 ft. (2 m) from the tip of its tail to its snout. It uses its strong front claws to tear open ant and termite nests.

▲ *Anteaters live in the tropical forests and swamps of South America. They are active only at night.*

Antelope

Antelopes are grazing animals with horns and hoofs. They look a lot like DEER, but are actually related to the goat and the ox. Most antelopes live on the African plains. They are fast runners and often live in large herds, fleeing suddenly at any hint of danger. Some of the best known are the impala, the waterbuck, the hartebeest, the gnu, the eland, and the little dikdik, hardly bigger than a rabbit.

▼ *A male waterbuck, native to the area of Africa south of the Sahara.*

Antibiotics

Antibiotics are substances, produced by living things, that are poisonous to harmful bacteria. For a long time it was thought that any medicine that was able to kill a particular microbe would also kill the patient. Then, early in this century, scientists began to discover drugs that would kill bacteria but do the patient no harm. The most important of these drugs was penicillin, a drug produced by a mold. Penicillin was a "wonder drug" that saved many lives. It was especially useful against pneumonia. The antibiotic streptomycin has almost gotten rid of the disease tuberculosis. Scientists have found many more useful antibiotics that can fight diseases such as whooping cough and typhus.

Antibiotics do not work against viruses, organisms that cause the common cold, flu, mumps, measles, AIDS, and other diseases.

The word "antelope" comes from the Greek *antholopos*, meaning brightness-of-eye. Antelopes' eyes are very large and bulging. This allows the animals to look around without moving their heads.

Antigua and Barbuda

This country is made up of two tiny islands in the Caribbean Sea. Antigua and Barbuda gained inde-

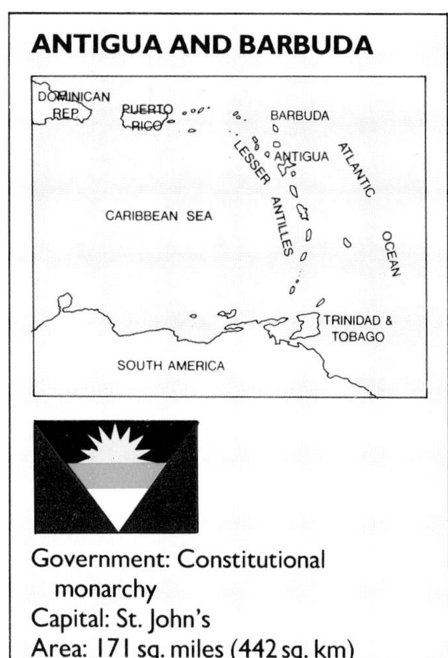

Government: Constitutional monarchy
Capital: St. John's
Area: 171 sq. miles (442 sq. km)
Population: 77,000
Language: English
Currency: East Caribbean dollar

pendence from Britain in 1981, but Queen Elizabeth II is still head of state. The capital is St. John's.

Antigua was discovered by Columbus in 1493, and it was colonized by the British in 1663.

Apartheid

The word "apartheid" is used by the white rulers of SOUTH AFRICA to describe their policy for the separate development of the white and non-white peoples of South Africa. The word is Afrikaans for "apartness." The South African government said apartheid would help the non-whites to be better off by helping themselves. But many people feel that this cannot happen while most power belongs to the whites.

Strict apartheid laws kept whites and non-whites apart, but by the late 1980s the government had taken steps to grant a greater share of government to all sections of the population.

Ape

Apes are our closest animal relatives. We share the same kind of skeleton and have the same kind of blood and catch many similar diseases. Their thumbs are "opposable," as in human hands. This means that they can grasp and pick up objects easily. Apes have large brains, but even the gorilla's brain is only half the size of a person's. Unlike monkeys, apes have no tails. There are four kinds of ape: the GORILLA and CHIMPANZEE are African; ORANGUTANS live

▼ *Apes have highly developed hands and fingers and enjoy swinging from branches.*

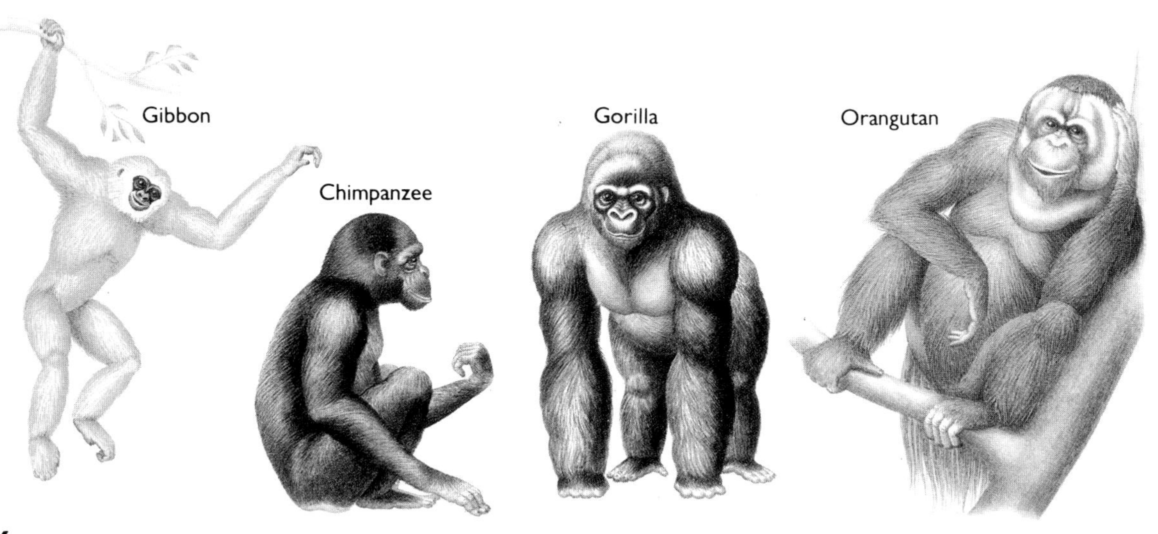

in Borneo and Sumatra; gibbons live in Southeast Asia and the East Indies. Scientists are now agreed that people and apes have evolved from the same ancestors millions of years ago.

The average adult chimpanzee is about as intelligent as a human child before the child learns to take its first steps.

Aquarium

An aquarium is a place where fish and other water animals are kept and studied. Many large public aquariums have become famous for their expertly trained performing animals, such as DOLPHINS and WHALES. A home aquarium is a small tank for fish and other water life, including plants. It is usually made of glass or has a glass side through which its contents can easily be seen. Many people keep beautiful TROPICAL FISH in aquariums that are specially heated to keep the water warm. These fish need very special care and attention.

SEE IT YOURSELF

You can keep many pond creatures at home in a simple glass or plastic aquarium. Put some clean sand or gravel and a few stones on the bottom of the tank (not a fish bowl), together with a few plants. Stand the tank in the light, but not in the full sun, and fill it with pond water. Sticklebacks do well in a simple aquarium. You can add most of the common pond creatures as well, but avoid dragonfly nymphs and the great diving beetle. Feed with fish food and, as a treat, give them water fleas from time to time.

Arabs

Arabs were originally those people who lived in Arabia. But from the A.D. 600s Arabian Arabs, inspired by their new faith, ISLAM, swept through western Asia and North Africa, conquering and settling a huge area. They taught the inhabitants the Arabic language and their Islamic religion. Today an Arab is anyone whose mother tongue is Arabic. This

The Arabic language is spoken by more than 100 million people. Arabic calligraphy (writing) is given a high rank among the arts. In fact, those who excelled in the art of writing far outnumber other artists.

includes Arabic-speaking peoples from countries such as Algeria, Syria, Iraq, and Libya. Muslims in Iran, India, and Pakistan pray in Arabic, but do not use it in everyday speech, so they are not considered Arabs.

The Arabs ruled North Africa and southwest Asia for 900 years, until they were defeated by the Turks in the 1500s. They lived under Turkish rule until World War I. After World War II many Arab countries became extremely rich from the production of huge quantities of valuable OIL. There have been several attempts to unify the Arab nations, but in recent years conflict with Israel has caused a split in the Arab ranks. The oil-producing countries hold great power in the world because of their control of important oil resources.

▲ *The Bedouin Arabs move from place to place with their animals seeking fresh water and pasture. Many Bedouins are now giving up their nomadic life and are being encouraged to live in settlements.*

Archaeology

Archaeology is the study of history through the things that people have made and built. They may include tools, pottery, houses, temples, or graves. Even a garbage pit can help to reveal how people lived. Archaeologists study all these things, from the greatest of monuments to the tiniest pin. Modern archaeology began during the RENAISSANCE, when people became interested in the cultures of ancient

▼ *Excavations in progress on the Greek island of Kithira. Archaeology began in the Mediterranean area, and a lot of work is still being done there.*

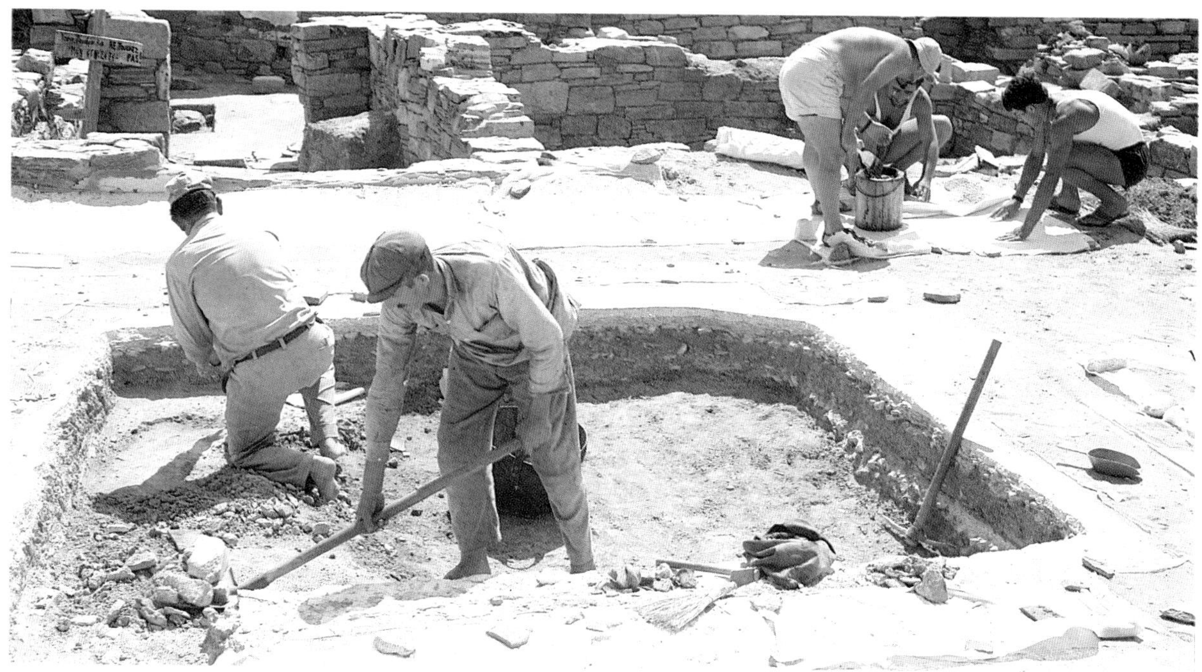

GREECE and ROME. At first, archaeological sites were ransacked for the treasures they contained. But by the early 1800s archaeologists had begun to uncover sites carefully, noting all they found and where they found it. Many exciting and important discoveries were made, including the remains of ancient TROY (1871); the early Greek civilization at Mycenae (1876); and the tomb of the pharoah TUTANKHAMUN in Egypt (1922).

Today, science helps the archaeologist in his work. RADIOCARBON DATING and *dendrochronology* (dating by tree rings) help tell us when particular objects were made. INFRARED and X-RAY photography can show up designs under the rotted surface of a bronze bowl. Archaeology has even gone under the sea. With modern diving equipment, archaeologists can explore sunken wrecks and other long-lost remains of the past.

Archery

Archery is the use of the bow and arrow, once for hunting and warfare, now mostly for sport. No one knows when bows and arrows were first used, but prehistoric man certainly used them to shoot animals for food and to protect himself. Until the discovery of gunpowder, the army with the best archers usually won the battle.

Today, archery is a popular sport. In target shooting the target is 4 ft. (1.2 m) across. The length of the arrow is about 28 ins. (71 cm) for men and slightly shorter for women. Bows are usually made of laminated wood or fiberglass.

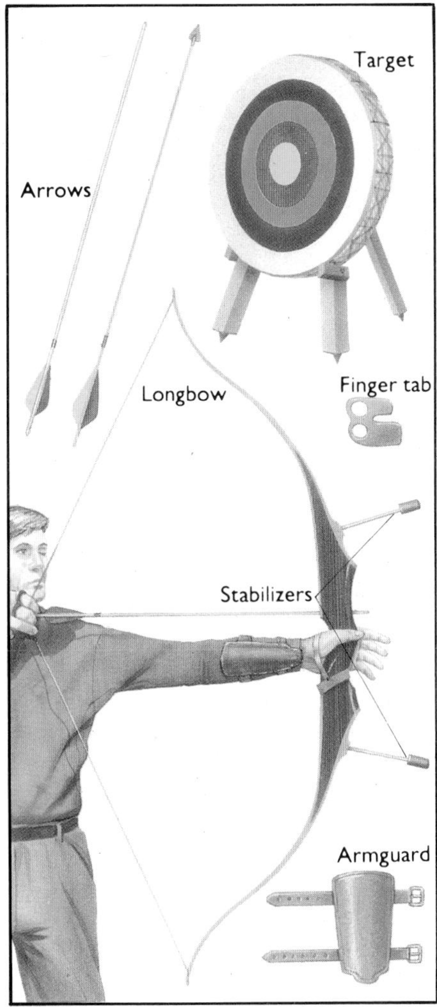

▲ *A variety of equipment is needed for the sport of archery. The armguard is to protect the arm from the bowstring.*

Archimedes

Archimedes (282–212 B.C.) was a famous Greek scientist who lived in Sicily. Among many other things, he discovered Archimedes' Principle, which tells us that if we weigh an object in the air and then weigh it again submerged in a liquid, it will lose weight equal to the weight of the liquid it displaces. Archimedes is supposed to have discovered this when he stepped into a bath full to the brim, and water spilled onto the floor. (See VOLUME.)

Archimedes is supposed to have played a part in the construction of one of the Seven Wonders of the Ancient World. It was the Pharos of Alexandria, a lighthouse designed by Ptolemy I of Egypt. The lighthouse was about 400 ft. (122 m) high, and at the top, fires were kept burning. The fires were reflected by mirrors designed by Archimedes so that they could be seen 30 miles (50 km) away at night.

Ancient Egyptian style (2000–500s B.C.—Temple of Amon at Luxor

Ancient Roman style (100s B.C.–A.D. 400s) —Pont du Gard aqueduct, Nîmes, France

Ancient Greek style (600s–100s B.C.) Temple of Artemis at Ephesus

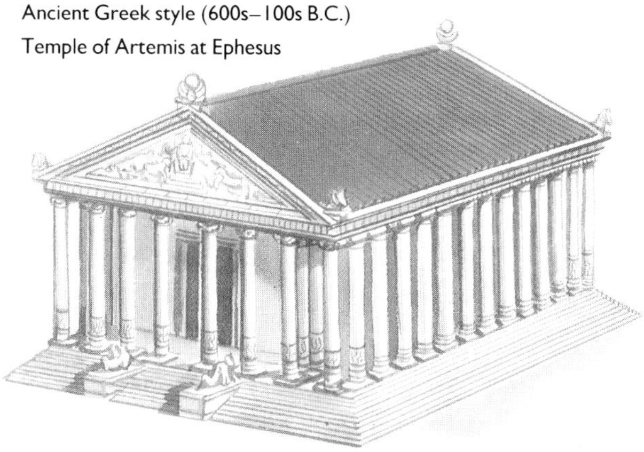

Byzantine style (A.D. 400s–1453) —Santa Sophia church, Istanbul, Turkey

GREEK CAPITALS

These are the three main styles of ancient Greek capital (the decorated top of columns used in their buildings).

Architecture

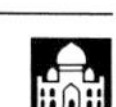

Architecture is the art of designing buildings. If we look at old buildings still standing we can learn a great deal about the people who built them.

Architecture as we know it began about 5,000 years ago in ancient Egypt. The Egyptians built huge pyramids as tombs for their kings, and many of these pyramids still stand.

Greek architecture began to take shape about 600 B.C. and developed into the beautiful styles we can see today on the Acropolis at Athens.

When the Romans conquered Greece they copied Greek architecture. But they soon discovered how to make an arch, so they could build larger, stronger buildings. They also began to make domes for the first time.

About A.D. 800 the Romanesque period of architecture began in Europe. Romanesque architecture at first imitated the style of ancient Rome, but soon took on a style of its own—a style that was strong and heavy. This style was followed by the Gothic. Most of the fine old cathedrals are in the Gothic style. They

Gothic style (mid 1100s–1400s)—Notre Dame cathedral, Paris, France.

Georgian style (1725–1800)—row houses, London, England.

Renaissance style (1400s–1500s)—Florence cathedral, Italy.

Seagram Building, New York, (1950s).

have graceful pointed arches over doors and windows, and in the roof as well. The roof of a Gothic cathedral is usually made of a series of crisscross arches which take the weight of the ceiling. Roofs like this are called *vaulted* roofs.

In about 1400 a new style of architecture began in Italy. This was during the RENAISSANCE (the word means rebirth) and it spread all over Europe. Renaissance architects paid almost as much attention to public buildings and people's houses as they did to churches.

Later, many famous architects changed the building styles to fit the times in which they lived. Sir Christopher WREN (1632–1723) designed St. Paul's Cathedral and many other London churches.

Today people still build with brick and stone, but they also have new materials which have changed the way in which buildings are constructed. Concrete and steel, glass and plastic are shaping the new world in which we live. Architects are designing offices, factories, and sports arenas so as to make the best use of these new materials. They even have the opportunity sometimes to design whole new cities.

▼ *An example of modern architecture. This building is in Munich in Germany.*

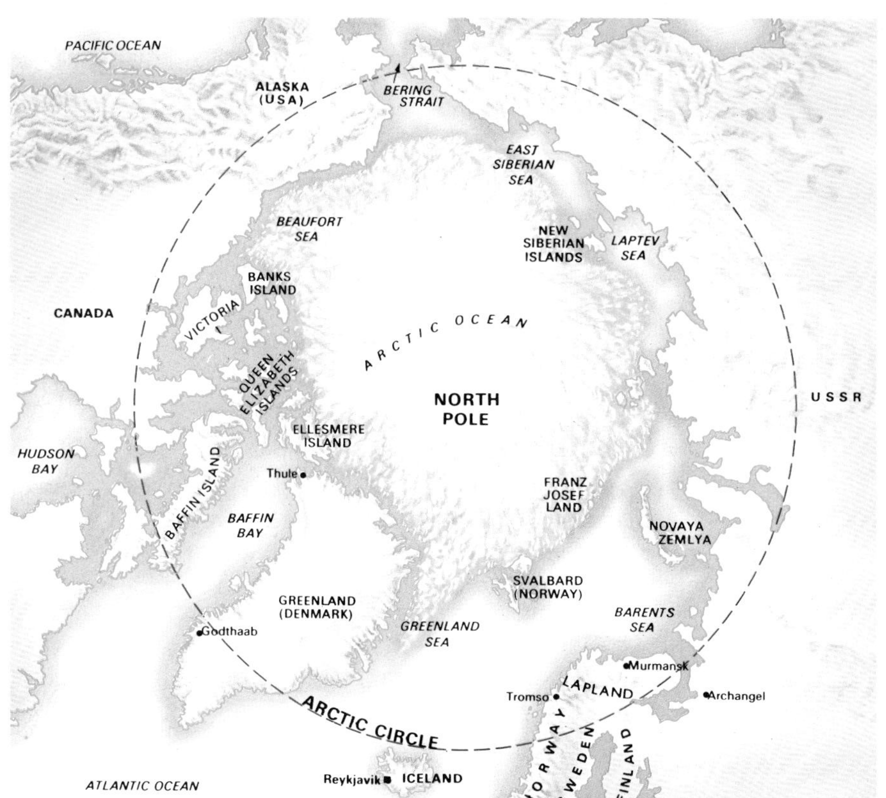

▲ *The Arctic tern is the world's migration champion. It breeds on seacoasts along the Arctic Ocean and in August migrates to the Antarctic at the other end of the world.*

Arctic

The Arctic is the region around the NORTH POLE. At the North Pole itself there is no land, only a huge area of frozen sea. The land in the Arctic region is frozen solid for most of the year. In the short summer the surface soil thaws, and some plants can grow, even brightly colored flowers. There are now more people in the Arctic than there used to be. This is because valuable minerals and oil have been found there. You can find the Arctic Circle at $66^1/_2$ degrees north on a map.

It is cold near the North Pole because the Sun never rises high in the sky. In winter there are days when it does not rise at all. In summer there are days when it can be seen all day and night.

ARGENTINA

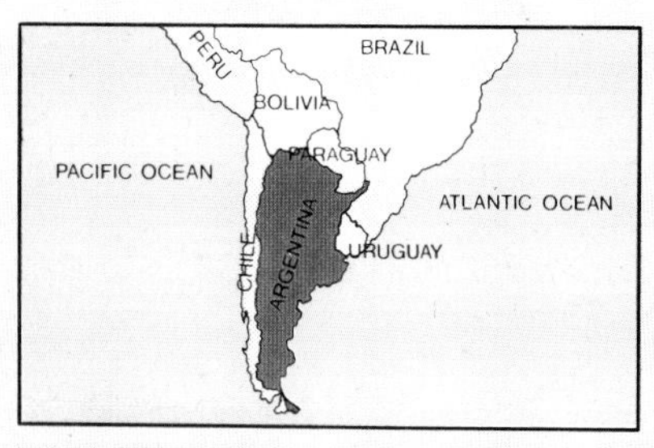

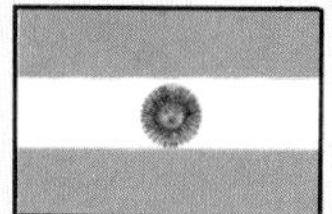

Government: Republic
Capital: Buenos Aires
Area: 1,065,189 sq. miles (2,578,826 sq. km)
Population: 32,322,000
Language: Spanish
Currency: Peso

Argentina

Argentina is the second largest country in SOUTH AMERICA. Most of the country's people are farmers and ranchers, for much of Argentina's wealth comes from livestock and crops. Argentina is one of the world's top producers of beef and veal, fruit, wheat, millet and sorghum, and wool. The chief farming region is on the *pampas*, a Spanish word meaning "plains." The pampas lie to the northwest and south of Argentina's capital, Buenos Aires. Here, vast farms raise millions of cattle and sheep which graze on the rich pasture. Northern Argentina is an area of tropical forests and is little developed. In the far south, near the tip of South America, is Patagonia, a desert waste. The western part of the country is dry, and the land rises to the Andes Mountains, including Aconcagua, at 22,834 ft. (6,960 m) the highest peak in South America. Argentina was ruled by Spain from 1535 to 1810. Today most Argentinians are descended from Europeans, though there are still about 20,000 native Indians.

▲ *Gauchos are South American cowboys of the pampas region.*

Arizona

The state of Arizona lies in the southwestern United States. Once thought of as an almost worthless desert, Arizona has become one of the nation's fastest-growing areas.

More than half the state is covered by mountains and plateaus. Large herds of sheep and cattle graze there. In northwestern Arizona is the greatest scenic attraction of the United States—the Grand Canyon of the Colorado River. This and other scenic attractions such as the Petrified Forest and the Painted Desert attract millions of visitors each year.

Dams provide water to irrigate large areas of Arizona and also generate electricity. Manufacturing is the state's most important industry, especially electrical, communications, and aeronautical products.

ARIZONA

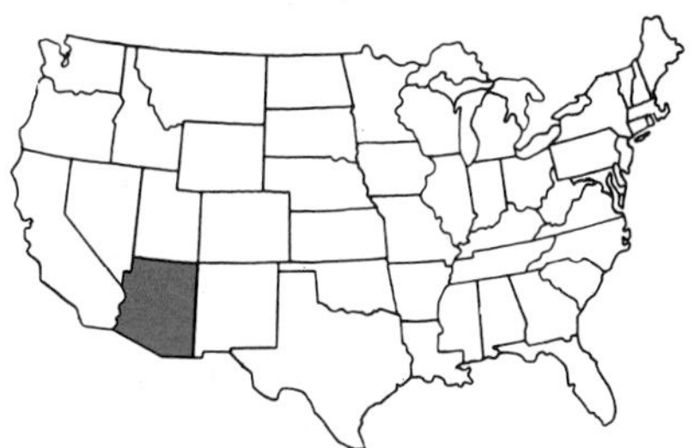

Capital: Phoenix
Population: 3,665,228
Area: 114,000 sq. mi. (295,260 sq. km)
State flower: Flower of Saguaro Cactus
State bird: Cactus Wren
State tree: Palo Verde
Statehood: February 14, 1912
48th state

Arkansas

Arkansas is a state in the south-central United States. It lies on the west bank of the Mississippi River. Arkansas was French territory until the United States bought it as part of the Louisiana Purchase in 1803.

► *The Hoover Dam on the Colorado River stands on the state line between Arizona and Nevada.*

ARKANSAS

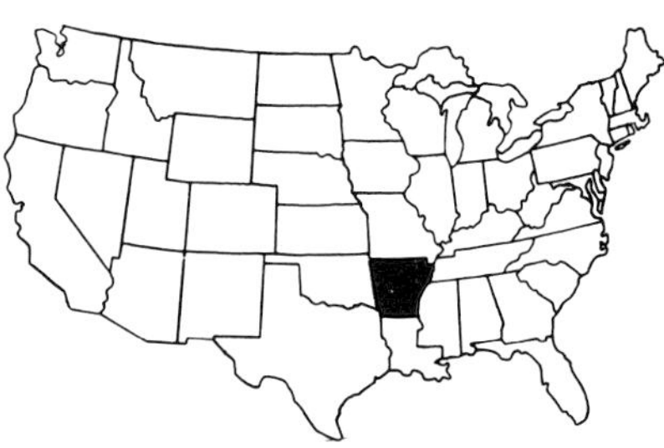

Capital: Little Rock
Population: 2,350,725
Area: 53,187 sq. mi. (137,754 sq. km)
State flower: Apple Blossom
State bird: Mockingbird
Statehood: June 15, 1863
25th state

The state is a leader in the manufacture of food products, lumber, cotton, rice, and soybeans. Arkansas also produces most of the nation's bauxite, the ore from which aluminum is made. There are also important oil and natural gas wells.

Millions of tourists visit Arkansas every year to enjoy boating and fishing on the state's beautiful lakes. The only diamond mine in the United States is near Murfreesboro. Fort Smith and the Little Rock-North Little Rock area are the state's most important manufacturing areas.

Armor

Armor is covering used to protect the body in battle. It was first worn at least 5,000 years ago and was originally made of tough leather. Then men made metal breastplates, helmets, and shields. But the rest of the body was still protected by leather or chain mail, many small iron rings linked together to form a flexible metal coat. In the MIDDLE AGES, knights rode into battle encased from head to toe in plate armor which weighed up to 70 pounds (30 kg). When firearms were invented, armor was no longer worn, except for the helmet.

Today, lightweight metals and plastics are used in armored jackets worn by soldiers and police.

Art

▲ *Giotto's painting shows St. Francis driving out the devils. It dates from the 13th century.*

Since the very earliest times people have painted and made sculptured objects. We can still admire cave paintings that were drawn over 20,000 years ago. Beautiful wall paintings and sculptures from ancient EGYPT, GREECE, and ROME still survive.

The Christian religion has had a great influence on art. During the MIDDLE AGES painters worked on religious scenes, often in a rather stiff way. But when the RENAISSANCE came in the 1400s art began to flower and artists became famous for their work. Painters such as LEONARDO DA VINCI and MICHELANGELO began to make their subjects more lifelike. Great Dutch painters such as REMBRANDT painted portraits and everyday scenes. In the 1700s and 1800s many artists went back to making their work look something like early Greek and Roman art.

Later, painting became more real looking, but by the 1870s a new style called IMPRESSIONISM was starting. Artists such as Monet (1840–1926) and Renoir (1841–1919) painted with little dabs of color, making soft, misty outlines. Painting in the 1900s became even freer. Styles included Abstract Art and Cubism, with famous painters Jackson Pollock (1912–1956) and PICASSO (1881–1973).

The ancient Egyptians made very fine sculptures between 2,000 and 4,000 years ago. Many of them were huge statues of kings and queens. Some of the world's most beautiful carving was done by the sculptors of ancient Greece and Rome, in what is known as the Classical period. During the Renaissance, especially in Italy, the art of sculpture advanced by leaps and bounds. Michelangelo carved superb statues such as his famous David.

Modern sculptors often create sculptures in which the general shape is more important than showing the likeness of a figure.

▲ *A prehistoric painting of a bison from the caves at Altamira in Spain.*

▲ *Picasso's* Weeping Woman, *a fine example of modern art.*

Arthur, Chester A.

Chester A. Arthur (1830–1886) was the twenty-first president of the United States. He became president when President GARFIELD was shot. Many people thought that Arthur would do whatever the Republican Party wanted, but they were proved wrong. He got rid of many dishonest politicians and tried to do what he thought was right for the country. President Arthur also modernized the Navy and stopped corruption in the Post Office.

The Republican leaders did not like Arthur because he would not do what they wanted. They did not nominate him for president in 1884, and he retired to his New York home. But Chester Arthur was respected by the people.

CHESTER A. ARTHUR

Twenty-first President 1881–1885
Born: Fairfield, Vermont
Education: Union College, Schenectady, N.Y.
Occupation: Teacher and lawyer
Political Party: Republican
Buried: Albany, New York

Asia

Asia is the largest of all the continents. It also has more people (3,172,000,000) than any other continent. Places such as the Ganges-Brahmaputra delta, the river valleys of CHINA, and the island of Java are

Continued on page 48

ASIA

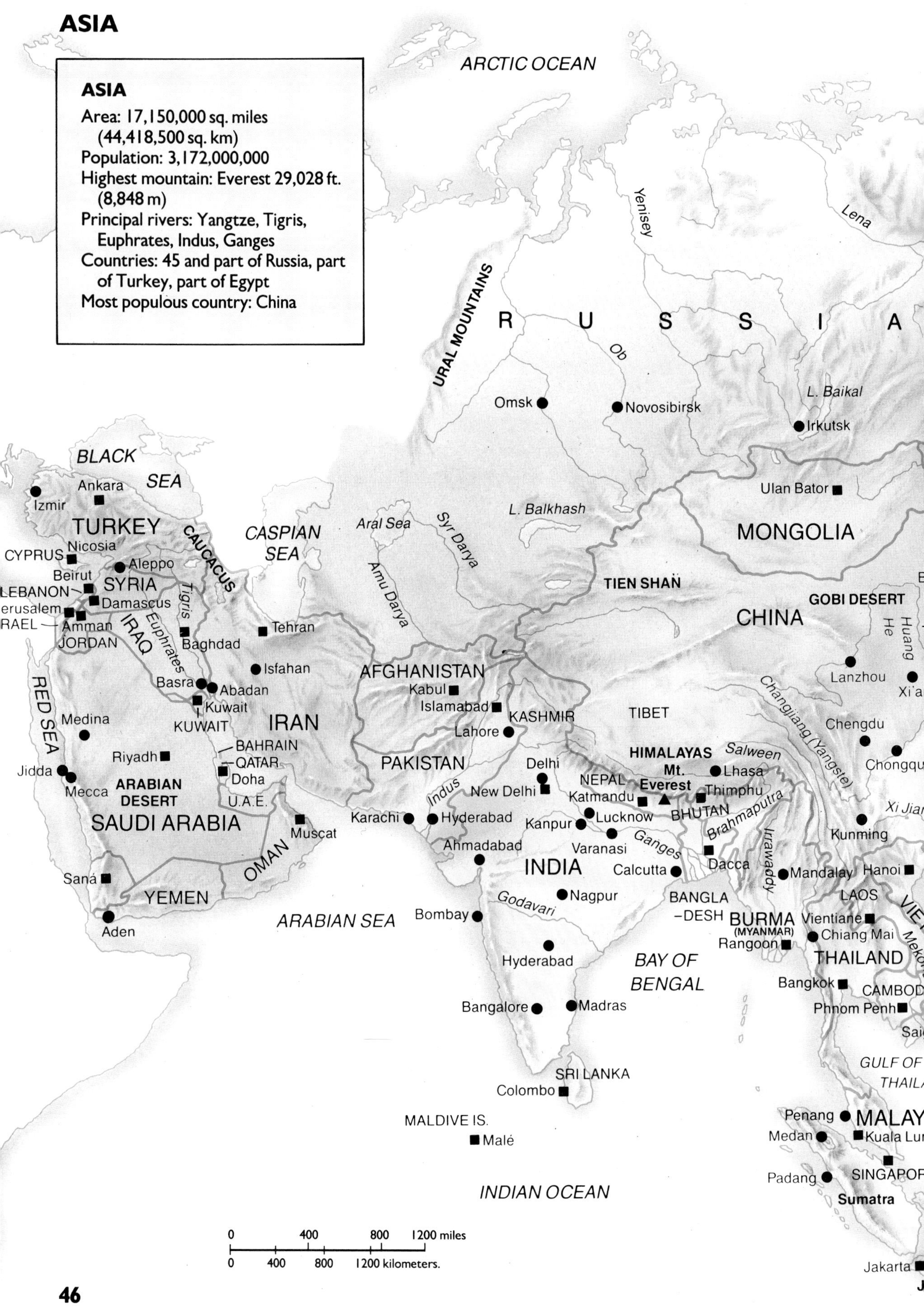
ASIA
Area: 17,150,000 sq. miles (44,418,500 sq. km)
Population: 3,172,000,000
Highest mountain: Everest 29,028 ft. (8,848 m)
Principal rivers: Yangtze, Tigris, Euphrates, Indus, Ganges
Countries: 45 and part of Russia, part of Turkey, part of Egypt
Most populous country: China
ARCTIC OCEAN
Yenisey
Lena
URAL MOUNTAINS
R U S S I A
Ob
Omsk
Novosibirsk
L. Baikal
Irkutsk
BLACK SEA
Ankara
Izmir
TURKEY
CAUCASUS
CASPIAN SEA
Aral Sea
Syr Darya
L. Balkhash
Ulan Bator
MONGOLIA
CYPRUS
Nicosia
Aleppo
Beirut
SYRIA
LEBANON
Damascus
Tigris
Amu Darya
TIEN SHAN
GOBI DESERT
Jerusalem
ISRAEL
Amman
JORDAN
IRAQ
Euphrates
Tehran
Baghdad
CHINA
Huang He
Isfahan
AFGHANISTAN
Kabul
Lanzhou
Basra
Abadan
Kuwait
KUWAIT
Islamabad
KASHMIR
TIBET
Changjiang (Yangste)
Chengdu
RED SEA
Medina
IRAN
Lahore
BAHRAIN
QATAR
Doha
Riyadh
PAKISTAN
HIMALAYAS
Salween
Jidda
Mecca
ARABIAN DESERT
Delhi
NEPAL
Mt. Everest
Lhasa
Chongqu
U.A.E.
Indus
New Delhi
Katmandu
Thimphu
SAUDI ARABIA
Karachi
Hyderabad
Lucknow
BHUTAN
Brahmaputra
Muscat
Kanpur
Irrawaddy
Kunming
OMAN
Ahmadabad
Varanasi
Ganges
Dacca
INDIA
Calcutta
Mandalay
Hanoi
Saná
YEMEN
Godavari
Nagpur
BANGLA-DESH
LAOS
Aden
ARABIAN SEA
Bombay
BURMA (MYANMAR)
Vientiane
Chiang Mai
Rangoon
Hyderabad
BAY OF BENGAL
THAILAND
Bangkok
Bangalore
Madras
Phnom Penh
SRI LANKA
Colombo
GULF OF THAIL
MALDIVE IS.
Malé
Penang
Medan
Padang
Sumatra
INDIAN OCEAN
0 400 800 1200 miles
0 400 800 1200 kilometers.
Jakarta

► *Asia is a vast continent. It is bigger than Europe and Africa put together. And it is so wide that the Sun rises almost 11 hours earlier in the east of the continent than in the west.*

▲ *There is a huge variety of animals in Asia, ranging from elephants to pandas. The giant panda is found in Tibet and southern China. Much of eastern Asia is so crowded with people that few totally wild animals live there.*

▲ *Tokyo, the capital of Japan, today resembles many Western cities.*

among the most thickly populated places in the world.

Northern Asia is a cold, desolate tundra region. In contrast, the islands of INDONESIA are in the steamy tropics. The world's highest mountain range, the HIMALAYAS, is in Asia, and so is the lowest point on land, the shores of the Dead Sea. And all the world's great religions began in Asia—JUDAISM, CHRISTIANITY, ISLAM, BUDDHISM, HINDUISM, CONFUCIANISM, and SHINTO.

Most Asians are farmers, and many are very poor. The chief food crops are wheat and rice. Other crops are exported; they include tea, cotton, jute, rubber, citrus fruits, and tobacco. Many nations such as China are developing their industries, but JAPAN is the only truly industrialized nation.

Asia was the birthplace of civilization, and was the home of many great civilizations, including those of Mesopotamia, BABYLON, China, and the Indus Valley, in what is now PAKISTAN. Europeans began to visit Asia in the 1400s, and trade quickly grew up between the two continents. Later, for several centuries, China and Japan closed their doors to trade with Europe. By the late 1800s most of the rest of Asia was ruled by European powers. But after World War II, during which Japan occupied parts of east Asia, most European-ruled colonies became independent. In 1949 the Chinese Communists took control of mainland China. In 1975 Communists took over VIETNAM, LAOS, and CAMBODIA, after a seven-year war for control, fought mainly in Vietnam.

Asia has the deepest lake in the world—Lake Baikal in Siberia. It has a maximum depth of 5,314 feet (1,620 m)—more than three times the height of the Sears Tower in Chicago, the world's tallest building. Lake Baikal also contains more fresh water than any other freshwater lake—one-fifth of all the fresh water on the Earth's surface.

► *Elephants are used in the logging industry in several Asian countries.*

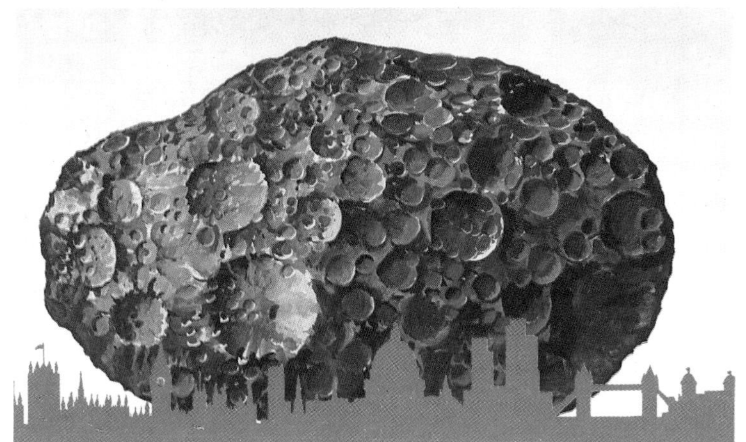

◀ *A very small asteroid, compared in size with part of London. There are probably thousands of bodies of this size in the solar system.*

Asteroid

Asteroids are countless thousands of tiny planets left over from the time when the Sun and planets were being formed. Most of them can be found in the wide gap between the orbits of MARS and JUPITER. Asteroid collisions formed the craters that can be seen on the MOON and MERCURY. The largest asteroid is Ceres, about 600 miles (1,000 km) across, but most of the 30,000 asteroids big enough to be photographed are less than a tenth of this size.

Astrology

Astrology is the art of foretelling the future by observing the movements of the Sun, Moon, planets, and stars. Ancient peoples believed that the heavenly bodies influenced people and their affairs. This led to the growth of a priesthood of astrologers, men and women who claimed to be able to read the future in the heavens. Throughout history, kings, generals, and other powerful leaders have listened to their advice. Today, some people still follow the predictions of astrologers.

Astronomy

Astronomy is the scientific study of the heavenly bodies, and is the oldest science in existence. Early observations of the heavens enabled people to divide the year into months, weeks, and days, based on the movements of the SUN, EARTH, and MOON. The development of the calendar helped early astron-

▼ *Astrology is based on the* zodiac, *an imaginary circle in the sky in which the Sun, Moon, and planets move. Also in this circle are the 12 constellations or groups of stars that look like different shapes. Each shape is a sign of the zodiac and occupies a month in the astrologer's calendar. Some people believe that persons born under each sign have special character traits.*

SIGNS OF THE ZODIAC

♑ CAPRICORNUS	December 22–January 19
♒ AQUARIUS	January 20–February 18
♓ PISCES	February 19–March 20
♈ ARIES	March 21–April 19
♉ TAURUS	April 20–May 20
♊ GEMINI	May 21–June 20
♋ CANCER	June 21–July 22
♌ LEO	July 23–August 22
♍ VIRGO	August 23–September 22
♎ LIBRA	September 23–October 22
♏ SCORPIUS	October 23–November 21
♐ SAGITTARIUS	November 22–December 21

▲ *During the Middle Ages, the Arabs were very interested in astronomy, studying the planets and stars.*

omers to forecast the appearance of COMETS and the dates of ECLIPSES. For many centuries people believed that the Earth was the center of the UNIVERSE, until, in the 1540s, Nicolaus COPERNICUS revived the idea that the Sun was at the center of the SOLAR SYSTEM. Around 1550 Leonard Digges invented the TELESCOPE, an important new tool for astronomers. Today, big optical telescopes are aided by radio telescopes which collect radio waves sent out by objects in space, such as PULSARS and QUASARS.

Athens

Athens is the capital of GREECE, but it was once the center of the world's civilization and learning. It was already an important city when its citizens took a leading part in driving the powerful Persians from Europe in 479 B.C. After this, Athens quickly rose to become the most important city in Greece under a leader called Pericles (490–429 B.C.). Pericles built many magnificent buildings, especially on the hill called the ACROPOLIS. Even after the Romans conquered Greece, Athens remained famous as a center of culture.

Athletics *See* Olympic Games, Track and Field

Atlantic Ocean

The Atlantic Ocean is the second largest ocean in the world, after the PACIFIC OCEAN. It lies between Europe and Africa in the east and the Americas in the west. Its average depth is more than 11,000 ft. (3,350 m). There are a number of strong currents in the Atlantic. The best known is the GULF STREAM, which carries warm water toward the coasts of Europe. It is this current that keeps Europe comparatively warm in the winter months.

The Atlantic began to form about 150 million years ago, when the Americas began to separate from Africa. This separation continues today along the Mid-Atlantic Ridge. This is a long chain of underwater mountains that runs from Iceland southward almost to the tip of South America.

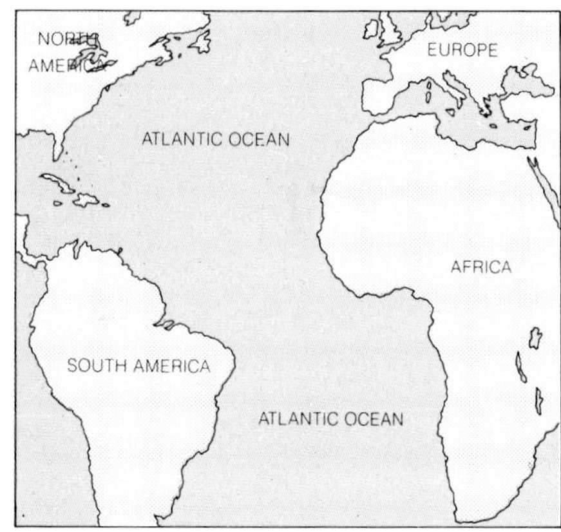

Atlantis

According to PLATO, a famous ancient Greek philosopher, Atlantis was a large island somewhere west of the Pillars of Hercules (Gibraltar). Atlantis had a powerful army that invaded countries around the Mediterranean Sea more than 10,000 years ago. But Plato tells that great earthquakes destroyed Atlantis and all its people. Atlantis may never have existed, but some people think it may have been an island that was blown apart by a terrible volcanic eruption.

Atlas

An atlas is a book of maps or charts. The first person to call a book of maps an atlas was Gerhardus Mercator, a Flemish mapmaker. He called it this because at that time people always put a picture of the Greek god Atlas at the beginning of map books. Atlas is always shown carrying the Earth on his shoulders.

Atmosphere

The blanket of air that surrounds our planet is called the atmosphere. Nothing on Earth could live without it and the oxygen it contains. It keeps the Earth's temperature at just the right level, and it holds out most of the Sun's harmful rays. The layer of atmosphere closest to the Earth holds most of the air that we need. This layer is called the *troposphere*. Above the troposphere the air gets thinner and thinner. The second layer, the *stratosphere*, begins about 10 miles (16 km) up. Jet airplanes fly in the lower stratosphere where it is usually calm, above the wind and the rain. Higher up still, in the *ionosphere*, some radio waves are reflected back to Earth to give us long distance radio reception. Here also flickering colored lights called the *aurora borealis* can be seen sometimes in the northern hemisphere.

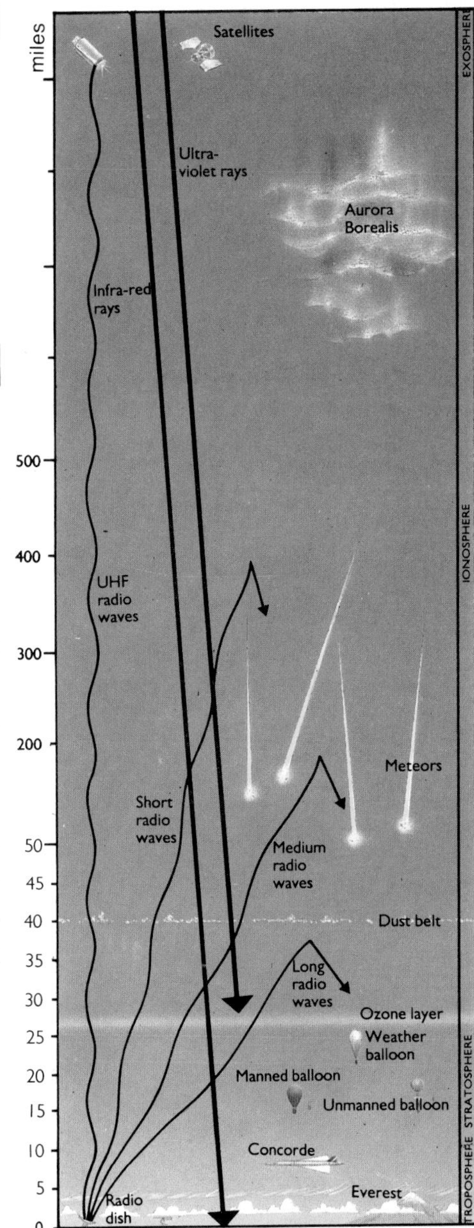

► *Air surrounds the Earth like a transparent shell. We could not live without this atmosphere. It gives us oxygen to breathe and keeps the Earth's temperature at just the right level. It also shields us from most of the Sun's dangerous rays. The atmosphere reflects most radio signals back to Earth.*

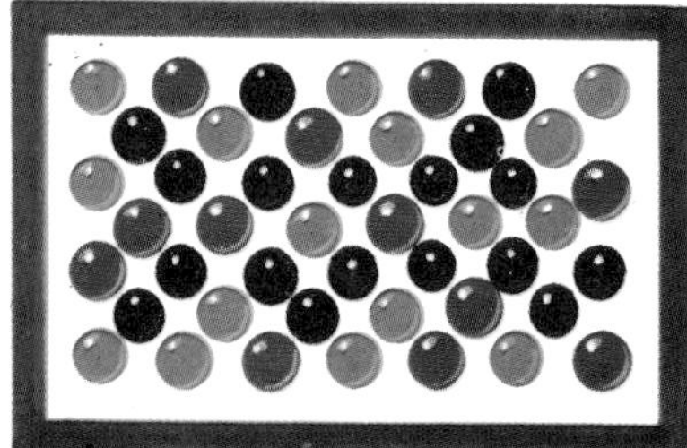

In a solid, atoms pack tightly.

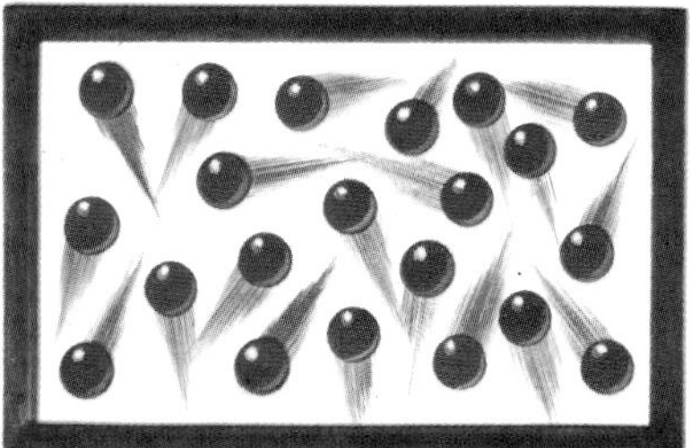

In a liquid, atoms move around

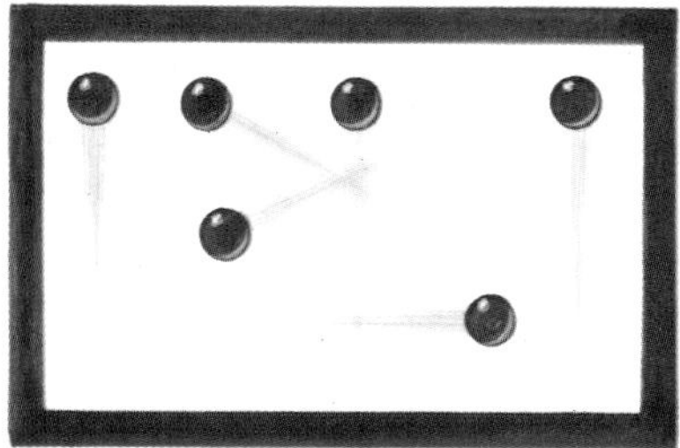

In a gas, atoms move around a lot.

Atom

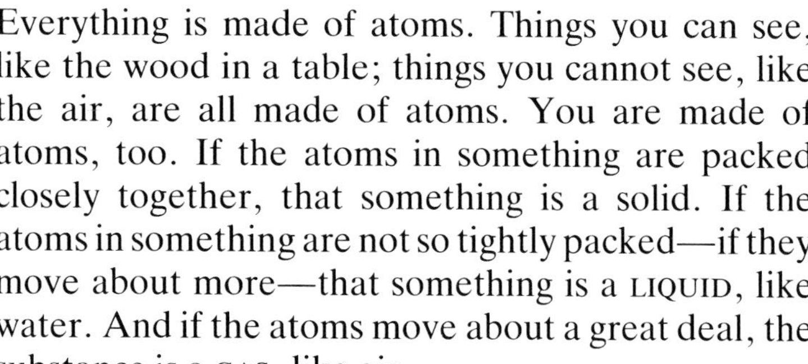

Everything is made of atoms. Things you can see, like the wood in a table; things you cannot see, like the air, are all made of atoms. You are made of atoms, too. If the atoms in something are packed closely together, that something is a solid. If the atoms in something are not so tightly packed—if they move about more—that something is a LIQUID, like water. And if the atoms move about a great deal, the substance is a GAS, like air.

It is very difficult to imagine how small an atom is. We cannot see them—they are far too small. Look at the period at the end of this sentence. It has in it about 250,000 *million* atoms! But even atoms are made up of smaller pieces. The simplest atom is that of the light gas HYDROGEN. The center is a tiny body called a *proton*. Around it spins an even smaller *electron*. Other atoms are much more complicated than the hydrogen atom. The carbon atom, for example, has at its center 6 protons and 6 other particles called *neutrons*. Around these spin 6 electrons.

Scientists have discovered other tiny particles, all much smaller than the atom. They think, for instance, that protons and neutrons are themselves made up of particles called *quarks*.

The British astronomer James Jeans proposed one way of grasping the size of an atom. There are three atoms in every molecule of water. If the molecules in a pint of water were arranged in a single line, they would encircle the Earth more than 20 million times.

Atomic Energy *See* Nuclear Energy

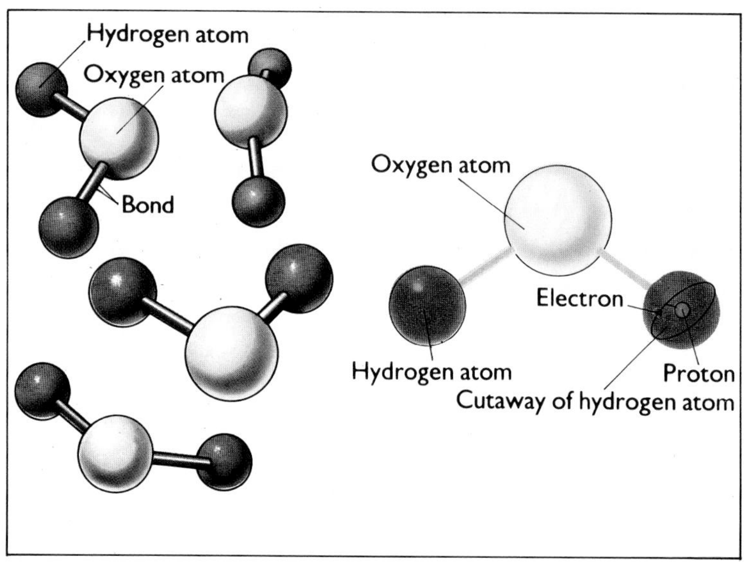

► *Water is made up of tiny molecules. Each molecule contains two atoms of hydrogen and one of oxygen. One of the hydrogen atoms in this picture is cut away to show its central proton and the single electron spinning around about it.*

Attila the Hun

Attila (about 406–53) was the leader of the HUNS, a warlike group of tribes from central Asia that terrorized Europe in the A.D. 400s. In 434 Attila and his brother Bleda became joint rulers of the Huns, but Attila murdered his brother to become sole ruler. Attila led his forces from the Danube to the Mediterranean, killing and burning along the way. Then he tried to conquer the eastern Roman Empire, but was stopped by the strong walls of its capital, CONSTANTINOPLE. In A.D. 451, Attila invaded Gaul (now France), but he was defeated by an army of Romans and Visigoths at Chalons.

When Attila had recovered from his defeat he turned his attention to Italy. As he neared Rome he was met by Pope Leo I. The Pope persuaded Attila to turn back, so saving Rome from destruction.

▲ *One-third of all the wool used in the world comes from Australia. Sheep stations cover thousands of square miles.*

Austen, Jane 

Jane Austen (1775–1817) was a famous English writer. She wrote six novels, four being published during her lifetime without her name being mentioned, and the other two after she died. Her *Pride and Prejudice* is one of the best-known novels ever written. All her stories are about ordinary people in ordinary situations, and seem very real and lifelike.

Australia 

Australia is the world's smallest continent and a large country. It is a huge landmass, nearly as big as the United States, excluding Alaska. It was the last continent to be discovered and settled by Europeans; its first inhabitants were the ABORIGINES.

Much of Australia is dry, flat desert. Most of its people live along the coasts, especially in the four large cities—Sydney, Melbourne, Brisbane, and Perth. Sheep and cattle farming are important, as well as mining and manufacturing.

Australia's first European settlers came from Britain, but today the population includes people from other parts of Europe and Southeast Asia. The country is a member of the British COMMONWEALTH.

Government: Democratic, federal state system
Capital: Canberra
Area: 2,966,200 sq. miles (7,682,450 sq. km)
Population: 17,086,000
Language: English
Currency: Australian dollar

STATES and TERRITORIES	CAPITAL
New South Wales	Sydney
Victoria	Melbourne
Queensland	Brisbane
South Aust.	Adelaide
Western Aust.	Perth
Tasmania	Hobart
Aust. Capital Territory	Canberra
Northern Terr.	Darwin

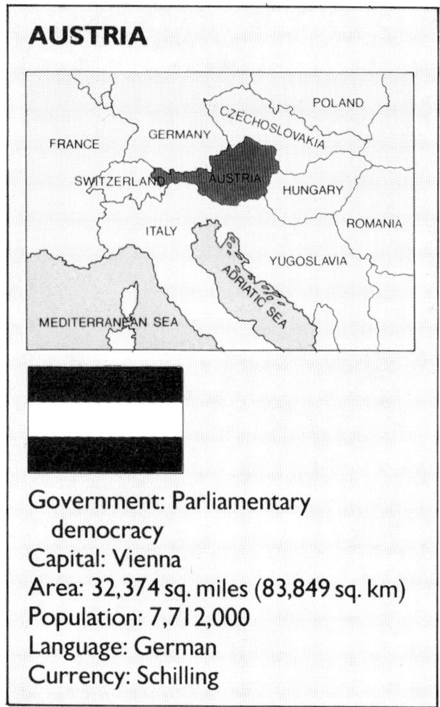

Government: Parliamentary democracy
Capital: Vienna
Area: 32,374 sq. miles (83,849 sq. km)
Population: 7,712,000
Language: German
Currency: Schilling

Austria

Today, this small country is hardly as big as the state of Maine. But once it was one of the largest and most powerful nations in Europe.

For almost 700 years, from 1278 to 1918, Austria was ruled by a dynasty of kings and queens called the Hapsburgs. Their lands covered most of central Europe. They included Hungary, Czechoslovakia, large parts of Italy, Yugoslavia, Poland, and Germany.

The Austrian Empire collapsed after World War I. But there are many relics of the rich court life of the Hapsburg emperors. Vienna, the capital city, where $1\frac{1}{2}$ million Austrians live, is filled with castles, beautiful buildings and churches, statues, and parks.

Automobile

In about a hundred years the automobile has changed the world. It has also itself been changed. The clumsy "horseless carriage" has become the fast, comfortable, reliable car of today.

In 1885 two German engineers, working independently, produced vehicles which were the forerun-

▼ A cutaway of a modern motor car showing the main parts. Power produced by the engine is transmitted to the driving wheels. For most cars these are the rear wheels, although some cars use the front or all four as driving wheels.

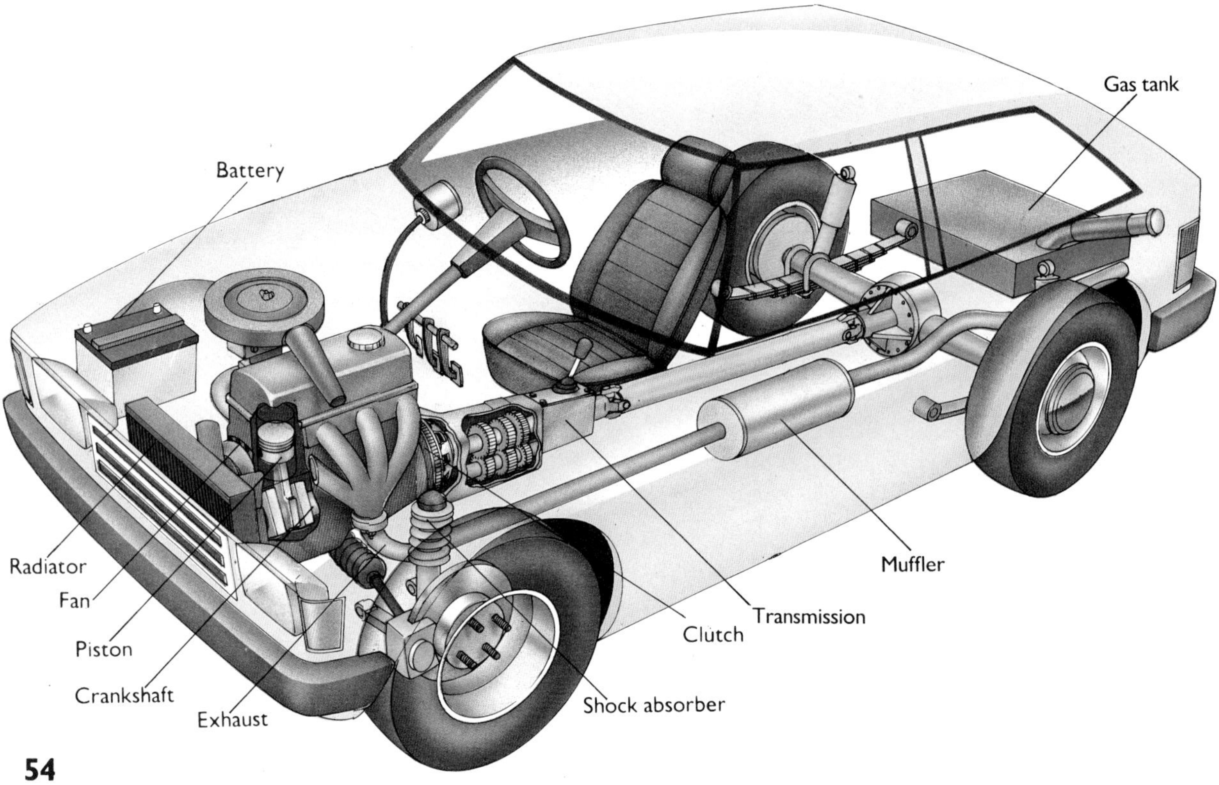

ners of today's cars. These men, Karl Benz and Gottlieb Daimler, used INTERNAL COMBUSTION ENGINES fueled by gasoline.

In 1913 Henry FORD introduced the first successful way of producing cars quickly and cheaply. The cars moved down a line of workers who each added a certain part. Cars are still made in this way except that it is now robots that do the assembling in many factories.

The power for the car comes from an internal combustion engine which burns a mixture of gasoline and air in cylinders. Most engines have four or six cylinders. Inside the cylinders are pistons, which are forced down by the burning gases and turn a crankshaft. At one end of the crankshaft is a heavy flywheel which smooths out the motion of the engine. From the crankshaft, the power goes to the transmission, which takes the power to the shaft that is made to drive the wheels. (The wheels that are driven can be either at the front or the back.) The driver can use gears to make the car go faster or slower for the same engine speed, and to reverse. Most cars have automatic transmission which changes gear automatically. All cars need a BATTERY, which is charged from the engine. The battery provides power for the starter motor, the lights, the horn, and other accessories. Some cars and trucks have a DIESEL engine, which burns diesel oil.

The electric automobile is not new. At the beginning of this century, about 40 percent of the automobiles in the United States were driven by electricity. Forty percent were driven by steam and only 20 percent by gasoline.

Aztecs

The empire of the Aztecs was a great Indian civilization in Mexico and Central America when Spanish soldiers discovered it. A Spanish commander by the name of Hernando Cortés landed with 600 men on their shores in 1519. Within two years he had smashed the Aztec empire forever.

Montezuma was the last ruler of the Aztecs. He was captured by Spanish soldiers soon after a small army of them arrived in his capital city. By holding him hostage, they were able to control his subjects, even though they were greatly outnumbered.

The Aztecs were famous for their grim religious practices. One of their gods had human beings sacrificed to him regularly in front of his temple.

▼ *An Aztec warrior. Not until he had captured three prisoners could a warrior wear his hair in a tuft.*

Babbage, Charles

Charles Babbage (1792–1871) was a British inventor and mathematician who is often called "the father of the computer." In 1833 he began working on an "analytical engine" which was intended to do any arithmetical calculation. Although Babbage's engine worked by using wheels and levers, it contained the main parts of a modern computer—including a memory. Numbers and instructions were to be fed in on punched cards.

But Babbage's invention was never completed, and the partially finished machine can be seen in the Science Museum in London, England.

Babylon

Babylonia was one of the greatest civilizations of the ancient world. It rivaled EGYPT in its splendor. Babylonia lay between the fertile valleys of the Tigris and Euphrates rivers in a region that is today called IRAQ. The first signs of civilization appeared about 3000 B.C.—almost 5,000 years ago. At first Babylonia was a collection of small cities, each with its own ruler. Then the city of Babylon grew more powerful and

▼ *A typical Babylonian house, showing how simply the people lived. Note the burial chamber on the left with the mummified figure.*

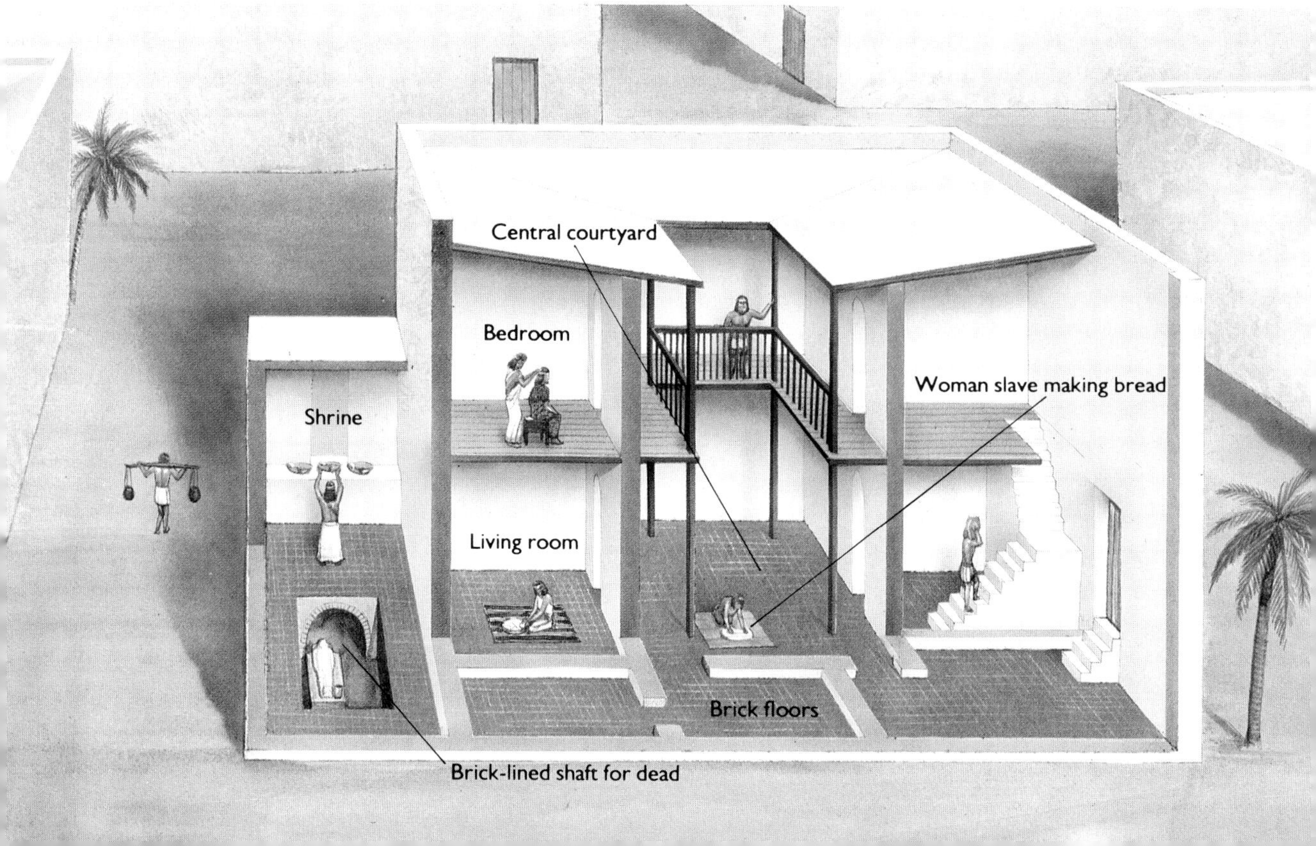

began to dominate its neighbors. Under the rule of its great king Hammurabi it became the capital of Babylonia in the 1700s B.C. Hammurabi was a scholar and a poet. He drew up fair laws for his people. These set out the rights of women and children as well as many other laws.

When Hammurabi died, other tribes raided and lived in Babylon. A new king called Nebuchadnezzar built magnificent temples and palaces. He also built the Hanging Gardens of Babylon, one of the SEVEN WONDERS of the ancient world.

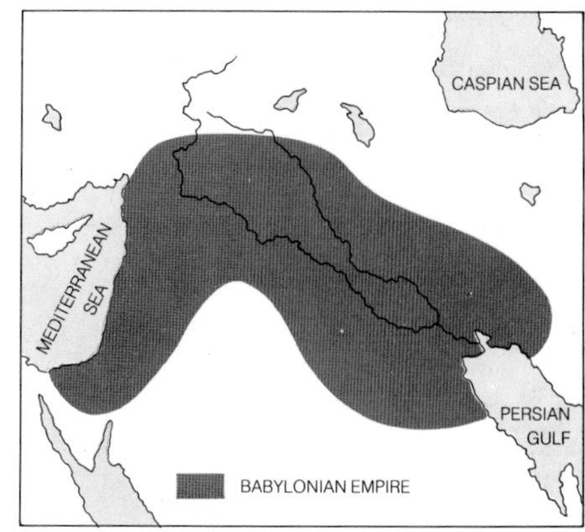

Bach, Johann Sebastian

Johann Sebastian Bach (1685–1750) was one of the greatest composers of all time. He was born at Eisenach in Germany, and all his family were musical. In fact, there were more than sixty musical Bachs before the family died out in the 1800s. From an early age Bach played the violin and the viola. He studied music passionately, often creeping out of bed to copy music from his brother's collection.

At the age of 38 Bach moved to Leipzig, where he lived for the rest of his life. Here he wrote some of his greatest pieces of music—mostly music for singing and for the organ.

When Bach died, his music was almost at once forgotten. No one put up a monument to him. Almost a hundred years passed by before people began to realize what a genius Johann Sebastian Bach had been.

▲ *Bach's most famous pieces of music include the* Brandenburg Concertos, *the* Passions, *and the* B Minor Mass.

Bacon, Roger

Roger Bacon (*c.* 1214–1292) was a famous scientist of the MIDDLE AGES. He was born in England, but spent some time living and studying in Paris. Bacon taught that it is better to see and try things for yourself than believe everything that other people tell you. He was always experimenting.

His scientific studies were a great success. He invented the magnifying glass and described how it might be used in both microscopes and telescopes, although neither had yet been invented. He foretold that the time would come when people would make flying-machines.

In 1242 Roger Bacon produced a secret formula for gunpowder. He said that it should be made up of 41.2 parts saltpeter, 29.4 parts charcoal, and 29.4 parts sulfur. Because he wanted to keep his formula secret he wrote it in the strange form of a Latin anagram that was very difficult to decipher.

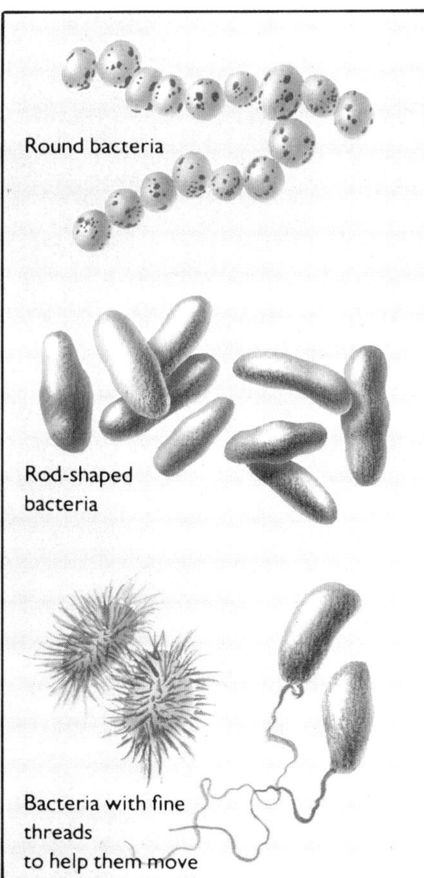

▲ *There are many different kinds of bacteria. A few of them are shown here. There are now drugs, such as penicillin, that destroy bacteria, but because they multiply so quickly, new kinds soon develop that are not affected by the drugs.*

▶ *This picture of a bacterium was taken through a very powerful microscope. The bacterium is about to divide in two.*

Bacteria are measured in micrometers. A micrometer is one-millionth of a meter or one-thousandth of a millimeter. Some bacteria are only 1 micrometer long. The tip of a sharp pencil would cover at least 1,000 of even the largest bacteria.

Bacteria

Bacteria are tiny living things—so tiny that they cannot be seen by your naked eye. They are some of the simplest kinds of life.

Bacteria are more like plants than animals. They come in various shapes and sizes. Under a good MICROSCOPE it is possible to see that some are rod-like, some spiraled, and others round in shape.

There are thousands of different kinds of bacteria. They are found in huge numbers almost everywhere you care to look. Some live in the SOIL. They help to break down animal and vegetable matter and thus make the soil rich. Bacteria also take the gas nitrogen from the air and turn it into forms that help plants to grow. Some bacteria even live inside our bodies. They help with the digestion of our food.

Although most bacteria are quite harmless, some can cause diseases. These kinds are known as germs. Pimples and boils are caused by bacteria. A few are even deadly once they get inside the human body.

Bacteria multiply very quickly. Some of them can divide into two every 20 minutes. From a single bacterium there can be millions in only a few hours.

We now have drugs that kill bacteria. *Sulfonamides* are chemicals that stop bacteria growing. ANTIBIOTICS such as penicillin destroy bacteria. But

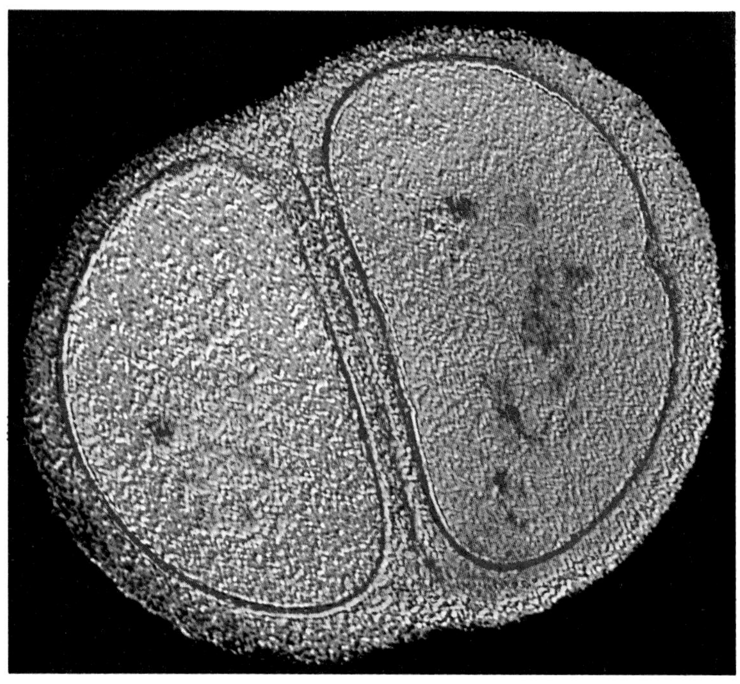

because bacteria multiply so quickly, they soon develop new kinds that are not affected by the drugs that formerly killed them. Then new drugs have to be made to kill the new kinds of bacteria.

The famous French chemist Louis PASTEUR was the first to study bacteria. It was he who found out that it was bacteria that made food go bad. However, we also use bacteria to make pleasant food flavors. Cheeses and some meats are improved by "ripening." Harmless bacteria live in them for a while and make, for example, the green or blue parts in certain cheeses. When we put food in a refrigerator, the cold slows down the action of bacteria. The colder it is, the longer we can keep food fresh.

Among the most dangerous kinds of bacteria are those that we cannot smell or see and that damage our food. These bacteria can cause "food poisoning." Listeria is caused by bacteria of this kind, so we must be very careful how we handle our food.

Bacteria are found everywhere and can live in conditions that would kill any other organism. They have been found in the almost airless upper atmosphere; they have been found 6 miles (10 km) deep in the ocean. They can live in frozen soil and in boiling hot springs. Some bacteria cannot be killed except by boiling in high-pressure steam for hours!

Badger

Badgers are big, weasel-like animals. They are common in North America, Europe, and Asia.

Badgers are MAMMALS. They have thickset bodies, long blunt claws used for digging, sharp teeth, and powerful jaws. A fully grown adult badger measures about 2 ft. (60 cm) from nose to tail.

People rarely see badgers during the day. They are night creatures. After sunset they emerge from their underground dens to begin feeding. They browse on plant roots and hunt mice, rats and voles, insects, frogs, and other small animals.

Badgers build elaborate underground burrows. A burrow has several entrances, a system of long tunnels, and a number of rooms. Here, the badger couple makes its home and raises from two to four young at a time.

▲ *The American badger, shown here, is smaller than the European one.*

Bahamas

The Bahamas consist of about 700 long, narrow islands in the WEST INDIES. The islands stretch for 750 miles (1,200 km) southeastward from Florida. Most of the islands are uninhabited because the soil is

BAHAMAS

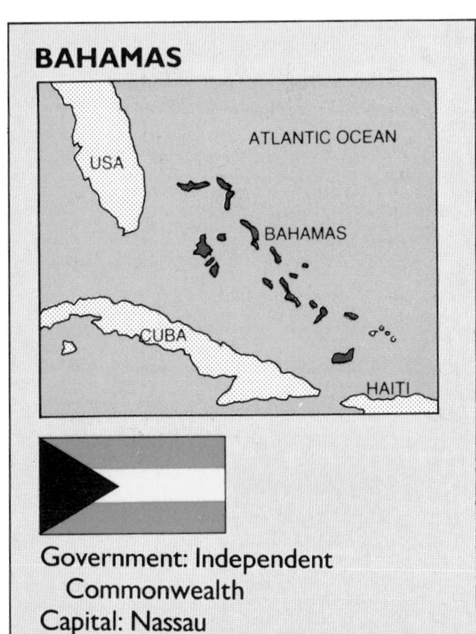

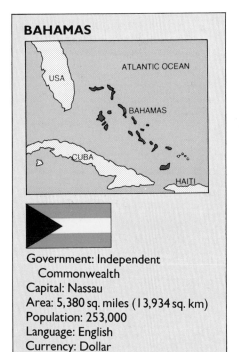

Government: Independent Commonwealth
Capital: Nassau
Area: 5,380 sq. miles (13,934 sq. km)
Population: 253,000
Language: English
Currency: Dollar

poor and there are no minerals. The inhabitants earn their living by tourism. The climate is pleasant, and there are many beautiful beaches of white sand.

In 1973 the Bahamas became an independent country in the COMMONWEALTH of Nations.

Bahrain

Bahrain is an independent country made up of 33 islands in the Persian Gulf. From 1820 to 1971 Bahrain was under British protection. Most of the people are employed in the oil industry, the main source of Bahrain's wealth.

BAHRAIN

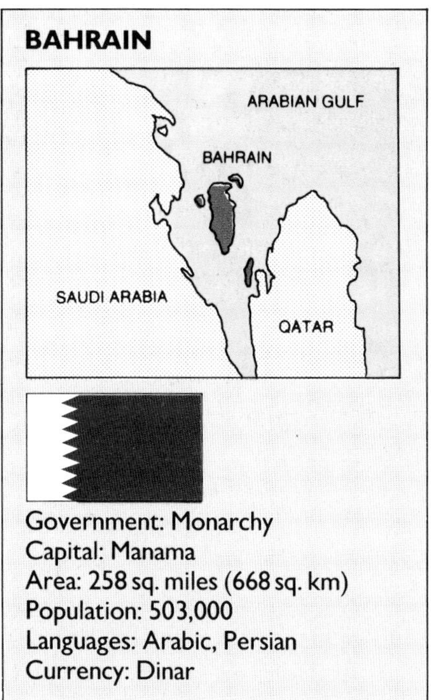

Government: Monarchy
Capital: Manama
Area: 258 sq. miles (668 sq. km)
Population: 503,000
Languages: Arabic, Persian
Currency: Dinar

Balboa, Vasco Núñez de

Vasco Núñez de Balboa (1475–1519) was a Spanish soldier and explorer who was the first European to set eyes on the Pacific Ocean in the New World.

Balboa joined a Spanish expedition to South America in 1501, exploring the north coast of the continent. After living in two Spanish colonies there, Balboa led an expedition across the Isthmus of Panama. There, from a mountaintop, he looked down upon the Pacific Ocean.

Vasco Balboa was a very determined man. It took 24 days for his party of 200 Spaniards and 1,000 native Indians to cross 50 miles (80 km) of dense jungle before they reached the Pacific Ocean. Balboa expected to be hailed as a great explorer and dreamed of glory back in Spain. Unfortunately, a man named Pedrarias Dávila had been made the new governor of Darién. Pedrarias grew increasingly jealous of Balboa and accused him of treason. The explorer was found guilty and sentenced to death. Balboa was beheaded in the public square of Acla in January, 1519.

Balkans

The Balkan peninsula is a mountainous region of southeastern EUROPE. It includes the countries of GREECE, ALBANIA, YUGOSLAVIA, ROMANIA, BULGARIA, and the European part of TURKEY.

The Turks ruled much of this region for 500 years, from the 1300s to the 1800s.

It was in the Balkans that Archduke Ferdinand of Austria was assassinated in 1914. This event triggered WORLD WAR I.

Ball

Most balls used in games are round, but a few are not. Footballs and the balls used in lawn bowling are not *spherical*. Balls used for each sport have a standard size and weight, and some must have a standard bounce. Many nowadays have plastic covers.

▲ *Swan Lake, by the Russian composer Tchaikovsky, is a favorite ballet of many people.*

Ballet

Ballet is a precise and beautiful form of dancing that is performed in a theater. A kind of ballet first appeared in Italy in the 1400s, but ballet as it is danced today began in France. During the reign of King LOUIS XIV, in the 1600s, it was officially recognized as a form of art. The French Royal Academy of Dance was founded in 1661 to promote ballet.

Traditional, or *classical*, ballet follows strict rules and traditions. There are standard positions for the arms, legs, and hands, and special movements that make the dance flow smoothly.

Classical ballet uses orchestras, elaborate scenery, and splendid costumes. Many ballets tell a story, but the dancers do not speak any words. They MIME (act out) the story, using their bodies. The person who arranges the dance movements is called the *choreographer*.

Some ballets are very famous and have been danced for many years. *Giselle*, a story of a tragic young village girl who dies in love-stricken grief, was first performed in 1841. Two other long-time favorites are *Swan Lake* and *Sleeping Beauty*. These two ballets are as famous for their music as for their dancing. Famous dancers include Anna Pavlova, Waslaw Nijinsky, Mikhail Baryshnikov, Natalia Makarova, Margot Fonteyn, and Rudolf Nureyev.

Modern ballets often look very different from classical ones. They include freer, more natural dance steps. Sometimes, instead of telling a story, they dwell on certain moods or themes. Special effects may be produced with lighting, rather than scenery.

▼ *Modern ballet often uses striking costumes and poses like this one to achieve a stunning effect.*

▲ *This brightly colored balloon, built by the Montgolfier brothers, was the first one to carry passengers.*

▼ *Airships like this one were popular in the 1920s but they were slow, clumsy, and often dangerous. They were popular because they could fly long distances, but fire was a constant danger.*

Balloons and Airships

Balloons and airships use lighter-than-air gases to fly. Balloons can only drift in the wind, but airships can be flown and steered.

The first manned balloon was a hot-air craft launched in 1783. It was built by two French brothers, the Montgolfiers. Their balloon was an open-ended bag. A fire was burned under the opening to fill it with hot air.

In the same year, the first gas-filled balloon took to the air. The gas used was HYDROGEN, and it was a simpler craft to fly. To go down, one simply opened a valve and let some gas out.

In the 1800s, manned balloons were used by the military for observations. Today, balloons are used to study the weather. Hot-air ballooning is a popular sport.

Airships

Most airships are bigger than balloons. The simplest kind looks like a cigar-shaped bag, under which is slung a cabin and engines. More advanced airships have a rigid skeleton covered with fabric.

The first successful airship flew in 1852. It was pow-

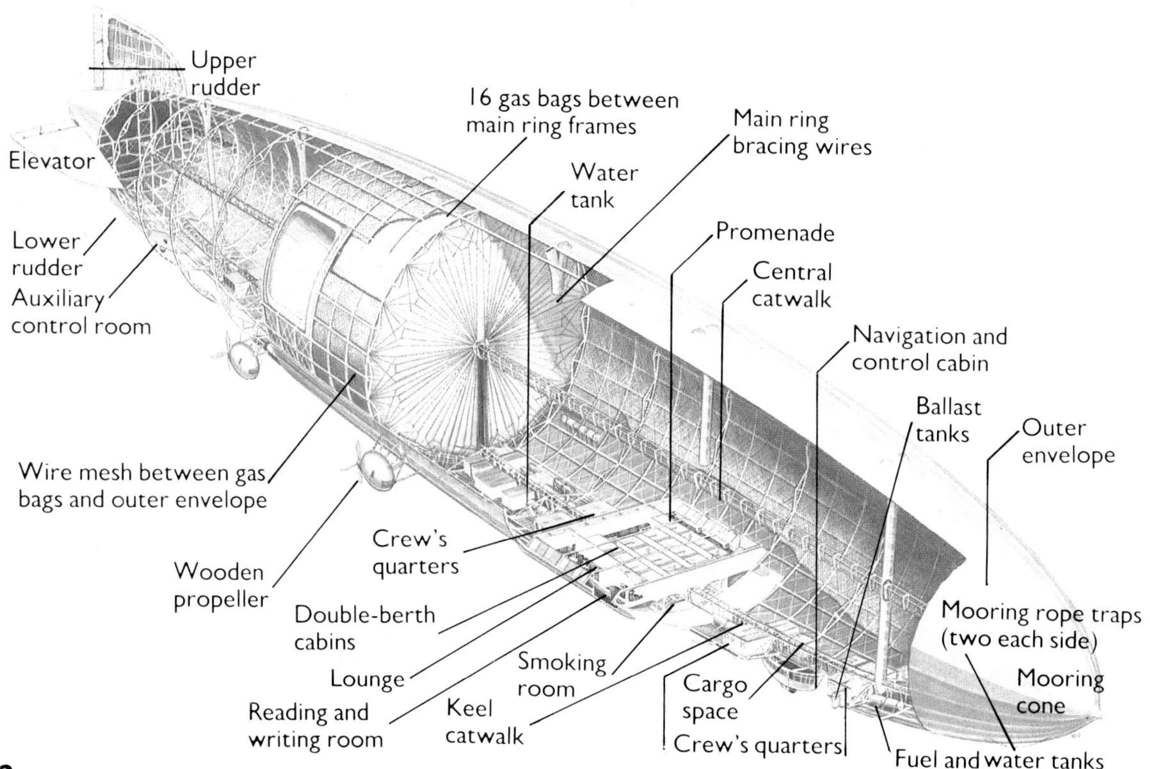

ered by a steam engine and could manage a speed of 5 mph (8 km/h). During World War I, airships were used to bomb cities. In 1919, the British-built R34 made the first Atlantic crossing. In 1929 the famous *Graf Zeppelin* of Germany flew around the world. But a series of disasters brought the building of airships to an end. They were simply not safe enough for regular passenger use because they were filled with dangerous hydrogen gas. Today's airships are lifted by helium, a gas that is safer because it does not catch fire. They are used for special purposes such as advertising and filming.

Baltic States

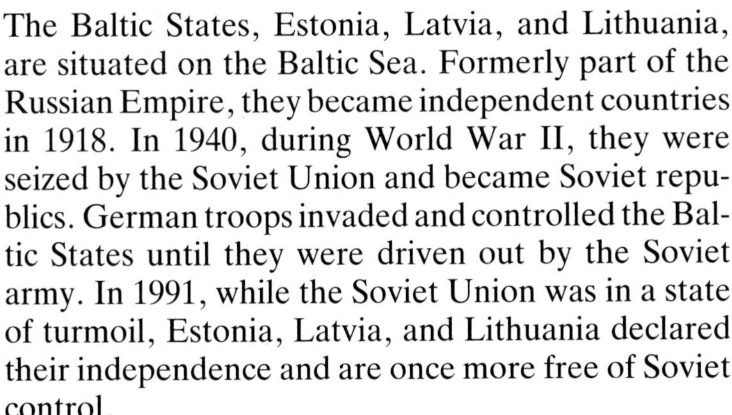

The Baltic States, Estonia, Latvia, and Lithuania, are situated on the Baltic Sea. Formerly part of the Russian Empire, they became independent countries in 1918. In 1940, during World War II, they were seized by the Soviet Union and became Soviet republics. German troops invaded and controlled the Baltic States until they were driven out by the Soviet army. In 1991, while the Soviet Union was in a state of turmoil, Estonia, Latvia, and Lithuania declared their independence and are once more free of Soviet control.

The Baltic States have kept their own languages, literature, and traditions. Estonia has textile, shipbuilding, and mining equipment industries. Latvia is an important producer of railroad passenger cars and telephone exchanges. Lithuania produces cattle, hogs, and electric appliances.

ESTONIA

Government: Republic
Capital: Tallinn
Area: 17,413 sq. miles (45,100 sq. km)
Population: 1,600,000
Languages: Estonian, Russian

LATVIA

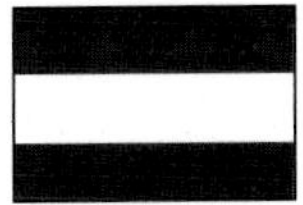

Government: Republic
Capital: Riga
Area: 24,595 sq. miles (63,700 sq. km)
Population: 3,340,000
Languages: Latvian, Russian

LITHUANIA

Government: Republic
Capital: Vilnius
Area: 25,170 sq. miles (65,000 sq. km)
Population: 3,700,000
Languages: Lithuanian, Russian

Bangladesh

Bangladesh is an Asian country that came into being in 1971. Before that it was part of Pakistan. It is one of the world's most densely populated countries, and most of the people are very poor. In the rainy season, branches of the Ganges and Brahmaputra rivers flood the flat land. A cyclone in 1991 killed 125,000 people. Rice, jute, tea, and sugarcane are the main crops. The people of Bangladesh have been promised democratic rule, but military rule, imposed in 1982, still exists.

BANGLADESH

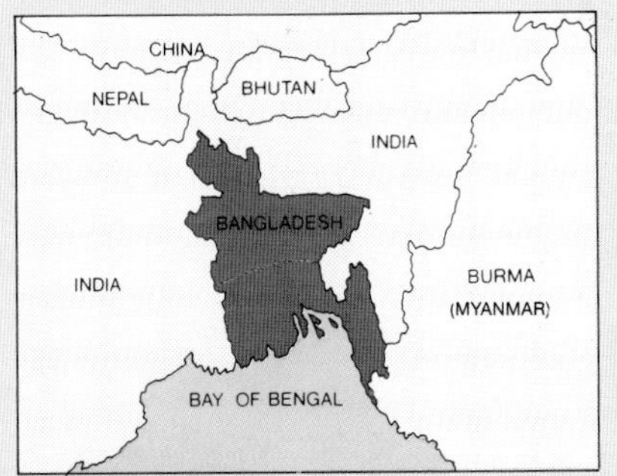

Government: Martial law
Capital: Dhaka
Area: 55,598 sq. miles (143,998 sq. km)
Population: 115,594,000
Language: Bengali
Currency: Taka

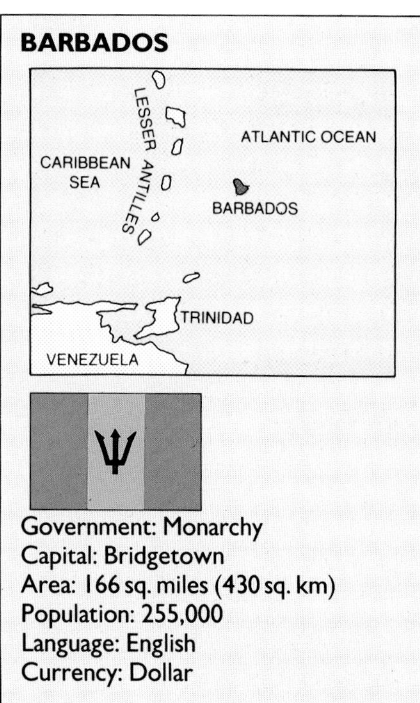

Government: Monarchy
Capital: Bridgetown
Area: 166 sq. miles (430 sq. km)
Population: 255,000
Language: English
Currency: Dollar

Bank

Banks are companies that take people's money for safekeeping. When someone's money is first put in the bank, this is called "opening an account." Every time you put more money in, you make a *deposit*. If you wish to take some out, you make a *withdrawal*.

Banks do not only hold money in safety. They also make loans to people and provide other ways of making saving and spending easier.

Baptist

The Baptists are one of the largest Protestant religious groups in the world. Most Baptists live in the United States. They do not believe in baptising babies. They think that before people are baptised they should be old enough to make up their own minds about their religion. They also believe in total immersion (dipping under water) at baptism.

Barbados

Barbados is the most easterly island in the West Indies. It is almost surrounded by coral reefs. The country is an independent state within the Commonwealth, having gained its independence from Britain in 1966.

Most of the people earn their living from the sugar industry. The cane is made into sugar, molasses, or rum. The island attracts many tourists to enjoy its excellent climate.

▼ *A bar-code reader in use at a supermarket checkout.*

Bar Code

You will have noticed a pattern of black and white stripes on many cartons, packages, and books. The stripes make a number in binary code, and each product that you buy has a different number. At the store's checkout a machine reads the bar code and turns it into a signal that goes to the store's computer. The computer finds the price of each item and prepares the sales check. It also works out how many products have been sold and orders new supplies when necessary.

Bardeen, John

John Bardeen (1908–1991) was an American scientist who was best known for his invention of the TRANSISTOR with William Shockley and Walter Brattain. The three were awarded the Nobel Prize in physics in 1956 for this work. Today's radios, televisions, and computers can contain hundreds of transistors.

Bardeen won a second Nobel Prize in 1972, with John Schrieffer and Leon Cooper, for his work on SUPERCONDUCTIVITY.

SEE IT YOURSELF

You can collect bark rubbings of different kinds of trees. You need some large sheets of fairly heavy paper and a thick wax crayon. Make sure the paper can't move, then rub the crayon firmly over it. Watch the bark pattern appear. Label your rubbing with the tree's name.

Bark

The outer layer of WOOD on the trunk and branches of a TREE is the bark. Bark is dead wood. It is tough and waterproof and protects the living wood underneath. In this way it has the same purpose as the outer layers of skin on our bodies.

As trees grow, they form layers, or rings, of new wood and become thicker. When this new wood is formed inside a tree it pushes against the dead bark and makes it crack and peel off.

The most useful bark is probably CORK, which comes from the cork oak, a tree found in southern Europe. The cork is carefully removed from the tree and used for many different purposes.

Barometer

Put simply, high air pressure is a sign of good weather. Low air pressure is a sign of changing and bad weather. The barometer is used to measure such changes.

There are two kinds of barometer, the aneroid and the mercury. The aneroid is more widely used. Inside it is a flat metal box. The air inside the box is at very low pressure. The metal walls of the box are so thin they will bend very easily. They do not collapse because a spring keeps them apart.

As air pressure drops, the spring pushes the sides of the box apart. As air pressure rises, the sides of the box are squeezed together. These movements are picked up by levers and gears that move a pointer around to show the air pressure.

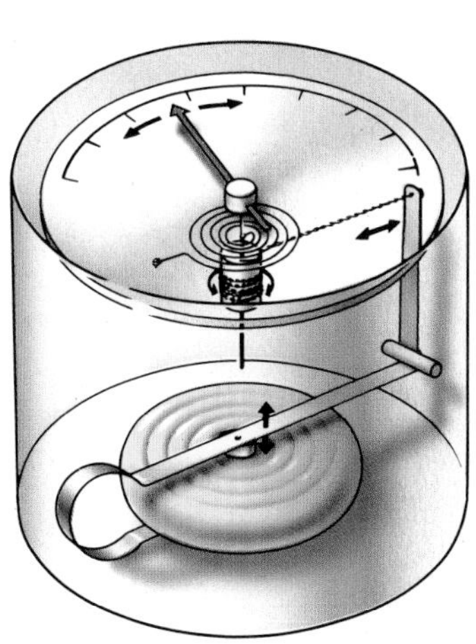

▲ *If you have a barometer at home it is probably an aneroid barometer. If the air pressure rises, it pushes in the sides of the thin metal (yellow) box. This moves the pointer around.*

▼ *Major-league baseball bats cannot be more than 42 inches (106 cm) long nor more than 2¾ inches (7 cm) in diameter at the thickest point.*

Baseball

Baseball is the national sport of the United States. No one knows quite how it began. It may have come from a similar English game called rounders. In 1845 Alexander Cartwright set up the Knickerbocker Baseball Club of New York. The rules as he laid them out established a game of nine innings, with teams of nine players each. The baseball diamond would have four bases 90 feet (27.4 m) apart.

Today, baseball is played with a bat not more than 2¾ inches (7 cm) in diameter and 42 inches (106 cm) in length. The ball is 9 inches (23 cm) in circumference.

Professional baseball today is big business. Each year millions of fans watch the teams of the two major leagues (American League and National League) battle for a chance to play for the championship in the World Series, held in October. The champions must win four out of seven games.

Baseball is also popular at many other levels and is enjoyed by girls and boys through Little League and other junior leagues. Outside the United States, baseball is played in Latin America and is also popular in Japan and the Philippines.

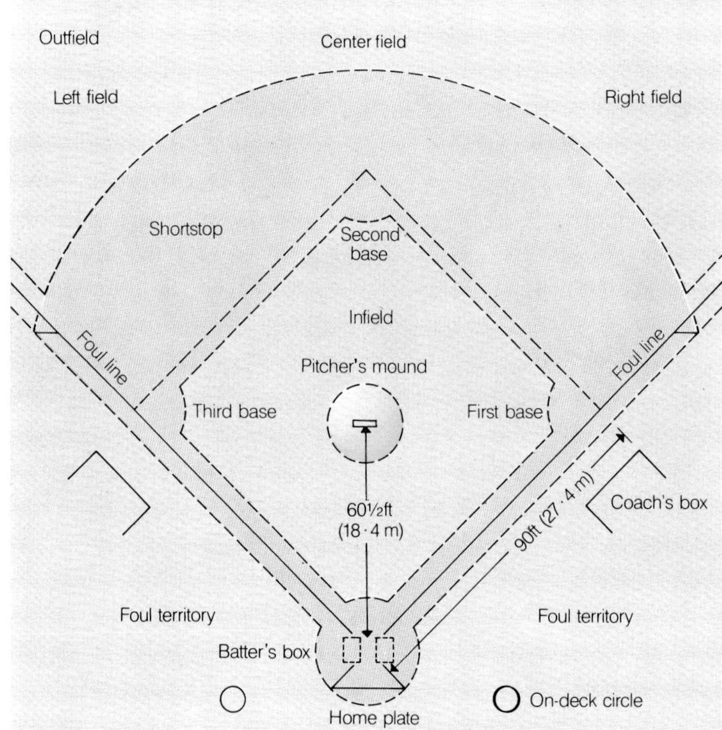

► *Baseball is played on a large field on which is marked a square. The square, known as the "diamond," has sides 90 feet (27.4 m) long. At the base of the diamond is home plate, a five-sided white rubber slab.*

Basketball

Basketball is an American game that has won popularity all over the world. It was invented in 1891 and quickly became popular as an indoor winter sport. Basketball is played in many countries and has been an Olympic sport since 1936.

Professional basketball is played by two teams of five players each. Each team tries to score points by shooting a ball into a basket. In men's basketball the basket is 10 ft. (3 m) from the floor and 18 inches (45.7 cm) in diameter at the top. The professional court is 94 ft. (28.6 m) long and 50 ft. (15.2 m) wide.

The ball can be advanced by bouncing it along the floor (dribbling) or by passing it to a teammate. A player cannot take more than one step while holding the ball. The opposing players try to block each other without making physical contact. A field goal counts two points. Free throws count one point.

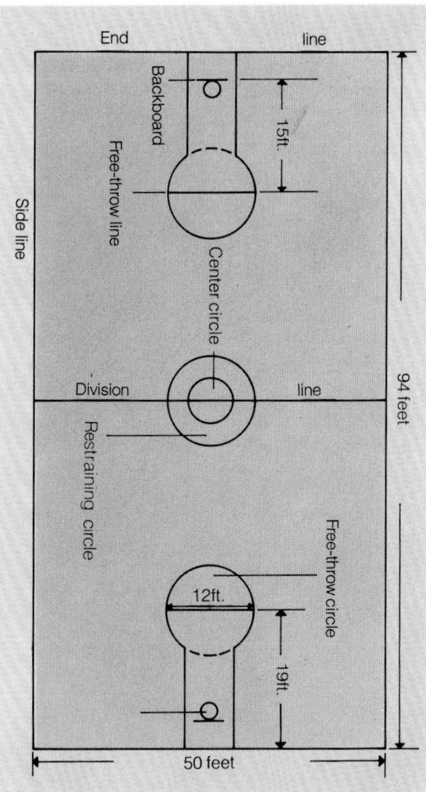

▲ *Professional basketball is played on a court measuring 94 ft. (28 m) long by 50 ft. (15 m) wide. The basketball measures 30 inches (76 cm) in circumference and weighs from 20 to 22 ounces (567 to 624 grams).*

Bat

Bats fly like birds, yet in fact they are MAMMALS. They are the only mammals than can truly be said to fly. Their wings do not have feathers, but are made of a thin sheet of skin stretched between the long "finger" bones. In most bats the wings are also joined to the legs and tail.

There are more than 2,000 different kinds of bat. Most live in the tropics and warm parts of the world.

The biggest of all bats are the fruit-eaters or flying foxes. One, the kalong, has a wingspan of 5 ft.

◀ *Free-tailed bats in Bracken Cave, Texas.*

▼ *The greater horseshoe bat gets its name from the shape of its nose. It is the largest bat in Europe, about 2½ inches (70 mm) long.*

▲ *As a bat flies, it utters a series of squeaks that are so high-pitched that few people can hear them. The sound waves from these cries bounce off objects and echo back to the bat's ears. From these echoes, the bat can tell where the objects are.*

(1.5 m). The insect-eaters are usually smaller. Their wingspan is rarely as much as 12 inches (30 cm). They live in most parts of the world. Where winters are cold they HIBERNATE.

Most bats are nocturnal—they sleep in the day and fly at night. Scientists have shown in experiments that bats do not need good eyesight for flying. They find their way in the dark by using a "sonar" system. They make high-pitched shrieks that few human ears can hear, and use the echoes bouncing off objects to tell where they are.

Battery

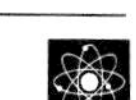

Batteries make electricity from chemicals stored inside them. Dry batteries such as those used in some transistor radios, flashlights, and calculators make electricity for only a limited time. Car batteries can be recharged with electricity and used again and again. They contain pairs of lead and lead oxide plates bathed in dilute sulfuric acid. As the battery is used, the chemicals in the plates change until no more electricity is produced. But feeding an electric current into the battery changes the chemicals in the plates back to their original state. When the battery's positive and negative terminals are joined by a conductor an electric current flows once more.

▼ *Dry batteries are useful for supplying small quantities of electricity for flashlights, transistor radios, and electric bells, In dry batteries, a pastelike chemical mixture is packed around a carbon rod. When the chemicals are used up the battery cannot be recharged.*

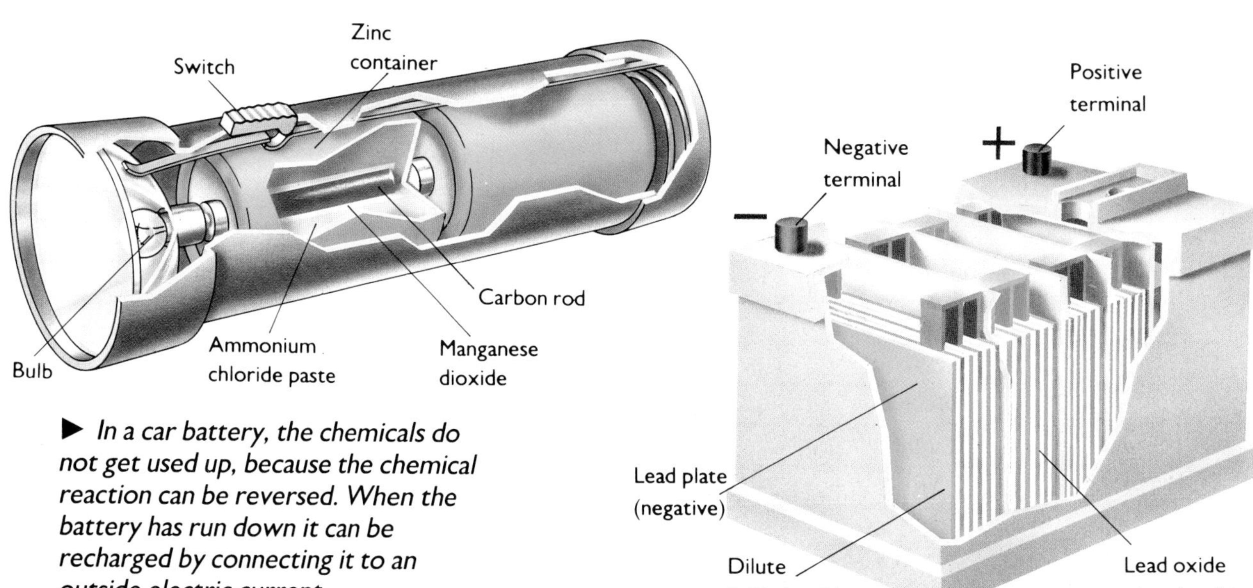

► *In a car battery, the chemicals do not get used up, because the chemical reaction can be reversed. When the battery has run down it can be recharged by connecting it to an outside electric current.*

Battles

Some battles have played an important part in the history of the world. Others are important only to the countries that fought them. Some of the important battles that affected many countries are shown on pages 70 and 71.

▼ *The pictures in the Bayeux Tapestry were worked in eight different colored yarns on strips of linen. Then they were sewn together into one long strip. The embroidery is kept under glass in a museum at Bayeux, France.*

Bayeux Tapestry

After WILLIAM THE CONQUEROR invaded England in 1066, one of his relatives had an embroidery made to record the conquest. This is known as the Bayeux Tapestry (although it is sewn, not woven). It is a piece of linen 230 ft. (70 m) long. There are 72 colorful scenes on it telling the story of William's victory. Latin words explain what is happening.

Bean

Beans belong to a family of plants called legumes. They are grown all over the world and have been eaten for thousands of years. There is evidence that beans were being eaten over 10,000 years ago by prehistoric people in Switzerland.

Beans are one of the cheapest and most widely eaten foods of all. They are rich in PROTEINS. Some kinds are used for animal fodder.

There are hundreds of different kinds of beans. A few of the best known varieties are kidney, lima, and soybeans. Some, such as SOYBEANS, are used to make vegetable oil. They are also used in making soaps and varnishes.

SEE IT YOURSELF

Put some bean seeds in a jam jar lined with blotting paper. Keep the paper moist. Soon a young root will burst from the seed. Then the young shoot will appear and grow upward, unfurling the first leaves as it goes. These start to make food as soon as they reach the light. You can plant the seedlings in the yard when you have watched the early stages of growth.

BATTLES

War and battles are as old as mankind. It was in the Middle East, more than 3,500 years ago, that the first effective armies appeared. In the ancient world the warriors of Egypt, Assyria, Greece, and Rome were feared by their enemies. Until modern times infantry (foot soldiers) made up the bulk of most armies. The armored corps of the armies of the past were knights on horseback, protected by metal and leather armor.

The invention of gunpowder and cannon made warfare more destructive. The Chinese used gunpowder rockets before A.D. 1000; in Europe, cannon were in use on the battlefield by the 1300s. Later, after the Industrial Revolution of the 1800s, came mechanized warfare—battles between war machines. Modern weapons such as missiles, aircraft, and tanks have made the battlefield even more terrible than in ancient times, when armies met in hand-to-hand combat.

Battles have been fought on land, in the air, and both on and beneath the sea. The most successful military commander is not always the person leading the largest force. Many famous victories have been won against seemingly hopeless odds. Some battles have decided the course of history and the destiny of nations.

◀ *The sea battle of Salamis was fought in 480 B.C. between the Greeks and Persians. The Greeks, with 380 ships, defeated a Persian fleet of up to 1,000 oared galleys.*

SOME FAMOUS BATTLES

Marathon 490 B.C. *10,000 Greeks defeated 60,000 Persians*
Tours A.D. 732 *Franks defeated Arabs.*
Hastings 1066 *Normans led by William defeate[d] Saxons and conquered England.*
Agincourt 1415 *English led by Henry V defeate[d] much larger French army.*
Constantinople 1453 *Turks overran Byzantine Empire.*
Armada 1588 *English fleet defeated Spanish invasion.*
Lexington-Concord 1775 *First engagement o[f] the Revolutionary War.*
Yorktown 1781 *Americans, helped by French, defeated British to win independence.*
Trafalgar 1805 *Nelson's British fleet defeated combined French-Spanish fleet.*
Waterloo 1815 *Napoleon's final defeat by Allies led by Wellington.*
Alamo 1836 *Heroic defense by Texans against Mexicans.*
Gettysburg 1863 *North defeated South in cruc[ial] battle of Civil War.*
Marne 1914 *World War I battle that ended Germany's hopes of a quick victory.*
Somme 1916 *Bloodiest battle of World War I.*
Battle of Britain 1940 *Britain's RAF defeated German Luftwaffe over southern England.*
Alamein 1942 *Montgomery's British army drove Rommel's German army out of North Africa: World War II.*
Midway 1942 *The first clear U.S. victory over Japan in World War II.*
Stalingrad 1942-43 *Germans failed to capture city from Russians.*
Leyte Gulf 1944 *Largest sea battle of World W[ar] II between U.S. and Japanese navies. U.S. broke Japanese sea power.*
Dien Bien Phu 1954 *Vietnamese defeated French.*

RECORD BATTLES

Longest siege: *Leningrad (U.S.S.R.), 880 days from August 1941 to January 1944.*
Largest retreat: *Dunkirk, May 1940: 338,000 Allied troops evacuated from France.*
Bloodiest: *First battle of the Somme, 1916: more than one million casualties.*
Longest war: *Hundred Years' War, 1346–1453 between England and France.*
Shortest modern war: *Six Day War, June 5–10, 1967, between Israelis and Arabs.*

▲ *The Battle of Gettysburg, fought in 1863 between North and South in the Civil War, was a turning point in the war.*

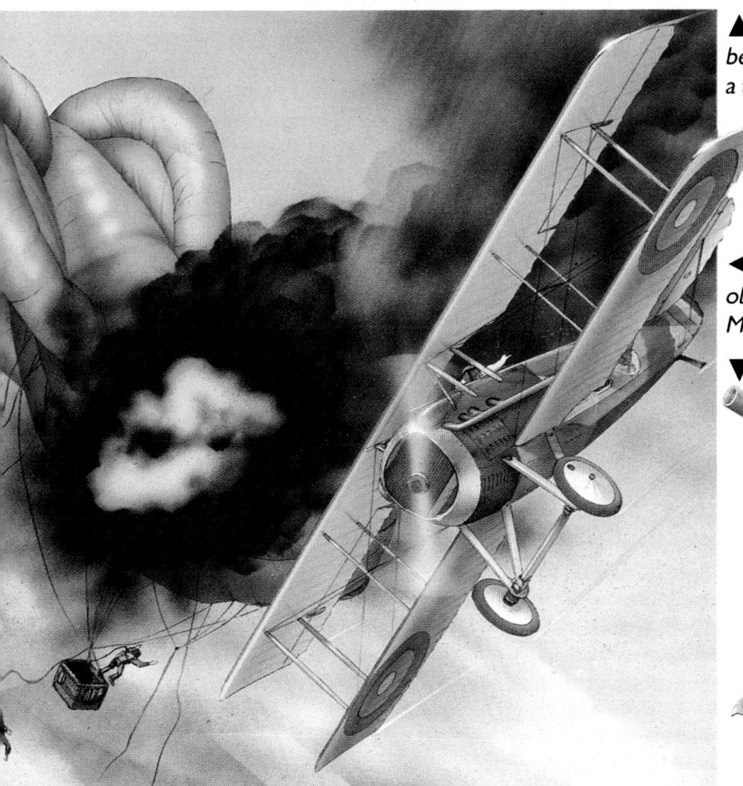

◀ *An American pilot destroys a German observation balloon during the Battle of the Marne in World War I.*

▼ *A modern Swedish self-propelled gun.*

For more information turn to these articles: CIVIL WAR; CRIMEAN WAR; REVOLUTIONARY WAR, AMERICAN; WORLD WAR I; WORLD WAR II.

▲ *The sloth bear, also called the honey bear, lives in the forests of India and Sri Lanka.*

▲ *Black bears are the most common species in North America. They are also the smallest.*

▲ *The polar bear lives in the Arctic. It is one of the biggest bears.*

Bear

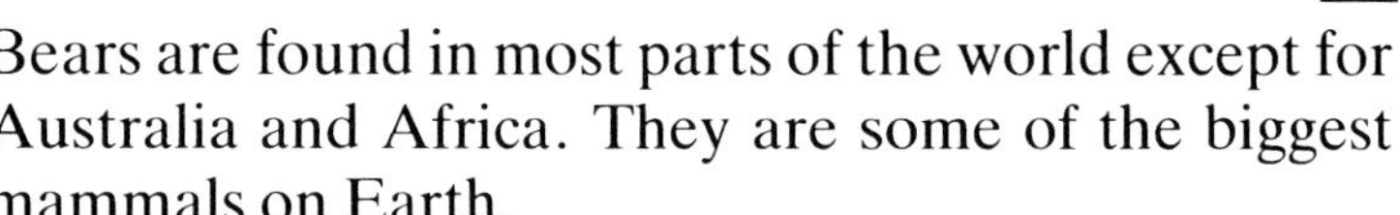

Bears are found in most parts of the world except for Australia and Africa. They are some of the biggest mammals on Earth.

The largest of all bears are the brown bears of Alaska. These can reach a weight of over 1,650 pounds (750 kg). Other giants include the polar bear of the Arctic and the grizzly of western North America.

The only bear that lives in South America is the small spectacled bear. Its name comes from the ringlike markings around its eyes.

The smallest bear in the world is the sun bear of the jungles of Southeast Asia. It weighs no more than 145 pounds (65 kg).

Bears can be slow, lumbering beasts. They have short, powerful limbs and heavy, broad heads with powerful jaws. They also have long, dangerous claws for digging and tearing.

Their eyesight is not very sharp, but their sense of smell is very good. Although they look clumsy, all but the biggest bears can climb trees.

Bears eat almost anything. They browse on leaves, roots, berries, fruit, and nuts. They enjoy eating honey and ants and often attack beehives and anthills. They also eat other insects, and catch fish and small animals.

Most bears are shy, but if they are disturbed and cornered they will attack fiercely.

Beaver

Beavers are big RODENTS more than 3 ft. (1 m) long, including the tail, and weighing more than 55 pounds (25 kg). They live in woods by the side of lakes and rivers and are good swimmers. Beavers are able to stay under water for up to 15 minutes. They have a broad, flat tail covered with scaly skin. This is used for steering with when they swim.

Beavers need pools in which to build their homes, and often block up, or dam, streams with mud and sticks to make one. They cut down small trees with their sharp teeth and drag them to the pool to strengthen the dam.

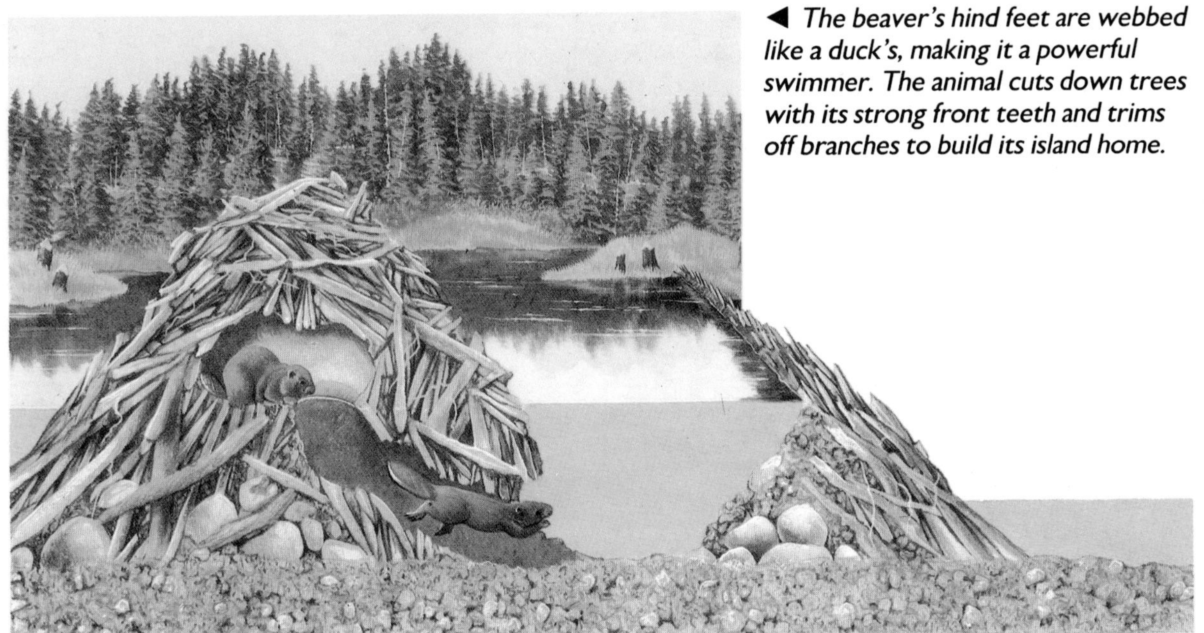

◀ *The beaver's hind feet are webbed like a duck's, making it a powerful swimmer. The animal cuts down trees with its strong front teeth and trims off branches to build its island home.*

Beavers build a home of mud and sticks by the side of the pool. This home, called a lodge, has an underwater entrance and an escape hole. Inside, there is a nest above water for the young beavers.

Beavers eat bark, mainly from alder and willow trees. They store twigs in their homes to feed on during the winter. Beavers have thick fur which keeps them warm. They live in many parts of North America.

Becket, Thomas à

Thomas à Becket (1118–1170) was an archibishop of Canterbury who angered King Henry II of England by demanding special rights for the Church. He was exiled but returned later and once more angered the King. Four knights mistakenly thought the King wanted Becket killed, and murdered him in Canterbury Cathedral in 1170. He was made a saint in 1173.

Bee

There are many different kinds of bee, but the best known kind is the honeybee. Honeybees live in hives or colonies of about 50,000 worker bees. Worker bees are female, but they do not breed. Each colony also has a queen bee, which breeds, and a few hundred stingless drones, which are male.

A bee can see the colors green, blue, and ultraviolet, the last of which is invisible to us. But pure red is no color to a bee. It sees red objects as black.

A bee must visit over 4,000 flowers in order to make a tablespoon of honey.

Worker bee

Queen bee

Drone bee

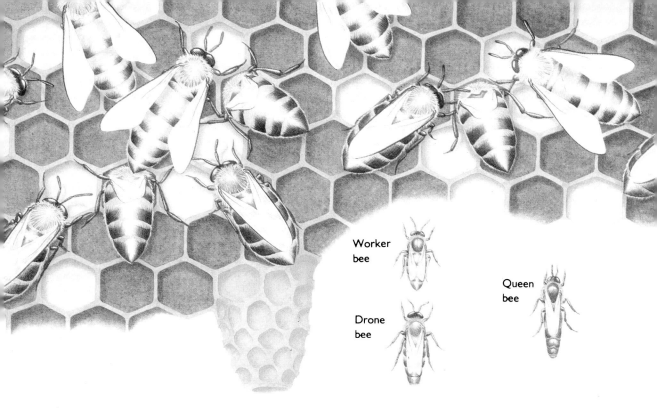

▲ *Inside the hive of the honeybee are cells made of wax. The queen lays eggs in the cells. Larvae hatch out of the eggs and are fed by the workers. Worker bees collect nectar and pollen from flowers. The nectar is made into honey, which is stored in the hive for food.*

The worker bee's life is very short, usually about four weeks, so the queen has to lay many eggs to provide enough bees. She can lay up to 1,500 eggs in one day. From time to time a new queen is born. The old queen then leaves the hive with a *swarm* of about half the workers to seek another home.

The workers collect *pollen* and nectar from flowers. The nectar is made into honey. It is stored in the hive to feed the bees in winter. Beekeepers carefully remove the honey from the hive. They give the bees sugar syrup to replace the honey they take.

There are other types of bee that do not live in large colonies. These are called solitary bees. They produce a small family of a few hundred bees which die each winter. The queen hibernates and produces a new family the following year.

▲ *When Beethoven was young he studied under Mozart and Haydn.*

Beethoven, Ludwig Van

Ludwig van Beethoven (1770–1827) was a German musician who composed some of the greatest music ever known. This included symphonies, concertos, and choral and chamber music. When he was young, Beethoven was well known as a pianist and was admired by many famous people. He began to go deaf at the age of 30 but continued to compose music even when he was totally deaf.

Beetle

Beetles are INSECTS. There are over 300,000 species of beetle known.

Some beetles are as small as a pinhead. Others are very large. The giant African goliath beetle measures up to 4 inches (10 cm) long and can weigh $3^{1}/_{2}$ ounces (100 grams).

In prehistoric times all beetles had two pairs of wings. But over millions of years the front pair changed, or *evolved*, into hard, close-fitting coverings for the second pair underneath. All beetles used to be flying insects, but now many of them live on the ground.

Beetles start their lives as eggs which hatch into grubs, or larvae. The larvae then turn into chrysalises, or pupae, before the adult beetles emerge.

Many beetles and their larvae are destructive pests. Woodworms, weevils, wireworms, cockroaches, and Colorado and flea beetles do great damage to crops, trees, and buildings.

Some beetles can be very useful. Ladybugs are small beetles that eat harmful insects such as aphids. Dung beetles and burying beetles clear away dung and dead animals.

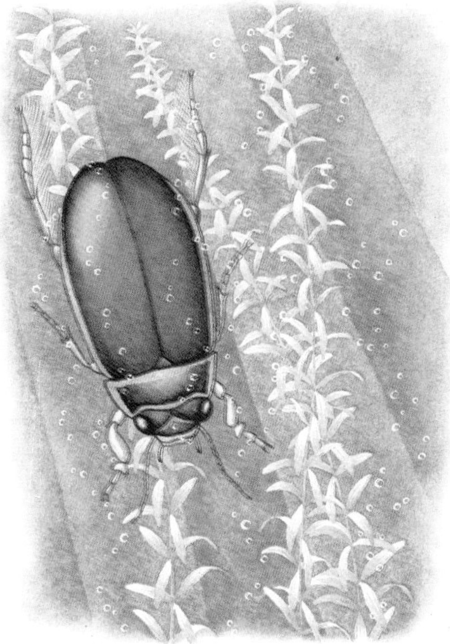

▲ *The great diving beetle catches its prey at the bottom of ponds and streams.*

▲ *The Colorado beetle, also called the potato bug, is a pest that ruins potato crops.*

◀ *Burying beetles bury the corpses of small birds and mammals by digging soil from under them. They lay their eggs on the buried animal, and the grubs feed on it.*

Beijing (Peking)

Beijing, formerly called Peking, is the capital of China. In A.D. 1267 the Mongol conqueror Kublai Khan made it the capital of his empire. In the center of the city is the walled Forbidden City containing the palace of the ancient Chinese emperors. Modern Beijing is a center of industry and learning. Its population is more than 7,000,000.

In 1267 Beijing was called Khanbalik ("City of the Khan"). In 1421 it was given the name Peking ("Northern Capital"). In the modern system used for translating Chinese "Peking" is written "Beijing."

BELGIUM

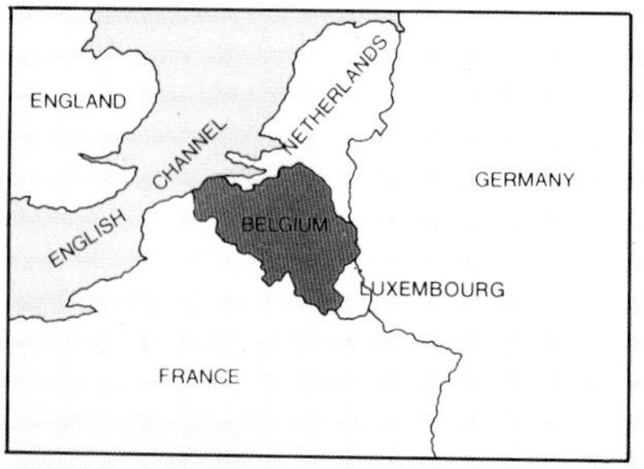

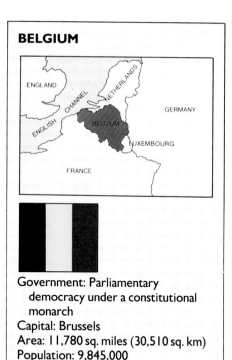

Government: Parliamentary democracy under a constitutional monarch
Capital: Brussels
Area: 11,780 sq. miles (30,510 sq. km)
Population: 9,845,000
Languages: Flemish; French
Currency: Belgian franc

Belgium

Belgium is a small country sandwiched between France, Germany, and Holland. Its capital is Brussels. Belgium's population is made up of two main groups: the Germanic Flemings of the north and the French-speaking Walloons of the south. Because of its central and strategic position, Belgium has been invaded and fought over throughout the course of European history. Today Belgium is an international center. The headquarters of the EUROPEAN COMMUNITY (EC) and NATO are both in Brussels.

Belize

Belize is a small country on the east coast of Central America. It was Great Britain's last colony on the American mainland, and achieved its independence in 1981. Belize was formerly named British Honduras. The main export is sugar.

Bell, Alexander Graham

Alexander Graham Bell (1847–1922) is remembered as the inventor of the TELEPHONE. Bell was the son of a Scottish teacher who went to Canada with his family in 1870. Two years later Alexander set up a school for teachers of the deaf in Boston, Massachusetts. Through his work with devices to help the deaf, Bell became interested in sending voices over long distances. On March 10, 1876, the first sentence was transmitted by telephone. The historic words were spoken by Bell to his assistant: "Mr. Watson, come here; I want you."

BELIZE

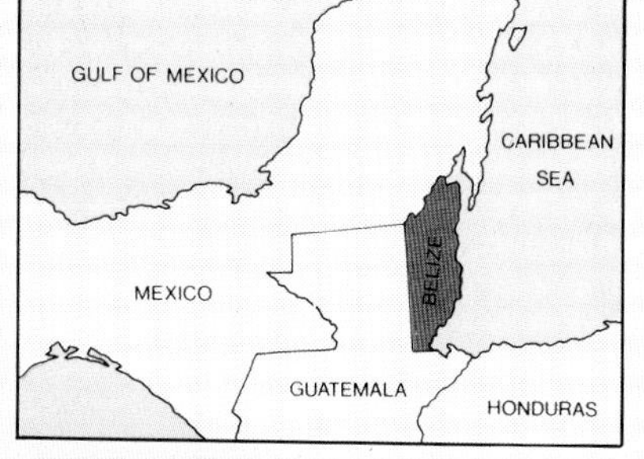

Government: Parliamentary
Capital: Belmopan
Area: 8,867 sq. miles (22,965 sq. km)
Population: 188,000
Languages: English; Spanish
Currency: Belize dollar

Bells

Bells come in many sizes for many uses. Some large bells are famous; these include the Liberty Bell in Independence Hall, Philadelphia, Big Ben in the clock tower of the Houses of Parliament in London, and the largest in the world, the Kolokol in Moscow, which weighs 193 tons.

The "bells" in the percussion section of orchestras are in fact metal tubes struck by mallets.

Benin

Benin is a small country in West Africa, known from 1960 to 1975 as Dahomey. It is slightly smaller than Pennsylvania. The climate is mostly hot and humid, and the people are poor. Most of them live in the south. Benin's economy depends very largely on one crop: the palm kernel. Benin became independent from France in 1960.

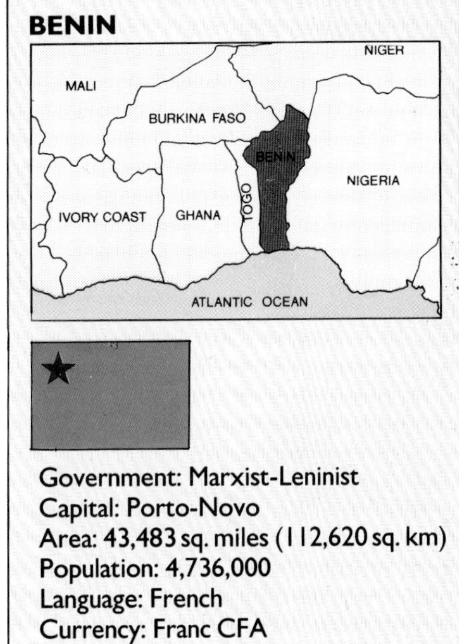

Government: Marxist-Leninist
Capital: Porto-Novo
Area: 43,483 sq. miles (112,620 sq. km)
Population: 4,736,000
Language: French
Currency: Franc CFA

Berlin

Berlin is the largest city in GERMANY and, since reunification, is the capital of all of Germany. In 1945, when Germany was divided into two countries, East and West, Berlin was divided into four zones between the Americans, British, French, and Russians.

In 1948 the Russians quarreled with the other allies and blockaded the city by cutting its road and rail links with West Germany. But Britain and the U.S. flew in supplies to keep the city going. After a year the Russians gave up and reopened the roads and railroads. Berlin was largely destroyed by bombing during World War II, but at the end of the war rebuilding was rapid.

Today West and East Berlin are almost completely rebuilt. The Berlin Wall, built by the communists in 1961 to divide the eastern and western parts of the city, was broken down by the East German authorities in 1989.

The Berlin zoo is one of the oldest and most famous in the world. It was opened in 1844 and leads all the world's zoos in the number of species it contains. There are more than 2,000 species and more than 13,000 animals.

◀ *The Brandenburg Gate is in the former Soviet sector of Berlin. This picture was taken when Berlin was a divided city. The notice reads:* Warning! You are now leaving West Berlin.

BHUTAN

Government: Monarchy
Capital: Thimphu
Area: 18,147 sq. miles (47,000 sq. km)
Population: 1,517,000
Language: Dzongkha
Currency: Ngultrum

Bermuda

Bermuda is a British colony in the North Atlantic Ocean, about 700 miles (1,130 km) southeast of New York City. There are about 300 islands in the group, but only 20 of them are inhabited. Bermuda's pleasant climate and beautiful beaches attract tourists all the year round. The capital is Hamilton.

Bhutan

Bhutan is a mountainous country lying on the slopes of the Himalayas between China and India. The government is under a king, a position handed down from father to son. The country became independent from Britain in 1949. India now helps Bhutan with foreign relations and money. Most people farm in isolated mountain valleys.

Bible

The Bible is the sacred book of Judeo-Christian religion. It is in two parts. The first part is called the Old Testament and records the history of the Jewish people and the teachings of their prophets before the birth of JESUS. The second part, the New Testament, records the life and sayings of Jesus and his disciples.

▶ *The caves at Qumran, on the shores of the Dead Sea, in which over a hundred scrolls of Old Testament books have been found.*

The Bible has always been the world's best-selling book. More than 212 billion copies have been sold since 1816. It has been translated into more than 1,500 languages.

Bicycle

The bicycle is a two-wheeled vehicle powered by its rider, who turns two pedals by foot. The earliest bicycles, called "dandy-horses," were invented in the 1700s. They were simply two wheels joined by a rod, with a seat on top. The rider pushed it along the ground by foot.

The first bicycle with pedals did not appear until 1865. These machines were known as "bone-shakers" because the seats had no springs. The next important development was the "high-wheeler" or "penny farthing," which had an enormous front wheel and a tiny rear wheel. The modern style of bicycle appeared in the 1880s. It has a chain-driven rear wheel and air-filled tires. This basic style has changed very little since then.

▲ *In 1817 Karl von Drais built his "dandy horse," or "draisine." It had no pedals, and the rider pushed it along by foot.*

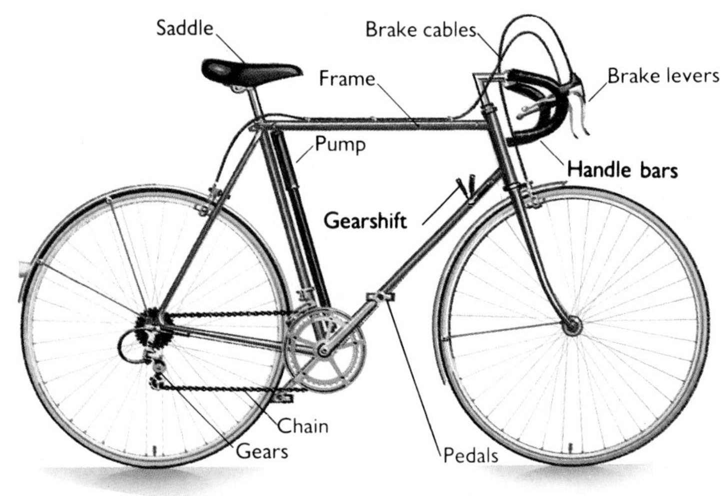

▲ *The Matchless ordinary bicycle, produced in 1883, was a "high-wheeler" or "penny farthing." It had solid tires and a step to help the rider get on.*

◀ *A modern bicycle may have as many as 15 or 20 gears.*

Binary System

The binary system is a number system that uses only two numerals—0 and 1. Our everyday *decimal system* uses ten numerals—0 to 9. In the decimal system you multiply a number by 10 by moving it one place to the left—2, 20, 200 etc. In the binary system, when you move a numeral one place to the left you multiply its value by two. A 1 by itself is 1. Move it a place to the left and it becomes 1 times 2, or 2. It is written 10. Move it another place to the left and it becomes 1 times 2 times 2, or 4. It is written 100. The binary for 93 is 1011101—one 1, no 2s, one 4, one 8, one 16, no 32s, and one 64.

0	Ø	Ø	Ø	Ø
1	Ø	Ø	Ø	1
2	Ø	Ø	1	Ø
3	Ø	Ø	1	1
4	Ø	1	Ø	Ø
5	Ø	1	Ø	1
6	Ø	1	1	Ø
7	Ø	1	1	1
8	1	Ø	Ø	Ø

▲ *A diagram of the binary system, in which the numerals 1 and 0 are used to represent all numbers.*

Biochemistry is a vast subject. Some biochemists are busy designing new drugs. Others are searching in the muscles to find molecules that expand and contract like tiny rubber bands. Still others are trying to find out which chemicals existed in the oceans when the Earth was new. They want to find out how life first began.

Biochemistry

Biochemistry is the study of the chemical reactions that take place inside tiny cells that make up all living things. Biochemists find out about the food people must eat to be healthy. They help fight disease by making chemicals that kill harmful bacteria. They also help farmers by finding out what foods are needed by plants and animals.

Biochemists also study special molecules in living things called *nucleic acids*. One kind of nucleic acid—DNA (deoxyribonucleic acid)—is found in the nucleus of cells. It carries and passes on the plan of a living thing from one generation to the next. It is the substance that makes each human being different from any other person that has ever lived. Biochemists are finding out more and more about the chemistry that makes us what we are.

Biology

Biology is the study of living things, from the tiniest ameba, which consists of just one CELL, to a mighty oak tree or a human being. The part of biology that deals with the PLANT world is called BOTANY. The study of ANIMALS is called zoology. One of the earliest biologists was the ancient Greek thinker Aristotle, who was the first to dissect, or cut open, and classify animals.

There was little interest in biology for more than a thousand years, until the RENAISSANCE, when scholars and artists such as LEONARDO DA VINCI tried to discover how living things grew and worked. At

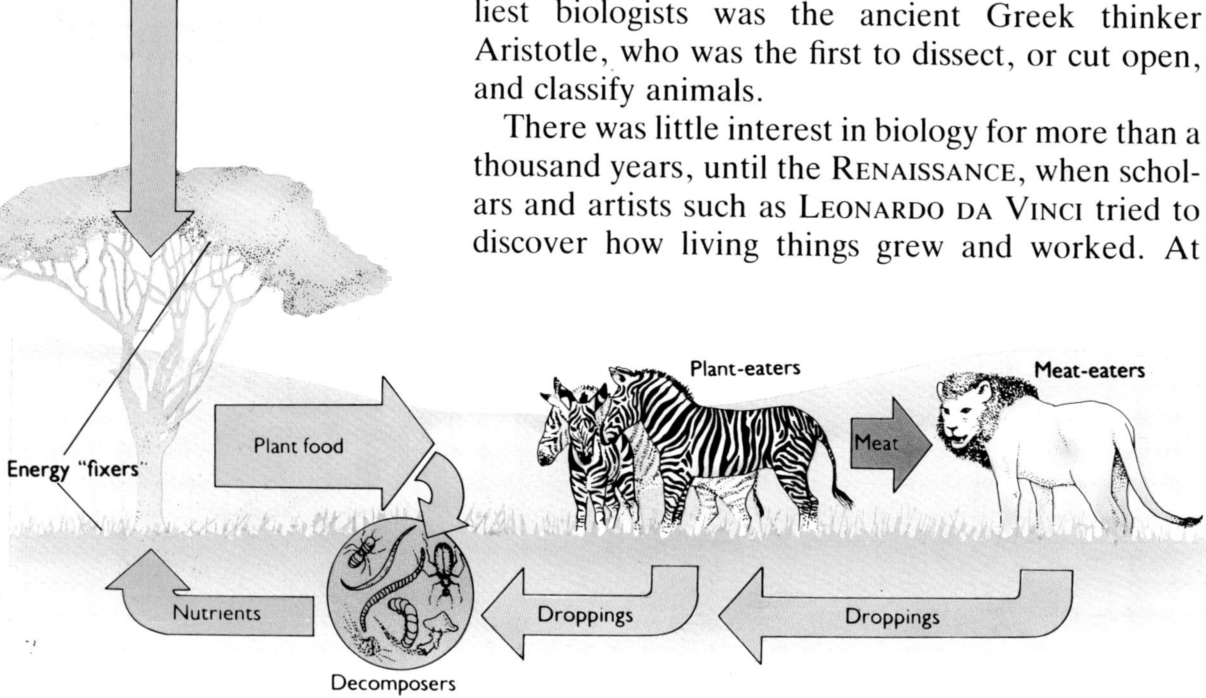

▼ *Biologists study all living things and how they are related to each other. Green plants store energy in the form of food, which is eaten by animals. Dead leaves are recycled in the soil. The droppings of plant-eating animals are also recycled. Nothing is wasted in the system. Even the lion is recycled when it dies.*

first the study of the human body by dissection was frowned upon by the Church. But this changed after the 1500s, and William HARVEY was able to show how the BLOOD travels around the body, and other people were able to compare the structure of various animals with that of people.

The invention of the MICROSCOPE in the 1600s opened up whole new areas of study for biologists. They were able to learn more about the animal and plant cells that are the building blocks of life. The study of other microscopic organisms, such as BACTERIA, helped people like Louis PASTEUR understand more about disease and how to prevent it.

In the 1800s, the English naturalist Charles DARWIN revolutionized biology with his theory of EVOLUTION. Today biology is divided into dozens of separate sciences. Biologists can spend their entire careers studying one tiny part of living matter.

Bird

Birds come in all shapes and sizes, but they all have wings and feathers. Some birds can fly thousands of miles. Others, such as the OSTRICH and the PENGUIN, cannot fly at all. The ostrich is the largest bird. It

▼ There are many different kinds of bird. Tropical birds, such as the macaw and the bird of paradise, are often brightly colored. The emperor penguin is a flightless bird but an excellent swimmer. It finds its food underwater, as does the flamingo, a wading bird.

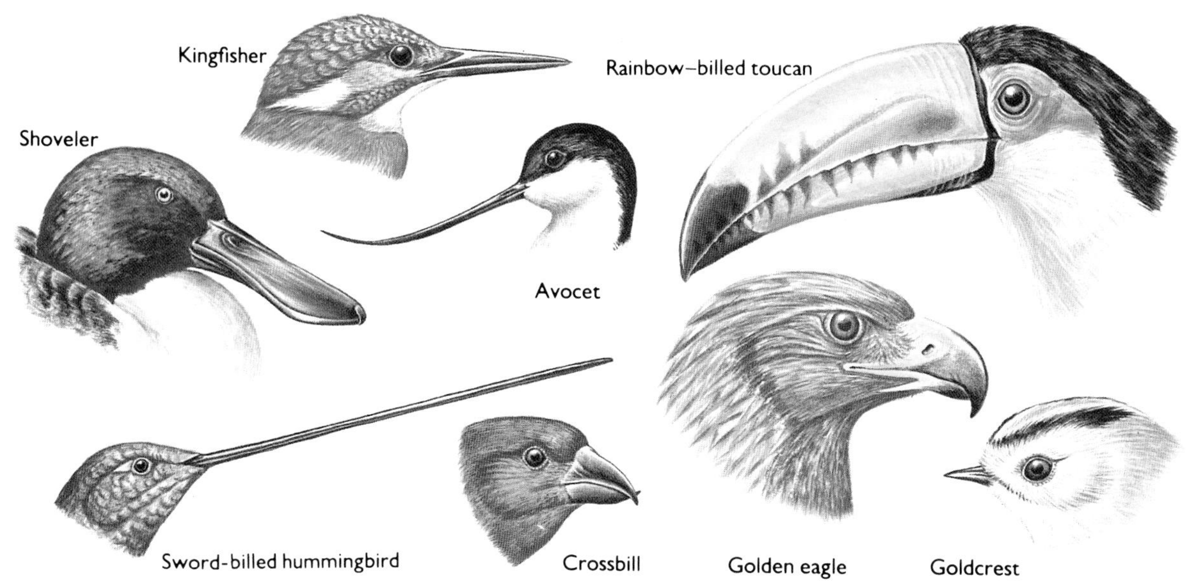

▲ *Birds' beaks are well suited to their feeding habits. The hummingbird, for example, probes for nectar, the crossbill cracks seeds, and the golden eagle tears flesh with its beak.*

can weigh more than 300 lbs. (150 kg). The smallest bird, a HUMMINGBIRD, weighs less than .07 oz. (2 g).

Birds developed from scaly REPTILES that lived 180,000,000 years ago. Their scales changed over millions of years into feathers, and their front legs became wings. Birds have hollow bones for lightness in the air and strong breast muscles for working their wings. Large birds can flap their wings slowly and float, or hover, on air currents. Small birds need to flap their wings fast to stay in the air.

All birds lay EGGS. Most birds are busy parents who work hard to rear their young. Some, like the CUCKOO, lay their eggs in other birds' nests for foster parents to rear. Other birds bury their eggs in warm places and leave them. Most birds are wild, but some, such as chickens, pigeons, and canaries, have been tamed or *domesticated*. Some birds are bred on farms for their eggs and meat.

Birds' beaks have many different shapes. Sparrow hawks have hooked beaks for tearing up their prey. Chickadees have short beaks for eating small nuts, seeds, and insects. The nuthatch has a powerful, pointed beak for breaking open nuts.

Blackbirds have sharp beaks for digging up worms and slugs. The strange-looking crossbill has a crossed beak for tearing open pine cones to reach the kernels inside. Nightjars have short, wide beaks for snapping up moths and other night-flying insects on the wing.

SEE IT YOURSELF

A bird table will attract lots of birds to your backyard. Try making one for yourself. The tray should be about 6 ft. (2 m) from the ground to prevent cats from leaping onto it. Put the table near a window so you can watch it from inside. You can hang up a bit of fresh coconut for the chickadees.

Wading birds, such as the oyster-catcher, have long, thin beaks for probing in the mud. Many birds have beaks adapted for one kind of food only, but others such as the sparrow and the thrush thrive on a mixed diet.

▲ *A bird skeleton, with hollow and lightweight bones. The breastbone is deep and large.*

Birth Control

Birth control is the means by which people can choose the number of children they have. It is sometimes known as "family planning." Birth control has been used since ancient times, but modern methods did not become widespread until the 1800s and 1900s.

There are many methods of birth control. Some of them work by stopping the seed, or *sperm*, of the male from fertilizing the EGG, or *ovum*, of the female. This is known as *contraception*.

Some people are forbidden by their religion to use certain kinds of birth control. However, birth control is now encouraged in many countries with large populations.

Bison

The bison is a large animal of the cattle family. Its head and humped shoulders are covered in long shaggy hair. It is also called the BUFFALO.

There are two kinds of bison, the American and the European. There used to be great herds of bison in North America. The Indians were the first people

▼ *Once huge herds of bison roamed the prairies of North America. They were hunted by Plains Indians, who depended upon them for food, clothing, and for their "buffalo-hide" tepees. Bison have quick tempers, so it has been impossible to tame them. This picture shows a duel between two bulls.*

to hunt them. When Europeans went to America, they killed great numbers of bison until, by 1889, there were only about 500 left. Today, there are no bison living in the wild in America or Europe. Those that survive all live in parks and zoos.

A black hole turns space inside out. From the outside it might appear to be a round black object only a few miles across. But if you were inside it, it would seem as big as a universe. You could not see anything outside it.

Black Hole

Stars are made up mostly of HYDROGEN. It is the turning of this hydrogen into helium that makes stars like our SUN shine and give out heat. When a massive star uses up all its hydrogen fuel, it collapses. This collapse is called a *supernova* explosion. All that is left after such an explosion is a tiny star only a few miles across—a *neutron star*. The material in a neutron star is so squashed together—so dense—that a pinhead-sized piece of it would weigh as much as a large building! The GRAVITY of some neutron stars is so great that even light waves find it impossible to escape from them. As the light waves cannot get out, we call them *black holes*. Because these strange objects are entirely black, astronomers have never actually seen one, but they have found stars that could have an invisible black hole nearby.

Each year, the Elizabeth Blackwell Medal is awarded to a woman who has contributed to the advancement of the role of women in medicine.

Blackwell, Elizabeth

Elizabeth Blackwell (1821–1910) was the first woman doctor in the United States. She was born in

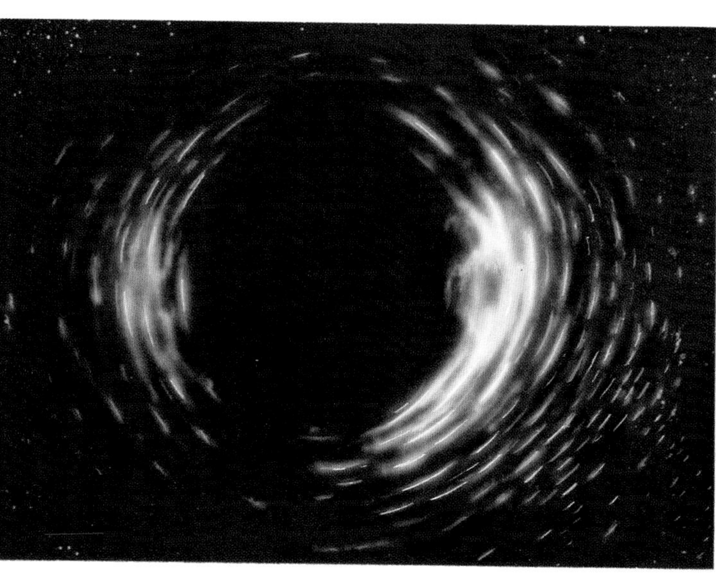

▶ *A close-up view of a black hole might appear like this—a pattern of bright light around its edge. The light, coming from distant stars behind the black hole, has been "bent" by the extra strong gravitational force around the hole.*

England, but grew up in New York. She decided to be a doctor, something that no woman had ever been before. Many colleges turned her down, but she eventually obtained her doctor's degree at the Geneva (New York) College of Medicine. Dr. Blackwell could not get a job, so she started a clinic for poor people in New York. Later she went to England to open a school of medicine for women.

▼ *Louis Blériot made his epic flight across the English Channel in a monoplane which he had designed and built, powered by an Anzani engine.*

Blériot, Louis

Louis Blériot (1872–1936) was a famous French airman. He was a pioneer of aviation and designed and built a number of early airplanes. On July 25, 1909, he took off from Calais in one of his own AIRCRAFT. Twenty-seven minutes later, he touched down at Dover, becoming the first man to fly the English Channel. In doing so, he won a prize of £1,000 offered by the London *Daily Mail* newspaper. Blériot went on to design other aircraft and became the owner of a large aircraft company.

Blood

Blood is the fluid that nourishes our bodies and removes waste products. It takes in food from the digestive system and OXYGEN from the LUNGS, and carries them to all the CELLS in the body. Each cell takes exactly what it needs from the blood, and the blood carries away cell waste, including water and

▼ *Blood is made up of red and white blood cells. Red cells carry oxygen to all parts of the body. White cells fight harmful bacteria. Platelets help blood to clot in a wound, stopping bleeding and sealing the wound against bacteria.*

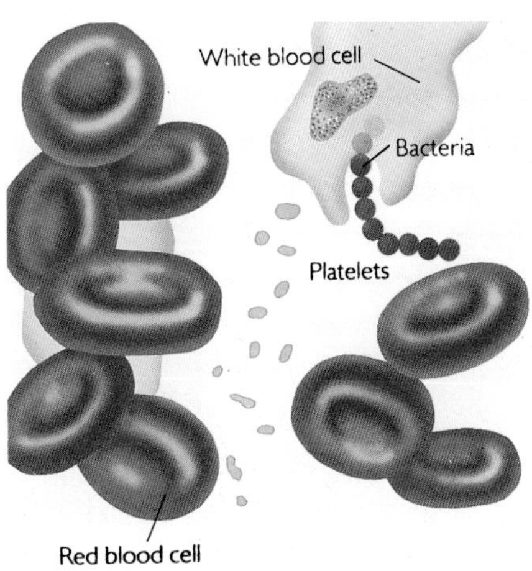

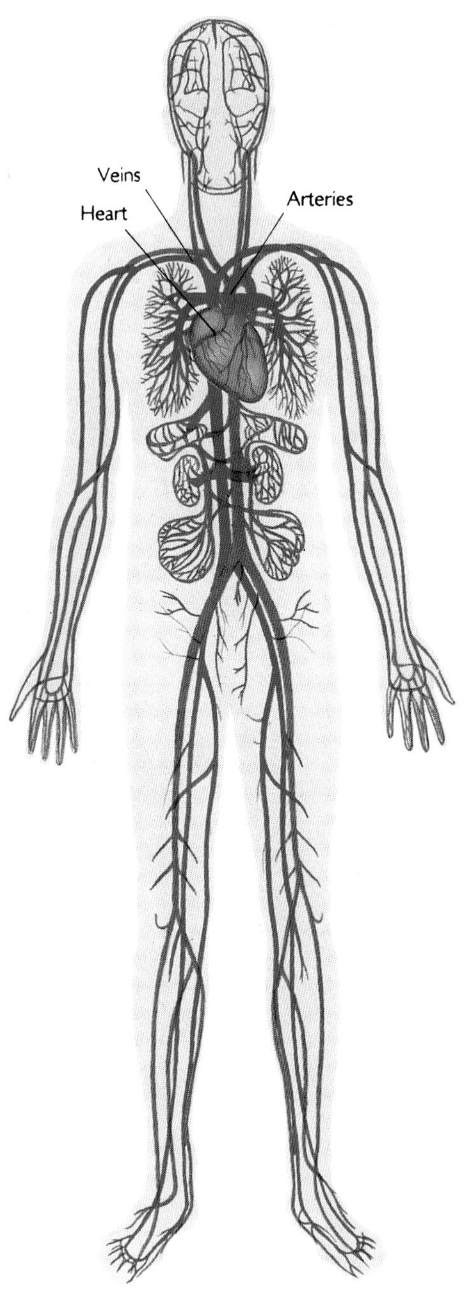

▲ *The heart pumps blood around the body, through a system of arteries, veins, and capillaries.*

carbon dioxide. Blood also carries special body chemicals to where they are needed. And it kills germs and keeps the body at the right temperature.

Blood is made in the marrow of the bones. The adult human body contains about 5 qts. (4.7 l) of blood. This blood is made up of a pale liquid called *plasma* and millions of cells, or *corpuscles*. Corpuscles are tiny red disks that give the blood its color. The blood also contains white corpuscles. There are about 5 million red corpuscles and between 5,000 and 10,000 white corpuscles in every tiny cubic millimeter of blood.

Fighting Disease

White corpuscles attack germs that enter the body by absorbing them. Often many white corpuscles are killed in the fight against disease or infection. Large numbers of dead white corpuscles collect as *pus*. Other blood particles, called *platelets*, help our blood to clot when we bleed. This helps scratches and other wounds to heal more quickly.

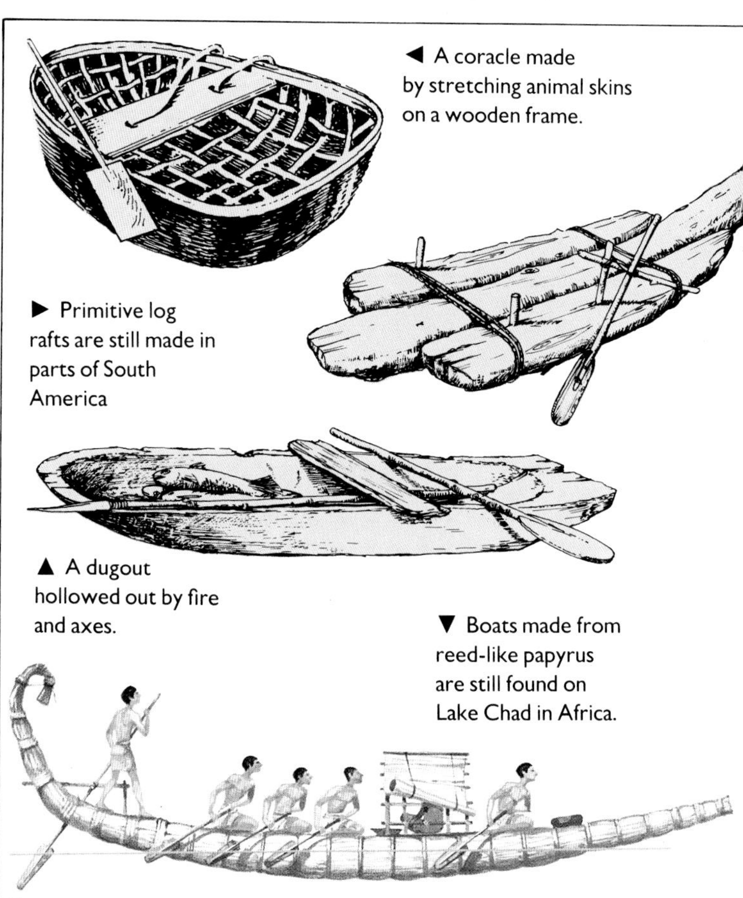

◀ A coracle made by stretching animal skins on a wooden frame.

▶ Primitive log rafts are still made in parts of South America

▲ A dugout hollowed out by fire and axes.

▼ Boats made from reed-like papyrus are still found on Lake Chad in Africa.

We can all be classified into blood groups A, B, AB, or O, according to the type of blood we have. Blood groups are important when patients are given blood transfusions. Transfusions are given to replace either diseased blood or blood that has been lost through an injury. The blood a person is given is generally the same blood type as their own.

Our red blood cells live for about 127 days. About 8,000 of them are destroyed and replaced every hour. An adult's body contains about 5 quarts (4.7 l) of blood, running through more than 60,000 miles (96,000 km) of blood vessels. One cubic centimeter of blood contains as many as 512 billion red cells and about 11 million white cells.

Boat

Boats, unlike SHIPS, are usually small, open craft, although the name is sometimes given to larger vessels such as the motor torpedo boat. The first boats date back to prehistoric times and were simply floating logs or driftwood paddled with the hands. The first real boats appeared later. One was the dugout canoe, which was a log hollowed out by fire or stone tools. Another was a raft made of logs or bundles of reeds tied together. When there were no logs or reeds, boats were made of skins stretched over a light framework. Small round boats called coracles

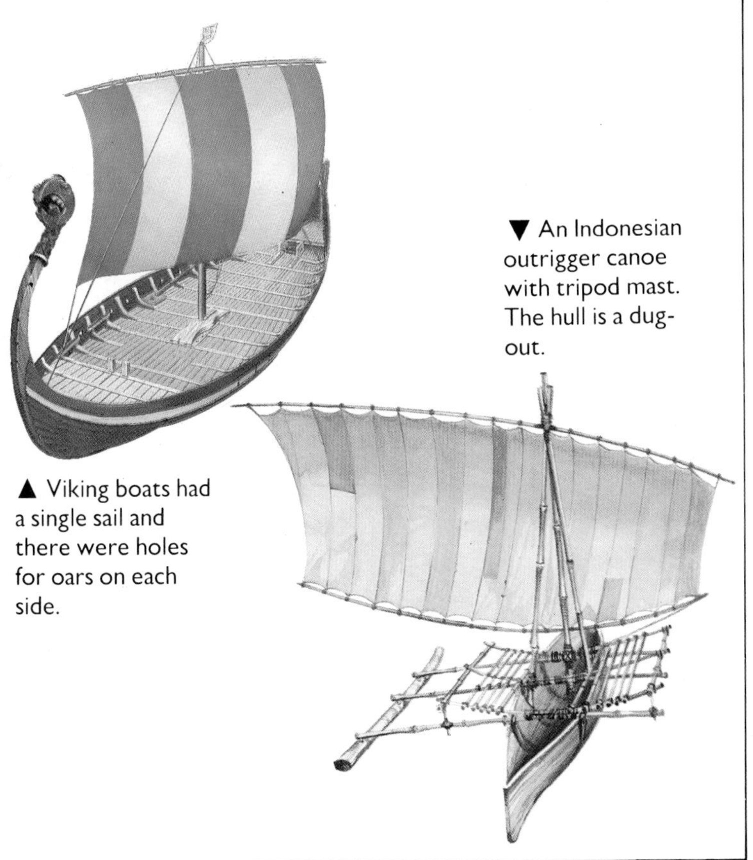

▼ An Indonesian outrigger canoe with tripod mast. The hull is a dugout.

▲ Viking boats had a single sail and there were holes for oars on each side.

Sailing boats can, given the right conditions, achieve very high speeds. The world sailing record is 41.5 mph (66.8 km/h) over a 500-meter (547-yard) course, achieved by an outrigger craft in 1980. Even higher speeds have been reached by windsurfers.

▲ *Some fishing boats change little over the years. These are at Mevagissey in Cornwall, England.*

and Eskimo kayaks were made in this way.

After a while, the dugout and the raft were built up with sides of wooden planks to make them drier and sturdier. A keel was added at the bottom to make the boat more seaworthy. Different types and shapes of sails were fitted to catch as much wind as possible. Until the 1800s, all boats were driven by sails, oars, or poles, but the invention of the STEAM ENGINE made paddle wheels and propellers possible. Today, motorboats, sailboats, canoes, and rowboats are used by people all over the world for pleasure as well as work.

Robert Baden-Powell was in command of the town of Mafeking during its 217-day siege by the Boers during the Boer War. When the town was freed, Baden-Powell returned to England a hero. In 1910 he retired from the army and devoted the rest of his life to the Scouting movement.

Boer War

The Boer War (1899–1902) was fought in SOUTH AFRICA between the Boers—settlers of Dutch descent—and the British. The slow and badly-led British troops were no match for the fast and lightly armed Boers in the early days of the war. But in the end Britain's overwhelming strength won. There were about 450,000 soldiers in the British armies during the Boer War, and only about 60,000 Boers.

Bolivia

Bolivia is a land-locked country in central SOUTH AMERICA, west of Brazil. Most of Bolivia is an enormous plain stretching from the Brazilian border to the eastern foothills of the ANDES Mountains. High in the Andes lies the great Bolivian plateau, over 13,000 ft. (4,000 m) high. Two-thirds of Bolivia's people live here. The capital is La Paz, the highest capital in the world, and Lake Titicaca, at 12,500 ft. (3,810 m) above sea level, is one of the highest lakes in the world.

Spain ruled Bolivia from 1532 until 1825. It gained freedom from Spain with the help of Simón Bolívar, a Venezuelan general, after whom Bolivia is named. More than half the people are Indians, a third are *mestizos* (people who are part European, part Indian) and the rest are direct descendants of Europeans. Bolivia is the world's second largest producer of tin, and mining is the country's most valuable industry.

BOLIVIA

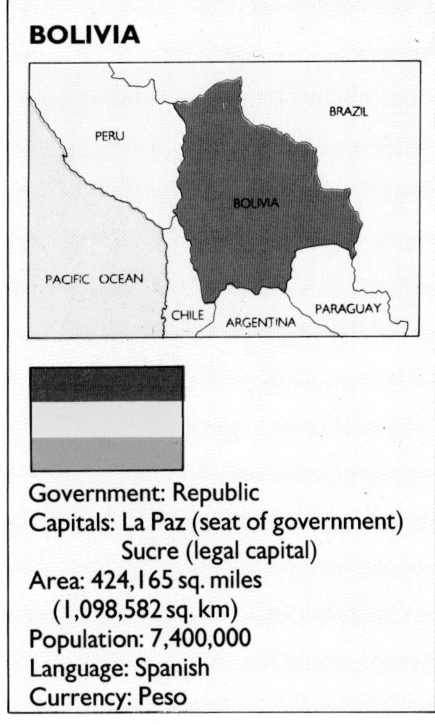

Government: Republic
Capitals: La Paz (seat of government)
Sucre (legal capital)
Area: 424,165 sq. miles
(1,098,582 sq. km)
Population: 7,400,000
Language: Spanish
Currency: Peso

Bone

Bones make up the hard framework that supports the flesh and organs of all vertebrates (animals with backbones). All bones are made up of the same thing, mostly calcium. Bones are hard on the outside, but soft on the inside. Bone *marrow*, in the hollow center of the bone, is where new red BLOOD cells are made.

The human skeleton has four kinds of bones: long bones, such as arm and leg bones; flat bones, such as the skull; short bones, including ankle and wrist bones; and irregular bones, such as those that make up the backbone. If bones are broken, they will knit together again if they are rejoined or *set* properly. The cells in the broken ends of the bone produce a substance that helps the ends to grow together again so that the mended bone is as strong as it ever was.

As human beings get older, their bones become more brittle and will break more easily. Children's bones, on the other hand, are able to bend a little and are not so easily broken or injured. Adults have about 206 bones in their skeleton.

▼ *Bones may look lifeless, but they are a mass of living cells. The Haversian canals contain blood vessels.*

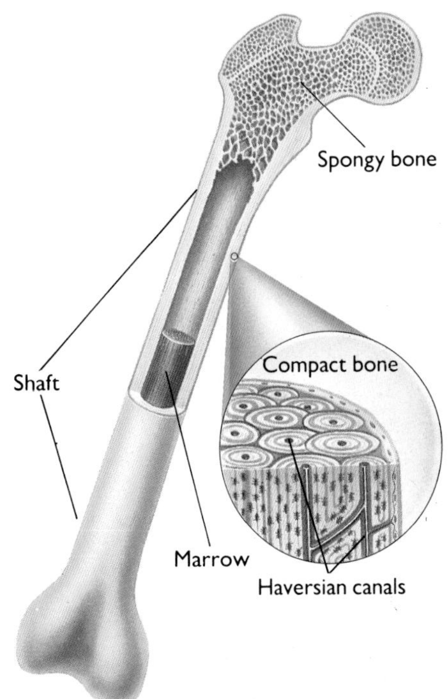

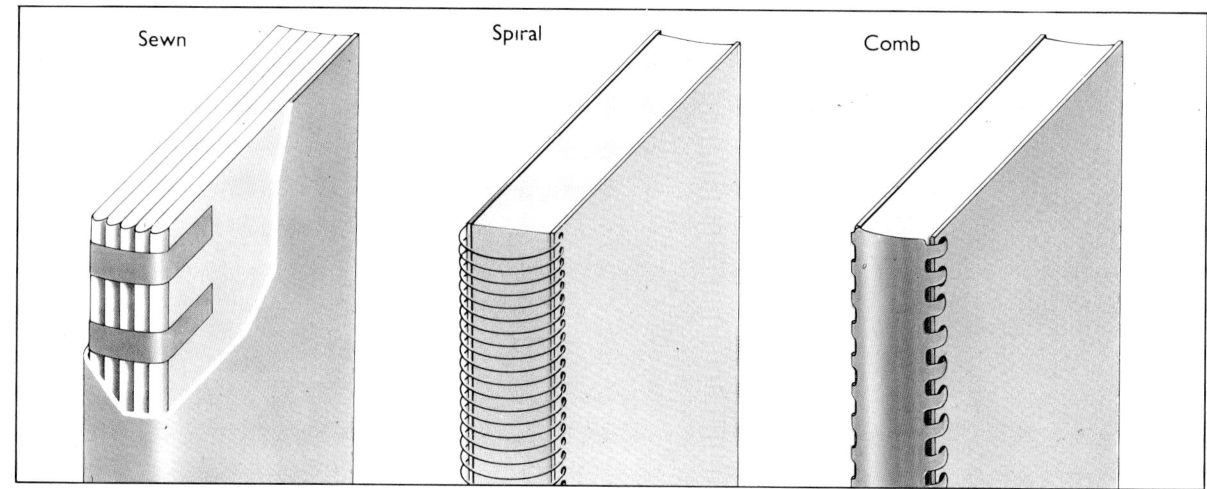

▲ *Three ways of binding a book. In a sewn binding, the gathered sections, or signatures, of the book are sewn individually and then joined to each other by thread. The cover is then glued on. Spiral and comb bindings both allow the pages to lie completely flat when open. Another kind of binding is perfect binding, in which the folded pages have the spine edge trimmed off and roughened to form a better bond when they are glued.*

▼ *A medieval illuminated manuscript. Before the invention of printing, books were copied and often elaborately decorated by hand.*

Book

Books are used for storing and passing on all kinds of knowledge, ideas, and stories. Some of the earliest books were made by the ancient Egyptians. They were written by hand on rolls of paper made from the papyrus plant.

By the time of the Roman Empire, many books were handwritten on parchment or *vellum*, made from animal skin. It was cut into sheets to look much the same as a modern book.

During the MIDDLE AGES, monks made many beautiful books. They were decorated, or *illuminated*, by hand with bright colors and sometimes gold and silver. In the 1400s PRINTING on paper was introduced to Europe. At first this was very slow because much of the work still had to be done by hand. Then Johannes GUTENBERG invented a machine with movable type which could print books quickly. Today, many millions of books are produced every year, in all the languages of the world.

Boone, Daniel

Daniel Boone (1734–1820) was a well-known frontiersman of colonial America. He grew up in Pennsylvania and learned the skills of survival from the Indians. In 1775 he led settlers into Kentucky and built a fort at Boonesboro. Boone was captured several times by Indians but always escaped. In later years he became a respected lawmaker in West Virginia and Missouri.

▲ *The Boston Tea Party and its aftermath made the colonists even more determined to end British rule in America.*

Boston

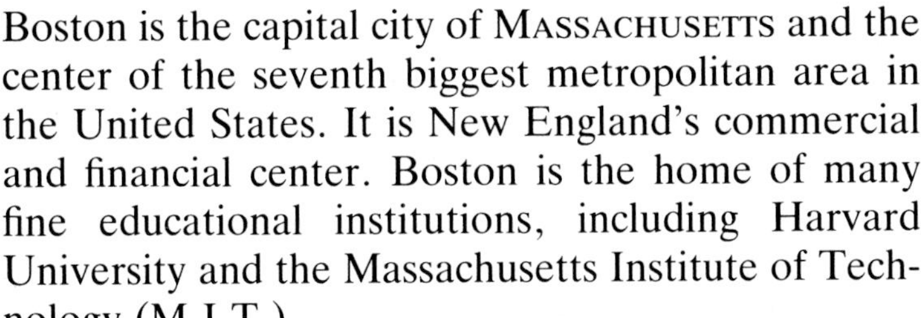

Boston is the capital city of MASSACHUSETTS and the center of the seventh biggest metropolitan area in the United States. It is New England's commercial and financial center. Boston is the home of many fine educational institutions, including Harvard University and the Massachusetts Institute of Technology (M.I.T.).

Boston was settled in 1630 by Puritans from England. Before the Revolutionary War the city was a leading center of opposition to British rule. Several of the incidents leading up to the war took place here, including the Boston Massacre (1770) and the Boston Tea Party (1775).

The Boston Tea Party was an act of protest against the British tax on tea. In 1773, the British decided to raise money by sending more tea to America and making the colonists pay a tax on it. The colonists were furious and asked the British governor to send all ships carrying tea back to England. When he refused, a group of Bostonians disguised themselves as Indians, boarded a ship in Boston harbor and dumped the cargo of tea overboard. This incident helped to fuel the flames that started the REVOLUTIONARY WAR.

The early settlers of Boston held very strict religious beliefs. No plays were allowed to be staged; Christmas was not allowed to be celebrated. Cooking on Sunday was sinful, so the women of Boston baked enough beans on Saturday to last them through Sunday. This is why Boston has been named Beantown.

SEE IT YOURSELF

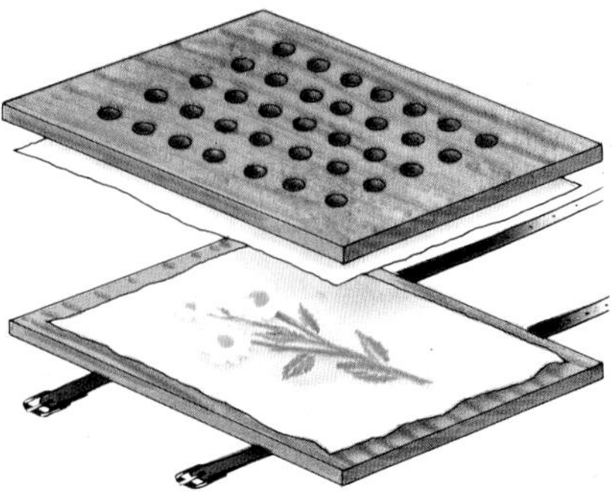

Make a wildflower collection by pressing them. Make sure the flowers are clean and dry. Put them carefully between two sheets of absorbent paper. You can make a flower press from two pieces of plywood or masonite and two straps. Put the flowers and the paper between the boards and strap them tightly together. The flowers should be quite dry in two weeks. If you drill some holes in the boards, it will help to let the moisture escape.

Botany

Botany is the study of PLANTS and how they grow. There are more than 300,000 different kinds of plant. They vary from tiny *algae* that can be seen only with a microscope, to giant redwood trees nearly 300 ft. (100 m) high. New plants are being discovered all the time.

Without plants there would be no animals, because animals depend on plants for all their food. There would be no cattle for us to eat if there was no grass for the cattle to eat. Animals also breathe the gas OXYGEN that plants give out.

By studying the way in which the qualities of one generation of plants are passed on to the next generation, scientists are able to grow bigger and better crops. They can breed varieties that are better at fighting plant disease.

In 1753, Carl von Linné (known as Linnaeus), a Swedish botanist, invented the first real system for naming plants. He gave every plant a name made up of two Latin words.

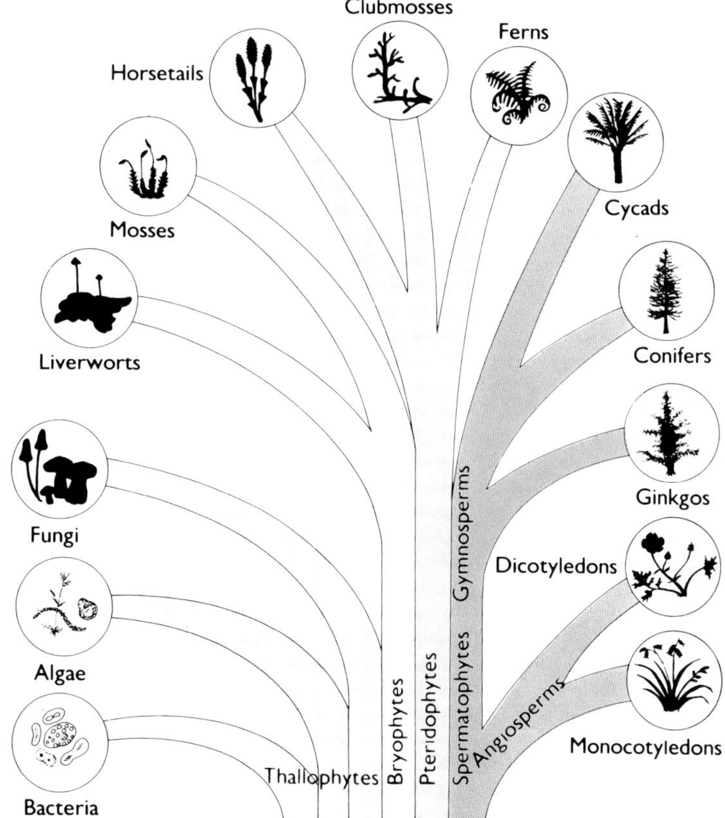

▶ *Plants are classified, or grouped, into four main divisions, which are further subdivided. For example, the flowering plants, or angiosperms, are divided into two groups—dicotyledons and monocotyledons—according to the number of seed leaves they have.*

Botswana

Botswana is an African country that lies far from the sea. It is bordered by Zimbabwe, South Africa, and Namibia. In 1885, the country, then called Bechuanaland, came under British control. Independence came in 1966. Botswana is a hot, dry country. Cattle raising and mining are the main industries. Most of western Botswana is covered by the Kalahari Desert.

BOTSWANA

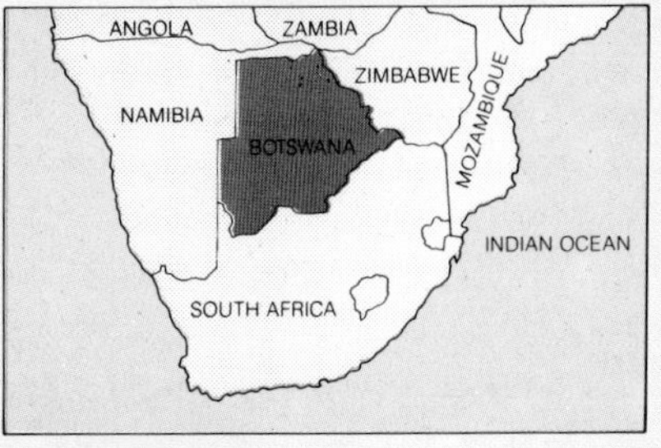

Government: Republic, parliamentary democracy
Capital: Gaborone
Area: 231,800 sq. miles (600,372 sq. km)
Population: 1,291,000
Language: English, Setswana
Currency: Pula

Bowie, James

James Bowie (1796–1836) was a frontiersman who settled in Texas in the days when it was still part of Mexico. He lived a wild life, but he was a brave man, too. He was killed at the Alamo, fighting for Texan independence from Mexico. Some say he also invented the Bowie knife, a sharp hunting knife with a single-edged blade.

Bowling

Bowling is one of the most popular sports in the United States. It is played indoors in bowling alleys. But this is only one form of one of the oldest games in the world. In tenpin bowling, the winner is the person who knocks down the most pins. If you knock down all the pins with one ball, you get a "strike." Twelve strikes in a row gives you a perfect score of 300 points.

Boxing

People have fought with their fists since ancient times. But boxing as we know it began in 1867 when the Marquess of Queensberry drew up a set of rules. Boxers today are divided into weight categories, from 112 lb. (51 kg) flyweights to heavyweights over 175 lb. (79.4 kg). Points are awarded after each 3-minute round for skill in attack and defense. Amateur contests usually consist of 3 rounds of 3 minutes each, with 1 minute rests between rounds. Professional contests can be any number of rounds up to 12 or even 15.

BOXING WEIGHT LIMITS

Professional
Flyweight: 112 lb. (50.8 kg)
Bantamweight: 118 lb. (53.5 kg)
Featherweight: 126 lb. (57.1 kg)
Lightweight: 135lb. (61.2 kg)
Welterweight: 147 lb. (66.7 kg)
Middleweight: 160 lb. (72.6 kg)
Light-heavyweight: 175 lb. (79.4 kg)
Heavyweight: any weight

Amateur
Light-flyweight: 107 lb. (48 kg)
Flyweight 112 lb. (51 kg)
Bantamweight: 119 lb. (54 kg)
Featherweight: 125 lb. (57 kg)
Lightweight: 132 lb. (60 kg)
Light-welterweight: 139 lb. (63.5 kg)
Welterweight: 147 lb. (67 kg)
Light-middleweight: 156 lb. (71 kg)
Middleweight: 166 lb. (75 kg)
Light-heavyweight: 178 lb. (81 kg)
Heavyweight: no limit

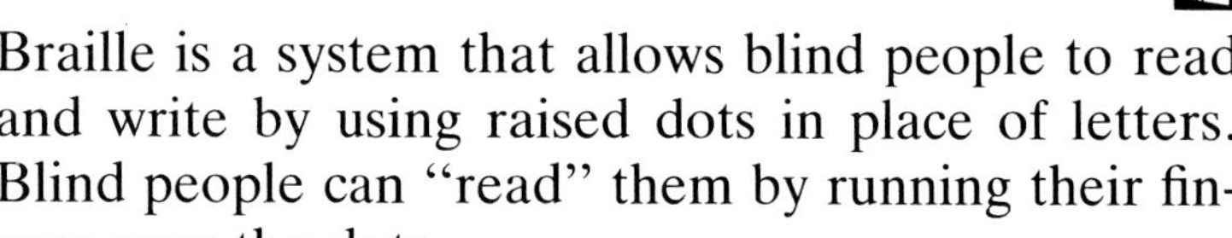

Braille

Braille is a system that allows blind people to read and write by using raised dots in place of letters. Blind people can "read" them by running their fingers over the dots.

Brain

The brain controls all the other parts of the body. In some tiny insects it is no bigger than a speck of dust. Even in some mighty dinosaurs it was no bigger than a walnut. But MAMMALS have big brains in relation to their size, and a human has the biggest brain of all. The human brain is largely made up of gray and white matter. Gray matter contains NERVE cells, and white matter contains the nerve fibers that carry messages from the nerve cells to the body. These nerve fibers leave the brain in large bundles and reach out to all parts of the body. Messages from the body are traveling back along the fibers to the brain all the time.

Different parts of the brain control different parts of the body. For example, most thinking is done in the front part. Sight, on the other hand, is controlled from the back of the brain.

The size and weight of our brains are in proportion to our body size and weight. Men have slightly heavier brains than women. Tall people have heavier brains than short people, but it has been found that there is very little connection between a large head and intelligence. Doctors have discovered that the average man's brain has increased in weight from 48 oz. (1,360 g) in 1860 to 50 oz. (1,420 g) today. The average woman's brain has increased from 44 oz. (1,245 g) to 45 oz. (1,275 g).

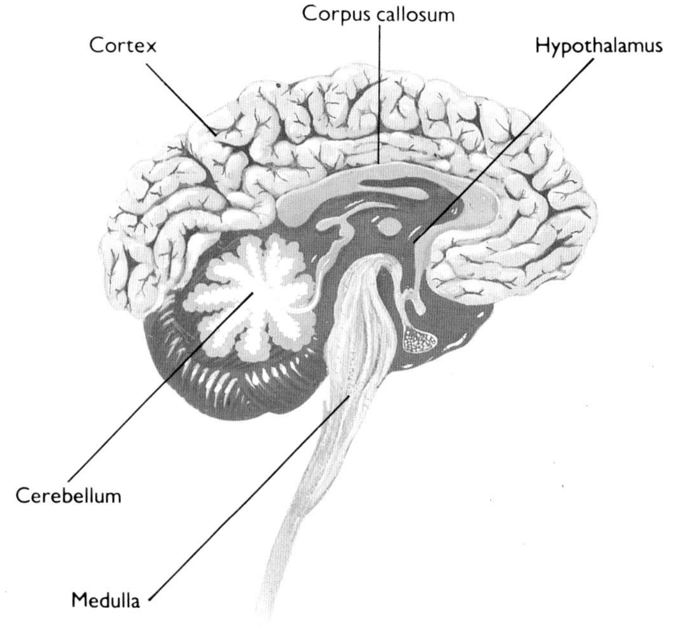

► *The brain is the body's control center. It uses a fifth of all the energy produced in the body. The medulla and hypothalamus control involuntary activities such as breathing and blood pressure. The cerebellum controls muscles and organs of balance. The cortex, the largest area, controls conscious feeling and voluntary movements such as writing and running. The corpus callosum is a band of nerves linking the two halves of the cortex.*

▲ *Rio de Janeiro is a beautiful city lying among bays, islands, and rounded hills.*

Brazil 

Brazil is by far the largest country in SOUTH AMERICA and the fifth largest country in the world. Much of Brazil is low-lying. It contains the huge basin of the AMAZON River and the world's largest rain forest. Until recently, only tribes of Indians lived here. Today, the government is trying to open up the Amazon region, but some scientists fear that this may destroy the fragile balance of the great forest.

Over half of Brazil's people live in cities that include Rio de Janeiro, Saõ Paulo, Belo Horizonte, and Recife. Brasilia, a specially built modern city, has been the capital of Brazil since 1960.

Brazil was ruled by Portugal from the early 1500s until 1822, and most people still speak Portuguese. About three-fourths of the people are descended from Europeans; most of the rest are of mixed European, Indian, and African ancestry. Most Brazilians work on farms. The country leads the world in producing coffee, and oil is now also becoming a more important product. Brazil is also one of the biggest producers of beef, cocoa, cotton, corn, sugarcane, and tobacco. Most of Brazil's great mineral wealth is still undeveloped.

BRAZIL

Government: Federal republic
Capital: Brasilia
Area: 3,286,470 sq. miles
(8,511.965 sq km)
Population: 150,368,000
Language: Portuguese
Currency: Cruzeiro

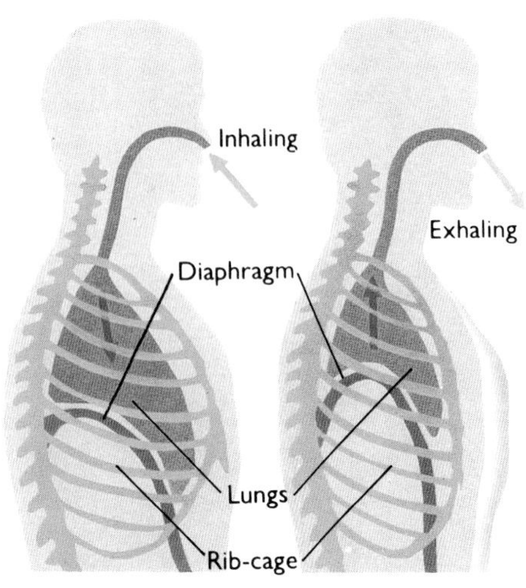

▲ *When you breathe in, your rib cage is pulled upward and the diaphragm is lowered. Air is sucked into your lungs. These actions happen in reverse when you breathe out.*

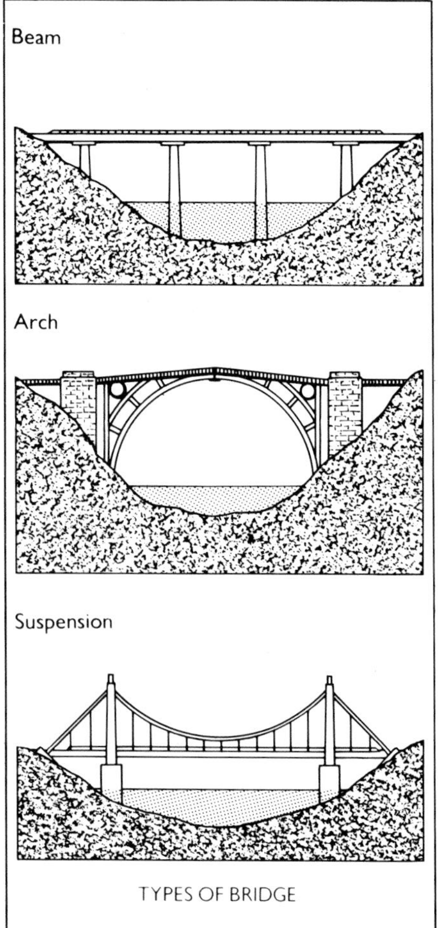

TYPES OF BRIDGE

Bread

Bread is one of our oldest foods, dating back to at least 2000 B.C. It may be made from wheat, corn, oats, barley, or rye flour. At first, bread was flat, but the Egyptians added YEAST to make the dough rise. Today most bread is baked with yeast.

Breathing

Breathing is something we rarely have to think about. As soon as a baby is born, its starts to breathe, and we go on breathing all our lives. It is the OXYGEN in the air that we need. Like all other animals, we must have oxygen to stay alive. This oxygen is used with the food we eat to give us energy to move about and keep our bodies going.

We draw air into our LUNGS. From there it goes through tiny tubes which allow the oxygen to pass into the blood vessels. So oxygen goes all around our bodies in the blood. We breathe out another type of gas called carbon dioxide. An adult normally breathes in and out about 20 times a minute (children usually breathe faster than this).

Bridge

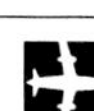

Bridges are used to take roads, paths, and rail tracks over rivers, valleys, or other obstacles. People have been building bridges for thousands of years.

The first simple bridges were probably fallen tree trunks placed across a river or small valley. Later, they may have been supported underneath by stones or logs. Another kind of simple bridge is the rope bridge made from long pieces of rope slung across a river.

The Romans were among the first great bridge builders. Some of their stone bridges are still standing today. In the MIDDLE AGES, bridges in towns often had shops and houses built on top of them.

Today there is a great variety of bridges. They have to be carefully planned and built. The weight of the bridge must be balanced so that it does not fall down. It must also be strong enough to carry traffic and stand up to the force of the wind.

There are three main kinds of bridge. These are the *beam*, the *arch*, and the *suspension* bridge. Some are fixed and others can be moved.

Different kinds of bridge

A modern beam bridge works in the same way as a simple tree trunk bridge. It is made of strong girders, or beams, which stretch from one bank to the other. Sometimes the middle of the bridge rests on pillars. Railroad bridges are often girder bridges.

An arch bridge may have one arch or more. In the past, it was usually built from stone, but today some are made of steel, like the Sydney Harbour Bridge in Australia. It has a span (the distance from one side to the other) of 1,650 ft. (503 m). Others, such as Waterloo Bridge in London, are made of CONCRETE.

▲ *The Romans were expert bridge builders. They built many arched bridges all over their empire. A number of these bridges still remain. This bridge crosses a river in Syria.*

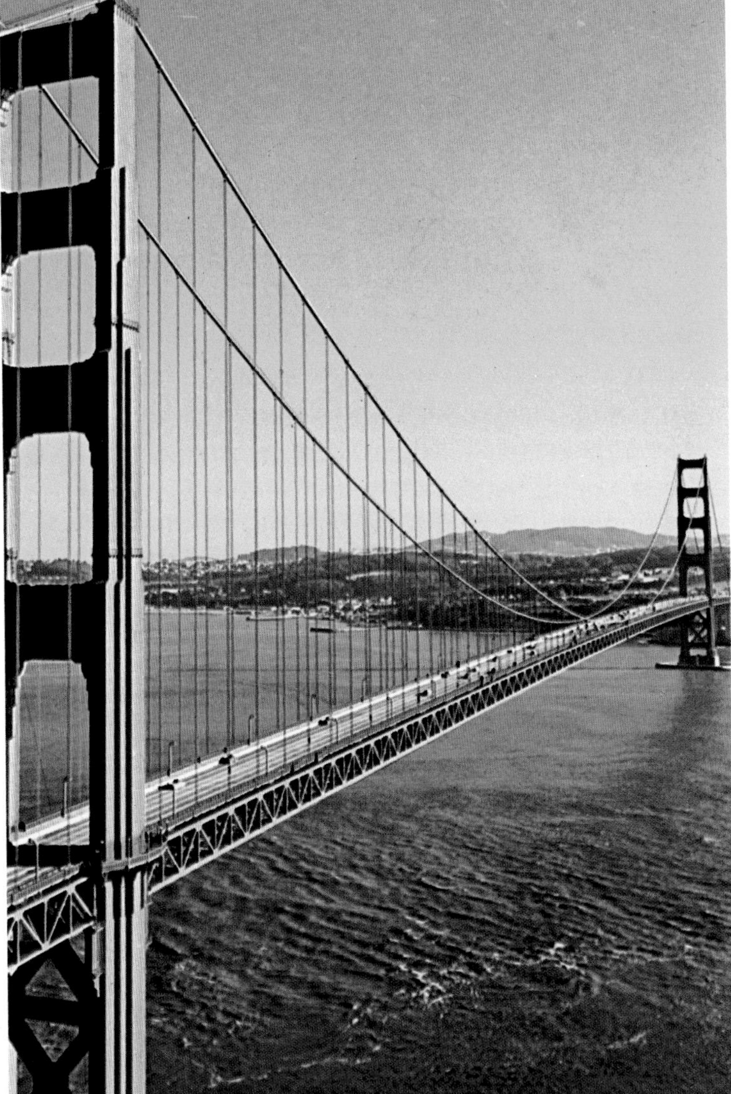

◀ *The Golden Gate suspension bridge in San Francisco was finished in 1937. It has a span of 4,200 feet (1,280 meters). Each main cable is over 3 feet (92 cm) thick, and is made up of 25,570 separate wires.*

▼ *Tower Bridge across the Thames River in London has a roadway carried on bascules, or arms, which are pivoted. They lift to allow ships to pass beneath it.*

Perhaps the most famous of all bridges is London Bridge—there have really been several of them. The Romans built the first bridge across the Thames River at London. Then, built between 1176 and 1209, came the bridge of nursery rhyme fame (London Bridge is falling down...). It was loaded with houses and shops, many of which stuck out over the river. In the 1840s, the old bridge was replaced by a new one. Then, in the 1960s, it in turn was replaced by the London Bridge of today. The 1840s bridge was taken apart stone by stone and shipped across the Atlantic. Today it is a tourist attraction at Lake Havasu City, Arizona.

▲ *Alpine lake, British Columbia.*

BRITISH COLUMBIA

Capital: Victoria
Population: 3,138,900
Area: 358,971 sq. mi. (929,730 sq. km)
Entry into confederation: July 20, 1871

LONGEST BRIDGE SPANS

Akashi-Kaikyo, Japan (suspension)	5,840 ft. (1,780 m)
Humber Estuary, England (suspension)	4,626 ft. (1,410 m)
Verrazano Narrows, New York (suspension)	4,260 ft. (1,298 m)
Golden Gate, California (suspension)	4,200 ft. (1,280 m)
Mackinac Straits, Michigan (suspension)	3,800 ft. (1,158 m)
Second Bosporus, Turkey (suspension)	3,576 ft. (1,090 m)
First Bosporus, Turkey (suspension)	3,524 ft. (1,074 m)
George Washington, New York (suspension)	3,500 ft. (1,067 m)
Tagus River, Portugal (suspension)	3,323 ft. (1,013 m)
Forth Road, Scotland (suspension)	3,300 ft. (1,006 m)
Severn, England–Wales (suspension)	3,240 ft. (988 m)
Tacoma Narrows, Washington (suspension)	2,800 ft. (853 m)
Kanmon Strait, Japan (suspension)	2,336 ft. (712 m)
Transbay, California (suspension)	2,310 ft. (704 m)

Suspension bridges are hung by strong steel cables from tall towers. The towers also have cables fixed to the ground.

Some beam bridges over rivers can be moved to let ships pass through. Tower Bridge in London is a *bascule* bridge. Both sides of the bridge can be lifted up in the middle, like drawbridges. *Swing* bridges are on pivots and can be swung sideways.

Modern bridge building began with IRON bridges in the 1700s. Later, many of these were built for the railroads. The first modern suspension bridge was built by Thomas Telford at Menai in North Wales.

By the end of the 1800s, steel was being used. Brooklyn Bridge in New York, finished in 1883, was one of the first steel suspension bridges. It has a span of 1,594 ft. (486 m). The longest suspension bridge in the world is the Akashi-Kaikyo bridge in Japan, 5,840 ft. (1,780 m).

British Columbia

British Columbia is the westernmost province of CANADA, and one of the largest. Its capital city is Victoria, but the largest and richest city is Vancouver. Both cities are on an island in the south of the province—Vancouver Island, named after a British sailor, George Vancouver. More than half of all British Columbians live in the Vancouver–Victoria region. The climate here is always warm because of the closeness of the Pacific Ocean.

Inland, British Columbia is wild and rugged, with towering mountains and huge forests. It can be very cold in winter and hot in the summer.

The first white men to settle in British Columbia were fur trappers and traders. Today, logging, mining, and fishing are the major industries of the province.

The population of British Columbia has increased dramatically over the years. In 1870 there were only 36,000 people in the province. By 1950, the population had increased to over a million. Today, it is over three million and still growing.

Brontë Sisters

Brontë was the name of three English sisters who became famous writers. Charlotte Brontë (1816–1855), Emily Brontë (1818–1848), and Anne Brontë (1820–1849) wrote novels that are among the classics of English literature.

In 1847, all three produced their first novels. *Jane Eyre* by Charlotte was largely based on her own life and it became an immediate success. Emily's *Wuthering Heights* was too shocking for its time, but today is considered a great book. Anne's novel was entitled *Agnes Grey*. The sisters published these and later works under pen names because few people in the 1800s would buy books written by women.

▲ *Charlotte Brontë is best known for her novel* Jane Eyre.

Bronze Age

Bronze is the ALLOY of COPPER and TIN. It was first made in the countries at the eastern end of the Mediterranean in about 3000 B.C. It took another thousand years to reach Europe.

Bronze changed the lives of the STONE AGE people in Europe. With bronze they could make better tools and weapons much more quickly. Bronze weapons were much stronger and sharper than their old stone or flint axes and knives. Bronze swords were sharp on both sides, so that warriors no longer used the points only.

The Bronze Age people used their new tools to make other objects more quickly. These included pots, shields, helmets, and ornaments. As the Stone Age gave way to the Bronze, huts were replaced by towns, and people began to build palaces and temples.

The Bronze Age lasted until about 800 B.C. At

By varying the amounts of tin and copper, it is possible to change the qualities of bronze completely. The more tin that is used, the harder and more brittle the alloy will be. Because bronze is easily cast in large shapes, it is used in making big bells. It also has a fine ringing quality when struck. The bronze used in bell-making has a lot of tin in it—sometimes as much as one part tin to four parts copper. Bronze for statues, on the other hand, may have as little as one part tin to ten parts copper.

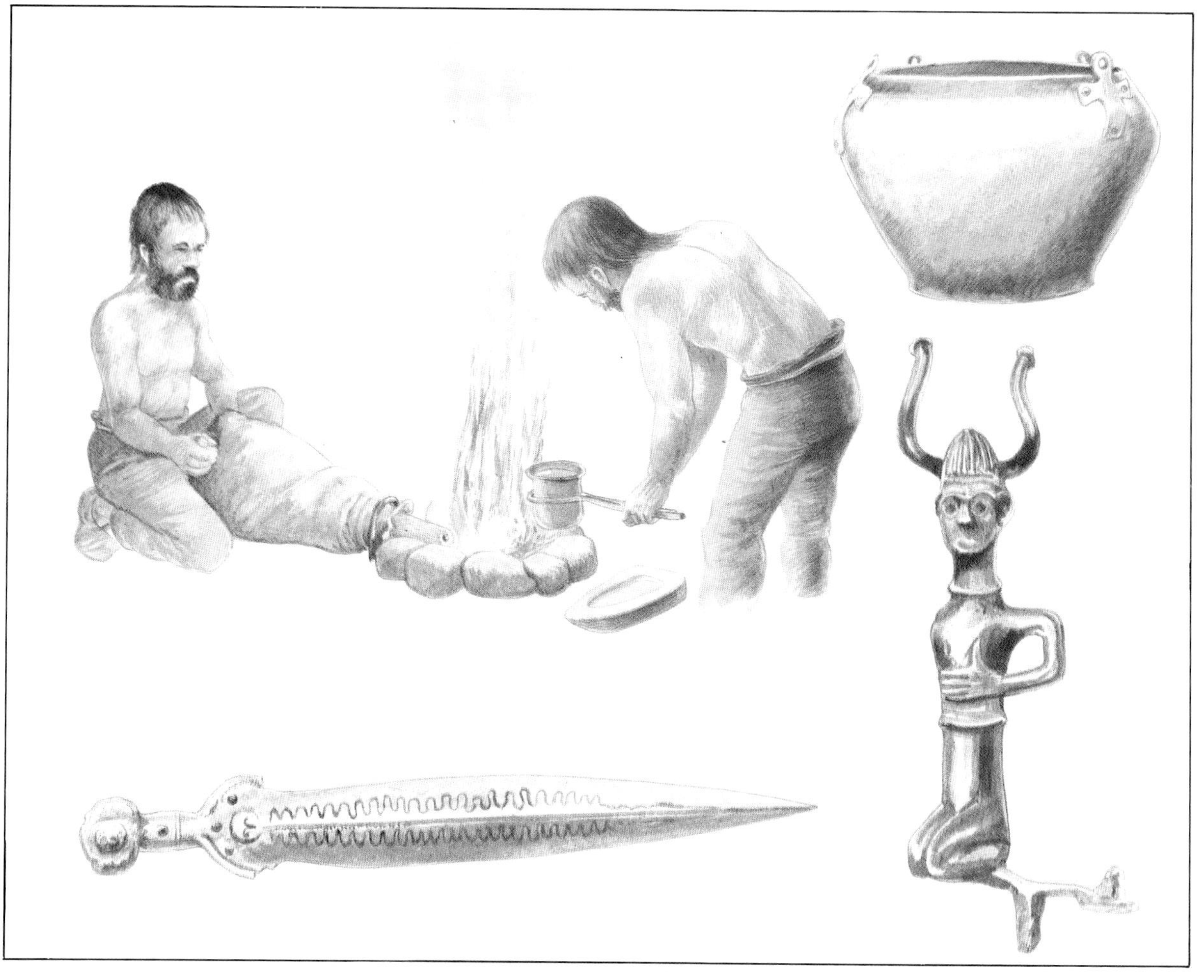

▲ *Bronze Age people used bronze to make swords and tools. This useful metal could also be cast into shape by heating it until it melted and pouring it into a mold.*

In many parts of the world, the Bronze Age came after a period sometimes called the Copper Age. This was when people had discovered copper and its uses, but had not learned to mix it with tin to make the stronger bronze. Other parts of the world did not have a Bronze Age at all. In certain parts of Africa, for example, people went straight from the use of stone to the use of iron.

this time, iron started to be used in Europe. Iron became important because it was even more useful than bronze. But bronze was still used in England 400 years later, and for hundreds of years after this in Scotland and Ireland.

Many Bronze Age tools and ornaments are still found today. Some of them are kept in museums and may be seen there.

Statues made of bronze weather to a brown or green coating or *patina* which protects the metal.

Brown, John

John Brown (1800–1859) was a fierce opponent of slavery in the years before the CIVIL WAR. He was hanged after trying to steal guns to give to slaves. After he died, many people who hated slavery saw him as a symbol of their fight. He is still remembered in the song *John Brown's Body*.

Brunei

Brunei is a tiny country on the northwestern coast of the island of Borneo. Is is only about twice the size of Rhode Island. The country's chief exports are oil, rubber, and hardwood. About 90 percent of Brunei's revenue comes from oil exports. During the 1800s, Brunei was a stopping place for British ships traveling to China, and the country came under British protection in 1888. Brunei achieved full independence under a sultan in 1984.

BRUNEI

Government: Independent sultanate
Capital: Bandar Seri Begawan
Area: 2,226 sq. miles (5,765 sq. km)
Population: 266,000
Language: Malay
Currency: Brunei dollar

Buchanan, James

James Buchanan (1791–1868) was the 15th president of the United States, and held office between 1857 and 1861. These were the years leading up to the Civil War, and the problems that caused it dominated his presidency.

Buchanan was a congressman, a senator, and then secretary of state before he became president. When he was president, his biggest problem was slavery. Many people in the North said that slavery should be stopped. People in the South wanted it to continue. Buchanan was cautious. He said that North and South should try to understand each other better and should respect the law. But this was not enough to prevent the war.

Buchanan was the only president who never married. He was succeeded by Abraham Lincoln.

JAMES BUCHANAN

Fifteenth President 1857–1861
Born: near Mercersburg, Pa.
Education: Dickinson College, Carlisle, Pa.
Occupation: Lawyer
Political Party: Democratic
Buried: Lancaster, Pa.

Bud

A bud is an undeveloped shoot of a plant. There are two kinds of bud, flower buds and leaf buds. If the covering of the bud is peeled off, the tightly-packed flowers or leaves can be seen inside. Some buds are eaten as food. These include asparagus, brussels sprouts, and globe artichokes.

Buddha

The word Buddha means "Enlightened One." This name is given to great teachers of Buddhism.

The first Buddha was Siddhartha Gautama. He

▲ *Buddha in a characteristic pose, with legs folded. His restful expression reflects the Buddhist ideal state of complete happiness and peace.*

was born about 563 B.C. in northern India. For most of his life, he traveled around India teaching people. Buddha taught his followers that the only way to true happiness was to be peaceful and kind to other people and animals, and to avoid evil.

Like the HINDUS, Buddhists believe that after they die they are born again as an animal or human being. If they are very good, they are not born again, but live in a kind of heaven called *Nirvana*.

Buffalo

The buffalo is a large relative of the cow. The Asian buffalo originally came from India, where it has been used as a work animal for many centuries. Today the buffalo is used to plow and pull loads all over the Far East and also in Syria, Turkey, Hungary, and the Balkans. It is often called the water buffalo because it loves to wallow in the mud by the side of rivers or at water holes. The water keeps away flies and keeps the animal cool.

Another kind of buffalo lives by the swamps and rivers of central and southern Africa. It is wild and has never been tamed by man. This buffalo can be very dangerous and will charge without warning. The North American BISON is often called a buffalo, but it is not a close relative.

▼ *A buffalo pulls a plow on a farm in Asia. This strong animal has been a beast of burden for centuries.*

▼ *The great pyramids of ancient Egypt were early engineering feats. Huge blocks of stone were cut and hauled up ramps by hundreds of men.*

▲ *Early shelters were made from the most easily available materials—in this case animal bones and hide.*

Building

Early people built with the materials they found around them—stones, branches, mud, and turf. In Europe, poor people usually lived in houses made of wattle and daub. Wattle was a wickerwork of branches, which was plastered over with a "daub" of wet mud. When this "plaster" hardened, it made quite a strong wall.

Because in some areas certain materials were easily available, buildings look quite different in different places. Where there was plenty of clay, people built with bricks; where there was plenty of limestone or sandstone, people built their houses with those.

Today, houses being built everywhere look very much the same. Large buildings have a framework of steel girders or reinforced *concrete* which takes all the weight of the building. The walls can be light and there can be plenty of windows.

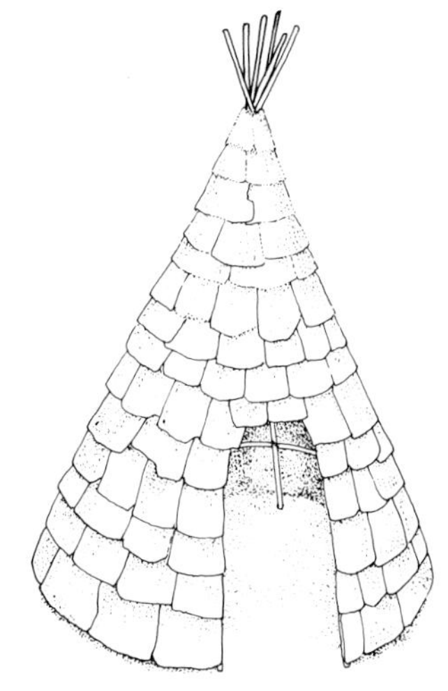

▲ *An early North American Indian tepee made of birchbark laid over a framework of birch poles.*

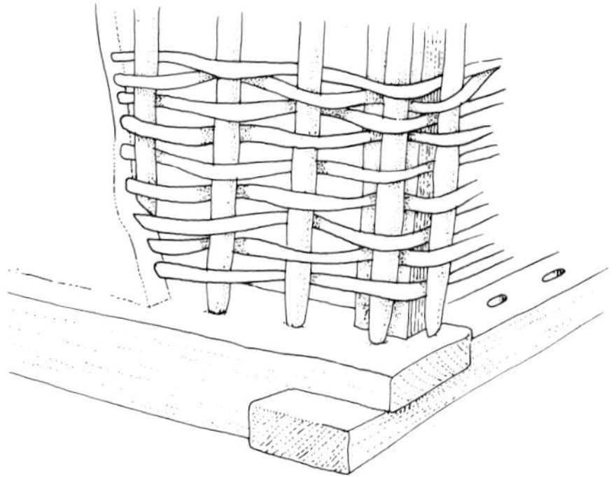

▲ *Early houses in Europe had walls of woven branches, or wattle, filled in with lumps of mud, or daub.*

▶ *Modern buildings are constructed using reinforced concrete and prefabricated sections. Towering cranes make the job of moving building materials fast and efficient.*

All buildings, especially tall ones, have to be built on firm foundations. If they are not, they may collapse or sink into the ground like the Leaning Tower of Pisa in Italy.

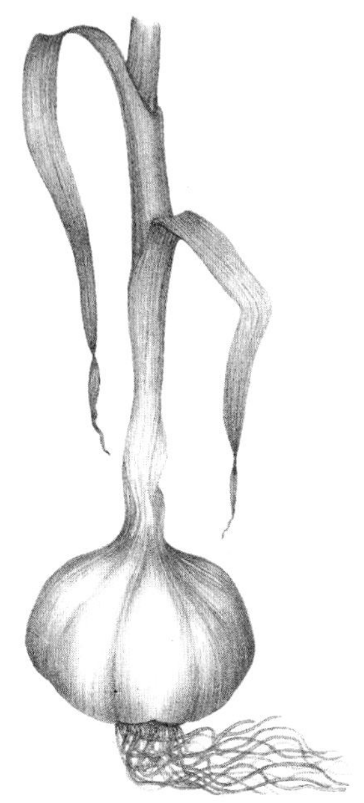

▲ *The garlic we use in the kitchen is actually the bulb from which the garlic plant grows. Each "clove" of garlic is one of the bulb's fleshy scales.*

Bulb

Many PLANTS, such as tulips, daffodils, and onions, grow from bulbs. The bulb is the underground part of the plant where food is stored during the winter months. When the plant has finished flowering, the bulb begins to grow under the ground. Then the leaves above the ground wither away, leaving only the bulb. It is made up of fleshy scales packed tightly together. The scales feed the bud as it grows.

Bulgaria

Bulgaria is a country in Eastern EUROPE about the size of Ohio. Like several of its European neighbors, in 1990 parliament voted to drastically reduce the role of the Communist Party. As in other east European countries, the government is becoming more democratic.

In the north of Bulgaria are the Balkan Mountains. To the east is the BLACK SEA, where many people spend their vacations. In the center of Bulgaria is a big valley with many farms. The farmers grow fruit, flowers, vegetables, grain, and tobacco. There are also many factories and mines in Bulgaria. About two-thirds of the people live in cities.

BULGARIA

Government: Multiparty system
Capital: Sofia
Area: 42,823 sq. miles (110,912 sq. km)
Population: 9,011,000
Language: Bulgarian
Currency: Lev

Burkina Faso

Burkina Faso is an inland republic in West Africa. It used to be called Upper Volta, but the name was changed in 1984. The country was controlled by France from 1896. Full independence came in 1960. Most people are farmers and raise cattle, sheep, and goats. Millet, corn, and rice are grown. There are valuable deposits of minerals including gold and bauxite, but they have not yet been developed. Burkina Faso is about the size of Colorado. It depends largely on foreign aid.

BURKINA FASO

Government: Military
Capital: Ouagadougou
Area: 105,869 sq. miles (274,200 sq. km)
Population: 9,001,000
Languages: French
Currency: CFA franc

Burma (Myanmar)

Burma is a country in SOUTHEAST ASIA. It is nearly as large as Texas and has mountains, forests, and rivers. The biggest river is the Irrawaddy, which is 1,292 miles (2,080 km) long. Most of the people are farmers. They grow rice, teak, rubber, and jute. Nearly all Burmese follow the Buddhist religion.

Britain ruled Burma as part of India until 1937, when the country became self-governing.

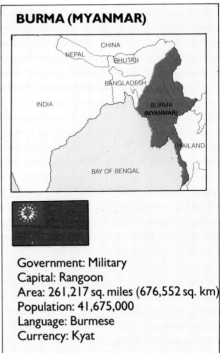

BURMA (MYANMAR)

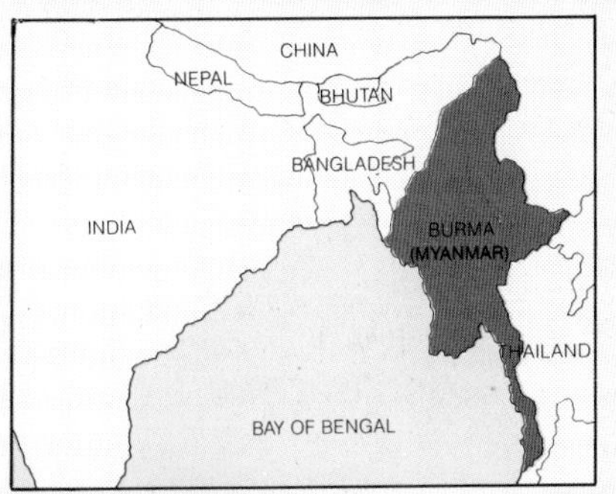

Government: Military
Capital: Rangoon
Area: 261,217 sq. miles (676,552 sq. km)
Population: 41,675,000
Language: Burmese
Currency: Kyat

◀ *Two fierce lions guard the entrance to a golden-roofed pagoda in Burma. Most Burmese are Buddhists, though in the countryside many still worship the* nats*—spirits of forests and mountains.*

BURUNDI

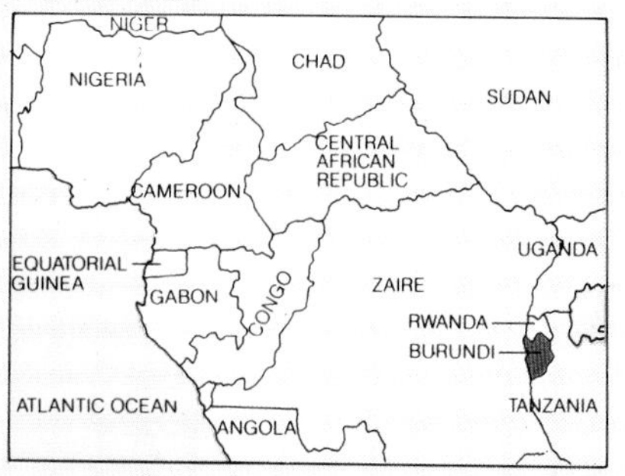

Government: Republic
Capital: Bujumbura
Area: 10,747 sq. miles (27,834 sq. km)
Population: 5,458,000
Languages: French, Rundi
Currency: Burundi franc

Burundi

Burundi is a small country in the center of Africa. It is sandwiched between Zaire, Tanzania, and Rwanda. Most of the people are Bantu peasant farmers. Burundi is one of the poorest and most densely populated countries in Africa. It became independent from Belgium in 1962.

Bush, George Herbert Walker

George Bush (1924–) was elected President of the United States in 1988, having served as vice president under Ronald Reagan for two terms.

During World War II, Bush served as a fighter pilot in the United States Navy and was decorated for heroism. After graduating from Yale University, he entered the oil industry, in which he prospered.

In 1964, Bush became a Republican candidate for the U.S. Senate, but he was defeated. Then, in 1966, he was elected to the House of Representatives as a Texas Republican. He served two terms in the House. President Nixon appointed him U.S. ambassador to the United Nations in 1970. Two years later he became chairman of the Republican National Committee just before the Watergate scandal which led to the resignation of President Nixon. In 1975, Bush was appointed head of the CIA; in 1980 he sought presidential nomination.

The Allied victory against Iraq in the Gulf War in 1991 gave Bush one of the highest presidential approval ratings in history.

GEORGE BUSH

Forty-first President 1989–
Born: Milton, Mass.
Education: Yale University
Occupation: Businessman
Political Party: Republican

Butterfly

Butterflies are flying INSECTS. There are about 17,000 kinds of butterfly. They are related to MOTHS, and live in most parts of the world, even as far north as the Arctic Circle.

Butterflies have many colors and sizes. One of the smallest, the dwarf blue of South Africa, has a wingspan of only half an inch (14 mm). The largest, the Queen Alexandra birdwing, has a wingspan of 11 inches (28 cm).

All butterflies begin their lives as CATERPILLARS

which hatch from eggs. The caterpillars spend their lives eating the plant they were hatched on. They change their skins several times as they grow. When a caterpillar is fully grown, it changes into a chrysalis with a hard skin. Inside, the chrysalis changes into an adult butterfly. When ready, the butterfly breaks out and flies away to mate and lay eggs of its own.

Some butterflies *migrate*. They fly from one part of the world to another at certain times of the year. One of the most famous migrating butterflies is the monarch butterfly in North America. In the summer it lives all over the United States and Canada. In the fall, the butterflies gather together in groups. They fly south to Mexico, Florida, and southern California for the winter. Sometimes thousands of monarchs are seen flying together. In spring, they fly north again.

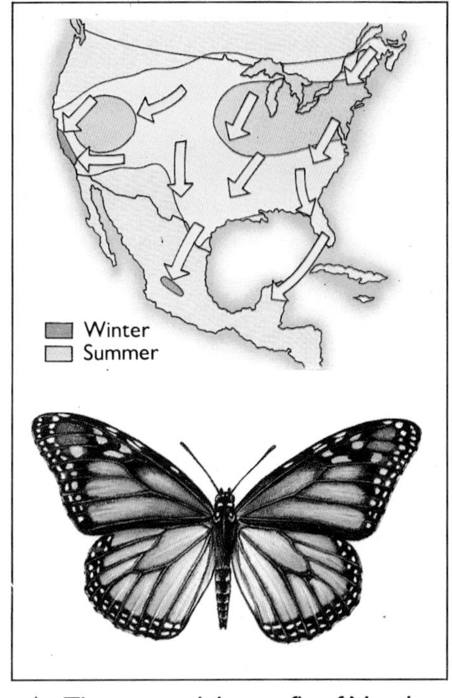

▲ *The monarch butterfly of North America travels thousands of miles to winter in Mexico and southern California.*

▼ *Butterflies are found in virtually every part of the world except for the polar regions. They come in a variety of sizes and colors. Some live only a few weeks; others live for nearly a year. Once they emerge from the chrysalis, they do not grow.*

▶ *Cacti come in all shapes and sizes, from small pincushion-sized specimens to the giant saguaro cactus which may reach 50 ft. (15 m) in height.*

▼ *Julius Caesar was a military genius. During his nine years campaigning in Gaul, he lost only two of the battles in which he took part.*

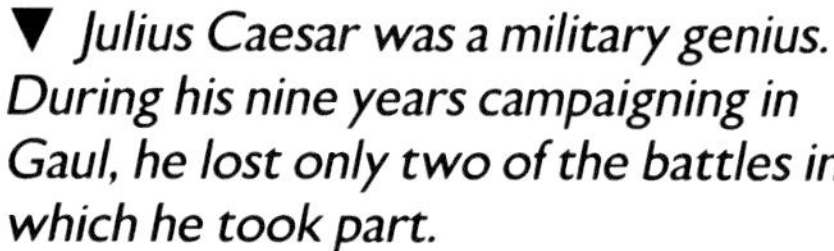

Cactus

Although there are hundreds of different cacti, they all have one thing in common. They are able to grow in hot DESERT climates. Cacti can do this because they store water in their fleshy stems. They are covered with prickly spines instead of leaves. The spines protect the plant's store of water from the desert animals.

Caesar, Julius

Julius Caesar (c. 102–44 B.C.) was a great leader of the ROMAN EMPIRE. He is most famous for his part in turning the Roman Republic into an empire ruled by one man.

He first became powerful when he commanded an army that conquered what is today France, the Netherlands, and Germany. In 55 B.C., he crossed the English Channel and invaded Britain. He rebelled against the Roman Senate (the government) when he led his victorious armies into Italy itself. He captured Rome without a struggle, and in 48 B.C. he defeated Pompey, his main rival for power. Caesar then became the sole ruler of Rome.

Caesar made many enemies who hated what he was doing to the Republic. A group of them plotted to kill him. On the "Ides of March" (the 15th of the month), 44 B.C., they stabbed him to death in the Roman Forum.

Calculator

About 5,000 years ago, someone invented the ABACUS. This was the first calculator. Then in 1642, the French scientist Blaise Pascal built the first machine for adding numbers. It worked by turning dials. After this, mechanical adding machines were used for years in offices and stores. They were useful but slow, and could not do difficult calculations.

Everything changed in the 1970s when the SILICON CHIP was invented. Soon everyone could have a small pocket-sized electronic calculator. These calculators can add, subtract, and divide as fast as we can press the keys. More advanced calculators can also do the more difficult calculations needed in science.

Although they are electronic, not all calculators need batteries. Some are solar-powered—they get their power from sunlight.

Electronic cash registers are very important in stores. They add up the price of goods, print out a receipt, and calculate your change.

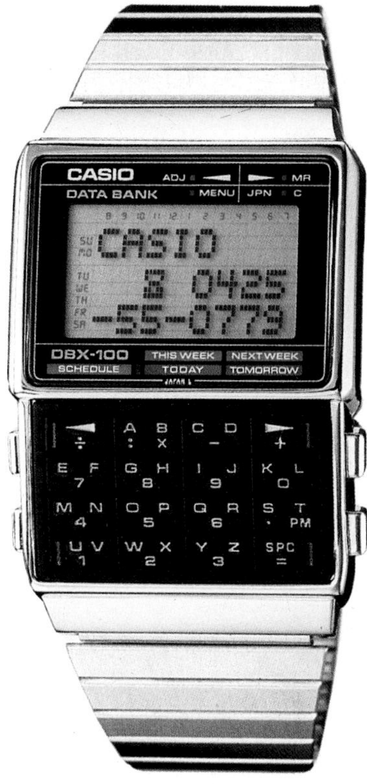

▲ *This modern electronic watch, calculator, and data bank will store personal data (such as your Social Security number) and telephone numbers. It can also store appointments, and the watch will beep and display a message at a preset time as a reminder.*

◀ *Pascal's adding machine of 1642 looks ungainly and primitive next to a modern electronic pocket calculator.*

CALIFORNIA

Capital: Sacramento
Population: 29,760,021
Area: 158,706 sq. mi. (411,049 sq. km)
State flower: Golden Poppy
State bird: California Valley Quail
State tree: California Redwood
Statehood: September 9, 1850
31st state

CAMBODIA

MYANMAR
LAOS
THAILAND
CAMBODIA
VIETNAM
SOUTH CHINA SEA

Government: Coalition
Capital: Phnom Penh
Area: 69,898 sq. miles (181,035 sq. km)
Population: 8,246,000
Language: Khmer
Currency: Riel

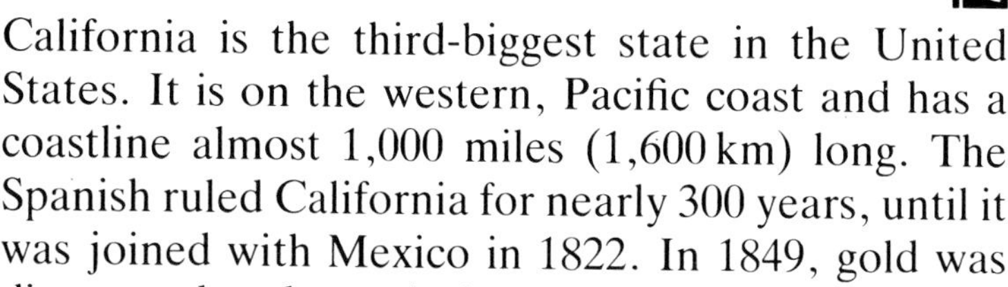

California

California is the third-biggest state in the United States. It is on the western, Pacific coast and has a coastline almost 1,000 miles (1,600 km) long. The Spanish ruled California for nearly 300 years, until it was joined with Mexico in 1822. In 1849, gold was discovered and people flocked to California.

The best-known cities are LOS ANGELES and SAN FRANCISCO. Both are on the San Andreas fault, a weak line in the Earth's crust that causes earthquakes.

California is one of the richest states. Much of its money comes from farming. But there are many important industries, too, including film and wine production. Today, many people live in California because of its warm climate and relaxed lifestyles.

Cambodia

Cambodia is a country in SOUTHEAST ASIA. It changed its name from Cambodia to Kampuchea in 1976 and back to Cambodia in 1988. Most of Cambodia's people live in small villages and grow rice, fruit, and vegetables. The country was formerly part of the French colony of Indochina. It became independent in 1955. Since then, Cambodia has seen bitter civil war and starvation. In 1991 the country's warring factions signed a peace treaty.

▶ *The single-humped camel on the right is an Arabian. The two-humped one on the left is the Bactrian camel of Asia.*

Camel

The camel is one of the few creatures that can stand up to extreme heat and still do work carrying heavy loads. They are ideally suited for the job of making long journeys across the deserts. Their wide padded feet grip well on loose sandy ground. They are powerful and swift and can go for days without eating or drinking, living off the fat in their humps.

When a thirsty camel finally gets a chance to drink, it can swallow as much as 20 gallons (76 l) of water at one time.

Camera

Modern cameras work in much the same way as those of a hundred years ago. A shutter opens to let light from the scene being photographed pass through a glass lens to fall on the film. The amount of light that gets through can be varied by adjusting the size of the hole through which the light passes—the "aperture." Apertures are measured in "f-numbers." A high f-number such as 16 or 22 means a small aperture. With a low f-number such as 2 or 2.8, the aperture is large. The light forms an upside-down image of the scene on the film. The film is then treated with chemicals (developed). The image on the developed film is printed onto a special type of paper. The result is a photograph.

Today, most cameras have a lot of different parts to help us take photographs in many kinds of light.

Taking pictures with the early cameras was a slow process. The first real camera, invented by the Frenchman Louis Daguerre at the beginning of the 19th century, needed a very long exposure time. The subject had to sit motionless for as much as ten minutes, usually with his or her head in a clamp to keep it still. Some modern cameras have shutter speeds as fast as one thousandth of a second to take pictures of fast-moving objects.

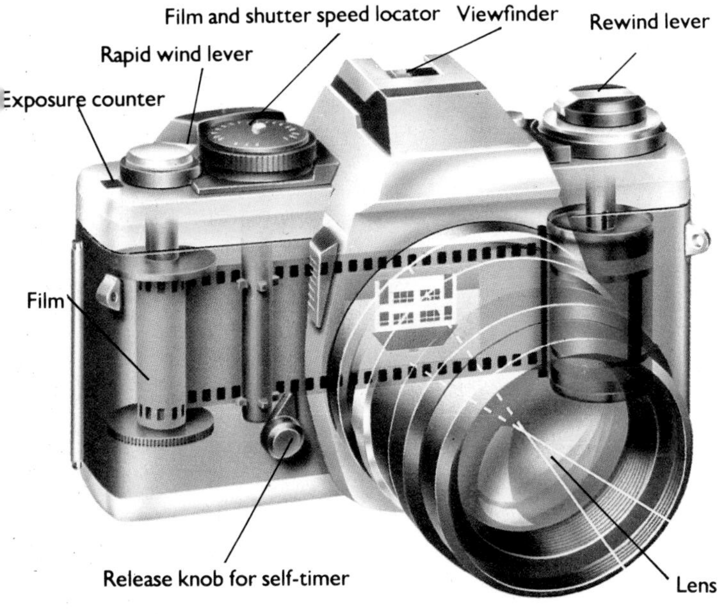

Film and shutter speed locator
Viewfinder
Rewind lever
Rapid wind lever
Exposure counter
Film
Release knob for self-timer
Lens

◀ *To take a picture, the shutter opens and light passes through a lens into a small aperture—the iris. From there it is focused onto the film by a second set of lenses. The image formed is upside down.*

CAMEROON

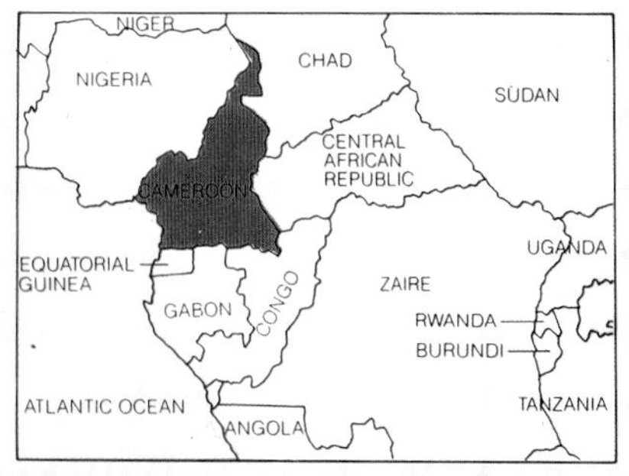

Government: Independent republic
Capital: Yaoundé
Area: 183,568 sq. miles (475,442 sq. km)
Population: 11,834,000
Languages: English, French
Currency: CFA franc

Cameroon

Cameroon is a republic on the west coast of Africa. It is slightly larger than California. Most of the country's people live in scattered tribal villages and are farmers. Cocoa, coffee, peanuts, bananas, and cotton are the chief crops. Oil is produced and is exported to help Cameroon's economy.

Canada

Canada is the second biggest country in the world and covers almost four million square miles.

In the ARCTIC, Canada reaches almost as far north as Greenland. To the south, it extends to the same latitude as southern France. The distance from the Pacific coast in the west to the Atlantic in the east is farther than that from North America to Europe. In the east are the GREAT LAKES which lie on the border with the U.S. These huge inland seas empty into the St. Lawrence River, which links them with the Atlantic Ocean. In spite of Canada's size, two-thirds of all Canadians live in a narrow belt of land no more than 120 miles (200 km) from the U.S. border. The two largest cities are Montreal, in the east, and

▼ Some of the most spectacular scenery in North America can be seen in the Canadian Rockies in Jasper National Park, Alberta.

Toronto, in the center. The capital is OTTAWA.

In the past, both France and Britain ruled all or parts of Canada. The country still has strong ties with both, especially Britain. For example, Queen Elizabeth II is also queen of Canada, and Canada is a member of the Commonwealth. At the same time, 18 percent of all Canadians speak only French. In the province of Quebec, over 80 percent of the people speak French.

Because it is so large, Canada has enormous natural resources. Its huge forests have made it the world's largest producer of "pulpwood" for paper-making. Its many rivers and lakes have enabled enormous hydroelectric power plants to be built. And the huge interior has important mineral reserves, especially of oil and iron, that have helped make Canada one of the ten most important industrial nations in the world.

CANADA

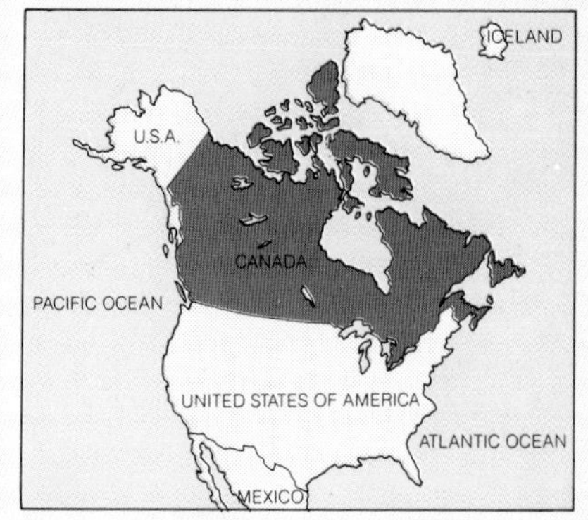

Government: Confederation with parliamentary democracy
Capital: Ottawa
Area: 3,849,000 sq. miles (9,970,610 sq. km)
Population: 26,522,000
Languages: English, French
Currency: Canadian dollar

▼ *Farms in central Canada can cover thousands of acres. The House of Commons sits in session in the Canadian Parliament in Ottawa. Its members are elected, while those of the Senate are appointed.*

CANADIAN PROVINCES

1 Alberta
2 British Columbia
3 Manitoba
4 New Brunswick
5 Newfoundland
6 Northwest Territory
7 Nova Scotia
8 Ontario
9 Prince Edward Island
10 Quebec
11 Saskatchewan
12 Yukon Territory

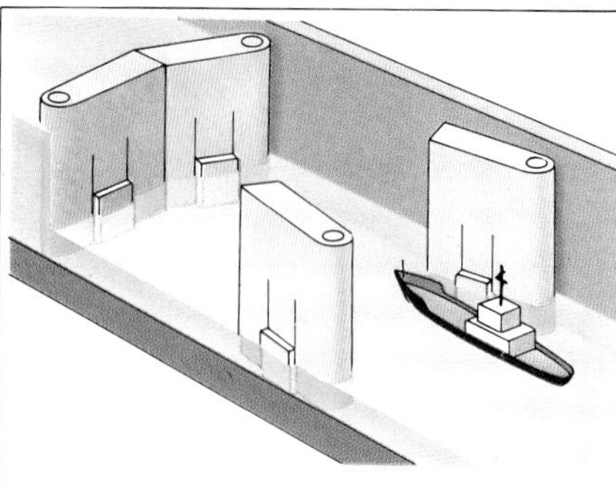

The gates open to allow a ship into the lock before closing again.

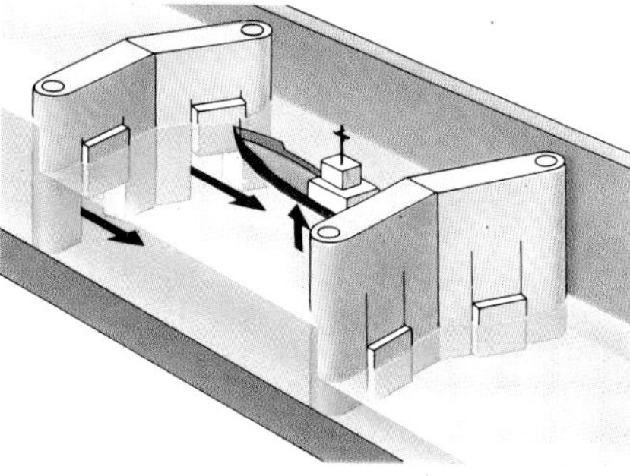

Openings in the upper gates release water into the lock.

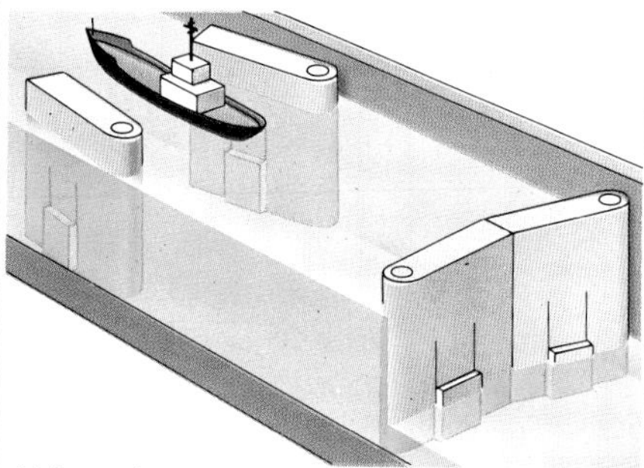

When the water level inside the lock is the same as that above the gates, they are opened to allow the ship to pass through.

▲ *How a canal lock works. Before the ship can enter, the level of water in the lock must be the same as that in the lower pool.*

► *A ship negotiates one of the three sets of locks on the Panama Canal, whose 50 mile (80 km) length links the Atlantic and Pacific oceans.*

Canal

A canal is a manmade waterway built to carry water traffic.

Until the 1500s, canals could be built only across flat country. With the invention of canal locks, however, they could be built across high ground, too.

Early canals could be used only by narrow, shallow-bottomed boats. These boats were pulled along by horses that walked on tow paths running alongside the canal. Some canals, like the SUEZ CANAL and the PANAMA CANAL, are big enough to let ocean liners pass through them.

Cancer

Cancer is a disease that causes cells in the body to grow uncontrollably. These cells can form a "tumor." A severe tumor is called "malignant," and can often lead to death. No one yet understands why this happens, though treatments for it can sometimes be successful. Finding a cure for cancer is one of the greatest challenges facing medicine, and doctors all over the world are working hard at it. Cancer is especially likely to affect older people. There are about a hundred different kinds of cancer.

Cape Verde

The 15 islands of the tiny African republic of Cape Verde lie in the Atlantic Ocean about 400 miles (650 km) west of Senegal. They were formed by volcanic eruptions. The people farm and fish. The islands were discovered by the Portuguese in 1456, and Cape Verde became independent in 1975.

CAPE VERDE

CAPE VERDE ISLANDS
AFRICA
ATLANTIC OCEAN

Government: Republic
Capital: Praia
Area: 1,557 sq. miles (4,033 sq. km)
Population: 370,000
Language: Portuguese
Currency: Escudo

Carbon

Carbon is an important ELEMENT that is found in every living thing—both plant and animal. Many of the things we use every day, such as sugar and paper, have carbon in them. Forms of carbon also exist as COAL, OIL, graphite (the lead in our pencils is graphite), and DIAMONDS.

Caribbean Sea

The Caribbean Sea is bounded by the West Indies, the east coast of Central America and the north coast of South America.

In the 17th century, British and French pirates sailed the Caribbean to attack and plunder Spanish possessions. After the completion of the Panama Canal in 1914, the sea became one of the busiest waterways in the world. It lies on the route between the Atlantic and Pacific Oceans.

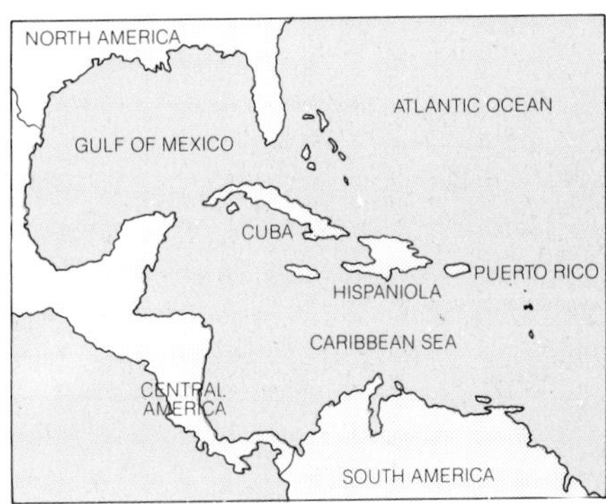

Carnivore

Carnivores are a group of MAMMALS that feed mainly on the flesh of other animals.

Although carnivores mainly live on meat, they will sometimes eat insects and plants. But what they all have in common is a set of very powerful jaws for chopping up their food, deadly curved claws for tearing, and long sharp teeth for seizing, stabbing, and killing their victims.

Carnivores include CATS, DOGS, FOXES, RACCOONS, weasels, and HYENAS. All have good eyesight, smell, and hearing and are fast, intelligent, and skilled at hunting down other animals. Some carnivores, like wild dogs and hyenas, hunt in packs. In

Cats are very efficient carnivores. They are well known for their hunting skills, their stealthy stalking of their prey, their final pounce with deadly teeth and claws. This applies to all the cat family, from lions and tigers to our domestic animals. All cats are very similar inside. For instance, it is almost impossible to tell the difference between the skull of a lion and that of a tiger.

▲ *Foxes are carnivores. They like eating rabbits and often scatter bones and feathers around their dens.*

this way they can kill animals much larger than themselves. Other carnivores, like the LEOPARD and the JAGUAR, hunt alone.

Carpets and Rugs

The first people to make carpets were the ancient Egyptians. Carpetmaking spread from Egypt across Asia all the way to China. The finest carpets were made in Turkey, Persia (Iran), and the north of India. Today, people in these countries still make carpets by hand, but in may other countries rugs and carpets are made in factories, using wool or synthetic fibers.

Carroll, Lewis

Lewis Carroll (1832–1898) was the pen name of an English writer whose real name was Charles Dodgson. He was a mathematics professor at Oxford University in England, but is best known today for his strange children's stories. The two most famous are *Alice's Adventures in Wonderland* and *Through the Looking-Glass*. The stories were written for the daughter of a fellow professor and contain characters such as Humpty Dumpty, Tweedledum and Tweedledee, and the Mad Hatter.

***Through the Looking-Glass* contains Lewis Carroll's famous poem "Jaberwocky." It is written in nonsense words and begins:**

'Twas brillig and the slithy toves
Did gyre and gimble in the wabe;
All mimsy were the borogroves,
And the mome raths outgrabe.

Carter, James Earl

Jimmy Carter (1924–) was the 39th president of the United States, and held office between 1977 and 1981. He was born in Plains, GEORGIA. In 1962 he was elected to the Georgia Senate, and in 1970 he became Governor of Georgia. When he decided to run for president in 1976, few thought he would win.

Jimmy Carter was respected for his hard work and belief in human rights. But many problems faced him. At home, rising oil prices pushed inflation up to high levels. Overseas, the overthrow of the Shah of Iran by the Ayatollah Khomeini and the invasion of Afghanistan by the Soviet Union were his most difficult problems. His greatest success was to bring Israel and Egypt together as friends. Jimmy Carter was defeated in 1980 by Ronald REAGAN.

JIMMY CARTER

Thirty-ninth President 1977–1981
Born: Plains, Georgia
Education: Georgia Tech; U.S. Naval Academy
Occupation: Businessman
Political Party: Democratic

Cartoon

Most people think of short, funny films with talking creatures and plants when they speak of cartoons. But originally, cartoons were rough sketches of the design for a PAINTING or a TAPESTRY. These sketches were drawn to the same size as the finished work. Another kind of cartoon is the comic strip.

Cartoon films are made by joining together a series of drawings. Each drawing is a little different from the one before. When they are shown one after another at a very fast speed, it looks as if the scene is moving.

▲ *To create a cartoon, the original sketch is drawn on sheets of transparent film, called "cels." These are then photographed on film.*

Carver, George Washington

George Washington Carver (1864–1943) was a black scientist who was born in MISSOURI just before the end of the CIVIL WAR. Both his parents were slaves. His father was killed soon after the baby was born and his mother was kidnapped. Carver worked hard as a boy, and in 1890 he went to college, where he studied agriculture. In 1896, Carver moved to ALABAMA, and stayed there for the rest of his life. His work on agriculture, especially on peanuts, won praise from experts all over the world. Carver also worked hard to help other black people.

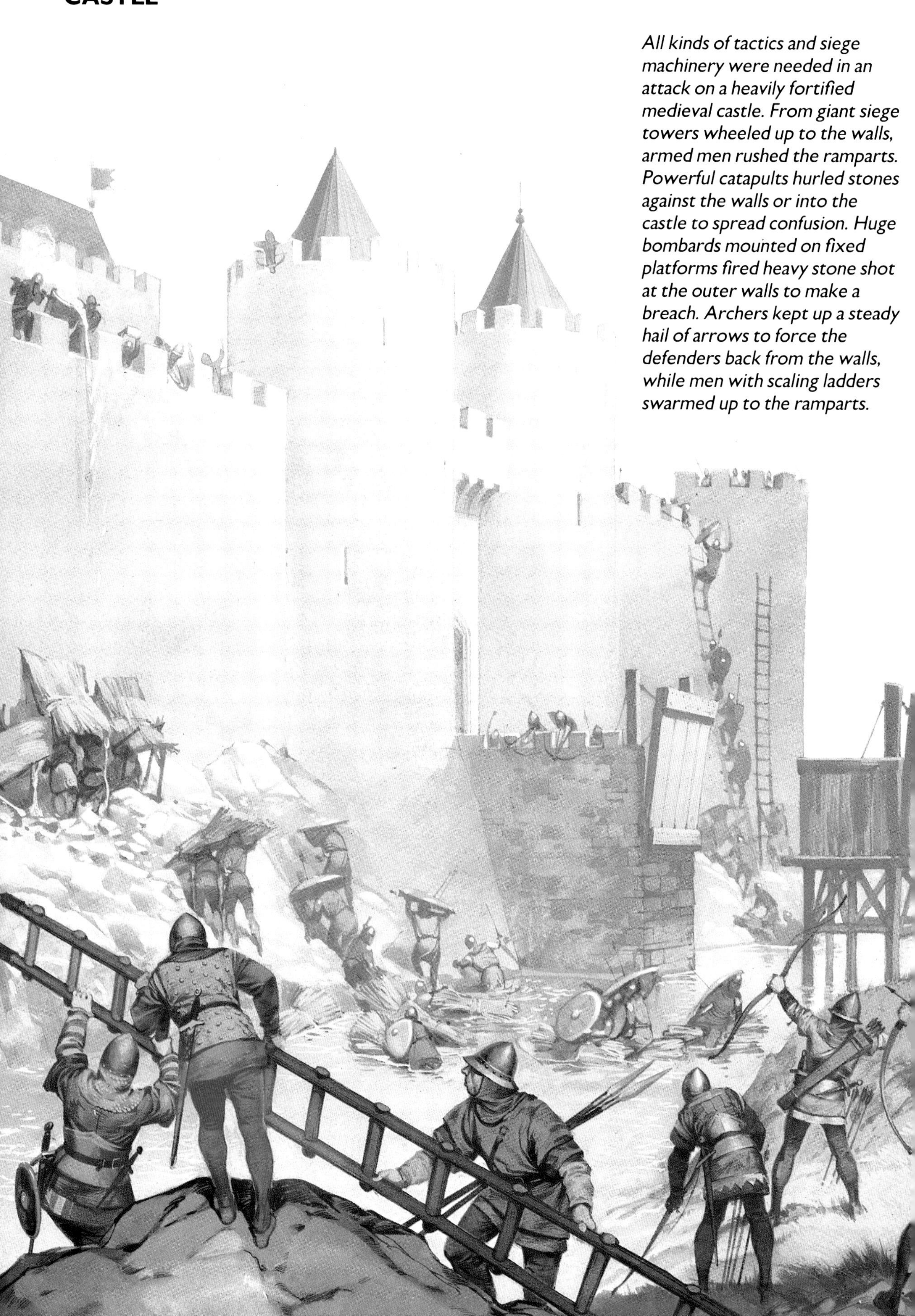

All kinds of tactics and siege machinery were needed in an attack on a heavily fortified medieval castle. From giant siege towers wheeled up to the walls, armed men rushed the ramparts. Powerful catapults hurled stones against the walls or into the castle to spread confusion. Huge bombards mounted on fixed platforms fired heavy stone shot at the outer walls to make a breach. Archers kept up a steady hail of arrows to force the defenders back from the walls, while men with scaling ladders swarmed up to the ramparts.

Castle

One of the few places where kings and lords in the MIDDLE AGES could feel safe was behind the thick stone walls of their castles. There, they and their men could fight off attacks by roving bandits and sit out long sieges by invading armies.

As castles developed, they became larger and more comfortable. Instead of all the living quarters being crowded into the main keep, small "villages" of huts and buildings sprang up inside the castle walls.

Castles had high, thick stone walls. A wall-walk ran right around the top, and through each tower.

▲ *This castle in southern Germany, built with tall, rounded towers, is much like the castle of fairy tale and fable.*

What do the cat, the camel, and the giraffe have in common? Very little, except one surprising fact. Other animals move their front leg on one side at the same time as the back leg on the other side. The cat, the camel, and the giraffe move their front and back legs on the same side at the same time, then the front and back legs on the other side.

Soldiers could run from one point of attack to another without ever showing themselves to their enemies.

Rounded towers could stand up to battering rams and hurled rocks much better than square towers. The towers jutted out from the main wall. This gave the defenders a better chance to fire on the attackers and stop them from reaching the castle walls.

Cat

A cat belongs to the group of MAMMALS called the feline family. Although the cat family ranges in size from domestic breeds to TIGERS, they all have many things in common. Cats have short, rounded heads, long face whiskers, sharp teeth that serve as deadly weapons for grabbing and biting their prey to death, and powerful claws. All cats except the cheetah can pull their claws back into a sheath of skin when they are not in use. Their long tails help them balance and make them superb at jumping and climbing. LIONS and cheetahs live in families. All other cats live mostly alone.

▼ *Cats come in all sizes, from the house cat to the powerful lion and tiger. On the front row with the tabby cat are, left to right, a wildcat, a lynx, a black panther, and a snow leopard.*

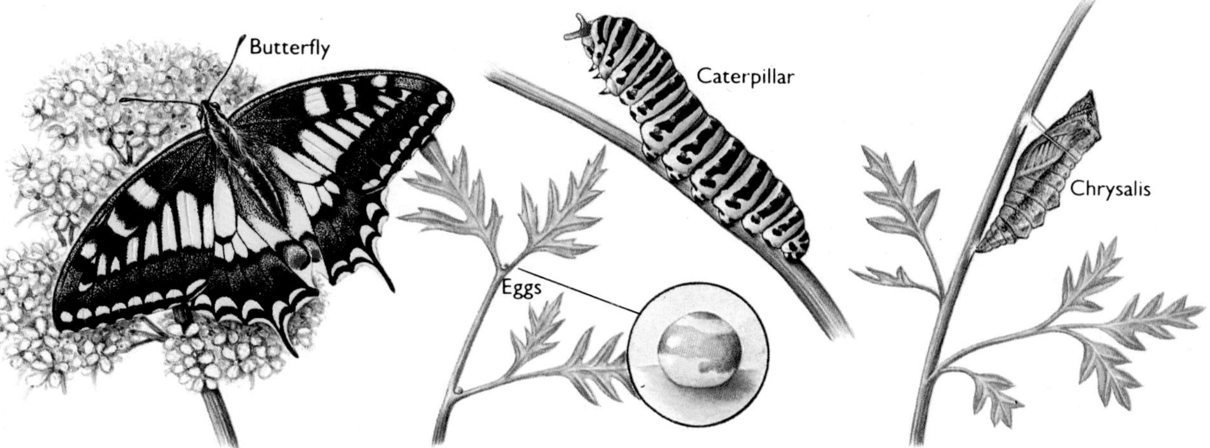

▲ *From egg to winged beauty—the life cycle of a butterfly. In very cold regions, some species take two or three years to pass from the egg to the butterfly stage.*

Caterpillar

The middle or "adolescent" stage in the lives of BUTTERFLIES and MOTHS is when they are called caterpillars.

Butterflies and moths usually lay their eggs on plants. After they hatch, small, soft, wormlike creatures—the caterpillars—emerge. Some are smooth-skinned. Others are spiny or hairy.

Caterpillars spend their whole life feeding. Their only purpose in life is to eat and grow and prepare for the change into adulthood. For this reason they have powerful jaws for chewing up plants. Many feed on crops and can cause great damage.

As caterpillars grow, they become too big for their skins. After a while, the skin stretches and splits and they emerge with a new one. This happens several times. The last "skin" is quite different from the others. It forms a hard layer which makes it impossible for the caterpillar to move. In this state it is called a *chrysalis*. Inside the chrysalis, the caterpillar changes into a butterfly. A moth caterpillar will spin a cocoon around itself before turning into a chrysalis. Caterpillars take almost a year to grow to full size.

Cathedral

Cathedrals are CHURCHES—only bigger. They are the grandest and most impressive kinds of Christian church ever to be built. A cathedral is the home church of a bishop. It is the center from which he looks after all the other churches under his care.

SEE IT YOURSELF

Caterpillars are easy to rear if you have plenty of the right food plant. A box or a big glass jar makes a good container. Cover the front with fine netting. The food plant can be anchored in moist Oasis, or you can put it in a small jar of water. Put in fresh food plants each day. Watch the caterpillars turn into pupae and butterflies.

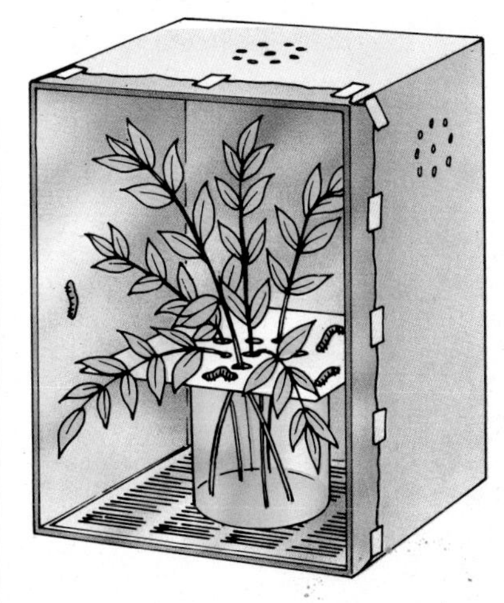

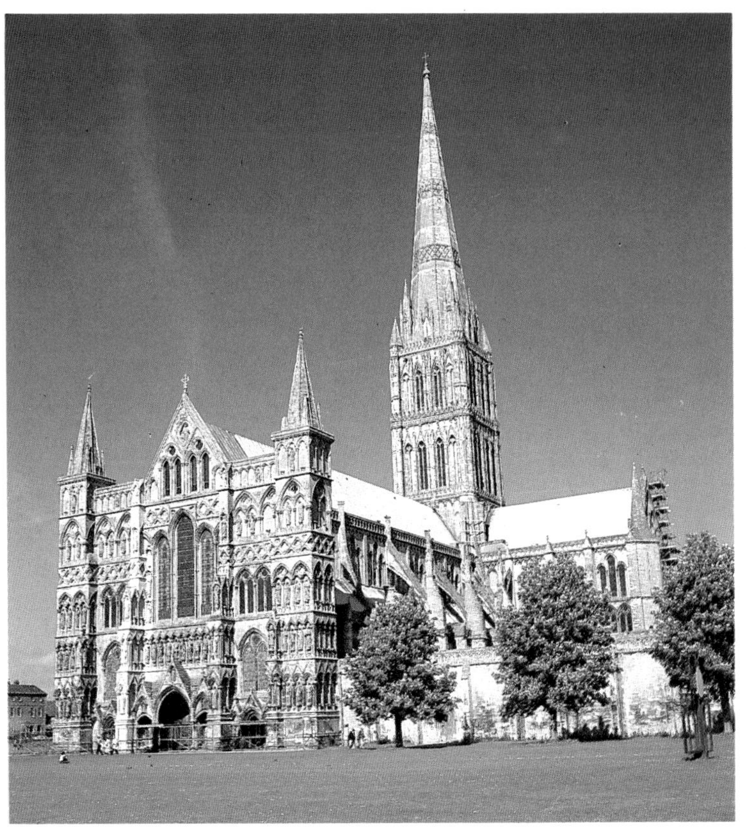

► *Salisbury Cathedral in Wiltshire, built in the 1200s, is a splendid example of Early English Gothic style. Its magnificent 404 ft. (123 m) spire is the tallest in England.*

Cathedrals are also places of worship. Most can hold large numbers of people, as well as having room for choirs, organs, chapels, statues, paintings, stained glass windows, and other religious items of decoration. Cathedrals were built with great splendor as they were built in honor of God. There are many styles of cathedral ARCHITECTURE.

Cattle *See* Cow

Cave

A cave is an underground hollow or passage that is formed when slightly ACID waters flow or seep through limestone rocks. The water slowly dissolves the rock, sometimes leaving behind a whole network of caves, like a huge decayed cavity deep down in the Earth.

After a cave has been formed, water may go on dripping through the walls and ceiling. This often results in odd-shaped deposits known as *stalactites* and *stalagmites*.

▼ *How limestone caves are formed. 1. Water seeps through cracks in the rocks. The acid in the water gradually widens the cracks into passageways and caverns. 2. The water forms an underground stream, which further widens the caverns. 3. Over the years, dripping water forms stalactites and stalagmites.*

1

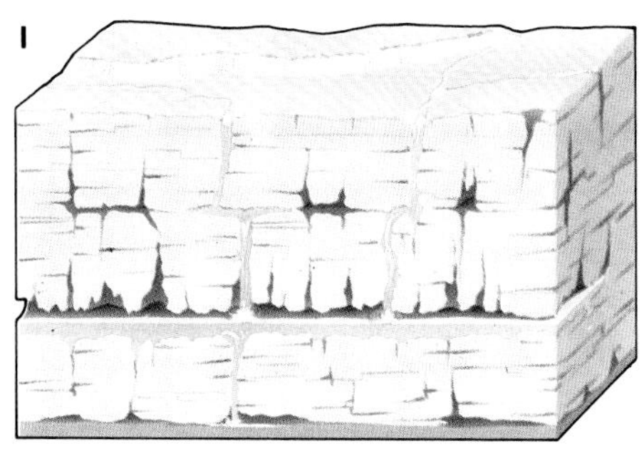

2

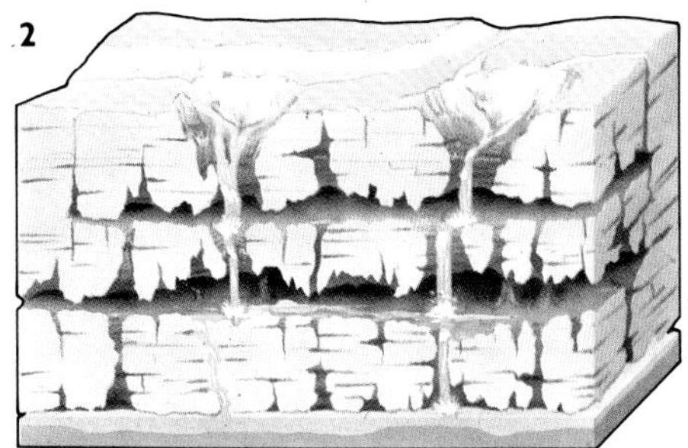

3

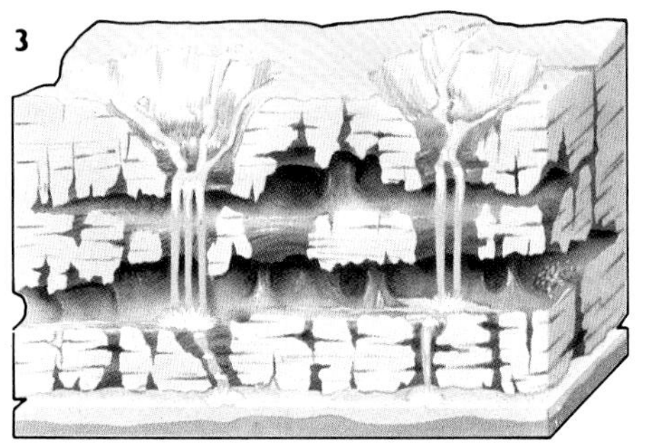

Cave Dweller 

Anybody who lives in a cave could be called a cave dweller. But what we usually mean are people who were the ancestors of modern man. Caves are natural places in which to shelter from the weather and from wild animals. They were some of the first dwelling places used by human beings.

The mouth of a cave is often dry, and it is possible to build a fire inside when the weather is cold. In hot weather, caves give shelter from the sun. Also, with walls all around them, the cave people could fight off dangerous animals from the cave mouth. The remains of ancient cave dwellers have been found in sites all around the world—in China, southern Asia, Europe, and Africa. Here, bits and pieces of their tools and weapons have been dug up, along with bones of the animals they hunted. Remains of their fires have also been found. Deep toward the back of the caves, graves of cave people have been unearthed. On the walls of some caves, paintings of animals have been found. From all these things, archaeologists have been able to piece together a great deal about the way of life of these people of long ago.

▼ *People of long ago built shelters in the entrances to caves. The dark interiors were often used only for ceremonies and rituals.*

▼ *Every living thing—plant or animal—is made up of cells. They differ in shape, size, and function. The diagrams below are "typical" cells only in that they show the characteristics of plant and animal cells. The nucleus is the control center of the cell. Most of the cell's energy is produced in the mitochondrion. Plant cells have a cell wall containing cellulose, a stiffening substance. They also have chloroplasts, which contain the green substance chlorophyll used in photosynthesis.*

Cell

Cells are the smallest living parts of plants and animals. Single cells can be seen only under a MICROSCOPE. Even a tiny bit of human skin contains millions of them.

Cells are usually round in shape. A few are spiraled, and some, like nerve cells, have sprawling treelike branches.

In 1665, a scientist named Robert Hooke looked at a piece of cork under a microscope and saw that it was made up of tiny compartments. He named them cells, and this term has been used ever since.

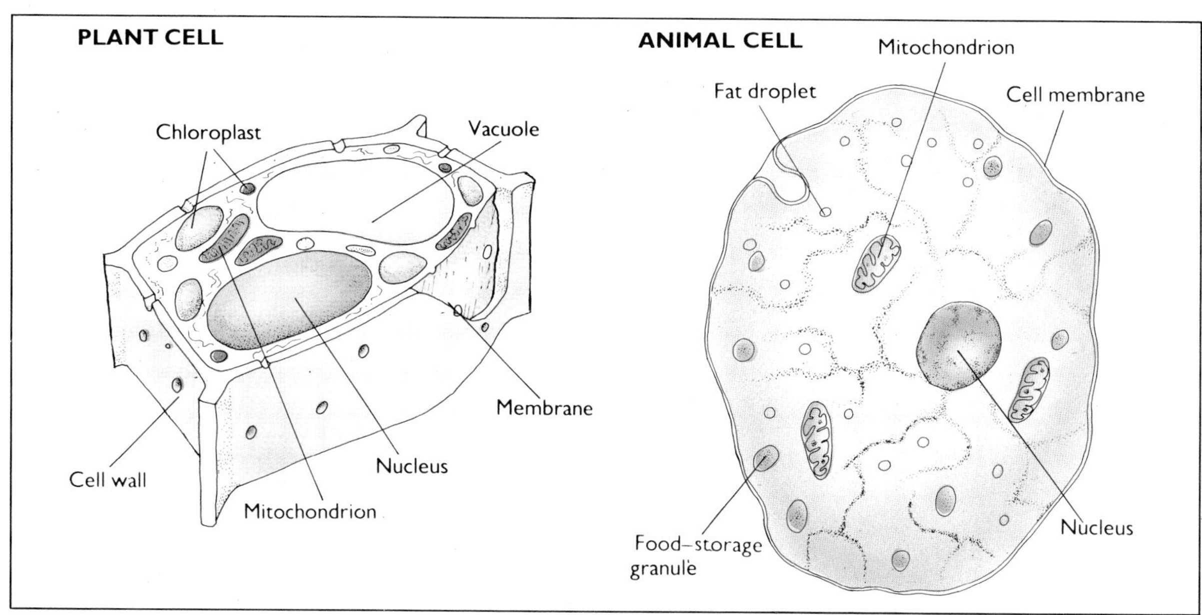

Celts

The Celts were an ancient people of northwestern Europe. At one time, over 2,000 years ago, they lived all over Britain, France, and parts of Spain and Germany. In about 400 B.C. they even crossed into Italy and attacked Rome.

The Celts were tall, fair, and very warlike. They lived in tribes made up of a chief, nobles, free men, and slaves. The tribes often fought each other. They were good metal workers and liked to decorate their weapons and armor with bright designs and strange creatures. And they were gifted musicians and poets. The Celtic religion was known as Druidism, and their priests were called druids.

The Celtic priests called druids have long been associated with the great standing stones of Stonehenge, near Salisbury in England. However, it is now known that Stonehenge was built well over a thousand years before the first Celts reached Britain in 550–450 B.C.

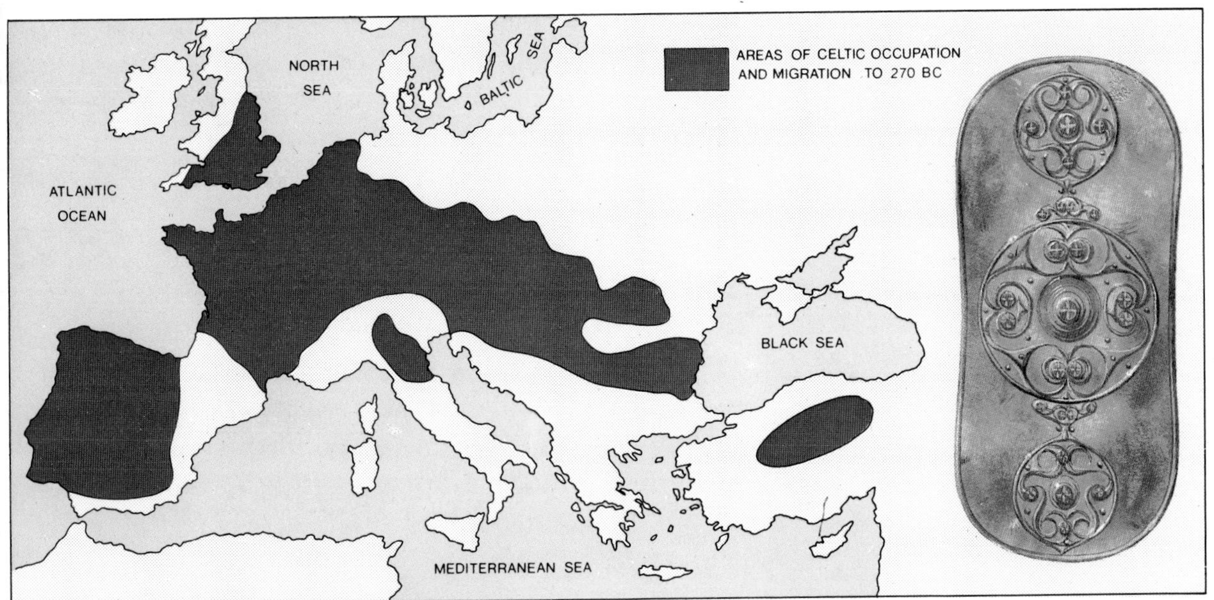

▲ *At one time the Celtic occupation of Europe had spread as far as Italy. Typical of the Celtic type of metalwork is this bronze shield, which was found in the River Thames in London.*

When the armies of the ROMAN EMPIRE spread out, many Celts fled to remote regions. In the lands they had once conquered, the Celtic way of life was soon lost. It was only in the far-off corners of Europe that their language and way of life survived.

Celtic speech was very common in Ireland, Cornwall, Wales, Scotland, and Brittany up until a few hundred years ago. Today, although less common, Celtic speech can still be heard. Irish and Scottish Gaelic, and Welsh are Celtic languages.

Census

Nearly all countries of the world regularly count the number of people living in them. This population count is called a census. Most countries take a census every ten years. A census also gives important facts about how much money people earn, what kind of homes they live in, whether they are married or single, and how many children they have.

The 1990 census found the U.S. population to be 249,632,692.

The word "census" comes from the Latin word *censere*, meaning to tax. In ancient Rome, census takers made lists of people and their property, chiefly for purposes of taxation. When William the Conqueror invaded England in 1066, his officials made a count of the country's land and property. This census was listed in the Domesday Book.

Centipede

Centipedes are long, worm-like creatures. Their bodies are made up of many parts, often up to 100 or more. Each part has a pair of clawed legs. The

The largest known centipede is a 46-legged giant that lives in the forests of South America. It is about 10 in. (25 cm) long and 1 in. (2.5 cm) thick!

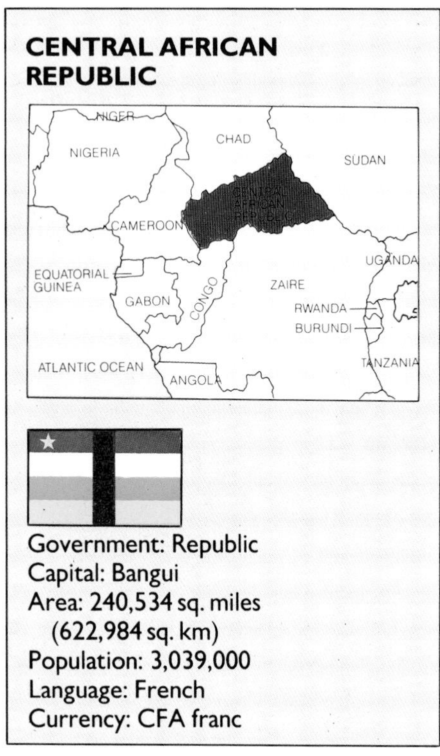

Government: Republic
Capital: Bangui
Area: 240,534 sq. miles (622,984 sq. km)
Population: 3,039,000
Language: French
Currency: CFA franc

head has long feelers, powerful jaws, and two stinging claws that are able to inject poison into their prey. Centipedes are found all over the world. They feed mainly on worms, insects, and snails.

Central African Republic 

This African country is slightly smaller than Texas, but there are only about 3 million people living there. The Central African Republic has a warm climate. Rain falls nearly every day during the rainy season. At other times the country is hot and dry. Most of the people are poor. Some of them raise cattle. Others are farmers who grow cotton, coffee, and grain.

The country was once part of French Equatorial Africa. It became independent in 1960 and is one of the least developed countries in Africa.

Central America 

Central America forms a land bridge between the continents of North and South America. It consists of the independent republics of COSTA RICA, EL SALVADOR, GUATEMALA, HONDURAS, NICARAGUA, PANAMA, and BELIZE.

This land bridge was created many millions of

▼ *Buildings in Guatemala City reflect the Spanish colonial style. Guatemala, Honduras, El Salvador, Nicaragua, and Costa Rica became independent republics in 1838.*

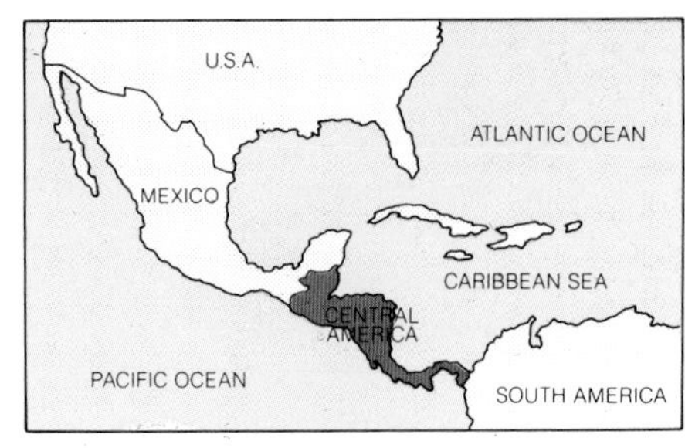

◀ *Many people outside the cities in Central America live in primitive one-room huts of adobe and grass, farming small plots on the surrounding hillsides.*

years ago by volcanic activity. In the east, Central America has a flat coast covered with jungle. Central America is a hot area. Most of the large cities are in the cooler highlands.

Central America, along with Mexico and the West Indies, is said by many people to be the tropical part of North America. Also, most of this "tropical" area, along with much of South America, is often called Latin America. This is because the people there speak Spanish or Portuguese, which come from ancient Latin.

Most of the people of Central America are of Indian, Spanish, or mixed origin. Spanish is the main language, but many Indians still speak their native language. Central Americans farm tropical crops such as sugar, bananas, cotton, and coffee.

Cereal

Cereals are the SEEDS of a group of plants that belong to the GRASS family. Throughout human history they have been the most important of all types of FOOD. In ancient times, cereals were collected from wild plants. Later, when they began to be grown on farms, they became the most important food of early civilizations.

Some cereals, such as RICE and corn, are eaten in their natural form. Others, such as WHEAT and rye, are ground into flour before being baked or cooked. Cereals are also used to make alcoholic drinks and to feed farm animals.

▼ *Cereals are all members of the grass family which are grown for food. Wheat, rice, and rye are grown mainly for people to eat, while barley, oats, corn, and millet are more often grown as animal feed. Rice is the major food crop for half the world's population.*

CHAD

Government: Republic
Capital: N'Djamena
Area: 495,752 sq. miles (1,284,000 sq. km)
Population: 5,679,000
Language: French
Currency: CFA franc

Chad

Chad is a large landlocked country in the center of Africa. It is named after Lake Chad, which lies on the western border of the country. This shallow lake can be as large as 10,000 sq. miles (26,000 sq. km) during the wet season. North Chad is part of the great Sahara Desert. The southern part gets plenty of rain and is covered with grass and trees. Chad became a French colony in French Equatorial Africa in 1913 and gained its independence in 1960. It is one of the least developed countries.

Chalk

Chalk is a pure white, soft, and crumbly form of limestone. Land that is rich in chalk is found in the south of England, in France, and in parts of North America.

Most chalk was formed between 135 and 65 million years ago. It is made up of the crushed shells of countless tiny sea creatures. When these creatures died, their shells built up in thick layers at the bottom of warm, shallow seas. As the shape of the Earth's surface changed, these layers were lifted out of the seas to become land.

We usually think of chalk as something that we use to write with, but it is also used in many other ways. Mixed with other things, chalk is used to make paints, medicines, rubber, paper, ink, and toothpaste.

▼ *The famed white cliffs of Dover are made of thick layers of chalk formed during the Cretaceous Period, 100 million years ago.*

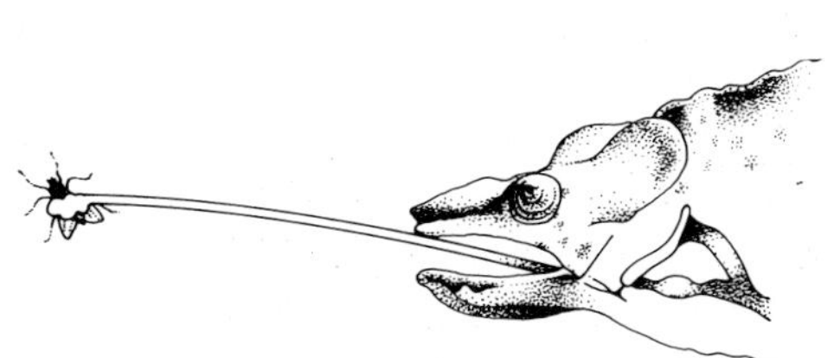

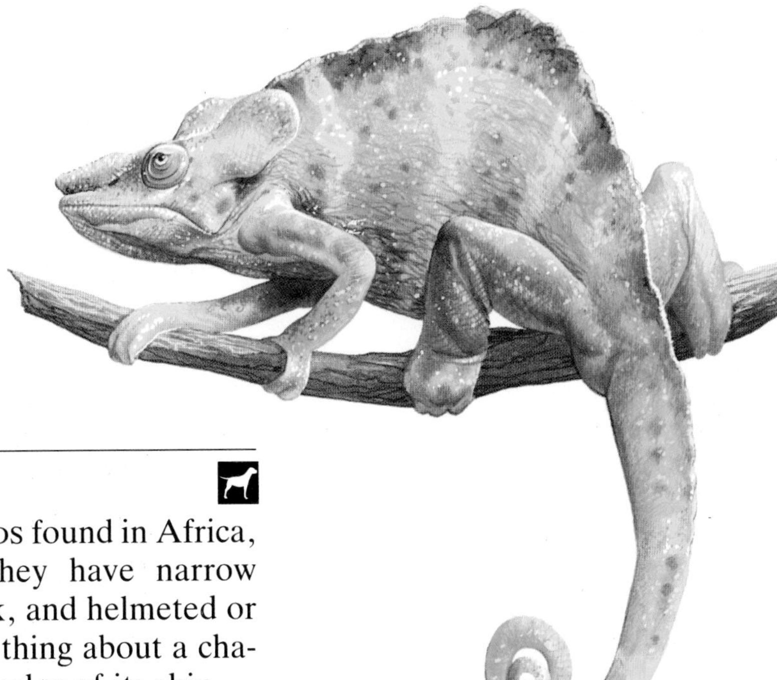

▶ *The chameleon shoots out its long tongue to snare its prey. The sticky, knoblike tip of the tongue swells up to trap the insect.*

Chameleon

Chameleons are a group of LIZARDS found in Africa, Asia, and parts of Europe. They have narrow bodies with a crest along the back, and helmeted or horned heads. The most unusual thing about a chameleon is that it can change the color of its skin.

Chameleons live in trees. They move very slowly and will sit on branches for hours, as still as a statue, waiting until insects come close to them.

Chanukah

Chanukah is a Jewish holiday that lasts for eight days each December. Jewish families light candles and exchange presents on each night of Chanukah to celebrate an ancient miracle. Long ago, one day's supply of oil for their temple lasted for eight days until the Jewish people could get a new supply.

Chaplin, Charles

Charlie Chaplin (1889–1977) was one of the most famous comic MOTION PICTURE actors of all time. He is best known for his role as the gentle, well-meaning tramp who was always making mistakes and getting into trouble.

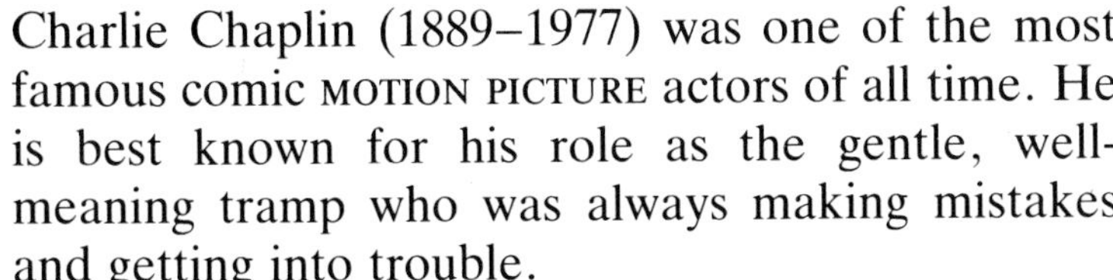

▼ *Charlie Chaplin, seen below in his famous role as the Little Tramp, was one of the most versatile people in movie history. He wrote and directed many of his films, and he composed the music for all his sound films.*

Charlemagne

Charlemagne (A.D. 742–814) was a great military leader. In the 700s, he founded an empire that covered most of western Europe.

In the year 768, Charlemagne became the king of

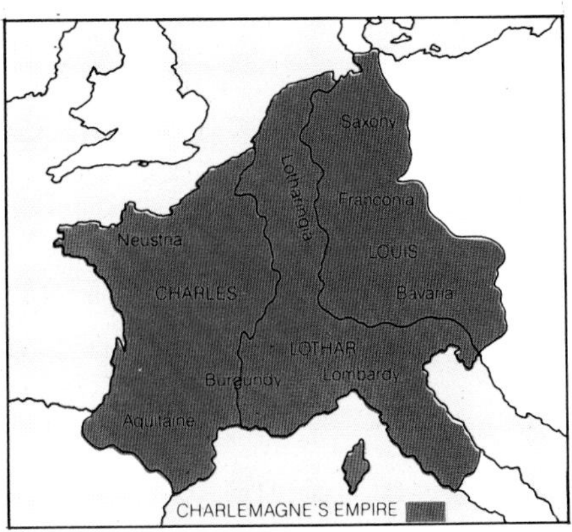

▲ *This map shows the extent of Charlemagne's empire at its height. When he died, his sons fought among themselves. Eventually Charlemagne's empire was divided between his grandsons, Charles, Louis, and Lothar.*

the Franks, a people who lived in the country we now call France. Through his skill in war, he soon took over northern Spain, Italy, and Germany. He fought for the Catholic Church in Rome, and in return, the POPE crowned him Holy Roman Emperor on Christmas Day in the year A.D. 800.

▲ *Charles I defied Parliament and was ultimately convicted of treason and beheaded.*

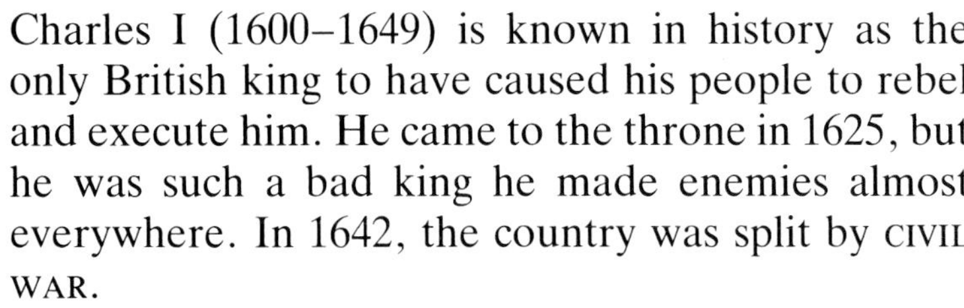

Charles I

Charles I (1600–1649) is known in history as the only British king to have caused his people to rebel and execute him. He came to the throne in 1625, but he was such a bad king he made enemies almost everywhere. In 1642, the country was split by CIVIL WAR.

Charles II

As King of Britain, Charles II (1630–1685) was liked as much as his father was disliked. He spent most of his youth in exile in Europe, while CHARLES I fought to save his crown and his life, and lost both.

In 1660, after being ruled by Oliver CROMWELL

for ten years, the English invited Charles II to return and take back the crown. He was a wise ruler, and he was very careful in the way in which he treated his people and PARLIAMENT. His court was very lively and exciting and his personal charm won him many friends. His subjects called him the "Merry Monarch."

▲ *After the stark years of Puritan rule under Cromwell, Charles II won the hearts of the people with his great personal charm.*

Chaucer, Geoffrey

Geoffrey Chaucer (*c.*1340–1400) was a great English poet. He was one of the first people to write in the ENGLISH LANGUAGE rather than in Latin. His best known work is *The Canterbury Tales*. It is a collection of stories told by an imaginary group of pilgrims as they traveled to Canterbury Cathedral.

◀ *A detail from an early illustration from* The Canterbury Tales. *Chaucer wrote the work in Middle English, the form of English used from about 1100 to 1450.*

Cheese

Most cheese is made from cows' MILK, but it can be made from the milk of goats, sheep, buffalo, and even reindeer. To make cheese, the milk is turned sour so that it will *curdle*.

The solid parts, called the *curds*, are taken away from the liquid, or *whey*, and are pressed into a more solid form and dried. The cheese is then left to ripen.

The greatest cheese-eaters are the French. They eat more than 40 lb. (18 kg) per person every year. There are over 240 different kinds of French cheese.

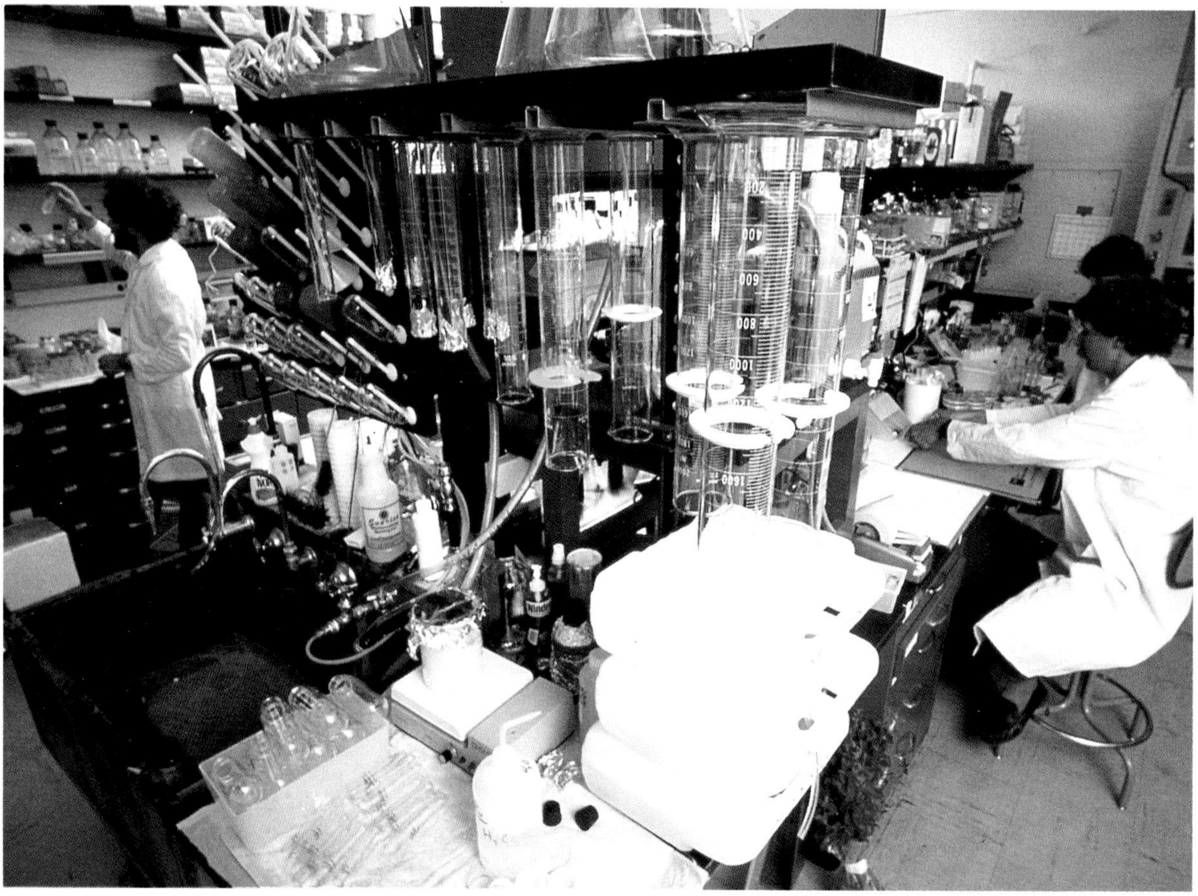

▲ *Research into cancer at a biochemistry laboratory in the United States. Growth, genetics, and reproduction are all of great interest to biochemists.*

Our bodies contain many different chemicals. More than half the atoms in the body are hydrogen. Next in abundance comes oxygen. Then there is carbon, making up one-tenth of the body's weight. That is enough carbon, if it were pure, to fill 3,000 pencils!

Chemistry

Chemistry is the study of materials—solids, liquids, and gases. A chemist finds out what things are made of and how they are joined together. If a piece of wood is burned in a fire, this is a *chemical reaction*. The wood turns to ash, and at the same time, heat and light are given off. It took chemists a long time to find out that burning is the joining together of the wood with the gas oxygen from the air. There are lots and lots of chemical reactions.

The true science of chemistry as we know it began only in the 1600s. Chemists at this time began to find out how chemicals really work. Then they discovered the ELEMENTS, simple substances that make up all the millions of different substances on Earth. There are only about a hundred elements, each of them made up of tiny ATOMS. The atoms of elements often join together to make different substances. The salt you put on your food is made up of atoms of the elements sodium and chlorine. An atom of sodium joins with an atom of chlorine to make a molecule of salt.

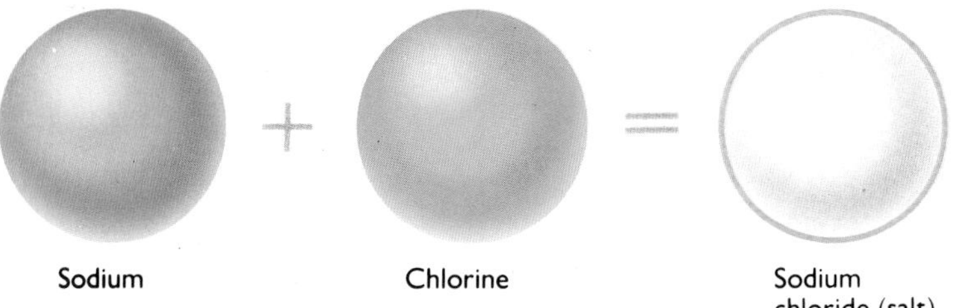

Chemistry is today a very important science, and chemists work in a vast number of industries.

▲ *A chessboard, showing the opening positions of the pieces. The line-up is always the same, with a white or light-colored square in the bottom right-hand corner.*

Chess

Chess is a game that has been played for hundreds of years. It is played by two people on a board with 64 black and white squares. Each of the two players has 16 pieces which they line up on opposite sides of the board. Every piece can be moved around the board only in a special way. They are used to attack and retreat and to defend each other, and can be captured and taken out of play. The most important piece for each player is the "king." The game is won when one player manages to capture the other player's king.

Chess pieces

Chicago

Chicago is one of the most important cities in the United States. It is important because of its location on the southern shore of Lake Michigan and at the edge of the rich prairie lands of the Midwest. This made it a natural center for goods from the east to be sent to the west and for produce from the west to be sent to the east. Today, many industries are based in the city. There is often a breeze from the Lake, so Chicago has been called "Windy City."

▼ *Looking toward Lincoln Park and the skyscrapers of Chicago. Lake Michigan is on the left.*

CHILE

Government: Republic
Capital: Santiago
Area: 292,257 sq. miles (756,945 sq. km)
Population: 13,173,000
Language: Spanish
Currency: Peso

Chile

Chile is a narrow country that lies along 2,650 miles (4,265 km) of the western coast of South America. Its habitable area is made narrower by the Andes Mountains, which lie along its eastern border.

Chile has over a quarter of the world's copper resources, as well as other minerals. Its people are Spanish-speaking and are mainly Roman Catholics. In 1973, a military government seized power in Chile, but in 1988 the Chilean people voted for an end to military rule.

Chimpanzee

Chimpanzees are the most human-looking of all the APES. Fully grown, they are about 4 ft. (1.3 m) tall and are able to walk upright, although they often use their hands to help push themselves along the ground. Chimpanzees come from the jungles of Africa. They live in family groups and are very fond of their young and take good care of them. They are playful and intelligent animals. Tame chimpanzees have been taught to behave like humans in many ways. They can even learn simple sign language.

In the wild, chimpanzees live in forested areas. They travel in groups, but males sometimes travel alone. They sleep in nests in trees.

Chimpanzees are among the noisiest of all animals. They scream and shriek, drum on trees, slap the ground, and keep up an almost constant hooting and muttering. But when a human appears, they usually fall silent and disappear into the forest.

► *A chimpanzee infant watches as an adult probes a termite nest with a stick. Chimpanzees are intelligent animals capable of using simple tools.*

China

China is the third biggest country in the world, and it has a population larger than that of any other country. A fifth of all the people on Earth are Chinese—over one billion. (See pages 136–137.)

Chlorophyll

This is a chemical substance that is found in the leaves and stems of almost all PLANTS. It gives them their green color. Chlorophyll is found inside plant CELLS in tiny bodies called *chloroplasts.*

Plants need chlorophyll to make their food. Sunlight is also necessary. It falls on the leaves and acts with the chlorophyll to turn carbon dioxide from the air and water, which the plant's roots suck up from the soil, into food made up of SUGARS and STARCHES. At the same time, the plant's leaves give out OXYGEN. This whole process is called *photosynthesis.* It is a very important part of life on our Earth, as all living things need oxygen in order to breathe.

SEE IT YOURSELF

Plants need light to make green chlorophyll. You can prove this for yourself by attaching a piece of black paper to part of a leaf. If you leave the plant for a few days, you will see a pale patch begin to appear under the paper. No light, no chlorophyll.

Chocolate

The chocolate we eat is made from the beans of the cacao tree. The beans grow inside pods, which hang from the trunk and the branches of the tree.

To make chocolate, the beans are first roasted and then ground up to give an oily liquid called "chocolate liquor." Other things may then be added to the liquor. The chocolate candy we buy, for example, has milk and sugar added to it.

▼ *Cacao trees grow huge pods which are cut off with a large knife. The beans inside are dried to make chocolate and cocoa.*

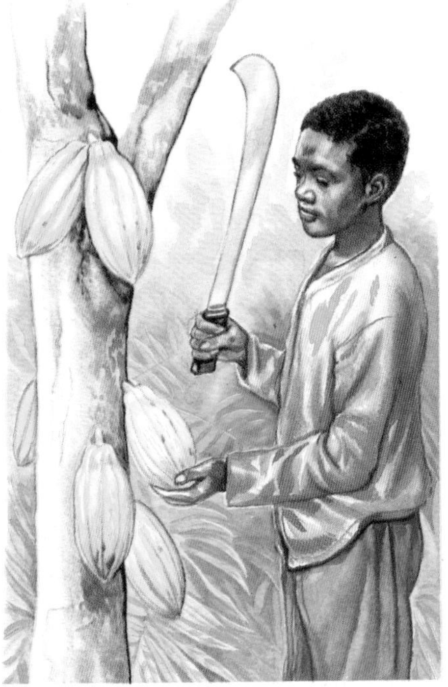

Christianity

Christianity is one of the world's major RELIGIONS. More than a billion people call themselves Christians. These are people who follow the teachings of JESUS, and who believe that he is the son of God who came to Earth in human form.

Christianity is almost 2,000 years old. In fact, we date our calendar from the year in which it was thought that Jesus was born. Christians accept the BIBLE as their holy book. Sunday is their holy day,

Continued on page 138

CHINA

China is the third largest country on Earth, and the nation with the greatest population. There are more than a billion Chinese—a fifth of the Earth's people. China has the oldest continuous civilization of any country.

Natural barriers, including the Himalaya Mountains and great deserts, cut off China from its neighbors on the Asian mainland. In the east are great plains and rivers, including China's longest river, the Chang Jiang (or Yangtze Kiang) and the slightly shorter Huang Ho, or Yellow River. It is here that most of the people live. Many Chinese are city dwellers, working in factories. Others till the soil, as their forefathers have done for centuries.

For more than 3,000 years China was an empire. Chinese inventions included paper, printing, silk, porcelain, and gunpowder—all discovered long before such things were known in Europe. Since 1912, the country has been a republic. A bitter civil war between Nationalists and Communists ended in 1949 with the Communists victorious. Under Mao Tse-tung (1893–1976) Communist rule was often harsh, and China became isolated from the rest of the world. Later leaders have "opened up" China to new ideas and Western trade, but young Chinese want a more democratic rule.

CHINA

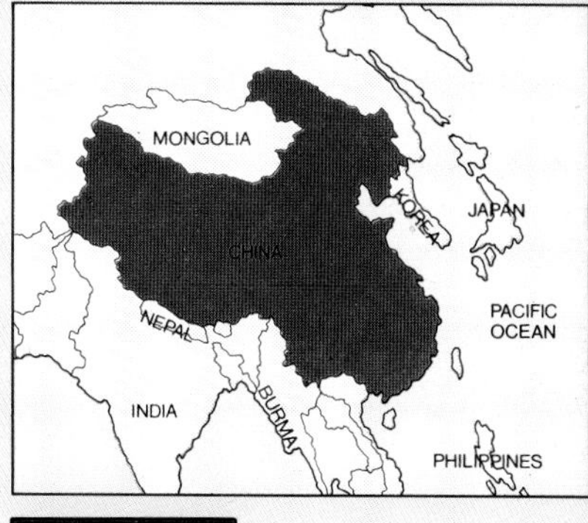

Government: People's republic
Capital: Beijing (Peking)
Area: 3,696,100 sq. miles (9,573,000 sq. km)
Population: 1,139,060,000
Language: Mandarin Chinese
Currency: Yuan

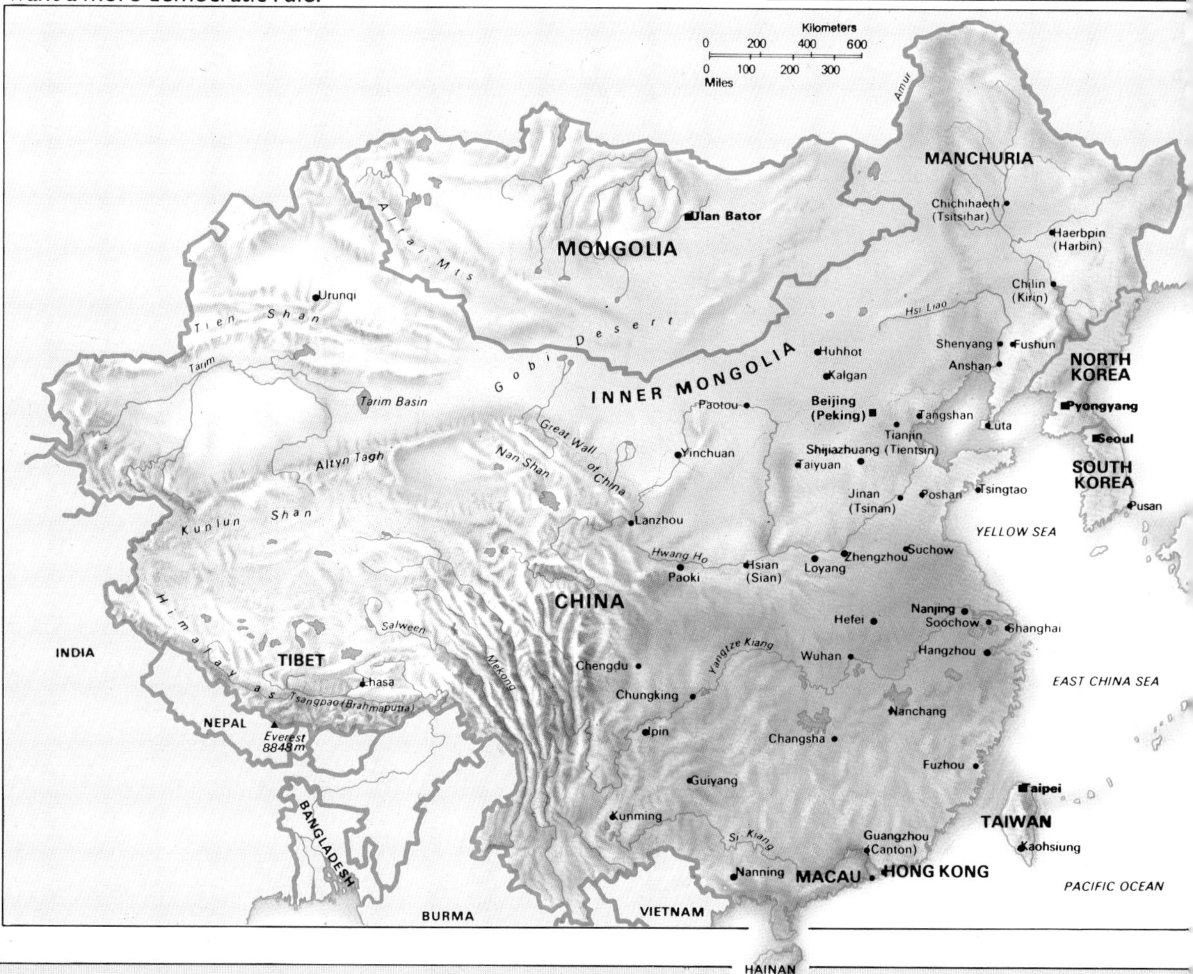

我要马上找医生
我这里痛上
请别理得太短

THE CHINESE LANGUAGE

Iore people speak Chinese than ny other language. Chinese is vritten in picture-signs or :haracters. A Chinese person can nanage perfectly well using about ,000 characters. But there are nany more: a dictionary in 1716 isted more than 40,000! To spell he sounds of Chinese in the Vestern alphabet, the Chinese use a system known as Pinyin. In Pinyin, he old name for the capital of China, Peking, becomes Beijing. Another city, Canton, becomes Guangzhou, and so on. Pinyin is based on Mandarin, the standard orm of the language taught in China.

► *The Great Wall of China stretches for more than 1,500 miles (2,400 km) and is the longest fortification ever built. It was begun about 200 B.C. to keep out the invading Tartars.*

► *China covers such a vast area that transportation is not yet well developed. Its rivers are still important "highways" for people and goods.*

▼ *The giant panda, a native of China, is now a rare and protected species.*

THE HISTORY OF CHINA

700 to 1000 B.C. *Shang dynasty*: bronze tools used and writing developed.
000 to 256 B.C. *Chou dynasty*: Confucius and foundation of Chinese civilization.
00 B.C. *Barbarians invade China.*
21 to 207 B.C. *Ch'in dynasty*: China becomes an empire. The Great Wall is built.
02 B.C. to A.D. 221 *Han dynasty*: invention of paper.
89 to 618 Sui dynasty.
18 to 906 *T'ang dynasty*: invention of printing. Poetry and painting flourish.
07 to 960 Period of unrest, with weak rulers.
60 to 1279 *Sung dynasty*: movable printing type invented. Cities are built, firearms invented.
215 Mongol ruler Genghis Khan conquers China.
275 Marco Polo reaches China.
280 to 1368 *Yuan dynasty*: Kublai Khan is great ruler and science flourishes. Mongols are driven out.
1368 to 1644 *Ming dynasty:* European traders and missionaries visit China. Splendid temples, palaces, and tombs built, beautiful porcelain made.
1644 to 1912 *Ch'ing dynasty*: China gradually becomes weak and dominated by foreign traders.
1839 to 1860 Opium Wars: Europeans force Chinese to open their ports to foreign trade, including the harmful drug opium.
1900 Boxer Rebellion against foreigners.
1912 *End of dynasties*: China becomes a republic.
1927 Chiang Kai-shek seizes power.
1930s War with Japan and civil war between Chiang Kai-shek's Nationalists and Communists.
1949 China becomes a Communist republic, led by Mao Tse-tung.
1976 Death of Mao. New rulers restore order and begin modernization of China.
1989 Army sent to disperse students' pro-democracy demonstration in Tiananmen Square, Beijing.

or more information about China, turn to the following articles which you will find elsewhere in the encyclopedia: ACUPUNCTURE; UDDHA; COMMUNISM; CONFUCIUS; EVEREST, MOUNT; GENGHIS KHAN; GREAT WALL OF CHINA; HIMALAYAS; MAO TSE-TUNG; MARCO POLO; PANDA.

We know very little about the early part of Christ's life. He grew up in Nazareth, learning to be a carpenter. The only recorded event of Jesus' youth took place when he was 12 years old. We are told he went to the temple in Jerusalem and discussed questions about God with the wise men. When Jesus next appears, he is a man of about 30.

when they go to church, pray, and observe other religious traditions.

In some ways, Christianity grew out of the religion of JUDAISM. But the teachings of Jesus upset the Jewish and Roman leaders of the time, and in A.D. 29 he was crucified. After his death, the followers of Jesus, the disciples, spread his teachings far and wide. Today, there are many different forms of Christianity.

Christmas

This festival, celebrated by Christians on December 25, marks the birth of JESUS. It is not known if Jesus was actually born on this date. In fact, the first mention of a festival of Christmas comes from a Roman calendar over 300 years after his death. However, there were a number of Roman festivals held on this day, and early Christians may have thought that celebrating the birthday of Jesus on the same day would show that this festival was just as important. The customs of decorating Christmas trees and sending Christmas cards did not begin until the 1800s.

▼ *An illustration from a Victorian Christmas card. The sending of cards at Christmastime is a tradition dating back to the 1840s.*

Church

Christian churches are as varied as the countries in which they are found. They come in all shapes and sizes—from tents and tiny wooden huts to towering stone CATHEDRALS. But all churches are used for the same purposes. They serve as places of prayer, as settings for holding religious services, and as places that house all kinds of religious objects.

Larger churches, especially traditional Catholic ones, were usually built in the shape of a cross. In most, the altar is built at the east end. It is found at the end farthest away from the main door.

Throughout the ages, churches have been built in many different styles of ARCHITECTURE, depending on the period of history and which country they were built in. Many churches adopted the Romanesque style of architecture. They all had wide, rounded arches and low round DOMES. In the MIDDLE AGES in western Europe, a style known as *Gothic* appeared. After the 1000s, cathedrals with pointed spires, narrow soaring arches, richly stained glass windows, and lots of stone carvings became very popular. These churches were cool and dark on the inside. The huge space inside them helped to give churchgoers a sense of awe at being in the presence of God.

Most cathedrals were laid out in the same way on the inside. The worshipers sat in the center, in a section called the *nave*. They faced the altar and the place where the choir sang. On either side were the wings, called *transepts*, which gave the church its cross shape.

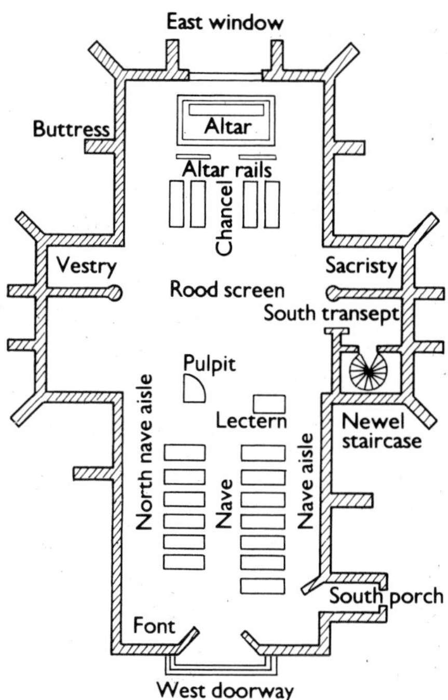

▲ *The ground plan of many English parish churches, including the one shown above, is cruciform—shaped like a cross. The nave and the chancel form the upright beam of the cross, and the transepts form the arms. The altar is usually at the eastern end.*

▲ *Building a big church in the Middle Ages was an enormous task that went on for many years. In this picture workmen are building a Gothic abbey.*

Churchill, Winston

Sir Winston Churchill (1874–1965) was a great British prime minister, war leader, and writer. Although he was a senior minister in PARLIAMENT before and during World War I, he was not very powerful. But in 1940, when World War II threatened Britain, the country chose him as its prime minister. As a leader during wartime, he showed great courage and determination. His rousing speeches helped the people of Britain to fight on

▲ *Sir Winston Churchill was Britain's greatest wartime leader. His speeches and courage inspired the country.*

when they stood alone against Germany and her allies. He told the people, "I have nothing to offer but blood, toil, tears, and sweat."

Circus

The Romans first used the word "circus" to describe a large open-air space where exciting displays of horsemanship, acrobatics, chariot racing, and wrestling were held. The modern type of circus began in the 1700s, and circus acts today include jugglers, clowns, acrobats, and all sorts of trained animals, even bears and lions.

Civil Rights

People have always fought for the right to govern themselves. But this does not always mean that people have freedom in their own lives, and sometimes they must fight for this freedom—for their civil rights. The most important of these rights are freedom to follow your own religion, freedom to say what you like in speech and in newspapers, equality in law, and the right to elect and dismiss a government. In the United States, civil rights became an important issue for blacks in the 1950s.

Civil War

The Civil War was fought between the states of the North and the South from 1861 to 1865. It began mainly because the Southern states wanted to keep their slaves and old-fashioned, agricultural way of life. The Northern states felt that slavery was wrong and that slaves should be set free. This lead to arguments over whether a state that disagreed with the others should have the right to leave, or "secede" from, the Union.

When the war came, it divided the country terribly. The North won because of its greater industrial strength, but it was a struggle that cost the lives of hundreds of thousands of people and destroyed many towns. After the war, many in the South felt great bitterness.

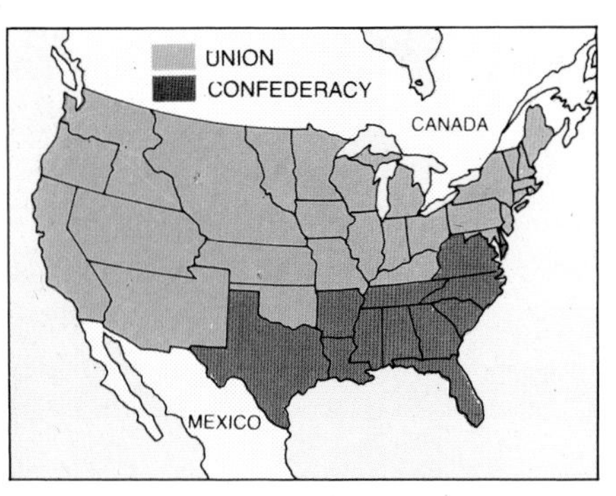

▲ *When the Civil War broke out, 11 states left the Union to form the Confederacy. The North had much more industry than the South, and that in the end decided the war.*

The war began in April 1861 when six Southern

◀ *The battle of Williamsburg, May 5, 1862. The Confederates withdrew after heavy fighting.*

states left the Union. Five more states soon joined them to form the Confederate States of America. Twenty-three states fought on the Union side. At first, the Confederate states did well. Their armies were well organized and won several important victories. But then the power of the Union began to tell. In 1863, the Confederate army was defeated at Gettysburg, Pennsylvania. After this, it became clear the Union would win.

The Civil War destroyed the prosperity of the South. Many felt, however, that it was more important that slavery be ended and the Union be preserved.

When the Civil War broke out, President Lincoln thought that he would need only 75,000 volunteers to put down the Southern uprising in three months. In the end, four million men fought in a war that went on for four years.

▼ *The Civil War was one of the first wars to be photographed. This gun crew must have had to stand very still.*

▲ *Animal figures being fashioned out of clay. Clay that has been fired (baked in a kiln) is called terracotta, which simply means "baked earth."*

Clay

Clay is rock which has been broken down by millions of years of weathering. It is made of tiny particles that make a thick, sticky paste.

Clay particles are so small and closely packed together that a layer of them is waterproof. When a thick layer of clay lies underground; rain that seeps down through the soil cannot go through it. The water forms an underground pool, or *reservoir*. People can get the water out by digging wells. London, England, lies over a layer of clay like this and still gets some of its water from wells.

Clay is easy to mold and can be baked hard in an oven, or *kiln*. People began making pots from clay in prehistoric times. Today even the finest porcelain is made from clay. Clay is also used to make bricks for houses and other buildings.

Clay, Henry

Henry Clay (1777–1852) was one of the most important American politicans of the early 1800s. Yet, though he ran for president five times, he was never elected. Clay was called the "Great Compromiser" because of his skill in settling disputes. Most of the arguments he helped settle were about slavery, and whether it should be allowed in the new states of America as the country grew.

Cleopatra

Cleopatra (69–30 B.C.) was a queen of Egypt. She was made ruler with her brother at the age of 17, but her brother's supporters soon drove her from the throne. When Julius CAESAR visited Egypt, he fell in love with Cleopatra and helped her to become queen again. Cleopatra followed Caesar back to Rome and lived in his house until he was murdered in 44 B.C. Then, she went back to Egypt.

Three years later, Cleopatra met Mark Antony, who ruled the Roman Empire with Octavian. Antony also fell in love with Cleopatra and left his wife, the sister of Octavian, to live with her. Octavian did not trust Cleopatra or Antony and started a

Cleopatra was the name of seven queens of ancient Egypt. The famous queen we mention here was Cleopatra VII. Historians are not quite sure as to which kind of snake Cleopatra allowed herself to be bitten by. The most likely snake was the Egyptian cobra. Its bite causes death quite quickly.

war with them. He defeated them in a naval battle at Actium in Greece in 31 B.C.

Cleopatra and Antony fled to Alexandria in Egypt. They were followed there by Octavian and his army. Cleopatra began to realize that she could never beat the Romans. She and Antony decided to kill themselves. Antony stabbed himself first and died in Cleopatra's arms. Cleopatra then died from a poisonous snake bite.

▲ *Cleopatra was one of the most fascinating women of all time. Although queen of Egypt, she was a Greek, one of the Ptolemy line that Alexander the Great had set on the throne of Egypt.*

Cleveland, Grover

Grover Cleveland (1837–1908) twice served as president of the United States: from 1885 to 1889 and from 1893 to 1897. He was the 22nd and 24th president. He was known for his common sense and his refusal to grant special privileges to those who demanded them. This sometimes made him unpopular, but it also helped the United States to grow into the most powerful nation on earth. He understood how important it was in a time of such rapid change that the country have firm and steady government. His friends called him Uncle Jumbo because he was a large and friendly man.

GROVER CLEVELAND

Twenty-second President 1885–1889
Twenty-fourth President 1893–1897
Born: Caldwell, New Jersey
Education: Public schools
Occupation: Lawyer
Political Party: Democratic

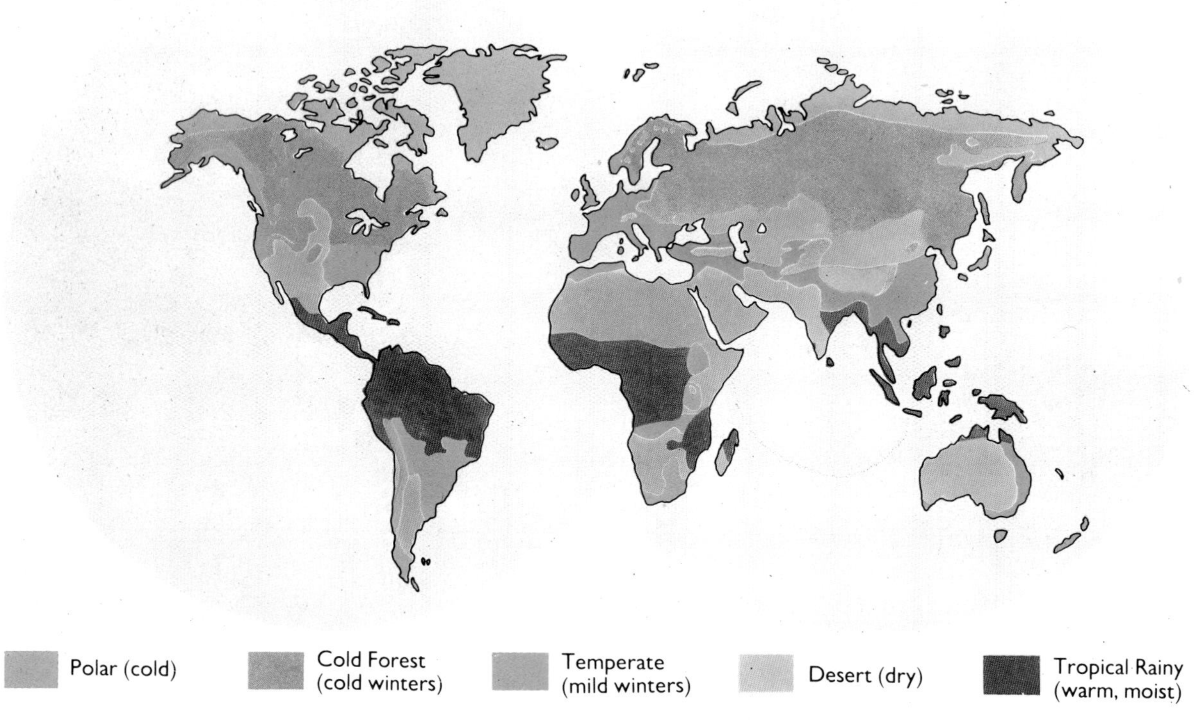

▲ *The Earth can be roughly divided into five climatic zones. Within each zone there are variations because climate is determined by altitude as well as by latitude.*

▼ *The Poles get less heat than the equator because the Sun's rays have to travel farther through the Earth's atmosphere. The rays also reach the Poles at a slant because the Earth is round.*

Climate

Climate is the usual WEATHER of a place over a long period of time. The weather can change from day to day, but the climate stays the same.

The Sun has the greatest influence on the climate. It heats the land, the seas, and the air. Countries near the equator get more of the Sun's rays and usually have a hotter climate than places farther north or south. The Sun's rays do not get to the Arctic and the Antarctic easily. They have very cold climates.

When the Sun heats the air, it causes winds which can make the climate hotter or colder. The winds may also carry rain or dry air which can make the climate wet or dry.

Mountains also affect the climate. On a mountain top, the air is thinner. It does not soak up the heat of the Sun as much as air at the bottom of mountains or in valleys.

The United States, with its vast area, contains examples of the main types of world climates. But much of the United States has a temperate climate. There is regular rainfall and temperatures are not extreme during most of the year.

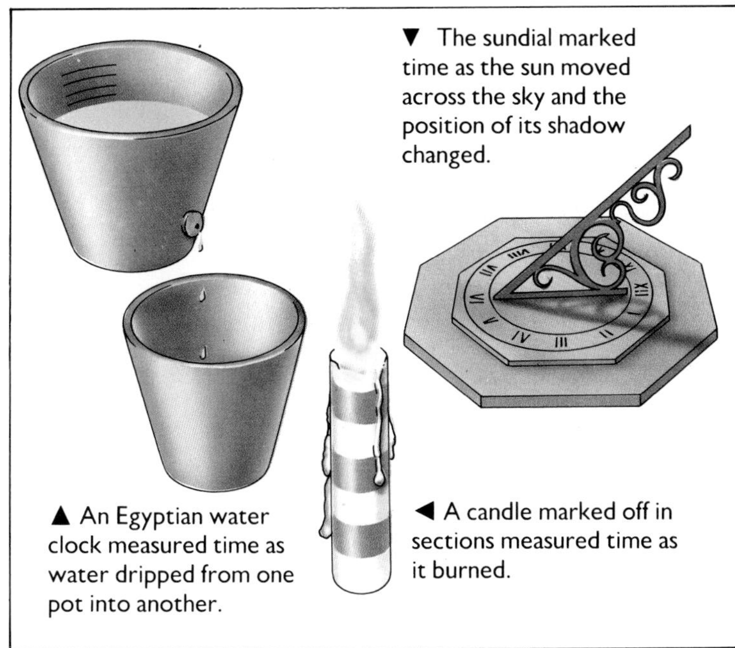

▼ The sundial marked time as the sun moved across the sky and the position of its shadow changed.

▲ An Egyptian water clock measured time as water dripped from one pot into another.

◀ A candle marked off in sections measured time as it burned.

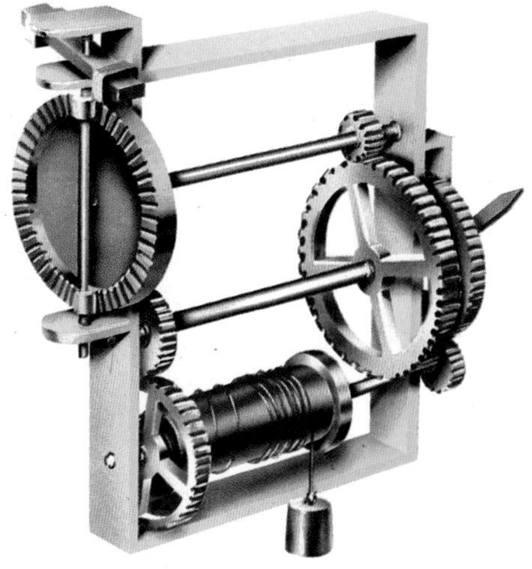

▲ *Early mechanical clocks in Europe were driven by a weight on the end of a cord wound around a drum. As the drum rotated, it turned the hands of the clock.*

Clock

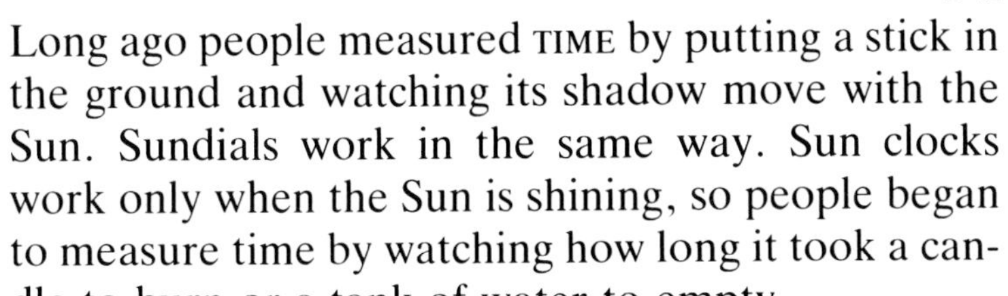

Long ago people measured TIME by putting a stick in the ground and watching its shadow move with the Sun. Sundials work in the same way. Sun clocks work only when the Sun is shining, so people began to measure time by watching how long it took a candle to burn or a tank of water to empty.

The first mechanical clocks were made in Europe in the 1200s, although the Chinese probably had clocks as early as the 600s. European clocks were first used in churches and abbeys to mark the time of services. A clock in Salisbury Cathedral, England, dates from 1386.

Early clocks like these were bad timekeepers and could lose or gain an hour a day. In 1581, the great astronomer Galileo discovered that the PENDULUM could be used to measure time. This helped people to make much more accurate clocks. From then on, improvements were made, and ordinary clocks are now accurate to within a few minutes a year.

Today's scientists need very accurate clocks. They invented first the electric and then the quartz crystal clock. The most accurate clock today is at the United States Naval Research Laboratory in Washington, D.C. It is an atomic hydrogen maser clock, accurate to one second in 1,700,000 years.

▼ *One of the most famous clocks in the world is at the Houses of Parliament in London. It is often mistakenly called Big Ben—this is actually the name of its biggest bell.*

Clothing

Everybody wears some sort of clothing. What they wear depends on many things: the climate (how hot or cold it is); work and rest (people often wear different clothes when they go to work—it might be a uniform or it might be because they have to dress up for the office); and fashion (we don't just wear clothes to protect us but because we want to look good in them).

The earliest clothes were crude, probably no more than animal skins. When people learned how to sew, they began to make more complicated clothes. Then men and women learned how to make their own cloth, using "yarn" from plants. By the time of the ancient Egyptians and Greeks, clothes had become much more sophisticated. Even rich people wore only loose draped tunics to keep cool. The Romans called these "togas." By the MIDDLE AGES in Europe, the clothes of poorer people remained simple, but the wealthy dressed in fine clothes. They often used expensive materials such as silks and damasks that had been brought from the East. Until the 1900s, clothing remained either very lavish if you were rich or simple if you were poor. Then clothing began to become more practical, especially for women. Today in the West, clothing and fashion are big businesses, with styles changing

▲ *Popular clothing styles over four centuries. Modern fashion reflects the change in lifestyle in this century—designs are practical and clothes are sewn from manmade fabrics that are easy to care for.*

▼ *Clothing styles from prehistoric to medieval times. The ancient Greeks and Romans wore loosely-draped tunics and togas. Costume became more elaborate after rich silks and muslins were imported from the East.*

◀ *Fashion is big business. Every season brings shows where models display the latest top fashion designs.*

▼ *Elizabeth I led the fashion of her day. When she died, she is said to have left 3,000 dresses in her closet.*

from year to year. The top fashion designers are very important to the way we live. Many clothes now are made with artificial materials that are inexpensive and hard wearing. In other parts of the world, many people still wear traditional dress, but more and more people are wearing Western-style clothes.

Cloud

Clouds are great clusters of tiny water droplets or ice crystals in the air. A cloud may float more than 33,000 ft. (10,000 m) up, or drift so low that it touches the ground, when it is known as mist or fog.

There is always a certain amount of water *vapor* in the air. It is made up of tiny specks of water. Warm air that contains water vapor often rises and cools. Since cool air cannot hold as much water as warm air, the vapor particles start to form droplets (condense) around bits of dust, pollen, and salt.

As more water vapor condenses, the droplets grow in size and clouds begin to form. At first, they are white and gauzy. As they become heavy with water, they become thick and gray. Finally, the droplets become so heavy that they clump together and fall to the earth. If the temperature is high enough, they come down as rain. Otherwise, they land as hail or snow.

Most clouds form along the boundaries between cold and warm air masses. By watching how they

A large cloud can contain more than a billion billion raindrops. And each raindrop is made up of about a hundred million tiny water droplets.

▶ *Different types of cloud bring different weather. The high cirrus clouds are made of ice and are sometimes called "mares' tails." Puffy cumulus clouds often mean good weather. Low, gray, stratus clouds bring rain and the towering cumulonimbus are thunder clouds.*

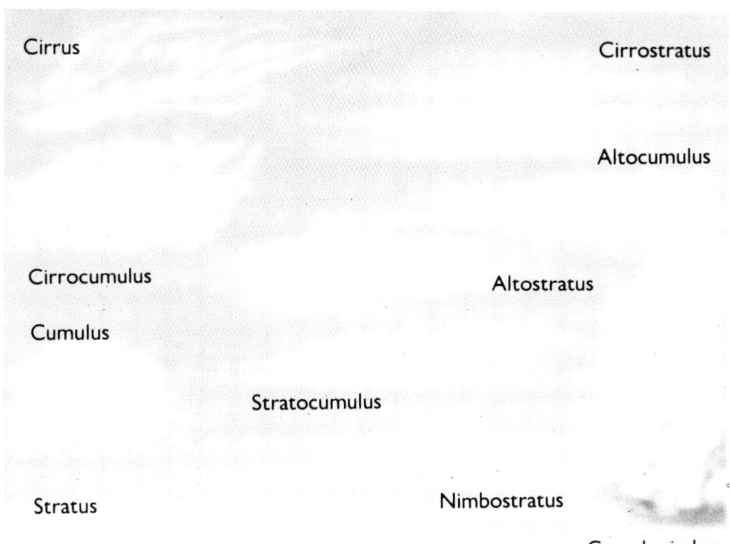

build and move, it is possible to tell what sort of weather is coming. Different types of clouds tell weather forecasters different things. Clouds are one of the best ways we have of predicting the WEATHER.

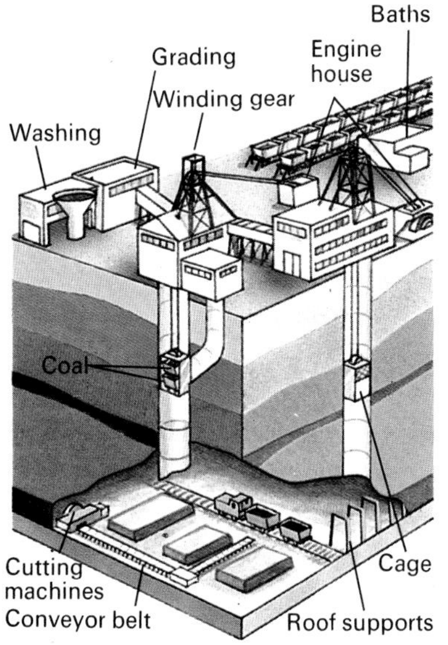

▲ *Most coal is now cut by machines. The workings may stretch for miles underground.*

Coal

Coal is a FUEL that is found under the ground in layers, or "seams." It is called a FOSSIL fuel because it was made millions of years ago from plants that were "fossilized" after they died. The energy they absorbed from the Sun is released in the form of heat when coal is burned.

People discovered long ago that coal could be burned to produce heat. Its most important uses were to power factories and to warm homes. Today, most coal is used to make electricity.

Coffee

Coffee is a drink made from the beans of the coffee plant. The coffee tree can grow as high as 40 ft. (12 m), but it is kept trimmed to only 6 to 10 ft. (2 or 3 m), so that the fruit can be reached easily. The trees bear red berries which contain two seeds or beans in yellow pulp, surrounded by a tough skin. The skin and pulp are removed and the beans dried and roasted until they are brown. Then they are ground to brew the coffee we drink.

▼ *Coffee comes from beans that are found inside the fruit of the coffee tree. These berries are red when ripe. The beans are roasted to bring out the coffee flavor.*

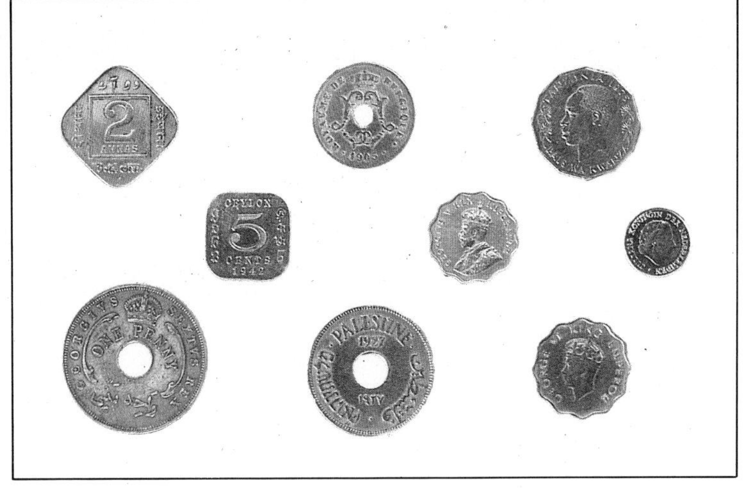

Nearly all American coins are struck (made) at the Philadelphia or Denver mints. Coins made at the Philadelphia mint are stamped with a small P. Coins made at the Denver mint have a small D. Pennies do not have mint marks.

◀ *Coins are made in different shapes and in different metals. Collecting coins can be a satisfying hobby.*

Coin

The first metal coins were minted (made) about 800 B.C. Before then, all trade had been done by barter—by exchanging goods. For a long time, coins were made of precious metals, particularly gold and silver. Then people realized that any metal would do as long as everybody agreed that each coin was a symbol for a certain value.

Colombia

Colombia is a country in northwestern South America. Much of the land is hot, dry jungle. Most of the people live in the northwest, where the highlands are fertile. Coffee is Colombia's most important crop, and it accounts for half of the country's exports. Other crops are rice, corn, and cotton.

The Colombians won their independence from Spain in 1819 under the leadership of Simón Bolívar. The country has many economic problems.

COLOMBIA

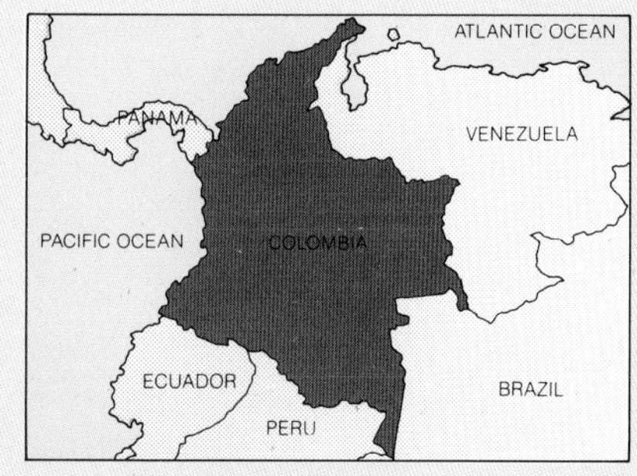

Government: Republic
Capital: Bogotá
Area: 439,735 sq. miles (1,138,914 sq. km)
Population: 32,987,000
Language: Spanish
Currency: Peso

Color

The first man to find out about colored light was Isaac Newton. He shone sunlight through a piece of glass called a *prism*. The light that came out of the prism was broken up into all the colors of the rainbow—red, orange, yellow, green, blue, and violet. Newton had found out that ordinary white light is made up of many colors added together.

When sunlight falls on rain or spray from a garden

▼ *Colored light behaves differently from colored pigment (the substances in inks and paints). All the colors in light (1) combine to make white. Mixing colored paints (2) results in black.*

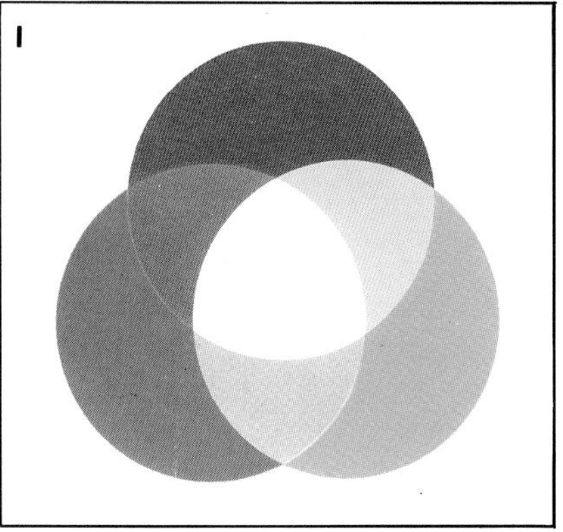

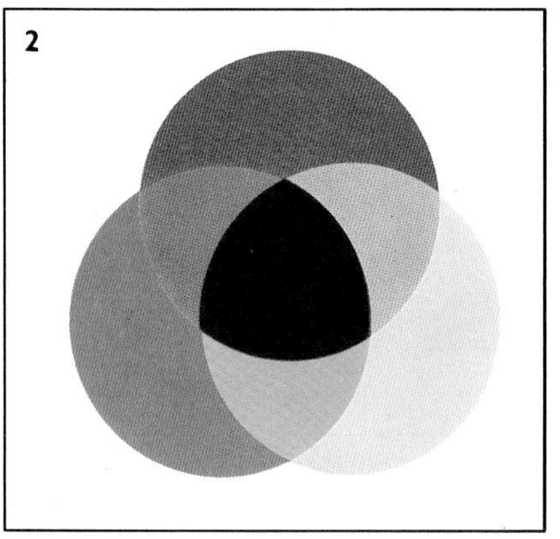

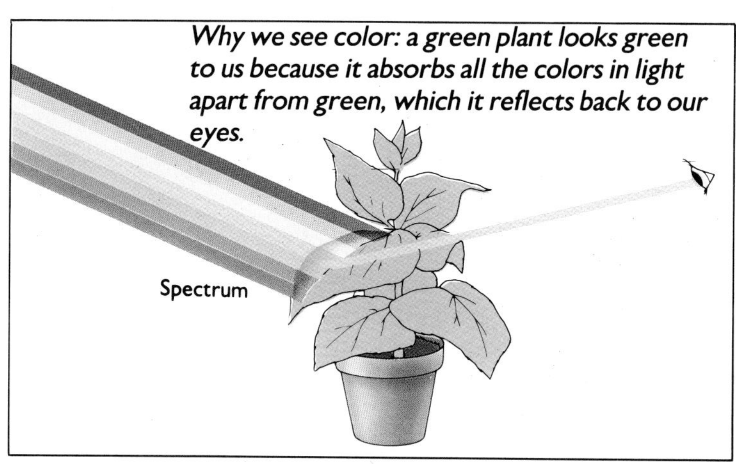

Why we see color: a green plant looks green to us because it absorbs all the colors in light apart from green, which it reflects back to our eyes.

hose, we sometimes see a rainbow. Rainbows are caused by drops of water behaving like tiny prisms. They break up the Sun's light into a *spectrum* of colors. The colors are always in the same order, from red to violet.

A red flower is red because it takes in all the other colors and throws back only red. A white flower gives back to our eyes all the colors of light. We know that all the colors of the rainbow added together make white.

Colorado

Colorado is one of the country's most beautiful states. The towering Rocky Mountains that run down through the state are one of the natural wonders of America. People come to ski in winter and

▼ *Night falling over Denver, Colorado.*

to hike and sightsee in summer. But Colorado is also one of the most prosperous and dynamic states. Its capital is Denver—"the mile-high city"—and it has become an important center for businesses such as finance. The state also produces oil. Probably the most famous industry is mining. It was mining that brought white men to Colorado in the 1800s. In 1894, the largest silver nugget ever found in the United States was dug up in Aspen. It weighed 1,840 pounds (838 kg). Colorado is called the Centennial State because it joined the Union exactly 100 years after the Declaration of Independence.

COLORADO

Capital: Denver
Population: 3,294,394
Area: 104,091 sq. mi. (269,595 sq. km)
State flower: Rocky Mountain Columbine
State bird: Lark Bunting
State tree: Colorado Blue Spruce
Statehood: August 1, 1876
38th state

Colosseum

The Colosseum of ROME was a giant sports stadium built by the ancient Romans. It could hold more than 50,000 people and was the largest building of its kind in the Roman Empire. It was dedicated in A.D. 80 and still stands in the center of Rome, but it is partly in ruins.

The floor, or *arena*, was used for GLADIATOR combats, battles between men and animals, and fights

Although the Colosseum has suffered several earthquakes much of it still stands. Only a portion of the outer masonry remains, however, because it served as a handy quarry during the Middle Ages. Much of the stone that was used to build St. Peter's Basilica in Rome was taken from the Colosseum.

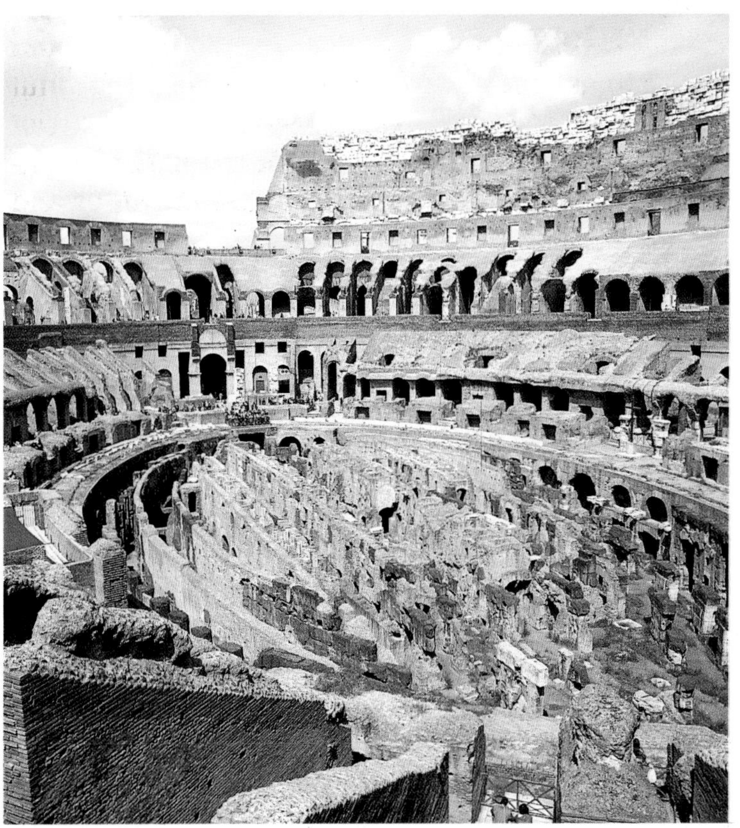

◀ *The Colosseum, now a ruin, was a great open-air arena where the ancient Romans watched displays and combat.*

between different kinds of animal. It was also used for showing rare wild creatures. The floor could also be flooded so that sea battles could be fought on it. Underneath the arena were pens in which were kept the wild beasts. When the Colosseum was finished, it was opened with a ceremony in which 5,000 animals were killed.

Columbus, Christopher 

Christopher Columbus (1451–1506) was a sailor and explorer. He discovered America for Spain in 1492. Although Columbus returned to America three more times, he died believing that the land he had reached was Asia.

Like many people of his time, Columbus knew that the Earth was not flat but round. Sailors from Europe used to sail east to the "Indies" (Asia). They brought back rich cargoes of gold, spices, and treasure. Columbus thought that if he sailed west instead he could reach the Indies quicker. The queen and king of Spain gave him ships and money to make this voyage.

▲ *Christopher Columbus made four voyages to the Americas, first landing in San Salvador. His flagship on the first voyage, the 100-ton caravel* Santa Maria, *ran aground and had to be abandoned.*

In 1492, Columbus sailed west with three small ships, the *Santa Maria*, the *Pinta*, and the *Niña*. The ships sailed for three weeks without seeing any land and the crews became afraid. Then on October 12, they reached an island in the Americas. Columbus named it San Salvador—an island in the Bahamas. When he returned to Spain, Columbus had a hero's welcome.

Columbus thought he had sailed to the Indies. This is why the people he met in America were called Indians. The islands he first reached are still known as the West Indies.

He made four voyages to the Americas. On the third, he landed on the mainland of South America, on the coast of Venezuela. It was probably the first time for 500 years that Europeans had set foot on the American continent. But the colony he had founded on Hispaniola on his second voyage rebelled. This revolt by the colonists put him in disgrace. He died without regaining his fortune or his prestige, but today his voyages are recognized as being among the most important events in history.

Columbus died thinking that the lands he had discovered were part of China or Japan. During his first voyage he actually sent men inland in the hope that they would reach the Chinese capital, Beijing.

Comet

Comets travel around the SOLAR SYSTEM in long paths, or ORBITS. Sometimes they pass close to the Sun. At other times, they move far beyond the path of Pluto, the outermost planet. A complete orbit by a comet is called its period. Encke's Comet has the shortest period of all. It lasts for three years and four months. Others have periods of centuries or even thousands of years.

Comets are clouds of frozen gases, ice, dust, and rock. The biggest are only a few miles across, but their bright tails may be millions of miles long.

Most of the time, comets cannot be seen, even through the biggest telescopes. But whenever their orbits bring them back into the middle of the solar system, they flare up and look very bright.

As a comet travels slowly toward the Sun, the Sun's rays knock particles out of the comet and push them away to make a long tail, which always points away from the Sun. So, when the comet moves away from the Sun, the tail is in front. The tail is made of glowing gas and dust. But the tail is so fine that a rocket passing through it would not be harmed. The Earth has passed through the tails of several comets. One of the most famous comets is named after the astronomer Edmond HALLEY. In 1682, he studied the path of a bright comet and accurately forecast when it would return.

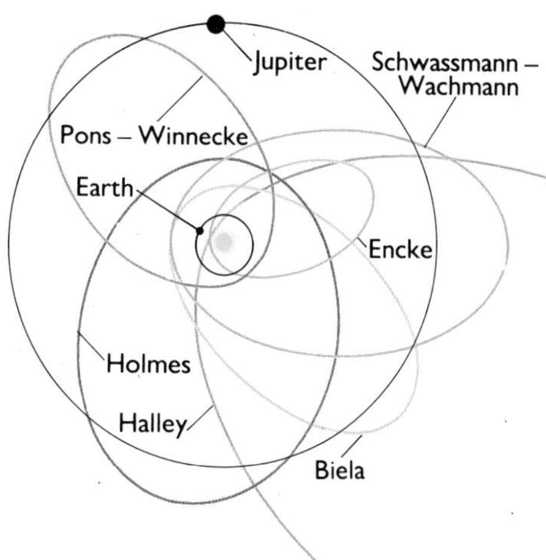

▲ *Some of the comets that return regularly to the Sun every few years. Part of the much bigger orbit of Halley's Comet is also shown. Encke's Comet has the smallest period. It passes close to the Sun every three years and four months, although it cannot be seen without a telescope. Comets are usually named after those who discovered them. They were once thought to foretell the coming of harmful events, since they appeared so unexpectedly and dramatically.*

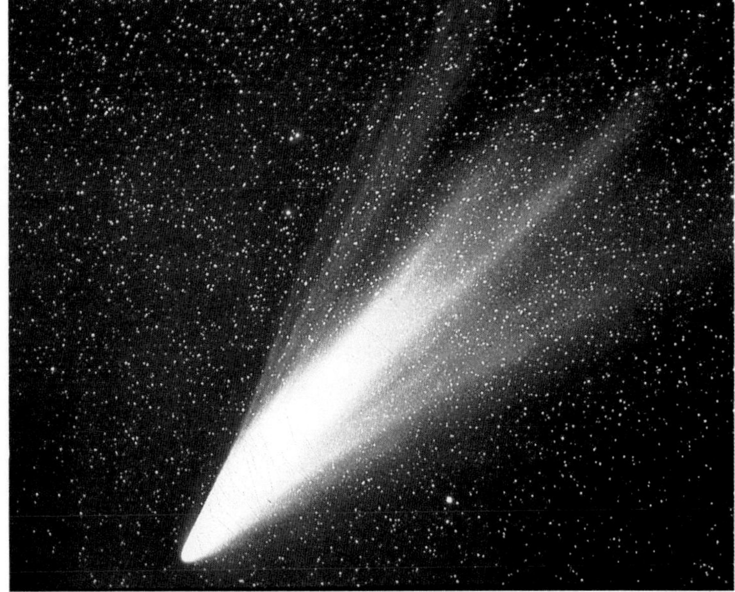

◀ *Comet West, photographed on March 9, 1976, showing its dust tail (white) and its gas tail (blue).*

▲ *Commercial artists prepare advertisements for magazines and newspapers. This old advertisement for a German airline is a good example.*

MEMBERS OF THE BRITISH COMMONWEALTH

Antigua and Barbuda	New Zealand
Australia	Nigeria
Bahamas	Papua New Guinea
Bangladesh	Western Samoa
Belize	Seychelles
Botswana	Sierra Leone
Brunei	Singapore
Canada	Solomon Islands
Cyprus	Sri Lanka
Dominica	St. Kitts-Nevis
The Gambia	St. Lucia
Ghana	St. Vincent and the Grenadines
Grenada	Swaziland
Guyana	Tanzania
India	Tonga
Jamaica	Trinidad and Tobago
Kiribati	Tuvalu
Lesotho	Uganda
Malawi	United Kingdom
Malaysia	Vanuatu
The Maldives	Zambia
Malta	Zimbabwe
Mauritius	
Nauru	

Commercial Art

Commercial art is the art that has to do with business—the word "commerce" means business. Commercial artists are usually trained in an art school, where they learn to design, draw, and paint. They learn to "lay out" books and magazines—that is, to arrange pictures and text on a page. They prepare advertisements for newspapers and magazines, and illustrate books. Fashion designers design clothing; industrial designers design products and appliances. Nearly everything manmade that we see has been "designed" in some way or other.

Common Cold

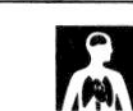

The common cold is the most widespread disease. Many people miss several days of work or school each year because of it. The disease is caused by tiny organisms called viruses. The viruses are carried through the air by coughs and sneezes. Anyone nearby can catch a cold if the viruses enter the eyes, nose, or mouth. That is why it is very important to cover your nose and mouth when you cough or sneeze.

There are more than a hundred different cold viruses known, and many more may exist. This is one of the reasons why scientists have not so far found a cure for the common cold.

Commonwealth

A commonwealth is a group of countries or people who are friendly and help each other. The Commonwealth of Nations is made up from most of the countries that were once ruled by Britain. Most of these countries now have their own governments and laws, but many of them still have the queen or king of Britain as their monarch.

The Commonwealth came into being at a meeting held in 1926. Commonwealth countries share some of the same beliefs and TRADE with each other. The heads of Commonwealth countries that have their own governments meet together often. They talk about their problems and try to help each other.

Communication

Communication is the exchange of ideas—through words, pictures, and numbers. We learn by communication with other people. And it is by means of communication that civilization has grown. Imagine a world without any way of storing and recording information (such as a printed book). Each new generation would have to rediscover things for itself, relying on word of mouth and memory alone to pass on wisdom and knowledge.

Communication began with the first human languages and with the cave paintings of Stone Age people. The first writing, using picture-signs, was invented more than 5,000 years ago. But it is in the last 500 years that the communications "explosion" has taken place. The invention of printing made books available to everyone who could read. Since the Industrial Revolution in the 1800s, communications science has changed our lives, bringing amazing new ways of sending and storing messages. Inventions such as photography, sound recording, radio, telephones, television, and computers have brought about the modern communications revolution.

▲ *Before the invention of printing, books were copied by hand. Printing began in Europe in the 1400s.*

▲ *Hammond's typewriter of 1880. A hammer hit the back of the paper, pressing it against a letter on a fixed cylinder.*

IMPORTANT INVENTIONS

► *The Polaroid camera takes "instant" photos that are exposed and developed in a single process.*

◄ *A telephone of 1905. It had no dial—all calls had to be connected by an operator.*

► *The gramophone, which played flat disks, was invented by a German, Emile Berliner, in 1887.*

◄ *Home video recorders allow us to watch recorded programs.*

▼ *An early Daguerreotype camera.*

·–	A	····	H
–···	B	··	I
–·–·	C	·–––	J
–··	D	–·–	K
·	E	·–··	L
··–·	F	––	M
––·	G	–·	N

▲ *The Morse code was once the main way of sending signals along wires or by radio.*

► *Small portable cassette players make it possible to listen to sound recordings almost anywhere.*

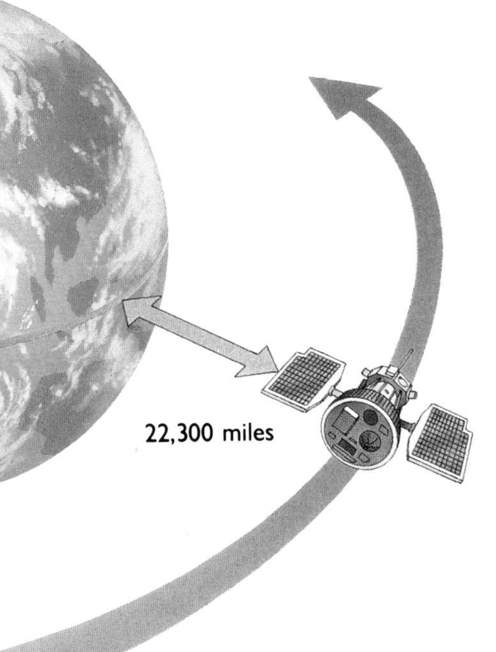

▲ *Geostationary satellites orbit the Earth once every 24 hours in the same time it takes the Earth to spin once on its axis, so that they remain in the same spot above the Earth's surface. They are used to receive telephone and television signals and retransmit them over long distances.*

COMOROS

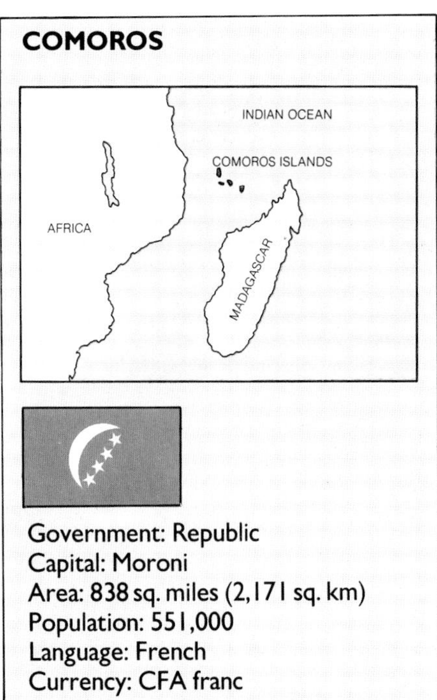

Government: Republic
Capital: Moroni
Area: 838 sq. miles (2,171 sq. km)
Population: 551,000
Language: French
Currency: CFA franc

Communications Satellite

Communications satellites are vital for mass communication around the world. They are spacecraft that are sent into orbit and then used to send many different types of message around the Earth. Television programs, radio messages, and telephone calls can all be sent through them. They work when messages are sent up to them from one part of the Earth and then sent back down to another part of the Earth from the satellite.

Communism

Communism is a set of ideas about the way a country should be run. The main idea of communism is that people should share wealth and property. This makes people more equal because nobody is very rich or very poor. In most communist countries the people own the factories and farms, but it is usually the government that runs them. The government controls almost everything, and personal freedoms are restricted. However, during the 1980s, the then U.S.S.R. under Mikhail Gorbachev adopted a freer form of communism, and by the end of 1991, Communism was dead. In 1989, the peoples of most eastern European communist countries also demanded and obtained more democratic government.

The countries who became communist in the 1900s included the Soviet Union, China, and Cuba, and some countries in Eastern Europe and the Far East. LENIN and MAO TSE-TUNG were among the great communist leaders of the twentieth century.

Comoros

The Comoro Islands are a cluster of volcanic islands in the Indian Ocean between Madagascar and Africa. Most of the people are poor and live on small farms. France took the islands from the Arabs in 1886, and in 1975, the islands declared their independence. However, one island, Mayotte, voted to remain French. Comoros is one of the poorest nations. It has no major industry and no minerals.

Compass

A compass is an instrument for finding the way. A magnetic compass always points to the Earth's magnetic poles, which are close to the North and South poles. The magnetic compass has been used for centuries by sailors and explorers to find the right direction.

A magnetic compass works by MAGNETISM. It has a magnetic needle fixed to a pivot so that it is free to swing around. The needle always points north and south when it is at rest. With a compass showing where north and south are, it is easy to travel in a straight line in any direction you wish to go.

The needle always points north and south because the Earth itself is a big magnet. The compass needle lines up parallel with the Earth's magnetic field.

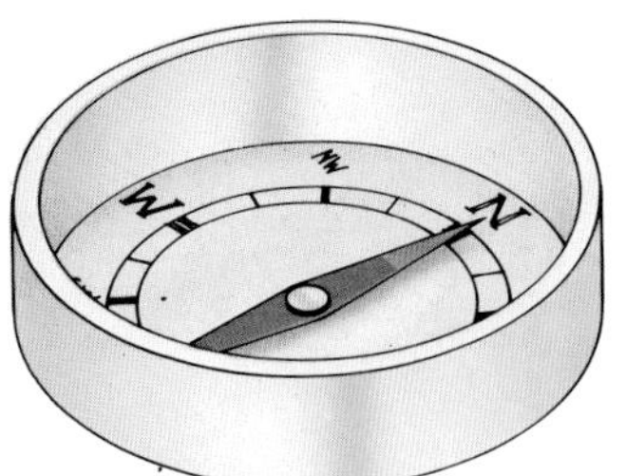

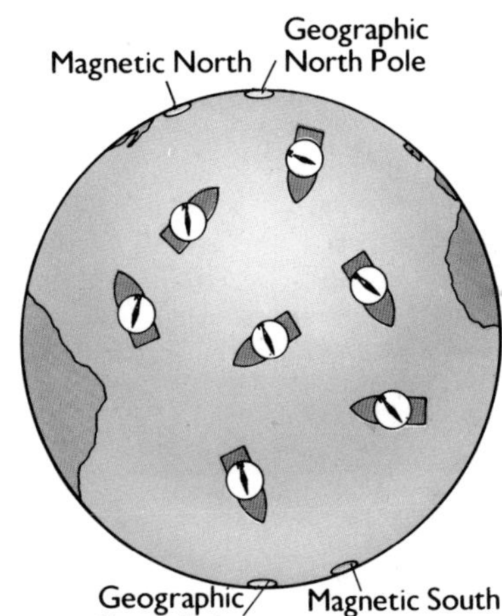

▲ *A compass does not point directly at the North Pole. This is because the Earth's magnetic field does not line up with the geographic poles. The difference between the geographic and magnetic poles is called the "magnetic variation."*

Compound

Compounds are chemicals that are made up of two or more ELEMENTS. For example, salt is a compound made up of the elements sodium and chlorine.

Compounds are formed when elements come together and make a new substance which is completely different from the elements. Water is a compound of the gas elements hydrogen and oxygen, and it is very different from either of them.

There are millons of compounds in the world. They can be very simple, like water (with three ATOMS in each molecule), or complex, like some plastics with hundreds of atoms in their molecules.

Computer

Computers are playing a bigger and bigger part in all our lives. They can play a game of chess with you, guide a spacecraft, check fingerprints, and draw a map of Australia. They can do all these things, and many more, merely because they can add, subtract, and compare one number with another. Computers are special because they can do millions of calculations in a second.

Although the computer works with numbers, the information it uses does not have to start off as

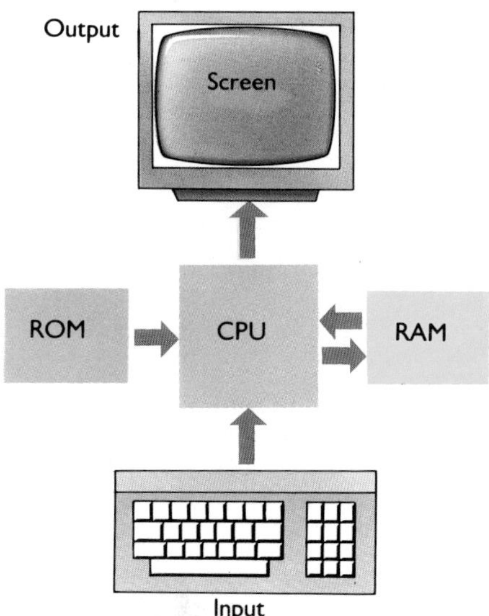

▲ *A computer has four basic parts, the "input" (keyboard), memory (RAM and ROM), central processing unit (CPU), and "output," a screen or printer.*

► *Computer programs and data can be stored on a cassette or on a floppy disk. Floppy disks are more efficient. They store information in concentric tracks, which make data easy to locate quickly.*

▲ *The American computer ENIAC was completed in 1946. Early computers such as this filled large rooms, but they were no more powerful than a small modern pocket computer.*

One disadvantage of concrete is that it can be very heavy. The ancient Romans knew this, so they mixed cement with lightweight substances to lighten their building materials. The great dome of the Pantheon in Rome, larger than that of St. Paul's in London, was made with concrete mixed from pumice stone—lightweight volcanic ash—from the slopes of Mount Vesuvius.

numbers. We can feed almost anything into it, but the first thing the computer does is to turn everything into numbers. But the numbers it uses are not quite the same as ours. We use the numbers 0 to 9. All the computer needs is 0 and 1. In fact, it can only count up to 1! This is called the BINARY SYSTEM. The computer uses the binary system because it has been designed to work with electrical currents. It can recognize the difference between a big current and a small current flow. If there is a big current, it registers 1; if there is a small current, it registers 0. When we type on the keys of a computer keyboard, we are making little electrical currents flow through tiny circuits in microchips. It is these tiny currents that give us the answers we need.

Concrete

Concrete is a mixture of cement, gravel, and sand, together with water. The paste-like concrete sets hard and is used to make buildings, roads, bridges, and dams. The cement that is the starting point for concrete is usually made from limestone and clay, but chalk and sand may also be included. These materials are crushed and mixed, then heated in a

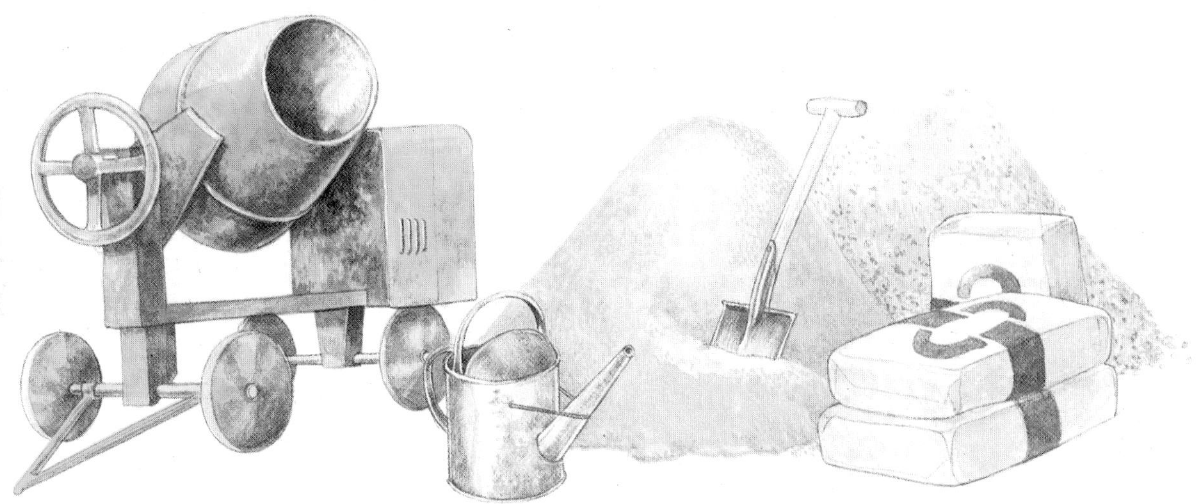

kiln. When cool, the mixture is ground into cement powder. Concrete is often strengthened by placing steel rods in it when it is soft. This *reinforced* concrete is very, very strong.

▲ *To make concrete, cement is mixed with sand, gravel, and water. Too much water will weaken the concrete, and mixing concrete of good quality is a highly skilled job.*

Confucius

Confucius (551–479 B.C.) lived nearly 2,500 years ago in China. He was a famous thinker. He taught people how to live and behave in a good way. The Chinese people followed his teaching for centuries.

The most important rule made by Confucius was that people should think of others, and not do anything to others that they would not like done to themselves.

Congo

The Congo is a country in the west of central AFRICA. It was formerly part of a huge French colony and became independent in 1960. It is nearly as big as Montana.

The Congo is a hot, wet country. It has huge forests and swamps, and a low grassy plain on the coast. The Congo produces timber, diamonds, oil, cocoa, and coffee.

Along the Congo's border with its larger neighbor, Zaire, runs a great river. This river used to be called the Congo, but is now called the Zaire River. It is 2,900 miles (4,667 km) long, one of the longest in the world.

CONGO

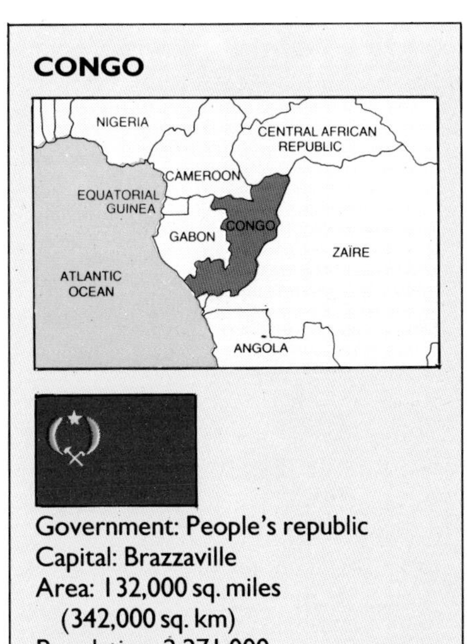

Government: People's republic
Capital: Brazzaville
Area: 132,000 sq. miles (342,000 sq. km)
Population: 2,271,000
Language: French
Currency: CFA Franc

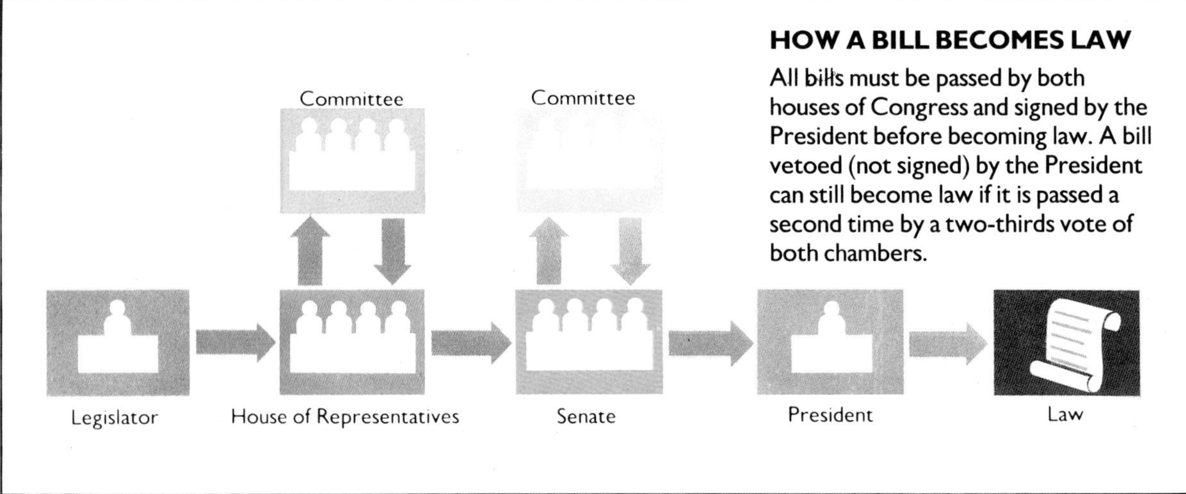

HOW A BILL BECOMES LAW

All bills must be passed by both houses of Congress and signed by the President before becoming law. A bill vetoed (not signed) by the President can still become law if it is passed a second time by a two-thirds vote of both chambers.

Congress

Congress is the legislature of the United States of America. It is the part of the government which makes laws.

Congress is made up of two chambers: the House of Representatives and the Senate.

To make a new law, a "bill" is introduced by a member into one of the chambers. It is discussed by groups, or *committees*, and then voted on by the members of the chamber. The bill then goes to the other chamber. When it has been passed by both chambers, the president signs it and it becomes law.

Conifer

Conifers are TREES and shrubs that have cones instead of flowers for making pollen and seeds. Many of them are found in the cool parts of the world. Some even grow north of the Arctic Circle.

Scotch pine

▲ *Conifers include pines, spruces, larches, and cedars. Most have needle-like leaves which they do not lose in winter.*

Connecticut

Connecticut is one of the most historic and one of the smallest states. But despite its size, Connecticut is also one of the most important industrial regions of the United States. Many of the inventions and industries that made America rich came from here. Tourism is important to Connecticut, too.

The first Europeans to travel to Connecticut were Dutch. But in 1674 the British defeated them and settled here. In the REVOLUTIONARY WAR, Connecticut played an important part in defeating Britain. After the war, it also played a very important role in writing the U.S. CONSTITUTION. That is why Connecticut is called the Constitution State.

CONNECTICUT

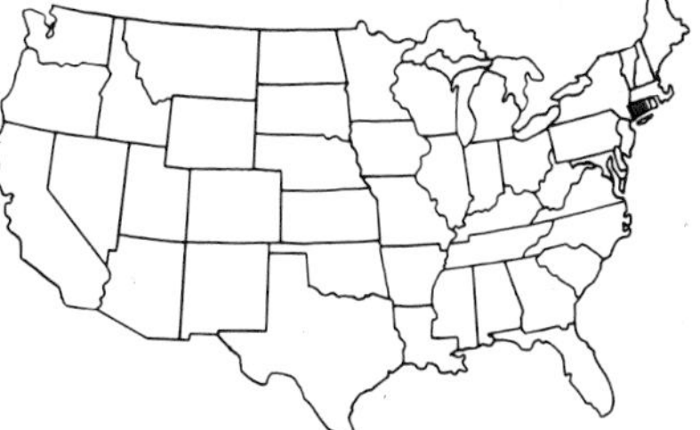

Capital: Hartford
Population: 3,287,116
Area: 5,018 sq. mi. (12,977 sq. km)
State flower: Mountain Laurel
State bird: American Robin
State tree: White Oak
Statehood: January 9, 1788
5th state

Conservation

Human beings use plants, animals, soil, water, and minerals for nearly everything they make. Often they waste and destroy those natural resources. Conservation means using these resources wisely and protecting them. It also means preserving areas of natural beauty.

▼ *Felling trees to meet the world demand for paper and wood has destroyed thousands of acres of forest land. Conservation means careful use of such resources.*

▲ *When the Turks captured Constantinople in 1453, mosques such as this one replaced the Christian churches.*

► *Some constellations of the Northern Hemisphere (opposite, top)*

1 *Equuleus, Colt*
2 *Delphinus, Dolphin*
3 *Pegasus, Flying Horse*
4 *Pisces, Fishes*
5 *Cetus, Sea Monster*
6 *Aries, Ram*
7 *Triangulum, Triangle*
8 *Andromeda, Chained Maiden*
9 *Lacerta, Lizard*
10 *Cygnus, Swan*
11 *Sagitta, Arrow*
12 *Aquila, Eagle*
13 *Lyra, Lyre*
14 *Cepheus, King*
15 *Cassiopeia, Lady in Chair*
16 *Perseus, Champion*
17 *Camelopardus, Giraffe*
18 *Auriga, Charioteer*
19 *Taurus, Bull*
20 *Orion, Hunter*
21 *Lynx, Lynx*
22 *Polaris, (North Star)*
23 *Ursa Minor, Little Dipper (Little Bear)*
24 *Draco, Dragon*
25 *Hercules, Kneeling Giant*
26 *Ophiuchus, Serpent-Bearer*
27 *Serpens, Serpent*
28 *Corona Borealis, Northern Crown*
29 *Boötes, Herdsman*
30 *Ursa Major, Big Dipper (Great Bear)*

Today the need to conserve wildlife and natural resources is a world problem. It involves the study of ECOLOGY, the branch of BIOLOGY that deals with the relationship between all living things and their surroundings. People must avoid upsetting Nature's balance.

Constantinople

Constantinople is the old name for the city of Istanbul in TURKEY. It lies between Asia and Europe.

Constantinople was the most important city in the western world for more than a thousand years. It was named after the Roman emperor Constantine. In A.D. 330, Constantine founded the city on the site of the ancient Greek town of Byzantium. He divided the Roman Empire into two to make it easier to manage. Constantinople was the capital of the eastern half, which became known as the Byzantine Empire.

After the last Roman emperor was overthrown in A.D. 476, Constantinople and the Byzantine Empire continued to be powerful. The city was a great center of Christianity, trade, and western learning until it was invaded by the Ottoman Turks in 1453.

The Byzantines built many beautiful buildings. One of these is the famous Cathedral of Saint Sophia, which was begun in the reign of Constantine. It was first a Christian church and then a Muslim place of worship, or *mosque*. Today it is a museum containing fine pieces of Byzantine art.

Constellation

Constellations in early times were simply patterns of stars in the sky. They were named after ancient gods, heroes, animals, and everyday objects whose shapes people saw in the patterns—Orion the Hunter, Leo the Lion, Lyra the Lyre. There are now 88 constellations over the whole sky. Twelve of them form a wide track where the Sun appears to travel in the course of the year, and where the planets are usually found. These are the constellations of the Zodiac.

31 Gemini, Twins
32 Cancer, Crab
33 Canis Minor, Little Dog
34 Hydra, Sea Serpent
35 Leo, Lion
36 Leo Minor, Little Lion
37 Canes Venatici, Hunting Dogs
38 Coma Berenices, Berenice's Hair
39 Virgo, Virgin

About 45 constellations were first named thousands of years ago. But there is a large group of "modern" constellations, particularly in the southern sky, which were not charted until the great sea voyages of the 17th and 18th centuries.

◄ Some constellations of the Southern Hemisphere (below)

1 Cetus, Sea Monster
2 Sculptor, Sculptor
3 Aquarius, Water Bearer
4 Picis Austrinus, Southern Fish
5 Capricornus, Sea Goat
6 Grus, Crane
7 Phoenix, Phoenix
8 Fornax, Furnace
9 Eridanus, River Eridanus
10 Hydrus, Little Snake
11 Tucana, Toucan
12 Indus, Indian
13 Sagittarius, Archer
14 Aquila, Eagle
15 Corona Australis, Southern Crown
16 Pavo, Peacock
17 Octans, Octant
18 Dorado, Swordfish
19 Pictor, Painter's Easel
20 Columba, Dove
21 Lepus, Hare
22 Orion, Hunter
23 Monoceros, Unicorn
24 Canis Major, Great Dog
25 Puppis, Stern
26 Carina, Keel
27 Volans, Flying Fish
28 Chamaeleon, Chameleon
29 Apus, Bird of Paradise
30 Triangulum Australe, Southern Triangle
31 Ara, Altar
32 Scorpio, Scorpion
33 Serpens, Serpent
34 Ophiuchus, Serpent-Bearer
35 Lupus, Wolf
36 Centaurus, Centaur
37 Crux, Southern Cross
38 Musca, Fly
39 Vela, Sails
40 Pyxis, Compass
41 Hydra, Sea Serpent
42 Sextans, Sextant
43 Crater, Cup
44 Corvus, Crow
45 Libra, Scales
46 Virgo, Virgin

The opening words of the United States Constitution are: "We, the people of the United States, in order to form a more perfect Union, establish justice, insure domestic tranquility, provide for the common defense, promote the general welfare, and secure the blessings of liberty to ourselves and our posterity do ordain and establish this Constitution for the United States of America."

▲ *The Constitution was signed at the Pennsylvania State House, now called Independence Hall, in Philadelphia.*

There are several points around the world where the continents nearly touch. Asia is 56 miles (90 km) away from North America at the Bering Strait, which separates the Pacific and Arctic oceans. Europe and Africa are only 8 miles (13 km) apart at the Strait of Gibraltar.

Constitution, United States

The Constitution of the United States is the document that sets out all the basic laws under which the country is governed. It defines the relationship between the federal, or national, government and the state governments; it sets out the exact form of the federal government; and it explains the rights, the freedoms, and the duties of individual people. Most important, it also establishes the goals and purposes of government. It is a guarantee of democracy and liberty.

The Constitution was written after the REVOLUTIONARY WAR ended in 1783. Though Britain had been defeated, the new states had no common form of government. They argued among themselves, and some refused to accept that there should be a new central government. In 1787, ALEXANDER HAMILTON and GEORGE WASHINGTON managed to persuade the 13 states to send representatives to meet in PHILADELPHIA to discuss a new form of government. They talked and argued all summer. Only in September was the Constitution agreed. Even then many held out against it. Only when a series of amendments to it had been agreed did all the states accept the Constitution. These amendments are known as the Bill of Rights.

Continental Shelf

Continents do not end where their coasts meet the sea. Their true edge lies far out under the sea. Each continent is ringed by a gently sloping shelf of land under the sea called the continental shelf. This shelf sometimes stretches hundreds of miles from the shore. Beyond the continental shelf is the deep ocean floor.

In the past, the sea level was lower, and much of the continental shelf was dry land. Rivers flowed through it to the sea and made valleys or canyons. These canyons are still there, but today they are under the sea.

Most sea life is found on the continental shelf. Sunlight shines through the water, helping plants, fish, and other animals to grow.

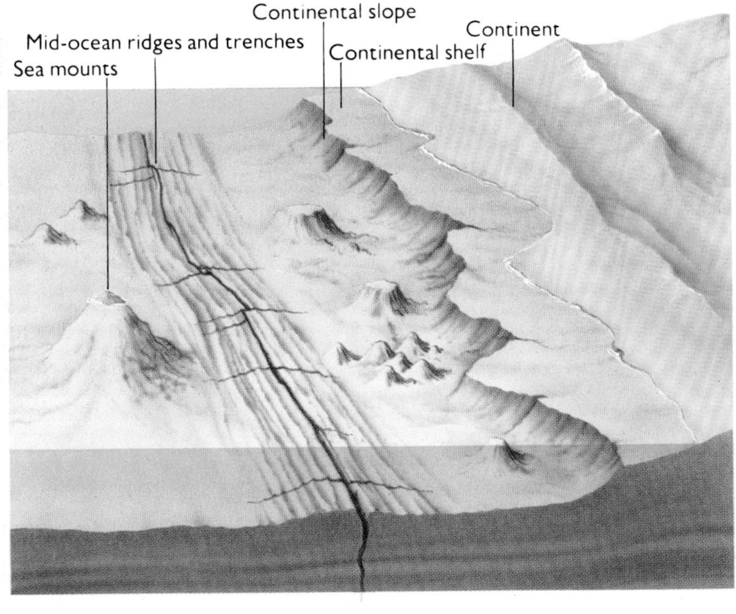

◀ *Most of the continental shelf lies under about 460 ft. (140 m) of water. At its edge, the seabed falls steeply to the deep ocean floor.*

Continents

Continents are large areas of land. The Earth has seven continents: Africa, Antarctica, Asia, Australia, Europe, North America, and South America. Some people say that because Europe and Asia are joined, they are one big continent called Eurasia.

The continents are not fixed. They are made of lighter rock than the rock on the ocean floor. The great heat in the center of the Earth has made the surface rocks break into huge pieces called *plates*.

▼ *Continental drift at various stages in the Earth's history. Over millions of years, the single continent we call Pangaea broke up to produce the pattern of continents we know today.*

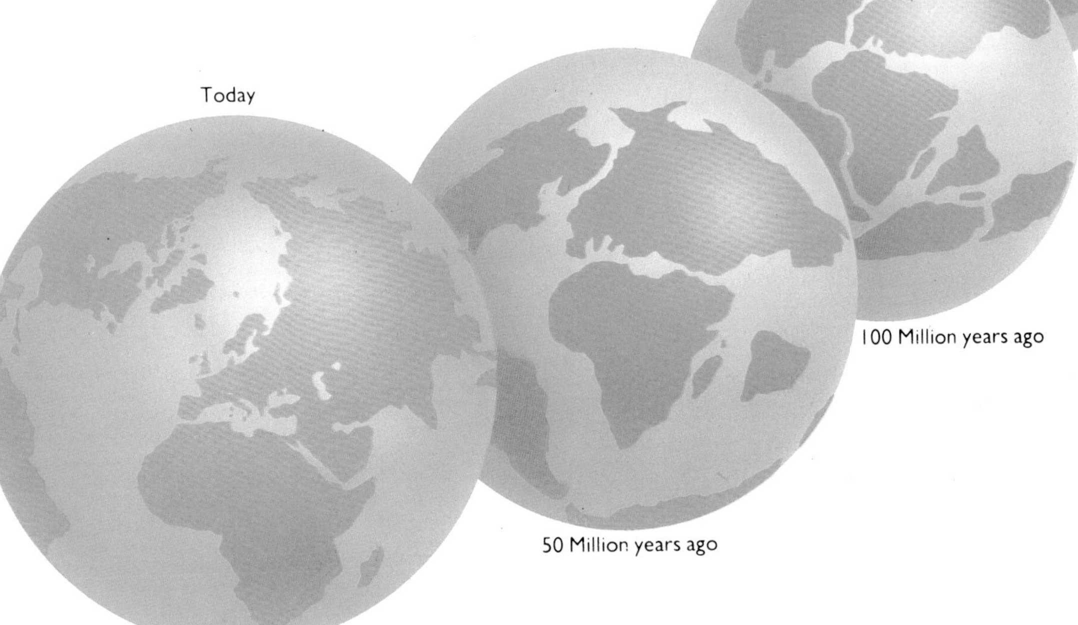

During the Ice Age, the northern and southern parts of the world were covered by great ice caps. So much water became ice that the sea level dropped by as much as 500 ft. (150 m). This meant that vast areas of the shallow continental shelf became dry land. It has been estimated that a total area of about 11,000,000 sq. miles (30,000,000 sq. km) of sea became dry land—an area bigger than Russia, the biggest country in the world.

When the plates move, they move the continents with them. This movement is very slow. A continent moves only a few inches in one century.

A hundred years ago, some people saw that the shapes of America, Europe, and Africa looked like jigsaw pieces that would fit closely if they were pushed together. This gave them the idea that the continents used to be one big piece of land which broke up. This idea is called continental drift. Continental drift was first suggested in 1912 by Alfred Wegener. He found evidence to show that America was once in contact with Africa. Today, people who study GEOLOGY believe this idea is true.

Geologists think that the movements of the continents pushed up some pieces of land to make mountains such as the Alps and the Himalayas.

Cook, James

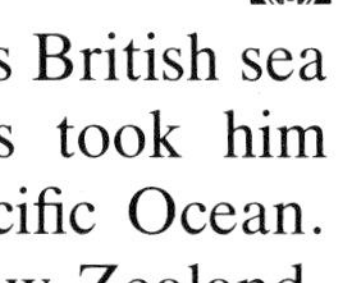

James Cook (1728—1779) was a famous British sea captain and explorer. His expeditions took him around the world and all over the Pacific Ocean. Cook's discoveries led to Australia, New Zealand, and many South Pacific islands becoming British colonies.

After serving in the Royal Navy for 13 years, Cook was put in command of an expedition to Tahiti in 1768. After Tahiti, Cook went on to New Zealand. He sailed around both North and South Islands, and then went to Australia.

In 1934, the cottage in which James Cook lived as a boy, in England, was presented to the government of Victoria in Australia. It was carefully taken apart and re-erected in Fitzroy Gardens, Melbourne.

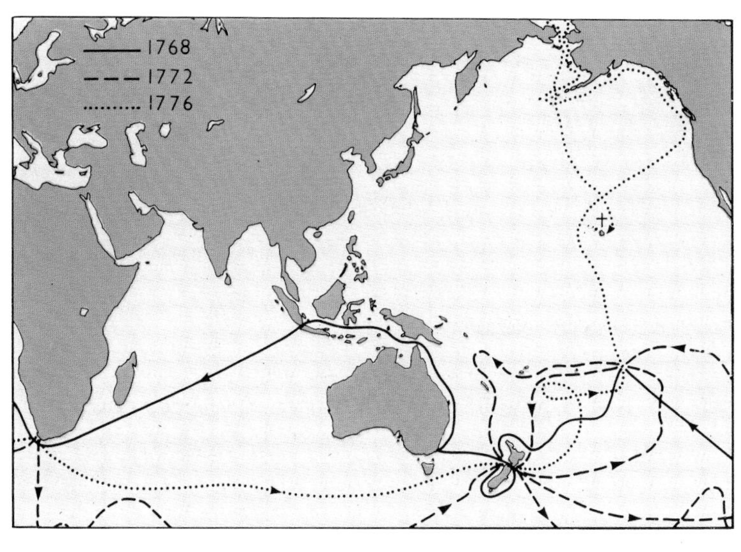

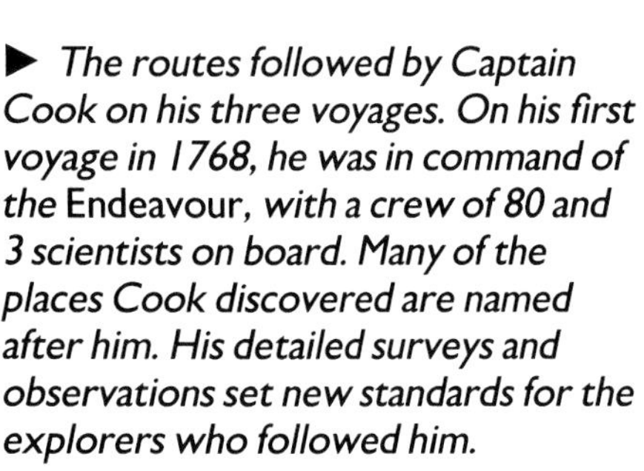

▶ *The routes followed by Captain Cook on his three voyages. On his first voyage in 1768, he was in command of the* Endeavour, *with a crew of 80 and 3 scientists on board. Many of the places Cook discovered are named after him. His detailed surveys and observations set new standards for the explorers who followed him.*

Coolidge, Calvin

Calvin Coolidge (1872–1933) was the 30th president of the United States. He held office from 1923 to 1929. He first became president when serving as vice-president, on the death of the then president, Warren HARDING. In 1924, Calvin Coolidge was elected president himself.

Though he was president during a time of great prosperity, when many Americans thought they were going to get richer and richer, Coolidge himself was a shy and modest man. He advocated personal as well as national economy. He also did much to help industry and business. His most famous saying was, "The chief business of the American people is business." His quiet manner and dignity made him popular across the country. After he retired, his last years were made unhappy by the Great Depression of the '30s.

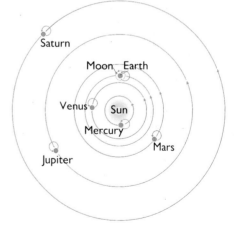

CALVIN COOLIDGE

Thirtieth President 1923–1929
Born: Plymouth, Vermont
Education: Amherst College
Occupation: Lawyer
Political Party: Republican
Buried: Plymouth, Vermont

Cooper, James Fenimore

James Fenimore Cooper (1789–1851) was one of the earliest strictly American writers. He wrote a number of novels describing life on the American frontier in the 1700s. His most famous books describe a frontiersman named Natty Bumppo, or Leatherstocking, who, though a simple man, understood the wilderness in which he lived and the Indians who lived there, too. Cooper contrasted Bumppo with other white settlers. He showed that though they brought order to the frontier, they also helped to corrupt it and mistreated the Indians. His most famous book was *The Last of the Mohicans*.

Copernicus, Nicolaus

Nicolaus Copernicus (1473–1543) was a Polish scientist. He is sometimes called the father of modern ASTRONOMY.

Copernicus showed that the Earth is not the center of the UNIVERSE, as people used to believe. Instead, the Earth and PLANETS revolve around the Sun. Copernicus also showed that the Earth itself moves around, or *rotates*, each day.

▲ *Copernicus realized that the Earth-centered universe theory was not supported by the actual movements of the planets. He correctly showed that all the planets revolved around the Sun. But, he wrongly thought that all the planets also move in small circles.*

▲ *Aaron Copland helped develop a music that is clearly American.*

Copland, Aaron

Aaron Copland (1904–1990) was born in New York. He was a composer who wrote many different types of music, including music for movies. He is most famous for having blended folk music from many parts of the United States and from Mexico with traditional forms of classical music. He also incorporated jazz into his work at a time when many thought it unsuitable for serious composers.

Copper

Copper is a reddish-brown METAL. It was probably one of the first metals that people used. About 7,000 years ago, the ancient Egyptians and people in Iraq began to use copper for their tools and weapons. They also made copper ornaments. At first, they used pure copper which they found in the ground. But most copper is found with other metals and minerals in a mixture called ore. Most U.S. copper is mined in Arizona.

Copper is very soft when it is pure. But if it is mixed with other metals, it makes ALLOYS such as brass and BRONZE, which are harder and better for making tools. If copper is exposed to the air for a long time, it becomes coated with a green film called *patina*, which protects it against corrosion.

Copper is the second most widely used metal. More than half the world output is used to make copper wires. Copper is very pliable (ductile) and is easily drawn into wires of any thickness. It can also be rolled into sheets so thin that light can shine through it.

► *Nearly three-fourths of the world's copper is mined in only six countries: the U.S.A., Russia, Zambia, Chile, Canada, and Zaire. Copper is the world's second most widely used metal after iron.*

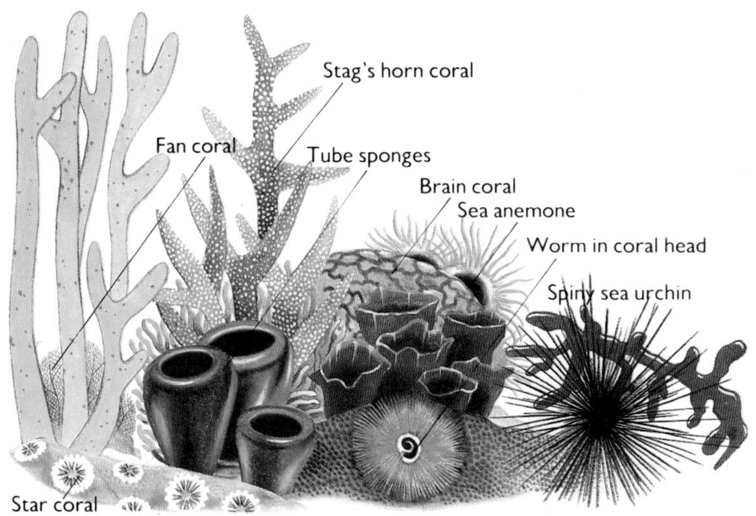

◀ *Coral reefs provide homes for many sea animals that find shelter in crevices or burrow into the soft coral rock.*

Copper can be beaten into sheets or pulled out into wire. It lets heat and electricity pass through it very easily, so it is often used for making pots and pans and electric wires.

Coral

Coral is a kind of limestone found mainly in warm, shallow seas. It is made by tiny animals, called coral polyps, that build limestone "shells" around themselves for protection. Most coral polyps live in groups, or colonies. These may take many shapes, from lacy fans to stubby branches, all in beautiful colors. Other colonies form thick underwater walls known as reefs.

Along some reefs, waves may throw up bits of sand and coral which gradually build up on top of the reef until it is above water. The reef then becomes an island. One kind of coral island is the atoll, a ringed reef that encloses a central lagoon.

Cork

The cork that is used to make bottle stoppers comes from the smooth bark of the cork oak tree of the Mediterranean. It is a light, spongy material that forms a thick layer about 1 in. (3 cm) deep around the trunk of the tree.

Cork is stripped from cork oaks once every nine or ten years until the trees are about 150 years old.

HOW AN ATOLL IS FORMED

Coral grows in the warm waters surrounding an island; in this illustration an island that has been formed by volcanic action.

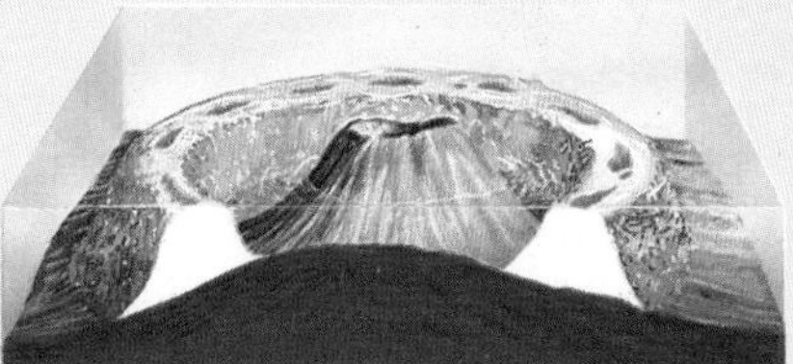

Coral continues to grow on the reefs as the island sinks or the sea rises.

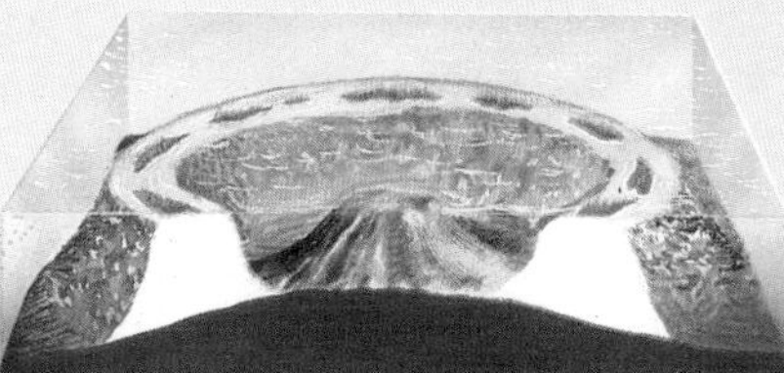

Once the island has completely disappeared, the coral reefs remain, forming a typical atoll.

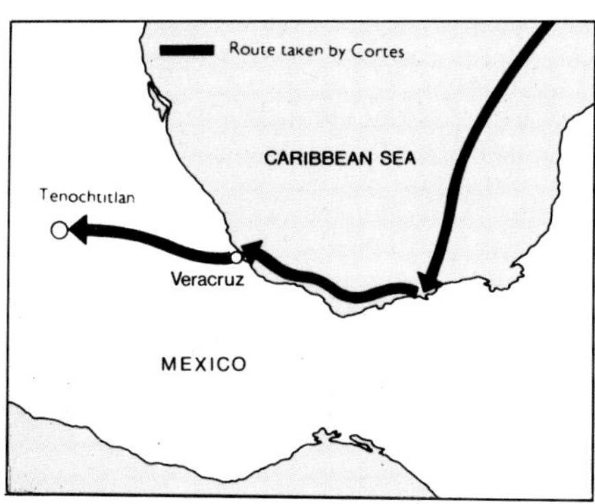

▲ *Cortés founded the town of Veracruz on the coast of Mexico. There he dismantled his ships and set out to explore the country, arriving in the Aztec capital, Tenochtitlán, in November, 1519.*

Cortés, Hernando

Hernando Cortés (1485–1547) was a Spanish soldier and explorer who in 1519 landed on the coast of Mexico. With a force of only 600 men and a few horses, he conquered the great AZTEC empire. His horses and guns helped convince the Aztecs he was a god. Cortés marched on their capital, captured the Aztec emperor Montezuma and, by 1521, had taken control of Mexico.

Cosmetics

Cosmetics have been used since prehistoric times, when cave people decorated their dead with dyes and paints. Lipstick, eyeshadow, nail polish, rouge, and hair dyes were used widely by the ancient Egyptians. The Greeks and Romans bathed with many kinds of scented oil and wore perfumes to make their bodies and clothing smell sweet.

Today, cosmetics are big business. Modern cosmetics are used for cleaning the skin and for coloring and decorating the face and body in countless ways.

The ancient Egyptians used many different kinds of cosmetics. They edged the underside of their eyes with a green paste made from ground malachite rock and outlined their eyes with a mixture of ground ants' eggs. Rouge, whitening powder, and lipstick were used daily by both men and women.

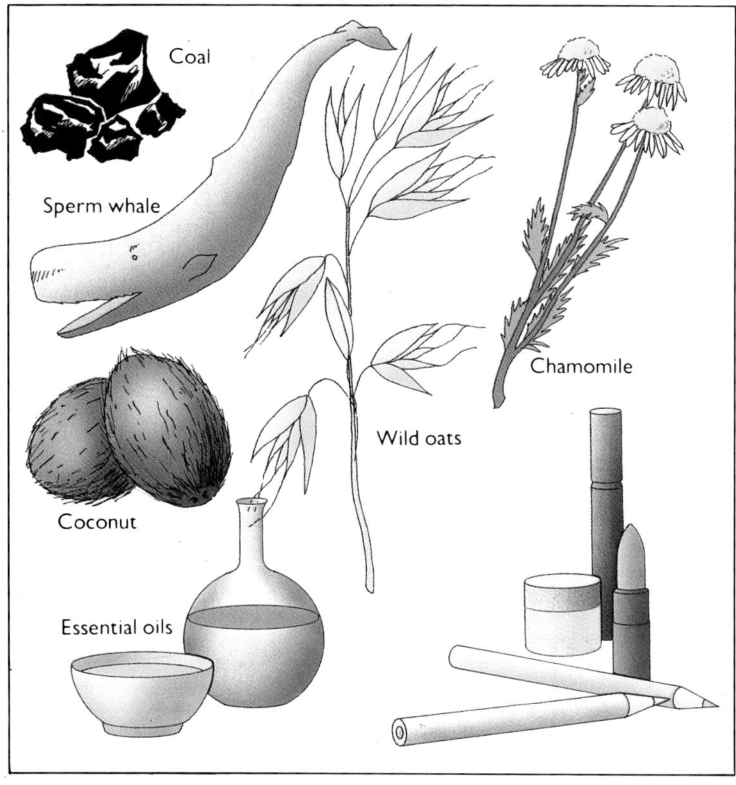

► *Most modern cosmetics are made from a base of fats and oils, to which a variety of substances, natural and man-made, are added.*

◀ *Grass-roofed huts in a Costa Rican village. In country areas, the highlight of the year is the coffee harvest.*

Costa Rica

Costa Rica is a Spanish-speaking country lying between Nicaragua and Panama in Central America. It is largely an agricultural country; the chief crops are coffee, bananas, sugar, and cocoa. More than 90 percent of Costa Ricans can read and write, a higher percentage than in any other Central American country.

Costa Rica was a Spanish colony from 1530 to 1821 and became an independent republic in 1848.

COSTA RICA

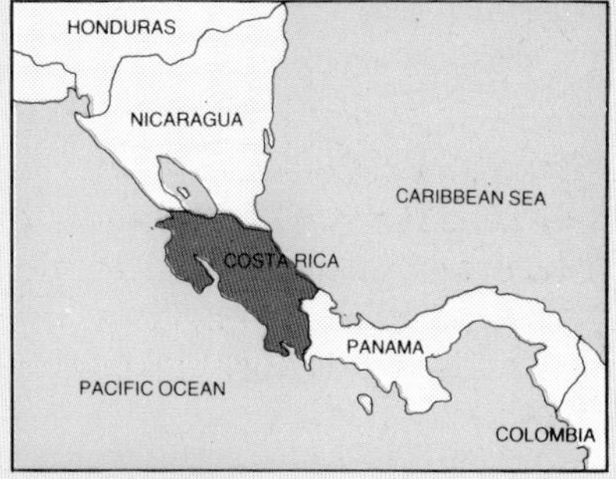

Government: Democratic republic
Capital: San José
Area: 19,575 sq. miles (50,700 sq. km)
Population: 2,994,000
Language: Spanish
Currency: Colón

Côte d'Ivoire (Ivory Coast)

Côte d'Ivoire is a republic in West Africa. It is slightly larger than New Mexico. The country's major products are cocoa, coffee, and timber. Formerly a French territory, Côte d'Ivoire became independent in 1960. It is the most prosperous of tropical African nations.

CÔTE D'IVOIRE

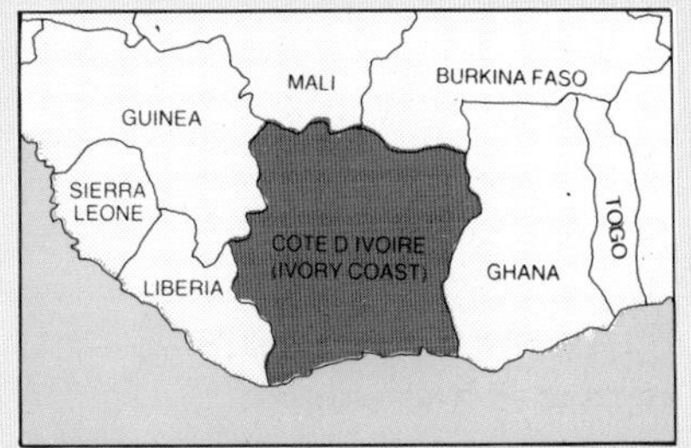

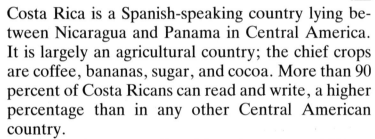

Government: Republic
Capital: Abidjan
Area: 124,500 sq. miles (322,463 sq. km)
Population: 11,998,000
Language: French
Currency: CFA Franc

Cotton

Cotton grows in warm and tropical places all over the world. It is one of the most important plants grown by people; its fibers and seeds are both used. The fibers are made into cloth, and the seeds are used for oil and cattle feed. The oil is used in soaps, paints, and cosmetics.

Cotton has green fruits called bolls. When they

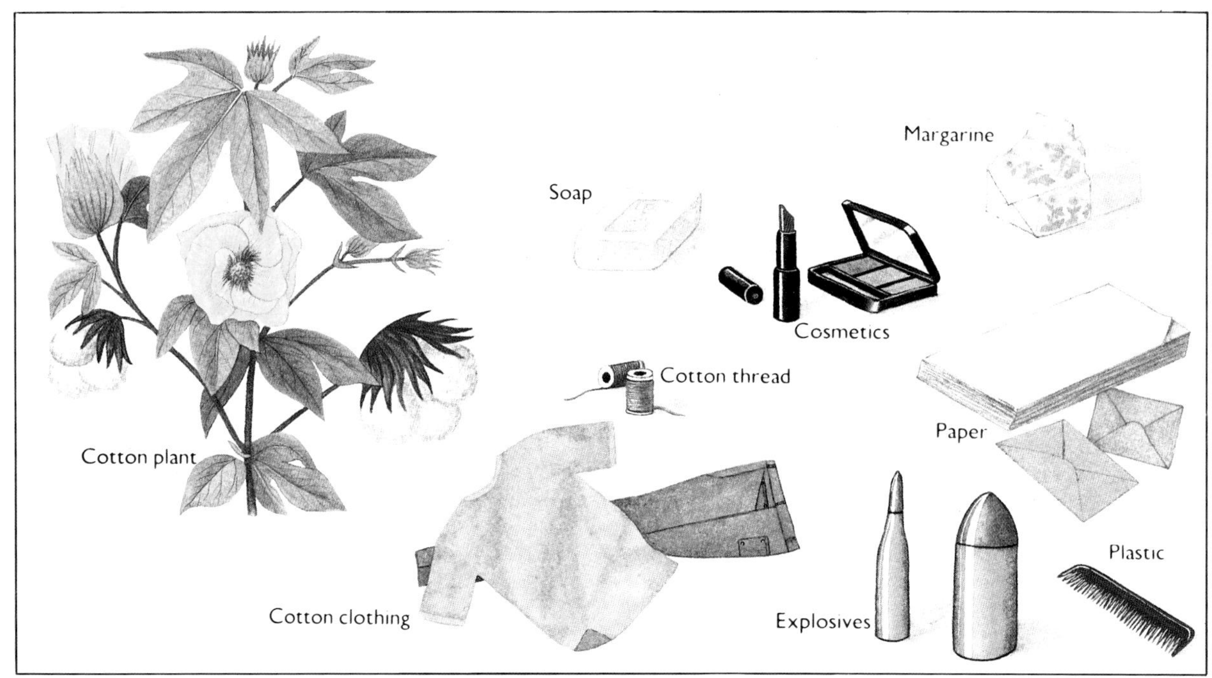

▲ *Cottonseed oil goes into cooking oil, margarine, soap, and cosmetics. The seed itself is a source of cellulose for making explosives, paper, and plastics.*

are ripe, the bolls split open. Inside them is a mass of white fibers and seeds. The bolls are harvested, and the fibers are separated from the seeds. The fibers are spun into yarn and then woven into cloth.

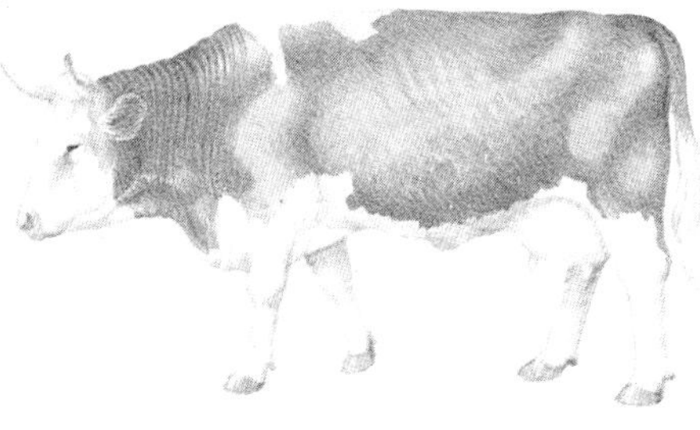

▲ *The Swiss Simmental is bred for both milk and meat.*

Cow

The cow, which gives us milk, is a member of the cattle family. Cattle are large, grass-eating animals. Grass is difficult to digest, and all cattle have four stomachs to make it easier. During digestion, the food is returned to the mouth to be chewed and

▲ *The Jersey is a small cow that produces very rich milk and cream.*

► *The Hereford is a popular beef breed throughout North America.*

swallowed again. When a cow does this, we say it is "chewing the cud." The farm cow is descended from an extinct wild cow called an *aurochs* and has been tamed by people for about 6,000 years.

▲ *There are more Holstein-Friesian cattle in the United States than any other breed.*

▲ *The dairy shorthorn, bred for meat, is red, white, or roan.*

Cowboy

There are still many people in the American West who ride horses and herd cows, but the great days of the cowboys lasted only 40 years, from the 1860s to 1900.

At that time, there were open grasslands stretching from Texas to Canada. Cattle grazed there and were then driven in great herds by cowboys to the railroad stations.

A cowboy's life was simple and hard. Out on the grassland, or *range*, he was his own boss. He often stayed in the wild for many months. There was usually no one to help him except other cowboys, so each cowboy had to know how to do many things.

Because of the roaming life they led, cowboys traveled light. Usually they owned nothing more than

▼ Cowboys Roping a Steer, *an oil painting by Charles M. Russell.*

their horse, saddle, bedroll, and the clothes they wore. Although many cowboys had guns, they never carried pistols when they worked. The pistols were too heavy and got in the way.

Crab

Most people think that crabs live only in the sea, but there are some kinds that live in fresh water (rivers or lakes) and some tropical kinds that make their home on land.

Crabs belong to a group of animals called CRUSTACEANS. They have hard, thick shells that cover their flat bodies.They also have long, spidery legs for walking underwater, swimming, and burrowing. The first pair of legs have pincers, which are used for attacking and holding prey. Crabs' eyes stick out on the end of short stalks. They can be pulled into the shell for safety.

▼ The cantilever crane is most often used in shipyards and on construction sites. It is used for heavy loads and usually works by electricity. The shorter side of the cross frame jib always carries the balancing weight.

Crane

Cranes are long-necked, long-legged birds. They live in marshes or rivers and eat mainly berries, fruits, and fish. Cranes have a loud cry that can be heard from a long distance away, and the big birds fly in large flocks. The whooping crane of North America is in danger of dying out.

Crane

A crane is a piece of machinery that is used for lifting heavy objects. It usually has a long arm, or *jib*. Cranes may be fixed in one place, like the giant cranes erected on construction sites. Sometimes they are mounted on special wheels, railroad flatcars, or on the backs of trucks so they can be moved around.

Modern jib-cranes have a powerful motor that winches the hook, raises and lowers the crane's arms, and moves the driver's cab around.

Some of the biggest cranes are traveling ones. The hook hangs from an overhead arm that can move back and forth along a set of rails. These cranes can lift hundreds of tons at a time.

Crimean War

The Crimean War (1854–56) was a struggle between Russia on one side and Turkey, France, and Britain on the other. At that time, the Turkish Empire was very weak. Russia hoped to make its own power greater in the eastern Mediterranean by taking CONSTANTINOPLE. The British, French, and Turks pushed the Russian army back into the Crimean peninsula, where the war was fought. There was much suffering.

▼ The British light cavalry rode to their deaths at the battle of Balaclava in the Crimea. The poet Tennyson commemorated the battle in his poem "The Charge of the Light Brigade."

For the first time, newspaper reporters and photographers went to the battlegrounds. They reported the terrible conditions of the soldiers to the newspapers.

Crockett, Davy

Davy Crockett (1786–1836) was the most famous frontiersman of the 1800s. He was also a clever and successful politican who served three terms as a congressman for Tennessee. Like JAMES BOWIE,

▲ *Oliver Cromwell held strict views on religion. He was a Puritan and believed that people should be forced to be good.*

Davy Crockett was killed at the Alamo, fighting for Texan independence from Mexico. There have been many stories, songs, TV programs, and movies about his skills as a hunter and tracker. He once claimed to have killed 105 bears in less than a year.

Crocodile *See* Alligator and Crocodile

Cromwell, Oliver

Oliver Cromwell (1599–1658) was the only ruler of Britain never to have been a king or queen. He came to power after the civil war of the 1640s. Cromwell was a member of PARLIAMENT. He fought against CHARLES I with the army of Parliament and became its leader.

After Charles I was executed, Cromwell became the head of the country, but he never made himself king. From 1653, he was called the "Lord Protector." Two years after Cromwell died, Britain became a monarchy again.

Only once has anyone tried to steal the British crown jewels. In 1671, Colonel Thomas Blood, disguised as a parson, gained the confidence of the keeper of the jewels. When the keeper showed Blood the jewels, he was seized by Blood and his friends and stabbed. They escaped with the crown, scepter, and orb, but were captured on the banks of the Thames. Blood was pardoned by Charles II, who admired his audacity.

Crown Jewels

Crown jewels belong to the kings and queens of some nations. They show that the queen or king is head of the country. Some of them are worn by the monarch when he or she is being crowned.

The crown jewels of Britain include crowns, scepters, staffs, spurs, swords, and bracelets. They are

▶ *The British crown jewels contain some of the most famous gems in the world. Shown here are the St. Edward's crown, used to crown the monarch in the coronation service, two scepters, the coronation ring and the Sovereign's orb.*

made of gold, and precious stones such as diamonds, rubies, emeralds, and sapphires. The Imperial State Crown, made for Queen VICTORIA, has in it a huge ruby, called the Black Prince's Ruby. The jewels are all kept in the Tower of London. Other countries also have crown jewels on display. The crown jewels of France can be seen in the Louvre in Paris. The Secular Treasury in Vienna houses the crown jewels of the Holy Roman emperors. The crown jewels worn by Danish monarchs are in Rosenborg Castle, Copenhagen.

Crusades

The Crusades were wars between Christians and Muslims in the MIDDLE AGES. They took place in Palestine, the Holy Land. In 1071, Turkish Muslims captured the city of Jerusalem in Palestine. The Muslims stopped Christians from visiting the holy places in Palestine.

The Christian rulers in Europe were very angry about this. A few years later, the Byzantine emperor in CONSTANTINOPLE asked the Pope to help him drive the Turks from the Holy Land. The Pope started the first Crusade. He said he would forgive the sins of all the people who went and fought in the Holy Land.

▼ *To attack the strong walls of cities and castles, the Crusaders used catapults and battering rams. They built tall towers from which they could fire arrows and climb over the walls.*

CRUSADES
First Crusade (1095–99) resulted in the capture of Jerusalem.
Second Crusade (1147–49), led by Louis VII of France and Conrad III of Germany, failed to take Damascus.
Third Crusade (1189–92), led by Philip Augustus of France and Richard I of England, failed to recapture Jerusalem from Saladin.
Fourth Crusade (1202–04) ended in the brutal sack of Christian Constantinople.
The Children's Crusade (1212), a tragic crusade in which thousands of children died or were made slaves.
Sixth Crusade (1228–29), led by Emperor Frederick II, recovered Jerusalem by negotiation, but it was finally lost in 1244.
Seventh and **Eighth Crusades** (1248–70), led by Louis IX of France, gained nothing.

The armies of the first Crusade were successful. They took Jerusalem from the Muslims in 1099. The Crusaders set up Christian kingdoms along the coast of Palestine and Syria and built strong fortresses to defend their new lands.

There were seven more Crusades after the first one. Many of them failed because the Crusaders quarreled with each other. The Muslims took back much of the Holy Land from the Christians. When the Muslims took Jerusalem in 1187, the third Crusade set off from Europe. When they got to the Holy Land, the Crusaders were defeated by the Muslims who had a new general, named Saladin.

Later, the Crusaders forgot that they were fighting for their religion. Many of them went to Palestine hoping to take the land and become rich. By 1291, the Muslims had taken the last remaining Christian city at Acre.

During the Crusades, European people learned more about the eastern parts of the world. When they returned to Europe, they took back with them many new things including foods, spices, silk clothes, and paper. They learned about medicine, mathematics, and astronomy from the Arabs, and trade between east and west began to grow.

Crustacean

Crustaceans are a large group of about 10,000 animals. They include sandhoppers, wood-lice, waterfleas, barnacles, crayfish, shrimp, prawns, CRABS, and LOBSTERS. All have hard, jointed bodies and jointed legs. Most crustaceans live in the sea.

Crustaceans are *invertebrates* (animals with no backbones). Most have SHELLS around their bodies. This keeps their soft bodies safe. Many have a set of claws, or pincers, on their front legs. They use these to defend themselves and to grab their prey.

Crustaceans begin life as EGGS. They hatch into tiny *larvae*, which make up much of the floating *plankton* which other sea animals eat. As each larva grows, it sheds its shell and grows a new one which is bigger. This is called *molting*. When the larva becomes an adult, it continues to grow and molt.

The best-known crustaceans are the large shellfish

The heaviest crustacean is the North Atlantic lobster. Specimens weighing more than 44 lb. (20 kg) and over 3 ft. (1 m) long have been caught. This lobster is also the longest-lived crustacean. Some may be 50 years old.

such as lobsters, shrimp, crabs, and crayfish. They all have ten jointed legs, including the pair with pincers. Except for crayfish and some crabs, they all live in the sea. Many of them are very good to eat.

Barnacles live on rocks, on pieces of wood, and often on the bottom of boats. They open their shells and put out long, feathery hairs which trap food floating in the water.

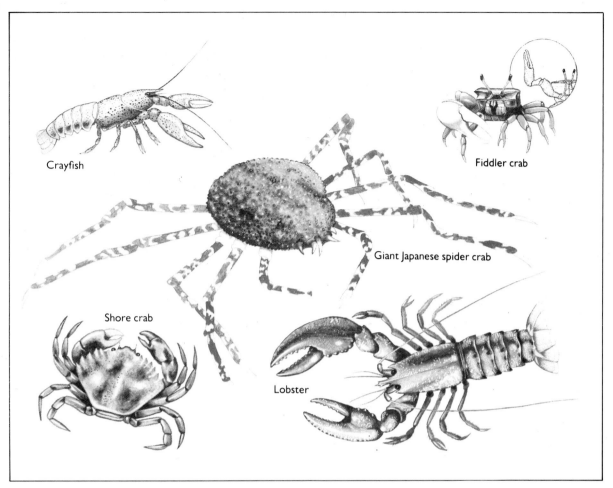

▲ *The creatures above are all crustaceans. The male fiddler crab (see inset) uses its large claw to signal aggression.*

Crystal

If you look closely at sugar through a magnifying glass, you will see that it is made up of thousands of tiny glassy pieces with flat sides. They are sugar crystals. SNOW is made up of tiny crystals of frozen water. So are the beautiful patterns on a frosty window. Some crystals are so small they can be seen only through a microscope. Others can grow to be as big as a person.

All crystals have a definite shape. They have

▼ *Crystals can be many different shapes. Some are combinations of two or more patterns, making complicated designs.*

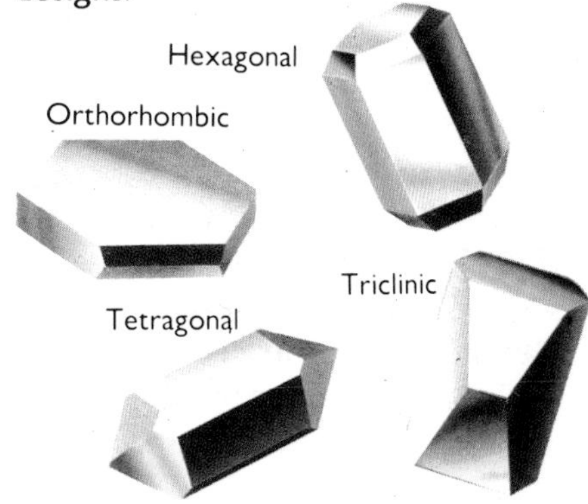

SEE IT YOURSELF

You can grow crystals yourself, using minerals such as salt or baking soda. Pour hot water into a bowl and add the mineral little by little, stirring all the time. Eventually, no more mineral will dissolve. Now let the solution cool. Hang a thread in the solution, and crystals will form on the end.

smooth, flat sides that meet in sharp edges. The shape of any one type of crystal never changes, but there are many different crystal shapes. The differences between them are caused by the ATOMS in the crystals arranging themselves in different ways.

For example, the salt you eat is made up of two different kinds of atoms—sodium atoms and chlorine atoms. The tiny sodium and chlorine atoms are arranged in cube patterns. If you look at salt grains through a magnifying glass, you will see that most of them are little CUBES. All salt crystals are built in the same way.

Cuba

Cuba is an island country in the Caribbean Sea. It is part of the WEST INDIES.

Part of the island is hilly, with high mountains in the southeast. In the center are large cedar and mahogany forests. Cuba has big sugarcane plantations and tobacco farms.

The climate is warm and pleasant, but Cuba lies in the path of HURRICANES which blow fiercely through the West Indies every year. Hurricanes are very strong winds which travel fast and often damage buildings and farms.

Cuba was ruled by Spain after Christopher COLUMBUS went there in 1492. The United States

CUBA

USA
ATLANTIC OCEAN
GULF OF MEXICO
BAHAMAS
CUBA
DOMINICAN REPUBLIC
MEXICO
HAITI
BELIZE
JAMAICA
HONDURAS
CARIBBEAN SEA

Government: Communist state
Capital: Havana
Area: 44,218 sq. miles (114,524 sq. km)
Population: 10,609,000
Language: Spanish
Currency: Peso

► *Modern Havana, the capital of Cuba, has many new buildings, but retains some built in the colonial style.*

took Cuba from Spain in 1898. In 1902, the island became independent. Cuba became a communist country in 1959 under its leader, Fidel Castro. Relations between Cuba and the United States have been poor since Castro came to power.

Cube

A cube is an object with six square sides. All the edges are the same length. Sugar and ice are often made in cubes.

The space a cube fills is called its volume. You can find the volume of a cube by multiplying the length of a side by itself and then by itself again. If the length of a side is 2 in. (5 cm), the volume of the cube is $2 \times 2 \times 2 = 8$ cubic in. ($5 \times 5 \times 5 = 125$ cubic cm).

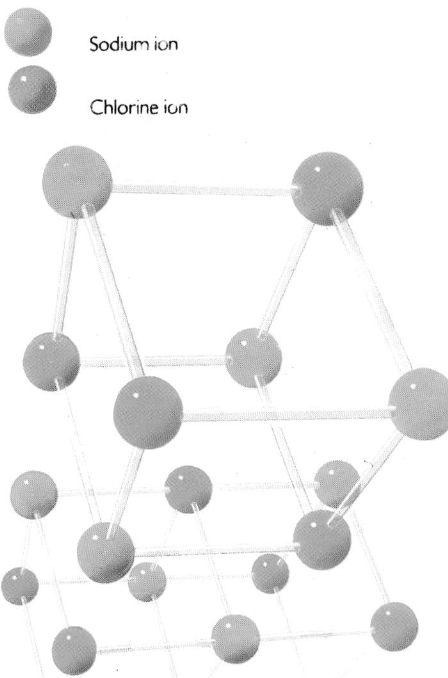

▲ *The atoms in a crystal of salt are all arranged in cube patterns. Thousands and thousands of these tiny cubes join together to make one grain of salt, which is also a cube.*

Cuckoo

Cuckoos are a family of birds. There are many kinds of cuckoo. They are found in many countries, but most live in the warm parts of the world. Cuckoos that live in cool countries fly to warm places for the winter. European cuckoos are large birds about 12 in. (30 cm) long. They do not build nests, but lay their eggs in the nests of other birds. When the young cuckoo hatches, it pushes the other eggs or baby birds out of the nest. The foster parents feed the cuckoo until it is ready to fly away.

◀ *Young European cuckoos grow quite large before they leave the nest. This young cuckoo is already much bigger than its foster parent, a willow warbler.*

▲ *Pierre and Marie Curie devoted their lives to their research, spending their money on equipment and often living in conditions of hardship.*

Curie, Marie and Pierre

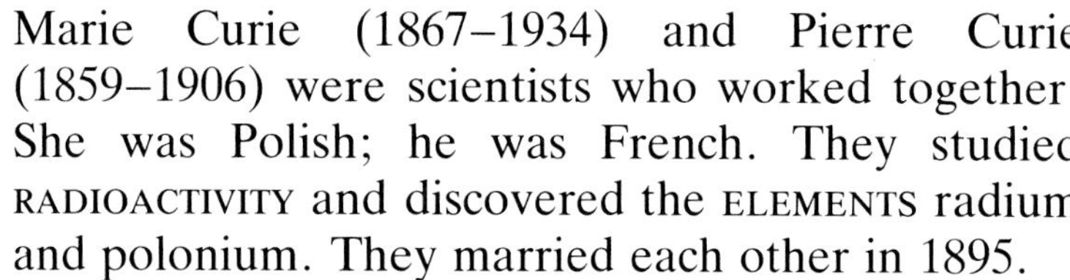

Marie Curie (1867–1934) and Pierre Curie (1859–1906) were scientists who worked together. She was Polish; he was French. They studied RADIOACTIVITY and discovered the ELEMENTS radium and polonium. They married each other in 1895.

For their work on radioactivity and their discovery of radium in 1898, they were given the NOBEL PRIZE for physics in 1903. When Pierre was killed three years later, Marie took over his job as professor at the Sorbonne University in Paris. In 1911, she was given a second Nobel Prize, this time for chemistry.

Current, Electric

Electric current is the movement, or flow, of ELECTRICITY. Current must always be flowing before electricity can work. Electricity is usually made in a GENERATOR at a POWER PLANT. From there, the current travels through wires to your home. Before it reaches your home, a *transformer* reduces its force, or *voltage*, so that it does not burn up the wires and

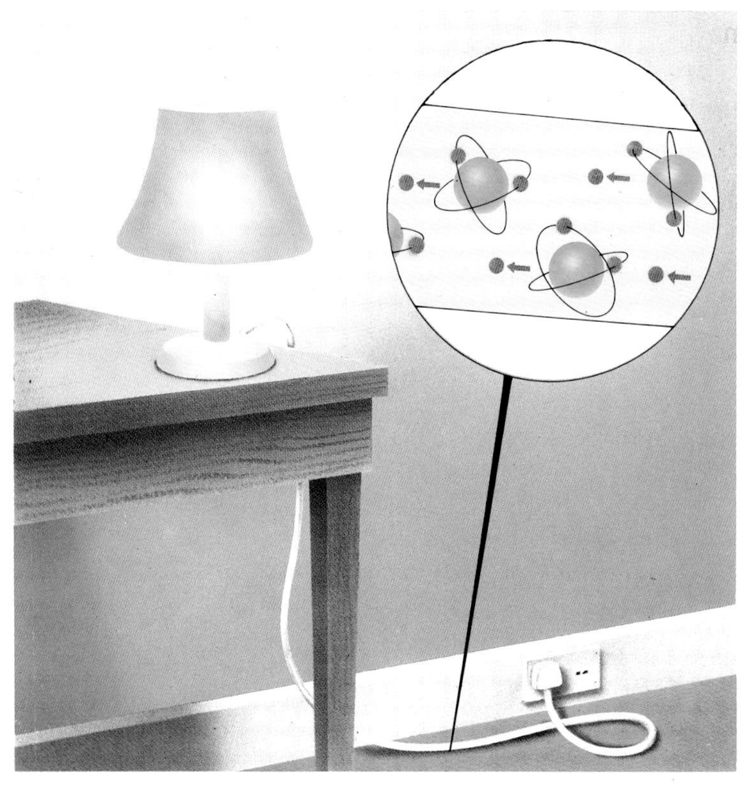

▶ *Electricity flows along a wire when electrons jump from one atom to the next. Electrons are tiny units of negative electricity. The protons in the center of the atoms are positive.*

electric equipment in your home or school.

The current flows out of the sockets in the walls of your house and through the equipment you are using. Then it returns to the generator in the power plant through another set of wires.

Electricity in houses flows in one direction and then in the opposite direction. It is called *alternating* current. Each movement back and forth happens very quickly (about 60 times a second). This is too fast for us to notice, for example, that lights flicker.

Electricity from *batteries* flows in only one direction. It is called *direct* current.

The unit of electric current is the amp, short for ampere. The current in one of our nerves to make us raise an arm is about one hundred thousandth of an amp. A lightning flash can peak at about 20,000 amps. A nuclear power plant can deliver 10 million amps.

Custer, George Armstrong

George Armstrong Custer (1839–1876) was a dashing young cavalry officer who gained great success in the CIVIL WAR, fighting for the North. He was made a general when he was still only 26. But he is most famous for the Battle of the Little Bighorn. In it, Custer and his force of over 200 men were killed by a large army of Sioux and Cheyenne Indians led by Crazy Horse and Sitting Bull.

No one is really sure what happened at the battle, and arguments about who was to blame raged for many years. Perhaps because he had been so successful when he was young, Custer had many enemies in the U.S. Army. Some of them said that Custer had been reckless at the battle and that he had disobeyed orders. His friends said that other soldiers had refused to come to his aid and that they were to blame.

▲ *George Custer died with all his men at Little Bighorn.*

Cyclone *See* Hurricane

Cyprus

Cyprus is a large, mountainous island in the eastern Mediterranean. It has a sunny climate, and many tourists visit the country to enjoy its historic sites and scenery. Farmers grow grapes, lemons, oranges, grains, and olives.

Cyprus was ruled by Turkey for 300 years until 1878, when Britain took it over. It gained full

CYPRUS

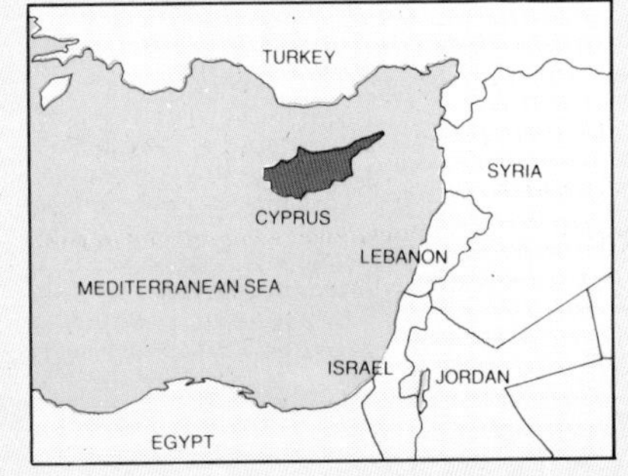

Government: Republic
Capital: Nicosia
Area: 3,572 sq. miles (9,251 sq. km)
Population: 702,000
Languages: Greek and Turkish
Currency: Pound

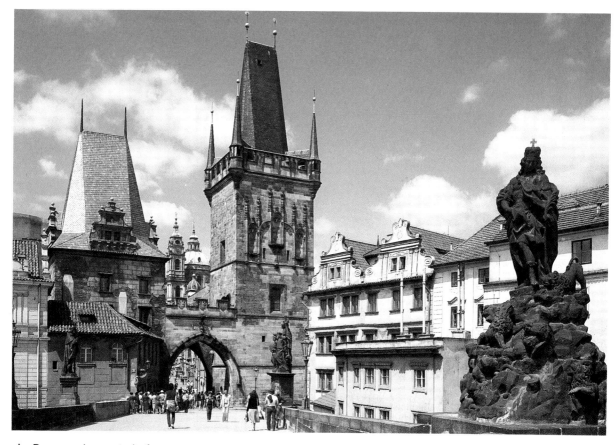

▲ *Prague, the capital of Czechoslovakia, is steeped in history and has many beautiful old buildings.*

independence in 1960. The people are Greek Cypriots, who are Christian, and Turkish Cypriots, who are Muslim. These two groups often quarreled, and in the 1960s there was a civil war. Today, Cyprus is split into two parts, one part ruled by Greek Cypriots, the other by Turkish Cypriots.

Czechoslovakia

Czechoslovakia is a country in eastern EUROPE. It is surrounded by Germany, Poland, the Ukraine, Hungary, and Austria. The country is about the same size as Louisiana.

Much of Czechoslovakia is covered by hills and mountains, and there are some big forests. Many of the people are farmers. Czechoslovakia also has coal and iron and an important steel industry.

The capital of Czechoslovakia is Prague. It is a medieval city with many fine churches and old buildings. Most of the people speak either Czech or Slovak. In 1989 the people demanded, and obtained, more freedom from the communist government.

CZECHOSLOVAKIA

Government: Multiparty system
Capital: Prague
Area 49,370 sq. miles (127,860 sq. km)
Population: 15,662,000
Languages: Czech and Slovak
Currency: Koruna

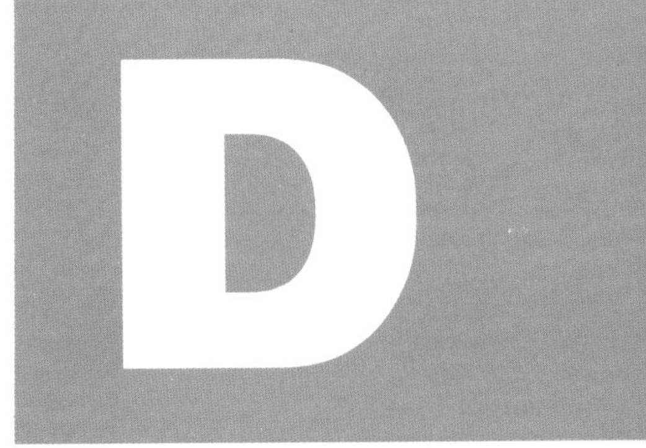

Dam

A dam is a barrier built across a river or stream to control its flow. There are many reasons for building dams. The most common is to make a *reservoir*. A reservoir is a manmade lake in which water is stored and sent across the country in pipes so that people can use it for drinking, washing, and cooking.

Another reason for building dams is to store water for irrigating fields in the dry season. People have been doing this in hot countries for hundreds of years.

Whenever water is at a height from which it can fall, it can be made to do work. Dams are built to harness this power. In the past, small dams were built to force streams of water into narrow channels. The rushing stream turned water wheels that drove machinery. Today, huge dams build up an enor-

▼ *Dams are among the biggest structures built by people. This dam in Morocco is an arch dam. The curved shape makes the water press against the sides of the canyon instead of pushing against the dam wall.*

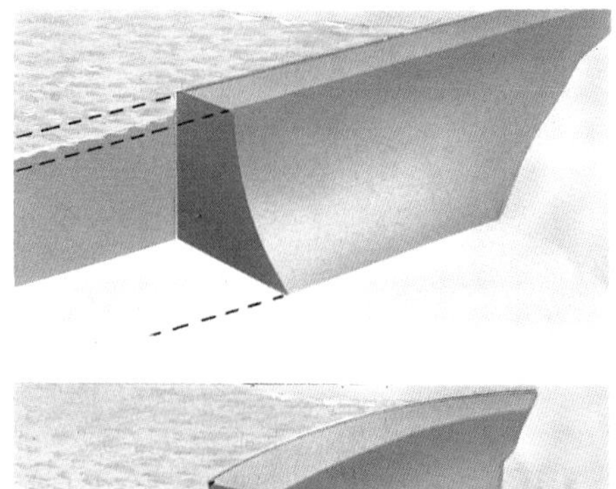

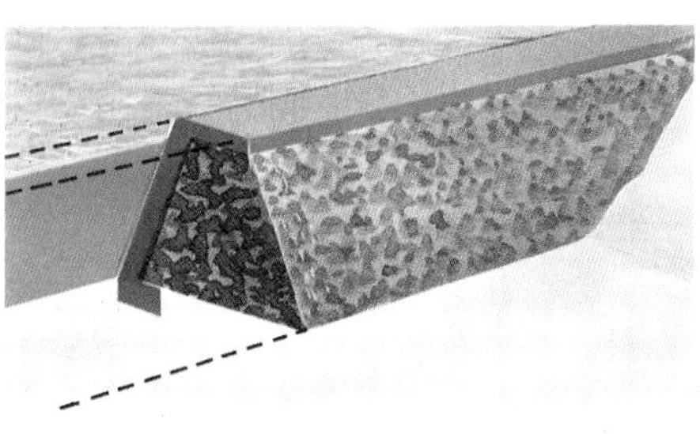

▲ *A* gravity *dam (1) made of stone or concrete blocks that take the whole weight of the water. An* arch *dam (2) is curved so that the weight of water pushes against the sides of the canyon instead of against the dam wall. An* embankment *dam (3) is just a heap of rocks and earth, with an outside layer of concrete.*

HIGHEST AND LARGEST DAMS

Highest	Location	Type	feet	(m)	Completed
Nurek	Russia	earthfill	1,046	(317)	1980
Grande Dixence	Switzerland	gravity	937	(284)	1962
Inguri	Russia	arch	898	(272)	1980
Vajont	Italy	multi-arch	865	(262)	1961
Mica	Canada	rockfill	799	(242)	1973
Mauvoisin	Switzerland	arch	782	(237)	1958

Largest	Location	cu. yd.	(cu. m)	Completed
New Cornelia	Arizona	272,357,800	209,506,000	1973
Tabela	Pakistan	192,400,000	148,000,000	1979
Fort Peck	Montana	124,800,000	96,000,000	1940
Oahe	S. Dakota	91,000,000	70,000,000	1963
Mangla	Pakistan	85,345,000	65,650,000	1967
Gardiner	Canada	85,215,000	65,550,000	1968
Oroville	California	78,000,000	60,000,000	1968

mous pressure of water that falls through big pipes. The rushing water hits the blades of turbines, making them spin and turn generators. From the generators comes ELECTRICITY.

Dance

Dance is probably the oldest of the arts. People have always danced to express their feelings. Today there are many different kinds of dancing. (See pages 188–189.)

Dark Ages

Early scholars gave the name "Dark Ages" to the period in Europe after the fall of the great Roman Empire in the A.D. 400s. During this period, barbarian Goths, Vandals, and Huns swept down on Europe from the north and east. They destroyed many fine buildings and works of art that had existed during Roman times. This is why the time was called the Dark Ages. It lasted for about 500 years.

During the Dark Ages, knowledge survived only in monasteries, and there were very few schools. Many of the old arts and crafts were lost.

At this time, however, people were still writing and thinking and making fine works of art in other

One country did not experience the Dark Ages. What for most of Europe was a period of decay was a golden age for Ireland. At this time religious art and learning flourished in Ireland. Beautiful illuminated manuscripts such as the Book of Kells, one of the world's finest examples of Christian art, were produced.

parts of the world. The eastern Roman Empire was not conquered by the barbarians. There, the arts still flourished. And in China and India, great civilizations grew and spread.

In the A.D. 1000s, Europe began slowly to recover from its artistic darkness. The lost knowledge of the ancient Greeks and Romans was found again. There was a new interest in learning, and the richer life of the MIDDLE AGES began.

▲ *During the Dark Ages, Viking raiders from Scandinavia threatened much of Europe. They were also settlers and traders, founding colonies from North America to Russia.*

Darwin, Charles

Charles Darwin (1809–1882) was an English biologist. In 1859, he published his great book, *On the Origin of Species*. Before this, almost everyone believed that the world was created by God exactly as the Bible described. Darwin put forward the theory that all living things *evolved* from earlier forms. They were alive because they had won the struggle to survive.

Within any species of living thing, there would be small variations in shape, size, or habit. Some of these variations would increase the living thing's chance of survival. For example, a giraffe with a long neck could reach leaves which a giraffe with a shorter neck could not. In times of famine, the taller giraffe would survive, while the shorter one would

Continued on page 190

▲ *Darwin's theory of evolution stirred up much controversy. Here he is mocked in a cartoon of the time.*

DANCE

Dance is one of the most ancient human arts. Thousands of years ago, people acted out stories in dance. Dance became part of religion: people danced to bring rain to make crops grow and to guarantee good hunting. Warriors danced war dances to make themselves feel brave before a battle.

People all over the world dance. Dancing is usually done to a rhythmic beat, and some music is written especially for dancing. Every country has its own folk dances, with traditional steps and costumes.

Ballet developed in the 1600s from court dancing in Europe. Ballroom dancing became widespread in the 1800s, with popular dances such as the waltz and, later, the tango, which was borrowed from a South American folk dance. Today, in the theater, on film and television, and in the disco, dance is enjoyed in different styles.

Dancing is excellent exercise. Everyone can enjoy dance; by moving your body in time to music, you can express your feelings and have fun. What's more, in today's disco, you can dance either with a partner, in a group, or by yourself.

▲ *Dancing figures have been found in the wall paintings of ancient Egypt.*

▼ *Terpsichore was one of the nine Muses, who represented the arts in ancient Greek mythology. She was the Muse of Dance and Poetry.*

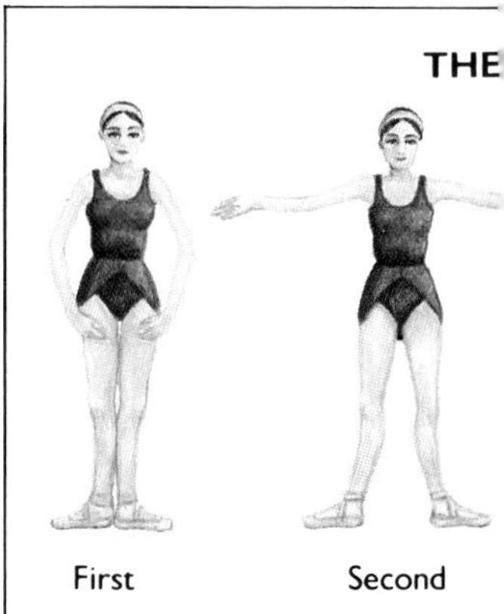

SOME WORDS USED I BALLET

ballerina female solo ballet dancer
barre exercise bar used in training
corps de ballet main grou of dancers
entrechat leap in which dancer rapidly crosses ar uncrosses feet in the air
jeté leap from one foot to another
pas de deux dance performed by two peop
pirouette spin on one foot

◀ *Stars such as Fred Astaire popularized modern dance, including tap dancing, in films.*

◀ *The ballet positions from which all movements begin.*

ances performed by the Cossacks of a require both energy and agility.

orris dancing is a form of English folk , usually performed by men.

▶ *Dancers in a chorus line wear identical costumes and dance the same steps in a well-drilled line.*

▲ *In formation ballroom dancing, a team of couples move in patterns across the floor.*

SOME FAMOUS DANCERS

Isadora Duncan (1878–1927) An American, she studied ancient Greek dance and performed wearing flowing classical-style costumes. Her dancing helped make new ideas about dance more popular.

Margot Fonteyn (1919–1991) British ballerina, who studied at the Sadler's Wells school and became a star of the British Royal Ballet. Best known for her performances in *Swan Lake* and *The Sleeping Beauty*.

Vaslav Nijinsky (1890–1950) Russian dancer, remarkable for his dramatic performances and amazingly high leaps (elevation). He danced with the famous Ballets Russes run by the Russian impresario Serge Diaghilev.

Rudolf Nureyev (born 1939) Russian dancer who left the Kirov Ballet in 1961 to dance in the West. He formed a much-admired partnership with Margot Fonteyn.

Anna Pavlova (1882–1931) Russian ballerina, famous for solo performances, especially as the Dying Swan. Trained at the Imperial School of Ballet in St. Petersburg, she became an international star.

more information turn to these articles: BALLET; GYMNASTICS; LOUIS, KINGS; MOTION PICTURES; MUSIC; POP MUSIC; PREHISTORIC PEOPLE; TING; THEATER.

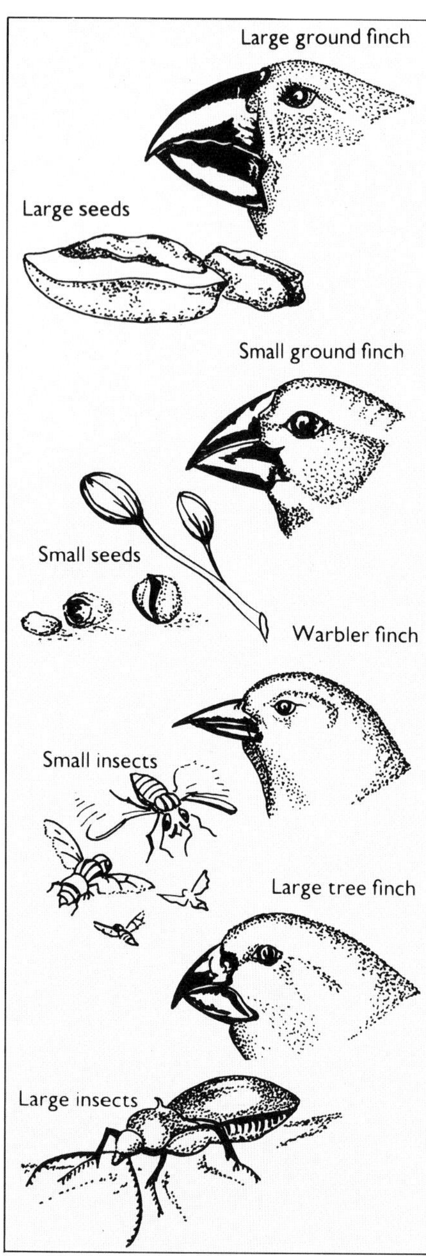

▲ *Darwin discovered a variety of finches on the Galapagos Islands, each species of which had evolved different beaks suited for eating different foods. All had originally come from a South American finch that had reached the islands long before.*

die. The taller giraffe that survived would, in time, replace the variety with the shorter neck.

This theory outraged many people. They thought it was against the teaching of the Bible. But today people accept the idea of Darwin's theory, and many churches have decided that it does not threaten their religious beliefs.

Day and Night

The Earth turns on its own axis as it moves around the Sun. So the part of the Earth facing the Sun is light while the part facing away from the Sun is dark. The lighted part is "day" and the dark part "night." Because the Earth turns around, day and night follow each other continually.

Scientists have another way of describing a "day." They say it is the time it takes the Earth to complete one full turn on its axis. If you measure how long it takes from one sunrise or one sunset to the next, you will find that it takes almost exactly 24 hours.

The length of time that any particular part of the Earth is in daylight varies, depending on where it is on the globe. This is because the axis of the Earth is tilted at an angle to its path around the Sun. This also means that some parts of the Earth have differ-

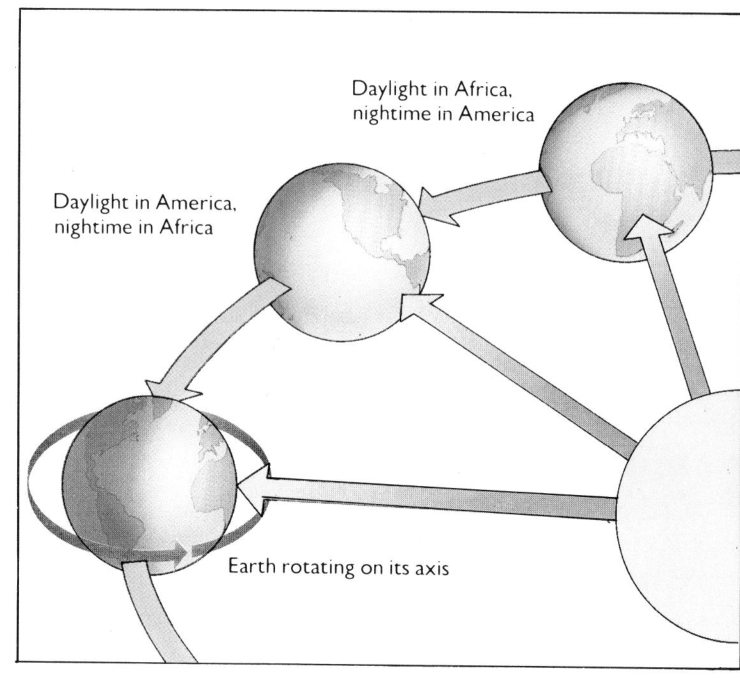

► *Day and night happen because the Earth spins like a top as it circles the Sun. Only one half of the Earth faces the Sun at any one time.*

SEE IT YOURSELF

If you shine a flashlight on a globe, you will see why we have day and night. The Earth rotates from west to east. As we travel eastward on the revolving Earth, we pass into sunlight. We see the Sun first in the east in the morning. In the evening, the Sun disappears (sets) in the west. It takes the Earth 24 hours (a day) to complete one turn on its axis.

ent amounts of day and night at certain times of the year. For instance, in June in the Arctic, it is always daylight. In the Antarctic, it is always night. In December, it is the other way around—dark all the time in the Arctic and light in the Antarctic.

Because the Earth turns all the time, it is always day in one place when it is night somewhere else. The world is divided into "time zones." There is no single time, such as "noon," for the whole world. When it is noon in New York it is midnight in Western Australia.

To make a clear difference between one day and the next, an imaginary line was drawn from the North to the South Pole. On one side it is one day, and on the other side, the day following. This line, known as the "dateline," runs through the Pacific Ocean. It has a strange effect: if you cross the dateline going eastward you gain a day, while those traveling westward miss a day.

D-Day

D-Day was the day of the Allied landings in Normandy, France, during WORLD WAR II. It took place on June 6, 1944, and led to the defeat of Hitler's Germany. On this famous day, about three million men—Americans, British, and their allies—and 11,000 ships and aircraft crossed the English Channel. It was by far the greatest invasion force the world had ever seen. The supreme commander of this force was General Dwight EISENHOWER. At the same time, the Russians attacked from the east, and the Germans had to retreat on all fronts. They surrendered on May 7, 1945.

▼ *Before D-Day, the Germans were led to believe that the Allied landings would take place across the Straits of Dover. Instead, they were on the Normandy coast between Cherbourg and Le Havre.*

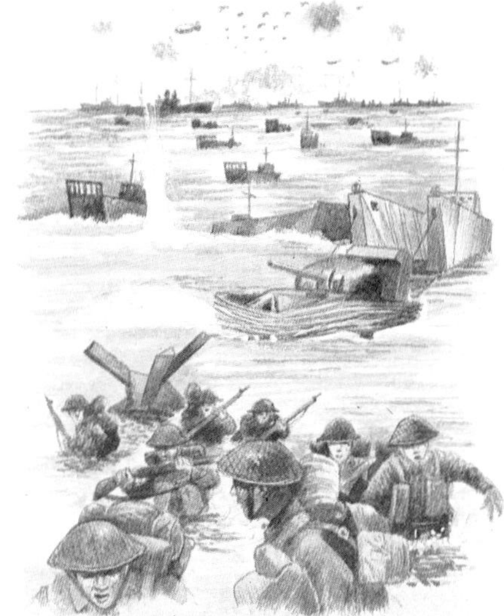

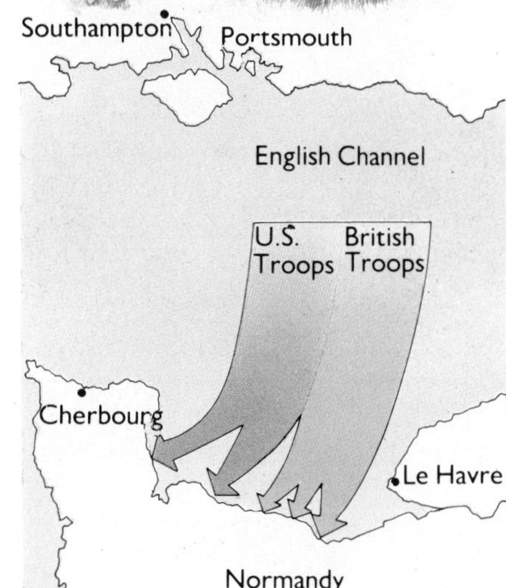

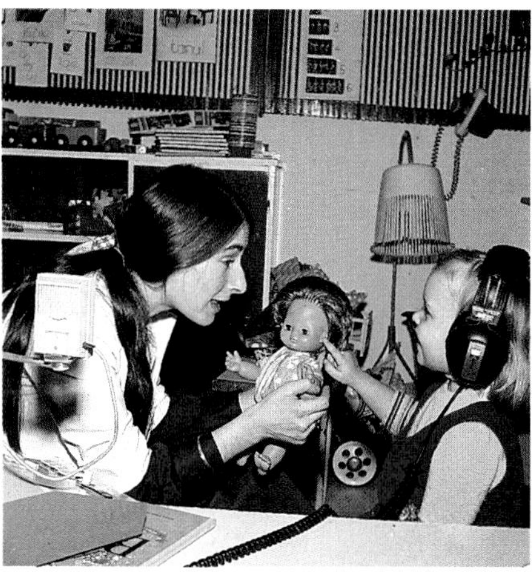

▲ Electronic aids are used in teaching deaf children today.

Deafness

There are many different kinds of deafness, or hearing loss. We all lose some hearing as we get older—but some people are born deaf, and some go deaf as children or later in life from illness or accident. There are many ways of communicating if you are deaf. Sometimes it is difficult for deaf people to use their voice if they have never heard spoken language, and they may use sign language, speaking mainly with their hands and body rather than with their voice. There are many famous and successful deaf people.

Fifty-six members of the Continental Congress signed the parchment copy of the Declaration of Independence. Most of them signed on August 2, 1776.

Declaration of Independence

The Declaration of Independence, along with the United States CONSTITUTION, is the bedrock of American democracy and government. It is a document whose influence has been immense. It is admired across the world for its simple statement of the nature of government and the rights of the American people.

It was written in 1776, and adopted by the American Congress in Philadelphia on July 4 that year, Independence Day. At that time, though the 13 colonies were already at war with Britain, few people thought they should become completely independent. But anger at the British grew so much that the Congress decided it should cut all its links with Britain. Five of the members were asked to write a formal "declaration of independence." Among them was THOMAS JEFFERSON, who was one of the representatives from VIRGINIA. He wrote nearly all of the original document, though others later made some changes.

▲ On June 10, 1776, a committee of five was appointed to write a declaration of independence. The five were, left to right, Thomas Jefferson, Roger Sherman, Benjamin Franklin, Robert R. Livingston, and John Adams. The committee asked Thomas Jefferson to write the first draft of the declaration. He finished it in two weeks.

The Declaration of Independence describes the form of government Jefferson thought the new country should have. Its most important parts state that, "all men are created equal," and have the right to, "Life, Liberty, and the Pursuit of Happiness." If a government fails to meet these goals, "it is the Right of the People to alter or abolish it." The original document is on view at the National Archives Building in WASHINGTON, D.C.

Deep-Sea Life 

Most of the animals and plants that live in the sea stay in the top 650 ft. (200 m). Below this, conditions become less and less suitable for living things. At a depth of half a mile it is very cold and very dark. No sunlight gets down that far. Plants cannot live there because they need light to make their food. Some animals do, however, live at great depths. Their bodies are specially designed to withstand the enormous pressure deep down. Most of them are quite small, often with enormous jaws, teeth, and eyes. Many deep-sea fish have light-producing organs. These lights may help them to recognize their own kind in the darkness and may also act as lures for their prey.

▼ *Strange fish live at the bottom of the ocean. No daylight reaches these depths, and many of the animals, such as the deep-sea angler and the lantern fish, give out light of their own.*

Deep-sea angler

Hatchet fish

Lantern fish

Viper fish

Scientists have brought up tiny bacteria from a depth of 36,000 ft. (11,000 m)—nearly 7 miles (11.25 km). They look very much like the bacteria we have on land, but they cannot live at a pressure of less than a thousand atmospheres! These creatures of the deep live with a pressure of about 1,000 lb. pressing in on every square inch of their bodies.

Deer  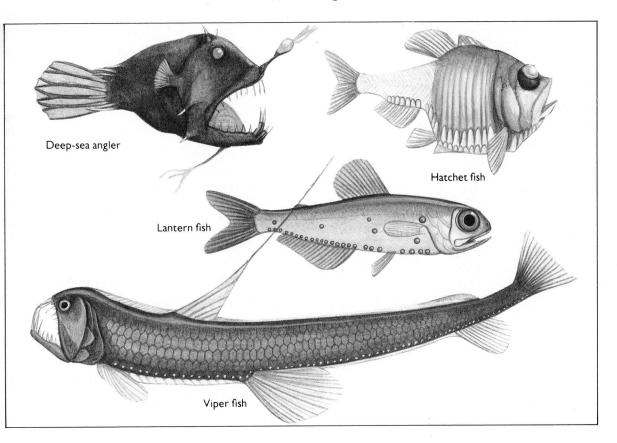

Deer are animals related to cattle and antelopes. They are different from their relatives because they have antlers instead of permanent horns. Male deer

▲ *The moose is the largest of all deer. The reindeer is well adapted to life in northern latitudes, while the fallow deer is often found in parks. The red deer is a widespread species. The little muntjac is about 18 in. (45 cm) tall and barks like a dog.*

Deer have a common origin with giraffes. They became separated from the giraffes about 20 million years ago. Fossil bones show that prehistoric people often dined on deer meat. Deer hides were used for clothing, and antlers were made into weapons and tools.

grow new antlers every year. Female deer, except for reindeer, do not grow antlers.

Every year in early spring, a lot of blood starts to flow into two bony lumps on the male deer's forehead. The blood carries a bony substance that makes the antlers grow quite rapidly. At first, they are covered with a soft, hairy skin known as velvet. In early summer, the antlers are fully grown. The blood supply is then cut off, and the velvet dies. The male deer rubs off the velvet until his antlers are hard and shiny. Some antlers are enormous. One red deer's antlers weighed as much as 77 lb. (35 kg). A moose's antlers have measured 6 ft. (2 m) across.

Deer are found mainly in the Northern Hemisphere. But there are some species in South America and Asia.

De Gaulle, Charles

Charles De Gaulle (1890–1970) was a French general and statesman. He went to the Military Academy at St. Cyr. He fought in World War I. In 1916, he was badly wounded. After the war, he continued his army career. When World War II broke out in 1939, he was put in command of a tank division. After the Germans occupied France in 1940, De Gaulle went to Britain and formed the Free French Movement, which fought very bravely.

In 1944, he returned to France as head of government. But two years later, he resigned when the political parties could not agree. By 1958, France was in desperate political trouble. The French settlers in Algiers and the French army were rebelling. De Gaulle became president of France in 1959 and settled the Algerian problem. He stayed in office until 1969 when he retired from politics.

▲ *Charles De Gaulle was one of the founders of the European Community, and in its early days he dominated it.*

Delaware

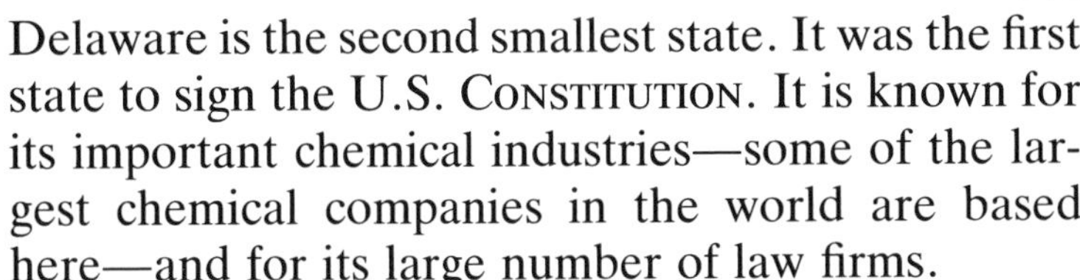

Delaware is the second smallest state. It was the first state to sign the U.S. CONSTITUTION. It is known for its important chemical industries—some of the largest chemical companies in the world are based here—and for its large number of law firms.

Because it is on the east coast of the country, Delaware was one of the first areas of America to be settled by Europeans. The first white man to visit it was Henry Hudson, in 1609. Later, the Dutch had a settlement in Delaware. But in 1664 Britain took it over and gave it to William Penn, the English founder of PENNSYLVANIA. Delaware played an important part in the REVOLUTIONARY WAR, and its soldiers fought successfully against Britain.

DELAWARE

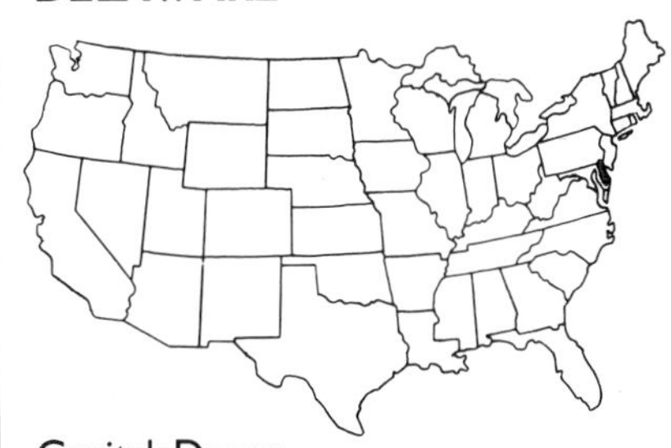

Capital: Dover
Population: 666,168
Area: 2,045 sq. mi. (5,296 sq. km)
State flower: Peach Blossom
State bird: Blue Hen Chicken
State tree: American Holly
Statehood: December 7, 1787
1st state

Delta

When a river flows across a flat plain into the sea, it flows very slowly. On its way, it deposits soil and sand on the plain. In time, this sediment begins to form mudbanks. The river flows through these in many channels, often changing direction. This wide, blocked-up mouth with many channels is called a delta. This is because its shape is often like the Greek letter *delta* Δ.

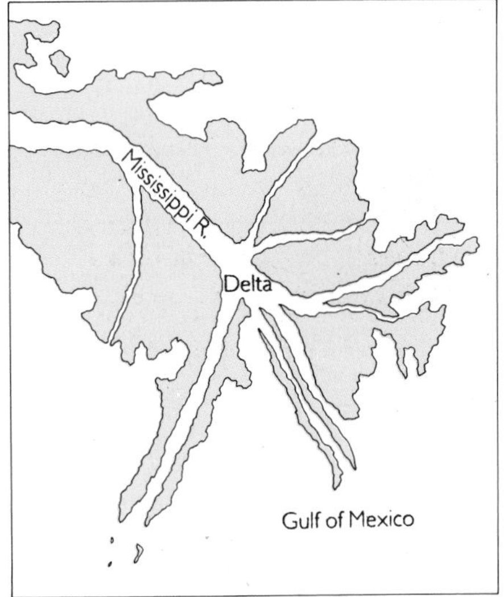

▶ *The Mississippi Delta stretches 200 miles (320 km) into the Gulf of Mexico and is still growing at the rate of half a mile every 20 years.*

► *The Statue of Liberty stands at the entrance to New York Harbor as a symbol of freedom under American democracy.*

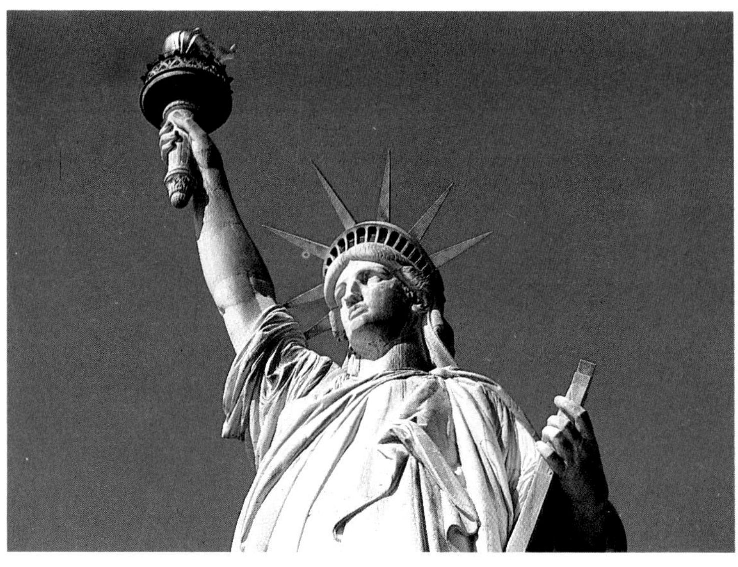

Abraham Lincoln described democracy as "government *of* the people, *by* the people and *for* the people." He meant that in a democracy everyone takes part in making the laws that everyone then has to obey.

Democracy

Any government in which the people have supreme power is a democracy. In a democracy, people elect their own government. Representatives of different political parties run for office, and people vote for the one they prefer. The people can also dismiss their government if they want to. In a democracy, people can say and read what they like. They cannot be put into prison without a proper trial.

There are many different kinds of democracy. The British form is a monarchy with an elected PARLIAMENT. The American form is a republic with an elected president and an elected CONGRESS. There is no one perfect democracy in the world, but all free nations are trying to work toward a perfect democracy.

DENMARK

Government: Constitutional monarchy
Capital: Copenhagen
Area: 16,633 sq. miles (43,080 sq. km)
Population: 5,140,000
Language: Danish
Currency: Krone

Denmark

Denmark is a small Scandinavian country in the north of EUROPE. It consists mainly of a peninsula called Jutland, surrounded by 600 islands. In the west is the North Sea, to the east is the Baltic Sea, and to the south is Germany. The capital is Copenhagen. Denmark is a flat country whose soil and climate are ideal for agriculture. Dairy and pig farming are especially important. Denmark is a member of the EUROPEAN COMMUNITY. It exports butter and bacon.

Desert

Not all deserts are hot and sandy. Some are cold, and some are rocky. But all are very dry. Some scientists say that a desert is any area where less than 3 in. (8 cm) of rain falls in a year. Other scientists call a place a desert when there is more rain than this, but where it evaporates quickly in the sun or sinks rapidly into the ground.

Many big deserts are in the tropics, often inland on large continents where rainbearing winds cannot reach them.

There are three main types of desert. The first is rocky, where any soil is blown away by the wind. The second has large areas of gravel. The third is made up of great sand dunes, burning hot by day and bitterly cold at night.

Cold deserts are found in northern Canada, Greenland, northern Russia, and Antarctica. Very few plants and animals can survive in these regions because they are so cold and icy. Cold deserts are dry because they have no liquid water—it is all in the form of ice.

It is difficult for plants and animals to live in desert conditions. Some plants, like the CACTUS, store

LARGEST DESERTS

	sq. miles	(sq. km)
Sahara	3,500,000	(9,100,000)
Gt. Australian	1,500,000	(3,900,000)
Libyan	500,000	(1,300,000)
Gobi	500,000	(1,300,000)
Rub'al Khali	250,000	(650,000)
Kalahari	225,000	(580,000)
Kara Kum	120,000	(310,000)
Atacama	25,000	(65,000)
Mohave	15,000	(39,000)

▼ *Wind-sculpted dunes in the Sahara Desert in Morocco. Not all deserts are sandy; many are stony and barren.*

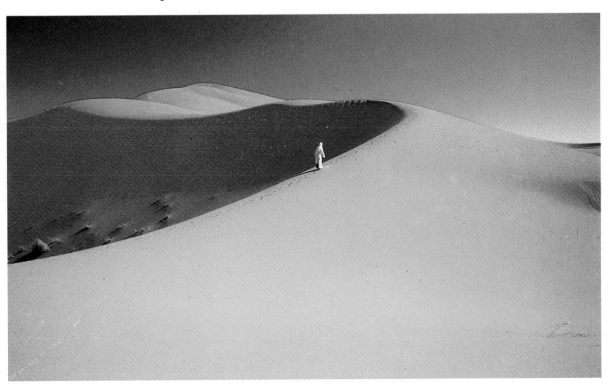

▼ *Many animals keep cool in the desert by hiding away during the daytime, coming out after the Sun sets. To conserve water, desert animals sweat very little.*

▼ The sand grouse soaks its feathers in a waterhole and takes the water to its thirsty young.

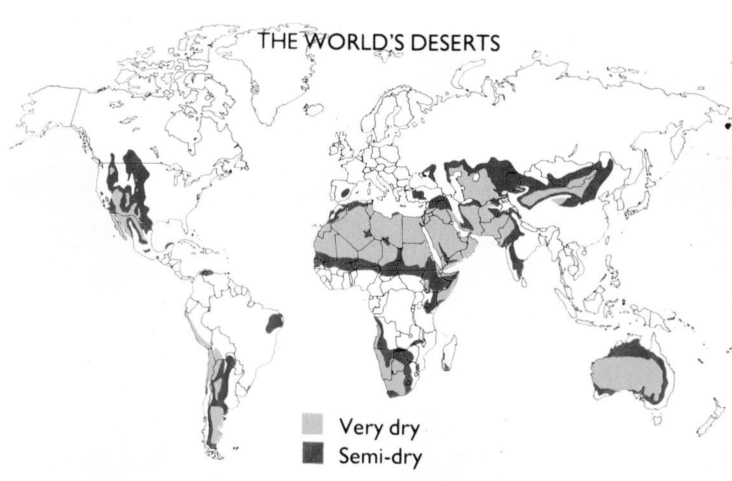

◀ The peregrine falcon preys on small desert animals. It is one of the fastest flying birds.

moisture in their fleshy stems. Others have seeds that lie apparently lifeless in the ground for long periods. When a shower of rain falls, they burst into life and can flower and produce new seeds within weeks. Many desert animals shelter from the sun by day and come out only at night. Some never drink, but get all the moisture they need from their food.

The world's largest desert is the SAHARA in Africa. The driest desert is the Atacama in South America, where it may not rain for several years. The Mohave Desert and the Painted Desert lie in the western United States.

▲ The Gila monster is a poisonous lizard. Its poison travels along grooves in its teeth while it is biting its victim.

▼ There are two types of camel, the Bactrian (two-humped) of the Gobi Desert and the Arabian (one-humped).

▲ Dingoes are wild dogs, descended from dogs brought to Australia by the first settlers to arrive there.

Detergent

The word *detergent* means any substance that will clean things. *Soap* is a detergent. But today the word detergent usually means synthetic, or man-made, detergents such as most washing powders. Detergents are similar to soap, but soap leaves behind filmy deposits, such as the familiar bathtub ring. Detergents can reach soiled areas better than soaps and do not leave deposits.

Detroit

Detroit, Michigan, is one of the most important cities in the country, and one of the largest. It is the home of the American automobile industry. Many of the biggest car manufacturers have factories there. Because Detroit is on the GREAT LAKES, it is easy to transport the raw materials that are needed to make cars to it. Detroit was built first by the French, but the British captured it in 1760. It became an American city only in 1796, 13 years after the REVOLUTIONARY WAR.

Diamond

Diamonds are CRYSTALS. They are harder than anything else in the world. They are formed by great heat and pressure deep beneath the surface of the earth. Diamonds are made of pure CARBON, the same mineral that is found in ordinary coal. They are usually colorless and have to be cut in a special

◀ *A cut and uncut diamond. The finished diamond has usually lost about 50 percent of its original weight after cutting and polishing.*

The Cullinan diamond, named after its finder, Thomas Cullinan, was the largest ever found. It was discovered in 1905 near Pretoria, South Africa. The huge uncut stone was about 5 in. (13 cm) across and weighed more than 1½ lb. (.75 kg). In 1908, the diamond was cut by expert diamond cutters in Amsterdam and finished up as 105 separate stones. One big diamond cut from the Cullinan is called the Star of Africa. It is in the British royal scepter. Another is in the State Crown, and others are in jewelry worn by Queen Elizabeth II.

The world's most famous colored diamond is the large Hope diamond. It is deep blue and came originally from India. The Hope is now in the gem collection of the Smithsonian Institution in Washington, D.C. Although diamonds are usually colorless, they are found in a variety of colors in shades of blue, yellow, pink, and champagne.

way to catch the lights and "sparkle." A diamond cutter is very skilled and uses tools tipped with diamonds, for only another diamond is hard enough to cut a diamond. Diamonds are used in industry for drilling and cutting.

▲ *Charles Dickens wrote all his novels in weekly or monthly installments for magazines.*

▼ *An illustration from Charles Dickens' novel* Oliver Twist, *which portrayed the harsh conditions suffered by orphans in Britain at the time.*

Dickens, Charles

Charles Dickens (1812–1870) was a great English writer. His books give us a vivid picture of life in Victorian England in the middle 1800s. Several of his stories are about children, especially poor children and orphans. Dickens tried to improve the lives of the poor by making their suffering more widely known through his books. He also created some of the liveliest and best-known characters in English literature. Some of his most famous books are *Oliver Twist*, *David Copperfield*, *Great Expectations*, and *A Christmas Carol*.

Dickinson, Emily

Emily Dickinson (1830–1886) was one of America's greatest poets and one of the most important of the 1800s. Her poems can be hard to understand. She wrote about the difficulty of understanding the world, and of how quickly and strangely life passes. She was a very reserved person, who refused to publish any of her poems during her life and who never married. She lived all her life at her parents' home in Massachusetts. Few certain facts about her solitary life are known.

Dictator

A dictator is the leader of a country who rules with absolute power and authority. In ancient Rome, a dictator was a magistrate who was given absolute power to deal with emergencies, when decisions had to be made quickly. Today the term is used to describe a tyrant who takes away people's rights and freedoms and rules by force. Often those who try to oppose a dictator are killed, imprisoned, or forced to leave the country until a time when the dictator is overthrown.

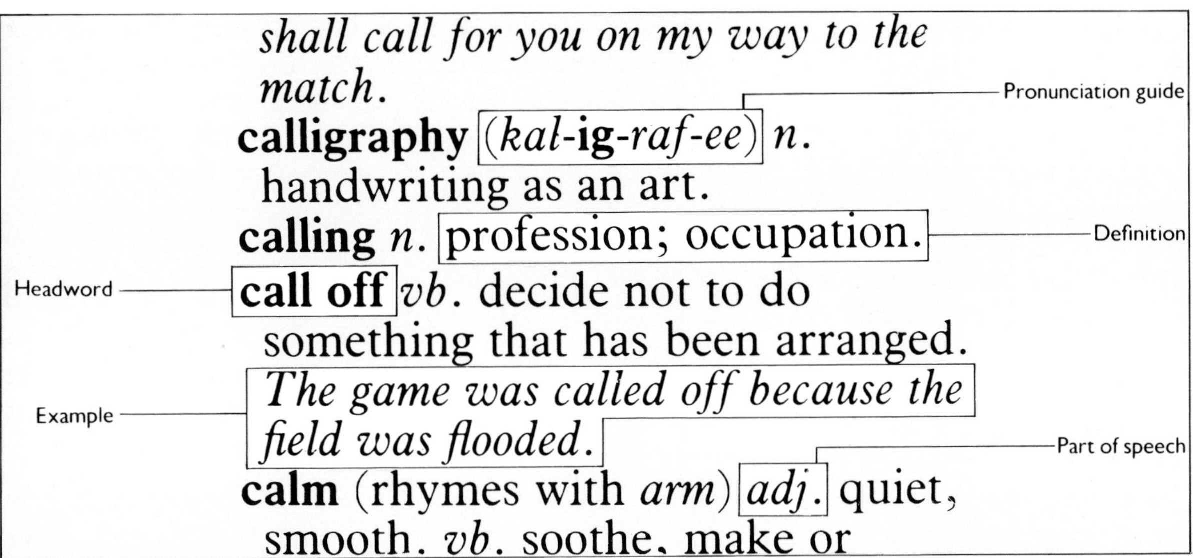
shall call for you on my way to the match.
calligraphy (*kal*-**ig**-*raf-ee*) *n.* handwriting as an art.
calling *n.* profession; occupation.
call off *vb.* decide not to do something that has been arranged. *The game was called off because the field was flooded.*
calm (rhymes with *arm*) *adj.* quiet, smooth. *vb.* soothe, make or

▲ *A dictionary definition has a number of standard parts, though not every dictionary includes them all. After the word itself, called the* headword, *comes a pronunciation guide and the part of speech, usually abbreviated* (n., adj.). *Next comes the definition, or what the word means. Finally, other forms of the same word may be listed.*

Dictionary

A dictionary is a book that tells us what words mean. The words are arranged in alphabetical order from A to Z. Often the meanings, or definitions, include the history of the words and how they are used and pronounced. Dictionaries may vary in size from many volumes to dictionaries small enough to slip into your pocket. Dr. Samuel Johnson (1709–84) made one of the first large dictionaries of English words.

Diesel Engine

Diesel engines are a type of INTERNAL COMBUSTION ENGINE in which fuel is burned inside the engine. Diesel engines are named after their inventor, Rudolf Diesel, who built his first successful engine in 1897 to replace the steam engine. Diesel engines use a cruder, heavier fuel oil than gasoline. They are cheaper to run than gas engines, but they are heavier and more difficult to start, so until recently they were not widely used in cars. They are used to drive heavy machines such as trains, tractors, ships, buses, and trucks. A properly-working diesel engine causes less pollution than a gasoline engine.

A diesel engine is similar to a gas engine. But instead of using a spark from a spark plug to ignite the fuel, the diesel engine uses heat that is made by a piston squeezing air inside a cylinder. When air is

▼ *London taxis are driven by diesel engines, which are cheaper to run and cause less pollution.*

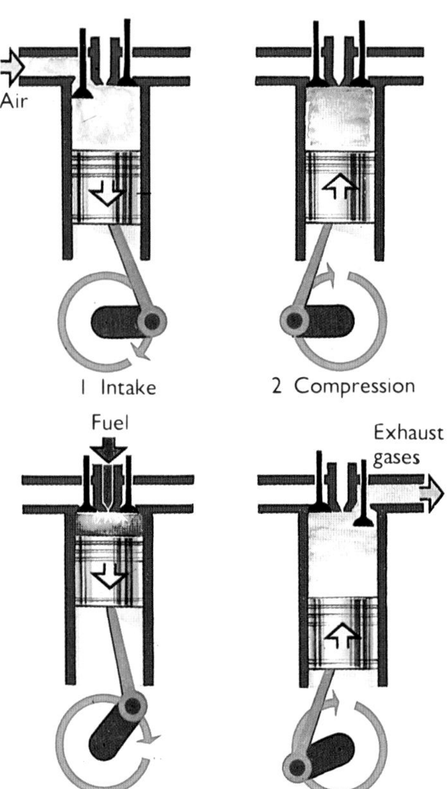

▲ *How a diesel engine works. As the piston goes down (1), air is drawn into the cylinder. When the piston goes up, the air is squeezed and becomes very hot (2). When the piston gets to the top, oil is squirted in and bursts into flame. The hot gases expand and push the piston down (3). When the piston goes up again, it pushes the spent gases out through the exhaust valve.(4).*

very tightly compressed, or pushed into a much smaller space than it filled before, it gets very hot. This heat sets fire to the diesel oil, which burns instantly, like a small explosion. The burning oil heats the air and forces it to expand again to push the piston down and thus drive the engine.

Many RAILROADS began using diesel engines after World War II. European railroads badly damaged in the war took the opportunity to modernize their engines and replaced the old steam locomotives with diesel ones. Diesel engines were first used regularly on the railroads of the United States in the 1930s. Today, diesel-electric locomotives are in use all over the world. In these engines, the diesel motor is used to make electricity. The electricity then drives the train.

Digestion

Digestion is the way in which the food we eat is broken down into substances that can be used by the body. It takes place in the digestive tract, or *alimentary canal*, a long tube that runs from the mouth to the anus. Digestion starts in the mouth, where the teeth and special chemicals in the saliva help to break down the food. The food then passes down a

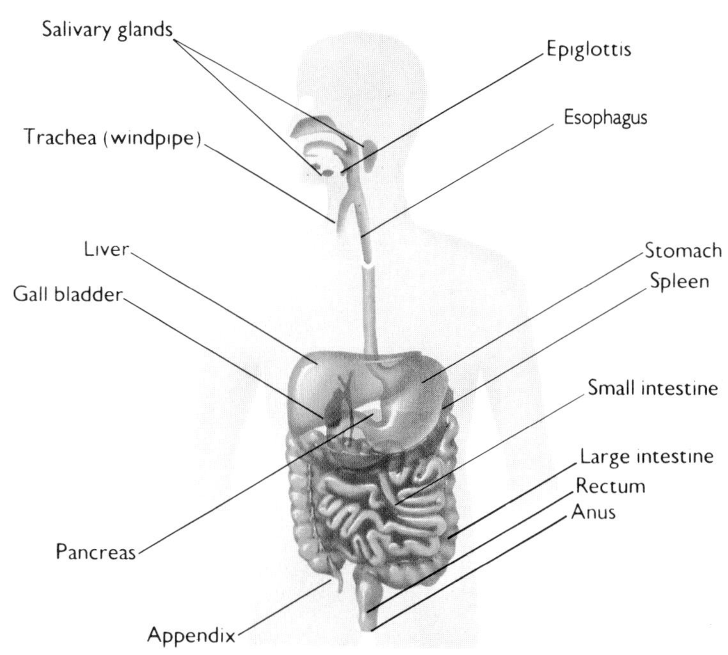

▶ *The human digestive tract. The alimentary canal in an adult is 25 to 35 ft. (8 to 10 m) long.*

tube called the *esophagus*. Muscles in the esophagus push and squeeze the food down into the STOMACH. There, acids and more chemicals help to turn the food into a creamy liquid. Then a muscle at the lower end of the stomach opens from time to time to release food into the small intestine.

Inside the small intestine, bile from the LIVER and juice from the pancreas help to break down the food still further. Much of it passes through the thin walls of the intestine into the bloodstream. The remainder goes into the large intestine. There, liquids and salts are absorbed until only solid waste material is left. Bacteria in the large intestine digest any remaining food products. The final waste product is passed out of the body as *feces*.

Indigestion is a pain in the stomach which some people feel after eating. It may be caused by eating too fast or by the stomach producing too much acid. People who worry a lot tend to produce a lot of acid in their stomach. Some of this may rise up in their throat and cause a burning feeling. This acid may also damage the lining of the stomach and lead to stomach ulcers (open sores).

Dinosaur

The word *dinosaur* means "enormous lizard." These creatures lived between 65 and 225 million years ago, long before there were any people on earth. They developed from primitive REPTILES.

There were two main groups of dinosaurs—the *saurischians* and the *ornithischians*. The ornithischian dinosaurs were all plant-eaters and most of them moved on all fours. Some of these, like *Stegosaurus* and *Triceratops*, were large and lumbering, but had bony armor to protect them from the teeth and claws of the great meat-eating dinosaurs.

The saurischian group contained both plant-eaters and meat-eaters. The plant-eaters included the largest dinosaurs, the biggest of which scientists are calling "*Ultrasaurus*." The remains of this creature are incomplete, but they include a huge arm and shoulder girdle which show that it was about 26 ft. (8 m) tall at the shoulder—four times the height of a tall man! It probably weighed as much as 130 tons, even heavier than the blue whale. But these great beasts were harmless plant-eaters.

Perhaps the most famous of the dinosaurs are the great carnivores, or meat-eaters. *Tyrannosaurus*, which was 45 ft. (14 m) from snout to tail, stood on its hind legs. Its toes had claws as long as carving knives. Saber-like teeth—some nearly the length of

During the age of the dinosaurs, 200 million years ago, the continents were all joined together in one great land mass. This is why dinosaurs have been found in every continent except Antarctica. About 300 different species of dinosaur have been found, but some of these are known only from a single tooth or a small bone fragment.

The largest flying creature that we know about was a pterosaur that glided over parts of North America about 70 million years ago. Scientists calculate from its fossil remains that it had a wingspan of about 36 ft. (11 m)—more than half the distance from home plate to the pitcher's mound!

Triceratops

Tyrannosaurus

▲ *Many of the dinosaurs of the late Cretaceous Period could survive an attack from great meat-eaters such as* Tyrannosaurus. *The ostrich dinosaurs such as* Struthiomimus *could run very fast, while the ceratopsian* Triceratops *and the ankylosaur* Ankylosaurus *had strong armor and weapons such as spikes and clublike ends to their tails.*

a man's hand—lined the jaws. No flesh-eating beasts that ever lived on land were larger or more menacing than these monsters.

No one knows why all the dinosaurs, great and small, died out about 65 million years ago.

Discrimination

There are a few harmless forms of discrimination, but most kinds are bad. If you have a photographic club, anyone who is not interested in photography is excluded. That is harmless discrimination. The oldest form of discrimination is in religion. People who did not belong to the popular religion were punished. For example, until 1829, Roman Catholics in Britain could not vote or sit in Parliament.

Other forms of discrimination are being fought today. One kind is *racism*—discriminating against people because of their race. In the United States blacks were discriminated against for many years. South African *apartheid* is a kind of discrimination.

Ankylosaurus

Struthiomimus

Another form of discrimination is by sex. In some countries, women are still barred from some jobs just because they are women.

Disease

Diseases make us ill. Some diseases are caused by BACTERIA, or germs, that invade our bodies. Other diseases are caused by VIRUSES. Sometimes diseases can be passed down from parents to their children in the genes that they are born with.

Our bodies fight against diseases through our immune systems. Special CELLS, such as white blood cells, fight the invading organisms. Our bodies also produce antibodies to fight diseases such as measles and chicken pox. These antibodies stay in our systems when we catch these diseases and prevent us from having the same diseases again. This means that we are immune to these diseases.

Doctors have developed many ways of helping us fight diseases with drugs and inoculations.

HOW DISEASES ARE SPREAD

Bacteria and viruses are often spread when we cough or sneeze.

Hands should always be washed thoroughly before preparing food.

▲ *A monorail at the Epcot Center at Disney World amusement park in Orlando, Florida. Walt Disney opened the first of his parks, Disneyland, in California in 1955.*

Disney, Walt

Walt Disney (1901–1967) was an American filmmaker best known for his cartoons and films for children. Disney characters, especially Mickey Mouse and Donald Duck, are famous all over the world. Walt Disney began his work in the 1920s. His cartoon artists, or animators, produced characters and settings that moved realistically. Full-length Disney cartoon features such as *Snow White and the Seven Dwarfs*, *Pinocchio*, and *Bambi* are still popular everywhere.

▲ *Walt Disney, shown here with his most famous creation, Mickey Mouse, began as a commercial artist and made the first of his short films with sound,* Steamboat Willie, *in 1928.*

Distillation

When water boils, it turns into steam. When the steam cools, it turns back into water again. The steam from a boiling pot *condenses* into drops of water when it hits a cool window. But the water on the window is not quite the same as the water in the kettle. It is *pure* water. When salt seawater is boiled, pure fresh water condenses from the steam. The salt is left behind in the boiler. This boiling and cooling of liquids to make them pure is called distillation. An apparatus used for distilling is called a still. Large stills are used in some places to turn seawater into fresh water.

Distillation is often used to separate liquids that are mixed together. The mixture is heated, and the

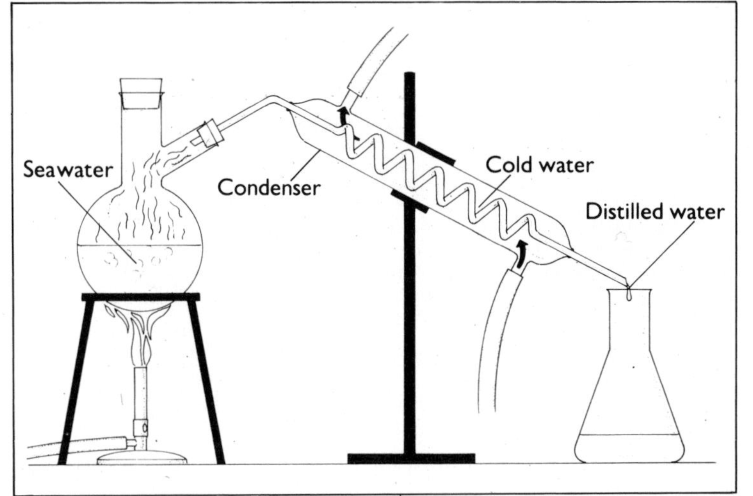

◀ *To distill water in a simple laboratory experiment, the water in the flask is heated. Steam rises into the cold condenser. Cold water circulating around the condenser cools the steam, which turns back into a liquid and collects as distilled water in the beaker.*

liquid that boils at the lowest temperature evaporates first and is separated from the other liquids. Then the liquid with the next lowest boiling point is condensed off, and so on. This is called *fractional distillation*, and it is used to separate the materials in the crude OIL that comes from oil wells. Distilling is also used in making alcoholic drinks such as whiskey.

Two thousand years ago, Greek sailors made drinking water from seawater by distillation. They boiled seawater and hung sponges in the steam. Then they squeezed pure distilled water out of the sponges.

District of Columbia

The District of Columbia is the site of the city of WASHINGTON. It has been the capital of the United States since 1800. Because it is under the control of the Federal Government, it is the only part of the country that does not belong to any state. All the important offices of the government are here: the WHITE HOUSE, where the president lives; the CONGRESS, where the House of Representatives and the Senate meet; and the Supreme Court. The Lincoln Memorial, the Washington Monument, and the Jefferson Memorial honor three great presidents.

The city was chosen as the capital by GEORGE WASHINGTON in 1791. To honor the first president, the city was named after him.

DISTRICT OF COLUMBIA

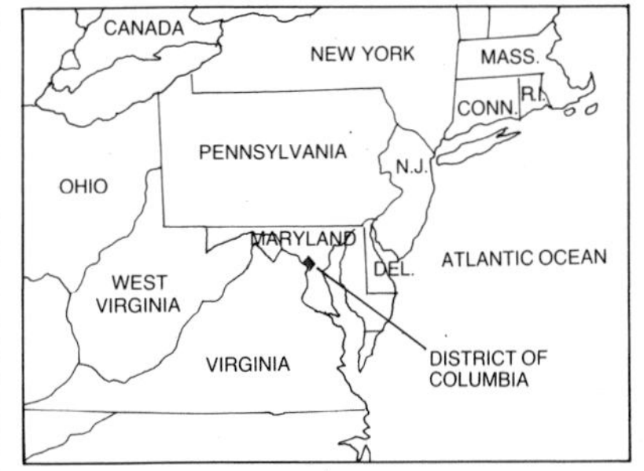

Population: 606,900
Area: 69 sq. miles (179 sq. km)
State flower: American beauty rose
State bird: Wood thrush
State tree: Scarlet oak
Founded: 1791

Djibouti

The small republic of Djibouti is in northeastern Africa beside the Red Sea. It is about the size of Massachusetts. Much of the country is desert, and

DJIBOUTI

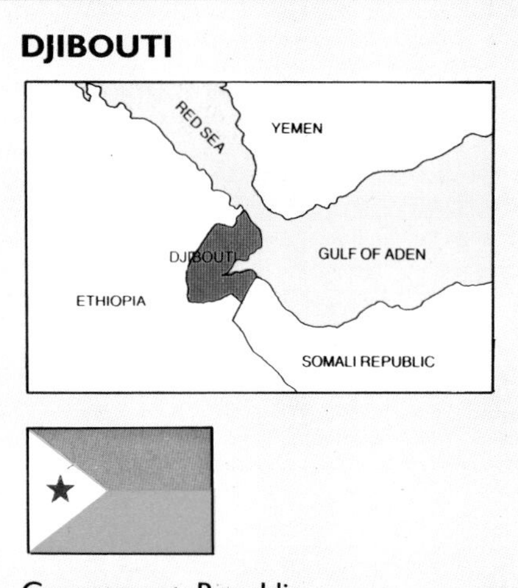

Government: Republic
Capital: Djibouti
Area: 8,500 sq. miles (22,000 sq. km)
Population: 409,000
Language: French
Currency: Djibouti franc

there are few natural resources. About a third of the people are nomads who rear goats, cattle, and camels. The country's capital, also called Djibouti, is a port that handles exports from neighboring ETHIOPIA. Djibouti gained independence from France in 1977.

Dodo

About 400 years ago Dutch explorers landed on Mauritius, a lonely island in the Indian Ocean. They found doves, fish, and large flocks of birds as big and as fat as turkeys. These birds had no true wings and could not fly. In time, people called them dodos, from the Portuguese word *doudo*. This word means "simpleton" or stupid person.

Sailors quickly learned that dodos were good to eat. Ships that visited Mauritius sailed off with holds full of salted dodo meat. Rats and dogs from the ships started eating dodo eggs and chicks.

By the 1690s, all the dodos were dead. Only drawings, bones, and one stuffed bird remained.

▲ *The dodo was said to have a cry like a gosling. It laid one white egg in a nest of grass.*

Dog

People have been keeping dogs for perhaps 10,000 years. Most dogs are kept as pets, but some do useful work like herding sheep or guarding buildings.

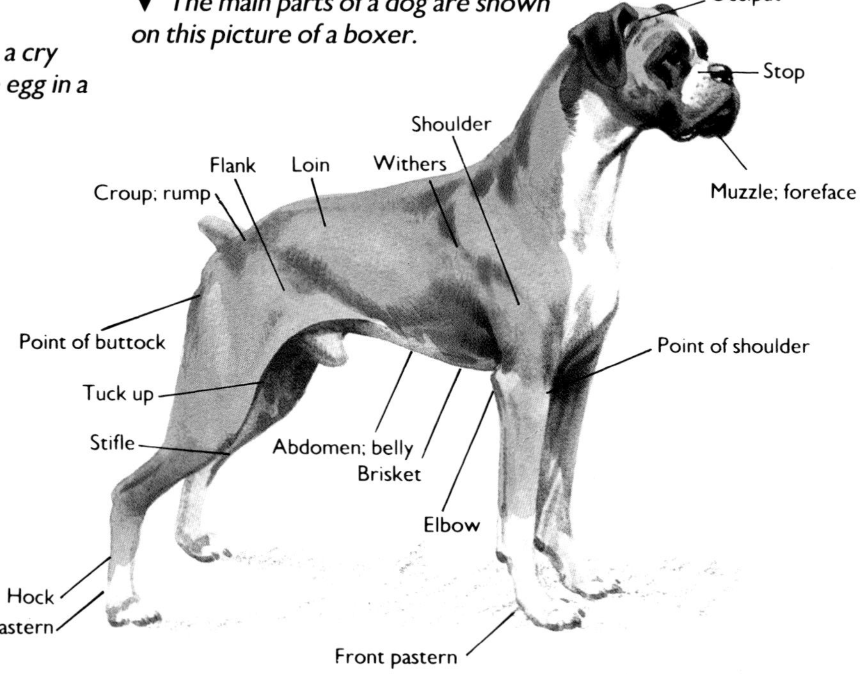

▼ *The main parts of a dog are shown on this picture of a boxer.*

The first dog was probably descended from a WOLF and looked much like a wolf. Today there are more than 100 breeds of dog of many colors, shapes, and sizes. The St. Bernard is the largest breed. A St. Bernard may weigh nearly twice as much as a man. The Yorkshire terrier is one of the smallest dogs. A fully grown Yorkshire terrier may weigh less than a small jar of jelly.

Most of the modern breeds of dog were developed to be good at special kinds of work. Airedales and other terriers make fine rat hunters. Labrador retrievers bring back ducks shot by hunters and also make excellent guide dogs for blind people. Collies round up sheep. Dachshunds were once used for hunting badgers. Dobermans are ferocious guard dogs.

All puppies are born blind and helpless, and at first feed only on their mother's milk. But small dogs are fully grown in a year or so. Most kinds of dog live for about 12 years.

Dogs are nearsighted and can see only a few of the colors we can see. But a dog's sense of smell is thousands of times better than ours. Customs officers use specially trained dogs to sniff out illegal drugs. It is not necessary to open cases or crates—one sniff is enough for a dog, even if the drugs are packed in metal containers.

Doll

Children all over the world play with dolls. Dolls may be made of wood, china, plastic, or many other substances. The very first doll may have been just a forked twig that looked a bit like a human being. Homemade dolls can cost nothing, but doll collectors pay a lot of money for rare old dolls.

Dolphin and Porpoise

Dolphins are small whales. Although they never leave the sea, they are mammals. They breathe air and are warm-blooded. They have sharp teeth, and their heads end in beaklike mouths. Porpoises, close relatives of the dolphins, have no beak and the front of the head is rounded. Because the dolphin is a friendly creature, it has been well known since ancient times. Dolphins are intelligent and communicate with each other by means of whistles and clicks. Tame dolphins can learn many tricks.

► *Dolphins and porpoises are small whales. The bottle-nosed dolphin has a shorter, more upturned beak than the common dolphin.*

▲ *Domes, large and small, decorate the church of Santa Maria della Salute in Venice. The word dome comes from the Latin* domus, *meaning "house."*

Dome

Domes are roofs like giant upturned mixing bowls. Some domes are made from bricks or stones. Other domes are made of concrete, steel, or plastic. Domed roofs cover famous churches such as St. Sophia in Istanbul, St. Peter's in Rome, and St. Paul's Cathedral in London, and non-religious buildings such as the Capitol in Washington. The world's largest dome is the Louisiana Superdome in New Orleans. It is as wide as the length of two football fields.

The Romans were the great dome builders. In A.D. 112 they built the Pantheon in Rome. Its dome is 142 ft. (43 m) in diameter and 142 ft. (43 m) high.

▼ *The Domesday Book recorded who owned land, how much land they owned, how many people worked the land, how many animals they owned, and how many pastures, mills, and fish ponds they had.*

Domesday Book

Twenty years after the Norman Conquest of England, William the Conqueror ordered that a great survey of property owners in England should be made. It was called the Domesday Book (or Doomsday), because it spared no one and there was no appeal from it. William wanted to find out how much land people held so that he could be sure that he was getting all the taxes that were due him. The survey was completed in 1086 and can be seen in the Public Record Office in London.

Dominica 

This small island country in the Caribbean Sea was a British colony until it became independent in 1978. The main products are bananas, coconuts, and citrus fruits.

Dominican Republic 

The Dominican Republic occupies the larger part of the island of Hispaniola in the Caribbean Sea. The rest of the island is occupied by Haiti. The main crop is sugar. About 75 percent of the people are of mixed black and white descent. Most of them live and work on farms.

Donkey 

Donkeys are small and sturdy relatives of the HORSE. They are descended from the wild asses of Africa. A donkey has a large head with long ears. It has a short mane, and its tail ends in a tuft of hair.

Donkeys are surefooted and can carry heavy loads over rough ground. They have long been used as pack animals and are still at work in southern Europe, North Africa, Asia, and Latin America.

DOMINICA

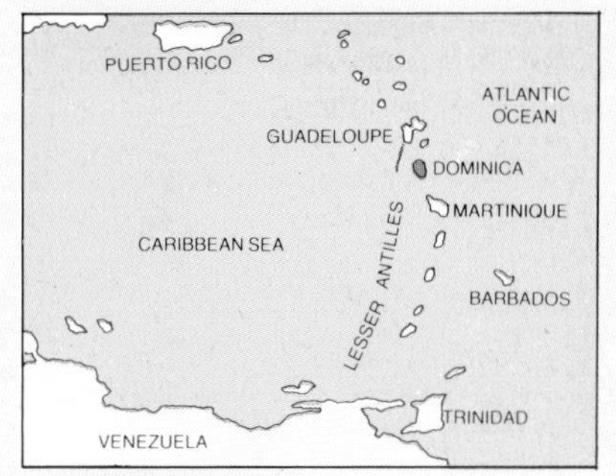

Government: Republic
Capital: Roseau
Area: 290 sq. miles (751 sq. km)
Population: 83,000
Language: English
Currency: East Caribbean dollar

DOMINICAN REPUBLIC

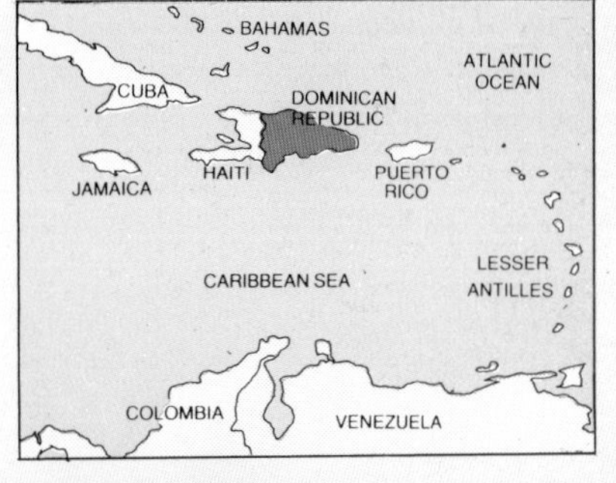

Government: Republic
Capital: Santo Domingo
Area: 18,816 sq. miles (48,734 sq. km)
Population: 7,170,000
Language: Spanish
Currency: Peso

◀ *Donkeys can carry very heavy loads for their size. They are patient and hardworking, and have been used as pack animals for centuries.*

► *One of the best known legendary dragons was the one said to have been slain by St. George, the patron saint of England. The story inspired this painting by Paolo Uccello.*

Dragon

Dragons are storybook monsters, but once many people believed that they really lived. Artists showed them as huge snakes or lizards with wings of skin and terrifying claws. They were supposed to breathe fire and swallow people and animals whole.

Fighting dragons called for great bravery. Legends tell how Hercules, St. George, and other heroes killed these evil monsters.

Not everyone thought dragons were wicked. The Chinese looked upon the creatures as gods.

When we read about Sir Francis Drake's exploits, it is hard to imagine how small his ships were. When he set out to pillage Spanish possessions in the West Indies, his two ships weighed just 71 tons and 25 tons. The *Golden Hind*, in which he sailed around the world, was a large merchant ship of its day—it displaced about 100 tons. The *John F. Kennedy* aircraft carrier displaced 87,000 tons.

Drake, Francis

Sir Francis Drake (about 1540–1596) was a sea captain who helped to make England a great sea power. In the 1570s, he led sea raids against Spanish ships and ports in the Caribbean Sea. He also became the first Englishman to sail around the world. In 1588, he helped to destroy the Spanish Armada.

▲ *Sir Francis Drake got his first command as captain of a ship at the age of 24.*

Drawing

Drawings are pictures or designs, usually made as lines with pencil, pen, or some similar material other than paint.

Drawing has been a natural human activity since prehistoric times, when people began to express

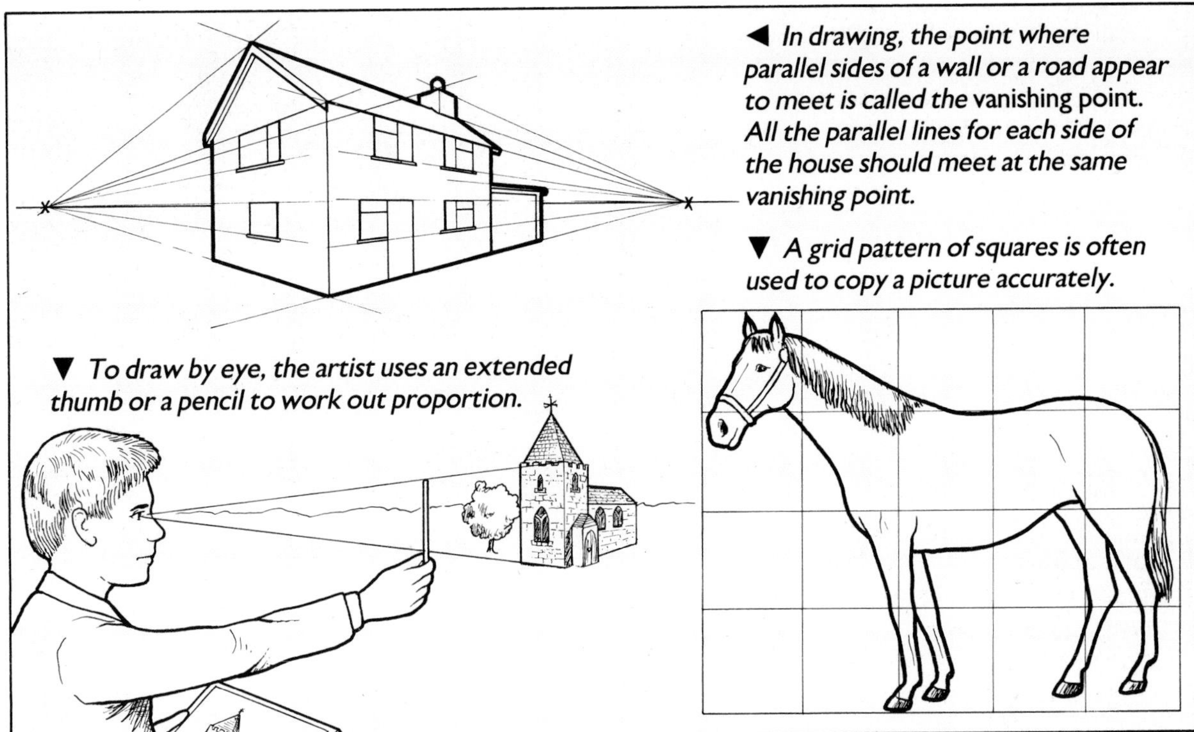

◀ *In drawing, the point where parallel sides of a wall or a road appear to meet is called the vanishing point. All the parallel lines for each side of the house should meet at the same vanishing point.*

▼ *A grid pattern of squares is often used to copy a picture accurately.*

▼ *To draw by eye, the artist uses an extended thumb or a pencil to work out proportion.*

their thoughts and ideas on the stone walls of caves. All children draw naturally. Many famous artists have included drawings in their best work. Some drawings are very precise and realistic. Every detail is picked out. In others, a powerful effect is produced by using very few lines and little detail. LEONARDO DA VINCI made scientific drawings and sketches for his paintings. Other painters who were also expert at drawing include Pieter Bruegel (the Elder), Paul Cézanne, and Pablo PICASSO.

Dream

Dreams occur when our brains are active while we are asleep. Some dreams are of everyday occurrences. Others may be just a series of jumbled images. On waking, we may or may not remember what we have dreamed. A frightening dream is called a nightmare.

We do not know exactly why people dream. Dreams may be sparked off by indigestion or a similar physical cause, such as a cramped sleeping position. External noises may also cause dreams. Some dreams are very common. These include dreams of falling, or being chased, or of lakes or water.

▼ *A profile of an armored warrior drawn by Leonardo da Vinci in about 1480. Leonardo did numerous sketches and studies from nature.*

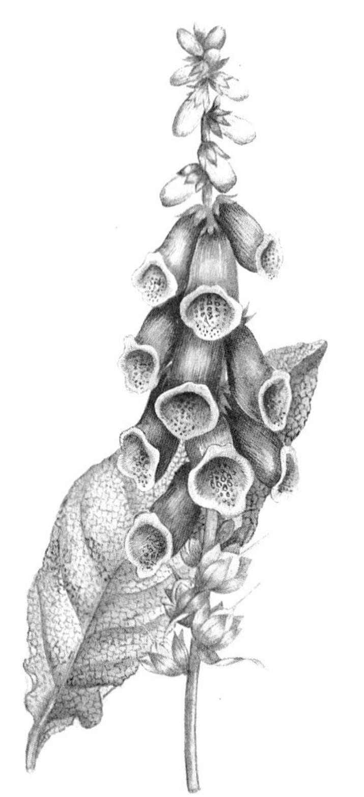

▲ *Foxgloves are still cultivated for the drug digitalis, which is used in the treatment of heart disease.*

Drug

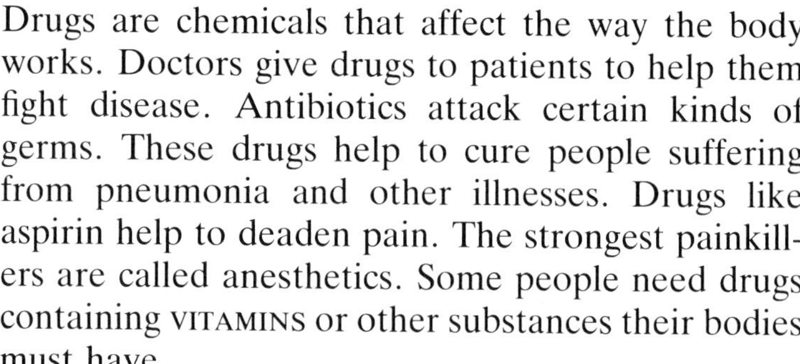

Drugs are chemicals that affect the way the body works. Doctors give drugs to patients to help them fight disease. Antibiotics attack certain kinds of germs. These drugs help to cure people suffering from pneumonia and other illnesses. Drugs like aspirin help to deaden pain. The strongest painkillers are called anesthetics. Some people need drugs containing VITAMINS or other substances their bodies must have.

Certain drugs come from plants or animals. For instance, the foxglove gives us a drug called digitalis. This makes weak hearts beat more strongly. Many other drugs are made from MINERALS.

Some people take drugs such as cocaine, cannabis, or alcohol just because they give a pleasant feeling. Some of these drugs can be addictive (habit-forming) and cause illness or even death.

Drum

Drums are the most important of those MUSICAL INSTRUMENTS that are played by being struck. The sound is made by hitting a tightly stretched sheet of skin or plastic called a drumhead. A kettledrum has one drumhead stretched over a metal basin. A bass drum or a snare drum has two drumheads, one across each end of a large open "can."

▼ *Tribal drums were once used in Africa to send messages in a drum code from village to village. Today they are used chiefly for ceremonial occasions.*

Duck

These web-footed water birds are related to swans and geese. Ducks look somewhat like small geese with short necks.

The two main groups of ducks are dabbling ducks and diving ducks. Dabbling ducks feed on the surface of the water. They may put most of their body under the water, but they do not dive. Dabbling ducks include the mallards that swim on pools and rivers in the northern half of the world. (Farmyard ducks were bred from mallards.) Other dabbling ducks include teal and widgeon, and the pretty wood duck.

Diving ducks dive completely underwater in their

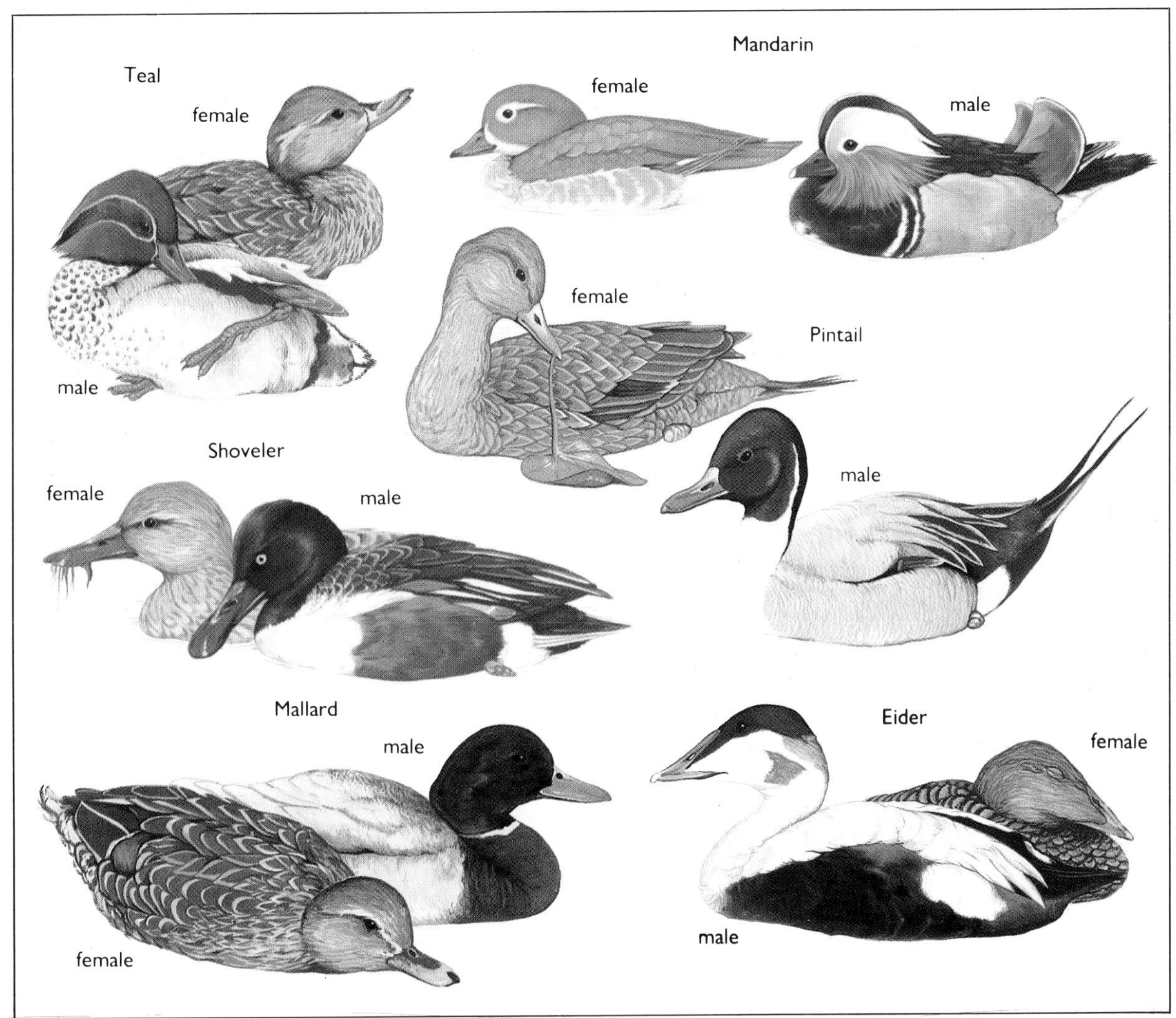

hunt for food. Most diving ducks live at sea. These ducks include the eider duck from which we get eiderdown. Sawbills are also diving ducks. Their long, slim beaks have inside edges like the teeth of a saw. Sawbills are good at grasping fish. The long-tailed duck is a diving duck that can fly at 70 miles (112 km) an hour.

▲ *The best known of the surface-feeders, or dabbling ducks is the mallard. The teal is another suface-feeder and is the smallest European species. The shoveler is characterized by its spoon-shaped bill. The male pintail has a long, pointed tail, and the eider duck gives us the soft breast feathers known as eiderdown. The mandarin originated in China and is now found wild in other parts of the world.*

Dye

Dyes are substances that people use to color TEXTILES and other materials. Some dyes come from plants. Cochineal, a red dye, comes from the cochineal insect. Most dyes are now made from chemicals. To dye an object, dip it in water containing dissolved dye. If the dye is *fast*, the object will keep its dyed color no matter how often you wash it.

Eagle

Eagles are large birds of prey. Most hunt small mammals and birds. Some catch fish or reptiles. The harpy eagle and the monkey-eating eagle catch monkeys. Each of these great birds measures more than 6 ft. (2 m) across its outspread wings. These eagles are the largest in the world.

Many eagles soar high above the ground. Others perch on a tree or rock. When an eagle sees its prey, it swoops suddenly and pounces. It seizes its prey with its sharp claws and tears off pieces of flesh with its strong, hooked beak.

The short-toed eagle, below and left, has white underparts. The booted eagles, left, show the light and dark forms of the bird. The bald eagle is the symbol of the United States.

Booted eagle

Short-toed eagle

Bald eagle

Ear

Our ears help us to hear and to keep our balance. Each ear has three main parts. These are the outer ear, middle ear, and inner ear.

The outer ear is the part we can see, and the tube leading from it into the head. Sounds reach the outer ear as vibrations, or waves, in the air. The cup-like shape of the ear collects these sound waves and sends them into the tube.

Next, the sound waves reach the middle ear.

Here, the waves make the *eardrum* move to and fro. This is the thin "skin" across the entrance of the middle ear. The moving eardrum sets tiny bones vibrating in the middle ear.

The vibrations travel on into the inner ear. Here they make liquid in the *cochlea* move. The cochlea looks like a snail's shell. The nerves inside it turn vibrations into messages that travel to your brain. The inner ear also has three hollow loops containing liquid. These loops send signals to the brain to help you keep your balance.

Ears are delicate and easily damaged. Hitting or poking into an ear can cause injury and may lead to DEAFNESS.

If you spin around quickly and stop suddenly, the liquid in the hollow loops in your inner ear keeps on spinning for a while. The nerve cells in your ear send confusing messages to your brain, and you feel dizzy. The dizziness ends when the liquid in the loops stops moving.

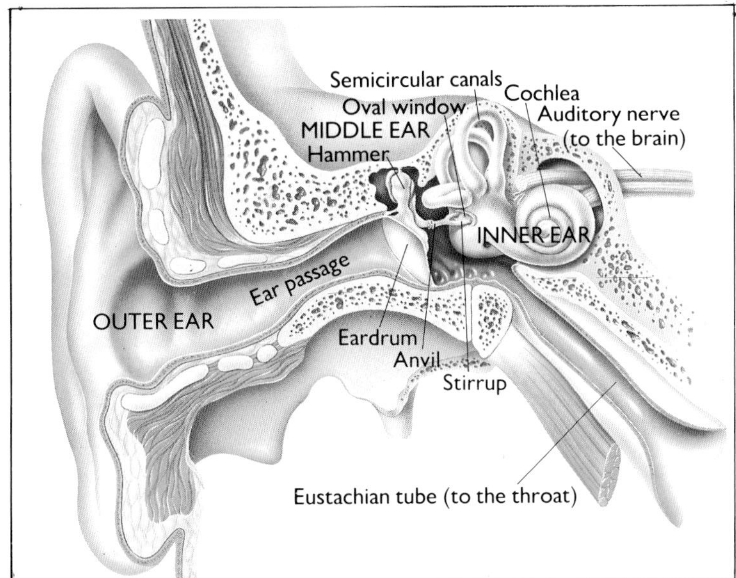

◀ *This picture shows the main parts of the outer, middle, and inner ear. The eustachian tube helps to keep air pressure the same on both sides of the eardrum.*

Earth

Our Earth is the fifth largest of the PLANETS that move around the SUN. Seen from space, the Earth looks like a giant ball. Land and WATER cover the surface, and AIR surrounds the Earth. (See pages 218–219.)

Earthquake

In some places, buildings sometimes topple over because the ground starts trembling. This trembling is called an earthquake. About half a million earthquakes happen every year. Most are so weak that

Continued on page 220.

FAMOUS EARTHQUAKES
Shensi Province, China, 1556: Over 800,000 people perished—more than in any other earthquake.
Lisbon, Portugal, 1755: About 60,000 people died, and shocks were felt as far away as Norway.
San Francisco, 1906: An earthquake and the fires it caused destroyed the center of the city.
Kwanto Plain, Japan, 1923: Some 570,000 buildings collapsed. This was the costliest earthquake ever when measured by damage to property.
Northwest Armenia, 1988: More than 55,000 people died.

EARTH

As far as we know, the Earth is the only planet that supports life. Our world is a medium-sized planet, orbiting a star (the Sun) along with eight other planets. What makes our Earth unique are its atmosphere and its water. Together, they make possible a rich variety of animal and plant life. Seen from space, Earth can look mostly covered by ocean, wreathed in swirling clouds. Land covers only about one quarter of the planet's surface. Beneath the surface is an intensely hot, dense core.

If the Earth were the size of a basketball, the highest land masses such as the Himalayas would be no higher than a coat of paint on the ball. The deepest ocean trenches would be almost invisible scratches in the paint.

Although the Earth is between 4 and 5 billion years old, no rocks that old have ever been found. It is thought that the Earth's original rocks have all been worn away. Rocks found in the United States have been dated at about 3,800,000,000 years old.

EARTH'S VITAL STATISTICS

Age: about 4.6 billion years
Weight: about 6,000 million million tons.
Diameter: from Pole to Pole through the Earth's center: 7,926 miles (12,756 km); across the Equator through the Earth's center: 7,927 miles (12,757 km)
Circumference: around the Poles: 24,860 miles (40,007 km); around the Equator: 24,900 miles (40,070 km)
Area of water: about 139,500,000 sq. miles (361 million sq. km) – 71 percent
Area of land: about 57,400,000 sq. miles (149 million sq km) – 29 percent
Volume: 4,440,064 million cu. miles (1,084,000 million cubic km)

INSIDE THE EARTH

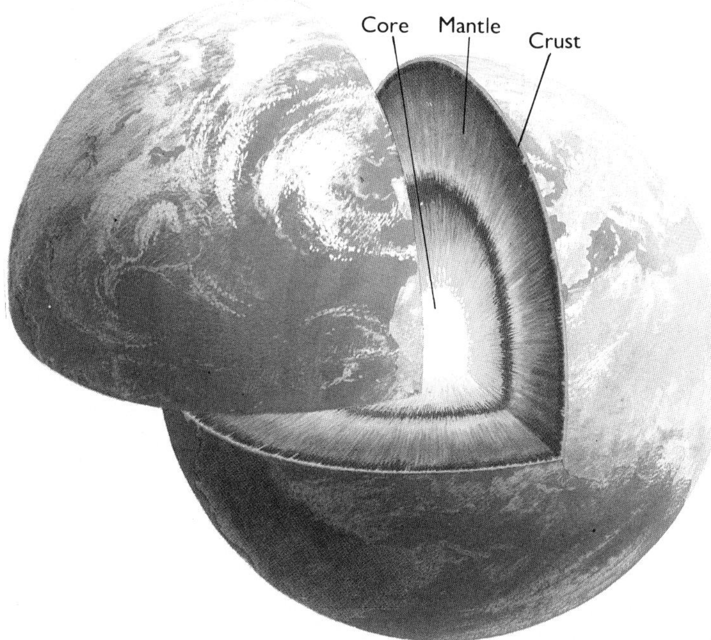

The Earth's **outer core** lies below the mantle and above the inner core. It is 1,400 miles (2,240 km) thick. The outer core is made mainly of metals, under enormous pressure and so hot they are molten (melted). Four-fifths of it may be iron and nickel. The rest is probably silicon.

The **inner core** is a solid ball, about 1,516 miles (2,440 km.) across. Like the outer core, it may be made mainly of iron and nickel. The core temperature 6,692°F (3,700°C) and the pressure there is 1,900 tons per sq. inch (3,800 tons per sq. cm).

The **mantle** lies beneath the crust and above the outer core. Nearly 1,800 miles (2,900 km) thick, the mantle is made up of hot rocks. Temperature and pressure here are lower than in the core. Even so, much of the mantle rock is semi-molten.

The **crust** is the Earth's solid outer layer. It is up to 20 miles (30 km) beneath mountains, but only 3¾ miles (6 km) thick under the oceans. Its rocks float on the denser rocks of the mantle.

◀ *The Earth photographed from space. Cloud "swirls" are depressions—areas of low atmospheric pressure where warm tropical air meets cold polar air. Such views help weather experts to plot the paths of hurricanes and so give warning of dangerous storms. Astronauts see the Earth outlined by a black sky.*

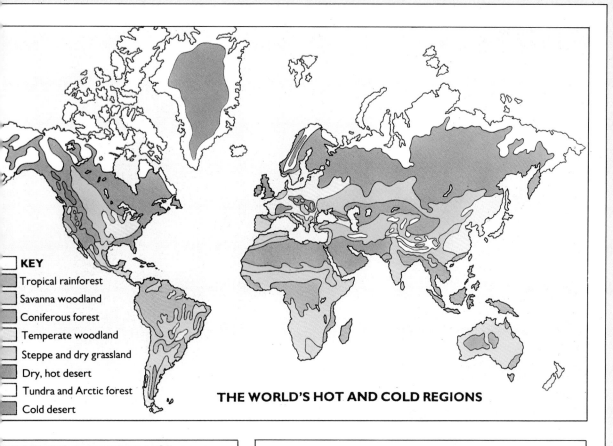

KEY
Tropical rainforest
Savanna woodland
Coniferous forest
Temperate woodland
Steppe and dry grassland
Dry, hot desert
Tundra and Arctic forest
Cold desert

THE WORLD'S HOT AND COLD REGIONS

VORLD FACTS AND FIGURES

Iighest mountain: Everest (Asia) 29,028 ft. 3,848 m)

.ongest river: Nile (Africa) 4,160 miles (6,695 km)

Greatest ocean depth: Marianas Trench (Pacific)cean) 36,198 ft. (11,033 m)

.argest desert: Sahara (Africa) 3,500,000 sq. miles),100,000 sq. km)

.argest ocean: Pacific 64,100,000 sq. miles 166,000,000 sq. km)

Iighest navigated lake: Titicaca (South America) 2,500 ft. (3,810 m) above sea level

.argest lake: Caspian Sea (Asia) 143,244 sq. miles 371,000 sq. km)

Iighest waterfall: Angel Falls (Venezuela, South merica) 3,212 ft. (979 m)

Iottest place: Al'Aziziyah in Libya, where 136°F 58°C) was recorded in 1922

Coldest place: Vostok, Antarctica, where -128.6°F -89.2°C) was recorded in 1983

Vettest place: Mt. Waialeale, Hawaii, with 460 ıches (11,680 mm) of rainfall a year

Driest place: Atacama Desert, Chile, with an verage rainfall of only 0.03 inch a year

HOW MOUNTAINS ARE FORMED

Fold mountains (below right) are thrown up when huge forces buckle rock layers into giant wrinkles. The Rocky Mountains and the Andes were formed in this way when the Earth's crustal plates collided. Some rocks were folded over onto others, and over millions of years, a new mountain range was born. Other kinds of mountains are formed when faults (breaks) in the Earth's crust take place.

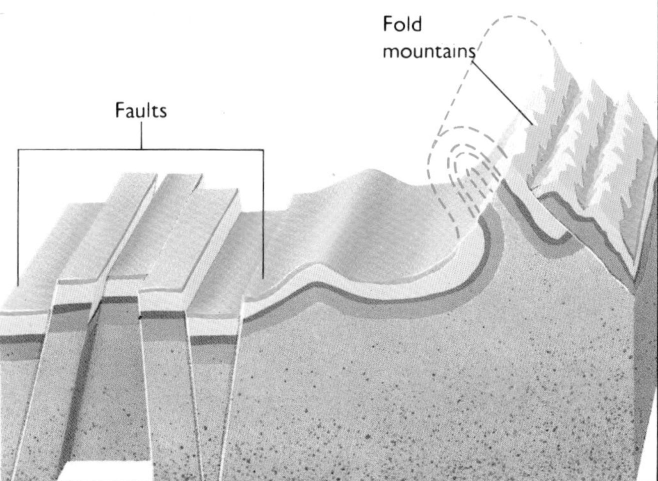

or more information turn to these articles: CONTINENTS; DESERT; GEOGRAPHY; GEOLOGY; ISLAND; LAKE; MOUNTAIN; OCEAN; RIVER; SOLAR 'STEM; VOLCANO; WEATHER.

▶ *A devasting earthquake in Alaska in 1964 was followed by a tsunami (tidal wave) that was almost as destructive.*

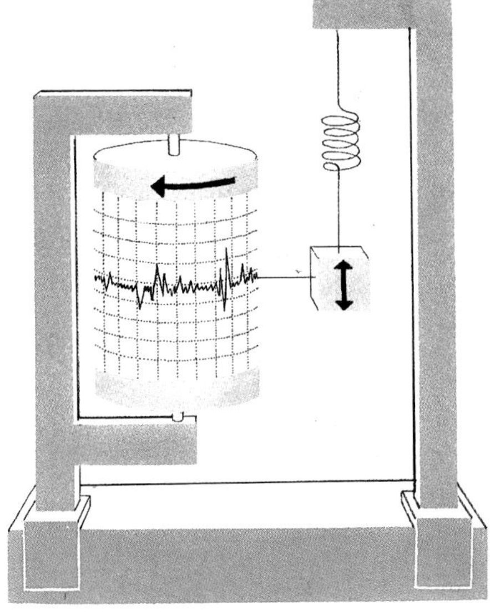

▲ *A seismograph shows earth tremors as wriggles in a line traced on a turning drum. A tremor vibrates the weight that holds the tracer.*

only special instruments called *seismographs* show that they have happened. Only one earthquake in 500 does any damage. But some earthquakes can cause terrible damage and suffering. Three-quarters of a million people are thought to have died when an earthquake hit the northeastern Chinese city of Tangshan in 1976.

Small tremors can happen when VOLCANOES erupt, when there is a landslide, or when the roof of an underground cave falls in. The largest earthquakes occur when one huge piece of the Earth's crust slips suddenly and crashes against another piece. This slipping may take place deep underground. But the shock travels up through the crust and sets the surface quaking.

A seabed earthquake may set off a huge ocean wave called a *tsunami*. These can rise higher than a house and travel faster than the fastest train. They occur most often in the Pacific Ocean.

We have eggs at Easter because they tell us of the new life that returns in nature at about this time. People have been exchanging eggs at Easter since ancient times. The Egyptians and Persians dyed eggs and gave them to their friends. The Persians believed that the Earth had hatched from a giant egg.

Earthworm *See* Worm

Easter

Easter is the day when Christians remember the resurrection of JESUS. Most Christians celebrate Easter on the Sunday following the first full moon that occurs after the first day of spring in the northern half of the world.

Echo

An echo is a SOUND bounced back from a wall or some other object. Sound travels at a known, fixed speed, so we can use echoes to find how far away some objects are. A ship's SONAR uses echoes to find the depth of the sea. Echoes help BATS to fly in the dark. RADAR depends on echoes from radio signals.

▲ *When you hear an echo, you hear the sound twice, or more. This is because the sound waves that reach your ears also bounce off nearby cliffs or walls. These waves reach your ears a second or two later, and you hear an echo.*

Eclipse

An eclipse happens when the shadow of one planet or moon falls on another. If the shadow hides all of the planet or moon, there is a total eclipse. If the shadow hides only a part, there is a partial eclipse.

The only eclipses you can easily see without a telescope take place when the Sun, Moon, and Earth are in line. When the Earth lies between the Sun and the Moon, the Earth's shadow falls on the Moon. This is an eclipse of the Moon. When the Moon lies between the Earth and the Sun, the Moon's shadow falls on a part of the Earth. An eclipse of the Sun, or solar eclipse, can be seen from that part.

The center of the shadow of a solar eclipse is called the *umbra*. It is a dark circle only about 170 miles (270 km) across. Inside the umbra, the eclipse is complete—the Moon completely hides the Sun. Around the umbra is a lighter shadow about 1,865 miles (3,000 km) across, in which part of the Sun can be seen.

▼ *A solar eclipse is caused as the Moon's shadow falls on the Earth, and a lunar eclipse as the Earth's shadow falls on the Moon. Only the umbra—the dark middle part of the Moon's shadow—is shown for a solar eclipse.*

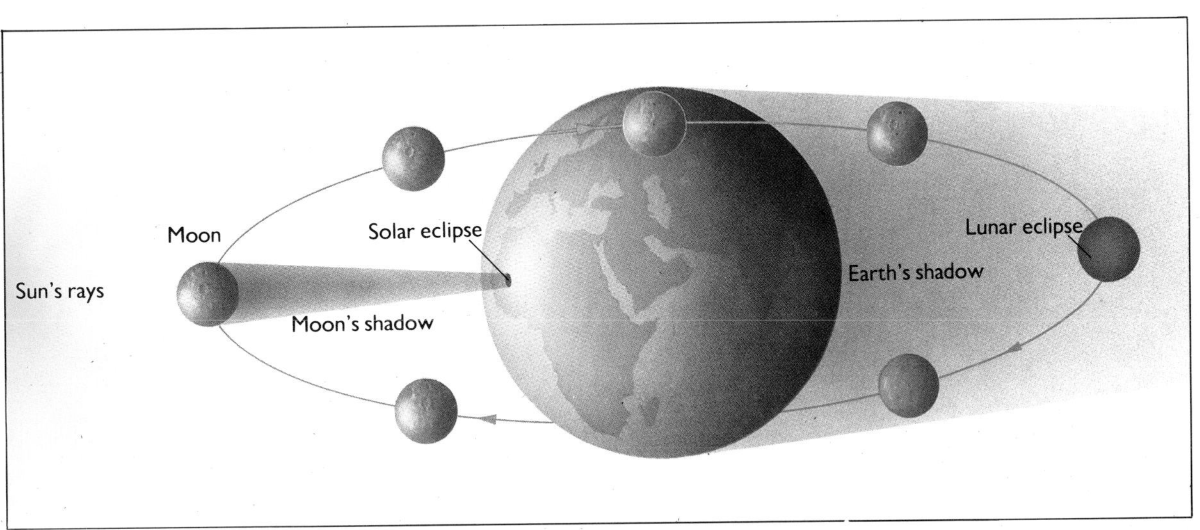

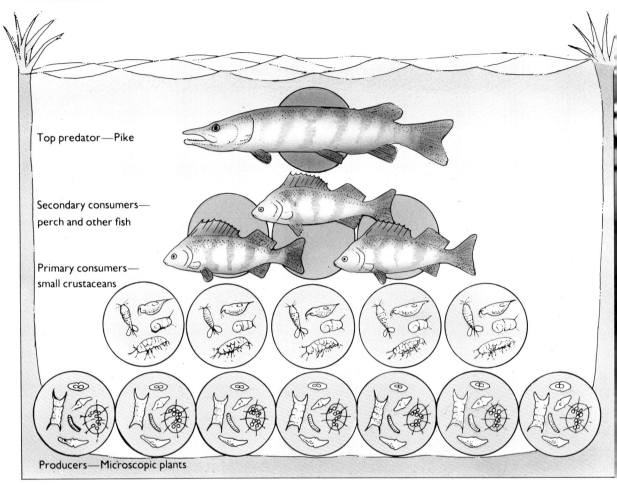

Top predator—Pike

Secondary consumers—perch and other fish

Primary consumers—small crustaceans

Producers—Microscopic plants

▲ *The food pyramid above gives some idea of just how much food it takes to keep the creatures in a pond alive and healthy. About 2,200 lbs. (1,000 kg) of plant life is needed to feed the animals that feed the fish that in turn feed just 2 lb. (1 kg) of pike.*

The introduction of animals from foreign lands can have harmful effects on the balanced ecology of a place. In 1850, three pairs of European rabbits were turned loose in Australia. With no natural enemies, the rabbits multiplied so quickly that they became a plague to farmers. Only the introduction of a disease that was fatal to rabbits halted the plague.

Ecology

Ecology is the study of living things and their surroundings. Scientists called ecologists try to find out how living things and their surroundings affect each other. Ecology shows us that most plants and animals can live only in a special set of surroundings such as a pond, field, forest, or desert. Within each place live plants that are suited to a certain soil, temperature, and so on. All the animals living there eat the plants, or each other. So the plants and animals are linked in what ecologists call a food web. If some kinds die out, those that eat them lose their food and may die too.

Everything in the world changes. Human inventions and discoveries are causing rapid changes. Sometimes the air is being filled with poisons; waterways are being polluted. Ecologists can help us to use the inventions and discoveries without making the world sick.

Economics 

Economics is the study of people's needs, such as food, clothes, and housing, and the ways in which people fill these needs. Economists study trade and money, and the ways in which a community's needs can be met. No country has enough resources to supply all the things that its people want. It has to decide the best way of using the resources that it has. Many economists believe that deciding how to economize (spend less) is the most important decision nations must make.

▲ *Business as usual on the Tokyo stock exchange. The buying and selling of shares is a basic part of the capitalist economic system, in which land, resources, and industries are owned by private individuals and companies, rather than by governments.*

Ecuador 

Ecuador is a country slightly bigger than Colorado, but only about eleven million people live there. It is in northwestern South America and lies on the equator. Its name is Spanish for *equator*. More than half of the people live in the high mountain valleys where sheep and llamas graze. The chief products are bananas, oil, coffee, rice, and sugar. The Galapagos Islands, 600 miles (960 km) off the Pacific coast of South America, belong to Ecuador.

Ecuador has been torn by many rebellions in its history and has been ruled by civilian and military dictatorships. Since 1979, the country has been governed by a democratic civilian government.

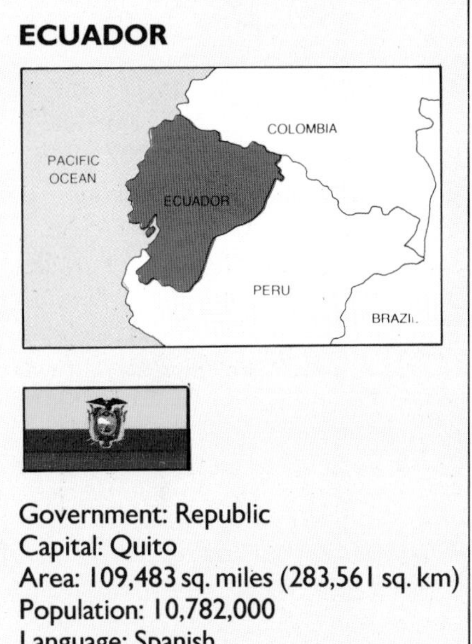

Government: Republic
Capital: Quito
Area: 109,483 sq. miles (283,561 sq. km)
Population: 10,782,000
Language: Spanish
Currency: Sucre

◀ *A woman sells leeks and plantains in a market in Ecuador. Indians and mestizos (of mixed Indian and European ancestry) make up about 80 percent of the population.*

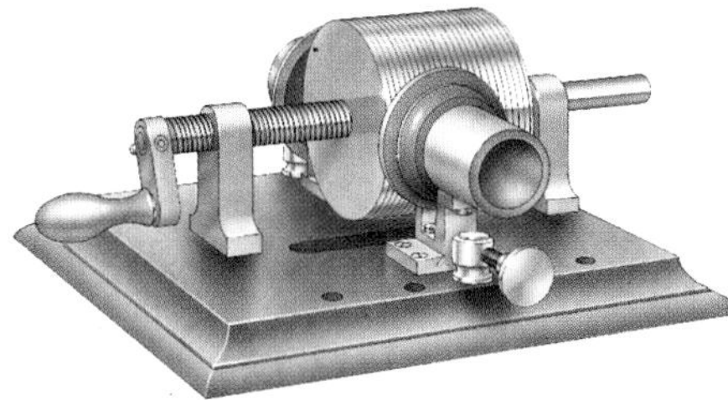

▲ *In 1877, Edison produced a hand operated "phonograph" that made recordings on tinfoil cylinders.*

► *Edward VIII and Mrs. Simpson, the American divorcee for whom he abdicated (gave up the throne).*

Edison, Thomas

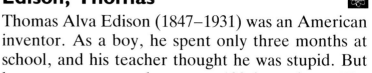

Thomas Alva Edison (1847–1931) was an American inventor. As a boy, he spent only three months at school, and his teacher thought he was stupid. But he went on to produce over 100 inventions. The most famous were the electric light and the phonograph for RECORDING and playing back sounds.

Edwards (Kings)

Nine kings of England were named Edward. Edward "The Confessor" (about 1002–1066) founded Westminster Abbey. Edward I (1239–1307) brought Wales under English rule. Edward II (1248–1327) was the first English Prince of Wales. Edward III (1312–1337) began the Hundred Years' War. Edward IV (1442–1483) took the crown from Henry VI in the Wars of the Roses. Edward V (1470–1483) was murdered in the Tower of London. Edward VI (1537–1553) reigned as a boy for only six years. Edward VII (1841–1910) was Prince of Wales for 60 years. Edward VIII (1894–1972) gave up the throne to marry Mrs. Wallis Simpson, a divorced American.

▲ *Two English kings named Edward: Edward the Confessor ruled from 1042 to 1066, before the Norman conquest. Edward VII was the eldest son of Queen Victoria.*

Eel

Eels are long, slim fish with fins like narrow ribbons. Some eels have tiny scales. Some are covered with slime. European and American freshwater eels swim thousands of miles to spawn far out in the

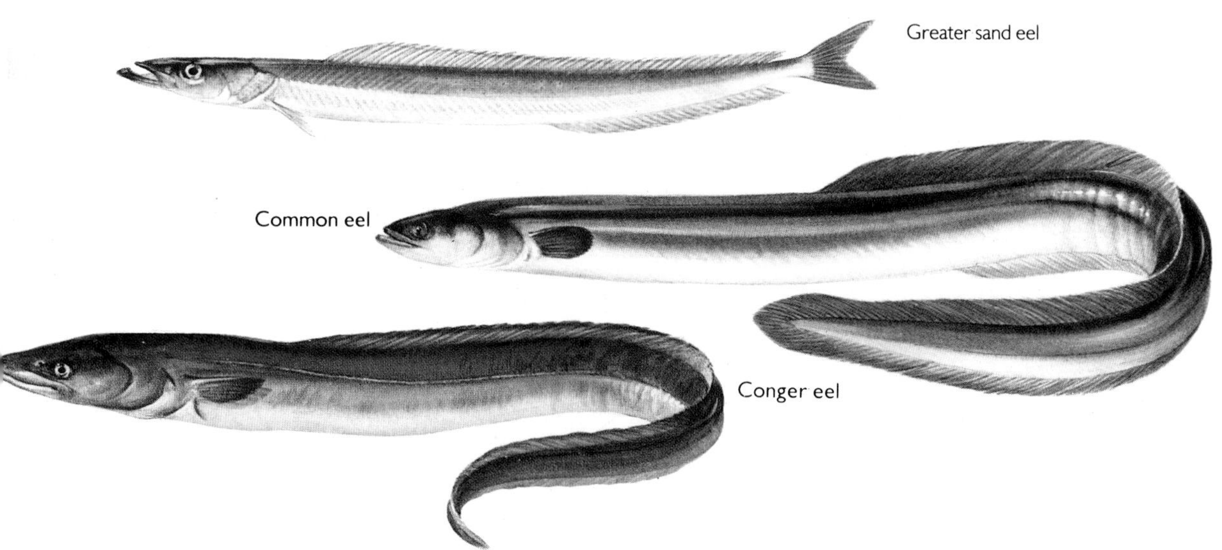

Atlantic Ocean. Then they die. The tiny, transparent young that hatch look nothing like their parents. These babies find their way all the way back to their parents' homes in America and Europe. There, they travel up rivers and streams. The young eels grow up in fresh water and stay there until they are ready for their long journey back across the Atlantic.

▲ *Eels look like snakes, but are actually fish. The common eel lives in lakes and rivers, but returns to the sea to breed. The conger eel and the greater sand eel both live in the sea.*

Egg

An egg is a female CELL that will grow into a new young plant or animal. Most eggs grow only if they are joined with, or fertilized by, male cells. In most MAMMALS, the fertilized eggs grow inside the mother's body, but birds and most reptiles and fish lay eggs that contain enough food to help the developing young grow inside the egg.

Egypt

Modern Egypt dates from A.D. 642 when Egypt was conquered by Muslim soldiers from Arabia. Egypt is now a Muslim, mainly Arab, country. It has over 50 million people, more than any other nation in Africa. No other African city is as large as Cairo, Egypt's capital. But Egyptians still depend upon the waters of the NILE River, which made Egypt great.

In 1979, Egypt signed a peace treaty with ISRAEL. This agreement was disliked by other Arab states, leaving Egypt isolated from its Arab neighbors.

EGYPT

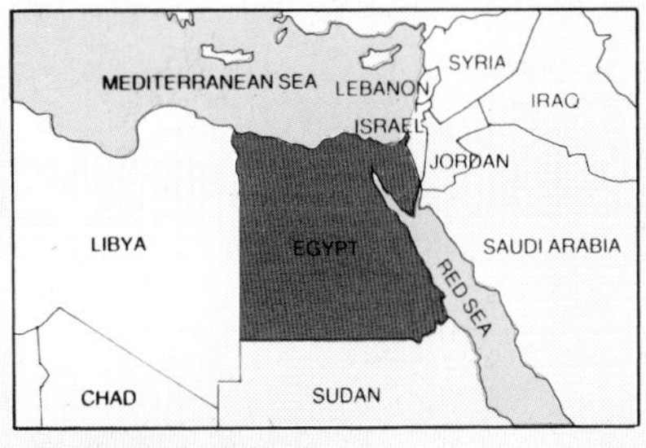

Government: Republic
Capital: Cairo
Area: 386,650 sq. miles (1,001,449 sq. km)
Population: 53,153,000
Language: Arabic
Currency: Egyptian pound

Egypt, Ancient

About 5,000 years ago, the ancient Egyptians began to build one of the world's first great civilizations. For the next 2,500 years, ancient Egypt was one of the strongest, richest nations on Earth.

The people who made Egypt great were short, slim, dark-skinned men and women with dark hair. They probably numbered no more than six million. Scarcely any of them lived in the hot sand and rock deserts that cover most of Egypt. Almost all the people settled by the NILE River, which runs from south to north across the land.

Each year, the river overflowed and left rich mud on nearby fields. Farmers learned to dig and plow the fields. They could grow two crops a year in the

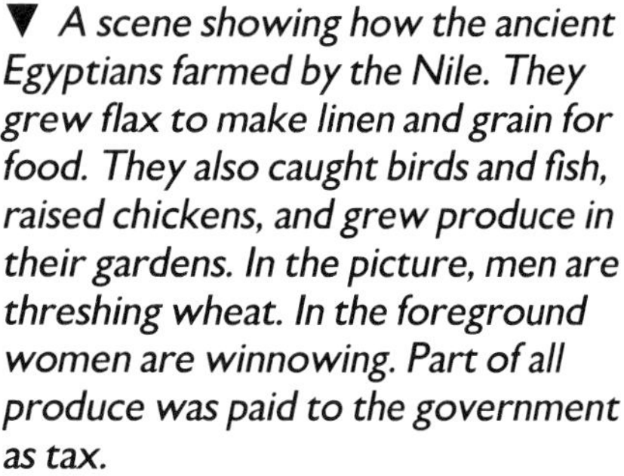

▼ *A scene showing how the ancient Egyptians farmed by the Nile. They grew flax to make linen and grain for food. They also caught birds and fish, raised chickens, and grew produce in their gardens. In the picture, men are threshing wheat. In the foreground women are winnowing. Part of all produce was paid to the government as tax.*

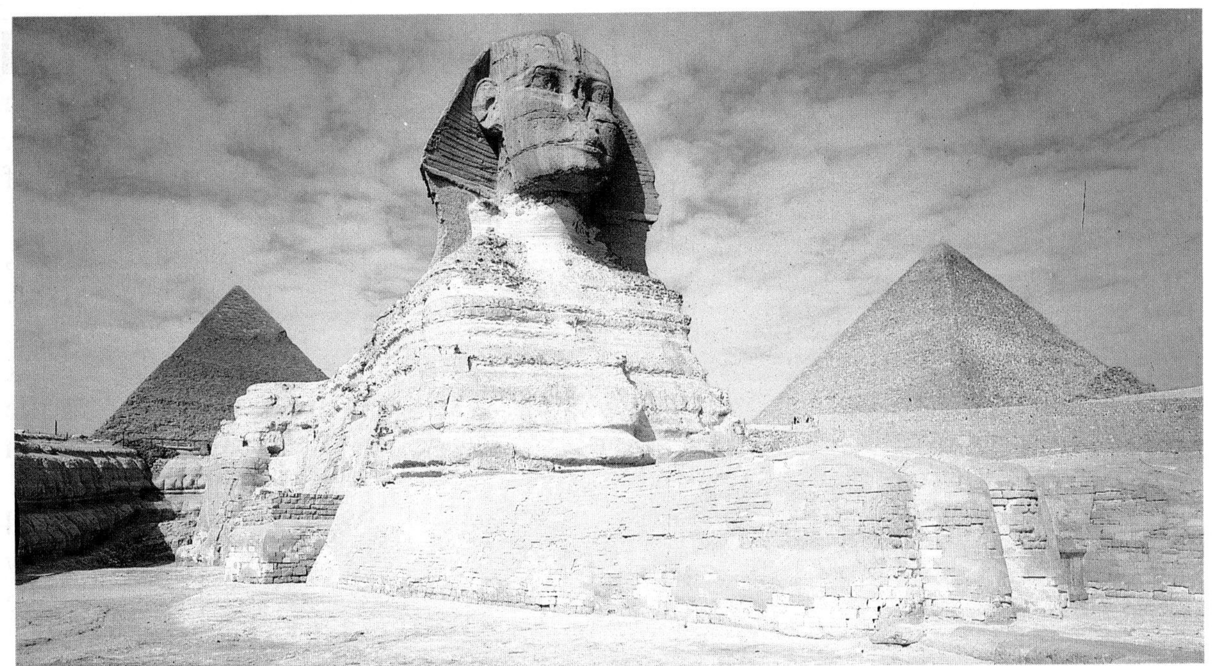

warm, fertile soil. The farmers grew more than enough grain, fruit, and vegetables to feed themselves. The rest of the food helped to feed Egyptian craftsmen, miners, merchants, priests, noble families, and the PHARAOHS who ruled over the entire land.

Most Egyptians were poor and lived in mud-brick huts with palm-leaf roofs. Rich Egyptians lived in large, well-furnished houses and had meat and cakes to eat. They wore fine clothes and jewels.

The most splendid buildings in the land were tombs and temples. Thousands of workers toiled for years to build the mighty PYRAMIDS. In each such tomb, Egyptians would place the mummy (preserved body) of a pharaoh. They believed the dead went on living, so they buried food and furniture beside each mummy. Thieves later emptied almost all the tombs. But the boy pharaoh TUTANKHAMUN'S tomb shows us what royal burials were like.

The dry Egyptian air has preserved HIEROGLYPHICS written on fragile paper made from the papyrus plant. Paintings and hieroglyphics tell us a great deal about how the ancient Egyptians lived. They also left many fine statues.

In time, foreign armies using iron weapons defeated the Egyptians. Their land fell under foreign rule after 525 B.C.

▲ *The sphinx is an imaginary creature found in the folk tales of many ancient peoples. Egyptian sphinxes combined the body of a beast—usually a lion—with the head of the ruling pharaoh. The most famous sphinx is the one shown above. It guards the great pyramid of Khafre at Giza, 6 miles (10 km) from Cairo. It is 240 ft. (73 m) long and about 66 ft. (20 m) high. Unfortunately, the sphinx's nose is missing. It was used by soldiers for target practice.*

Several times during the Twentieth Egyptian Dynasty, the workmen building a tomb for the pharaoh were not paid their food and other goods on time. The men went on strike. They marched to the temple where supplies were kept and sat down outside calling for bread. They soon got what they wanted, because it was unthinkable that the pharaoh's tomb should not be finished on time.

Einstein, Albert

Albert Einstein (1879–1955) was a great scientist who was born in Germany. His theory of relativity was a new way of looking at time, space, matter, and ENERGY. Einstein showed that a small amount of matter could be changed into a vast amount of energy. This made it possible for people to use NUCLEAR ENERGY.

Eisenhower, Dwight David

Dwight D. Eisenhower (1890–1969) was the 34th president of the United States. He served from 1953 to 1961. He was also a successful soldier. He was the commander of the Allied forces in WORLD WAR II. His most important job was the D-DAY invasion in 1944, when American and British soldiers landed in France to defeat the Germans. Later, he was head of NATO, a military union between the Western powers against the Soviet Union. As president, his biggest problems were with the Soviet Union. This was the Cold War, when the United States and the Soviet Union were fierce opponents. He had fewer problems at home. All through his presidency, the country prospered.

DWIGHT D. EISENHOWER

Thirty-fourth President 1953–1961
Born: Denison, Texas
Education: U.S. Military Academy, West Point, New York
Occupation: Army officer
Political Party: Republican
Buried: Eisenhower Center Chapel, Abilene, Kansas

Elasticity

When you pull a rubber band, it stretches. When you let it go, it springs back to its original size. It is elastic—it has elasticity. If you drop a rubber ball, the part of the ball that hits the ground is flattened. Then the ball springs back into its original round shape. As this happens, the ball pushes on the ground and it jumps up—it bounces. The ball has elasticity.

Elasticity happens because the molecules that make up the elastic material like to stay at a certain distance from each other. If they are squeezed more tightly together, they immediately push apart. If they are pulled apart, they want to get together again. All solids and liquids have some elasticity. Even a steel ball bounces a little when it hits a concrete floor.

SEE IT YOURSELF

Air has elasticity, too. It can be squeezed into a container, and the energy stored in it can be used to drive machines such as pneumatic drills and hammers. You can feel the elasticity of air by putting your thumb over the end of a bicycle pump and pushing the pump handle.

Electricity 

Electricity is the kind of ENERGY that powers electric trains, vacuum cleaners, radios, television sets, and many more devices.

The electricity that we use flows through wires as electric CURRENT. Current flows when tiny particles called electrons jump between the ATOMS that make up the metal in the wire. Current can flow only if a wire makes a complete loop called a circuit. If a gap is made in the circuit, the current stops flowing. Switches are simply devices that open and close gaps in circuits.

BATTERIES produce electric current that can be used to start cars, light flashlight bulbs, and work radios. But most of the electricity we use is produced in POWER PLANTS. In a power plant GENERATOR, coils of wire are made to rotate between powerful magnets. This makes electric current flow through the coils of wire. This current then flows through other long wires to our homes.

In 1752, the American scientist and statesman Benjamin Franklin wondered whether lightning and thunder were caused by electricity. During a thunderstorm, he flew a kite with a metal tip joined to a silk string. He attached a key to the string at a point near the ground. In a few seconds, Franklin had the answer to his question. When he touched the key, there was a spark. He could *feel* the electricity. But don't try this; it is very dangerous!

▼ *Electricity travels from a power station through a network of high-voltage power lines. It passes through transformers and substations, where the current is changed to the lower voltage used in homes and factories.*

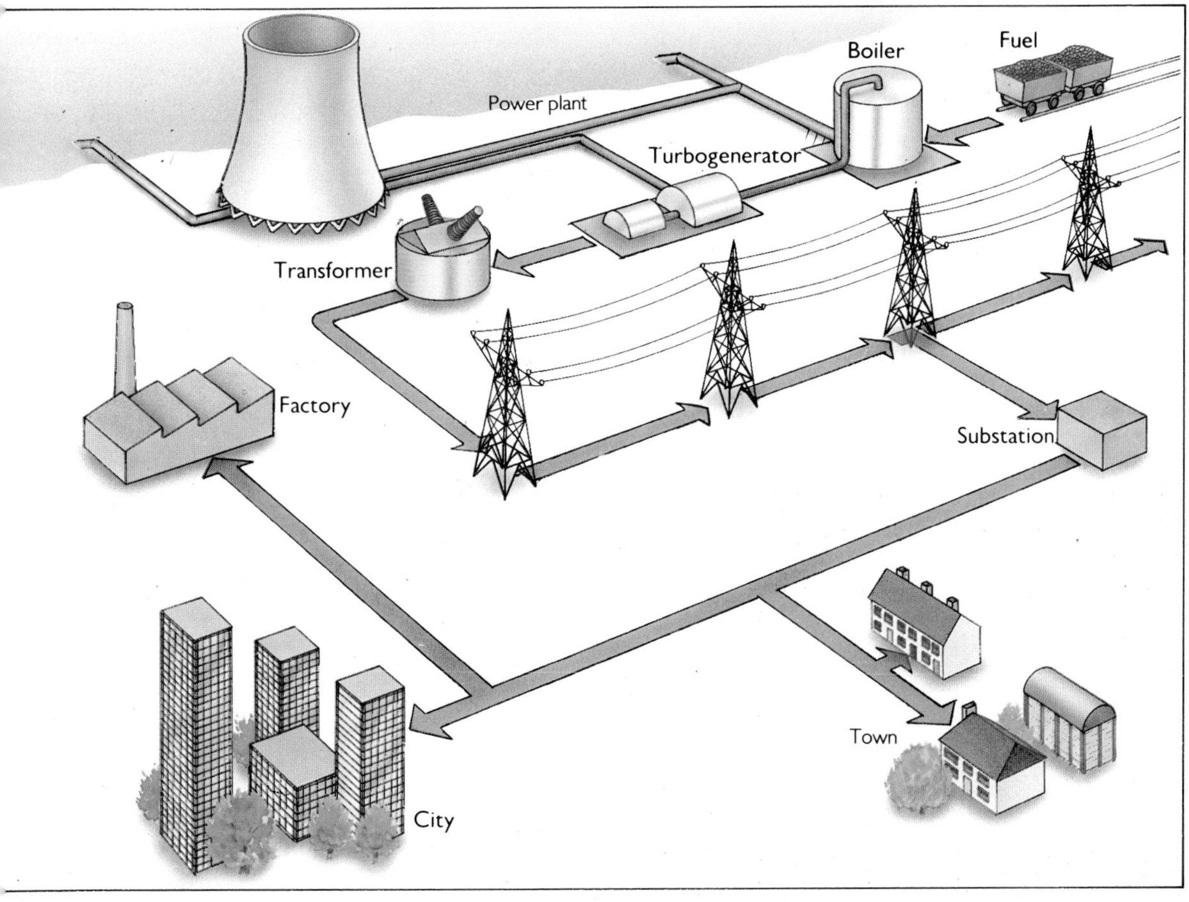

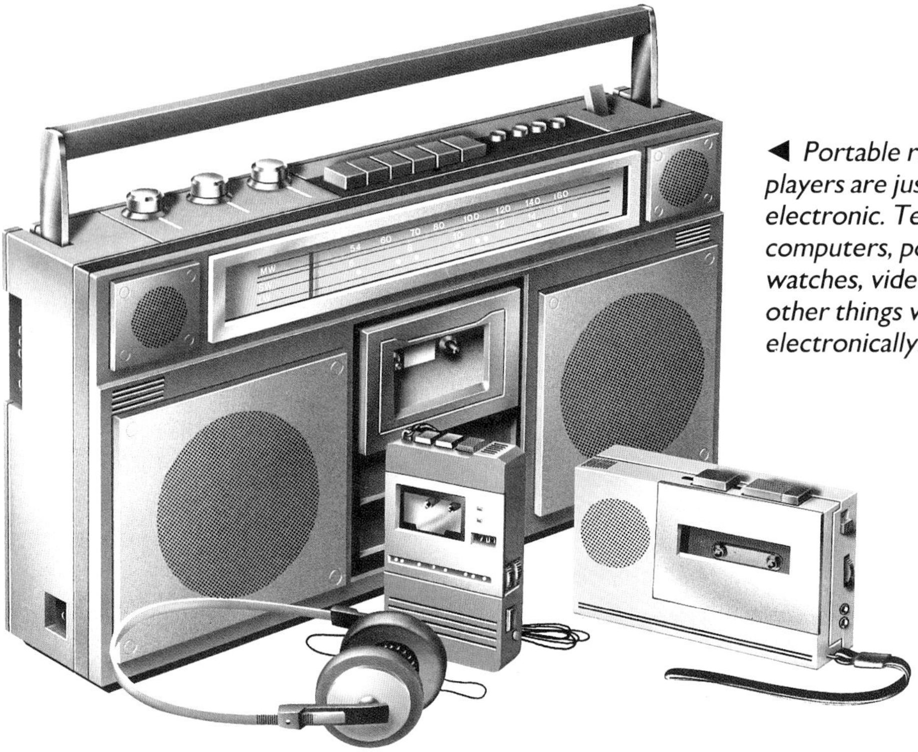

◀ *Portable radios and cassette players are just two devices that are electronic. Television sets, home computers, pocket calculators, digital watches, video recorders, and many other things we use every day work electronically.*

Electronics

Electronics is an important part of the study of ELECTRICITY. It deals with the way in which tiny particles called electrons flow through certain CRYSTALS, GASES, or a VACUUM. Electronic devices like TRANSISTORS and SILICON CHIPS are used in such things as COMPUTERS, RADAR, television sets, and radios. Electronics help us to see the smallest living things, to guide planes, and to do difficult sums instantly. Without electronics, space travel would be impossible.

▼ *This pellet of the element plutonium shines from the glow of its own radioactivity. Plutonium (Pu) does not occur in nature except in tiny quantities from the decay of Uranium-238.*

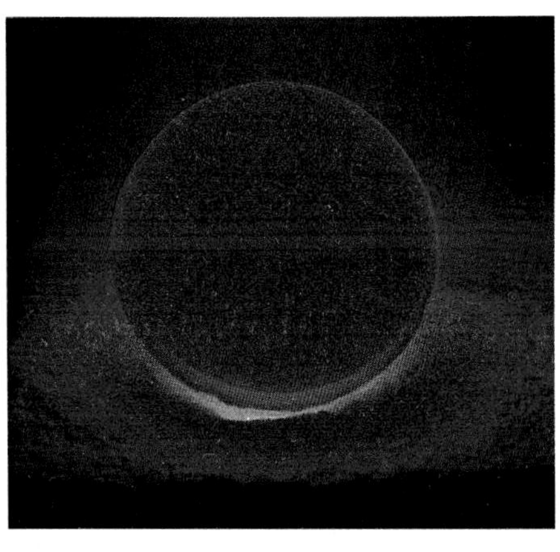

Element

Your own body and everything you see around you is composed (made up) of chemical ingredients called elements. In each element, all the ATOMS are of the same kind. You can join different elements to make more complicated substances called COMPOUNDS, but you cannot break an element into a simpler kind of substance.

Chemists have found more than 100 differen

elements. Ninety-two of these occur naturally. Scientists have produced other elements in laboratories. At ordinary temperatures, some elements are *gases*, some are *liquids*, and some are *solids*.

OXYGEN is the most plentiful element on Earth. Half of the Earth's crust and most of your body is made of oxygen.

Elephant

Elephants are the largest living land animals. A big bull (male) elephant may stand twice as high as a man and weigh as much as seven family cars. An elephant has larger ears, thicker legs, a longer nose, and longer teeth than any other creature. Its skin is nearly as thick as the heel of a man's shoe.

Baby elephants stand no taller than big dogs. Elephants are fully grown after 20 years. They live almost as long as people.

Indian elephants can be trained to move heavy loads. African elephants are harder to tame. Many thousands have been killed just for the IVORY of their tusks. Today, most are protected by law.

▲ *The African elephant has larger ears and tusks than the Indian, or Asiatic, elephant. It also has a different-shaped back.*

▼ *The African elephant protects the herd with an aggressive display—ears forward and trunk raised.*

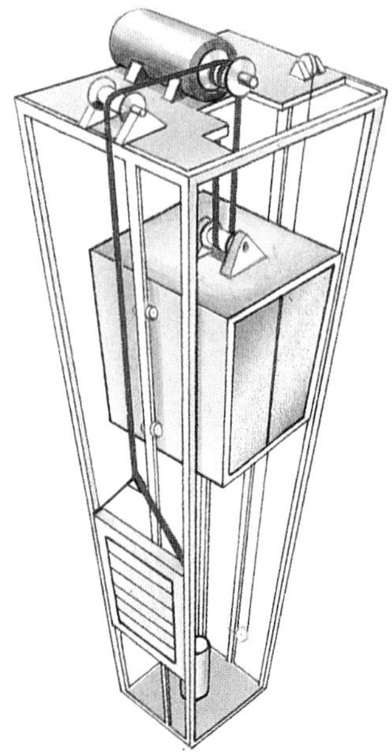

▲ *Modern elevators are complex machines, often controlled by computers. But all elevators have the basic parts shown in the diagram. The car is wound up and down by an electric motor. A counterweight at the other end of the steel cable balances the weight of the car. A safety rope connected to the car operates a governor. Should the car fall, the governor throws a switch which causes the car to grip the guide rails and stop.*

▼ *Escalators can move as fast as 13 ft. (4 m) a second. The steps are joined to a continuous, moving chain. At the end, the steps go underneath the escalator and back to the beginning.*

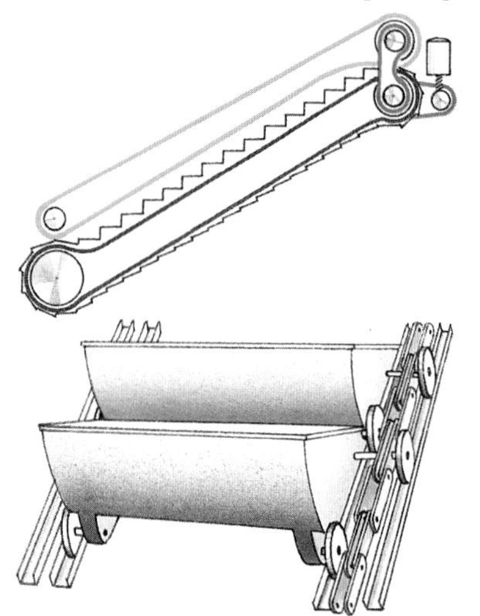

Elevators and escalators

Elevators and escalators are machines for transporting people or goods upstairs—or downstairs.

Elevators are metal cars like boxes that travel vertically in shafts. Their doors open and close automatically. They are used in many office and apartment buildings. Some elevators can travel at more than 500 ft. (150 m) per minute, There are many different types of elevator, but most are powered by electricity. All have important safety features in case of accident. The first elevators were invented in the 1800s. They were powered by steam, but were not very reliable. Electric elevators were introduced in the 1890s. The first completely automatic elevators were invented in the 1950s.

Escalators are moving stairways. As they reach the top or bottom, the steps flatten to let people on or off. They are used in department stores and malls, at airports, and at subway stations. The first escalator was installed in 1900. Today, they are used throughout the world.

El Greco

El Greco (1541–1614) was a Greek painter who was born on the island of Crete during the RENAISSANCE. His real name was Domenikos Theotokopoulos—El Greco simply means "the Greek." He soon left Crete and went to Venice. Later, he lived in Spain, in a town called Toledo. His paintings have strange, swirling compositions and bright colors.

Eliot, Thomas Stearns

T.S. Eliot (1888–1965) was a poet, playwright, and critic. Some say he was the most important poet of the 20th century. Though he was born in the United States, he spent most of his life in England. In 1927 he became a British citizen.

His most famous poem is called *The Waste Land*. In it, Eliot wrote of the need for people to have strong moral and religious beliefs. The poem is complex and combines references to myths, history, and literature, as well as scenes of modern life.

Elizabeth I

Elizabeth I (1533–1603) was a famous English queen. She never married, but she reigned for 45 years with the help of wise advisers. She worked for peace between quarreling religious groups, but had her rival, MARY QUEEN OF SCOTS, put to death. Elizabeth's seamen crushed the Spanish Armada and made England powerful at sea. Great English playwrights, poets, and scholars lived in her reign. People often call it "the Elizabethan Age."

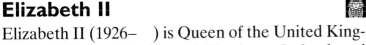

▲ Elizabeth I reviews her troops at Tilbury before the arrival of the Spanish Armada. With the defeat of the Armada, England gained in wealth and confidence.

Elizabeth II

Elizabeth II (1926–   ) is Queen of the United Kingdom of Great Britain and Northern Ireland and head of the COMMONWEALTH. Her husband is the Duke of Edinburgh. Her eldest son is Charles, Prince of Wales.

EL SALVADOR

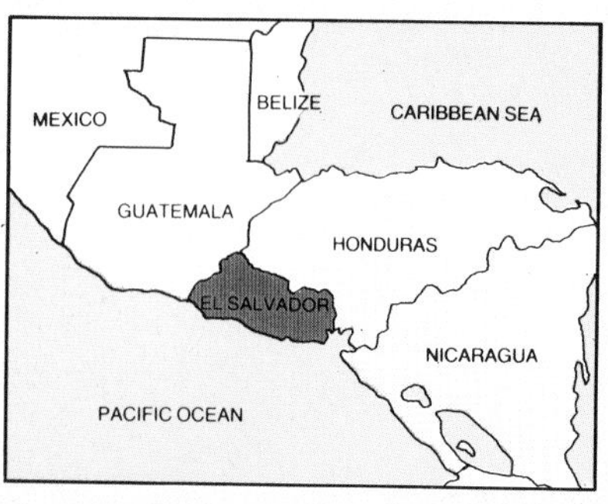

Government: Republic
Capital: San Salvador
Area: 8,124 sq. miles (21,041 sq. km)
Population: 5,000,000
Language: Spanish
Currency: Colón

El Salvador

El Salvador is Central America's smallest country, but it has more people per square mile than any other country in Central America. Most of the people are *mestizos* (of mixed Indian and European descent). Their main occupation is farming. Leading crops are coffee, cotton, corn, and sugar. The capital is San Salvador.

El Salvador has had several clashes with its neighbor Honduras, and there is a continuing struggle in El Salvador between government forces and left-wing guerrillas.

▶ *Despite their political troubles, the people of El Salvador still enjoy their festivals.*

▼ *This photograph of Ralph Waldo Emerson was taken in 1876.*

Emerson, Ralph Waldo

Ralph Waldo Emerson (1803–1882) was a critic and writer whose work was important for the development of many American thinkers and writers in the 1800s. He also wrote many poems.

He was born in Boston in a poor family. His father died when he was young, and two of his brothers also died young. Another was insane.

Emerson took his ideas from many sources, but he always wanted to show that men must be strong and not afraid to do what they believed in.

Emu

The ostrich is the only bird that is larger than this big Australian bird. An emu is as tall as a man, but not as heavy. Emu feathers are thick and dark. Its wings are small, and an emu cannot fly. But it can run as fast as a horse on its long, strong legs.

Emus eat leaves and insects. Big herds of emus sometimes attack farm crops.

Each female lays up to 10 green eggs on the ground. The male sits on the eggs and later guards the chicks.

▲ *Emus are now rare in their native Australia, though they are being bred successfully in captivity.*

Energy

Having energy means being able to do work. MUSCLES and machines have mechanical energy—they can move loads. Energy exists in several forms. There are two main kinds—*potential energy* and *kinetic energy*. Potential energy is the energy of position—stored energy. For example, the water in a high dam has potential energy. Then, when the water falls through pipes and works turbines to make electricity, it has kinetic energy—energy of movement. Other forms of energy are electrical, heat, chemical, sound, radiant, and nuclear. These forms can be changed into each other. For example, the chemical energy of gasoline is turned into kinetic energy as it moves a car's pistons; to electrical energy in the car's generator to work the head-

▼ *When an archer draws back a bow, he or she gives it a store of potential energy. As the arrow is released, the potential energy is turned into kinetic (moving) energy.*

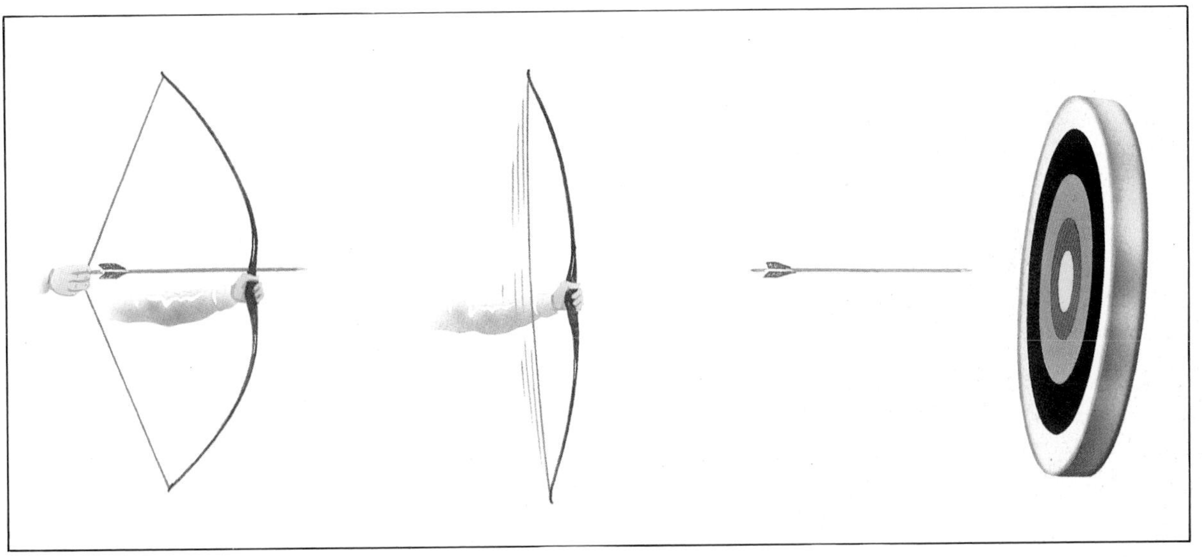

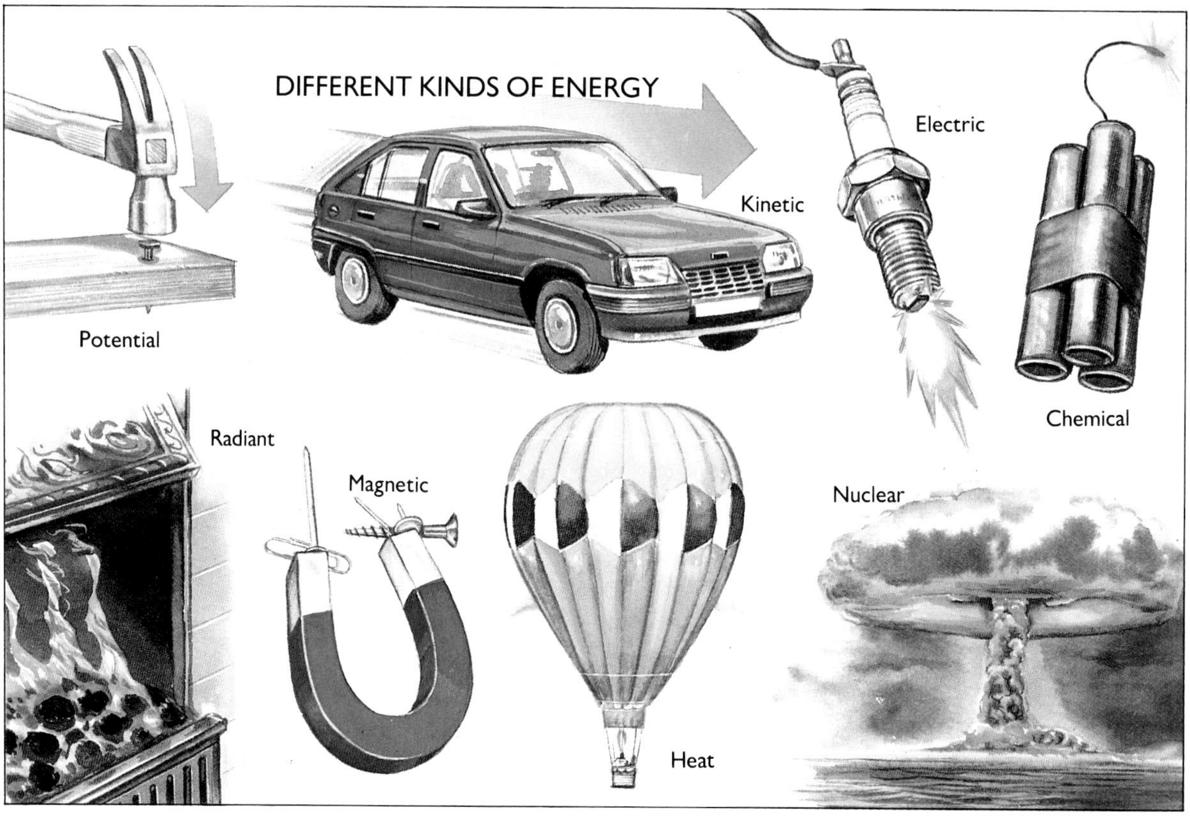

DIFFERENT KINDS OF ENERGY

Potential

Kinetic

Electric

Chemical

Radiant

Magnetic

Heat

Nuclear

▲ *Energy can exist in many forms. All forms of energy can do work.*

lights and sound the car's horn, and so on. At every stage, some energy is turned into heat.

Radiant energy from the Sun gives us most of our energy on Earth. Coal, oil, and natural gas—the fossil fuels—were formed from plants and animals that depended for their life on the Sun's light and warmth.

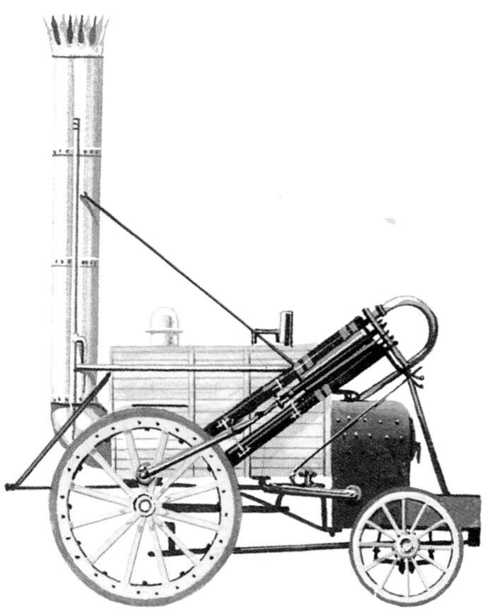

▼ *Stephenson's* Rocket *(1829) was the first locomotive to use steam power successfully as a means of fast travel.*

Engine

Engines are devices that change potential (stored) energy into useful energy that does work. People have used simple engines such as windmills and water wheels for hundreds of years.

In the 1700s, the STEAM ENGINE took over to drive everything from ships, trains, and cars to all kinds of factory machinery. Steam still drives many machines—such as the steam turbines in nuclear power plants.

INTERNAL-COMBUSTION ENGINES—gasoline engines and DIESEL ENGINES—are easier to handle than steam engines and light enough to be fitted in aircraft. After them came JET and ROCKET engines.

Engineering

Engineers do a great many different types of jobs. Mining engineers find useful MINERALS and take them from the ground. Metallurgical engineers separate METALS from unwanted substances and make them usable. Chemical engineers use chemicals to make such things as explosives, paint, plastics, and soap. Civil engineers build bridges, tunnels, roads, railroads, ports, airports, and so on. Mechanical engineers make and use machines. They design JET ENGINES and factory machinery. Electrical engineers work with devices that produce and use electricity. Some specialize in building a particular type of GENERATOR. Others, such as those who design and build computers, are known as electronic engineers. Electronic engineers form the newest branch of electrical engineering. Power engineers maintain machinery in power plants. Most kinds of engineering fall into one or other of these groups.

The ancient Egyptians were the first real engineers. When the pyramids were being built about 2500 B.C., Egyptian workmen were already using tools such as the lathe. They smelted and cast metals. Their quarrying and stoneworking techniques were so advanced that they could fit blocks of stone weighing 2½ tons so closely together that a hair couldn't be passed between them.

▼ *Engineers design big machines such as this excavator to save time, labor, and cost. One such machine can do more work in an hour than a hundred men using hand tools could do in a day.*

▲ *As an island nation, the English have had a long association with the sea. This is a small fishing village in Yorkshire.*

England 

England is the largest country in the UNITED KINGDOM of Great Britain and Northern Ireland. If Great Britain were divided into five equal parts, England would fill three of them. England's neighbors are Scotland and Wales, but most of England is surrounded by sea. Green fields spread over the plains and low hills that cover most of the country. In the north and west, there are mountains with moors and forests. Most English people live and work in big cities like London, Birmingham, Liverpool, and Manchester.

England gets its name from the Angles, a Germanic people who, like the Saxons, sailed to the island and settled there about 1,500 years ago.

ENGLAND

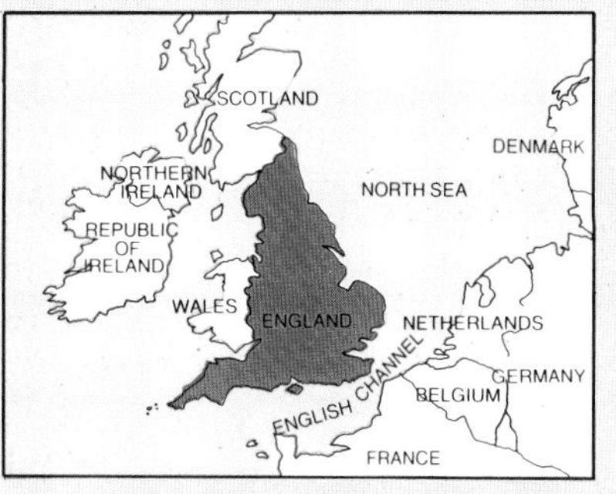

Area: 50,858 sq. miles (131,722 sq. km)
Population: 49,000,000
Highest point: Scafell Pike 3,224 ft. (982 m)
Greatest width: 322 miles (518 km)
North to south: 356 miles (570 km)
Longest rivers: Thames 216 miles (348 km) Severn 211 miles (338 km)
Largest lake: Windermere

English Language 

More people speak English than any other language except Chinese. English is the main language spoken in the United Kingdom, Ireland, Australia, New Zealand, Canada, the United States, and some other countries. Altogether, more than 450 million people speak English as their everyday language. Another 100 million or more speak at least some English. Most English words come from old Anglo-Saxon, French, or Latin words.

Equator

The equator is an imaginary line around the world, halfway between the North Pole and the South Pole. A journey around the equator covers 24,900 miles (40,070 km). The word "equator" comes from an old Latin word meaning "equalizer." The equator divides the world into two equal halves. The half north of the equator is called the Northern Hemisphere. The half south of the equator is the Southern Hemisphere. Distances north and south of the equator are measured in degrees of latitude. The equator has a latitude of 0 degrees.

On the equator, nights are always as long as days. At noon, the sun always shines from directly or almost directly overhead. So all places on the equator are warm all through the year.

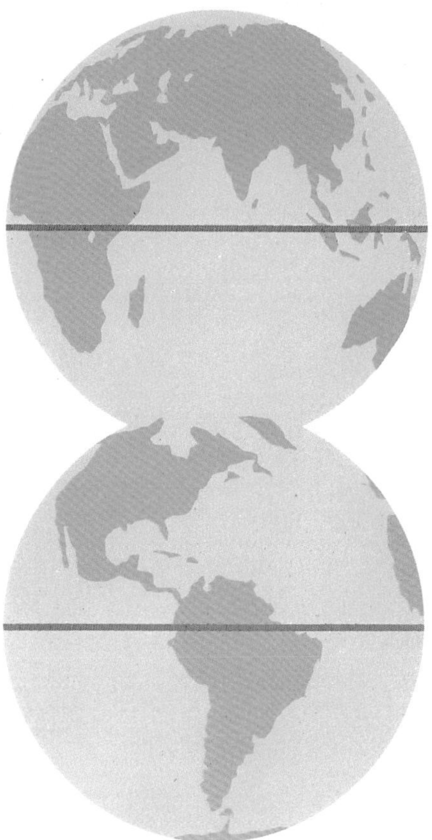

▲ *Europe and North America both lie north of the equator; Australasia and much of South America lie south.*

Equatorial Guinea

Equatorial Guinea is a small country on the west African coast. The largest territory is on the mainland, and there are several offshore islands. The largest island is Bioko, which has the country's capital. Most of the people speak Spanish, for the country was a Spanish possession until 1968.

EQUATORIAL GUINEA

NIGERIA
CAMEROON
EQUATORIAL GUINEA
GULF OF GUINEA
GABON

Government: Republic
Capital: Malabo
Area: 10,832 sq. miles (28,055 sq. km)
Population: 348,000
Language: Spanish
Currency: Ekuele

Ericson, Leif

Leif Ericson (11th century) was a Norse sailor who led what was probably the first European expedition to North America. According to old Norse stories, Leif first went ashore at a place where grapes were growing. He named it Vinland (Wineland). Some people think that Vinland was in northern Newfoundland.

Eskimo

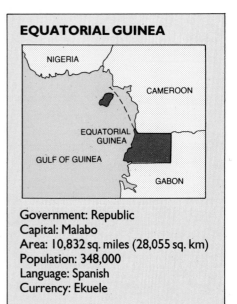

Eskimos are hardy people who live in the cold, Arctic lands of Greenland, North America, and northeast Asia. They have slanting eyes, a wide flat face, and a short, thick body with short arms and legs. This shape helps to keep them warm in the cold Arctic climate.

Eskimos once wore only fur clothes. Some lived in tents in summer and built snow homes called igloos for the winter. They made bows and arrows and harpoons, and hunted seals, whales, fish, seabirds, and deer. Eskimos paddled skin BOATS and canoes called kayaks. Many Eskimos no longer lead this kind of life. They now live and work in towns. Eskimos call themselves by words that mean "people"—*Inuit* or *Yuit*.

► *Nomads in Eritrea, in northeastern Ethiopia. One of the poorest of Ethiopia's provinces, Eritrea has been torn by civil war and famine since the 1960s.*

Estonia *See* Baltic States

Ethiopia

Ethiopia covers a huge area of the northeastern part of AFRICA. It was formerly called Abyssinia. Much of Ethiopia consists of high, cool tablelands. Here, Ethiopian farmers grow grain and coffee. The RED SEA coast in the north is one of the hottest places on Earth. Among Africa's countries, only Egypt and Nigeria have more people. Most Ethiopians are Christian. For years, Ethiopia has suffered from CIVIL WAR and drought. Famine is widespread, and there has been a worldwide campaign to raise money for relief and aid. In 1991, rebel armies took possession of the capital and announced plans for a coalition government.

ETHIOPIA

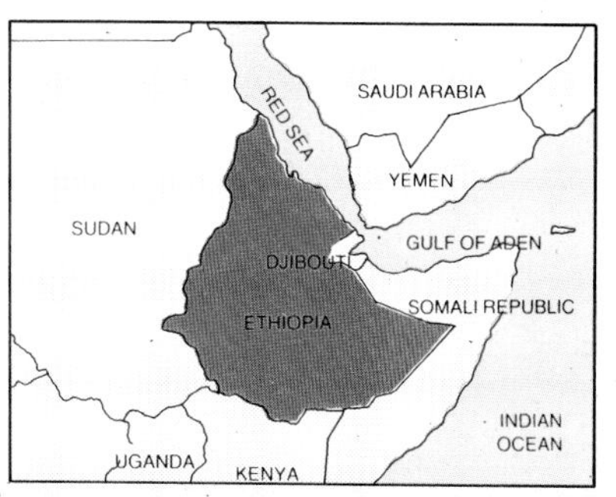

Government: Military
Capital: Addis Ababa
Area: 471,776 sq. miles (1,221,900 sq. km)
Population: 49,241,000
Language: Amharic
Currency: Ethiopian dollar

Europe

Europe is a peninsula sticking out from the western end of Asia. Some small peninsulas jut from the main one, and there are many offshore islands. Australia is the only continent smaller than Europe, but Europe holds more people than any continent except Asia.

European people have settled in the Americas, Australia, New Zealand, South Africa, and Siberia. European ideas and inventions helped shape the way of life of many people all around the world.

Mountains cross the countries of southern Europe. From west to east, there are the Pyrenees, Alps, Apennines, Balkans, Carpathians, Caucasus, and other ranges. The Caucasus has Mount Elbrus, Europe's highest peak.

In northern Europe, low mountains cover much of Iceland, Ireland, Scotland, Wales, Norway, and Sweden. Between the mountains of the north and south lies a great plain. Here flow Europe's longest rivers. The Volga, in Russia, is the longest of them all (2,300 miles/3,700 km).

All of Europe lies north of the hot tropics, and most of it lies south of the cold Arctic. So most of Europe does not have extremes of temperature. But Mediterranean lands have hot summers, and countries in the north and east have long, cold winters.

Shrubs and flowering plants grow in the far north. Next come the great northern forests of CONIFERS. Farther south lie most of Europe's farms and cities.

▲ *Europe has more advantages for people than any other continent. It has scarcely any desert, and a greater proportion of the land can be farmed than in any other continent. It is rich in coal and iron, essential for industry. Its climate is seldom either too hot or too cold.*

▼ *Like much of Mediterranean Europe, Italy's coast has wide bays and rocky headlands. Behind lie volcanic mountains, and hills cut into terraces for vineyards and olive groves.*

EUROPE

ARCTIC OCEAN
NORWEGIAN SEA
NORTH SEA
ATLANTIC OCEAN
BALTIC SEA
BLACK SEA
ADRIATIC SEA
MEDITERRANEAN SEA
English Channel
ICELAND
Reykjavik
FAROE IS.
SHETLAND IS.
ORKNEY IS.
Murmansk
Narvik
Arkhangelsk
KJOLEN MOUNTAINS
Trondheim
SWEDEN
FINLAND
L. Onega
Tampere
Vyborg
L. Ladoga
Sundsvall
NORWAY
Helsinki
St. Petersburg
Bergen
Oslo
Stockholm
Vänern
Stavanger
Novgorod
Yaroslavl
Aberdeen
Vättern
ESTONIA
Glasgow
Gothenburg
Edinburgh
Riga
LATVIA
Moscow
Belfast
UNITED KINGDOM
DENMARK
IRELAND
Dvina
Copenhagen
Malmö
LITHUANIA
Smolensk
Dublin
Manchester
Cork
NETHER-LANDS
Hamburg
Kaliningrad
RUSSI
Birmingham
Gdańsk
Vistula
Minsk
Cardiff
London
Amster-dam
Elbe
Poznań
Warsaw
Thames
Berlin
Rhine
Kharkov
Brussels
Bonn
GERMANY
POLAND
Kiev
Brest
Le Havre
BELGIUM
Frankfurt
Dnepr
Paris
LUX-EMBOURG
Prague
Kraków
Dneprpetrovsk
Seine
Dnestr
Nantes
Loire
Stuttgart
CZECHOSLOVAKIA
CARPATHIANS
ALPS
Vienna
Prut
Munich
Odessa
Saône
Bern
Zurich
Budapest
FRANCE
AUSTRIA
La Coruna
Bordeaux
Geneva
SWITZ-ERLAND
HUNGARY
Lyon
LIECHTENSTEIN
ROMANIA
Santander
Zagreb
Bilbao
Toulouse
Rhône
Turin
Po
Milan
Venice
Trieste
Bucharest
Oporto
Valladolid
Ebro
MONACO
Belgrade
Douro
ANDORRA
SAN MARINO
PYRENEES
Marseille
Nice
YUGOSLAVIA
Danube
PORTUGAL
Florence
BULGARIA
Lisbon
Madrid
Tagus
Corsica
ITALY
Dubrovnik
Sofia
Barcelona
Ajaccio
Rome
Istanbul
Guadiana
Valencia
ALBANIA
TURKEY
Tirana
Bari
Naples
SPAIN
Seville
Sardinia
Thessaloniki
Taranto
BALEARIC IS.
Cagliari
GREECE
Cádiz
Málaga
GIBRALTAR
Palermo
Messina
Sicily
Athens
MALTA
Crete
Capital Cities
0 100 200 300 400 miles
0 200 400 600 kilometers

▲ *This valley along the Moselle River in the Rhineland in Germany is one of the chief wine-producing regions in Europe. Vineyards can be seen on the hillside in the foreground.*

Much of Europe's wealth comes from its factories, farms, and mines. Europe's richest nations include Germany and Switzerland. The largest European country is Russia. It is also the largest country in the world. The smallest European country is the Vatican, in Rome.

European Community

This is a group of western European nations that work together to help goods, people, and money travel between countries in the Community. Its members are Belgium, Denmark, France, Germany, Ireland, Italy, Greece, Luxembourg, the Netherlands, Portugal, Spain and United Kingdom. The 12 nations aim to unite their economies and bring about political union of the democratic states.

Everest, Mount

Mount Everest is the world's highest peak. It rises 29,028 ft. (8,848 m) above sea level. The mountain stands in the HIMALAYAS on the borders of Nepal and Tibet. Gales and falling masses of rock and snow sweep the steep, cold slopes. Many climbers tried to reach the top before two finally succeeded in 1953. They were the New Zealander Edmund Hillary and Tenzing Norgay, a Nepalese Sherpa.

EUROPE

Area: 4,066,263 sq. miles (10,531,623 sq. km) 7 percent of the world's land area
Population: 500,000,000 (9.3 percent of world total)
Highest point: Mount Elbrus, 18,480 ft. (5,633 m)
Lowest point: Caspian Sea, 92 ft. (28 m) below sea level
Longest river: Volga, 2,300 miles (3,700 km) long
Biggest lake: Lake Ladoga in Russia, 7,100 sq. miles (18,388 sq. km)
Northernmost point: North Cape, Norway
Southernmost point: Cape Tarifa, Spain
Westernmost point: Dunmore Head, Ireland
Easternmost point: Ural Mountains

▲ *The modern horse evolved from an animal no bigger than a dog, with four toes on its front feet and three on its hind feet.*

Evolution

The theory of evolution states that today's plants and animals are descended from other forms that lived long ago. This slow process of change has been going on for millions and millions of years—ever since life first appeared on earth—and is still happening. Much of the evidence for evolution comes from FOSSILS. Rocks contain the remains of extinct plants and animals and so help to build up a family tree for species now living.

The theory of evolution says that plants and animals must adapt to their surroundings if they are to survive. Those which adapt best are most likely to survive.

Charles DARWIN, an English naturalist, first put forward the theory of evolution in 1859, in a book entitled *On the Origin of Species*.

▲ *Jogging is a good form of exercise. It keeps the heart and lungs fit.*

Exercise

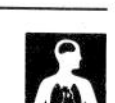

Exercise usually means activities that strengthen the muscles and improve health. Nearly all sports are good ways to exercise, but it is better to take regular mild exercise than to take strenuous exercise only once in a while. Brisk walking is one of the best exercises.

Exercise helps the blood to circulate through our bodies, cleaning out waste and supplying plenty of oxygen. When people want to lose weight, they should take exercise as well as dieting.

On April 30, 1978, Neomi Uemura, a Japanese explorer, became the first person to reach the North Pole alone. During his 54-day dogsled trek over the ice, Uemura survived several attacks by a polar bear.

Explorer

Explorers are people who travel to find out about unknown places. There have always been explorers. The Stone Age men and women who wandered across continents were, in a way, explorers. Phoenician seamen sailed the Mediterranean about 2,600 years ago. ALEXANDER THE GREAT, in the 300s B.C., explored and conquered all of the Middle East as far as India. In the Middle Ages, MARCO POLO reached China from Europe.

But the great age of exploration began in the 1400s. Sailors like Vasco da GAMA, Christopher

Continued on page 246

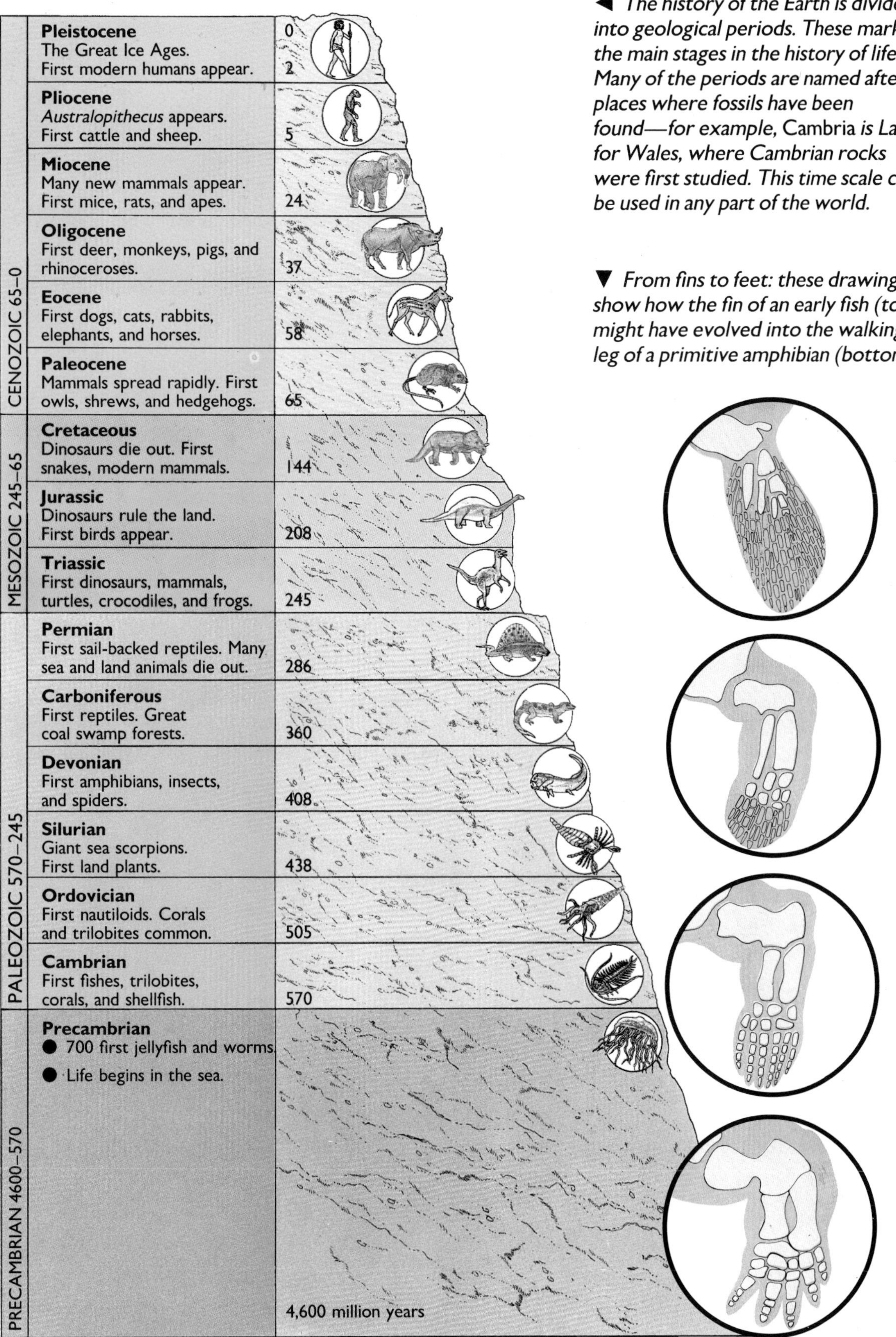

Millions of Years
CENOZOIC 65–0
Pleistocene
The Great Ice Ages.
First modern humans appear.
0
2
Pliocene
Australopithecus appears.
First cattle and sheep.
5
Miocene
Many new mammals appear.
First mice, rats, and apes.
24
Oligocene
First deer, monkeys, pigs, and rhinoceroses.
37
Eocene
First dogs, cats, rabbits, elephants, and horses.
58
Paleocene
Mammals spread rapidly. First owls, shrews, and hedgehogs.
65
MESOZOIC 245–65
Cretaceous
Dinosaurs die out. First snakes, modern mammals.
144
Jurassic
Dinosaurs rule the land.
First birds appear.
208
Triassic
First dinosaurs, mammals, turtles, crocodiles, and frogs.
245
PALEOZOIC 570–245
Permian
First sail-backed reptiles. Many sea and land animals die out.
286
Carboniferous
First reptiles. Great coal swamp forests.
360
Devonian
First amphibians, insects, and spiders.
408
Silurian
Giant sea scorpions.
First land plants.
438
Ordovician
First nautiloids. Corals and trilobites common.
505
Cambrian
First fishes, trilobites, corals, and shellfish.
570
PRECAMBRIAN 4600–570
Precambrian
● 700 first jellyfish and worms.
● Life begins in the sea.
4,600 million years

◀ *The history of the Earth is divided into geological periods. These mark the main stages in the history of life. Many of the periods are named after places where fossils have been found—for example,* Cambria *is Latin for Wales, where Cambrian rocks were first studied. This time scale can be used in any part of the world.*

▼ *From fins to feet: these drawings show how the fin of an early fish (top) might have evolved into the walking leg of a primitive amphibian (bottom).*

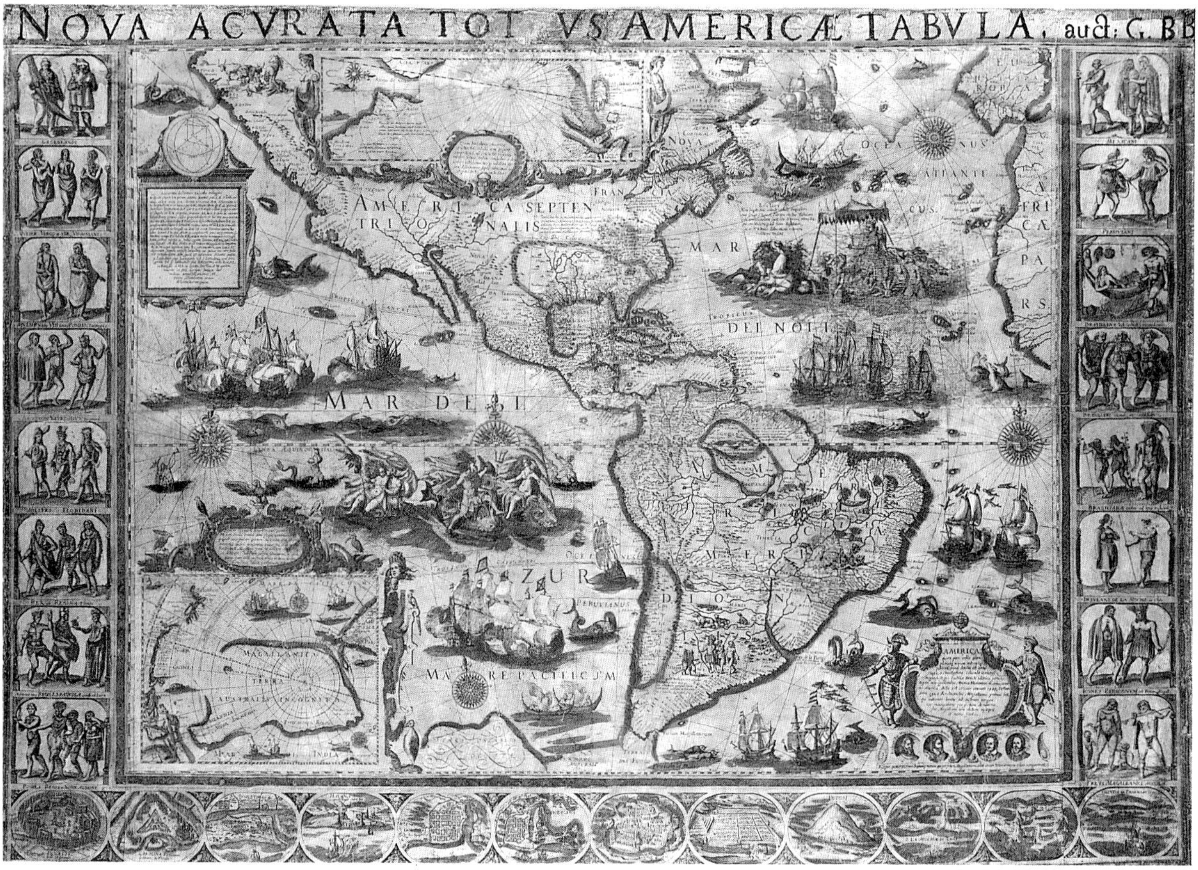

▲ *This Dutch map of newly-explored America was originally drawn in 1608 and updated in 1655.*

▲ *Robert Peary, the American naval officer who reached the North Pole in 1909.*

Columbus, Ferdinand Magellan, and James Cook discovered the shape, size, and position of continents and oceans. Later, David Livingstone, Roald Amundsen, and others explored wild, untamed continents. The world's highest peak, Mount Everest, was climbed by Edmund Hillary and Tenzing Norgay in 1953. Space exploration now takes people beyond the Earth, and the explorations of the next century will probably make all past discoveries seem minor by comparison.

Explosive

Explosions happen when people heat or strike certain solid or liquid substances. These suddenly turn into hot gases. The gases fill more space than the solids or liquids, so they rush violently outward. High explosives like dynamite explode faster and do more damage than low explosives like gunpowder. Engineers use explosives to break up rocks and old buildings. Armies use explosives to destroy vehicles and cities.

Eye

Our eyes show us the size, shape, and color of objects in the world around us. Our eyes can see something as small and near as a tiny insect crawling on this page, or as far off and large as the Moon or stars.

A human eye is much larger than the part you can see. The eye is a ball bigger than a marble. It works much like a camera. Both bend LIGHT rays to form a picture of the object that the rays are reflected from.

Light rays enter the eye through a layer of transparent skin called the *conjunctiva*. The rays pass through a hard, transparent layer called the *cornea*. This bends the rays. The LENS brings them into focus on the *retina* at the back of the eye. But you do not "see" the picture formed there until light-sensitive nerve endings on the retina send the brain a message along the *optic nerve*.

To see properly, all the parts of the eye have to work correctly. For example, the *iris* (the eye's colored part) can open and close to let more or less light through the *pupil*.

Human eyes have a better sense of color than those of any other animal. We can distinguish 250 different pure colors, from red to violet, and about 17,000 mixed colors. We are also able to distinguish about 300 shades of gray between black and white.

The animal with the largest eye is the giant squid. One big specimen has eyes nearly 16 in. (40 cm) in diameter. The biggest whales have eyes about 4 in. (10 cm) across.

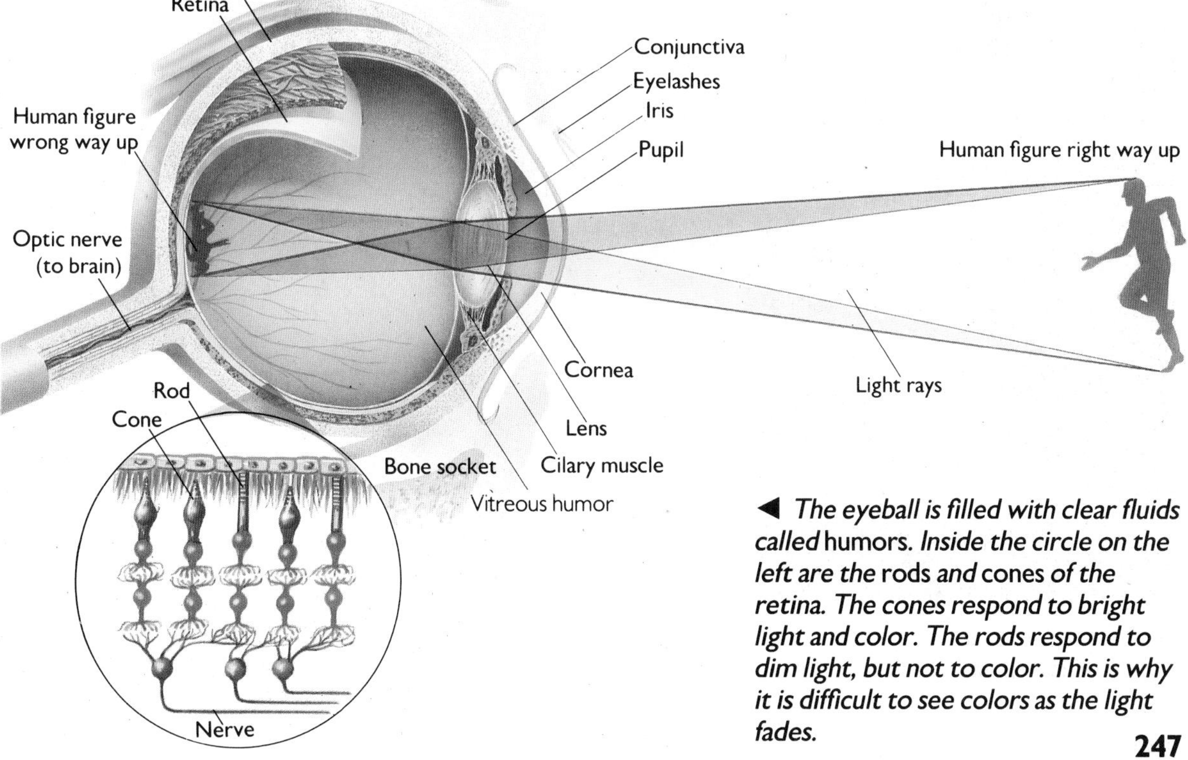

▼ *Inside the eye, the image on the retina is upside down, but the brain turns it over so that we see things the right way up.*

◀ *The eyeball is filled with clear fluids called* humors. *Inside the circle on the left are the* rods and cones *of the retina. The cones respond to bright light and color. The rods respond to dim light, but not to color. This is why it is difficult to see colors as the light fades.*

Fable

Fables are short tales in which the main characters are usually animals that can speak and act like human beings. Fables always teach a lesson. Some of the most famous are those of AESOP, an ancient Greek storyteller. His fables of the fox and the crow, and of the grasshopper and the ant, are told to this day.

Falcon

Falcons are a group of birds of prey that are found all over the world. They can be recognized by the dark markings around their eyes and by their pointed wings. Falcons use their large, hooked beaks for tearing flesh, but they kill their prey with their sharp claws. Falcons swoop down on their victims from above, hitting them with their claws. This act is called "stooping." It is used to kill smaller birds in mid-flight and also to take RODENTS and other small animals on the ground.

The biggest of all falcons is the gyrfalcon of the Arctic. It may reach over 24 inches (60 cm) in size. The American kestrel is the smallest and most common North American falcon. It is about 8 inches (20 cm) long.

▲ *The merlin is one of the smallest of the falcons. It flies low and fast as it chases smaller birds.*

Falkland Islands

This group of cold, windy islands form a British colony in the stormy South Atlantic Ocean. They lie about 480 miles (770 km) northeast of the tip of South America. Sheep farming is the main occupation.

Argentina claims the islands, although 97 percent of the inhabitants are of British origin. In 1982, Argentine troops invaded the Falklands, but they were defeated by British forces.

FALKLAND ISLANDS

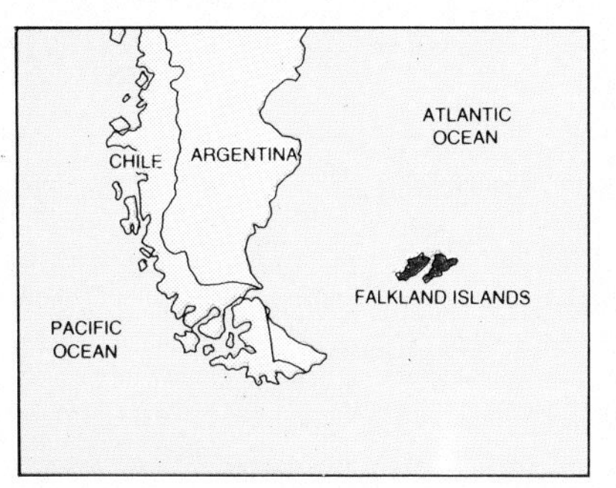

Area: 4,633 sq. miles (12,000 sq. km)
Capital: Stanley
Population: 2,000
Average temperature: 6°C

Famine Relief

Sometimes, a country does not have enough food to feed the people who live there. People may even starve to death. This is famine. Many of the

developing countries of Africa and Asia are subject to famine, often because there has not been enough rain to grow enough food for an increasing population. This is when famine relief is needed. Richer countries organize a supply of food for the starving people, but getting the food to the places where it is needed most is seldom easy. There are usually transportation problems and in some cases civil war. To prevent future famines, help with irrigation and farming methods is needed.

▲ *Ethiopian children receive food during one of the terrible droughts of the 1980s, when thousands of people died of starvation and disease.*

Faraday, Michael

Michael Faraday (1791–1867) was a brilliant English scientist. His studies of chemistry and physics made him world famous. Faraday is best known for his experiments with ELECTRICITY. He showed that it could be made to flow in a wire when the wire was passed between the poles of a magnet. Today this is how most electricity is produced in big generators.

▲ *For many years, Michael Faraday gave science lectures for children. One of the best-known lectures is called "The Chemical History of a Candle."*

Farming

Farming is the world's most important human activity. More people work at it than at any other job. (See pages 250-251.)

FARMING

Farming began somewhere in the Middle East about 9,000 years ago. Today, about half the world's people are farmers. Many are *subsistence* farmers, growing just enough to feed themselves. Others grow *cash crops* to sell.

Farming has become more and more scientific. In the 1600s, turnips and clover were introduced to feed farm animals in winter. Before, they had always been killed as winter approached. So, breeders could keep good stock longer and develop larger, fatter breeds of cattle, sheep, and pigs. New World plants, such as potatoes and tomatoes, became widespread. In the 1800s, steam engines and motor tractors replaced horses and oxen.

Today, most farms in developed countries are mechanized. Few people are needed to work on them. Poultry and calves are often raised indoors, as if in a factory. The rich countries produce more food than they need. But despite the success of the "green revolution," which has brought new crops and new farm methods to the Third World, many people in poor countries still starve. In Africa, Asia, and South America, most farms are small, and the work is done mainly by hand.

STRIP FARMING

In early times, people shared fields. They each had a narrow strip. The strips were plowed up and down the slope of the field, seldom across. Thus the strips of one group ran in one direction, those of a neighboring group in another.

CROP ROTATION

In the 17th century, it was found that fodder crops put goodness back into the soil. In the four-course method of farming, cereals such as wheat and barley alternate with clover and root crops such as turnips.

THE HISTORY OF FARMING

7000 B.C. Farming begins when people discover how to grow grain and raise domestic animals.

4000 B.C. Irrigation of crops in Mesopotamia and Egypt.

500 B.C. Iron tools and heavy ox-drawn plows in use.

A.D. 600 Open-field system common in northern Europe. Peasants share fields, growing crops in narrow strips.

1400s Enclosure (fencing or hedging) of open fields. Sheep-rearing important.

1500s New plants introduced to Europe from America.

1600s Improved breeds of farm animals developed in Europe.

1700s New machinery, such as Eli Whitney cotton gin (1793).

1800s Steam power, threshing, and reaping machines, new fertilizers; North America and Australia become important farming regions.

1900s Wide use of chemicals as fertilizers and insecticides; new strains of plants able to resist disease; factory farming and the "green revolution" improve food production.

IMPORTANT FARM CROPS

Bananas grow in the tropics. Plantains (cooking bananas) are eaten in Asia, Afric and the Americas.

Barley is an important cereal grown in temperate climates.

Cassava is a tropical root crop.

Maize (corn) grows well in warm, moist conditions.

Oats are grown in North America and Europe.

Potatoes are an important crop in Europe

Rice is the main food of half the world's people. It grows best in warm, wet areas.

Sorghum is grown for food by people in Asia and Africa.

Sugar comes either from sugarbeet, grow in cool climates, or from sugarcane grow in the tropics.

Vegetable oils come from coconuts, cotton seed, peanuts, sunflowers, soybeans, olives, and maize.

Wheat is a cereal grown worldwide in areas with moist, mild winters and warm, dry summers.

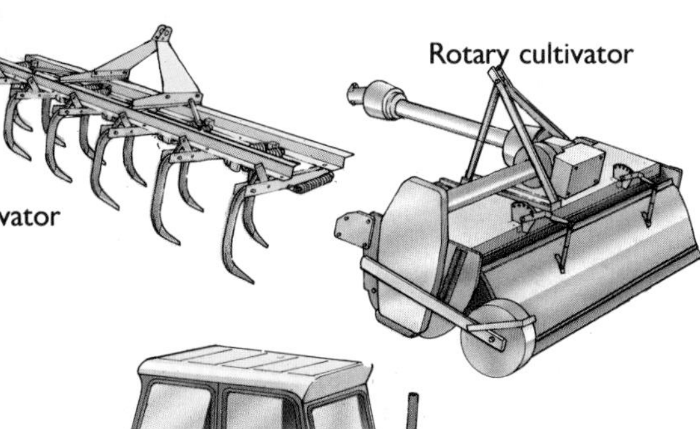

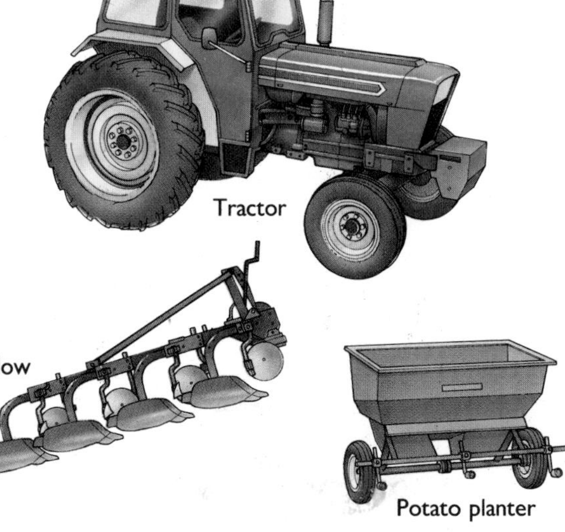

some parts of the world, old farming methods are still Modern machinery is slowly taking over.

▲ *In battery farming, poultry is reared to produce more eggs in less time and at a low cost.*

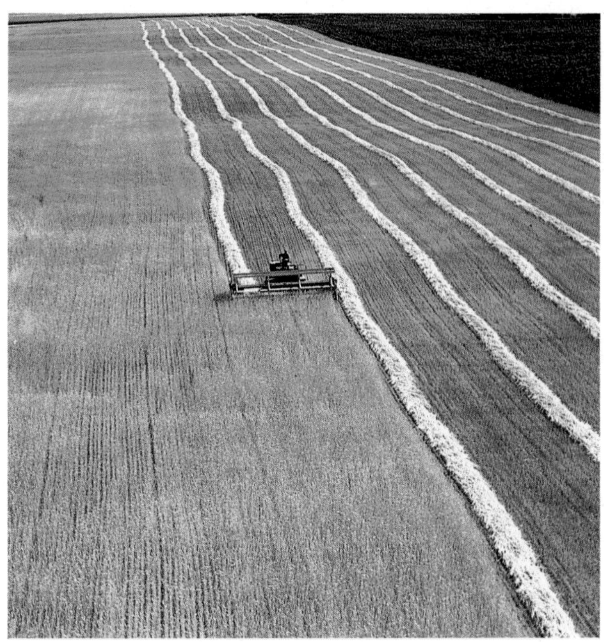

▲ *A combine harvester at work on a prairie wheatfield in the Midwest.*

more information turn to these articles: BEANS; CEREAL; COFFEE; COTTON; COW; FERTILIZER; FOOD; GOAT; HORSE; IRRIGATION; OLIVE; PIG; POTATO; ULTRY; RICE; SHEEP; SUGAR; TEA; VEGETABLE; WHEAT.

► *The Fascist followers of the Italian dictator Mussolini adopted black shirts as an official uniform.*

Fascism

Fascism is a political belief. It was founded in Italy in the 1920s by Benito MUSSOLINI. Mussolini seized power in 1922 as DICTATOR of Italy and head of the Italian Fascist Party. Fascism takes its name from the Roman *fasces*, the bundle of rods and the ax that were the symbol of authority in ancient Rome.

Fascist political ideas include the belief that the government of a country should be all-powerful. Its citizens must work hard and obey the government for the good of the nation. Fascists believe in strict discipline and training for all people, including children, and in the wearing of military-style uniforms.

Anybody opposed to a Fascist government is made an outlaw. In Fascist Italy, many people were jailed, exiled, or put to death because they did not agree with the Fascists. All the other political parties were made illegal.

Fat

Fat is an important food for both animals and plants. The tissue of these living things contains fat. Fat in a pure state can take the form of a liquid, such as vegetable oil, or a solid such as butter or lard.

Fat is a store of ENERGY. A unit of fat contains twice as much energy as the same amount of PROTEIN

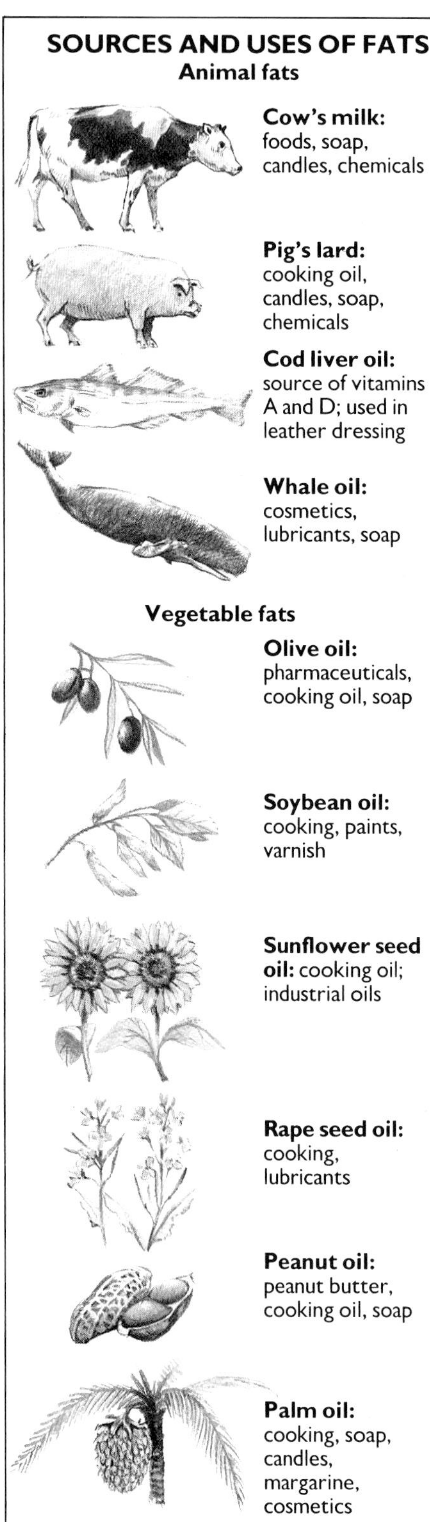
SOURCES AND USES OF FATS
Animal fats
Cow's milk: foods, soap, candles, chemicals
Pig's lard: cooking oil, candles, soap, chemicals
Cod liver oil: source of vitamins A and D; used in leather dressing
Whale oil: cosmetics, lubricants, soap
Vegetable fats
Olive oil: pharmaceuticals, cooking oil, soap
Soybean oil: cooking, paints, varnish
Sunflower seed oil: cooking oil; industrial oils
Rape seed oil: cooking, lubricants
Peanut oil: peanut butter, cooking oil, soap
Palm oil: cooking, soap, candles, margarine, cosmetics

or STARCH. Fats play an important part in our diet. Vitamin A, which is necessary for growth, and Vitamin D are both contained in most fats.

We get most vegetable fats from the seeds and fruits of plants, where it is stored. In animals and human beings, fat is stored in tiny "droplets" in a layer under the skin and in the CELLS of the body. Pigs and cattle are our main sources of animal fats.

Some people do not use up all the fat they eat, so they gain too much weight. Some fats cause cholesterol to build up in the bloodstream. Both conditions can be unhealthy.

Fathers of the Confederation

The Fathers of the Confederation were a group of Canadian politicans in the mid-1800s who wanted to bring together all the separate parts of what is now Canada into one country. Until then, Canada was a group of separate colonies, each part of the British Empire.

The Fathers of the Confederation first met in 1864. They agreed that, like the United States, Canada should be a "federation" of states, or provinces. They wanted it to become a self-governing nation, but they also wanted it to stay a part of the British Empire, with the British king or queen as its head.

The British government supported them. It thought that a united Canada would be easier to defend from attacks from overseas and that trade between Canada and other countries could increase. In 1867, the British Parliament passed the British North America Act, and Canada was born.

Feather

The only animals with an outer layer of feathers are BIRDS. Feathers protect birds and keep them warm. They give their bodies a smooth, streamlined shape. Feathers also form the broad surface area of the wings that allows birds to fly.

Feathers are replaced once or twice a year. This process is called molting. Old feathers that are worn and broken fall out. New ones grow in their place.

▲ *A close-up of part of a feather, showing the thread-like barbs which are "glued" together by smaller hooked fibers called barbules.*

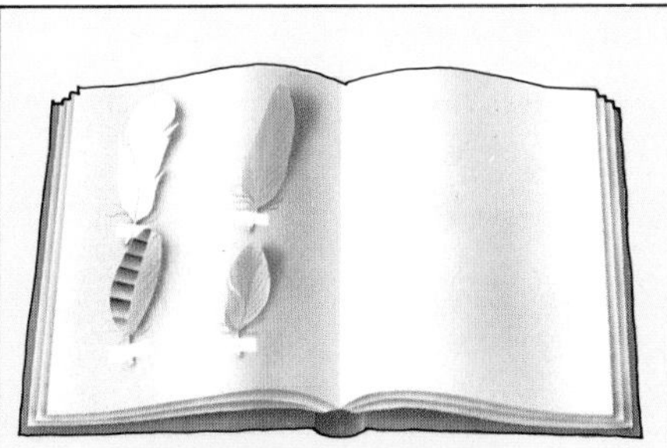

SEE IT YOURSELF

Collect feathers in the woods and look at them with a magnifying glass to see how they are made. "Unzip" part of the flat vane to see the tiny hooked branches that fit neatly together to form it. Mount your feathers in a notebook, and label them with the birds' names if you know them.

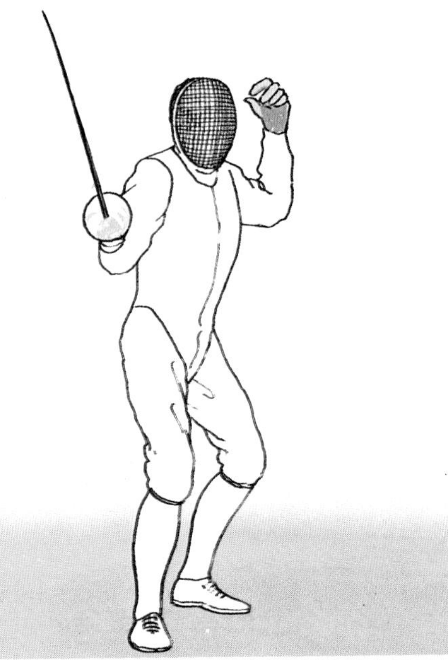
▲ *Fencers wear wire mesh masks, thick jackets, and a glove for the weapon hand.*

Fencing

Fencing can be described as the sport of "friendly dueling." Fencers wear a special glove, padded jacket, and a face mask. They fight with blunted swords. The winner is the one who scores the most points by touching his opponent with his sword.

Today, fencing is a popular sport and an OLYMPIC GAMES event. The three weapons used in fencing are the foil, the épée, and the saber.

Fermentation

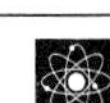

Milk goes sour, bread dough rises, grape juice turns into wine. All these are examples of fermentation. Fermentation is caused by the work of very tiny living BACTERIA, YEASTS, and MOLD. These tiny things break up substances into simpler forms. People have been using fermentation since the earliest times to make bread, beer, wine, and cheese. But it was not until the 1800s that the French scientist Louis PASTEUR found out how fermentation really works.

Fermi, Enrico

Enrico Fermi (1901–1954) was a great Italian scientist. His studies of the ATOM were rewarded by the NOBEL PRIZE in 1938.

In 1942, during World War II, Fermi built the first atomic reactor. He constructed it in an empty squash court under a football stadium in Chicago. Here he set off the first manmade nuclear chain reaction. Later, Fermi helped to develop the atom bomb.

▼ *The common polypody grows on rocks and walls in damp woods. The small adder's tongue looks more like a leaf than a fern. Its spores develop on the slender spike.*

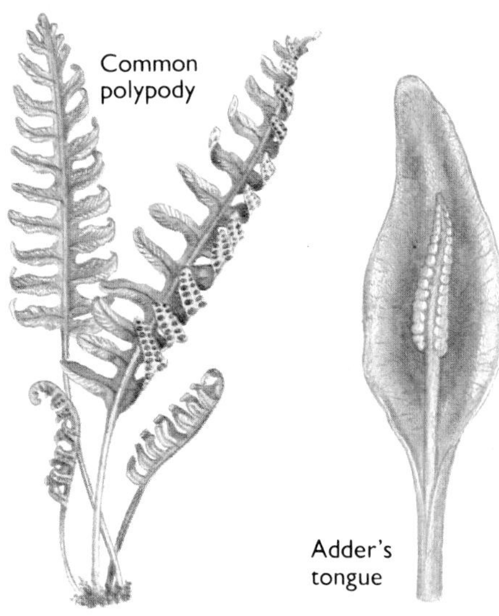

Fern

The primitive ferns were some of the earliest land plants. Today their delicate, feathery leaves look much the same as they did millions of years ago.

About 10,000 different kinds of ferns live on the Earth today. They are found all over the world, usually in damp shady places. In the tropics, giant tree-ferns grow to over 50 ft. (15 m) high.

Ferns do not have FLOWERS OR SEEDS. Instead, they form spores from which new ferns develop.

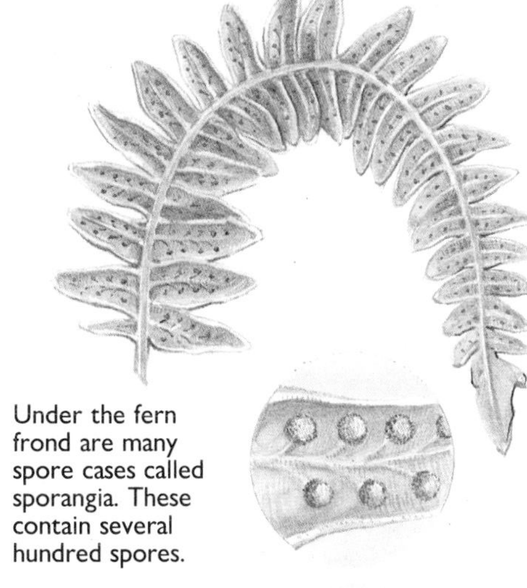

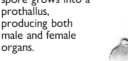

Under the fern frond are many spore cases called sporangia. These contain several hundred spores.

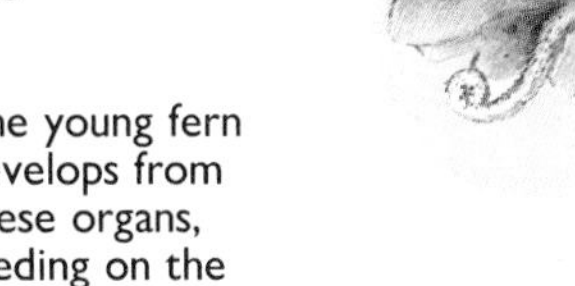

The sporangia burst, and the spores are carried by the wind. When they settle on damp ground, each spore grows into a prothallus, producing both male and female organs.

The young fern develops from these organs, feeding on the prothallus. The leaves unroll as the plant grows.

▲ *Ferns reproduce themselves from spores rather than seeds. It can take several years before a fern is able to produce spores.*

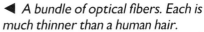

Fertilizer

Fertilizers are chemicals. They are dug into the SOIL to nourish it. In this way, fertilizers help plants to grow bigger and healthier by giving them the chemical nutrients, or "foods," they need to grow. The most important fertilizers are calcium, phosphorus, potassium, and SULFUR.

Fertilizers are usually added to soils that do not contain enough natural nutrients. This can happen if the same crops have been planted in the soil year after year, or if the rain has washed out all the nutrients.

Fiber Optics

An optical fiber is a flexible glass strand thinner than a human hair. Along this fine fiber, a beam of light can travel very easily. The light can be used to carry telephone conversations and television pictures, or allow doctors to see inside our bodies. The fibers are made of especially pure glass designed to reflect the light in toward the center of the strand. Using LASER light, signals can be sent for more than 30 miles

◀ *A bundle of optical fibers. Each is much thinner than a human hair.*

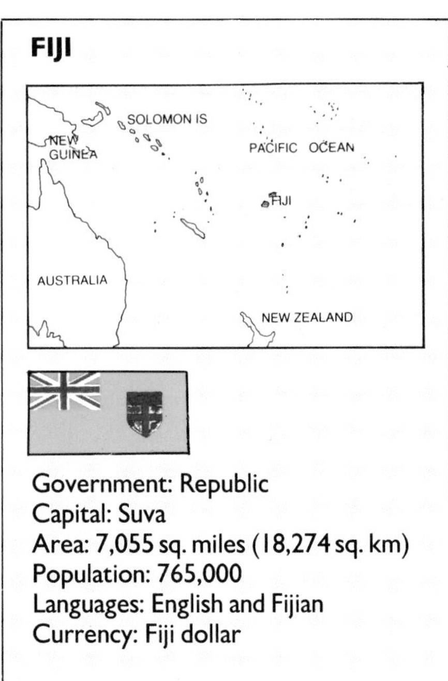

Government: Republic
Capital: Suva
Area: 7,055 sq. miles (18,274 sq. km)
Population: 765,000
Languages: English and Fijian
Currency: Fiji dollar

(50 km) before they have to be amplified. This means that optical fibers are much more efficient than copper cables and much thinner and lighter. A pair of fibers can carry hundreds of telephone conversations at the same time.

Fiji

Fiji is a country made up of hundreds of islands in the Pacific Ocean. The biggest island is Viti Levu. Fiji became a British possession in 1874, but gained its independence in 1970. The main product of the islands is sugar. In 1879, peasants from India were brought to the islands to work on the sugar plantations. The offspring of these Indians now outnumber the original Fijians, and tension between the two groups led to an army takeover in 1987. A civilian government was later restored.

► *Ceremonial dancers on the little island of Taveuni, now a Fijian national park.*

MILLARD FILLMORE

Thirteenth President 1850–1853
Born: Cayuga County, N.Y.
Education: Rural schools
Occupation: Lawyer
Political Party: Whig
Buried: Buffalo, New York

Fillmore, Millard

Millard Fillmore (1800–1874) was the 13th president of the United States. He came from a poor family and was a clothmaker's apprentice. He became vice president in 1848 and president after the death of the then president, Zachary TAYLOR. Though he was in office for less than three years, Fillmore played an important part in the argument about slavery. Though he opposed slavery, he knew that to outlaw it, as many in the North wanted to do, would bring war. This realistic view cost him the support of many people in the North.

Fingerprint

Fingerprints are marks we leave behind whenever we touch something. You can see them by pressing your fingertips into an ink pad and then onto a sheet of white paper. Everybody has patterns of lines and swirls on their fingers. But each person's fingerprints are different from everybody else's. Because of this, police officers use fingerprints to help identify criminals. They keep files of thousands of different prints. By comparing those on file with those found at the scene of a crime, they can often trace the guilty person. Computers can now hold details of the fingerprints of half a million people. In a few seconds, the computer will match any of these prints with those of a suspect.

SEE IT YOURSELF

Press your fingertips gently but firmly onto an ink pad. The ridges on the skin of your fingertips will be covered with ink.
Transfer your fingerprints onto a clean piece of white paper and examine them through a magnifying glass. Can you tell which fingerprint group you belong to?

► *All fingerprints can be divided into four main types – the arch, the whorl, the loop, and the composite.*

In many hospitals, the footprints of babies are taken shortly after birth. Footprints, like fingerprints, never change, so the person will always be known by these prints. The owners of valuable dogs sometimes have nose prints made of their animals in case they should stray.

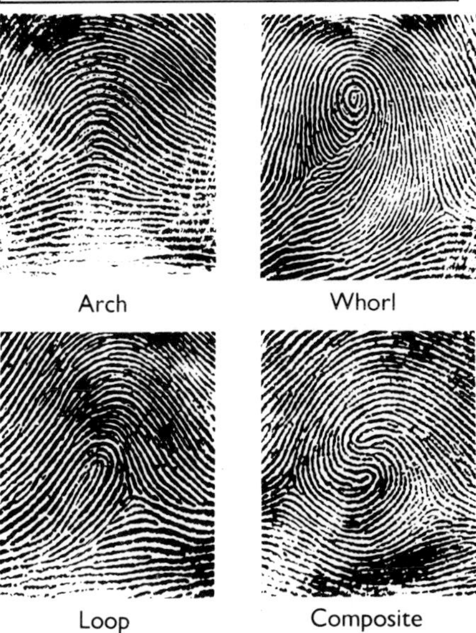

Finland 

Finland is a country in northern EUROPE tucked between Scandinavia and Russia.

The thousands of lakes and rivers that dot the Finnish landscape form a great inland waterway. About 75 percent of the land is covered by thick forests of spruce, pine, and larch trees. The main industries of Finland are logging and the making of wood products, such as paper.

Russia controlled the country from 1809 until 1917, when Finland became independent.

FINLAND

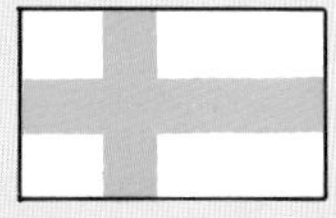

Government: Constitutional republic
Capital: Helsinki
Area: 130,120 sq. miles (337,009 sq. km)
Population: 4,986,000
Languages: Finnish and Swedish
Currency: Markka

▲ *The coast of Norway is broken by hundreds of fiords, some with steep, rocky sides several hundred feet high.*

Fiord (Fjord)

Along the coasts of NORWAY and GREENLAND are a series of steep-sided valleys called fiords. Here the sea has invaded the land. Narrow tongues of water wind inland in narrow mountain gorges.

Fiords were formed when the great glaciers of the ICE AGES gouged out valleys as they flowed to the sea. When the ice melted, the sea flooded the valleys. Fiords are very deep and make perfect shelters for large ocean-going ships.

Fire

The ability to make and use fire is one of the great advantages people have over animals. Primitive people found fire frightening, just as animals do. But once they learned to make and control fire, it became a necessary part of life. It kept out the cold, lit up the dark, cooked food, kept people warm, and scared away animals. But even today, fires that get out of control cause terrible damage and suffering.

▼ *In ancient times, people found that two flints struck sharply together produced a spark. Later, a flint was struck against a piece of steel to make a spark which could be used to light an easily-burned material called tinder.*

Fireworks

Fireworks are devices that produce spectacular displays of lights, colors, smoke, and noise in the night sky. They were invented in China centuries ago, and only became known in Europe in the 1300s.

Fireworks are often launched in ROCKETS. They are shot in the air and made to explode by a black powder called *gunpowder*. The brilliant colors of fireworks come from burning different chemicals.

In 1749, George Frideric Handel wrote his *Fireworks Music* for a display in London's Green Park. A report written at the time says: "Although Signor Servandoni's display of fireworks was not a complete success, Mr. Handel's music was enthusiastically received."

Fir Tree *See* Conifer

Fish

There are more fish than all the other backboned animals put together. The fish shown on pages 260–261 are just a few of more than 30,000 different kinds.

Fishing

Fishing is one of the world's most important activities. In one year, about 60 million tons of fish are taken from the seas, rivers, and lakes.

Although fish are a good source of food, much of the catch ends up as animal feed or FERTILIZER. Oil

Continued on page 262

▼ *Some of the ways in which fish are caught. From left to right: fish such as cod and haddock are caught by their gills in gill nets; in long-line fishing, a series of baited hooks are attached to a long main line; in purse seine fishing, a net is drawn around a school of fish; lobsters are caught in traps; the otter trawl net has boards or buoys which keep the net open as it is dragged over the seabed, trapping bottom fish. The diagram also shows some important food fish.*

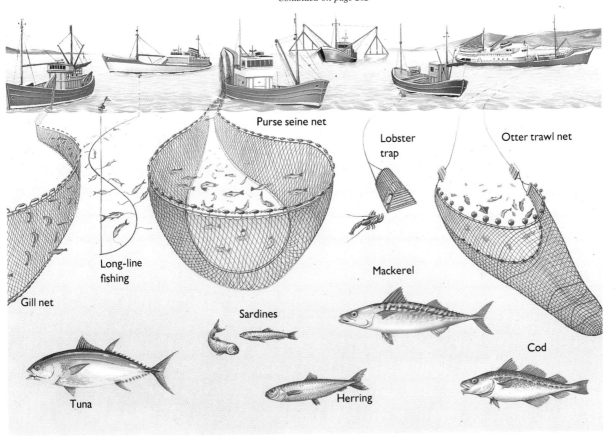

FISH

Fish were the first animals with backbones (vertebrates) to develop on Earth. They are the animals best adapted to life in water. They breathe by means of gills, and they swim by using their fins and tails. Fish are found in salt and fresh water, from the cold polar seas to the warm tropics.

Scientists divide fish into three groups. The *cartilaginous* fish have gristly, rather than bony, skeletons, and leathery skins, not scales. They include the sharks and rays. The *bony* fish make up the next, and largest, group. All these fish have bony scales covering their body. The third, and smallest, group are the *lungfish*, which are unusual in being able to come out on land and breathe air.

People have eaten fish since earliest times. Today, the world's fishing fleets catch millions of tons of fish every year.

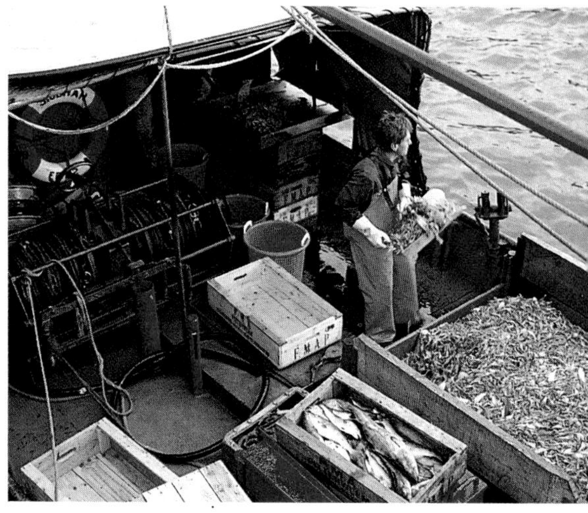

▲ *A catch is sorted on a trawler. Trawlers fish in waters as fa away as Greenland and the Arctic Ocean. Some stay at sea for weeks at a time, storing their catches in deep freezers on boar*

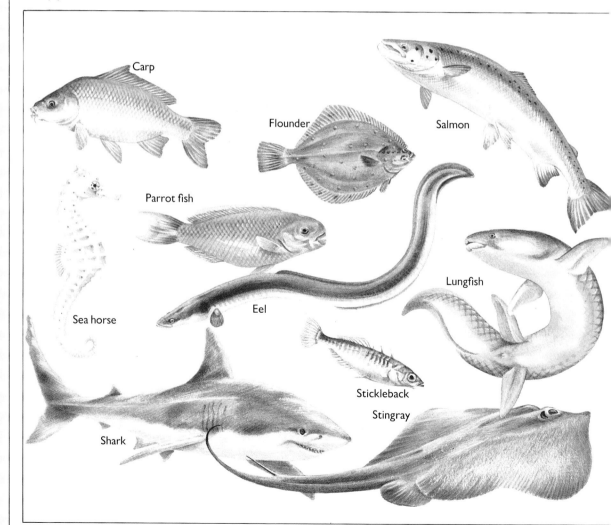

Carp
Flounder
Salmon
Parrot fish
Sea horse
Eel
Lungfish
Stickleback
Stingray
Shark

WHAT IS A FISH'S SIXTH SENSE?

Fish have an organ called the lateral line, found in no other animal. It detects vibrations in the water through sensors beneath the fish's scales. Using this sixth sense, a fish can detect another fish before it comes into view.

HOW DOES A FISH BREATHE?

A fish breathes by means of gills on each side of its head. It takes in water through its mouth and, as the water passes over the gills, the gills extract oxygen from the water. The oxygen enters the fish's bloodstream. Fish are cold-blooded.

HOW DOES A FISH SWIM?

Most fish swim by beating their tails from side to side. They use their fins for steering and balance.

WHY CAN'T SEA FISH LIVE IN FRESH WATER?

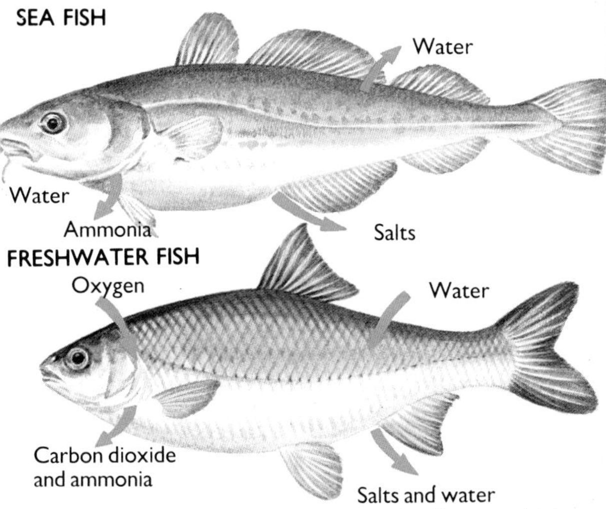

Sea fish are constantly losing water, so they have to drink a lot. Unwanted salt is excreted in their urine. Freshwater fish take in water through their skin. They excrete large volumes of water. Regulation of the amount of salt in a fish's body is also carried out by the gills and the kidneys.

SOME INTERESTING AND UNUSUAL FISH

Archer Fish This river fish catches insects by squirting water at them.

Catfish, like other bottom-dwelling fish, have feelers or "barbels" to help them find food.

Cleaner fish remove parasites and food scraps from the jaws of fierce barracuda.

Eels have an amazing life cycle, migrating from Europe and America to the Sargasso Sea to breed.

Flatfish A baby flounder swims upright. But as it grows, one eye travels across its head, and its body twists until the fish is lying on its side.

Flying Fish glide, using their long stiffened fins as wings. They take to the air to escape pursuing enemies.

Mudskippers use their leg-like fins to crawl over the mud to find food.

Pilot Fish often swim with sharks. They feed on the sharks' leftovers.

Porcupine Fish have prickly skins and blow themselves up like balloons to baffle a hungry enemy.

Salmon swim upriver to breed, often returning to the spot where they were born.

Scorpion Fish This fish is one to keep away from, for it has poisonous spines.

Sea Horse This curious-looking fish carries its young in a pouch.

For more information turn to these articles: EEL; FISHING; GOLDFISH; LAKE; OCEAN; RIVER; SALMON; TROPICAL FISH; TUNA.

The United States flag, or "Stars and Stripes," has had the same basic design since 1777, during the Revolutionary War. It has 13 horizontal stripes which represent the original 13 colonies that rebelled against British rule. Fifty white five-pointed stars, representing the 50 states of the Union, appear on a dark blue field in the *canton*, the rectangular area in the top corner near the staff, or pole.

from fish is used to make SOAPS or for tanning—turning animal skins into leather.

Often the catch is made far from the home port. The fish must be preserved, or they will quickly spoil. In the past, fish were often dried, smoked, or salted, because there were no refrigerators. Today they are packed in ice or frozen. Some fishing fleets include large factory ships. They take fresh fish straight from the other ships and can them or package them on the spot.

The best places to fish at sea are where the sloping sea bottom is no more than 600 ft. (180 m) deep. Here, fish can be found feeding in huge numbers. The Grand Banks off the coast of Newfoundland is one such region. It has been fished for hundreds of years.

Flag

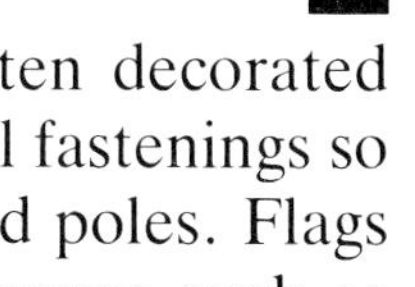

Flags are pieces of colored cloth, often decorated with bold markings. They have special fastenings so that they can be flown from masts and poles. Flags are used by countries, armies, and groups such as marching bands and sports teams.

Flags have been used as emblems since the time of the ancient Egyptians. Their flags were flown on long poles as battle standards, held by "standard-bearers." Flying high in the air, flags helped soldiers to find their companions as they plunged into

▼ *International signal flags used by ships at sea include a flag for each letter of the alphabet as well as for the numerals one to ten, shown below. On the right, the basic patterns in flag design are shown. The* canton *design is seen in the United States flag above. The* quarterly *is used on the flag of Panama; the* triangle *is seen in the flags of Guyana and Jordan. The* serration *appears in Qatar's flag, the* border *in Grenada's.*

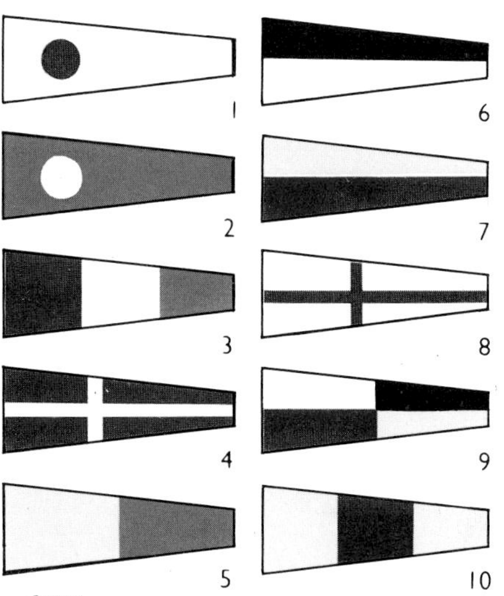

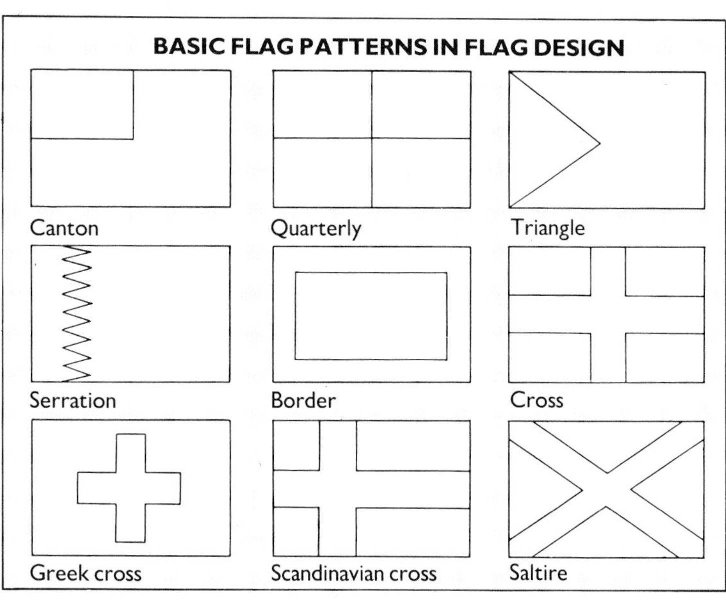

1

2

3

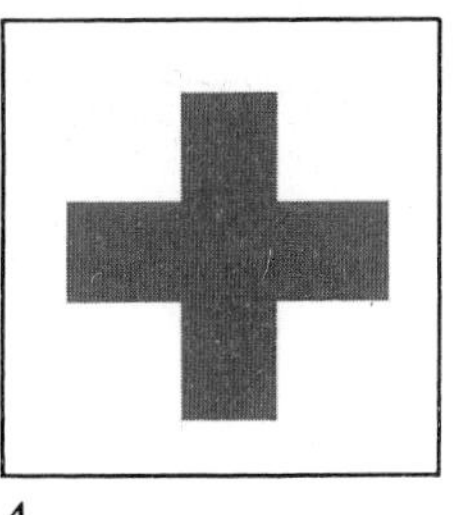
4

▲ *The World Scout flag (1) and the flag of the Red Cross (4) both represent organizations. The Japanese naval ensign (2), flown from the stern of a ship, is a recognized flag of nationality. The personal standard of Britain's Queen Elizabeth II (3) is just one of the royal standards.*

battle. And they showed which soldiers belonged to which king or general.

Today, national flags are flown as a symbol of a country's history, its power, and its importance, or *prestige*.

Flags are also used for signaling. Since 1857, there has been an international code for flag signals. It is used by ships. A yellow flag, for example, means that a ship is in quarantine because of illness on board. For thousands of years, flags have been important as a way of identifying ships at sea.

Other well known signals are a white flag—a sign of truce—and a flag raised to half-mast—a sign that people are mourning someone's death.

Flame

When something is heated enough to make it burn, it will also often burst into flames. These flames are gases that are given off during burning. Bright flames that give off plenty of light, such as those of candles, wood, or coal, have tiny CARBON particles in them that glow brightly. Flames are not all equally hot. Wood fires burn at about 1,800°F (1,000°C). The flames of acetylene WELDING torches are about 5,400°F (3,000°C).

Flamingo

Flamingos are tropical birds found in huge flocks in many parts of the world. The bright color of their feathers ranges from pale to deep pink. Flamingos live in marshes and shallow lakes, wading on their stilt-like legs. A flock of thousands of these splendid birds is a wonderful sight.

The flamingo's body is not much bigger than that of a goose, but its long legs and neck can make it up

▼ *Flamingos are timid birds and usually live together in large colonies on the edges of lakes and marshes.*

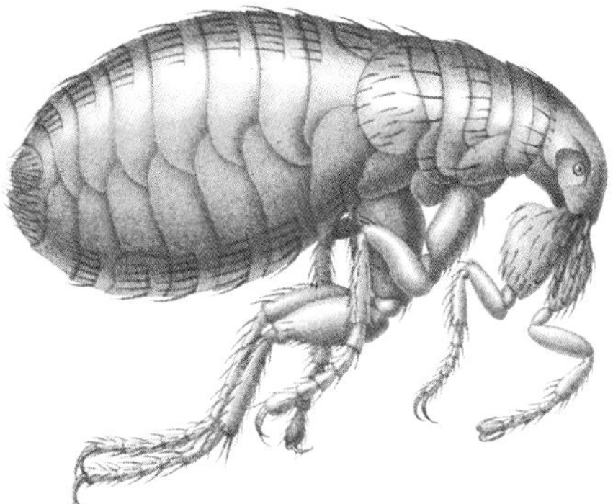

▲ *This greatly magnified body of a flea shows the large abdomen where blood is stored.*

to 6 ft. (1.8 m) tall. These elegant birds feed on tiny plants and animals that are found in shallow waters. When feeding, they tuck their heads right under the water and use their broad, hooked beaks like strainers to filter their food from the water and mud.

Flea

Fleas are tiny wingless insects less than 1/8 in. (3 mm) long. They live on the bodies of birds, animals, and human beings. Fleas are PARASITES, and they feed on their hosts by biting through the skin and sucking the blood. Fleas can carry germs from one host to another. Rat fleas, for example, can give bubonic plague to people.

▲ *Sir Alexander Fleming, the British bacteriologist who discovered penicillin.*

Fleming, Alexander

Sir Alexander Fleming (1881–1955) was a British doctor who discovered the antibiotic drug penicillin. It is one of the most important drugs known. Penicillin fights infections caused by many kinds of germs and BACTERIA. Although the drug fights the infection, it does not usually harm the body. Penicillin has saved thousands of lives.

Fleming discovered the drug by accident in 1928. He found an unknown kind of mold growing in his laboratory. From it, he was able to make pencillin. For his work, Fleming shared the 1945 Nobel Prize in medicine with Howard W. Florey and Ernst B. Chain, the doctors who found a way to produce penicillin in large quantities.

▼ *A pointed flint tool and a tool for scraping, both made by Neanderthal people about 50,000 years ago.*

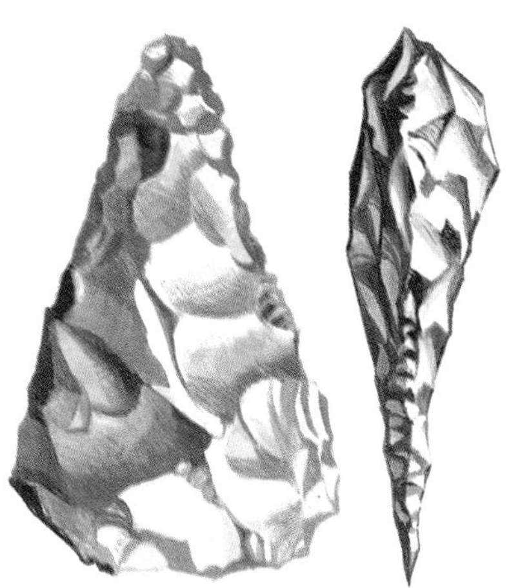

Flint

Flint is a glassy MINERAL that is a form of QUARTZ. It is found in beds of chalk and limestone. A lump of flint is dull white on the outside and shiny gray to black on the inside.

Flint is very hard, but it can be easily chipped into sharp-edged flakes. Stone Age people made tools and weapons out of flint. Because it will give off a spark when struck against iron, it can be used to start a FIRE. A spark from a flint also ignited the powder in a flintlock GUN.

Flood

There are two main kinds of floods: those caused by rivers overflowing their banks, and ocean floods caused by high tides and strong winds blowing from the ocean toward the land. Rivers usually flood in the spring, when spring rains add to water produced by melting snow and ice. The water overflows, causing much destruction in the area of the river.

Throughout history, three great rivers have flooded regularly—the Nile in Egypt, the Yellow River in China, and the Mississippi.

▼ *Below left: Florida's seaquarium in Miami was the first center of its type in the world when it was built in 1938. Below: Palms and slash pines at the Lower Keys Wildlife Refuge, off the Florida coast.*

Florida

Florida is the most southerly state. It is located on the east coast and juts out into the sea, with the Atlantic Ocean to the east and the Gulf of Mexico to the west. It has more coastline than any state other than Alaska. Tourism is the most important industry. Miami Beach and Walt Disney World are just two of the major attractions. Florida's warm climate attracts visitors all year round, and many retired people live here, too. The sunny weather also encourages agriculture, and many kinds of fruit and vegetable are grown.

Florida was discovered by the Spanish as early as 1513. In 1763 the British captured it, but it returned to Spain soon afterward. In 1821 it passed to the United States.

FLORIDA

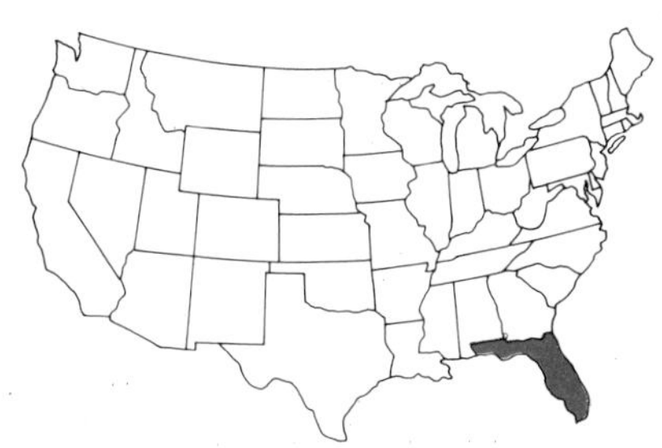

Capital: Tallahassee
Population: 12,937,926
Area: 58,664 sq. mi. (151,939 sq. km)
State flower: Orange Blossom
State bird: Mockingbird
State tree: Palmetto Palm
Statehood: March 3, 1845
27th state

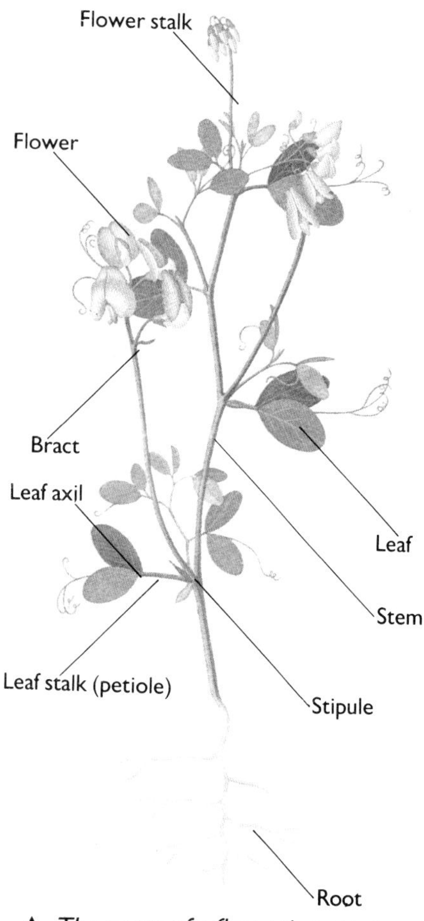

Flower

There are about 250,000 different kinds of flowering plants in the world. Their flowers come in a dazzling array of colors, sizes, and shapes. Some grow singly. Some grow in tight clusters. Many have showy colors, a strong scent, and produce a sweet nectar. Others are quite drab and unscented.

Whatever they look like, flowers all have the same part to play in the life of the plant. Flowers help plants to reproduce themselves. Inside a flower are male parts, called *stamens*, and female parts

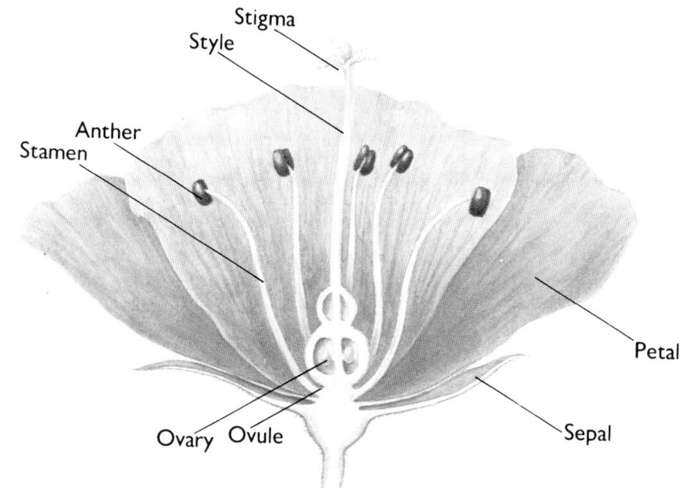

▲ *The parts of a flowering plant.*

► *A flower cut away to show its parts. Fertilization occurs when pollen from the anther unites with an ovule in the ovary. The ovule becomes a seed from which a new plant will eventually grow.*

known as *pistils*. The stamens contain hundreds of powdery grains of pollen. These fertilize the pistil. Then a FRUIT begins to form and grow. Inside the fruit are the SEEDS for a new generation of plants. The seeds are scattered in different ways. They may be blown by the wind, or carried off by birds and animals. From them, new plants will grow.

▼ *Houseflies lay their eggs in decaying matter. The life cycle can be complete in a week in warm weather. The sponge-like mouth is drawn in the circle.*

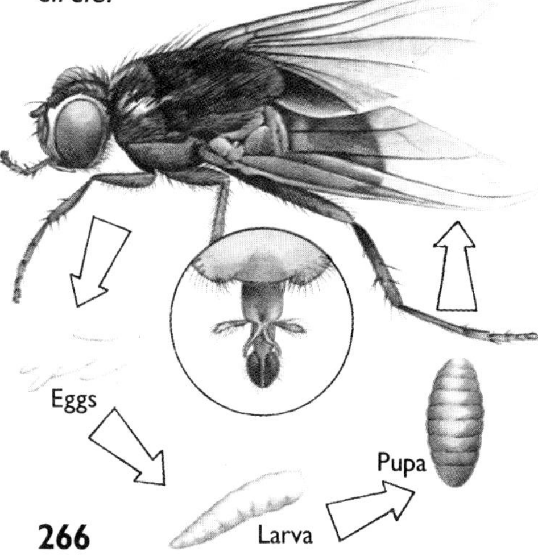

Fly

Flies are winged insects. They are one of the largest groups of insects in the world. There are more than 750,000 different kinds of flies. They have two pairs of wings, one pair for flying and a smaller set behind the main pair to help them to balance in flight.

Many flies are dangerous. They spread deadly diseases such as cholera and dysentery. They pick up germs from manure and rotting food and carry them into homes, where they leave them on our food.

Some flies bite and feed on the blood of animals. Horseflies and gadflies attack cattle and horses in great swarms. Tsetse flies, which live in the tropics, spread sleeping sickness among domestic animals and humans. Blowflies lay their eggs in open wounds on the skin of animals. The maggots that hatch from the eggs eat into the flesh and cause great harm.

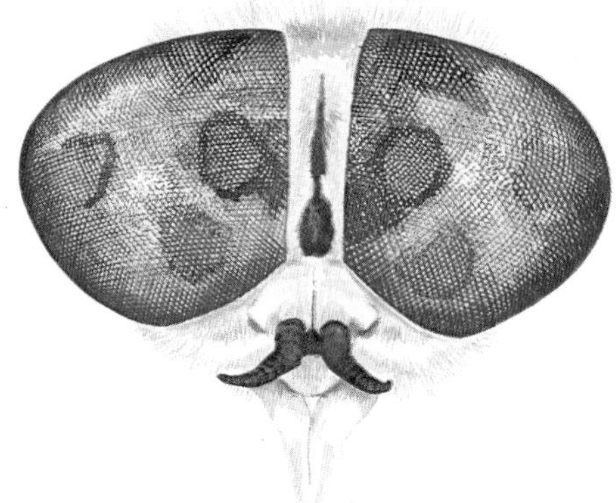

▲ *A fly has two huge compound eyes made up of thousands of six-sided lenses.*

Fog

What we call fog is simply a low-lying bank of CLOUD. Fog forms when warm, moist air comes into contact with cold ground. As the air cools, the moisture it contains forms the tiny droplets that make up any cloud.

Fog may form when warm air currents blow across chilled water or land. This kind is common around the coast. Another kind occurs on still, clear winter nights, when the cold ground chills the air above it and there is no wind to blow the resulting fog away.

The famous "London fogs" of Sherlock Holmes's day are now a thing of the past. They were not really fogs, but smogs. Smog is caused by drops of water condensing on smoke particles or the exhaust gases of cars or factories. Air pollution is a serious problem in many large cities.

Food

Anything that people eat can be called food. But it makes more sense to talk of it as being only those plant and animal products people enjoy eating.

Primitive and ancient peoples often ate insects and animals raw, or only very lightly cooked.

Monday				
Tuesday				
Wednesday				
Thursday				
Friday				
Saturday				
Sunday				

SEE IT YOURSELF

You can find out whether you are eating enough healthy foods by making a chart like the one on the left. Draw pictures at the top to show the four main food groups—fruit, meat or fish, bread or rice, and vegetables. Every day, check the box under each group when you have eaten something in that group. After a few days, look to see how you have done. If you have at least one check in each box, you are probably eating a healthy diet.

You can judge a country's standard of living (how rich or poor people are) by the amount of cereals that people eat. (Cereals are wheat, rye, barley, oats, corn, and rice.) In rich countries such as the United States, cereals provide only about a third of all foods eaten. In parts of Europe, cereals provide about half of the food eaten. In most of Asia, three-fourths of the people's food is rice.

Today, food may be very skillfully prepared, decorated, and cooked before being eaten. Much of our food is prepared in factories. It is bottled, canned, frozen, or dried before it is sold to us.

Food is essential for life. It gives us the energy to move around and stay warm, and keeps our bodies healthy. A "balanced diet" is necessary for good health. The three main kinds of food are carbohydrates, PROTEINS, and FATS. We also need certain MINERALS and VITAMINS.

Food Chain

When you eat a piece of fish, such as bass, you are taking part in a food chain that began somewhere in the sea. There, the tiny floating plants and animals called plankton were eaten by tiny fish. The tiny fish were eaten by bigger fish, and these bigger fish were eaten by even bigger fish such as your bass.

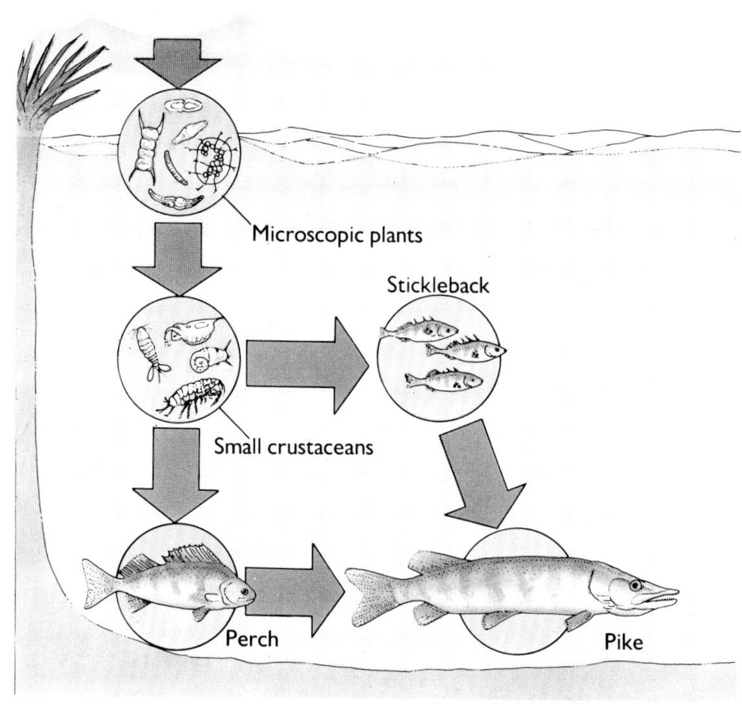

▶ *In this diagram, arrows show how food energy is passed along a typical food chain. Here, there are two possible chains—one from plants to crustaceans to perch to pike, and the other taking a different route—plants to crustaceans to stickleback to pike. There are many other possible food chains.*

At each stage in any food chain, energy is lost. This is why food chains seldom extend beyond four or five links. In overpopulated countries, people often increase the total food supply by cutting out a step in the food chain. Instead of eating cows that eat plants, the people themselves eat the plants. Because the food chain is made shorter, the total amount of energy available to the people is increased.

Every living thing has its place in one or many food chains. The chain begins with green plants. They make their own food from water, chemicals in the soil, and air and sunlight. Animals cannot make their own food as plants can. Instead, they eat plants or other animals. When animals or plants die, tiny BACTERIA that live in the soil break down the animal or plant tissues. The chemicals that make up the animals or plants are released into the soil. These chemicals act as FERTILIZERS to enrich the soil and help the green plants to grow. And so the food chain begins all over again.

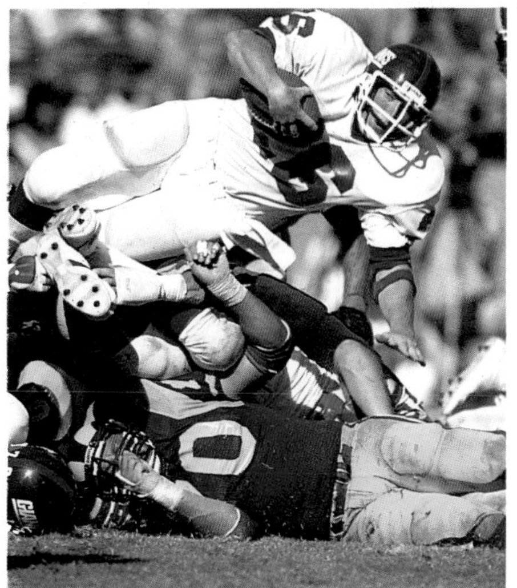

▲ *In football, the players carry or throw the ball much more than they kick it.*

Football

This American sport is played in schools, colleges, and by professional teams. Unlike BASKETBALL and BASEBALL, which are played in other parts of the world, football, until recently, has been uniquely American.

The game is played on a field 100 yards (91 m) long from goal line to goal line, by 160 feet (49 m) wide. End zones extend 10 yards (9 m) behind each goal line. The field is marked with white lines every 5 yards (4.5 m) along its length.

A football game lasts 60 minutes and is divided into four 15-minute quarters. The team kicking off kicks the ball from its 35-yard line in professional football. The receiver on the opposing team tries to run up the field without being tackled. He is *downed* if he is touched by an opponent while any part of his body other than his feet and one hand is in contact with the ground. The teams then take up positions facing each other on the line of *scrimmage* where the ball carrier has been downed.

In four downs the team must advance the ball at least 10 yards. If they succeed they have a *first down* and can try for another 10 yards. If they fail, the defending team gains possession of the ball. Points are scored either by carrying the ball over the opponent's goal line (a *touchdown*), or by kicking the ball over the goalpost from any part of the field (a *field goal*). A touchdown is worth 6 points; a field goal 3 points. After a touchdown, the scoring team tries for a *conversion* point.

▼ *A football field marked for the amateur game. In professional football the goal posts are on the goal line.*

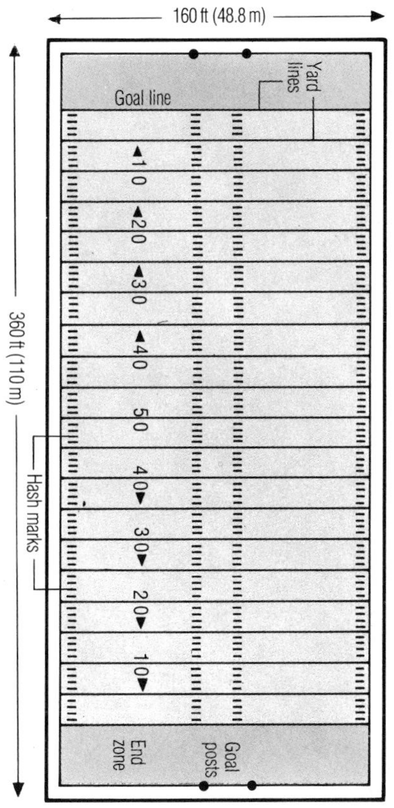

GERALD R. FORD

Thirty-eighth President 1974–1977
Born: Omaha, Nebraska
Education: Michigan University
Occupation: Lawyer
Political Party: Republican

Force

Force is a motion or an action that affects an object, causing it to move or to change shape. If you push something so that it moves, you have applied force to it. How much force you need to move an object depends on how big it is and how much it weighs. There are many kinds of force, and many complicated rules controlling them. These rules govern the way objects behave throughout the universe.

Ford, Gerald Rudolph

Gerald Ford (1913–) was the 38th president, and the only president to come to office after the resignation of a president. He was a Michigan Republican who was elected to the House of Representatives 13 straight times. Ford became president in 1974 when Richard NIXON resigned. Nixon was unpopular because of the Watergate scandal. Many people welcomed Ford because they thought he would be a reliable president. Though he brought stability to the government, he also faced problems with the economy and the Vietnam War.

Ford, Henry

Henry Ford (1863–1947) was a pioneer automobile maker. He was the first to use assembly lines. By building his cars from standard parts, he was able to turn out hundreds a day. His cars were so cheap that many people could afford to buy them. Ford's biggest success was the Model T. His Detroit factories turned out 15 million Model T's during the 19 years it was in production.

▲ *The Ford family of automobiles spans nearly a century, from the production of the first Model T to the cars of today.*

Forest

Forests are large areas of tree-covered land. Tropical rain forests are found near the EQUATOR. In this hot and steamy climate, many kinds of trees and plants grow very quickly. In some places, the trees grow so close together that the sunlight cannot reach the dark, bare forest floor.

Coniferous forests are nearly always found in cold

northern lands. These forests are made up mainly of one kind of tree, such as spruce, fir, or pine. Few other plants grow there. In temperate lands like the U.S., Europe, and the cooler parts of Africa, there are deciduous forests with trees like oak and beech which shed their leaves. Most Australian forest trees are eucalyptus.

▼ *Five layers can be seen in a tropical forest. At ground level, fungi, moss, and ferns grow in the rich leaf litter. Then comes a layer of tree ferns, shrubs, and lianas. Above this is a layer of young tree crowns and then the thick canopy, the crowns of mature trees. The topmost layer consists of the few trees that stand above the canopy.*

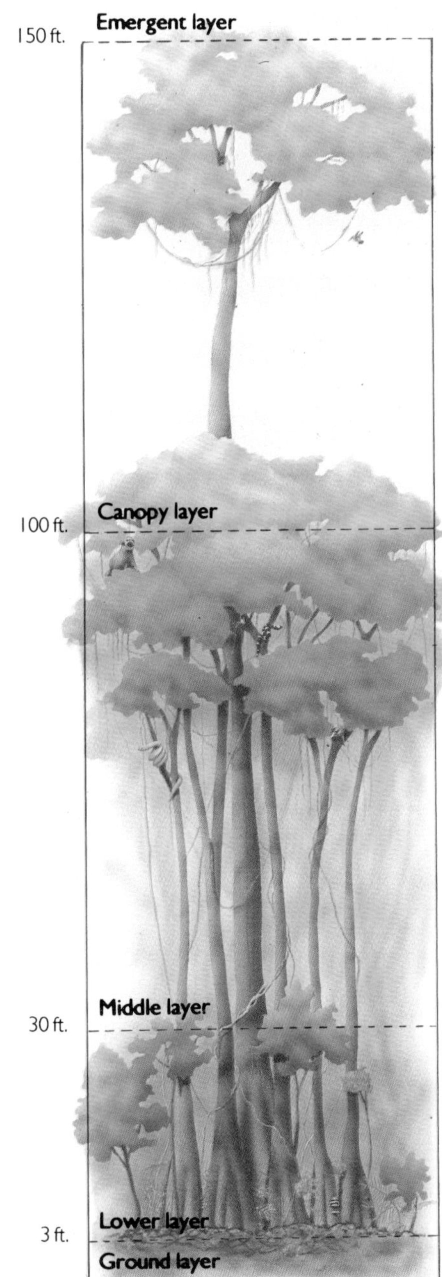

Fossil

Fossils are the hardened remains or impressions of animals and plants that lived a very long time ago. A fossil may be a shell, a bone, a tooth, a leaf, a skeleton, or even sometimes an entire animal.

Most fossils have been found in areas that were once in or near the sea. When the plant or creature died, its body sank to the seabed. The soft parts rotted away, but the hard skeleton became buried in the mud. Over millions of years, more and more mud settled on top of the skeleton. Eventually, these layers of mud hardened into rock, and the skeleton became part of that rock. Water seeping through the rock slowly dissolved away the original skeleton. It was replaced by stony MINERALS which formed exactly the same shape.

These fossils lay buried until movements in the Earth's crust pushed up the seabed and made it dry land. In time, water, ice, and wind wear away the rock, and the fossil is exposed. The oldest known fossil is over three billion years old.

HOW FOSSILS ARE FORMED

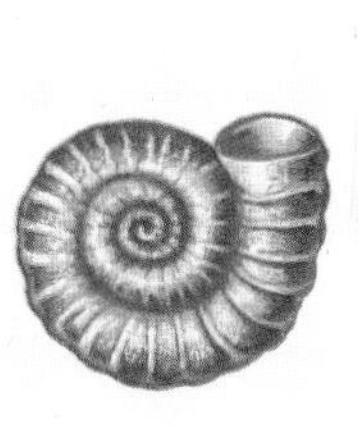

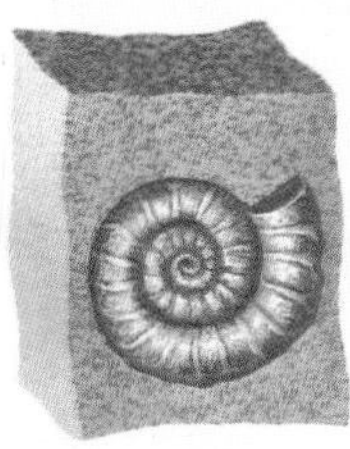

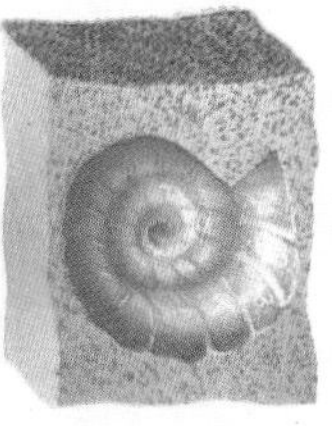

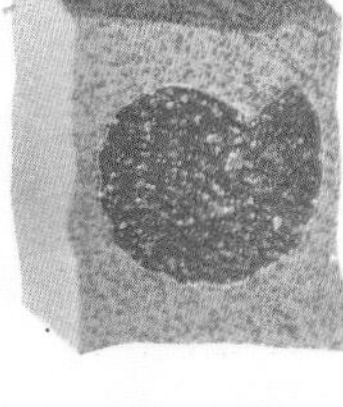

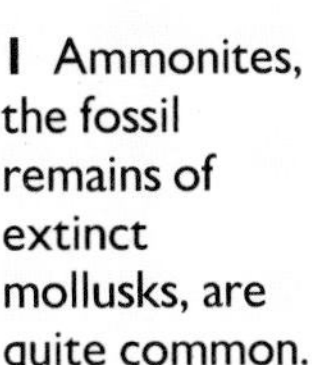

1 Ammonites, the fossil remains of extinct mollusks, are quite common.

2 When the ammonite died, it was buried on the seabed.

3 The animal dissolved away to form a hollow fossil mold.

4 If the mold was filled by sediment, a cast was formed.

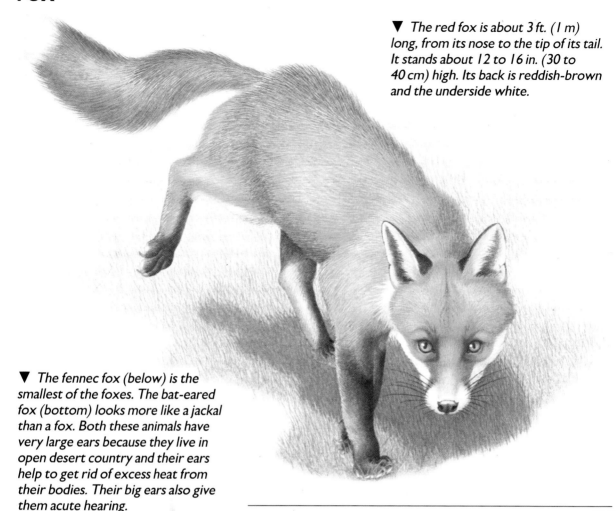

▼ The red fox is about 3 ft. (1 m) long, from its nose to the tip of its tail. It stands about 12 to 16 in. (30 to 40 cm) high. Its back is reddish-brown and the underside white.

▼ The fennec fox (below) is the smallest of the foxes. The bat-eared fox (bottom) looks more like a jackal than a fox. Both these animals have very large ears because they live in open desert country and their ears help to get rid of excess heat from their bodies. Their big ears also give them acute hearing.

Fox

Foxes belong to the same animal family as dogs. The most common kind is the red fox, which is found in Europe, North Africa, North America, and parts of Asia. It eats small birds, animals, and insects, and occasionally poultry or lambs.

Foxes live in holes called "dens," which they either dig themselves or take over from rabbits or badgers. Recently, more and more foxes have been found in cities. They live under the floors of buildings or in any hidden place they can find. They eat scraps from trash cans.

Foxes are very cunning animals. Sometimes they catch rabbits and other prey by chasing their own tails very fast. This fascinates the rabbit, who watches without realizing that the fox is gradually getting nearer and nearer. When the fox gets close enough, it suddenly straightens out and grabs its dinner.

Fraction

If you cut a cake into equal parts, each part is a fraction of the whole cake. We can write this as a number, too. If the cake is cut into two, each half can be written like this: $^1/_2$. If the cake is cut into four, each quarter is written $^1/_4$. The number above the dividing line in a fraction is called the *numerator*. The number below is called the *denominator*.

Until fractions were invented, people had to manage with just *whole* numbers. It was not possible to express a length or weight between two whole numbers.

Fractions help us to divide things. They can be used to mean a part of one: a half of one is a half ($^1/_2 \times 1 = {}^1/_2$). They can also be used to divide numbers greater than one. A box of eggs has 12 eggs in it. Half the box has 6 eggs ($^1/_2 \times 12 = 6$).

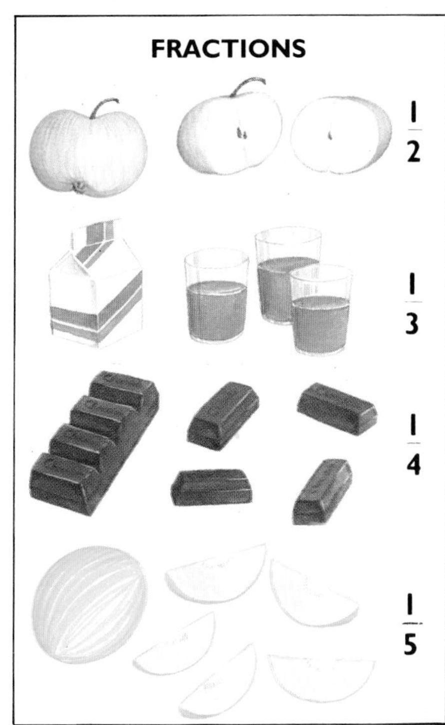

France

France is the largest country in western EUROPE. The capital city is PARIS, on the River Seine. In ancient times, France was inhabited by CELTS, but Julius CAESAR conquered it, and for 500 years it was part of the Roman Empire. The Franks, from whom the country got its name, invaded in the A.D. 400s. France was once divided into hundreds of small parts. There was no standard language until the founding of the French Academy in the 1630s.

France is a very varied and beautiful country. It has a temperate climate and is very fertile. Farmland covers about half the country, and many of the people are employed in farming, fishing, or forestry. France produces a lot of grain, fruit, and vegetables, and it is famous for its WINES.

The history of France is long and turbulent. For centuries, the French and English were enemies and fought many wars. The French people suffered under the rule of greedy kings and nobles. Then in 1789, the people started the FRENCH REVOLUTION. They overthrew their king and made France a republic.

But the country was soon taken over by NAPO-

FRANCE

ENGLAND
NETHERLANDS
BELGIUM
GERMANY
LUXEMBOURG
FRANCE
SWITZERLAND
BAY OF BISCAY
ITALY
SPAIN
ANDORRA
MEDITERRANEAN SEA

Government: Republic
Capital: Paris
Area: 220,668 sq. miles (571,530 sq. km)
Population: 55,000,000
Language: French
Currency: French franc

▶ *The Tour de France, an annual bicycle race around France, is an internationally popular event.*

▼ *Three well-known French monuments—from top to bottom, the Eiffel Tower, Sacré Coeur, and the Arc de Triomphe. The Arc de Triomphe, in Paris, was built by Napoleon. The white-domed church of Sacré Coeur is a landmark on Montmartre, the tallest hill in Paris. The Eiffel Tower was erected for the Paris Exhibition of 1889.*

LEON, who made himself emperor. He went to war and conquered most of Europe before he was finally defeated at Waterloo in 1815. Later, France became a republic once again.

Today, France is one of the wealthiest nations in Europe. It was one of the first members of the EUROPEAN COMMUNITY.

The island of Corsica in the Mediterranean is an official region of France.

Francis of Assisi

St. Francis (1182–1226) was born in Assisi in central Italy. When he was 22, he suffered a severe illness. Afterward, he decided to devote his life to the service of God. He lived in poverty and gathered around him a band of monks who became known as the Franciscans. St. Francis was very fond of birds and animals, whom he called his brothers and sisters.

Franklin, Benjamin

Benjamin Franklin (1706–1790) was a gifted American politician and scientist. He was born in Boston, the youngest of 17 children. Franklin became a printer and then began to publish a yearly almanac, which made him his fortune.

He became involved in the REVOLUTIONARY WAR, which brought the United States freedom from British rule. He was one of the men who signed the

Declaration of Independence and helped draw up the peace treaty at the end of the war.

His scientific inventions include bifocal eyeglasses and the lightning conductor, a rod that protects buildings from lightning.

▲ *By flying a kite in a thunderstorm, Benjamin Franklin proved that lightning was electricity.*

French and Indian Wars

The French and Indian Wars were fought in the 1600s and 1700s between Britain and France for control of North America. They ended in 1763 with victory for Britain and the American colonies. Before that, France had controlled large areas of Canada and along the Mississippi. There were four separate wars, but the most important was the last, fought between 1754 and 1763. After it, France lost almost all her huge North American empire.

French Revolution

In the 1700s, the poor people of France suffered under the rule of their kings and nobles. Rich people built themselves lavish palaces and mansions

▼ *On July 14, 1789, a Paris mob stormed the Bastille, a prison, and sparked off the French Revolution.*

while many others starved in misery. French kings forced the peasants and shopkeepers to pay taxes to support their extravagant way of life and to finance the wars they were always fighting.

There was no parliament to stop the king from treating his subjects badly, and eventually, in 1789, the French people's anger exploded into revolution. King Louis XVI was imprisoned, but tried to escape. Violent leaders like Danton, Robespierre, and Marat directed the Revolution, and the king and queen and many nobles were beheaded.

Then followed the "Reign of Terror," when the revolutionary leaders began to quarrel among themselves, and many of them were beheaded, too. The people grew tired of bloodshed, and in 1795, they set up a government called "The Directory." But it ruled the country badly, and in 1799, it was overthrown by Napoleon

▲ *Sigmund Freud, whose theories did much to advance the study of nervous diseases.*

Freud, Sigmund

Sigmund Freud (1856–1939) was an Austrian doctor who made a great contribution to our understanding of the human mind.

Freud received a degree in medicine from the University of Vienna in 1881 and began to devote himself to the study of mental illness. He taught that the *subconscious*—the thoughts and memories we are not aware of—held the key to a person's mental state. To open up the subconscious, he developed the system of *psychoanalysis*, a kind of clinical examination of the mind. Freud published several books on this and other subjects.

Friction

Without friction, the world would be a strange place. We could not walk because our shoes would not grip the ground. Cars would stand still no matter how fast their wheels turned. Nails and screws would not hold.

When two things rub together, it causes friction. Friction makes it hard to move something across a surface. Smooth objects cause much less friction than rough objects, so when things need to go fast, we try to reduce friction. This is why the wheels of a train and the rails of the track are smooth. When we want things to slow down, we add friction; for example, putting on the brakes in our cars. If two things rub together at great speed, the friction

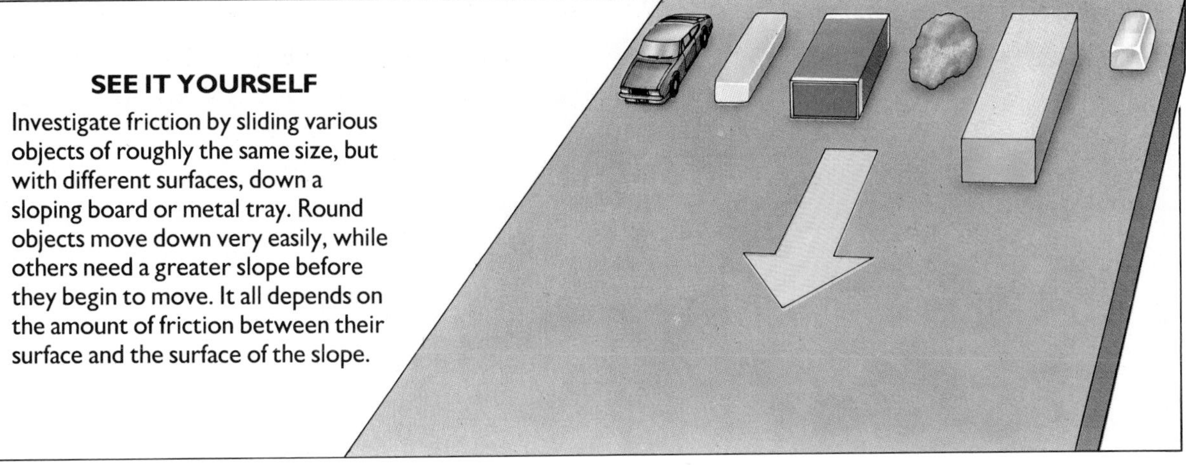

SEE IT YOURSELF

Investigate friction by sliding various objects of roughly the same size, but with different surfaces, down a sloping board or metal tray. Round objects move down very easily, while others need a greater slope before they begin to move. It all depends on the amount of friction between their surface and the surface of the slope.

produces HEAT. If you rub your hand hard against your leg, you can feel the heat made by the friction.

Frog and Toad

Frogs and toads are AMPHIBIANS. This means that they can live both on land and in water. Frogs and toads are found all over the world, except in very cold lands that are always frozen. There are hundreds of different kinds. The biggest is the Goliath frog of Central Africa. This frog can be over 12 in (30 cm) long and weigh over $6\frac{1}{2}$ lbs. (3 kg). The smallest is a tree frog native to the U.S., which is less than $\frac{3}{4}$ inch (2 cm) long.

Frogs and toads breathe through their skins as well as their LUNGS. It is important that they keep their skins wet, because if the skin became too dry, they could not breathe and would die. This is why you will never find a frog very far away from water.

Common frogs feed on insects, grubs, and slugs. They catch their food with a long, sticky tongue

▼ *These are just a few of the world's 2,500 different species of frogs and toads. The brightly colored arrow-poison frogs of South America are among the most poisonous of all. Indians of the Amazon basin use their poison to tip hunting arrows. Tree frogs have pads on their fingers and toes which help them to climb trees. Gliding frogs have webs on their feet which they use as "wings."*

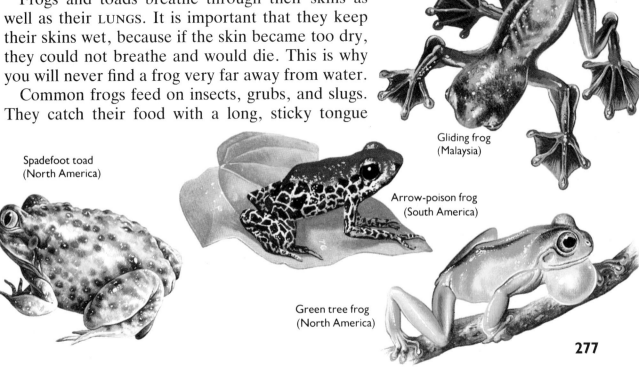

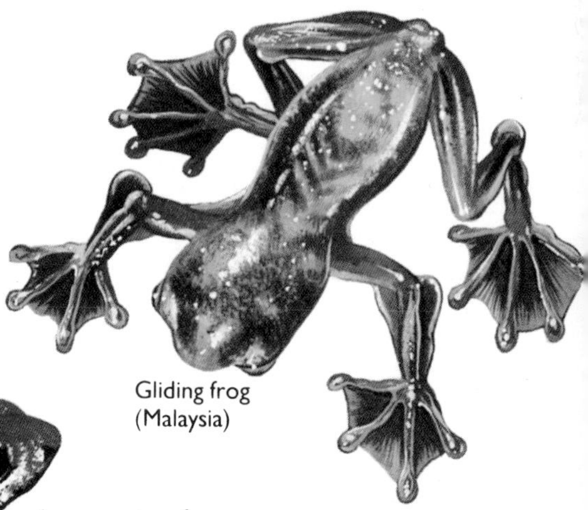

Gliding frog (Malaysia)

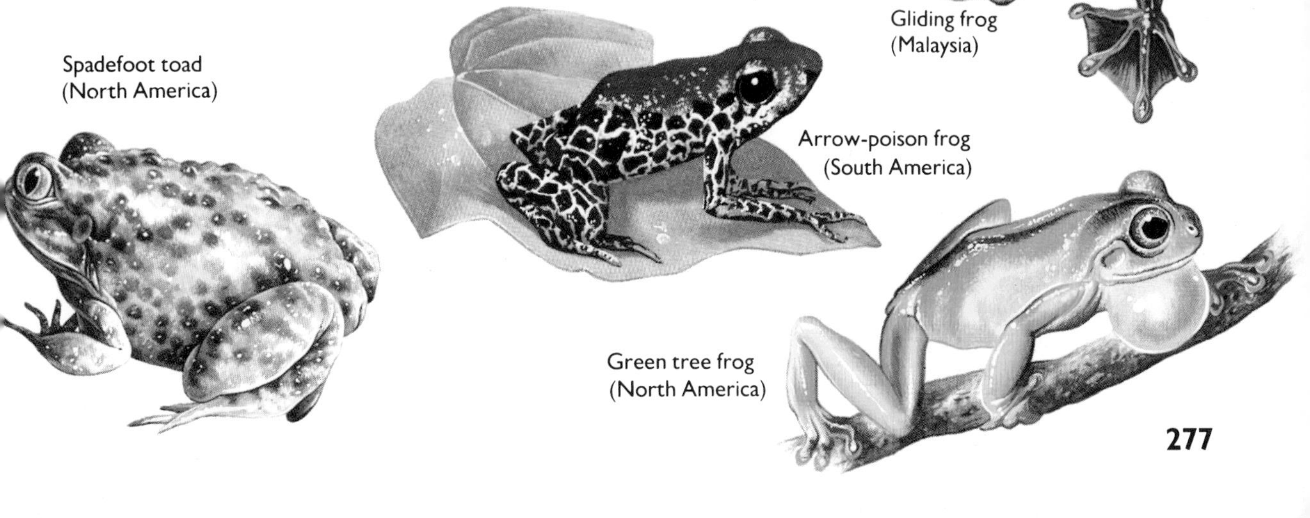

Spadefoot toad (North America)

Arrow-poison frog (South America)

Green tree frog (North America)

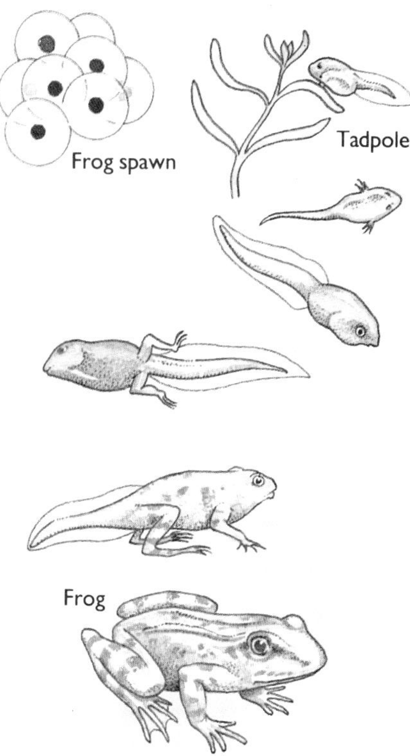

▲ *The life cycle of a frog: The jelly-like eggs, or* spawn, *are laid in a pond and hatch into tadpoles. The tadpoles gradually develop legs, and their tails shrink. They develop lungs instead of gills. They become adult frogs in about 3 years.*

▼ *In many plants, the seeds are enclosed in fleshy fruits. Many fruits are good to eat. As the fruits develop from the flowers, the sepals and petals wither and finally drop off.*

which is attached to the front of the mouth. A frog can flick its tongue in and out in a fraction of a second. Really big frogs eat snakes, small animals, and other frogs, as well as insects.

Toads' skins are rough, dry, and lumpy. They can live in drier places than frogs can.

Frost

Frost is a covering of tiny CRYSTALS of ice that form on cold surfaces. There are three kinds of frost. Hoarfrost forms when tiny drops of water in the air freeze as they touch cold objects. Hoarfrost makes lacy patterns on windowpanes. Glazed frost forms when rain falls on a cold road and covers the surface with a glassy coat. Rime frost is white ice that forms when cold fog or drizzle freezes on surfaces such as cold aircraft wings.

Fruit

To most of us "fruit" means juicy foods which grow on certain plants and trees. Apples, oranges, and pears are three examples. These fruits taste good and are important in our diet. They give us mineral salts, sugar, and VITAMINS. The water, skins, and seeds of fruit help our DIGESTION.

To scientists who study plants, fruits are the ripe SEED cases of any flowering plant. The fruits protect the seeds as they develop and help spread them when they are ripe. Some fruits scatter seeds. Others are eaten by birds and animals that spread the seeds.

Tomato

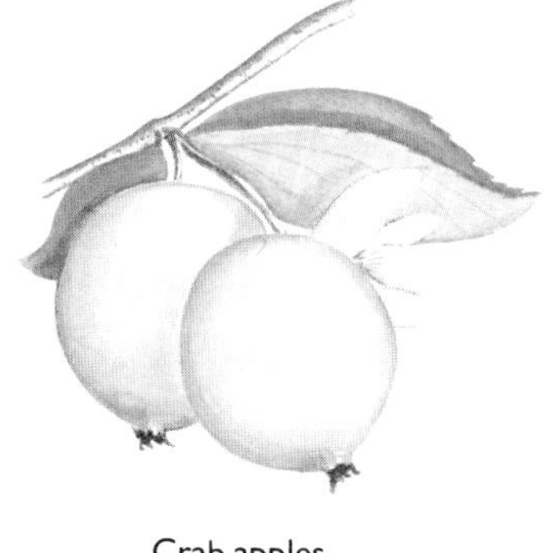

Crab apples

Blackberries

◀ *Coal is a solid fuel. Like other fuels, it is a combination of three chemical elements—carbon, hydrogen, and oxygen.*

Fuel

Fuels are substances that give off heat when they burn. Fuels provide our world with the ENERGY we use for heating, cooking, powering ships, planes, cars and machines, and producing electricity.

The most important fuels are COAL, OIL, and NATURAL GAS. They were formed underground from the remains of prehistoric plants or animals. People often call them fossil fuels.

Some fuels give out more heat than others. A pound of coal gives nearly three times as much heat as a pound of wood. Oil gives nearly four times as much, and HYDROGEN gas ten times as much. But URANIUM can give more than half a million times as much heat as hydrogen.

As fossil fuels are used up, we shall have to make more use of atomic energy, SOLAR ENERGY, and wind and water power.

Fuel Cell

A fuel cell is a special kind of electric battery that keeps on making electricity as long as fuel is fed into it. The main use for the fuel cell is in spacecraft. Fuel cells supplied electricity in the Apollo spacecraft that flew to the Moon in 1969–72. These cells used oxygen and hydrogen as fuel. Inside the cells, the oxygen and hydrogen combined together to produce electricity and water. The astronauts drank the water.

FUELS

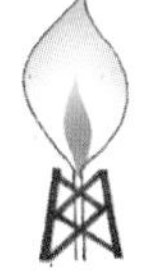

Natural gas is a fuel that is widely used for cooking and heating. It is found deep underground close to oil pools.

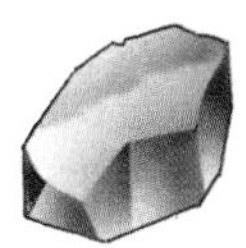

Coal is still used to produce most of the world's electricity. For a century and a half, it has been the most important fuel for producing heat to make steam.

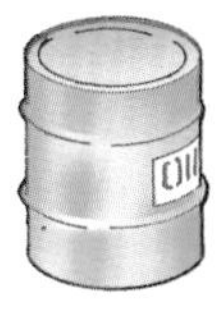

Oil, or petroleum, comes from oil wells sunk deep into the Earth. Gasoline, kerosene, and diesel oil are all separated from petroleum.

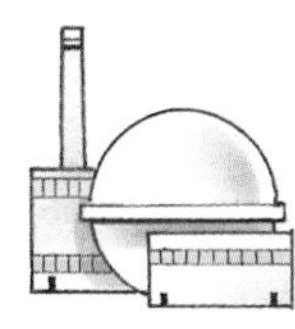

Nuclear fuel is usually uranium. It is put into nuclear reactors and produces great amounts of energy. Nuclear reactors generate electricity.

Solar energy — energy from the Sun— is radiant energy, energy that travels in waves. It gives us light and heat. It is also the source of most of the energy on Earth.

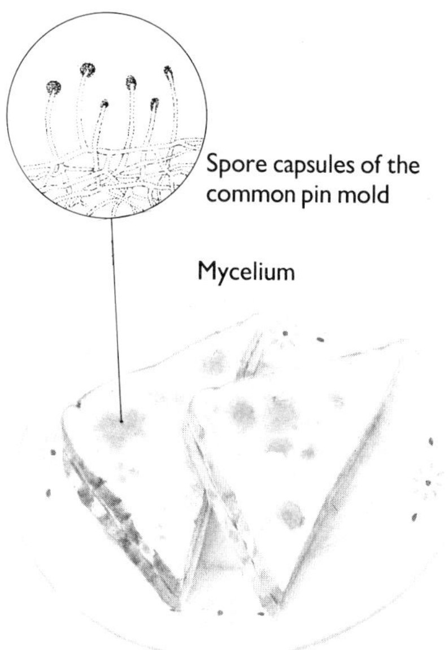

▲ *The fungus family includes molds. Uncovered food offers a perfect place for molds to grow. The tiny, thread-like growths (inset) spread quickly.*

Fulton, Robert

Robert Fulton (1765–1815) was an American inventor who designed and built one of the earliest steamboats, the *Clermont*. It sailed between New York City and Albany. He also designed the first steam-powered warship, which he called *Fulton the First*. Among his other important inventions were a new type of canal boat and a machine for cutting canals. Though it was never a complete success, Fulton also designed a type of submarine.

Fungus

A fungus is a simple PLANT with no true roots, stem, or leaves. Fungi do not have the chlorophyll that helps green plants to make food. So fungi have to find a ready-made supply of food. Some feed as parasites on living plants or animals. Others feed on animal and plant remains.

There are more than 50,000 kinds of fungus. Some have only one CELL. Other fungi are chains of cells. These produce tiny, threadlike growths that spread through the substance they feed on. Many fungi grow a large fruiting body that sheds spores to produce new fungus plants. The MUSHROOMS we eat are the fruiting bodies of a fungus. Some fungi are useful. Pencillin, the ANTIBIOTIC drug, and YEAST are both fungi.

▼ *Throughout history, furniture has often been beautiful as well as useful. Below are some very individual pieces of everyday furniture from 4,000 years ago to the 20th century.*

▲ A highly-decorated queen's bathtub from the early Greek civilization at Knossos, on the island of Crete (1500 B.C.).

▼ This chair dates from 2690 B.C. and is an example of the fine wooden furniture made by the ancient Egyptians.

▲ A French writing desk from the 1700s. French furniture from this period was often ornate and elaborately decorated.

Furniture 

Furniture is used for resting things on and for storing things in. Beds, chairs, and tables all support some kind of load. Chests and closets hold things such as sheets and china. But as well as being useful, furniture can also be beautiful. People have always tried to make furniture attractive to look at as well as useful.

The first pieces of furniture were simple slabs of stone and roughly carved wood. As people became more sophisticated and wealthy, so furniture became more complex. The ancient Egyptians had carefully carved and painted tables and beds as much as 4,000 years ago. The Romans used bronze and marble as well as wood to make furniture. Their furniture was often very skillfully made. After the RENAISSANCE, furniture-making in Europe became a great craft. In the 1700s especially, furniture-makers produced work that many people think has never been surpassed, and many people prize their work highly today. In the 1800s, people began to use new materials to make furniture. Furniture began to be mass produced and less expensive. This meant that more and more people were able to buy at least some pieces of furniture. Today, furniture is made from many different materials in many styles. A lot of modern furniture has clean, simple lines.

Furniture was so scarce in Europe during the Middle Ages that it was quite common for a visitor to bring along his or her bed and other pieces of furniture.

In England until the 17th century, the three-legged stool was still widely used. People thought that a chair should be used only by the lord of the manor.

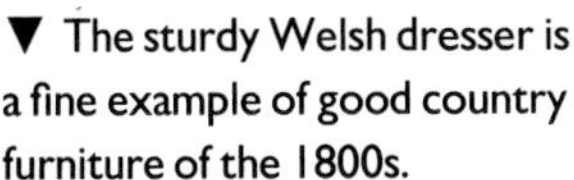

▼ The sturdy Welsh dresser is a fine example of good country furniture of the 1800s.

▼ An American parlor bed, dating from 1891, which folded away when not in use.

► A light and elegant chair designed by Charles Rennie Mackintosh, a Scottish architect and designer.

Gabon

Gabon is a country on the west coast of Africa. It lies on the equator, so it is hot and rainy there. Gabon is a land of high plateaus, mountains, and dense tropical forests. The country is rich in mineral resources, and trees are cut down for export. Most of Gabon's people are farmers who live in villages along the coast or along the rivers.

GABON

CAMEROON
EQUATORIAL GUINEA
GABON
CONGO
ATLANTIC OCEAN
ZAIRE
ANGOLA
ANGOLA

Government: Republic
Capital: Libreville
Area: 103,346 sq. miles (267,667 sq. km)
Population: 1,069,000
Language: French
Currency: CFA Franc

Gagarin, Yuri

Yuri Gagarin (1934–1968) was the first human being to travel into space. The Soviet cosmonaut was rocketed upward in *Vostok I* on April 12, 1961. He circled the Earth once in 108 minutes and landed by parachute within 6 miles (10 km) of the planned spot. After his famous flight, Gagarin continued to train as a cosmonaut, but he was killed in a plane crash in March, 1968.

Galaxy

Someone once called galaxies "star islands" in space. A galaxy is made up of a huge group of STARS. Our SUN is just one star of about 100,000 million stars that belong to the Milky Way galaxy. A beam of light would take about 100,000 years to shine from one side of the Milky Way to the other. Yet the Milky Way is only a middle-sized galaxy.

Beyond our galaxy, there may be as many as 10,000 million more. The nearest large galaxy is

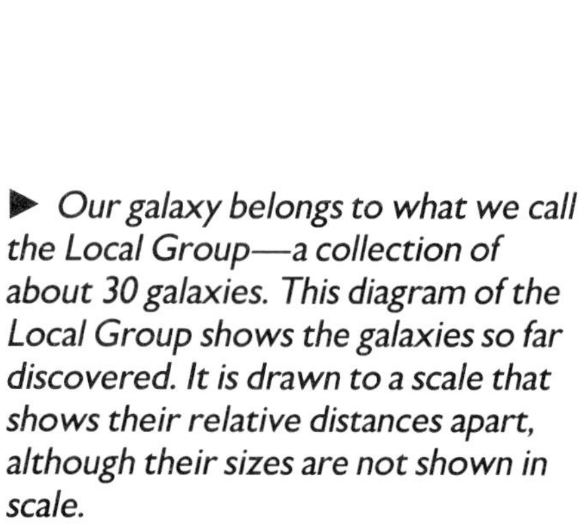

▶ *Our galaxy belongs to what we call the Local Group—a collection of about 30 galaxies. This diagram of the Local Group shows the galaxies so far discovered. It is drawn to a scale that shows their relative distances apart, although their sizes are not shown in scale.*

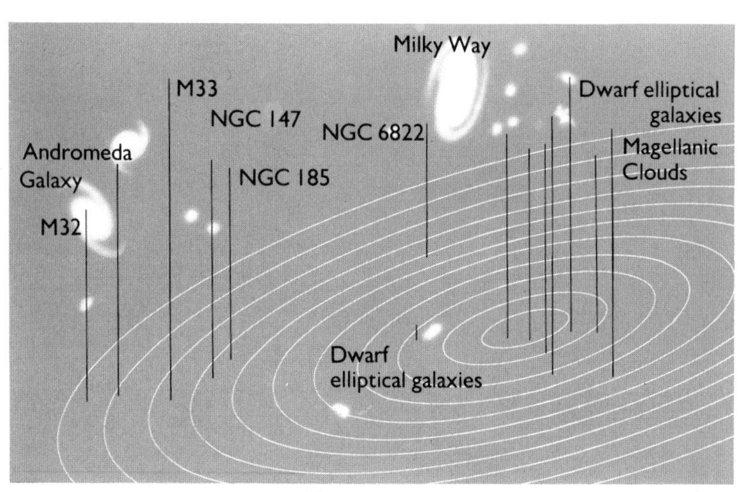

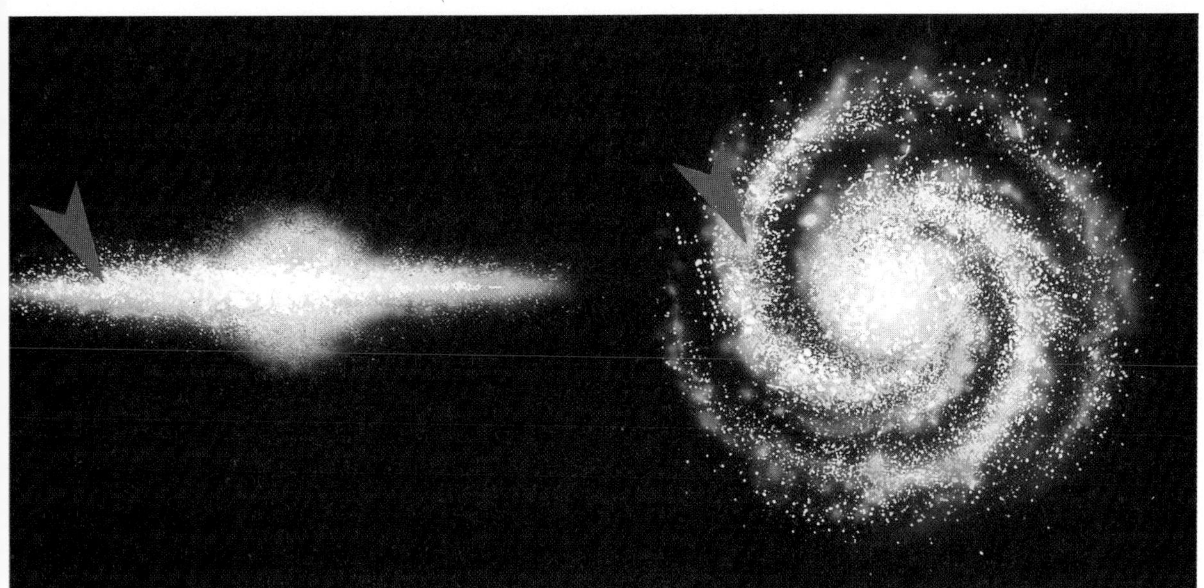

called Andromeda. The light we see it by took more than two million years to reach us.

Some galaxies have no special shape. Others have spiral arms made up of many millions of stars. The Milky Way and Andromeda galaxies both look like this. There are also galaxies that look like saucers or balls. Astronomers used to think that these changed into galaxies with spiral arms. Now some astronomers believe that the spiral galaxies shrink into the other kind instead.

RADIO ASTRONOMY has shown that radio waves are sent out from many galaxies. Strong radio waves also come from strange starlike objects known as QUASARS. Quasars are very powerful energy sources. Some people think that a quasar may be the beginning of a new galaxy. Scientists think that galaxies may form where GRAVITY pulls huge clouds of gas together.

▲ *Edge on, our Milky Way galaxy looks like a flat disk with a swollen middle—the nucleus. From above, it looks like a whirlpool of stars. The position of our solar system is marked by the red arrows.*

Galileo

Galileo Galilei (1564–1642) was an Italian mathematics teacher and one of the first true scientists. Instead of believing old ideas about the way the world worked, Galileo made careful experiments to find out for himself. He learned that a PENDULUM took the same time to make a long swing as it did to make a short one. He showed that light objects fell as fast as heavy ones when pulled toward the Earth

▲ *Galileo was a mathematician, astronomer, and physicist, and one of the first true scientists.*

▲ *A galleon sets sail. A gang of seamen unfurl the mainsail, and others in the main top adjust the running rigging.*

by what we know as GRAVITY. He built a TELESCOPE and became the first man to use this tool for studying the Moon and PLANETS. What he saw made Galileo believe COPERNICUS's idea that the Earth was not the center of the UNIVERSE. The Church punished him for his belief in this idea. But later scientists like Isaac NEWTON built new knowledge on Galileo's discoveries.

Galleon

This kind of heavy, wooden sailing ship was used for carrying fighting men and cargoes over oceans in the 1500s. A galleon was four times as long as it was wide. It had a special deck to carry cannons. There were square sails on its two front masts and three-cornered *lateen* sails on its one or two rear masts. Lateen sails helped galleons to sail against the wind. Galleons were faster and easier to manage than some other ships, but some Spanish galleons were clumsy and top-heavy.

INSIDE A GALLEON

1 Forecastle
2 Gun deck
3 Orlop
4 Bitts
5 Anchor cable locker
6 Stone ballast
7 Cookhouse
8 Pump
9 Cannonball store
10 Capstan
11 Sail locker
12 Hold
13 Rudder
14 Tiller
15 Whipstaff
16 Captain's cabin

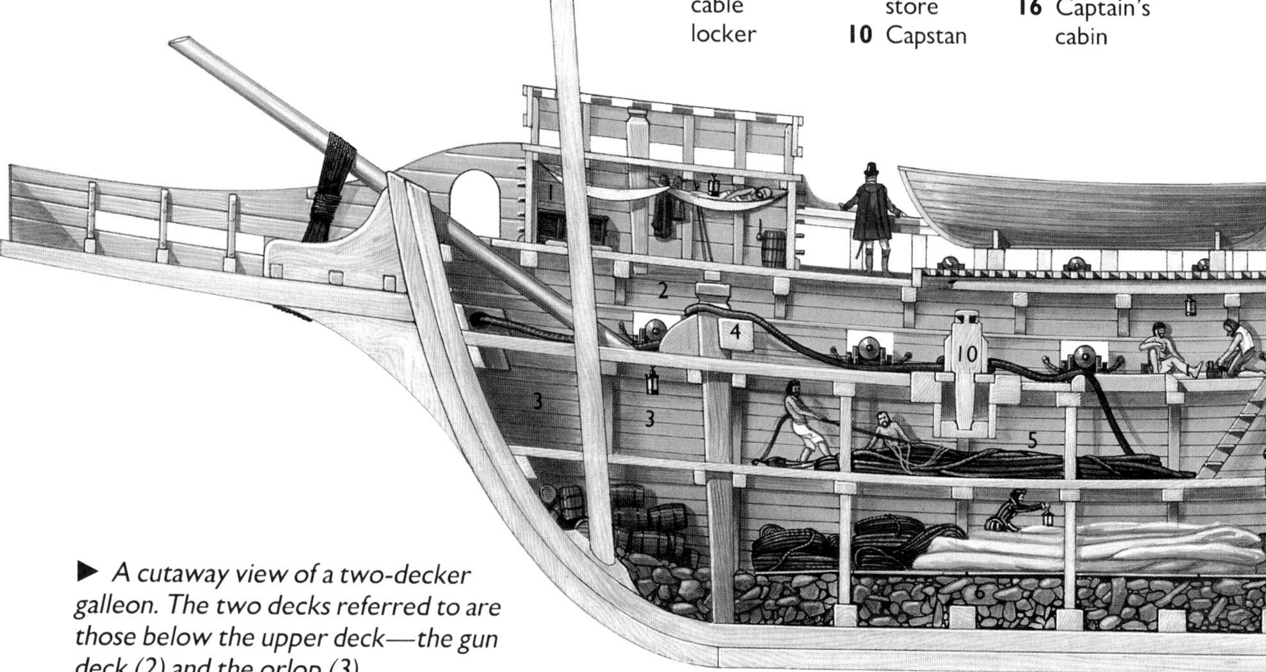

► *A cutaway view of a two-decker galleon. The two decks referred to are those below the upper deck—the gun deck (2) and the orlop (3).*

Gama, Vasco da

Vasco da Gama (about 1469–1524) discovered how to sail by sea from Europe to India by way of southern Africa. This Portuguese navigator left Lisbon with four ships in July, 1497. In East Africa, he found a guide who showed him how to sail across the Indian Ocean. Da Gama reached Calicut in southern India in May, 1498. But Arab traders who were jealous of the Portuguese tried to stop him from trading with the Indians. On the journey home, 30 of his 90 crewmen died of scurvy, and only two of the four ships got back to Lisbon.

But da Gama had found a way to reach the spice-rich lands of the East.

Gambia, The

The Gambia is Africa's smallest country. It is on the west coast and is about half the size of Massachusetts. Most Gambians are poor and earn their living as farmers. Peanuts are the main crop. In recent years, tourism has increased. Once a British colony, Gambia became independent in 1965.

THE GAMBIA

MAURITANIA
ATLANTIC OCEAN
SENEGAL
MALI
GAMBIA
GUINEA-BISSAU
GUINEA

Government: Republic
Capital: Banjul
Area: 4,360 sq. miles (11,295 sq. km)
Population: 861,000
Language: English
Currency: Dalasi

▲ *Gandhi was called the* Mahatma *by his followers, which means "Great Soul."*

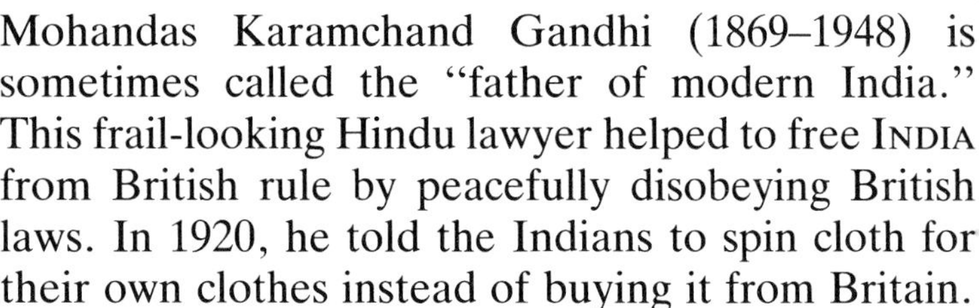

Gandhi

Mohandas Karamchand Gandhi (1869–1948) is sometimes called the "father of modern India." This frail-looking Hindu lawyer helped to free INDIA from British rule by peacefully disobeying British laws. In 1920, he told the Indians to spin cloth for their own clothes instead of buying it from Britain.

People admired Gandhi's beliefs, his kindness, and his simple way of life. He was called the Mahatma, meaning "Great Soul." In 1947, Britain gave India independence. Soon after, one of his fellow HINDUS shot Gandhi for preaching peace between Hindus and Muslims, followers of ISLAM.

Gandhi, Indira

Indira Gandhi (1917–1984) was prime minister of India from 1966 until 1977 and from 1980 until her death. Her father, Jawaharlal Nehru, supported GANDHI and became India's first prime minister after independence. In 1942, Indira married a lawyer, Feroze Gandhi. For years, she helped her father. Then she went into politics herself. In power, Mrs. Gandhi fought for economic progress, social reforms, and national unity. In 1984, she was killed by two Sikhs, members of an Indian religious group. Her son Rajiv succeeded her as India's prime minister, but he was assassinated in 1991.

▼ *The Ganges rises in the Himalayas and flows southeast to join the Brahmaputra River at its delta.*

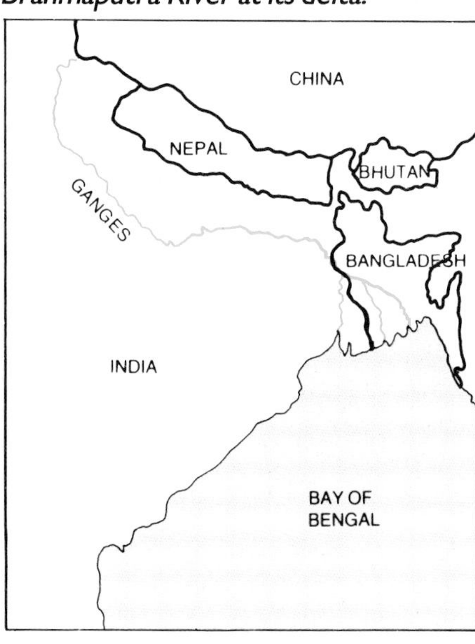

Ganges, River

The Ganges is the greatest river in INDIA. It flows for about 1,560 miles (2,500 km) and drains an area three times the size of Spain. The river rises in the HIMALAYAS and winds across northern India and BANGLADESH, then through a DELTA to the Bay of Bengal. Rich farmlands and great cities line its banks. HINDUS believe the river is sacred.

Garden

Gardens are pieces of land kept especially for growing lawns, flowering plants, fruits, vegetables, and other attractive shrubs and trees.

Rich people in ancient Egypt had gardens 4,500 years ago. The city of Babylon was later famous for hanging gardens. In the Middle Ages, many monasteries also had gardens. New types of gardens with fountains, pools, terraces, steps, and pathways were developed during the Renaissance in Italy. In the 1600s and 1700s, the French developed this type of garden, making it larger and more formal. In England, people preferred gardens that seemed more natural looking, with large lawns and trees around big houses. In the 1800s, cities laid out gardens where anyone could walk. Today, many houses have some sort of garden or yard.

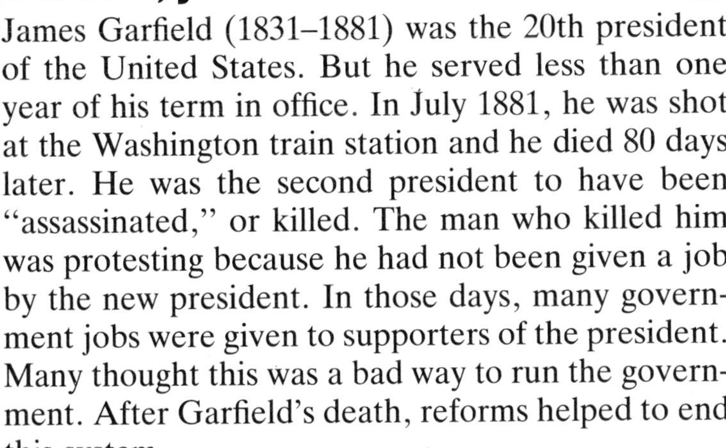

Garfield, James Abram

James Garfield (1831–1881) was the 20th president of the United States. But he served less than one year of his term in office. In July 1881, he was shot at the Washington train station and he died 80 days later. He was the second president to have been "assassinated," or killed. The man who killed him was protesting because he had not been given a job by the new president. In those days, many government jobs were given to supporters of the president. Many thought this was a bad way to run the government. After Garfield's death, reforms helped to end this system.

Garfield was a college professor and a soldier before he became a politican. He served bravely in the Civil War for the North and was made a general when he was only 31.

JAMES A. GARFIELD

Twentieth President Mar.–Sept. 1881
Born: Orange, Ohio
Education: Williams College, Mass.
Occupation: Teacher
Political Party: Republican
Buried: Cleveland, Ohio

Garibaldi, Giuseppe

Giuseppe Garibaldi (1807–1882) was an Italian patriot who helped to turn Italy from a collection of small states into a united and independent country. After two periods of exile in the U.S., Garibaldi led his followers, known as Redshirts, against the Austrians, who then controlled Italy. In 1860, he gained control of Sicily and southern Italy. Then he invaded mainland Italy and captured the important city of Naples. This victory helped make possible the uniting of Italy under King Victor Emmanuel.

▲ *Giuseppe Garibaldi, who helped to create the modern state of Italy, began his career as cabin boy on a ship.*

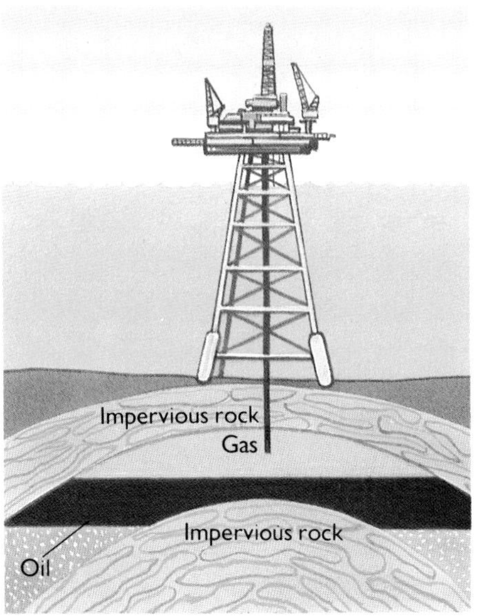

▲ *Oil and natural gas collect in porous rocks (rocks that allow liquids to soak through). They are trapped between impervious rocks (which will not allow liquids to pass through).*

Gas

Gases are substances with no special shape or size. They take up the size and shape of any container that holds them. This can happen because a gas is made of ATOMS moving freely in space. When a gas becomes cold enough, it turns into a liquid. Liquids have a fixed size, but no fixed shape. If that liquid becomes much colder still, it turns into a solid. Solids have a fixed shape and size. AIR, HYDROGEN, and OXYGEN are gases at normal temperatures.

The gas some people use to cook and heat homes with is called NATURAL GAS. This gas is found beneath the Earth's surface in many parts of the world.

Gasoline

Gasoline is made from an oil called petroleum, and is used to power cars and trucks. It is one of the most important fuels. It is made by "refining" the elements that make up petroleum. Though it is so important, gasoline also pollutes the air when it is burned. Its use has to be controlled carefully.

▼ *Gear wheels turn at different speeds in proportion to the number of teeth they possess. The small wheel turns twice as fast as the large one if it has half the number of teeth.*

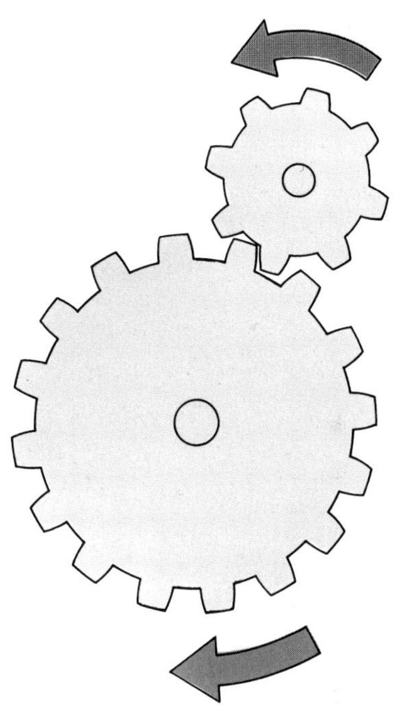

Gear

A gear is a wheel with teeth along its rim. These teeth can fit into the teeth of other gear wheels. Metal rods, or *axles*, are fitted into the center of each gear. If one axle is turned, its gear turns and makes the second gear turn. This makes the second axle turn, too.

Gears are used to increase or decrease the *speed* at which wheels turn. They are also used to increase or decrease the *turning power* of wheels.

In the picture on the left, the large gear wheel has twice as many teeth as the small wheel. If the small wheel is turned by an engine, the big wheel will turn at only half the speed of the small wheel, and the big wheel will turn in the opposite direction to the small wheel. But the big wheel will have twice the turning power of the small wheel. When a car is in low gear, this is what happens. The car goes quite slowly, but it has plenty of power for starting or going up hills.

Inside an AC generator, a coil of wire is turned between the poles of a magnet. Halfway through each turn, the coil becomes positioned for an instant at a right angle to the magnet. This causes the direction of the current to change.

ALTERNATING CURRENT

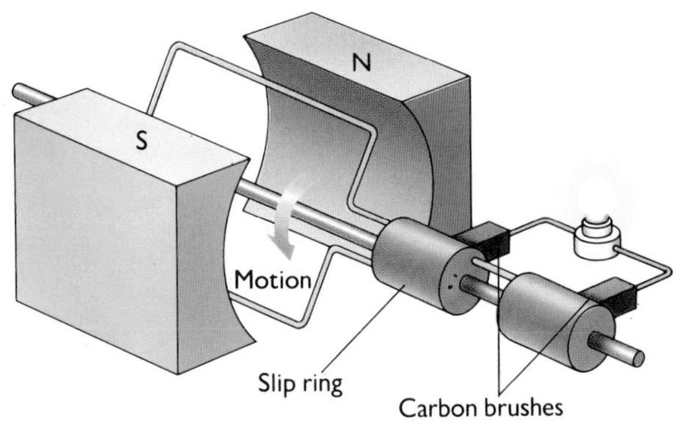

DIRECT CURRENT

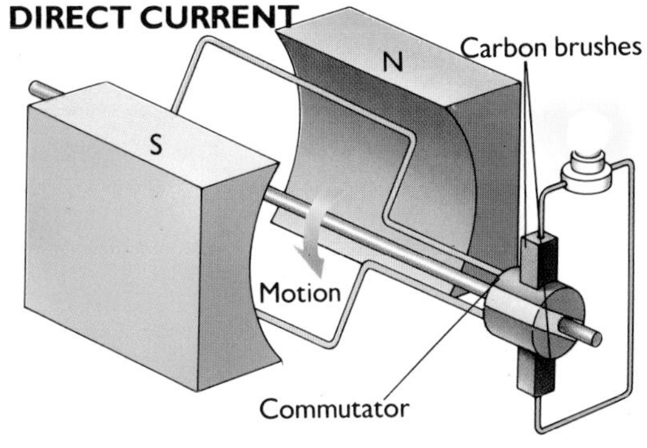

Direct current, such as that from a battery, can be obtained from a generator by using a device called a commutator. This makes the current flow continuously in the same direction.

▲ *An AC and a DC generator. Each has a wire coil held between the poles of a magnet.*

Generator

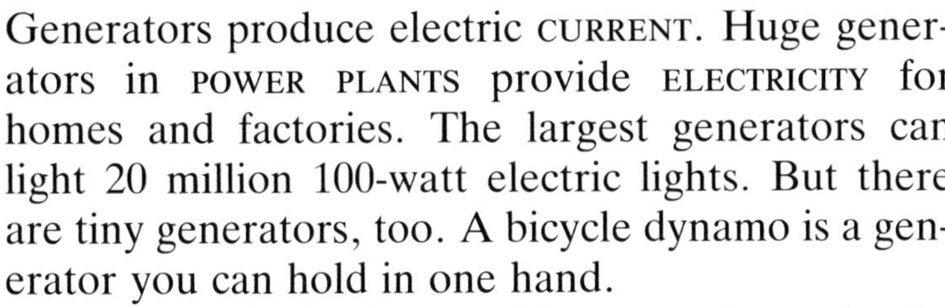

Generators produce electric CURRENT. Huge generators in POWER PLANTS provide ELECTRICITY for homes and factories. The largest generators can light 20 million 100-watt electric lights. But there are tiny generators, too. A bicycle dynamo is a generator you can hold in one hand.

If a loop of wire is turned between the ends of a horseshoe-shaped magnet, an electric current flows in the wire. Generators work like this. They change the ENERGY of motion into electrical energy. The energy to work a generator's moving parts can come from wind, flowing water, or steam produced by heat from FUELS such as oil or coal. Big generators have thousands of coils of wire which are made to turn very quickly between powerful magnets.

Genetics

Each animal or plant passes on certain characteristics to its offspring. For example, we say that someone has "his father's eyes" or "her mother's hair." The science of genetics explains why living things look and behave as they do.

Heredity works in an amazing way. Each individ-

▼ *Albino animals such as this hedgehog are born white, with no coloring matter in their skin or hair. They have pink eyes. Albinos inherit their colorless condition from their ancestors' genes. An albino parent may produce normal young, and the young may later produce albinos.*

The chances of a baby being a girl or boy are about the same. But one in 16 families with four children is likely to have four boys, while another such family will have four girls. Much longer strings of boys or girls have been recorded. One French family had nothing but girls—72 of them—in three generations.

ual produces sex cells. If a male and female cell join, the female cell grows into a new individual. Inside every cell there are tiny chromosomes, largely made of a chemical called DNA. Different parts of each chromosome carry different coded messages. Each of these parts is called a *gene*. The genes carry all the information needed to make a new plant or animal look and behave as it does. They decide its sex and also every other characteristic it inherits from its parents.

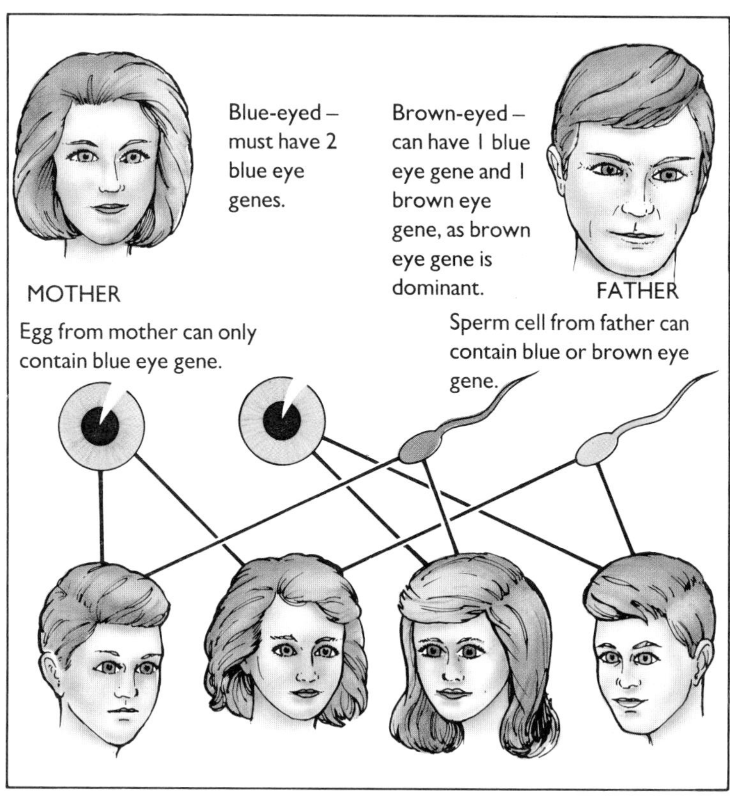
Blue-eyed – must have 2 blue eye genes.
Brown-eyed – can have 1 blue eye gene and 1 brown eye gene, as brown eye gene is dominant.
MOTHER
FATHER
Egg from mother can only contain blue eye gene.
Sperm cell from father can contain blue or brown eye gene.

▶ *Each of us has two genes for a characteristic such as eye color, one from each parent. If the two genes are different, one may have a stronger influence than the other. It is called the* dominant *gene. If someone inherits one brown eye gene and one blue eye gene, they will have brown eyes because the brown eye gene is dominant. The blue eye gene is called the* recessive *gene. If someone inherits two blue eye genes, one from each parent, he or she can only have blue eyes.*

Genghis Khan

Genghis Khan (1167–1227) was a Mongol chief who cruelly attacked many Asian peoples and won a mighty empire. His real name was Temujin ("iron-smith").

At 13, he took his dead father's place as chief of a small Mongol tribe of nomads. He soon won power over nearby tribes as well. In 1206, he became known as Genghis Khan, "Very Mighty King." Genghis Khan formed a huge army of tough, hard-riding nomads on the great grasslands of central Asia. Then he set off to conquer the lands around

▼ *At its height, the Mongol empire under Genghis Khan stretched from China in the east right across Asia.*

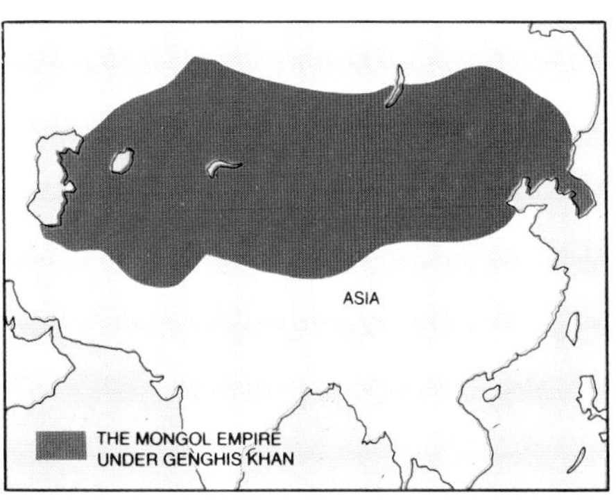
ASIA
THE MONGOL EMPIRE UNDER GENGHIS KHAN

him. His troops pushed southeast to Beijing in China, and south into Tibet and what are now Pakistan and Afghanistan. In the southwest, they invaded Persia (Iran) and southern Russia.

After he died, other Mongol rulers won more land and made the empire even larger.

▲ *Genghis Khan put together a huge, organized army. Each man had five ponies, ridden in turn so that they would not get tired. When the Mongols besieged a city, most of the inhabitants were killed, and the land around was laid waste.*

Geography

Geography is the subject we study when we want to learn about the surface of the Earth. Geographers study everything on the Earth—the land, sea, air, plants, animals, and people. They explain where different things are found, how they got there, and how they affect one another.

There are many different areas, or branches, of geography. For instance, physical geography describes things liks mountains, valleys, lakes, and rivers. Meteorology describes weather. Economic geography deals with farming, mining, manufacturing, and trade. Human geography divides the peoples of the world into *cultures*.

MAPS AND CHARTS are the geographer's most useful tools.

Ptolemy of Alexandria was the most famous ancient geographer—he lived about A.D.150. Ptolemy drew a map of the then-known world that is remarkably accurate, considering what was known about the Earth in those days. His eight-volume *Guide to Geography* consisted of a list of all known places, each with its latitude and longitude, a system Ptolemy devised.

▶ *Geologists study rocks, which tell them about the Earth's structure. There are three kinds of rock:* igneous, *formed when molten rock is pushed up from deep inside the Earth;* sedimentary, *which is hardened layers of sediment; and* metamorphic, *which is igneous or sedimentary rock that has been changed by heat and pressure inside the Earth. Of the rocks shown here, obsidian (1) and granite (2) are igneous rocks, marble (3) and slate (4) are metamorphic rocks, and coal (5), limestone (6), and sandstone (7) are sedimentary rocks. Conglomerate (8) is made up of stone stuck together in a sedimentary "concrete."*

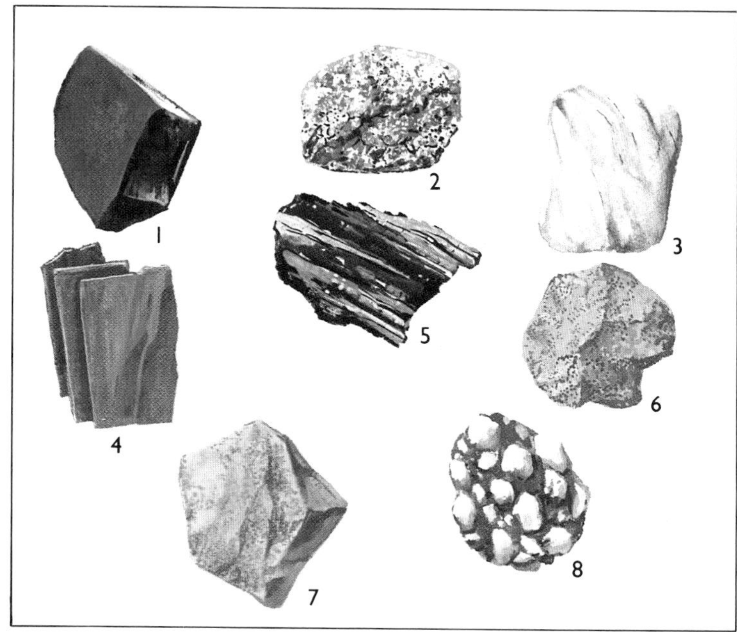

For a long time, people have tried to work out the age of the Earth. In the 1600s, an Irish archbishop named Ussher decided from reading the Scriptures that the world was created in 4004 B.C. It was not long, however, before geologists realized by examining the rocks that this date was very wrong. We now know that the Earth was formed about $4\frac{1}{2}$ billion years ago.

Geology

Geology is the study of the Earth itself. Geologists discover what things the Earth is made of, where they are found, and how they got there. Geologists study the chemicals in ROCKS and MINERALS. They also try to find out how rocks are formed, and how they are changed by movements beneath the surface of the Earth. VOLCANOES and EARTHQUAKES give us useful clues about movements deep down underground.

Geologists also study the history of the Earth. They have found rock 3.8 billion years old and FOSSILS showing that EVOLUTION began over 3.4 billion years ago.

Geologists help engineers to choose where to build a road or tunnel. They help miners to find coal, oil, or gas beneath the ground. By studying rocks brought back by astronauts, they were able to tell us what the Moon is made of.

In geometry, we learn that the three angles of any triangle add up to 180 degrees—a straight line. You can prove this by cutting out a triangle from a piece of paper. Tear off the three angles and rearrange them so that the sides, angles and corners are together. They make a straight angle of 180°.

Geometry

Geometry is a branch of MATHEMATICS. It can help you to find out the shape, size, and position of an object, or how much a container holds. People draw lines and measure ANGLES to help them solve geometric problems.

Georgia

Georgia is a southern state, and one of the 13 original states. Farming is important to it, but many modern "service" industries help to make Georgia prosperous today. Some people think Georgia one of the most beautiful states. Its lush vegetation, especially its pine trees and magnolias, are famous.

Georgia was named in 1732 for King George II of England. But the first Europeans to visit it were Spaniards, in 1540. Later, Frenchmen settled here, too. But by the mid-1700s, Georgia was an English colony. There was fierce fighting here in the Revolutionary War before the British were driven out.

In the 1800s, Georgia's prosperity was based on cotton and slaves. It was one of the first states to leave the Union before the Civil War. Union troops destroyed huge areas of the state and burned the capital, Atlanta. For many years afterward, Georgia was one of the poorest states.

GEORGIA

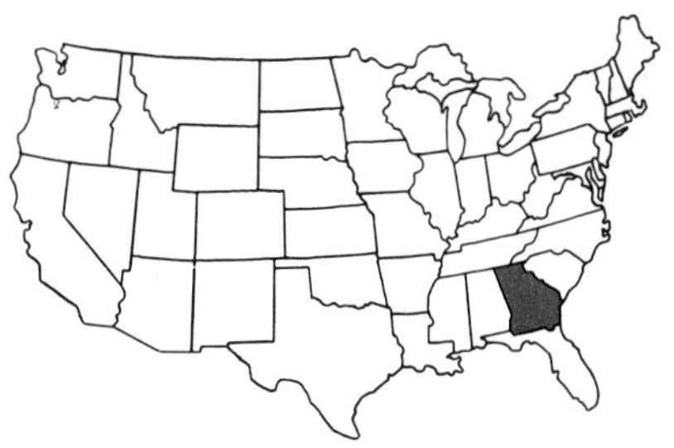

Capital: Atlanta
Population: 6,478,216
Area: 58,910 sq.mi. (152,576 sq.km)
State flower: Cherokee Rose
State bird: Brown Thrasher
State tree: Live Oak
Statehood: January 2, 1788
4th state

▲ *The Okefenokee National Wildlife Refuge at Folkston, Georgia.*

Germ *See* Bacteria; Virus

Germany

Before World War II Germany was one nation, but after the war the land was divided into two countries: West Germany and East Germany. East Germany was a Communist country, closely allied to the Soviet Union. The two Germanys remained separate until 1990, when they were finally reunited

◀ *The German city of Dresden was almost totally rebuilt after being heavily bombed in World War II.*

▶ *Traditional buildings line this street in Lohr-am-Main in Germany.*

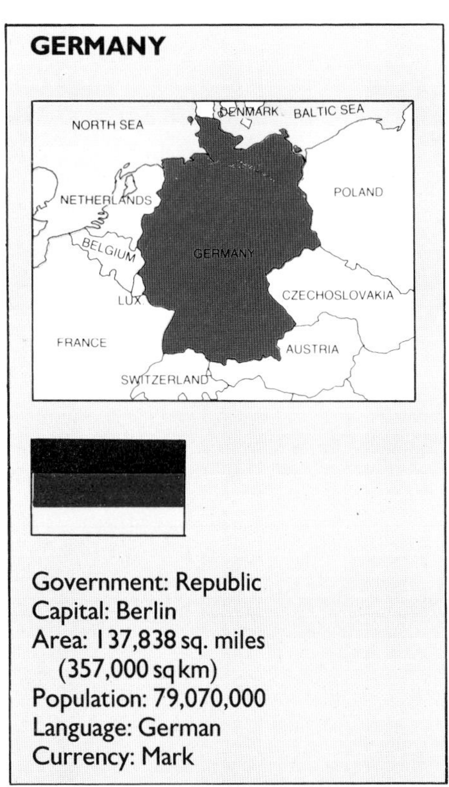

Government: Republic
Capital: Berlin
Area: 137,838 sq. miles (357,000 sq km)
Population: 79,070,000
Language: German
Currency: Mark

under a federal government. The capital is once more BERLIN.

Germany lies in the middle of Europe and has the largest population of any western European nation. Farms and cities stand on a low, flat plain to the north; the south is a region of wooded mountains. In the far south the tall peaks of the Alps rise thousands of feet above sea level. Germany's major rivers are the Rhine, the Elbe, and the Oder. They flow north toward the North Sea and the Baltic Sea.

Before reunification, West Germany was the richest nation in Europe. Its mines and factories produced more coal, steel, cars, and television sets than any other western European nation. East Germany, less than half the size of West Germany, had mines and factories, too, but much of its industry was old-fashioned and unproductive. Now that the rich West and the poorer East are united there are problems to be faced, but the German people are working together to overcome them.

Gershwin, George and Ira 

George (1898–1937) and his brother Ira (1896–1983) were two of the most important American songwriters of the 20th century. George wrote the music, Ira wrote the words. Their most famous works include the opera *Porgy and Bess* and songs such as *I Got Rhythm*. George also wrote many orchestral works. The best known and most influential is *Rhapsody in Blue*.

Geyser

Geysers are hot springs that now and then squirt out steam and scalding water. They work like this. Water fills a deep crack in the ground, often near VOLCANOES. Hot rock heats the water deep underground, but the weight of the water above it stops the hot water from boiling until it is much hotter still. Then it turns to steam, which forces the water upward, emptying the crack. The next eruption happens when the crack is full again.

There are many geysers in some parts of Iceland, the United States, and New Zealand. The tallest geyser ever known was the Waimangu Geyser in New Zealand. In 1904, it squirted steam and water nearly 1,520 ft. (460 m) into the sky.

▲ *A geyser seems to work in a similar way to a pressure cooker. The higher the pressure, the hotter the water has to be to boil. The super-heated steam and water is pushed out as a powerful jet. When enough water has seeped back and heated up, the process starts again.*

Ghana

Ghana is a nation in West AFRICA. It is a little smaller than Oregon. The country is hot, with plenty of rain in the south where Ghana meets the Atlantic Ocean. The land here is low, with tropical

▼ *Women sell pineapples in a market in Ghana. Two-thirds of Ghana's people live in the southern third of the country.*

GHANA

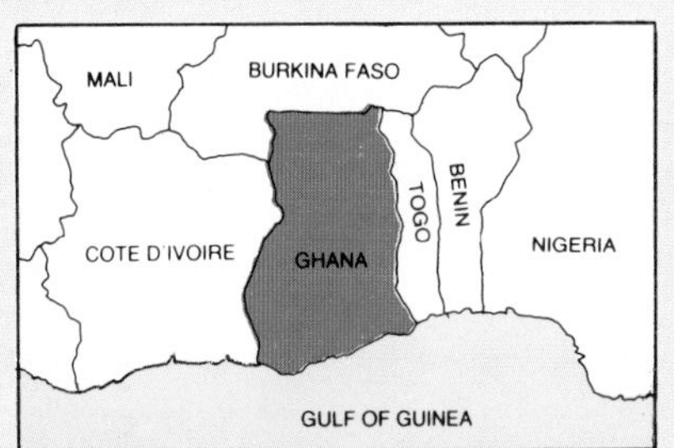

Government: Military
Capital: Accra
Area: 92,100 sq. miles (238,537 sq. km)
Population: 15,028,000
Language: English
Currency: Cedi

forests and farms. The north is drier and grassy.

Most of Ghana's 13 million people are farmers. They grow cocoa and mine diamonds and gold. Lake Volta provides water power to make electricity. This manmade lake covers a greater area than any other manmade lake in the world.

▼ *A giraffe's long neck and legs enable it to eat the leaves from branches that are far above the reach of other browsing animals.*

Giraffe

Giraffes are the tallest animals. An adult male may stand three times taller than a tall man. They have long legs and a long neck. Yet this neck has only seven bones, the same as any other MAMMAL. Giraffes live in the hot grasslands of Africa and feed on leaves from shrubs and trees.

Glacier

Glaciers are rivers of ice. Most form high up in mountains where snow falls and never melts. As snow piles up, the lower layers are crushed and turn to ice. This begins to flow very slowly downhill through valleys. Most glaciers take a year to flow as far as you can walk in five minutes. The rocks they

▼ *Glaciers move faster at the center than at the sides. This creates huge gaps, or crevasses.*

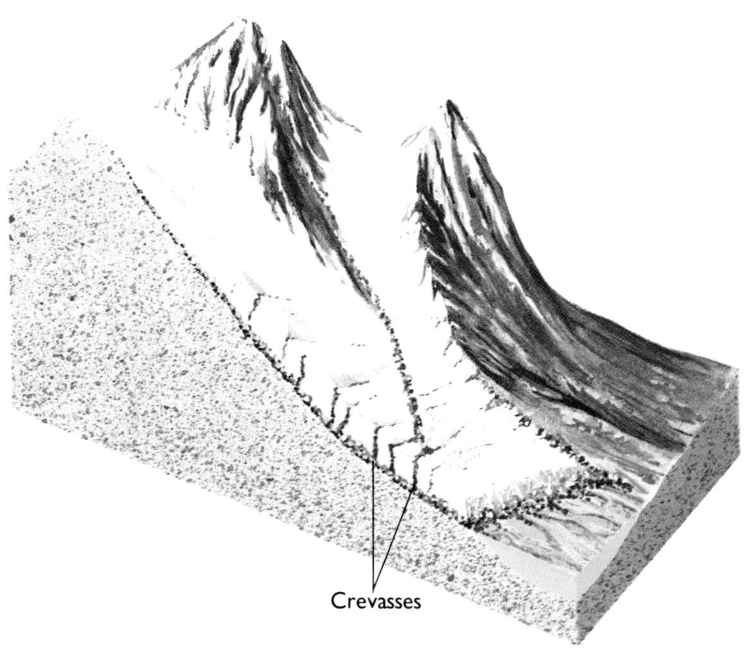

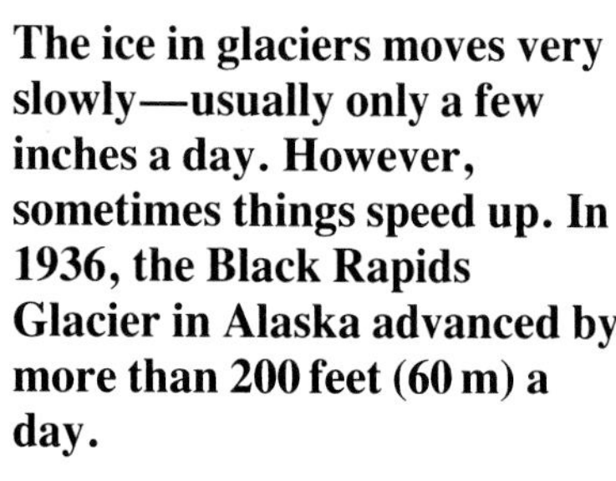

The ice in glaciers moves very slowly—usually only a few inches a day. However, sometimes things speed up. In 1936, the Black Rapids Glacier in Alaska advanced by more than 200 feet (60 m) a day.

carry grind against the sides and floor of each valley until they make it deep and wide.

During ICE AGES, glaciers spread beyond the mountains. When the weather warms up, they melt, leaving a valley behind. Many valleys in the ALPS and ROCKY MOUNTAINS once held glaciers.

Gladiator

Gladiators were men trained to fight to the death in shows to entertain crowds in ancient Rome. Many gladiators were criminals, prisoners of war, or slaves. Some fought with a sword and shield. Others had a three-pronged spear and a net. Most fights ended when one gladiator killed the other.

▲ *Successful gladiators became famous in Rome. They were carefully fed and received medical care.*

Gland

Glands are organs that produce special substances needed by the body. There are two kinds—*endocrine* and *exocrine* glands. Endocrine glands send their substances, called *hormones*, directly into the bloodstream. One main endocrine gland is the *thyroid*. Its hormone controls the rate at which the body uses energy.

Exocrine glands release their substances through tubes, either into the intestines or onto the skin. Sweat, tears, and saliva come from exocrine glands.

THE ENDOCRINE GLANDS

Pituitary gland	The small "master gland" that produces at least nine hormones, including those that control growth and reproduction
Thyroid gland	Controls the rate at which food is converted into energy. The tiny **parathyroids** regulate the amount of calcium in your bones and blood
Ovaries	Produce estrogen and progesterone, which control female characteristics. Also produce the ova, or egg cells
Testes	Produce testosterone, which controls the production of sperm cells and male characteristics
Pancreas	Produces insulin, which controls the level of glucose, a source of energy
Adrenal glands	Produce adrenaline, the "emergency" hormone that speeds up heartbeat and breathing rate when danger threatens.

▼ *Endocrine glands produce hormones that control such things as growth and reproduction.*

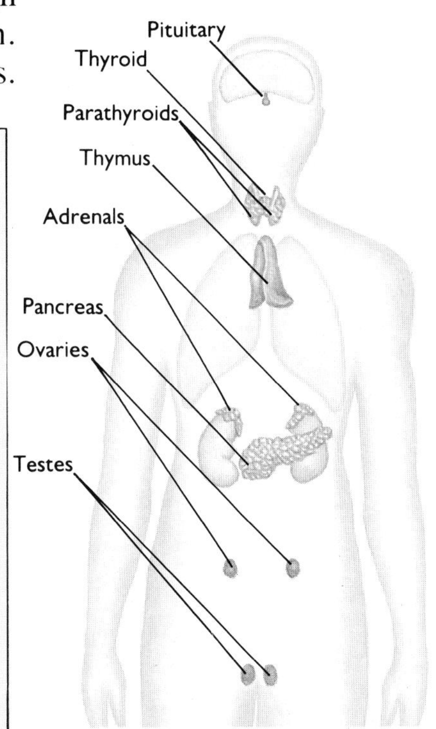

▲ *Hang gliding is a popular sport. The glider's design was the result of NASA research into spacecraft re-entry as part of the U.S. space program.*

Glass

People use glass in windows, eyeglasses, mirrors, tumblers, bottles, electric light bulbs, and many other objects. (See pages 300–301.)

Glenn, John Herschel, Jr.

John Glenn was the third American to go into space and the first to orbit the Earth. His flight was in 1962. It lasted less than five hours but it reassured America that it was keeping pace with the Soviet Union in the space race. Afterward, he became a politician, and in 1975 was elected a senator.

Gliding

Gliding is flying without using engine power. Gliding AIRCRAFT called sailplanes have long narrow wings. This gives them extra *lift*. The glider is launched by a winch or a towing aircraft. Once it is aloft, it loses height very gradually, kept up by rising air currents.

In 1853, the first glider to carry a man flew just across a valley. Modern sailplanes can do much more than that. In 1986, one sailplane reached a

To become a glider pilot in the U.S., a person must be 14 or older, and to get a private glider pilot's license he or she must be at least 16.

height of 37,730 feet (11,500 m) over California.

Hang gliding is a sport in which the pilot is suspended from the glider by a harness and a trapeze-like bar. The wing is light—usually 48 to 100 lbs. (22 to 44 kg) in weight—so that it can be carried and launched by one person. Takeoff is from a hill, cliff, or mountain steep enough to achieve flight. While in the air, pilots use their body weight to control the glider.

Goat

Goats are taller, thinner, and more agile animals than their close relatives, the SHEEP. Goats have hoofs and hollow horns; the male has a beard.

Wild goats, found in the mountains of central Asia and the Middle East, live in herds and eat grass and leaves. Domestic goats are kept in many lands. They provide milk, meat, hair, and skins. Two kinds, Angora and Cashmere goats, are famous for their silky wool, which is woven into fine cloth.

Gold

This is a yellow metal that never gets rusty. It is so soft that you can beat it into thin sheets, or pull it out into a wire.

Continued on page 302

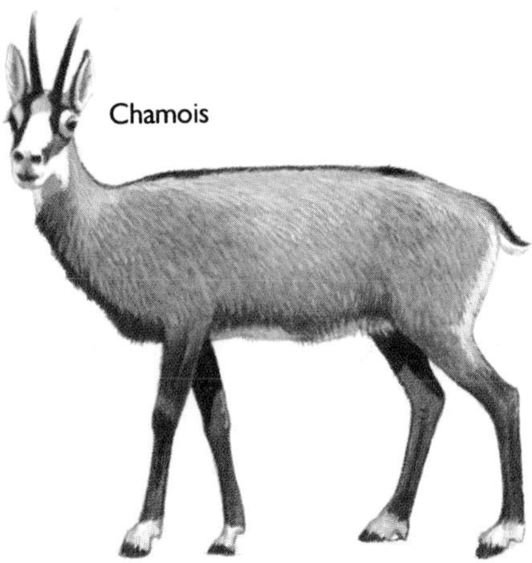

▲ *The Alpine ibex is a wild goat that lives above the treeline in alpine meadows and hillsides. It was hunted almost to extinction and is now protected by law. The chamois is a small mountain goat known for its leaps. Its soft hide is used for polishing.*

◀ *These gold bars in a Swiss bank are checked for purity with a machine that can "look" inside them by using sound.*

The biggest gold nugget ever found weighed about 471 lbs. (214 kg). It was discovered in New South Wales, Australia, in 1872. When refined, it yielded about 187 lbs. (85 kg) of pure gold.

GLASS

Glass is one of our most useful materials. It is easy to shape and cheap to make. It is also transparent, so you can see through it. Glass can be made as flat sheets, thick castings, or delicate wafers. It can be made into curved lenses for cameras, microscopes, and other optical instruments. It can be blown into bottles, or drawn out into tubes, wires, and very thin fibers.

Glass is made from mixing and heating sand, limestone, and soda ash. When these ingredients melt, they become glass. Special ingredients can be added to make glass that is heat-proof, extra-tough, or colored. Although glass looks like a solid, it is really a "supercooled" liquid. Glass is a good electrical insulator as it does not conduct current easily. It also resists common chemicals and nuclear radiation.

METHODS OF MAKING GLASS

Blowing Once done only by hand, glass-blowing is now also done by machines to make such things as bottles and light bulbs.

Pressing This is done by pushing partly melted glass into a mold, then cooling it. Ovenware and insulators are made by this method.

Drawing To pull out glass into tubes or wires, molten glass is drawn over a series of pulleys while air is blown through or around it. Drawn glass makes fluorescent tubes and pipes.

Casting This is done by pouring hot, molten glass into molds. The big optical telescopes used by astronomers have cast-glass lens disks.

Rolling A series of rollers squeeze molten glass into flat sheets (like rolling out dough).

Floating This is a method of making sheet glass by floating the molten glass across a bath of molten tin.

STAINED GLASS

Some of the most magnificent decorative stained glass was made in Europe during the Middle Ages. You can see examples in many churches and cathedrals, especially in Britain, France, Germany, and Italy.
The art of making stained glass flourished from the 1100s. By this time, glassmakers were able to make glass in many colors, and windows could be made much larger than before. Artists fitted pieces of colored glass together with lead to make beautiful designs for windows. Often medieval stained glass illustrates a Bible story, illuminated by the light streaming through the glass. Modern stained glass artists continue the craft, using similar techniques.

▼ *Sparkling crystal glassware has been made in England and Ireland since the 1700s Lead is used instead of limestone to give crystal its shine.*

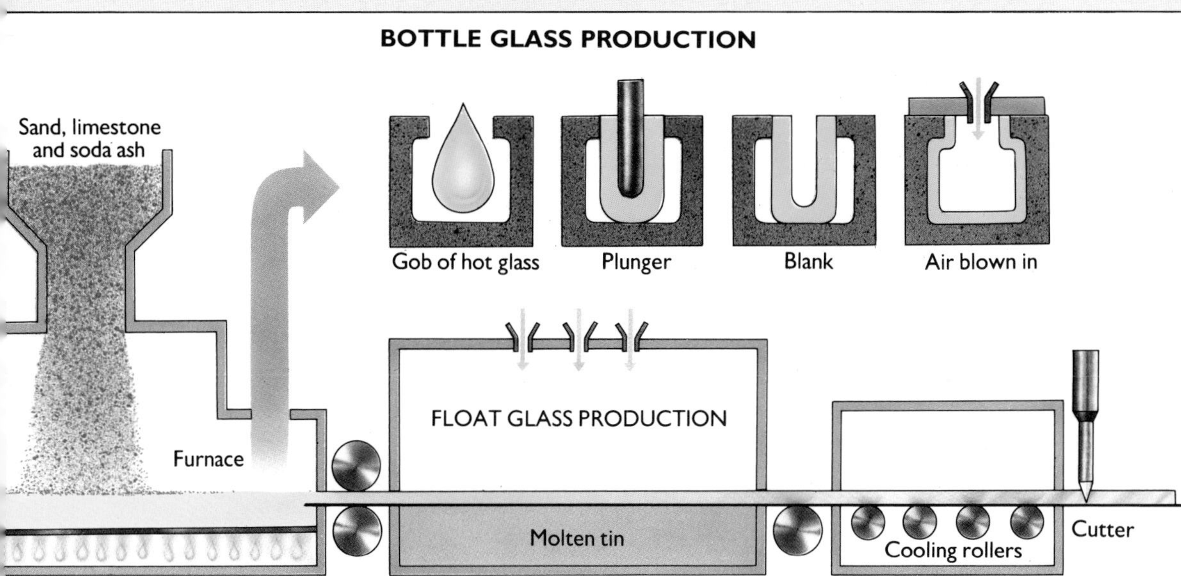

In glass manufacture, sand, soda ash, and limestone are loaded into the furnace, ...g with "cullet"—old pieces of glass. Molten glass from the furnace may either be ...ded and blown into hollow shapes (above), or shaped into flat sheets by the "float ...s" method (below). In the float glass process, molten glass is floated on a "bath" of ...ten tin and then cooled and cut into lengths.

The edges of float glass are automatically trimmed as it moves over rollers. Glass-...ving (inset) is the traditional way of making glass objects. "Gobs" of molten glass are ...ed on the end of a long tube. Blowing down the tube produces a bubble that can be ...ed before it cools.

GLASS FIBER

Glass can be drawn out into long threads by pouring red-hot molten glass through the bottom of a furnace. One important use for this thread is in fiberglass. For this, it is combined with plastic to give an easily molded, light and strong substance ideal for making boat hulls.

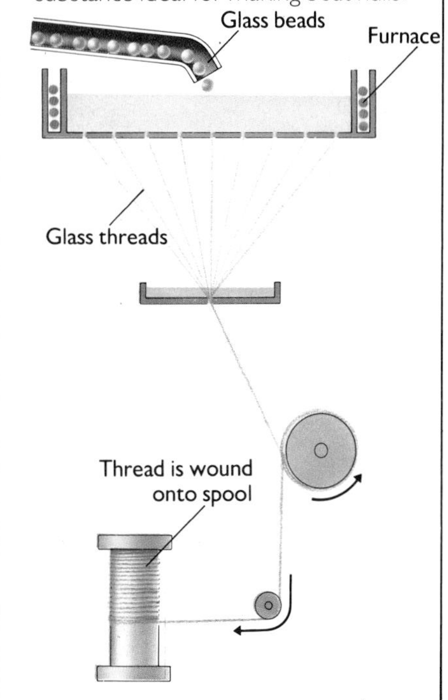

For more information turn to these articles: ARCHITECTURE; BUILDING; CATHEDRAL; LENS; LIGHT; TELESCOPE.

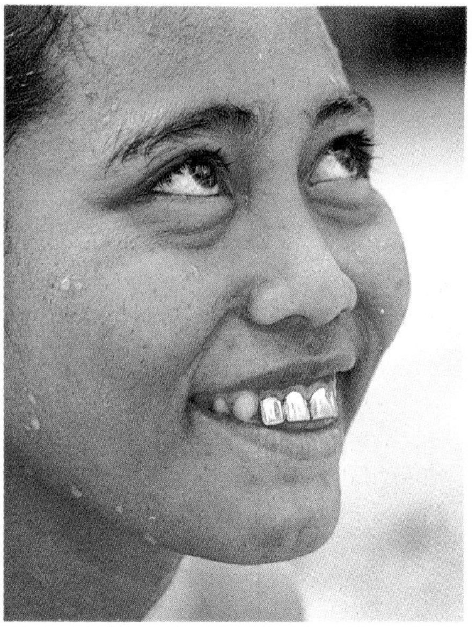

▲ *The gold used for crowning teeth is normally at least 20 karats—nearly pure gold.*

People find thin veins of gold in cracks in certain rocks. It was formed long ago by hot gases and liquids rising from deep underground. If water washes the gold out, lumps called nuggets may collect in the beds of streams and rivers. Half of the world's gold is mined in just one part of South Africa.

Because gold is beautiful and scarce, it is also very valuable. Most of the world's gold is kept in brick-shaped bars (called ingots) in BANKS. People make jewelry from gold mixed with other substances to make it harder. But gold is useful, too. Dentists sometimes put gold fillings in people's teeth.

Goldfish

Goldfish are a type of carp that are usually gold, gold and black, or gold and white in color. They are easy to keep as pets in tanks or ponds. Goldfish came originally from China. They can grow up to 12 in. (30 cm) long and may live for 20 years or more.

Gorbachev, Mikhail

▼ *Under Mikhail Gorbachev's leadership, the U.S.S.R. became a more open society.*

Mikhail Gorbachev was general secretary of the Soviet Communist Party and president of the Soviet Union from 1985 until 1991. He attempted many reforms of the Soviet Union to make it a more prosperous and democratic country. The most famous was "perestroika." It meant reconstruction. "Glasnost," or openness, was also an important part of his plan to make the Soviet Union more free. Gorbachev also took steps to reduce the number of the Soviet Union's nuclear weapons. He signed an "arms reduction treaty" with President Reagan in 1987, and held arms talks with President Bush.

At home, Gorbachev faced growing opposition to his policies, and in August 1991 a coup took place in which he was placed under house arrest. The coup failed and led to the breakup of the communist party. It became apparent that he would have to share decision-making with Boris YELTSIN, the Russian republic's president. At the end of 1991, Gorbachev resigned and the U.S.S.R. ceased to exist.

Gorilla

Gorillas are the largest of the APES. A big male may be as tall as a man. Gorillas live in family groups in the warm forests of central Africa. They eat fruit, roots, tree bark, and leaves. Every night, they make beds of twigs in the low branches of trees.

▲ *Gorillas live in family groups. The leading male defends the group if danger threatens and takes charge of nest building.*

Government

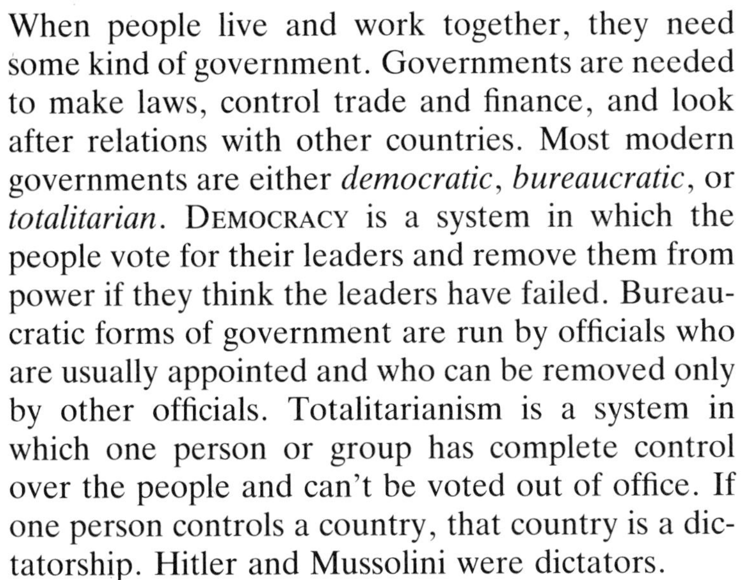

When people live and work together, they need some kind of government. Governments are needed to make laws, control trade and finance, and look after relations with other countries. Most modern governments are either *democratic*, *bureaucratic*, or *totalitarian*. DEMOCRACY is a system in which the people vote for their leaders and remove them from power if they think the leaders have failed. Bureaucratic forms of government are run by officials who are usually appointed and who can be removed only by other officials. Totalitarianism is a system in which one person or group has complete control over the people and can't be voted out of office. If one person controls a country, that country is a dictatorship. Hitler and Mussolini were dictators.

There are different kinds of democracies. Great Britain is a democratic monarchy with a king or queen as head of state. The country is, however,

Gorillas in zoos are normally heavier than those in their natural surroundings. It is not unusual for male gorillas in captivity to weigh as much as 570 lbs. (260 kg), four times the weight of a man. They can reach a height of 6 ft. (1.8 m). Females are shorter and weigh about half as much as the males.

▲ *The Palace of Westminster in London is the seat of government where both houses of the parliament of the United Kingdom meet.*

FORMS OF GOVERNMENT

System	Ruled by
Anarchy	No rule of law
Aristocracy	Privileged people
Autocracy	One person, absolutely
Bureaucracy	Officials
Democracy	The people
Matriarchy	A mother, or mothers
Meritocracy	The most able
Monarchy	A hereditary king or queen
Patriarchy	A male head of family
Plutocracy	The wealthy

governed by PARLIAMENT. The United States is a republic with a president as head of state. The U.S. government is divided into three branches. Congress makes the laws. The executive, with the president in charge, proposes and enforces the laws. The judicial branch decides which laws are constitutional (agree with the Constitution).

Grammar

Words must be arranged in special ways to make sentences that are understood. Grammar is the study of the ways in which words are formed and arranged to make sentences.

Words are usually classified as *parts of speech*, according to what they do in a sentence. There are four main kinds of words: VERBS (action words). NOUNS and pronouns (naming words), ADJECTIVES (describing words for nouns or pronouns), and adverbs (describing words for verbs and adjectives). Words can change from one part of speech to another. "Clean" can be a verb or an adjective. "Can" can be a noun or a verb.

If someone says "I see the cat," he or she is speaking of something happening now. If they say "I saw the cat," it happened in the past. The word "see," changes to "saw." Changes like this are called *inflections*.

The order of words in a sentence is very important. "The dog bites the girl" means something quite different from "The girl bites the dog," but exactly the same words are used. It is usual in English for the subject of a sentence—"dog" in the first example, "girl" in the second—to come before the verb—"bites." Exceptions to this rule are called *idioms*—"There goes the boy."

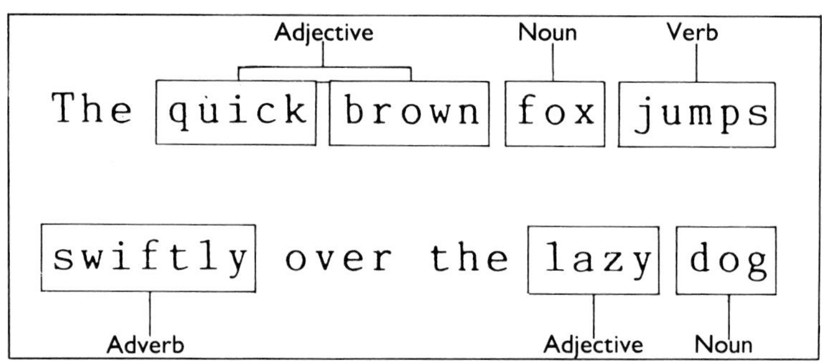

▶ *Every sentence can be broken down into its parts of speech. To be a sentence, it must have a subject (noun) and a verb.*

Grand Canyon

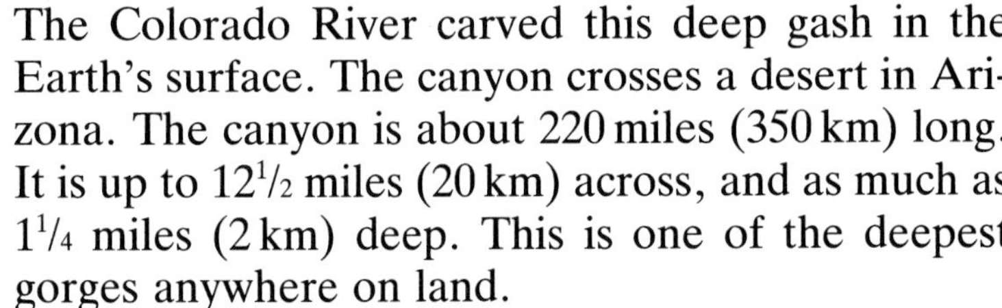

The Colorado River carved this deep gash in the Earth's surface. The canyon crosses a desert in Arizona. The canyon is about 220 miles (350 km) long. It is up to $12\frac{1}{2}$ miles (20 km) across, and as much as $1\frac{1}{4}$ miles (2 km) deep. This is one of the deepest gorges anywhere on land.

▲ The layers of rock in the Grand Canyon show the Earth's history over millions of years.

Granite

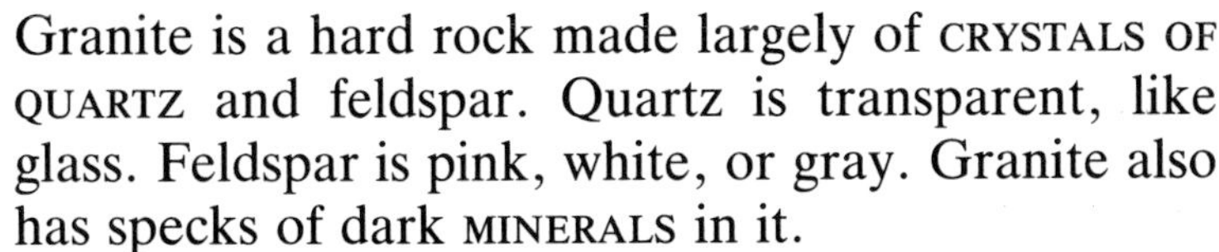

Granite is a hard rock made largely of CRYSTALS OF QUARTZ and feldspar. Quartz is transparent, like glass. Feldspar is pink, white, or gray. Granite also has specks of dark MINERALS in it.

Granite was once a mass of hot, melted rock underground. As the rock cooled, it hardened. Then movements of the Earth's crust forced it up to the surface. The weather very slowly breaks down granite into sand and clay.

Builders use granite when they need a hard, strong stone. People also use granite to make polished stone monuments, because they last longer than those made of limestone.

▼ Granite quarried in Scotland was used to build this castle near Fort William. Large blocks of granite for building are often blasted with gunpowder instead of dynamite, as it causes less of an explosion.

ULYSSES S. GRANT

Eighteenth President 1869–1877
Born: Point Pleasant, Ohio
Education: U.S. Military Academy, West Point, New York
Occupation: Army officer
Political Party: Republican
Buried: Grant's Tomb, Riverside Drive, New York City

Grant, Ulysses Simpson

Ulysses S. Grant (1822–1885) was the 18th president of the United States, in office from 1869 to 1877. Before that, he was the commander of the victorious Union forces during the last years of the Civil War. To many people, Grant is better known as a soldier than as a politician. He secured many important victories for the Union forces in the war. The commander of the Confederate forces, Robert E. Lee, surrendered personally to him in 1865 to end the war. Grant's presidency was not always successful. Though he helped greatly in the "reconstruction" of the South after the war, and was popular there, many scandals involving corruption of high officials affected his time in office.

Grass

Grasses are flowering plants with long, thin leaves growing from hollow stems. Bamboo is as tall as a tree, but most grasses are short. Sheep and cattle eat grass. We eat the seeds of cultivated cereal grasses like wheat and rice.

Common reed   False oat   Meadow foxtail

▲ *Three of the more than 10,000 species of grass. The flowers, and later the grains, are contained in scaly spikelets (inset).*

Grasshopper

These insects have feelers, wings, and long back legs. A grasshopper can jump 20 times its own length. Grasshoppers eat leaves, and those called locusts damage crops. Many males "sing" by rubbing their back legs on their wings.

Gravity

Gravity is the pull that tries to tug everything toward the middle of the Earth. It is gravity that makes objects tend to fall, stops us from flying off into space, and keeps the Moon circling the Earth. When we weigh something, we are measuring the force with which gravity pulls that object down. The more closely packed the substances in an object are, the heavier it seems.

Not just the Earth, but all planets and stars exert a pulling force. Scientists call this gravitation.

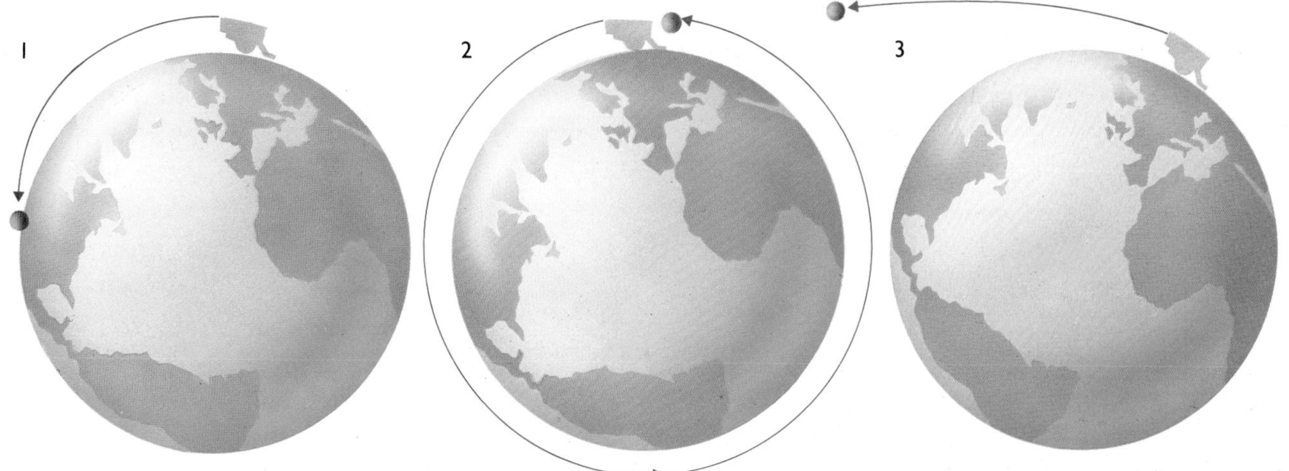

The larger and denser a star or a planet is and the nearer it is to other objects, the more strongly it pulls them toward it. The SUN is far from the planets, but it is so huge that its gravitation keeps the planets circling around it. The Moon is small, and its gravitation is weak. An astronaut on the Moon weighs far less than he weighs on Earth, although his *mass* stays the same.

▲ *A small body, such as the cannonball above, balances its speed against the gravitational pull. The speed in this path is too low, and it falls to the ground (1). When it is fired at a greater speed, it is attracted toward the surface at the same rate as the surface curves away, and it will go into orbit (2). If its speed is too fast, gravity cannot hold it, and it escapes into space (3).*

Great Britain *See* United Kingdom

Great Lakes

This is the world's largest group of freshwater lakes. They extend from New York to Minnesota. Lake Michigan lies in the UNITED STATES. Lakes Superior, Erie, Huron, and Ontario are shared by the United States and CANADA. The largest lake is Superior. The lakes were formed when a huge sheet of ice melted 18,000 years ago.

Eight states of the United States touch the Great Lakes. These eight states make more than half of the country's manufactured goods. Two-thirds of Canada's population and most of its factories lie on the Great Lakes or on the St. Lawrence River. A ship can go from the Atlantic up the St. Lawrence River and through the lakes to the western end of Lake Superior, halfway across the continent of North America.

◀ *Lakes Erie and Ontario are on two different levels, linked by the 165 ft. (50 m) Niagara Falls and the Niagara River. Ships avoid this route by using the Welland Canal.*

▲ *The sun-baked buildings of this town on the Greek island of Santorini, also known as Thera, perch on the remains of an exploded volcano.*

Rivers and canals connect the lakes to each other and to the Atlantic Ocean. Ships can reach the sea from lake ports that lie 1,000 miles (1,600 km) inland. Lots of factories are built around the lakes. Most of the goods that the factories produce are taken to other parts of the country by boat.

Great Wall of China

More than 2,000 years ago, the first emperor of CHINA, Shih Huang Ti, built this wall to keep out China's enemies from the north. The Great Wall is the longest wall in the world. It stretches for 1,500 miles (2,400 km) from western China to the Yellow Sea.

The wall is made from earth and stone. Watchtowers were built every 660 feet (200 m) along it. Chinese sentries sent warning signals from the towers if anyone attacked the wall. The signal was smoke by day and a fire at night.

Greece

Greece is a country that lies in southeastern EUROPE. Mountains cover most of the land, and peninsulas poke out into the sea like giant fingers. Greece includes the island of Crete and many smaller islands in the Aegean and Ionian seas. Greek summers are hot and dry. Winters are mild and wet.

Greek farmers produce lemons, grapes, and olives. Millions of tourists visit Greece every year.

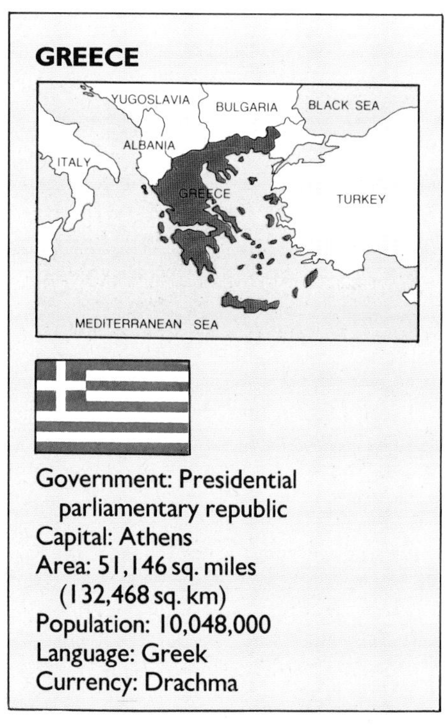

GREECE
YUGOSLAVIA
BULGARIA
BLACK SEA
ALBANIA
ITALY
GREECE
TURKEY
MEDITERRANEAN SEA
Government: Presidential parliamentary republic
Capital: Athens
Area: 51,146 sq. miles (132,468 sq. km)
Population: 10,048,000
Language: Greek
Currency: Drachma

Greece, Ancient

The first great people in Greece were the Minoans and the Mycenaeans. The Minoans lived in Crete. They had rich cities and farms and led a peaceful life. The Mycenaeans lived on the mainland of Greece. They were warriors and sailors. The heroes of HOMER's poems were probably Mycenaean. Both these civilizations ended in about 1200 B.C.

Around this time, new groups of people began to move into Greece. They came from the north, but spoke Greek. Instead of making Greece one kingdom, they built separate cities. They often fought wars with each other. Sometimes, they joined together to fight foreign enemies, such as the Persians. Two of the strongest cities were Athens and Sparta. In the 400s B.C. Athens was ruled by a DEMOCRACY. It became very powerful.

The Greeks loved the theater, art, and poetry. They had many great thinkers, or *philosophers*, including ARISTOTLE, PLATO, and Socrates. Greek cities had many graceful buildings. They were decorated with beautiful SCULPTURE. The Greeks also started the first OLYMPIC GAMES. In 339 B.C. Greece was conquered by Philip, the father of ALEXANDER THE GREAT.

▲ *The marketplace, or agora, of a Greek town was an open area surrounded by temples and public buildings. Storage jars such as the one at the top of the picture were often decorated with figures or scenes.*

GREEK GODS

God	Title
Apollo	God of the Sun
Artemis	Goddess of the Moon and Hunting
Athena	Goddess of Wisdom
Demeter	Goddess of Agriculture
Dionysus	God of Wine
Eros	God of Love
Hades, Pluto	God of the Underworld
Hera	Goddess of Marriage
Hermes	Messenger of the Gods
Hestia	Goddess of the Hearth
Hephaestus	God of Fire
Poseidon	God of the Sea and Waters
Zeus	Leader of the Gods

Greek Mythology

The ancient Greeks, like all peoples who lived thousands of years ago, invented gods and goddesses to explain the world around them. Stories about these *deities* are called *myths*. In Greek mythology, many of the gods lived on Mount Olympus. There they ate a special food called *ambrosia* and drank *nectar* to make them immortal. The greatest god was Zeus. When he was angry, he made thunder. Zeus had many children. One, Athena, was the goddess of wisdom. The city of Athens is named after her. Another, Apollo, was the sun god. He drove the sun's chariot across the sky each day.

► *Fishing boats lie at anchor in the coastal town of Jakobshavn in Greenland. Fishing and processing fish are Greenland's chief activities.*

Greenland

Greenland is the world's largest island. VIKINGS discovered it nearly 1,000 years ago. It lies northeast of Canada, but belongs to DENMARK, a small European country. Since 1979, Greenland has enjoyed home rule. It is 50 times the size of Denmark, but it holds no more people than a large town. This is because Greenland is so cold. Most of it lies in the ARCTIC. Thick ice covers seven-eighths of the island. Bare mountains make up much of the rest. The capital is Godthaab.

Most Greenlanders live in villages of wooden houses near the coast. Some are Danes, many are ESKIMOS. A few Eskimos hunt seals, but many Greenlanders are fishermen.

GREENLAND

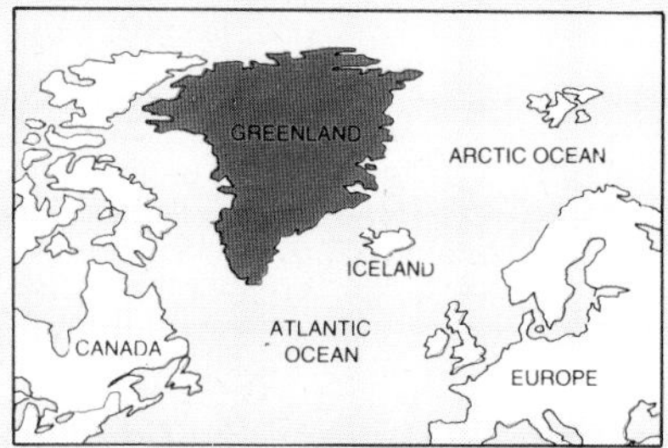

Government: Part of Denmark, but with home rule
Capital: Godthaab (Nuuk)
Area: 839,782 sq. miles (2,175,600 sq. km)
Average ice depth: 4,950 ft. (1,500 m)
Highest point: Gunnbjornsfjaeld, 12,214 ft. (3,700 m)
Official name of Greenland: Kalaallit Nunaat
Population: 57,000

Grenada 

Grenada is the smallest nation in the western hemisphere. It is a group of small islands in the south Caribbean Sea. Grenada was a British colony until 1958 and gained full independence within the Commonwealth in 1974. The nation is a leading producer of nutmeg and other spices.

Guam 

Guam is the largest of the Marianas Islands in the Pacific Ocean. It has a tropical climate with heavy seasonal rainfall. The country depends largely on income from U.S. military installations. Guam became United States territory after the Spanish-American War. The people have U.S. citizenship, but are self-governing.

Guatemala 

More people live in Guatemala than in any other Central American country. Nearly half of them are Indians, descendants of the MAYAS. Guatemala is a land of dense jungles, volcanoes, dry deserts, and sparkling lakes. Most of the people earn their

GRENADA

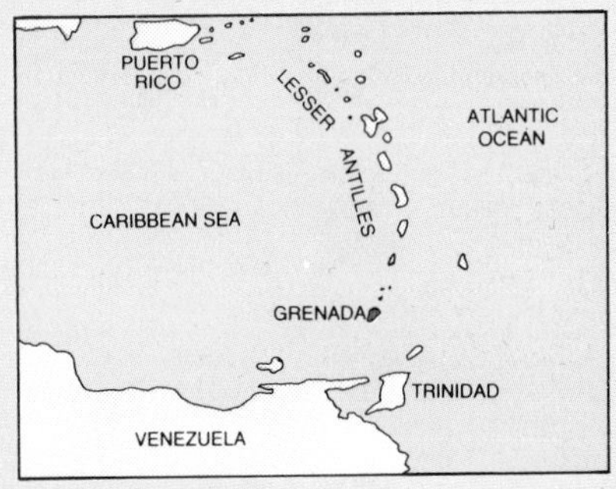

Government: Independent British colony
Capital: St. George's
Area: 133 sq. miles (344 sq. km)
Population: 85,000
Language: English
Currency: East Caribbean dollar

GUAM

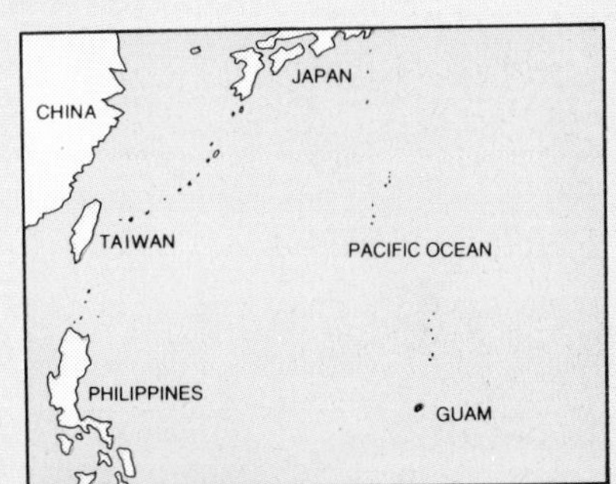

Government: Self-governing U.S. territory
Capital: Agana
Area: 209 sq. miles (541 sq. km)
Population: 119,000
Language: English
Currency: Dollar

◀ *This magnificent temple at Tikal in Guatemala was once part of the Mayan Empire, a civilization dating back to the A.D. 100s.*

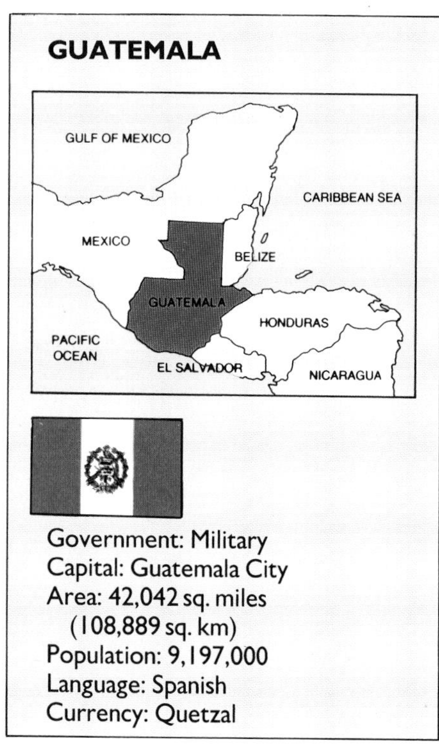

living by farming—coffee, cotton, and bananas are the main products. The country was conquered by the Spanish in 1524, declared its independence in 1821, and became a republic in 1839.

Guerrilla Warfare

Guerrillas are "hit and run" fighters. Often they do not wear regular uniforms, and they live in the countryside, relying on help from friendly local people. The word "guerrilla" is Spanish for "little war." Guerrilla tactics are most often used by small groups of people who are fighting against a larger and more organized force. Guerrillas usually live in places where they can easily hide, such as forests or mountains. Urban guerrillas operate in cities and towns.

Guided Missile

A guided missile is usually a rocket-powered missile armed with an explosive warhead. The missile is guided to its target by radio or radar commands from Earth or by a device inside the missile. A *ballistic missile* follows a path that is partly outside the Earth's atmosphere. It is guided as it goes up, but

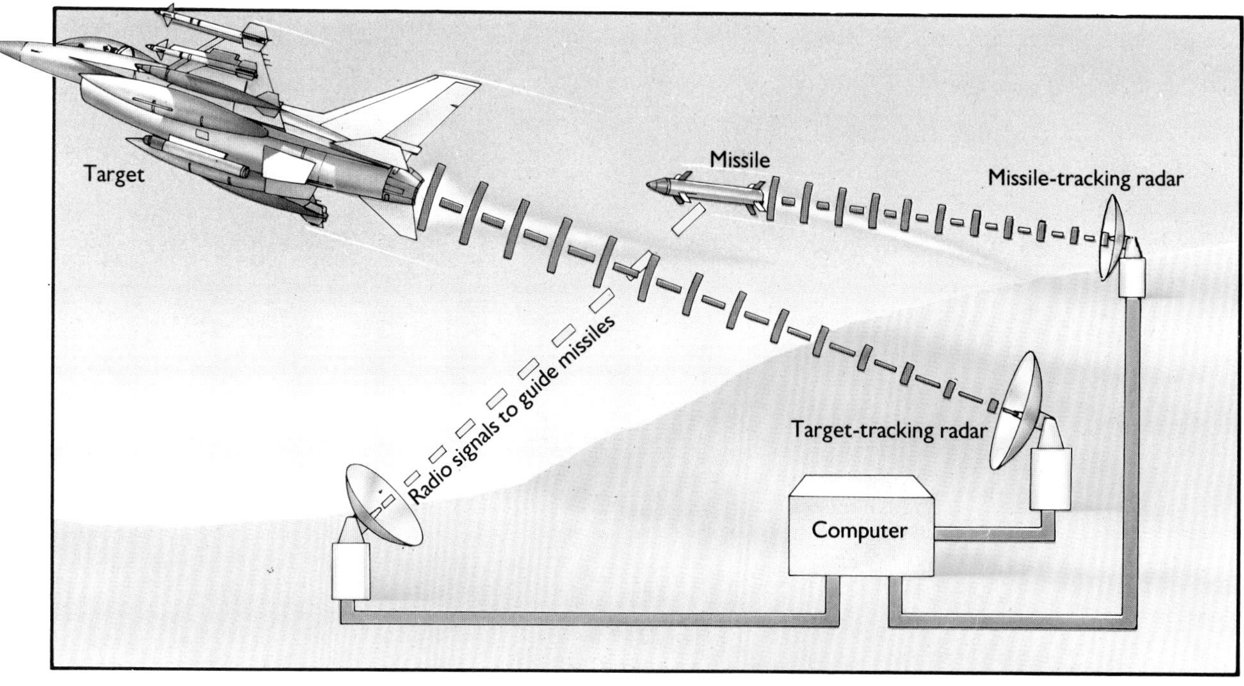

▼ *A radar system may track both the missile and its target. A computer reads the radar signals and controls the missile's guidance system to guide it to the target by radio.*

when its rocket engine burns out, it returns to Earth in an unguided path. The only defense against a ballistic missile is to fire another missile at the incoming missile to destroy it before it hits its target. Such defensive missiles are called *antiballistic missiles*. However, modern missiles are armed with warheads that split up into several separate nuclear warheads as they descend. This makes defense much more difficult.

Guinea

Guinea is a country on the western coast of Africa. Some of the world's largest deposits of bauxite are in Guinea. Bauxite is the ore from which aluminum is made. Guinea was a colony of France from the late 1800s until 1958, when it became an independent nation.

GUINEA

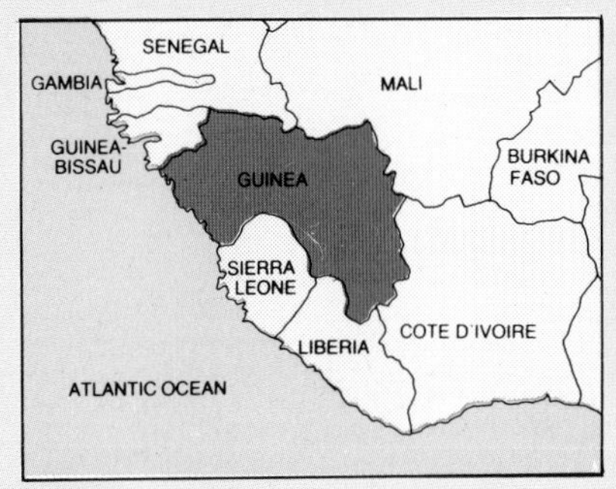

Government: Republic under military committee
Capital: Conakry
Area: 94,964 sq. miles (245,957 sq. km)
Population: 5,756,000
Language: French
Currency: Syli

Guinea-Bissau

The small country of Guinea-Bissau is on the west coast of Africa. Most of the 900,000 people who live there earn their living by farming. The main crops are peanuts, coconuts, and rice. Guinea-Bissau gained its independence from the Portuguese in 1974.

GUINEA-BISSAU

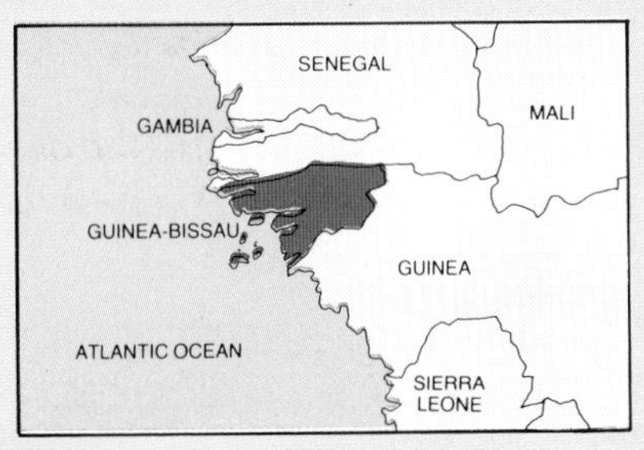

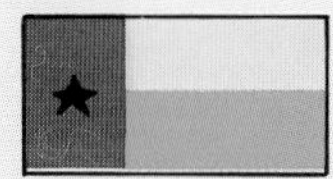

Government: Republic
Capital: Bissau
Area: 13,948 sq. miles (36,125 sq. km)
Population: 965,000
Language: Portuguese
Currency: Escudo

Guinea Pig and Hamster

The guinea pig is a RODENT, not a pig, and it comes from Peru, not Guinea. It is also called a cavy. Guinea pigs are up to 12 in. (30 cm) long and have no tail. They may be brown, white, black, gray, or a mixture. Some have long, silky hair, or hair that

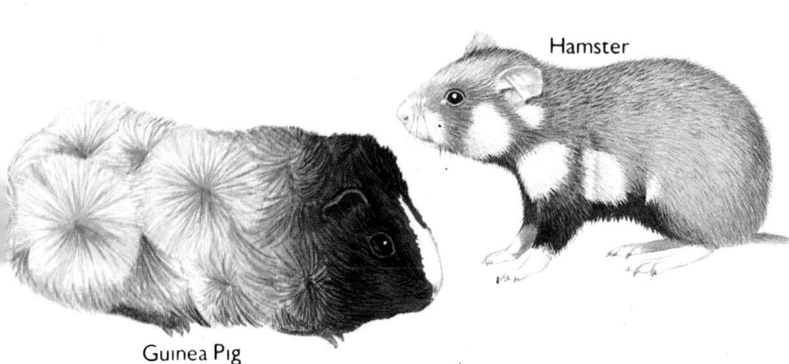

◀ *The tame guinea pig is descended from the grizzled brown cavy of the Andes. Hamsters' nearest relatives are gerbils and voles.*

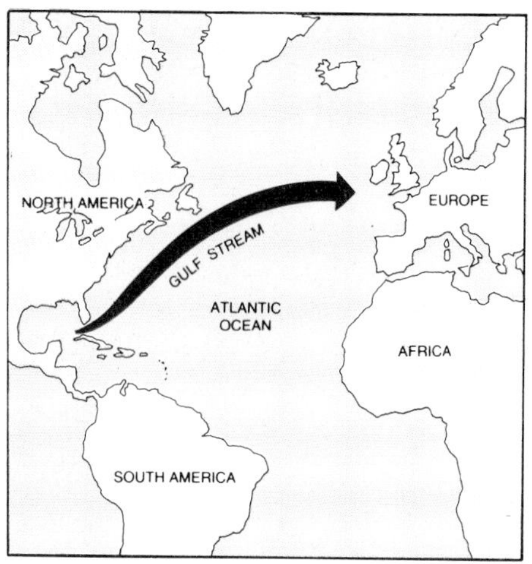

▲ *East of Newfoundland, the Gulf Stream is more correctly known as the North Atlantic Drift.*

forms rosettes. Scientists use guinea pigs in experiments, and many people keep guinea pigs as pets. They eat grass and hay and need a dry cage with clean bedding on the floor.

Hamsters are smaller than guinea pigs and have short tails. They have big pouches in their cheeks where they store food. Most hamsters are light brown on top and white or black underneath.

Gulf Stream

This ocean current is like a giant river flowing through the sea. It carries warm water from the Gulf of Mexico northward along the eastern coast of the United States. The Gulf Stream is up to 38 miles (60 km) wide and 1,970 ft. (600 m) deep. The current separates. One branch crosses the ATLANTIC OCEAN and brings warm water to northwestern Europe. If it were not for the Gulf Stream, winters in countries from France and Britain to Norway would be much more severe.

Gull

Few birds are more graceful than gulls gliding and soaring over the sea. They have webbed feet and swim well, but most do not stray far from land. They can catch fish, but also eat food scraps washed up on the shore.

Gulls breed in noisy crowds called colonies. Their nests are built on the ground. Many gull colonies live on islands. This helps to keep their eggs safe from rats and foxes.

▼ *Despite its name, the common gull is not the most numerous gull. The herring gull and the black-headed gull are often seen inland, but the larger glaucous gull is found only on coasts and in harbors.*

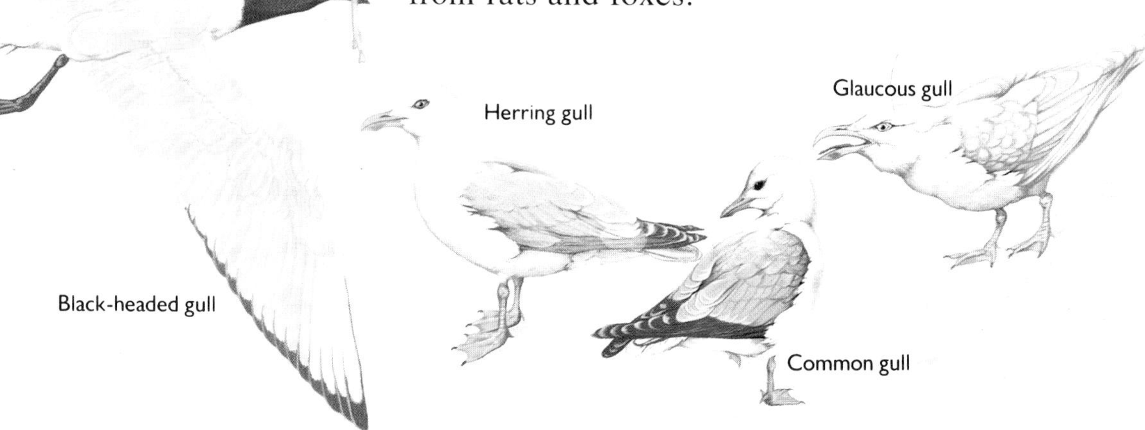

◀ *This breech-loading cannon of the 1400s fired solid balls which could knock down the thickest castle walls.*

▼ *The Gatling gun was the first successful machine gun. Invented in 1861 and first used during the Civil War, it had up to 10 barrels rotated by a hand crank.*

Gun

Guns are weapons that fire bullets or other missiles from a tube which is open at one end.

Guns were probably invented in the 1200s. By the 1300s, guns were firing missiles that could pierce armor and break down castle walls.

Early guns were large weapons, far too heavy for one man to carry. The first gun was a big bucket with a small hole in the bottom. Soldiers put gunpowder into the bucket. Then they piled stones on top. They lit the gunpowder through the hole. When the gunpowder exploded, the stones flew out. The large, long guns called cannons were first used in about 1350. Cannons fired big metal cannonballs. In the 1800s came guns which fired pointed shells that exploded when they hit their target. A spiral groove cut in the gun barrel made the shells spin as they flew through the air. Soldiers could fire such shells farther and hit their targets more often than with cannonballs.

▲ *This modern antiaircraft gun can destroy attacking aircraft from the ground.*

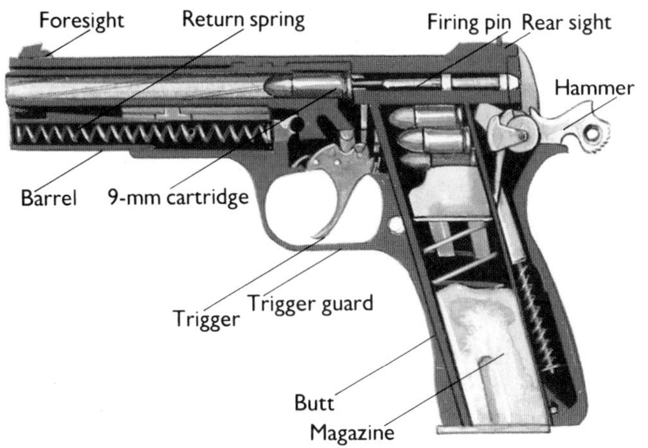

◀ *This cutaway view of a Browning self-loading pistol of 1968 shows the pistol when loaded.*

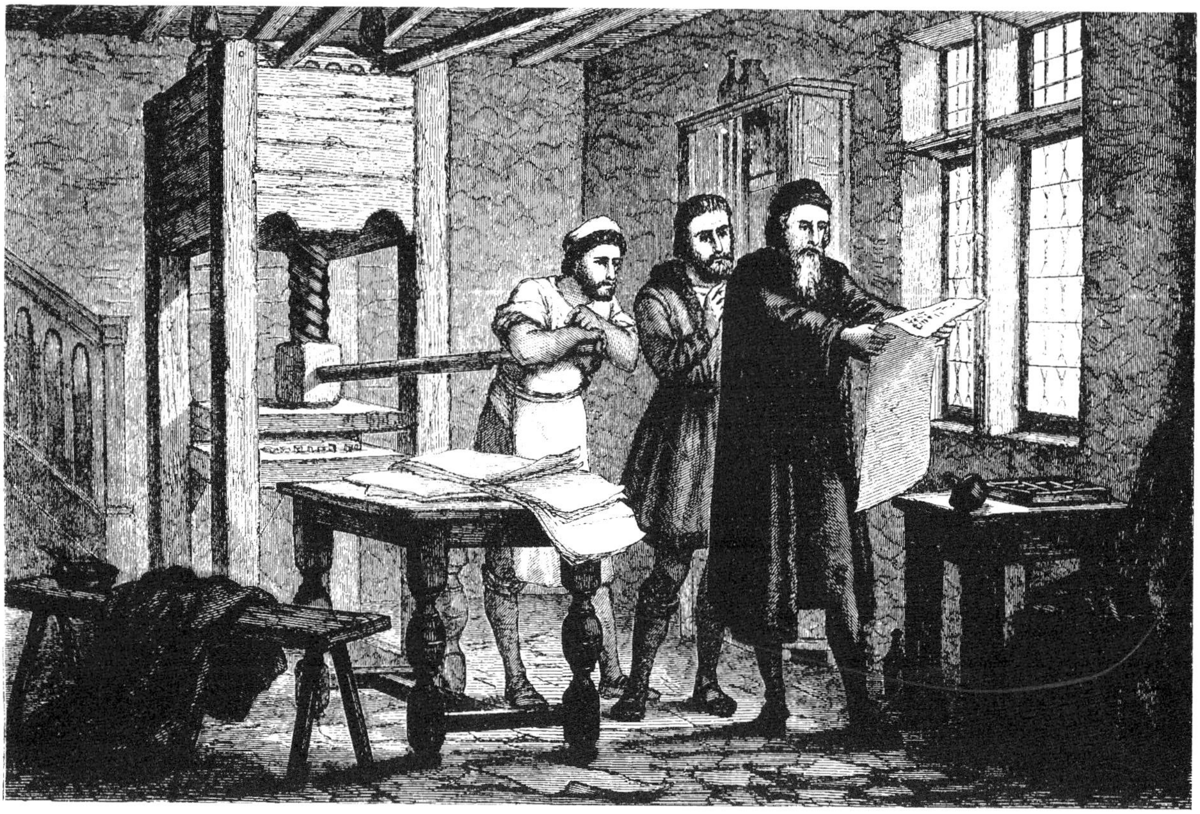

▲ *Johann Gutenberg inspects a printed sheet that has just come off his new press. Despite the importance of his achievement, he never made much money from it.*

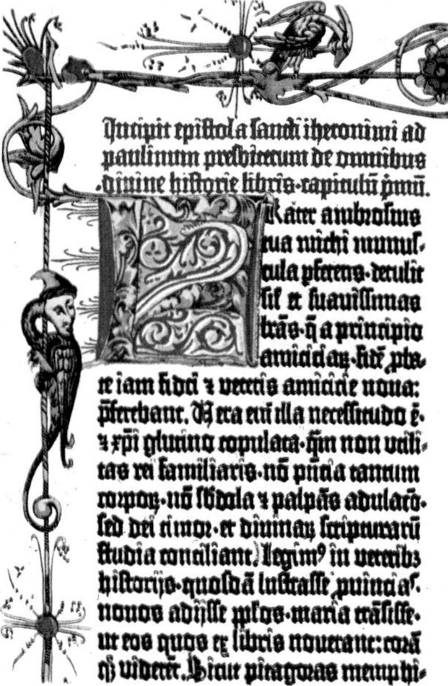

Incipit epistola sancti iheronimi ad
paulinum presbiterum de omnibus
divine historie libris-capitulū pmū.
Frater ambrosius
tua michi munus-
cula pferens-detulit
sil et suavissimas
lrās-q̄ a principio
amiciciarū-fidē pba-
te iam fidei et veteris amicitie nova:
pferebant. Vera enī illa necessitudo ē.
et xpi glutino copulata-q̄m non utili-
tas rei familiaris-nō pñcia tantum
corporū-nō subdola et palpās adulacō-
sed dei timor-et divinaꝝ scripturarū
studia conciliant. Legim⁹ in veterib;
historijs-quosdā lustrasse pvincias-
novos adijsse pplos-maria transisse-
ut eos quos ex libris noverant:corā
q̄ viderent. Sicut pitagoras memphi-

▲ *One of Gutenberg's first books was a Bible printed in Latin in 1455.*

Troops first used small arms in the 1300s. Small arms are guns that one man can carry. Inventors developed short-barreled pistols and revolvers for firing at nearby targets. They developed muskets, rifles, and machine guns for long-distance shooting. In modern guns, a hammer sets off an explosion that drives a shell or bullet from the barrel.

Gutenberg, Johann

Johann Gutenberg (about 1395 to about 1468) was a German goldsmith sometimes called the father of PRINTING. In his day, people slowly copied books by hand or printed them from wooden blocks on which each letter of every page had to be carved separately. About 1440, Gutenberg learned to make metal letters called type. He could pick them up and place them in rows to build pages of type. Each page was held together by a frame. Gutenberg fixed the frame to a press and quickly pressed the inky surface of his type onto sheets of paper. Gutenberg's movable type helped him to make copies of a book faster and more cheaply than ever before.

Guyana

Guyana is a hot, rainy country on the northeastern coast of South America. Most of the people live along the coast in a narrow strip of flat land about 12 miles (20 km) wide. Sugarcane and rice are grown there. Valuable minerals, including gold and diamonds, are found in the hilly region inland. Guyana produces bauxite to make aluminum. A vast forest covers more than three-fourths of the country.

Guyana was once a British colony. It is the only country in South America that has English as its official language. The colony became independent in 1966 and a republic in 1970.

GUYANA

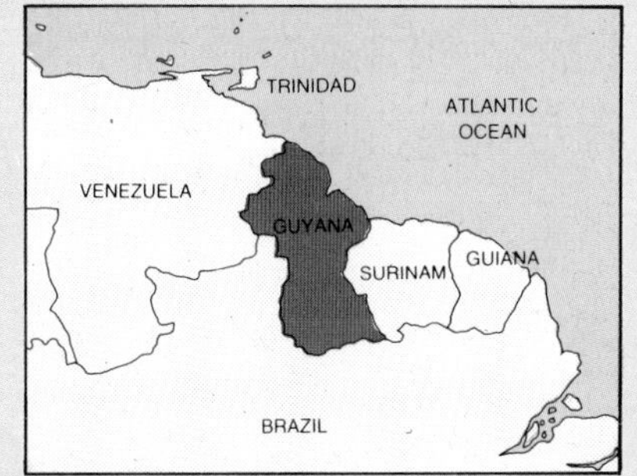

Government: Republic
Capital: Georgetown
Area: 83,000 sq. miles (214,970 sq. km)
Population: 796,000
Language: English
Currency: Guyanese dollar

Gymnastics

Gymnastics are exercises that help to make and keep the body fit. The OLYMPIC GAMES have separate gymnastic exercises for men and women. Women perform graceful steps, runs, jumps, turns, and somersaults on a narrow wooden beam. They hang from a high bar and swing to and fro between

▼ *Modern competitive gymnastics developed from German and Swedish systems of exercise.*

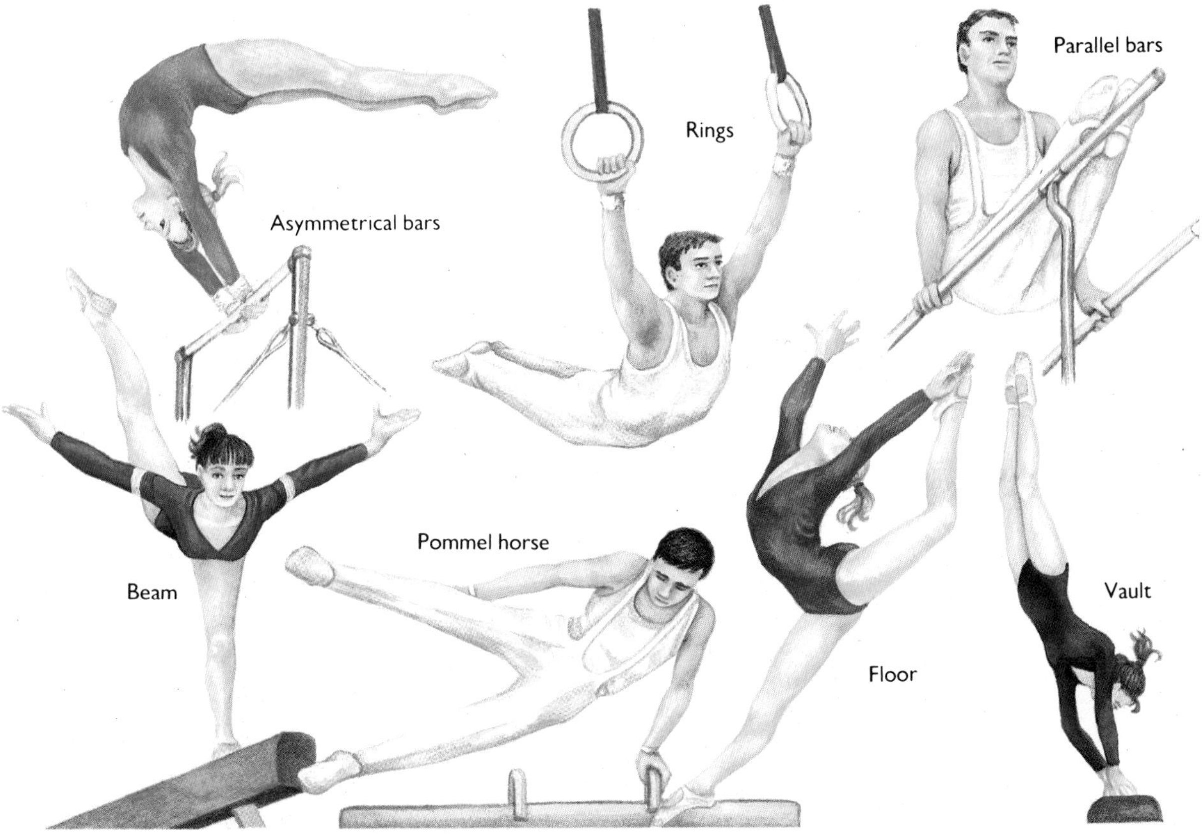

Asymmetrical bars
Rings
Parallel bars
Beam
Pommel horse
Floor
Vault

Modern gymnastics grew considerably in popularity because of the performance of tiny Olga Korbut of the Soviet Union in the 1972 Olympics. The widespread television coverage of her dramatic performance increased interest in the sport almost overnight.

it and a lower one. They leap over a vaulting horse. Women also perform floor exercises to music.

Men hang from a high bar and from rings, swinging up and down, to and fro, and over and over in giant circles. Using two parallel bars, they swing, vault, and do handstands. They grip hoops that jut up from a leather-covered pommel "horse" and swing their legs and body. They leap over a vaulting horse. Simpler exercises are done by children and adults in gymnastics classes.

► *The traditional, brightly-painted gypsy caravan is now a rarity. Most traveling gypsies live in modern trailers.*

Gypsy

Gypsies are an interesting group of people found in Europe and North America. They have dark hair, skin, and eyes. Many speak a language called Romany. Some live in houses; others travel all the time and live in trailers. Gypsies deal in cars and horses and make metalwork or tell people's fortunes. They are famous for their songs and dances.

The name "gypsy" probably comes from the word Egyptian. It was thought gypsies came from Egypt, but they probably came from India 600 years ago.

▼ *No matter how much the gyroscope is tilted or twisted, the wheel axle will continue to point in the same direction.*

Gyroscope

A gyroscope is a wheel that spins in a special frame. No matter how the frame tilts, the wheel's axle points in the same direction. Even GRAVITY and the Earth's MAGNETISM do not affect the axle.

On a ship or aircraft, a COMPASS made from a gyroscope always points north. Gyroscopes can also keep an aircraft on course without the pilot steering.

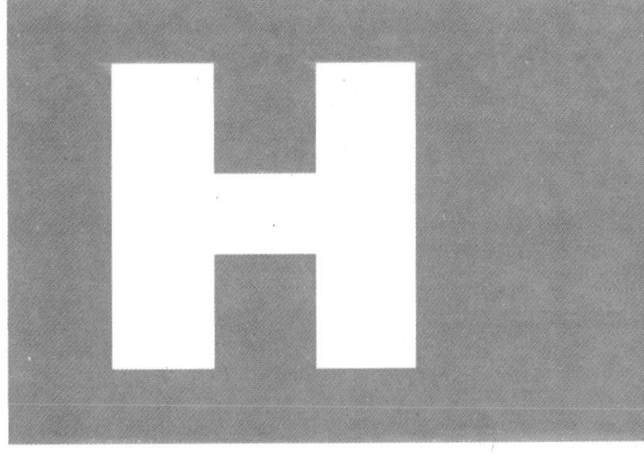

Hail *See* Rain and Snow

Hair

Hair grows like living threads from the skins of MAMMALS. It has the same ingredients that make nails, claws, hooves, feathers, and reptiles' scales. Hair helps to keep the body warm and protects the skin. There are several kinds of hair. Cats have plenty of soft, thick fur. Porcupines are protected by sharp, stiff hairs called quills.

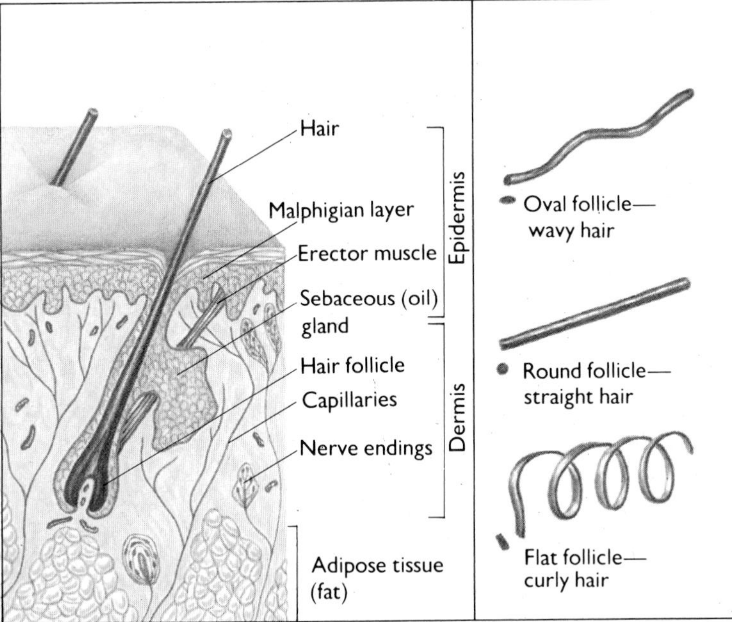

◀ *Each hair root is enclosed in its own follicle, which has a blood supply, a tiny erector muscle, and a gland. The type of hair you have depends partly on the shape of your hair follicles.*

Haiti

Haiti is a small country in the western part of the island of Hispaniola in the West Indies. Much of the country is covered by rugged mountains, but there are fertile valleys and coastal plains where coffee and other crops are grown. Nine-tenths of the people are descended from African slaves.

A French colony from 1677, Haiti became independent in 1804, following a rebellion. Dr. François Duvalier became president in 1957. Upon his death in 1971, he was succeeded by his son, Jean-Claude. This family dictatorship came to an end in 1986 when Jean-Claude was forced to flee the country. Political unrest continues.

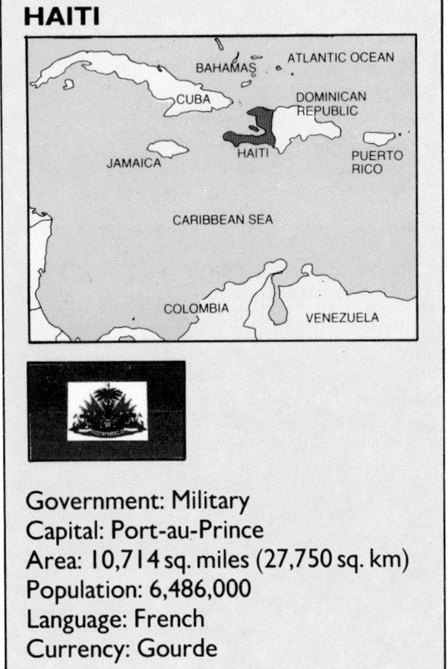

Government: Military
Capital: Port-au-Prince
Area: 10,714 sq. miles (27,750 sq. km)
Population: 6,486,000
Language: French
Currency: Gourde

▶ *When Halley's Comet passed near the Earth in 1985, its center was discovered to be a peanut-shaped mixture of rock, dust, and ice about 1 ¼ miles (2 km) long. Each return to the Sun leaves the nucleus with a smaller store of ice and dust, and eventually the comet will "die."*

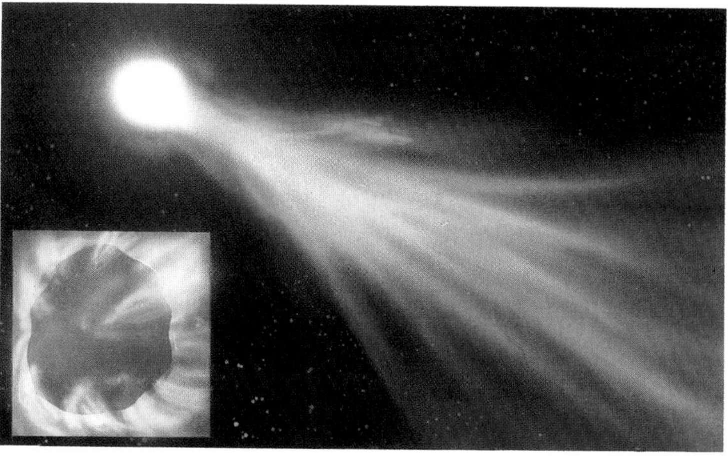

Edmond Halley was a friend of Isaac Newton, the great scientist. He encouraged Newton and helped him with money to publish his most famous work, *Mathematical Principles of Natural Philosophy*.

Halley, Edmond

Edmond Halley (1657–1742) was an English astronomer who is best known for his study of comets. In 1676, at the age of 20, he went to the island of St. Helena to catalog the stars of the Southern Hemisphere, something that had never been done before. He became interested in comets and noticed that the path followed by a comet he had seen in 1682 was very much like those reported in 1607 and 1531. He decided that these sightings must be of the same comet and predicted that it would return in 1758. On Christmas Day, 1758, it did, and Halley's Comet reappears regularly every 76 years.

Hamilton, Alexander

Alexander Hamilton (1755–1804) was a key figure in the development of the United States. He was a supporter of independence, and a close friend of George WASHINGTON. He played an important role in the writing of the U.S. CONSTITUTION. He then became the first Secretary of the Treasury. Hamilton was killed in a duel with a political opponent.

Hancock, John

John Hancock (1737–1793) is famous as the first man to sign the DECLARATION OF INDEPENDENCE. People today still sometimes call a signature a "John Hancock." He was an important figure in the REVOLUTIONARY WAR.

▼ *John Hancock was the first to sign the Declaration of Independence because he was then president of the Continental Congress.*

Handel, George Frideric

George Frideric Handel (1685–1759) was a German-born British composer, famous for the oratorio *Messiah* and the orchestral *Fireworks Music* and *Water Music*. He wrote about 21 oratorios.

▲ *Handel was born in Germany, but made England his home. He became a British subject in 1726.*

Hang Gliding *See* Gliding

Hannibal

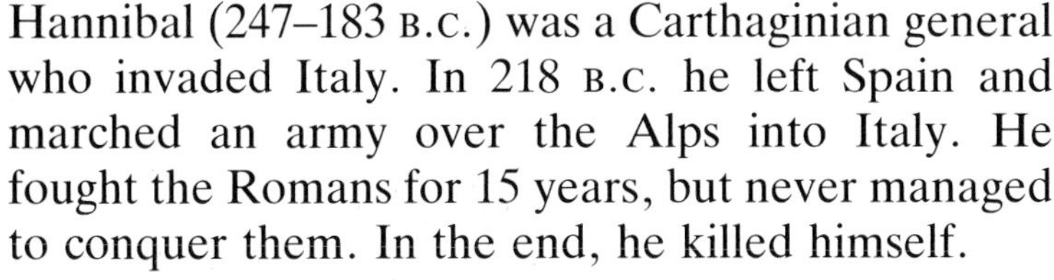

Hannibal (247–183 B.C.) was a Carthaginian general who invaded Italy. In 218 B.C. he left Spain and marched an army over the Alps into Italy. He fought the Romans for 15 years, but never managed to conquer them. In the end, he killed himself.

Harding, Warren

Warren Gamaliel Harding (1865–1923) became president of the United States after World War I. He grew up in central Ohio, and when he was 19 he bought a bankrupt weekly newspaper and turned it into a prosperous daily newspaper. He was elected to several state offices and then to the U.S. Senate before becoming president.

When Harding became president, he appointed several able men to his cabinet. To other offices, however, he appointed his personal friends. Some of these men used their positions of power to cheat the government. Harding's Secretary of the Interior, Albert B. Fall, was sent to prison for selling government lands to oil companies for large sums of money. The President became aware of this corruption. This may have hastened his death in San Francisco in 1923.

WARREN G. HARDING

Twenty-ninth President (1921–1923)
Born: Corsica, Ohio
Education: Ohio Central College, Iberia, Ohio
Occupation: Newspaper editor
Political Party: Republican
Buried: Marion, Ohio

Hare

Hares look like large RABBITS with very long ears and long legs. They live in wide open fields and do not burrow. By day, they just crouch in a dip in the ground. At night, they come out to eat grass and other plants.

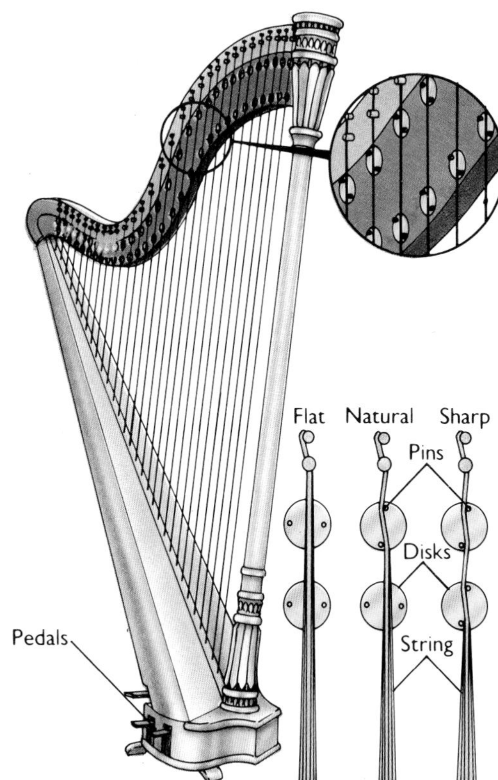

▲ *Moving the harp's pedals up and down gives the harpist more notes. The pedals turn small disks at the top of the strings. As the disks turn, pins make the lengths of string that vibrate shorter or longer. This gives sharp or flat notes.*

► *Harpsichords make a rich sound, but it cannot be made loud or soft as easily as the sound from a piano. So when pianos were invented, harpsichords were forgotten for more than a century.*

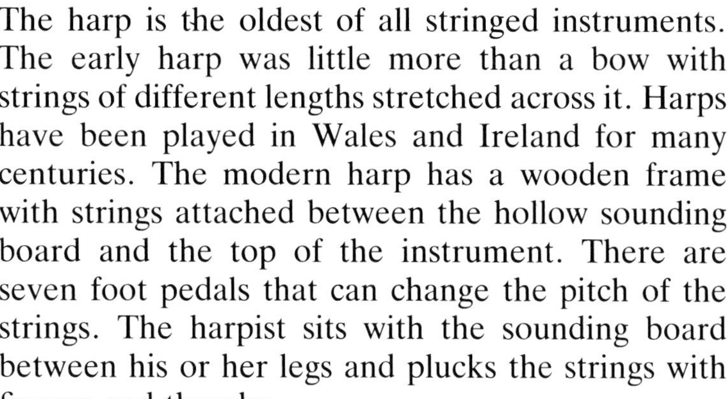

Harp

The harp is the oldest of all stringed instruments. The early harp was little more than a bow with strings of different lengths stretched across it. Harps have been played in Wales and Ireland for many centuries. The modern harp has a wooden frame with strings attached between the hollow sounding board and the top of the instrument. There are seven foot pedals that can change the pitch of the strings. The harpist sits with the sounding board between his or her legs and plucks the strings with fingers and thumbs.

Harpsichord

A harpsichord looks like a HARP laid on its side and put in a box with legs. The first successful harpsichords date from the 1500s. Harpsichords have a keyboard that looks like a PIANO's. When a key is pressed, it lifts a piece of wood called a jack. A quill or piece of leather fixed to the jack plucks a string inside the harpsichord. Harpsichords were popular during the 1700s, but by the 1800s they began to be replaced by pianos.

Harrison, Benjamin

Benjamin Harrison (1833–1901) was the 23rd president of the United States. His grandfather was William Harrison, the 9th president, and his father was a congressman. Benjamin Harrison was a general in the Civil War. In 1881, he became a senator. He became president during a time of great changes. The United States was growing rapidly and becoming a leading industrial power. Six states joined the Union during Harrison's administration. Industry had to be regulated; trade barriers, or tariffs, had to be controlled; the navy had to be expanded. Farmers faced different sorts of problems when prices fell and they needed government help. Harrison was the first president to say that the Stars and Stripes should fly over government buildings and schools.

BENJAMIN HARRISON

Twenty-third President 1889–1893
Born: North Bend, Ohio
Education: Miami University
Occupation: Lawyer
Political Party: Republican
Buried: Indianapolis, Indiana

Harrison, William Henry

William Harrison (1773–1841) was the 9th president of the United States. His time in office was short; he died only 30 days after becoming president—the first president to die in office.

Harrison was born to a rich Virginia family. After serving in the army, he became secretary of the Northwest Territory. Though he tried hard to protect the Native Americans living there, he also angered many of them by taking their land for settlement. When the native peoples rose against him in 1811, Harrison defeated them at the Battle of Tippecanoe. After the war of 1812, Harrison moved to Ohio, and in 1825 he became a senator.

WILLIAM H. HARRISON

Ninth President March–Apr. 1841
Born: Berkeley, Virginia
Education: Hampden-Sydney College, Virginia
Occupation: Soldier
Political Party: Whig
Buried: North Bend, Ohio

Hawaii

Hawaii is a group of more than 20 islands in the Pacific Ocean. The islands lie more than 2,000 miles (3,000 km) southwest of the United States. They became the 50th state in 1959. The Hawaiian Islands were formed as volcanoes built up from the ocean bed. Two volcanoes are still active.

The islands have beautiful beaches and in places there are tropical rain forests filled with unusual flowers. The Hawaiians are descended from the

HAWAII

Capital: Honolulu
Population: 1,108,229
Area: 6,471 sq. mi. (16,759 sq. km)
State flower: Hibiscus
State bird: Hawaiian Goose
State tree: Candlenut
Statehood: August 21, 1959
50th state

people who have settled on the islands. These include the early Polynesians, and later Americans, Europeans, Filipinos, and Puerto Ricans. Thousands of tourists flock to Hawaii every year.

The United States entered World War II because Japanese aircraft attacked its base at Pearl Harbor in Hawaii.

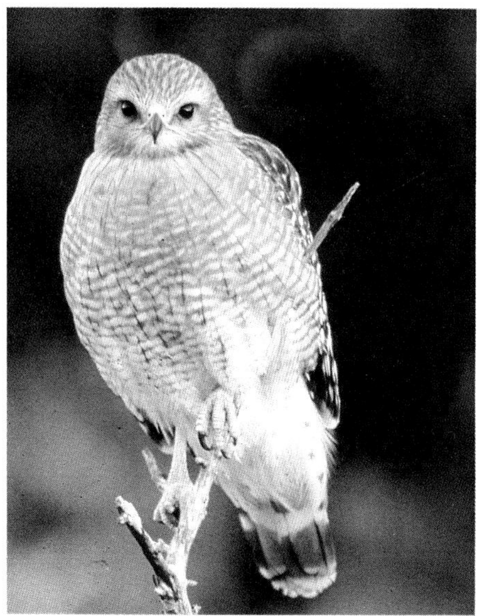

▲ *The red-shouldered hawk is common in the southeastern United States. It hunts for rodents, insects, and small birds.*

Hawk

Hawks are birds of prey in the same family as the VULTURES and all EAGLE species. Hawks are not as large as these relatives. Many look rather like FALCONS, but have broader wings with more rounded ends. Broad wings and a long tail help a hawk to fly fast and nimbly through trees. Hawks hunt birds and small mammals.

Hawthorne, Nathaniel

Nathaniel Hawthorne (1804–1864) was one of the most important American writers of the 1800s. His most famous books are *The Scarlet Letter* and *The House of the Seven Gables*. He wrote many stories for children, too. His best stories can be hard to understand, but all have a strong sense of the world he lived in—the little towns of New England in the 1800s.

▼ *The goshawk is widely used in falconry, as it is strong enough to catch game birds and rabbits.*

Haydn, Franz Joseph

Franz Joseph Haydn (1732–1809) was an Austrian composer known as the "father of the symphony." For 30 years he wrote music at the court of Prince Esterhazy. He wrote 104 symphonies. Many of them used the ORCHESTRA in a powerful new way. He also wrote fine pieces for the piano, and quartets for four stringed instruments. MOZART and BEETHOVEN both studied Haydn's work. Later, this helped them compose some of their most splendid music.

▲ *Haydn made two long visits to England, where he wrote his last 12 symphonies. He spent his last years in Vienna.*

Hayes, Rutherford B.

Rutherford B. Hayes (1822–1893) was the 19th president of the United States. His presidency was important because it ended the bitter "reconstruction" of the South after the Civil War. He also stopped the corruption over government jobs that had become commonplace during the presidency of Ulysses S. GRANT.

Hayes was elected president only after a special "electoral commission" decided that many of the votes for his opponent, Samuel Tilden, were fraudulent. Later, his decisions to withdraw federal soldiers from the South and to give government jobs to Southerners angered many in the North but helped heal the wounds of the Civil War. Hayes was widely respected for his honesty.

RUTHERFORD B. HAYES

Nineteenth President 1877–1881
Born: Delaware, Ohio
Education: Kenyon College, Gambier, Ohio
Occupation: Lawyer
Political Party: Republican
Buried: Fremont, Ohio

Health

Good health is one of the most important things in life. It is something that allows a person to lead a happy, useful, and successful life. There are certain rules which help us to stay healthy.

We should eat a balanced diet of the right kinds of FOOD and drink plenty of water. All foods are fattening if we eat too much of them, but this applies especially to starchy foods, fats, and sweets.

We should have regular EXERCISE, if possible in the open air, and get enough sleep. The number of hours' sleep we need depends on our age. Young babies sleep from 20 to 22 hours each day; older people only need between 6 and 7 hours.

▲ *The range of vibrations that can be heard varies in different animals. In humans, the range is from about 20 (very low-pitched) to 20,000 cycles per second. A bat and a dog can hear high-frequency sounds that the human ear cannot detect. The frog cannot hear high-pitched sounds.*

We should keep ourselves clean. Regular washing is important, especially of the hands after we have used the toilet. Teeth, of course, should be brushed night and morning.

Hearing

Hearing is the sense that allows us to pick up SOUND. The sense organ making this possible is the EAR. Some people cannot hear; they are *deaf*. Either they were born without hearing or, at some time, their ears became damaged by an illness or accident. Deaf people can "talk" by using special sign language.

Like people, all animals with backbones have hearing organs. Some can hear much better than people. CATS and DOGS, for example, pick up more sounds than we can. BATS hunt by sound, listening for echoes bounced back off flying insects.

Heart

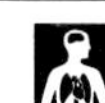

The heart is a muscle in the body. It pumps BLOOD around the body through VEINS and ARTERIES. In an adult person, the heart goes on working at between

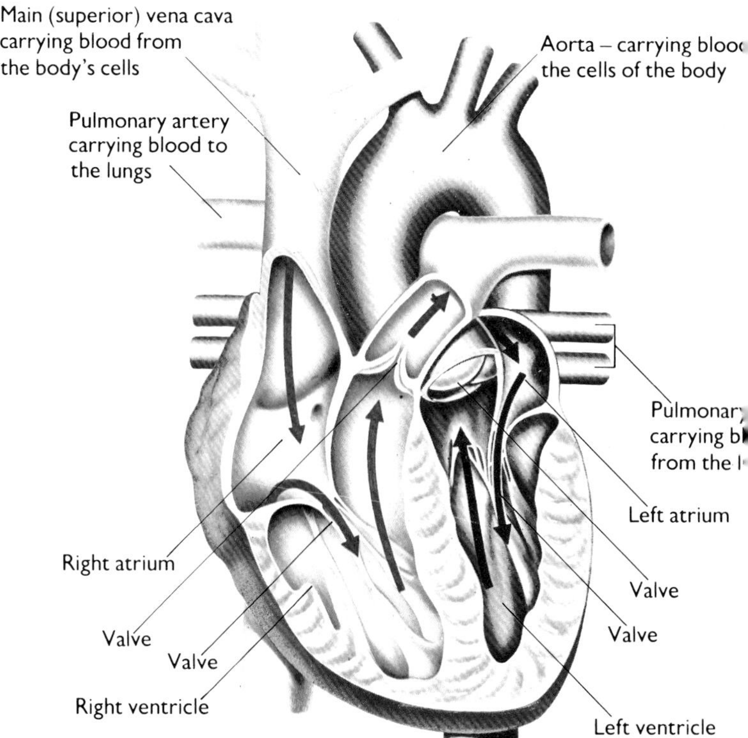

► *Your heart is about the same size as your clenched fist and is made of strong muscle. It constantly pumps blood around your body, so that each cell gets the food and oxygen it needs. The areas shown in red in the illustration indicate where oxygen-rich blood travels. The areas shown in blue show where blood low in oxygen travels back to the lungs. The* atria *(plural of* atrium*) collect the blood flowing into the heart. The* ventricles *are strong muscles that pump blood into the arteries.*

70 and 80 beats a minute until death. It was the English doctor, William Harvey (1578–1657), who discovered how the heart works.

The blood carries OXYGEN from the LUNGS and energy from the food we eat. Arteries carry this rich red blood to feed the body. Veins carry away waste products and return the dark "tired" blood to the heart to be "recharged" with oxygen from the lungs.

When the heart stops beating, the body is starved of oxygen and quickly dies. But doctors can sometimes massage a stopped heart back to life. People with diseased hearts can be given "spare parts" to repair them and even a new heart, transplanted from someone who has just died.

Heat

Heat is a form of ENERGY. We can feel it, but we cannot see it. We feel heat from the SUN, or when we sit in front of a fire. When something burns, heat is produced. The Sun gives out enormous amounts of heat, which is produced by atoms joining together, or "fusing," inside the Sun. This same kind of energy can be released by a hydrogen bomb on Earth. It is because we get just the right amount

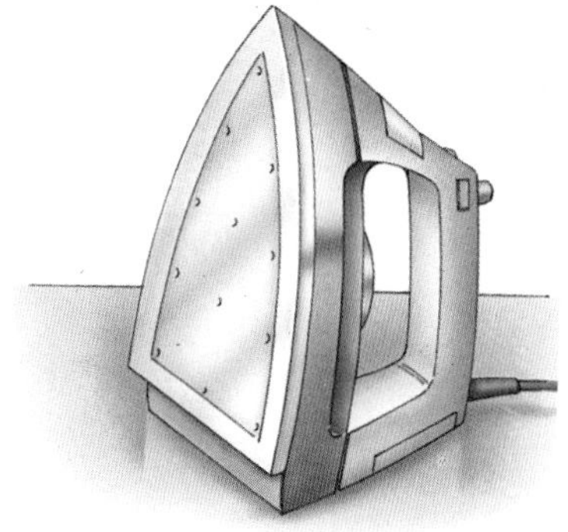

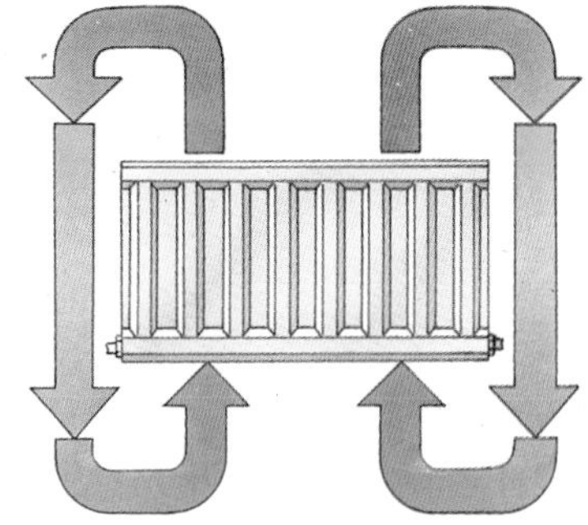

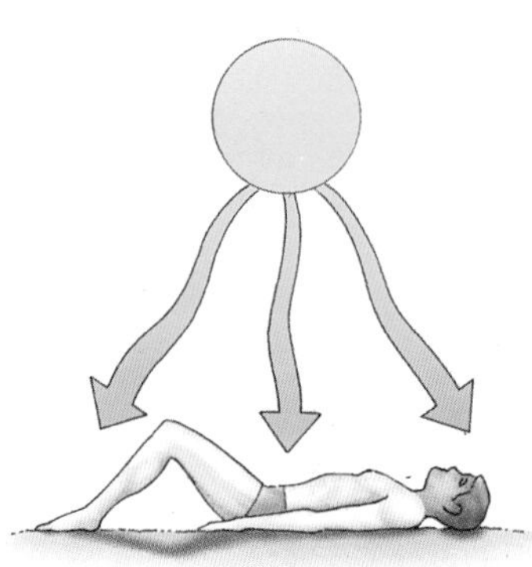

▲ *Heat travels in three ways—by conduction, convection, and radiation. A conductor, such as a metal iron, allows heat to pass through it. When heat is carried from a radiator by convection, molecules in the air move, taking the heat with them. Heat from the Sun travels by radiation in the form of electromagnetic waves.*

◄ *The energy in heat can be used in many different ways. This picture shows a solar-powered car that converts the Sun's energy and uses it to drive along.*

We need fuel to keep our body warm. This fuel is the food we eat. The human body contains a surprising amount of heat. It gives out about 100 calories of heat an hour. This is about the same as a 120-watt electric bulb. You can see, therefore, why it can become quite hot if a lot of people are gathered in a room.

of heat from the Sun that our Earth and ourselves are what they are. A few degrees less heat from the Sun, and our world would be a lifeless waste. A few degrees more heat, and life could not exist.

Most of the heat we use comes from burning fuels. But heat can also be made by FRICTION, or rubbing. Heat is also produced when electricity travels through a coil of wire. This is what makes the coils inside a toaster glow red.

We can measure how hot a thing is by finding its temperature. This is done with a THERMOMETER. When a substance gets hot, the molecules, or tiny particles, of which it is made move around more quickly. Often the substance expands (gets bigger) as this happens. Metals expand the most when they are heated.

Hebrews

In the early days of their history, the Jewish people were known as the Hebrews or Israelites. There were 12 tribes, descended from Abraham. The greatest Hebrew leader was Moses, who led his people out of slavery in Egypt to the Promised Land of Canaan. Hebrew is the national language of modern Israel.

Hedgehog

Like the American PORCUPINE, the European hedgehog has a coat of spines to protect it. When frightened, it curls up into a prickly ball.

▼ *Hedgehogs need to fatten themselves up if they are to survive their period of hibernation in the winter. They are carnivorous and like dog or cat food.*

Hedgehogs amble along snuffling for snails, slugs, worms, and insects to eat. They will often visit people's yards. During the winter, hedgehogs HIBERNATE. They live in northern Europe, Asia, Africa, and New Zealand.

▲ *King Menelaus of Sparta with his wife, Helen of Troy. The war that started because of her went on for ten years, according to the story told by Homer.*

Helen of Troy

Helen of Troy was said by the ancient Greeks to be the most beautiful woman in the world. She was the wife of Menelaus, King of Sparta, but ran away with Paris, Prince of Troy. Menelaus followed with a great army and so began the TROJAN WAR. The story is told by the poet HOMER.

Helicopter

The helicopter is an unusual and useful aircraft. It was invented in the 1930s, and today, it is used for all kinds of jobs, especially sea and mountain rescue. Helicopters can take off and land vertically and can therefore work in areas too small for ordinary aircraft. Helicopters can fly in any direction and hover in mid-air. Instead of fixed wings, they have a moving wing called a rotor, which acts as a wing and a propeller. The pilot controls the craft by changing the angle, or "pitch," at which the blades of the rotor go through the air. A smaller rotor on the tail keeps the helicopter from spinning around. Helicopters are also used for carrying passengers over short distances and for transporting troops to remote areas.

▼ *The UH-1* Iroquois *was used by the United States Army in the Vietnam War. A similar type is still being made today. The Ka-26* Kamov Hoodlum *is mainly used for farming purposes, although it is also used as an air ambulance. It has two sets of main rotors rotating in opposite directions.*

▲ *Ernest Hemingway was a war correspondent in the Spanish Civil War, and was fascinated by bullfighting.*

Hemingway, Ernest

Ernest Hemingway (1899–1961) was one of the most important American writers of the 20th century. He was a larger-than-life figure, and was almost as well known for his noisy personality as for his writing. He loved hunting, fishing, and traveling, and spent much of his life in other countries. His most famous books include *The Sun Also Rises*, *For Whom the Bell Tolls*, and *The Old Man and the Sea*. Many of his stories have a simple and vivid quality that few other writers have succeeded in capturing.

Henry (kings)

Eight English kings have been called Henry. They were: Henry I (1069–1135), the youngest son of William the Conqueror; Henry II (1133–1189), the first of the Plantagenet kings; Henry III (1207–1272), a weak king ruled by powerful barons; Henry IV (1367–1413), or Henry Bolingbroke; Henry V (1387–1422), who was a brilliant soldier; Henry VI (1421–1471), the last of the Lancastrian kings; Henry VII (1457–1509), the first of the Tudors and a shrewd ruler; and Henry VIII (1491–1547), who had six wives.

▼ *Henry VI was a quiet and religious king, very different from his strong-willed wife, Margaret of Anjou. The Wars of the Roses were fought during his reign.*

◀ *These simple designs found on old heraldic shields are called* charges, or ordinaries. *The designs of many modern flags are based on these shapes.*

Heraldry

In the MIDDLE AGES, a knight in full ARMOR was hard to recognize, for his face was hidden by his helmet. So knights began to use special designs worn on their surcoats and shields. These designs became special family emblems, which no one else could wear. They were called coats-of-arms.

Heralds were officials who kept records of coats-of-arms and awarded new ones. The College of Heralds in London still does this. There are special names for the colors and patterns used in heraldry.

Herb

Herbs are plants with soft, rather than woody, stems. But the name herb is also given to certain plants which are added to food during cooking. They are valued for their scent and flavor. A common herb is mint, which can be bruised and used in iced tea.

Other herbs used in cooking include sage, thyme, parsley, garlic, chervil, rosemary, basil, fennel, and

SEE IT YOURSELF

You can preserve herbs by drying them. Spread them out in a warm, dry, dark place for 3 to 5 days. Place them in a strainer over a sheet of clean paper and rub the herbs through the strainer with the flat of your hand. Throw away the stalks, and pour the rubbed herbs back into the strainer. Do this until there are no more stalks. Store your dried herbs out of direct light in sealed glass jars.

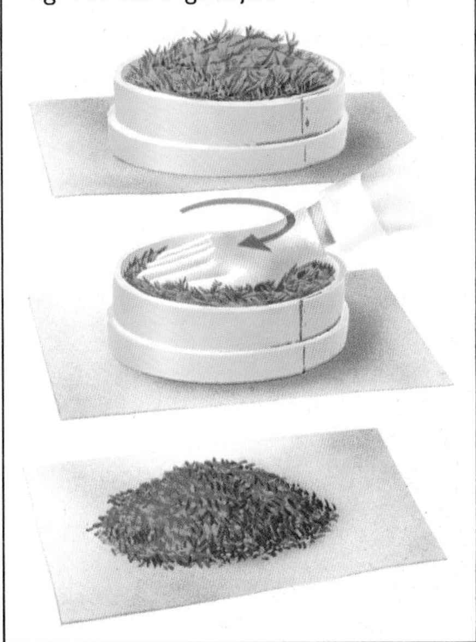

▼ *These herbs are easy to grow and make attractive garden plants as well as being useful in cooking.*

Tarragon

Rosemary

Sweet marjoram

chives. Most can be grown quite easily, although they came originally from the warm, sunny lands of the Mediterranean region.

Hercules

Hercules was a famous hero of ancient stories told by the Greeks and Romans. He was the son of the chief god, Jupiter, and a mortal princess. He was amazingly strong. As a baby, he strangled two snakes sent by Jupiter's jealous wife to kill him.

Later, Hercules went mad and killed his wife and children. To make amends, he had to perform twelve tasks, or labors. They included killing the Nemean lion and the many-headed Hydra; and washing clean the stables of King Augeas, where 3,000 oxen lived. In the end, Hercules was killed when he put on a poisoned shirt.

▲ *Slaying the Hydra was the second of the twelve tasks of Hercules. As soon as Hercules cut off one of its heads, two more grew in its place.*

Heredity *See* Genetics

Hibernation

When an animal hibernates, it goes to sleep for the winter. It does this because, in winter, food is scarce. Going to sleep during the cold weather saves certain animals from starving to death.

Before hibernating, animals eat as much food as they can find. The woodchuck, for example, stuffs itself until it is fat and round. As fall approaches, it makes a snug nest, curls into a ball, and falls into a sound sleep. In fact, its heart beats so slowly, the woodchuck looks dead. Its body uses hardly any energy during hibernation, in order to make its store of fat last as long as possible. In spring, a thin and hungry woodchuck wakes up and comes out of its nest to look for food.

In cold countries, many animals hibernate. Not all sleep right through the winter.

A hibernating marmot may slow down its breathing from 16 to 2 breaths a minute, and its heartbeats from 88 to 15 per minute. In a test, the temperature of a hibernating ground squirrel fell to almost freezing. The creature later woke up unharmed.

Hieroglyphics

Hieroglyphics were an ancient form of writing. Our alphabet has 26 letters. However, 5,000 years ago,

▲ *Hibernating animals have to find a warm, safe place to spend the winter. They need to reserve their energy until the weather warms up.*

the ancient Egyptians used picture-signs instead of letters. Later, these signs became hieroglyphics—marks which stood for things, people, and ideas. Egyptian hieroglyphics were sometimes written from right to left, and sometimes from left to right. Hieroglyphic writing was very difficult, and only a few people could do it. When the Egyptian empire died out, the secret of reading it was lost. No one could understand the hieroglyphics carved on stones and written on papyrus scrolls. Then, in 1799, a Frenchman found the Rosetta Stone, which is now in the British Museum in London. On it was something written in two known languages and also in hieroglyphics. By comparing the known languages with the hieroglyphics, experts were able to understand and translate the signs.

▲ *Many examples of hieroglyphic writing carved in stone have survived over thousands of years and can now be understood.*

High Holy Days

The High Holy Days are the two most important Jewish holidays. The first is Rosh Hashanah, the first day of the new year on the Jewish calendar, which is about 6,000 years old. Yom Kippur, 10 days later, is the solemn Day of Atonement, when Jews ask forgiveness for any wrongdoings of the past year. Both holidays occur early each fall.

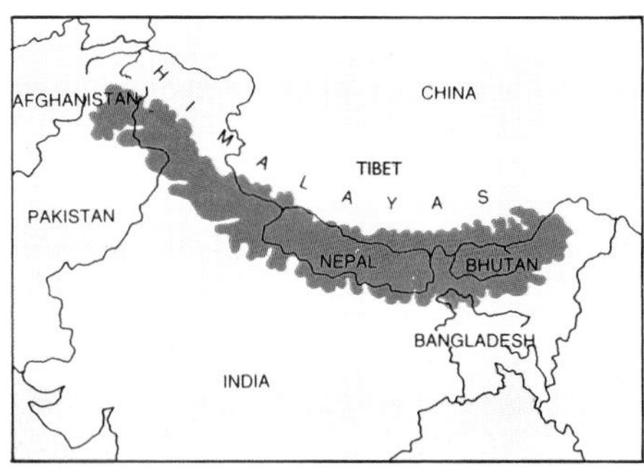

▶ *The Himalayas form a great natural barrier between India and the large plateau of Tibet. The passes that run through the Himalayas are among the highest in the world. Few are lower than 16,500 feet (5,000 m).*

Himalayas

The highest range of mountains in the world is the mighty Himalayas. The name means "land of snow." The Himalayas form a great barrier range across ASIA, dividing INDIA in the south from TIBET (part of CHINA) in the north. Many of Asia's greatest rivers rise among the Himalayas, fed by the melting snows.

Until aircraft were invented, few outsiders had ever been into the Himalayas. There are no roads or railroads. The only way to travel is on foot, over steep mountain tracks. Horses, yaks, goats, and even sheep are used to carry heavy loads.

The highest mountain in the world lies in the Himalayas. This is Mount EVEREST, 29,028 feet (8,848 m) high.

Hinduism

Hinduism is one of the world's great religions. Most Hindus live in ASIA, and particularly in INDIA. Their religion has grown over a period of 4,000 years.

Hindus believe that God is present in all things. Only priests (Brahmans) can worship the supreme God. Ordinary people worship other gods, such as Vishnu, God of Life. The most important holy books of Hindus are the *Vedas*. Hindus believe that certain animals, such as the cobra and the cow, are sacred and must never be killed or eaten.

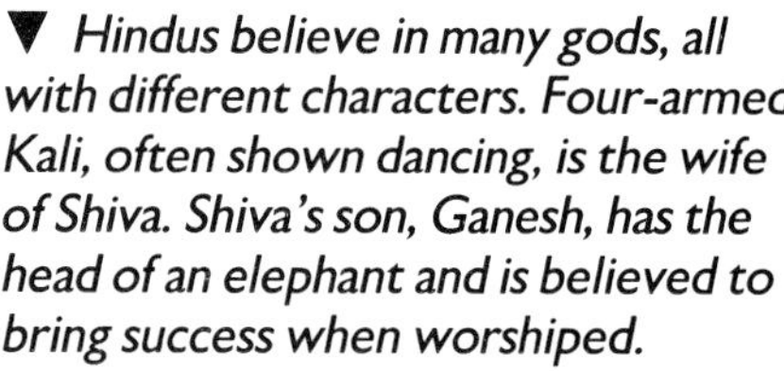

▼ *Hindus believe in many gods, all with different characters. Four-armed Kali, often shown dancing, is the wife of Shiva. Shiva's son, Ganesh, has the head of an elephant and is believed to bring success when worshiped.*

▲ *Hippopotamuses have eyes on the tops of their heads so they can stand under water and peep out without being seen. They can stay submerged for almost ten minutes without coming up for breath.*

Hippopotamus

The name hippopotamus means "river horse," but in fact, the hippo is related to the pig, not the horse. It is a huge, heavy animal and lives in Africa. Of all land animals, only the elephant is bigger.

Hippopotamuses live near rivers and lakes. They spend most of their time in the water and are good swimmers. In spite of their fearsome-looking jaws, hippopotamuses eat only plant food. They browse on water weeds and grasses, and at night, they often come ashore to feed.

These animals are not usually dangerous if left alone, but they can inflict serious wounds with slashes from the tusks in their lower jaws.

History

History is the story of the past. The people who write down history are called historians. They usually write about important events such as wars, revolutions, and governments, because these affect nations. However, historians are also interested in the lives of ordinary people and in what they did and thought about.

Nowadays, we think of history as being written down in history books. But in earlier times, before books and printing, history was passed on by word of mouth. People told stories about their kings, their wars, their adventures, and also about their

Continued on page 338

▼ *The history of ancient civilizations has to be pieced together from clues that have come to us over the years. This is a bronze head of a king who lived almost 4,500 years ago.*

AFRICA

B.C.

3,000,000	Australopithecus is early ancestor of modern man
30,000	Human hunters in Africa
5000	Stone Age craftworkers in Nile Valley
4500	Metal working in Egypt
2780	First pyramid in Egypt
1400	Golden age of Egypt's power
500	Kushite kingdom in Africa
146	Romans destroy power of Carthage, a great North African city-state

A.D.

500	Kingdom of Ghana
850	Building of citadel at Great Zimbabwe
980	Arabs begin to settle on east coast
1000	Moslems control all of North Africa; Ife bronze art at its peak in West Africa
1307	Empire of Mali in central Africa reaches its height under Munsa Mali
1498	Vasco da Gama begins Portugese trade along east coast
1500	Empire of Gao
1591	Fall of Songhai empire (which had succeeded Mali)
1652	Europeans led by Jan van Riebeeck settle at Cape of Good Hope
1713	Height of slave trade between West Africa and the New World
1818	Chaka founds the Zulu empire
1821	Liberia (West Africa) founded as free state for ex-slaves from U.S.A.
1835–37	Great Trek by Boers to found Transvaal
1869	Opening of Suez Canal creates shorter sea route from Europe to Asia
1884	Berlin Conference allows European powers to divide Africa between them
1899–1902	Boer War; Britain defeats Boers
1936	Italy conquers Ethiopia, Africa's oldest independent African nation
1949	South Africa adopts policy of apartheid (separation of the races)
1956	President Nasser of Egypt nationalizes the Suez Canal; this leads to a brief war with Britain and France
1960	Civil war in Congo
1960s	Many former European-ruled states become self-governing
1963	Formation of Organization of African Unity
1967	Civil war in Nigeria after Biafra breaks away
1974	Portugal gives up its last African colonies
1980	Zimbabwe (Rhodesia) becomes independent
1980s	Apartheid eases in South Africa; civil war in parts of the continent; drought and famine are serious problems
1991	Apartheid law repealed in South Africa

ASIA

B.C.

9000	Beginnings of agriculture in "fertile crescent"
7000	Jericho is world's first town
3500	Copper working in Thailand
3100	Earliest known writing, cuneiform script from Sumer
2300	Mohenjo-daro civilization in the Indus River valley (modern Pakistan)
2100	Abraham migrates from Ur
1500	Chinese master the skills of bronze working
1230	Peak of Assyrian power
565	Birth of Buddha
551	Birth of Confucius
221–210	Reign of Chinese emperor Shihuangdi, builder of the Great Wall: China is the world's largest empire

A.D.

4?	Birth of Jesus Christ
570	Birth of Muhammad
1000	Perfection of gunpowder in China
1100	Temples of Angkor Wat in Cambodia
1190	Genghis Khan begins to conquer an empire for the Mongols
1275	Marco Polo at the court of Kublai Khan
1405–33	Chinese fleets led by Cheng Ho make voyages of exploration in Pacific and Indian oceans
1498	Vasco da Gama sails from Portugal to India
1520s	Mogul empire in India
1600	Shogun Ieyasu becomes ruler of Japan
1760	French and British fight for power in India
1854	Japan is forced to sign trade treaty with U.S.A
1857	Indian Mutiny
1868	Meiji government begins to "westernize" Japan
1900	Boxer Rebellion in China
1905	Japan defeats Russians in war
1912	Sun Yat-sen leads new Chinese republic
1930s	Rise of Japan as a military power
1939–45	World War II: first atomic bombs dropped on Japan
1947	India gains independence from British rule
1948	Creation of the state of Israel
1949	Mao Tse-tung's Communists win civil war in China
1954	French pull out of Indochina: beginnings of Vietnam War
1976	Vietnam War ends with victory for North Vietnam
1979	Shah of Iran overthrown; Iran becomes an Islamic republic
1980s	Civil war in Lebanon: war between Iran and Ir (ends 1988); China becomes more open, but clamps down on democratic students
1990	Iraq invades Kuwait
1991	War in the Persian Gulf

EUROPE

B.C.

5000	Planting crops and animal husbandry reach Europe from Asia
2000	Minoan bronze age civilization of Crete
1193	City of Troy destroyed by Greeks
331	Alexander the Great leads Greeks to victory over the Persian Empire
509	Foundation of the Roman republic

A.D.

313	Christian religion tolerated throughout Roman Empire
330	Roman emperor Constantine founds Constantinople
476	Roman Empire collapses
732	Charles Martel leads Franks to victory over Moors
800	Charlemagne is crowned first Holy Roman Emperor
1066	William of Normandy conquers England
1096	First of six crusades by Christian armies against the Islamic rulers of the Holy Land (Palestine)
1215	English barons draw up Magna Carta
1300s	The Renaissance in arts and sciences
1348	The Black Death kills millions
1453	Constantinople is captured by the Turks
1517	Martin Luther's protest begins the Reformation
1522	First circumnavigation by Europeans (Magellan's fleet)
1588	English defeat the Spanish Armada
1642	Civil War in England
1700s	Revolutions in agriculture and industry; beginning of the Age of Machines
1789	French Revolution
1854–56	Crimean War
1870–71	Prussia defeats France in Franco-Prussian War
1914–18	World War I: Germany and its allies are defeated by Britain, France, U.S.A., Russia and others. More than 10 million soldiers are killed
1917	Communist revolution in Russia
1933	Hitler becomes ruler of Germany
1936–39	Civil war in Spain
1939–45	World War II: Allies defeat Germany and Italy in Europe
1957	Treaty of Rome establishes European Community (E.C.)
1980s	E.C. moves toward free market (1992); Gorbachev government brings new ideas in U.S.S.R. Eastern bloc countries move toward democracy
1991	Serbs and Croats fight in Yugoslavia Soviet Union breaks up into independent states
1992	Soviet Union ceases to exist

AMERICA AND AUSTRALASIA

B.C.

100,000?	Ancestors of Aborigines reach Australia
40,000	Ancestors of North American Indians migrate across "land bridge" from Asia
20,000	Indians complete settlement of South America
8400	First domesticated dog (Idaho)
3372	Earliest date in Mayan calendar (Mexico)

A.D.

1100	Maoris sail to New Zealand from Pacific islands
1400	Inca empire in Peru
1492	Columbus sails to "discover" America
1500	Cabral claims Brazil for Portugal
1518	Cortes begins conquest of Mexico, defeating Aztecs
1533	Pizarro conquers Inca empire for Spain
1584	Raleigh founds English colony in Virginia
1620	Voyage of the Pilgrim ship *Mayflower*
1626	Dutch found New Amsterdam (New York)
1642	Abel Tasman discovers Tasmania; French found Montreal in Canada
1763	Britain gains control of Canada after defeating France
1770	Cook explores coast of Australia and New Zealand
1776	American Declaration of Independence
1783	End of American War of Independence
1788	First British settlement in Australia
1789	George Washington first U.S. President
1824	South American republics break free from Spanish rule
1840	New Zealand becomes British colony
1861–65	American Civil War; Northern states defeat the South
1867	Canada becomes self-governing dominion
1901	Australia and New Zealand are independent
1917	U.S.A. enters World War I
1930s	Depression and unemployment in U.S.A.
1941	Japanese attack on Pearl Harbor brings U.S.A. into World War II
1959	Fidel Castro leads Communist revolution in Cuba
1963	President John F. Kennedy is assassinated
1965	U.S. troops fight in Vietnam
1969	U.S. astronauts land on the Moon
1975	Last U.S. forces leave Vietnam
1980s	U.S.A. is the strongest world power; civil war in Nicaragua (Central America); Australia and New Zealand make new trade partners in Asia
1991	U.S. recognizes and offers help to ex-Soviet states as they break apart.

▶ *Historic moments are well documented today. Future historians will have no difficulty piecing together the past from pictures like this one, of Soviet leader Gorbachev and President Reagan signing a treaty.*

▲ *We know a great deal about the history of Europe, even in the Middle Ages. This type of ship, called a caravel, was used in the 15th century for voyages of discovery.*

own families. It was in this way that the stories of ancient Greece were collected by the poet HOMER to form the *Iliad* and the *Odyssey*. Some early stories such as these were made up in verse and sung to music. This made it easier for people to remember the stories correctly.

In ancient Egypt, scholars recorded the reigns of the PHARAOHS and listed the victories they won in battle. Often, these accounts were written in HIEROGLYPHICS on stone tablets. The Chinese, Greeks, and Romans were also very interested in history. It was they who first took the writing of history seriously, and they wrote of how their civilizations rose to power. The history of America starts with the history of the native American Indians.

During the MIDDLE AGES in Europe, many people could not read or write, and printing had not been invented. The priests and monks preserved ancient books and kept the official records and documents. History became an important branch of study in the 1700s and 1800s. Famous historians include Edward Gibbon (1737–1794) and Lord Macaulay (1800–1859).

Historians get their information from hidden remains such as things found buried in old graves, as well as from old books. The study of hidden remains is called ARCHAEOLOGY. But history is not just concerned with the long distant past. After all, history is *our* story. What is news today will be history tomorrow. So modern historians are also interested

It is sometimes said, "Those who fail to learn the lessons of history are destined to repeat them." One of the best-known and most incorrect statements about history came from the famous American car manufacturer Henry Ford. He said: "History is bunk."

in recording the present. They talk to old people about the things they remember, and they keep records on film and tape, often made for television news programs, of the events of today.

Hitler, Adolf

Adolf Hitler (1889–1945) was the "Fuhrer," or leader, of Germany during World War II. An ex-soldier, born in Austria, he became leader of the Nazi Party which took over Germany in 1933.

Germany was still weak after its defeat in World War I. The Nazis promised to avenge this defeat and create a new German empire. In 1939, Hitler led Germany into World War II and conquered most of Europe. Millions of people were killed in Nazi death camps. But, by 1945, Germany had lost the war. Hitler killed himself in the ruins of Berlin to avoid capture.

▲ *Hitler used to organize rallies, attended by thousands of people, to spread his ideas.*

Hobby

People today have more and more leisure time. Most people work fewer hours and have longer holidays than people did in the past. They retire at an earlier age and live longer. Housework takes less time because of modern household appliances. All this means that people have more free time for their

SEE IT YOURSELF

The hobby of paper-folding is called *origami*, a Japanese word. To make a paper penguin, follow the steps below: 1 and 2. Fold and crease a square along the dotted lines so C meets D. 3. Fold point B up. 4. Fold point B down along dotted line. 5. Fold and crease so that point F meets point E. 6. Fold point F along dotted line to make penguin's foot. 7. Turn over and fold point E to match other foot. 8. Fold point A down along dotted line to make head. 9. Unfold so head points up again. Separate folds of head and push inward along central crease. Cut to separate tail. Fold tail pieces back so penguin will stand. 10. Draw eyes.

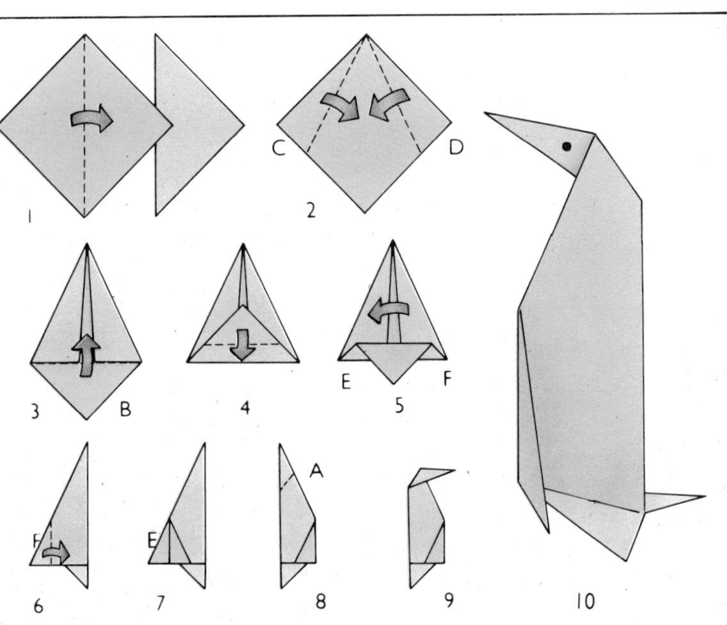

Most famous people have hobbies. George Washington collected different kinds of tea. Winston Churchill loved bricklaying. There is a long wall in the grounds of his former home built by the great man himself.

hobbies. Any activity that is enjoyed during your spare time is a hobby. It can be collecting things such as stamps, butterflies, bottles, or rocks. It can be a creative hobby, such as weaving, knitting, drawing, painting, or photography. Or it can be a playing hobby such as tennis, swimming, fishing, sailing, or chess. Part of the fun of any hobby is sharing it. The friendships that people gain from their hobbies are an important part of their interest.

Hockey

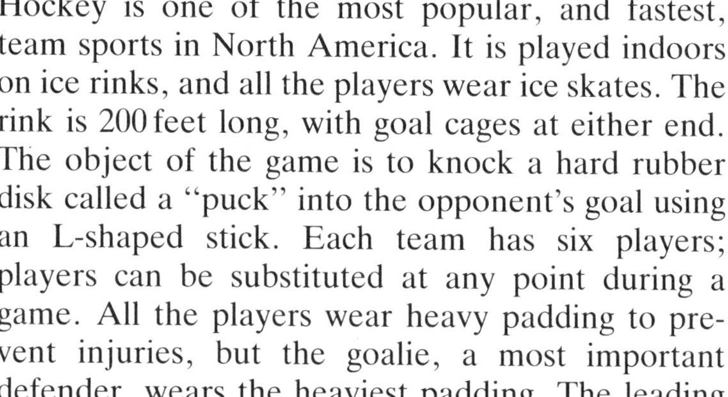
Hockey is one of the most popular, and fastest, team sports in North America. It is played indoors on ice rinks, and all the players wear ice skates. The rink is 200 feet long, with goal cages at either end. The object of the game is to knock a hard rubber disk called a "puck" into the opponent's goal using an L-shaped stick. Each team has six players; players can be substituted at any point during a game. All the players wear heavy padding to prevent injuries, but the goalie, a most important defender, wears the heaviest padding. The leading professional league is the National Hockey League.

▲ *Ice hockey players, and particularly the goalkeeper, have to wear special padded clothing to protect them against injury.*

Holography

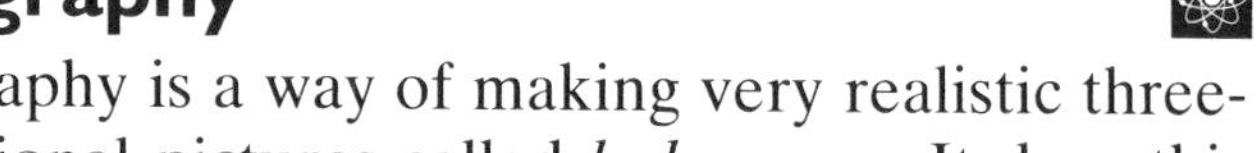
Holography is a way of making very realistic three-dimensional pictures called *holograms*. It does this

► *Holograms look very realistic because they are three-dimensional images. You can walk past a hologram and view it from different angles. Unfortunately, we cannot print a picture of a hologram in three dimensions here.*

by using LASER light instead of a camera.

To make a hologram, a laser beam is split into two; one beam hits the object and is reflected onto a photographic plate; the other beam, angled by mirrors, strikes the plate directly. The photographic plate is developed, and a black-and-white pattern, the hologram, appears. When the hologram is lit by a laser beam and viewed from the other side, it produces a three-dimensional image of the original object. The image seems real, with width, depth, and height.

One of the amazing things about a hologram plate is that it can be cut into pieces and each piece will give, not a part of the picture, but the whole picture.

Holy Roman Empire

For many years, a large part of Europe was loosely united as the Holy Roman Empire. At different times, it included Italy, Germany, Austria, and parts of France, the Netherlands, and Switzerland.

On Christmas Day in the year 800, Pope Leo III crowned CHARLEMAGNE as the first "Emperor of the Romans." The word "holy" was not added to the emperor's title until years later. After a while, the popes began to have more trouble than help from the emperors, and by the end of the thirteenth century, the emperor always came from the HAPSBURG family, the rulers of powerful Austria.

Homer

Homer was a Greek poet and storyteller. He probably lived around 800 B.C., but we know nothing else about him. All we have are two great poems said to be by Homer: the *Iliad* and the *Odyssey*.

▼ *Homer's stories are full of excitement. In the* Odyssey, *Odysseus and his men encountered many dangerous monsters, including the Sirens, three bird-women whose beautiful voices lured sailors to their doom on the rocky shores. Odysseus had himself tied to the mast, and his men plugged their ears so they would not be tempted.*

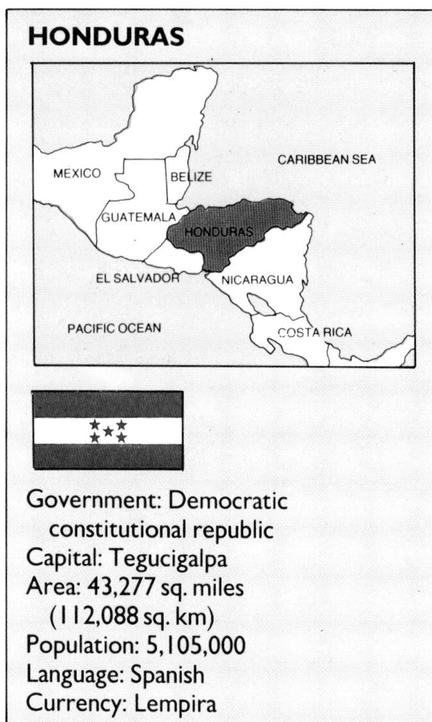

Government: Democratic constitutional republic
Capital: Tegucigalpa
Area: 43,277 sq. miles (112,088 sq. km)
Population: 5,105,000
Language: Spanish
Currency: Lempira

HONG KONG

Government: British Crown colony
Capital: Victoria
Area: Island 29 sq. miles (75 sq. km)
New Territories, etc.
375 sq. miles (971 sq. km)
Population: 5,801,000
Highest point: Tai Mo Shan 3,140 ft. (957 m)
Climate: Tropical monsoon
Rainfall average: 85 in. (2160 mm)

These poems tell us much of what we know about ancient Greek history and legend. The *Iliad* tells the story of the TROJAN WAR. The *Odyssey* tells of the adventures of Odysseus, a Greek hero, as he made his long journey home after the war.

Honduras

Honduras is a mountainous country in Central America. It has a long coastline with the Caribbean Sea and a short one along the Pacific. Most of the people are farmers. They live mainly in small villages in the west of the country and in the large banana plantations on the north coast. Columbus discovered Honduras in 1502. The country won its independence from Spain in 1821 and became a republic in 1838.

Hong Kong

Hong Kong is a tiny British colony off the coast of China. Part of it is a small island, and the rest is a narrow strip of land called the New Territories which is actually part of mainland China. Hong Kong has been governed by Britain since 1842. It is due to be handed over to Chinese rule in 1997.

Hong Kong has a fine harbor surrounded by

▶ *The name Hong Kong means "fragrant harbor." It is a crowded, busy place, and the famous Tiger Balm Gardens are a popular retreat.*

mountains. The capital is Victoria, and another busy city is Kowloon. Hong Kong is a fascinating mixture of East and West. The people live by trade, fishing, and farming. Tall apartment buildings have been built to house them, but there is still little room for the millions of people who crowd this small colony.

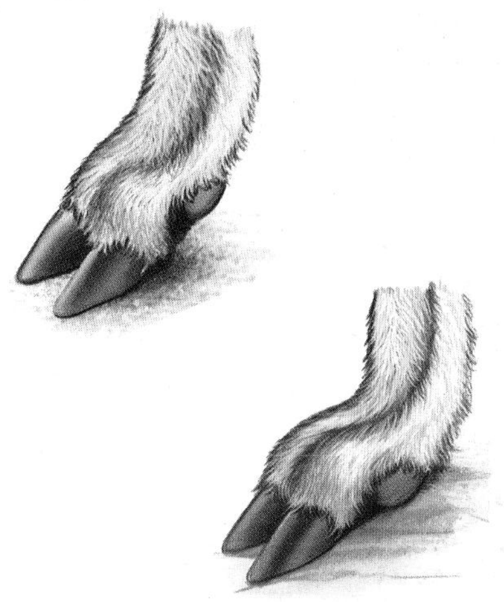

▲ *The ibex is a kind of wild goat. It has dual claws that can be brought down to give extra grip when scrambling up smooth rock faces.*

Hoof

A hoof is the hard covering of horn-like material that protects the feet of many animals. Animals that have hooves are divided into two main groupings: those that have an even number of toes; and those that have an odd number of toes. Those animals that have an even number of toes include DEER, GOATS, CAMELS, and SHEEP. All of these animals have either two toes or four toes. Animals that have only one toe include HORSES and zebras. All domesticated, or tame, horses have their hooves cut and trimmed and wear horseshoes. These are metal semicircles that are held in place by nails and that give valuable extra protection to the horse's hoof.

Hoover, Herbert Clark

Herbert Hoover (1874–1964) was president of the United States from 1929 to 1933. His presidency was dominated by the stock market crash of October 1929 and the Great Depression that followed it. The depression was the most severe in the history of the United States. Millions of people lost their jobs.

When Hoover became president, the United States had never been more prosperous. Most people expected that Hoover, who was a successful businessman, would help it to become richer still. Everyone was taken by surprise when the stock market fell only nine months after Hoover had become president. Few people knew what to do. Because Hoover believed that a country's economy should be allowed to regulate itself, he refused to give help to businesses or to pay unemployment to people who had lost their jobs. He became unpopular and was defeated in the next election by Franklin Roosevelt.

HERBERT C. HOOVER

Twenty-first President 1929–1933
Born: West Branch, Iowa
Education: Stanford University, Calif.
Occupation: Mining engineer
Political Party: Republican
Buried: West Branch, Iowa

▲ *Hormones can affect how much—or how little—people grow. This jockey, shown here with his trainer, is exceptionally small.*

Hormone

Hormones are chemical messengers found in all animals and plants. In many animals, hormones are produced in organs called GLANDS. Glands are found in several parts of the body. From these glands, the different hormones are carried in the blood to other parts of the body. There, they make the parts do certain jobs.

The pituitary gland in the center of the head produces several hormones. These "master" hormones control the hormone secretion of several other glands. The thyroid gland in the neck, for example, is stimulated by the pituitary gland to make a hormone that controls how fast food is used up by the body. Too little of this hormone makes people overweight. The hormone adrenaline is controlled by nerve messages. When it flows, the heart beats faster, blood pressure rises, and the body prepares itself for strenuous physical exertion.

Many hormones can now be made in the laboratory and used to help people suffering from diseases caused by lack of certain hormones. Insulin is a hormone used in the treatment of diabetes, a disease in which too much sugar stays in the blood.

Horn

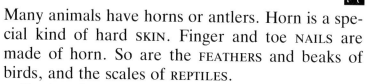

Many animals have horns or antlers. Horn is a special kind of hard SKIN. Finger and toe NAILS are made of horn. So are the FEATHERS and beaks of birds, and the scales of REPTILES.

Cattle, sheep, goats, and most ANTELOPES have curved horns. These are bony growths covered with a layer of horn, and they are fixed to the animal's skull. DEER have branched antlers, made of bone covered with skin. Every year, the antlers fall off, and the deer grows a new set.

▲ *The horns of some animals are very distinctive and decorative.*

Horse

The horse was one of the first wild animals to be tamed. Today, there are very few wild horses left. Many so-called "wild" horses are actually descended from domestic horses which have run wild.

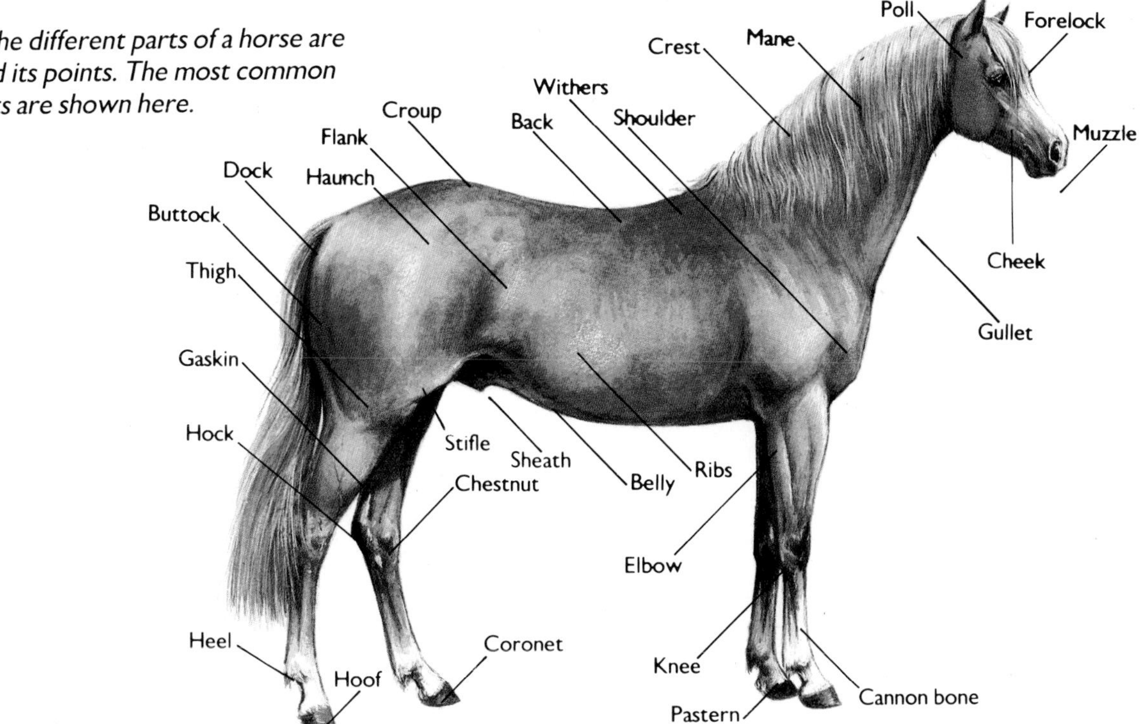

▼ *The different parts of a horse are called its points. The most common points are shown here.*

The horse is valued for its speed and strength. But the first horse was a small, rather doglike creature, with a way of life quite unlike that of modern horses. Called *Eohippus*, or "dawn horse," it lived millions of years ago. It had four toes on its front feet and three toes on its back feet, and it probably hid from its enemies in the undergrowth.

Later, horses came out to live on the wide grassy plains. There was no undergrowth to hide in, so they escaped from enemies by running away. Gradually, their legs grew longer, and they lost all their toes except one. Finally, after millions of years of EVOLUTION, the modern horse appeared. It, too, has only one toe, and actually runs on tiptoe. Its toe has become a tough nail or HOOF.

Today, horses are measured in hands from the ground to the highest point of the withers. A hand is 4 inches (10 cm), the width of a man's palm. But in the past a hand was only a little more than 3 inches because people's hands used to be smaller. Early horses were probably a lot smaller than those of today, seldom reaching 14 hands. Some of today's horses are over 17 hands and may even reach 20 hands.

Hospital

Hospitals are places where sick people, or patients, are cared for. Doctors and nurses look after the patients and try to make them better.

There are two types of hospital. One, the general hospital, deals with everything from accidents to contagious diseases. The other type of hospital specializes in certain conditions. For example, there

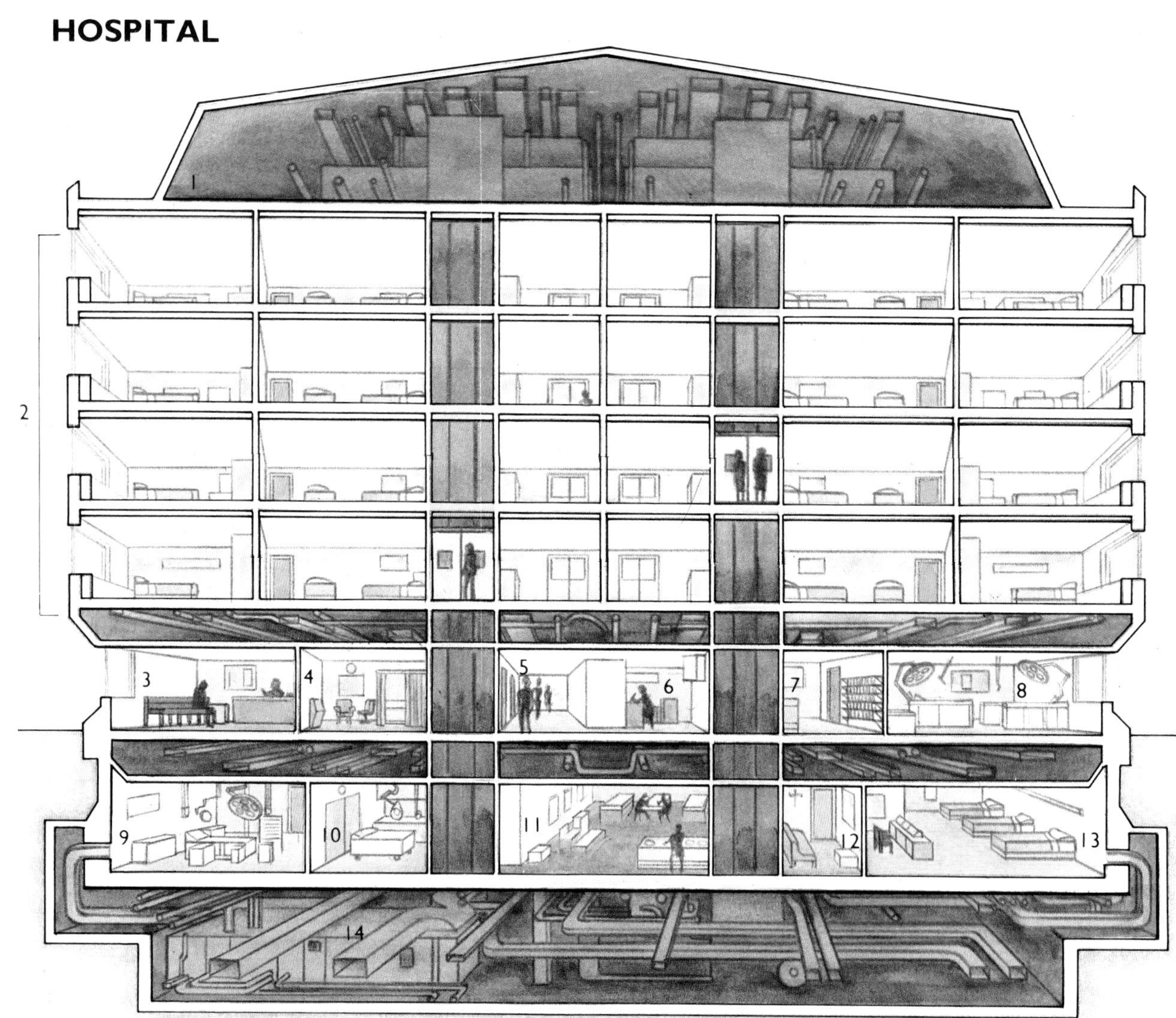

▲ *The modern hospital is designed so that the needs of both patients and staff can be met in the most efficient way possible. Some of the most important parts are:*
1 Heating and air conditioning
2 Patient floors 3 Waiting area
4 Consulting room 5 Corridor
6 Administration 7 Administration
8 Operating room 9 Operating room 10 Operating room
11 Staff restaurant 12 Chapel
13 Recovery room 14 Heating and air conditioning.

are *psychiatric* hospitals for people who are mentally ill; *maternity* hospitals where women have their babies; and *pediatric* hospitals that treat only children. In hospitals attached to medical schools, student doctors can gain experience through treating real patients.

In the ancient world, temples dedicated to the gods of healing used to have a hospital area. Sick people came there to pray and be treated. Later, in the Middle Ages, hospitals were attached to monasteries and run by monks and nuns. But in the last 200 years, non-religious hospitals have become the most common. In some countries, hospitals organized by the government provide inexpensive or free medical treatment for all people. Most hospitals are either owned by the community, the government, or are private and run like a business. Modern hospitals have a wide range of technical equipment.

Hotel

Hotels are places where travelers or people on vacation can stay. Before 1800, there were no hotels as we know them. Travelers spent the night at taverns or inns. Wherever people traveled, there were inns that gave food and shelter to the traveler and his horse.

Today, large hotels are like small towns. They provide people who are on business trips or are traveling for pleasure with all the comforts—swimming pools, television, restaurants, shops, travel agencies, and beauty salons.

Another kind of hotel is the "motel." This gives overnight housing for people who are traveling by car. Motels are found along major roads. Guests can usually drive their car right up to the door of their room.

▲ *Hotel kitchens are usually run with great efficiency and discipline. In large hotels, the work is very specialized, with one person in charge of making sauces, for example, while someone else only makes desserts, etc.*

House

Houses date back to prehistoric times. Some of the first were built in the Middle East. They were simple little boxes with flat roofs. Often, doors and windows were simply open spaces in the walls. (See pages 348–349.)

Hovercraft (Air Cushion Vehicle)

Depending on how you look at one, a hovercraft is either a plane with no wings or a ship that rides out of the water.

A hovercraft rides on a cushion of air, blown

Continued on page 350

▼ *The cushion of air produced by powerful fans inside a hovercraft provides a fast ride across water or land.*

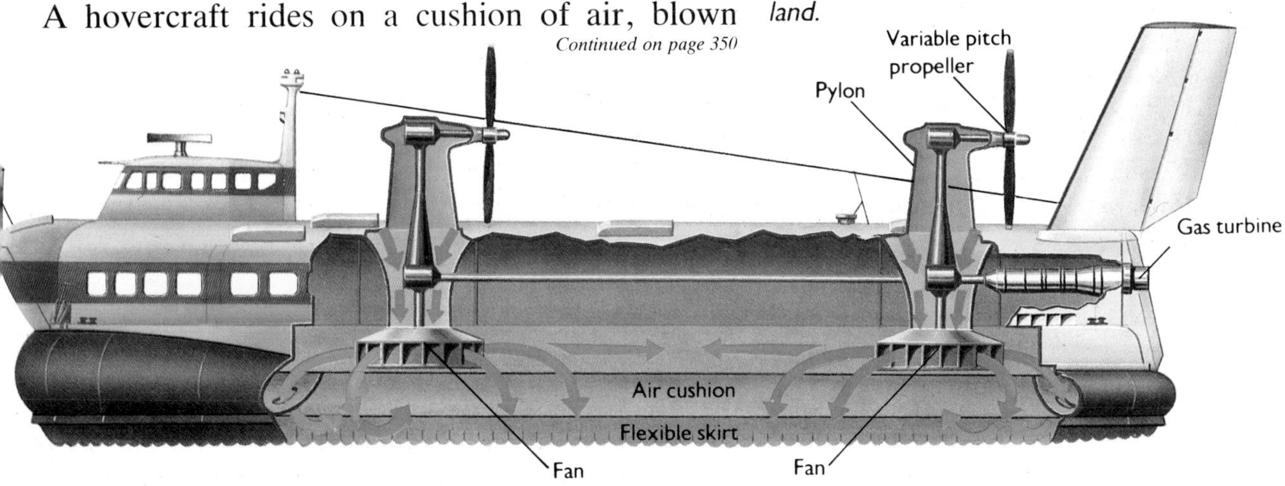

HOUSE

Prehistoric people lived in caves. The first houses were rough shelters, made of mud, branches, and leaves. Later, people learned how to make bricks by drying wet clay in the sun. Brick, wood, and stone were for thousands of years the materials from which almost all houses were built.

The modern house is built to keep out the cold and wet, and to keep in warmth. Insulation in the roof and walls helps to do this. Many homes have central heating and, in hot climates, air conditioning.

In most countries, a house is lived in by either a single family or a family group. A number of houses joined together form a row. Two houses joined side by side are called duplexes. A number of homes built on top of one another form an apartment building. In many big cities, there are not enough houses to provide homes for everybody. In some countries, poor people live in slums and shanty towns.

HOUSES AROUND THE WORLD

► *Although houses in cities around the world now look very much the same, there are still lots of differences in the way houses are built. Houses in North Africa and Arabia, for example, have thick mud-brick or cement walls and small windows. This helps to keep them cool. In Southeast Asia, many people live in houses built on stilts over the water. In Borneo, a whole village may live in one big dwelling called a long-house. In Canada, the U.S., and Scandinavia, many houses are built of wood, whereas in parts of Britain, you will see houses made of local stone, perhaps with a roof of thatch (reeds).*

HOW HOUSES AND APARTMENTS ARE BUILT

Houses are built in a different way from apartments. Both must have foundations, with pipes for water and sewage, and cables for electricity. A house often has walls of brick, covered on the inside with plaster or wallboard. The floors are made of concrete or wood. The roof is usually sloped, so that rain runs off easily and is covered with rows of shingles. An apartment building has a framework of steel girders to give extra strength. The walls may be factory-made panels, lifted into place by a crane. It will have an elevator, as well as stairs, and it may have a flat roof.

▲ *Traditional building techniques using timber, bricks, and tiles are still widely used, particularly for housing.*

▲ *Large-scale building projects often rely on advanced techniques and materials.*

Sudanese mud huts

Indonesian stilt house

Modern apartment building

English thatched cottage

Suburban house

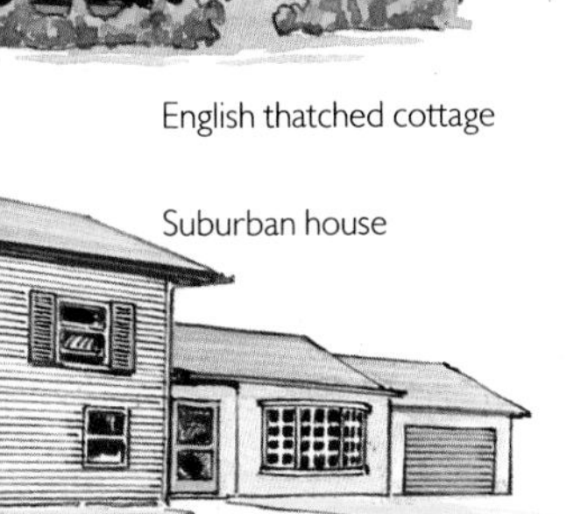

HISTORY OF THE HOUSEHOLD

100 A.D. Wealthy Romans lived in houses with running water and underfloor heating.
1200s Only rich people could afford glass in their windows.
1500s The water closet was invented, but few people had real toilets until the 1900s.
1830 Edwin Budding invents lawnmower.
1840s Gas lighting replaced oil lamps and candles.
1858 Ferdinand Carré invents the refrigerator, allowing people to keep food fresh for later use.
1879 Electric light bulb invented.
1880s Gas stoves introduced to replace the old kitchen range.
1900s Invention of the vacuum cleaner.
1910 First electric washing machine.
1930s Electric stoves become popular.
1950s First dishwasher invented.
1953 Microwaves appear in the U.S. They cook food much faster than normal methods.
2000 The home run by a computer?

▼ ***The Xanadu experimental house in Florida could be the shape of things to come. Built for maximum energy efficiency, it combines convenience with concern for the environment.***

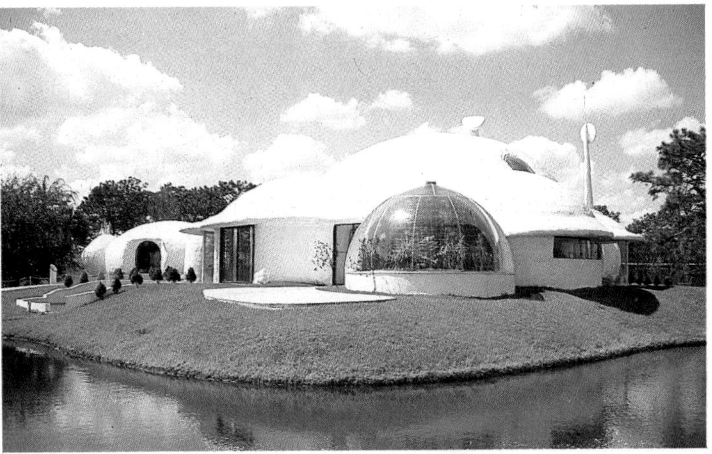

BUYING AND RENTING HOUSES

People wanting to buy a house usually need to borrow most of the money, because houses are expensive. In the U.S., house buyers can borrow money from a bank or from a savings and loan. This is called taking out a mortgage. They have to repay the loan over a number of years. They will probably visit a realtor to see what houses are for sale.

Not all houses are owned by the people who live in them. Many people live in rented houses or apartments. They pay rent to the owner.

For information about how houses are built see ARCHITECTURE; BUILDING. For interesting and unusual houses, turn to AMERICAN INDIANS; CAVE DWELLER; ESKIMO; GYPSY. For the insides of houses, see FURNITURE; TAPESTRY.

A well-known use of the hovercraft principle is the "hovering" rotary lawnmower. The engine, besides rotating the grass-cutting blade, creates a cushion of air that raises the machine to the right height above the ground.

downward by fans, and held in by a skirt or side wall around the hovercraft. They work best over flat surfaces like water, but can also cross beaches and flat land. The only danger is that rough ground may snag their bottoms.

Hovercraft are much faster than ships. Since they do not have to push against any water, but simply skim smoothly through the air, they can easily manage speeds of 75 mph (120 km/h). Their advantage over planes is the size of the load they can carry. A large craft can load dozens of cars and up to 400 passengers. And of course they do not need harbors or runways to land. They simply climb up the beach to settle on a simple concrete landing pad.

The hovercraft was invented in 1955 by a British engineer, Christopher Cockerell. The first working model appeared four years later and had soon crossed the Channel from England to France. Today, fleets of hovercraft shuttle back and forth every day carrying hundreds of cars and passengers.

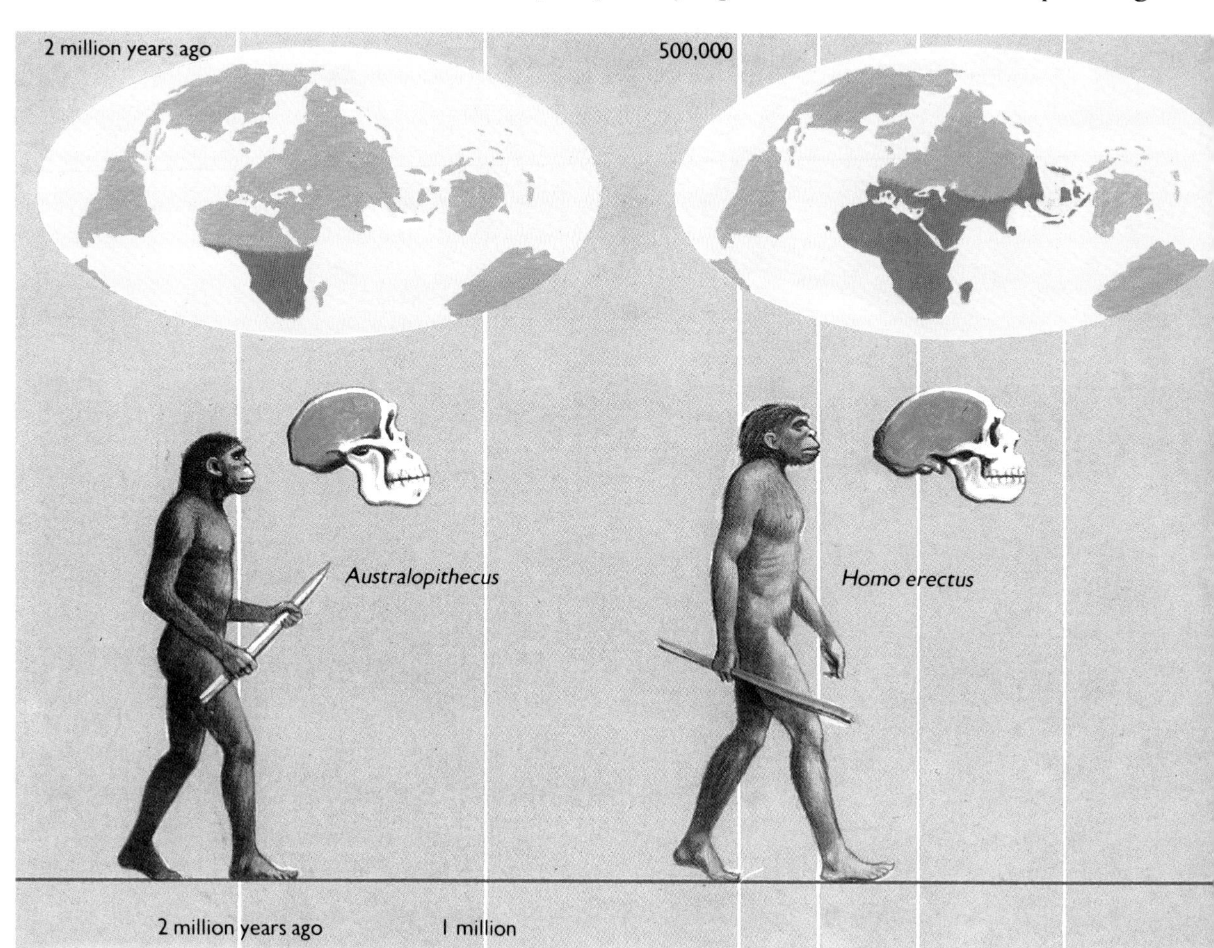

Human Beings  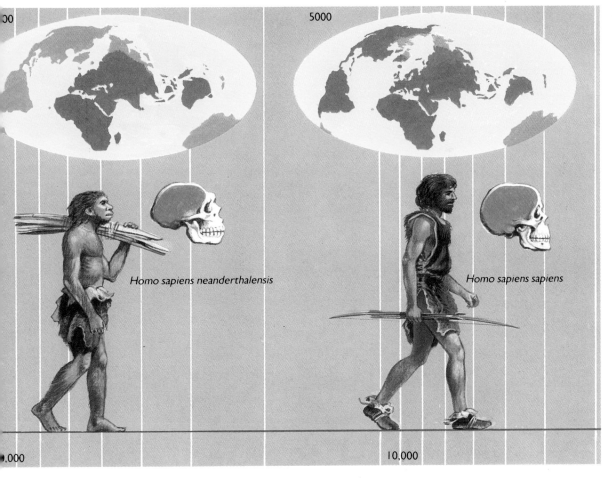

Human beings are mammals, but rather clever ones. They are very like their relatives, the apes. They have the same kind of bones, muscles, and other parts inside their bodies. But the main difference between people and any other animal is the size of their brain. The human brain is enormous, compared to body size. Some animals are stronger than human beings, others can run faster, hear and smell more acutely. But people use their brain to think things out, and when they have found an answer to a problem, they can talk about it with other people.

Scientists now agree that our ancestors were ape-like creatures who slowly, over millions of years, evolved (changed) into people. People something like ourselves have probably lived on Earth for about 500,000 years.

Today, all people belong to the same *species* (kind of creature). This creature is classified as

▼ *Our ancestors of two million years ago were very different from us, but the world, too, was very different. A series of ice ages meant that huge glaciers covered much of the northern half of the Earth. One of the most important events in the development of people took place about one million years ago, when our ancestors started to make tools. By about 10,000 B.C. people were beginning to understand how to grow and harvest crops. The red areas show how people spread all over the world.*

5000

Homo sapiens neanderthalensis

Homo sapiens sapiens

10,000

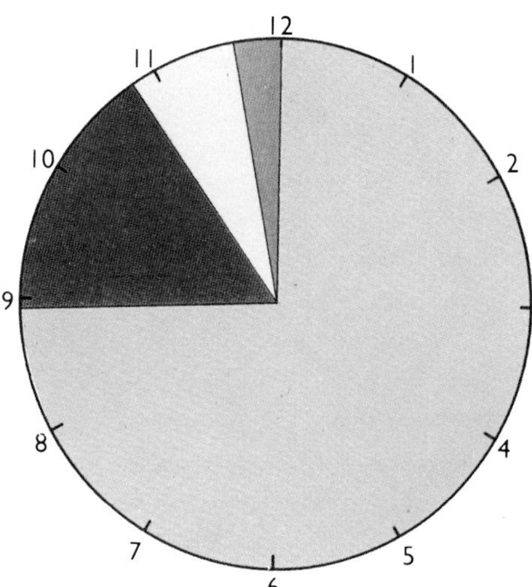

▲ *If the history of the Earth to the present day were condensed into twelve hours, the earliest life in the sea would have begun just before nine o'clock. Life moved onto land at a quarter to eleven, and mammals appeared at twenty to twelve. Humans would have arrived just before the stroke of twelve.*

Homo sapiens ("thinking man"). All people, in every country on Earth, whether black, white, brown, or yellow, are *Homo sapiens*.

Scientists divide human beings into three main *races*. The *Caucasoid* people are fair-skinned like the people of Europe and America or dark-skinned like the people of India, and others. The *Mongoloid* group takes in most of the yellow-skinned peoples of Asia, plus the American Indians. The *Negroid* group consists of the dark-skinned peoples of Africa and other regions.

Human Body

Your body is a wonderful machine with many parts. Each part has a special job, and all the parts work together to keep you alive and healthy. Like all machines, your body needs fuel—food. The OXYGEN you breathe in from the air helps turn the food you eat into energy. This energy allows you to play, work, think, and grow.

Your body is made up of millions of tiny cells—many different kinds of cells. A group of cells that work together is called a *tissue*. For example, cells that allow you to lift things are called muscle tissue. Tissues that work together make up an *organ*. The HEART is an organ that pumps blood. Other organs are the LIVER, the LUNGS, the STOMACH, and the SKIN.

▼ *The body works through a series of interconnected systems that function all the time to keep us going.*

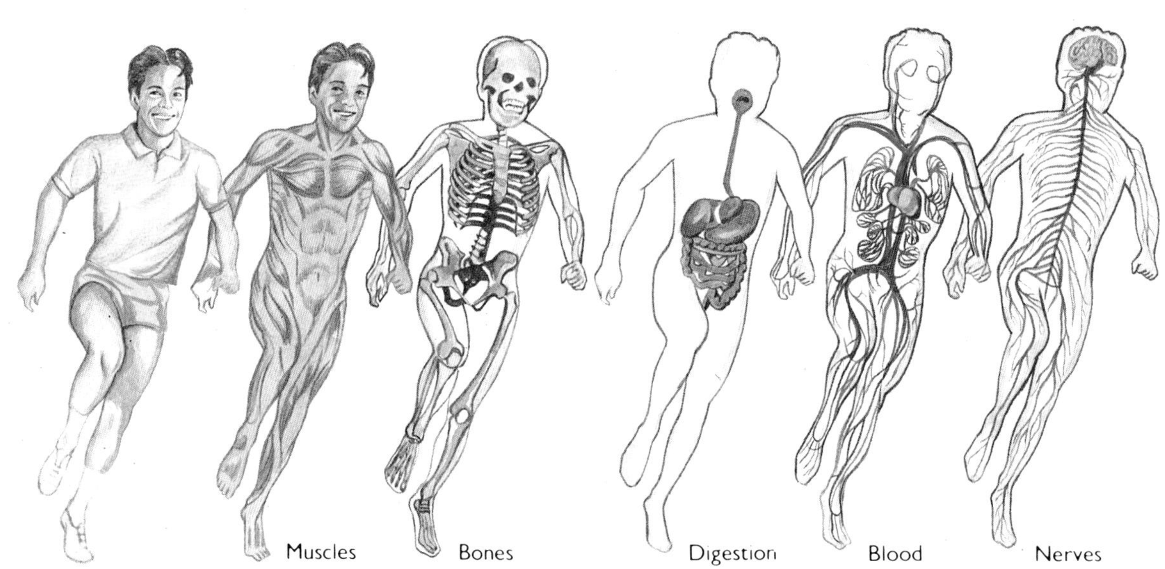

Organs that work together are called *systems*. You have a *digestive system* (mouth, stomach, and intestines), a *circulatory system* (heart, arteries, and veins), and a *nervous system* (brain and nerves). The study of the body is called *anatomy*.

Humidity

All air has some water in it, although we cannot see it. Humidity is the amount of water in the air. If the air contains only a little water vapor, the humidity is low. When air holds a lot of moisture, we say the humidity is high. The warmer the air, the more moisture it can hold. Humidity affects the way we feel. When the humidity is high, we feel "sweaty" and uncomfortable. This is because the sweat does not evaporate easily from our skin. But too low a humidity is not very good for us. Some people use *humidifiers* in their homes to put more moisture into the air.

SEE IT YOURSELF

Scientists calculate the humidity with the help of an instrument called a hygrometer. You can make one by taping two identical outdoor thermometers to a brick. Cut a narrow strip about 8 inches (20 cm) long from an old towel and wrap it around the bulb of one thermometer. Fill a pan with water and put the other end of the strip in it. After a while, take the difference between the temperatures shown on the two thermometers in the shade outdoors. The less the difference, the higher the humidity. Keep a record of the humidity in your area.

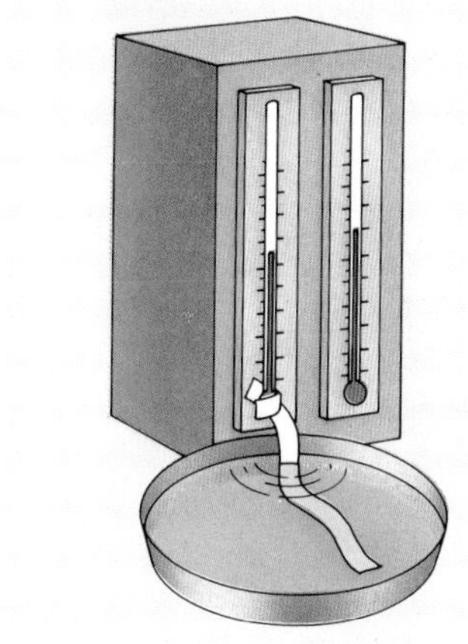

Hummingbird

These birds are among the smallest in the world. They are found only in the western hemisphere, from Canada to the tip of South America. The tiniest of the 320 kinds lives in Cuba. It is less than 2 inches (5 cm)—hardly bigger than a large bumblebee.

▲ *The tiny hummingbird has a specially developed beak and tongue that enable it to feed from deep inside flowers.*

Some tiny hummingbirds spend 20 hours in the air and make journeys of up to 500 miles (800 km) over water.

The feathers of hummingbirds are colored in brilliant metallic hues of blue, green, red, and yellow. The colors flashing in the sun make hummingbirds look like glittering jewels on the wing.

Hummingbirds can beat their wings up to 70 times a second. This is what causes their distinctive humming sound. It also lets them hover in mid-air and fly backward and sideways like a helicopter. In this way, they dart from flower to flower and feed while flying. They take nectar and tiny insects from deep within the cups of flowers.

Hungary

Hungary is a small, central European country. It covers an area about the size of Maine.

Hungary has no coastline. The mighty Danube River flows across the country on its way to the Black Sea, dividing it almost in two. Ships can sail up the river as far as Budapest, the capital and biggest city.

Hungary is low-lying and fairly flat. In the east, it becomes a vast grassy plain. Here herds of sheep, cattle, and horses graze. The climate is hot and dry in the summer, and bitterly cold in the winter. Agriculture is important, but more Hungarians work in industry than on farms. There are also rich sources of coal, oil, and bauxite for making aluminum.

HUNGARY

Government: Multiparty system
Capital: Budapest
Area: 35,910 sq. miles (93,030 sq. km)
Population: 10,553,000
Language: Hungarian
Currency: Forint

► *The capital of Hungary is actually made up of two cities—Buda and Pest, separated by the Danube.*

After World War I and the collapse of the Austro-Hungarian Empire, Hungary became an independent republic. After World War II, it had a communist government and was closely linked with the Soviet Union. But, in 1989, the people demanded and achieved a more democratic form of government.

In 1991 the last Soviet troops left Hungary.

Huns

These were a group of fierce wandering warriors who swept into Europe in about A.D.400 from the plains of Central Asia. They conquered large parts of Germany and France. Their famous general, Attila, attacked Rome and nearly destroyed the Roman Empire. However, the Huns' power grew less after his death in A.D.453.

When Attila, the great leader of the Huns, died in 453, his body was taken out into the plains and buried with much of his treasure. All those who had been at Attila's burial were put to death afterward so that his grave might never be discovered.

Hunting

In prehistoric times, hunting was the main way by which people lived. Nowadays, most hunting is done as sport or to keep down pests.

Big game hunting is the sport of tracking, stalking, and killing large wild animals. This kind of hunting is dying out, since people now want to preserve animals, not kill them. Another kind of hunting is with packs of hounds. The hunters may follow on foot or on horseback as the dogs chase deer, foxes, or hares through the countryside. Foxhunting is the most popular kind of hunting in the British Isles. In the United States, most hunting is done with guns.

▼ Hunting on horseback was a popular sport in ancient China. Cheetahs, dogs, and falcons were used in the chase.

▲ *Satellite pictures can help to predict the route a hurricane will take. Hurricane Allen is shown here over the Gulf of Mexico. You can clearly see the "eye" in the center of the storm.*

Hurricane

A hurricane is a severe storm. To be called a hurricane, a storm must have wind speeds of at least 75 miles (120 km) an hour. People who live around the Pacific Ocean call hurricanes *typhoons*. People who live on the Indian Ocean call them *cyclones*. Hurricane winds whirl around in a huge circle and can reach speeds of over 200 miles (320 km) per hour. The largest hurricanes have measured 1,000 miles (1,600 km) across. Hurricanes form over oceans near the Equator, where the air is very moist. The center of a hurricane is a narrow column of air that spins very slowly. This is the "eye" of the hurricane.

Hydroelectric Power

More than a quarter of the world's electricity is produced by using the energy of fast flowing water. This is called hydroelectric power. Most hydroelectric plants are found below dams, but some are powered by waterfalls.

Water is heavy. When it falls down through large pipes from a high dam, it can be made to turn TURBINES with paddle-shaped blades. Shafts connected to the blades turn electric generators, as in ordinary coal- or oil-fired POWER PLANTS.

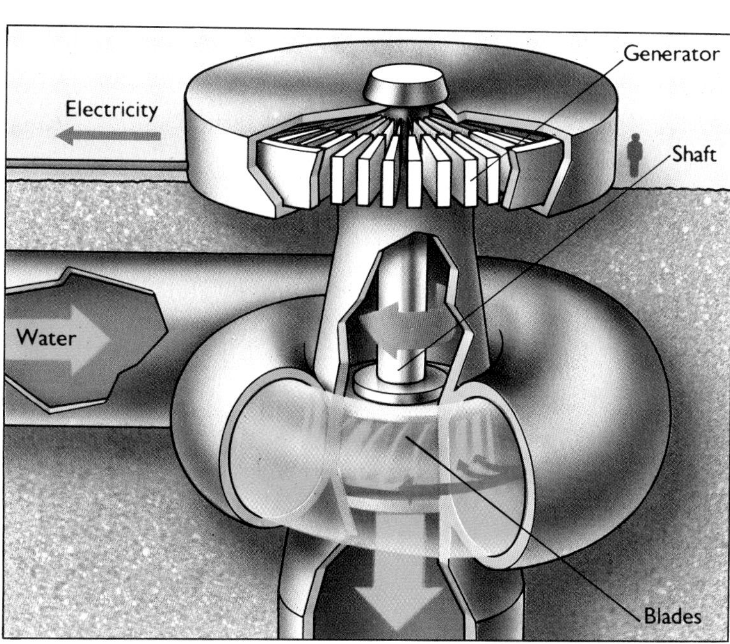

▶ *The huge turbine blades in a hydroelectric power plant are turned by water as it flows down from a dam. They in turn rotate a shaft connected to generators, which produce electricity in the same way as in ordinary power plants.*

Hydrofoil

Much of a ship's engine power goes into overcoming the drag of the water around the ship's hull. A hydrofoil solves this problem by lifting the ship right out of the water. It does this with a set of underwater struts attached to the hull of the craft at the bow and stern. These "water wings" can lift the hull as the ship gathers speed. As the water's drag grows less, the craft shoots ahead, traveling far faster than an ordinary vessel can.

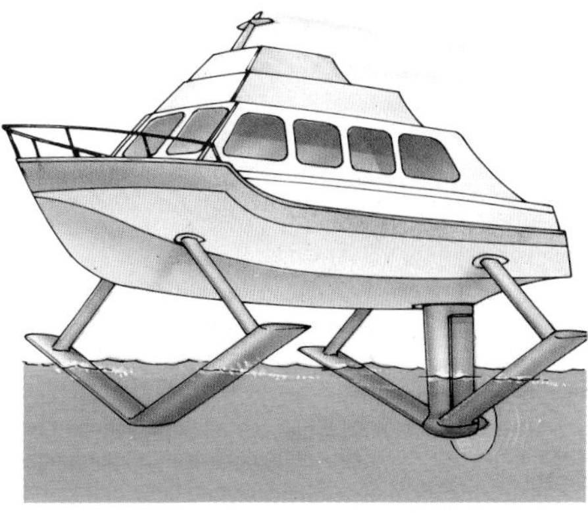

▲ *At rest, a hydrofoil lies in the water like a normal ship, but once it starts moving, the hull rises up and the vessel is supported on its underwater struts.*

Hydrogen 

Hydrogen is a gas. It is thought to be the most abundant ELEMENT in the whole universe. It is the single most important material from which stars, including our SUN, are made.

Hydrogen is the lightest of all elements. It is more than 14 times as light as air. It is colorless and has no smell and no taste. Hydrogen burns very easily. Great masses of hydrogen are always being burned in the Sun. It is this fierce burning that gives us light and heat from the Sun.

Coal, oil, and natural gas all contain hydrogen. It is also a very important part of all plant and animal bodies.

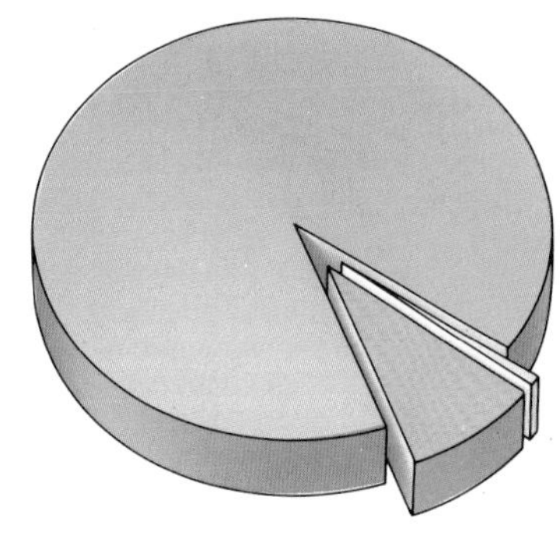

▲ *This pie chart shows the proportions of the gases that make up our Sun. Hydrogen is the main component by a long way.*

Hyena 

Hyenas are a small group of flesh-eating MAMMALS. Although they look a lot like dogs, they are more closely related to the cat family.

Hyenas feed on dead flesh, or carrion. They scavenge their meals from the kills of other animals such as lions. They have very powerful teeth and jaws for crushing the bones and making the most of their source of leftover food. Hyenas hunt in packs. They feed at night. By day, they sleep in holes and caves.

The spotted hyena lives in southern Africa. It is famous for its wild laughing cry, which resembles a hysterical human laugh, and is sometimes known as the laughing hyena. The striped hyena lives in India, southwest Asia, and northeast Africa.

▼ *A pack of hyenas can drive away most hunting animals from their kill, which the hyenas then finish off.*

► *The glaciers that spread over large parts of the Earth during the Ice Ages carried huge rocks and boulders with them as they went. Geologists can trace the path of the glaciers by studying these rocks and figuring out where they came from.*

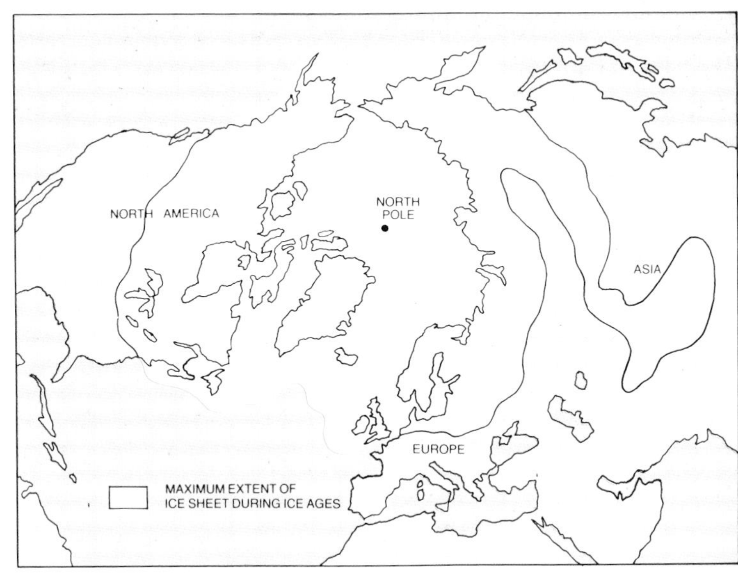

Ice Ages

The Ice Ages were times when vast sheets of ice covered parts of the Earth. Each period lasted for thousands of years. In between were warmer periods. The last Ice Age ended about 10,000 years ago, but the ice might return again.

During the Ice Ages, the weather was very cold. Endless snow fell, and GLACIERS grew and spread. At times, the glaciers covered much of North America and Asia, and Europe as far south as London. In some places, the ice piled up 3,300 feet (1,000 m) high. This made the sea level lower than it is today. A land bridge was formed between Asia and North America. The first people in America came across this land bridge from Asia.

▼ *Huge icebergs float in the sea because, when water freezes, it expands, so ice is less dense than water.*

Iceberg

Icebergs are pieces of GLACIERS and ice shelves that have broken away and float in the sea. They are found in the waters of the ARCTIC and the ANTARCTIC.

Icebergs can be very big. Some weigh millions of tons. Most of an iceberg is hidden under the surface of the sea. Some icebergs may be 90 miles (145 km) long. They can be 400 feet (120 m) high above water. An iceberg this high would be another 3,200 feet (960 m) deep under water.

Icebergs are dangerous to ships. Some icebergs

float south from the Arctic into the Atlantic Ocean. In 1912, a ship called the *Titanic* hit an iceberg in the Atlantic. It sank, and 1,500 people in it were drowned.

Iceland

Iceland is a small, mountainous island. It was first discovered by VIKINGS in A.D.874. The island lies just south of the Arctic Circle in the north Atlantic, between Greenland and Norway. Warm waters from the GULF STREAM keep most of the harbors free of ice all year round.

Iceland has many VOLCANOES. About 25 of its volcanoes have erupted. There are many hot springs, too. Some are used to heat homes. The north of Iceland is covered by GLACIERS and a desert of stone and lava (cooled volcanic matter).

◀ *These two volcanic hills rising out of the landscape are typical Icelandic features.*

Most people live in the south and east where the land is lower. They live by farming and fishing. It is light almost 24 hours a day in June, and dark nearly all the time in December.

Iceland became an independent country in 1944 after breaking its ties with Denmark.

ICELAND

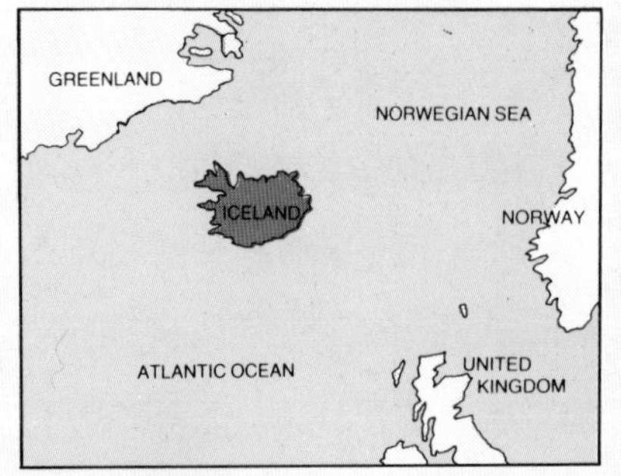

Government: Constitutional republic
Capital: Reykjavik
Area: 39,768 sq. miles (103,000 sq. km)
Population: 255,000
Language: Icelandic
Currency: Krona

Idaho

Idaho is one of the most spectacularly beautiful states. It is in the northwest of the country, on the Canadian border, and is dominated by the northern

IDAHO

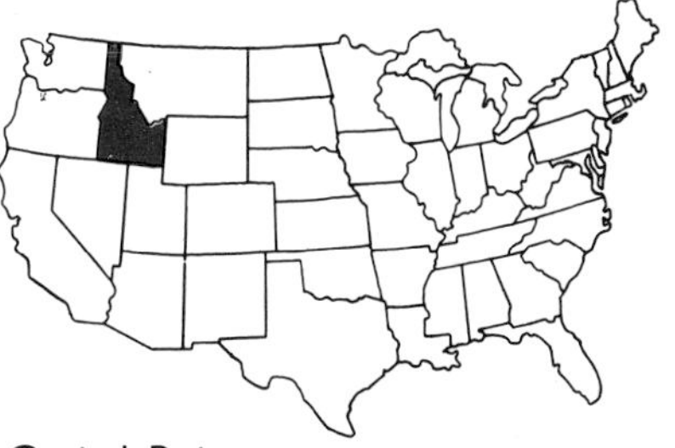

Capital: Boise
Population: 1,006,749
Area: 83,564 sq. mi. (216,432 sq. km)
State flower: Idaho Syringa
State bird: Mountain Bluebird
State tree: White Pine
Statehood: July 3, 1890
43rd state

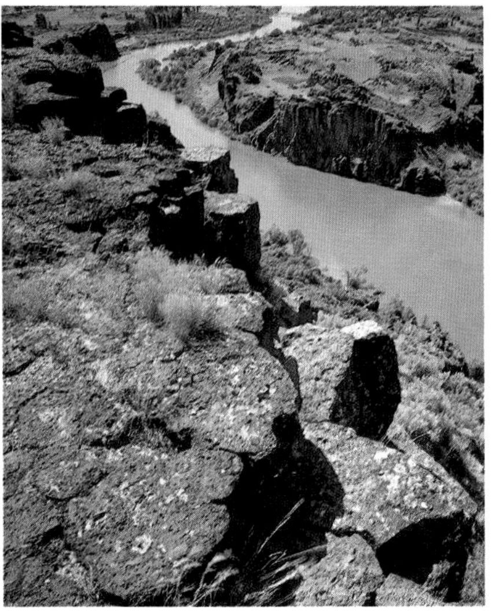

▲ *Snake River Gorge, Idaho.*

end of the Rocky Mountains. In the south is the rushing Snake River. It flows through Hells Canyon, which is 7,900 feet (2,400 m) deep, deeper than the Grand Canyon.

Idaho's most famous product is potatoes, but many other important agricultural products are grown, too, including wheat, peas, hops, and sugar beets. Almost 40 percent of the state is forested. Paper, which is made from wood, is one of the state's most important products. Idaho also has enormous mineral reserves, and produces more silver than any other state. Minerals for industry are also produced.

Illinois

ILLINOIS

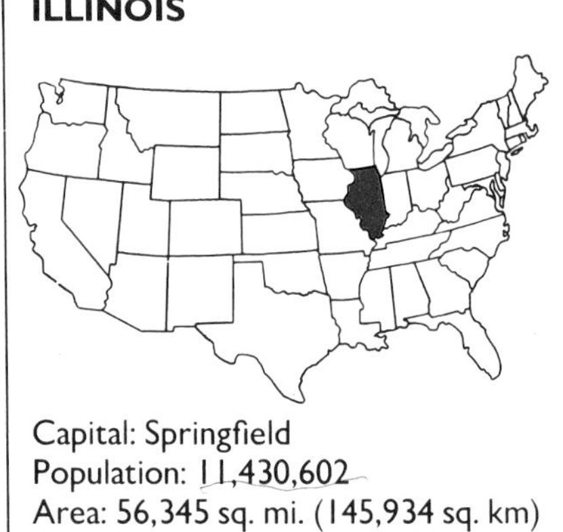

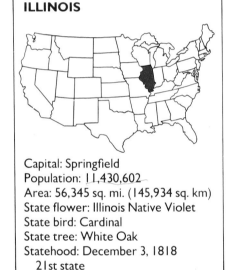

Capital: Springfield
Population: 11,430,602
Area: 56,345 sq. mi. (145,934 sq. km)
State flower: Illinois Native Violet
State bird: Cardinal
State tree: White Oak
Statehood: December 3, 1818
21st state

Illinois lies in the center of the Midwest. It is one of the most important industrial and agricultural states. Most industry is centered in and around Chicago, the largest city; over one half of the population lives in this area. Much of the rest of Illinois is rich agricultural land. The rolling prairie lands produce high-quality beef, pork, and dairy goods. With the Great Lakes to the north and the Mississippi running south, Illinois also lies in the center of many important transportation routes.

The French were the first Europeans to settle Illinois. In 1763 it was taken over by the British. It became a U.S. territory in 1783. European settlers flooded into the state in the 1800s.

▼ *Lincoln's house in Springfield, Illinois.*

Immunity

You have probably been vaccinated against the disease called polio. The substance the doctor or nurse put into your body contained polio germs, but these germs had been made harmless, so you only caught a very mild case of polio. Your body did not know that the polio germs had been weakened, and it got to work fighting them. Your body produced *antibodies*—substances that attack certain disease-causing germs. These antibodies stay in your body to stop more of the same kind of germs from invading your body again. This kind of long-term protection against diseases is called immunity.

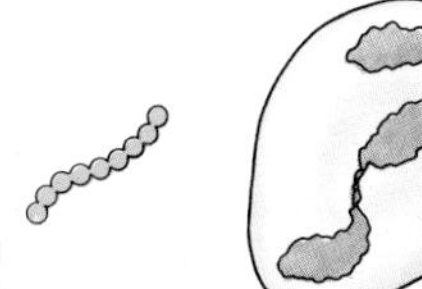

1. A white blood cell is moving to attack a bacterium.

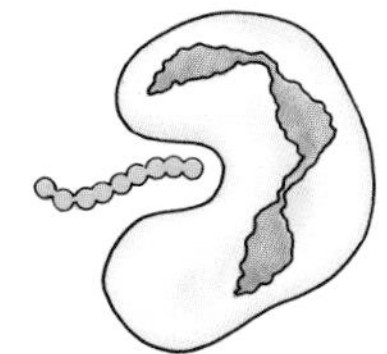

2. It surrounds the bacterium and takes it in.

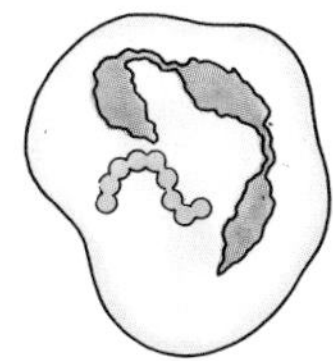

3. The bacterium is killed by chemicals inside the cell.

4. The bacterium is expelled in the form of pus.

▲ *The presence of bacteria in the body stimulates the white blood cells, which are always present to move in to attack them.*

People also have *acquired* immunity to disease. This happens when they have a disease and produce antibodies to fight it off. After that, the antibodies are waiting to ward off these germs if they appear again. If you had measles, you are unlikely to get measles again.

However, some diseases are very difficult or impossible to vaccinate against. Your body stops making antibodies against the common cold almost as soon as you are over it. The VIRUS that causes AIDS damages the body's immune system so that it stops making antibodies against any diseases.

Impressionism

In the 1860s in France, some young artists began to paint in a new way. Most artists worked indoors, but these young men began to paint outdoors. They

The Impressionists were so interested in light that they never used black. Black is the absence of light. If you look at an Impressionist painting, some things seem to be black, but look closely and you will see that they are dark brown, green, or blue.

◀ *Some of Monet's most famous paintings are of his garden at Giverny.*

◀ *The Incas worshiped the Sun and other nature gods in elaborate ceremonies, at which their priests would offer sacrifices of animals.*

painted scenes from nature and tried to catch the ever-changing light.

In 1874, the group held an exhibition in Paris. Their work was laughed at, and one newspaper poked fun at a painting called *Impression: Sunrise* by Claude Monet. It called the group "Impressionists," and the name stuck.

Now, people recognize the Impressionists as being among the greatest artists of all time. In addition to Monet, the most important Impressionists were Edouard Manet, Camille Pissarro, Edgar Degas, Alfred Sisley, and Pierre Auguste Renoir.

▼ *The Inca empire, when the Spaniards first encountered it, stretched for about 2,000 miles (3,200 km) north to south on the west coast of South America.*

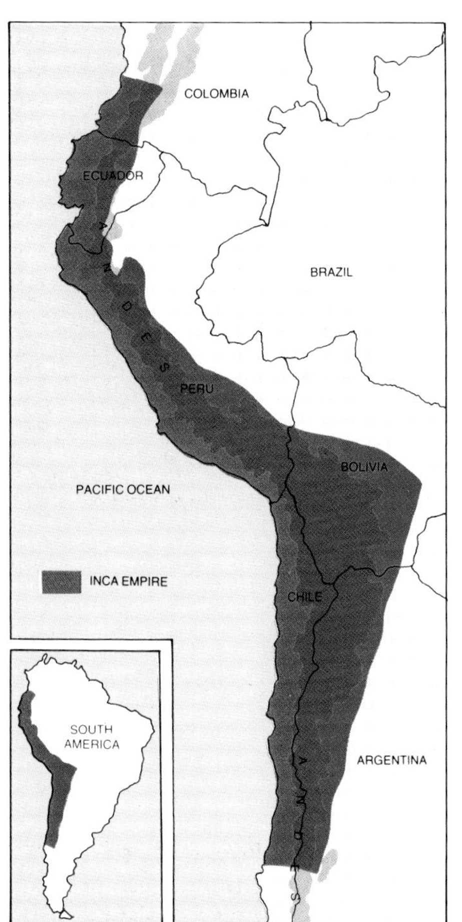

Incas

The Incas were people who lived in SOUTH AMERICA. They ruled a great empire from the 1200s until the 1500s. The center of their empire was in PERU. In the 1400s, the empire grew. It stretched thousands of miles, from Chile in the south to Ecuador in the north.

The Inca king and his nobles ruled over the people in the empire. They were very strict and told the farmers and craftsmen what to grow and make. The Incas built many roads through the empire.

In the 1500s, Spanish soldiers led by Francisco Pizarro reached South America. They captured the Inca king Atahualpa and said they would free him in return for gold. Incas brought their treasure to free the king, but the Spanish still killed him. By 1569, the Spaniards had conquered the whole Inca empire.

Independence Day

Independence Day—July 4—is one of the most important holidays in the United States. It commemorates the acceptance of the Declaration of Independence by the Continental Congress in Philadelphia on July 4, 1776. It was first celebrated in Philadelphia on July 8, 1776, the day the Declaration of Independence was read in public. It was not until after the War of 1812 that people across the country began to celebrate Independence Day. And it was only in 1941 that Congress made it a national holiday. Today, people celebrate Independence Day with parades, parties, and fireworks.

John Adams, the second president, said that Independence Day "ought to be solemnized with pomp and parade, with shows, games, sports, guns, bells, bonfires, and illuminations, from one end of the continent to the other, from this time forward for evermore."

India

India has a population of over 800 million. It has more people than any other country except China. India is part of ASIA.

In the north of India are the HIMALAYAS. Many people live in the fertile northern plains, which are crossed by the great Ganges and Brahmaputra rivers. The south is high, flat land, with mountains called the Ghats along the coast.

India is very hot and dry in summer. Parts of the country are almost DESERT. But winds called *monsoons* bring heavy rain to the northeast every year.

Most Indians are farmers. They live in small villages and grow rice, wheat, tea, cotton, and jute.

INDIA

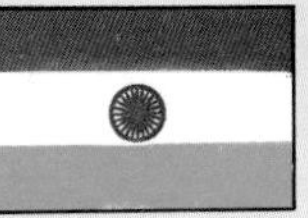

Government: Federal republic
Capital: New Delhi
Area: 1,266,595 sq. miles
(3,280,466 sq. km)
Population: 827,057,000
Languages: Hindi, English
Currency: Rupee

◄ *The Ganges River is sacred to Hindus because, in legend, it flows from the head of the god Shiva.*

India has some of the wettest places in the world. The Shillong Plateau in eastern India has an average of 427 in. (1,087 cm) of rain each year. New York has about 39 in. (99 cm).

India is also a fast-growing industrial country. Cities such as Calcutta and Bombay are among the world's biggest.

Hindi and English are the two main languages, but there are hundreds of others. Most Indians practice HINDUISM, but many follow the religion of ISLAM. There are also many other religions in India.

Indiana

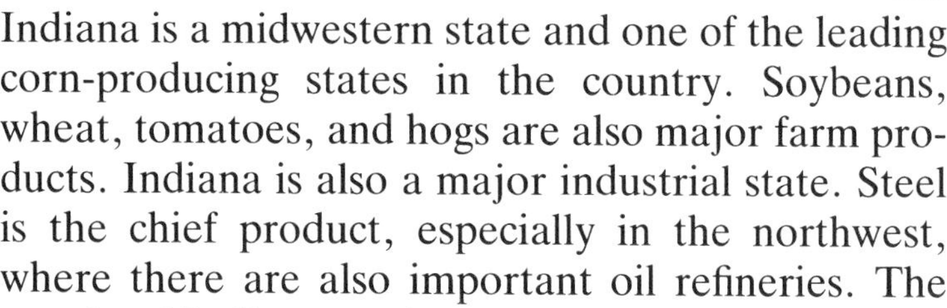

Indiana is a midwestern state and one of the leading corn-producing states in the country. Soybeans, wheat, tomatoes, and hogs are also major farm products. Indiana is also a major industrial state. Steel is the chief product, especially in the northwest, where there are also important oil refineries. The people of Indiana are known as "Hoosiers," though no one really knows why.

Like other Midwestern states, Indiana was settled first by the French, then by the British. It became a U.S. territory in 1783. In 1811, William Harrison fought an important battle against the Indians, the Battle of Tippecanoe. After this, many people settled in the state. Many famous writers have come from Indiana, including Theodore Dreiser and Booth Tarkington.

INDIANA

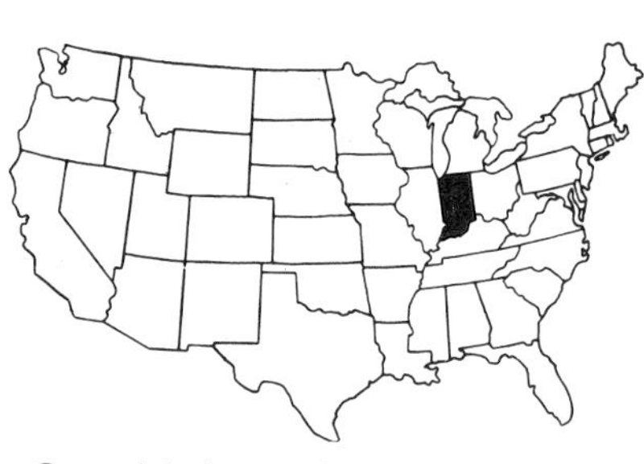

Capital: Indianapolis
Population: 5,544,159
Area: 36,185 sq. mi. (93,720 sq. km)
State flower: Peony
State bird: Cardinal
State tree: Tulip Tree
Statehood: December 11, 1816
19th state

► *Indiana's most famous annual event is the Indianapolis 500 automobile race.*

Indian Ocean

The Indian Ocean is the third largest ocean, with an area of 28,350,000 sq. miles (73,426,500 sq. km). Two very large islands lie in the ocean—Madagascar, off southern Africa, and Sri Lanka, off the southern tip of India. Strong winds from the ocean called *monsoons* bring moisture to Southeast Asia each summer.

Indian Wars

The Indian Wars were the struggles between European settlers and native Americans for control of the United States. The wars began almost as soon as Europeans landed in America in the 1600s. They continued until about 1900, when the Indians across the country were demoralized and defeated. As settlers moved farther west, the fighting moved west, too. Many people today believe that the settlers were cruel to take the tribal lands, and they claim that the native people should have been respected because they had lived in America for thousands of years. But at the time, the settlers thought they were savages who had to be defeated. Because many Indians often seemed cruel and fought for their land, white settlers felt that force was the best way to get rid of them. Because the settlers usually outnumbered the Indians, and had better guns and equipment, they were able to defeat them.

When Europeans first came to America, about one million Indians lived there. By 1900 there were only about 200,000 Indians left in the whole United States.

Indonesia

Indonesia is a country in Southeast ASIA. It is a chain of about 3,000 islands around the EQUATOR. The islands stretch over a distance of 3,000 miles (4,800 km).

Indonesia has about 180 million people. More than half of them live in Java. Java is the biggest island. The capital city, Jakarta, is in Java. Most Indonesians are farmers. They grow many things, including rice, tea, rubber, and tobacco. Indonesia also produces minerals, including petroleum, and timber from its forests. Once ruled by the Dutch, Indonesia fought for and won independence in 1949.

INDONESIA

Government: Independent republic
Capital: Jakarta
Area: 735,268 sq. miles (1,904,335 sq. km)
Population: 179,300,000
Language: Bahasa Indonesian (Malay)
Currency: Rupiah

▼ *The spinning machine was invented during the Industrial Revolution. It altered work methods that had not changed for hundreds of years.*

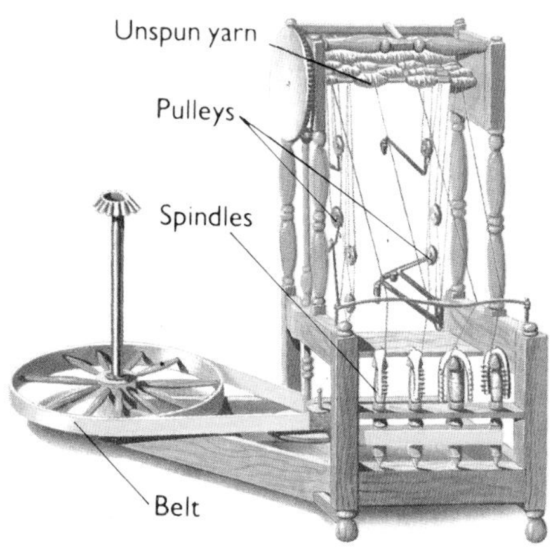

Industrial Revolution

The Industrial Revolution was a great change which took place in the 1700s and 1800s. People began to make things on machines in factories. The new machines were run by STEAM ENGINES. They made things much faster than people could by hand. Mining and metalworking became more important, and the RAILROADS began. Many people moved from the countryside and began to work in factories in the towns.

Inflation

Inflation is a word used to mean rapidly rising prices. Every time prices go up, MONEY is worth less, because people need more money to buy the same things. In turn, people ask for higher wages. If wages rise, then the cost of making things in factories goes up. This often makes prices rise again. Because prices and wages affect each other like this, inflation is hard to stop. There are many reasons why inflation starts. If inflation becomes very bad, money can become worthless.

▼ *Enormous social changes took place in the 1800s in Europe. Improved farming methods replaced traditional ways, and many peasant farmers had to move to towns where the conditions were crowded and unhealthy.*

Infrared Rays

When you feel the heat from a fire or the Sun, you are feeling infrared rays. They are also called *heat*

rays. Although you cannot see infrared rays, they behave in the same way as light rays. They can be reflected and refracted. Photographers use film that is sensitive to infrared rays to take pictures in total darkness.

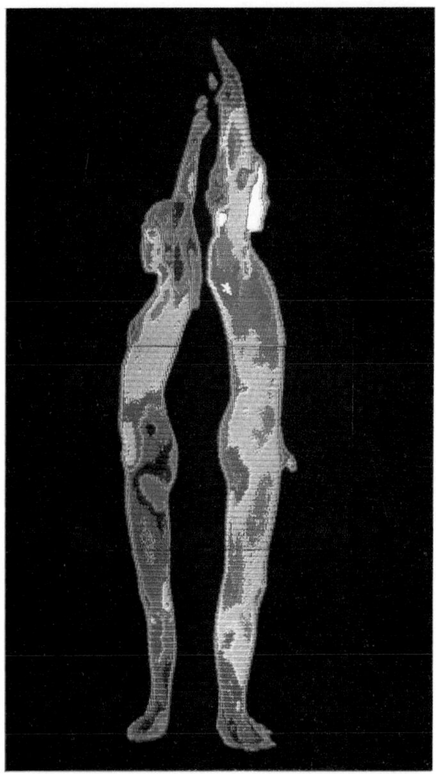

▲ *Infrared sensitive film can be used to take pictures in which areas of heat and cold show up as different colors. White areas are the hottest, and blue are the coolest.*

Inoculation

Inoculation is a way of protecting people from disease. It is also called *vaccination*.

Inoculation works by giving people a very weak dose of a disease. The body learns to fight the GERMS which cause the disease. In this way, the body becomes protected, or *immune*, from the disease.

IMMUNITY from a disease may last from a few months to many years, depending on the kind of disease and vaccine. There are many kinds of inoculation. They are used against diseases such as typhoid, cholera, measles, and polio. Many people used to become ill and die from these diseases. Now more people are saved every year through inoculation. A pioneer of inoculation was Edward JENNER (1815–1898).

▼ *Inoculation programs are vital in Third World countries, where diseases can be prevented and thousands of lives saved.*

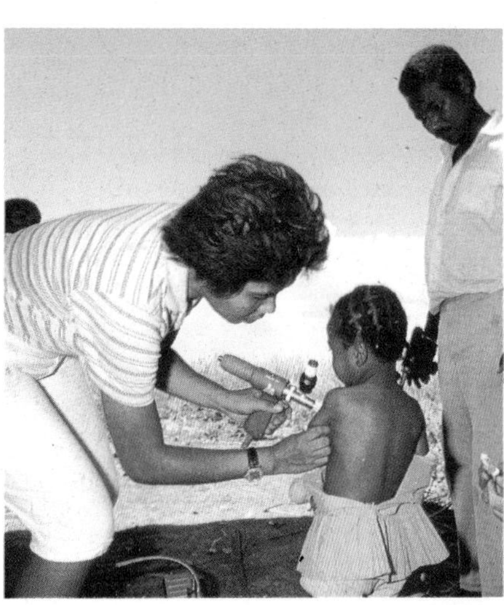

Insect

There are millions of different kinds of insects in the world. Every year, thousands of new kinds are found. (See pages 368–369.)

INSECTS

Insects live all over the world. They are by far the most numerous of all animal species. More than 850,000 different kinds of insects are known. Roughly eight out of ten of all the Earth's animals are insects!

Insects range in size from tiny fleas which can be seen only through a microscope to beetles as big as your hand. Many have interesting life stories, or cycles. Some insects, such as the desert locust of Africa, are destructive pests. But many others are helpful. Without bees and other flying insects, flowering plants would not be pollinated, and fruit trees would not bear fruit.

Among the most fascinating insects are the social insects, which live in highly organized communities or colonies. These include ants, bees, and termites. Many insects make regular journeys. Some butterflies, beetles, and dragonflies migrate at certain times every year.

▼ *These are just a few of the hundreds of thousands of different kinds of insects alive on Earth. Their success as a living species is due to the fact that they are small, they can adapt to many environments, and they reproduce rapidly.*

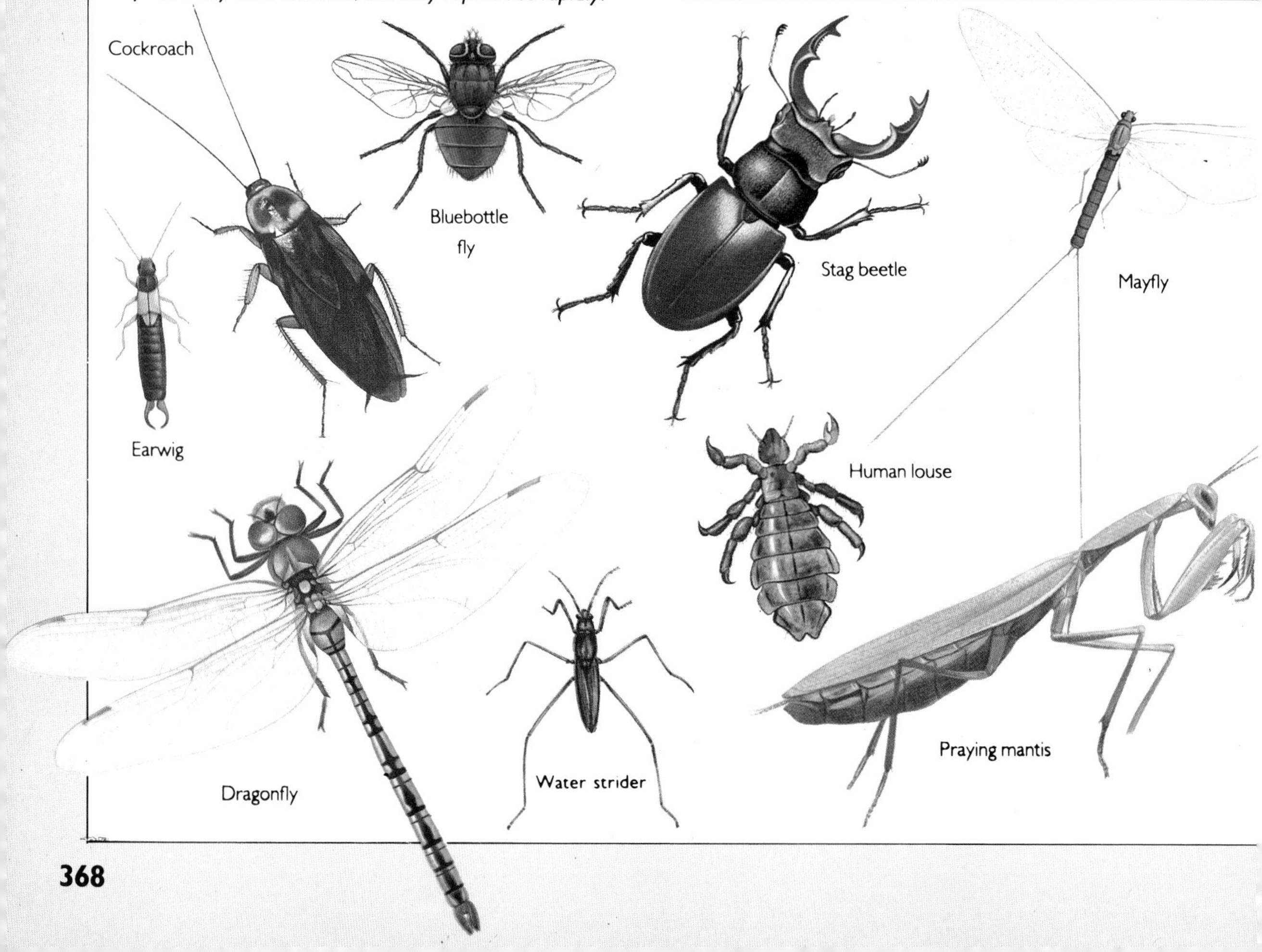

Cockroach
Bluebottle fly
Stag beetle
Mayfly
Earwig
Human louse
Dragonfly
Water strider
Praying mantis

INSECT HELPERS

pful insects include bees, which pollinate flowering
its and also give us honey. The silkworm (the larva of
silk moth) is reared for the silk it spins when turning
a pupa. Ladybugs are the gardener's friends because
y prey on the aphids which attack roses and other
its. Insects such as the ichneumon wasp prey on
er insects, controlling pests. Scavenging insects, such
burying beetles, feed on dead matter and help to
ke the soil fertile.

The seven-spot ladybug feeds on aphids,
ts in our gardens.

INSECT PESTS

mful insects are those that carry disease and
troy food grown by farmers. The mosquito
ich carries malaria) and the tsetse fly (which
eads disease in people and cattle) are pests. Flies,
fleas, and cockroaches live close to people, often
de houses, damaging food and spreading disease.
Colorado beetle destroys potato crops. Locusts
feared by farmers in Africa because they swarm
uch vast numbers that they blacken the skies. The
usts eat every plant in their path.

The locust travels long distances in
tructive swarms.

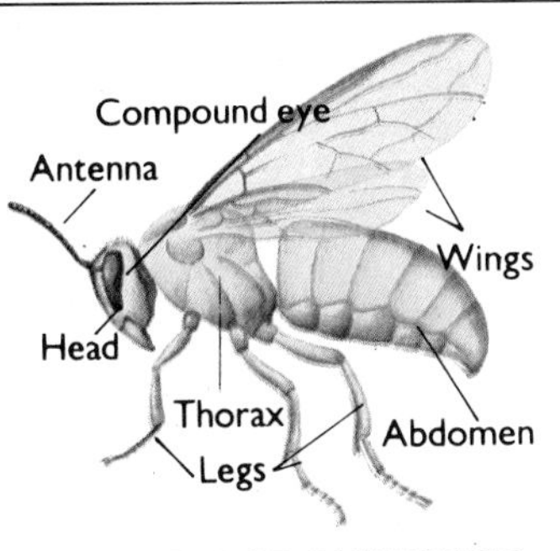

THE BODY OF AN INSECT

All insects have a similar body plan. An insect's body is in three parts: a head, thorax, and abdomen. The head has eyes, jaws, and feelers (antennae). The middle part, or thorax, carries three pairs of jointed legs and sometimes wings. The abdomen contains the stomach, reproductive organs, and breathing tubes called spiracles.

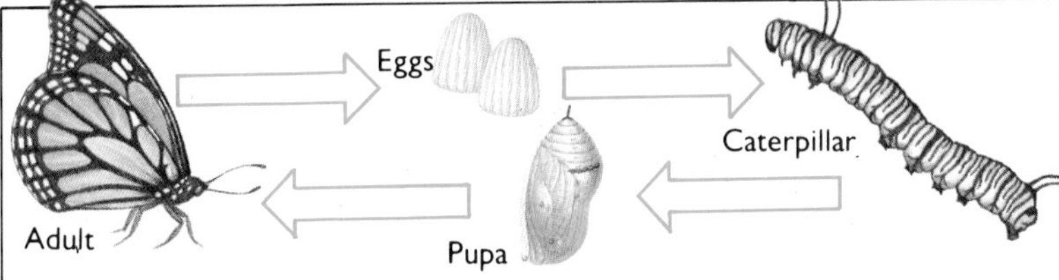

THE LIFE CYCLE OF INSECTS

All insects start life as eggs. In the most advanced insects, there are four stages in the life cycle. The egg hatches into a larva or grub. This larva grows by shedding its skin and finally turns into a pupa or chrysalis. The pupa looks lifeless, but inside many changes are taking place. The pupa finally splits apart, and a fully-formed adult insect emerges.

Some insects, such as grasshoppers, hatch from eggs not as larvae, but as nymphs. Grasshopper nymphs do not yet have wings, but otherwise look much like their parents. Nymphs grow by molting their skins. The most primitive insects, such as silverfish, hatch from the egg looking exactly like adults, only much smaller, and shed their skins many times as they grow.

For more information turn to these articles; ANT; BEE; BEETLE; BUTTERFLY; FLEA; FLY; GRASSHOPPER; LOCUST; PARASITE; TERMITE.

Instinct

People have to learn to read and write, but bees do not learn how to sting. They are born knowing how to sting when there is danger. This kind of behavior is called instinct. Parents pass on instincts to their young through HEREDITY.

Animals do many things by instinct. Birds build nests this way. Simple animals, such as insects, do almost everything by instinct. They have set ways of finding food, attacking enemies, or escaping. Animals that act entirely by instinct do not have enough INTELLIGENCE to learn new ways of doing things and cannot easily change their behavior.

▼ *Instinctive behavior is seen in humans and animals alike. Three examples are shown below. Bees sting as an instinctive reaction to danger, a newborn baby will grasp tightly enough with its hands to support its own weight, and a weaver bird makes an elaborate hanging nest out of grasses.*

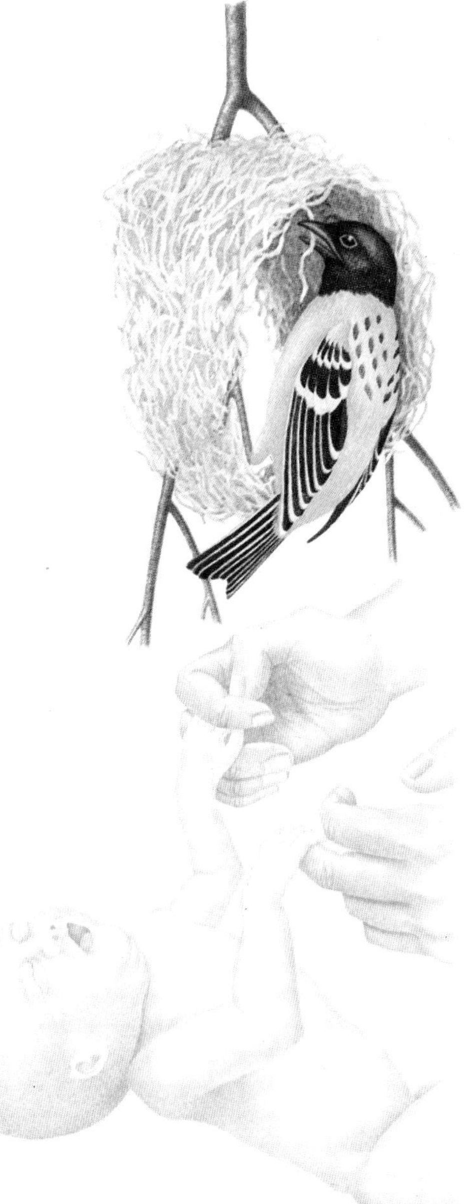

Insulin

Insulin is a HORMONE that controls the body's use of sugar. It is produced in a part of the pancreas GLAND. When not enough insulin is produced, the body cannot use or store sugar properly. This condition is called *diabetes*. Many people with diabetes have to be given insulin daily.

Insurance

Insurance is a way of safeguarding against loss or damage. A person with an insurance *policy* pays a little money to an insurance company every year. If they lose or damage something they have insured, the company gives them money to replace it or to pay for its repair.

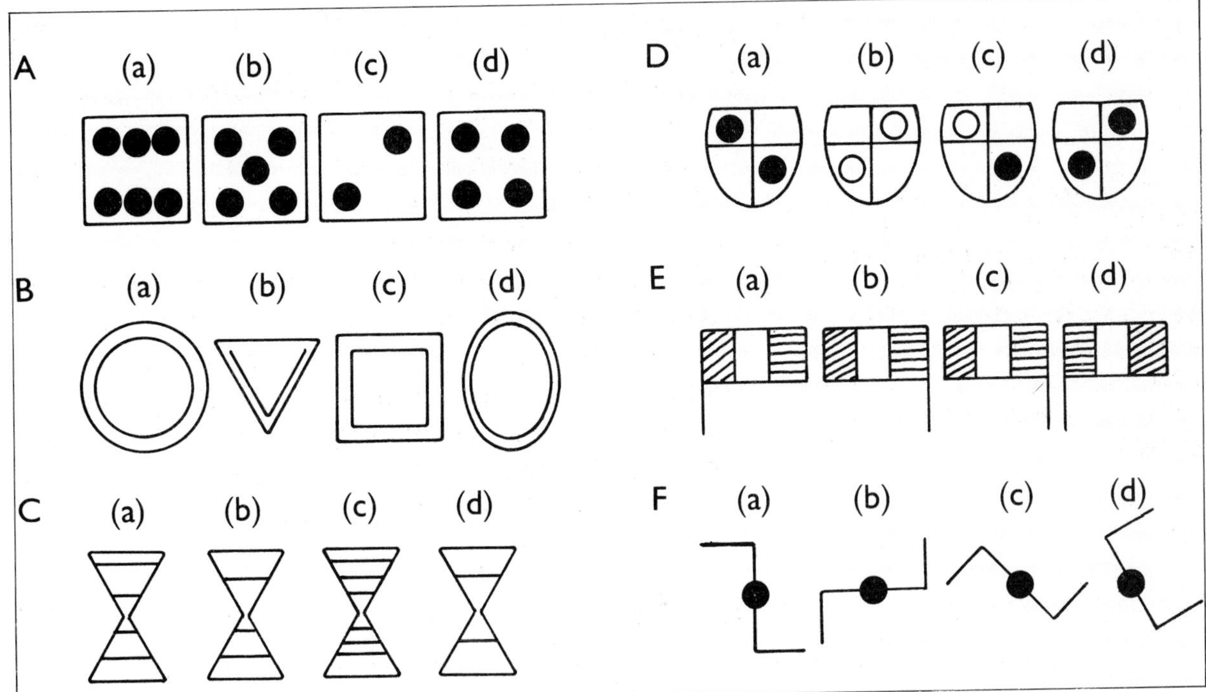

▲ *An example of a test for measuring intelligence. The idea of this reasoning problem is to spot the "odd-one-out" in each group. Answers on page 373.*

Intelligence

Intelligence is our ability to think and to learn. Creatures that act only by INSTINCT lack intelligence.

Human beings are the most intelligent animals. Apes and whales are also quite intelligent. No one knows why some people are more intelligent than others, or why some people are better at some subjects. Some people think that our environment—where we live—determines intelligence. Others think that intelligence is something that individual people have when they are born. Some think, too, that it can be inherited from our parents. A person's intelligence can be measured by an IQ test, but not very accurately.

A person's intelligence quotient, or IQ, is a number based on the person's score compared with others on the same test. The value of 100 is given to the average score and people tested are given IQs above or below 100.

Internal Combustion Engine

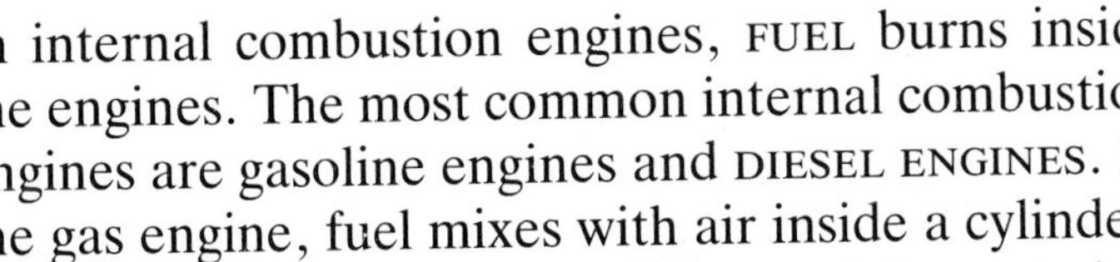

In internal combustion engines, FUEL burns inside the engines. The most common internal combustion engines are gasoline engines and DIESEL ENGINES. In the gas engine, fuel mixes with air inside a cylinder. A spark sets the mixture alight, and it explodes. This happens over and over again. Hot gases from the explosions push a piston to and fro inside the cylinder. Most engines have several cylinders. The

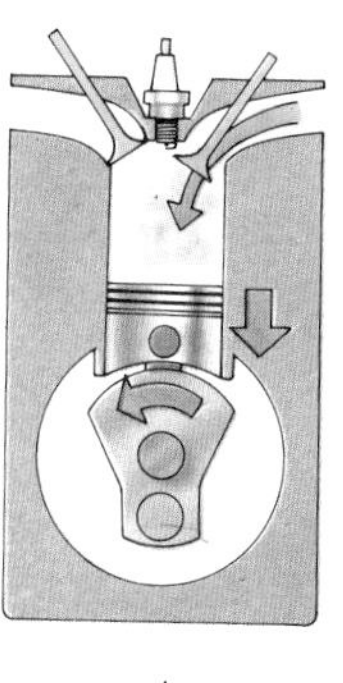

1

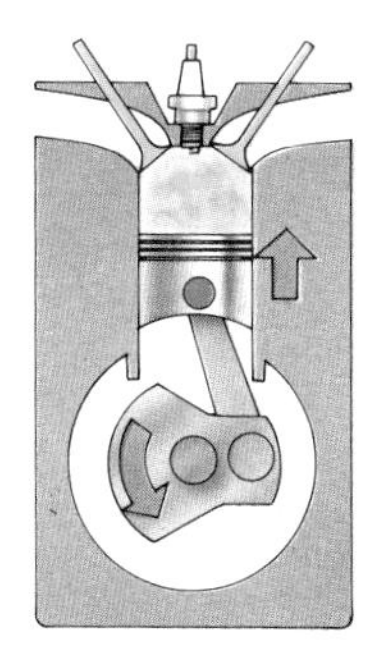

2

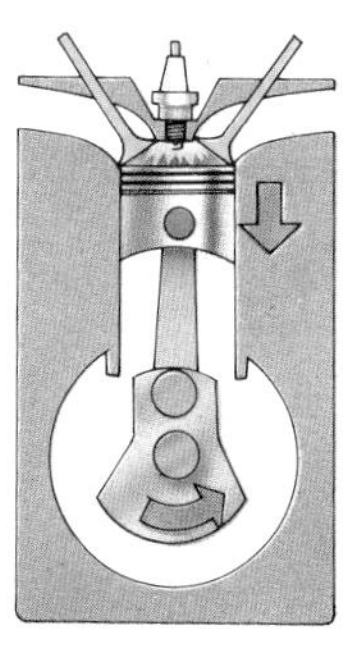

3

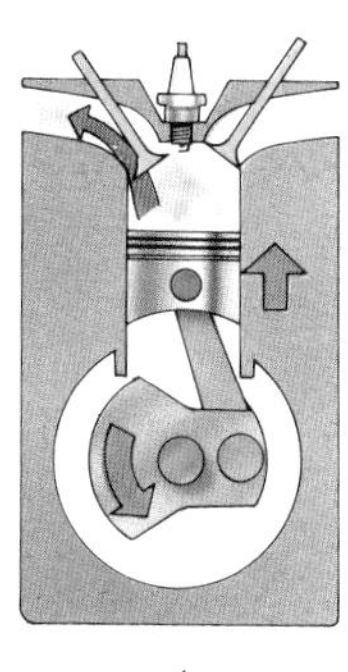

4

THE FOUR-STROKE ENGINE

In a four-stroke engine, the inlet valve opens (1) and the fuel mixture is drawn into the cylinder by the downward movement of the piston. Then both valves close, and the mixture is compressed (squeezed) (2) by the rising piston. The spark plug ignites the mixture (3) forcing the piston down. Finally, the exhaust valve opens and the rising piston pushes out the burned gases (4).

GREAT INVENTIONS

A.D. 105 Paper (from pulp) *(Chinese)*
1100 Magnetic compass *(Chinese)*
1440 Printing press *Johannes Gutenberg (Ger.)*
1608 Telescope *Hans Lippershey (Neth.)*
1765 Condensing steam engine *James Watt (Scot.)*
1822 Camera *Joseph Niepce (Fr.)*
1831 Dynamo *Michael Faraday (Eng.)*
1837 Telegraph *Samuel F. B. Morse (U.S.)*
1876 Telephone *Alexander Graham Bell (U.S.)*
1877 Phonograph *Thomas Edison (U.S.)*
1888 Kodak camera *George Eastman (U.S.)*
1895 Radio *Guglielmo Marconi (It.)*
1903 Airplane *Wilbur & Orville Wright (U.S.)*
1925 Television *John Logie Baird (Scot.)*
1948 Transistor *John Bardeen, Walter Brattain, & William Shockley (U.S.)*
1960 Laser *Theodore Maiman (U.S.)*

pistons work very quickly in turn. They move the crankshaft. This movement turns WHEELS or propellers.

Gasoline and diesel engines are used in AUTOMOBILES and trucks, and in ships and some planes.

Invention

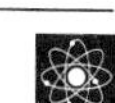

An invention may be the creation of something completely new or an improvement of something that someone else has produced. Many important inventions have come from the work of one person; others have been created by many people working as a team. We will never know who thought of many of the very early inventions, such as the wheel and the plow.

Invertebrate

Invertebrates are animals that have no spine, or backbone. There are more than a million different invertebrates. They include all the WORMS from the flat worms and round worms to the worms with joints, or segments, like earthworms, SHELLFISH, OCTOPUSES, INSECTS, SPIDERS, CRABS, STARFISH, and many others.

Iowa 

Iowa is a Midwestern state and among the most important agricultural states in the country. Its rich prairie lands grow corn, oats, and soybeans. Hogs and cattle are also raised in large numbers. There is little major industrial activity. Most industries supply farming equipment. Because it is such an important agricultural state, Iowa has a relatively low population for its size.

Iowa became a part of the United States in the Louisiana Purchase of 1803. But few settlers lived there until the 1830s, when much of the state was purchased from Indians after the Black Hawk War. Many of its settlers came from Scandinavia and Germany. It quickly developed into the important agricultural region it is today.

IOWA

Capital: Des Moines
Population: 2,776,755
Area: 56,275 sq. mi. (145,753 sq. km)
State flower: Wild Rose
State bird: Eastern Goldfinch
State tree: Oak
Statehood: December 28, 1846
29th state

Iran 

Iran is a country in ASIA. It lies between the Caspian Sea in the north and the Persian Gulf in the south. The country is a little bigger than Alaska. It has a long coastline along the Persian Gulf and the Arabian Sea. Deserts, snowy mountains, and green valleys cover most of the land. Much of the country has hot, dry summers and cold winters.

Iranians speak Persian. (Persia is the old name for Iran.) Their religion is ISLAM. Tehran is the capital.

ALEXANDER THE GREAT conquered Persia about 330 B.C. Later, the country was ruled by ARABS and MONGOLS. During this century, Iran was ruled by emperors, or *shahs*. In 1979, the government of Iran changed, and the shah left the country. Religious leaders now rule this Islamic Republic.

In 1980, Iran went to war against IRAQ, and this bitter war lasted for eight years.

IRAN

Government: Islamic republic
Capital: Tehran
Area: 636,293 sq. miles (1,648,000 sq. km)
Population: 54,608,000
Language: Farsi (Persian)
Currency: Rial

Iraq 

Iraq is an ARAB country in southwestern ASIA. Much of Iraq is a dry, sandy, stony plain. It is cool in winter and very hot in summer. The Tigris and Euphrates rivers flow through the plain to the Persian Gulf. Their water helps the farmers to grow

Answers to Intelligence Test on p.371: A(b); B(b); C(b); D(c); E(a); F(d).

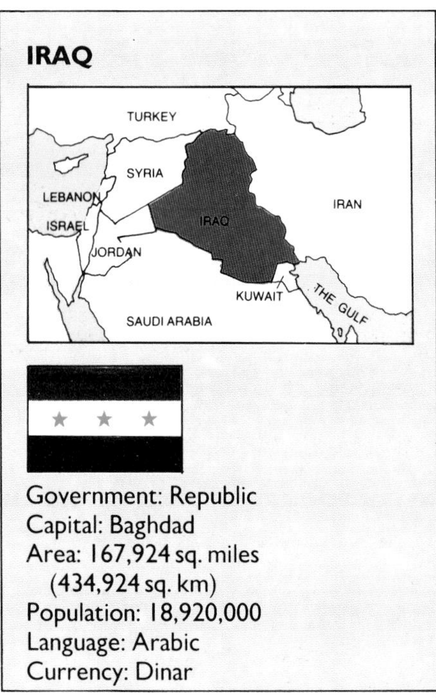

Government: Republic
Capital: Baghdad
Area: 167,924 sq. miles (434,924 sq. km)
Population: 18,920,000
Language: Arabic
Currency: Dinar

rice, cotton, wheat, and dates. Iraq is also one of the biggest oil producers in the world. Pipelines carry the oil from the north of the country across the desert to ports in Syria and Lebanon. Many Iraqis are NOMADS. They live in the deserts with their sheep and goats. But nearly 4 million people work in Baghdad.

Some of the first cities in the world were built near Iraq's big rivers. Ur was one of the earliest cities. It was built by a BRONZE AGE people called the Sumerians. Later, the Babylonians built their famous city, BABYLON, in Iraq. Modern Iraq is a republic and it was at war with IRAN from 1980 until 1988. In 1990 Iraq invaded KUWAIT but was forced to leave after being defeated by the U.S. and her allies in the Gulf War.

Ireland

Ireland is the second largest island of the BRITISH ISLES. Mountains rim the edges. The middle is a low plain. Through this flows the Shannon, the longest river in the British Isles. Irish weather is often mild and rainy. Meadows and moors cover much of the land. Southern Ireland is the Republic of Ireland, or Eire. It occupies five-sixths of the island. Its capital city is Dublin. Northern Ireland is part of the United Kingdom of GREAT BRITAIN and Northern Ireland. Its capital city is Belfast.

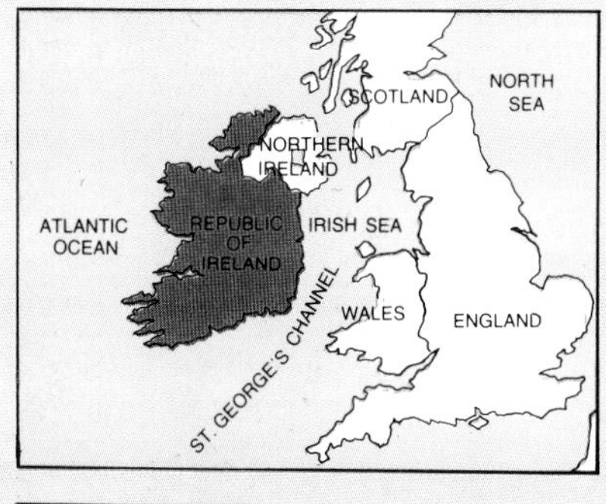

Government: Parliamentary republic
Capital: Dublin
Area: 27,136 sq. miles (70,283 sq. km)
Population: 3,557,000
Languages: English, Irish (Gaelic)
Currency: Irish pound (punt)

Iron and Steel

Iron is the cheapest and most useful of all metals. Much of our food, clothes, homes, and cars are made with machines and tools made from iron.

Iron is mined, or *quarried*, as iron ore. The ore is melted down in a blast furnace. The iron is then made into cast iron, wrought iron, or mixed with a small amount of CARBON to form steel.

Cast iron is hard, but not as strong as steel. Molten cast iron is poured into molds to make such things as engine blocks. Wrought iron is softer, but tough. Steel is hard and strong. Steel ALLOYS containing metals such as tungsten and chromium are used to make many things, from bridges to nails.

The shaduf was used for irrigation, as long ago as 5000 B.C.

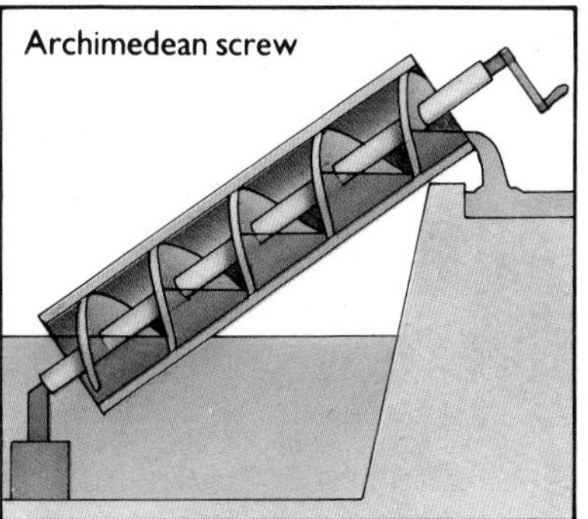

The Archimedean screw uses a rotating spiral to raise water.

King Sennacherib of ancient Assyria built canals for irrigation.

Irrigation

Farmers and gardeners who water plants are irrigating them. Irrigation makes it possible to grow crops and flowers in dry soils, even in a DESERT. Farmers

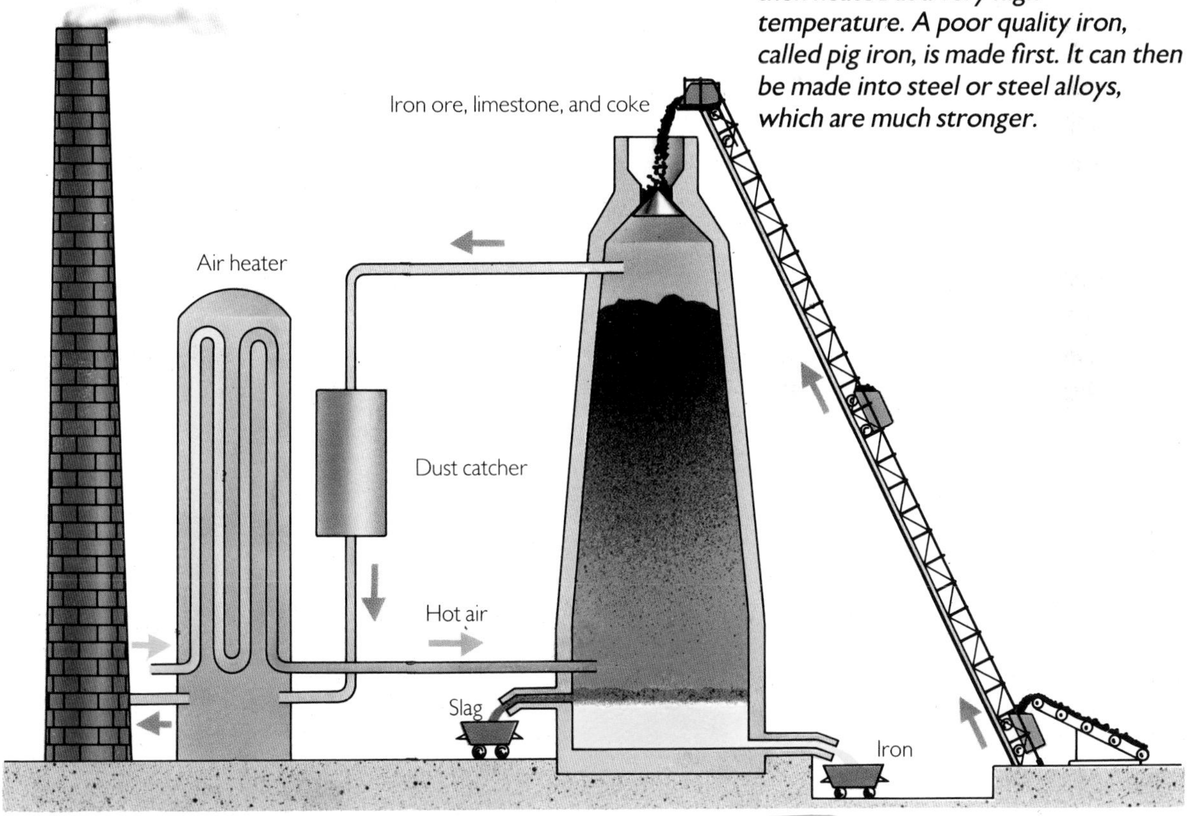

▼ *To produce iron from iron ore, the ore is mixed with coke and limestone, then heated at a very high temperature. A poor quality iron, called pig iron, is made first. It can then be made into steel or steel alloys, which are much stronger.*

Iron ore, limestone, and coke

Air heater

Dust catcher

Hot air

Slag

Iron

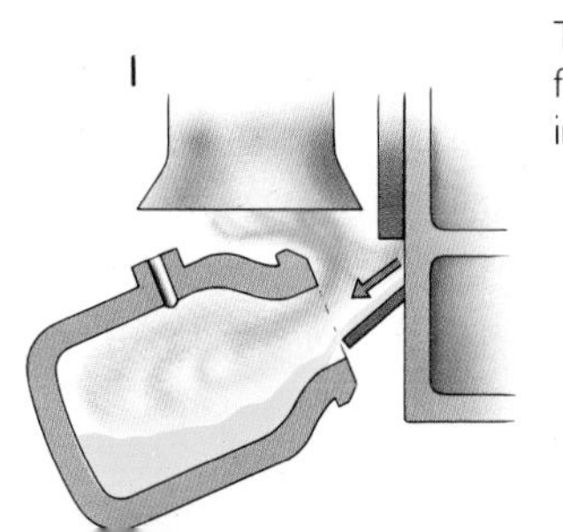

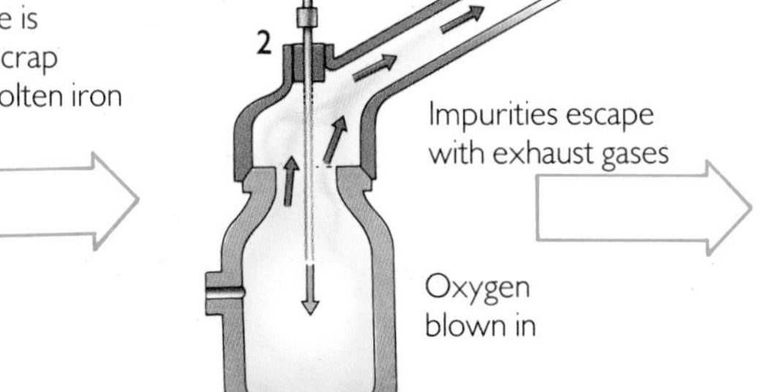

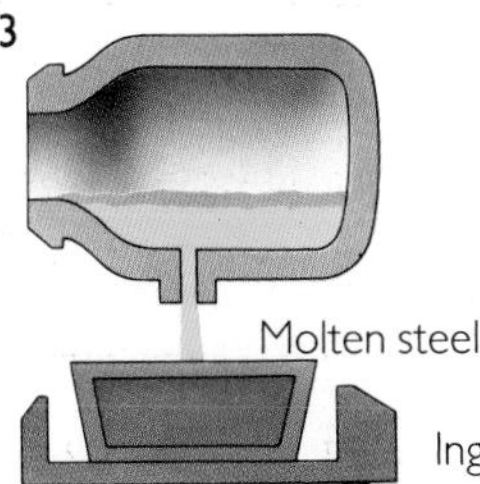

▲ *Islamic styles of building are very graceful and well suited to hot climates. Mosques, the Islamic places of worship, often have a high tower from which a priest calls the people to prayer.*

in China, Egypt, and Iraq have been irrigating large areas of land for thousands of years.

Many countries store water in lakes made by building DAMS across rivers. CANALS take water from the lakes to farms. One irrigation canal in Russia is 530 miles (850 km) long. Ditches or pipes carry water from each canal to the fields. In each field, the water flows between the rows of plants. Sometimes it spurts up from holes in the pipes. It sprinkles the plants like a shower of rain.

Islam

Islam is a religion started in A.D.622 by MUHAMMAD. It has more followers than any other religion except Christianity. Islam means "submission." Its followers are called Muslims. Muslim means "submissive one." Muslims believe they must submit, or give in, to God's will. They believe in one God and in Muhammad as his prophet. Muslims pray five times a day and give gifts to the poor. They go without food until dark for one month a year and try to visit Mecca, Muhammad's birthplace, before they die. They also try to obey the rules for good living set out in the KORAN, the holy book of Islam.

Islam began in Arabia. Today it is the main religion in North Africa and most of southwest Asia.

Israel

Israel is a country in southwest Asia, on the shores of the Mediterranean Sea. Though people have lived here for thousands of years, Israel itself is a modern nation. It was founded in 1948 as a homeland for Jewish people from around the world. Its short history has been difficult. Many Arabs lived in what is now Israel, and they fiercely opposed the Jews who wanted to settle there. The Israelis have had to fight wars to survive, and violence continues over the Israeli occupation of the West Bank and the Gaza Strip. Israel is a holy land to Jews, Christians, and Muslims. More than half the land is desert. On the rich lands by the sea, farmers grow oranges, cotton, and grain. There are important industries here, but Israel imports more than it exports.

ISRAEL

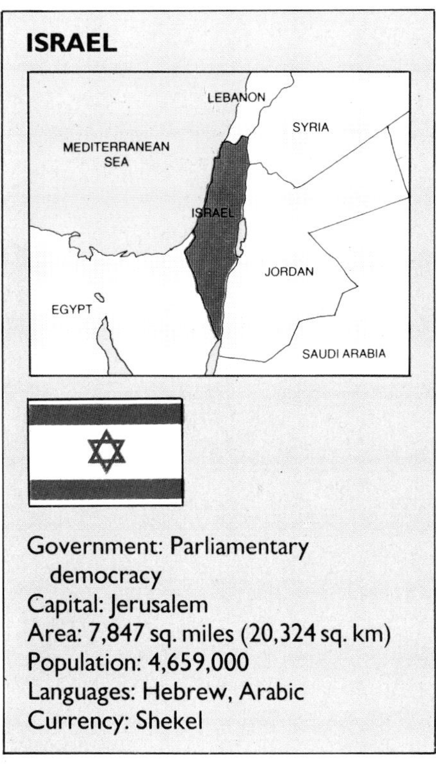

Government: Parliamentary democracy
Capital: Jerusalem
Area: 7,847 sq. miles (20,324 sq. km)
Population: 4,659,000
Languages: Hebrew, Arabic
Currency: Shekel

Italy

Italy is a country in southern EUROPE. It is shaped like a boot stuck out in the Mediterranean Sea to kick the island of Sicily. Sicily and Sardinia are Italian islands.

Much of Italy is mountainous. The sharp, snowy peaks of the ALPS cross northern Italy. The Apennines run like a backbone down the middle. Between the Alps and Apennines lies the plain of Lombardy. Italy is famous for its hot, sunny summers. Rain falls mostly in winter.

Crops grow on almost half the land. Italy produces more pears and olives than any other country. The farmers also grow a lot of grapes, lemons, wheat, rice, and oranges. Big factories in northern Italy make cars, chemicals, and machines.

The capital is ROME. Many tourists visit Rome to see the VATICAN and ruins of the ROMAN EMPIRE.

◀ *Venice was a wealthy trading city in the 16th and 17th centuries. This beautiful city of canals is full of art treasures.*

ITALY

Government: Republic
Capital: Rome
Area: 116,303 sq. miles (301,225 sq. km)
Population: 57,663,000
Language: Italian
Currency: Lira

Italy is the world's largest producer of wine, with nearly 2 billion gallons a year out of a world production of 35 billion bottles. Italians drink more wine than any other nation—over 24 gallons (90 liters) per head of the population in a year.

Ivan the Terrible

Ivan IV, the Terrible (1530–1584), was the first emperor, or *tsar*, of RUSSIA. He was a cruel man who killed his son with his own hands. But he helped to make Russia great. During his reign, Moscow became the Russian capital, and Russia began trading with Western countries.

Ivory Coast *See* Côte d'Ivoire

Jackson, Andrew

Andrew "Stonewall" Jackson (1767–1845) was the 7th president of the United States. He was one of the most influential presidents of the 1800s, and changed the style of American politics in several important ways. He was the first president to come from one of the frontier states, (as they then were) Tennessee. And he was the first president who was elected through a modern democractic system. People talk of "Jacksonian democracy" to describe the new political ideas introduced under him. Jackson had been a successful soldier before he became president. The popularity he gained then helped him when he ran for president. In office, he was tough and resolute. His biggest problem was the rights of individual states as opposed to the federal government. Though his political opponents said he behaved more like a king than a president, he remained popular.

ANDREW JACKSON

Seventh President 1829–1837
Born: Waxhaw, South Carolina
Education: Mostly self-educated
Occupation: Lawyer
Political Party: Democratic
Buried: Nashville, Tennessee

Jaguar

No other American wild CAT is as heavy or perhaps as dangerous as the jaguar. From nose to tail, a jaguar is longer than a man and may be nearly twice his weight. The jaguar is yellow with black spots. The LEOPARD also has spots, but many of the jaguar's spots are in rings. Jaguars live in the hot, wet forests of Central and South America. They leap from trees onto wild pigs and deer. They also catch turtles, fish, and alligators.

► *Jaguars look like the leopards of Asia and Africa but they are heavier.*

Jamaica

Jamaica is a tropical island in the Caribbean Sea. The name Jamaica means "island of springs." It is a beautiful island, with hundreds of streams flowing from springs on the sides of its green mountains.

There are more than two million people in Jamaica. Most of them are of African ancestry. Many work on farms that grow bananas, coconuts, coffee, oranges, and sugarcane. Jamaica also mines bauxite. The country's beautiful beaches and pleasant climate attract many tourists.

JAMAICA

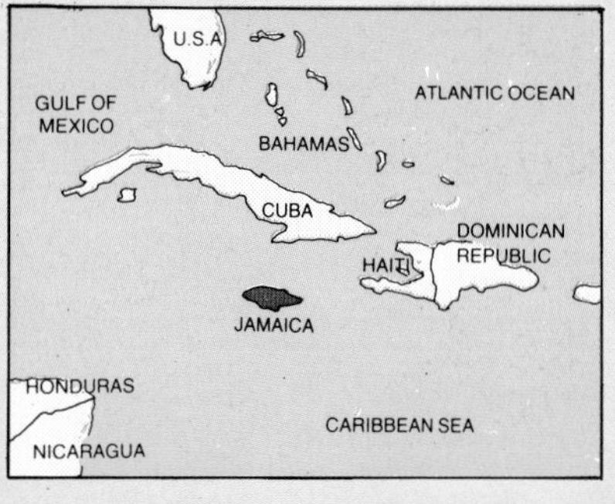

Government: Constitutional monarchy
Capital: Kingston
Area: 4,323 sq. miles (11,200 sq. km)
Population: 2,420,000
Language: English
Currency: Jamaican dollar

James (kings)

James was the name of two kings of Great Britain. James I (1566–1625) was the son of Mary, Queen of Scots. He was the first king of Scotland and England. James II (1633–1701), the grandson of James I, tried to restore the Roman Catholic Church to Britain, but was forced to resign his throne in 1688.

Japan

Japan is a long, narrow string of islands off the mainland coast of Asia. Altogether they make a country slightly smaller than California.

▼ *There is very little spare land in Tokyo, so overhead trains are an ideal way of coping with commuter travel.*

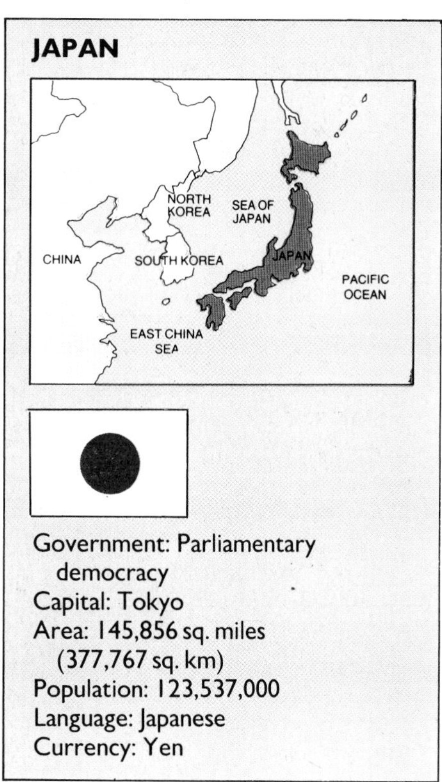

Government: Parliamentary democracy
Capital: Tokyo
Area: 145,856 sq. miles (377,767 sq. km)
Population: 123,537,000
Language: Japanese
Currency: Yen

Mountains cover most of Japan. The highest is a beautiful volcano called Fujiyama, or Mount Fuji. Parts of Japan have forests, waterfalls, and lakes. Northern Japan has cool summers and cold winters. The south is hot in summer and mild in winter.

Japan is a crowded country. It has more than 120 million people. To feed them, farmers grow huge amounts of rice and fruit. The Japanese eat a lot of fish and seaweed. They catch more fish than any other country.

Japan does not have many minerals, so the Japanese buy most of their minerals, such as iron ore, from other countries. But no other country makes as many ships, television sets, radios, videos, and cameras as Japan does. The Japanese also make a lot of cars.

Jazz

Jazz is a kind of music. The players use unexpected rhythms. They can play any notes they like, but they must fit the music made by the rest of the band. In this way, jazz musicians often *improvise*, or make up music as they go along. Jazz began in the United States in the 1800s.

THOMAS JEFFERSON

Third President 1801–1809
Born: Albemarle County, Virginia
Education: College of William and Mary, Williamsburg, Virginia
Occupation: Planter and lawyer
Political Party: Republican
Buried: Charlottesville, Virginia

Jefferson, Thomas

Thomas Jefferson (1743–1826) was the 3rd president of the United States, and one of the most important founders of the country. He was a champion of democracy and liberty and is best remembered because he wrote the Declaration of Independence. But he was more than just a politician. He was interested in many things—architecture, farming, music, painting, philosophy, and science. Though he said he disliked politics, he spent most of his life as a politician. He was governor of Virginia, a Congressman, ambassador to France, secretary of state, and vice president. His most important acts as president were the LOUISIANA PURCHASE of 1803, which doubled the size of the country, and keeping the country out of the Napoleonic Wars in Europe. He retired to his home in Virginia. In 1819, he founded the University of Virginia.

Jenner, Edward

Edward Jenner (1749–1823) was a British doctor and the first man to discover how INOCULATION works. He inoculated a young boy with cowpox germs. Cowpox is a disease like smallpox, but less dangerous. Then Jenner injected the boy with smallpox germs. Because the cowpox germs protected the boy, he did not develop smallpox. Today, millions of people all over the world are inoculated against many diseases.

Jerusalem

Jerusalem is the capital of ISRAEL. It is a holy city of the Jews, Christians, and Muslims. David, Jesus, and other famous people in the Bible lived or died here. Jerusalem stands high up in hilly country. It has many old religious buildings. Huge walls surround the city's oldest part. In 1948, Jerusalem was divided between Israel and Jordan, but Israel took the whole city during a war in 1967.

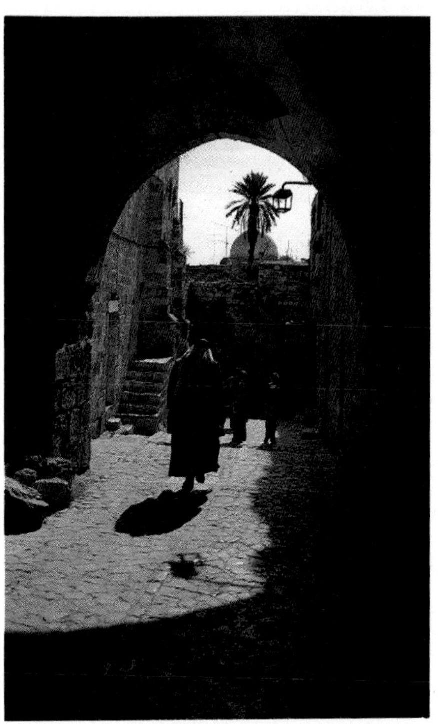

▲ *An old street in Jerusalem. In the distance is the Dome of the Rock, a Muslim shrine built on the spot where Muhammad is said to have ascended to heaven.*

▼ *The* Baptism of Christ *was painted by the Italian Renaissance artist Piero della Francesca in the 1400s. Many masterpieces of Western art have had the life of Jesus as their inspiration.*

Jesus

Jesus was a Jew who started CHRISTIANITY. The New Testament of the BIBLE says that Jesus was God's Son. He was born in Bethlehem. His mother was called Mary. When he grew up, he traveled around, teaching and healing sick people. Some Jewish priests were jealous of Jesus. They told their Roman rulers that he was making trouble. The Romans killed Jesus on a cross, but the New Testament says that he came to life and rose to heaven. Followers of Jesus spread his teachings worldwide.

Jet Engine

A swimmer swims forward by pushing water backward. A jet engine works in a similar way. It drives an AIRCRAFT forward by pushing gases backward. Engines that work like this are called *reaction* engines. ROCKETS are also reaction engines. The main difference between jets and rockets is that jets take in oxygen from the air to burn their fuel, but

▶ *Jet engines provide a powerful thrust to drive both passenger and military planes.*

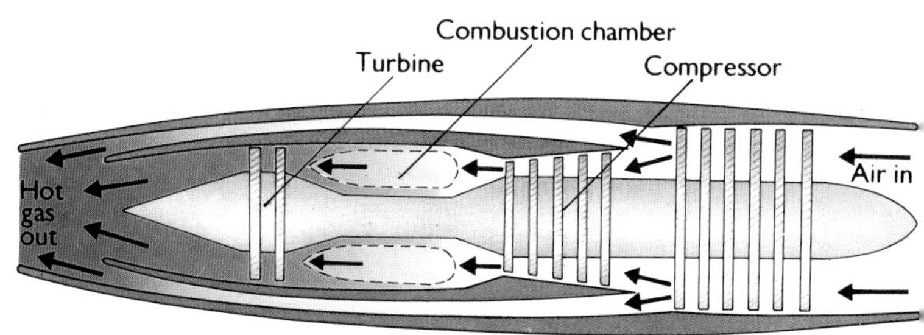

▲ *Joan of Arc successfully took on the role of soldier to lead the French into battle against the English.*

rockets have a supply of oxygen in their fuel.

There are four main kinds of jet engine. These are turbojets, turboprops, turbofans, and ramjets.

Jet engines have replaced propeller-driven piston engines in many kinds of plane. There are many reasons for this. Jet engines weigh less than piston engines. They also break down less often. Their moving parts spin instead of moving to and fro. This stops the plane from shaking. Jet engines burn cheap kerosene instead of costly gasoline. Jet engines can also carry planes faster and higher than piston engines can.

Joan of Arc

Joan of Arc (1412–1431) was a French girl who believed that God told her to free France from its English invaders. At 17, she left the farm where she worked, and persuaded France's King Charles VII to let her lead his army. She won five battles. Then she was captured and burned as a witch. But she had saved France. In 1920, the Pope made her a SAINT.

Johnson, Andrew

Andrew Johnson (1808–1875) became president of the United States when Abraham Lincoln was assassinated. He was immediately faced with serious problems arising from the division of the nation after the Civil War. Congress opposed many of Johnson's policies and accused him of being too friendly with the South. The division became so wide that the Representatives voted to impeach the president (charge him with conduct unworthy of his position). Eventually, the Senate found Johnson "not guilty."

Andrew Johnson came from a very poor family

ANDREW JOHNSON

Seventeenth President 1865–1869
Born: Raleigh, North Carolina
Education: Mostly self-educated
Occupation: Tailor
Political Party: National Union-Republican
Buried: Greeneville, Tennessee

and he received little schooling. People are still undecided whether he was a good or bad president.

Johnson, Lyndon Baines

Lyndon Johnson (1908–1973) became president of the United States after the assassination of John F. Kennedy. He ran again for the presidency in 1964 and was elected by a large majority. Johnson set about the task of fighting poverty, improving education, and enforcing civil rights laws.

Johnson faced problems in foreign affairs, especially the war in Vietnam, which he supported. The war aroused opposition throughout the country, and in 1968 Johnson announced that he would not seek re-election and urged peace talks. "LBJ" retired to his ranch in Texas.

LYNDON B. JOHNSON

Thirty-sixth President 1963–1969
Born: Stonewall, Texas
Education: Southwest Texas State Teachers College
Occupation: Teacher and legislator
Political Party: Democratic
Buried: LBJ Ranch, Stonewall, Texas

Jordan

Jordan is a small Arab country in the northwest corner of the Arabian Peninsula. Most of the country lies on a plateau 3,300 feet (1,000 m) above sea level. The Jordan River and the salty Dead Sea lie west of the plateau. The Jordanians and the Israelis have for many years been unfriendly neighbors. In 1967, Israel captured Jordanian land west of the Jordan River. This land is known as the West Bank.

JORDAN

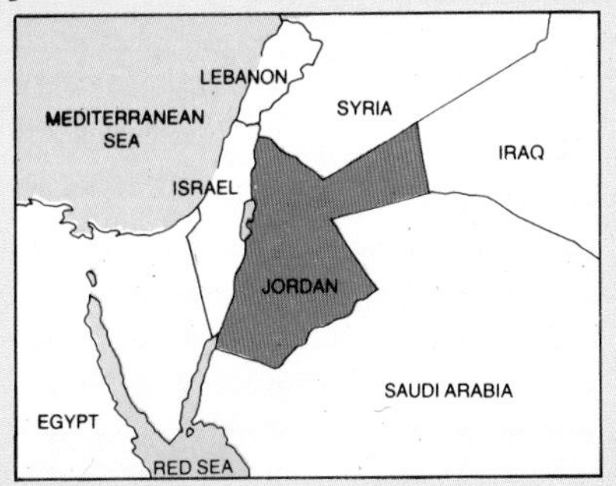

Government: Constitutional monarchy
Capital: Amman
Area: 37,737 sq. miles (97,738 sq. km)
Population: 4,009,000
Language: Arabic
Currency: Jordanian dinar

Judaism

Judaism is a religion that believes in one God and has as its holy book the Bible. The Hebrew Bible

◀ *Many Jewish religious traditions, such as those involved in this wedding, are very ancient.*

The total number of Jews in the world is estimated to be 16,000,000. Nearly half of that number, 7.3 million, live in North America. There are 2 million Jews in the New York area alone. In Israel, there are nearly 3.5 million, while the British Jewish population is nearly 400,000.

consists of the first five books of Moses (the Torah), historical accounts of the tribes of Israel, and books written by prophets and kings. (Christians include all this material in their Bible, calling it the Old Testament.) Judaism's followers are called Jews. They observe the Ten Commandments. They believe God gave the Law to Moses on top of Mount Sinai after Moses led their ancestors out of Egypt, where they had been slaves. The commemoration of this Exodus from Egypt is one of Judaism's most important festivals and is called PASSOVER. Today, Jews live all over the world, but regard Israel as their spiritual and historical home.

JUPITER FACTS
Average distance from Sun: 483 million miles (778 million km)
Nearest distance from Earth: 391 million miles (630 million km)
Average temperature: −238°F (−150°C)
Diameter across equator: 88,700 miles (142,800 km)
Atmosphere: Hydrogen, helium
Number of moons: 16 known
Length of day: 9 hours 50 minutes
Length of year: 11.9 Earth years

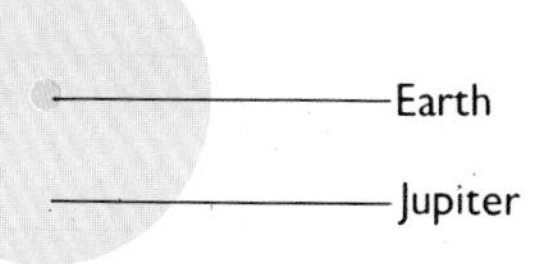

Jupiter

Jupiter is the largest of the PLANETS in our SOLAR SYSTEM. It is twice the size of all the other planets put together. You could fit 1,300 planets the size of the Earth into the space filled by Jupiter. Jupiter's force of GRAVITY is great. Anyone on Jupiter would weigh twice as much as on the Earth. Astronomers believe that most of Jupiter is hot, liquid HYDROGEN. Jupiter is so hot that it would be a glowing star if it were ten time larger. It has 16 moons.

Jupiter spins so fast that a day and night last less than ten Earth-hours. But a YEAR on Jupiter is 12 times longer than one of ours. This is because Jupiter is farther from the SUN than we are.

If an astronaut managed to "land" on Jupiter, he or she would find that there are no seasons. The faint Sun, so distant as to be just a flickering star, would rise and set every nine and three-quarters hours. Jupiter's biggest moon, Callisto, is bigger than the planet Mercury.

▶ *The planet Jupiter appears to have light and dark belts around it in its atmosphere.*

Kaleidoscope

A kaleidoscope is a toy containing mirrors that make regular patterns. it consists of a tube with two or three long mirrors running the length of the tube. The mirrors are fixed at an angle to each other. One end of the tube is covered by a piece of ground glass, the other end has a peephole. Small pieces of colored glass or plastic in the tube tumble around and are reflected to make patterns.

Kangaroo

Kangaroos are MARSUPIALS that live in New Guinea and Australia. Most of them live on grassy plains and feed on plants. They move around in troops, springing along on their big, powerful hind legs and large feet. Their long tails help them to balance.

There are more than 50 kinds of kangaroo. Red and gray kangaroos are the largest. A red kangaroo may be taller and heavier than a man. Gray kangaroos can bounce along at 25 mph (40 km/h) if chased. Wallabies are smaller kinds of kangaroo. The smallest of all are rat kangaroos. They are about the size of a rabbit. Tree kangaroos live in New Guinea.

▲ *Each time the kaleidoscope is shaken, a new pattern appears.*

◀ *Kangaroos are considered pests in Australia, and to keep their numbers down, they are sometimes hunted.*

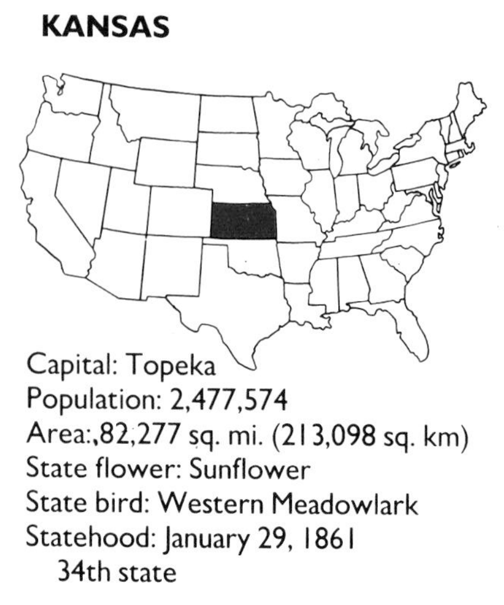

KANSAS

Capital: Topeka
Population: 2,477,574
Area:,82,277 sq. mi. (213,098 sq. km)
State flower: Sunflower
State bird: Western Meadowlark
Statehood: January 29, 1861
34th state

▲ *A restoration of Front Street, Dodge City, Kansas.*

JOHN F. KENNEDY

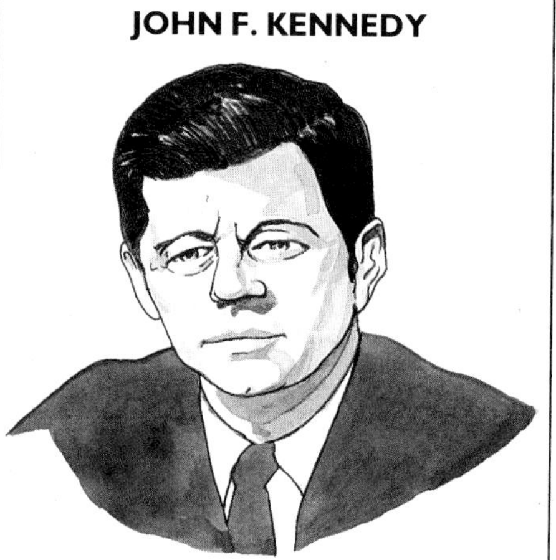

Thirty-fifth President 1961–1963
Born: Brookline, Massachusetts
Education: Harvard University
Occupation: Author and legislator
Political Party: Democratic
Buried: Arlington National Cemetery, Arlington, Va.

Kansas

The state of Kansas, located in the heart of the continental United States, is the breadbasket of America. Agriculture has always been its mainstay, either crop growing, or, especially in its early days, cattle rearing. In the 1860s and '70s, the cowboys of Kansas were famous. This was the Wild West, when thousands of cattle passed through Kansas towns such as Dodge City and Abilene on their way from Texas to the East. Lawmen such as Wild Bill Hickok and Wyatt Earp became well known. Before it became a state, people argued fiercely about whether Kansas should allow slavery. There were so many violent battles that Kansas became known as "bleeding Kansas." In the end, it was decided that slavery should not be allowed.

Kennedy, John Fitzgerald

John F. Kennedy (1917–1963) was the 35th president of the United States. He was only 43 when he was elected, the youngest man ever to win the office. When he was killed, he was the youngest president to die in office. The "Kennedy era" was a time of great optimism and prosperity in the United States. To many people, Kennedy was a symbol of this strength. His death was seen as the end of a vigorous period, as well as a great tragedy. The greatest challenge he faced as president was with the Soviet Union. It wanted to put nuclear missiles in Cuba. Kennedy bravely forced it not to. Afterward, relations with the Soviet Union improved. Kennedy also agreed with the Soviet Union to stop testing atomic bombs. He was assassinated in Dallas, Texas.

Kentucky

The state of Kentucky is known for tobacco, bourbon, whiskey, coal mining, and horseracing. It lies just to the west of the Appalachian Mountains and was one of the first frontier areas to be settled in the late 1700s. After it became a state in 1792, people began to breed horses in the lush pastures of the

◀ *Abraham Lincoln's birthplace near Hodgenville, Kentucky.*

bluegrass region. By the 1830s, tobacco and cotton became major crops. These tied it closely to the industries of the South. Kentucky suffered badly in the Civil War. Though it fought on the Union side, many people supported the South. After the war, the economy slumped. Coal became an important industry around 1900.

KENTUCKY

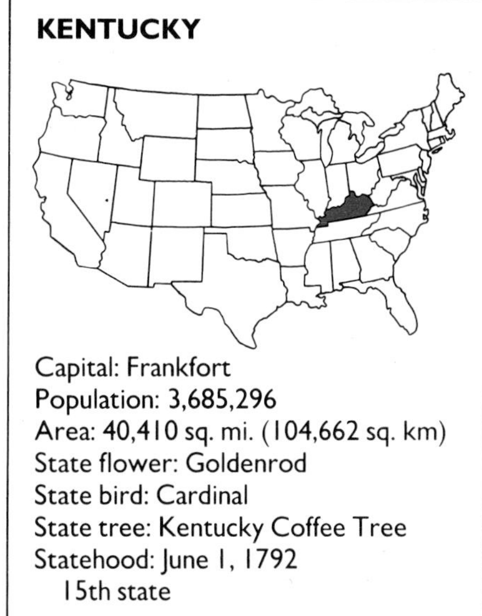

Capital: Frankfort
Population: 3,685,296
Area: 40,410 sq. mi. (104,662 sq. km)
State flower: Goldenrod
State bird: Cardinal
State tree: Kentucky Coffee Tree
Statehood: June 1, 1792
15th state

Kenya

Kenya is a country in east AFRICA. It is just a little smaller than Texas. The southwest border touches Lake Victoria. The Indian Ocean is on the southeast. The EQUATOR goes across the middle of the country. Much of the land is covered by mountains and flat-topped hills. The rest looks like a huge open park. It is a hot, dry country.

KENYA

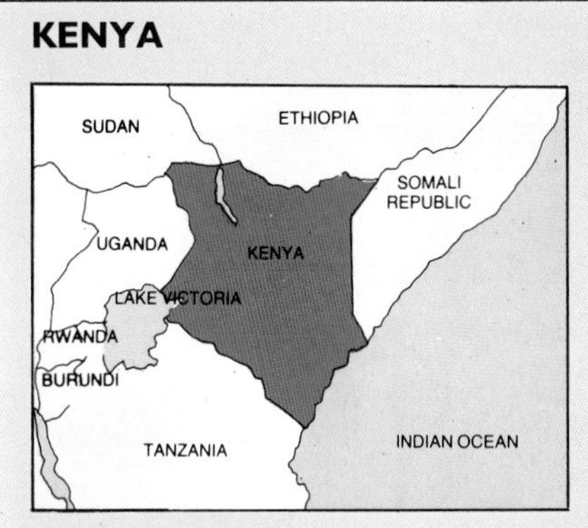

Government: Republic
Capital: Nairobi
Area: 224,960 sq. miles (582,646 sq. km)
Population: 24,032,000
Languages: Swahili, English
Currency: Shilling

◀ *Sisal, used to make rope, is made from the agave plant, which is widely grown in Kenya.*

▼ *The kidneys are part of a vital system for cleaning the blood of impurities and excess liquid. They are drained off through the ureters into the bladder and leave the body as urine. Blood flows in through the renal artery and back to the heart through the renal vein.*

Kenya is a member of the British COMMONWEALTH. Most of the 24 million Kenyans are African. They belong to a number of different tribes. Some tribes, like the Masai, keep cattle. Kenyan farmers grow corn, tea, and coffee. Kenya sells a lot of tea and coffee abroad. Many tourists visit Kenya to see the wild animals roaming the huge nature reserves. Britain ruled Kenya until it became independent in 1963.

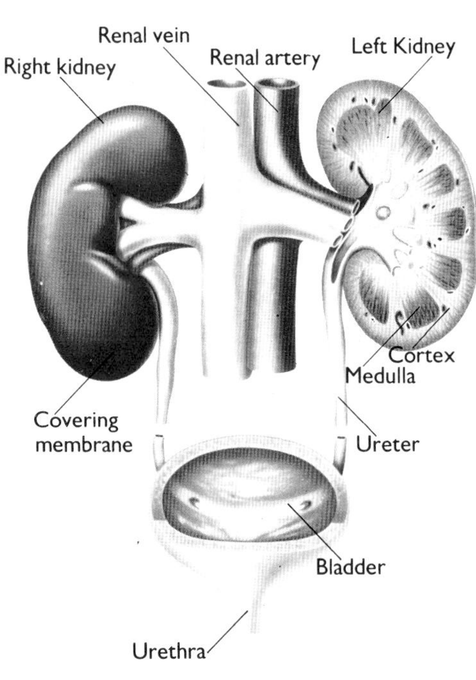

Kidney

All VERTEBRATES (animals with a backbone) have two kidneys. Kidneys look like large, reddish-brown beans. Human kidneys are about the size of a person's fist. They lie on each side of the backbone, just about waist level.

Kidneys clean the BLOOD. They filter out waste matter and strain off any water that the body does not need. Blood pumped from the HEART flows into each kidney through an artery. Each kidney contains tubes that act as filters. Blood cells, tiny food particles, and other useful items stay in the blood to be used by the body. Filtered blood flows out of the kidney through a vein. All the waste matter and extra water mix together to make urine.

King, Martin Luther

Martin Luther King (1929–1968) was an American civil rights leader who worked for racial justice through peaceful means. He was born in Altanta, Georgia, and became a Baptist minister like his father. It was in Montgomery, Alabama, where he was pastor, that he began his CIVIL RIGHTS crusade. One of King's first actions was to organize a boycott of buses in Montgomery in 1956 as a protest against unfair treatment of black passengers. During the next ten years, he led many peaceful demonstrations and meetings all over the country. Success came when Congress passed CIVIL RIGHTS laws in 1964 and 1965.

In 1964, King won the Nobel Peace Prize for his campaigns of nonviolence. In 1968, at the age of 39, he was assassinated in Memphis, Tennessee.

▼ *When Martin Luther King, Jr., was assassinated, President Johnson declared a day of national mourning.*

Kiribati

Kiribati is one of the smallest countries in the British Commonwealth. It is a string of islands in the Pacific Ocean, northeast of Australia. The islands were a British protectorate from 1892 until 1979, when they became independent. The people live simply, fishing and growing coconuts.

KIRIBATI

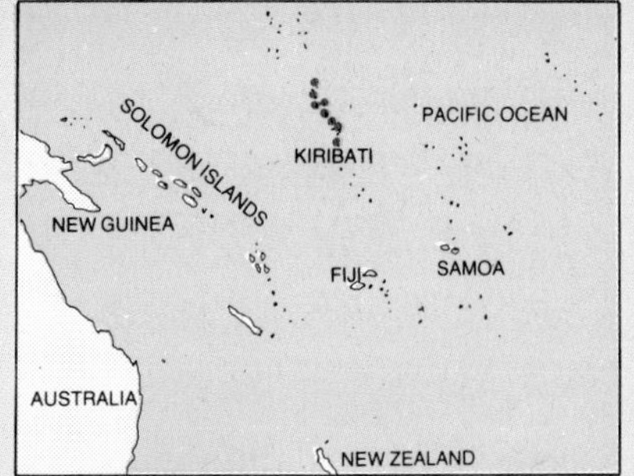

Government: Republic
Capital: Tarawa
Area: 266 sq. miles (689 sq. km)
Population: 66,000
Languages: Gilbertese, English
Currency: Australian dollar

Kiwi

This strange bird from New Zealand gets its name from the shrill cries made by the male. The kiwi is a stocky brown bird as big as a chicken. It has tiny wings, but cannot fly.

Kiwis are shy birds that live in forests. By day, they sleep in burrows. At night, they hunt for worms and grubs. Kiwis can hardly see. They smell their food with the help of nostrils at the tip of their long beaks. The females lay very large eggs.

Knot

Knots are a way of fastening rope, cord, or thread. They are especially important for sailors and climbers. But everyone needs to tie a knot at some time.

Knots are used to make a noose, tie up a bundle, or join the ends of small cords. There are also *bends* and *hitches*. A bend is used to tie the ends of a rope together; a hitch is used to attach a rope to a ring or post. Common knots are the square knot and bowline, both true knots; the clove hitch, half hitch, and sheet bend. Rope ends can also be joined by weaving them together. This is called a *splice*.

▼ *There are many different types of knots for various purposes. Choosing the right knot is half the skill of knot-tying.*

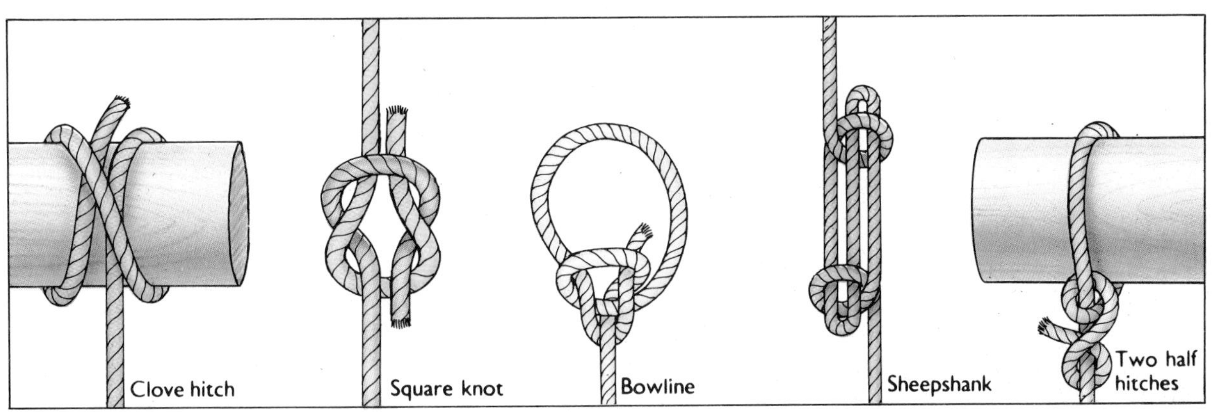

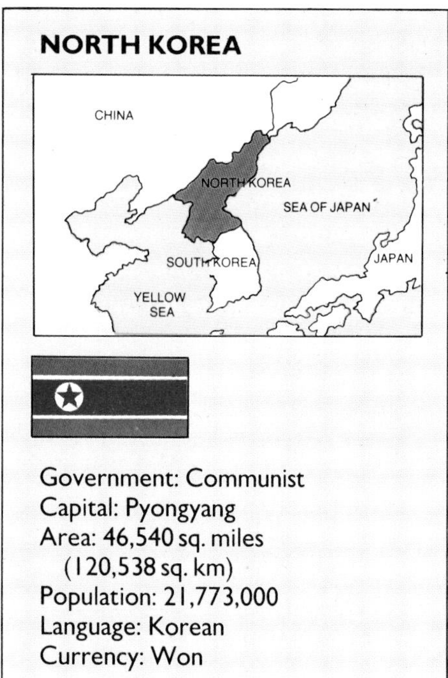

Government: Communist
Capital: Pyongyang
Area: 46,540 sq. miles (120,538 sq. km)
Population: 21,773,000
Language: Korean
Currency: Won

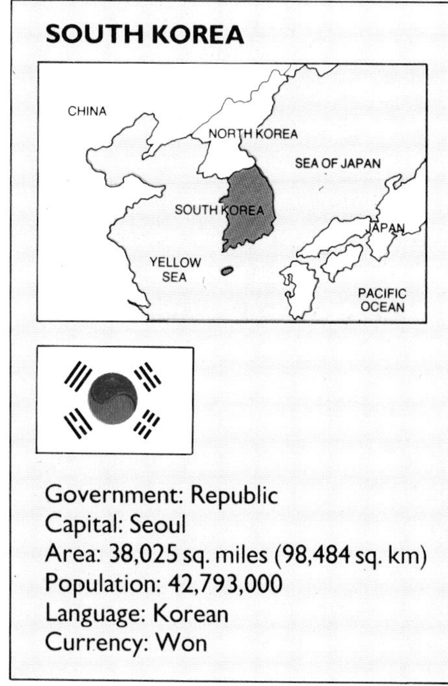

Government: Republic
Capital: Seoul
Area: 38,025 sq. miles (98,484 sq. km)
Population: 42,793,000
Language: Korean
Currency: Won

Koran

The Koran is the sacred book of ISLAM. Its name means "a recitation." It has 114 chapters of Arabic verse and teaches that there is one God whose prophets (messengers) included Abraham, JESUS, and MUHAMMAD. The book teaches Muslims to be humble, generous, honest, courageous, and just. It is said that the Koran was revealed to Muhammad through the angel Gabriel. Parts of the Koran resemble the Bible. The way it is written has influenced Arab literature.

Korea

Korea is a peninsula in ASIA which juts out from CHINA into the Sea of Japan. The land has many mountains and small valleys. Forests cover most of the country. Korean farms produce much rice and silk. Korean factories make steel and other products.

Korea was divided into two separate nations in 1945. They are known as North Korea and South Korea.

War between North and South Korea broke out in 1950, with Soviet and Chinese forces supporting the North and United Nations (mostly American) forces helping the South. There is now an uneasy peace between the two countries.

► *The Olympic Stadium in Seoul was the location of the 1988 games. Superbly equipped, it saw many record-breaking achievements.*

◀ *The view across Red Square to the Kremlin and St. Basil's Cathedral must be one of the most impressive in the world.*

Kremlin

This is the oldest part of Moscow. Some of its buildings date from the 1100s. The Kremlin was once the fortress home of Russia's *tsars*. Inside the high wall that surrounds it stand old palaces and cathedrals crowned by golden domes. For most of its history, the Kremlin has been the seat of the Russian government; it still is today.

▼ *The fifth chief Khan of the Mongol race, Kublai Khan, established the Mongol dynasty in China. Although he was a Buddhist, he was interested in Christianity and allowed missionaries to come to China.*

Kublai Khan

Kublai Khan (1216–1294) was the grandson of GENGHIS KHAN. Kublai became Great-Khan in 1259. Under his rule, the Mongol empire reached its peak of power. He conquered CHINA and set up his capital at Cambulac, modern Beijing. It was the first time that China had been completely overcome by outside forces. Neighboring countries in Southeast Asia were forced to recognize Kublai as their ruler. He also tried to conquer Japan and Java, but failed. Kublai encouraged art, science, and trade. Among his many foreign visitors was MARCO POLO.

Kuwait

The tiny nation of Kuwait is one of the richest in the world because it is an important supplier of oil. IRAQ invaded KUWAIT in 1990, but was forced to leave after the Gulf War in 1991. Except for the capital city, Kuwait, the country is almost all desert.

KUWAIT

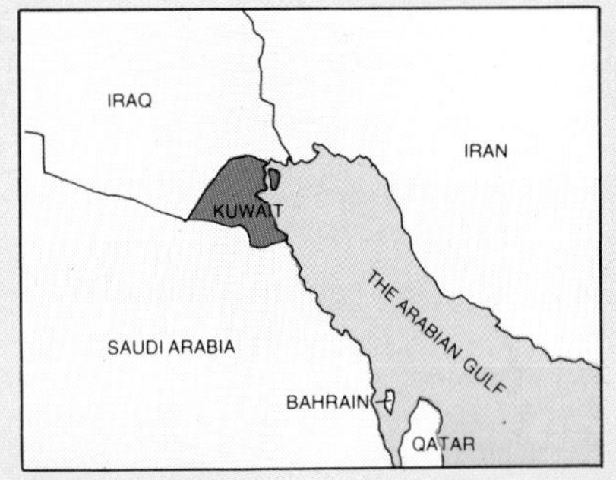

Government: Constitutional monarchy
Capital: Kuwait
Area: 6,880 sq. miles (17,819 sq. km)
Population: 2,143,000
Language: Arabic
Currency: Dinar

Lake

Lakes are large areas of water surrounded by land. The world's largest lake is the salty Caspian Sea. It lies between Europe and Asia, east of the Caucasus Mountains. The largest freshwater lake is Lake Superior, one of the GREAT LAKES.

Many lakes were formed in the ICE AGES. They began in valleys made by glaciers. When the glaciers melted, they left behind mud and stones that formed DAMS. The melted water from the glaciers piled up behind the dams.

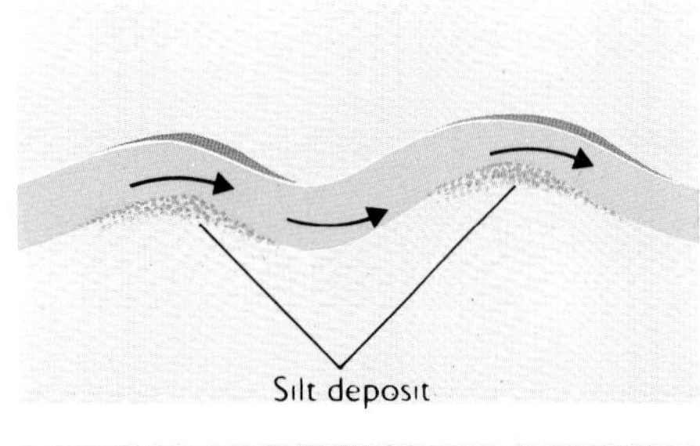

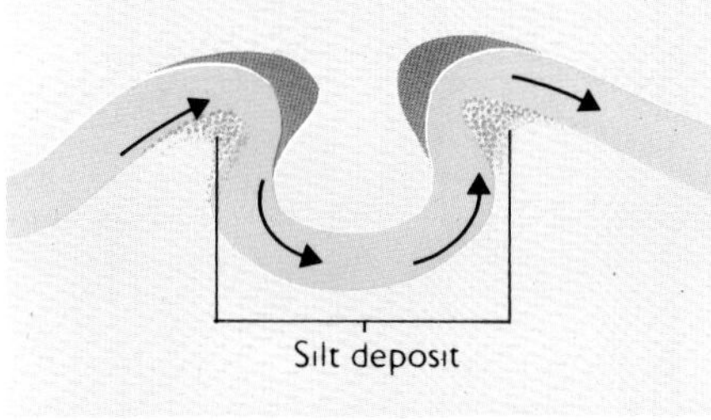

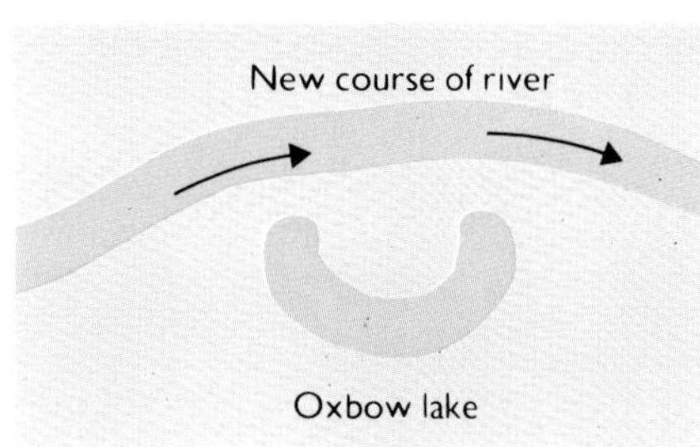

▲ *Rivers can gradually form bends by erosion of one bank and a buildup of material on the other. After a time the river cuts a straight channel through the neck of the bend. The loop of leftover water is called an oxbow lake.*

Language

Language is what we use to talk to, or communicate with, one another. Many animals have ways of communicating. These may include special body movements and sounds. But the speaking of words is something that so far only human can do. Spoken language came first; later people invented a way of writing it down. This is known as written language. Language is always changing, as some words are forgotten and others are added.

Today, there are about 3,000 languages in the world. They can be grouped into a number of language families. Some of the most widely spoken languages are English, French, German, Russian, Chinese, Hindi, Arabic, and Spanish.

► *This bewildering array of newspapers from countries all over the world gives an indication of how difficult international relations can be when people are divided by alphabet, language, and culture.*

Laos

Laos is a country in Southeast Asia. It is slightly smaller than Wyoming. The country's capital and largest city is Vientiane on the Mekong River. Most of Laos is covered with forests and mountains. Nearly all the people earn their living by farming—especially rice. Laos became a French protectorate in 1893, but gained its independence in 1949.

LAOS

BURMA (MYANMAR)
CHINA
VIETNAM
LAOS
THAILAND
CAMBODIA
SOUTH CHINA SEA
INDIAN OCEAN

Government: Democratic Republic
Capital: Vientiane
Area: 91,428 sq. miles (236,800 sq. km)
Population: 4,139,000
Language: Lao
Currency: New kip

Lapland

Lapland is a region in the ARCTIC. It lies in the far north of Sweden, Norway, Finland, and Russia.

Some Lapps are nomads. They travel with herds of reindeer. They sleep in tents and eat reindeer meat. Other Lapps are fishermen or farmers. They live in small huts in villages. Lapps speak a language related to Finnish. They keep warm by wearing clothes made from wool and reindeer skins. Their clothes are brightly colored.

Laser

A laser is a device that strengthens light and makes it shine in a very narrow beam. Many lasers have a ruby CRYSTAL or gas inside them. Bright light, radio waves, or electricity are fed into the laser. This

▼ *In this Los Angeles studio, experiments are being carried out into the use of lasers in games for the future.*

Laser light is being used more and more to carry telephone conversations. A narrow cable containing 144 hairlike glass fibers can carry 40,000 telephone conversations at the same time.

makes the ATOMS of the crystal or gas jump around very quickly. The atoms give off strong light.

The light of lasers can be used for many things. Doctors use small laser beams to burn away tiny areas of disease in the body. They also repair damaged eyes with laser beams. Dentists can use lasers to drill holes in teeth. Some lasers are so strong they can cut through DIAMONDS. Lasers are used in factories to cut metal and join tiny metal parts together.

Lasers can also be used to measure distance. The laser beam is aimed at objects far away. The distance is measured by finding the time it takes for the light to get there and back. Laser beams can also carry radio and television signals. One laser beam can send many television programs and telephone calls at once without mixing them up.

Latitude and Longitude

Every place on Earth has a latitude and a longitude. Lines of latitude and longitude are drawn on MAPS. Lines, or *parallels*, of latitude show how far north or south of the *equator* a place is. They are measured in degrees (written as °). The equator is at 0° latitude. The North Pole has a latitude of 90° north, and the South Pole is 90° south.

▼ *Lines of longitude are measured in degrees. Greenwich, in London, England, is at 0° longitude. A place halfway around the world from Greenwich is at 180° longitude. Some of the lines of latitude and longitude are marked on globes or atlases. They form a kind of network that can be used to pinpoint specific places.*

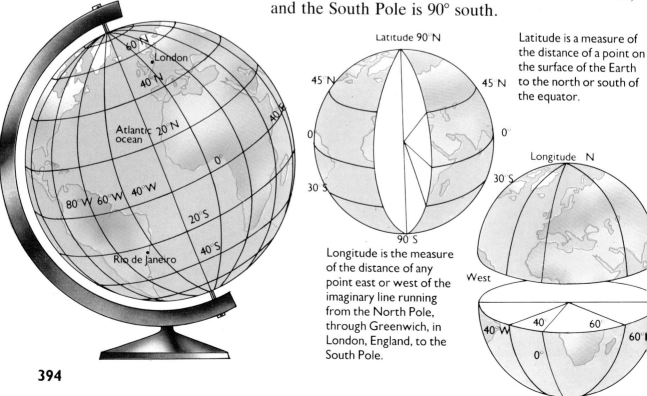

Latitude is a measure of the distance of a point on the surface of the Earth to the north or south of the equator.

Longitude is the measure of the distance of any point east or west of the imaginary line running from the North Pole, through Greenwich, in London, England, to the South Pole.

Lines, or *meridians*, of longitude show how far east or west a place is.

Latvia *See* Baltic States

Law

Laws are rules made by a country's leaders. Laws are made to help people live together in peace. They control many of the things people do. The laws of each country are often different. Some countries have very strict laws about things which other countries do not worry about. Every country has judges and POLICE. They help to make sure that people obey the law. When people break the law, they are often punished. They may have to pay money (fines) or go to prison. Sometimes people are put to death for breaking laws.

The people of BABYLON had written laws over 3,000 years ago. The ancient Greeks and Romans also made laws. In Europe, many important laws were made by kings and the Church. Today, laws are made by governments.

▲ *This carved stone block dates from about 1800 B.C. and is inscribed with laws made up by a king of Babylon called Hammurabi.*

Lead

Lead is a soft, heavy, blue-gray metal. It does not RUST. Lead is used for many things, but its greatest single use is in car batteries. Lead shields protect ATOMIC ENERGY workers from dangerous radiation. Lead is mixed with TIN to make pewter or *solder*. Solder is used for joining pieces of metal. Many items are now made without lead, because lead can become poisonous.

▼ *In the past, lead was often used to make toys and, in particular, model soldiers, but for reasons of safety, it is no longer used.*

Leaf

Leaves are the food factories of green PLANTS. To make food, leaves need light, carbon dioxide, and water. Light comes from the Sun. Carbon dioxide comes from the air. Air enters a leaf through little holes called *stomata*. Water is drawn up from the ground by the plant's roots. It flows up the stem and into the leaf through tiny tubes called veins. Inside

▶ *Leaves come in many shapes, sizes and even colors. You can identify a tree by looking at one of its leaves, once you learn a little about them.*

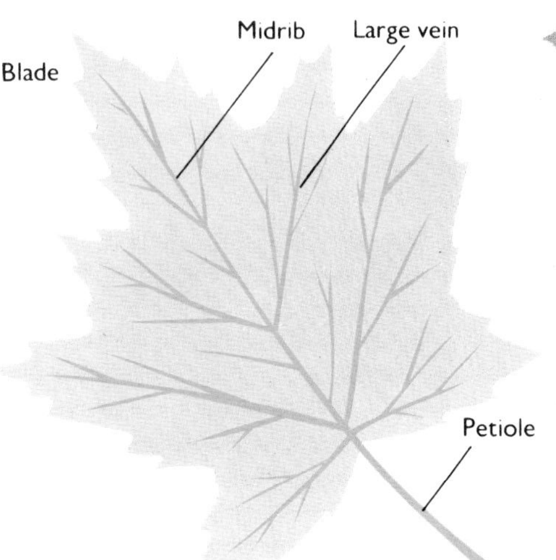

▲ *Most leaves have the same basic parts. Of great importance are the veins that carry water and food to all parts of the plant.*

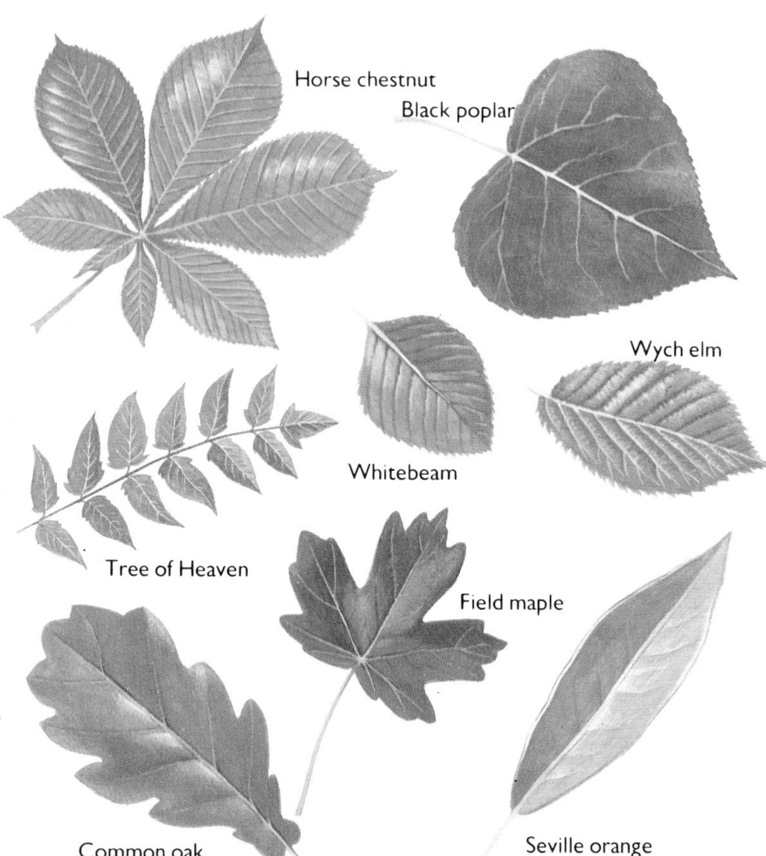

SEE IT YOURSELF

Make a leaf print by rubbing the back of a leaf lightly with shoe polish or paint. Lay the leaf, painted side down, on a clean sheet of paper and cover it with another sheet. Rub over the whole area of the leaf, and you will have a clear picture of the veins. To make a leaf rubbing, lay a clean sheet of paper over a leaf and rub firmly all over with a crayon or soft pencil. The leaf pattern will gradually appear.

the leaf is a green coloring called chlorophyll. The chlorophyll uses light, water, and carbon dioxide to make SUGAR. The way it does this is known as *photosynthesis*. The sugar then passes through tubes to the other parts of the plant.

In the fall, many trees lose their leaves. First they shut off the water supply to the leaves. This destroys the green color and gives the leaves yellow, red, and orange tints.

Leather

Leather is made from the skin, or hide, of animals. The skins are treated to make them strong and waterproof (for the soles of shoes) or flexible (for furniture and luggage). The process of treating them is called *tanning*. Before tanning, the skins are *cured* by being soaked in salt water. Then, the remaining hair and meat is taken off. Next, the skins are treated with a chemical called *tannin*, which comes from tree bark. Then, the leather is oiled to soften it and dyed different colors. It is now ready to be cut, shaped, and stitched or glued into the final product.

Lebanon

Lebanon is a Middle Eastern country bordering on the Mediterranean Sea. It is sandwiched between Syria and Israel. Lebanon's coast is flat, but most of the country inland is mountainous.

Lebanon has been a trading center for centuries. Ancient Lebanon was part of the Phoenician empire. The Phoenicians were great traders all over the Mediterranean. Later, Lebanon became part of the Byzantine empire, ruled from Constantinople. It was famous for the fine cedar wood that came from its forests.

In recent years, the country has become a battleground for a number of religious and political opponents.

LEBANON

Government: Parliamentary republic
Capital: Beirut
Area: 4,015 sq. miles (10,400 sq. km)
Population: 2,701,000
Language: Arabic
Currency: Lebanese pound

◀ *Lebanon has a rich and exciting history. This fortress at Sidon was built during the Crusades.*

Lee, Robert E.

Robert E. Lee (1807–1870) was the commander of the Confederate forces in the Civil War, and the most skillful general in the war. He was admired in both the North and the South for his dignity, his military skills, and his bravery.

Lenin, Vladimir

Vladimir Ilyich Lenin (1870–1924) helped to make Russia the first communist country in the world. Before his time, Russia was ruled by emperors, or

▲ *Lenin's revolutionary ideas united the group of communists called Bolsheviks, who overthrew the Russian government in 1917.*

tsars. Like Karl MARX, Lenin believed in COMMUNISM. He wanted every country run by the workers and no longer split into rich and poor groups. For many years, Lenin lived outside Russia. He wrote books and articles for communist newspapers. In 1917, he went back to Russia. He became the leader of a group of communists called Bolsheviks, who overthrew the government. Lenin then ruled Russia until he died.

Lens

Lenses are used to make things look bigger or smaller. They are usually made of glass or plastic. The lens inside your EYE is made of PROTEIN. Sometimes, eye lenses do not work properly. Then people cannot see clearly. The lenses in glasses make people's eyesight better. The lenses in MICROSCOPES, binoculars, and TELESCOPES make faraway things or small things seem much larger.

Each lens has two smooth sides. Both sides may be curved, or one may be curved and the other flat. There are two main kinds of lens. Lenses where the edges are thicker than the middle are called *concave* lenses. Concave means "hollowed out." When LIGHT rays pass through a concave lens, they spread out. If you look at something through a concave lens, it looks smaller than it really is.

Lenses where the middle is thicker than the edges

NEARSIGHTEDNESS

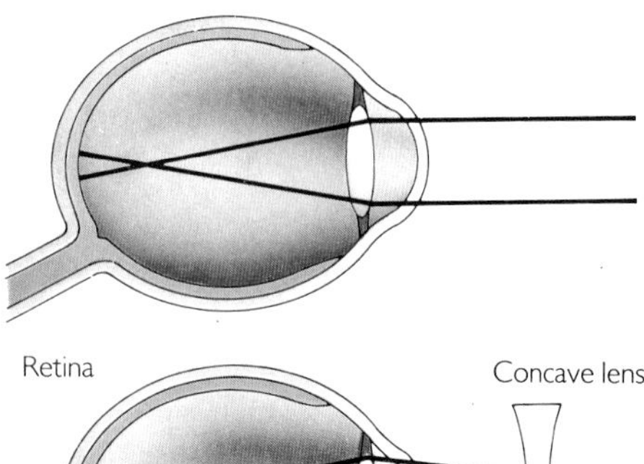

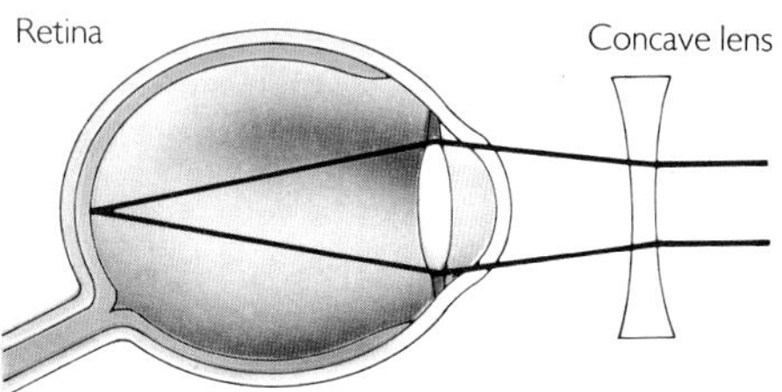

FARSIGHTEDNESS

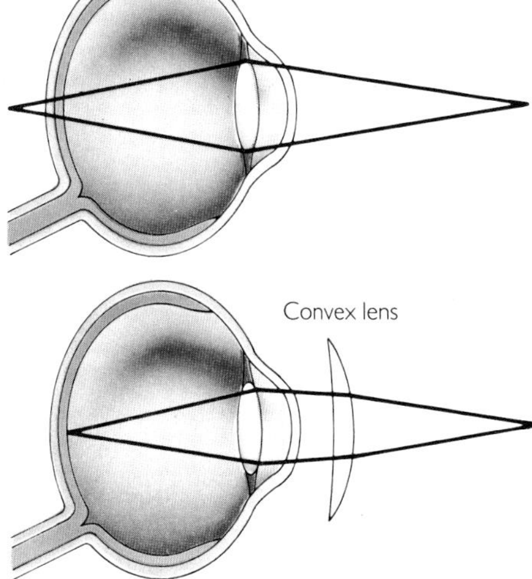

▲ *When people are nearsighted, light from a distant object is focused by the lens of the eye before it reaches the back of the eye, or retina. This means the object looks blurred. When people are farsighted, light from nearby objects is focused at a point beyond the retina, so they appear blurred. Corrective lenses in glasses make the images focus on the retina, so they look sharp and clear.*

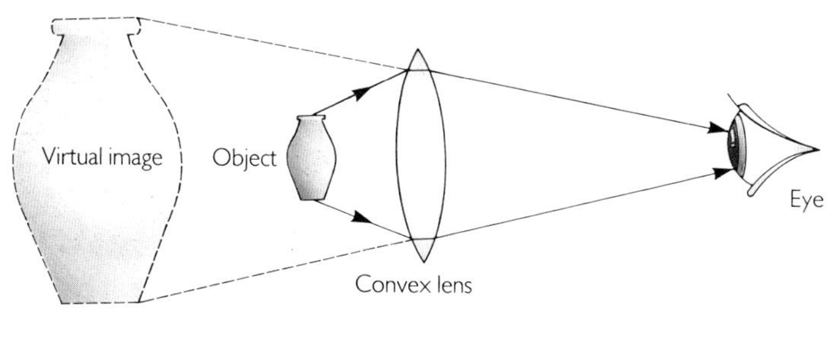

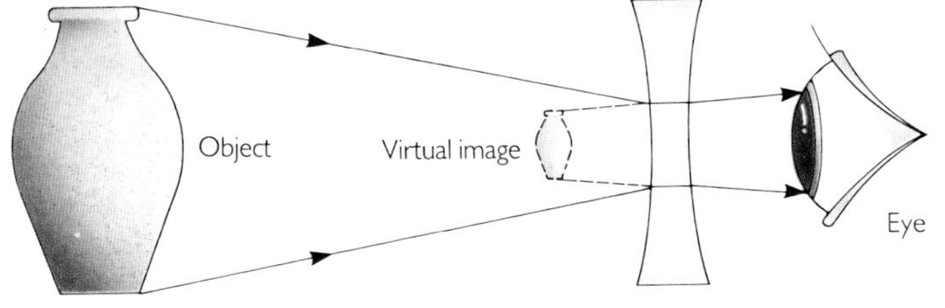

▶ *Light rays passing through a convex lens bend outward, making the virtual image appear larger than it really is. The virtual image is what we see. A concave lens bends the rays inward, and the image looks smaller.*

are called *convex* lenses. Convex means "rounded." When light rays pass through a convex lens, they come together. If you look at things through a convex lens, they seem larger.

Craftspeople who make lenses know exactly how to shape them for various uses. They may fit different lenses together or shape each side of a lens differently. Nearsighted people use lenses with a concave and a convex side. But the concave side is curved more than the convex side.

The "burning glass" for producing fire from the Sun's rays has been known since ancient times. The magnifying property of a simple lens was recorded by Roger Bacon in the 1200s. Lenses were first used in the 1300s, and by the 1500s, eyeglasses were commonly used. Benjamin Franklin invented the bifocal lens in 1760.

Leonardo da Vinci

Leonardo da Vinci (1452–1519) was an Italian artist and inventor. He lived during the RENAISSANCE. One of his most famous paintings is the *Mona Lisa*. It is a picture of a woman who is smiling mysteriously. Many people have wondered what she was smiling at. Leonardo made thousands of drawings of

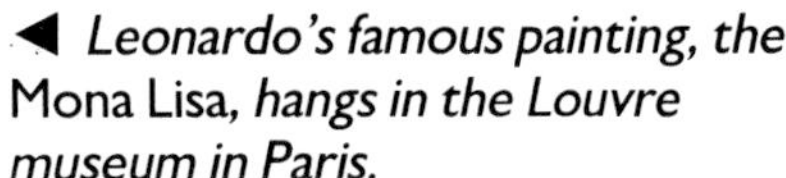

◀ *Leonardo's famous painting, the* Mona Lisa, *hangs in the Louvre museum in Paris.*

▼ *Leonardo's self-portrait, drawn in about 1512, is the only known authentic likeness of the artist.*

Leonardo often smoothed in the paint with his fingers to get a special effect. The result is that several of the great artist's paintings have clearly visible fingerprints somewhere on their surface. These fingerprints have been used to prove without doubt that certain paintings are the work of Leonardo.

Leonardo wrote in a strange way. He wrote his lines from right to left, and each letter was reversed. This is called "mirror writing" because viewed in a mirror it looks quite normal.

human bodies, water, plants, and animals. He left more than 7,000 pages of notebooks with scientific ideas and sketches.

Leonardo worked as an engineer for Italian nobles and for the French king. He designed forts and canals. The canals had locks so that boats could travel up and down hills. Leonardo also drew ideas for things long before they were invented. His drawings include a helicopter, a flying machine, and a machine gun.

Leonardo was interested in many other things, including music and architecture. He was also a good musician and singer.

Leopard

Leopards are large, wild cats a little smaller than LIONS. They live in Africa and southern Asia. Most leopards are spotted like jaguars, but some are nearly black. These are called panthers.

Leopards are very fierce, strong, and agile hunters. They catch and eat antelopes, goats, dogs, and sometimes people. They often hunt from trees, lying in wait on a branch. If they cannot eat all their catch at once, they may haul the carcass high up into a tree. This is to stop lazier hunters such as lions or hyenas from stealing it.

▼ *Although they are fierce hunters, female leopards are good mothers and take good care of their young until they can fend for themselves.*

Lesotho

The kingdom of Lesotho is a small country completely surrounded by South Africa. Most of the people farm corn, wheat, and sorghum, or raise sheep, goats, and cattle. Nearly half of Lesotho's adults work in South Africa's mines, industries, and farms. Lesotho, once called Basutoland, became a British protectorate in 1868. It gained its independence in 1966.

LESOTHO

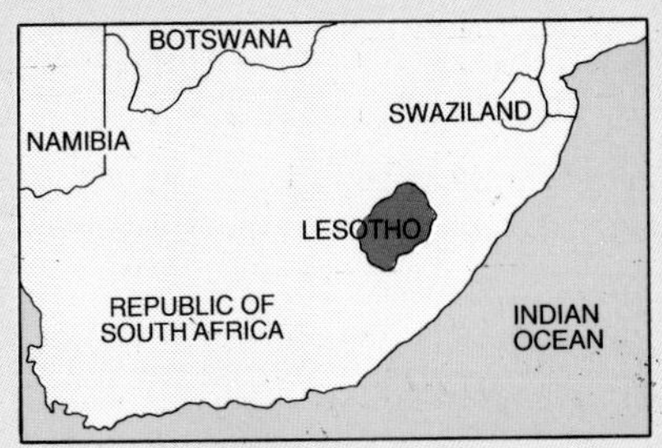

Government: Constitutional monarchy
Capital: Maseru
Area: 11,720 sq. miles (30,355 sq. km)
Population: 1,774,000
Languages: Sesotho and English
Currency: Loti

Liberia

Liberia is one of the oldest independent African countries. It has never been controlled by a European country. Liberia was founded in 1822 as a home for freed slaves from the United States. It is on the west coast and is about the size of Tennessee. It is easy to register ships in Liberia, so many countries do so there. Iron ore is Liberia's chief export. More than half the country's people became refugees as the result of a civil war that ended in 1991.

LIBERIA

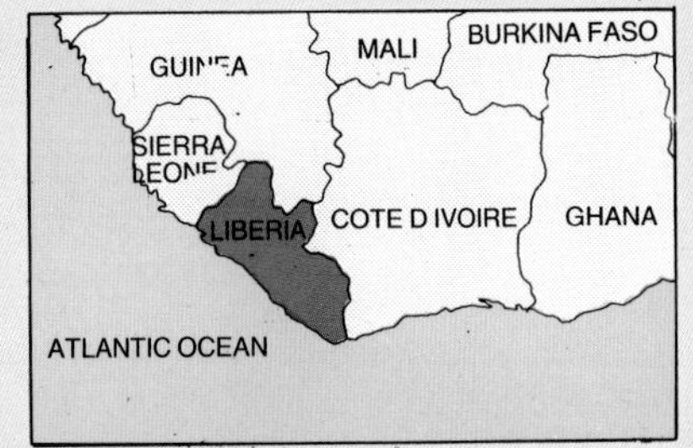

Government: Republic
Capital: Monrovia
Area: 43,000 sq. miles (111,370 sq. km)
Population: 2,607,000
Language: English
Currency: Liberian dollar

Liberty Bell

The Liberty Bell is one of the most famous symbols of American independence. It was made in England, in 1752, for what is now Independence Hall in Philadelphia. The bell cracked when it reached America, and had to be recast. It was rung when the DECLARATION OF INDEPENDENCE was signed in 1776. Until 1835, when it cracked again, it was rung every July 4. Today it hangs in the Liberty Bell Pavilion.

Liberty, Statue of

The Statue of Liberty is a famous symbol of America. It is 152 feet (46 m) tall on a 150-foot (45 m) pedestal and stands on Liberty Island in NEW YORK harbor. The statue was a gift from the government of France to the United States to mark the first centennial of America, in 1876. It was made in Paris in separate pieces, and was shipped to New York, where it was put together again. Inside, the statue is

The Statue of Liberty is made of 300 sheets of copper, each $^{3}/_{32}$ inch (2 mm) thick. The sheets are riveted together.

▲ *The Library of Congress in Washington is one of the great libraries of the world. It has more than 80 million items in its vast collection.*

supported by an iron framework designed by Gustave Eiffel (1832–1923), the designer of the Eiffel Tower in Paris.

Library

A library is a place where books and documents are stored. There are different kinds of libraries. In some, you borrow books to take home. In others, students and scholars use the books and documents for their work. People have used libraries for as long as men have known how to write.

Libya

Libya is a large country in North Africa. It is nearly three times the size of Texas, but very few people live there. This is because most of Libya lies in the Sahara Desert.

Most Libyans are Arabs who farm the land. Libya is also rich in oil. The country became part of the Turkish Ottoman Empire in the 1500s, and was a colony of Italy from 1912 to the end of World War II. It became an independent monarchy in 1952. In 1969, army officers overthrew the king and took control, and Colonel Muammar al-Qaddafi became head of the government. Since that time, Qaddafi has led a revolution in Libyan life and the leaders of many nations have accused him of interfering in other countries' affairs.

LIBYA

TUNISIA
MEDITERRANEAN SEA
ALGERIA
LIBYA
EGYPT
NIGER
CHAD
SUDAN

Government: Islamic Arab Socialist
Capital: Tripoli
Area: 679,359 sq.miles (1,759,540 sq. km)
Population: 4,545,000
Language: Arabic
Currency: Libyan dinar

▶ *The Libyan port of Tripoli, on the Mediterranean, used to be called Medina. Its long history as a trading city dates back to biblical times.*

Lichen

A lichen is a simple PLANT. It has no roots, leaves, or flowers. Some lichens grow as crusty patches on rocks, trees, or walls. They grow very slowly. A patch no larger than your hand may be hundreds of years old. Other lichens grow as shrubby tufts. Lichens can live in places that are too bare, dry, cold, or hot for any other plant.

Scientists use lichens to find out how much sulfur dioxide there is in the air. (Sulfur dioxide is a poisonous gas that is harmful to living things.) Lichens are very sensitive to harmful gases in the air. They do not thrive in cities where there is smoke, dust, and exhaust fumes.

◀ *A lichen is actually made up of two plants—a fungus and an alga—growing together. Reindeer moss, though called a moss, is actually a lichen.*

Liechtenstein

Liechtenstein is one of the smallest countries in the world. It lies between Switzerland and Austria in the Alps. Liechtenstein is a prosperous country. Many international companies have their headquarters there. Tourism brings money into Liechtenstein. Switzerland runs the postal and telephone systems, and the two countries use the same money. Liechtenstein is ruled by a prince.

LIECHTENSTEIN

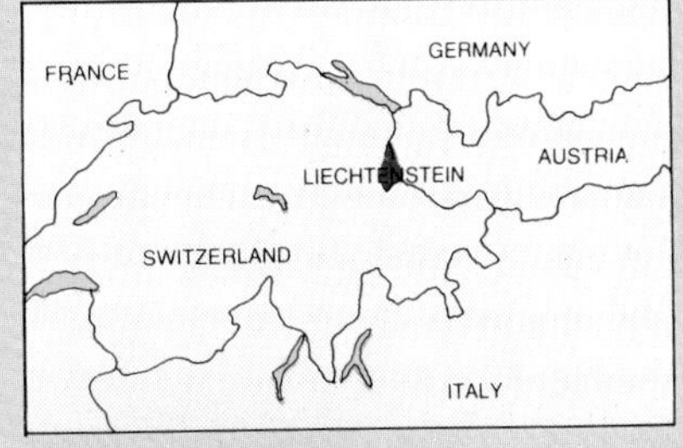

Government: Constitutional monarchy
Capital: Vaduz
Area: 62 sq. miles (160 sq. km)
Population: 29,000
Language: German
Currency: Swiss franc

Light

Light is a kind of ENERGY that we can see. Some objects—stars, lamps, certain chemicals—produce light. Most things do not produce light. We can see them only because they reflect light. For example, we can see the MOON and planets such as VENUS and JUPITER in the sky only because they reflect light from the SUN.

Sunlight is the brightest light we normally see. Summer sunlight can be as bright as 10,000 candles

► *A prism splits white light into a spectrum of colors. When the sun shines through rain, the raindrops act as a prism to make a rainbow.*

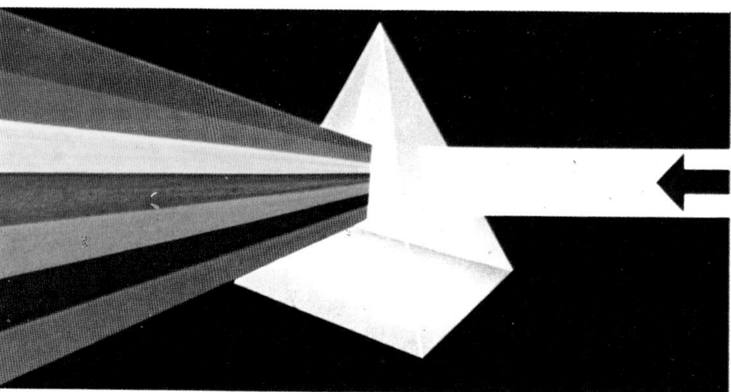

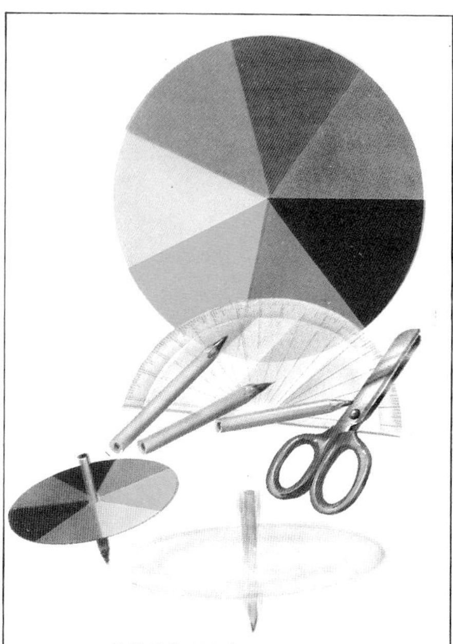

SEE IT YOURSELF

Here is a way to show that white light is made up of the seven colors of the rainbow. Cut a disk from cardboard, and divide it into seven equal sections. Color each section as shown. Make a small hole in the middle of the disk and push a sharp pencil or stick through. Spin the disk quickly. What do you see?

▼ *When light rays travel through different substances, in this case air and water, they are bent so the image looks distorted.*

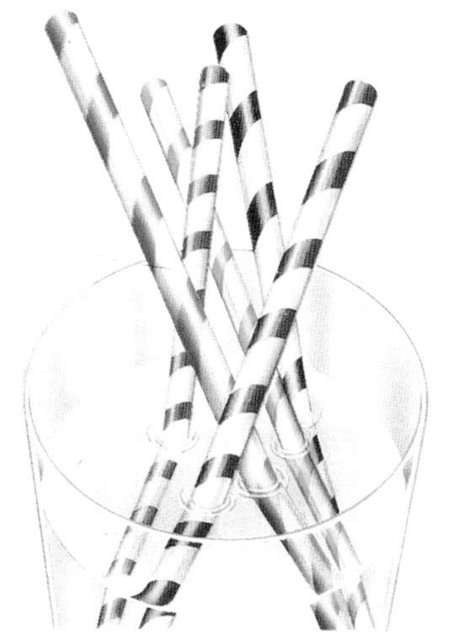

burning close enough to touch. Bright sunlight seems white, but it is really made up of the colors of the RAINBOW. Isaac NEWTON showed this. He made a sunbeam shine through a specially shaped chunk of glass called a prism. Red, orange, yellow, green, blue, indigo, and violet rays of light came out of the prism.

The prism had split the sunbeam into separate beams, each with its own *wavelength*. This is easy to understand if you think of light traveling in waves. The distance between the tops of the waves is the wavelength. We see each wavelength as a different color. Long waves are red, short waves are violet, and wavelengths in between show up as all the other colors in the rainbow.

Light travels very fast, more than 186,000 miles (300,000 km) each second. Even so, it takes eight minutes for the light from the Sun to reach Earth, a distance of 93,000,000 miles (150 million km). A light year is the total distance a beam of light travels in one year—5,884,000,000,000 miles (9,470,000,000,000 km). Scientists use light years to measure how far away STARS are. Some are millions of light years away.

Lightning

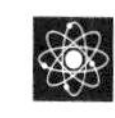

Lightning is ELECTRICITY that is generated in storms. It is the sudden flow of huge amounts of electricity between two clouds; between a cloud and the ground; or between two parts of a single cloud.

There are three types of lightning. Streak lightning is a single line of lightning that flashes between a cloud and the ground. Forked lightning is caused

◀ *Lightning is caused by a buildup of static electricity in the atmosphere. When it discharges, it causes a flash and the bang we know as thunder.*

when the lightning divides, or forks, to find the quickest route to the earth. Sheet lightning happens inside a cloud, which it lights up, like the flashbulb on a camera.

Lincoln, Abraham

Abraham Lincoln (1809–1865) was the 16th president of the United States. He was elected for two terms, but was assassinated just three months into his second term. Many people believe Lincoln, who was president in the CIVIL WAR, was America's greatest president. His wisdom, dignity, and deep love of democracy not only helped the North to win the Civil War, but strengthened democracy in the United States. His speeches and writings helped many to a better understanding of American democracy. Though Lincoln hated the war for the suffering it brought, he knew that it had to be fought to save the Union and to end slavery. He also showed himself to be a brilliant military leader. But because he urged compassion to the South, many in the North distrusted him. And because he defeated them, many in the South feared him.

ABRAHAM LINCOLN

Sixteenth President 1861–1865
Born: near Hodgenville, Kentucky
Education: Self-educated
Occupation: Lawyer
Political Party: Republican
Buried: Oak Ridge Cemetery, Springfield, Illinois

Lindbergh, Charles

Charles Lindbergh (1902–1974) was the first man to fly single-handed nonstop across the Atlantic. His flight made him an international hero. The Atlantic had been flown before, but not single-handed.

Lindbergh knew he would need a special kind of plane to succeed, one that could carry all the fuel he

▲ *Lindbergh's historic flight across the Atlantic inspired many other pioneering aviators.*

needed. He took off from New York, in his plane named the *Spirit of St. Louis*, on May 20, 1927. Thirty-three hours and 3,500 miles (5,600 km) later, he landed in Paris, France, to a hero's welcome.

Lion

Lions are large, tawny-colored wild CATS. An adult male weighs about 400 pounds (180 kg) and measures about 9 ft. (2.7 m) from nose to tail. Females (lionesses) are slightly smaller and have no mane.

Lions usually live in groups called prides. A pride has one male, several females, and all their cubs. Lions often hunt as a team. No other big cats seem to do this. They hunt mainly antelope and zebra. Lionesses do most of the hunting.

Liquid

A liquid can flow and change its shape. Liquids include water, milk, mercury, and oil. When liquid is poured into a container, it takes the shape of the container, but its volume remains the same. As a liquid gets hotter, the atoms or molecules in it move faster. They begin to leave the liquid. A GAS is formed. At the boiling point, the liquid boils, and in time, all of it turns into gas.

When a liquid gets colder, the atoms or molecules in it slow down. At the freezing point, they settle into rows, and the liquid becomes a solid.

▼ *When lions are not hunting, they spend long periods resting to conserve their energy. Lions used to roam wild over southern Europe, India, and Africa. Now they live only in South and East Africa and a tiny part of India. Many lions today lead protected lives on nature reserves.*

Lister, Joseph

Joseph Lister (1827–1912) was an English surgeon who found a way to stop his patients from dying of infection after operations. He used antiseptics to kill germs on surgeons' hands and instruments.

Lithuania *See* Baltic States

Liver

Your liver is a flat, triangular organ tucked under your right ribs. It is larger than your stomach. The liver is a kind of chemical factory and storage cabinet. It produces the digestive juice that burns up the fat you eat. It makes the PROTEINS used in blood. It gets rid of any poisonous substances in the blood or changes them so that they are harmless. Minerals and VITAMINS are stored in the liver until the body needs them.

Lizard

Lizards are REPTILES with dry, scaly skins and long tails. Most have four legs, but some have none. These look like snakes. Some lizards are born live like MAMMALS, but most of them hatch from eggs.

There are about 3,000 kinds of lizard. Most live in hot countries. Lizards that live in cooler places spend the winter in HIBERNATION. Lizards mainly eat insects.

SEE IT YOURSELF

The surface of water is held together by a force called "surface tension," which makes water appear to have a thin, elastic "skin" all over it. To show that sugar breaks this "skin," float some matches carefully on the surface of a bowl of water as shown. Now dip a lump of sugar in the middle. The sugar absorbs some of the water, and a small current of water flows toward the sugar, pulling the matches with it.

▼ *Lizards are usually small, very active reptiles. They live mostly in hot countries and can be anything from a few inches to 10 feet (3 m) in length.*

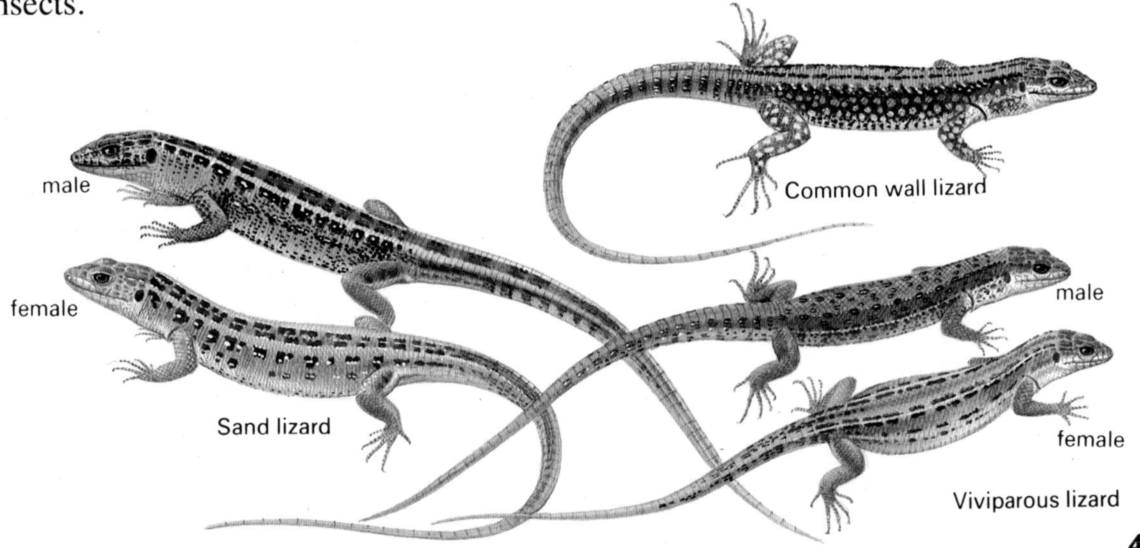

▲ *Llamas are hardy animals, well-adapted to the harsh conditions of the Andes Mountains.*

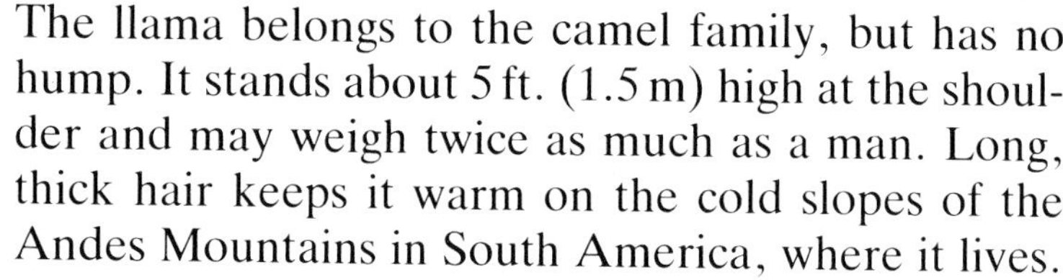

Llama

The llama belongs to the camel family, but has no hump. It stands about 5 ft. (1.5 m) high at the shoulder and may weigh twice as much as a man. Long, thick hair keeps it warm on the cold slopes of the Andes Mountains in South America, where it lives.

All llamas come from wild ancestors who were tamed at least 4,500 years ago by the INCAS. Today, South American Indians still use llamas to carry heavy loads. They make clothes and ropes from the llama's wool and candles from its fat.

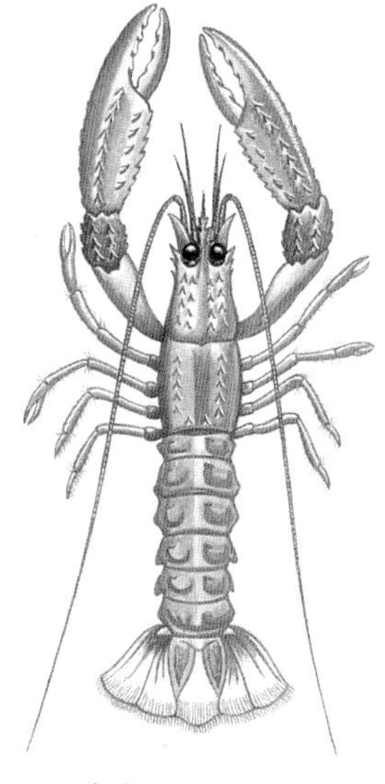

▲ *Norway lobsters are usually known as scampi or prawns.*

Lobster

Lobsters are CRUSTACEANS. They are related to shrimps and CRABS. One kind of lobster can weigh up to 44 lbs (20 kg). The lobster's body has a hard SHELL. It has four pairs of legs for walking and a pair of huge claws for grabbing food. When a lobster is afraid, it tucks its tail under its body. This drives water forward and pushes the lobster backward to escape.

Lobsters hide among rocks on the seabed. They feed on live and dead animals. A female lobster can lay thousands of eggs.

The earliest locks and keys were large wooden instruments. We can get some idea of the size of the keys from an Old Testament reference in Isaiah: "And I will place on his shoulder the key of the house of David." This probably shows how people carried their keys.

Lock and Key

There are two main kinds of lock. In the simplest kind, when the key is turned, a piece of metal, called a bolt, moves out and fits into a slot. The key has a few notches that have to match similar notches in the lock. The Yale lock was invented in 1860. In it, the key can turn a cylinder when all the little pins in the lock are pushed to the right height by the notches on the key.

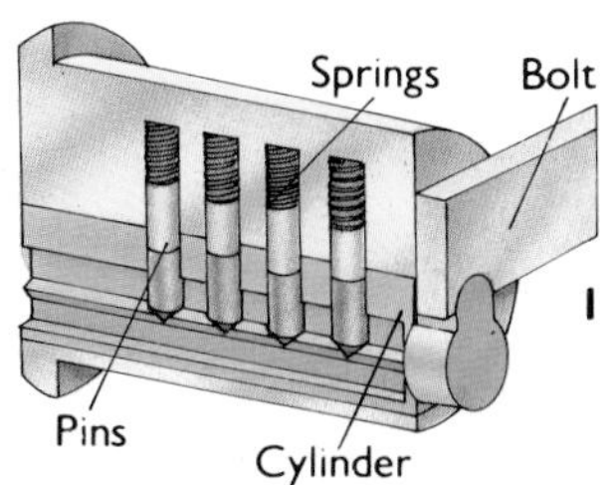

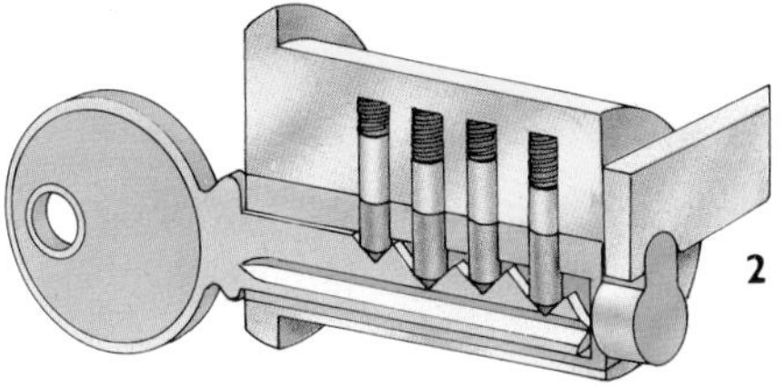

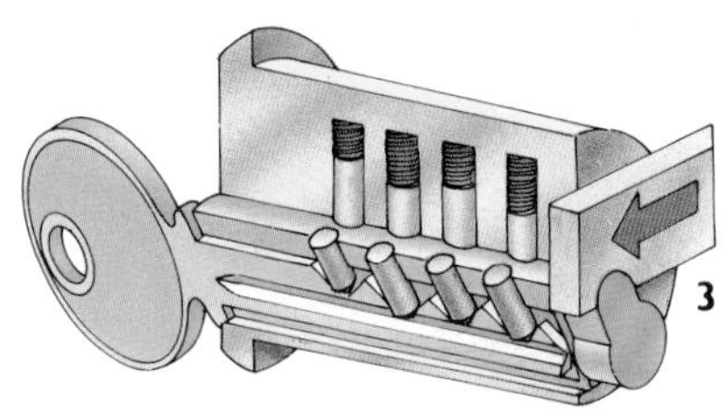

▲ *In a Yale lock, there are many combinations possible for the heights of the pins. Before the key is inserted, all the pins are level and held in place by springs (1). The key slides into the lock, and its jagged edge pushes the pins to different heights (2). When the right key is used, the pins are pushed to the heights that will allow the cylinder to be turned, opening the lock (3).*

Locust

Locusts are GRASSHOPPERS that sometimes breed in huge numbers. They fly far across land and sea to find new feeding places. A big swarm may have hundreds of thousands of locusts. When they land, the locusts eat everything green. Swarms of locusts have destroyed many farms in warm lands.

Locusts swarm and fly away only when there are too many of them. Farmers try to kill the young locusts before they are able to fly.

London

London is the capital of the UNITED KINGDOM. It has about seven million people. The River Thames runs through London.

People from all over the world visit London to see Buckingham Palace, the Houses of PARLIAMENT, Westminster Abbey, and the Tower of London. There are many museums, theaters, and parks in London, as well as offices and factories.

◄ *The Tower of London has been the site of a fortification since Roman days. It has seen some of the most turbulent moments of British history.*

London is very slowly sinking into its foundations and the level of the River Thames is slowly rising. As a result, extra-high tides could flood a large part of London. To prevent this from happening, a great barrier has been built across the Thames at Woolwich. If very high tides happen, the barrier can be raised, and London will be safe.

London began as a Roman settlement called *Londinium*. The PLAGUE came to London in the 1600s, followed by the Great Fire of 1666. The city was badly bombed in WORLD WAR II.

Longfellow, Henry Wadsworth

Henry Longfellow (1807–1882) was an American poet, and one of the most famous writers of the 1800s. He wrote a number of very long poems such as *The Song of Hiawatha* and *The Courtship of Miles Standish*, as well as shorter poems such as *The Wreck of the Hesperus* and *Paul Revere's Ride*. Today, some people think his poetry is old fashioned and prefer other writers of the period. But his achievement in making people around the world take American poetry seriously was important. Longfellow was also a university professor.

Los Angeles was founded in 1781 by Felipe de Neve, the Spanish governor of California. Although there were only about 40 people living there, de Neve gave the little settlement a very long name—*El Pueblo de Nuestra Señora la Reina de Los Angeles de Porciuncula*, which means The Town of Our Lady Queen of the Angels of Porciuncula.

Los Angeles

Los Angeles is the second-largest city in the UNITED STATES. More than 14 million people live in the Los Angeles area. The city lies in the sunny countryside of California. On one side of Los Angeles is the Pacific Ocean. Behind it are the San Gabriel Mountains.

There are thousands of factories and a big port in Los Angeles. Visitors go to see Disneyland and Hollywood. More movies and television programs are made in Los Angeles than in any other city.

▶ *The air pollution in Los Angeles is sometimes so severe it can actually be seen. The smog forms a thick haze over the city, particularly in hot, dry weather.*

Loudspeaker

A loudspeaker turns electric signals into SOUND waves. The sounds that we hear on RADIO, TELEVISION, record players, and tape recorders all come from loudspeakers.

A moving coil loudspeaker has a cone fixed to a wire coil. Inside the coil is a magnet. Electric signals flow through the coil. The signals make the coil move to and fro. The tiny movements of the coil make the cone shake, or vibrate. Air around the cone also starts to vibrate. These air vibrations reach our ears, and we hear sounds.

▼ *When sound is recorded, it is turned into electrical signals. The loudspeaker turns these signals back into sound waves that we can hear. The signals are fed to a coil that is attached to a plastic cone and positioned between the poles of a circular magnet. The signals cause the coil to vibrate, which vibrates the plastic cone. The vibrating cone produces sound.*

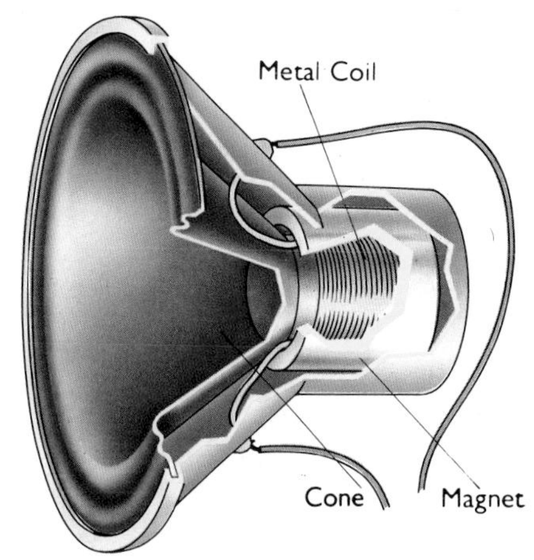

Louis (French kings)

Eighteen French kings were called Louis.

The first was Louis I (778–840). Louis IX (1214–1270) led two CRUSADES. Louis XI (1423–1483) won power and land from his nobles. Louis XIII (1601–1643) made the French kings very powerful. Louis XIV (1638–1715) ruled for 72 years. He built a great palace at VERSAILLES. All the French nobles had to live in his palace. Louis XVI (1754–1793) was beheaded after the FRENCH REVOLUTION.

Louisiana

Louisiana is a Southern state. It is important chiefly because of the MISSISSIPPI RIVER, which flows through it. Much trade passes along the river and reaches right into the heart of the United States. Large ships can sail as far as 250 miles (400 km) up the Mississippi. Louisiana has been ruled by many different peoples. Frenchmen and Spaniards have left their colorful mark, especially in New Orleans, the state's largest city and the birthplace of jazz. Its French-style restaurants draw many visitors.

LOUISIANA

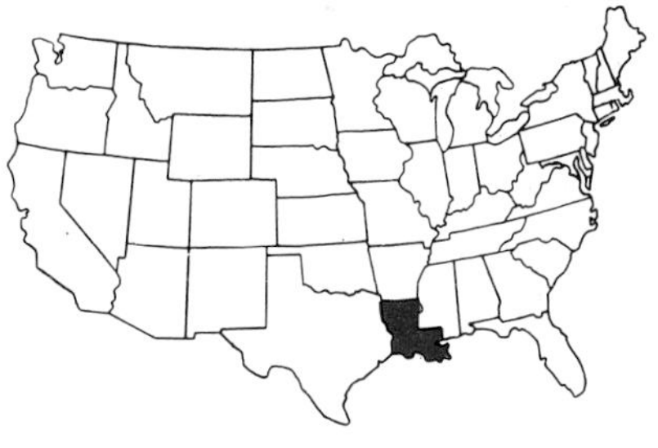

Capital: Baton Rouge
Population: 4,219,973
Area: 47,752 sq. mi. (123,677 sq. km)
State flower: Magnolia
State bird: Brown Pelican
State tree: Bald Cypress
Statehood: April 30, 1812
18th state

Louisiana Purchase

The Louisiana Purchase took place in 1803, and was an important event in the early life of the United States. Under it, the country bought a huge area of land west of the MISSISSIPPI RIVER from France for $15 million. It doubled the size of the country and allowed settlers to move rapidly west. Fifteen states were formed from the land. Thomas JEFFERSON was responsible for the purchase.

Lung

Lungs are organs for BREATHING. People have lungs, and so do many animals. Lungs bring OXYGEN to the body from the AIR. They also remove waste carbon dioxide from the BLOOD.

Your lungs are two large, sponge-like masses in your chest. They fill with air and empty as you breathe in and out.

You breathe in air through the nose. The air flows down the windpipe, or *trachea*. Where the lungs begin, the trachea divides into two hollow branches called bronchial tubes, or *bronchi*. Each divides into smaller tubes called *bronchioles*. These end in cups called air sacs, or *alveoli*. This is where the lungs give oxygen to the blood and take away carbon dioxide.

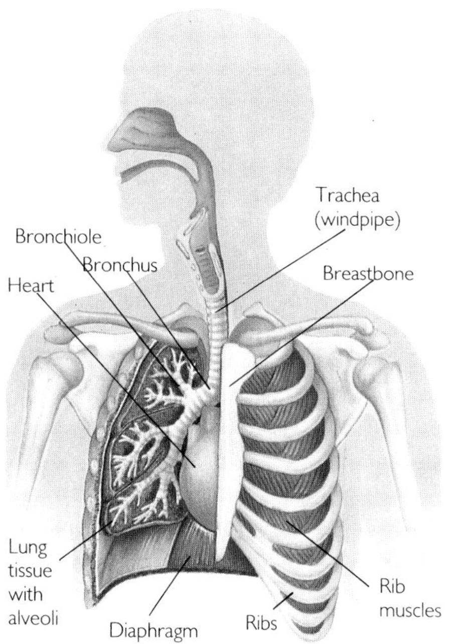

▲ *The soft, fragile lungs are well protected inside the rib cage, which expands and contracts to allow for the movements of breathing. The movement of the lungs is controlled by the diaphragm. As you breathe in, it contracts, increasing the volume of the lungs. As you breathe out, it rises to push the air out.*

Luther, Martin

Martin Luther (1483–1546) was a German priest who quarreled with the ROMAN CATHOLIC CHURCH. He started the Protestant REFORMATION.

Luther did not like the way priests forgave people's sins in return for money. He also believed that God's teachings lay in the BIBLE. The Bible was more important to Luther than what the POPES said.

Under Luther's leadership, a large number of Christians split away from the Roman Catholic Church.

Luxembourg

Luxembourg is one of the smallest countries in EUROPE. Around it are Belgium, France, and Germany. Luxembourg has low mountains with large forests. There are farms in the hills. There are also iron mines and towns that make steel. The European Parliament has offices in Luxembourg.

LUXEMBOURG

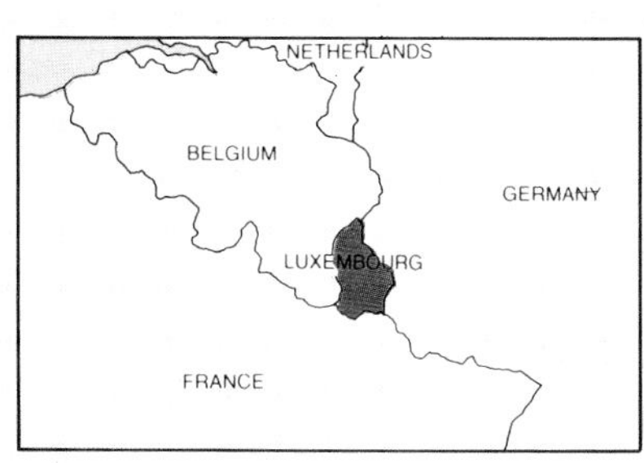

Government: Constitutional monarchy
Capital: Luxembourg
Area: 998 sq. miles (2,586 sq. km)
Population: 373,000
Languages: French and Letzeburgesch
Currency: Luxembourg franc

Machine (Simple)

Some machines are very large and have many moving parts. Other machines are very simple. All the machines we see working around us are related to one or other of six simple machines. These machines were among people's oldest and most important inventions.

A machine is stronger than a person. It uses a greater *force*. When a force is used to move something, we can say that *work* is done. Machines make work easier. The *wedge*, for example, helps us to split things. A wedge hammered into a small crack in a tree trunk will split the trunk in two. Chisels, knives, nails, and axes are all different forms of wedges.

The SCREW can pull things together or push them apart. With a jackscrew, a man can quite easily lift a car weighing far more than himself. There are many kinds of *levers*. The simplest is a long pole, pivoted or balanced on a log and used to lift a heavy rock. The lever changes a small downward force into a bigger upward force.

The *inclined plane* makes it easier to raise heavy loads to higher levels. It is easier to pull a load up a slope than to lift it straight up. The PULLEY also makes lifting easier. A simple pulley is used in the winding mechanism that raises water from a well. A more complicated machine is the block and tackle, which has several sets of ropes and pulleys.

Probably the most important of all simple machines is the *wheel and axle*. This is used not only for moving loads, but also in all sorts of machines—such as clocks and cars.

▼ *Machines make it easier for us to do work. When we operate them, we do a little work over a long distance so that the machine can do a lot of work over a short distance. For example, in the jackscrew shown below, you have to turn the lower bar many times to raise the upper bar only a little, but this bar can raise a very great weight.*

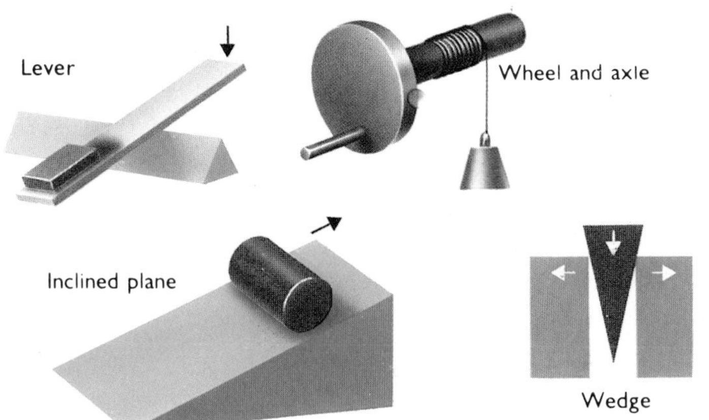

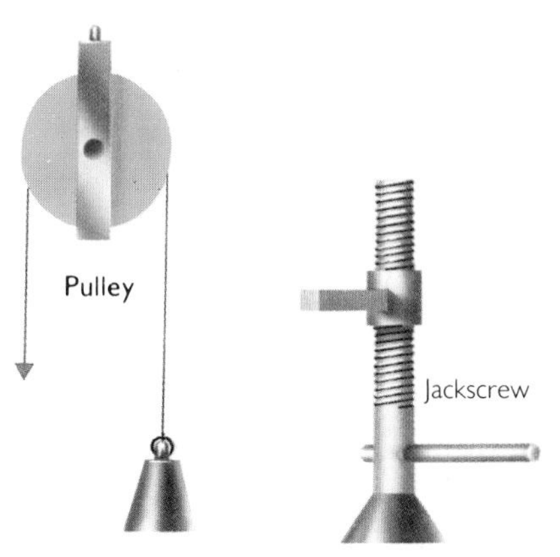

WILLIAM MCKINLEY

Twenty-fifth President 1897–1901
Born: Niles, Ohio
Education: Allegheny College, Meadville, Pennsylvania
Occupation: Lawyer
Political Party: Republican
Buried: Canton, Ohio

McKinley, William

William McKinley (1843–1901) was the 25th president of the United States. He was elected to serve two terms, but was assassinated six months after the start of the second. During his presidency, the United States became a major industrial power as well as an important world power. Cuba, Puerto Rico, and the Philippines all became American dependencies, and Hawaii became a United States territory. At home, the success of American industry brought problems, too. McKinley believed that U.S. businesses should be protected from foreign competition by high tariffs. Many of his political opponents were against these tariffs. McKinley was a politician all his adult life. Despite his cold personality, he was popular with many people.

Madagascar

Madagascar is the fourth largest island in the world. It is in the Indian Ocean, off the east coast of Africa. The country of Madagascar has fertile coastal plains, a rugged central plateau, and a warm, tropical climate. Coffee, rice, sugar, and vanilla are among the leading crops.

Between the 800s and 1300s, Arab colonies were set up in Madagascar. In the 1800s, the island came under French control. It gained independence from France in 1960. The government is socialist.

MADAGASCAR

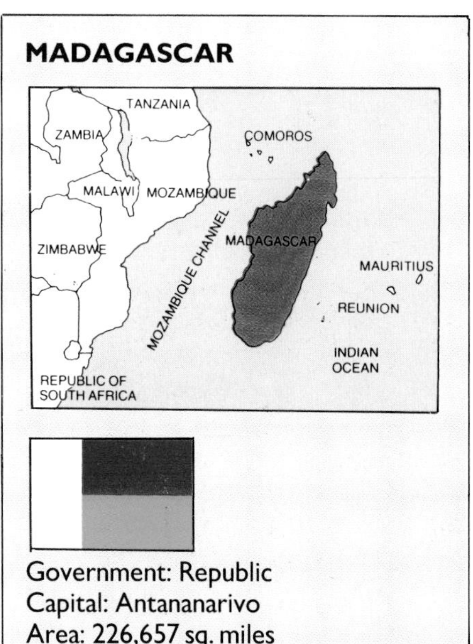

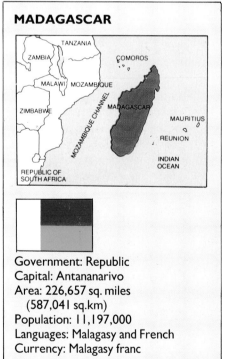

Government: Republic
Capital: Antananarivo
Area: 226,657 sq. miles (587,041 sq.km)
Population: 11,197,000
Languages: Malagasy and French
Currency: Malagasy franc

Madison, James

James Madison (1751–1836) was the 4th president of the United States. As president, his major problem was to keep the United States out of the Napoleonic Wars in Europe. Both Britain and France seized American ships, each believing that U.S. trade was helping the other. Many people in the United States were angry at this, and in 1812 Britain and America did go to war, despite all Madison's efforts to avoid fighting. Earlier, Madison played an important part in writing the U.S. CONSTITUTION. His writings on the nature of federal power influenced many people.

Magellan, Ferdinand 

Ferdinand Magellan (1480–1521) was a Portuguese sailor and explorer. In 1519 he sailed west from Spain, around Cape Horn, and into the Pacific Ocean. Magellan was killed by natives in the Philippines. But one of his five ships returned safely to Spain, having completed the first voyage around the world. Of the crew of 265 who set sail with Magellan, only 16 survived the voyage.

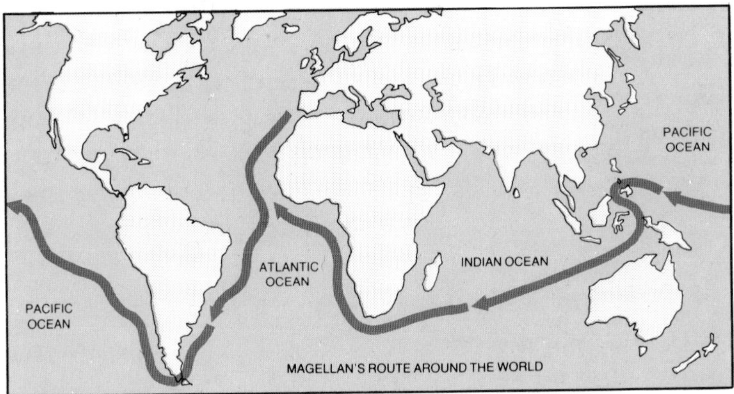

◀ *Magellan set out to find a new sea route to Asia, heading west and rounding the tip of South America.*

JAMES MADISON

Fourth President 1809–1817
Born: Port Conway, Virginia
Education: College of New Jersey (now Princeton University)
Occupation: Lawyer
Political Party: Democratic-Republican
Buried: Montpelier, Virginia

Magic 

Many primitive peoples used magic. It was their way of trying to control what happened around them.

SEE IT YOURSELF

Here is a magic trick using three loops of paper. Take three strips of paper, each about 3 ft. (1 m) long and 2 in. (5 cm) wide. Take the first strip and glue the ends together to form a loop (1a and b). Do the same with the second strip, but give it a complete turn (turn it over and over again) before joining the ends (2a and b). With the third strip, turn one end over once before gluing (3a and b). Now cut the three strips down the center. The first loop gives you two separate loops (1c). The second forms two linked loops (2c). The third becomes a single loop twice the size of the original (3c)! These magic loops were discovered by a famous German mathematician, Ferdinand Moebius, in 1858.

They said magic words, or danced special dances, or painted magic pictures.

All through history, people have believed that certain things (such as talismans or charms) or people (such as witches and sorcerers) have magical powers. Magic is often closely tied up with religion, but increased scientific knowledge has reduced people's dependence on magic. Most people today think of magic as the tricks performed by magicians on television, in the theater, or at parties.

▲ *In an electromagnet, a metal that is not normally magnetic, such as an iron bolt, can be made magnetic by passing an electric current through a coil of wire wrapped around it. As soon as the current is broken, the magnetic field ceases to exist. The bolt is no longer a magnet.*

Magnetism

A magnet attracts metals, particularly iron and steel. The Earth is a huge natural magnet. Invisible lines of magnetic force spread out around the planet, joining the North and South magnetic poles. We call this the Earth's *magnetic field*.

The needle in a COMPASS is a magnet. It always turns to face magnetic North. In ancient times, people noticed that a kind of iron ore called a lodestone suspended from a string would always swing to point in the same direction. A lodestone is a natural magnet. Another name for it is magnetite.

Maine

Maine is the most northeasterly state of the United States. It is known for its wild and rocky shore, its farming and fishing, and its forests—over 90 percent of Maine is forest. Paper is just one of the important

SEE IT YOURSELF

If you have two bar magnets, you can show the shapes of force-fields around the magnets. Put one of the magnets under a piece of plain paper and sprinkle some iron filings on top (1). The filings show the lines of force running between the north and south poles of the magnet. Now do the same thing using the two magnets. You will see why a north pole attracts a south pole (2), and why two north poles or two south poles push each other apart (3).

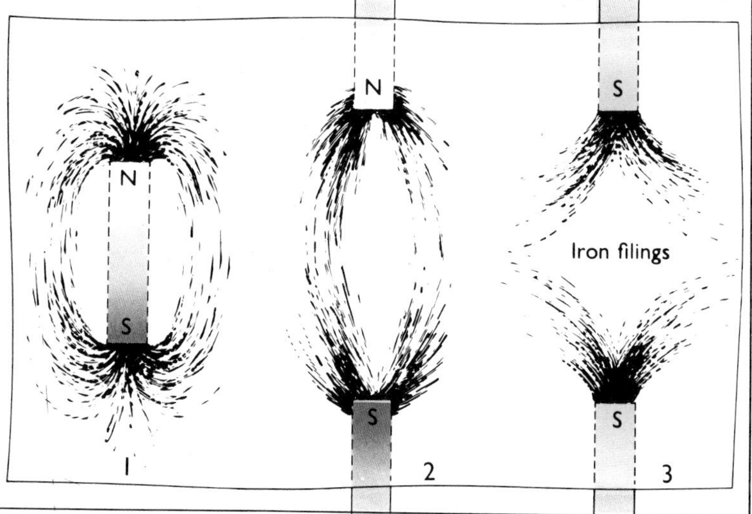

products which depend on the wood from Maine's forests. Most people in Maine live in the southern half of the state. This is where the largest cities are located. Much of the northern part of the state is wild and empty. Many people visit Maine in the summer to enjoy its beautiful seashore and mild climate.

Maine was one of the first areas of the United States to be settled. English settlers landed as early as 1608. Maine played an important part in the Revolutionary War. Most Maine people were fierce opponents of slavery in the Civil War.

MAINE

Capital: Augusta
Population: 1,227,928
Area: 33,265 sq. mi. (86,156 sq. km)
State flower: White Pine Cone and Tassel
State bird: Chickadee
State tree: Eastern White pine
Statehood: March 15, 1820
23rd state

Malaria

Malaria is a common and deadly tropical disease. It is carried by the female *Anopheles* mosquito, which can infect the humans it bites. Drugs are used to treat malaria. Scientists try to destroy the mosquitoes and the swamps in which the insects breed.

◀ *In Malawi, traditional methods of farming and the village way of life still exist.*

Malawi

Malawi is a long, narrow country in eastern Africa. It is a little smaller than Mississippi. Most of Malawi's people live in small villages and grow their own food. Tobacco, tea, and sugar are grown.

In 1859, the explorer, David Livingstone, was the first European to come to the region of Malawi. In 1891, Britain took over the territory and set up the Protectorate of Nyasaland. Independence was granted in 1964. The name was changed to Malawi, the name of the people who once lived there.

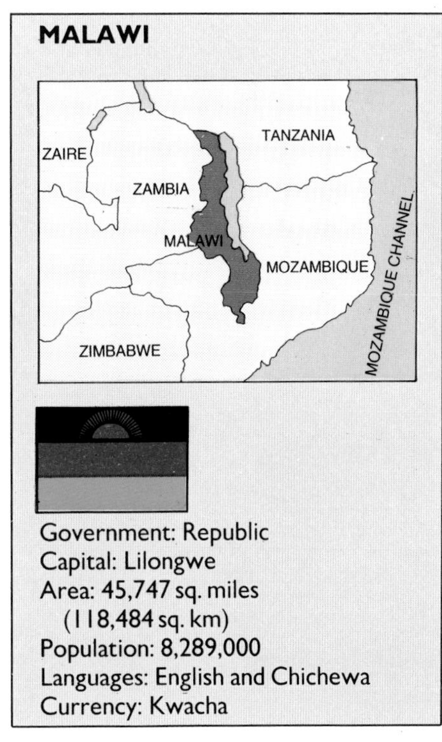

Government: Republic
Capital: Lilongwe
Area: 45,747 sq. miles (118,484 sq. km)
Population: 8,289,000
Languages: English and Chichewa
Currency: Kwacha

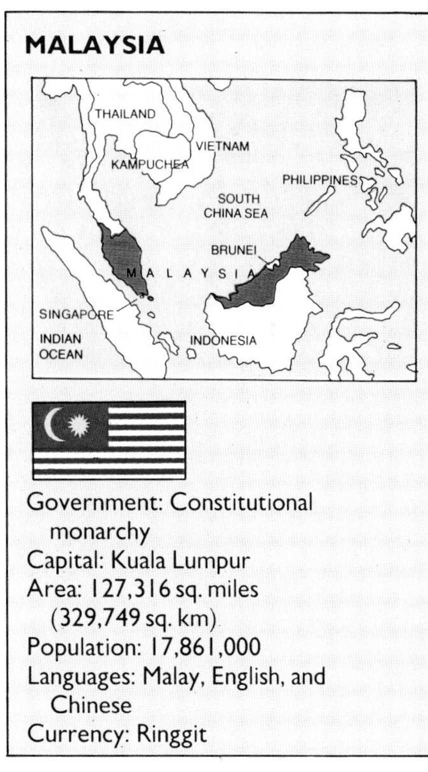

Government: Constitutional monarchy
Capital: Kuala Lumpur
Area: 127,316 sq. miles (329,749 sq. km)
Population: 17,861,000
Languages: Malay, English, and Chinese
Currency: Ringgit

Malaysia 

Malaysia is a country in SOUTHEAST ASIA. It is in two parts, West Malaysia on the Malay Peninsula, and East Malaysia, which is part of the island of Borneo. In 1965, SINGAPORE broke away from Malaysia to become an independent state.

Malaysia has about 18,000,000 people, mostly Malays and Chinese. Its main exports are rubber, timber, and tin.

Malaysia is a member of the British Commonwealth. It is ruled by a sultan, who is head of state, and a prime minister, who is head of government.

Maldives 

The Republic of Maldives is a chain of islands southwest of India in the Indian Ocean. Although there are about 2,000 islands, the total area is only half that of New York City. The climate is damp and hot, with heavy rainfall. Most of the people make their living by fishing.

The islands became a British protectorate in 1887 and gained complete independence in 1965. The Maldives is one of the world's poorest countries.

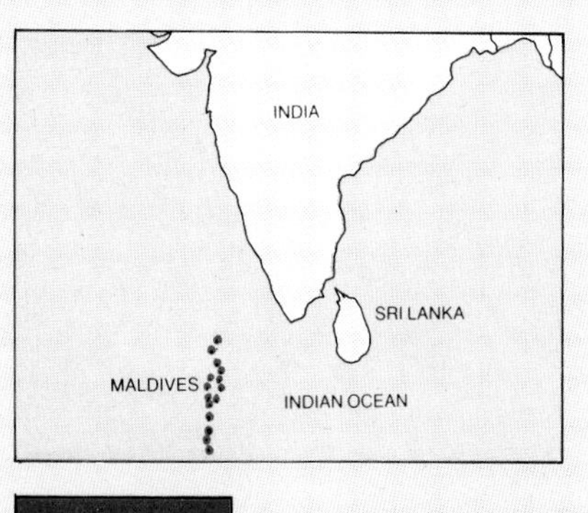

Government: Republic
Capital: Malé
Area: 115 sq. miles (298 sq. km)
Population: 215,000
Language: Divehi
Currency: Maldivian rupee

Mali 

The country of Mali is in northwest Africa. It is three times the size of California, but has only a third of its population. A large part of the country is in the Sahara Desert.

In the 1800s, Mali was occupied by the French and achieved independence in 1960. Famine and drought have plagued the country.

Malta 

Malta is an island in the MEDITERRANEAN SEA. It lies south of Sicily. Since ancient times, it has been a vital naval base, for it guards the Mediterranean trade routes to the East. For centuries, Malta was ruled by the Knights of St. John, but in 1813, it became British. During World War II, Malta survived heavy bombing raids.

◀ *Fishing boats at anchor in a harbor in Gozo. The Republic of Malta includes the island of Malta and its neighboring island, Gozo.*

Since 1962, Malta has been self-governing. Today, it is a republic. The capital is Valletta, with its splendid Grand Harbour.

MALI

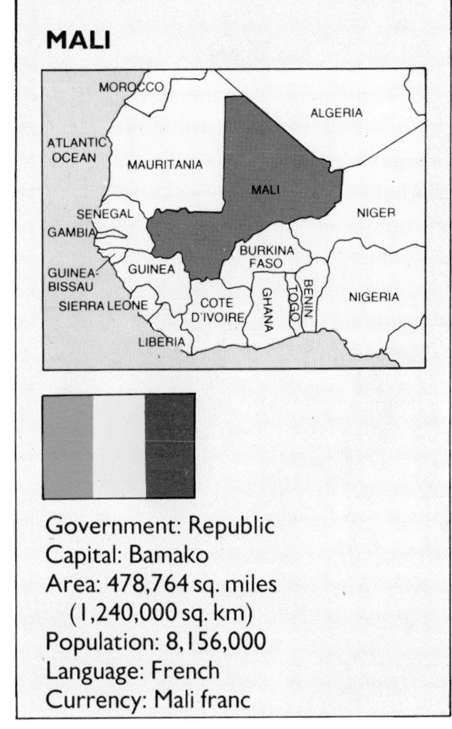

Government: Republic
Capital: Bamako
Area: 478,764 sq. miles (1,240,000 sq. km)
Population: 8,156,000
Language: French
Currency: Mali franc

Mammal

Mammals are not the largest group of animals on Earth. But they are the most intelligent and show a greater variety of forms than any other group of animals.

All mammals have warm blood and a bony skeleton. Many have hair or fur on their bodies to keep them warm. Female mammals give birth to live young, which they feed on milk from special glands in their bodies. Some mammals (such as mice) are born naked, blind, and helpless. Others (such as deer) can run within hours of being born.

Mammals were the last great animal group to appear on Earth. They came long after fish, amphibians, reptiles, and insects. When DINOSAURS ruled the Earth, millions of years ago, the only mammals were tiny creatures which looked like SHREWS. But after the dinosaurs died out, the mammals took over. During EVOLUTION, the mammals multiplied into many different forms which spread all over the world.

Scientists divide the mammals into three families.

MALTA

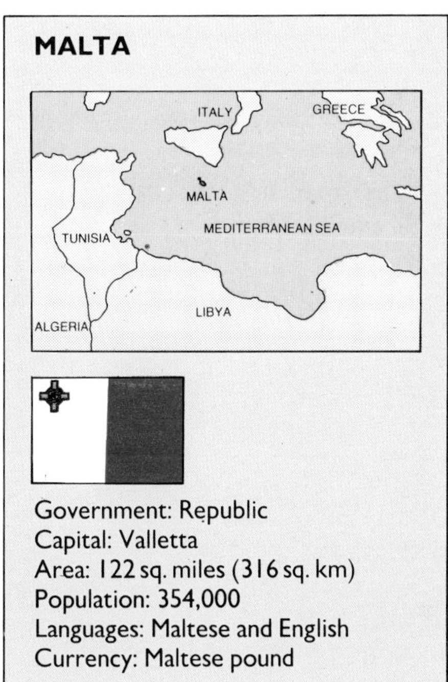

Government: Republic
Capital: Valletta
Area: 122 sq. miles (316 sq. km)
Population: 354,000
Languages: Maltese and English
Currency: Maltese pound

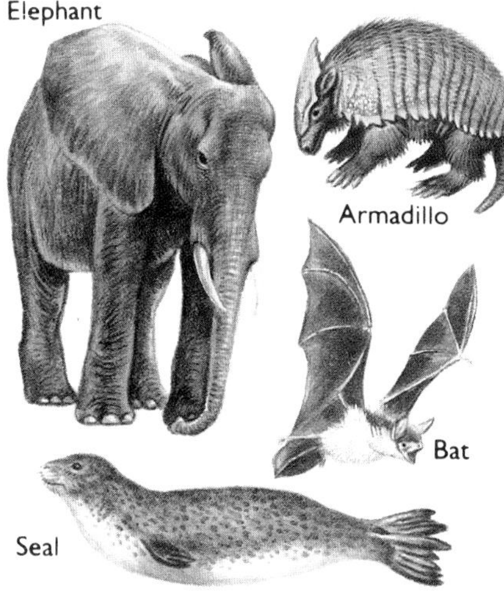

▲ *There are three families of mammals: egg-laying mammals, marsupials, and placental mammals. The placental mammals are the most advanced group.*

The most primitive mammals still lay eggs, like reptiles and birds. There are only two left in this family, the echidna and the PLATYPUS. Then come the MARSUPIALS. These mammals give birth to tiny, half-developed young which have to be carried in their mother's pouch until they are big enough to look after themselves. The best known marsupial is the KANGAROO. Almost all the marsupials live in Australia.

The "placental" mammals, the highest group of all, give birth to fully developed young. There are many different kinds, including flying mammals (BATS); gnawing animals or RODENTS; sea mammals (WHALES and DOLPHINS); and burrowing mammals (for example, moles). There are insect-eaters, plant-eaters, and flesh-eaters. The flesh-eaters, or CARNIVORES, include the powerful CATS, WOLVES, and BEARS. The most intelligent of all the mammals are the primates. This family includes MONKEYS, APES, and HUMAN BEINGS.

Mammoth

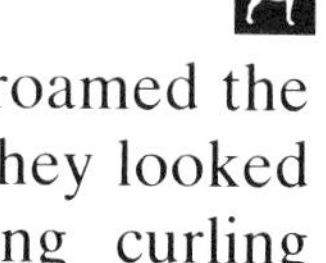

During the ICE AGES, wooly mammoths roamed the plains of Europe and North America. They looked like shaggy-haired elephants, with long curling tusks. But they lived in much colder climates than the elephants of today.

► *Wooly mammoths developed from a more primitive creature called the Mastodon, which was also the ancestor of the modern elephant.*

Mammoths lived together in herds, feeding on plants, grass, and leaves. Their enemies included the fierce saber-toothed tiger, wolves, and also CAVE DWELLERS, who hunted mammoths for food. Sometimes, a group of hunters drove a mammoth into a pit, where it could be killed with spears.

The frozen bodies of mammoths have been dug up by scientists in the icy tundra of Siberia. Mammoth remains have also been found in tar pits in California. The last mammoths died out about 30,000 years ago.

About 40 mammoths have been found frozen into the arctic ice of Alaska and Siberia. The meat of these great creatures was so fresh that it could be eaten by dogs after more than 30,000 years.

Manitoba

Manitoba is a province in Canada. It is located in the heart of the country, halfway between the Atlantic and Pacific oceans. The south of Manitoba has rolling prairie lands where farmers grow wheat and raise cattle. Winnipeg, the largest city in Manitoba, is in the south, too. More than half the population of the province lives in and around it. Winnipeg is an important industrial center. The north of Manitoba is wild and empty. Tourists like to visit it to discover its unspoiled beauty, and its lakes and rivers. There are important mineral reserves of gold, copper, and zinc.

MANITOBA

Capital: Winnipeg
Population: 1,090,700
Area: 211,723 sq. mi. (548,360 sq. km)
Entry into confederation: July 15, 1870

Maoris

The Maoris are the native people of NEW ZEALAND. These well-built, brown-skinned people came in canoes from Pacific islands to New Zealand in the 1300s. The Maoris were fierce warriors who fought with clubs made of bone or greenstone (a kind of jade). They fought many battles against the first white people who came to New Zealand. This war did not end until 1865, and there were some outbreaks of fighting for years afterward.

The Maoris were very skillful at weaving, dancing, and, above all, carving. Maori carving is full of decoration. Every inch of the surface of their work is covered with curves, scrolls, and spirals.

Today, the Maoris play an important part in the life of New Zealand. Their population is increasing at a faster rate than that of non-Maoris.

▲ *Tikis are an important part of Maori art and culture. This tiki, carved from jade, was worn for protection against the ghosts of stillborn children.*

▲ *Mao was chairman of the Communist Party in China for 27 years and brought about many radical changes in culture and economics.*

Mao Tse-tung

Mao Tse-tung (1893–1976) was a great Chinese leader. He was the son of a farmer and trained to be a teacher. In 1921, he helped to form the Chinese Communist Party and fought against the Chinese Nationalists under Chiang Kai-shek. In 1934, he led 90,000 Communists on a 368-day march through China to escape Nationalist forces. This feat was called the Long March. When Mao Tse-tung and the Communist armies beat the Nationalists, he became head of the Chinese government in 1949. He wanted CHINA to become as rich as America, but many of his plans for his country did not work. He resigned from his job as head of government in 1959, but continued as head of the Chinese Communists. He had many arguments with the Russian Communist Party. Mao also wrote poetry and books about guerrilla warfare.

After Mao's death, China's new leaders criticized his rule and brought in a less rigid and more Western-looking policy.

Map and Chart

Maps and charts are forms of pictures of parts of the Earth. They give us valuable information to help us move around and to tell us about other parts of the world. Maps show land, charts cover the sea. Charts can be used to give other kinds of information, too, such as business or school records.

There are several different kinds of map. Some show countries, towns, roads, and railroads. These are political maps. Physical maps show natural features such as mountains, plains, rivers, and lakes. Colors and contour lines can be used to show the shape and size of features such as mountains and valleys.

Maps are drawn to different scales. The scale of some is so big that you may even be able to find your house on one. On other maps, the scale can be so small that the whole world can be shown on just one page. On a small-scale map, one inch on the map may represent 100 miles, or even 10,000 miles. On a large-scale map, it may represent just one mile.

▼ *Early maps and globes show what a mysterious place the world once was. A lot of guesswork went into mapmaking in years gone by.*

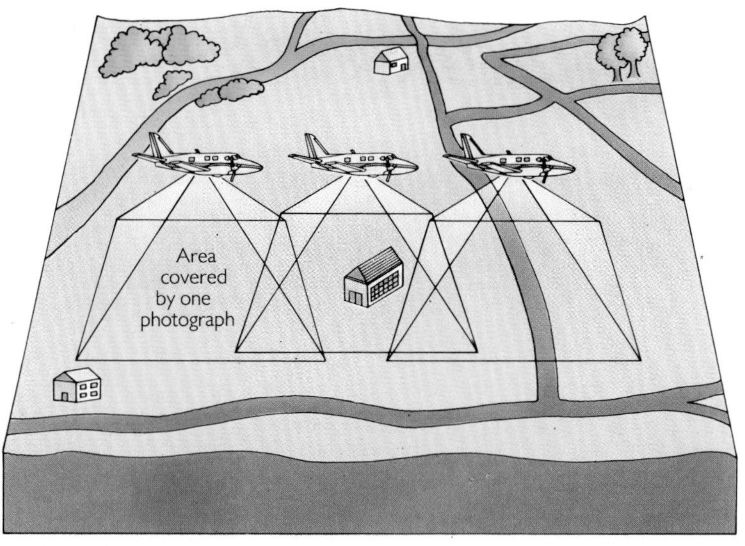

◀ *Today, aerial photographs are used to make accurate maps. The pictures are taken from a plane flying at a constant height. Each photo overlaps the next slightly, so no detail is lost.*

Charts tell sailors about the sea and help them to navigate. They show how deep the water is and where channels are, and they show important navigation aids such as lighthouses and buoys. Charts can use color, too, to help give this information.

Marathon Race

The Marathon is a very hard long-distance race of 26 miles 385 yards (42.19 km). It has been run in the OLYMPIC GAMES since 1896. It was named after a Greek soldier's run from the town of Marathon to Athens in 490 B.C. to bring news of a Greek victory over the Persians. In 1908, there was a famous finish to the Olympic Marathon. At the end of the race, a small Italian, Dorando Pietri, staggered into the stadium in the lead. He collapsed twice in the last 100 yards and had to be helped over the finish line. He was disqualified, but everyone remembers it as Dorando's Marathon.

▲ *Pheidippides was the soldier who ran with the news of Greek victory after the battle of Marathon.*

The official distance for the marathon is 26 miles 385 yards. The reason for this strange distance is that the British Olympic committee decided in 1908 to start the race from the royal castle at Windsor and finish in front of the royal box in the stadium in London. This was measured at 26 miles 385 yards, a distance that has remained standard ever since.

Marble

Marble is a rock that is formed when limestone is squeezed and made very hot inside the Earth. Pure marble is white, but most of the rock has other substances in it which give it different colors. If a piece of marble is broken, the broken faces sparkle like fine sugar. (The word marble means "sparkling.") Marble has long been used for making statues, as

▲ *Marble cut from a quarry (right) can be used to make beautiful patterns in a floor (left). The many different colors of marble are caused by impurities present when the rock was formed.*

well as for building. It is easy to shape and takes a high polish. The most famous marble for sculpture comes from quarries at Carrara in Italy. It is very white and has a very fine grain.

Marconi, Guglielmo

Guglielmo Marconi (1874–1937) was the man who, most people say, invented RADIO. His parents were rich Italians. When he was only 20, he managed to make an electric bell ring in one corner of a room, set off by radio waves sent out from the other corner. Soon he was sending radio signals over longer and longer distances. In 1901, he sent the first message across the Atlantic. In 1924, he sent signals across the world to Australia.

Marconi shared the Nobel Prize for physics in 1909 and was honored throughout the world.

▲ *Marconi left Italy to continue his experiments in England because he did not get enough encouragement from the Italian government.*

Marco Polo *See* Polo, Marco

Margarine

This is a food like butter. It is made from vegetable FATS and OILS. VITAMINS are usually added to make it nearly as nourishing as butter. Margarine was invented in 1867 by a French chemist called Mège-Mouries. He won a prize offered by the French government for finding a cheap substitute for butter. Many people now eat margarine and similar spreads because they are low in unhealthy fats.

Marie Antoinette

Marie Antoinette (1755–1793) was the Austrian-born wife of LOUIS XVI of France. A beautiful and vivacious young woman, she found her husband dull and boring, and hated her duties as queen. Instead, she spent money lavishly and cared little for the world outside the royal palace at Versailles. She became a symbol to the poor people of France of all they hated about the royal court. When the FRENCH REVOLUTION broke out in 1789, the king and queen were taken to Paris by force. They were executed on the guillotine in 1793.

▲ *Through her unthinkingly lavish spending, Marie Antoinette made the poor people of France hate her. She showed great courage at her trial, but was condemned to death and executed in October, 1793.*

Mars (God)

Mars was one of the oldest and most important of the Roman gods. He was the son of Jupiter and Juno and became the god of war. His son, Romulus, was supposed to have been the founder of ROME. The temples and festivals of Mars were important to the Romans. The month of March was named after him. It was the first month in the Roman year.

Mars (Planet)

The planet Mars is only about half the size of the Earth. It takes about two years to travel around the Sun. The surface of Mars has huge volcanoes and great gorges, far bigger than those on Earth. Most of Mars is covered with loose rocks, scattered over a dusty red surface. This is why Mars is called the "Red Planet." It has a North Pole and a South Pole, both covered with snow or frost.

Seen through a telescope, the red surface of Mars is crisscrossed by thin gray lines. Some early astronomers thought that these lines were canals which had been dug by intelligent beings. They said these canals had been dug to irrigate the soil, since Mars has very little water. But space probes to Mars in 1965, 1969, and 1976 found no trace of the canals.

MARS FACTS

Average distance from Sun: 142 million miles (228 million km)
Nearest distance from Earth: 48,700,000 miles (78 million km)
Temperature on sunlit side: 32°F (0°C)
Temperature on dark side: −274°F (−170°C)
Diameter across equator: 4,220 miles (6,794 km)
Atmosphere: Carbon dioxide
Number of moons: 2
Length of day: 24 hours 37 minutes
Length of year: 687 Earth days

Mars
Earth

► The dusty, red surface of Mars shows no trace of life. Viking space probes to the planet appear finally to have put an end to any ideas that there could be alien beings living there.

▼ The kangaroo, like other marsupials, gives birth to its young before they are fully formed: (1) Before the birth, the female cleans her pouch and the fur around it. When the joey, the baby kangaroo, is born, it crawls through the fur to the pouch (2). It attaches itself to one of the nipples (3) and stays in the pouch for about 190 days, until it is fully developed (4).

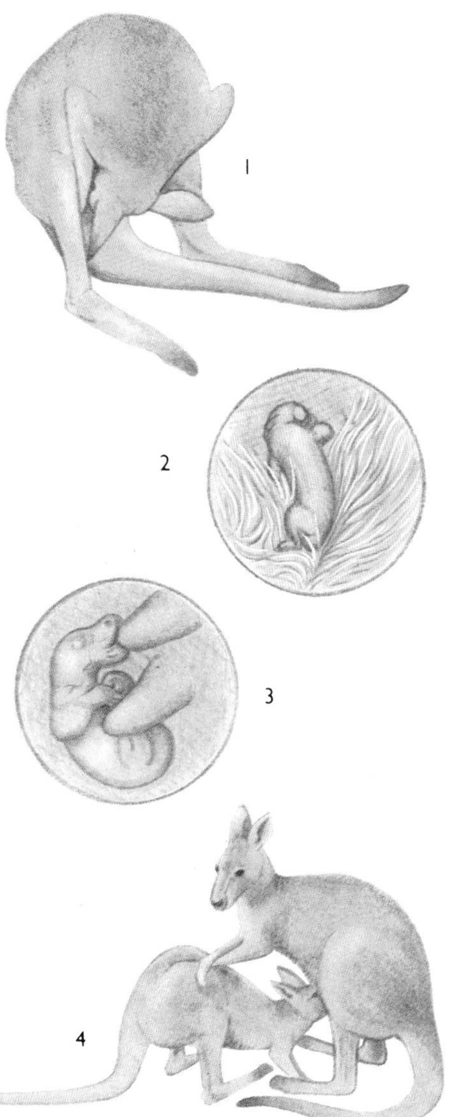

The American Viking spacecraft landed on Mars and took samples of the planet's soil, but it was unable to find any kind of life on Mars.

The planet has two tiny moons—Phobos and Deimos. Phobos, the larger of the two, is only about 15 miles (24 km) across.

Because Mars has a smaller mass than the Earth, things on its surface weigh only about 40 percent of what they would weigh on Earth. A day on Mars is about the same length as an Earth day.

Marsupial

Marsupials are MAMMALS with pouches—animals such as KANGAROOS, wallabies, bandicoots, koalas, and OPOSSUMS. They all live in Australia, except the American opossum. A newly born marsupial is very tiny. It crawls into its mother's pouch and stays there, feeding on her milk, until it can look after itself.

Martial Arts

The martial arts are various kinds of combat that come from the Orient. They include judo, karate, and aikido, all from Japan, and kung-fu, from China.

Judo, meaning "easy way," is probably the most

popular. It originally came from jujitsu, a violent practice that could maim or kill. Today, judo is a safe sport practiced by men, women, and children, which has been an Olympic sport since 1964. It is used in many parts of the world for self-defense. A trained student of judo can quickly unbalance an opponent and throw him or her to the ground.

In karate and kung-fu, the hands, elbows, and feet are used as weapons. Aikido, like judo, makes use of the opponent's strength to unbalance him. Kendo, another form of self-defense, is a kind of fencing using sticks instead of swords.

▲ *Although the martial arts were developed as methods of combat, they are now widely enjoyed as sport. Kendo, judo, and karate are all safe if practiced with proper supervision.*

Marx, Karl

Karl Marx (1818–1883) was a political thinker and writer whose ideas brought about great social and political changes. Marx was born in Germany, and his ideas were the starting point of COMMUNISM. He believed that people who own property, the capitalist class, keep those who work for them down so the owners can become richer. He also thought that the workers would one day rise against the capitalists and take control. Marx's ideas later inspired communist revolutions all over the world, notably the Russian Revolution.

◄ *Karl Marx (right), with Lenin (left) and Engels, heroes of communism. Between them, Marx and Engels developed the ideas that inspired Lenin to found the first communist state, in Russia.*

MARYLAND

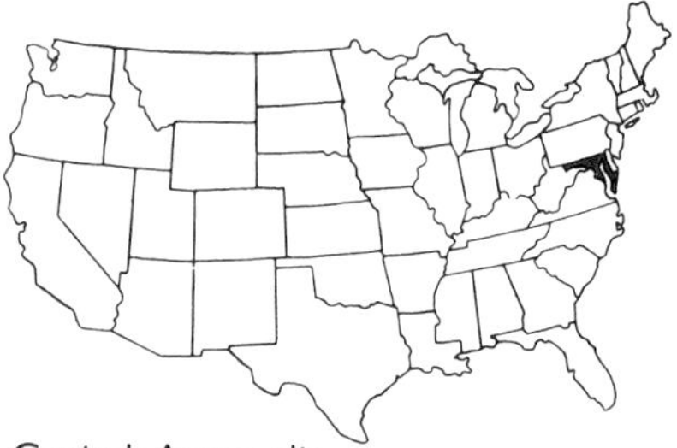

Capital: Annapolis
Population: 4,781,468
Area: 10,460 sq. mi. (27,092 sq. km)
State flower: Black-eyed Susan
State bird: Baltimore Oriole
State tree: White Oak
Statehood: April 28, 1788
7th state

▲ U.S.S. Constellation, *an early United States warship, is docked in the inner harbor area of Baltimore.*

▼ *Mary, Queen of Scots' determination to become Queen of England led to her execution.*

Maryland

The state of Maryland lies on and around Chesapeake Bay on the Atlantic coast of the United States. The east half of the state is called the Eastern Shore; the west half of the state is called the Western Shore. The sea has always been important to Maryland. Today, many people like to sail yachts on Chesapeake Bay, and the city of Annapolis is the home of the United States Naval Academy. Baltimore, the largest city, is one of the most important ports in the United States. Inland, more than 40 percent of the state is forest. The land is fertile, and there are many farms.

Mary, Queen of Scots

Mary, Queen of Scots (1542–1587) was the last Roman Catholic ruler of SCOTLAND. The daughter of James V of Scotland, she was educated in France, and did not return to Scotland until she was 19. By that time, she thought of herself as more French and Catholic than Scottish and Protestant.

Mary was the heir to the English throne after her Protestant cousin ELIZABETH I. In 1567, Mary was forced to give up the Scottish throne. Later, she was imprisoned for 20 years in England. People said she was plotting against Queen Elizabeth. She was executed on the queen's orders in 1587.

Massachusetts

Massachusetts is in New England. It is one of the most important and one of the most historic states. It is also one of the smallest. It was in Massachusetts, in 1620, that the Pilgrims arrived in the *Mayflower*. And it was in Massachusetts that many of the most important events in colonial America took place. Today, visitors from all over the world come to Massachusetts to see its colonial buildings and towns. Some of the most important events in the REVOLUTIONARY WAR happened in the state, including the first battles. Its capital city, BOSTON, is one of the oldest and richest in the country. It has many industries, as well as an important port. The people of Massachusetts opposed slavery before and during the CIVIL WAR.

MASSACHUSETTS

Capital: Boston
Population: 6,016,425
Area: 8,284 sq. mi. (21,456 sq. km)
State flower: Mayflower
State bird: Chickadee
State tree: Elm
Statehood: February 6, 1788
6th state

◀ *Cape Cod is a famous vacation area in Massachusetts. This is Provincetown, the town at the end of the peninsula.*

Mathematics

We all use mathematics every day. We add up the coins in our pockets to find out how much money we have. We look at a clock and figure out how much time we have left before going somewhere. In every business, people are constantly using some kind of mathematics; often, nowadays, with the help of calculators and computers. The branch of mathematics that deals with numbers is called arithmetic. ALGEBRA uses symbols such as *x* and *y* instead of numbers. GEOMETRY deals with lines, angles, and shapes such as triangles and squares.

Some numbers are magic! Take the quite ordinary-looking number 142857, for example. Try multiplying it by 2. You get 285714, the same digits in the same order, but moved along. Now try multiplying our magic number by 3, by 4, by 5, and by 6. (A calculator will make it easier.) See what happens! And there's more. Try dividing it by 2 and by 5.

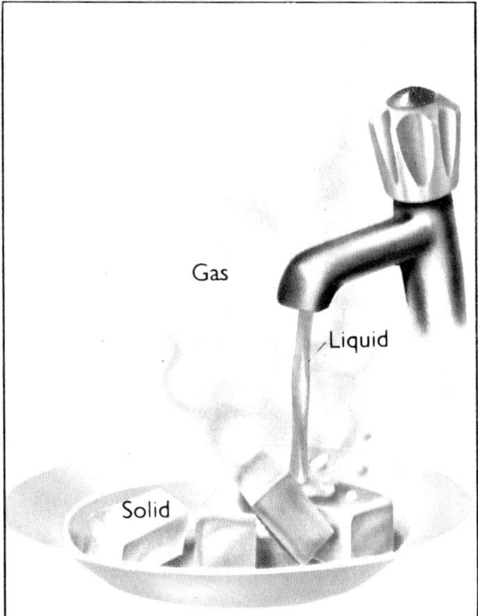

SEE IT YOURSELF

Every substance is either a solid, a liquid, or a gas at room temperature. But if the temperature changes, the substance can change its state. The picture shows the three states of water. Hot water in its normal liquid state is being poured onto ice cubes, which are water in its frozen, solid state. Rising above the melting ice is steam, which is water in its gaseous state.

Matter

Everything that you can see and touch has matter—and so do some things you can't. Matter is anything that has volume, or that takes up space. Scientists say that matter always has "mass." This seems like the same as weight, but it isn't. If you go to the Moon, your weight changes because there is less gravity. But your mass remains the same.

Matter comes in three main forms: solids, LIQUIDS, and GASES. These are the three "states" of matter. For example, iron is a solid, water is a liquid, and air is a gas. But most matter can exist in all three states, though not at the same time.

If you heat iron, it melts and becomes a liquid. This is how many manufacturing processes work. They turn raw materials such as iron into other goods by heating them. And if you heat iron even more, you can turn it into a gas. In the Sun, the hottest object in our solar system, many of our solids exist as gases. In the same way, if you cool a gas such as air, you can make it a liquid. And then if you cool a liquid, you can make it into a solid. Very cold water, for example, turns into ice.

All matter is made of tiny particles called ATOMS.

MAURITANIA

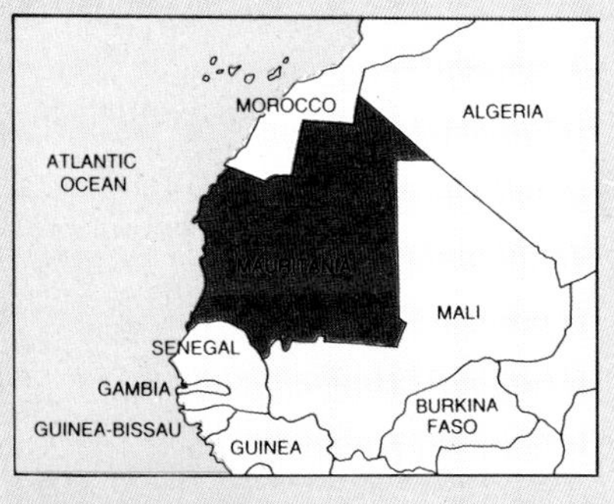

Government: Military republic
Capital: Nouakchott
Area: 397,954 sq. miles (1,030,700 sq. km)
Population: 2,025,000
Languages: French and Arabic
Currency: Ouguiya

Mauritania

Mauritania is an Islamic republic on the west coast of Africa. It is a very large country, but much of it is desert, where nomads keep cattle, sheep, and goats. The valley of the Senegal River and the southern coastal areas are the only fertile regions.

Mauritania became a French protectorate in 1903 and became independent in 1960. There is often a threat of famine.

Mauritius

Mauritius is a country on a small island in the Indian Ocean. Most of the island is surrounded by coral reefs. The island is thought to be the peak of an ancient volcano. Mauritius is one of the most densely populated places in the world. There are about

◀ *A view of the Rempart Mountains on the island of Mauritius, which has many volcanic hills.*

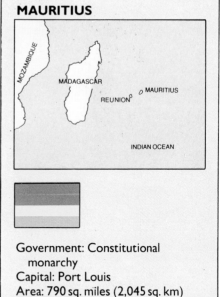

1,000 people for every square mile of the island. The chief crops are sugarcane and tea. Tourism is a growing industry.

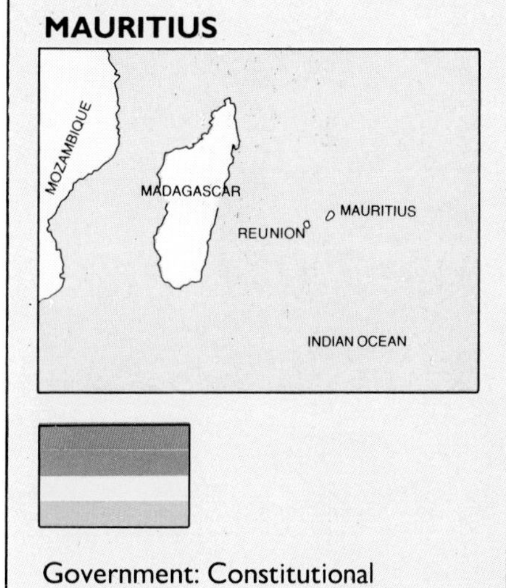

Government: Constitutional monarchy
Capital: Port Louis
Area: 790 sq. miles (2,045 sq. km)
Population: 1,075,000
Languages: English and French
Currency: Rupee

Maya

The Maya Indians first lived in Central America in the A.D. 400s. They grew corn and sweet potatoes and kept pet dogs. Later, they built cities of stone, with richly decorated palaces, temples, pyramids, and observatories. Even today, many of these wonderful buildings are still standing, hidden in the jungle. The Maya were also skilled in astronomy and mathematics, and they had an advanced kind of writing.

The Maya people did not have any metals until very late in their history. They built with only stone

▼ *A Mayan carving in serpentine, a kind of rock, showing the god Tlaloc.*

◀ *Mayan temples are huge and imposing buildings, showing skill in architecture and engineering.*

tools, and had no knowledge of the wheel. They worshiped a sun god, rain gods, soil gods, and a moon goddess who looked after women.

Measure *See* Weights and Measures

Mecca

Mecca is a city in SAUDI ARABIA. It is the holiest city in the Muslim world. All Muslims face Mecca when they pray, and all Muslims should make a pilgrimage to Mecca once. During the time of the pilgrimage more than a million Muslims pour into Mecca. Mecca is holy because the founder of the Muslim religion, the Prophet MUHAMMAD, was born there. The holiest site in Mecca is the Great Mosque. It contains the Kaaba, or "Black Stone." Muslims believe it was given to Muhammad by the Archangel Gabriel.

▲ *An old painting showing Abdul-Muttalib, Muhammad's grandfather, opening the Kaaba door.*

Medicine

When we first think of the word "medicine," perhaps we think about all the tablets, powders, pills, and liquids people take when they are not feeling well. But medicine also means the science of healing. It has taken a long time for medicine to become truly scientific.

In the early days, doctors relied on magic cures, prayers, and charms. But in the last few hundred years, medicine has advanced faster than in all of human history. The development of anesthetics in the last century was a vital step forward in progress in surgery. And in this century, progress has been fastest of all. Scientists have found out about VITAMINS; they have made all kinds of wonder drugs like penicillin; they have almost wiped out DISEASES such as tuberculosis and smallpox; they are finding out more and more about mental illness; and they can now give people spare parts for many parts of their bodies when these organs go wrong. But perhaps the most important area of a doctor's job is still *diagnosis*, finding out what is wrong with a patient by studying the symptoms.

ADVANCES IN MEDICINE

- 1590 **Microscope**—Zacharias Janssen
- 1593 **Thermometer**—Galileo
- 1628 **Blood circulation**—William Harvey
- 1796 **Vaccination**—Edward Jenner
- 1846 **Anesthetic**—William Morton
- 1865 **Antiseptic surgery**—Joseph Lister
- 1865 **Germs cause disease**—Louis Pasteur
- 1895 **X rays**—William Roentgen
- 1898 **Radium**—Pierre and Marie Curie
- 1922 **Insulin for diabetes**—Frederick Banting and Charles Best
- 1928 **Penicillin**—Alexander Fleming
- 1954 **Polio vaccine**—Jonas Salk
- 1967 **Heart transplant**—Christiaan Barnard

Mediterranean Sea

The Mediterranean is a large sea surrounded by three continents—Africa, Europe, and Asia. It flows out into the Atlantic Ocean through the narrow Strait of Gibraltar. It is also joined to the Black Sea by a narrow strait, or passage.

In ancient times, the Mediterranean was more important than it is now. In fact, it was the center of the Western world for a long time. The Phoenicians were a seafaring people who traveled around the Mediterranean from about 2500 B.C. Then the Greeks and Romans sailed the sea. The Romans were in control of the whole Mediterranean for nearly 500 years. They even called it *Mare Nostrum*, Latin for "our sea."

The SUEZ CANAL was opened in 1869. It cuts across Egypt, joining the Mediterranean to the RED SEA. The canal was very useful because it shortened the distance by sea between Europe and the East. It is still used by cargo ships.

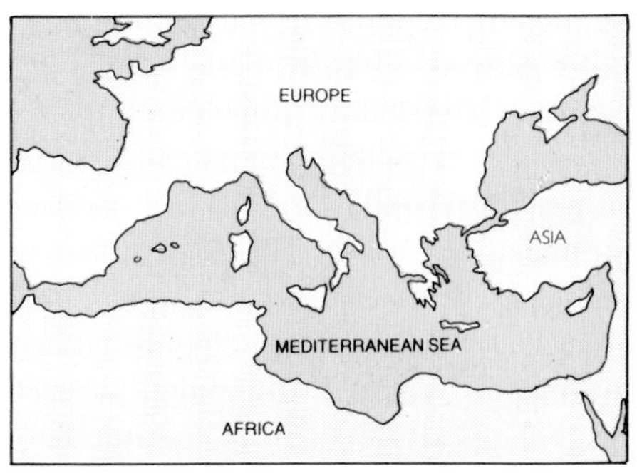

▼ *A 16th-century map of the port of Genoa, in Italy. The Mediterranean has long been of vital importance to trade and commerce, and thriving towns grew up around its natural ports.*

Melville, Herman

Herman Melville (1819–1891) was the most important American writer of the 1800s. His most famous book is called *Moby Dick*. It tells of a whaling captain and his search for a great white whale. Though Melville was already famous when he wrote *Moby Dick*, few people liked it at the time. Most people preferred Melville's earlier books. They described his life as a sailor.

▲ *Mendel's important findings were not believed at first. It was some years before his laws were generally accepted.*

Mendel, Gregor

Gregor Mendel (1822–1884) was an Austrian priest who became famous for his work on heredity. Heredity is the passing down of things such as eye color, skin color, and mental ability from parents to their children.

Mendel grew up on a farm, where he became interested in plants. When he entered a monastery, he began growing peas. He noticed that when he planted the seeds of tall pea plants, only tall peas grew. Then he tried crossing tall peas with short peas by taking pollen from one and putting it in the other. He found that again he had only tall plants. But when he crossed these new mixed tall plants with each other, three-fourths of the new plants were tall and one quarter were short. Mendel had found out that things like tallness are controlled by a pair of "factors" passed on from each parent. We now call these factors *genes*. Mendel also showed that some genes are stronger than others.

▼ *The god Mercury was supposed to look after writers, athletes, merchants, travelers, and thieves and vagabonds. In addition to being the messenger of the gods, he was a bringer of good luck and a protector of flocks and shepherds.*

Mercury (God)

Mercury was a Roman god who was the same as the Greek god Hermes. He was the messenger of the gods and is usually shown as a young man with winged sandals and wearing a winged hat.

Mercury (Metal)

Mercury, or quicksilver, is the only metal that is a liquid at ordinary temperatures. When mercury is poured onto a table, it forms little bead-like drops.

Most metals dissolve in mercury to make *amalgams*, used as fillings for teeth. Mercury is also used in THERMOMETERS and BAROMETERS.

Mercury (Planet) 

The planet Mercury is one of the smallest planets in the SOLAR SYSTEM. It is also the closest to the Sun. A day on Mercury lasts for 59 of our days. During the long daylight hours, it is so hot that lead would melt. During the long night, it grows unbelievably cold. Little was known about Mercury's surface until the space probe Mariner 10 passed within 500 miles (800 km) of the planet. It showed Mercury to have a thin atmosphere and big craters.

Mercury travels very fast through space—at between 23 and 35 miles (37 and 56 km) per second. This great speed and its nearness to the Sun give it the shortest year of all the planets (a year is the time it takes a planet to go once around the Sun). Mercury's year lasts only 88 of our Earth days.

▲ *Drops of mercury look like little round beads. This is because of the attraction between mercury's molecules.*

MERCURY FACTS

Average distance from Sun: 36 million miles (58 million km)
Nearest distance from Earth: 28 million miles (45 million km)
Temperature on sunlit side: 662°F (350°C)
Temperature on dark side: −275°F (−170°C)
Diameter: 3,030 miles (4,878 km)
Atmosphere: Almost none
Number of moons: 0
Length of day: 59 Earth days
Length of year: 88 Earth days

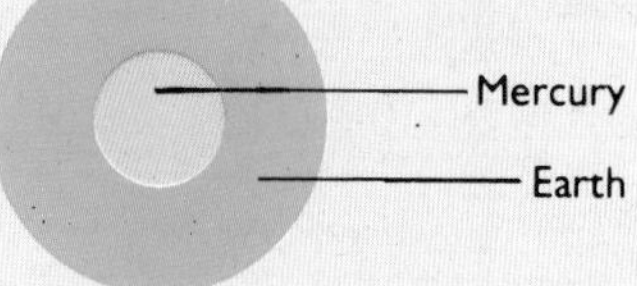

◀ *The Mariner 10 space probe passed Mercury three times in 1974 and 1975. It discovered that Mercury has a huge iron core, probably about three-fourths of the size of the planet.*

▲ *In legends, mermaids often lured ships onto the rocks. Seeing a mermaid was a sign of disaster to come.*

Mermaid

Mermaids are creatures of legend. There are many old stories about mermaids. They have long hair and the head and body of a woman. Their lower half is a long, scaly fish tail. They live in the sea.

In stories, mermaids sat on rocks on shores. They often sang sweetly. Sailors passing by in ships heard their lovely songs. They tried to follow the mermaids and wrecked their ships on the rocks.

Metal

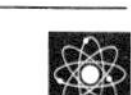

There are more than a hundred ELEMENTS on the Earth. About two-thirds of them are metals. The most important metals are IRON (for making steel), COPPER, and ALUMINUM.

People have used metals since early times. Copper, TIN, and iron were the first metals to be used. They were made into tools and weapons. GOLD and SILVER were also known very early. They are often made into jewelry.

Most metals are shiny. They all let heat and electricity pass through them. Copper and silver are the best for this. Nearly all metals are solid unless they are heated.

▼ *This map shows known metal deposits throughout the world, but there may be many more deposits waiting to be discovered.*

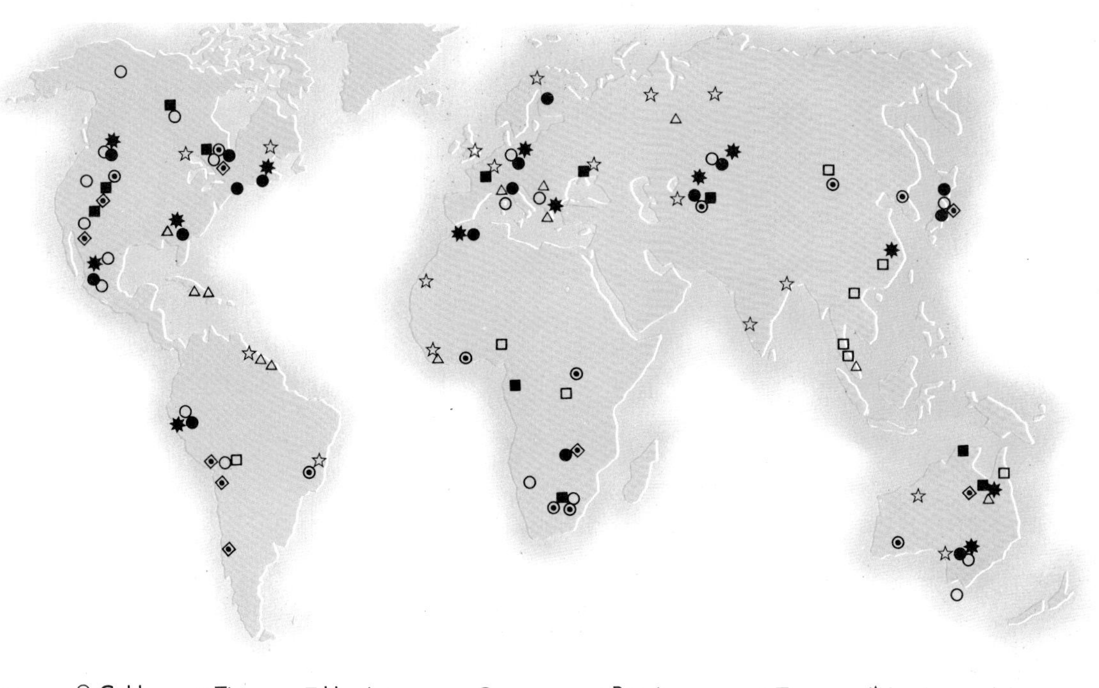

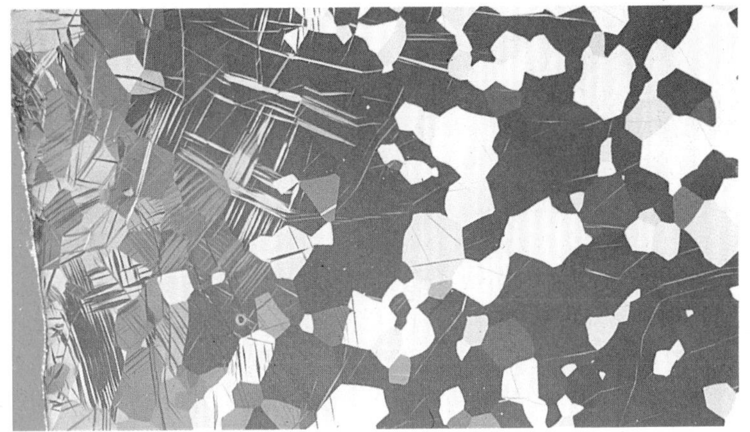

▲ *Metals in the form of ore, such as this lump of iron, are quite unrecognizable except to an expert. The photo of polished titanium (left) was taken through a very powerful microscope.*

Some metals are soft. They are easy to beat into shapes, and they can be pulled into thin wires. Other metals are *brittle*. This means they break easily. Some metals are very hard. It is difficult to work with them.

Metals can be mixed together to form ALLOYS. Alloys are different from their parent metals. Tin and copper are both soft. When mixed together, they form bronze. Bronze is a strong alloy. It is hard enough to make swords and spears.

Metals are found in the ground. Some are found pure. They are not mixed with other things. Many metals are mixed up with other elements in MINERALS. The minerals must be treated to get the pure metal out.

Metals vary so much that it is difficult to say exactly what a metal is. The metal lithium is so light it floats on water—it is only half the weight of the same volume of water. Osmium is 22 times as heavy as water—twice as heavy as lead. Pure gold is so soft that less than an ounce (20 grams) of it can be drawn out into a wire 31 miles (50 km) long.

Meteor

A meteor is a tiny piece of metal or stone. It travels through space at great speed. Millions of meteors fall toward the Earth every day. Most of them burn up before they reach the ground. On clear nights, you can sometimes see shooting stars. They are meteors burning up. When a large meteor reaches the ground it is called a meteorite. Meteorites sometimes make large holes called craters.

▼ *As a meteor enters the Earth's atmosphere, friction heats it and makes it glow.*

Metric System

The metric system is used for measuring weight, length, and volume. It is based on units of ten, or decimals. It was first used in France in the late 1700s. Now it is used in many parts of the world.

MEXICO

Government: Federal republic
Capital: Mexico City
Area: 761,604 sq. miles (1,972,554 sq. km)
Population: 86,154,000
Language: Spanish
Currency: Peso

Mexico 

Mexico is a country that borders the United States in the north and Central America in the south. Mexico is a tropical country with a wide range of climates. It has desert, fertile highlands, mountains, and the jungle-covered Yucatan Peninsula.

The first people in Mexico were Indians, such as the MAYAS and AZTECS. The Spanish conquered the Aztecs in 1521. Mexico won independence from Spain in 1821. From 1846–1848, the U.S. and Mexico fought a war over territory, and Mexico lost a large part of what is now the western United States.

Mexico has valuable oil, but many of the people live in poverty. Inflation and the drop in world oil prices caused economic problems in the 1980s.

▶ *Many Mexicans are Roman Catholics and they celebrate their religious festivals with processions and street parties.*

Michelangelo 

Michelangelo Buonarroti (1475–1564) was a painter and sculptor. He lived in Italy at the time of the RENAISSANCE. Michelangelo is famous for the wonderful statues and paintings he made of people. He spent four and a half years painting pictures in the Sistine Chapel in the VATICAN CITY. Many of his statues are large and very lifelike. His statue of David is 13 ft. (4 m) high. Michelangelo was the chief architect of St. Peter's Cathedral in Rome.

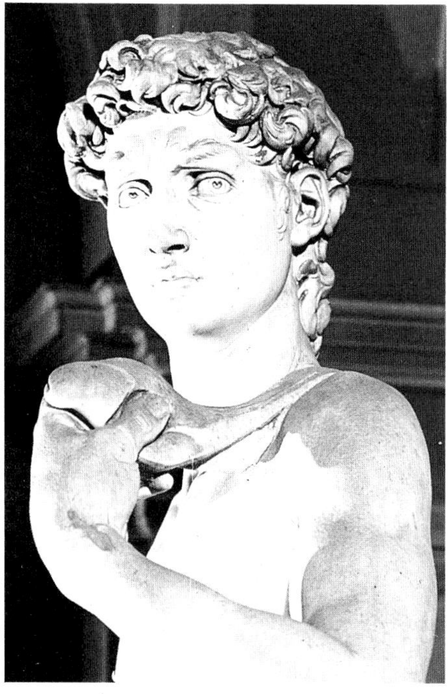

▲ *Michelangelo's statue of David is now housed indoors for protection at the Academy of Fine Arts in Florence.*

Michigan

Michigan has more shoreline than any other state except Alaska, and it isn't even on the sea. Michigan lies on the GREAT LAKES, between Canada and the United States. It has two separate areas, the Upper Peninsula and the Lower Peninsula. They are connected by the five-mile (eight-km) long Mackinac Bridge.

Michigan is most famous for making automobiles. Detroit, the largest city, is the most important automobile-manufacturing city in the country. But Michigan is also an important agricultural state. Many kinds of fruit are grown in the southern part of the state. Tourism is important, too. The forests, lakes, and rivers of Michigan draw visitors from all over the United States.

MICHIGAN

Capital: Lansing
Population: 9,295,297
Area: 58,527 sq. mi. (151,586 sq. km)
State flower: Apple Blossom
State bird: Robin
State tree: White Pine
Statehood: January 26, 1837
26th state

▲ *Renaissance Center in downtown Detroit, Michigan.*

Microphone

A microphone picks up SOUND waves and turns them into electric signals. The signals can be made into a RECORDING or sent out as RADIO waves. They can also be fed through an amplifier and loudspeakers. These make the sound louder. The mouthpiece of a TELEPHONE has a microphone in it that turns your voice into electric signals.

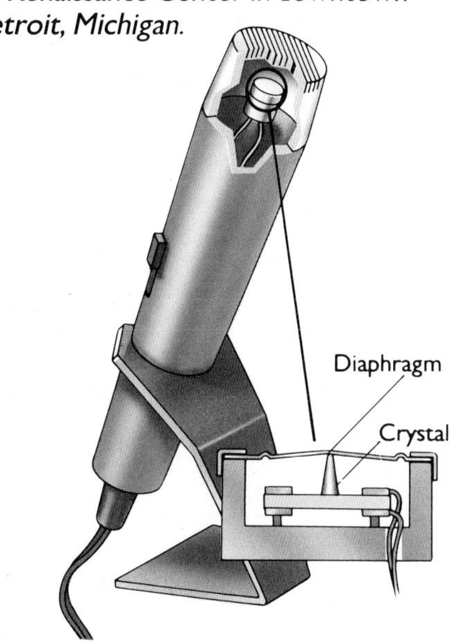

▲ *In this microphone, sound waves hit the flexible diaphragm and make it vibrate. These vibrations are picked up by a crystal and turned into electric signals.*

Microscope

A microscope is an instrument used for looking at tiny objects. It *magnifies* things, or makes them look bigger. Things that are invisible to the naked eye are called *microscopic*. Many microscopic plants and animals, including BACTERIA, can be seen if you look at them through a microscope.

Microscopes work by using LENSES. The simplest microscope is a magnifying glass. It has only one lens. The lenses in many microscopes work by bending light rays. Small microscopes can magnify 100 times. Big microscopes used by scientists may magnify up to 1,600 times. The electron microscope is very powerful. It can magnify up to 2,000,000 times. Instead of bending light rays, it bends beams of electrons. Electrons are parts of ATOMS.

▶ *This electron microscope image shows a dust mite, flakes of skin, soil particles, cat fur, and fibers, all taken from a vacuum cleaner.*

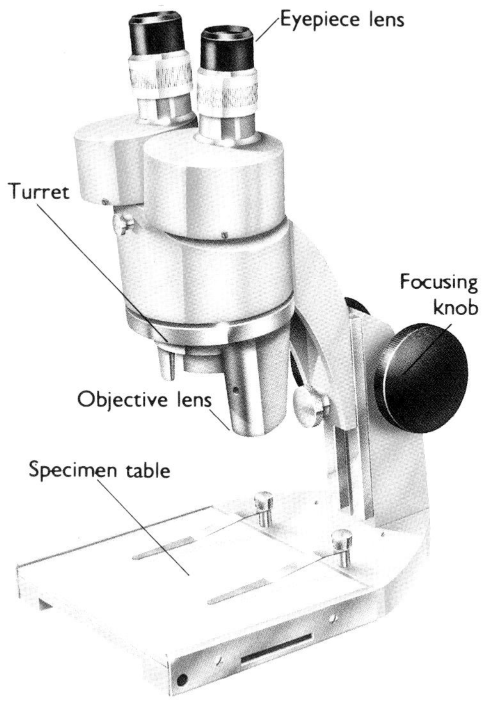

▲ *In an optical microscope, a group of lenses named the objective, focuses the light from the specimen to produce a much-enlarged image. The eyepiece lens magnifies the object still further.*

Anton van Leeuwenhoek, a Dutchman who lived in the 1600s, made one of the first microscopes. Using his microscope, he showed that fleas hatch from tiny eggs. Before this, people thought fleas came from sand or mud. They could not see the eggs.

Middle Ages

The Middle Ages was a period of history in Europe which lasted for a thousand years. The Middle Ages began when the ROMAN EMPIRE collapsed in the 400s. They ended when the RENAISSANCE began in the 1400s. (See pages 442–443.)

Migration

Many animals make long journeys to breed or find food. Most make the journey every year. Some make the journey only twice in their life. These journeys are called migrations. Animals migrate by INSTINCT. They do not have to plan their journey.

Birds are the greatest migrants. Swallows leave Europe and North America every fall. They fly south to spend the winter in Africa or South America. These places are warm and the swallows find food there. The trip may be 6,250 miles (10,000 km) long. In spring, they fly north again to breed. Birds are not the only animals that make long trips.

▲ *Monarch butterflies migrate from Canada and the U.S. to Mexico in huge numbers each year.*

◀ *Each year, the short-tailed shearwater travels from Tasmania and Australia toward the Pacific. Following the wind, the bird flies all the way to Arctic regions via the Asian coast before returning along the North American coast to its breeding ground. It is a round trip of 20,000 miles (32,000 km) and takes the bird seven months.*

Butterflies, fish, and mammals migrate, too. Whales and fish make long journeys through the sea to find food and breed. The EELS of Europe's lakes and rivers swim thousands of miles across the Atlantic Ocean to breed. After breeding, they die. The young eels take years to swim back to Europe. Monarch butterflies of North America fly south in great numbers for the winter.

Milk

Milk is a food that all baby MAMMALS live on. It comes from the breasts, or mammaries, of the baby's mother. The baby sucks the milk from its mother's nipple or teat.

At first, the milk is pale and watery. It protects the baby from diseases and infections. Later, the milk is much richer and creamier. It contains all the food the baby needs. Milk is full of FAT, SUGAR, STARCHES, PROTEIN, VITAMINS, and MINERALS. After a while, the baby starts to eat other kinds of food.

People use milk from many animals. These include cows, sheep, goats, camels, and even reindeer. The animals are kept in herds. Sometimes

Continued on page 444

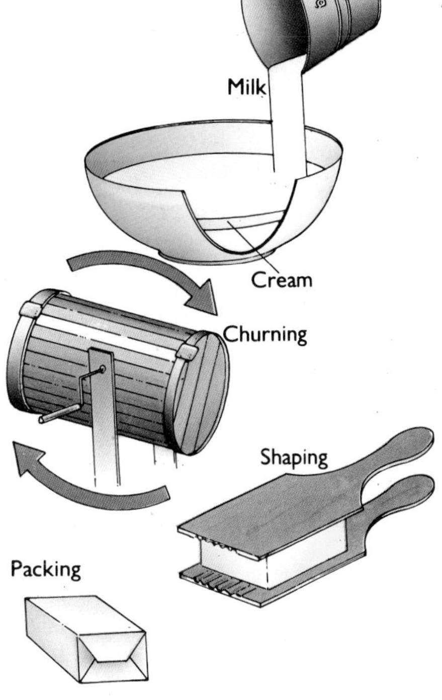

▲ *Traditional methods of making butter involved skimming the cream from milk and "churning" it by agitating it in a butter churn. This made the fat particles come together to form a thick yellow solid. It was patted into shape with wooden paddles, then wrapped and sold.*

MIDDLE AGES

The Middle Ages in Europe began with the collapse of the Roman Empire in the A.D. 400s and lasted for about 1,000 years. The "Roman peace" ended, and much of Europe suffered wars and invasions. The learning of ancient times was almost forgotten, surviving only in the monasteries. Kings and nobles struggled for power, while the mass of the people dwelt in poverty.

However, the Middle Ages also gave much to later generations. Great cathedrals were built. Universities were started. Painting and literature developed. With the 1400s came a rebirth of learning, the Renaissance, and the voyages of discovery to new lands. The Middle Ages were over.

THE CRUSADES

The Crusades were a series of wars between the Christian armies of Europe and the Muslims, who had conquered the Holy Land of Palestine. The First Crusade was in 1096, and there were six Crusades in all. The Crusaders captured Jerusalem in 1099, but lost it again in 1187. They were finally defeated by the Muslims in 1303.

Many knights went to the Holy Land, some seeking honor and glory, others riches and lands. Many died before they ever reached Palestine. An important result of these wars was that Europeans learned about Eastern medicine and science, and new trade routes were opened to Asia.

THE MONK

Monks lived in religious communities, or monasteries. They copied books by hand and spent much time in prayer. They also tended their farms, gardens, and fishponds.

THE KNIGHT

A knight was trained for war. He wore armor and rode a horse. Knights practiced fighting at mock battles called jousts. They were supposed to obey a code of knightly honor, known as chivalry.

THE PEASANT

Peasants worked on the land and lived in rough huts, which they often shared with their animals. They slept on straw mattresses on the floor. They tilled the fields with plows pulled by oxen.

IMPORTANT EVENTS OF THE MIDDLE AGES

476 Fall of Roman Empire
570 Birth of Muhammad, prophet of the Muslim religion, followed by Muslim conquests
732 Charles Martel defeats Muslims and prevents them from conquering Europe
800 Charlemagne is crowned first Holy Roman Emperor
896 Alfred, King of England, defeats Danish invaders
988 Christianity reaches Russia
1066 William of Normandy conquers England
1096 First Crusade to the Holy Land
1206 Genghis Khan founds Mongol Empire
1337 Start of Hundred Years' War between France and England
1347–51 Black Death (plague) in Europe

DID YOU KNOW...?

* In the Middle Ages, Latin was the language used by scholars throughout Europe.
* People in Europe did not have potatoes or sugar to eat, or tea and coffee to drink.
* The Black Death was spread by rats and killed 25 million people throughout Europe.

◀ *In the feudal system, society was organized in a sort of pyramid, with the clergy and nobles at the top and a great many peasants at the bottom. In the middle were the scientists, merchants, craftsmen, and yeoman farmers.*

THE SCIENTIST

Most medieval scientists practiced the mysteries of alchemy (trying to turn lead into gold). A few, such as Roger Bacon (1214–1294), studied the stars and realized that the Earth was round. Bacon also experimented with gunpowder.

THE MERCHANT

Merchants bought and sold goods such as furs and wool. Some became very wealthy and started the first banks. Merchants and craftsmen formed powerful associations called guilds. They sold their goods at fairs, at which people gathered to trade and have fun.

For more information turn to these articles : ALCHEMY; ARMOR; BACON, ROGER; CASTLE; CATHEDRAL; CHAUCER, GEOFFREY; HUNDRED YEARS' WAR; KNIGHT; MONASTERY.

► *Many different products can be made from milk by treating it in various ways.*

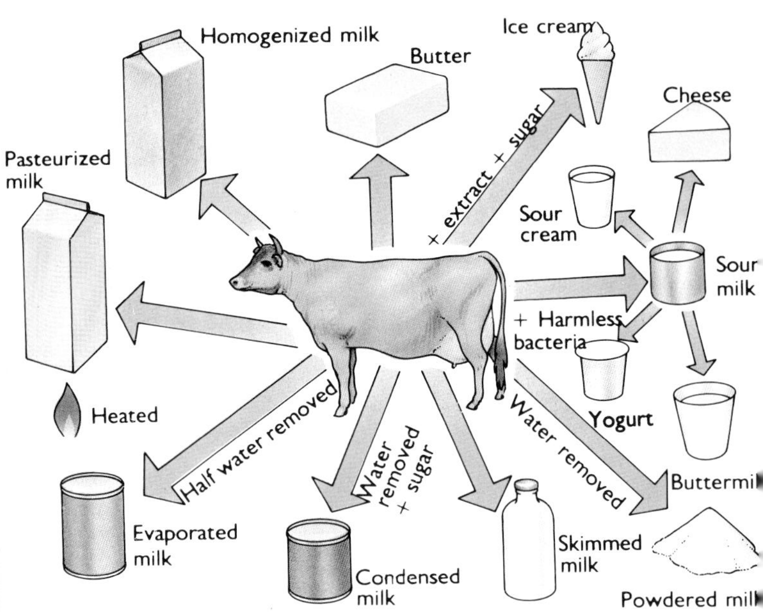

The average daily milk production per cow in the United States is about 4 gallons (16 liters). Each dairy cow needs about 50 pounds (23 kg) of food per day, and will take in about 15 gallons (57 liters) of water.

they live on farms. Reindeer do not live on farms, but wander about in the wild.

Milk is used to make many other foods. Cream, butter, yogurt, cheese, and some ice cream are all made from milk.

Milky Way

When you look at the sky on a clear, moonless night, you can see a pale cloud of light. It stretches across the heavens. If you look at it through binoculars or a telescope, you can see that the cloud is really millions of stars. All these stars, and most of the other stars we see, are part of our GALAXY. It is called the Milky Way.

Astronomers think that the Milky Way has about 100 billion million stars like our Sun. The Milky Way stretches over a distance of about 100,000 light-years. A light-year is the distance light travels in one year at a speed of 186,000 miles (300,000 km) a second. The distance between the stars in our part of the Milky Way averages about 5 light-years.

The Milky Way has a spiral shape. Its trailing arms turn slowly around the center. They take 200 million years to make a full circle. From Earth, we see the Milky Way through the arms of the spiral. The cloud of stars in the picture is what we might see from a great distance above the galaxy.

It is impossible to imagine the size of the Milky Way. It takes light from the Sun eight minutes to reach us. The Sun is 93,750,000 miles (150,000,000 km) away and light travels at a speed of 186,000 miles (300,000 km) per second. Light from the center of the Milky Way takes about 30,000 *years* to reach the Earth. From where we are in the solar system, it takes about 200 million years for the Earth to make just one trip around the Milky Way.

The Milky Way is not a special galaxy. There are thousands of other galaxies with the same shape. There may be millions and millions of other galaxies in the UNIVERSE.

▲ *The view above shows how the Milky Way might appear from a few hundred light-years above the galaxy.*

Mineral

The rocks of the Earth are made up of materials called minerals. There are many different kinds of mineral. Some, such as GOLD or platinum, are made up of only one ELEMENT. Others, such as QUARTZ and SALT, consist of two or more elements. Some minerals are metals, such as COPPER OR SILVER. Other minerals are non-metallic, like SULFUR.

Pure minerals are made up of ATOMS arranged in regular patterns, known as CRYSTALS. Minerals form crystals when they cool from hot GASES and LIQUIDS deep inside the Earth. Crystals can grow very large if they cool slowly. But large or small, crystals of the same mineral nearly always have the same shape.

Altogether, there are more than 2,000 minerals. Yet most of the Earth's rocks are made up of only 30 minerals. The most common mineral of all is quartz. Most grains of sand are quartz. Pure quartz is made up of large, well-shaped crystals and has a milky color. Mineralogists are scientists who study minerals. They look at crystals and try to understand their structure and origins.

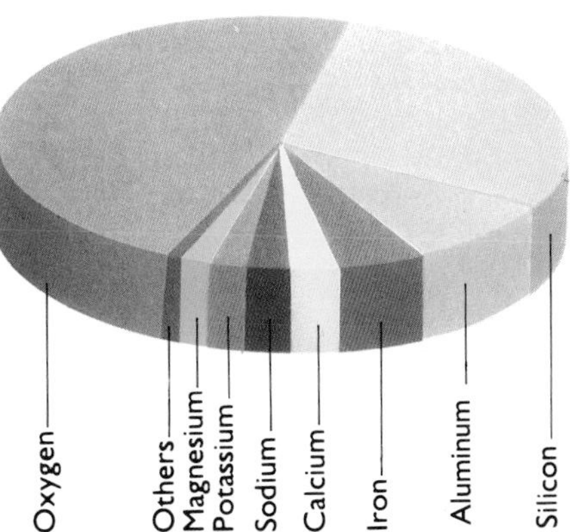

▲ *This chart shows the various elements, including minerals, found in the Earth's crust. They are shown in the proportions in which they occur.*

► *The Kennecott open-pit copper mine in Utah is the largest in the United States.*

The "Big Hole," at Kimberley, South Africa, is an old disused diamond mine that was dug in the last century by thousands of miners working with picks and shovels. They dug out more than 25 million tons of rock to make a hole 1,650 ft. (500 m) across and nearly 1,320 ft. (400 m) deep.

Mining

Mining means digging MINERALS out of the Earth. It is one of the world's most important industries. When minerals lie in one place in large quantities, they are known as ores. People mine minerals such as GOLD, SILVER, and TIN. They also mine COAL.

Mines can be open pits or underground tunnels. When the ore is close to the surface, the soil that lies on top of it is simply lifted away. Giant diggers then scoop up the rock that contains the minerals. Underground mines can be as deep as 2 miles (3 km) below the surface. Another form of mining is dredging. Here minerals are scooped up from the beds of rivers and lakes.

Minnesota

MINNESOTA

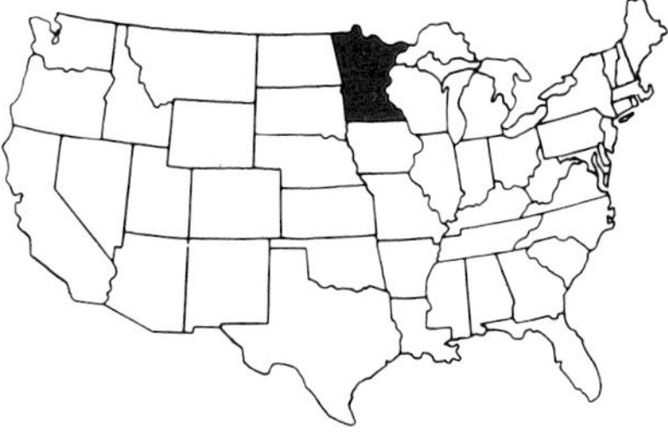

Capital: St. Paul
Population: 4,375,099
Area: 84,402 sq. mi. (218,601 sq. km)
State flower: Pink-and-white Lady's Slipper
State bird: Common Loon
State tree: Red Pine
Statehood: May 11, 1858
32nd state

Minnesota is a midwestern state that is known for agriculture and for industry. Its farms produce a wide range of products, including corn and soybeans. Cattle and hogs are also raised. Many of Minnesota's industries are based on farming and produce dairy products such as butter, milk, and cheese. But there are also important heavy industries. Because Minnesota has large deposits of iron ore, mining is important.

Minnesota is the largest midwestern state, and

contains huge areas of wilderness. Many are covered with forests. Campers, hunters, and fishermen are drawn by this dramatic scenery.

A large part of the state's population came from Germany and Scandinavia in the 1800s when Minnesota was settled.

▲ *Minneapolis is the largest city in Minnesota and a major midwestern center of finance and industry.*

◀ *This solar furnace in France uses a huge curved mirror to focus the Sun's rays and produce temperatures as high as 5,400°F (3,000°C).*

Mirror

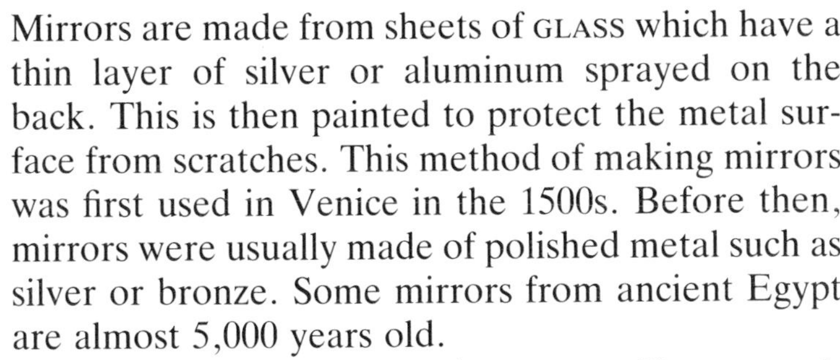

Mirrors are made from sheets of GLASS which have a thin layer of silver or aluminum sprayed on the back. This is then painted to protect the metal surface from scratches. This method of making mirrors was first used in Venice in the 1500s. Before then, mirrors were usually made of polished metal such as silver or bronze. Some mirrors from ancient Egypt are almost 5,000 years old.

LIGHT is reflected from (bounces off) a smooth surface. The reflection, called an image, is what we see when we look into a mirror, but the image is reversed. If you raise your left hand, the image raises its right hand.

A plane mirror has a flat surface. A convex mirror curves outward like the back of a spoon. It makes things look smaller. A concave mirror curves inward like a hollow bowl. It magnifies.

SEE IT YOURSELF

It is possible to see a reflection of a reflection. Lay a coin on a table. Take two mirrors and hold them next to each other with the edges touching as shown above. Now move the outer edges of the mirrors slowly forward, while keeping the inner edges together. How many coins can you see?

MISSISSIPPI

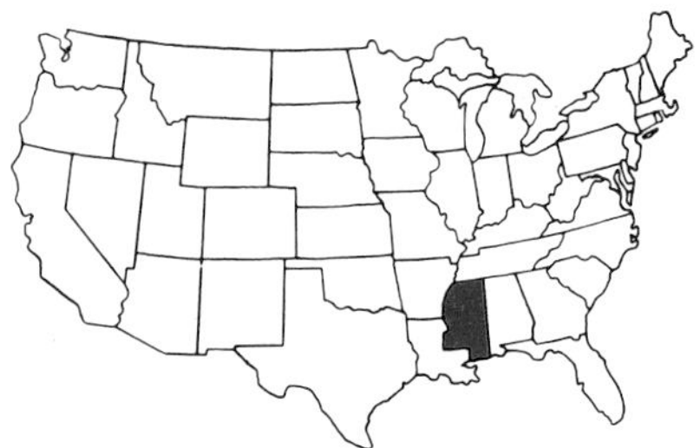

Capital: Jackson
Population: 2,573,216
Area: 47,689 sq. mi. (123,515 sq. km)
State flower: Magnolia
State bird: Mockingbird
State tree: Southern Magnolia
Statehood: December 10, 1817
20th state

Mississippi

Mississippi is a state in the Deep South. Its luxuriant magnolias and other flowers, its slow pace of life, and its handsome mansions give it a romantic quality that many visitors appreciate. There is a strong feeling in Mississippi of life in the South as it was before the CIVIL WAR. Its fertile soil and warm climate made Mississippi one of the most important cotton-growing states before the Civil War. It was one of the first Southern states to leave the Union. The Civil War destroyed Mississippi and made it one of the poorest states. Its reconstruction was slow and painful. Today, agriculture, fishing, tourism, and many forms of manufacturing have made Mississippi more prosperous.

▲ *Mississippi's stately homes are reminders of life in the old South. This one is in Natchez.*

Mississippi River

The Mississippi is the longest river in the United States and the country's most important inland waterway. It is 2,350 miles (3,780 km) long. It "rises" in MINNESOTA in the north and flows south to the Gulf of Mexico. Over 250 other rivers, or "tributaries," flow into it from as far away as the Appalachian Mountains in the east to the ROCKY MOUNTAINS in the west. Goods from many regions can be transported along the Mississippi. Because it is easier to travel along a river than overland, the Mississippi played an important role in the settling of the United States.

Missouri

Missouri is a Midwestern state at the heart of the nation. For many years in the 1800s it was the western frontier of the country. Both the Oregon Trail and the Sante Fe Trail began in Missouri. Many of the fiercest arguments over slavery raged in Missouri, which was then a slave state. After the Civil War, gangs of former Confederate soldiers roamed the country; among these outlaws was the famous Jesse James. Missouri today is a prosperous state. Much of its wealth comes from trade passing along the Mississippi and Missouri rivers. The north and

◀ *Gateway Arch, in St. Louis, Missouri, commemorates the city's part in the settlement of the West.*

west are rich agricultural lands, with large farms. Southern Missouri is empty and rugged. This region, which is in the Ozark Mountains, is a favorite vacation area.

MISSOURI

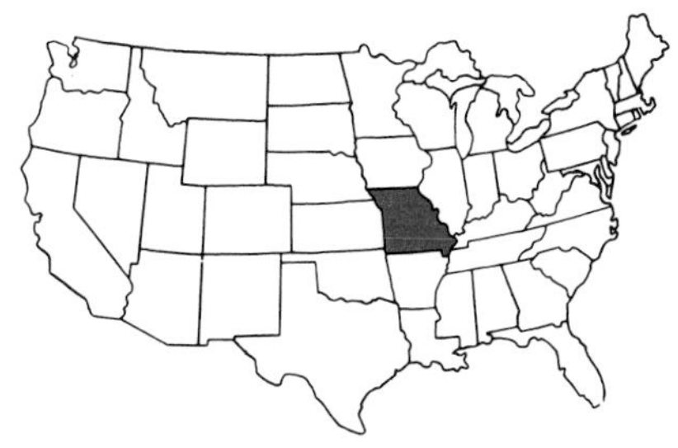

Capital: Jefferson City
Population: 5,117,073
Area: 69,697 sq. mi. (180,516 sq. km)
State flower: Dogwood
State bird: Bluebird
State tree: Hawthorn
Statehood: August 10, 1821
24th state

Mollusk

Mollusks are all members of one of the largest groups of animals in the world. There are over 70,000 different types of mollusks, making them the second-largest animal group. Only insects are more numerous. There are mollusks all over the world, from mountains to the oceans.

Most mollusks grow shells to protect themselves;

▼ *A great variety of mollusks are found in the sea, and some of them are good to eat.*

MONACO

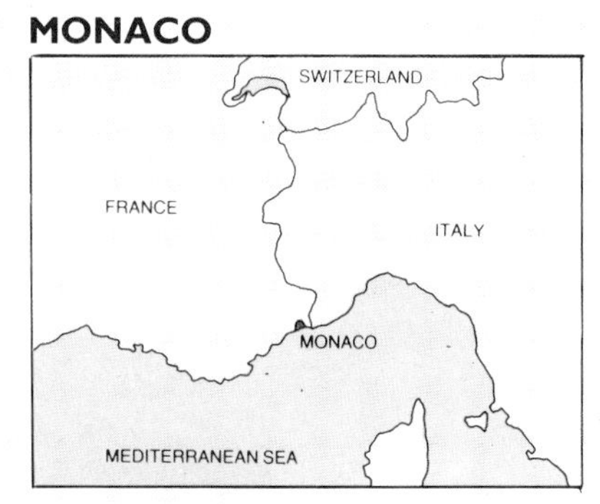

Government: Constitutional monarchy
Capital: Monaco-Ville
Area: 0.6 sq. miles (1.6 sq. km)
Population: 29,000
Language: French
Currency: French franc

The world's most famous monastery is that at Monte Cassino in central Italy. It was founded in A.D. 529 by St. Benedict, and it was there that he gathered around him the first group of Benedictine monks. The monastery has led a troubled life. It was stormed by the Lombards in 589, the Saracens in 884, and by the Normans in 1030. Each time it was rebuilt on the same site and became a great center of the arts and learning. During World War II, it was the scene of heavy fighting as the German army retreated before the Allied advance. Then, on February 15, 1944, the monastery was almost completely demolished by Allied bombers. Most of its valuable art collection was destroyed, but many treasured manuscripts were saved. The monastery has been rebuilt.

some have shells inside parts of their bodies; some have no shells at all. But all mollusks have soft bodies and no bones. And all mollusks have to stay moist to live.

Snails, slugs, oysters, octopuses, and squids are all mollusks. Some mollusks, such as snails, are only a few inches long; other mollusks, such as the giant squid, grow to be more than 40 feet (12 meters) long. Many mollusks, especially oysters and clams, are good to eat; others are poisonous.

Mollusks with shells grow them as they grow themselves. The shell is made of hard lime material that is formed from the food the mollusk eats. Shells have many beautiful patterns. Pearls, which are found in oysters, are a form of shell.

Monaco

The tiny country of Monaco lies on the French coast of the Mediterranean Sea. It has an area of less than a square mile. It is called a principality because it is ruled by a prince. Monaco's main industry is tourism. More than half of the people of Monaco are French.

Monaco has been ruled by the Grimaldi family since the 1200s.

Monastery

Monasteries are places where monks live in a community, or group. They lead a religious life and obey strict rules. Monasteries are especially important in the BUDDHIST and CHRISTIAN religions.

Christian monasteries began in Egypt around A.D. 300. Hermits were religious men who lived alone. A group of hermits came together and made rules for their way of life. Soon after, communities of monks began to grow up. The monks worked as farmers, laborers, and teachers, and helped the poor.

One of the most famous monks was St. Benedict. He founded the Benedictine order. Many groups of monks followed his rules for running a monastery. St. Benedict divided the day into periods of prayer, religious study, and work. The Benedictine order includes nuns.

THE DEVELOPMENT OF MONEY

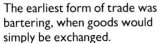

The earliest form of trade was bartering, when goods would simply be exchanged.

Money has been made in all shapes and sizes, but it must be easy to use and store.

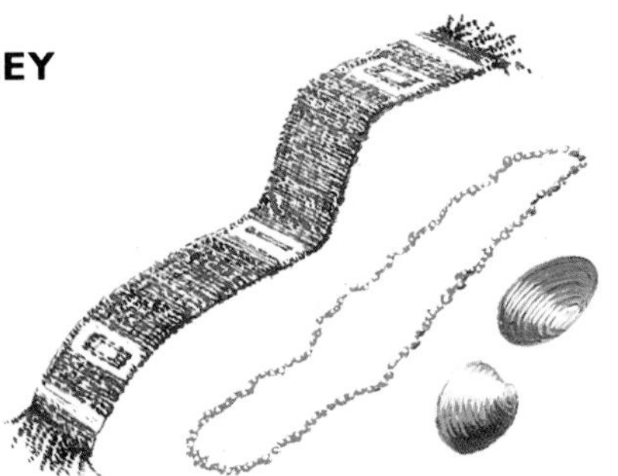

Native Americans used beads and shells, often made into decorative patterns, as money.

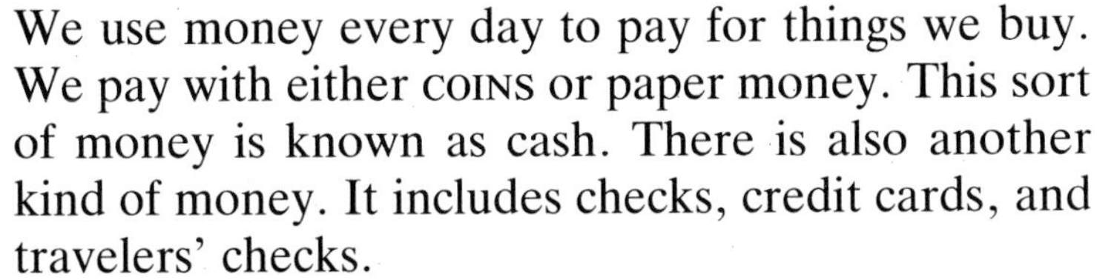

Money

We use money every day to pay for things we buy. We pay with either COINS or paper money. This sort of money is known as cash. There is also another kind of money. It includes checks, credit cards, and travelers' checks.

Almost anything can be used as money. In the past, people have used shells, beads, cocoa beans, salt, grain, and even cattle. But coins are much easier to use than, say, cattle. They are easy to store and to carry around.

Coins were first used in China. They were also used by ancient Greeks as early as 600 B.C. They were valuable because they were made of either gold or silver. They were stamped with the mark of the government or the ruler of the country for which they were made. The stamp also showed how much each coin was worth.

Later, people began to use coins made of cheaper metals. The metal itself had no value, but the coins were still worth the amount stamped on them. They also started to use paper money. It no longer mattered that the money itself had no real value. It was backed by the government and BANKS. This is the kind of money we use today.

Coins have remained popular for centuries. They are easy to produce and last a long time.

Bills, or bank notes, are a kind of promise, because they represent a sum of money.

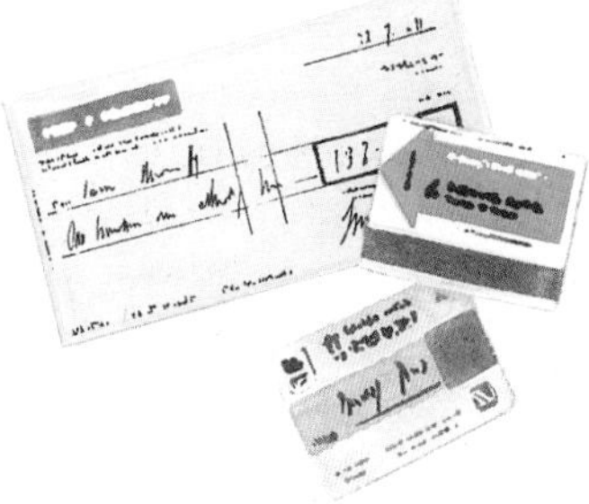

Credit cards and checks are useful because they can be used instead of cash.

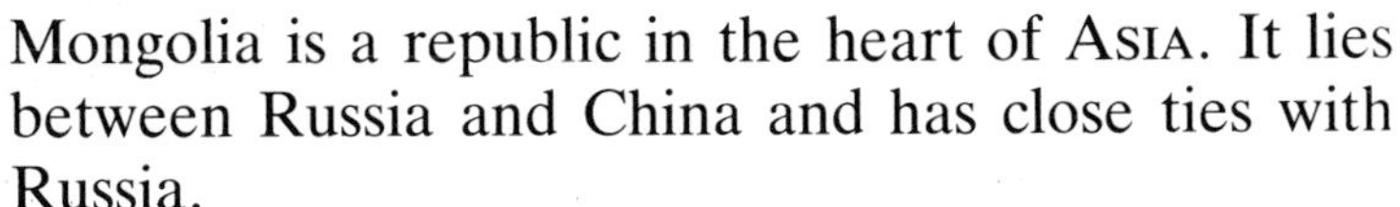

Mongolia

Mongolia is a republic in the heart of ASIA. It lies between Russia and China and has close ties with Russia.

MONGOLIA

Government: Socialist
Capital: Ulan Bator
Area: 604,247 sq. miles (1,565,000 sq. km)
Population: 2,000,000
Language: Mongolian
Currency: Tugrik

Mongolia is a high, flat country. It has mostly desert or rolling grassland, with mountain ranges in the west. The Gobi Desert covers a large part of the land.

The people of Mongolia are descended from the MONGOLS. Until recently a Communist state, Mongolia now has a socialist system.

Mongols

Mongols were nomads who lived on the great plains of central Asia. They herded huge flocks of sheep, goats, cattle, and horses, which they grazed on the vast grasslands of the region. They lived in tent villages that they could pack up quickly and take with them when they moved on to find new pastures.

The Mongols were superb horsemen and highly trained warriors. In the 1200s, they formed a mighty army under the great GENGHIS KHAN. Swift-riding hordes of Mongols swept through China, India, Persia, and as far west as Hungary.

Under Genghis Khan, and later his grandson, Kublai Khan, the Mongols conquered half the known world. But they were unable to hold their empire together. In less than a hundred years, the Mongol empire had been taken over by the Chinese.

▼ *Mongols were wanderers and expert horsemen. Their temporary shelters, known as* yurts, *were made of wood and hides.*

◀ *In a story by Rudyard Kipling, a mongoose called Rikki-Tikki-Tavi bravely kills a snake.*

Mongoose

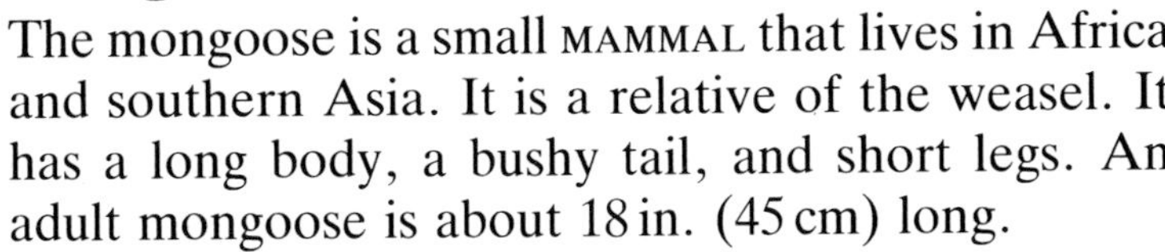

The mongoose is a small MAMMAL that lives in Africa and southern Asia. It is a relative of the weasel. It has a long body, a bushy tail, and short legs. An adult mongoose is about 18 in. (45 cm) long.

Mongooses live in burrows and feed on small birds, poultry, mice, and rats. Their fierceness and speed also helps them to kill dangerous snakes like the cobra.

Monkey

Monkeys are MAMMALS that belong to the same group of animals as APES and HUMAN BEINGS. Most monkeys have long tails and thick fur all over their body. Monkeys are usually smaller than apes. Their hands and feet are used for grasping and are very similar to those of humans.

There are about 400 different kinds of monkey. Most live in the tropics, especially in forests, in Africa, Asia, and South America. South American monkeys have long tails that they use like an extra arm or leg when swinging through the branches of trees.

On the ground, monkeys usually move around on all four limbs. But when they are using their hands to hold something, they can stand or sit up on two legs.

Monkeys live in family groups known as troops. They spend a lot of time chattering, playing, fighting, and grooming each other. Each troop of monkeys has its own territory where it lives and feeds. It will fight fiercely to defend this area against other invading groups.

▲ *The colobus and mandrill are both Old World monkeys living in Africa. The colobus has no thumb, and the mandrill is one of the largest monkeys. New World monkeys, including the spider and woolly monkeys, live in the forests of South America. They have long* prehensile *tails than can be used as an extra "hand."*

Monroe, James

James Monroe (1758–1831) was the fifth president of the United States. He served two terms. Monroe spent nearly all his adult life in the service of his country. He fought in the REVOLUTIONARY WAR when he was only 18. Later, he was a senator for Virginia, minister to France, governor of Virginia, secretary of state, and secretary of war. He was president during a time of stability and prosperity. The War of 1812 was over and American businesses were flourishing. The country was growing rapidly westward, too. This was "the era of good feeling." Monroe is most famous for the Monroe Doctrine. This stated that European countries no longer had the right to interfere with the business of any of the states in the American continent.

JAMES MONROE

Fifth President 1817–1825
Born: Westmoreland County, Virginia
Occupation: Lawyer
Political Party: Democratic-Republican
Buried: Richmond, Virginia

Monsoon

Monsoons are winds that blow from land to sea during winter, and from sea to land during summer. They occur mainly in southern Asia. The summer monsoon carries moisture from the sea, and rain falls over the land. Summer monsoons bring the rainy season. In India, about 67 in. (1,700 mm) of rain falls between June and September, and only another 4 in. (100 mm) in all the rest of the year.

▲ *Glacier National Park in northeastern Montana is an area of majestic mountain scenery and many lakes.*

Montana

Montana lies in the northwest of the country, on the Canadian border. It is a huge state. In the west, it is mountainous and rugged. In the east, there are rolling prairie lands where cattle graze in their thousands. Coal mining, oil, and agriculture are the main industries. Montana was settled from 1862, when gold was discovered and prospectors poured in. The mining towns that sprang up also drew outlaws from all over the country. Shootings and hangings were common in these wild days. Montana was also the site of some of the last battles of the Indian wars, including the Battle of the Little Bighorn. Today, many people visit Montana to explore its open spaces, and to go camping and hunting.

MONTANA

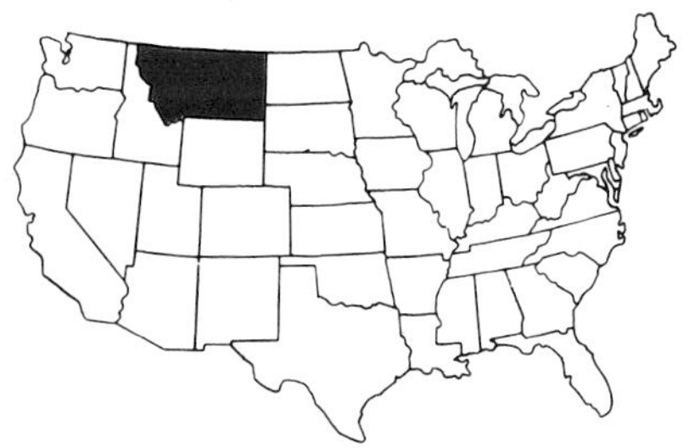

Capital: Helena
Population: 799,065
Area 147,046 sq. mi. (380,848 sq. km)
State flower: Bitterroot
State bird: Western Meadowlark
State tree: Ponderosa Pine
Statehood: November 8, 1889
41st state

Moon

The Moon is our nearest neighbor in space. It loops around the EARTH, never coming closer than 221,460 miles (356,400 km). It travels at about 2,274 miles (3,660 km) per hour and takes $27^1/_3$ days to complete the circuit. (See pages 456-457.)

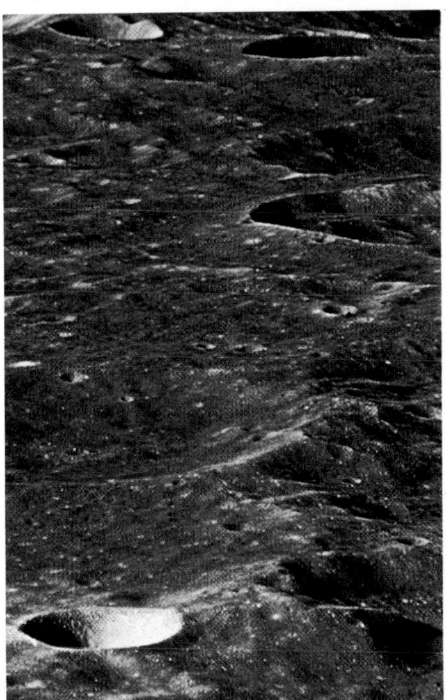

▲ *The lunar highlands, photographed by the* Apollo 8 *astronauts in December, 1968.*

Mormon

Mormons belong to a religious group founded by Joseph Smith in 1830. The name comes from the *Book of Mormon*, which Mormons believe is a sacred history of ancient American peoples. The Mormons began in New York, but were persecuted for their beliefs and driven out. They finally settled in Salt Lake Valley, Utah.

Morocco

Morocco is a country right at the top of northwestern AFRICA. It is slightly larger than California and has two coastlines. On the west is the Atlantic Ocean and to the north is the Mediterranean Sea.

Most of Morocco's 25 million people are farmers. They grow wheat, corn, fruit, olives, and nuts. Some keep sheep, goats, and cattle. Most of the people are Muslims. Casablanca is the largest city and main seaport. The country is ruled by a king.

MOROCCO

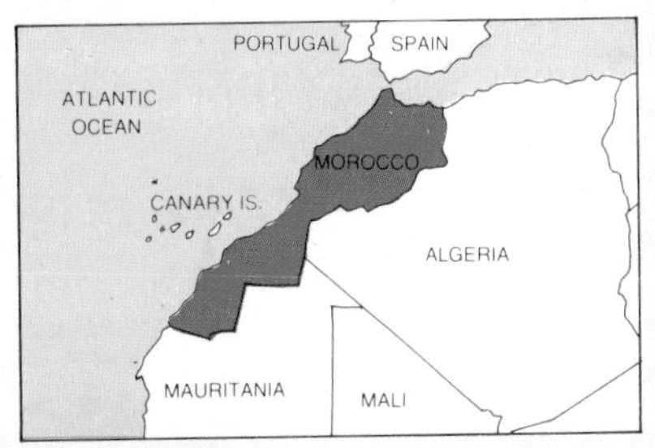

Government: Constitutional monarchy
Capital: Rabat
Area: 172,413 sq. miles (446,550 sq. km)
Population: 25,061,000
Language: Arabic
Currency: Dirham

Morse Code

Morse code is a simple way of sending messages. It is an alphabet of dots and dashes. Each letter has its own dot and dash pattern. The code was invented by Samuel Morse, an American artist, to send messages along a telegraph wire. The telegraph operator pressed a key at one end to send a signal along the wire to a sounder at the other end.

Mosaic

A mosaic is a picture made from small pieces of colored stone or glass set into cement. The pieces are arranged to make a design or a portrait.

Continued on page 458

MOON

People have worshiped the Moon, made wishes on the Moon (because of superstition), and even walked on the Moon. The Moon is our nearest neighbor in space. It is the Earth's only natural satellite and was probably formed at the same time as our planet. But the rocks on the Moon's surface are older than those on the Earth's surface because the Moon has not changed in over 4 billion years.

The Moon is a dry, lifeless world, without air. Gravity on the Moon is just one-sixth of gravity on Earth, yet the Moon's gravitational pull affects us every day. It is the Moon's pull that causes the rise and fall of the ocean tides. Astronauts landed to explore the Moon in 1969. One day in the future, permanent bases may be built there.

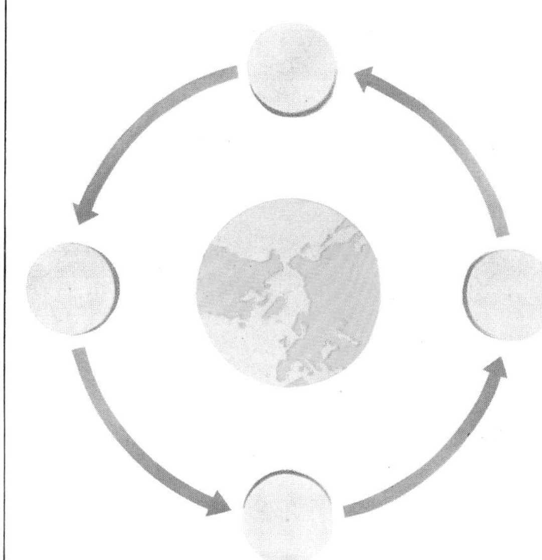

THE MOON'S FACE

When the Moon was newly formed, it was made of molte rock spinning around once in a few hours. As it cooled, a hard skin or crust formed on the outside. The Earth's gravity, pulling at this crust, slowed the spin down and rais a "bulge" a few miles high on one side. Now this bulge is always turned inward, and the Moon keeps the same face toward the Earth.

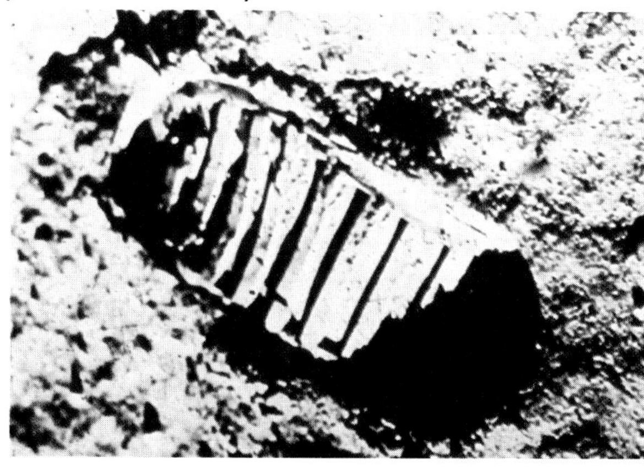

◀ *The Moon has no wind; in fact, no erosion of any kind. This footprint in the Moon dust, left by an Apollo astronaut, will remain undisturbed forever.*

THE PHASES OF THE MOON

The Moon takes just over 27 days to travel around the Earth. It also spins on its own axis, and it always presents the same face to us. The Moon has no light of its own; we see it because it reflects light from the Sun.

When the Moon is between the Earth and the Sun, we cannot see it, because the dark side is facing us. Gradually, a thin crescent Moon appears: the New Moon. The New Moon waxes (gets larger) and at Full Moon (halfway through its cycle), we see the whole face lit by sunlight. Then the Moon wanes (gets smaller). The interval between one New Moon and the next is 29½ days (longer than the time the Moon takes to orbit the Earth). This is because the Earth itself is moving in space, as it travels around the Sun.

Sun's light
First Quarter
New Moon
Earth
Full Moon
Last Quarter

EXPLORING THE MOON

1609 Galileo studies the Moon through the newly invented telescope.

1647 Johannes Hevelius maps the Moon.

1860s First photographs of the Moon.

1959 Russian Luna 2 crash-lands on lunar surface. Luna 3 flies around far side.

1966 U.S. Orbiter craft photograph Moon in detail to find best landing sites.

1968 U.S. Apollo 8 astronauts fly around the Moon.

1969 Apollo 11 astronauts land on Moon.

1972 Last Apollo Moon landing.

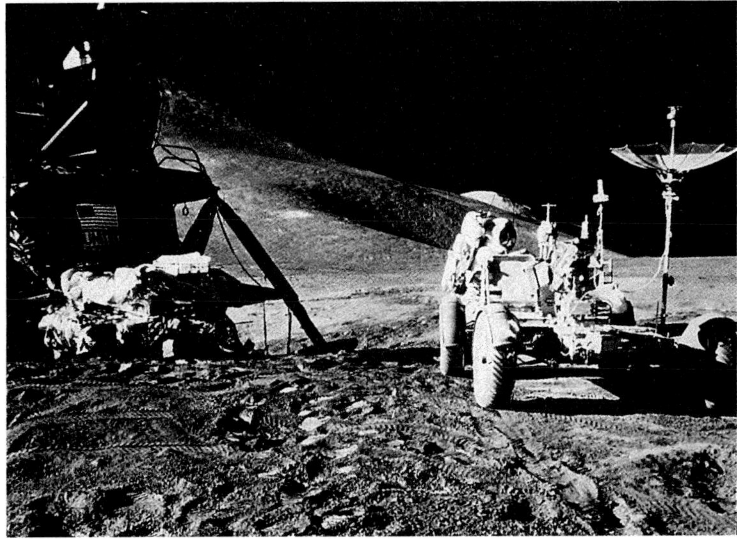

▲ *The Apollo astronauts explored the Moon on foot and with the aid of battery-powered "Moon buggies."*

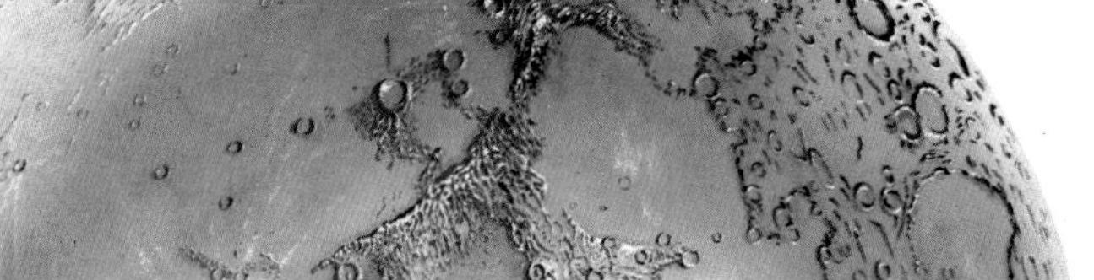

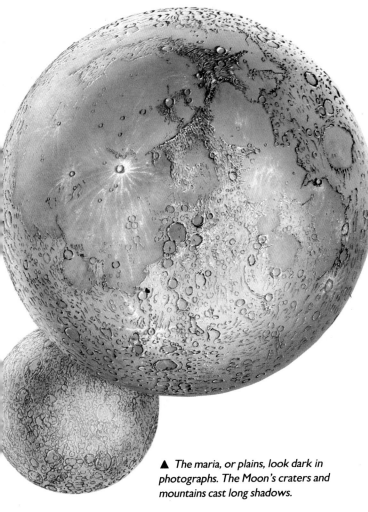

▲ *The maria, or plains, look dark in photographs. The Moon's craters and mountains cast long shadows.*

MOON FACTS

- The Moon is 238,860 miles (384,400 km) from the Earth.
- The Earth weighs 81 times as much as the Moon.
- The diameter (distance across) of the Moon is 2,160 miles (3,476 km).
- The oldest Moon rock is 4,600 million years old.
- The Moon has no seas. Its flat plains are called maria, because early astronomers mistook them for oceans and named them after the Latin *mare*, meaning "sea."
- The Moon's surface is pitted with craters. Almost all these holes were made by meteorites crashing into the Moon.
- The Latin word for the Moon is *luna*. From this, we get our word "lunar," meaning "of the Moon."
- The Moon once had active volcanoes, but almost all of its volcanoes are now dead.
- No one on Earth had seen the far side of the Moon until a spacecraft photographed it in 1959.

r more information turn to these articles : ECLIPSE; GALILEO; ORBIT; SATELLITE; SPACE EXPLORATION; TIDES.

SEE IT YOURSELF

You can make your own mosaic by using small pebbles, shells, pieces of broken china, or broken tiles. You will need a board or a very stiff piece of cardboard and some strong glue. Draw your design on the board and decide which colors you will use for each area of the design. Glue the pieces along the edge first and work toward the center. Glue the pieces as close together as possible. You can put some grout or filler in the spaces between the pieces. This will help to hold your mosaic together.

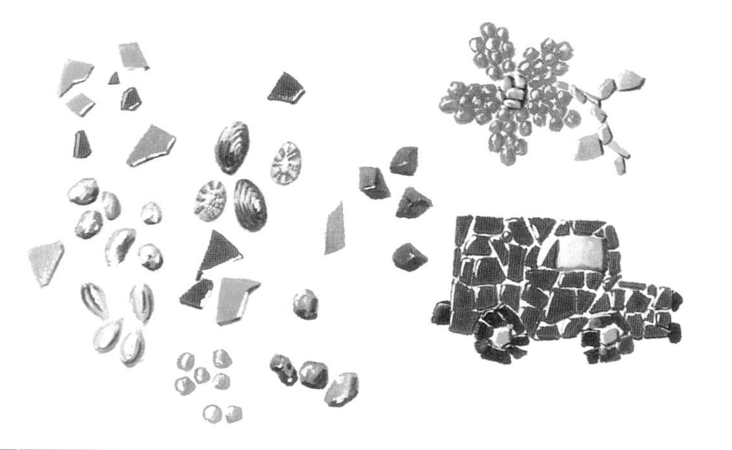

The world's largest mosaic adorns four walls in the National University, Mexico City. It shows historical scenes. The two largest mosaic-covered walls are each 1,435 sq. yds. (1,200 sq. m) in area.

Mosaic making is a very ancient art. The Sumerians made mosaics nearly 5,000 years ago. Mosaics are a very practical way of decorating floors and walls, as they can be washed without being spoiled. In ancient Rome, every villa and palace had dazzling mosaics showing scenes from everyday life.

Mosaics were also used to make pictures of saints, angels, and JESUS in churches all over Greece, Italy, and Turkey.

Moscow

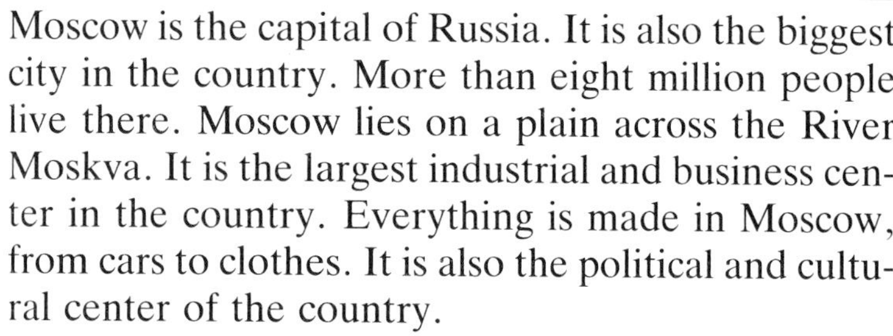

▲ *St. Basil's Cathedral is in one of the most historic parts of Moscow, near Red Square and the Kremlin.*

Moscow is the capital of Russia. It is also the biggest city in the country. More than eight million people live there. Moscow lies on a plain across the River Moskva. It is the largest industrial and business center in the country. Everything is made in Moscow, from cars to clothes. It is also the political and cultural center of the country.

Moscow was first made the capital of Muscovy in 1547, during the reign of IVAN the Terrible, the first *tsar* (emperor) of Russia. It grew up around the KREMLIN, an ancient fort from which the Muscovy princes used to defend their country. Moscow remained the capital of the tsars until 1712 when Peter the Great moved the capital to St. Petersburg. The city remained very important, even after it was nearly burned down during NAPOLEON's occupation of 1812.

After the Communist Revolution of 1917, Moscow became the seat of the Soviet government. In 1992 it became the capital of Russia again.

Mosquito

Mosquitoes are a small kind of FLY. They have slender, tube-shaped bodies, three pairs of long legs, and two narrow wings. There are about 1,400 different kinds. They live all over the world, from the tropics to the Arctic, but they must be able to get to water to lay their eggs.

Only female mosquitoes bite and suck blood. They have special piercing mouths. Males live on the juices of plants. When the female bites, she injects a substance into her victim to make the blood flow more easily. This makes mosquito bites itch.

Some kinds of mosquito spread serious diseases. Malaria and yellow fever are two diseases passed on by mosquitoes.

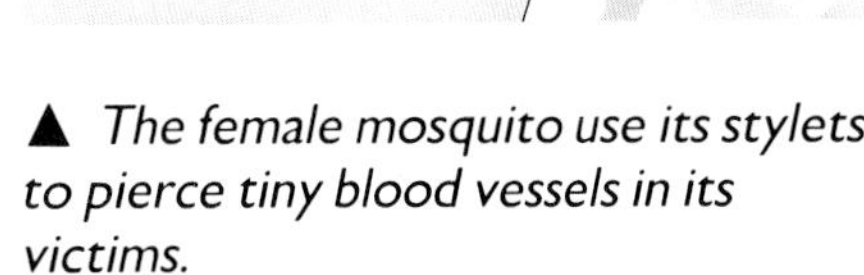

▲ *The female mosquito use its stylets to pierce tiny blood vessels in its victims.*

Moss

This is a very common kind of PLANT that grows in low, closely-packed clusters. There are more than 12,000 different kinds. They are very hardy plants and flourish everywhere, except in deserts, even as far north as the Arctic. Most mosses grow in damp places. They spread in carpets on the ground in shady forests, or over rocks and the trunks of trees.

Mosses are very simple kinds of plants, like LICHENS. They were among the first plants to make their home on land. They have slender creeping stems that are covered with tiny leaves. Instead of true roots that reach down into the soil, mosses simply have a mass of tiny hairs that soak up moisture and food. Mosses do not have flowers.

▼ *When mosses are ready to reproduce, they produce capsules containing tiny spores. They soak up moisture and nutrients through tiny root-hairs called rhizoids.*

Clothes moths do not really eat clothes. But they lay an enormous number of eggs from which larvae hatch. It is these that devour our clothes and carpets.

Moth

It can be hard to tell moths and BUTTERFLIES apart. These are the signs to look out for. Moths usually fly in the evening and at night, while butterflies can be seen in the daytime. Moths have plumper bodies than butterflies. Moths' antennae are like tiny combs or have feathery hairs on them. Butterfly antennae end in tiny knobs. When butterflies rest on a plant, they hold their wings upright. Moths spread their wings out flat.

Moths belong to one of the biggest insect groups. There are over 100,000 kinds of moth, and they are found all over the world. The smallest scarcely measure $^1/_8$ in. (3 mm) across. The largest may be bigger than a person's hand. Some moths have very striking colors that warn their enemies that they are poisonous or bad tasting. Moths have a very good sense of smell. They find their food by "sniffing" their way from plant to plant. A male moth can follow the scent of a female 2 miles (3 km) away.

Moths hatch from eggs, usually in the spring. They hatch into CATERPILLARS. The caterpillar feeds on leaves until it is fully grown. Then it spins itself a silk cocoon. This protects the caterpillar while its body changes into a moth. A few kinds of moth do not spin cocoons, but bury themselves in the ground or in piles of leaves until they grow into moths.

▼ *There is a great variety in the appearance of moths and their caterpillars.*

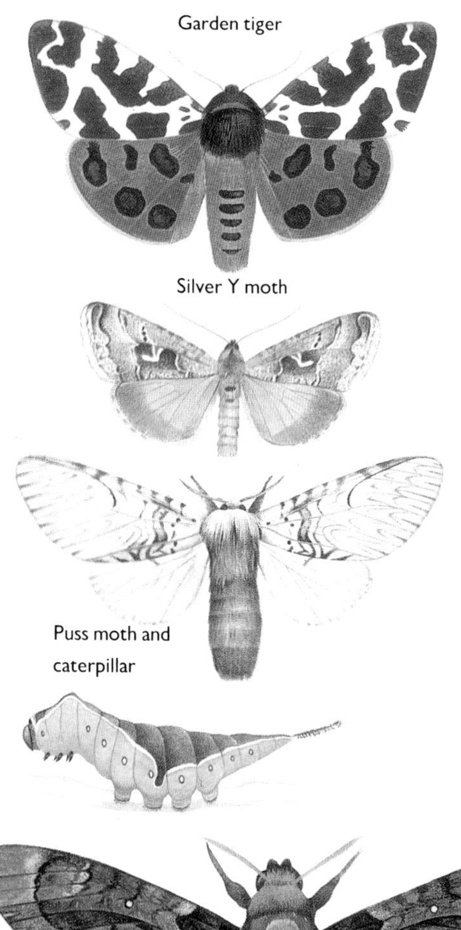

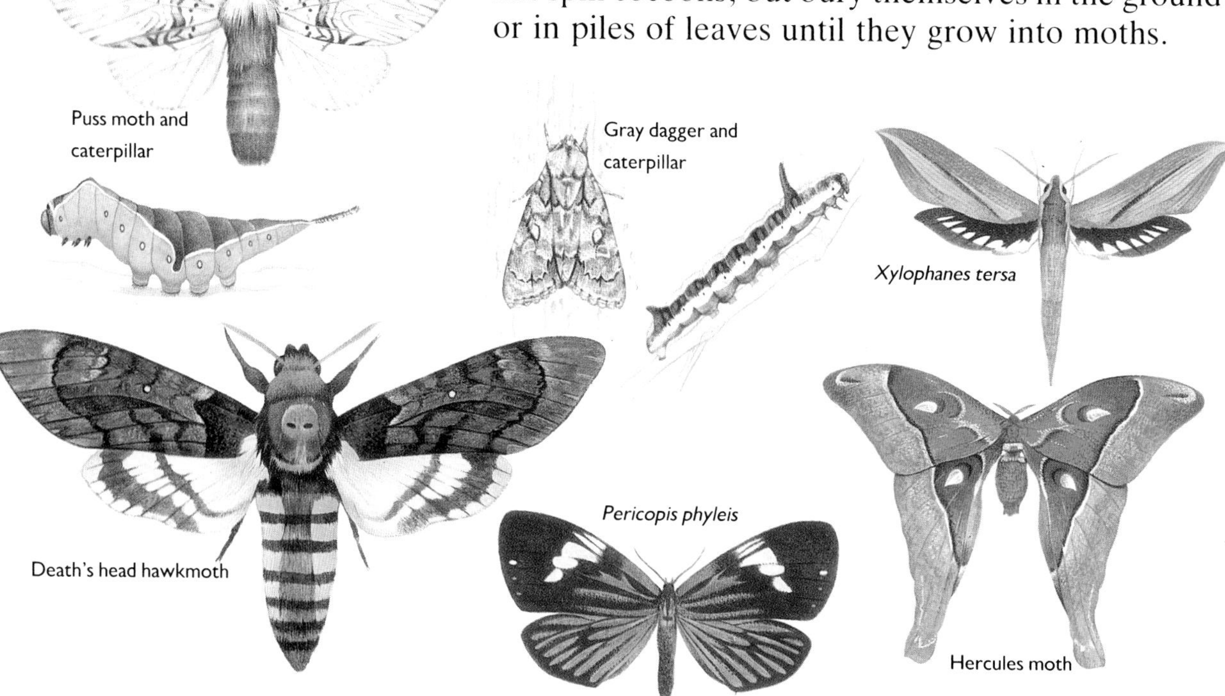

▲ *Left: Special effects play a big part in today's motion pictures. Model buildings are used in the making of* Supergirl. *Right: The making of* A Passage to India.

Motion Pictures

The art of making moving pictures came from an invention called the *kinetoscope*, built by an American, Thomas EDISON, in 1891. Soon after Edison's machine became known, two brothers, Auguste and Louis Lumière, built a similar machine of their own called a *cinématographe*. This machine projected pictures from a piece of film onto a screen. The pictures were shown one after the other so quickly that the images on the screen appeared to move. In 1896, in Paris, the Lumière brothers gave the world's first public film show. Soon, people all over Europe and North America were making films.

These early motion pictures did not look much like the ones we are used to seeing today. They were only in black and white, the movements were very

▲ King Kong *was perhaps the most famous of the early special effects films. At the time, amazed audiences didn't know how he had been brought to life.*

◀ Gone with the Wind, *made in 1939, was a Civil War epic that became one of the most popular motion pictures ever.*

▶ *The thrill-a-minute formula of* Raiders of the Lost Ark *depended heavily on special effects.*

Which story character has been a film hero more often than any other? The answer is Sherlock Holmes, Conan Doyle's famous detective. There have been 187 films about him between 1900 and the present time. And no doubt there will be lots more.

jerky, and they had no sound. At first, films were made to show news and real events, but by 1902, filmmakers began to make up their own stories, using actors to play the parts of imaginary people. These motion pictures were very popular in France and the United States, and Hollywood in California became the filmmaking center of the world. The first "talkie," or moving picture with sound, was shown in 1927. It was called *The Jazz Singer*.

The United States remained the leader in the film world. Huge amounts of money were spent on motion pictures that used hundreds of actors, singers, and dancers, lavish costumes, and specially designed "sets," or backgrounds. Europe also produced many important films, and after World War II, a more realistic type of film became popular, telling stories of everyday life.

Today, motion pictures are made all over the world, although the United States still produces most of the big feature films, using modern technology to create fantastic visual effects. Television has been a threat to the film industry since the 1960s, and there have been many experiments in recent years to develop new kinds of films.

▼ *Early motorcycles, such as this Daimler of 1885, were very simple, slow, and uncomfortable to ride.*

Motorcycle

The first motorcycle was built in 1885 by a German, Gottlieb Daimler. He fitted one of his gasoline engines to a wooden bicycle frame. Today's motorcycles are more complicated machines. The engine is similar to that of a car, but smaller. (See INTERNAL

COMBUSTION ENGINE.) It is either a two-stroke or a four-stroke engine, and it may have from one to four cylinders. The engine can be cooled by either air or water. It is started with an ignition button on the handlebars. This turns the engine and starts it firing. The speed is controlled by a twist-grip on the handlebars. The clutch works from a hand lever. The gears are changed by a foot lever. Another foot pedal works the brake on the back wheel. A chain or drive shaft connects the engine to the back wheel and drives it around.

Motor, Electric

There are electric motors all around us. Refrigerators, washing machines, electric clocks, vacuum cleaners, hairdryers, and electric mixers are all driven by electric motors. So are some trains and ships.

Electric motors work because the like poles of a magnet repel (push each other apart), and unlike poles attract each other. A simple motor consists of a coil of wire held between the poles of a magnet. When an electric current flows through the coil, the coil becomes a magnet with a north pole and a south pole. Since like poles repel and unlike poles attract, the coil swings around between the poles of the magnet, until its north pole is facing the south pole of the magnet and its south pole is facing the mag-

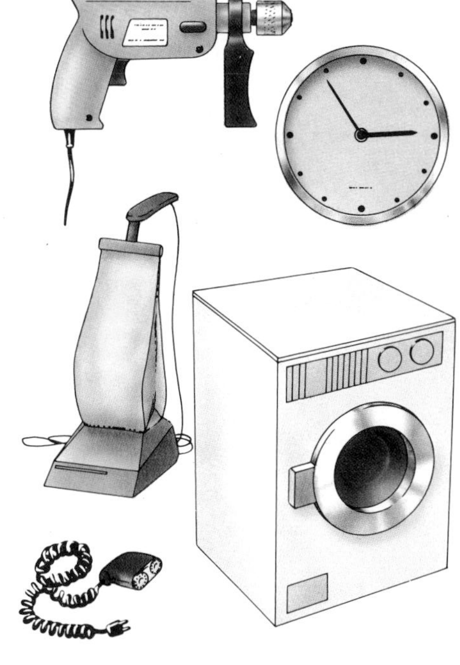

▲ *Many household appliances are run by electric motors.*

▼ *Today's motorcycles are designed to let the rider get the best performance in any situation. This Suzuki GSXR1100 has a maximum speed of 150 miles (240 km) an hour.*

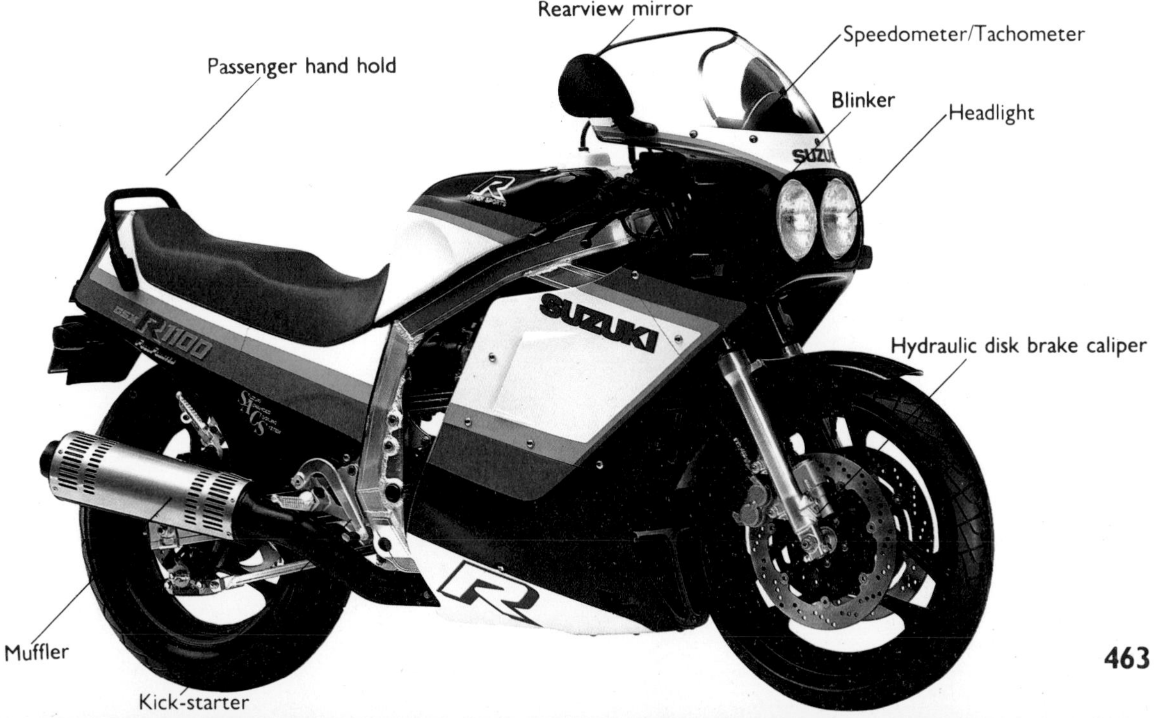

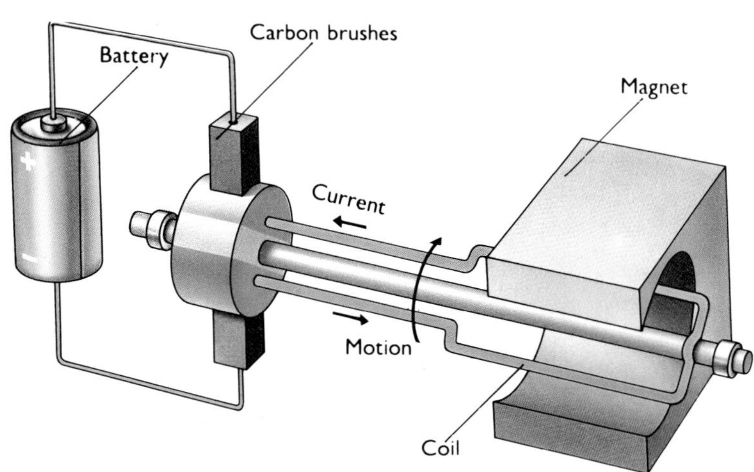

► *Simple motors change electric current into mechanical energy. A coil is held between the poles of a permanent magnet. When current flows from the battery, it turns the coil into an electromagnet. The poles of the permanent magnet repel those of the electromagnet, making it spin around. Motors such as these are clean and do not produce fumes.*

net's north pole. The direction of the current in the coil is then reversed so that the coil's poles are also reversed. The coil then has to swing around again to line up its poles with those of the magnet. So the electric motor keeps on turning because it keeps getting a series of magnetic pushes.

Mountain

A large part of the Earth's surface is covered by mountains. The greatest mountain ranges are the ALPS of Europe, the ROCKIES of North America, the ANDES of South America, and the HIMALAYAS of Asia. The Himalayas are the greatest of them all. They have many of the world's highest peaks, including the biggest, Mount EVEREST.

There are mountains under the sea, too. And sometimes the peaks of underwater mountains stick up above the sea's surface as islands. One mountain called Mauna Loa which rises from the floor of the Pacific Ocean is very much higher then Everest.

Mountains are formed by movements in the

▼ *Different plants grow at different altitudes in mountain areas. This is because the air gets thinner and colder the higher you go.*

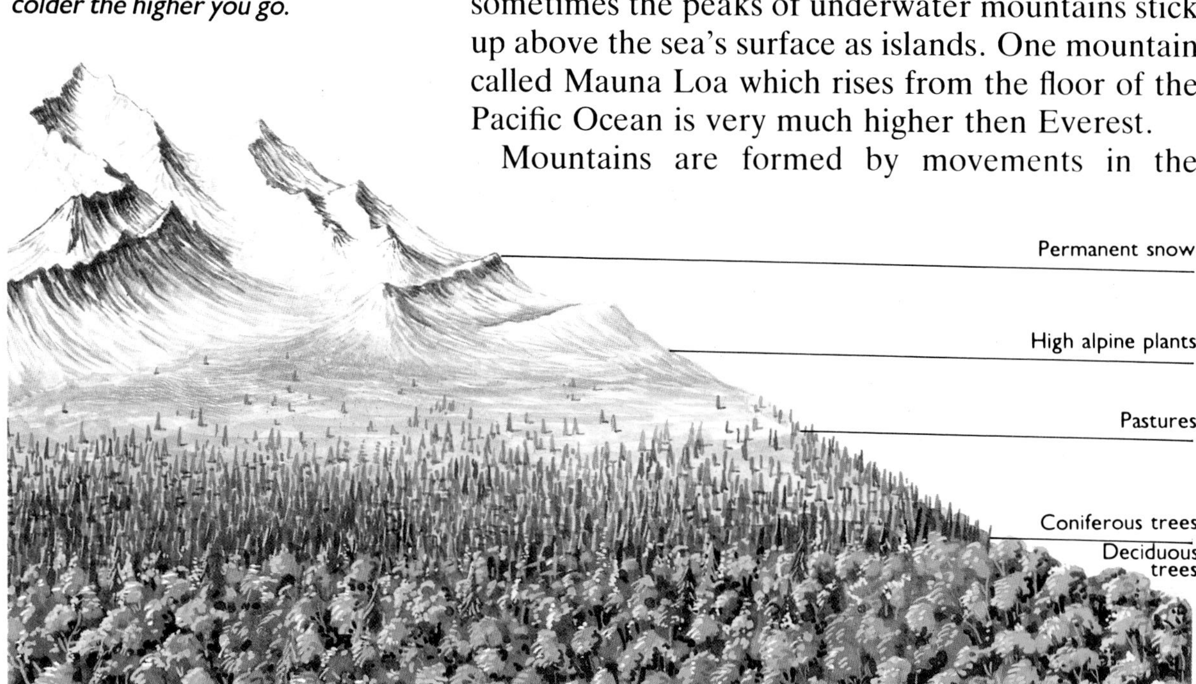

Earth's crust. Some mountains are formed when two great land masses move toward each other and squeeze up the land in between. The Alps were made in this way. Other mountains are VOLCANOES, great heaps of ash and lava that poured out when the volcano erupted.

But even the greatest mountains do not last forever. The hardest rock gets worn away in time by rain, wind, sun, and frost. RIVERS cut valleys, GLACIERS grind their way down, wearing away the mountains after untold centuries into gentle hills.

When the height of a mountain is given, it means the height above sea level. This can be a lot more than the height from the base.

WORLD'S HIGHEST MOUNTAINS

Peak	Range	Feet
Everest	Himalayas	29,028
Godwin Austen	Karakoram	28,250
Kanchen junga	Himalayas	28,208
Lhotse	Himalayas	27,923
Makalu	Himalayas	27,824
Dhaulagiri I	Himalayas	26,810
Manaslu	Himalayas	26,760
Cho Oyu	Himalayas	26,750
Nanga Parbat	Himalayas	26,660
Annapurna I	Himalayas	26,504
Gasherbrum I	Karakoram	26,470
Broad Peak	Karakoram	26,400
Gasherbrum II	Karakoram	26,360
Gosainthan	Himalayas	26,287
Gasherbrum III	Karakoram	26,089
Annapurna II	Himalayas	26,041
Gasherbrum IV	Karakoram	26,000
Kangbachen	Himalayas	25,925
Gyachung Kang	Himalayas	25,910
Himal Chuli	Himalayas	25,892
Disteghil Sar	Karakoram	25,868
Kunyang Kish	Karakoram	25,761
Dakum (Peak 29)	Himalayas	25,761
Nuptse	Himalayas	25,726

Mouse

A mouse is a RODENT, like its relative the RAT. And, like the rat, the house mouse is a pest to human beings. It can do a great deal of damage to food supplies, usually at night. One mouse can have 40 babies a year, and when the young are 12 weeks old, they can themselves breed. People have used cats to catch mice for thousands of years. The wood mouse, field mouse, harvest mouse, and dormouse are mice that live in the countryside. White mice can be kept as pets.

Mozambique

Mozambique is a country in East Africa. It was ruled by Portugal, but became independent in 1975. Farming is the most important industry in this hot, tropical country. Mozambique's ports of Maputo and Beira are important for importing and exporting goods to the African interior.

Most of the people of Mozambique are black

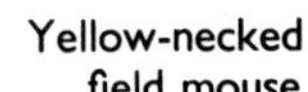

▲ *Mice are adaptable creatures and live in a variety of habitats.*

MOZAMBIQUE

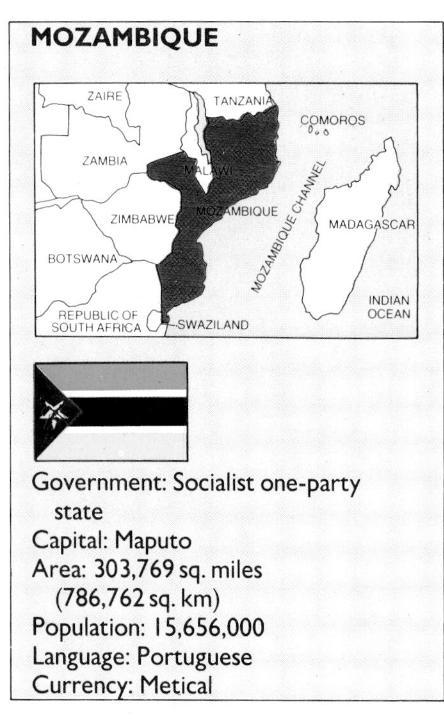

Government: Socialist one-party state
Capital: Maputo
Area: 303,769 sq. miles (786,762 sq. km)
Population: 15,656,000
Language: Portuguese
Currency: Metical

Africans who speak one of several Bantu languages. There are also some Portuguese and Asians.

In the 1980s, severe droughts and civil war caused hardship in the country.

Mozart, Wolfgang Amadeus

Wolfgang Amadeus Mozart (1756–1791) was an Austrian and one of the greatest composers of music that the world has known. He began writing music at the age of five. Two years later he was playing at concerts all over Europe. Mozart wrote over 600 pieces of music, including many beautiful operas and symphonies. But he earned little money from his hard work. He died in poverty at the age of 35.

Muhammad

Muhammad (A.D. 570–632) was the founder and leader of the RELIGION known as ISLAM. He was born in MECCA, in what is now Saudi Arabia. At the age of 40, he believed that God had asked him to preach to the ARABS. He taught that there was only one God, called Allah.

In 622, he was forced out of Mecca, and this is the year from which the Muslim calendar dates. After his death, his teachings spread rapidly across the world.

Muscle

Muscles are the things that make the parts of your body move when you pick up a book or kick a ball. There are two different kinds of muscles. Some work when your brain tells them to. When you pick up a chair, your brain sends signals to muscles in your arms, in your body, and in your legs. All these muscles work together at the right time, and you pick up the chair. These muscles are called *voluntary* muscles. Other kinds of muscles, called *involuntary* muscles, work even when you are asleep. Your stomach muscles go on churning the food you have eaten. Your heart muscles go on pumping blood. Your lung muscles go on making you breathe. The human body has more than 500 muscles.

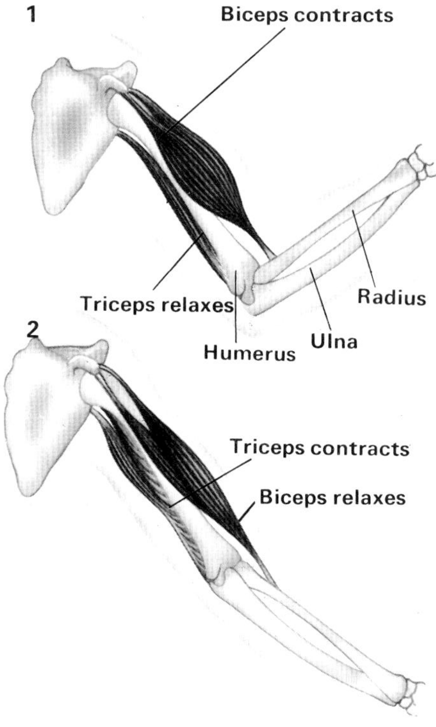

▲ *Muscles often work in pairs, with one contracting as the other relaxes. This is how the arm muscles work.*

Mushroom and Toadstool

Mushrooms grow in woods, fields, and on lawns—almost anywhere, in fact, where it is warm enough and damp enough. Some mushrooms are very good to eat. Others are so poisonous that people die from eating them. Many people call the poisonous ones toadstools. Mushrooms are in the FUNGUS group of plants. They have no green coloring matter (CHLOROPHYLL); instead they feed on decayed matter in the soil or on other plants.

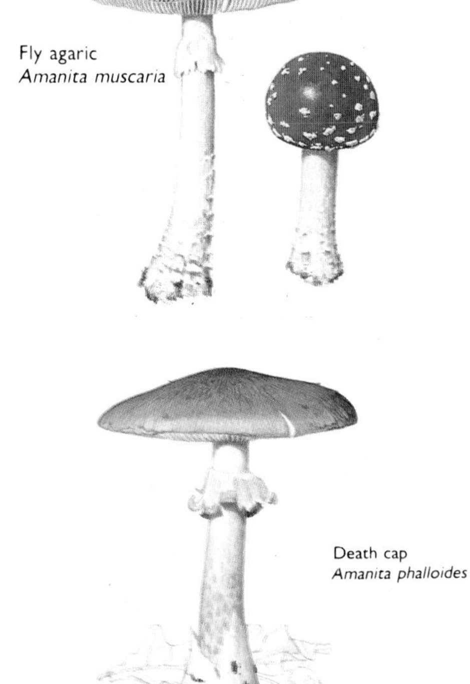

▲ *Poisonous toadstools like these sometimes look dangerous, but even some harmless-looking ones can kill.*

Music

People have been making some kind of music all through history. The very earliest people probably made singing noises and beat time with pieces of wood. We know that the ancient Egyptians enjoyed their music. Paintings in the tombs of the PHARAOHS show musicians playing pipes, harps, and other stringed instruments. The ancient Greeks also liked stringed instruments such as the lyre. But we have no idea what this early music sounded like, because there was no way of writing it down.

By the MIDDLE AGES, composers were writing music for groups of instruments. But it was not until the 1600s that the ORCHESTRA as we know it was born. The first orchestras were brought together by Italian composers to accompany their OPERAS. It was at this time that VIOLINS, violas, and cellos were first used.

As instruments improved, new ones were added to the orchestra. BACH and HANDEL, who were both born in 1685, used orchestras which played mainly stringed instruments like the violin. But they also had flutes, oboes, trumpets, and horns. Joseph HAYDN was the first composer to use the orchestra as a whole. He invented the *symphony*. In this form

▼ *These instruments are named the woodwinds because at one time they were all made of wood. Now they are made of metal or other materials.*

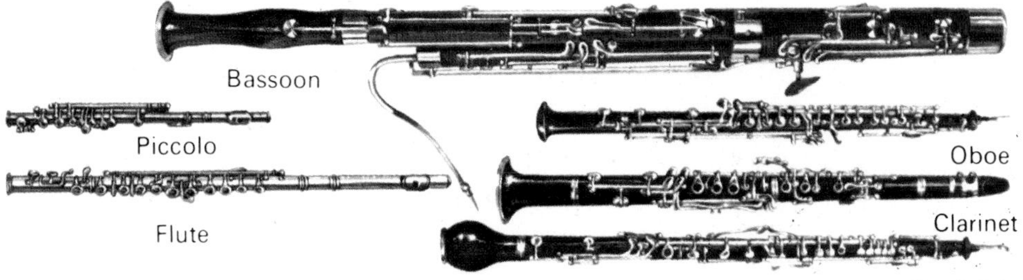

▶ *The layout of a modern symphony orchestra has been developed over many years.*

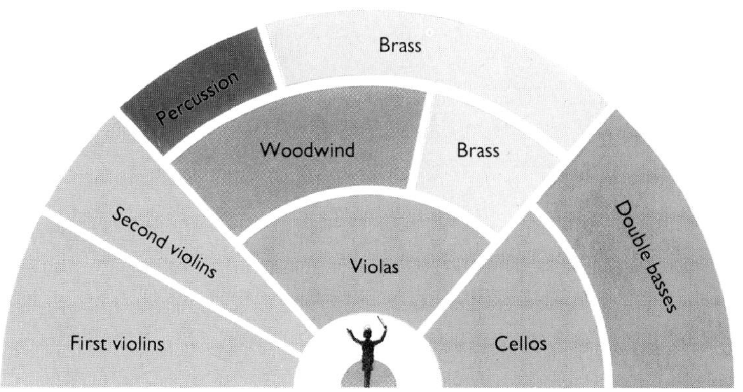

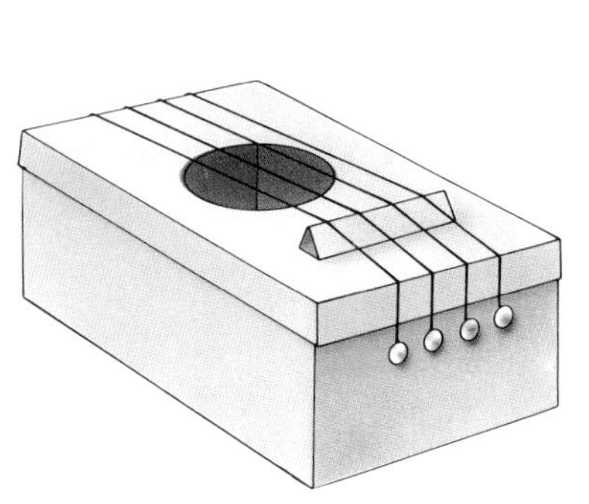

SEE IT YOURSELF

You can make a simple guitar from a cardboard box and some rubber bands. Cut a hole in the lid of the box and tack rubber bands of varying thickness tightly across it. Fit a wedge of wood beneath the rubber bands as shown. The bands will give out different notes when they are plucked.

of music, all the instruments blended together so that none was more important than the others.

A new kind of music began with the great German composer, Ludwig BEETHOVEN. He began writing music in which some of the notes clashed. This sounded rather shocking to people who listened to his music in his day. Later, musicians tried all kinds of mixtures of instruments. In the 1900s, new kinds of music were made by composers such as Igor Stravinsky and Arnold Schönberg. Others since then have used tape recorders and electronic systems to produce new sounds that are often rather strange to our ears.

But much music still has three things: *melody*, *harmony*, and *rhythm*. The melody is the tune. Harmony is the agreeable sound made when certain notes are played together. Often these notes form a *chord*, an arrangement of notes within a particular musical key. Rhythm is the regular "beat" of the music. The simplest kind of music is just beating out a rhythm on a drum.

What is probably the oldest kind of musical instrument has been found by archaeologists in Stone Age sites. It is a bull-roarer, consisting of a small oval-shaped piece of bone with a hole in one end in which a cord is tied. It is whirled around by the player and produces a buzzing sound – the faster it is whirled, the higher the buzz.

Musical Instrument 

There are four kinds of musical instrument. In wind instruments, air is made to vibrate inside a tube. This vibrating air makes a musical note.

All *woodwind* instruments such as clarinets, bassoons, flutes, piccolos, and recorders have holes that are covered by the fingers or by pads worked by the fingers. These holes change the length of the vibrating column of air inside the instrument. The shorter the column, the higher the note. In *brass* wind instruments, the vibration of the player's lips makes the air in the instrument vibrate. By changing the pressure of the lips, the player can make different notes. Most brass instruments also have valves and pistons to change the length of the vibrating column of air, and so make different notes.

Stringed instruments work in one of two ways. The strings of the instrument are either made to vibrate by a bow, as in the violin, viola, cello, and double bass; or the strings are plucked, as in the guitar, harp, or banjo.

In *percussion* instruments, a tight piece of skin or a piece of wood or metal is struck to make a note. There are lots of percussion instruments—drums, cymbals, gongs, tambourines, triangles, and chimes.

Electronic instruments such as the electric organ and the synthesizer make music using sounds produced by electronic circuits.

▼ *Percussion instruments are played by striking them. The note made by the timpani can be changed by tightening or loosening the skin.*

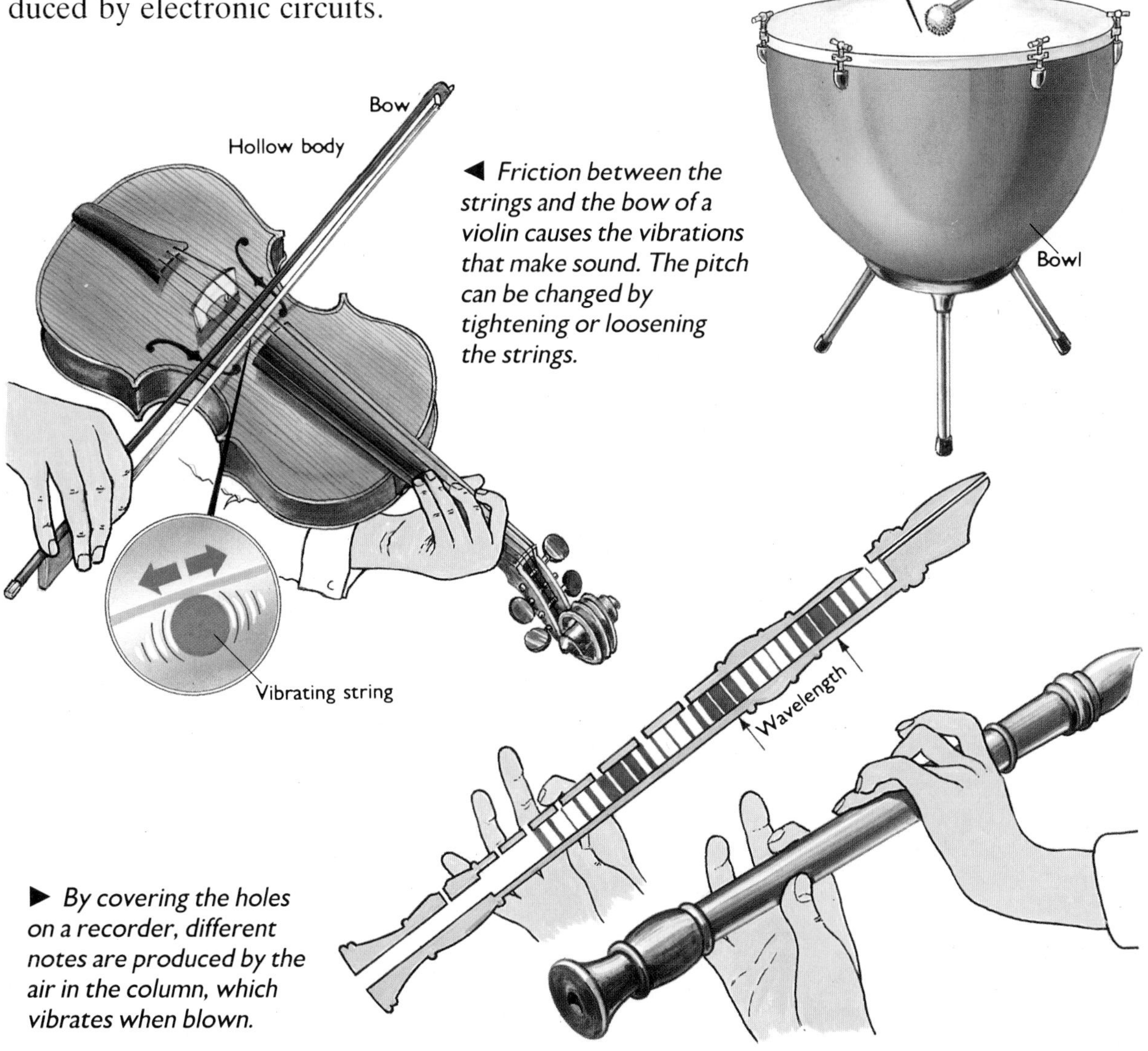

◀ *Friction between the strings and the bow of a violin causes the vibrations that make sound. The pitch can be changed by tightening or loosening the strings.*

▶ *By covering the holes on a recorder, different notes are produced by the air in the column, which vibrates when blown.*

▲ *Mussolini was known in his native Italy as* Il Duce, *which means "the leader."*

Mussolini, Benito

Mussolini (1883–1945) was a DICTATOR and leader of Italy's FASCISTS. In 1922, he bluffed the king of Italy into making him prime minister. Soon he made himself dictator. He wanted to make Italy great; he built many new buildings and created new jobs. But he also wanted military glory and led Italy into World War II on the side of HITLER. His armies were defeated by the Allies, and Mussolini was finally captured and shot by his own people.

Myth

In ancient times, people believed that the world was inhabited by many different gods and spirits. There were gods of war and thunder, the sea, wine, and hunting. The Sun and the Moon were gods, too. Stories that tell of the gods are called myths. The study of myths is called mythology.

Some myths tell of extraordinary human beings called *heroes* who performed great deeds. Others tell of the tricks the gods played on ordinary mortals. There are myths from all countries, but those of Greece and Rome have become the most familiar. Many of the Greek myths were adopted by the Romans. They even adopted some of the Greek gods.

Mythology teaches us much about the way people of long ago thought and lived.

▼ *The ancient Egyptians believed in many gods. Some were represented with the heads of animals considered sacred by the Egyptians. Osiris, god of the afterlife, was married to Isis, goddess of female fertility, and Horus was their son. Anubis escorted the dead to the afterworld, and Re was the Sun god.*

Horus

Anubis

Isis

Osiris

Re

Nail and Claw

Nails and claws are made of hard skin, like animal horns. They grow at the end of toes and fingers. When they are broad and flat, they are called nails, but if they are sharp and pointed, they are claws. Human nails are of little use. But BIRDS, MAMMALS, and REPTILES use their claws to attack and to defend themselves.

A close look at an animal's claws will tell you about its way of life. CATS and birds of prey have very sharp claws. They are hooked for holding onto and tearing prey. ANTEATERS have long, strong, curved claws for tearing apart termites' nests.

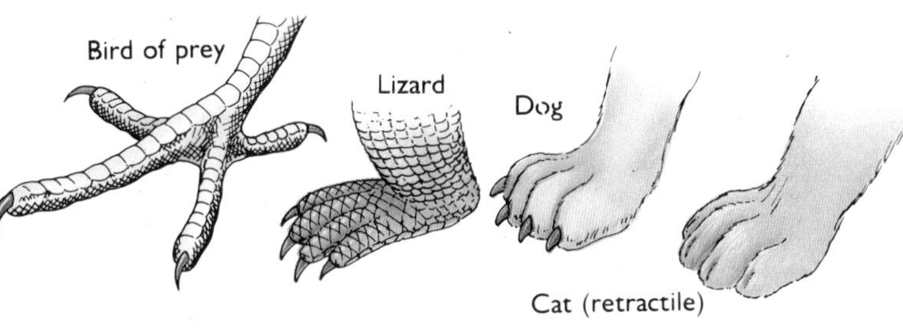

◀ *The claws of birds, reptiles, and mammals are all vital to their survival. The claw design of members of the cat family is particularly interesting. The claws can be retracted (pulled back) into the paws at will.*

Namibia

Namibia is in the southwest part of Africa. On some maps, the country is called South West Africa. Most of the country is a plateau more than 3,300 ft. (1,000 m) high. In the east is a part of the Kalahari Desert. There is not much good farmland. The main industry is mining.

In 1915, the country became a South African territory under the League of Nations. In 1946, the United Nations said that South Africa had no rights over Namibia, but South Africa disputed this. In 1989, it was finally decided that South Africa would hand over power to the black majority. Independence was achieved in 1990.

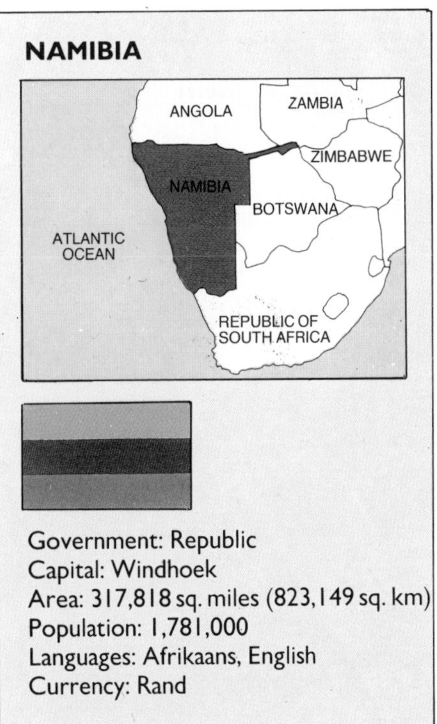

NAMIBIA
ANGOLA
ZAMBIA
ZIMBABWE
NAMIBIA
BOTSWANA
ATLANTIC OCEAN
REPUBLIC OF SOUTH AFRICA
Government: Republic
Capital: Windhoek
Area: 317,818 sq. miles (823,149 sq. km)
Population: 1,781,000
Languages: Afrikaans, English
Currency: Rand

Napoleon Bonaparte

In 1789, the people of France rebelled against the unjust rule of their king and his nobles. The FRENCH REVOLUTION was supported by a young man born on the island of Corsica 20 years before. His name was Napoleon Bonaparte (1769–1821).

► *Napoleon set out to conquer the whole of Europe. Shown here is the extent of his empire at the height of his power.*

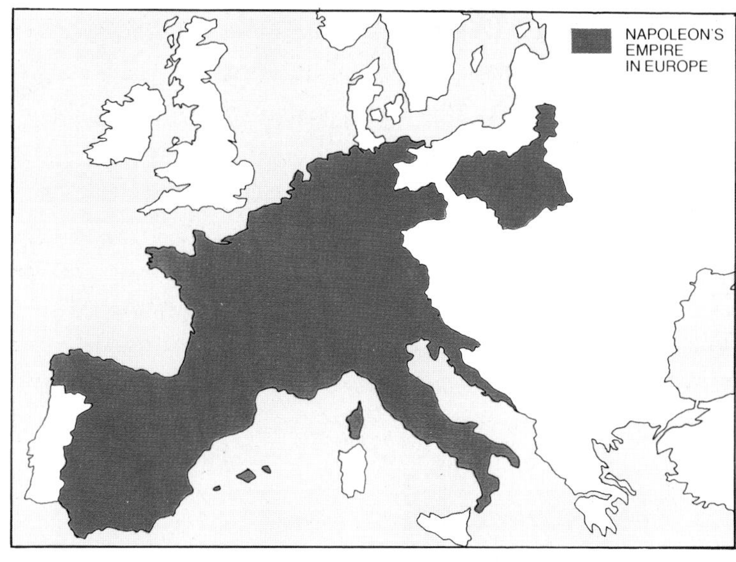

As the pope prepared to crown Napoleon emperor in Notre Dame Cathedral, Napoleon seized the crown from his hands and placed it on his own head, to show that he, Napoleon, had personally gained the right to wear it.

Napoleon went to the leading military school in Paris, and by 1792, he was a captain of artillery. Three years later, he saved France by crushing a royalist rebellion in Paris. Soon, Napoleon was head of the French army and won great victories in Italy, Belgium, and Austria. In 1804, he crowned himself emperor of France in the presence of the Pope. Then he crowned his wife, Josephine.

But Napoleon could not defeat Britain at sea. He tried to stop all countries from trading with Britain, but Russia would not cooperate. So Napoleon led a great army into Russia in the winter of 1812. This campaign ended in disaster. His troops were defeated by the bitter weather. Then he met his final defeat at the battle of Waterloo in 1815. There he was beaten by the British under Wellington and the Prussians under Blücher. He was made a prisoner by the British on the lonely Atlantic island of St. Helena, where he died in 1821.

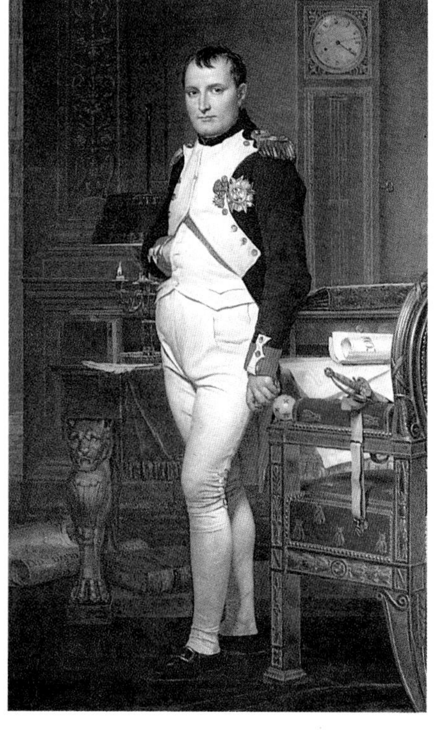

▲ *With political skills equal to his skills as a general, Napoleon reorganized the government of France.*

National Parks

The National Parks are part of the National Park System, an organization that was set up in 1916 to preserve areas of great natural beauty or of historic interest so that everyone can enjoy them. Some monuments and buildings, such as the Statue of LIBERTY and the WHITE HOUSE, are also part of the National Park System. Only Congress or the president can designate a new area or monument. Once they are part of the system, they must be preserved exactly as they are. Famous national parks include Yellowstone Park and the Grand Canyon.

▲ *Arches National Park, Utah, contains some of the world's most unusual rock formations.*

NATO (North Atlantic Treaty Organization)

NATO is a defensive alliance set up after World War II. In 1949, 12 countries signed a treaty in which they agreed that an attack on one member

◀ *The armed forces of NATO countries exercise together.*

should be considered an attack on them all. The 12 were Belgium, Canada, Denmark, France, Iceland, Italy, Luxembourg, the Netherlands, Norway, Portugal, the United Kingdom, and the United States. Greece and Turkey joined in 1951, West Germany in 1954, and Spain in 1982. In 1991, NATO forces were restructured as the Cold War came to an end. U.S. forces in Europe are being gradually cut.

In 1966, Charles de Gaulle announced France's withdrawal from NATO, though not from the Atlantic Alliance.

Natural Gas

Natural gas is a type of GAS which occurs naturally underground and does not have to be manufactured. It is usually found in OIL fields, but is sometimes found on its own. When there is only a little natural gas in an oil field, it is burned off. If there is plenty, it is piped away and used for cooking, heating, and producing ELECTRICITY.

It is found in large quantities in Russia, in Texas

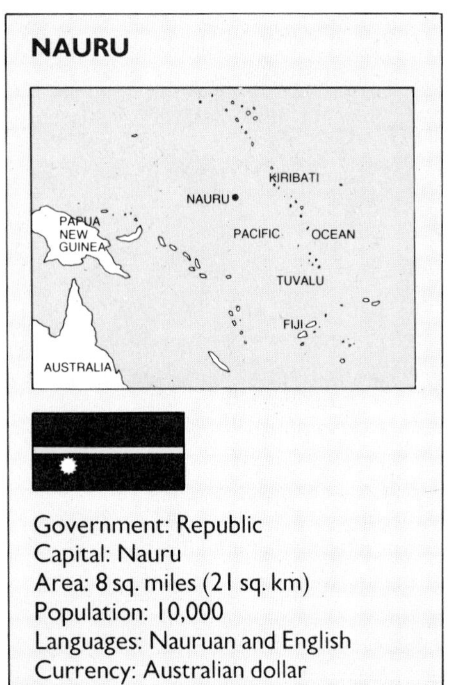

Government: Republic
Capital: Nauru
Area: 8 sq. miles (21 sq. km)
Population: 10,000
Languages: Nauruan and English
Currency: Australian dollar

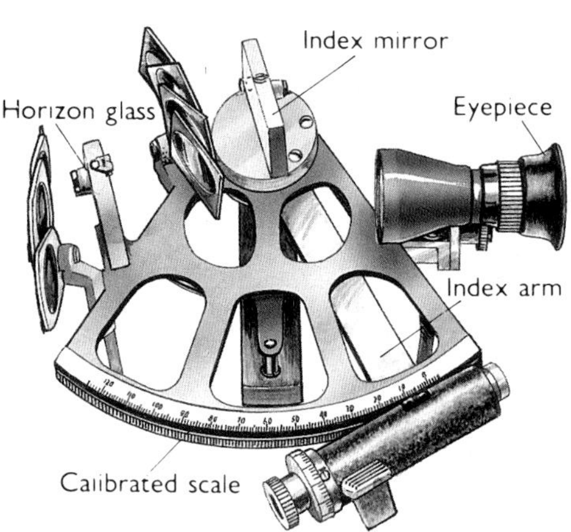

▲ *A sextant can be used to figure out a ship's position by measuring the angle between a star or the Sun and the horizon (see right).*

▶ *Once the angle has been measured, the star's position at that particular time can be looked up on a very accurate table. This allows the position of the ship to be calculated. By taking a series of sextant readings, the ship can be kept on the right course.*

and Louisiana in the United States, and in the NORTH SEA oil fields. Half the world's supply of natural gas is used by the United States.

Nauru

Nauru is a tiny island country in the Pacific Ocean. The only industry is mining for phosphate, but by the middle 1990s, there will be no phosphate left on the island. Nauru became independent in 1968 and is a member of the British Commonwealth.

Navigation

Navigation means finding the way, usually in a ship or an aircraft. For hundreds of years, navigators at sea used the changing positions of the Sun and stars to figure out their LATITUDE. Knowing the difference between the time on the ship and the time set at 0° longitude at Greenwich (G.M.T.) helped them to work out their position more precisely.

Today, many navigational instruments are electronic and are highly accurate. Radio beacons and SATELLITES send out signals from which a ship can find its position. Then the navigator uses a COMPASS to keep the ship on the right course. COMPUTERS help ships, aircraft, and spacecraft navigate so exactly that their position is known precisely.

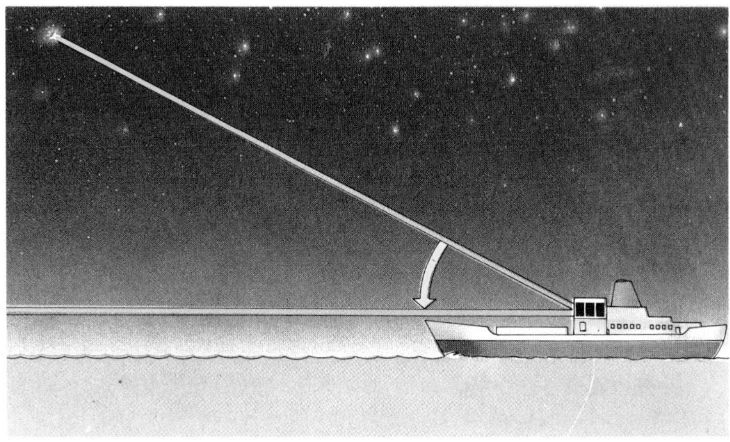

Nebraska

Nebraska is a western state that earns its living from farming. The first settlers thought it was an arid region—some called it a desert. But later settlers made it one of the most richly agricultural states in the country. Over 95 percent of Nebraska is farm land. In western Nebraska, there are huge fields of corn that roll on for mile after mile. Cattle are farmed in the central region on vast prairie lands. In the east, corn and soybeans are grown.

The Nebraskans have had to work hard to make the land so productive. In the 1860s and 1870s, when Congress encouraged people to move west to territories such as Nebraska, many found the conditions too tough. Droughts and plagues drove many settlers back east or on to the west coast. Those who stayed had to build houses out of soil, since there were so few trees.

NEBRASKA

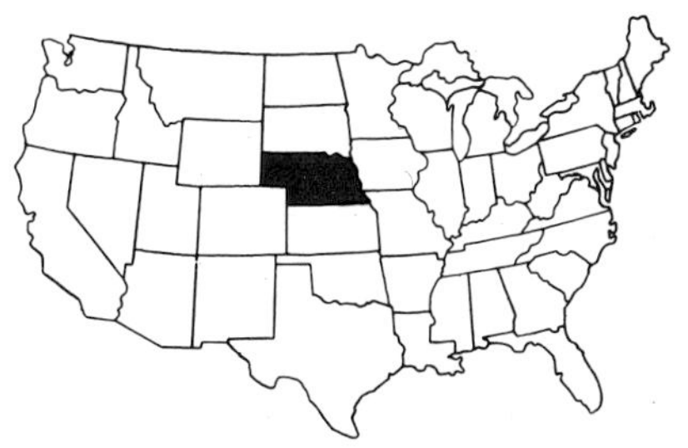

Capital: Lincoln
Population: 1,578,385
Area: 77,355 sq. mi. (200,350 sq. km)
State flower: Goldenrod
State bird: Western Meadowlark
State tree: Cottonwood
Statehood: March 1, 1867
37th state

Nepal

A country about the size of Arkansas, Nepal lies between India and Tibet and is very mountainous. The Himalaya Mountains lie in northern Nepal. Most of the people live in the fertile central valley. The country was almost completely closed to the rest of the world for centuries. Now there are roads and an air service to India and Pakistan.

NEPAL

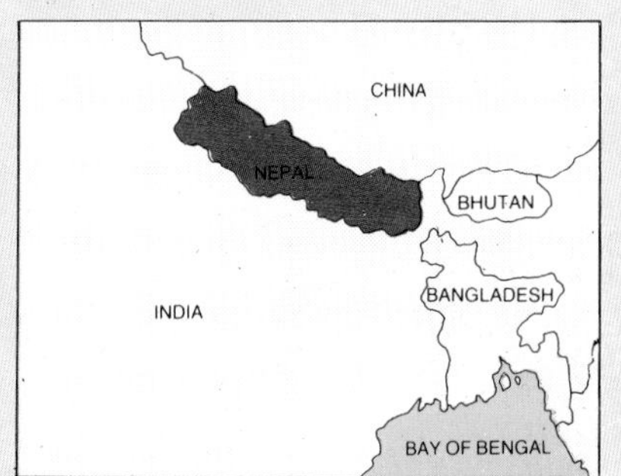

Government: Constitutional monarchy
Capital: Kathmandu
Area: 56,136 sq. miles (145,392 sq. km)
Population: 18,916,000
Language: Nepali
Currency: Rupee

Neptune

The PLANET Neptune is named after the Roman god of water and the sea. It is a large planet far out in the SOLAR SYSTEM. It is about 2.8 billion miles (4.5 billion km) from the SUN. Only PLUTO is farther away. It takes Neptune 165 years to circle the Sun. (The Earth takes 365 days.)

◀ *If we could observe Neptune from its large moon, Triton, it would probably look like this.*

NEPTUNE FACTS

Average distance from Sun:
2.8 billion miles (4.5 billion km)
Nearest distance from Earth:
2.7 billion miles (4.35 billion km)
Average temperature (clouds):
−400°F (−240°C)
Diameter across equator:
30,000 miles? (49,000 km?)
Atmosphere: Hydrogen, helium?
Number of moons: 6 known
Length of day: 18–20 hours?
Length of year: 165 Earth years

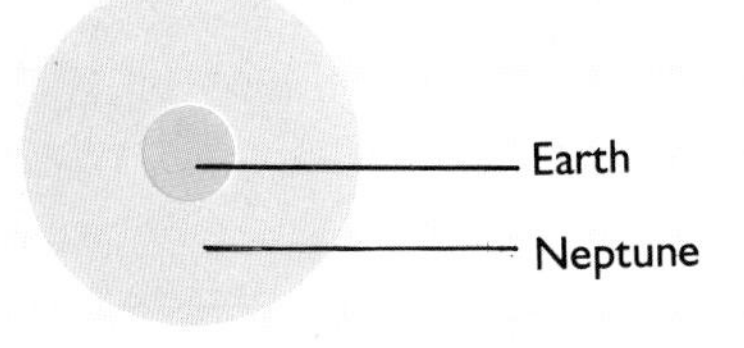

Being so far from the Sun, Neptune is a very cold place. Scientists think its atmosphere is similar to JUPITER'S, which is mostly made up of the gas HYDROGEN. Neptune has six moons. Triton is as large as the planet Mercury. It is a moon with icy plateaus, geysers, and volcanoes.

Early astronomers were unable to see Neptune, but they knew it had to be there. They could tell there was something affecting the ORBIT of the nearby planet URANUS. In 1845, two astronomers, Adams in England and Leverrier in France, used mathematics to work out where Neptune should be. Astronomers used this information the next year and spotted Neptune.

Nerve

Nerves are tiny fibers made up of CELLS. They reach all through the body. When a part of the body touches something, the nerves send a message through the spinal column to the BRAIN. If we feel PAIN, a message is sent back to make us move away from whatever is hurting. Nerves also carry the senses of sight, hearing, and taste. The sense organs have special nerve endings that respond to heat, light, cold, and other stimuli around us.

▼ *If the size of the various parts of your body corresponded to the number of nerve cells in them, you would look rather like this.*

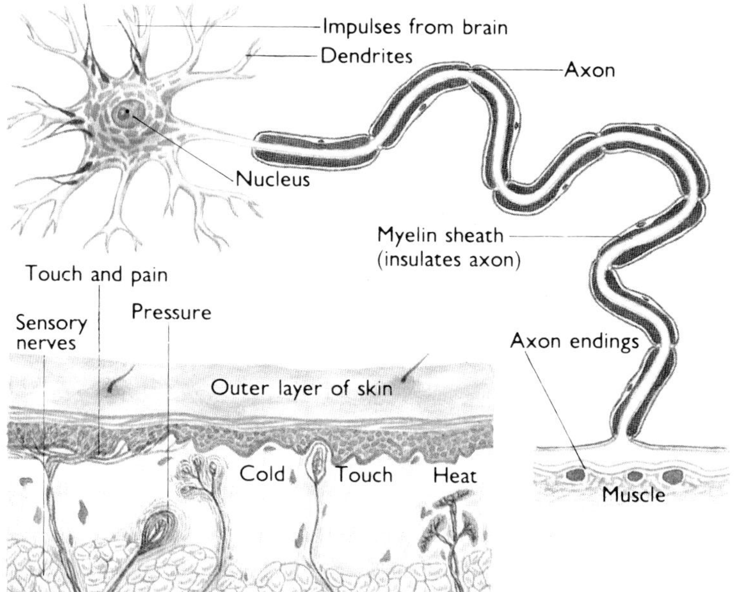

▼ *A motor nerve, with its many dendrites and long axon, carries messages from the brain or spinal cord to the muscles.*

► *Various receptors in the skin deal with different sensations. They transmit these sensations to the brain with the help of nerve cells.*

Nest

A nest is a home built by an animal, where it has its young and looks after them. BIRDS build nests when they are ready to lay EGGS. Sometimes the female builds the nest; sometimes the male will give her some help. Some nests are very complicated, and may be lined with wool, hair, or feathers. Others are simple or rather messy.

A few MAMMALS, such as MICE and SQUIRRELS, make nests for their young, but they are not as complicated as birds' nests.

Some INSECTS make the most complicated nests of all. They are not at all like birds' nests. They are often built for a whole group, or colony, of insects. There will be one queen, who lays eggs, and hundreds or even thousands of workers to look after them. Most BEES and WASPS make this kind of nest. Some wasps build their nests out of paper. TERMITES make huge mud nests.

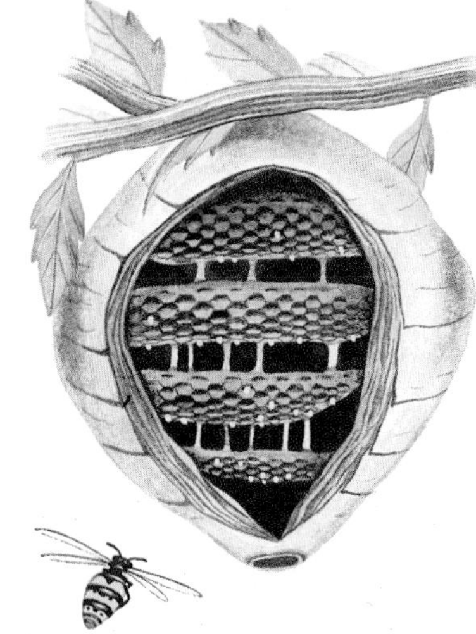

▲ *The complex pattern of cells in the hornet's papery nest makes a safe home for the young.*

▲ *Coots live on open stretches of water, but build their nests on piles of stones or sticks raised above the water.*

▲ *The South American oven bird builds a nest shaped like an old-fashioned oven from mud and bits of grass or straw.*

Netherlands

The Netherlands, or Holland, as it is also known, is a low-lying country in western EUROPE. The sea often floods the flat land near the coast, so sea walls have been built for protection against storms. Living so near the sea, the people of the Netherlands (who call themselves the Dutch) have a long and successful history of seafaring, trade, and exploring.

◀ *A lot of the inhabited land in the Netherlands was reclaimed from the sea and drained, using networks of canals.*

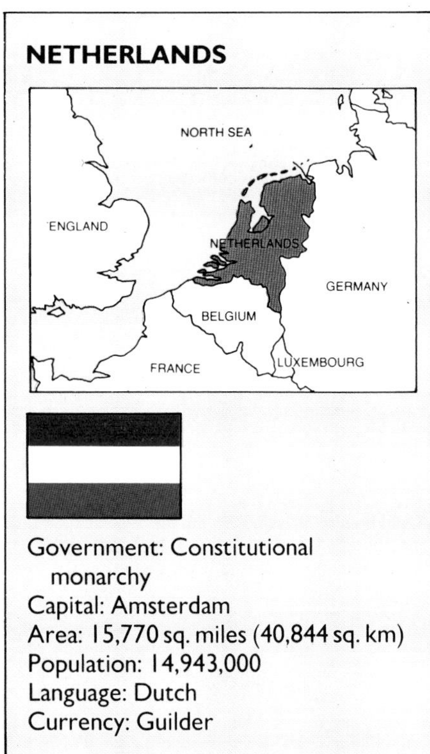

Government: Constitutional monarchy
Capital: Amsterdam
Area: 15,770 sq. miles (40,844 sq. km)
Population: 14,943,000
Language: Dutch
Currency: Guilder

The Netherlands is a land of canals, windmills, farms, and bulb fields, which burst into color in spring. It was once part of a group of countries called the Low Countries, but it became self-governing in 1759. Important cities are Amsterdam, the capital, and Rotterdam, which is the busiest port in Europe. The Netherlands is a prosperous country and one of the first members of the EUROPEAN COMMUNITY. It has a queen, but is governed by a democratic parliament.

Nevada

Nevada is a rugged, semi-desert state whose wild scenery and empty spaces attract visitors from all over the country. They come to explore its unspoiled mountain ranges, its clear lakes, and its pine forests. Many come to gamble, too: Nevada is the only state to allow most forms of gambling, and visitors pour into large resorts such as Las Vegas and Reno to gamble in the casinos there. The state also makes money from mining. Gold, silver, and oil are all mined in Nevada. It was the prospect of striking it rich that brought the many settlers and prospectors to Nevada in the 1860s and '70s. Today, visitors come to visit the old mining towns.

► *Red Rock Canyon, near Las Vegas, typifies the rugged desert land that covers much of the state.*

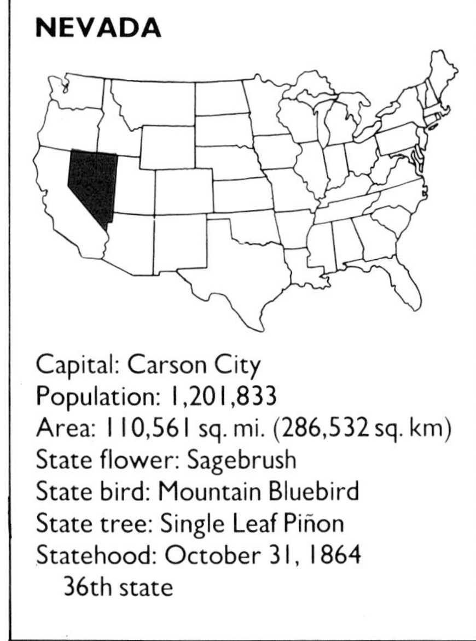

Capital: Carson City
Population: 1,201,833
Area: 110,561 sq. mi. (286,532 sq. km)
State flower: Sagebrush
State bird: Mountain Bluebird
State tree: Single Leaf Piñon
Statehood: October 31, 1864
36th state

New Brunswick

New Brunswick is a Canadian province in the east of the country, on the Atlantic coast. It was one of the four original provinces of Canada. Ninety percent of New Brunswick is forest, and wood and paper products are vital to its economy. The northeast of New Brunswick has huge mineral reserves, including copper, lead, zinc, and silver. Fishing is also an important industry. Lobster, herring, cod, crab, and shrimp are caught in the waters of the Bay of Fundy and the Gulf of St. Lawrence. The rich, rolling lands in the center of the province are heavily farmed. The empty interior, with its lakes and rivers, is popular with hunters and fishermen.

NEW BRUNSWICK

Capital: Fredericton
Population: 724,300
Area: 27,834 sq. mi. (72,090 sq. km)
Entry into Confederation: July 1, 1867

NEWFOUNDLAND

Capital: Saint John's
Population: 573,000
Area: 143,510 sq. mi. (371,690 sq. km)
Entry into Confederation: March 31, 1949

Newfoundland 

Newfoundland is Canada's newest province. It became a province in 1949 after years of discussion about joining the Dominion. The province consists of the island of Newfoundland off Canada's east coast and Labrador on the mainland. Fishing is one of the province's main industries. Fishing fleets from many nations come to fish the Grand Banks, southeast of Newfoundland. The province's extensive forests produce wood pulp and paper. Iron ore and other minerals are mined.

New Hampshire 

New Hampshire is a state in New England. It was one of the first areas of the country to be settled, and one of the 13 original states. When New Hampshire ratified the U.S. CONSTITUTION in 1788, the Constitution became law. It is a ruggedly beautiful area, with lakes, mountains, and forests. Its vivid fall foliage is famous across the country. New Hampshire has many modern industries, but farming and forestry are still important to it, as they were in the 1700s and 1800s. There are important shipbuilding ports on the coast. The state played an important part in the Revolutionary War. In the Civil War, New Hampshire was among the fiercest opponents of slavery and the South.

NEW HAMPSHIRE

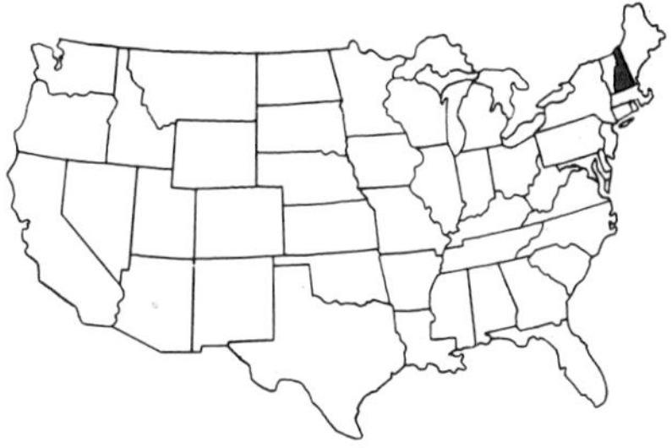

Capital: Concord
Population: 1,109,252
Area: 9,279 sq. mi. (24,032 sq. km)
State flower: Purple Lilac
State bird: Purple Finch
State tree: White Birch
Statehood: June 21, 1788
9th state

New Jersey 

New Jersey is one of the smallest states and one of the most important industrially. It also has the largest population, for its size, of any state. It is

NEW JERSEY

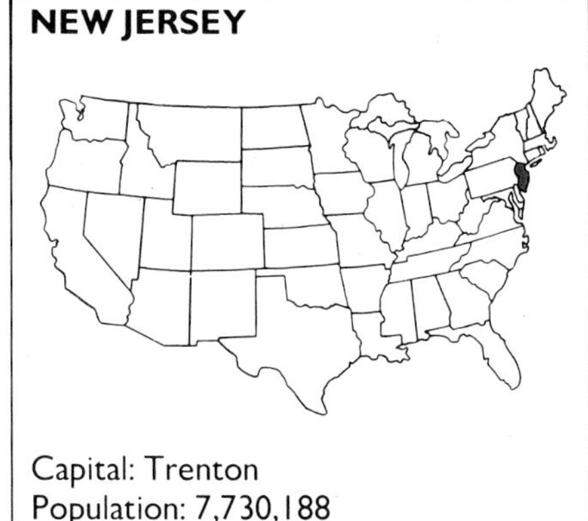

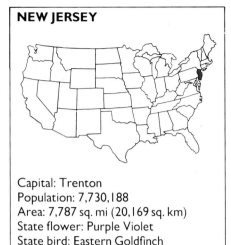

Capital: Trenton
Population: 7,730,188
Area: 7,787 sq. mi (20,169 sq. km)
State flower: Purple Violet
State bird: Eastern Goldfinch
State tree: Red Oak
Statehood: December 18, 1787
3rd state

located on the Atlantic coast, between the cities of New York and Philadelphia. Many people who live in New Jersey work in one of these cities. Though it is small, there are also many large cities in New Jersey. Most are major manufacturing centers, too, producing goods that are used across the country. Inland, there are many small farms that supply food to cities all along the Atlantic coast. The New Jersey shore is one of the most popular vacation areas in the country. Summer resorts with beaches line the coast.

New Mexico

New Mexico is one of the largest and most spectacular states. It also has one of the most colorful histories of any state. New Mexico is in the southwest. It has impressive mountain ranges and huge areas of semi-desert. Its low rainfall means that little agriculture is possible. It has large reserves of many important minerals, including natural gas and petroleum. It also has an important nuclear industry. It was in New Mexico, in 1945, that the first

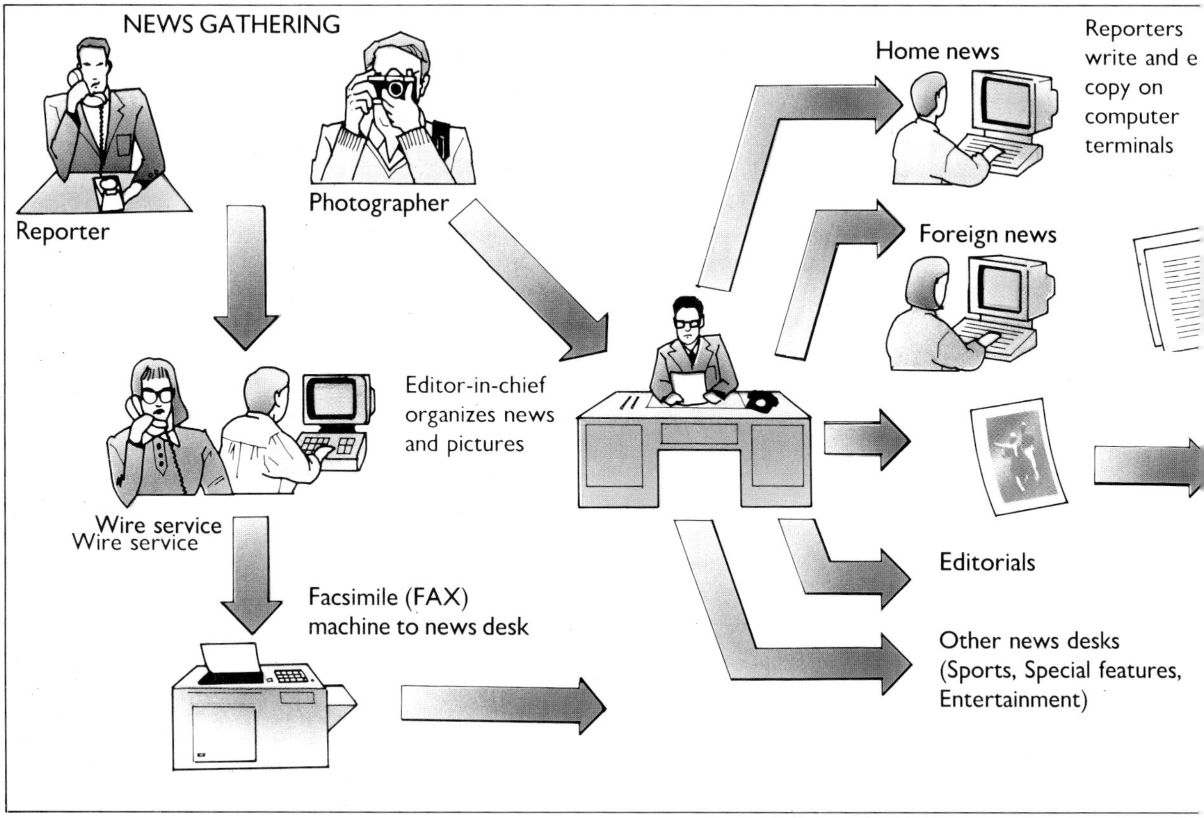

NEWS GATHERING

Reporter

Photographer

Wire service
Wire service

Facsimile (FAX) machine to news desk

Editor-in-chief organizes news and pictures

Home news

Reporters write and e
copy on computer terminals

Foreign news

Editorials

Other news desks (Sports, Special features, Entertainment)

atomic bomb was exploded. New Mexico was ruled for many years by Spain and then Mexico. And it was in New Mexico that some of the fiercest battles of the Indian wars took place in the 1800s.

NEW MEXICO

Capital: Santa Fe
Population: 1,515,069
Area: 121,593 sq. mi. (314,925 sq. km)
State flower: Yucca
State bird: Roadrunner
State tree: Piñon
Statehood: January 6, 1912
47th state

Newspaper

Newspapers are just what their name says they are—papers that print news. They first appeared in the 1400s, just after PRINTING began. Printers produced pamphlets telling people what was happening in the country and what they thought about it.

Modern newspapers first appeared in the 1700s. Today, there are newspapers in almost every country in the world, in many different languages. Some are printed every day, some every week.

One of the oldest newspapers is the *The Times* of London. It began in 1785. Other famous newspapers are the *New York Times* and the *Washington Post* in the United States, *Pravda* in Russia, and *Le Monde* in France. The first successful U.S. daily newspaper, the *Pennsylvania Packet and General Advertiser*, was published in 1784.

Artwork is prepared on computer graphic programs or by hand

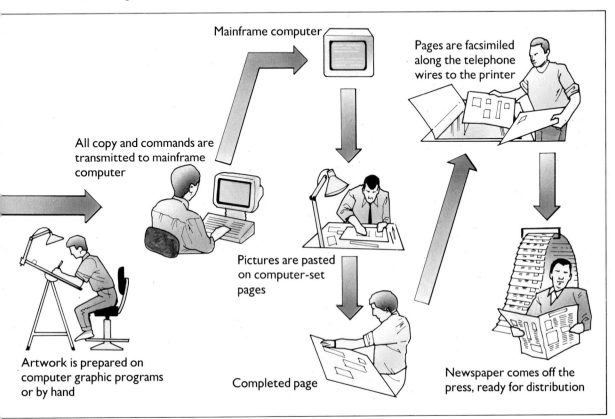

All copy and commands are transmitted to mainframe computer

Mainframe computer

Pictures are pasted on computer-set pages

Completed page

Pages are facsimiled along the telephone wires to the printer

Newspaper comes off the press, ready for distribution

▲ *Newton determined the laws of motion that are still used in physics today.*

Newton, Isaac

Sir Isaac Newton (1642–1727) was an English mathematician and scientist who made some of the world's greatest scientific discoveries. He left Cambridge University in 1665 when an epidemic of plague closed the University. In the 18 months before the University reopened, Newton did much of his most important work.

Newton's experiments showed that white LIGHT is a mixture of all the colors of the rainbow (the SPECTRUM). By studying the spectrum of light from a star or other glowing object, scientists can now find out what that object is made of. Newton's studies of light also led him to build the first reflecting TELESCOPE.

Newton also first thought about GRAVITY. He realized that the same kind of force that makes apples fall from trees also gives objects weight and keeps PLANETS revolving around the SUN.

NEW YORK

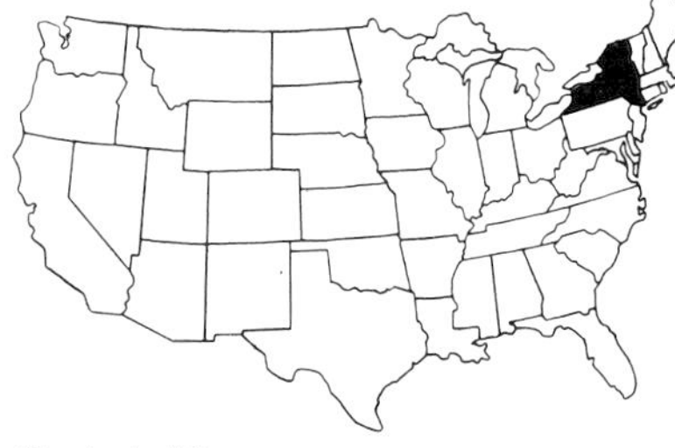

Capital: Albany
Population: 17,990,455
Area: 49,108 sq. mi (127,189 sq. km)
State flower: Rose
State bird: Bluebird
State tree: Sugar Maple
Statehood: July 26, 1788
11th state

New York

New York has always been one of the most important states in the country. It is home to the largest city in the United States, New York City. Its industries are world leaders in many fields. It is the most important financial state in the country. And, until the '60s, it had the largest population of any state. Though it is so heavily populated, New York is also a surprisingly rural area. Its wooded hills, its rivers and lakes, and its rich farming country are a contrast to its busy cities.

New York was settled first by the Dutch in the 1600s. In 1664, it was captured by Britain. The state played an important part in the Revolutionary War, and many battles were fought in it. In the 1800s, it became the leading industrial state.

New York City

New York City is the largest city in the UNITED STATES. More than 11 million people live in New York and its suburbs.

The city stands mainly on three islands that lie at

▲ *New York is home to some of the tallest buildings in the world.*

the mouth of the Hudson River. The island of Manhattan holds the heart of New York and many of its most famous sights. Some of the world's tallest SKYSCRAPERS tower above its streets. Fifth Avenue is a famous shopping street, and Broadway is known for its theaters. Perhaps New York's best-known sight is the Statue of LIBERTY, one of the largest statues on Earth. It stands on a small island in New York Harbor.

Ships from every continent dock at New York's port, which is the largest anywhere. New York is one of the world's great business centers. Its factories produce more goods than those of any other city in the United States.

▲ *The kiwi lives in the forests of New Zealand. Since it cannot fly, it does not need the strong, stiff feathers most birds have.*

New Zealand

New Zealand is a remote island nation in the Pacific Ocean, southeast of Australia.

New Zealand is actually two main islands. North

NEW ZEALAND

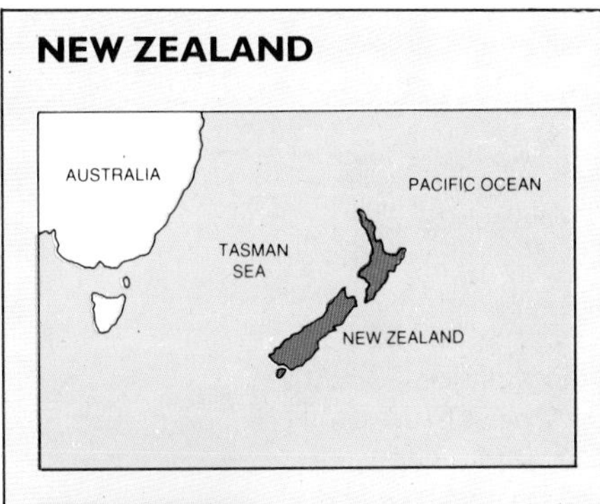

Government: Parliamentary
Capital: Wellington
Area: 103,736 sq. miles (268,676 sq. km)
Population: 3,346,000
Languages: English, Maori
Currency: Dollar

◄ *The Pohutu geyser on the North Island of New Zealand erupts because of the natural heat and pressure from underground springs.*

When the first European settlers arrived in New Zealand, the only mammals there were dogs and rats. All the country's cattle, sheep, pigs, deer, rabbits, and goats were brought in by Europeans.

Island is famous for its hot springs and volcanoes. South Island has a range of mountains, the Southern Alps, and many lovely lakes and waterfalls.

The country also has plains and valleys. Here, the mild climate helps farmers to grow grain, vegetables, and apples. They also raise millions of sheep and cattle. New Zealand is the world's third largest producer of sheep and wool.

There are over three million New Zealanders. Two out of three people live in a city or town. Auckland is the largest city, but the capital is Wellington.

New Zealand is a member of the British COMMONWEALTH. Many of its people are descended from British settlers. Other are MAORIS, descended from Pacific islanders, who lived in New Zealand before the British came.

NICARAGUA

BELIZE
GUATEMALA
HONDURAS
CARIBBEAN SEA
EL SALVADOR
NICARAGUA
PACIFIC OCEAN
COSTA RICA
PANAMA

Government: Republic
Capital: Managua
Area: 50,193 sq. miles (130,000 sq. km)
Population: 3,871,000
Languages: Spanish, English
Currency: Cordoba

Niagara Falls

The Niagara Falls are WATERFALLS on the Niagara River in North America. Water from most of the GREAT LAKES flows through this river. Each minute about 450,000 tons of water plunges about 165 ft. (50 m) from a cliff into a gorge.

The falls stand on the border between Canada and the United States. The water pours down on each side of an island. Most of it plunges down the Horseshoe Falls in Canada. The rest plunges down the American Falls in the United States.

People can gaze down on the falls from observation towers, or take a ship that sails up to the wild water below.

► *The sheer size of Niagara Falls has challenged people's courage and ingenuity for many years—Charles Blondin walked across the top of the falls on a tightrope on June 30, 1859.*

Nicaragua

Nicaragua is a country that stretches across Central America from the Pacific Ocean to the Caribbean Sea. Most of the people live on the western coast, where the land is flat and good for farming. A line of high mountains runs down the center of Nicaragua. Farming is the main occupation, with cotton, coffee, fruit, and sugar as the main products.

In 1938, Nicaragua became an independent republic dominated by the Somoza family. In 1979, Sandinista guerrillas took over the country, later opposed by the U.S.-backed "contras." In free elections held in 1990 the Sandinista government was defeated.

Niger

Niger is a West African country with no seacoast. The north of the country is part of the Sahara Desert. The south, through which flows the Niger River, is the agricultural region. The climate is hot and dry. Most of the people are herdsmen and farmers who grow peanuts and cotton. The mining of uranium is important.

Niger was a French colony that became independent in 1960. Severe droughts in the 1970s and 1980s led to great losses of crops and livestock. Many people starved.

NIGER

ALGERIA
LIBYA
MALI
NIGER
CHAD
BURKINA FASO
NIGERIA
BENIN
TOGO
GHANA
CAMEROON
CENTRAL AFRICAN REPUBLIC

Government: Republic
Capital: Niamey
Area: 489,189 sq. miles (1,267,000 sq. km)
Population: 7,732,000
Language: French
Currency: CFA Franc

Nigeria

This nation in West Africa is named after the Niger River that flows through it to the Atlantic Ocean. Nigeria has more people than any other nation in Africa.

All Nigeria is hot. Dry grass and scrubby trees are scattered across the country. But swamps and forests line the coasts.

There are a great number of different tribes, and many of them speak different languages.

Half the people believe in the religion of Islam. Most of the people grow corn, yams, or other food crops. Nigeria is one of the world's main cocoa growers, and one of Africa's top two oil producers.

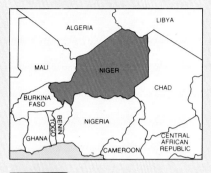

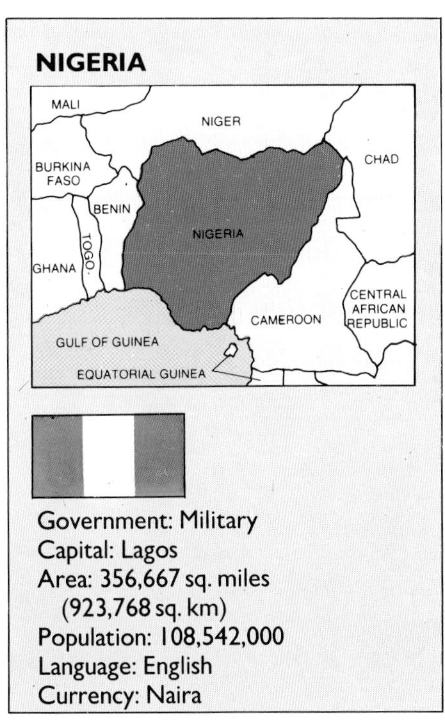

Government: Military
Capital: Lagos
Area: 356,667 sq. miles (923,768 sq. km)
Population: 108,542,000
Language: English
Currency: Naira

RICHARD M. NIXON

Thirty-seventh President 1969–1974
Born: Yorba Linda, California
Education: Whittier College and Duke University Law School
Occupation: Lawyer
Political Party: Republican

Nile River

The Nile River in Africa is generally thought to be the longest river on Earth. (Some people think that the AMAZON is longer.) The Nile has been measured at 4,160 miles (6,695 km). It rises in Burundi in central Africa and flows north through Egypt into the Mediterranean Sea. It is very important to farmers, who rely on it for irrigation.

Nixon, Richard Milhous

Richard Nixon (1913–) was the 37th president of the United States. He was the only president to be forced to resign. This happened in 1974 after the Watergate scandal. Officials working for the campaign to re-elect Nixon in the 1972 election broke into the headquarters of Nixon's opponents, the Democrats. When it became known that Nixon had helped in covering up the break-in, he resigned. Though

▼ *A ship unloads at the quay in an ancient Egyptian city. The civilization that grew up in ancient Egypt depended on the Nile for transport, so most large cities were built beside this great river.*

Watergate dominated Nixon's last years as president, he also achieved some successes in foreign policy. He ended U.S. involvement in the Vietnam War in 1972, and he improved relations between the United States and the Soviet Union and China.

Nobel Prizes

These money prizes are given each year to people who have helped mankind in different ways. Three prizes are given for inventions or discoveries in physics, chemistry, and physiology and medicine. The fourth is for literature. The fifth prize is for work to make or keep peace between peoples, and the sixth is for economics. Money for the prizes was left by the Swedish chemist, Alfred Nobel, who invented the explosive, dynamite.

▲ *When Alfred Nobel died in 1896, he left $9,000,000 to set up the prizes that now bear his name. The interest that this money earns each year forms the awards.*

North America

The continent of North America stretches north from tropical Panama to the cold Arctic Ocean, and east from the Pacific Ocean to the Atlantic Ocean. Only Asia is larger.

North America has the world's largest island (GREENLAND) and the largest freshwater LAKE (Lake Superior). It contains the second largest country (CANADA), the second longest mountain range (the ROCKY MOUNTAINS), and the third longest river (the MISSISSIPPI RIVER). North America's natural wonders include NIAGARA FALLS and the GRAND CANYON (the largest gorge on land).

The cold north has long, dark, frozen winters. No trees grow there. Farther south stand huge evergreen forests. Grasslands covered most of the plains in the middle of the continent until farmers plowed them up. Cactuses thrive in the deserts of the southwest. Tropical trees grow quickly in the hot, wet forests of the south.

Peoples from all over the world have made their homes in North America. First, from Asia, came the ancestors of the AMERICAN INDIANS and ESKIMOS. Later came Europeans, who brought black slaves from Africa. Most North Americans speak English, French, or Spanish, and are Protestant or

NORTH AMERICA

Area: 9,400,000 sq. miles (24,400,000 sq. km) 15.7 percent of world's land area
Population: 432,000,000—8 percent of world population
Coastline: 190,000 miles (305,000 km)
Highest mountain: Mount McKinley, Alaska, 20,320 ft. (6,194 m)
Lowest point: Death Valley, California, 282 ft. (86 m) below sea level
Principal rivers: Mackenzie, Mississippi, Missouri, St. Lawrence, Rio Grande, Yukon, Arkansas, Colorado
Principal lakes: Superior, Huron, Michigan, Great Bear, Great Slave, Erie, Winnipeg, Ontario
Largest city: Mexico City, 20,000,000
Busiest port: New Orleans

NORTH AMERICA

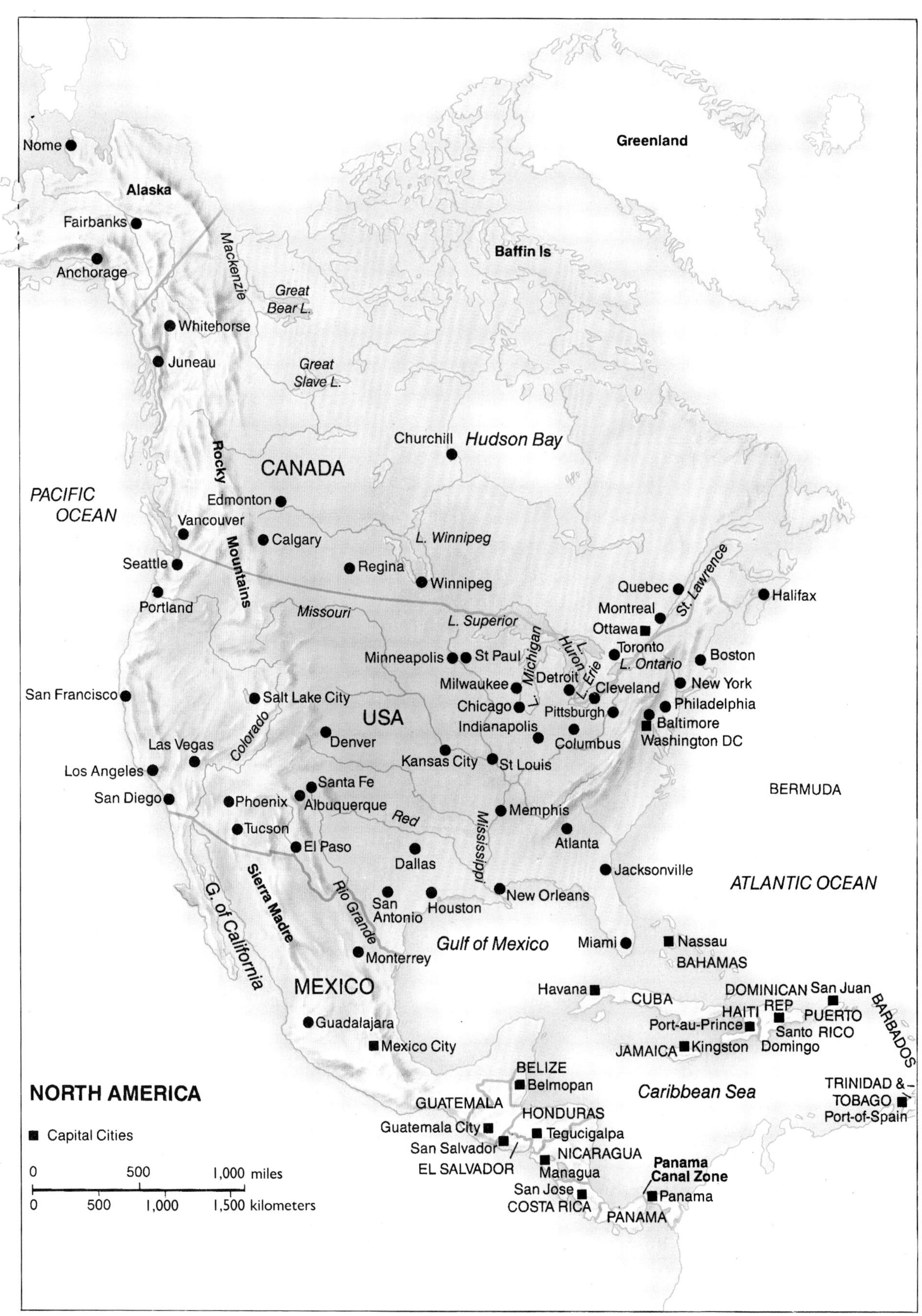

Roman Catholic Christians. They live in more than 30 nations. The UNITED STATES and CANADA are large, powerful, and rich. But many of the nations of CENTRAL AMERICA and the WEST INDIES are small and poor.

Only one person in every ten people in the world lives in North America.

North Carolina

North Carolina is a southern state on the Atlantic coast and one of the 13 original states. It was named for Charles I, king of England in the early 1600s. It was one of the first areas of the country to be settled: two English colonies were established as early as 1587, though neither survived. Tobacco farming is the most important business. The state's many forests are also carefully cultivated. But, though it is still largely an agricultural state, there are many industries, too. Furniture-making is important. North Carolina was one of the most prosperous cotton-growing states before the Civil War. Though it was destroyed economically in the war, it recovered quickly.

NORTH CAROLINA

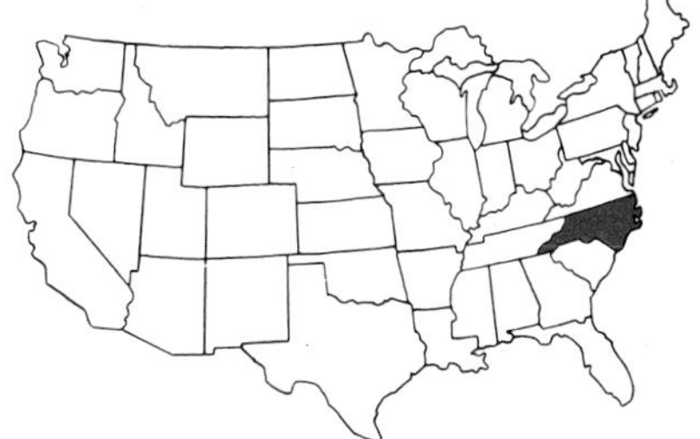

Capital: Raleigh
Population: 6,628,637
Area: 52,669 sq. mi. (136,413 sq. km)
State flower: Dogwood
State bird: Cardinal
State tree: Long leaf Pine
Statehood: November 21, 1789
12th state

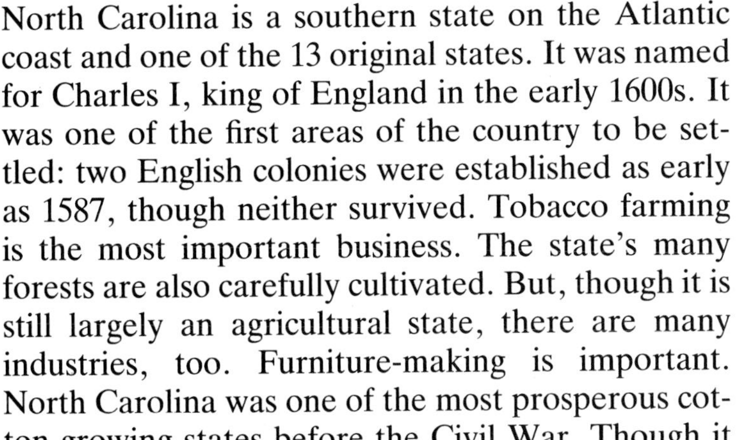

▲ *The Great Smoky Mountains in western North Carolina get their name from their hazy gray-blue color. In the foreground is Fontana Lake.*

North Dakota

North Dakota is the most westerly of the midwestern states and is located on the Canadian border. There are few large cities. More than half the population lives in rural areas. Farming is the most im-

◀ *Livestock and livestock products account for about a fourth of North Dakota's agricultural income.*

North Dakota is often called the Flickertail State because of the many flickertail ground squirrels that live there.

NORTH DAKOTA

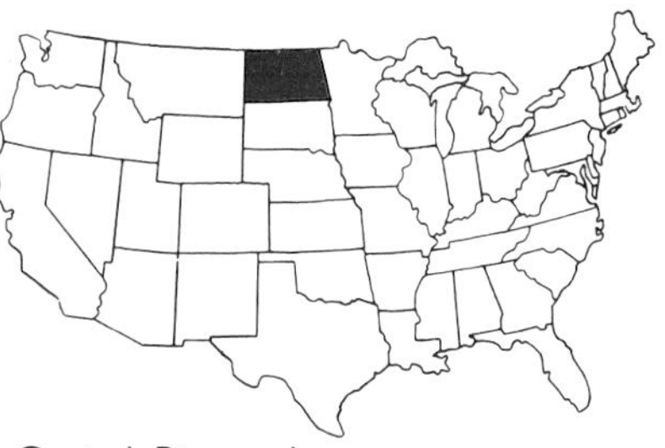

Capital: Bismarck
Population: 638,800
Area: 70,702 sq. mi. (183,119 sq. km)
State flower: Wild Prairie Rose
State bird: Western Meadowlark
State tree: American Elm
Statehood: November 2, 1889
39th state

portant industry. North Dakota's rich soil is used to grow a wide range of products. The most important is wheat, but oats, rye, sugar beets, and flaxseed are all grown, too. The state also has important mineral reserves, including coal and oil. Because it is so remote, and because the Native Americans there were thought to be especially fierce, North Dakota was one of the last states to be settled.

Northern Ireland

Northern Ireland is also called Ulster. It consists of six counties in the northeast corner of the island of Ireland. Northern Ireland was separated from the rest of Ireland in 1921, when the Republic of Ireland (Eire) won independence from Great Britain.

The leading industries are the manufacture of textiles and clothing, shipbuilding, and agriculture.

Political problems in Northern Ireland date back to the 1600s, when many English and Scottish Protestants settled there. In the 1960s, protests by the minority Catholics (outnumbered by Protestants in Northern Ireland) against unfair treatment led to civil disorder. Bombings, shootings, and other TERRORIST acts have led to great loss of life, though the British and Irish governments are trying to settle Northern Ireland's future peacefully.

▲ *The peaceful countryside around the Mountains of Mourne shows a more peaceful side of life in Northern Ireland than we usually hear about.*

North Pole

The North Pole is the place farthest north on EARTH. Its LATITUDE is 90° north. The North Pole is the northern end of the Earth's axis. This is an imaginary line around which the Earth spins.

The North Pole lies in the middle of the Arctic Ocean. Here, the surface of the sea is always frozen. The Sun does not rise in winter or set in summer for several weeks.

Northwest Territories

The Northwest Territories are one of Canada's two territories. The other is Yukon Territory. Northwest Territories is a vast area in the far north, covering about a third of Canada's total area. About half the territory lies north of the Arctic Circle. The population is quite small. About a third of the people are Eskimos and about a fifth are Indians. Minerals are the most valuable resource of the Northwest Territories. The fishing industry is also important, especially on Great Slave Lake. Fur trapping first drew whites to the Territories. This has now declined.

NORTHWEST TERRITORIES

Capital: Yellowknife
Population: 54,000
Area: 1,271,422 sq. miles (3,292,968 sq. km)
Created: 1870

Norway

Norway is EUROPE's sixth largest country. This long, northern kingdom is wide in the south, but narrow in the center and the north. Mountains with forests, bare rocks, and snow cover much of Norway. Steep inlets called FIORDS pierce its rocky coast.

Summers in Norway are cool and the winters long. It is very cold in the ARCTIC north, but the rainy west coast is kept fairly mild by the GULF STREAM. Norwegians catch more fish than any other Europeans, and their North Sea oil wells are among Europe's richest.

Norway has a king, and a prime minister who is head of the government.

NORWAY

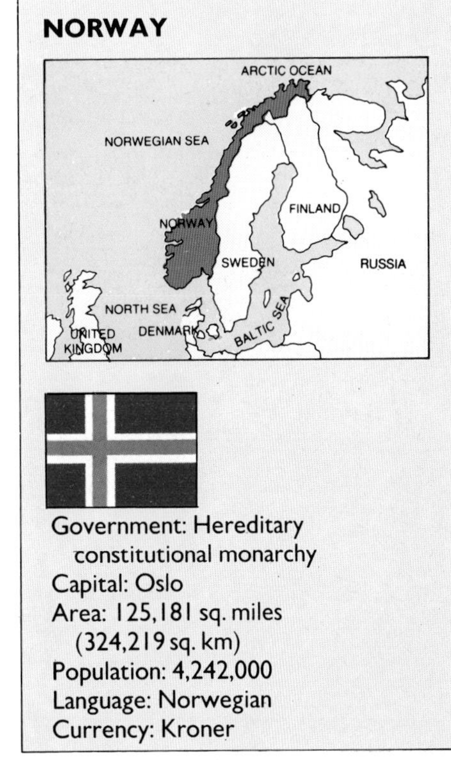

Government: Hereditary constitutional monarchy
Capital: Oslo
Area: 125,181 sq. miles (324,219 sq. km)
Population: 4,242,000
Language: Norwegian
Currency: Kroner

Noun

A noun is a word that names. The name of everything is a noun, whether it is a person (John); a place (China); a thing (book); a quality (kindness); or anything else. The *subject* of a sentence—what a sentence is about—is always a noun or a *pronoun*. A pronoun is a word that is used in place of a noun. The most common pronouns are *I*, *we*, *you*, *he*, *she*, *it*, and *they*.

Nova Scotia

Nova Scotia is one of the Atlantic provinces of Canada. The name means "New Scotland" and was given to the province by British settlers in the 1700s. The province is a peninsula, joined to the mainland by a narrow neck of land. No part of Nova Scotia is more than 35 miles (56 km) from the sea. The rise and fall of the tides in the province is greater than

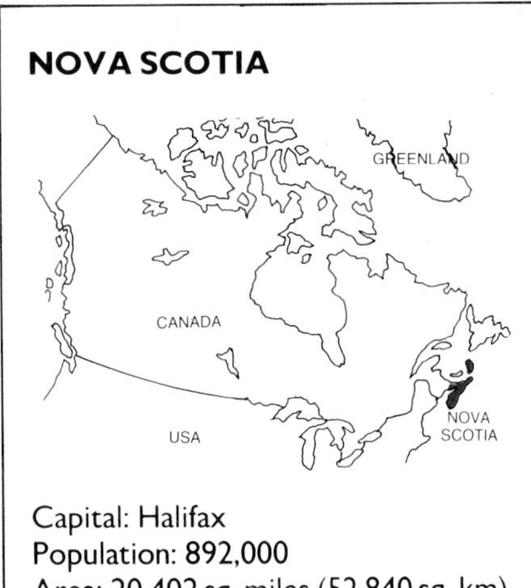

Capital: Halifax
Population: 892,000
Area: 20,402 sq. miles (52,840 sq. km)
Entry into confederation: July 1, 1867

anywhere in the world—more than 50 ft. (15 m) in the Bay of Fundy.

Nova Scotia's leading products are paper, food, and transportation equipment.

Novel

Novels are long written stories. There are many kinds. For instance, some are adventure tales, like *Treasure Island* by Robert Louis STEVENSON. There are horror novels like Mary Shelley's *Frankenstein*, science fiction novels, humorous novels like *Tom Sawyer* by Mark TWAIN, and satirical novels like Jonathan SWIFT's *Gulliver's Travels*, where Swift slyly pokes fun at mankind. Authors such as Sir Walter Scott wrote historical novels: novels set in the past.

Novels can be about people at any place or time. They are all meant to entertain us. But the best novels give us a new way of looking at life. Writers such as Charles DICKENS showed the harsh lives of poor people in England in the middle 1800s.

Novels grew out of short stories written in Italy in the 1300s. One of the first novels was *Don Quixote*, by the Spanish writer Cervantes. Some of the first English novels with believable stories were written by Daniel Defoe.

▲ *The "mushroom cloud" formed by the huge release of destructive energy from a nuclear explosion.*

Nuclear Energy

The tiny nucleus at the center of the atom contains the most powerful force ever discovered. This force gives us nuclear energy—sometimes called atomic energy. The most complicated ELEMENT that occurs in nature is URANIUM. The nuclear fuel used in nuclear power plants is a rare form of uranium called uranium-235.

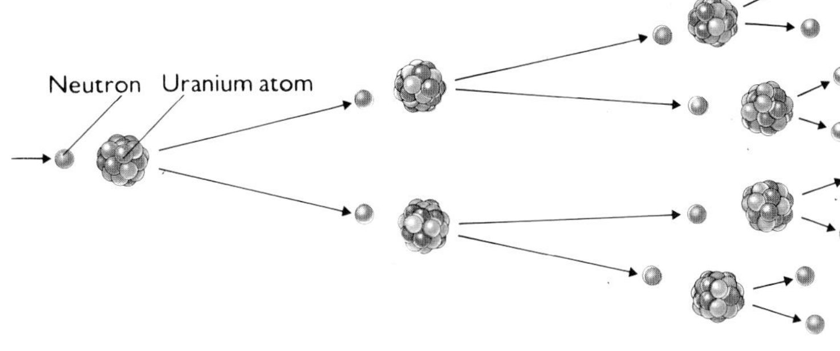

▶ *Bombarding an atom of uranium-235 with a neutron can start a chain reaction. As the nucleus of the atom splits, more neutrons are given out to split more atoms, and great amounts of energy are released.*

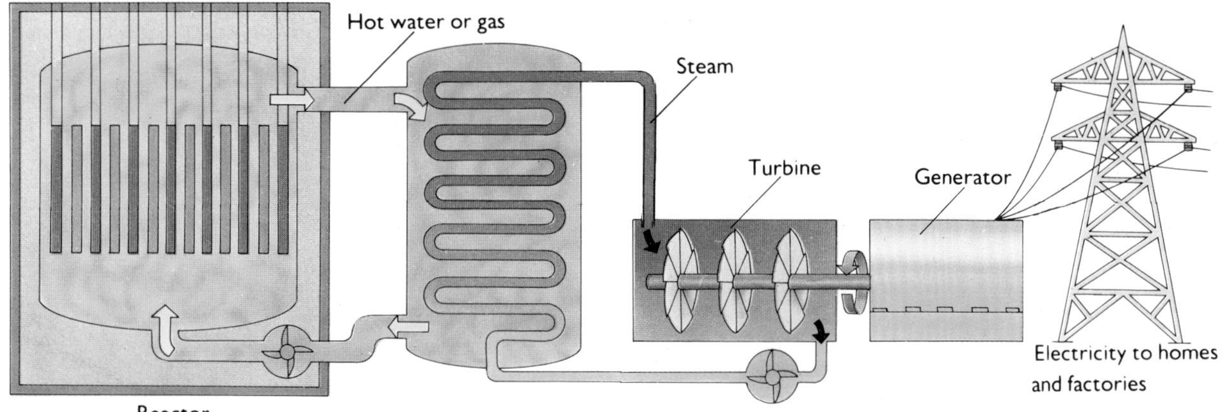

▲ *In a nuclear power plant, the energy from the controlled nuclear reaction, in the form of heat, is used to make steam. The steam drives turbines, which generate electricity in the same way as in any other type of power plant.*

When the nucleus of a uranium-235 atom is struck by a neutron (see ATOM), it breaks apart and more neutrons shoot out. These new neutrons strike other uranium nuclei, causing them to split and give out still more neutrons. In this way, more and more nuclei split, and many atoms give up their energy at once. If the action is not controlled, a tremendous explosion takes place—the atomic explosion that powers nuclear weapons.

Nuclear energy can be controlled to provide us with power. In a nuclear power plant, control rods are lowered into the reactor to keep the reaction in check. But the uranium still gets very hot, and so a coolant—a liquid or a gas—moves through the reactor. When the hot coolant leaves the reactor, it goes to a boiler to make steam. It is this steam that powers generators to make electricity for our homes and factories.

There are many very large numbers. The population of the world is very large. The number of blades of grass, and the leaves on the trees must be enormously large. The famous Greek scientist Archimedes estimated the number of grains of sand it would take to fill the universe. He did not know the number exactly, but he said it was *finite*. He also knew that some numbers are *infinite*. If we go on counting 1, 2, 3, 4, 5, . . . and so on, we will never come to the end. This set of numbers is infinite.

Number

In STONE AGE times, people showed a number like 20 or 30 by making 20 or 30 separate marks. In certain caves, you can still see the marks.

1	2	3	4	5	6	7	8	9	10		Arabic
𒁹	𒈫	𒐈	𒐉	𒐊	𒐋	𒑂	𒑄	𒑆	𒌋		Babylonian
Α	Β	Γ	Δ	Ε	Ζ	Η	Θ	Ι	Κ		Greek
I	II	III	IV	V	VI	VII	VIII	IX	X		Roman
一	二	三	四	五	六	七	八	九	十		Chinese
•	••	•••	••••	—	• —	•• —	••• —	•••• —	— —	(shell)	Mayan
१	२	३	४	५	६	७	८	९	१०	०	Indian

◀ *The earliest known written numbers were those used by the Babylonians about 5,000 years ago. All the great civilizations have had their own way of writing and using numbers.*

The word "nursing" comes from the Latin word *nutricia*, meaning "nourishing." Records from ancient Egypt and Greece mention various nursing practices, including the giving of herbal remedies. The Roman armies employed male nurses to care for the wounded.

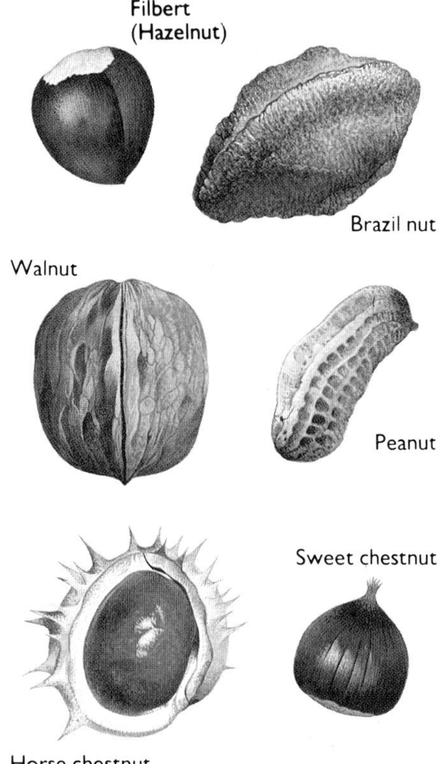

▲ *The filbert, or hazelnut, is cultivated in orchards in Oregon and Washington. The Brazil nut grows on large trees in northern South America. English walnuts grow in California, and in Italy, France, and Turkey. The American chestnut tree was almost completely wiped out by a bark disease in the early 1900s. Peanuts are not really nuts at all! They belong to the bean family.*

In time, people invented special signs or groups of signs to show different numbers. Such signs are called *numerals*. For centuries, many people used Roman numerals. But these are rather clumsy. For instance, the Roman numerals for 38 are XXXVIII. Our much simpler system uses Arabic numerals, which were first used in India.

Nursing

People who are very ill, old, or handicapped need nursing in their homes or in a HOSPITAL. Nursing can mean feeding, washing, and giving treatment ordered by a doctor. It is hard work and requires special skills. Men and women train for several years before becoming nurses. Modern nursing owes much to the example set by Florence Nightingale during the CRIMEAN WAR.

Nut

Nuts are FRUITS with a hard, wooden shell. The seeds are called kernels. The kernels of many nuts are good to eat and rich in PROTEINS and FAT. Peanuts are crushed and made into peanut butter. Some people bake bread from chestnuts ground into flour.

Nuts grow in temperate and tropical areas. Many widely grown nuts have been imported from countries around the world, such as the English walnut (which probably came originally from the Middle East) and the macadamia from Australia.

Nutrition

Nutrition is the process by which we take in and use food. We need food to keep our bodies running smoothly and to provide the energy for work and play. Malnutrition is a weakening of the body caused by eating too little food, or eating food that lacks enough of the nutrients that keep your body strong and healthy. Nutrients can be divided into six groups: PROTEINS, carbohydrates, FATS, VITAMINS, MINERALS, and WATER. No one nutrient is more important that another. Each has its own work to do. A well-balanced diet contains all of them.

Oak

Oaks are trees with NUTS called acorns. Some oaks measure over 36 ft. (11 m) around the trunk. They grow slowly and may live for 900 years. There are about 275 kinds of oak. Most have leaves with deeply notched (wavy) edges. But evergreen oaks have tough, shiny, smooth-edged leaves.

Oak wood is hard and slow to rot. People used to build sailing ships from it. Tannin from oak bark is used in making LEATHER. CORK comes from cork oak bark.

◀ *Most types of oak tree are deciduous; that is, they lose their leaves in the fall each year and grow new ones in spring. The fruit of an oak tree is called an acorn (above). Although squirrels eat them, humans cannot.*

Oasis

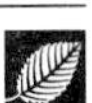

An oasis is a place where plants grow in a DESERT. It may be a small clump of palm trees, or much larger. Oases are found where there is water. This can come from rivers, wells, or springs. These may be fed by rain that falls on nearby mountains and seeps through rocks beneath the surface of the desert. People can make oases by drilling wells and digging IRRIGATION ditches.

▼ *This oasis in the Sinai Desert is the only source of water for miles around and supports varied plant and animal life.*

Ocean

Oceans cover nearly three-fourths of the surface of the Earth. If you put all the world's water in 100 giant tanks, 97 of them would be full of water from the oceans. The oceans are always losing water as water vapor, drawn up into the air by the Sun's heat. But most returns as RAIN. Rain water running

OCEAN FACTS

Arctic Ocean
Surface area 4,700,000 sq. miles (12,173,000 sq. km)
Average depth 3,250 ft. (990 m)
Greatest depth 15,100 ft. (4,600 m)

Indian Ocean
Surface area 28,350,000 sq. miles (73,426,500 sq. km)
Average depth 12,760 ft. (3,890 m)
Greatest depth 24,440 ft. (7,450 m)

Atlantic Ocean
Surface area 31,660,000 sq. miles (82,000,000 sq. km)
Average depth over 11,000 ft. (3,350 m)
Greatest depth 30,000 ft. (9,144 m)

Pacific Ocean
Surface area 64,100,000 sq. miles (166,000,000 sq. km)
Average depth 14,000 ft. (4,280 m)
Greatest depth 36,198 ft. (11,033 m)

WAVE, CURRENT, AND TIDE FACTS

Highest storm wave: 111 ft. (34 m)

Fastest waves: 300–500 mph (500–800 km/h) set off by earthquakes.

Largest ocean current: Antarctic Circumpolar Current. It carries 2,200 times more water than the world's largest river pours into the sea.

Fastest ocean current: Nakwakto Rapids, off Western Canada 19 mph (30 km/h)

Greatest range of tides on Earth: Bay of Fundy, Canada. A spring high tide can be more than 52 ft. (16 m) above a spring low tide.

off the land takes salts and other MINERALS to the oceans. For instance, enough sea water to fill a square tank half a mile long and half a mile high would hold four million tons of magnesium. The oceans supply most of the magnesium we use.

There are four oceans. The largest and deepest is the PACIFIC OCEAN. The second largest is the ATLANTIC OCEAN. This is only half as large as the Pacific Ocean. The Indian Ocean is smaller but deeper than the Atlantic Ocean. The Arctic Ocean is the smallest and shallowest ocean of all.

The oceans are never still. Winds crinkle their surface into WAVES. The GULF STREAM and other currents (some warm, others cold) flow like rivers through the oceans. Every day, the ocean surface

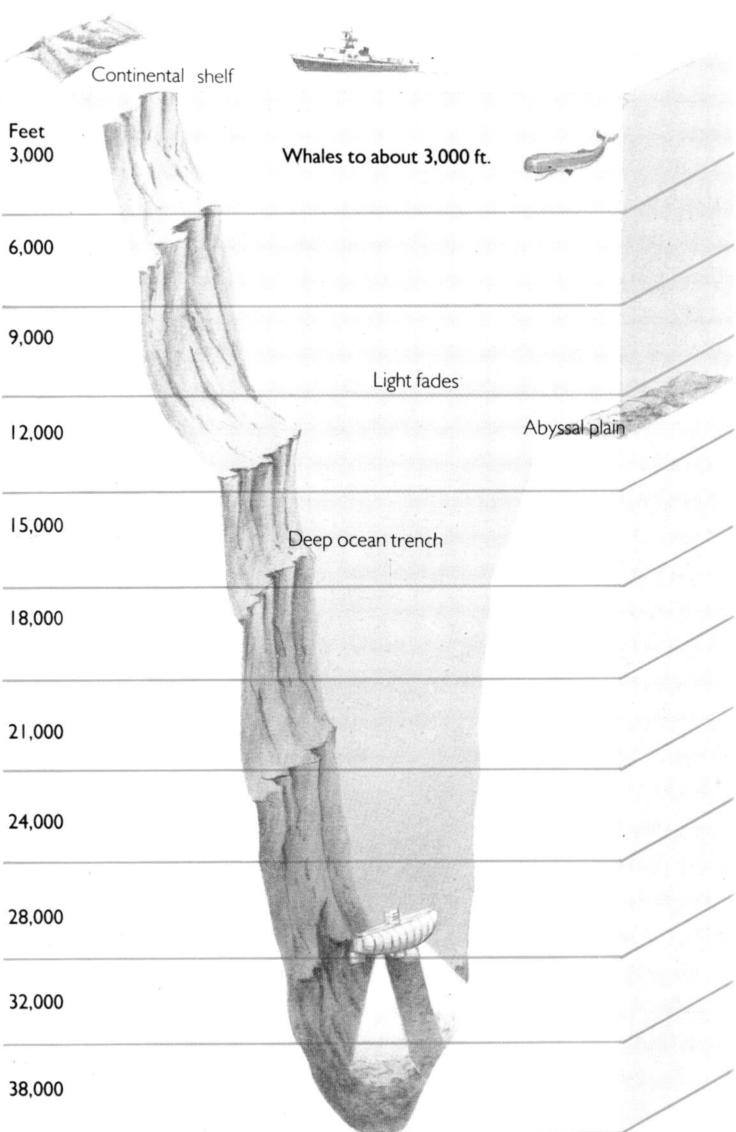

► *Most life in the sea exists in the top levels where sunlight can penetrate. The exploration of the deepest levels, more than 33,000 ft. (10,000 m) down, was first carried out using special underwater vehicles called bathyscaphes.*

falls and rises with the TIDES. In winter, polar sea water freezes over. ICEBERGS from polar seas may drift hundreds of miles through the oceans.

Oceans are home to countless living things. The minerals in sea water help to nourish tiny plants drifting at the surface. The plants are food for tiny animals. These animals and plants are called PLANKTON. Fish and some whales eat the plankton. In turn, small fish are eaten by larger hunters.

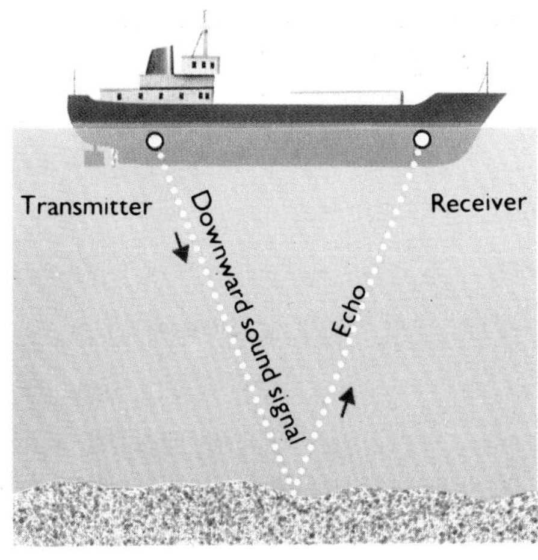

▲ *To figure out the depth of the water they are sailing in, ships use sonar devices. They send sound waves to the bottom of the sea and measure the time it takes for the echo to return.*

Octopus

There are about 50 kinds of octopus. They are soft-bodied MOLLUSKS that live in the sea. Octopus means "eight feet" but the eight tentacles of an octopus are usually called arms. The largest octopus has arms about 30 ft. (9m) across, but most octopuses are no larger than a person's fist. Suckers on the tentacles grip crabs, shellfish, or other prey. An octopus's tentacles pull its victim toward its mouth. This is hard and pointed, like the beak of a bird.

▼ *In many countries, particularly those bordering the Mediterranean Sea, octopuses are eaten regularly.*

Each octopus hides in an underwater cave or crevice. It creeps along the seabed searching for food. Its two large eyes keep a lookout for enemies. If danger threatens, the octopus may confuse its enemy by squirting an inky liquid. The ink hangs in the water like a cloud. An octopus can also dart forward by squirting water backward from a special tube in its body.

The octopus is the most intelligent of the animals without backbones. It can be trained to find its way through a maze and to solve simple problems, such as removing the stopper from a sealed jar containing food.

OHIO

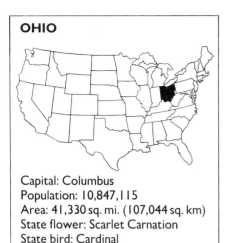

Capital: Columbus
Population: 10,847,115
Area: 41,330 sq. mi. (107,044 sq. km)
State flower: Scarlet Carnation
State bird: Cardinal
State tree: Buckeye
Statehood: March 1, 1803
17th state

Ohio

Ohio was the first state to be created from the huge Northwest Territory. Since the late 1800s, it has been a leading industrial area. Ohio factories produce many important goods, such as iron, steel, rubber, and truck and automobile components. But it is also an important agricultural area. Corn, soybeans, and hogs are all farmed on its fertile soil. There are many important minerals, too, such as coal and salt. Ohio became prosperous after the LOUISIANA PURCHASE in 1803. Merchants could then ship their goods down the Ohio River to the Mississippi and to New Orleans. When canals linking the state with the east were dug, trade increased again. Famous inventors from Ohio include Thomas EDISON and the WRIGHT BROTHERS.

▲ *The Ohio State Capitol in Columbus, the capital since 1816. Earlier capitals were Chillicothe and Zanesville.*

Oil

Oils are FATS and other greasy substances that do not dissolve in water. But when we say "oil" we usually mean mineral oil. Mineral oil was formed millions of years ago from dead plants and animals. The oil was trapped under rocks. Engineers drill holes down through the surface rocks to reach the mineral oil beneath. It gushes up or can be pumped up to the surface.

Oil refineries separate the oil to make gasoline, kerosene, and lubricating oil. Mineral oil is also used in making artificial fertilizer, many kinds of medicine, paint, plastics, and detergent. We may

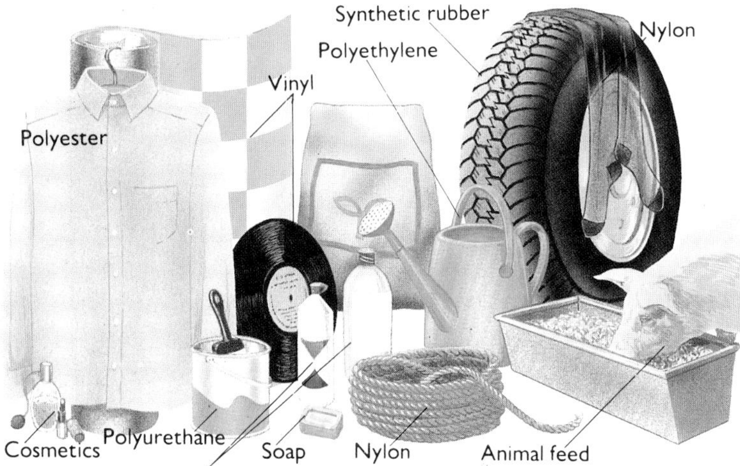

▶ *When petroleum oil is refined, it is separated into many different chemicals. In addition to gasoline and kerosene, oil by-products can be used to make plastics, perfumes, soaps, paints, and even animal feed.*

need to find new ways to make these things because the world's supplies of oil are running out. Scientists are working on new ways of extracting oil from shale, a kind of rock, and from tar sands.

The world's largest known oil deposits lie in the Middle East, in the countries of Saudi Arabia, Iran, Iraq, and Kuwait.

Oklahoma

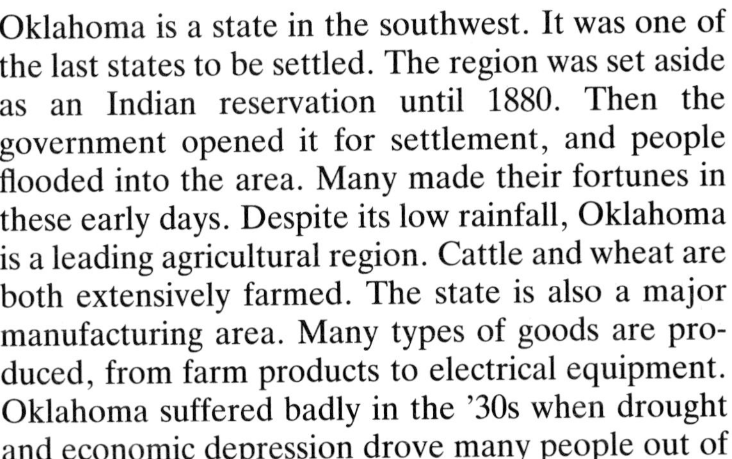

Oklahoma is a state in the southwest. It was one of the last states to be settled. The region was set aside as an Indian reservation until 1880. Then the government opened it for settlement, and people flooded into the area. Many made their fortunes in these early days. Despite its low rainfall, Oklahoma is a leading agricultural region. Cattle and wheat are both extensively farmed. The state is also a major manufacturing area. Many types of goods are produced, from farm products to electrical equipment. Oklahoma suffered badly in the '30s when drought and economic depression drove many people out of business.

OKLAHOMA

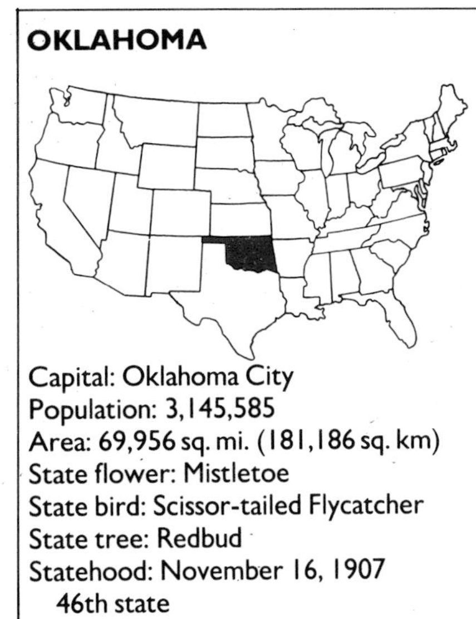

Capital: Oklahoma City
Population: 3,145,585
Area: 69,956 sq. mi. (181,186 sq. km)
State flower: Mistletoe
State bird: Scissor-tailed Flycatcher
State tree: Redbud
Statehood: November 16, 1907
46th state

◀ *The Oklahoma State Capitol stands on an oil field near the heart of the city. A well on the Capitol grounds was long a tourist attraction. It ended production in 1986.*

Olive

Olives grow on trees with slim, gray-green leaves and twisted trunks. Each FRUIT is shaped like a small plum. Farmers pick olives when they are green and unripe, or, when the fruit is ripe, they hit the trees with sticks to knock the olives onto sheets spread on the ground. Olives taste slightly bitter and have a hard pit in the middle. People eat olives and cook food in oil made from crushed olives.

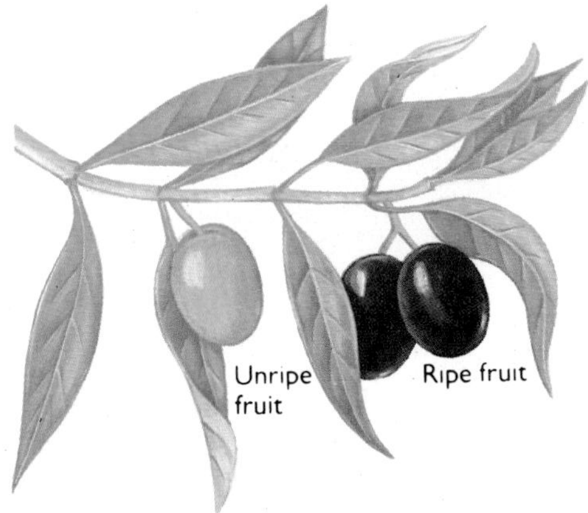

▲ *The oil we get from pressing olives is very useful. It can be used for cooking, in making medicine and soap, or as a salad dressing. Most olives come from Italy, Spain, and other countries on the Mediterranean Sea.*

OMAN

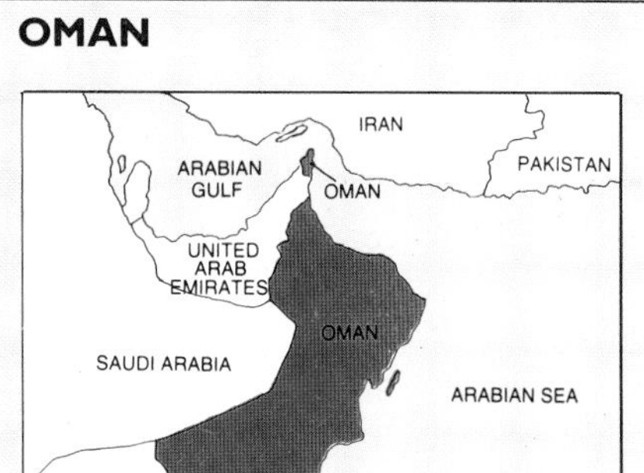

Government: Absolute monarchy
Capital: Muscat
Area: 82,030 sq. miles (212,457 sq. km)
Population: 1,502,000
Languages: Arabic, English, Urdu
Currency: Rial Omani

Olympic Games

This athletics contest is the world's oldest. The first known Olympic Games took place at Olympia in Greece in 776 B.C. The Greek Games ended in A.D. 394. The modern Olympic Games began in 1896.

They are held once every four years, each time in a different country. Athletes from different nations compete in races, jumping, gymnastics, ball games, yachting, and many more contests. The winners gain medals, but no prize money.

Oman

Oman is a country in southeast Arabia on the Persian Gulf. Most of Oman is desert, but on the fertile coastal plain, dates, fruits, and vegetables are grown. Oil is the main source of income. Many of Oman's people are nomads.

ONTARIO

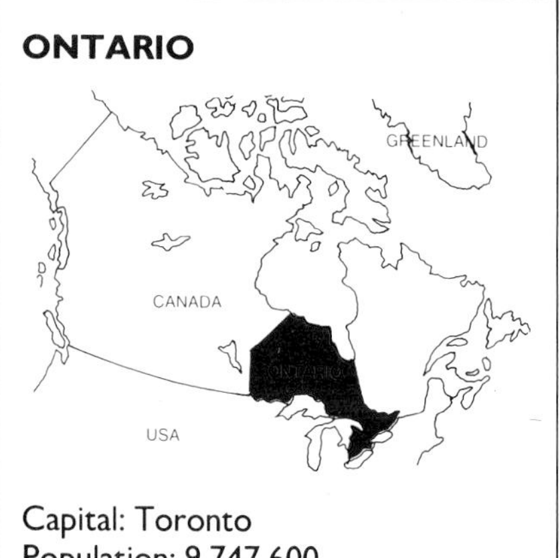

Capital: Toronto
Population: 9,747,600
Area: 344,090 sq. mi. (891,193 sq. km)
Entry into confederation: July 1, 1867

Ontario

Ontario is the most heavily populated and the richest province in Canada. It is the political and industrial center of the country. OTTAWA, the capital of Canada, is here, and Toronto, the capital of the province, is the most important industrial city in Canada. The province is the leading producer of iron and steel in Canada. It also has important reserves of nickel, gold, and uranium. There are many farms, too, producing dairy products, poultry, and fruit. Most people live in the south of Ontario.

Opera

An opera is a play with music. The "actors" are singers who sing all or many of their words. An ORCHESTRA accompanies them.

The first opera was performed in Italy, nearly 400 years ago. Famous composers of serious opera include MOZART, Verdi, Puccini, and WAGNER.

Light, short operas are called operettas. Operettas of the 1800s gave rise to the tuneful musical comedies of the 1900s.

Opinion Poll

Political parties and manufacturers want to know what people think of their party's policy or the goods they make. They employ a research firm to conduct an opinion poll—to ask questions and analyze the answers. It would be impossible to ask questions of everyone, everywhere, so a carefully selected group of people, called a *sample*, is chosen to represent a larger group. The sample may only be 1 percent of the larger group, but it must contain the same sort of people. For example, if 20 percent of the larger group are under 18 years of age, 20 percent of the sample group must also be under 18.

The questions may be asked by a trained interviewer or they may be printed on a *questionnaire*. The answers are then analyzed.

▲ *Papageno, the comic bird-catcher, from the 1816 Berlin production of Mozart's opera* The Magic Flute

SEE IT YOURSELF

You can take your own opinion poll. Choose the question you want to ask; then pick your sample group. It can be everyone in your class, or, better still, everyone in your grade. You do not have to record people's names, just their answers or whether they are undecided, and whether they are a boy or girl.

QUESTION: Do you prefer vanilla or chocolate ice cream?

TOTAL SAMPLE		ALL BOYS		ALL GIRLS	
Vanilla	40	Vanilla	18	Vanilla	22
Chocolate	50	Chocolate	28	Chocolate	22
Undecided	10	Undecided	4	Undecided	6
Total polled	100	Total polled	50	Total polled	50

FINDINGS: According to this poll, 50 percent of the sample pupils prefer chocolate ice cream, and 40 percent prefer vanilla. However, 56 percent of boys prefer chocolate and only 36 percent vanilla. The girls are equally divided between the two. What do you think would happen if the whole school were polled and divided into two age groups—those below 12 and those above?

▲ *Like all marsupials, the American opossum gives birth to its babies when they are still in a very immature state. After about three months, they are able to ride around on their mother's back.*

Opossum

Opossums are MARSUPIALS found in North and South America. Some look like rats; others look like mice. The common opossum is as big as a cat. This is North America's only marsupial. It climbs trees and can cling on with its tail. A female has up to 18 babies, each no larger than a honeybee at birth. If danger threatens, the common opossum pretends to be dead. If someone pretends to be asleep, we say he or she is "playing possum."

Orangutan

This big, red-haired APE comes from the islands of Borneo and Sumatra in Southeast Asia. Its name comes from Malay words meaning "man of the woods." A male is as heavy as a man, but not so tall. Orangutans use their long arms to swing through the branches of trees as they hunt for fruit and leaves to eat. Each night, they make a nest high up in the trees. A leafy roof helps to keep out rain.

Man is the orangutan's main enemy.

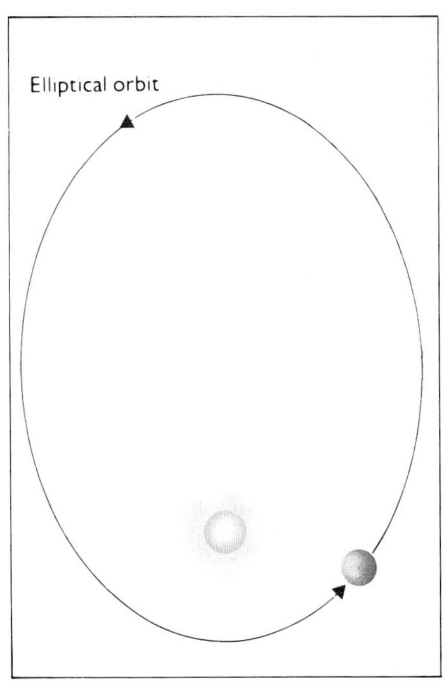

▲ *People used to think that planets moved in circular orbits, but actually their shape is more like a flattened circle, or ellipse.*

Orbit

An orbit is the curved path of something that spins around another object in space. Artificial SATELLITES and the MOON travel around the Earth in orbits. Each planet, including the Earth, has its own orbit around the SUN. Every orbit is a loop rather than a circle. An orbiting object tries to move in a straight line but is pulled by GRAVITY toward the object that it orbits.

Orchestra

An orchestra is a large group of musicians who play together. The word *orchestra* once meant "dancing place." In ancient Greek theaters, dancers and musicians performed in a space between the audience and the stage. When OPERA was invented, Italian theaters arranged their musicians in the same way. Soon, people used the word orchestra to describe the group of musicians.

◀ *Soloists rehearse with an orchestra. The conductor has the job of coordinating all the musicians in the orchestra, which may number over a hundred.*

The modern orchestra owes much to the composer HAYDN. He arranged its MUSICAL INSTRUMENTS into four main groups: strings, woodwind, brass, and percussion. Most orchestras have a conductor.

Oregon

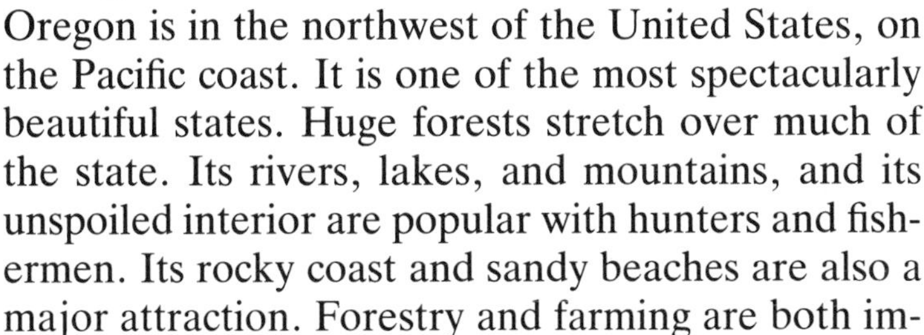

Oregon is in the northwest of the United States, on the Pacific coast. It is one of the most spectacularly beautiful states. Huge forests stretch over much of the state. Its rivers, lakes, and mountains, and its unspoiled interior are popular with hunters and fishermen. Its rocky coast and sandy beaches are also a major attraction. Forestry and farming are both im-

OREGON

Capital: Salem
Population: 2,842,321
Area: 97,073 sq. mi. (251,419 sq. km)
State flower: Oregon Grape
State bird: Western Meadowlark
State tree: Douglas Fir
Statehood: February 14, 1859
33rd state

◀ *Crater Lake in the Cascades, 1,932 feet (589 m) in depth, is the deepest lake in the United States. It lies in the crater of an extinct volcano in south-central Oregon.*

▲ *The Parliament buildings, Ottawa. Although Ottawa is the capital of Canada, the capital of its province, Ontario, is Toronto.*

portant industries. Oregon produces 10 percent of all the wood used in the United States. Thousands of people took the Oregon Trail from the east in the 1800s to settle in the state.

Ostrich

This is the largest living BIRD. An ostrich may weigh twice as much as a man and stand more than 6 ft. (2 m) high. Ostriches cannot fly. If an enemy attacks, an ostrich runs away. It can kick hard enough to rip a lion open.

Ostriches live in Africa. They roam in herds, led by a male. The females lay large, white eggs in nests dug in the sand.

Ottawa

Ottawa is the capital of CANADA and its third largest city. With its suburbs, Ottawa holds about 800,000 people. Ottawa stands in the province of Ontario in southeast Canada. The Ottawa and Rideau rivers flow through the city.

Ottawa's best-known buildings are the Parliament buildings, which stand on a hill above the Ottawa River. They include the tall Peace Tower, which contains 53 bells.

▼ *The number of otters in the wild is going down steadily, and they are now a rare sight. This could be due to pollution, but no one is sure.*

Otter

Otters are large relatives of the weasel. They have long, slender bodies and short legs. An otter is a bit heavier than a dachshund. It hunts in water for fish and frogs. Thick fur keeps its body dry. It can swim swiftly by waggling its tail and body like an eel and using its webbed hind feet as paddles.

Otters are wanderers. At night, they hunt up and down a river or roam overland to find new fishing grounds. They love to play by sliding down a bank of snow or mud.

Owens, Jesse

Jesse Owens (1913–1980) was a brilliant black American athlete. In the 1936 Olympic Games, he won four gold medals. These games were held in Berlin, Germany. The German leader, Adolf Hitler, was furious that a black man defeated his athletes.

Jesse Owens' real name was James Cleveland Owen. He was given the nickname "Jesse" because of his initials, J.C. He broke three world records and tied a fourth within 45 minutes at Ann Arbor, Mich., in 1935.

Owl

These birds of prey hunt mainly at night. They have soft feathers that make no sound as they fly. Their large, staring eyes help them to see in the dimmest light. Owls also have keen ears. Some owls can catch mice in pitch darkness by listening to the sounds they make. An owl can turn its head right around to look backward.

When an owl eats a mouse or bird, it swallows it complete with bones and fur or feathers. Later, the owl spits out the remains in a pellet. You can sometimes find owl pellets on the ground.

There are over 500 kinds of owl. Some of the largest and smallest owls live in North America.

▲ *The long-eared owl's tufted "ears" are not ears at all, just feathers. But they help in the recognition of this bird, which is found in most of Europe, northern Asia, and North America.*

◀ *Barn owls are far less common now than they once were. This may be because there are fewer deserted buildings and hollow trees in the countryside for them to use as nesting places.*

SEE IT YOURSELF

Nothing can burn without oxygen. To find out how much oxygen there is in the air, stand a candle in a bowl of water. Light the candle and cover it with a glass jar. Rest the jar on modeling clay so that water can get under the rim. Mark the level of water in the jar. As the candle burns, oxygen is used up and water rises to take its place. Soon the candle goes out—all the oxygen has gone. You will find that the water has risen about one-fifth of the way up the jar. A fifth of the air is oxygen.

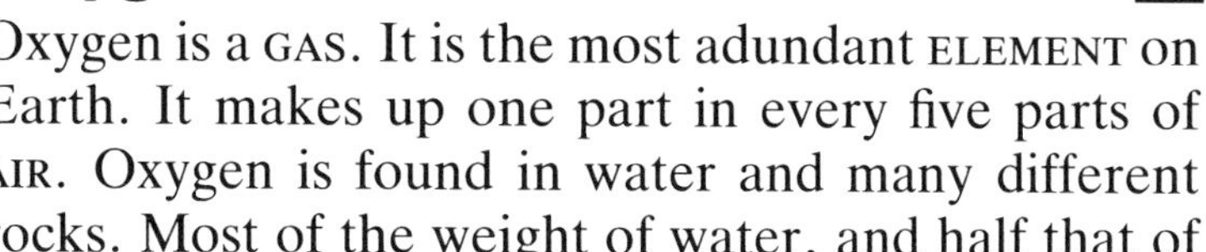

Oxygen

Oxygen is a GAS. It is the most adundant ELEMENT on Earth. It makes up one part in every five parts of AIR. Oxygen is found in water and many different rocks. Most of the weight of water, and half that of rocks, comes from the oxygen in them.

FIRE needs oxygen to burn. Almost all living things need oxygen for BREATHING and to give them the energy just to stay alive. Animals need extra oxygen to move around. PLANTS give out oxygen into the air.

Oyster

Oysters are MOLLUSKS with a soft body protected by a broad, hinged shell. This is rough on the outside. The inside of a pearl oyster's shell is smooth, shiny mother-of-pearl. Pearl oysters make pearls.

Several kinds of oyster are eaten as food. People farm oysters in shallow coastal water. Oysters cling to empty shells, rocks, or wooden posts on the seabed. When they have grown large enough, they are harvested.

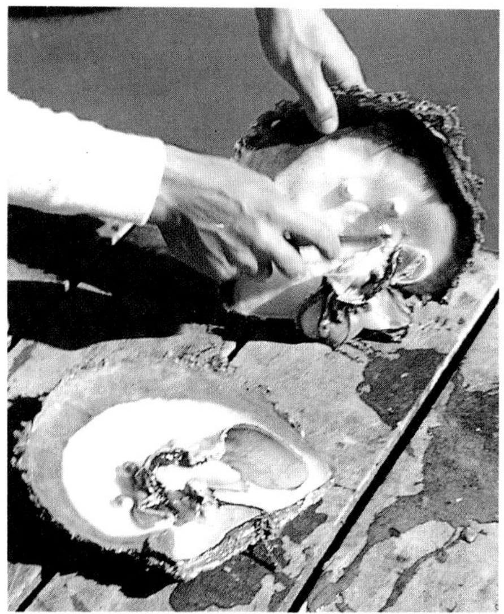

▲ *An oyster makes a pearl when there is a foreign object, such as a grain of sand, inside its shell. To stop the irritation caused by the sand, the oyster deposits a substance called nacre around it, which gradually builds up to form a pearl.*

Ozone Layer

The ozone layer is a layer of gases that surrounds the Earth and shields it from harmful radiation from the Sun. The layer is found in the region between 6 and 30 miles (10 and 50 km) above the Earth's surface. Ozone is a form of the gas oxygen, and although the ozone layer contains only a very small quantity of ozone, it shields us from most of the Sun's dangerous ultraviolet rays. Without the protection of the ozone layer, animals and plants probably could not live on Earth.

Recently, scientists have been worried about a thinning of the ozone layer, especially over polar regions. They believe this may have been caused partly by the use of substances called *chlorofluorocarbons*, or CFCs, in aerosol dispensers and refrigerators, and used to make the bubbles in foam plastic, and from the burning of fossil fuels such as gas, coal, and oil.

Pacific Ocean

This is the largest and deepest of all the OCEANS. Its waters cover more than one-third of the world. All the CONTINENTS would fit inside the Pacific Ocean with room to spare. Its deepest part is deep enough to drown the world's highest mountain.

The Pacific Ocean lies west of the Americas and east of Australia and Asia. It stretches from the frozen Arctic to the frozen Antarctic. There are thousands of tiny islands in the Pacific. Most were formed when VOLCANOES grew up from the seabed. Sometimes, earthquakes shake the seabed and send out huge tidal waves (tsunamis).

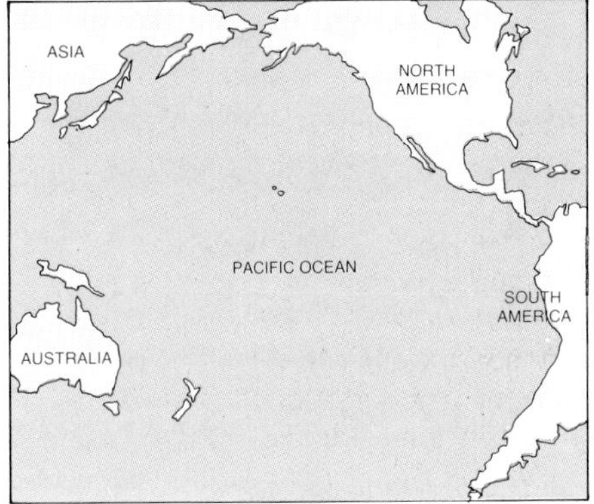

Pain

Pain is an unpleasant feeling. It is a warning that something is wrong somewhere in your body. You feel pain if something burns or presses hard on the ends of certain NERVES. Those parts of the body with the most nerve endings, such as your hands, feel pain most easily. The nerves carry the pain signals to the brain.

Sometimes pain is useful. It teaches you to avoid what caused it. If you prick yourself with a pin, you learn not to do it again. Toothaches tell you it's time to go to the dentist. Chemists have invented anesthetic drugs and other painkillers to deaden pain caused by disease and injury.

▼ When this girl touches the hot iron, special nerves in her finger send a warning signal to her central nervous system. A message is sent back to the nerves that control the muscles of her arm, making her jerk her hand away.

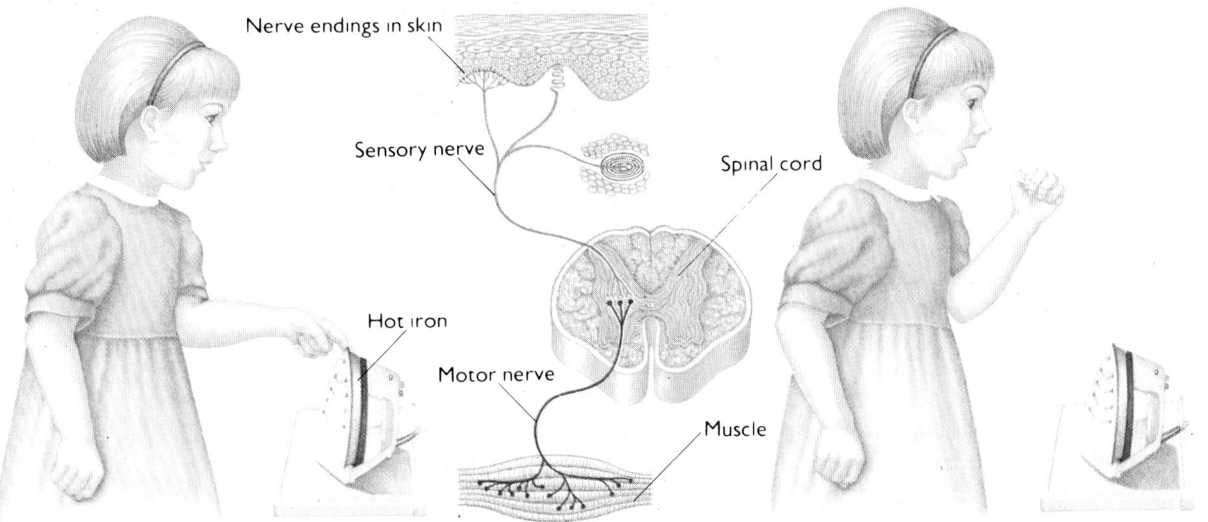

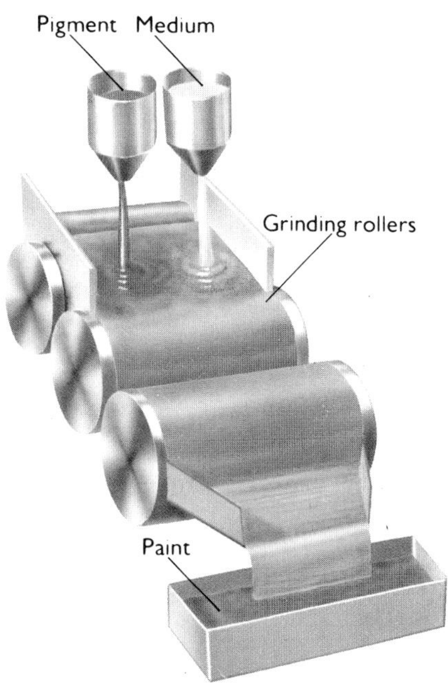

▲ *Paint is made by grinding colors called pigments, and a liquid medium (such as oil), between huge rollers.*

SEE IT YOURSELF

There are lots of fun ways to paint. Try this one: Put a spoonful of watery paint on a piece of white paper. Place one end of a drinking straw near the paint and blow gently through the other to spread out the paint. Using a clean spoon for each color, put some other colors onto the paper and blow them around too.

▶ *The cleaning and restoration of dirty or damaged old paintings is a delicate and highly skilled craft.*

Paint

Paint is colored powder mixed with a liquid. When it is spread over a solid surface, it forms a thin coat. This decorates the surface and protects it from rotting. OIL-based paints are colored powder in oil or resin. Emulsion paints are made of powder and drops of oil or resin in water.

Painting

Painting is a form of ART in which people use colored PAINT to make pictures on canvas, plaster, wood, or paper. Today most people paint for their own pleasure. But this was not always so.

STONE AGE hunters probably used painting as magic. They drew wounded wild beasts on their cave walls. They probably thought that such pictures would help them to kill real animals on their next hunt.

In the MIDDLE AGES, most artists worked for the Church. Their paintings showed scenes from Bible stories. Such paintings helped people who could not read to understand the Bible.

By the 1400s, Europe's rich princes and merchants were paying artists to paint pictures to decorate their homes. The pictures might be family portraits, still life scenes of flowers and fruit, or landscapes showing their cities and country estates.

In the 1800s, many artists began trying out new ideas. For example, some tried to give a feeling of the light and shade in a landscape. Others used bright, flat colors to bring out the patterns in still-lifes and landscapes. In the 1900s, Pablo PICASSO and other artists began to experiment with abstract paintings. These concentrate on the basic shapes, colors, and patterns of the things painted. Today, many artists are still experimenting.

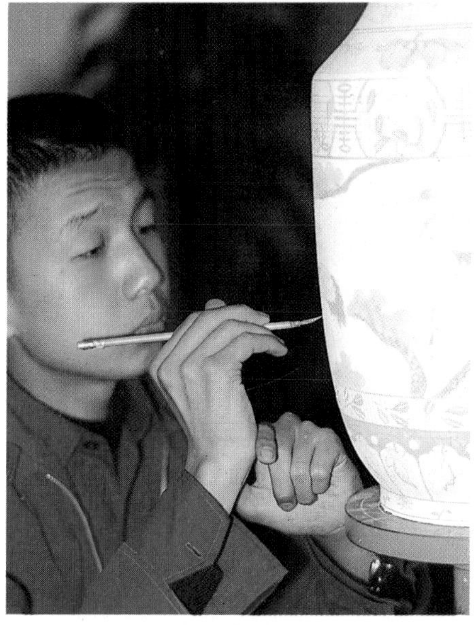

▲ *Once this boy has finished painting the design on this vase it will be glazed and fired in a kiln to complete the finish.*

Pakistan

Pakistan lies between India and Iran. It is about one-tenth the size of the United States. Most Pakistanis follow the religion of ISLAM.

Much of Pakistan is hot and dry, but crops such as wheat and cotton grow with the help of water from the Indus River. The Indus flows from the HIMALAYAS to the Arabian Sea. Until 1947, Pakistan was part of INDIA. It then broke away to become an independent Muslim republic. In 1971, East Pakistan broke away and became BANGLADESH. In 1988, Benazir Bhutto was elected prime minister, but her party was defeated in the 1990 elections.

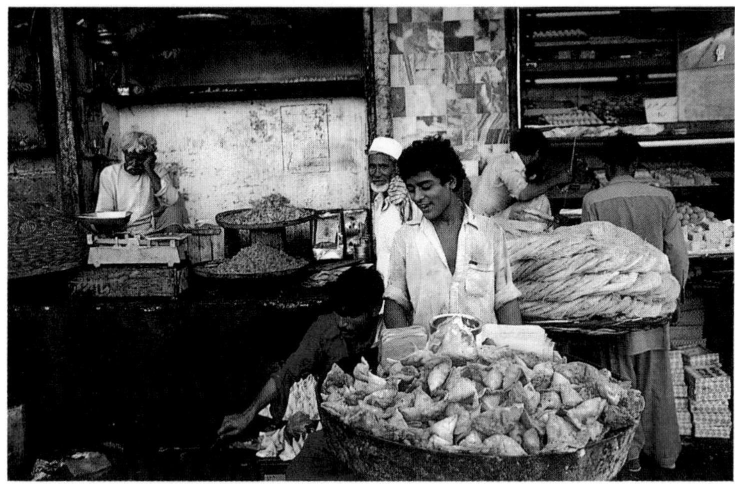

◀ *Street traders, selling all kinds of food, are a common sight in the city of Karachi in Pakistan.*

PAKISTAN

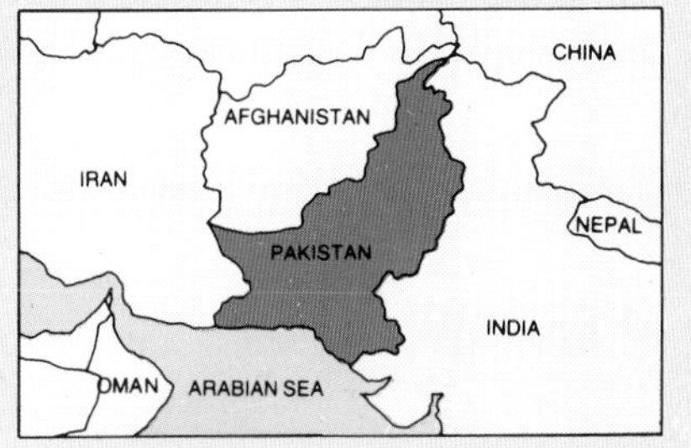

Government: Parliamentary democracy
Capital: Islamabad
Area: 310,403 sq. miles (803,943 sq. km)
Population: 112,050,000
Languages: Urdu and English
Currency: Rupee

Palestine

Palestine is a land on the eastern shore of the Mediterranean Sea. Most of the stories in the BIBLE took place there. Palestine gets its name from the Philistines who once lived in part of it.

Historic Palestine covers an area of only 10,400 sq. miles (27,000 sq. km), about the same size as Maryland. People lived in Palestine during the Old Stone Age, at least 200,000 years ago.

By 1800 B.C. the HEBREWS had made Palestine their home. Later they ruled it as two nations, called Israel and Judah. Both of these nations were then taken over by foreign rulers.

Today, most of what was Palestine lies in ISRAEL. The rest is part of Jordan, Lebanon, and Syria. Frequent clashes take place between Palestinians and Israeli police.

▲ *The coconut palm can grow as high as 100 ft. (30 m). Its fruit contains a hollow space filled with coconut "milk." The white meat, or kernel, inside the coconut is not only good to eat, but can also be used for making soap, wax, and oil. Dates are the fruits of the date palm. In the Middle East, they are eaten raw, or split and filled with butter.*

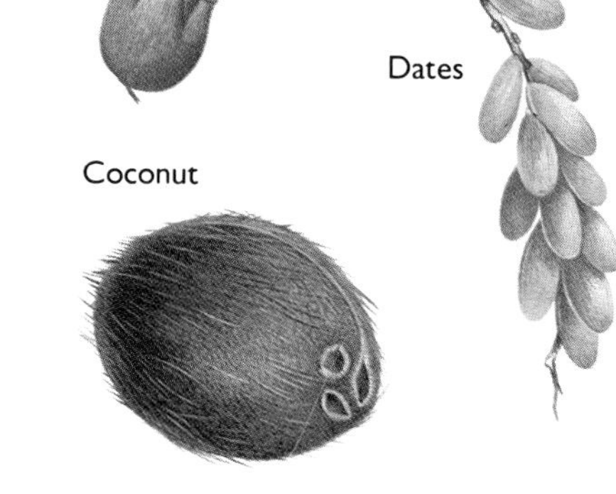

Palm

The most familiar palm tree has leaves that sprout straight out of the top of its trunk, rather like the fingers of an outspread hand. But there are more than 1,000 kinds of palm, and not all are trees. Some are shrubs, and others are vines. Most palms grow in warm climates.

Palms are useful plants. People make mats and baskets from their leaves. We eat the fruits of some palms, such as coconuts and dates.

Panama

Panama is a country about the size of South Carolina. It occupies the narrow neck of land that joins Central and South America. Panama has a damp, tropical climate. Rice, sugar, bananas, and pineapples are grown.

The Panama CANAL cuts the country in half. Much of Panama's wealth comes from the canal, and it has made Panama City an international finance center. Many ships are registered in Panama.

The world's shipping uses the Panama Canal as a short cut between the Atlantic and Pacific Oceans.

◀ *Many huge cargo ships pass through the Panama Canal every day.*

Sets of locks on the canal raise and lower ships as they cross the hilly countryside. In 1903, Panama granted the occupation and control of the canal to the United States. A new treaty in 1978 provided for the gradual takeover by Panama of the canal. The takeover will be completed in 1999.

PANAMA

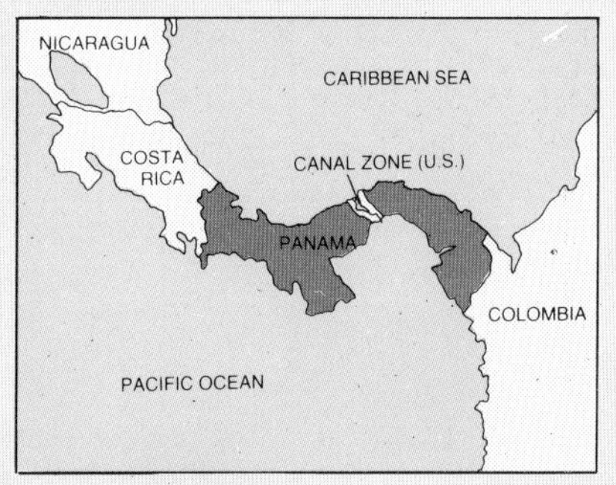

Government: Republic
Capital: Panama
Area: 29,208 sq. miles
(75,650 sq. km)
Population: 2,418,000
Languages: Spanish and English
Currency: Balboa

Panda

There are two kinds of panda. Both live in the forests of eastern Asia. The giant panda looks like a black and white bear. It lives in BAMBOO forests in China. The red panda is not much larger than a cat. It has a bushy tail and reddish fur. Both kinds eat plants. Their nearest relatives are the raccoons of North and South America.

Paper

Paper gets its name from papyrus, a plant that grows in swamps in Egypt. The ancient Egyptians made a kind of paper from papyrus. But the Chinese

▼ *The steps in making paper from softwood pulp.*

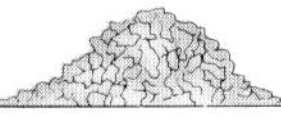

The chips are "cooked" with chemicals, and the pulp produced is washed, bleached, and beaten into finer fibers. It is mixed with resins and dyes, depending on the type of paper being made.

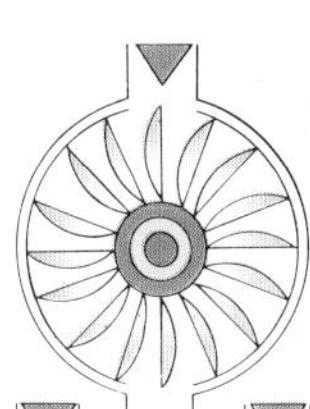

It is dried in steam-heated cylinders and polished in calender rollers

The pulp is passed through a series of rollers

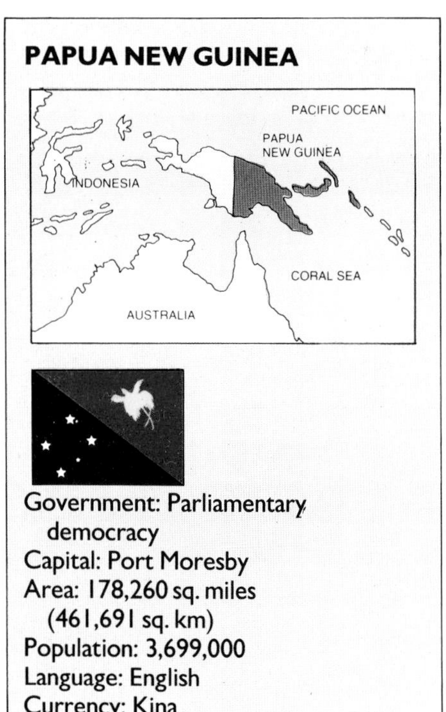

Government: Parliamentary democracy
Capital: Port Moresby
Area: 178,260 sq. miles (461,691 sq. km)
Population: 3,699,000
Language: English
Currency: Kina

invented paper as we know it. About 1,900 years ago, they learned to separate the fibers from mulberry bark. They soaked them and then dried them, making a flat, dry sheet that they could write on. Paper is still made of plant fibers. Some of the best paper is made from COTTON. Newsprint is made from wood.

Papua New Guinea

Papua New Guinea is a country that occupies the eastern half of the island of New Guinea, north of Australia. The western half of the island is Indonesian and is called Irian Jaya. Papua New Guinea is a hot, wet country. It gained its independence from Australia in 1975 and is a member of the British Commonwealth. The chief crops are coffee, coconuts, and cocoa.

Paraguay

Paraguay is a South American country with no seacoast. It is divided in half by the Paraguay River, and the eastern half contains most of the people. Most Paraguayans are *mestizos*, people of mixed Spanish and Indian descent. They farm soybeans, cotton, sugarcane, tobacco, rice, and fruits.

Spain ruled Paraguay until 1811, when the country declared its independence. Struggles for power between political groups continue.

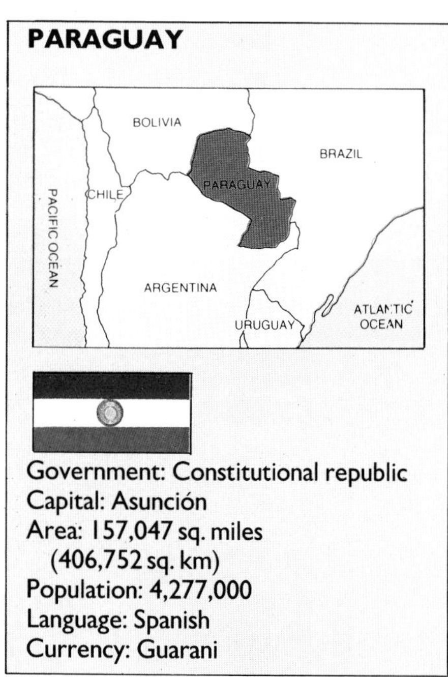

Government: Constitutional republic
Capital: Asunción
Area: 157,047 sq. miles (406,752 sq. km)
Population: 4,277,000
Language: Spanish
Currency: Guarani

► *Many of the people living in Paraguay are farmers, producing barely enough to feed themselves.*

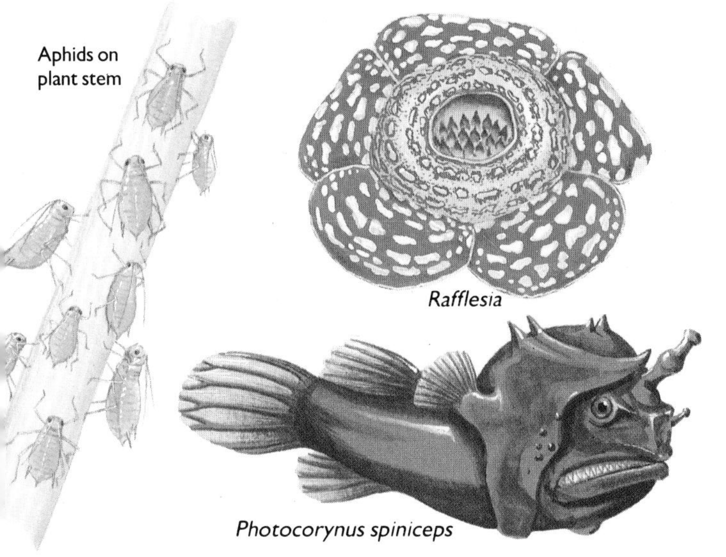

◀ *Aphids suck the sap of plants such as roses, and can spread diseases among plants.* Rafflesia *is a parasitic plant that produces the largest flower in the world—up to a yard across. The tiny male deep-sea fish,* Photocorynus spiniceps, *lives by attaching itself to the much larger female and sucking her blood.*

Parasite

Parasites are living things that live and feed on others larger than themselves.

Animal parasites include FLEAS, lice, ticks, and mites. Different kinds live on different birds and mammals. Most suck blood, and some spread germs that cause disease. Certain kinds of WORM get inside the body and live in the intestine or burrow into muscles.

Aphids and some other insects live as parasites on plants. Plant parasites include many kinds of FUNGUS that cause disease in plants or animals. Mistletoe is a parasite. It feeds on the trees on which it grows.

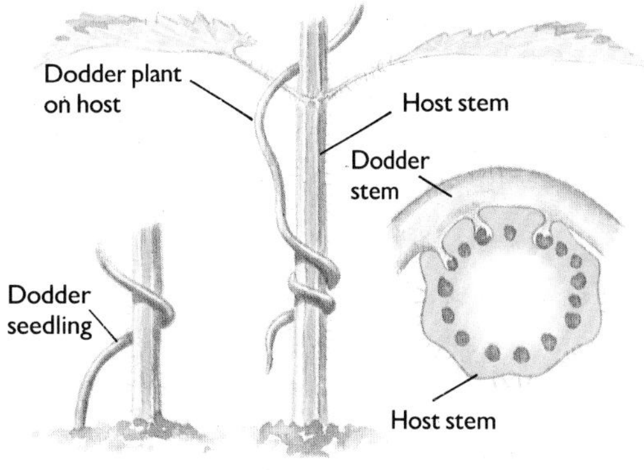

▲ *Dodder is a thread-like parasitic plant that twines around the host plant and "sucks" nourishment from it. It is very difficult to get rid of once it is established.*

Paris

Paris is the capital of FRANCE and France's largest city. More than two million people live there. The River Seine divides the city into the Left Bank and the Right Bank.

If you gaze down on Paris from the Eiffel Tower, you can see many parks and gardens, fine squares, and tree-lined avenues. Other famous landmarks are the cathedral of Notre Dame, the basilica of the Sacré Coeur, the Arc de Triomphe, and the Louvre Palace, now a famous museum.

Paris is famous for its fashions, jewelry, and perfume. Another important industry is car manufacturing.

▼ *Traffic skirts the Arc de Triomphe in Paris. Built by Napoleon I, it is one of the city's most famous landmarks.*

▲ *Black Rod is an usher of the Lord Chamberlain's department. Each year when Parliament opens, he comes to the House of Commons as the Queen's representative and has to knock on the door to be let in. This is part of the ceremony that surrounds much of the activity in the Palace of Westminster, the British Parliament.*

Parliament

A parliament is a meeting of people held to make a nation's LAWS. One of the first parliaments was Iceland's *Althing*, which was founded more than a thousand years ago.

In Great Britain, the Houses of Parliament stand by the river Thames in London. Members of Parliament elected by the people sit in the House of Commons. Peers (nobles) and churchmen (who are not elected) sit in the House of Lords. The British Parliament was started in 1265. It grew gradually out of a meeting of nobles who advised the king. In the 1300s, it was divided into the two Houses, and by the 1700s, Parliament had become more powerful than the king.

Parrot

These tropical birds have brightly colored feathers. They use their strong, curved beaks as "hands" to help them climb. Their beaks can also crack nuts open and bite off chunks of fruit.

There are hundreds of kinds of parrot. Cockatoos, macaws, and lovebirds all belong to the parrot family. Parakeets can learn to "talk" by imitating the sound of speech, and one African gray parrot could say more than 900 words.

► *A Cuban parrot. Parrots climb more than they fly, using their strong, hooked beaks to pull themselves from branch to branch.*

The building of the Parthenon began in 447 B.C. It was completed in 438 B.C., when the great gold and ivory statue of Athena was dedicated. Work on the carvings and decoration of the temple went on until 432 B.C.

Parthenon

The Parthenon is perhaps the world's most famous building. The ruins of this great white marble temple stand on the ACROPOLIS, a hill that overlooks the Greek capital of ATHENS.

The Athenians built the Parthenon around 440 B.C. in honor of Athena Parthenos, their patron goddess. Rows of columns like huge tree trunks held up its sloping roof. Everything was gracefully designed. Inside stood a huge statue of Athena.

The Parthenon has been damaged by an explosion and the effects of air POLLUTION, but its ruins still dominate Athens.

▲ *The decoration on the Parthenon was as grand as the building itself. This frieze, showing a boy fastening his master's belt, was one of a number removed from Greece by Britain's Lord Elgin between 1803 and 1812.*

◄ *The Passover feast, or seder, is a ritual that goes back many centuries. It is conducted by the head of the family on the first two nights of the eight days of Passover.*

Passover

This Jewish festival celebrates the Israelites' escape from slavery in Egypt. The BIBLE tells how God punished the Egyptians ten times before they freed the Israelites. The tenth time, an angel killed the eldest child in each Egyptian family, but *passed over* the Israelites' homes without harming them.

Pasteur, Louis

Louis Pasteur (1822–1895) was a great French scientist. He proved that BACTERIA and other germs cause diseases. He injected weakened germs into animals and people to stop them from catching the diseases those germs usually caused. He invented *pasteurization*, a way of heating milk and cooling it quickly to stop it from going bad. Pasteur also found out how tiny yeast cells turn sugar into alcohol.

▲ *Pasteur developed vaccines against cholera, rabies, anthrax, and other diseases.*

In Rome and later in medieval Europe, peacocks were raised for the table. The emperor Charlemagne is said to have served thousands of the birds at a single state banquet.

► *Only the male peafowl has a spectacular tail with its "eyes." The female is a duller bird with a short tail.*

Peacock

Peacocks are male peafowl. Peafowl are big birds that live in Asia. Peacocks attract their mates by spreading out the long, blue-green feathers that grow just above the tail. Big spots on the feathers look like rows of eyes. As the peacock struts before the female, it looks extremely proud—hence the expression "as proud as a peacock."

Pendulum

This is a hanging weight that is free to swing to and fro. When the weight is pulled to one side and then released, GRAVITY starts it swinging back and forth in a curved path called an *arc*. Each swing takes the same amount of time, no matter whether the swing is big or small. This makes pendulums useful for keeping time in CLOCKS. After a while, a pendulum stops. But a pendulum clock keeps its pendulum swinging with a device called an escapement. This makes the "tick-tock" sound.

▼ *In a pendulum clock, the movement of the pendulum is transmitted to the hands of the clock through the escapement, made up of an escape wheel and anchor, which also keeps the pendulum swinging.*

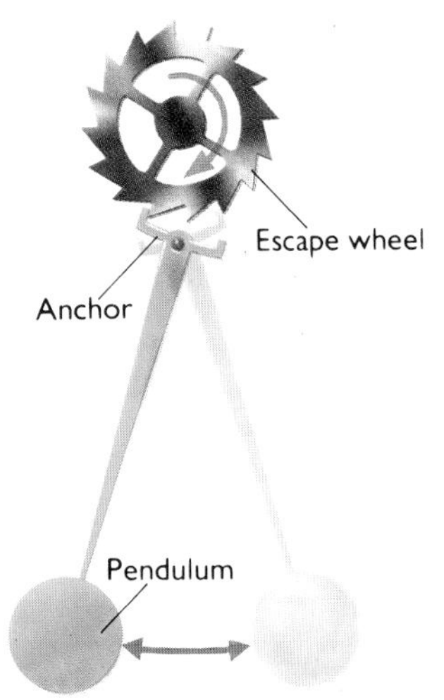

Penguin

Penguins are swimming birds. They cannot fly, because their wings are shaped as flippers. Penguins use their wings to "row" themselves through the sea. They swim and dive well. A penguin in the water can leap up nearly 6 ft. (2 m) to land on a rock or ice.

All penguins come from the southern part of the world. Emperor penguins live in the ANTARCTIC. In winter, each female lays one egg on the ice. Her mate rolls the egg onto his feet and warms it between his legs for two months until it hatches.

▼ *Four of the 18 different types of penguin.*

Pennsylvania

Pennsylvania is an eastern state and one of the 13 original states of the United States. It was founded in the 1600s by an Englishman named William Penn. He wanted it to be a place where all religions would be tolerated. Today, Pennsylvania is one of the leading industrial regions of the country. Huge coal reserves and many large factories producing a wide range of goods have made it prosperous. But much of the state is also fertile farming land. Poultry and cattle are raised and fruits and vegetables are grown. The largest city is PHILADELPHIA. It is one of the most historic cities in the country as well as an important port.

PENNSYLVANIA

Capital: Harrisburg
Population: 11,881,643
Area: 45,308 sq. mi. (117,348 sq. km)
State flower: Mountain Laurel
State bird: Ruffed Grouse
State tree: Hemlock
Statehood: December 12, 1787
2nd state

◀ *An Amish farm in Pennsylvania. The Amish are a Protestant group with a simple way of life. Members are forbidden to go to war, swear oaths, or hold public office.*

▼ *The main differences between the three major racial types are the facial features, hair type, and skin and hair coloring.*

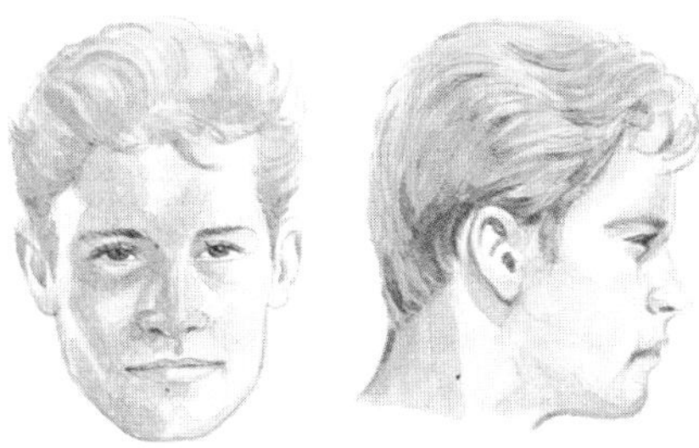

Caucasian

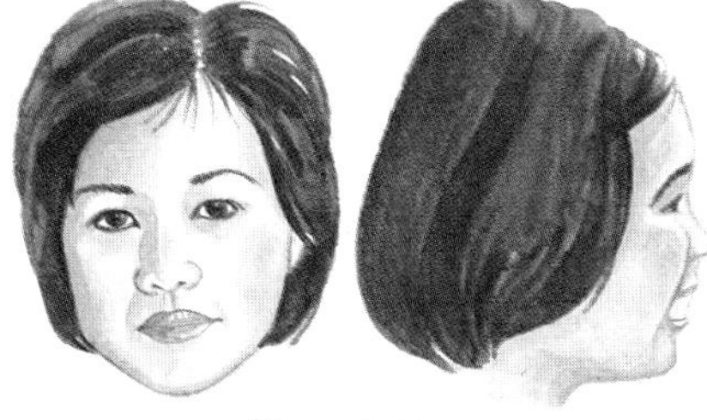

Mongoloid

Negroid

People of the World

All the people on Earth belong to the human race. But "race" also means any group of people who look alike in certain ways. Nobody knows for sure when and how the different races came into being, but the three main ones in the world are the Mongoloid, the Caucasian, and the Negroid.

The Mongoloid race is known for its straight dark hair, yellow-brown skin, and almond-shaped eyes. The Caucasian race has hair color ranging from blond and red to black, is mainly fair-skinned and round-eyed. The Negroid race has dark, tightly curling hair and dark brown skin color. In addition to these three main races, there are also a number of minor ones.

Thousands of years of migration, conquest, and marriage between races have mixed all the races into a great variety of groups. For this reason, it is not very sensible to speak of pure racial types.

Perfume

Certain substances that produce a pleasant smell are called perfumes. People use perfumes on their bodies. Factories add perfumes to SOAP, DETERGENT, and other products. Natural perfumes are oils squeezed from flowers, leaves, or stems and mixed with special animal substances like musk. Factories make synthetic perfumes from a variety of substances, including coal tar.

Peru

Peru is the third largest nation in SOUTH AMERICA. It is more than three times the size of California. There are more Indians in Peru than in any other South American country.

Peru touches five other countries. Western Peru is washed by the Pacific Ocean. The sharp, snowy peaks of the high ANDES MOUNTAINS cross Peru from north to south like a giant backbone. Between the mountains and the ocean lies a thin strip of desert. East of the mountains, hot, steamy forests stretch around the AMAZON RIVER.

Potatoes were an important food in Peru long before they were known anywhere else in the world. The Incas made a flour from the potato to bake their bread.

◀ *Lake Titicaca is the highest navigated lake in the world. Situated between Peru and Bolivia, it is 12,500 ft. (3,810 m) above sea level.*

Peruvians grow sugarcane and coffee. The sheep and LLAMAS in the mountains produce wool. Peru mines copper, iron, and silver. Its ocean fishing grounds usually hold plenty of fish.

People have been building towns in Peru for several thousand years. The most famous people were the INCAS, who developed a mountain empire. In the 1530s, the Spaniards seized Peru. Since the 1820s, Peru has been an independent nation.

PERU

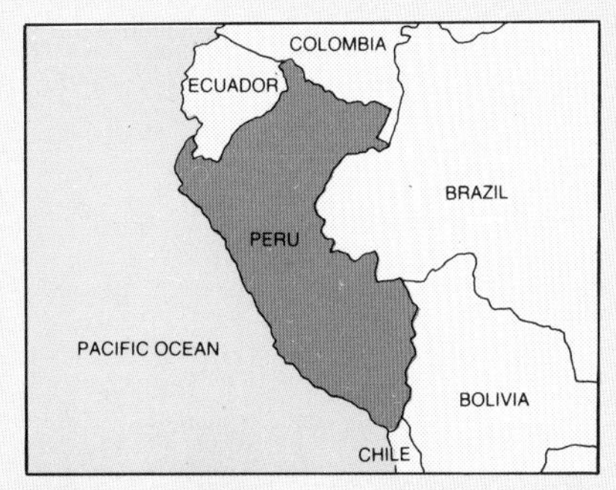

Government: Constitutional republic
Capital: Lima
Area: 496,222 sq. miles (1,285,216 sq. km)
Population: 22,332,000
Language: Spanish
Currency: Inti

Pharaoh

We use the word *pharaoh* to mean "king" when we talk of the kings of ancient EGYPT. (The ancient

▼ *The funeral procession of a pharaoh. Four yoked oxen pull the sled of the funeral boat, in which rests the coffin containing the mummy, the embalmed and wrapped body of the pharaoh.*

Egyptians gave their kings other titles as well.) "Pharaoh" comes from *peraa*, which means "great house." This was the palace where the pharaoh lived.

Egyptians believed that each pharaoh was the same god in the shape of a different man. He lived in certain ways said to have been determined by the gods. The pharaoh was said to look after all the needs of everyone in Egypt. He owned all the land. All of Egypt's nobles, priests, and soldiers were supposed to obey him. But in fact, the priests and nobles usually ran the country.

Philadelphia's Fairmount Park is the largest landscaped city park in the United States. It covers an area of more than 7,900 acres (3,200 ha) and contains the Philadelphia Zoo, colonial mansions, and a Japanese teahouse. The park was the site of the U.S. Centennial Exposition of 1876.

Philadelphia

Philadelphia is one of the largest and most historic cities in the United States. Both the DECLARATION OF INDEPENDENCE and the CONSTITUTION of the United States were adopted in Philadelphia's Independence Hall.

The city is in southeastern PENNSYLVANIA on the Delaware River. The word "Philadelphia" is Greek for "brotherly love," and the city was planned in 1681 by William Penn, an English QUAKER. Philadelphia is a busy port and manufacturing center.

PHILIPPINES

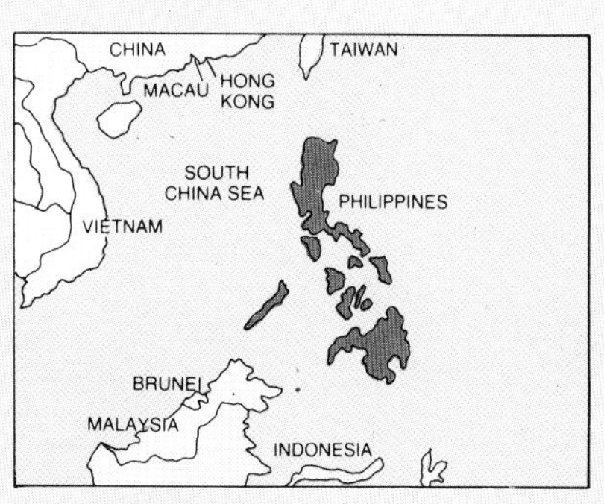

Government: Republic
Capital: Manila
Area: 115,830 sq. miles (300,000 sq. km)
Population: 61,480,000
Languages: Pilipino and English
Currency: Peso

Philippines

The Philippines is a large group of islands in southern Asia. The biggest islands are Luzon and Mindanao. Manila, the chief port and largest city, is the capital. Most of the people live in small villages and make their living from farming. They raise sugarcane, fruits, rice, coconuts, and vegetables.

Spanish explorers named the islands after King Philip II of Spain. In 1898, after the Spanish-American War, the islands were turned over to the United States. They became independent in 1946, but the Philippines still has close links with the United States.

Ferdinand Marcos, who was elected president in 1965, restricted the activities of his opponents. In 1986 he was forced to flee the country. The new government under Mrs. Corazon Aquino faced economic problems and widespread poverty.

Philosophy

The word *philosophy* comes from Greek words meaning "love of wisdom." Philosophers are thinkers who ask deep questions like these: How much can we really know about anything? When we say that God exists, what do we mean by "God" and what do we mean by "exists?" What is goodness? What is truth? What is beauty?

▼ *Modern copiers can make an unlimited number of duplicates from an original, each as good as the first.*

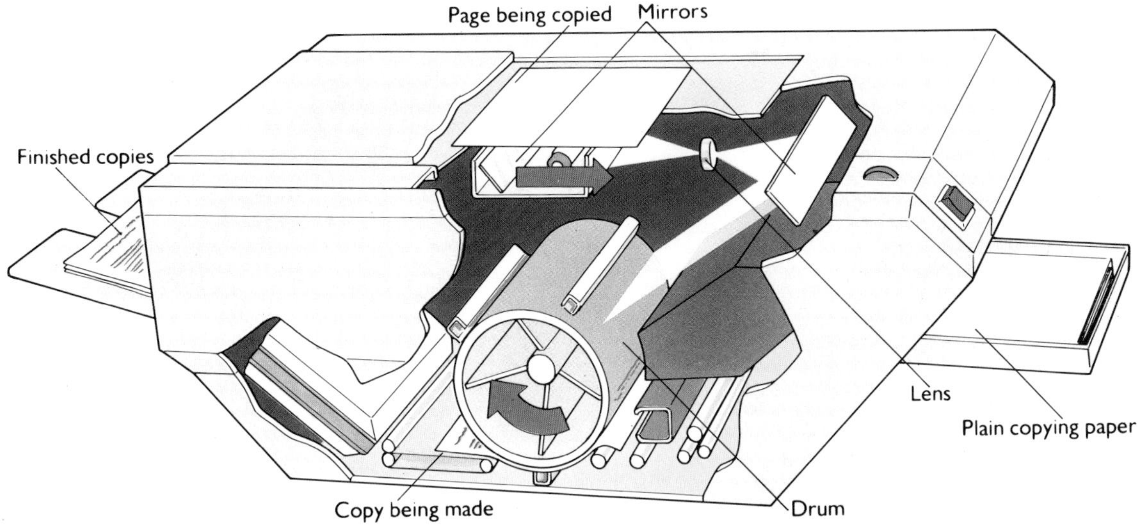

Photocopying

A photocopier is a machine that can copy a page of a book or a letter in a few seconds. When you press the button on a photocopier, a bright light comes on to light up the page. A lens inside the machine shines an image of the page onto a smooth metal drum. The drum is electrified all over. When the image shines on it, the light in the bright parts of the image destroys the electric charge. The dark parts of the drum are still electrified.

A black powder is dusted over the drum. This clings only to the parts of the drum's surface that are electrified. When a sheet of paper is pressed against the drum, the powder comes off onto the paper and produces a copy of the page. This process is called *xerography*.

▲ *The first photographs were very different from today's snapshots. They were made by exposing large metal plates covered in tar-like chemicals to light. Exposures for photos such as the one above could take minutes, during which time the subjects had to hold very still.*

Photography

The word *photography* comes from Greek words that mean "drawing with light." When you take a

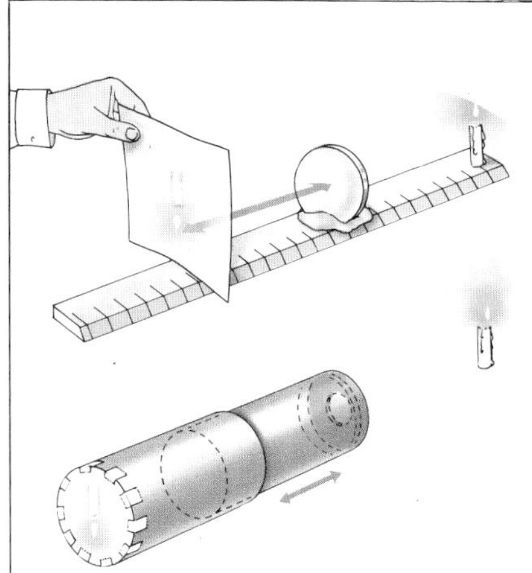

SEE IT YOURSELF

You can make a toy camera. Take the lens out of a magnifying glass. Using modeling clay, stand the lens upright on a ruler. Put a lighted candle in front of the lens. Hold a piece of white paper on the ruler behind the lens and move it backward and forward until you see a sharp image of the candle. Measure the distance between the lens and the paper. This is the focal length of that lens. Now take two cardboard tubes, one of which fits inside the other. Cover one end with tissue paper anchored with tape. Cover the other end with cardboard and make a hole about half an inch across. Anchor the lens here with clay or tape. Focus the camera by sliding the tubes in or out until you get a clear image on the tissue paper. The image will be upside down.

photograph, rays of LIGHT produce a picture on the film in your CAMERA. What happens is this: First, you look through a viewfinder at the subject you want to photograph. Then you press a button or lever, which opens a shutter to let light from the subject enter the camera. The light passes a LENS that produces an image of your subject on a film in the camera. But the image shows up only when the film is developed. A developed film is called a *negative*. This shows black objects white, and white objects black. From negatives, you can print *positives*, the final photos, either as paper prints or slides.

Physics

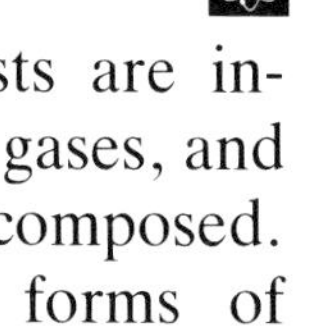

Physics is one of the sciences. Physicists are interested in *matter*—in solids, liquids, and gases, and in the tiny atoms of which all matter is composed. They are interested in the different forms of *energy*—electric energy, light energy, sound energy, mechanical energy, chemical energy, and nuclear energy.

Physicists try to find things out by doing careful experiments. They record the results of their experiments so that other people can try the same experiments if they want to. Physics is a very broad subject, and no one physicist today understands all the different parts of the subject. For example, nuclear physicists who study the tiny atom and its parts

► *A hair-raising experience: The steel ball is a Van de Graaf generator, which makes static electricity. When the girl puts her hand on it, her hair springs to attention! The generator is on display at the Science Center, Toronto, Canada.*

may know little about outer space and the movements of planets, stars, and galaxies as studied by astrophysicists. But one subject they must all understand is mathematics.

Two of the greatest physicists who ever lived were Sir Isaac NEWTON and Albert EINSTEIN.

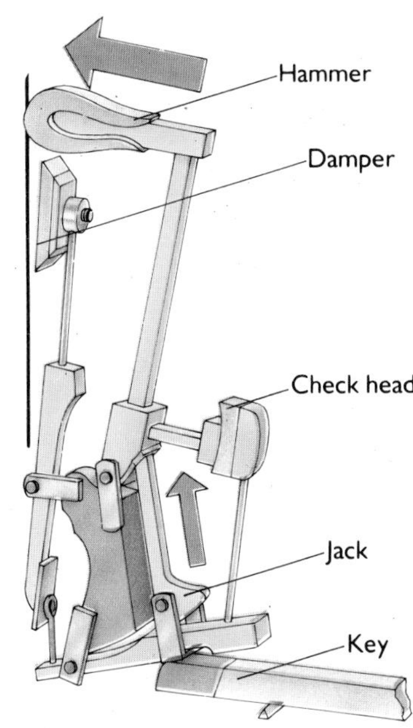

▲ *The action of a piano is based on a lever movement by the key, which is transmitted to a felt-covered hammer that strikes the piano string. A damper prevents the note from sounding after the key is released.*

Piano

Piano is short for the Italian word *pianoforte*, meaning soft and loud. The piano was invented by Bartolomeo Cristofori in 1709. It had great range compared to the harpsichord. The piano has 88 keys. When a key is struck, a system of wires makes a felt-tipped hammer strike a stretched wire. At the same time, a damper, which normally prevents the wire from vibrating, drops back from the wire and stays back until the key is released. The piano has pedals to soften and extend the notes.

◀ *This piano was given to the composer Beethoven by the piano maker Thomas Broadwood in 1818.*

Picasso, Pablo

Pablo Picasso (1881–1973) was the most famous artist of this century. He was born in Spain, but lived in France for most of his life.

People said Picasso could draw before he learned to talk. He disliked paintings that looked like pho-

▲ *Pablo Picasso was a very influential artist whose work changed the course of modern art.*

▶ *One of Picasso's cubist paintings,* The Three Musicians, *painted in 1921.*

tographs and admired the curving shapes of African sculpture. Picasso began painting people as simple shapes such as cubes. He also produced sculpture and pottery.

FRANKLIN PIERCE

Fourteenth President 1853–1857
Born: Hillsborough (now Hillsboro), New Hampshire
Education: Bowdoin College
Occupation: Lawyer
Political Party: Democratic
Buried: Concord, New Hampshire

Pierce, Franklin

Franklin Pierce (1804–1869) was the 14th president of the United States and served in office between 1853 and 1857. His presidency was dominated by the question of slavery and the events that led to the Civil War. While people in the North wanted to ban slavery, those in the South were determined to keep it. A fierce argument also raged about whether it was right to allow slavery in the new states of the West. Pierce was opposed to slavery, but he defended the rights of the South. He tried hard to avoid further conflict, but in the end the bitterness many felt overwhelmed his efforts to prevent the war.

▲ *The wild boar is a tough, fierce animal, unlike most of its domestic relatives.*

Pig

These farmyard animals have a long, heavy body; short legs ending in hoofed toes; a long snout; and a short, curly tail. Males are called boars. Females are called sows. The heaviest boars weigh over a ton.

Pigs provide us with bacon, ham, pork, and lard. Different parts of a pig's body are used to make brushes, glue, leather, and soap.

Domestic pigs, or hogs, are descended from the wild boar of Asian and European forests.

▲ *Most pigeons build their nest in trees. But one species, the Rock dove, nests on rocky cliffs or on the lower ledges and sills of buildings.*

Pigeon and Dove

Pigeons and doves are birds that eat seeds or fruit. Many make soft cooing sounds. Pigeons are larger than doves. The crowned pigeon is bigger than a chicken, but the diamond dove is almost as small as a blackbird.

Tame pigeons come from rock doves, which nest on cliffs. Pigeons and doves have become domesticated. Some are ornamental; others race. Homing pigeons fly great distances to return home. A bird once flew 815 miles (1,300 km) in one day.

Pigeons were the main source of fresh meat for the people of the Middle Ages.

Pilgrim Settlers

The Pilgrim settlers were not the first Europeans to make their homes in America, but they were the most influential. They were English Protestants of the early 1600s who believed that the Church of England was corrupt. Since they knew they could not change the Church, they decided to seek a new life in a new world—America. In 1620, they left England in a little ship called the *Mayflower*. Two months later, they arrived at Plymouth, Massachusetts, and set up Plymouth Colony. They are often considered the founding fathers of the United States.

Pine *See* Conifer

Pineapple

Pineapples earned their name because they look like large pine cones. Pineapples are big, juicy fruits from the tropics. They grow on top of short stems belonging to plants with long spiky leaves. Pineapple producers include Hawaii, Brazil, Mexico, and the Philippines.

▼ *The pineapple gets its name from the Spanish* piña, *meaning pine cone, because of the shape of the fruit.*

The nursery rhyme "Ring o' Roses" refers back to the time of the plague when the first sign of infection was a rosy rash. Herbs and fragrant posies were thought to protect against the disease. Once the victims started to sneeze—"Atishoo, atishoo"—they were almost certain to die—"all fall down."

Plague

Since ancient times, terrible epidemics of plague have swept through Europe, Asia, and Africa. Bubonic plague is one of the worst epidemic diseases. In the 1300s, a form of bubonic plague called the Black Death killed one-fourth of the people in Europe. In London alone, more than 150,000 people died from the plague during the first half of the 17th century. Plague is given to people chiefly by fleas from infected rats.

Planet

The word planet comes from a Greek word meaning "wanderer." Long ago, skywatchers gave this name to "stars" that appeared to move. We now know that planets are not STARS, but are heavenly bodies that travel around stars.

The EARTH and other planets of our SOLAR SYSTEM travel around the star we call the SUN. Each planet travels in its own ORBIT. But they all move in the same direction, and, except for Mercury and Pluto, they lie in the same plane (at about the same level).

The nine planets in the solar system are MERCURY, VENUS, EARTH, MARS, JUPITER, SATURN, URANUS, NEPTUNE, and PLUTO.

▼ *Despite their tiny size, plankton often have beautiful and complex structures. These diatoms have shells made of silica.*

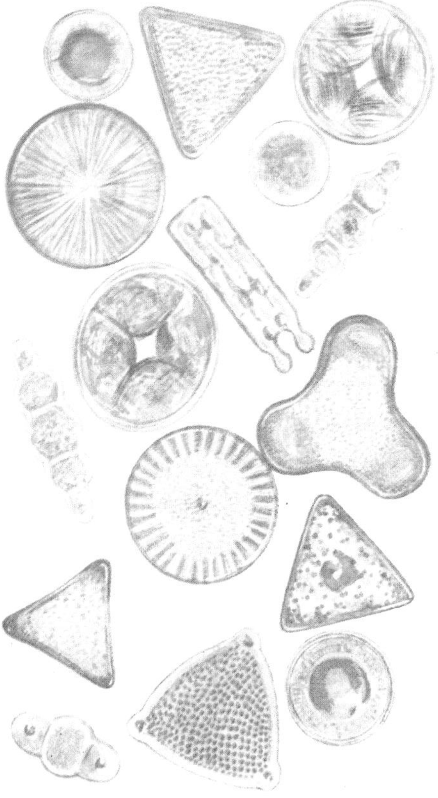

Plankton

Plankton is the mass of tiny plants and animals that drifts about in the sea and inland waters. Most plankton are so small they can be seen only with a microscope.

Planktonic plants are called *phytoplankton*. They live near the surface, where they find the light they need. Some tiny plants swim by lashing the water with little whip-like organs. Others have spiky shells that look like glass.

Planktonic animals are called *zooplankton*. Some live deep down and rise at night to feed. Zooplankton includes tiny one-celled creatures, and baby crabs, and fish.

Plankton is the base for the ocean FOOD CHAIN. All sea creatures depend on plankton.

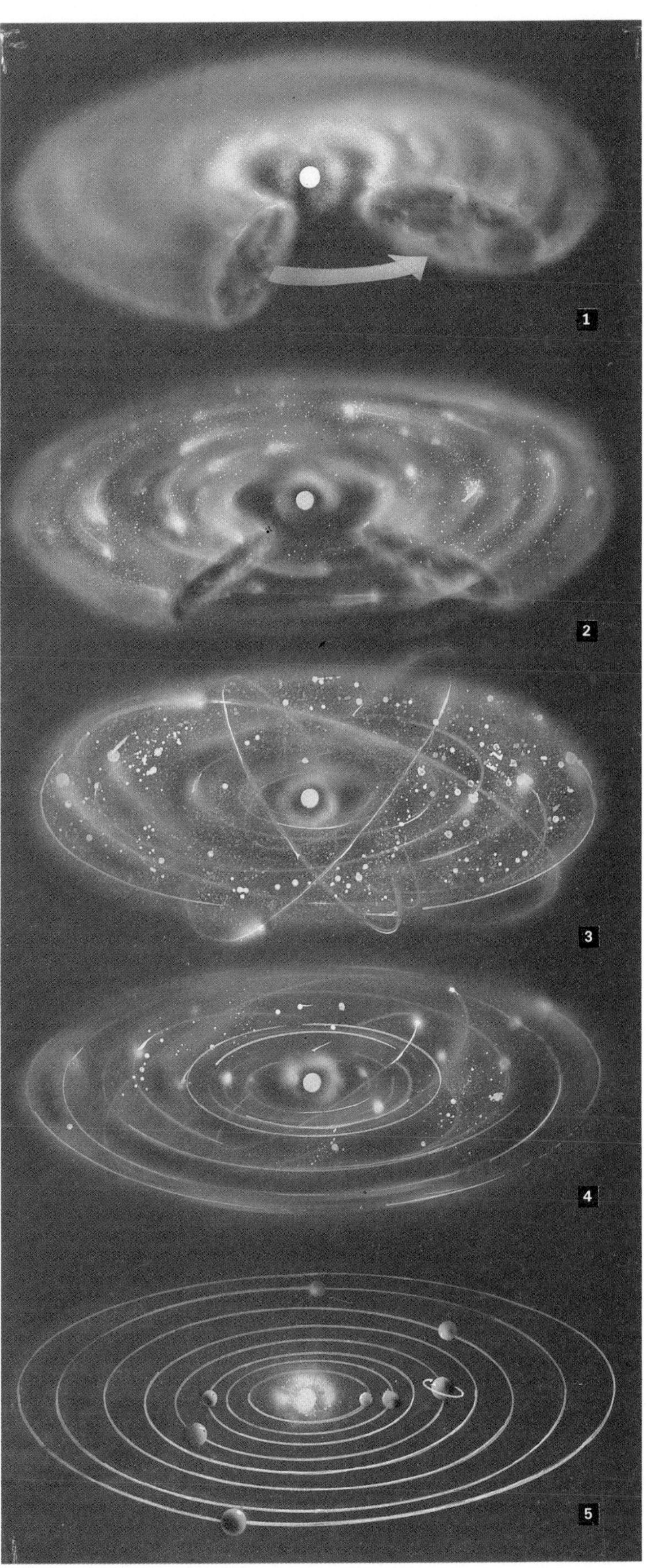

◀ *Scientists think the Sun was born about 4.6 billion years ago. The spare material around the Sun formed a ring, or "doughnut," of gas and dust, whirling around the Sun at high speed. The planets may have formed out of the "doughnut" something like this:*

1. To begin with, the doughnut was a spinning ring of gas and dust.

2. The solid particles began to strike each other and stick together, forming larger bodies. At first, they were mainly carbon and ice.

3. These particles rapidly grew to planetary size. As they grew larger, they began to "pull" against each other, which meant that if they passed too close to each other, they were pulled into a different orbit. Some of the very small carbon-ice bodies were pulled so violently by the larger ones that they were thrown right out toward the stars. Others found themselves pulled into very long orbits that carried them far beyond the planets and back again very near to the Sun. They are the comets.

4. Eventually, there were just a few large bodies going around the Sun in orbits that did not meet each other, and so there were no more collisions or near misses—the nine major planets were formed.

5. With the passage of thousands of millions of years, the planets continued to pull against each other, until their orbits have become almost level.

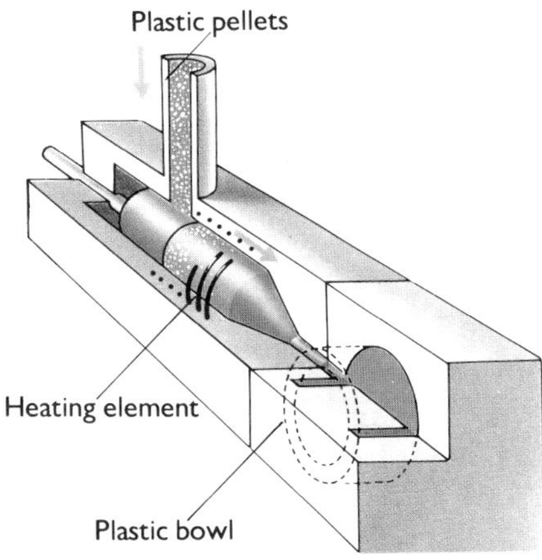

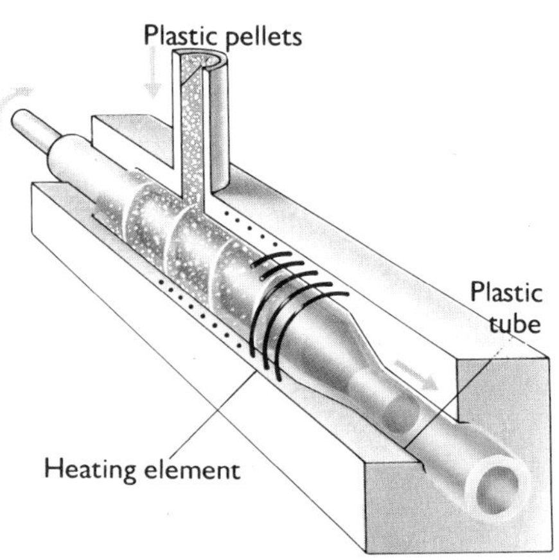

▲ *Hot plastic can be squeezed, or* extruded *(above) into a long, thin tube shape by forcing it through a specially shaped hole. A bowl (top) is made by "injection molding." Hot plastic is forced into a mold which is cooled to harden the plastic.*

Plant

Most living things are either animals or plants. Plants differ from animals in several ways. For example, green plants can make food with the help of CHLOROPHYLL. Each plant CELL has a wall of cellulose. But unlike animals, most plants cannot move around.

There are more than 300,000 kinds of living plant. (See pages 530-531.)

Plastic

Plastics are manmade substances that can be molded into many different shapes. They are used to make anything from furniture and car seats to shoes and bags or cups and plates.

Most plastics are made largely from chemicals obtained from petroleum oil. Coal, limestone, salt, and water are also used. Plastics can be hard, soft, or runny. They can be made to look like glass, metal, wood, or other substances.

Hard plastics are used in radio and camera cases. But fine threads of the hard plastic, nylon, make soft stockings.

Plastic bags and squeeze bottles are made of soft plastics like polyethylene. The first plastic was celluloid, discovered in the 1800s.

► *Bakelite, an early kind of hard plastic, was invented in 1908 by Leo Baekeland. It was used for many household objects.*

The word *Plato* was a nickname, meaning *broad-shouldered*. Plato's real name was Aristocles.

Plato

Plato (about 427–347 B.C.) was a great Greek thinker. His ideas were very important in the history of PHILOSOPHY. He believed that the things we see around us are only poor copies of the perfect things in an ideal world. He developed ideas like justice. In his book *The Republic*, Plato described his idea of a perfect nation.

The eyes, ears, and nostrils of the platypus shut completely when the animal is under water. Although the platypus is blind and deaf in the water, its soft rubbery bill is so sensitive it has no difficulty in finding small creatures to eat.

Platypus

The platypus is an Australian MAMMAL that lays eggs. Its name means "flat-footed." The platypus uses its webbed feet to swim in rivers and its duck-like beak to grub for worms and insects under water. It lives in a burrow in river banks. The female lays her soft-shelled eggs in a nest. They are as small as marbles.

◀ *The duck-billed platypus is just one of a number of very unusual animals found only in Australia and New Zealand. These land masses were cut off millions of years ago, when the continents drifted apart. The animals there evolved in isolation from those elsewhere.*

Pluto

The PLANET Pluto is named after the Greek god who ruled the dreary world of the dead. Pluto must be bitterly cold, because it is farther away from the Sun than any of the other planets. It is almost 40 times farther from the Sun than the EARTH is.

Continued on page 532

PLUTO FACTS

Average distance from Sun:
3,660 million miles
(5,900 million km)
Nearest distance from Earth:
3,583 million miles
(5,800 million km)
Average temperature: −370°F
(−220°C)
Diameter across the equator:
1,800 miles (3,000 km)
Atmosphere: None?
Number of moons: 1 known
Length of day: 6 days 9 hours
Length of year: 248 Earth years

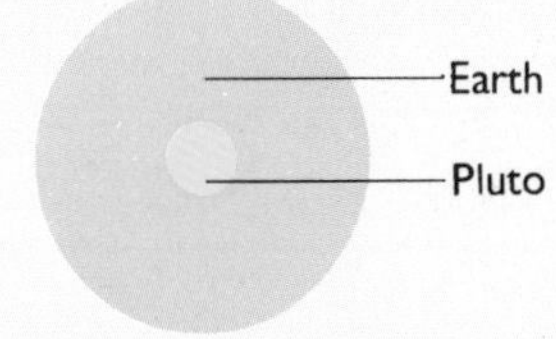

◀ *Pluto has one moon, Charon, which is about half as large as the planet it orbits. Many astronomers consider them a twin planet rather than a planet with a moon.*

PLANTS

We could not live without plants. Only plants are able to use sunlight to build up living matter. They use the carbon dioxide gas (breathed out as waste by animals) and "breathe out" life-giving oxygen. Without plants, there would be no animal life on Earth. Plants provide animals with food. People not only eat plants (and animals such as cattle that feed on plants), but also make use of plant products in all kinds of ways.

There are more than 300,000 different kinds of plant. Some trees may grow three hundred feet tall and live for hundreds of years. Other plants are so tiny they can be seen only through a microscope. Plants are found in the oceans, in deserts, on windswept mountains, and cold tundra plains. When people first learned how to cultivate plants, civilization began. Today, many wild plants are endangered because their habitats are under threat. It is important to protect wild plants and to save them for future generations.

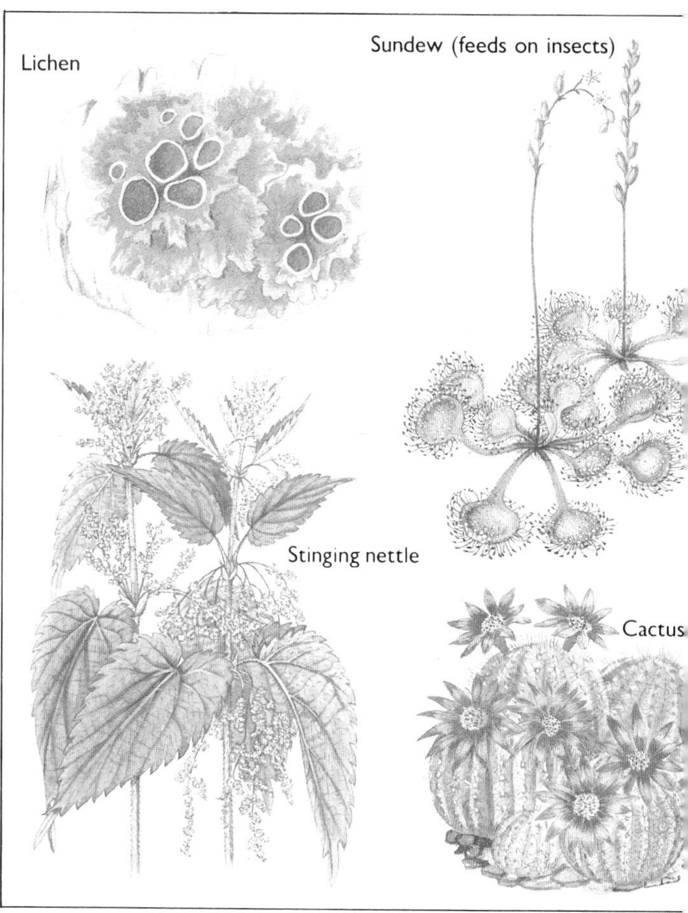

THE PARTS OF A PLANT

Flower: concerned with reproduction. Most flowers have male and female parts.
Leaf: concerned with food-making.
Stem: supports the leaves and flowers. Tubes in the stem carry, and also store, food and water.
Roots: anchor the plant in the soil. They also take in water and minerals through delicate hairs.

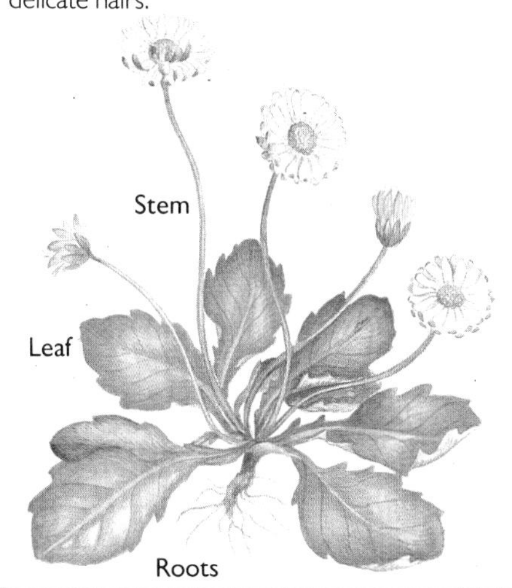

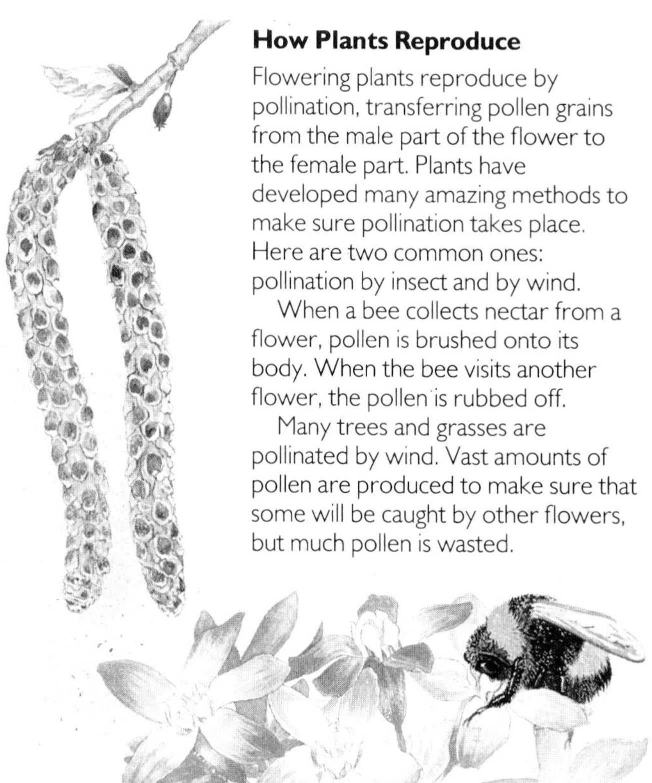

How Plants Reproduce

Flowering plants reproduce by pollination, transferring pollen grains from the male part of the flower to the female part. Plants have developed many amazing methods to make sure pollination takes place. Here are two common ones: pollination by insect and by wind.

When a bee collects nectar from a flower, pollen is brushed onto its body. When the bee visits another flower, the pollen is rubbed off.

Many trees and grasses are pollinated by wind. Vast amounts of pollen are produced to make sure that some will be caught by other flowers, but much pollen is wasted.

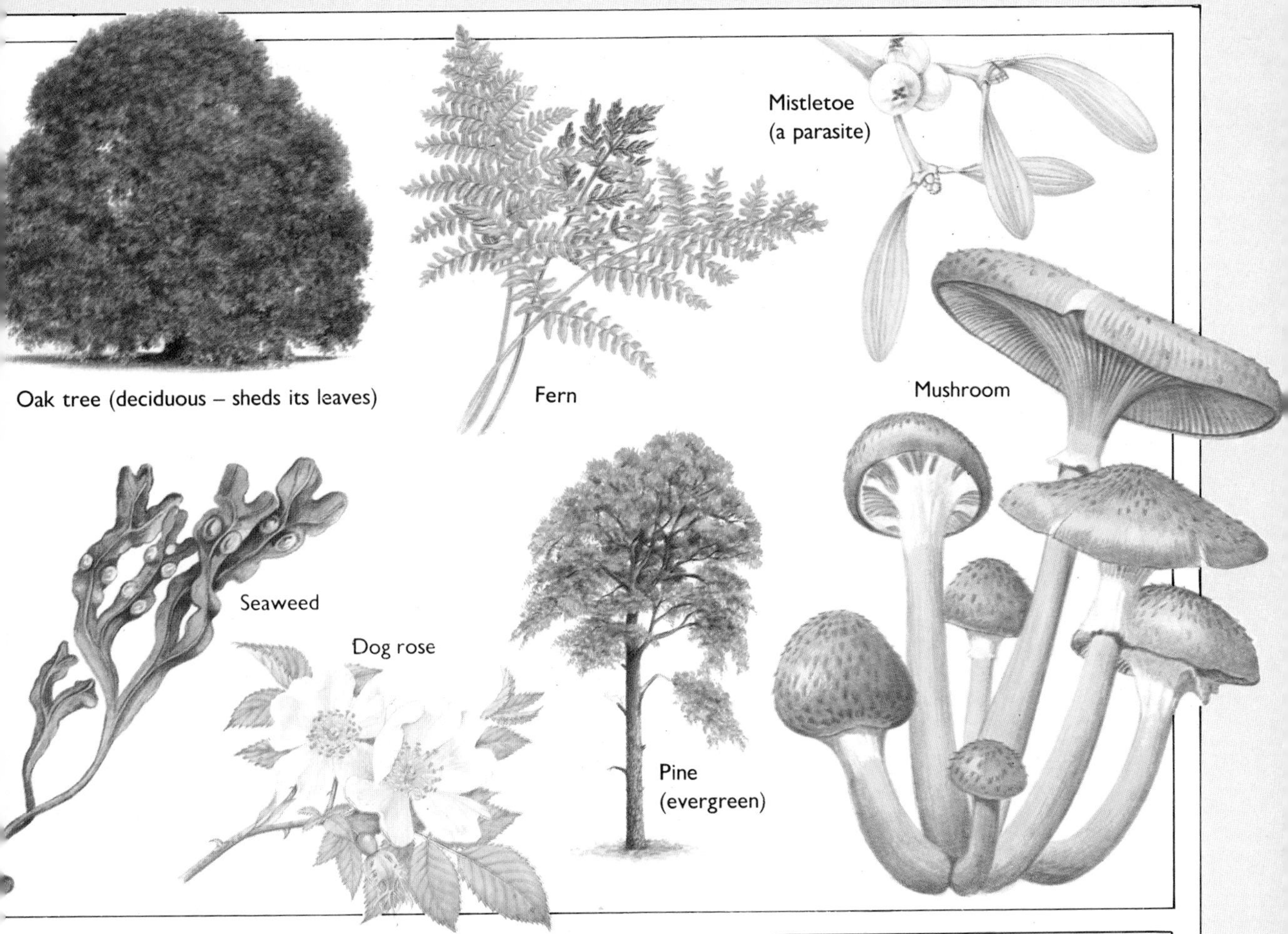

Oak tree (deciduous – sheds its leaves)

Fern

Mistletoe (a parasite)

Mushroom

Seaweed

Dog rose

Pine (evergreen)

IOW PLANTS FEED

'he leaves of green plants contain hlorophyll, a substance which bsorbs light energy from the Sun and ises it to make food for the plant. Vater from the plant's roots and :arbon dioxide gas (taken in from the ir by the leaves) are combined to nake glucose (sugar) and oxygen. The plant takes in the sugar as food or its cells. The oxygen is released nto the air. Plants are the only living hings on Earth which can do this.

Vater (shown blue) is taken in hrough the roots and travels through tubes (the xylem) to veins in the leaves. Some water is given off as vapor, the rest is used by the cells in photosynthesis. The glucose made by photosynthesis travels back around the plant through other tubes (the phloem) to feed the plant.

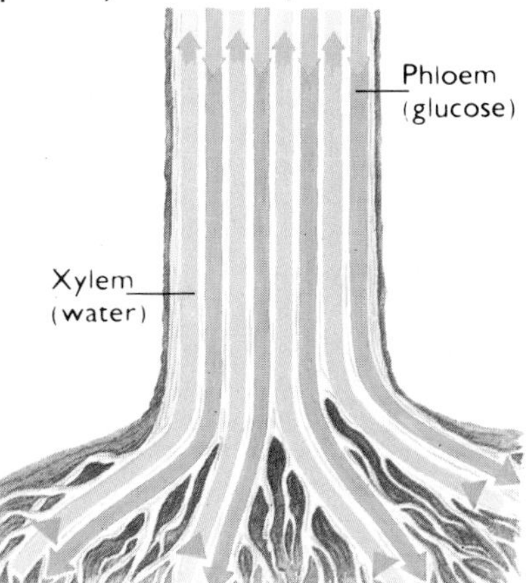

PLANT FAMILIES

Angiosperm: the most advanced plants, ranging from common garden flowers to trees such as the oak.

Gymnosperms: includes conifers (pines and other firs).

Pteridophytes: ferns, horsetails, and clubmosses. The simplest plants with roots, stems, and leaves.

Bryophytes: liverworts and mosses. These are the simplest land plants, without roots.

Fungi: mushrooms and toadstools have no chlorophyll and so feed on other living organisms or on dead matter. Lichens are a kind of fungi.

Algae: includes seaweeds and tiny single-celled plants called diatoms.

Bacteria and Blue-green Algae: the smallest and most primitive of all plants. Most have only one cell.

There are many articles on individual PLANTS in the encyclopedia. Use the Index to find them quickly. Useful information will also be found in BOTANY; BULB; CHLOROPHYLL; CONIFER; FLOWER; FOREST; FRUIT; FUNGUS; LEAF; NUT; SEAWEED; SEED; and TREE.

Pluto spins and moves around the Sun much more slowly than the Earth. A day on Pluto may equal nearly a week on Earth. One year on Pluto lasts almost 248 of our years.

Pluto is much smaller than the Earth and weighs one-sixth as much.

▲ *Edgar Allan Poe was the father of modern mystery and detective fiction.*

Poe, Edgar Allan

Edgar Allan Poe (1809–1849) was an American poet, critic, and short story writer. For many years, he was thought of as just a writer of suspense stories and mysteries. Today, many people believe that his work was much more important than that, and that his influence on many artists in the 1800s was very great. His best-known poem is "The Raven." His best-known stories are "The Murders in the Rue Morgue" and "The Fall of the House of Usher."

▼ *Alfred, Lord Tennyson (below) wrote his poem "The Charge of the Light Brigade" in 1854 after a tragic incident in the Crimean War when 247 men out of 637 were killed or wounded in a charge because of a misunderstood order (right).*

Poetry

Poetry is the oldest form of literature. Before people developed systems of writing words, they found that the best way to remember a story was to sing it or to put it in a rhyming pattern. When words rhyme, they can be easy to remember. This was the

way that poetry was born, long ago.

But poetry is more than just a way of telling a story. When words are put together so that they rhyme, they can suggest emotions, or feelings, in ways that ordinary words, or prose, never can. When we read a poem, we are able to come close to the poet's own feelings when he or she wrote the poem. Poetry can become like music, because it creates beautiful sounds.

There are many different types of poetry. Not all poems rhyme, for example, and many modern poets write poems without rhymes. But all poems have "meter," or internal rhymes. The best way to discover the rhythm of a poem is to read it aloud. You will hear the loud, soft, short, long variations.

▲ *An illustration for the poem "Jabberwocky" by Lewis Carroll. This poem, from the book,* Through the Looking Glass, *is a superb example of a nonsense rhyme.*

SOME POISONOUS SUBSTANCES

Many things around us—in our kitchens, our garages, or our toolsheds—can be poisonous if they are not used properly. These are just a few of them:

- Some **household substances** may be poisonous if swallowed. They include bleach, toilet cleaners, most detergents, furniture polish, gasoline, lighter fluid, kerosine, and household ammonia.
- Garden and farm **insecticides** and **weedkillers** can kill.
- **Carbon monoxide**, a gas given off by car exhausts, is poisonous, especially in badly ventilated areas. Car antifreeze is also a poison.
- Taken in excess, many **drugs and medicines** can be poisonous, including aspirin and sleeping pills.
- **Poisonous plants** include holly (berries), lily of the valley, hydrangea (leaves and buds), and deadly nightshade.

Poison

Poisons are chemical substances that kill or damage living things. Some poisons get into the body through the skin. Some are swallowed. Poisonous gases are harmful if someone breathes them in with air. Different poisons work in different ways. Strong ACIDS or alkalis "burn." NERVE poisons can stop the heart. Some other poisons can make the body bleed inside.

DRUGS called antidotes can cure people who are suffering from the effects of certain poisons.

▼ *The symbol for poisonous substances is a skull and crossbones.*

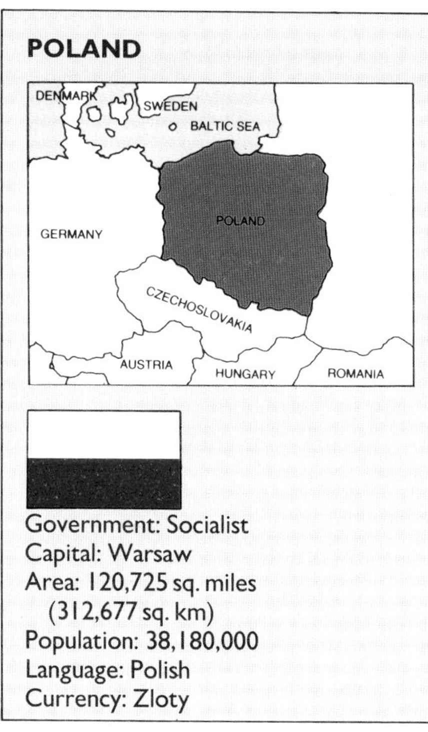

Government: Socialist
Capital: Warsaw
Area: 120,725 sq. miles (312,677 sq. km)
Population: 38,180,000
Language: Polish
Currency: Zloty

Poland

Poland lies in eastern Europe, south of the Baltic Sea, and is the seventh largest country in EUROPE. Most of Poland is low farmland, although forests sprawl across the Carpathian Mountains in the south. Poland's largest river is the Vistula. It rises in the mountains and flows into the Baltic Sea. Rivers often freeze in Poland's cold, snowy winters.

Poland used to be agricultural, but today, more than half the people live in cities. Most of them are Roman Catholics. Coal mining is important.

In 1989, Poland had the first free elections in 40 years. The independent trade union Solidarity swept into power and Poland became the first non-communist country in the Eastern bloc.

Police

Police work for a government to keep LAW and order in their country. Their main task is to see that everyone obeys their country's laws. Part of this job is protecting people's lives and property. Police also help to control crowds. They help people hurt in accidents and take charge of lost children.

Police officers try to prevent crime and track down and capture criminals. This can be dangerous, and sometimes officers are killed.

In 1829, Sir Robert Peel organized a body of paid and trained policemen for day and night duty in London. The public called these first policemen "peelers" or "bobbies," after Sir Robert, and the name bobbies is still used in England today.

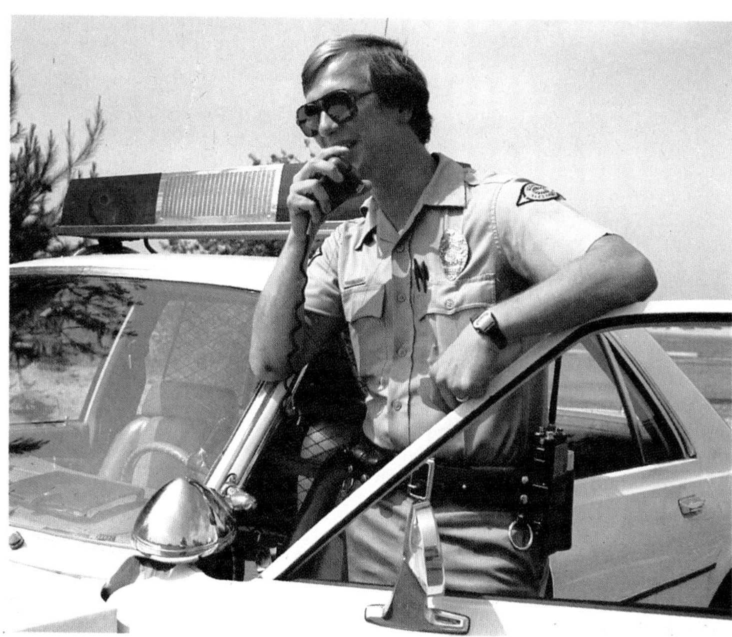

▶ *Modern policing relies heavily on fast and efficient communication. This officer in the highway patrol has a car radio, as well as a hand radio for instant contact away from the car.*

Polk, James Knox

James Polk (1795–1849) was the 11th president of the United States and served in office between 1845 and 1849. His term of office was one of the most successful of any president. America was expanding rapidly and becoming more prosperous all the time. But after he retired, Polk became unpopular. Some people came to dislike him because he was a cold and distant figure. Others thought he encouraged the slave states. During his presidency, the United States won the Mexican War, which allowed Texas to become a part of the Union. Businesses grew rapidly. Many felt that the country was on the verge of becoming a great power. During Polk's presidency, the first Women's Rights Convention was held.

JAMES K. POLK

Eleventh President 1845–1849
Born: Mecklenburg County, North Carolina
Education: University of North Carolina
Occupation: Lawyer
Political Party: Democratic
Buried: State Capitol, Nashville, Tennessee

Pollution

Pollution means the spoiling of air, soil, water, or countryside by wastes. Before the INDUSTRIAL REVOLUTION, most of the wastes produced by living things had been used by other living things. But today, people produce more wastes than nature can cope with.

Cars and factories pour smoke and fumes into the air. Chemical FERTILIZER and pesticides can kill wild plants and animals. Poor sewage disposal and spilled oil make seas and rivers filthy.

◄ Lichens that normally grow on trees in the countryside are sensitive to polluted air. As you get closer to towns, only certain types of lichen can survive. Where there are heavy concentrations of sulfur dioxide gas in the air, only a thin film of algae will grow on trees and stones.

▲ This plastic trash polluting a rocky shore must be cleared by hand—it will not decompose naturally.

Polo, Marco

Marco Polo (1254–1324) was an Italian traveler. He is famous for the long journey he made to faraway China at a time when the people of Europe knew little about the East. His father and his uncle were

▲ *Marco Polo and his companions were kindly received by Kublai Khan, who was interested in other countries and their customs.*

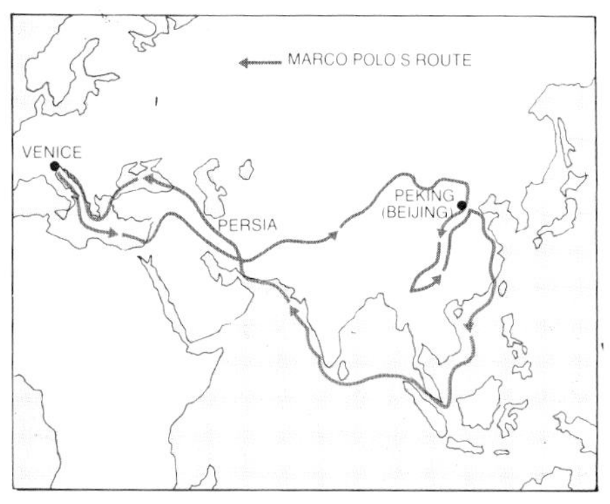

▲ *Even by modern standards, Marco Polo's journey was a long one, but in the 1200s, it was a tremendous achievement.*

The Roman writer, Pliny the Younger, described what happened when Vesuvius destroyed Pompeii. Pliny saw the ground shake, the sea sucked back and then hurled forward, and great tongues of flame spurt from the black cloud that boiled up from the volcano.

merchants from Venice, and they decided to take the young Marco with them when they set out for the East in 1271. They crossed Persia and the vast Gobi Desert. In 1275, they reached Peking (Beijing) and were welcomed by Kublai Khan, a great MONGOL conqueror. The Polos stayed for many years, during which Marco traveled all over China in the service of the Khan. They left China in 1292 and arrived home in Venice in 1295. Later, Marco's stories of his travels were written down. The *Travels of Marco Polo* is one of the most exciting books ever written.

Pompeii

Two thousand years ago, Pompeii was a small Roman city in southern Italy. A sudden disaster killed many of its citizens and drove out the rest. But the same disaster preserved the streets and buildings. Today, visitors to Pompeii can learn a great deal about what life was like inside a Roman city.

In A.D. 79, the nearby volcano of VESUVIUS erupted and showered Pompeii with volcanic ash and cinders. Poisonous gases swirled through the streets. About one citizen in every ten was poisoned by fumes or burned to death by hot ash. The rest escaped. Ash and cinders soon covered up the

▲ *Archaeologists have uncovered almost half of the city of Pompeii (above). Bodies of Pompeiians trapped while fleeing (left) have been recreated by making plaster casts of their imprints in the volcanic ash.*

buildings. In time, people forgot that Pompeii had ever been there.

For centuries, Pompeii's thick coat of ash protected it from the weather. At last, in the 1700s, people began to dig it out. The digging still goes on today. Archaeologists discovered buildings, streets, tools, and statues. They even found hollows left in the ash by the decayed bodies of people and dogs killed by the eruption. The archaeologists poured plaster into these hollows. They let the plaster harden, then they cleared away the ash. They found that the plaster had formed life-size models of the dead bodies.

Pope

The Pope is the head of the ROMAN CATHOLIC CHURCH. (The word "pope" comes from the Italian word *papa*, which means "father.") As head of the Catholic Church, the Pope is also the Bishop of Rome. He lives in Rome, in a tiny country called the VATICAN CITY.

The first pope was St. Peter. He was chosen by Jesus as his representative on Earth. Every later pope is also thought to be God's representative. As head of the church, the pope makes laws for the church, chooses bishops, and can declare people SAINTS. There have been many hundreds of popes since St. Peter. Whenever one dies, the cardinals of the church choose another.

▲ *As Pope, John Paul II is recognized by Roman Catholics as the representative of Jesus Christ on Earth. He is also head of the Vatican City State.*

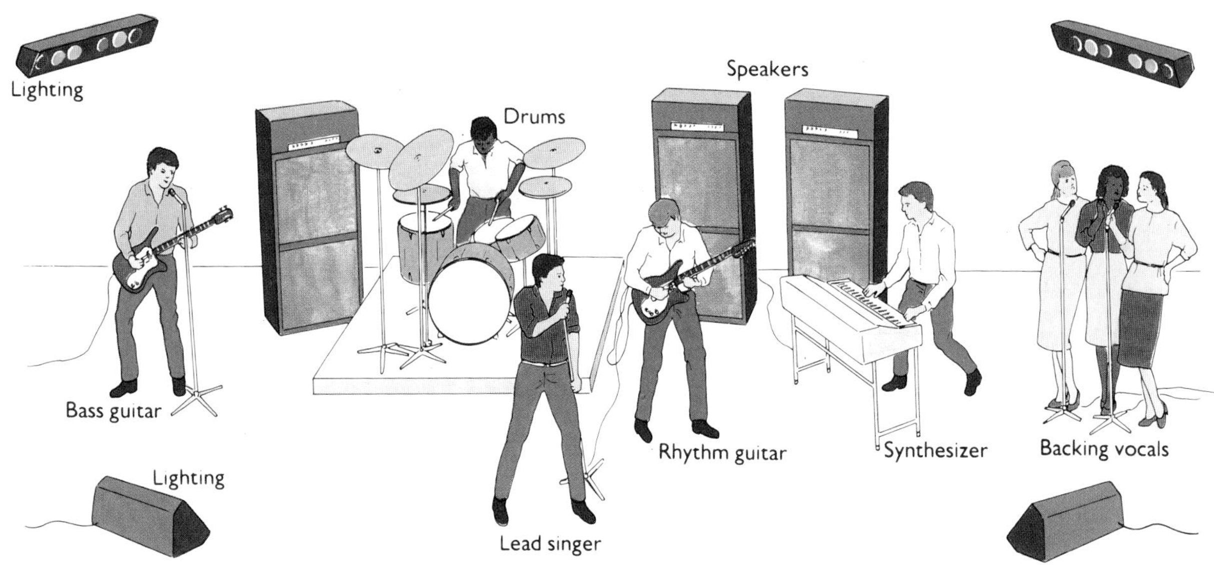

▲ *Many people start pop groups when they are still at school, and a few have achieved success by being "discovered" and given recording contracts. A common lineup for a band could consist of a drummer, a bass guitarist, rhythm guitarist, keyboard player, and vocalists.*

▲ *Elvis Presley was one of the first rock and roll stars to become a cult hero.*

Pop Music

"Pop music" is short for popular music. Modern pop music has strong, lively rhythms and simple, often catchy, tunes. Most pop tunes are songs. A pop group usually has one or more singers with musicians who play such instruments as electronic guitars, synthesizers, and electronic organs. Pop groups often need trucks to carry their equipment, as well as a crew to set it up, take it down, and repair it.

Famous pop groups and stars like the Beatles, the Rolling Stones, and Madonna have attracted huge audiences to concerts. Millions of people around the world watched the 1985 Live Aid pop music concert on television.

Population

All the people living in a place make up its *population*. That place may be a village, a city, a country, or the world.

In the STONE AGE, the whole world held only a few million people. Their numbers were kept low by lack of food, injury, and disease. As people have solved these problems, the population has increased.

Between A.D. 1 and 1650, the world's population doubled. It doubled again in only 150 years after 1650. Since then, it has risen even faster. In 1930,

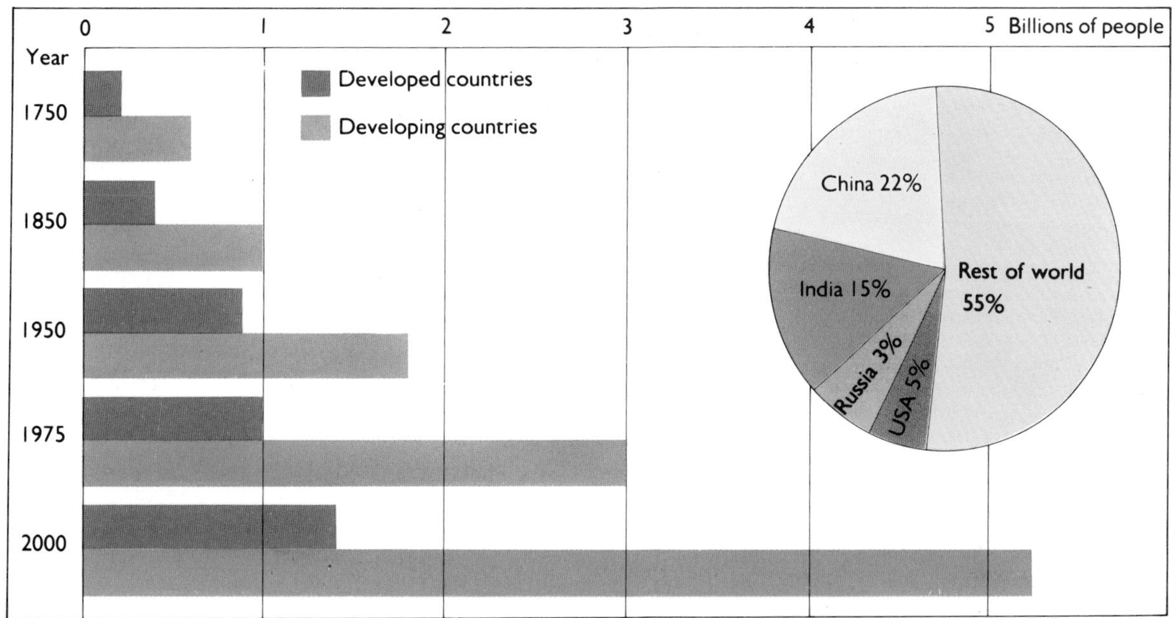

the world had 2 billion people. By 1980, there were over twice that many. The world's population is now over 5 billion and is still growing too quickly.

▲ *The bar chart shows how the populations of developed and developing countries have increased between 1750 and 1975 and estimates the population for the year 2000. The pie chart (inset) gives the percentage of the world's population in each of the largest countries.*

Porcupine

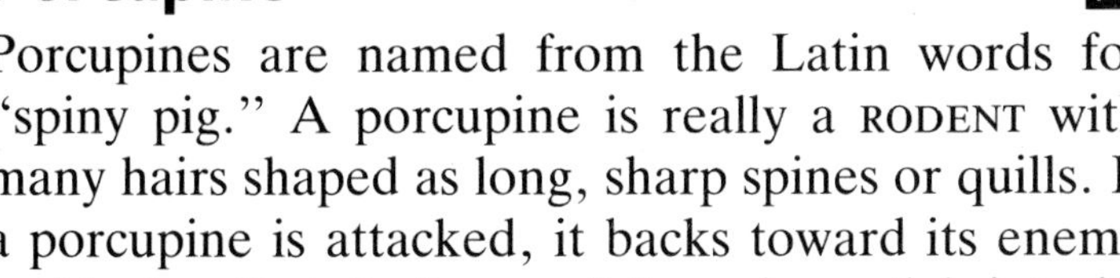

Porcupines are named from the Latin words for "spiny pig." A porcupine is really a RODENT with many hairs shaped as long, sharp spines or quills. If a porcupine is attacked, it backs toward its enemy and lashes its tail. Some of the spines stick into its enemy and cause painful wounds or even death.

North American porcupines spend most of their time in pine trees. They eat plants, but sometimes kill trees by eating the bark.

Portugal

This is a long, narrow country in southwestern EUROPE. It is sandwiched between the Atlantic Ocean and Spain.

Much of Portugal is mountainous. Rivers flow from the mountains through valleys and across plains to the sea. Portugal's mild winters and warm summers help its people to grow olives, oranges, and rice. Its grapes produce port, a wine named after the Portuguese city of Oporto. Portugal's woods yield more CORK than those of any other nation.

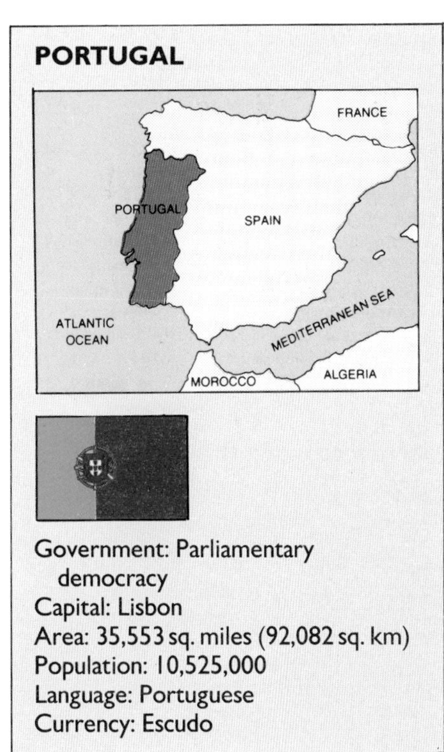

▼ *A hollow pot can be made by pouring "slip," or liquid clay, into a mold. Water seeps out of the slip into the mold and the clay next to the mold begins to thicken. When the required thickness of clay has hardened, the remaining slip can be poured away to leave a hollow shape.*

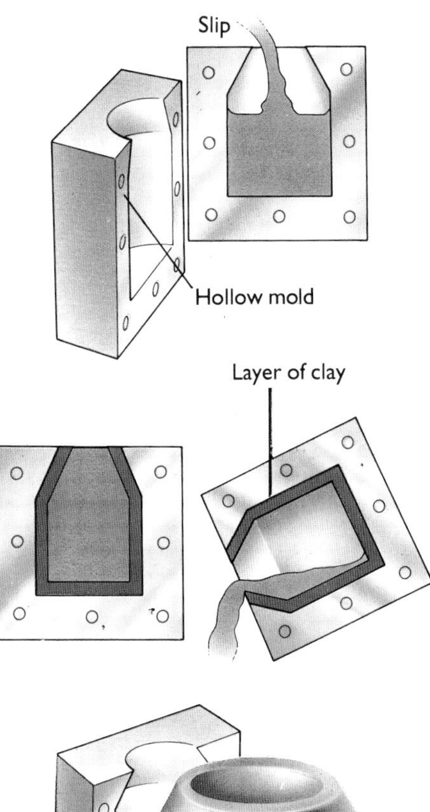

Potato

Potatoes are valuable foods. They are rich in STARCHES and contain PROTEINS and different VITAMINS. Potatoes must be cooked to give nourishment that we can use.

Potato plants are related to tomatoes. Each plant is low and bushy with a soft stem. Each potato grows on a root as a kind of swelling called a tuber. When its tubers have grown, the plant dies. But new plants spring up from the tubers.

Potatoes were first grown by South American Indians about 400 years ago. Spanish explorers brought potatoes back to Europe.

Pottery

All kinds of objects made of baked clay are called pottery. Many cups, saucers, plates, bowls, pots, vases, and other tools and ornaments are made of this useful substance.

People have been making pottery for thousands of years. Early pots were thick and gritty. They leaked, and they cracked if heated. In time, people learned to make pottery that was more useful and more beautiful. Today, the two main kinds of pottery are porcelain and stoneware. Porcelain is fine pottery made of white China clay. This porcelain lets the light show through. Stoneware is usually thicker than porcelain, and it does not let the light show through.

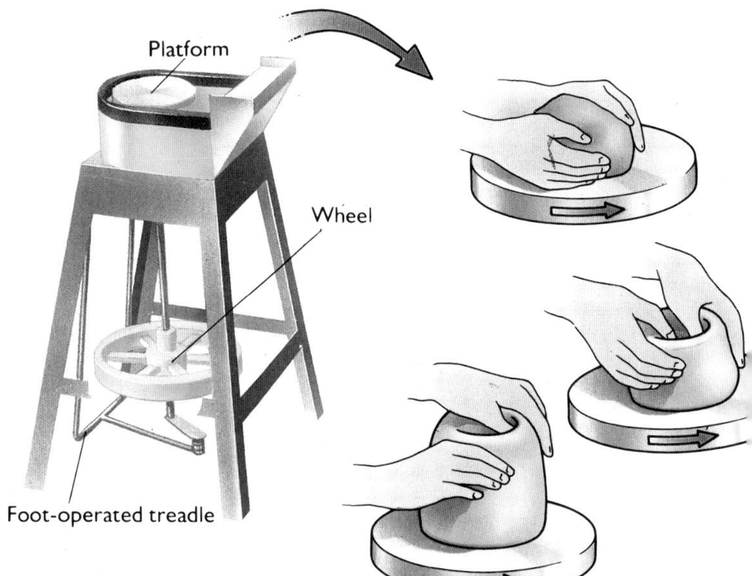

▶ *Making a pot on a potter's wheel is much more difficult than it looks. The lump of clay must be positioned centrally on the platform. It is rotated either by the action of the potter's foot or by electricity. By pressing both thumbs on top of the clay, the inside can be hollowed out as the platform spins.*

To make a pot, a potter puts a lump of moist clay on a spinning disk called a *wheel.* He uses his thumbs and fingers to shape the clay into a pot. He leaves this pot to dry. Next he may coat it with a wet mixture called a glaze. Then he fires (heats) the pot with others in an oven called a kiln. Firing makes the pots rock hard and turns their glaze into a smooth, hard, shiny coat.

▲ *Partridges are small game birds, about 12 inches (30 cm) long, with brown and chestnut markings. In the wild, they live on open farmlands and prairies.*

Poultry

All birds kept for meat or eggs are known as poultry. To most people, poultry means chickens, DUCKS, geese, and turkeys. But guinea fowl, OSTRICHES, partidges, PEACOCKS, pheasants, and PIGEONS can be kept as poultry, too.

Chickens outnumber other kinds of poultry. There are probably more chickens than people, and they lay enough eggs to give everyone on Earth several hundred eggs each year. Chickens also produce meat more cheaply than sheep or cattle. This is because it costs less in food to produce a pound of chicken meat than it costs to make a pound of beef, lamb, or mutton.

Power Plant

Power plants are places where the ENERGY in heat or in flowing water is changed into electrical energy for use in homes and factories. Most power plants obtain their energy from a FUEL which makes steam that works a GENERATOR or a group of generators.

These produce electric CURRENT that often travels overland through wires suspended between tall metal towers called pylons. First, the current passes

▼ *A coal-fired power plant transforms the energy locked in coal into electricity. Bituminous, or soft, coal is most commonly used as the fuel in power plants because it is cheaper and more plentiful than anthracite, or hard coal.*

through a transformer. This raises the pressure (voltage) of the current and so reduces the amount that leaks away as the current flows. The voltage is reduced again before it reaches our homes.

The first public power plant began operating in London, England, on January 12, 1882. Because it produced direct electric current at a low voltage, the area it supplied with electricity was very small. In those days, a single city was supplied by a dozen or more power plants.

Prehistoric Animals

Prehistoric animals are those that lived before history began, about 5,000 years ago. We know about them from their FOSSILS found in rocks. Different kinds of creatures lived at different times. Each kind developed from earlier kinds, by EVOLUTION. The first prehistoric animals probably looked like little blobs of jelly. (See pages 544–545).

▼ Homo habilis *was probably the first human being to make and use tools.*

Prehistoric People

Prehistoric people lived long ago before there were any written records of history. We know about them from the remains of their tools, weapons, and bodies. Prehistory is divided into the STONE AGE, the BRONZE AGE, and the Iron Age. The ages are named after the materials that people used to make their tools and weapons.

The Stone Age lasted for a long time. It began around 4 million years ago, when human-like creatures began to appear on the Earth. They were different from the ape-like animals that lived at the same time. They had larger brains, used stone tools, and could walk upright.

▼ *The evolution of human beings, from the ape-like* Ramapithecus *to modern man.*

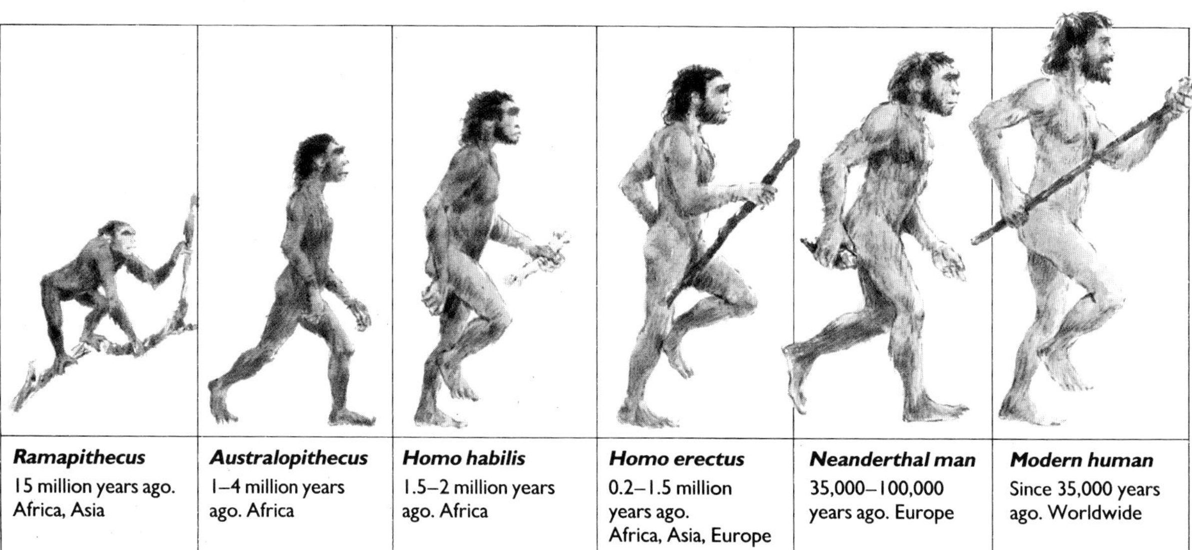

◀ *About 20,000 years ago, modern humans lived in caves or crude huts of wood or hides. They used tools of stone and bone for hunting and preparing food and for making clothing and shelters.*

Around $1^1/_2$ million years ago, a more human-like creature appeared. Scientists call this kind of early man *Homo erectus*. This means "upright man." *Homo erectus* is probably the ancestor of more advanced types of man, called *Homo sapiens*. This means "intelligent man." One kind of *Homo sapiens* was Neanderthal man, who appeared about 100,000 years ago. Modern man, called *Homo sapiens sapiens*, first appeared in Europe and Asia about 35,000 years ago.

Toward the end of the Stone Age, prehistoric people began to use metals. The first metal they used was copper. They made copper tools about 10,000 years ago. About 5,000 years ago, people invented bronze. Bronze is a hard ALLOY of copper and tin. This was the start of the Bronze Age, when the earliest civilizations began. The Bronze Age ended about 3,300 years ago in southeastern Europe, when people learned how to make iron tools. Iron is much harder than bronze. With iron tools, people could develop farming and cities more quickly than ever before.

It is difficult for us to imagine how few people there were in Stone Age times. It has been estimated that only a few thousand people lived in all of Africa and another few thousand in Asia. People moved around in small groups. During his or her whole lifetime, a Stone Age person might see only 25 to 50 other people.

Presbyterian

Presbyterians are PROTESTANTS whose churches are governed by ministers and elders, called *presbyters*.

A French religious thinker called John Calvin (1509–1564) led a reform movement in the Christian church, which gave rise to the Presbyterians. There are now about 50 million Presbyterians. Many of

Continued on page 546

▲ *John Calvin set up a Protestant church in Geneva, Switzerland, and became governor there in 1536.*

PREHISTORIC ANIMALS

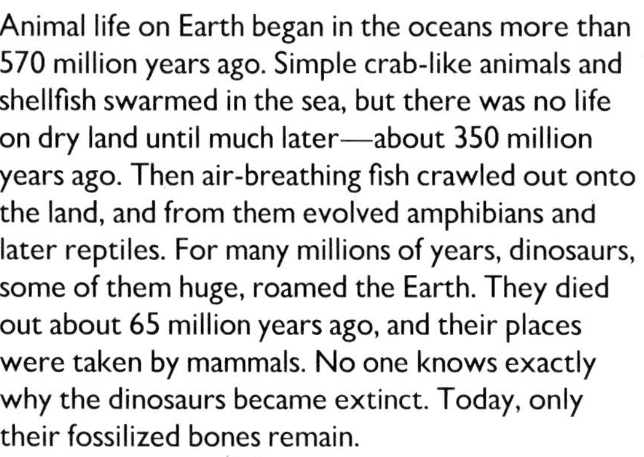

Animal life on Earth began in the oceans more than 570 million years ago. Simple crab-like animals and shellfish swarmed in the sea, but there was no life on dry land until much later—about 350 million years ago. Then air-breathing fish crawled out onto the land, and from them evolved amphibians and later reptiles. For many millions of years, dinosaurs, some of them huge, roamed the Earth. They died out about 65 million years ago, and their places were taken by mammals. No one knows exactly why the dinosaurs became extinct. Today, only their fossilized bones remain.

◀ *Trilobites were crab-like sea animals with jointed legs and hard bodies. They lived on Earth for more then 340 million years.*

▶ Ichthyostega *was one of the first amphibians. It had a fin-like tail, but walked on four legs.*

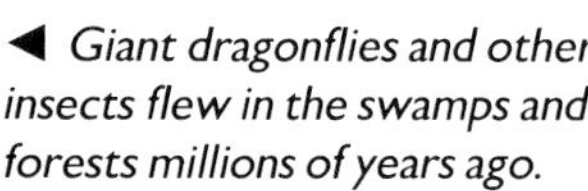

◀ *Giant dragonflies and other insects flew in the swamps and forests millions of years ago.*

▼ Triceratops *was an armored dinosaur. Its bony frill and horns protected it from enemies.*

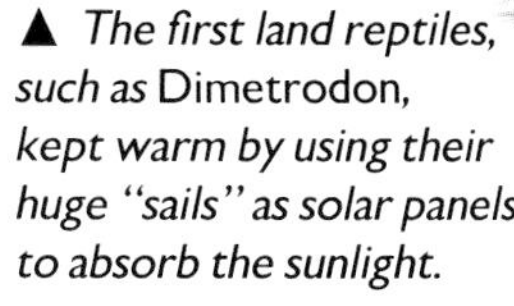

▲ *The first land reptiles, such as* Dimetrodon, *kept warm by using their huge "sails" as solar panels to absorb the sunlight.*

▼ *The plesiosaurs were marine reptiles. They used their limbs as paddles for swimming.*

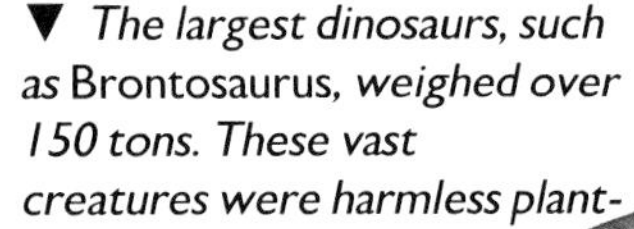

▼ *The largest dinosaurs, such as* Brontosaurus, *weighed over 150 tons. These vast creatures were harmless plant-eaters.*

◀ *Pterosaurs were flying reptiles with bat-like wings. It is thought most pterosaurs fed on fish, gliding over seas and rivers.*

▼ Archaeopteryx *was a feathered animal, halfway between reptile and bird. It probably used its wings to glide short distances.*

• Tyrannosaurus rex *"king of the tyrant* *:ards") was the fiercest* *:sh-eater of all time. It* *ood 20 ft. (6 m) high and* *easured 50 ft. (15 m)* *om jaws to tail.*

· *We know little about* *e first mammals. They* *ere small creatures that* *obably ate insects and* *orms.*

▼ *The wooly mammoth was an Ice Age relative of the elephant. Its thick, hairy coat kept it warm.*

▲ Toxodon *was a rhino-like plant-eater of the Pliocene epoch in South America.*

◀ *Humans and apes evolved from a common ancestor. This primitive manlike ape,* Dryopithecus, *lived 22 million years ago in Africa.*

The earliest mammals, tiny shrew-like animals, lived in the shadows of the great dinosaurs. After the dinosaurs died out, mammals developed and spread rapidly. From these early mammals (some of which were very curious-looking) developed the mammals of today. Some were much larger than their modern relatives. Animals that could not adapt to changing conditions (like the Ice Ages) died out. Others were hunted by human beings, the most intelligent of all animals, whose primitive ancestors first appeared on Earth some 35 million years ago.

For more information turn to these articles: DINOSAUR, EVOLUTION, FOSSIL, ICE AGES, and MAMMOTH. You will find lots of other useful references (such as Animal, Bird, Vertebrate) by looking in the Index.

THE PRESIDENTS OF THE UNITED STATES

President	Served
1. George Washington	1789–1797
2. John Adams	1797–1801
3. Thomas Jefferson	1801–1809
4. James Madison	1809–1817
5. James Monroe	1817–1825
6. John Quincy Adams	1825–1829
7. Andrew Jackson	1829–1837
8. Martin Van Buren	1837–1841
9. William H. Harrison	1841
10. John Tyler	1841–1845
11. James K. Polk	1845–1849
12. Zachary Taylor	1849–1850
13. Millard Fillmore	1850–1853
14. Franklin Pierce	1853–1857
15. James Buchanan	1857–1861
16. Abraham Lincoln	1861–1865
17. Andrew Johnson	1865–1869
18. Ulysses S. Grant	1869–1877
19. Rutherford B. Hayes	1877–1881
20. James A. Garfield	1881
21. Chester A. Arthur	1881–1885
22. Grover Cleveland	1885–1889
23. Benjamin Harrison	1889–1893
24. Grover Cleveland	1893–1897
25. William McKinley	1897–1901
26. Theodore Roosevelt	1901–1909
27. William H. Taft	1909–1913
28. Woodrow Wilson	1913–1921
29. Warren G. Harding	1921–1923
30. Calvin Coolidge	1923–1929
31. Herbert C. Hoover	1929–1933
32. Franklin D. Roosevelt	1933–1945
33. Harry S. Truman	1945–1953
34. Dwight D. Eisenhower	1953–1961
35. John F. Kennedy	1961–1963
36. Lyndon B. Johnson	1963–1969
37. Richard M. Nixon	1969–1974
38. Gerald R. Ford	1974–1977
39. James E. Carter	1977–1981
40. Ronald W. Reagan	1981–1989
41. George Bush	1989–

▼ *Postage stamp portraits of two 20th-century U.S. presidents.*

them live in France, Hungary, the Netherlands, Northern Ireland, Scotland, Switzerland, and the United States.

President of the United States

The president of the United States is the head of state and chief executive of the country. In many ways, the president is the most powerful person in the world. That is because he is the head of the richest and most powerful country in the world. The president has many responsibilities. He is the commander in chief of the country's armed forces. He decides the foreign policy of the country. He can attempt to have new laws passed. And in times of emergency, he can give executive orders—laws that do not have to be passed by Congress. He also represents the United States—he is a symbol of his country. When people talk about the dignity of the presidency, this is what they are referring to. But his power is also limited in important ways. When the CONSTITUTION was written, it was agreed that "checks" be placed on the president to make sure that he did not assume too much power. If Congress thinks the president has acted wrongly, it has the

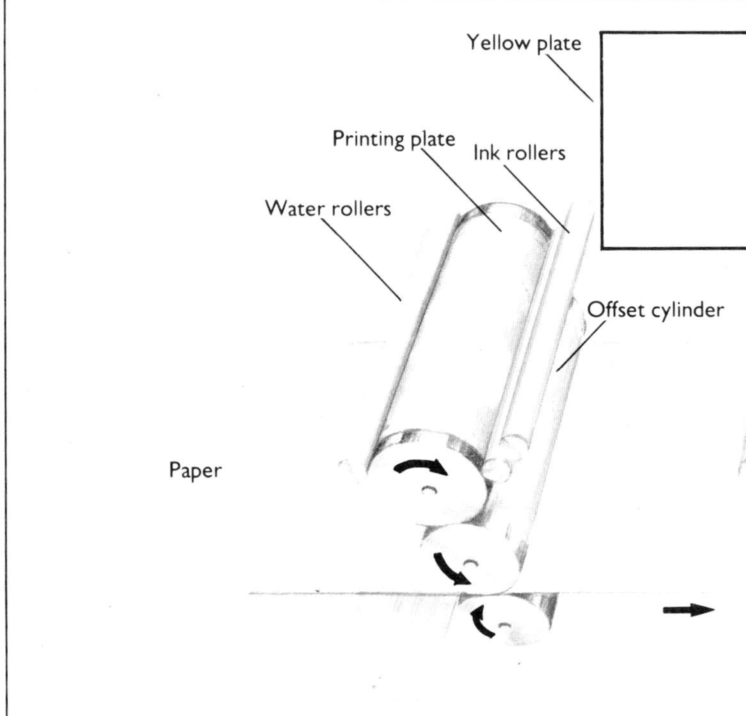

right to overturn his decisions. If it believes that he has broken the law, it also has the power to "impeach" him, to remove him from office.

Prince Edward Island

Prince Edward Island is the smallest, but most densely populated Canadian province. It is not one island, but many small islands in the Gulf of St. Lawrence on Canada's Atlantic coast. Because it is not connected with the rest of Canada, and transportation to it is difficult, industries have developed slowly. Instead, fishing, agriculture, and "service" industries are the most important businesses. It is also a vacation area.

PRINCE EDWARD ISLAND

Capital: Charlottetown
Population: 130,400
Area: 2185 sq. mi. (5660 sq. km)
Entry into confederation: July 1, 1873

Printing

Printing is a way of copying words and pictures by mechanical means. It is used to produce books, newspapers, magazines, and other items such as food can labels and printed shopping bags.

In *relief* printing, ink is put onto raised images, such as letters. The letters are then pressed against paper. The most common method is called *letter-*

▼ *When a color picture is printed, it is actually composed of tiny dots of the three primary colors—blue (cyan), yellow, and red (magenta)—and black. Four different printing plates are prepared for the picture, one for each color. In offset lithography, the images are not printed directly from the plate to the paper. The images are first transferred from the plate cylinder to a rubber cylinder which then presses on the paper.*

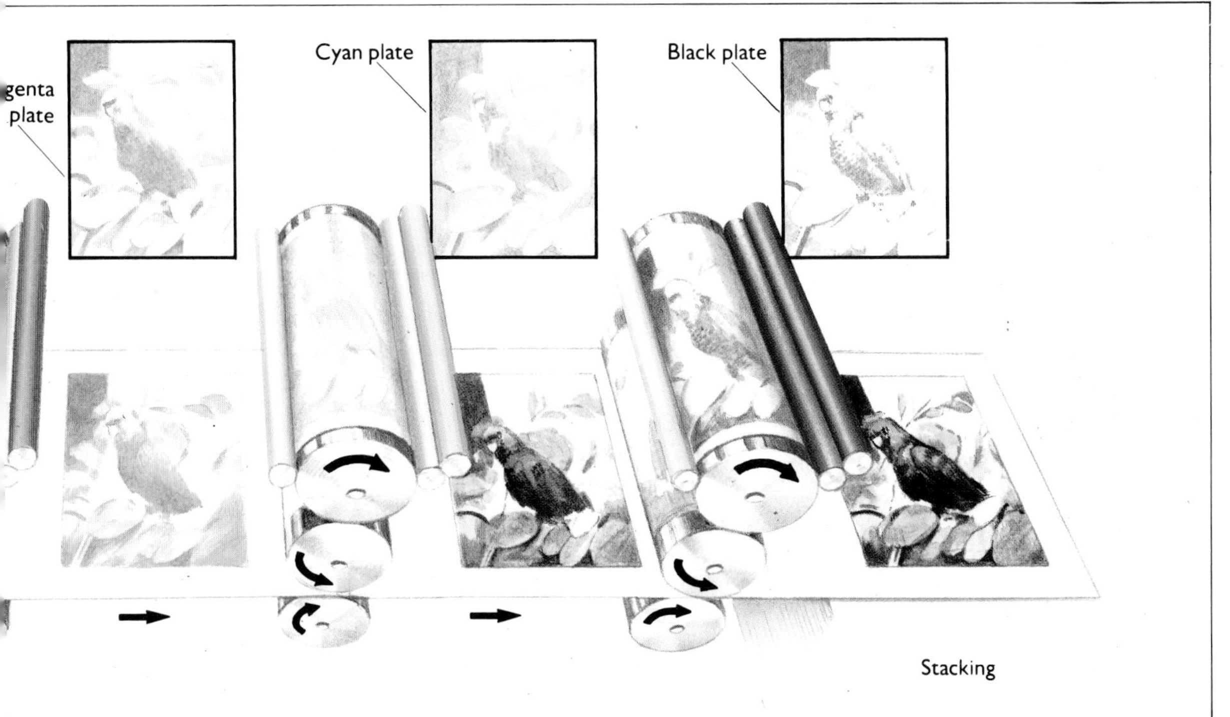

▲ *Meat, fish, eggs, cheese, and nuts are all rich sources of protein.*

▲ *John Bunyan, who wrote* The Pilgrim's Progress, *joined a Nonconformist (a kind of Protestant) church in 1653. He was arrested in 1660 for preaching without a license and spent almost 12 years in prison.*

► *In France, the fight between Protestants and Catholics was very bitter. In 1572, on the eve of August 24, St. Bartholomew's Day, thousands of Protestants known as Huguenots were murdered by Catholics. This terrible event became known as the St. Bartholomew's Day Massacre.*

press printing. In *intaglio* or *gravure* printing, the image is not raised, but cut away or etched.

In other kinds of printing, the ink is put onto a flat surface. *Offset lithography* uses printing plates that are made photographically. The plates are treated with chemicals so that the greasy ink sticks only to the images to be printed.

The earliest printing, using wooden blocks, was done in China, probably as early as the A.D. 500s. Johannes GUTENBERG of Germany founded modern printing, with movable type, in the 1400s.

Protein

Proteins are substances in food which are vital to life. They contain CARBON, HYDROGEN, OXYGEN, and nitrogen. They build up body tissue, especially muscle, and repair broken-down CELLS. They also give heat and energy, help us to grow, and help to protect us from disease. Our bodies do not store extra protein, so we must eat a regular supply.

Foods that come from animals provide most of our proteins. But some plant foods, such as nuts, peas, and beans, are also rich in protein.

Protestant

Protestants are Christians who do not belong to the Roman Catholic or the Eastern Orthodox churches.

Protestants believe that the things written in the BIBLE are more important than any rules made by church leaders. There are some passages in the Bible that can be explained in different ways. Protestants believe that people should make up their own minds about what these mean.

Protestantism began with the REFORMATION, when Martin LUTHER led a movement to change the ROMAN CATHOLIC CHURCH. In 1529, the Roman Catholic Church in Germany tried to stop people from following Luther's ideas. Luther's followers protested against this and were then called Protestants. Early Protestant groups included the Lutherans, Calvinists (PRESBYTERIANS), and Anglicans. Later groups included the Baptists, Congregationalists, Methodists, and QUAKERS.

Proverb

A proverb is a short sentence containing a piece of wisdom. The BIBLE contains a book called *Proverbs*. Proverbs are often easy to remember. One famous proverb is "A stitch in time saves nine." All peoples have proverbs. Many languages are rich in them. Typical African proverbs are "He who takes his time does not fall" (Somalia) and "The dog you do not feed will not hear your call" (Zaire).

Proverbs are often international, and very old. "A bird in the hand is worth two in the bush" is first found in English in a manuscript from about 1470. It says "Betyr ys a byrd in the hond than tweye in the wode." The Spanish version is "A sparrow in the hand is worth a vulture flying." The Germans say "A sparrow in the hand is better than a stork on the roof."

Pruning

Pruning is the cutting back of branches, shoots, buds, or roots of mainly woody plants. Careful pruning helps the plant to bear more fruit or flowers and to become stronger. Roses are often pruned in this way. Sometimes, gardeners prune plants so that they will grow to form special shapes.

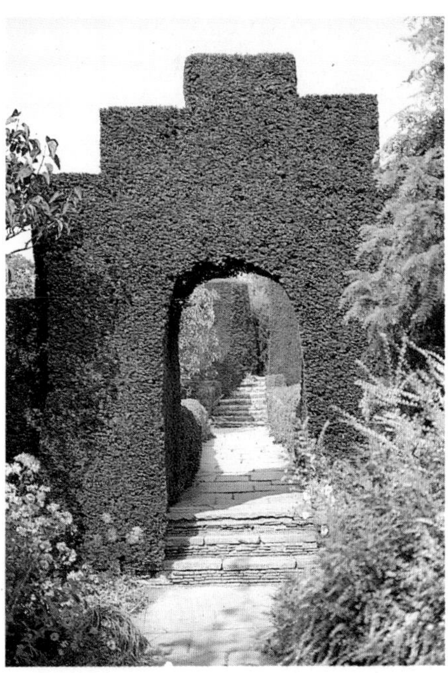

▲ *Shrubs and trees can be cut and trained to grow into special shapes. This pruning art is called "topiary."*

Psychology

Psychology is the study of the behavior of animals and people. Psychologists are interested in how the mind and senses work. They are able to measure some things, such as INTELLIGENCE, by using special tests.

There are several branches of psychology. For

▶ *Psychologists use tests to find out about people. You can test your short-term memory by looking at these objects for 30 seconds. Cover them up and see how many you can remember. Short-term memory becomes worse as you grow older.*

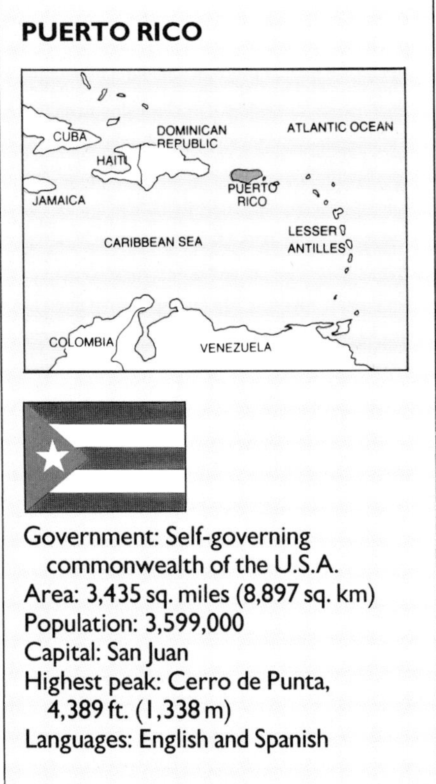

Government: Self-governing commonwealth of the U.S.A.
Area: 3,435 sq. miles (8,897 sq. km)
Population: 3,599,000
Capital: San Juan
Highest peak: Cerro de Punta, 4,389 ft. (1,338 m)
Languages: English and Spanish

▼ *The invention of the wheel led to a useful lifting device, the pulley. The pulley was invented in about 800 B.C.*

example, child psychology is the study of how children behave and what they can do at different ages. *Psychiatry* is a similar science. But psychiatrists are doctors who cure mental illness and abnormal kinds of behavior, such as drug addiction and depression.

Puerto Rico

Puerto Rico is an island in the WEST INDIES. It is a commonwealth that governs itself, but it has the military protection and some economic and political privileges of the United States. Puerto Ricans are U.S. citizens, but they cannot vote in American elections. The island is densely populated, and many people have emigrated to the United States. Puerto Rico means "rich port" in Spanish.

Pulley

A pulley is a simple MACHINE. You can lift heavy loads with a pulley. The weight of the load that can be raised depends on the number of wheels and the way they are connected together. If the pulley has one rope with a six-wheel pulley, you can lift a load six times heavier than you could without it. The reason for this is that the amount of rope that you pull is six times as long as the distance that the load is raised. This increases the amount of FORCE you apply to the load by six times.

However, the amount of work involved is just the same. You are merely spreading the work over a greater distance.

Pulsar

Sometimes a huge star, several times bigger than our Sun, becomes so hot that it explodes. For a few days, it sends out as much energy as a whole galaxy of stars. It has become a *supernova*. After a supernova explosion, all that is left is a very hot ball of matter a few miles across. It spins at a tremendous rate and sends out a beam of light and radio waves like a revolving searchlight. The beam seems to "pulse" on and off, so it is called a pulsar or neutron star. Most pulsars are too faint to be seen except with a very large telescope.

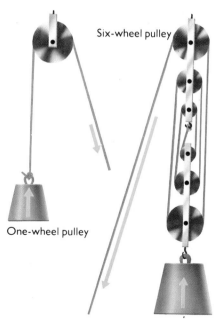

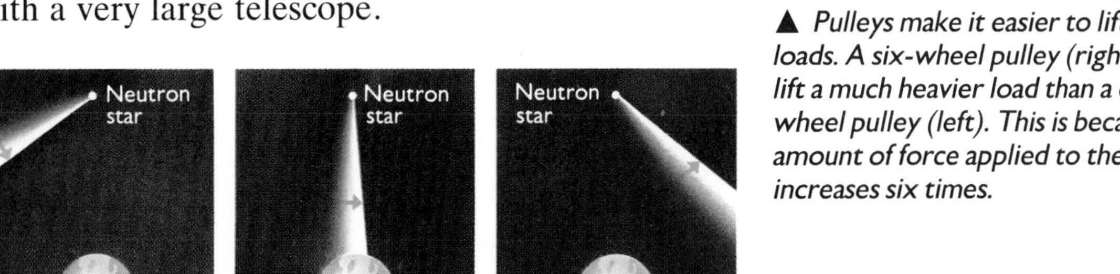

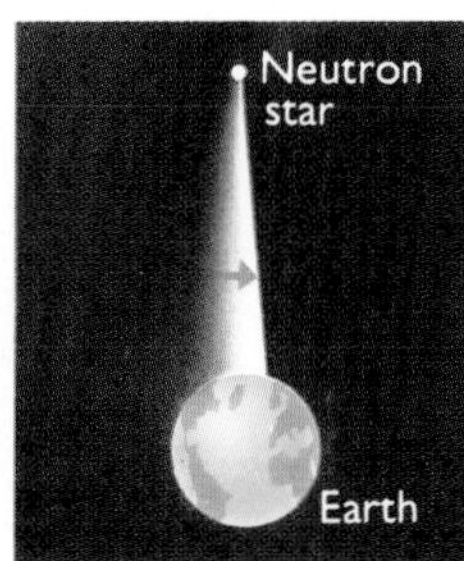

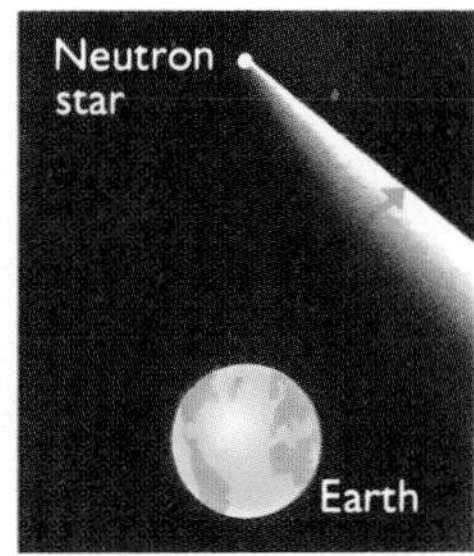

▲ *As a pulsar, or neutron star, spins, its signal sweeps through space like the beam of light from a lighthouse. The signal reaches the Earth once in every rotation, and can be photographed or picked up by radio. Over millions of years, pulsars slow down.*

Pulse

The pulse is a beating or throbbing in the body's arteries. These are BLOOD vessels that carry blood away from the HEART. A pulse beat occurs as the heart contracts and pumps blood into the arteries.

Doctors measure pulse rates to find out if the heart is beating normally. They usually feel the *radial artery* in the wrist. But the pulse can be felt wherever an artery passes over a bone. The normal pulse rate for men is 72 beats per minute. For women, it is 76 to 80 beats. But pulse rates between 50 and 85 are considered normal. Children have faster pulses than grown-ups.

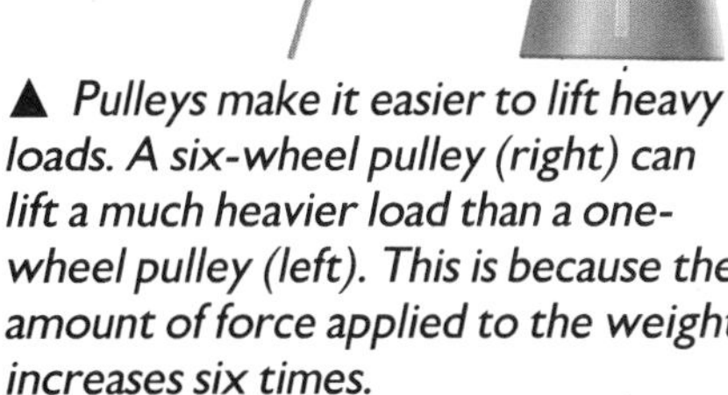

▲ *Pulleys make it easier to lift heavy loads. A six-wheel pulley (right) can lift a much heavier load than a one-wheel pulley (left). This is because the amount of force applied to the weight increases six times.*

SEE IT YOURSELF

Try taking your own pulse rate. Feel the inside of one of your wrists with the fingertips of the other hand. The best place is toward the edge of your wrist in line with the thumb. Use your watch to count the number of beats in one minute. Try measuring your pulse rate when you are doing various things that need different amounts of energy. Jot down the rates and compare them.

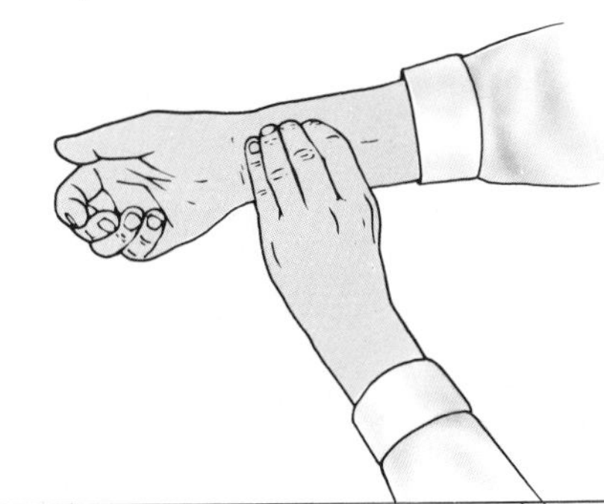

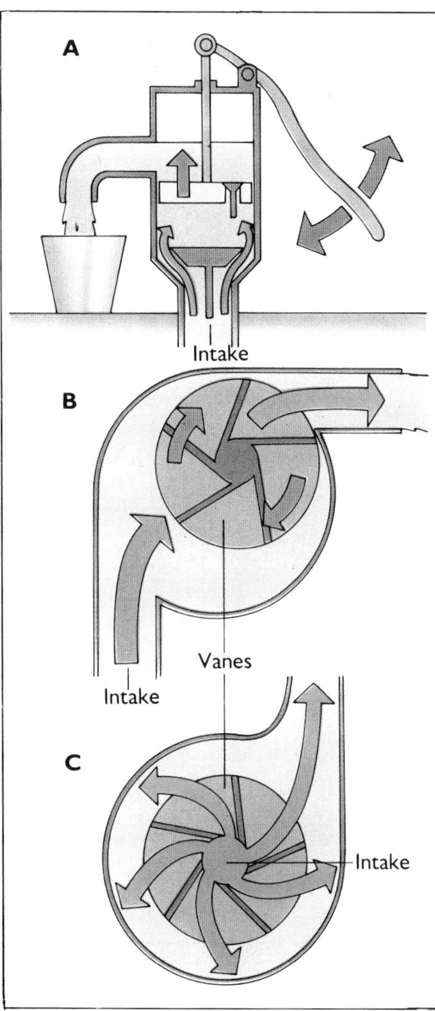

▲ *In a reciprocating pump (A), a piston forces liquid through an intake opening and out through a spout. A valve in the piston allows more liquid through as the piston is forced down. Rotary pumps (B) allow a steady flow of liquid, sucking the liquid in through the intake opening by means of a wheel instead of a piston. In a centrifugal pump (C), the liquid enters in the center and is whipped around and out by the spinning blades.*

Pump

Most pumps are used to move liquids, but some move gases or powders such as flour. There are several kinds of pumps. For example, a bicycle pump is a simple *reciprocating pump*. It has a piston which moves up and down inside a cylinder. A similar pump is the *lift pump*. This can raise water about 30 ft. (9 m) from the bottom of a well. It has an upright barrel with a close-fitting piston worked by a handle. *Force pumps* are used to raise water from greater depths.

Pyramid

Pyramids are huge, four-sided buildings. They have a square base. The sides are triangles that meet in a point at the top.

The Egyptians built pyramids as royal tombs. The first was built in about 2650 B.C. at Sakkara. It is 205 ft. (62 m) high. The three most famous pyramids are near Giza. The Great Pyramid, built in the 2600s B.C. by the PHARAOH Khufu, is 450 ft. (137 m) high. Khafre, who ruled soon after Khufu, built the second pyramid. It is 446 ft. (136 m) high. The third, built by Khafre's successor Menakaure, is 240 ft. (74 m) high. About 80 pyramids still stand in Egypt.

Central and South American Indians also built

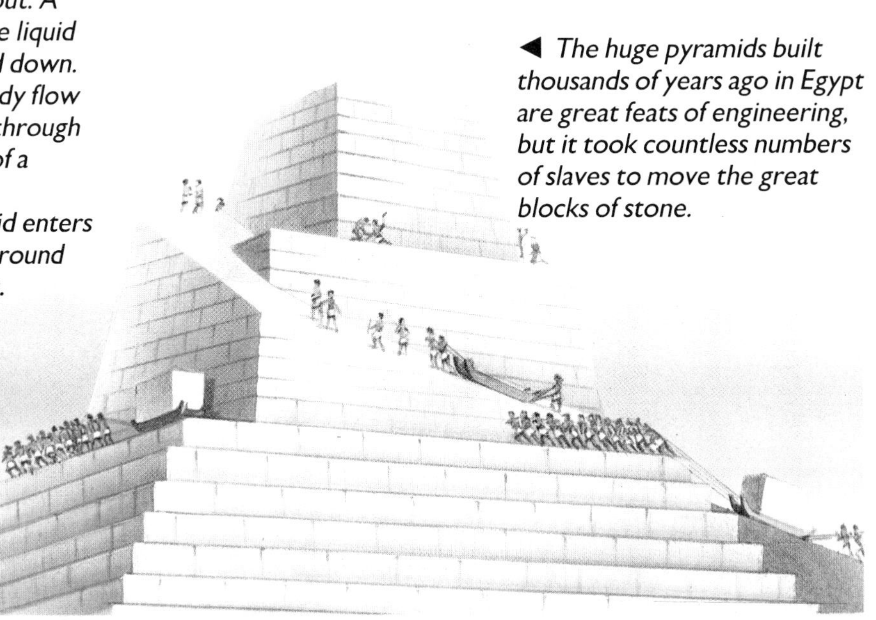

◀ *The huge pyramids built thousands of years ago in Egypt are great feats of engineering, but it took countless numbers of slaves to move the great blocks of stone.*

pyramids as temples during the first six centuries A.D. One huge pyramid is at Cholula, southeast of Mexico City. It is about 177 ft. (54 m) high.

Pyrenees

The Pyrenees are a chain of MOUNTAINS that lie between France and Spain. They stretch about 270 miles (435 km) from the Bay of Biscay to the Mediterranean Sea. Throughout history they have formed a natural barrier between France and Spain, so that most trade between the two countries has been by sea. Iron, lead, silver, and cobalt are mined in the mountains, and the beautiful scenery attracts many tourists.

The peaks of the Pyrenees rise to over 10,000 ft. (3,000 m), though most average about 3,600 ft. (1,100 m). The highest is Pico de Aneto at 11,168 ft. (3,404 m). On the southern slope of the eastern Pyrenees lies the tiny republic of ANDORRA.

▲ *A view of the Pyrenees along a green valley in France.*

Python

Pythons are large SNAKES. They live in Africa and southeastern Asia, and a few kinds are found in Australia. Some grow as long as 30 ft. (9 m). They are *constrictors*. This means they squeeze their prey to death, before swallowing it whole.

► *The reticulated python lives on the forest floor in Southeast Asia. Its pattern and coloring are well matched to its surroundings.*

Qatar 

Qatar is an *emirate*, a nation ruled by an emir, in Arabia. It is on the Persian Gulf, next to the United Arab Emirates. Revenue from oil has helped to modernize and develop agriculture and industry in Qatar.

QATAR

Government: Emirate
Capital: Doha
Area: 4,247 sq. miles (11,000 sq. km)
Population: 368,000
Language: Arabic
Currency: Riyal

Quaker 

The Quakers are also known as the Society of Friends. They are a PROTESTANT group that began in England during the 1650s.

They were called Quakers because some of them shook with emotion at their meetings. Early Quakers were often badly treated because of their belief that religion and government should not be mixed. Quakers have simple religious meetings and have elders, not priests.

Quantum 

We think of light and other forms of energy such as radio waves and X-rays as traveling in waves. Light can also be thought of as a stream of tiny quanta (the plural of quantum), or *photons*. The energy of each photon depends on the wavelength, and therefore the color, of the light. A photon of white light has more energy than a photon of red light. Scientists combine the two ways of thinking about light. They think of light streaming out in packets of waves, each packet being a quantum or photon. They also think that tiny particles of matter such as electrons behave like waves, as well as behaving like solid particles.

When you look at the light from a light bulb, it seems to be quite steady. Actually, light is not as steady as it seems. It is given off in a vast number of tiny packages of energy, like the bullets from a machine gun. Each package is a quantum.

Quark

Until the 1950s, scientists thought that ATOMS were made of tiny particles such as protons and neutrons. They thought that these particles were the basic bits of all matter. Then it was discovered that these "basic" particles were made up of even simpler particles. Scientists now think that the basic particles of protons and neutrons are tiny units which they call quarks. There are different kinds of quarks, and they always seem to exist in combination with other quarks. The different kinds of quarks have been given funny names such as "up quarks," "down quarks," "strange quarks," "bottom quarks," and "charmed quarks."

The world's largest quarry is Bingham Canyon copper mine in Utah. It is about 2,540 ft. (770 m) deep.

Quarrying

Quarries are huge pits where rocks are cut or blasted out of the ground. As long ago as prehistoric times, people had quarries where they dug up flint to make into tools and weapons.

Today, rock is quarried in enormous amounts. Explosives blast loose thousands of tons. This is scooped up by bulldozers and diggers, and taken to crushers. The rock is ground into stones for use in roads, railroads, concrete, and cement. Not all rock is removed in this way. Stone that is used in building and paving is cut out of the ground rather than blasted. Electric cutters, wire saws, and drills are used to cut the rock.

▼ *Rock is quarried for many uses: (1) In the quarry, workers prepare for blasting. (2) Dynamite or other explosives break up the rock, and diggers (3) load it into trucks for transporting (4) to the crushing plant (5). There, the rock is broken down still further for use on rail lines (6), road beds (7), and as cement for concrete buildings (8).*

1
2
3
4
5
6
7
8

▼ *Pure quartz crystals are colorless, but when they are mixed with other substances, they take on many different shades.*

Quartz

Quartz is one of the most common MINERALS in the world. It is found everywhere. SAND is made mainly of quartz, and many ROCKS have quartz in them.

Quartz forms six-sided CRYSTALS. It is very hard, harder even than steel. In its pure form, it has no color and is as clear as glass. But most is smoky white or tinted with various colors. Many semi-precious gems, such as agate, amethyst, opal, and onyx, are quartz.

Quartz is an important mineral. It is used in many things, including abrasives (such as sandpaper), lenses, and electronics.

▲ *Quebec lies on the St. Lawrence River. The Château Frontenac (above), helps give Quebec the charm of an old European city.*

Quasar

Quasars are very distant, very powerful objects farther out in space than the most remote GALAXIES. They may be galaxies with some extra-powerful energy source at their center. Quasars send out strong RADIO waves and X-RAYS. From Earth, they look like very faint stars because they are so far away. All quasars are millions of light-years away, and so we see them now as they were that length of time ago. Quasars were not discovered by astronomers until the 1960s.

Quebec

Quebec is the leading French-speaking province of Canada, and the largest province. Because it is a French province, Quebec is different in many important ways from the rest of the country. The people are proud of their French heritage and make many efforts to keep it alive. In fact, some of them feel that Quebec should be allowed to become a separate country. In the past, there have been disagreements between the rest of Canada, which is largely English speaking, and Quebec.

Most people in Quebec live in and around the cities of Montreal and Quebec itself. The north is empty and wild, but contains many important natural resources, including iron ore. These resources are important to Quebec's industries.

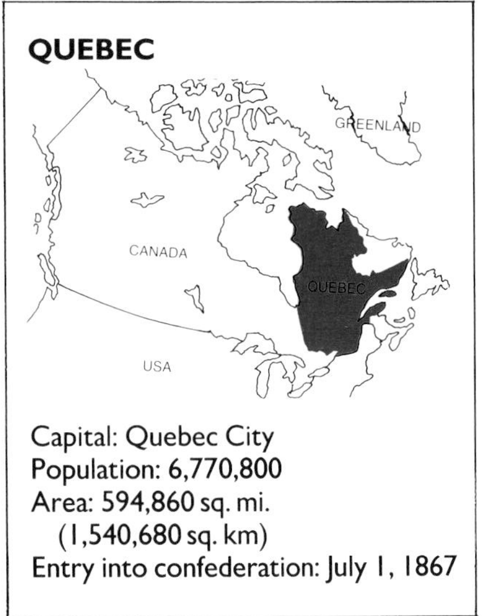

QUEBEC
GREENLAND
CANADA
QUEBEC
USA
Capital: Quebec City
Population: 6,770,800
Area: 594,860 sq. mi.
(1,540,680 sq. km)
Entry into confederation: July 1, 1867

Rabbit

Rabbits originally came from Europe. Today they are found all over the world. They are small MAMMALS with a short tail and long pointed ears. Rabbits live in burrows in the ground. Each burrow is the home of a single family. A group of burrows is known as a warren.

R

Raccoon

In North America, raccoons are common creatures of the wild. They have long gray fur, a short pointed nose, and a bushy tail ringed with black. They may grow to as much as 35 in. (90 cm) long.

Raccoons live in forests. They make their homes in tree holes and are good climbers. At night, they leave their hollows to hunt for food. They will eat almost anything: fruit and plants, eggs, insects, fish, birds, and small mammals. But their main food comes from rivers, so their tree holes are usually found close by.

► *Raccoons are often thought of as pests in the United States and are sometimes hunted. The frontiersman Davy Crockett's famous hat was made of raccoon fur, with the striped tail left hanging down at the back.*

▲ *All types of pet rabbit have been bred from wild rabbits. They now come in different sizes, colors, and even shapes. The tiny dwarf lop-eared rabbit has ears that droop. The Himalayan rabbit is not really from the Himalayas. It just means a certain type of coat marking with darker face, ears, legs, and tail.*

Radar

Radar is a device for tracking objects by RADIO beams. Because these beams work in the dark, in fog, and over distances well out of eyesight, radar is an enormously useful invention. It can detect objects thousands of miles away.

Radar works by sending out a narrow, high-powered beam about 500 times a second. It travels

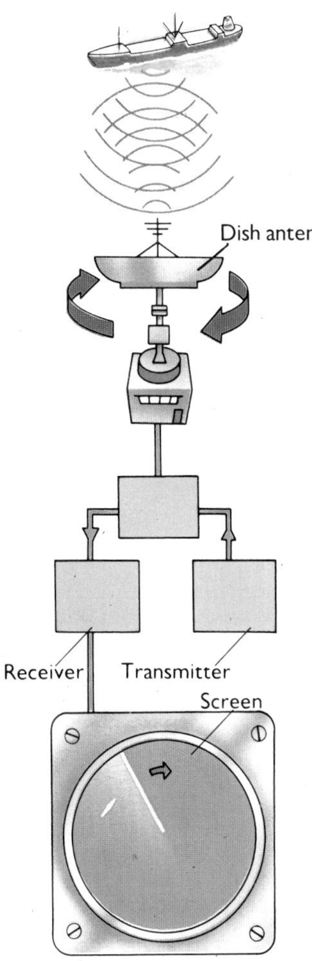

▲ *The name "radar" comes from the phrase "**ra**dio **d**etecting **a**nd **r**anging." The antenna that sends out the special radio signal usually acts as a receiver, too, detecting the signal as it bounces back. To do this, it has to change from one sort of operation to the other. This "changeover" is controlled from inside the radar installation. When the signals are displayed on the screen, objects detected by the radar show up as bright spots. Experienced operators can tell the direction and distance of objects from the "blips" on the screen, even though the "blips" look nothing like the objects in real life.*

at a steady 990 ft. (300 m) every millionth of a second. When the beam strikes an object, a faint echo bounces back. The echo is picked up and turned into a light "blip" on a screen. A radar operator can tell by studying the blip how far away the object is, in what direction it is moving, and at what speed. Radar is used by air traffic controllers at airports, by the armed forces to track missiles and planes, and by weather stations to find and follow the paths of storms. SATELLITES fitted with radar can map the ground.

Radio

The common household object we call a radio is only the receiving end of a great system of radio communications. Most of the system is never even seen.

A radio program begins in a studio. There, voices and music are turned into electronic signals. These are made stronger (amplified) and then sent out from tall masts as radio waves. They are picked up by the radio in your home and changed back into

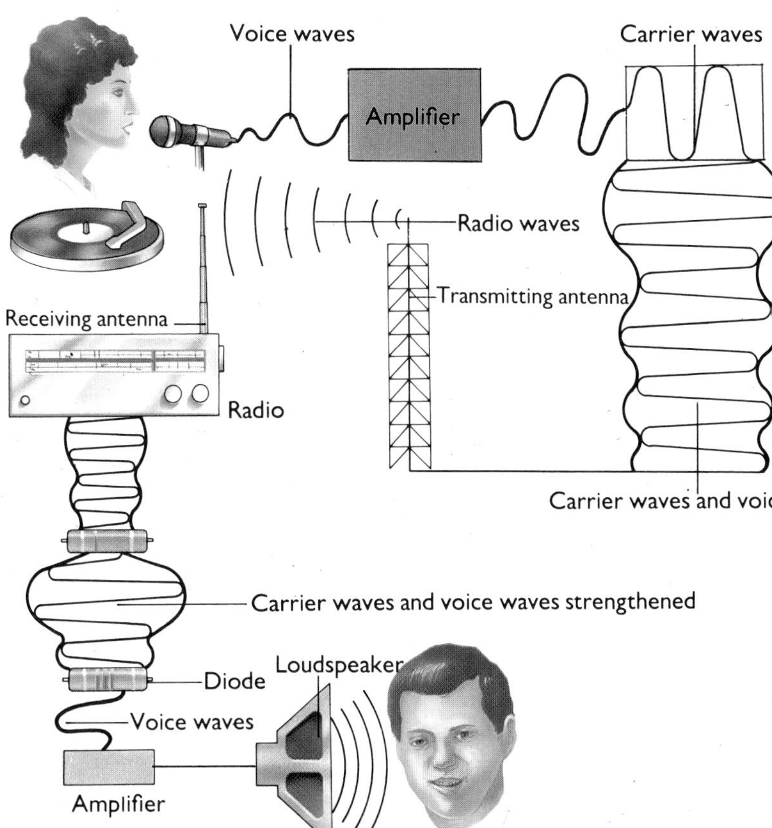

▶ *How a radio broadcast is carried to your radio. Inside the radio, the voice signals are separated from their carrier waves and turned back into sounds by the loudspeaker.*

sounds you can hear. Radio waves travel at the speed of light. This is so fast that a signal can circle the world 7½ times in one second.

The first person to generate radio waves was Heinrich Hertz in 1887. But it was Guglielmo MARCONI who sent the first messages in 1894. His first signals traveled only a few yards. Seven years later, he sent signals across the Atlantic.

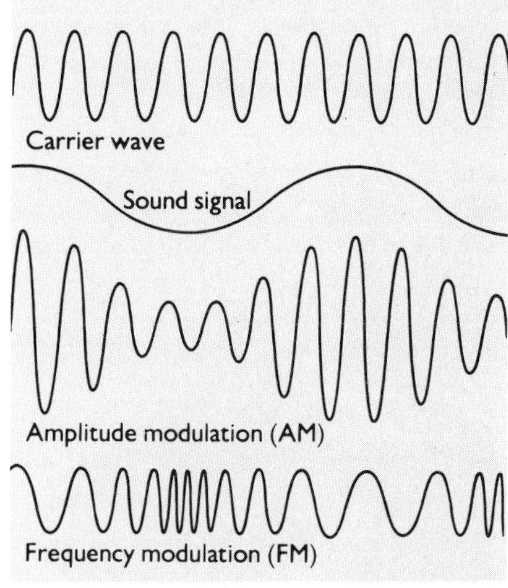

▲ *The station selector on your radio may have the initials AM and FM on it. These initials tell you how the carrier wave was joined with signals at the transmitter. AM stands for "amplitude modulation." This means that the amplitude (height) of the carrier wave was altered to match the signals. FM—"frequency modulation"—means that the frequency—the number of carrier waves passing each second—was changed to match the signal at the transmitter.*

Radioactivity

The atoms of some substances are always shooting off tiny particles and rays that we cannot see or feel. This is called radioactivity. These strange rays were discovered in 1896. It was soon found that nothing could be done to stop the rays from shooting out. It was also found that in time these radioactive substances changed into other substances, and that they did this at a steady rate. If a piece of radioactive uranium was left for millions of years, it would "decay" and turn into a piece of lead. Scientists measure the rate of decay in radioactive carbon in animal and plant remains to find out how many thousands of

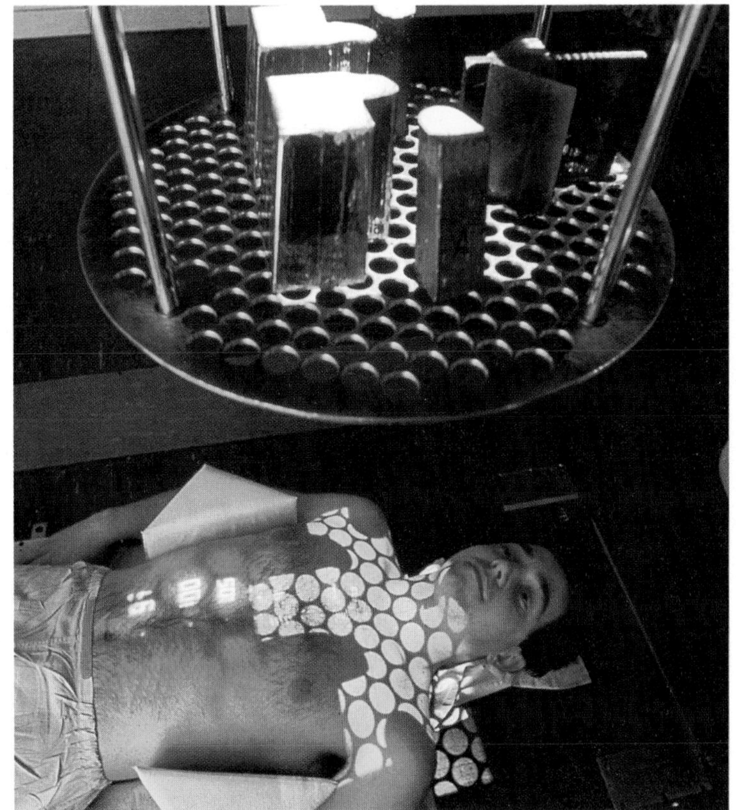

◀ *The power of radioactivity can be used to treat some types of illness, such as cancer. Radiotherapy can be used to destroy the cancer cells without harming the healthy cells. The illuminated disks above this patient's chest show the areas which are to receive radiation. The pattern can be altered by changing the position of the lead blocks (at the top of the picture) which shield the lungs from too much radiation.*

▶ *There are three types of radiation: alpha particles, beta particles, and gamma rays. Alpha particles are the least powerful. They cannot pass through paper. Beta particles can be stopped by a thin sheet of aluminum. But the power of gamma radiation can penetrate even thick blocks of iron.*

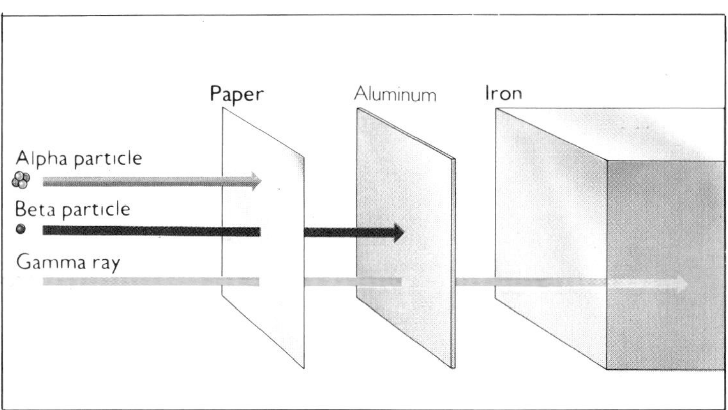

▲ *The international warning symbol used to label radioactive substances.*

years ago the animals and plants lived. Radioactive materials can be dangerous. A nuclear explosion causes dangerous levels of radioactivity.

Radio Astronomy

A heavenly body, such as a STAR, does not only give off LIGHT waves. It sends out many kinds of radio waves, too. Radio astronomers explore the UNIVERSE by "listening" to the radio signals that reach Earth from outer space. These signals are not made by other forms of life. They come from natural events, such as exploding stars or heated clouds of gases. By studying these signals, radio astronomers can find out many things about different parts of the universe.

▼ *The huge VLA (Very Large Array) radio telescope at Socorro, New Mexico, is made up of 27 dish antennas. Each of them is 82 ft. (25 m) in diameter, and they can be moved along a Y-shaped track to exactly the position the astronomers choose.*

Radio telescopes have giant antennas—often saucer-shaped. They pick up faint signals that have come from places much deeper in space than anything that can be seen by ordinary TELESCOPES. The first large radio telescopes were built after World War II. Today, the biggest in the world is at Arecibo in Puerto Rico. Its huge receiving dish has been built across an entire mountain valley. It is more than 1,000 ft. (300 m) wide.

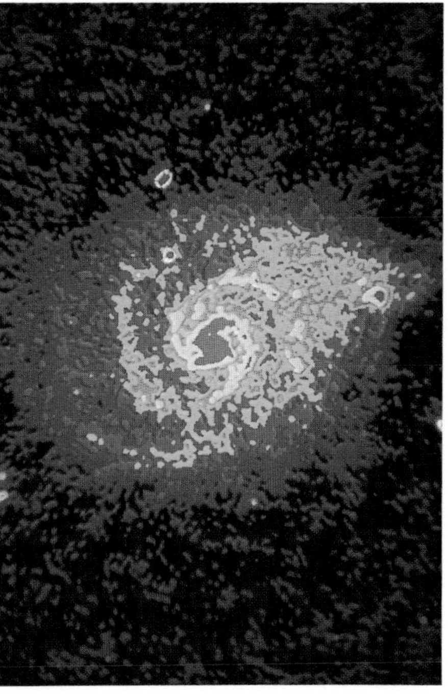

▲ *This image received by the Socorro radio telescope is of a galaxy 20 million light-years away from Earth. The colors are produced by computer and show how much energy is coming from each part. Red is the highest energy level, and purple is the lowest.*

Radiocarbon Dating

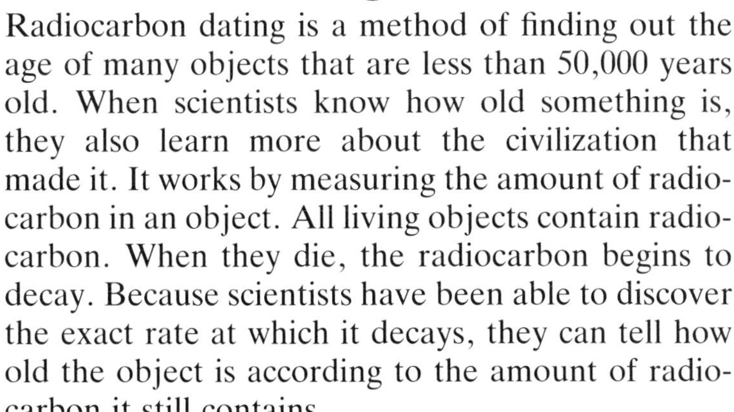

Radiocarbon dating is a method of finding out the age of many objects that are less than 50,000 years old. When scientists know how old something is, they also learn more about the civilization that made it. It works by measuring the amount of radiocarbon in an object. All living objects contain radiocarbon. When they die, the radiocarbon begins to decay. Because scientists have been able to discover the exact rate at which it decays, they can tell how old the object is according to the amount of radiocarbon it still contains.

Half the radiocarbon in an object disappears after 5,700 years. This is called radiocarbon's "half-life."

Railroad

Railroads have been in use since the 1500s. At first, rails were made of wood, and wagons were pulled by horses. Steam railroads were invented in the early 1800s. Railroads are useful because heavy loads can be pulled along them very easily. (See pages 562–563.)

Rain

When rain pours down, it is only the sky returning to Earth the same water that originally evaporated from the land and sea.

Rain forms when water vapor in the air starts to cool. As the vapor cools, it turns first of all into tiny droplets, which form wispy CLOUDS. The droplets grow, and the clouds thicken and turn a dull gray.

Continued on page 564

High mountains usually force rain out of any moist wind that strikes them. They force the air up to cooler heights, and as the moist air cools, it makes rain. Most rain falls on the slopes that face the wind. The other side of the mountain receives little rain. Waialeale Peak in Hawaii has the highest rainfall in the world—an average of 472 in. (1,200 cm) a year. Yet only a few miles away, on the other side of the peak, the average rainfall is less than 20 in. (50 cm).

RAILROADS

The railroad era began when an English engineer named Richard Trevithick drove a steam rail engine along a steel-plate track in south Wales. The year was 1804. The man who did more than any other to make the railroads an important form of transportation was another Englishman, George Stephenson. He built and equipped the first railroads to carry passengers on trains pulled by steam locomotives.

Today, the age of steam is over, though in some places you can still enjoy the thrill of riding on a steam train kept running by enthusiasts. Modern diesel and electric locomotives use less fuel and need less looking after. Railroads are particularly useful for carrying heavy freight and for taking commuters to and from their jobs in city centers.

▲ *George Stephenson's* Rocket *achieved the unheard-of speed of 36 miles (58 km) an hour at the 1829 Rainhill Trials. Its unrivaled power came from its multi-tube boiler.*

► *Before the steam engine, horses pulled rail wagons.*

▼ *Underground subway trains carry passengers beneath the stre of many of the world's cities. This is in Glasgow.*

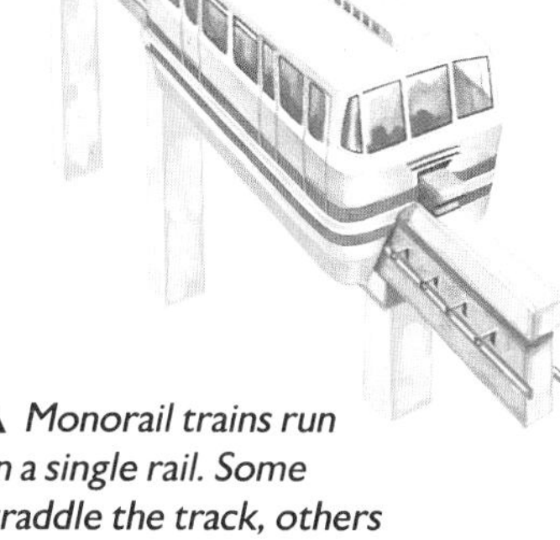

▲ *Monorail trains run on a single rail. Some straddle the track, others are suspended beneath it.*

▼ *A modern electric locomotive. It picks up electricity from overhead w through the hinged pantograph on th roof.*

▼ *A huge Union Pacific "Big Boy" locomotive of the 1940s. It weighed 534 tons.*

ION PACIFIC 4021

▲ Mallard *set the world speed record for a steam locomotive in 1938—126 miles (202 km) an hour.*

▼ *Japan's streamlined electr "bullet trains" run at an avera speed of more than 100 miles (160 km) an hour.*

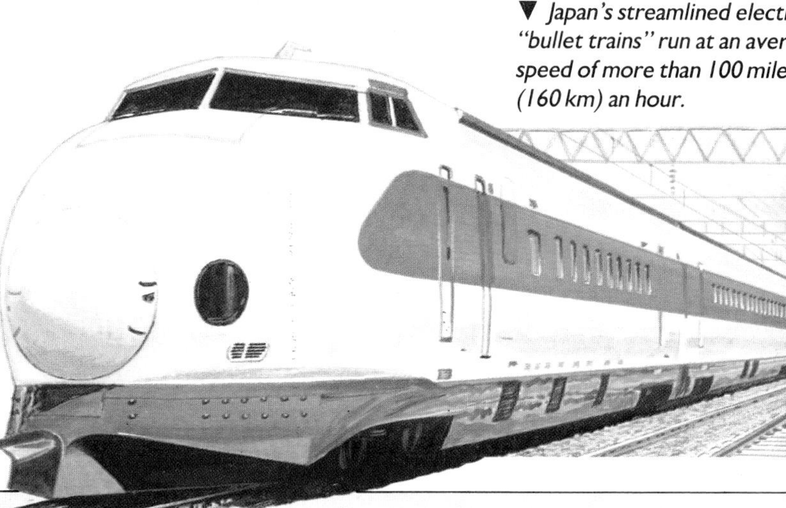

▲ *In some countries, steam locomotives can still be seen. This one is in daily use in Portugal.*

RAILROAD HISTORY

1765 Standard gauge (width of track) established at 4 ft. 8½in. (1,435 mm).
1804 Trevithick's first working locomotive.
1814 Stephenson's *Blucher* locomotive begins working at a coal mine.
1825 Opening of Stockton and Darlington Railway, first regular steam railroad.
1829 Stephenson's *Rocket* wins Rainhill Trials.
1830 Liverpool and Manchester Railway begins world's first passenger service using steam locomotives.
1830 First U.S. railroad, South Carolina.
1859 First Pullman sleeping cars (U.S.A.).
1863 First dining cars (U.S.A.).
1863 World's first underground rail system in London.
1869 Railroad across the U.S.A. is completed.
1879 First electric railroad (Germany).
1885 Completion of Canadian Pacific line across Canada.
1925 First diesel-electric locomotive (Canada).

THE RAILROADS AT WORK

◀ *A busy freight yard, where freight cars are sorted and assembled into trains.*

▼ *Each section of track (known as a block) is controlled separately. The signal operator checks that the track is clear and sets the signals and the switches. The engineer watches for a signal to tell him it is safe to proceed. On busy lines, computers control the smooth flow of trains.*

For more information turn to these articles: DIESEL ENGINE; ELECTRICITY; MOTOR, ELECTRIC; STEAM ENGINE.

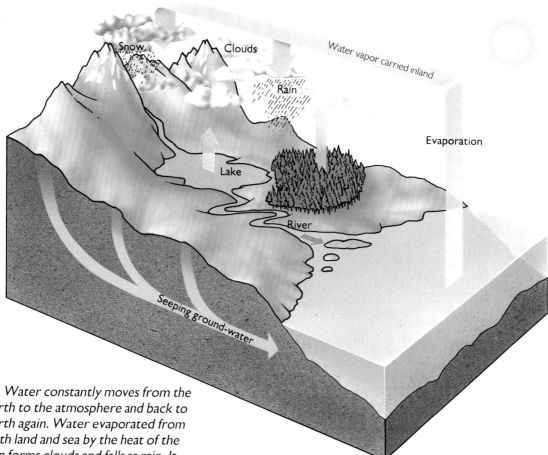

▲ *Water constantly moves from the Earth to the atmosphere and back to Earth again. Water evaporated from both land and sea by the heat of the Sun forms clouds and falls as rain. It flows into lakes and rivers and eventually into the sea, where it is turned into water vapor again, and so on. We call this movement of water the water cycle.*

At last, the drops become so heavy that they start to fall. If it is cold enough to freeze them, the drops hit the ground as either hail or snow.

The amount of rain that falls is widely different from place to place. In the Atacama Desert in Chile, less than 1 in. (25 mm) of rain falls in 20 years. But in eastern India, monsoon rains drop 424 in. (1,080 cm) every year.

An old fairy story says that there is a pot of gold at the end of a rainbow. Nobody has ever found the treasure because a rainbow really has no end. It is a full circle. The bottom half of the circle lies below the horizon and out of sight.

Rainbow

The gorgeous colors of a rainbow are formed by sunlight shining on drops of rain. The best time for rainbows is right after a shower, when the clouds break up and sunlight streams through.

Rainbows can be seen only when the Sun is behind you and low over the horizon. When the Sun's rays strike the raindrops, each drop acts as a prism and splits the LIGHT into a SPECTRUM of colors, ranging from red to violet. The lower the Sun, the higher the rainbow and the fuller its curved arch.

Raleigh, Walter

Sir Walter Raleigh (1552–1618) was an English knight at the court of ELIZABETH I. He was a soldier, explorer, historian, and poet. He tried unsuccessfully to set up a colony in Virginia, in the newly discovered land of North America. He introduced potatoes and tobacco smoking to the English. He was imprisoned on an unfair charge of treason during the reign of James I. After 13 years, he was freed from the Tower of London and sailed to find gold in South America. On his return, penniless, he was executed.

▲ *Sir Walter Raleigh was a great favorite of Elizabeth I. But when he married, she sent him and his wife away from court.*

Rat

Rats are RODENTS. They are found all over the world in enormous numbers and can live happily in towns and cities. They will eat almost anything. They are harmful to people because they spoil huge amounts of food and they spread diseases. Some rats carry a type of FLEA which can cause bubonic PLAGUE in human beings.

▼ *In the country, most rats live outside and do not represent much of a health risk. But rats in cities steal food intended for humans and are a major health hazard. They breed quickly and are very difficult to eliminate.*

Reagan, Ronald Wilson

Ronald Reagan (1911–) was the 40th president of the United States. He served two terms and was one of the most popular presidents in history. When he was reelected in 1984, he won more votes than any other previous president. People liked him for his easy charm and friendly manner. Some com-

RONALD W. REAGAN

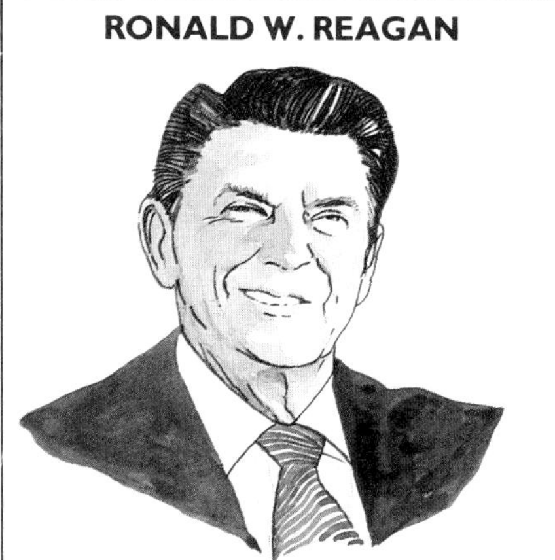

Fortieth President 1981–1989
Born: Tampico, Illinois
Education: Eureka College, Eureka, Illinois
Occupation: Actor and politician
Political Party: Republican

plained that he didn't always seem to know exactly what was happening in his administration, but few disliked him. Reagan was a successful Hollywood actor before he became a politician. From 1966 to 1975, he was governor of California. As president, Reagan oversaw a period of economic growth and prosperity. His most important achievement was improving relations with the Soviet Union. In 1988, he agreed a cut in U.S. and Soviet nuclear missiles.

Recording

Making a record is a complicated process. First, a microphone turns the voices and music into electronic signals. These are made stronger, or amplified, in order to make a sapphire "chisel" vibrate as it cuts a very fine groove into a smooth disc. This is the master disc.

A metal copy in reverse is made from the master disk so that the grooves stand out as ridges on the copy. Next, metal stampers are made. They are used to press thousands of records.

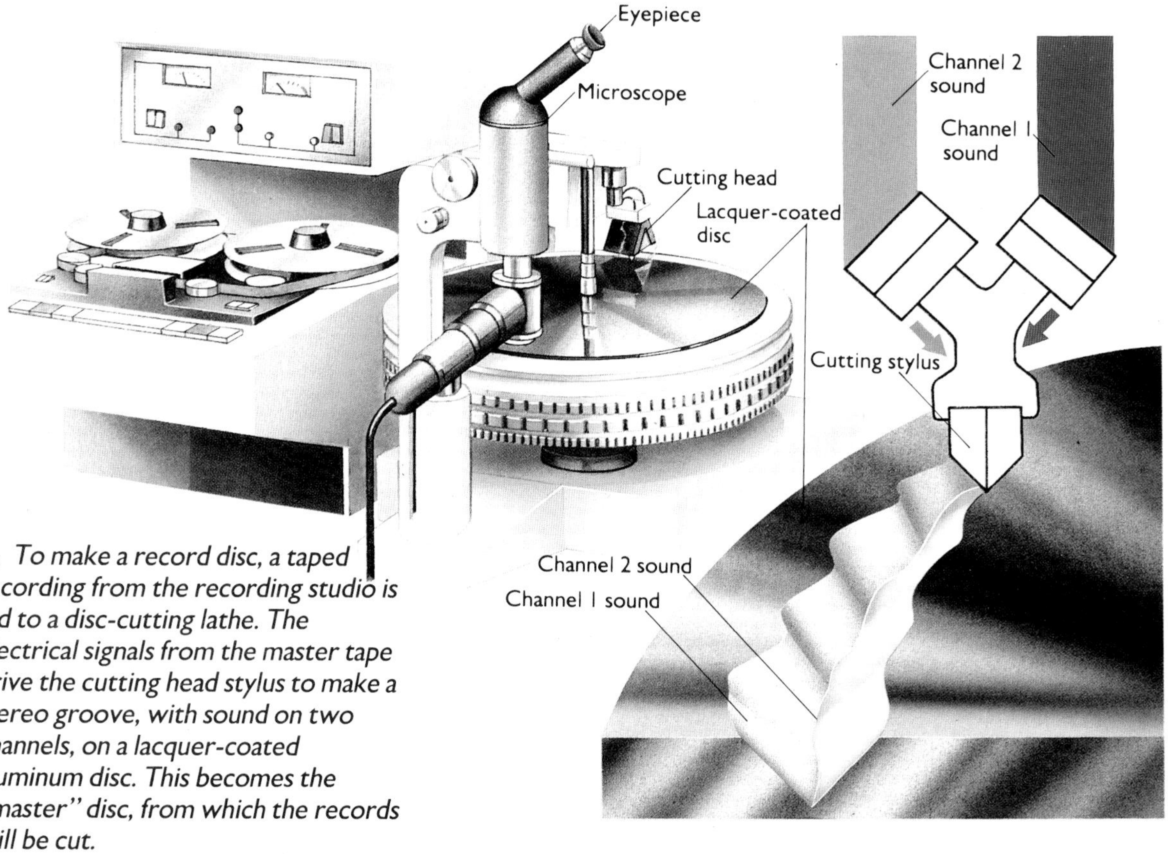

▲ *To make a record disc, a taped recording from the recording studio is fed to a disc-cutting lathe. The electrical signals from the master tape drive the cutting head stylus to make a stereo groove, with sound on two channels, on a lacquer-coated aluminum disc. This becomes the "master" disc, from which the records will be cut.*

A TAPE RECORDER works by changing sound waves into magnetism. The sound is recorded as a magnetic pattern along the recording tape. When the tape is played, the magnetic pattern is turned back into sound.

You can record a television program on a VIDEO cassette using a video recorder. The video cassette contains tape like a sound cassette. It records the electric signal coming from the television antenna. Sound recording was pioneered by Thomas EDISON.

As many as 48 separate sound recordings can be made on one tape in parallel paths called "tracks." Any single track is a "mono" recording. Two tracks are needed for stereophonic sound.

Red Cross

The Red Cross is an international organization that helps the sick, the hungry, and the suffering. It has its headquarters at Geneva in Switzerland. Its symbol is a red cross on a white flag.

The Red Cross was founded by Henri Dunant in 1863 after he had seen the terrible suffering of wounded soldiers. The organization helps the wounded of all armies—it does not take sides. Today, it is based in more than 70 countries and cares for soldiers and civilians all over the world.

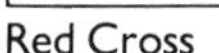

Red Cross

Red Crescent

Magen David

▲ *In other parts of the world, the Red Cross has different names and symbols. In some Muslim countries, for example, it is known as the Red Crescent; in Israel, the symbol is the Magen David.*

Red Sea

The Red Sea is a narrow arm of the Indian Ocean. It stretches for 1,180 miles (1,900 km), dividing Arabia from northeastern Africa. It has an area of about 170,000 sq. miles (440,300 sq. km). At its northern end, it is linked to the MEDITERRANEAN SEA by the SUEZ CANAL. Its southern end is guarded by the narrow straits of Bab el Mandeb.

The Red Sea is quite shallow. There are no major currents flowing through it, so it is warm and salty.

▼ *The Red Sea separates the African continent from southwestern Asia.*

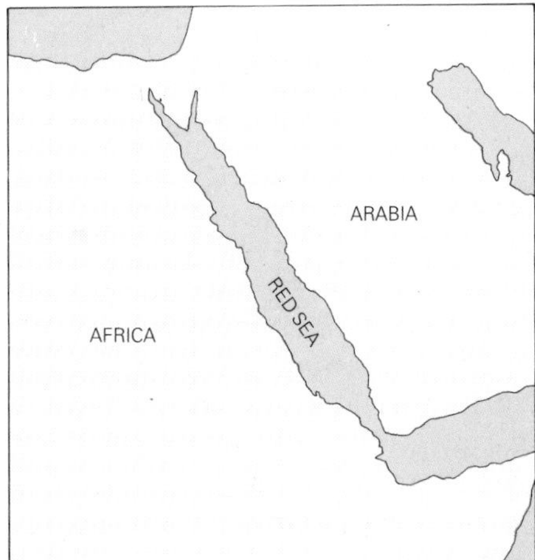

Reformation

The Reformation is the name given to the period of religious upheaval that began in Europe in the 1500s.

At that time, a revolt occurred in the ROMAN CATHOLIC CHURCH. In protest at what they saw as bad practice and errors in the Church, groups of people broke away to set up their own churches. These people became known as PROTESTANTS.

The Reformation saw the start of many long years of religious wars and persecution that have continued to this day. The Thirty Years' War was the result of rivalry between Catholics and Protestants. It began in Germany, but spread to involve most of the European countries. Most European countries now allow freedom of religion, but the two sides still think the other's beliefs are mistaken.

What many Protestants wanted was a simpler, more basic form of CHRISTIANITY, and one that allowed them greater freedom to worship as they chose. As the Protestant movement grew, many kings and rulers saw the new movement as a chance to widen their power at the expense of the Church. They were happy to support the Protestant cause, because in many ways the religious protest helped them to gain more influence. The Reformation led to wars between Protestants and Catholics.

Refrigerator

Refrigerators are used to keep food cold. The simplest ones are really just boxes with an electric motor running a cooling system. They are made from insulating material that keeps the inside cold for some time, even when the motor is not running. The average TEMPERATURE inside a refrigerator is 35 to 45°F (2 to 7°C).

The cooling system has a special gas in it. This gas is first compressed (squeezed) to turn it into a liquid. The liquid then flows through hollow tubes inside the refrigerator into an evaporator, which turns it back into gas. This gas is pumped on around the system. As it goes around the inside, it draws out heat from within the refrigerator.

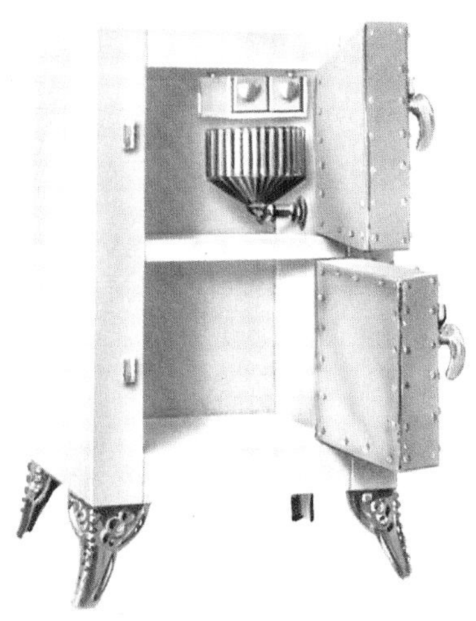

▲ *Refrigerators first came into use in the 1860s, but this is the type you would have been able to buy in 1927.*

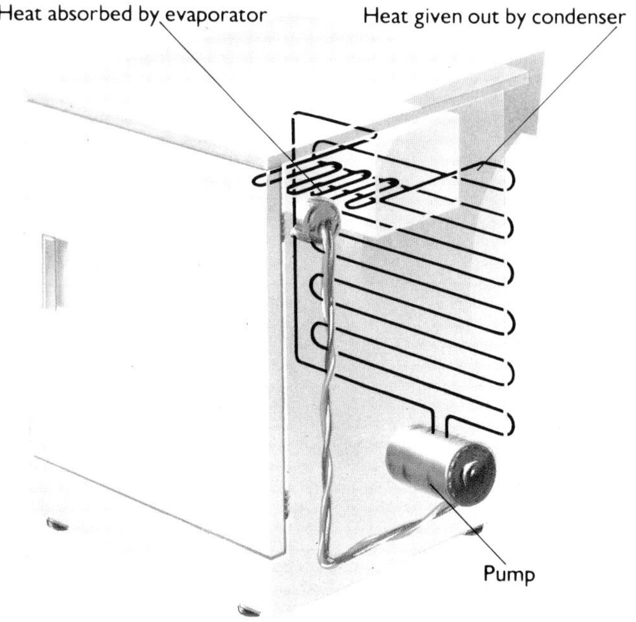

► *A modern refrigerator. In the evaporator, the liquid absorbs heat as it is turned into a gas. The cold vapor that flows through the pipes goes to a condenser. There, it gives out heat outside the refrigerator as it turns back into a liquid.*

When it is pumped outside the refrigerator, the gas is compressed again. This turns it back into a liquid, and it gives out the heat it picked up on the inside. The liquid is pumped around and around, turning from liquid to gas and back again. As this goes on, the air inside the refrigerator becomes colder, and the heat is taken to the outside. The process works like a sort of heat sponge.

We tend to think of the refrigerator as a comparatively recent invention. However, ice-making machines were slipped through the Union blockade of the South during the Civil War in the 1860s.

Relativity

If you are traveling in a car at 40 mph and you are passed by another car traveling at 50 mph, the second car pulls away from you at 10 mph. Its true speed relative to the ground is 50 mph, but its speed *relative* to you is 10 mph. This is the basic idea of relativity: assume that you are not moving and figure out the speed of something that is moving relative to you.

At the end of the last century, scientists discovered that the speed of light is always the same, no matter how fast the source of the light is moving. In 1905, Albert EINSTEIN put forward his *special* theory of relativity to explain this strange fact. His theory concerns, among other things, the effect of motion on time, length, and mass. For instance, the theory predicts that in a spaceship hurtling across the universe at nearly the speed of light, time would

▼ *Part of Einstein's theory of relativity was that gravity could make light rays bend. This means that, from the Earth, it would be easy to make a mistake about the real position of a distant star, because the rays of light coming from it could have been bent by the Sun's gravitational pull (below left). Another part of the theory of relativity says that time slows down for an object traveling at almost the speed of light. The example (below right) shows a rocket with a clock on board which takes off from Earth at 3 o'clock. As it nears the speed of light, its clock will be showing 5 o'clock. But time has slowed down on the rocket, and the clocks back on Earth will be showing 6 o'clock.*

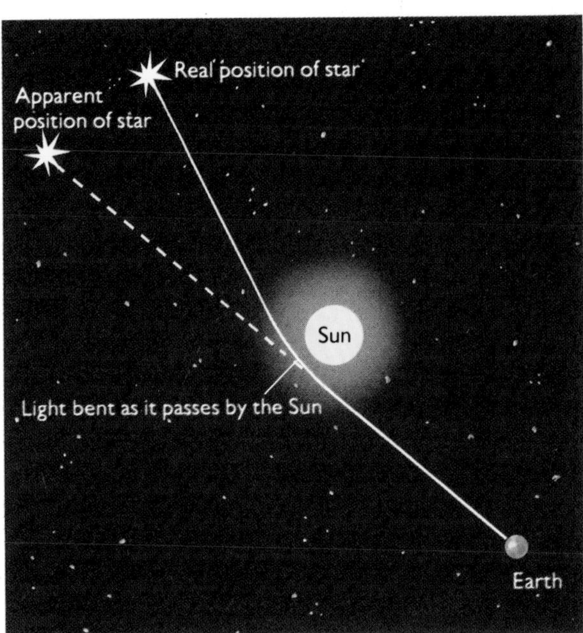

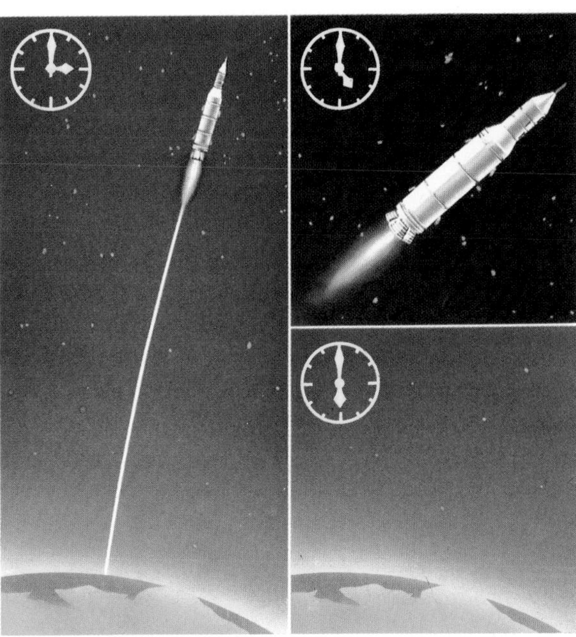

pass more slowly, the spaceship's length would become smaller, and its mass would become greater than on a similar spaceship stationary on Earth.

Later, in 1915, Einstein produced his *general* theory of relativity. This theory has helped scientists understand more about space, gravity, and the nature of the universe.

▲ *All the world's religions have special symbols and signs. The dancing goddess is a Hindu image; the candlestick, called a menorah, is Jewish; the temple is a feature of Shinto, a Japanese religion; the cross is a Christian symbol; the crescent moon is Islamic; and the statue represents Buddha.*

Religion

The greatest religions of today are Buddhism (based on the teachings of BUDDHA), CHRISTIANITY, HINDUISM (followed by Hindus), ISLAM (followed by Muslims), and JUDAISM (followed by Jews). All are very ancient. The most recent is Islam, which was founded about 1,300 years ago. The largest, Christianity, has well over a billion followers.

There are also some people today who follow ancient religions based on the worship of many gods and spirits. Often, these gods are part of nature. They may be rocks, trees, or lakes.

Buildings devoted to religious worship include splendid churches and magnificent shrines and temples. Statues and works of art showing religious figures are common. Specially trained priests and holy people say prayers and lead religious ceremonies. They also study the laws and teachings of the religion. These are often written down in holy books. Examples are the BIBLE and the KORAN.

MAJOR RELIGIONS: ESTIMATED WORLD MEMBERSHIP

	millions
Christians	1,759
Roman Catholics	996
Eastern Orthodox	167
Protestants	363
Muslims	935
Hindus	705
Buddhists	303
Taoists	20
Jews	17
Confucians	6
Shintoists	3

► *Jerusalem is a holy city to Jews, Christians, and Muslims. The Dome of the Rock is a Muslim shrine on the spot where Muhammad was said to have ascended into heaven.*

Rembrandt

Rembrandt Harmenszoon van Rijn (1606–1669) is one of the most famous of all Dutch painters. Helped by assistants, he produced hundreds of paintings and drawings.

Rembrandt is best known for his portraits of the wealthy townspeople of Holland. Unlike many painters, he became very successful while he was still alive. However, later in his career, many of the rich people no longer bought his pictures because they did not like the way his style of painting had changed. Although he became very poor, this was the time when he painted some of his best works.

▲ *Rembrandt painted this portrait of himself late in his career.*

Renaissance

The Renaissance is the name given to a period of about 200 years in the history of Europe. The word means "rebirth" in French, and the Renaissance

▼ *Goldsmiths working in Florence, Italy, during the Renaissance. Trading brought great wealth to the city.*

▼ *A statue of Perseus holding the head of Medusa, by the Italian Renaissance sculptor Cellini.*

was the time when people again became interested in every aspect of art, science, architecture, and literature, after the so-called Dark Ages.

Since the times of the ancient Greeks and Romans, there had been little interest in new ideas. Then, during the 1300s, Italian scholars began to take a fresh interest in the past. They also looked for new scientific explanations of the mysteries of the world and the universe. During the Renaissance, a great number of painters, sculptors, and architects were at work in Italy. The works of art of LEONARDO DA VINCI and MICHELANGELO are among the most famous products of this time. From Italy, the ideas of the Renaissance quickly spread to the rest of Europe.

At the same time as all these artistic and scientific ideas, there was a great growth in trade. Later, there were voyages to explore Africa and India; and in 1492, America was discovered by COLUMBUS.

► *Florence Cathedral is a supreme example of Renaissance architecture. The dome was designed by the artist Brunelleschi in 1420, but it was not completed until 1461, 15 years after his death.*

Reproduction

Reproduction is the process by which plants and animals make new plants and animals like themselves. Some plants and animals can reproduce on their own. Some just split in two. Many plants reproduce *asexually* by producing buds that drop off and start a new life of their own. Other plants produce spores that may be carried away by wind or water until they land in a suitable place to grow into new plants.

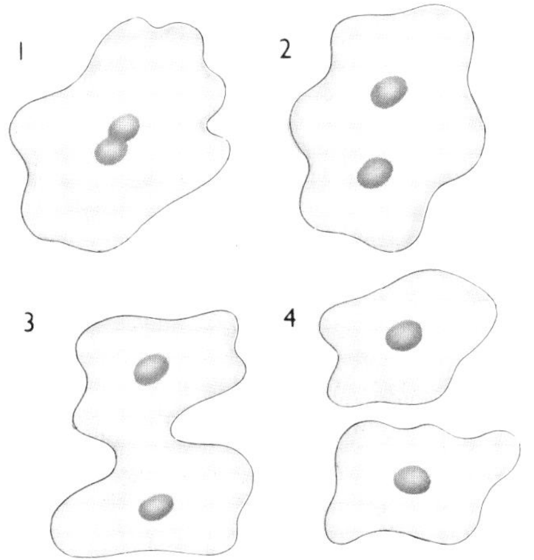

▼ *An amoeba is one of the simplest forms of life—a single-celled animal. It can reproduce on its own. First the nucleus, in the middle of the cell, divides in two. Then the cell splits apart to become two identical amoebas.*

◀ *Part of the egg rope of a perch. Once a female fish has laid her eggs and the male has fertilized them, the tiny fish embryos develop, one inside each egg. When they have used up the food stored in the egg, it is time for them to hatch.*

In *sexual* reproduction, a male cell, called a *sperm*, joins with, or fertilizes, a female cell, called an *ovum*, or egg, to form a new fertilized cell. This cell divides over and over again until a whole new organism has been formed.

Most female FISH lay their eggs in the water. Then the male swims over the eggs and releases his sperm on them. After fertilization, the embryo (developing) fish grows while using the store of food in the egg.

In most higher animals, fertilization takes place inside the female's body. After fertilization, the female BIRD OR REPTILE lays her eggs. The embryo then develops inside the egg until it is ready to hatch out.

In MAMMALS, fertilization also takes place inside the female, but the embryo develops inside its mother until it is ready to be born. The embryo

SEE IT YOURSELF

Some seeds grow in an amazingly short time. Buy a pack of parsley seeds. Put some potting soil or damp blotting paper in a shallow dish, and sow the seeds on top of it. It is fun to make the first letter of your name. After only a few days the seeds will start to grow, and soon the parsley will be ready to eat.

Take a leaf from an African violet or begonia and make cuts through some of the veins. Put the leaf on moist soil, and first roots and then a new plant will grow.

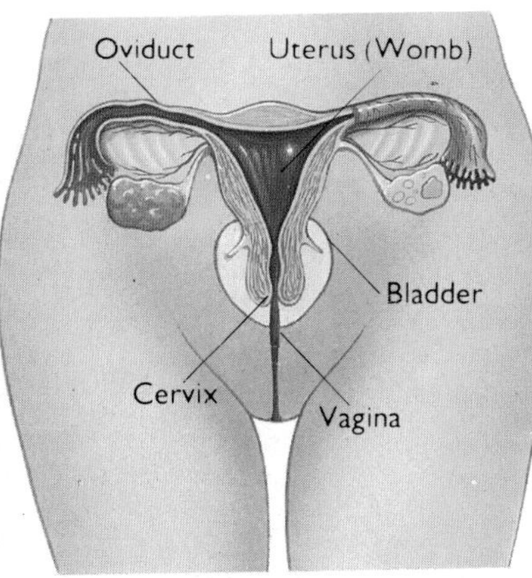

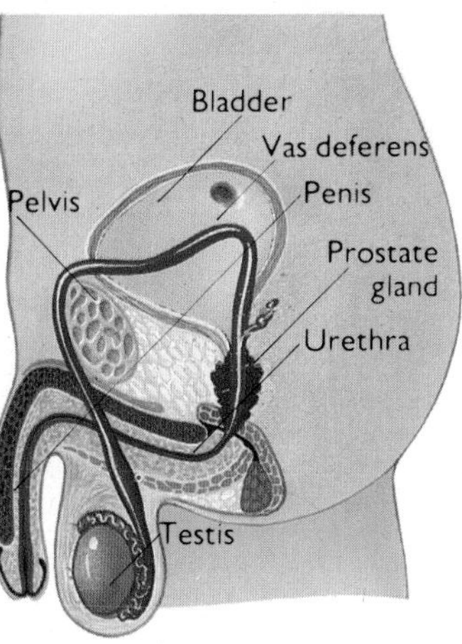

◀ *The reproductive parts of the body are very different in men and women. The woman produces eggs in her ovaries. These travel down the oviducts and, if fertilized by sperm provided by a man during sexual intercourse, may develop into a baby in the woman's uterus, or womb. Men produce millions of sperm in their testicles. The sperm and the egg each contain half of what is needed to make another human being.*

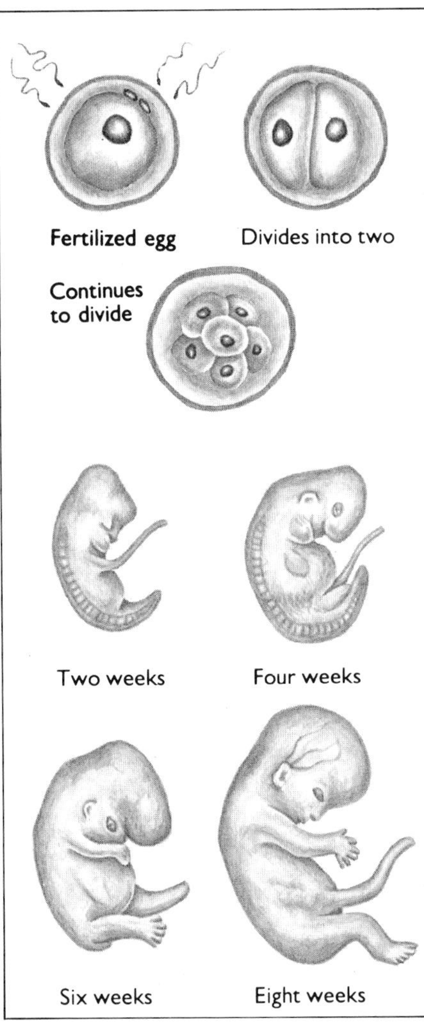

▲ *Once a human egg has been fertilized, it starts to divide to make countless new cells. At first, the baby looks strange—it even has a tail—but after a few weeks, it develops a human shape, with a face and tiny fingers and toes.*

receives food from its mother's bloodstream. After it is born, the mother feeds it with her milk.

The number of offspring a mother gives birth to at one time depends on the number of eggs fertilized. In human mothers, only one egg is usually fertilized. If more than one is fertilized, there may be twins, triplets, or even more babies.

Reptile

Reptiles are the most advanced of all cold-blooded animals. They live on land and in the sea.

Reptiles live in all parts of the world except for the North and South Poles. Most, however, live in warm regions. This is because they are cold-blooded and must get their warmth from their surroundings.

When it is cold, they become very sleepy and cannot move fast enough to catch food or escape from enemies. Most reptiles that live in cold places spend the winter in HIBERNATION.

Reptiles played an important part in the EVOLUTION of the Earth. About 360 million years ago, the first reptiles appeared. They soon became the strongest form of life on Earth. They ruled the planet for close to 100 million years. One group of reptiles, the DINOSAURS, were the most spectacular creatures ever to walk the land. The biggest weighed more than 100 tons.

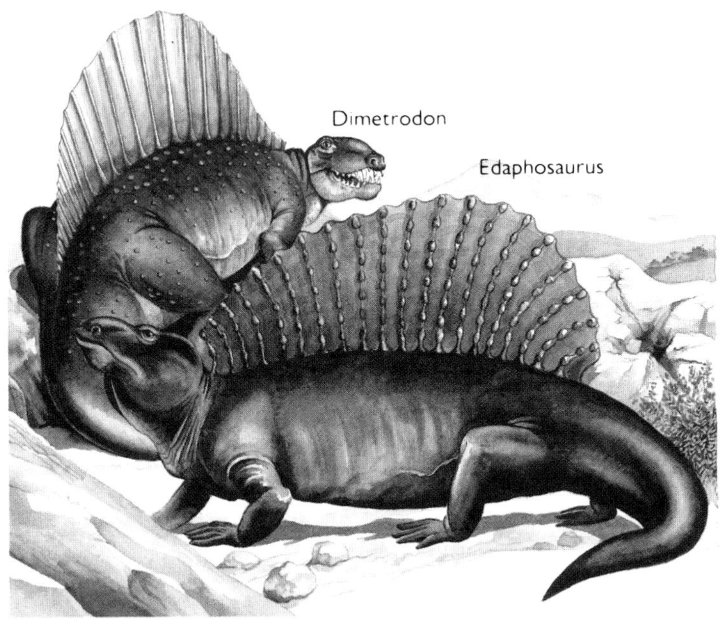

► *These primitive reptiles lived over 250 million years ago. They are called sailbacks because on their backs, they had bony spines covered in skin. They used these to help control their body heat. If they turned sideways to the Sun, the sails could absorb heat. If they turned their backs to the Sun, the sails gave out heat and the creatures cooled down.*

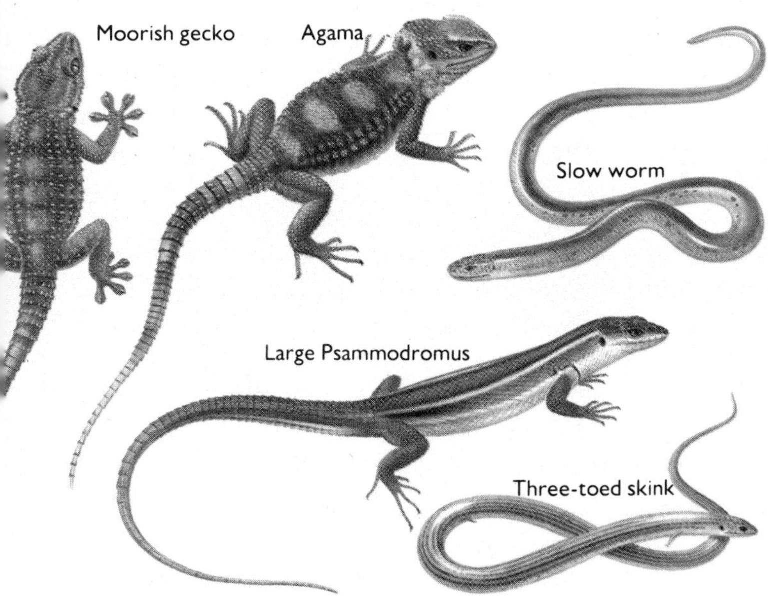

◀ *There are many different types of lizard, ranging in size from an inch to several feet. Lizards are far more ancient reptiles than snakes. Lizard fossils have been found dating from 200 million years ago, but snakes appeared only about 100 million years ago. The slow worm is in fact a lizard, though its legs have disappeared.*

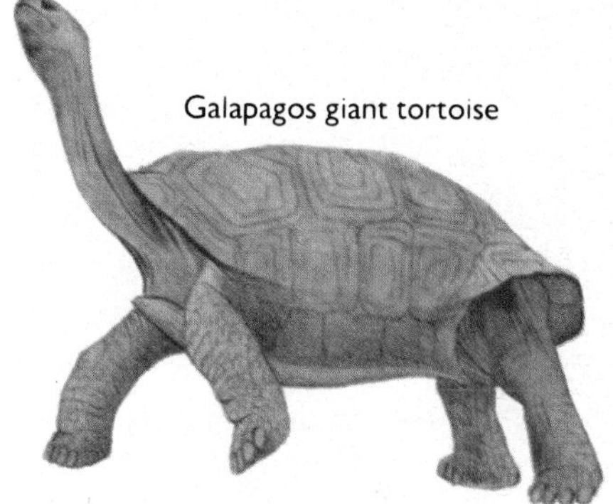

▲ *The Galapagos giant tortoise can have a shell over 5 ft. (1.5 m) long, and often weighs more then 440 lbs. (200 kg). Red-eared terrapins are found in fresh water in North America.*

Today, there are four main groups of reptiles: ALLIGATORS AND CROCODILES, LIZARDS and SNAKES, TORTOISES and TURTLES, and the rare tuatara. The biggest reptiles are the alligators and crocodiles. The estuarine crocodile of Southeast Asia grows to 20 ft. (6 m) in length, the biggest of them all.

There are over 5,000 kinds of lizards and snakes. They live everywhere, from deserts to jungles and faraway ocean islands. Some have poisonous bites with which they kill their prey. Turtles and tortoises are well protected by their hard shells. The biggest are the lumbering giant tortoises of the Pacific and Indian Ocean islands.

Republic

A republic is a form of government by which the people are supposed to rule themselves. Usually, they hold ELECTIONS to choose their leaders. Many republics have been formed to take over powers from kings who ruled unfairly.

The first republics were in ancient Greece and Rome, but many of the people in these countries were slaves. Today, some republics are run by people who have not been elected by the people. There are both Communist and Democratic republics.

Britain, Sweden, Norway, and Denmark have monarchs and are therefore not republics. But the people of these countries are freer to choose the people who govern them than are those of many of the world's republics.

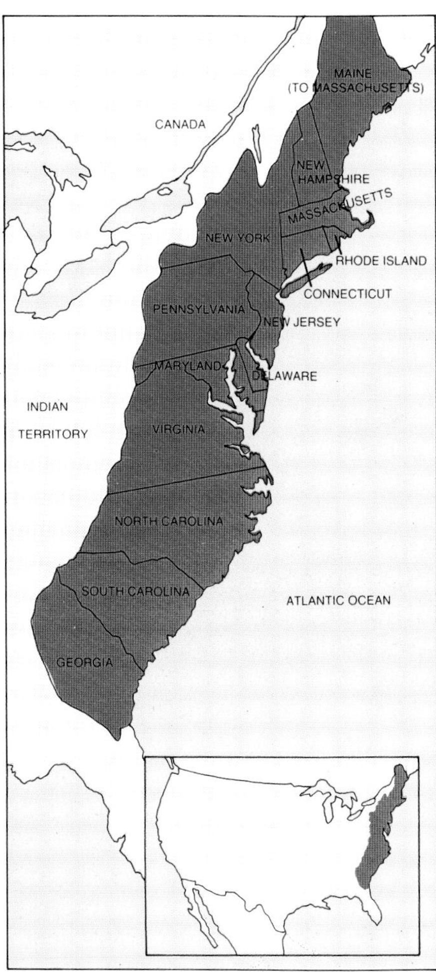

▲ *When the Revolutionary War broke out, only a small fraction of North America had been settled by people from Britain. The thirteen colonies were all situated along the eastern coast.*

Revolutionary War, American

The Revolutionary War was fought between Britain and her 13 American colonies from 1775 to 1783. The colonies won their independence from Britain and became a new nation, the United States of America. The war quickly became a symbol of a new way of thinking—that people should have the right to decide for themselves how they want to be governed.

For many years before the war, Britain and the American colonies had disagreed about a number of things, chiefly over taxes. The British tried to force the colonies to pay taxes, but would not allow the colonies any representation in the British Parliament. The colonies insisted on "no taxation without representation."

The first shot in the war was fired at Lexington, Massachusetts, on April 19, 1775. In July, George WASHINGTON was made commander of the American forces. On July 4, 1776, the colonies declared their independence.

At first, the war went badly for the Americans. The British soliders had good weapons and professional officers. But, because they were far from home, they had many problems transporting men

The Revolutionary War was a small war compared with modern ones. Large numbers of men were never involved. There were never more than 20,000 men in the American army at any one time. Britain sent about 60,000 men across the Atlantic during the entire six years of war.

► *This picture shows a detail from the painting "The Declaration of Independence" by John Trumbull. All the colonies agreed to the declaration.*

and weapons. In October, 1777, the British were defeated at the Battle of Saratoga, in New York. This was the turning point. On October 19, 1781, a British army under Lord Cornwallis surrendered to Washington at Yorktown, Virginia. The final peace treaty, the Treaty of Paris, was signed in 1783.

▲ *Backed by the French, the American army forced the British to surrender at Yorktown, Virginia, in 1781.*

Rhinoceros

Sometimes described as a "tank on legs," the rhinoceros is one of the largest and strongest of all land animals. A full grown male can weigh as much as 3.5 tons.

▼ *Although their poor eyesight may make them an easier target for hunters, rhinos have a good sense of hearing and smell.*

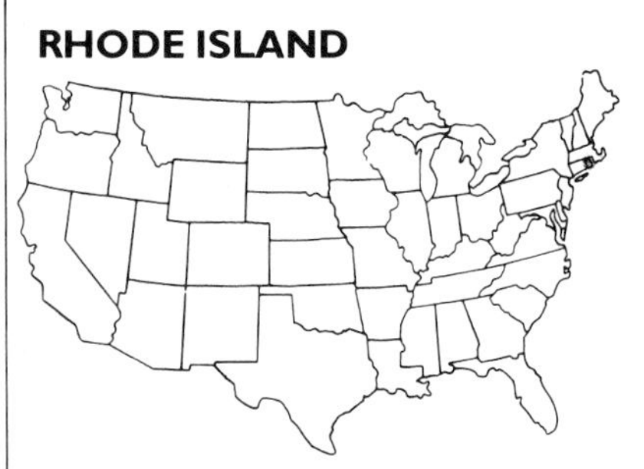

Capital: Providence
Population: 1,003,464
Area: 1,212 sq. mi. (3,140 sq. km)
State flower: Violet
State bird: Rhode Island Red
State tree: Red Maple
Statehood: May 29, 1790
13th state

This massive beast has a tough leathery skin and sprouts one or two horns (actually made of hair) on its snout. They may grow as long as 50 in. (127 cm).

The rhinoceros lives in Africa and in southeastern Asia. There, it feeds on leafy twigs, shrubs, and grasses.

Although an adult rhino has no natural enemies, it is so widely hunted for its horns that it has become an endangered species.

Rhode Island

Rhode Island is the smallest state and one of the 13 original states. It was also the last to ratify the U.S. Constitution. It agreed to do this only after the Bill of Rights had been added to it. Rhode Island is on the Atlantic Coast, in New England. It was settled as early as 1636. During the 1700s, it grew to become a prosperous colony. Fishing and farming were its major industries. In the 1800s, textile and jewelry production were begun, and these are still the most important industries. Tourism is important to Rhode Island, too.

Rice

Rice is a member of the GRASS family. Its grains are one of the most important CEREAL crops in the world. It is the main food of most Asian people.

Young shoots of rice are planted in flooded fields called *paddies*. Here they grow in 2 to 4 in. (5 to 10 cm) of water until they are ready to be harvested. Young rice has long narrow leaves and fine clusters of flowers that turn into the grains we eat.

▼ *Once rice is ready to be harvested, the stalks are cut and the seed heads are beaten on a hard surface to shake the rice grains out.*

Richard (kings)

Richard is the name of three English kings.

Richard I (1157–1199) was king for 10 years, but he spent only six months of them in England. The rest of his reign was spent on CRUSADES, battles against the armies of Islam in the Middle East. Richard and other European rulers wanted to capture the Holy Land.

Richard II (1367–1400) became king when he was

only 10 years old. Because he was so young, many scheming nobles fought against each other and him to gain more power. As he grew older, Richard tried to restore order, but he was never a clever ruler and in the end his enemies killed him horribly.

Richard III (1452–1485) was said to have gained the throne by treachery. Some people also believe he killed his two young nephews in the Tower of London. His many enemies, led by Henry Tudor, revolted against him, and Richard was killed in battle.

▲ *Clothes for riding do not have to be expensive, but they should be comfortable and practical.*

Riding, Horseback

People have been riding HORSES for many hundreds of years. Horses were one of the earliest forms of transport, but today, most people ride purely for pleasure. It takes a great deal of skill to ride a horse well. Some people test their skill by riding in competitions, in jumping, cross-country events, and various sports such as polo.

It takes a lot of patience and practice to ride well. One of the most important things a rider must learn is how to tell a horse what to do. There are two kinds of signals used for this. The first, known as natural aids, are given by hand, leg, and voice commands. The second are artificial aids. These include using riding crops and spurs.

Command signals must be given smoothly and correctly; otherwise, the horse will become con-

▼ *When you are learning to ride, it can be very useful to have a lesson with an experienced rider controlling your horse using a special long rein called a lunge-line.*

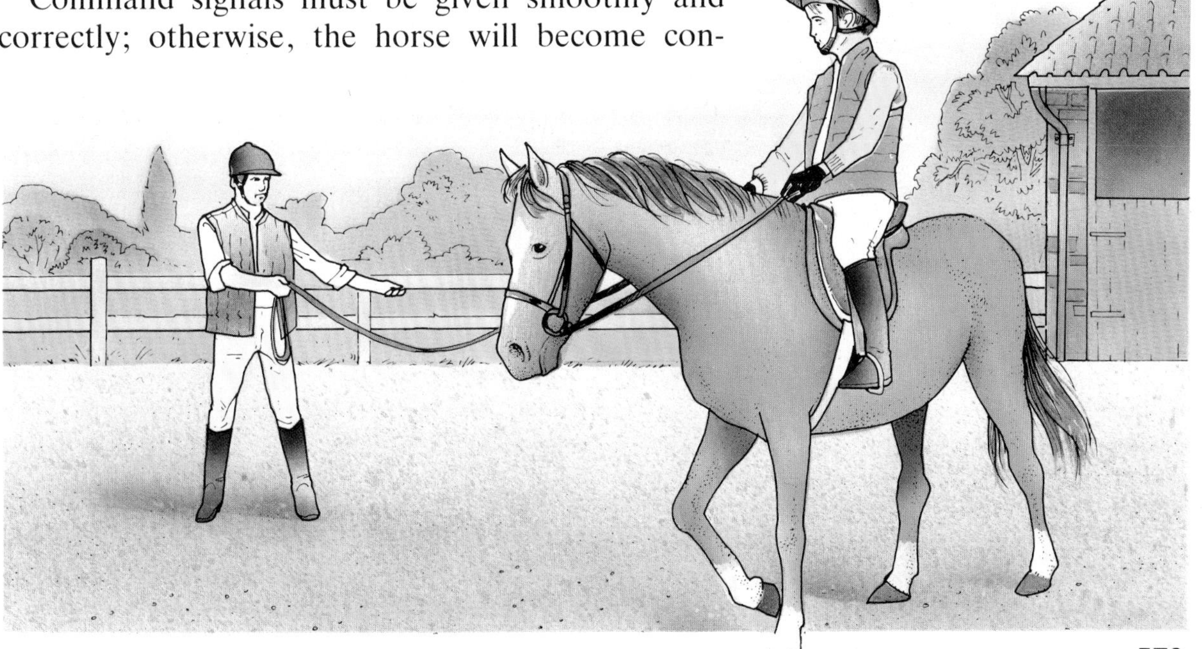

fused about what its rider wants to do. A horse must be taught exactly what each signal means, and it must learn to obey these signals promptly. There is no simple shortcut to learning how to control a horse, other than by hours of practice.

LONGEST RIVERS

	miles
Nile *Africa*	*4,160*
Amazon *South America*	*4,000*
Chang Jiang (Yangtze) *China*	*3,964*
Mississippi-Missouri *U.S.A.*	*3,710*
Ob-Irtysh *Russia*	*3,362*
Hwang Ho (Yellow) *China*	*2,903*
Zaire (Congo) *Africa*	*2,900*
Amur *Asia*	*2,744*
Lena *Russia*	*2,734*
Mackenzie *Canada*	*2,635*
Mekong *Asia*	*2,600*
Niger *Africa*	*2,590*

River

Rivers are one of the most important geographical features in the world. They range in size from little more than swollen streams to mighty waterways that flow for thousands of miles.

The greatest rivers in the world are the AMAZON, the MISSISSIPPI, and the NILE. They all drain huge areas of land. The basin of the Amazon, for example, stretches over an area larger than all of western Europe.

Some rivers serve as transport links that allow oceangoing ships to sail far inland. In tropical jungles, they are often the only way to travel. Rivers with DAMS supply us with electric power. Water from rivers is also used to irrigate farmland in desert lands and other dry parts of the world.

The first inhabitants of America nearly always settled beside rivers. The river gave them drinking water, water for cooking, and water for washing. They caught fish in the river, and by building boats and barges they could move about on it. When they began to raise crops, the river valley gave them fertile soil.

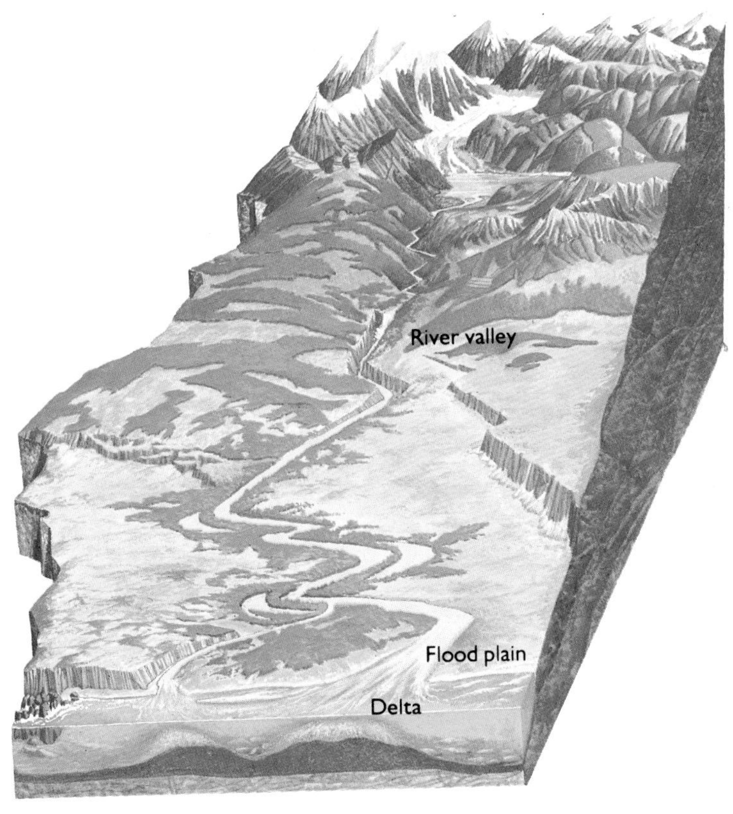

► *Over hundreds of years, rivers carve valleys out of the land as they flow toward the sea. From tiny mountain streams made from melted snow, they grow and swell, picking up mineral and other deposits as they flow through the landscape. These deposits sink to the bottom when the rivers slow down as they near the sea, forming great deltas.*

◀ *Complex road systems have to be planned to cope with ever-growing numbers of cars and other vehicles. In St. Louis, Missouri, this huge interchange had to be built where two major highways cross the Mississippi River.*

Road

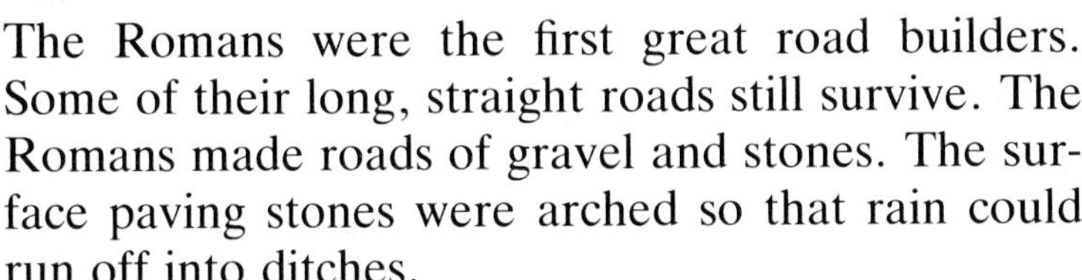

The Romans were the first great road builders. Some of their long, straight roads still survive. The Romans made roads of gravel and stones. The surface paving stones were arched so that rain could run off into ditches.

Modern road building began during the Industrial Revolution. In the early 1800s, a Scottish engineer, John McAdam, became the pioneer of modern road-making. But the stony surfaces of his roads were not good for vehicles with rubber tires. Later, tar-paved roads were built. They are covered with asphalt to make them smooth. Many roads, especially highways, are now made of concrete.

Robot

In films and books set in the future, robots often look like metal people, and they can walk, talk, and even think.

Real robots are very different. They are machines with arms that can move in several directions. Robots are *programmable* machines. This means they can be instructed to carry out different tasks. The instructions, or programs, are stored in the robot's computer brain.

Most robots work in industry and do jobs such as

▼ *Roman roads (below) were some of the first paved roads to be built in the world. They were built by the Roman army and had built-in gutters for drainage. Modern roads (bottom) are made of smooth layers of tar or asphalt over concrete or bitumen.*

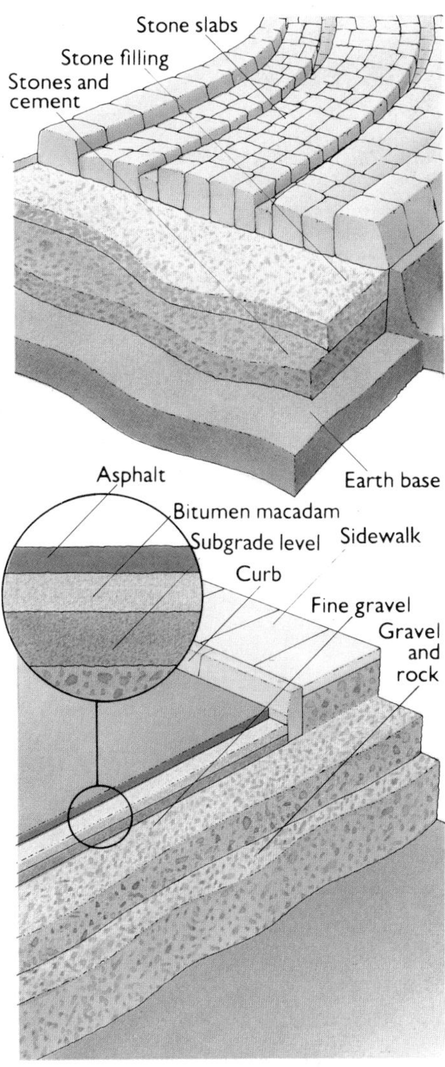

paint spraying, welding, and heavy lifting and loading. Some robots work in places that are dangerous for humans, such as nuclear power plants and outer space. Scientists are trying to develop robots with "artificial intelligence."

▼ *Unimate, made by the American firm Unimation, is one of the best-selling industrial robots. It can do a variety of jobs depending on how it is controlled. It can weld metal or move objects from place to place.*

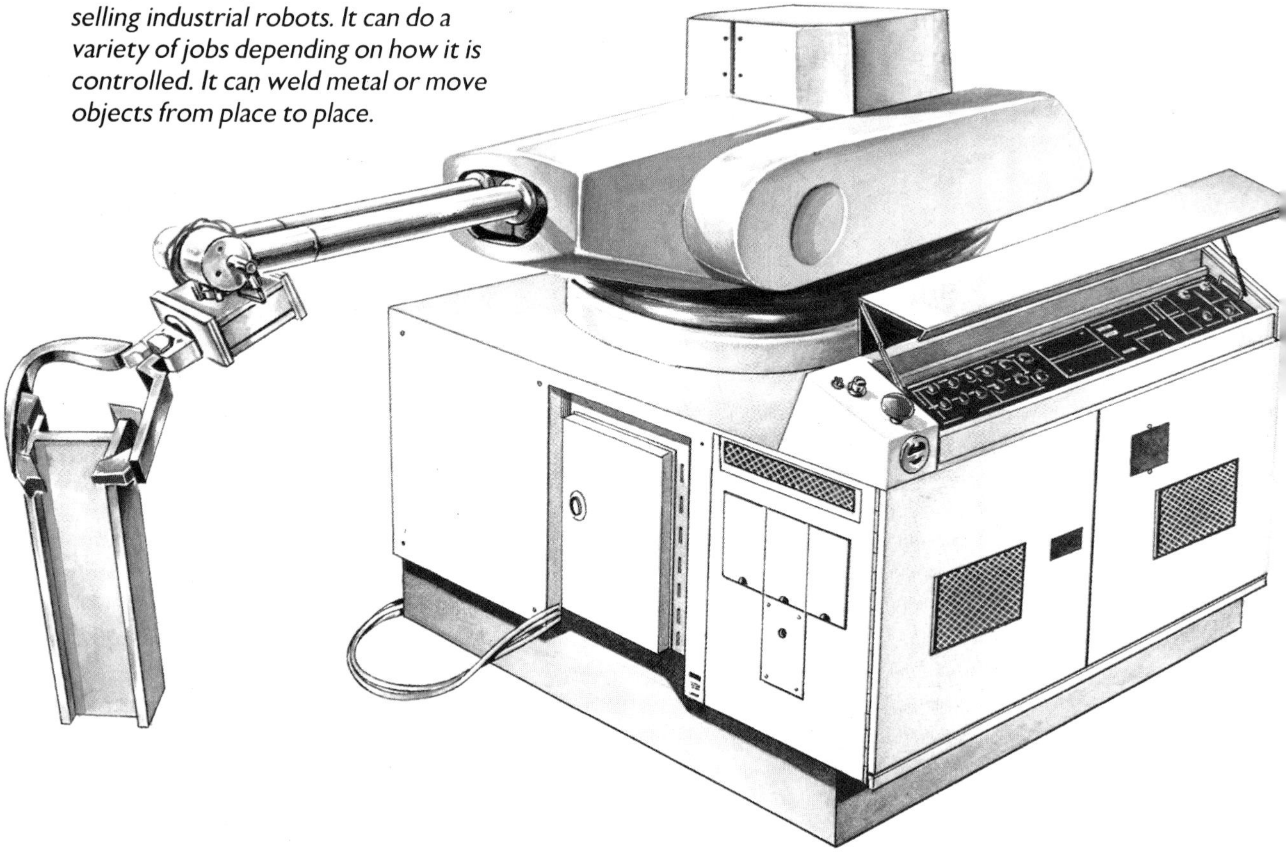

Rock

Rocks consist of grains of MINERALS. *Igneous rocks* form when magma (molten rock) hardens. Some harden on the surface to form rocks like basalt and obsidian. Some harden underground to form rocks like GRANITE. *Sedimentary rocks* are composed of sediments, like sand. For example, conglomerates are rocks made up of pebbles and sand. Many limestones are made of sediments formed mainly from the remains of dead plants and animals. *Metamorphic rocks* are igneous or sedimentary rocks that have been changed by great heat and pressure. For example, limestones may be *metamorphosed* (changed) into MARBLE.

Collecting rocks can be fun, and it will teach you much about the Earth. It is easy to find rocks, even

The whole Earth is covered by a crust of rock from 12 to 38 miles (20 to 60 km) thick. Most of this crust is covered by water or soil, but in many places the rocky crust is bare.

in a city. You can start by getting hold of a book that will tell you how to find and identify interesting rocks. Good hunting grounds for rocks are quarries, building sites, ocean cliffs, and the rocky sides of road cuts. But be careful.

All gems except pearls come from rocks. We eat one kind of rock every day—hallite or common salt.

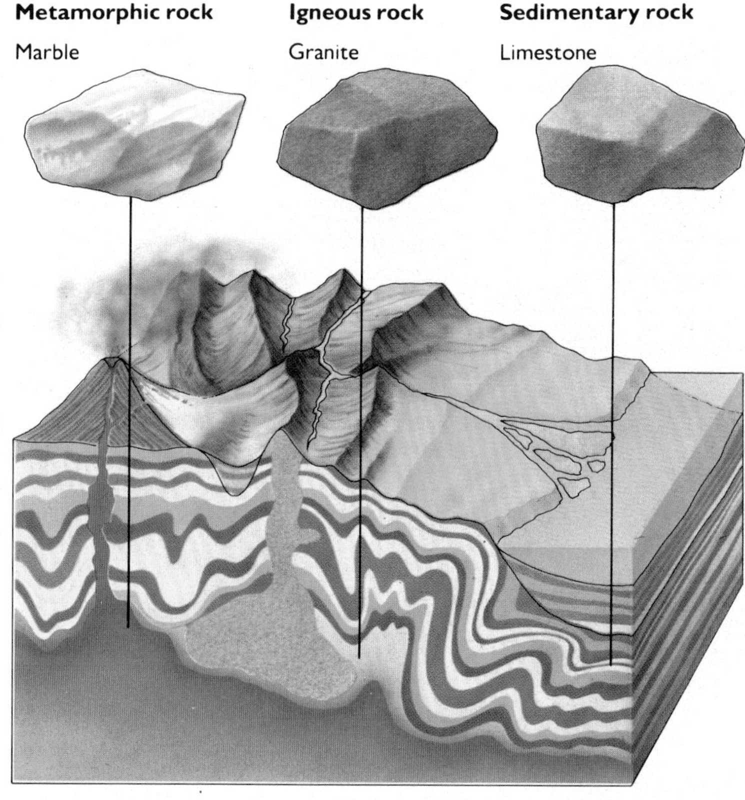

◀ *Granite is a rock that has hardened underground, and limestone is made from layers of sediment made up of dead sea creatures. Heat and pressure on limestone inside the Earth form marble, a metamorphic rock.*

Rocket

A fireworks rocket and the rockets that took astronauts to the MOON work in much the same way. Both burn fuel to produce hot gases. The gases shoot out backward. This creates a *reaction* force that thrusts the rocket forward. Rockets do not need air for their engines, unlike jets. So they are ideal for moving in space (where there is no air).

The Chinese used rockets as weapons as early as the 1200s. Rockets used to launch SATELLITES and spacecraft were developed after World War II. They are *multistage* rockets, which means several rockets joined together. Each stage fires in turn.

Fuel for early rockets, such as Germany's V2 in World War II, was kerosene and oxygen. Today's rockets use liquid fuels. Not only do liquid fuels give

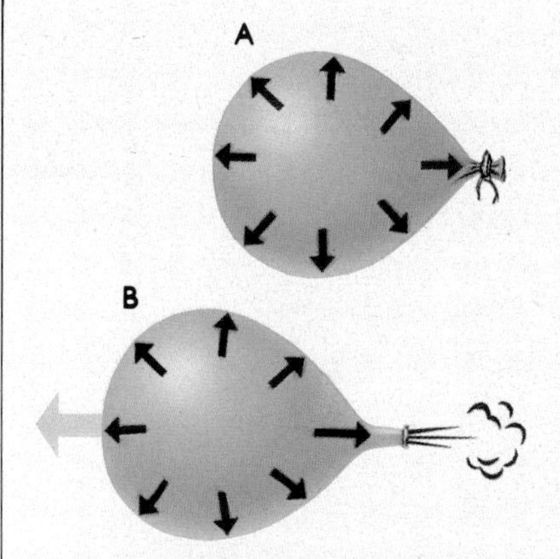

SEE IT YOURSELF

When air is let out of a balloon, it acts like a simple rocket. Fill a balloon with air. The balloon will stretch as you force a large amount of air into its small space. Once you close the mouth of the balloon (A), the air pushes equally in all directions. Now open the mouth (B). The balloon collapses as the air under pressure escapes. As this happens, the air pressure on the side opposite the mouth becomes greater than the pressure around the mouth, and the balloon flies in the direction of greater pressure. All rockets work on this principle.

▶ *Most engines run on fuel that burns in oxygen from the air, but out in space, there is no air. If the rocket fuel is going to burn, the rocket has to carry its own oxygen, in frozen liquid form. The rocket fuel is usually liquid hydrogen. Fireworks rockets burn gunpowder which pushes them up through the air. Chemicals in the tip of the rockets make the bangs and flashes.*

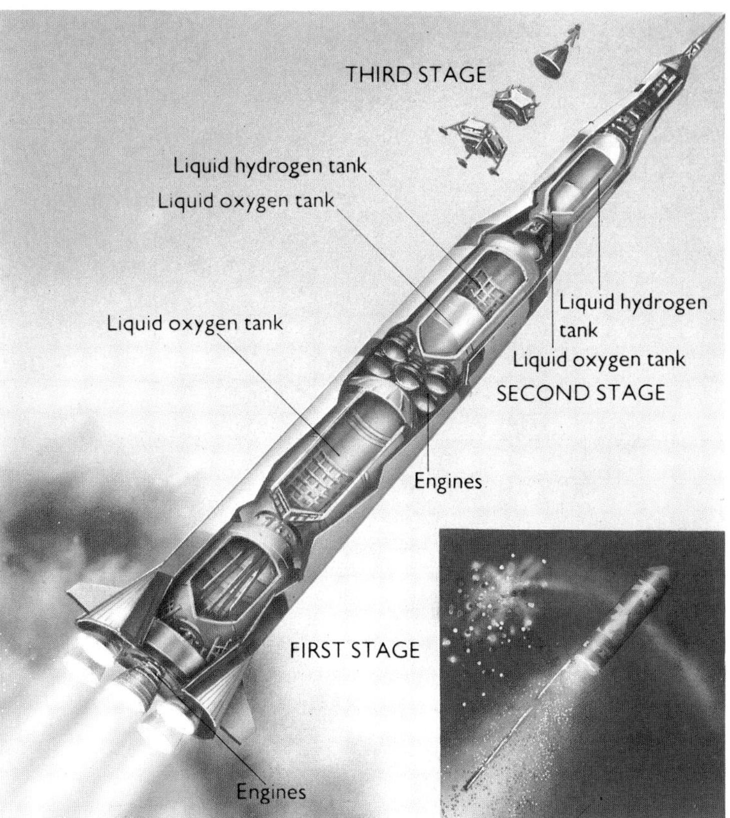

Today's space rockets use liquid fuels—usually a liquid called hydrazine or liquid hydrogen. In a liquid-fuel rocket, the fuel needs oxygen before it will burn. The fuel and the oxidizer are stored in separate tanks. When they are both pumped into a combustion chamber, they burn explosively and produce the gases that rush out of a nozzle and give lift. Liquid hydrogen and liquid oxygen have to be refrigerated to stay liquid, so space rockets need complicated systems of refrigeration pipes.

more energy, weight for weight, but they allow more control. The most powerful rocket in use today is the *Energia* rocket used in the Russian space shuttle.

▼ *A view of Mount Robson, the highest peak in the Canadian part of the Rocky Mountains.*

Rocky Mountains

The Rocky Mountains is a huge range of mountains in NORTH AMERICA. They stretch from Alaska through western Canada and the U.S.A., as far south as New Mexico. The highest peak, Mt. Elbert, is 14,433 ft. (4,399 m) above sea level. The Rockies have several national parks, and many wild animals live there. Rich veins of lead, copper, gold, silver, and zinc run through the mountains.

Rodent

Rodents are a group of gnawing animals. They have large, sharp front teeth that grow all the time. The animals wear these teeth down by gnawing their food. They also use their teeth to dig burrows in the ground for their homes and nests. BEAVERS even cut down good-sized trees with their gnawing teeth.

The 2,000 or so rodents also include MICE, RATS, PORCUPINES, and SQUIRRELS. The South American capybara is the largest rodent. It looks like a giant GUINEA PIG. It grows to a length of 4 ft. (1.25 m) and weighs over 100 lbs. (45 kg). The smallest rodent is the European harvest mouse. It grows only about 2½ in. (7 cm) long.

Rodeo

Rodeos are exciting shows where American COWBOYS show off their skills. In bareback riding, a cowboy rides a bronco (a half-wild or bad-tempered horse). In saddle-bronco riding, the cowboy rides one-handed, using one rein, a saddle, and a halter. Bull riding and calf roping are other events. In steer wrestling, the cowboy chases a young bull, or steer, on horseback, grabs its head, and pulls the steer down. A comic contest is catching a greased pig. The first recorded rodeo was held in 1869.

Roman Catholic Church

The Roman Catholic Church is the oldest and largest of all Christian churches. It has about 996 million members. The POPE is the head of the Church. He lives in VATICAN CITY in Italy.

▲ *Three of the many species of rodent. The flying squirrel does not actually fly, but glides with the help of extra flaps of skin between its fore and hind legs. The marmot and chipmunk are mainly ground dwellers.*

◀ *In the Roman Catholic Church, great importance is given to celebrations and ceremonies. Special saints' days and festivals are commemorated by processions and masses.*

Roman Catholics follow the teachings of JESUS Christ. The Church also helps its followers by giving them rules for good living. The main church service is called the Mass. Some Roman Catholics become nuns, monks, and brothers. They devote their lives to their faith in orders (societies) such as the Franciscans or Benedictines.

Roman Empire

The ancient Romans built up a vast empire around the Mediterranean Sea. ROME, in Italy, was the center of the empire. (See pages 588–589.)

Romania

Romania is a small country in southeastern EUROPE. It has beautiful mountains and many forests. Most people are farmers, but there are also mines, and oil is produced, too. In 1989, the people overthrew the corrupt communist government. They demanded democratic reforms and free elections.

ROMANIA

POLAND
CZECHOSLOVAKIA
UKRAINE
HUNGARY
ROMANIA
YUGOSLAVIA
BLACK SEA
BULGARIA

Government: Multiparty system
Capital: Bucharest
Area: 91,700 sq. miles (237,500 sq. km)
Population: 23,200,000
Languages: Romanian, Hungarian, German
Currency: Leu

Rome

Rome is the capital of ITALY. With a population of 2,800,000, it is also Italy's largest city. Rome stands on the River Tiber, about 17 miles (27 km) from the Mediterranean Sea. Many tourists visit Rome to see the great ruins of ancient Rome and the beautiful churches, fountains, palaces, and art galleries.

According to legend, Rome was founded by descendants of Aeneas, a Trojan who fled to Italy after the fall of Troy. Two of these descendants were Romulus and Remus. They were twin brothers who were abandoned at birth and suckled by a she-wolf. When they grew up, the brothers founded a town on one of Rome's seven hills and ruled it together. After a while, they quarreled, and Romulus killed his brother to become the sole ruler of Rome. Tradition says that Rome was founded on April 21, 753 B.C. The ancient Romans celebrated that day, and it is still a holiday.

▶ *A view over Rome from the dome of St. Peter's Basilica, looking over the colonnades in St. Peter's Square. On important holy days, the square is packed with people from all over the world.*

Roosevelt, Franklin Delano

Franklin Roosevelt (1882–1945) was the 32nd president of the United States. He was elected four times—more than any other president—and served in office from 1933 to 1945. He died 83 days after becoming president for the fourth time. Many people consider him one of the greatest U.S. presidents. He came to power during the worst economic depression the country has known, but guided the country through it skillfully. And he led the United States through most of World War II. Roosevelt had many political enemies. In the Depression, his "New Deal" was widely attacked by those who believed the government should not help the unemployed. And in the early days of the war, many claimed Roosevelt was leading the United States into a war it should stay out of.

FRANKLIN D. ROOSEVELT

Thirty-second President 1933–1945
Born: Hyde Park, New York
Education: Harvard University; Columbia University Law School, New York City
Occupation: Lawyer
Political Party: Democratic
Buried: Hyde Park, New York

Franklin D. Roosevelt entertained a great deal at the White House. In 1939, King George VI and Queen Elizabeth became the first British monarchs to visit the United States and stay at the White House.

Roosevelt, Theodore

Theodore Roosevelt (1858–1919) was the 26th president of the United States. He became president when William McKinley was assassinated. In 1904, he easily won the next election. Roosevelt had a huge personality. He loved the outdoor life—and he loved being president. The U.S. was already a great industrial power when he became president, but it had little military influence. Roosevelt increased the power of the country by expanding the navy. He called this his "big stick" policy. To help the navy sail ships quickly from the Atlantic to the Pacific, he had the Panama Canal cut. He also helped to break up monopolies in business.

THEODORE ROOSEVELT

Twenty-sixth President 1901–1909
Born: New York City
Education: Harvard University
Occupation: Lawyer, soldier, writer, explorer, public official
Political Party: Republican
Buried: Sagamore Hill, Oyster Bay, New York

Rowing

There are two main ways of using oars to drive a boat: *sculling* and *rowing*. In sculling, each oarsman or woman uses a pair of lightweight oars.

In rowing, each person has a single oar. Boats are built to take eight, four, or a pair of rowers. A boat for eight is always steered by a ninth crew member called the *coxswain*, or *cox*. There are races for fours and pairs, with or without a cox.

ROMAN EMPIRE

The story of the Roman Empire began about 2,700 years ago, in small villages on hills above the River Tiber in Italy. The people of these villages founded the mighty Roman Empire.

According to legend, Rome was founded by twin brothers called Romulus and Remus, who were reared by a wolf. About 590 B.C., the Romans set up a republic, and created a strong army. They began to conquer their neighbors.

The capital of this state was Rome, a city built on seven hills. Here was the Forum, or meeting place, and the Senate, or parliament. There were temples, markets, triumphal arches, and villas (large houses). The language of Rome was Latin.

In 45 B.C., the soldier Julius Caesar made himself dictator of Rome. In 27 B.C., his nephew Octavian (Augustus) became the first Roman emperor. The Romans ruled most of Europe and the lands around the Mediterranean. They brought peace and firm government. Roman ideas spread everywhere. The Romans were skillful engineers, and many remains of their roads, walls, forts, and other buildings can still be seen.

In A.D. 364, the empire was divided: the western half was governed from Rome, the eastern half from Constantinople (Byzantium). For a thousand years, Eastern Roman, or Byzantine, emperors ruled from Constantinople.

Rome was now in decline. Its army struggled to fight off attacks from barbarian tribes. Around 476, Rome itself fell, and the empire in the west collapsed. The eastern empire lasted (in name) until 1453, when Constantinople was captured by the Turks.

► *Two-wheeled Roman chariots were pulled by two, three, or four horses in races at the circus.*

▲ *The Arch of Constanti in Rome was built in A.D. 3 to mark the emperor Constantine's victory ove a rival.*

▼ *Roman engineers building an aqueduct for carrying water. The crane was a Roman invention. The Pont du Gard in southern France was built in this way. It has three tiers, and stands 158 ft. (48 m) high.*

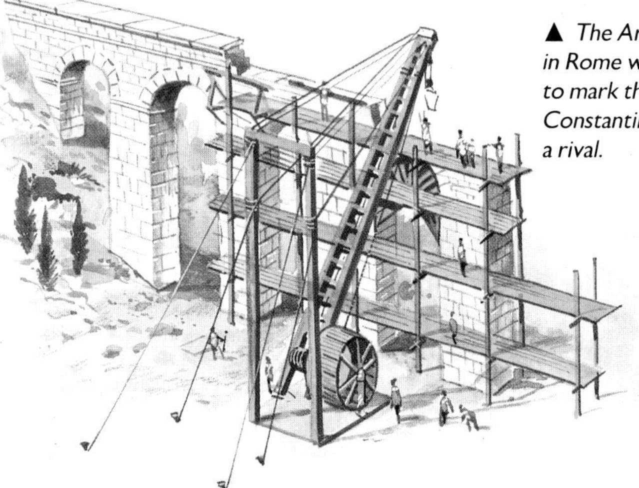

HISTORY OF ROME

753 B.C.	Founding of Rome (according to legend).
590 B.C.	Foreign kings driven from Rome and the republic set up.
264 B.C.	Punic Wars, against Carthage.
146 B.C.	Greece now controlled by Rome.
73 B.C.	Slaves revolt, led by Spartacus.
45 B.C.	Julius Caesar becomes dictator.
31 B.C.	Octavian (later called Augustus) defeats Mark Antony and Cleopatra.
A.D. 64	Emperor Nero blames Christians for setting fire to Rome.
A.D. 150	Peak of Roman power.
A.D. 330	Constantine, first Christian emperor, founds Constantinople.
A.D. 364	Division of the empire.
A.D. 378	Roman legions defeated at Adrianople by Goths.
A.D. 410	Alaric's Visigoths capture Rome.
A.D. 451	Attila the Hun attacks Rome.
A.D. 476	Fall of western empire.

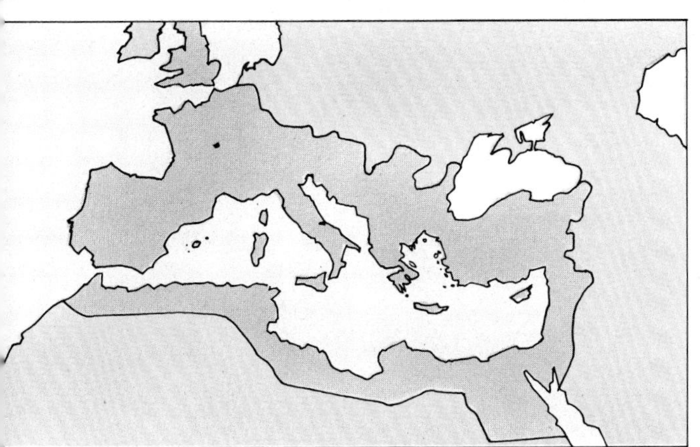

▲ *This map shows the Roman Empire when it was at its greatest, in* A.D. *117. At this time, it was ruled by the emperor Trajan.*

► *This sign was found in the ruins of the Roman town of Pompeii, buried when the volcano Vesuvius erupted in* A.D. *79. It says (in Latin): Beware of the Dog.*

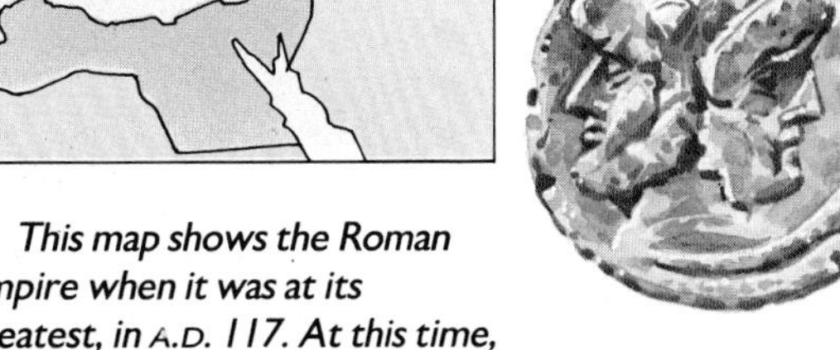

◄ *A Roman coin.*

► *A Roman senator. He is wearing the loose, flowing robe called a* toga. *The toga was made from an oval-shaped piece of material and had many folds. It was so difficult to drape that a special slave was sometimes employed to fix his master's toga. The color of togas depended on the wearer's rank and age.*

◄ *The Roman army conquered a vast area. In the center is a* legate *(a general); on the left is a cavalryman; and on the right is a* legionary *(an infantryman).*

THE ROMAN ARMY

Rome controlled its huge empire by means of a powerful and well-disciplined army. The backbone of the Roman army was the *legion*. Each legion had up to 6,000 foot-soldiers, divided into ten *cohorts*. The soldiers carried javelins, shields, and short swords. Each man was a Roman citizen (a high honor) and was trained to march long distances. The Roman army also had cavalry and siege artillery units equipped with giant crossbows and catapults.

For more information turn to these articles: CAESAR, JULIUS; COLOSSEUM; HANNIBAL; HOLY ROMAN EMPIRE; HUNS; POMPEII; ROAD.

Rubber was given its name by the scientist, Joseph Priestley. He noticed that this strange material could rub out pencil marks. The French name for rubber is *caoutchouc*. This word comes from a native American word meaning "the wood that weeps."

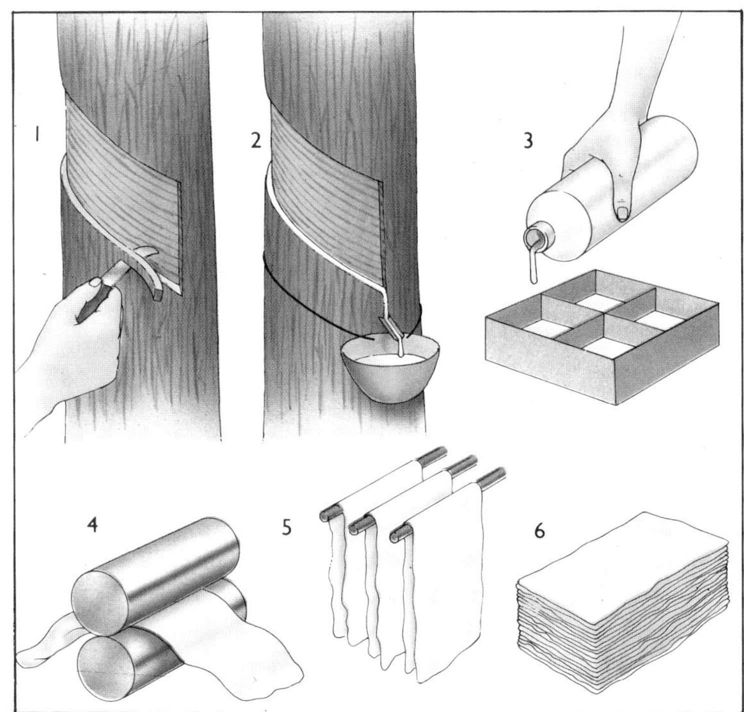

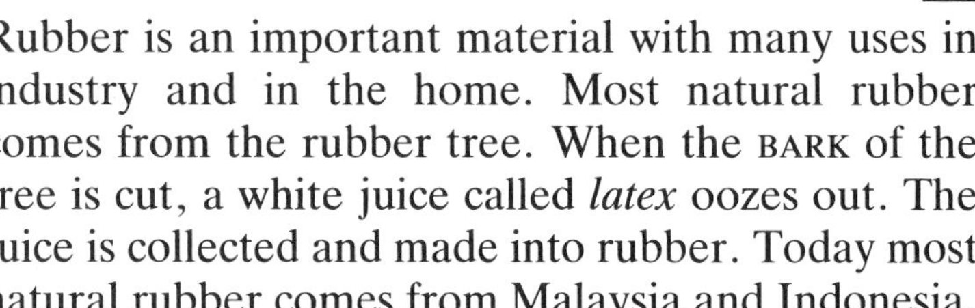

▶ *Steps in rubber production: (1) The rubber tree is tapped for latex. (2) Each tapping produces about 1 cup (.25 l) of latex. (3) Formic acid is added to the latex to make the rubber particles stick together (coagulate). (4) The rubber is rolled into sheets, which are hung up to dry (5). The crude rubber sheets (6) are dyed and treated, and shaped by machines into various products.*

Rubber

Rubber is an important material with many uses in industry and in the home. Most natural rubber comes from the rubber tree. When the BARK of the tree is cut, a white juice called *latex* oozes out. The juice is collected and made into rubber. Today most natural rubber comes from Malaysia and Indonesia.

Scientists found ways of making synthetic rubber during World War I. Synthetic rubber is made from oil and coal. About two-thirds of the rubber used today is synthetic rubber.

▼ *The faces on Mount Rushmore are, left to right, Presidents Washington, Jefferson, Theodore Roosevelt, and Lincoln.*

Rushmore, Mount

Mount Rushmore National Memorial is located in the Black Hills of South Dakota. It is a 500-ft. (150-m) cliff on which are carved the faces of four U.S. presidents: George Washington, Thomas Jefferson, Abraham Lincoln, and Theodore Roosevelt. They are the largest carvings in the world. Washington's head is 60 ft. (18 m) high. The faces were designed by a sculptor called Gutzon Borglum and took 14 years to carve, from 1927 to 1941. Many workers had to be hired to make them. They used dynamite and powerful drills to cut away the rock.

Russia

Russia is by far the largest of the countries that make up the Commonwealth of Independent States—the states that were the major part of the ex-U.S.S.R. It contains more people than all the other ex-Soviet states put together. It also has most of the great cities, including Moscow, the Russian capital, and St. Petersburg. Russia is rich in mineral resources and is industrially powerful. Farming—including such crops as grains, fodder, and cattle—is also important.

Boris YELTSIN was elected President of Russia in 1990, when he called for political and economic sovereignty for the republic. He was, however, faced with serious economic and food supply problems that threatened the stability of the country.

Rwanda

Rwanda is a small country in central Africa. Much of the country is mountainous; the climate is cool and pleasant. The people farm and raise cattle. Rwanda, which had been a part of the Belgian trusteeship of Ruanda-Urundi, became independent in 1962. The country is one of the most densely populated in Africa.

RWANDA

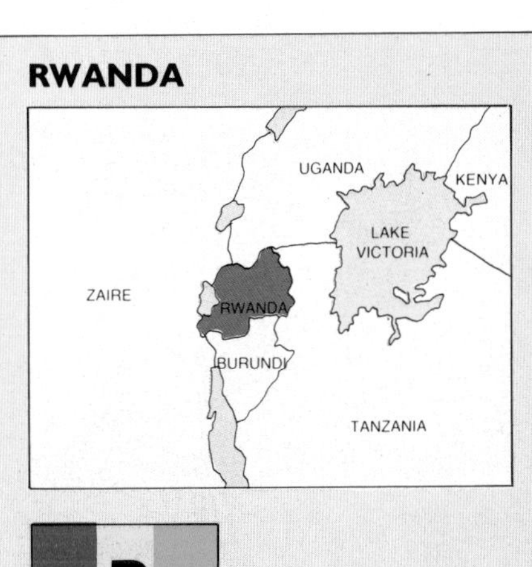

Government: Republic
Capital: Kigali
Area: 10,169 sq. miles (26,338 sq. km)
Population: 7,181,000
Languages: French, Kinyarwandu
Currency: Rwanda franc

◀ *Men fell trees in Rwanda, a country largely situated on a high plateau.*

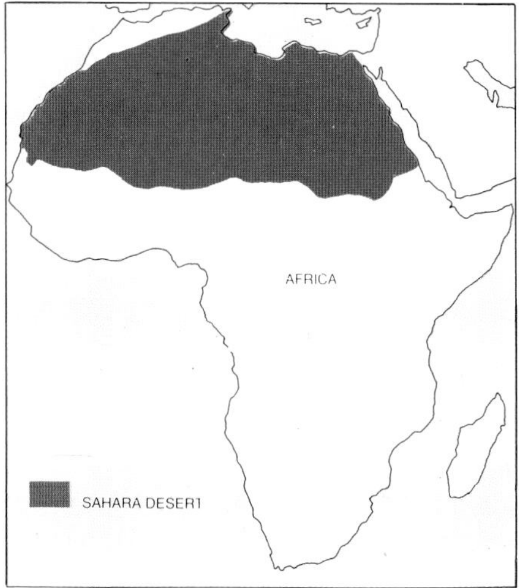

Sahara Desert

The Sahara is the world's largest hot DESERT. It covers about 3,500,000 sq. miles (9,100,000 sq. km) in North Africa. It extends from the Atlantic Ocean in the west to the Red Sea in the east. In the north, it stretches to the Mediterranean coast in Libya and Egypt. Recently, the lands south of the Sahara have had very little rain. Because of this, the desert is slowly spreading southward.

About a third of the Sahara is covered by sand. Other parts are covered by gravel and stones, or by bare rock. The Sahara is the hottest place on earth. The world's highest air temperature in the shade, 136°F (57.7°C), was recorded there.

Sailing

At one time, nearly all types of SHIPS used sails. But by the mid-1800s, sailing ships had been largely replaced by steamships. Today, sailing is done mainly for pleasure.

Sailing boats vary in size from small dinghies to large yachts. The *hull*, or body, of the boat may be made of wood, fiberglass, or molded plywood. Poles called *spars* support the sails. The sails are made of canvas or synthetic materials. They can be moved to catch the wind by pulling on ropes, called *rigging*. Sailing boats can sail in any direction, except straight into the wind.

▼ *The caravel (below) was used by the Portuguese to explore the African coast in the 1400s. The* Victory, *Nelson's flagship at the Battle of Trafalgar (1805), had 100 guns.*

The modern sport of sailing yachts began in Holland in the 1600s. Today, one of the most famous races is for the America's Cup, which began in 1870. Olympic sailing events were started in 1908.

▲ *This yacht has many features of modern sailing design.*

Saint

Saints are holy people. Christian saints are people who have been *canonized* (named as saints) by the ROMAN CATHOLIC CHURCH or the Eastern Orthodox churches. When someone is being made a saint, the Church looks at the person's life to see if he or she was very good. The saint must also have taken part in a miracle.

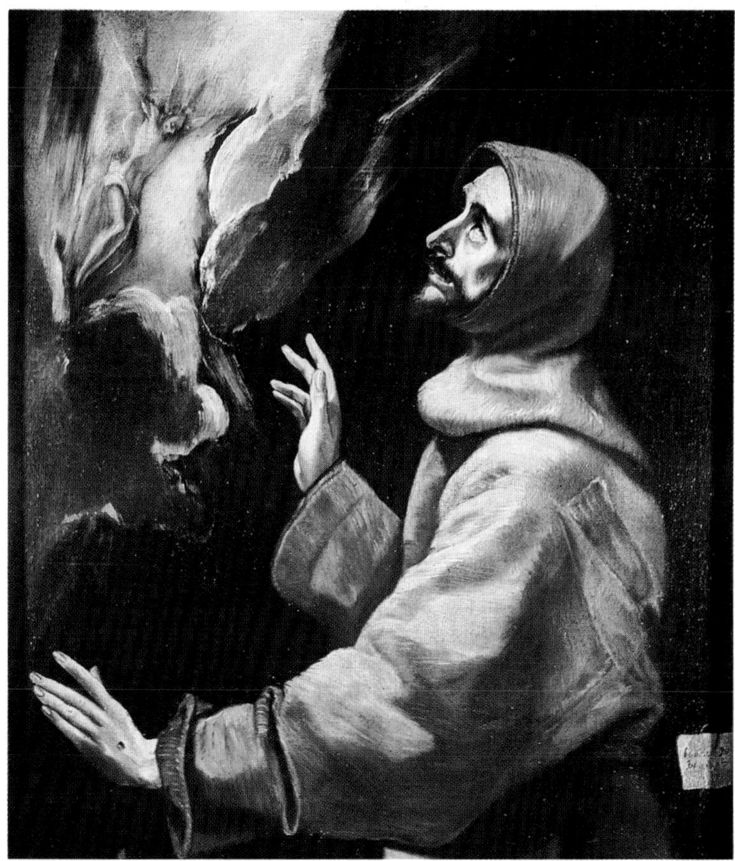

◀ *St. Francis of Assisi (1182–1226) believed that, to do God's work, he should give up everything he owned and lead a simple life of prayer and hard work. He formed an order of friars, called the Franciscans, that still exists today.*

St. Kitts and Nevis

These two tiny islands are in the Lesser Antilles in the Caribbean. They were settled by the British in 1623 and governed as a colony until they became fully independent in 1983. Sugar is the principal industry.

ST. KITTS AND NEVIS

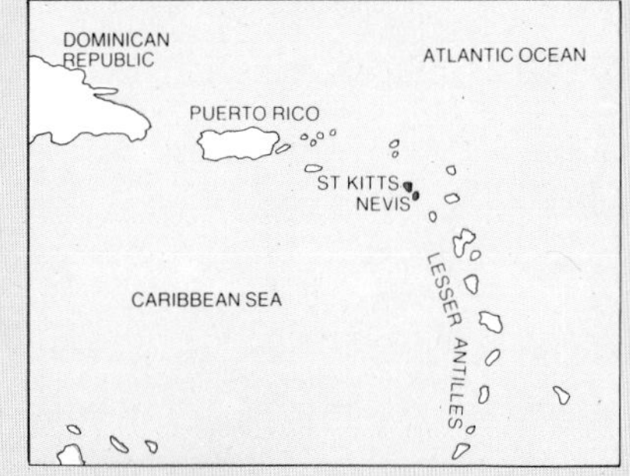

Government: Parliamentary democracy
Capital: Basseterre
Area: 101 sq. miles (262 sq. km)
Population: 44,000
Language: English
Currency: East Caribbean dollar

ST. LUCIA

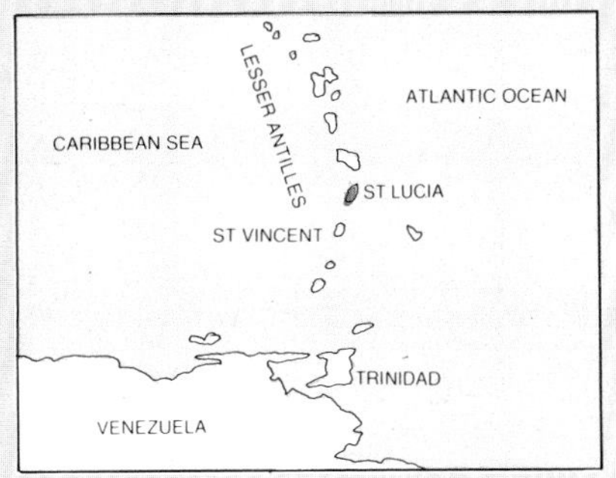

Government: Parliamentary democracy
Capital: Castries
Area: 238 sq. miles (616 sq.km)
Population: 151,000
Languages: English, French, Patois
Currency: East Caribbean dollar

ST. VINCENT AND THE GRENADINES

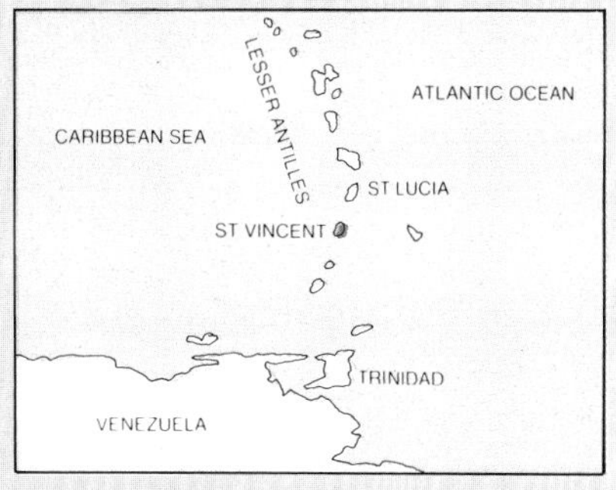

Government: Parliamentary democracy
Capital: Kingstown
Area: 150 sq. miles (388 sq. km)
Population: 116,000
Language: English
Currency: East Caribbean dollar

St. Lucia

St. Lucia in the Lesser Antilles is one of the Windward Islands. The people are farmers; the main crops are bananas, cocoa, coconuts, and citrus fruit. St. Lucia was given to Britain by France in 1814 and gained its independence in 1979.

St. Vincent and the Grenadines

These are islands in the Lesser Antilles in the Caribbean. St. Vincent is a forested volcanic island. The chief crops are bananas, arrowroot, and coconuts. Tourism is important. Columbus landed on St. Vincent in 1498. The islands were granted independence by Britain in 1979.

Salamander *See* Amphibian

Salmon

Salmon are fish which breed in shallow rivers. After the eggs hatch, the young fish swim down the river to the sea. They spend their adult life (about one to three years) in the sea. Then they return to their birthplace to breed. This may mean a journey of hundreds of miles. Most salmon die after laying their eggs.

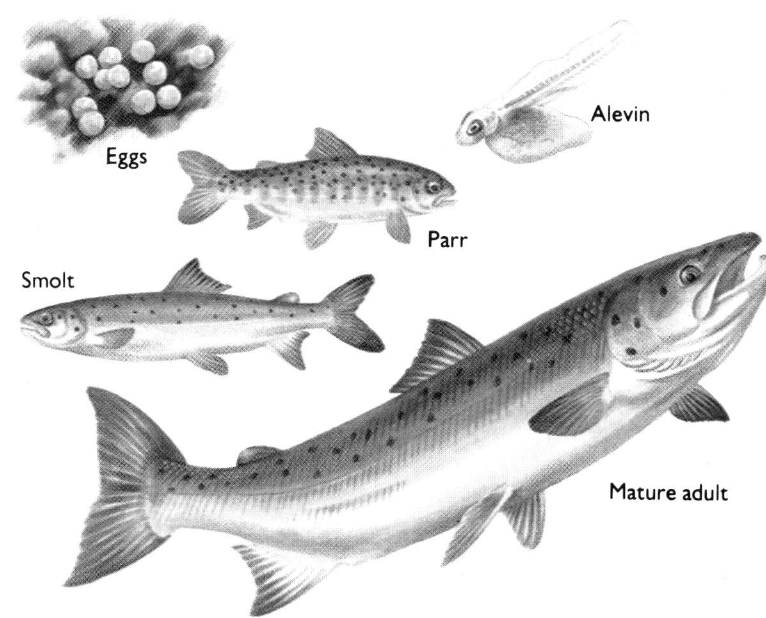

► *Salmon hatch from eggs laid in rivers. Newly hatched* alevins *live on the yolk attached to them. Young fish, called* parr, *become* smolts, *which migrate to the sea. Mature salmon return to the rivers to breed.*

◀ *Salt made from seawater, evaporated by the heat of the Sun, contains other minerals such as iodine.*

Salt

The chemical name for the salt we eat is sodium chloride. We need some salt to stay healthy, but not too much. Salt is also used to preserve foods, and it is important in many industries. Much of our salt comes from seawater, but some is mined from deposits in the ground.

▼ *A cable car climbs one of the steep hills in San Francisco, a major port and West Coast city.*

San Francisco

San Francisco is the second-largest city in California. Many people also think it one of the most beautiful. Its warm climate, spectacular location by the Pacific, steep hills, and busy cultural and business life have made it popular all over the world. The city was founded by the Spanish in 1769. In the 1800s, it was an important gateway to California, especially after gold was discovered in 1848. In 1906 and in 1989, it was hit by terrible earthquakes. Today, it is among the most prosperous cities in the United States.

San Marino

San Marino, in Italy, is the oldest and smallest republic in the world. It has made most of its money by frequent issues of its postage stamps and from the tourist industry. The people are ruled by two "captains regent" who are elected every six months. San Marino has had a treaty of friendship with Italy since 1862.

SAN MARINO

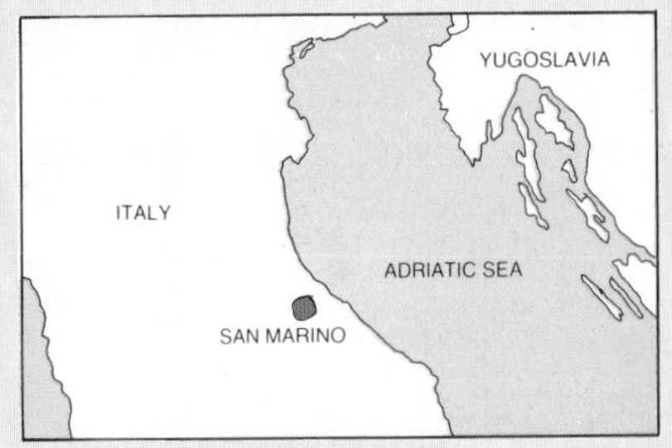

Government: Independent republic
Capital: San Marino
Area: 24 sq. miles (61 sq. km)
Population: 24,000
Language: Italian
Currency: Italian lira

São Tomé and Príncipe

These tiny volcanic islands are in the Gulf of Guinea off the coast of west Africa. They were discovered by the Portuguese in 1471, and slave trading became the main activity until coffee and cocoa-growing were introduced in the 1800s. The islands became independent of Portugal in 1975.

SÃO TOMÉ AND PRÍNCIPE

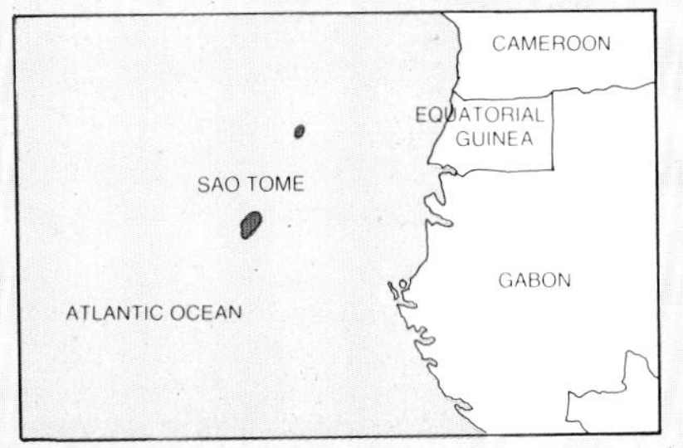

Government: Republic
Capital: São Tomé
Area: 372 sq. miles (963 sq. km)
Population: 121,000
Language: Portuguese
Currency: Dobra

Saskatchewan

Saskatchewan is the breadbasket of Canada. Over half the country's wheat is grown in the province. In the south, huge wheat fields roll on for mile after mile. There are important oil fields here, too, as well as potash mines. The north of the province is wild and rocky, and has many lakes and forests. Forestry and uranium mining are important.

SASKATCHEWAN

Capital: Regina
Population: 1,000,300
Area: 230,348 sq. mi. (596,600 sq. km)
Entry into confederation: September 1, 1905

Satellite

A body that moves in orbit around another body is called a satellite. The EARTH and the other planets are satellites of the SUN. The MOON is the Earth's satellite, but the Earth has many more satellites. They are the artificial satellites launched by rockets into fixed orbits. Weather satellites have cameras that send back pictures of cloud and storm formations. Communications satellites relay television and telephone signals around the world. They have radio and other equipment powered by batteries charged by the Sun's rays. The satellites receive a signal from the transmitting station on Earth, amplify it, and beam it down to another Earth station, which may be thousands of miles away.

▶ *The first satellite in space was the Soviet* Sputnik I, *launched in 1957.*

Satire

Satire is the use of wit or sarcasm to attack any kind of human behavior. Satire can be in prose or verse, in plays, in cartoons, in paintings, or motion pictures.

The best known satire in English is Jonathan Swift's *Gulliver's Travels*. Swift wrote the book to satirize the politics of his time, but it reads as a very good children's story.

Saturn

Saturn is the second largest PLANET in the SOLAR SYSTEM after JUPITER. It is about 75,000 miles (120,000 km) across. Saturn is famous for the rings that circle it. These rings are made of billions of icy particles. The rings are more than 170,000 miles (272,000 km) across, but they are very thin. The particles in the rings may be the remains of a moon that drifted too close to Saturn and broke up.

To the naked eye, Saturn looks like a bright star. The planet is actually made up mainly of light gases, and it is less dense than water, but scientists think

SATURN FACTS

Average distance from Sun: 887,000,000 miles (1,430,000,000 km)
Nearest distance from Earth: 800,000,000 miles (1,280,000,000 km)
Average temperature (clouds): -310°F (-190°C)
Diameter across equator: 75,000 miles (120,000 km)
Diameter of ring system: 170,000 miles (272,000 km)
Atmosphere: Hydrogen, helium
Number of moons: 24 known
Length of day: 10 hours 14 minutes
Length of years: 29.5 Earth years

Earth
Saturn

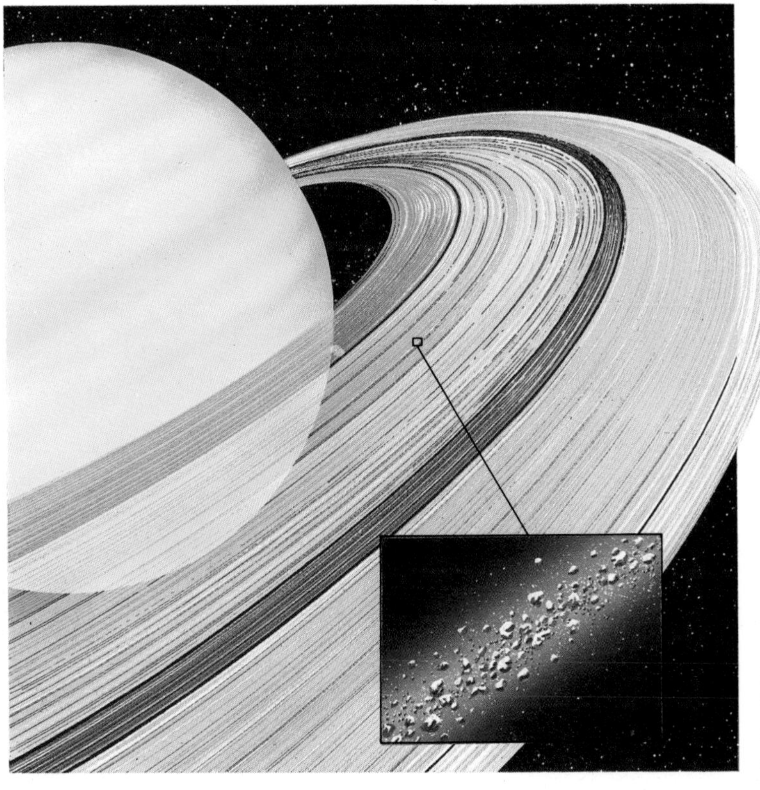

◀ *Saturn's rings are made up of pieces of ice, rock, and dust. They form a band that, measured across, is more than 20 times the diameter of the Earth.*

that it may have a solid core. Saturn has 24 satellites. The largest is Titan. It measures about 3,230 miles (5,200 km) across—larger than MERCURY. Titan is the only known moon to have an atmosphere—a layer of gases surrounding it.

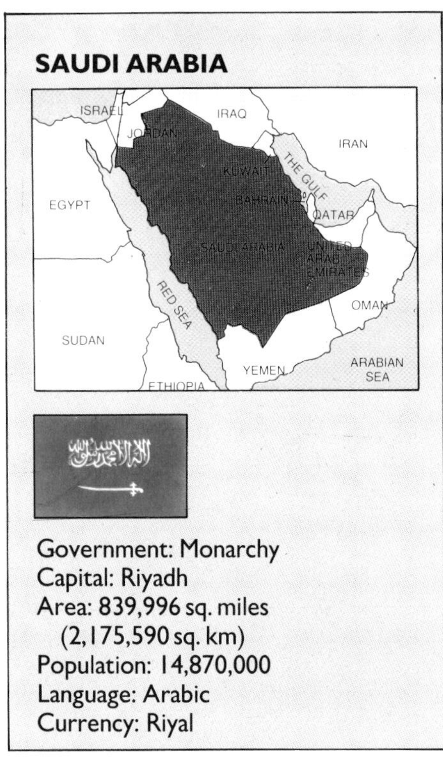

Government: Monarchy
Capital: Riyadh
Area: 839,996 sq. miles (2,175,590 sq. km)
Population: 14,870,000
Language: Arabic
Currency: Riyal

Saudi Arabia

Saudi Arabia is a large country that occupies most of the Arabian peninsula in southwestern Asia. It is named after the Saudi family which has ruled the country since it was founded in 1932. In 1933, oil was discovered along the Persian Gulf coast of Saudi Arabia, bringing vast wealth to the country. It is estimated that the country has about one-fourth of the world's oil reserves. During the Gulf War in 1990, Saudi Arabia was the base for the Allied forces' liberation of Kuwait.

School

Nearly all countries try to provide enough schools to give their children some education. In many countries, laws are passed by which children have to go to school between certain ages, such as between 6 and 16. But some poor countries do not have enough schools or teachers. They try to make sure that children go to school for long enough to learn to read, write, and use numbers. However, nearly a third of the world's people cannot read or write.

Schoolchildren may be surprised to learn that the word "school" comes from the Greek word *schole*, meaning leisure. The ancient Greeks thought learning was something to be done in a person's spare time.

▶ *In developing countries, schools such as this one in Lesotho have very little equipment. The pupils often have to walk many miles there and back.*

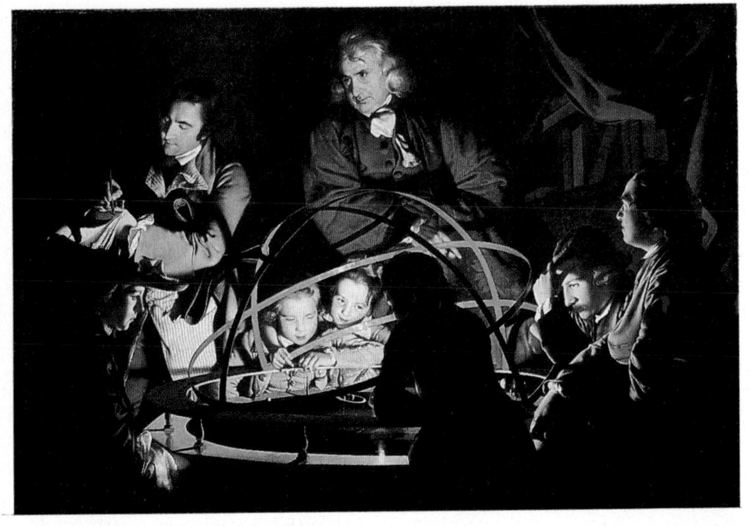

◄ *"The Orrery" by Joseph Wright. These working models of the planets in the solar system were very popular in the 1700s and 1800s.*

Science

The main divisions of science are ASTRONOMY, BIOLOGY, CHEMISTRY, GEOLOGY, MATHEMATICS, MEDICINE, and PHYSICS.

Modern scientists use the *scientific method*. First, they *observe*, or look at, something carefully to find out everything they can about it. Then they make a *theory* which explains what the thing is made of, or how it works. Then they test the theory with *experiments*. If the experiments agree with the theory, it becomes a *law* of science. Sometimes, a law is changed when scientists discover new facts about something. Science is always changing.

Scientific studies began in early times. Great

▲ *Democritus was a Greek scientist and philosopher who lived about 2,300 years ago. He taught that all things were made of atoms.*

SEE IT YOURSELF

Density measures how heavy a substance is compared to its size or volume. You can find out how dense some things are by carrying out the following scientific experiment. You will need some water, syrup, cooking oil, a tall glass jar, and a pitcher. Pour the liquids carefully into the glass jar, one after the other. Use a spoon so they do not mix. You will see that they separate into three layers. The syrup is more dense (or heavier) than the other two, and the oil is the least dense. Try floating some other objects on the different layers. What happens?

▶ *Scientific research is often aimed at making life easier and safer for people. This walking robot is used in the nuclear industry. It can be controlled remotely.*

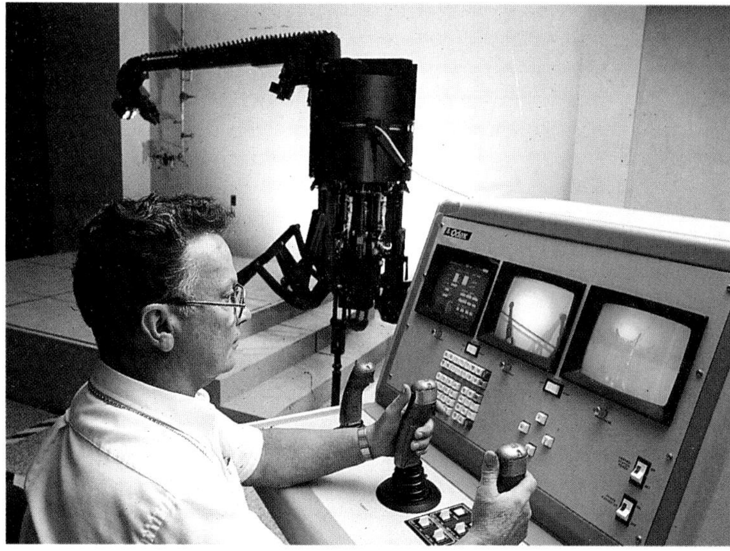

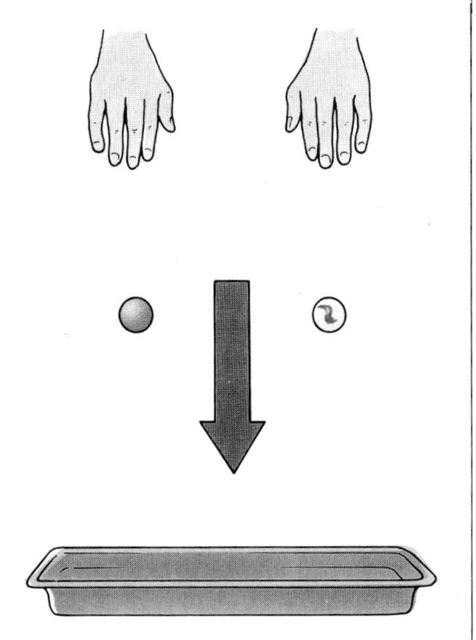

SEE IT YOURSELF

The famous scientist Galileo found out that objects always gather speed as they fall to the ground. Try dropping two objects onto a tray at the same time. Use objects which have the same shape, but different weight. Do they land together? Galileo proposed that objects of the same size and shape fall at the same speed no matter what they weigh.

advances were made during the first civilizations, especially in ancient Greece and China. Science nearly died out in Europe in the MIDDLE AGES, but during the RENAISSANCE, scientists began making discoveries that changed the way people thought and lived. This process speeded up during the INDUSTRIAL REVOLUTION, and scientific research has been increasing ever since.

Science Fiction

Imaginative stories which are set in the future or on other planets are called science fiction. The writers often use new scientific discoveries in their stories.

▶ *This is one artist's idea of how an alien spacecraft heading toward Earth might look. Many science fiction stories are set in outer space.*

They imagine how these discoveries might change the world in the future. Many of the stories are about space travel and time travel, and meetings between creatures from different planets. Some writers describe life in the future to show how many things they think are wrong in the world today.

Jules Verne (1828–1905) and H.G. Wells (1866–1946) were two of the first great science fiction writers. Recent writers include Isaac Asimov, Ray Bradbury, and Arthur C. Clarke.

Science fiction is not new. In the A.D. 100s, the Greek writer Lucian of Samosata described journeys to the moon and the strange creatures to be met there. Johannes Kepler, the famous astronomer who lived in the 16th century, wrote a book entitled *Somnium* in which he also described a trip to the Moon and the serpent-like creatures met by the hero.

Scorpion

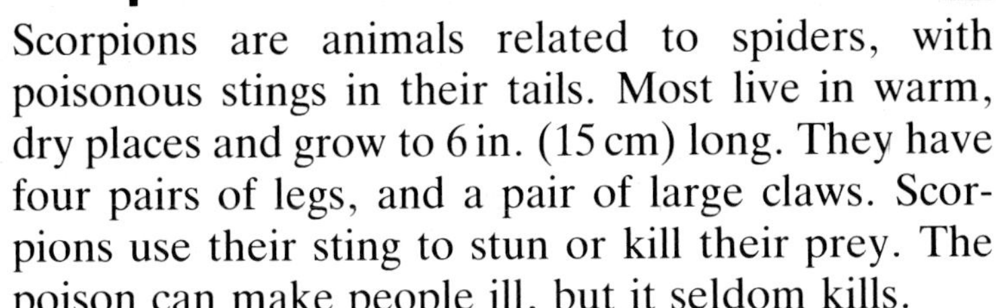

Scorpions are animals related to spiders, with poisonous stings in their tails. Most live in warm, dry places and grow to 6 in. (15 cm) long. They have four pairs of legs, and a pair of large claws. Scorpions use their sting to stun or kill their prey. The poison can make people ill, but it seldom kills.

▲ *When scorpions are frightened, they curl their tails up over their heads and may sometimes sting.*

Scotland

Scotland is part of the United Kingdom of Great Britain and Northern Ireland. Most Scots live in a narrow belt in the south where most industry is. In this belt are Glasgow, Scotland's largest city, and Edinburgh, the capital. The Highlands of Scotland have very few people and many beautiful mountains and lochs. The highest mountain in Britain is Ben Nevis, 4,432 ft. (1,343 m) high. There are many islands off the Scottish coast. They include the Hebrides, Orkneys, and Shetlands.

Scotland joined with England and Wales in 1707, but the Scots have kept many of their own traditions. Some Scots want their own government.

SCOTLAND

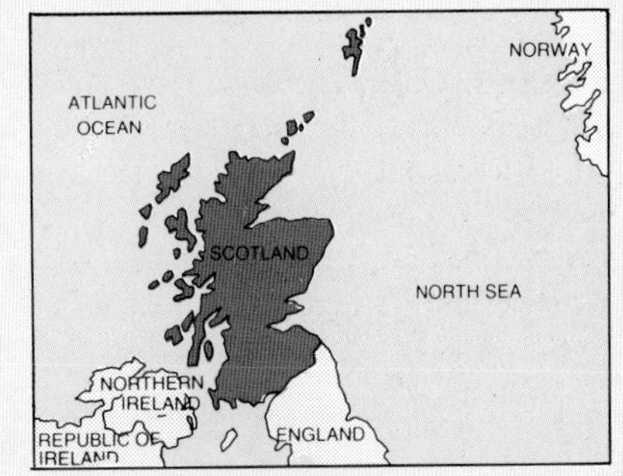

Area: 30,414 sq. miles (78,772 sq. km)
Population: 5,136,000
Agriculture: About 75% of land in use
Chief products: Barley, cattle, oats, sheep, wheat
Fishing: Crabs, herring, lobsters, and white fish
Chief industries: Iron and steel, motor vehicles, textiles, industrial machinery, chemicals, whisky, and shipbuilding

Scott, Robert Falcon

Captain Robert Falcon Scott (1868–1912) was an English naval officer and an explorer of the ANTARCTIC. His first expedition was in 1901–1904. With four companions, he began a march to the SOUTH POLE in 1911. After suffering great hardships, he reached the Pole on January 17, 1912. But he was disappointed to find that Roald AMUNDSEN of Nor-

▲ *Sir Walter Scott grew up on his grandfather's farm in the border country between England and Scotland. This area later became the location for many of his novels.*

way had been there just a month earlier. Scott and his companions died in a snowstorm on the journey back. They died only a short distance from a supply base where they would have been safe.

Scott, Walter

Sir Walter Scott (1771–1832) was one of the most popular of all story writers. He was born in Edinburgh, Scotland. He became a lawyer, but was more interested in Scottish history and folklore. He wrote several poems and many novels of historical adventures, including *Rob Roy* and *Ivanhoe*.

Scouting

Scouting is an international movement for boys and girls. It was founded in England in 1907 by Robert Baden-Powell for boys only. Three years later, a similar organization called the *Girl Guides* was founded for girls. The movement spread rapidly to other countries. Juliet Lowe started the U.S. Girl Scouts in 1912.

Young children from the age of 6 or 7 to 11 belong to the Cub or Brownie units. Young people from 15 up become Explorer Scouts or Senior Girl Scouts. One aim of scouting is to build character and self-reliance in young people. Another is to teach helpfulness to others.

▲ *Robert Baden-Powell was a soldier who served in both India and Africa. He wrote and illustrated many books.*

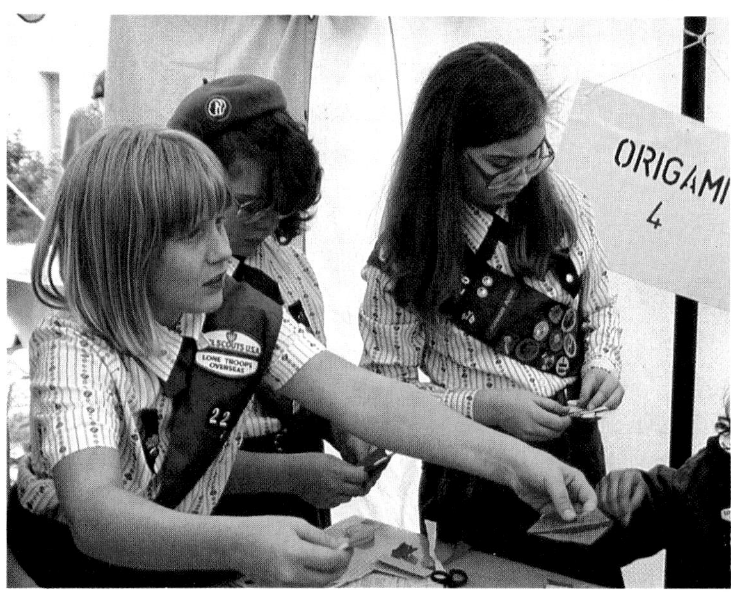

► *The scouting movement has spread to many countries, and there are now organizations to suit a wide range of age groups. Here, some Girl Scouts are doing origami.*

Screw

A screw is a simple machine. There are many kinds of screws, but those we know best are the metal ones used to join things together. The spiral part of a screw is called the *thread*. When a screw is turned around in a piece of wood, the thread pulls the screw into the wood.

When things are joined together with a screw, the squeezing force is very great. For example, if a wrench 12 in. (30 cm) long is turned with a force of $3\frac{1}{2}$ lbs. (1.5 kg) on an average screw nut and bolt, the nut and bolt are drawn together with a force of half a ton after one complete turn.

Sculpture

Sculpture is a way of making attractive models, statues, and objects as works of ART. They may be carved from stone or wood, or they may be made by *casting*. In making a cast, the sculptor first makes a

▼ *Sculpture is a very ancient art, as some of the earliest examples show.*

Female figure dating from about 5750 B.C., found in Anatolia.

Bronze head of an ancient Akkadian king, who ruled in Mesopotamia.

A Phoenician ivory carving dating from about the 800s B.C.

An ivory carving of a Byzantine empress from the A.D. 700s.

Neapolitan Fisherboy, a marble sculpture by Carpeaux.

A famous modern sculpture by Brancusi, called *The Kiss*.

▲ *The 19th century French artist Edgar Degas made a large number of paintings and sculptures inspired by ballet dancers.*

► *The angles and shapes in this modern sculpture by Jean Dubuffet are in sharp contrast to the flat New York skyscrapers that surround it.*

▼ *Sea anemones attach themselves to rocks with a suckerlike disk. The upper end of the column expands into the mouth opening.*

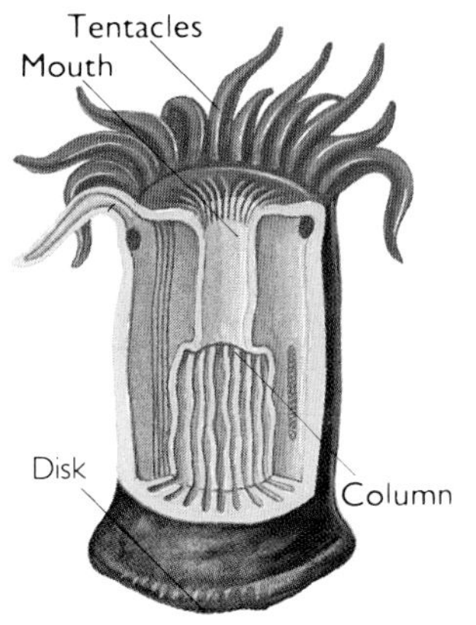

model in clay or wax. He or she uses this model to make a mold. Hot molten metal, such as bronze, is then poured into the mold. When the metal has cooled and hardened, it is taken out of the mold. The metal "cast" is a perfect copy of the original model.

Early Greek statues were models for RENAISSANCE sculptors such as MICHELANGELO, who was possibly the finest sculptor ever.

Modern sculptors have moved away from lifelike figures. Great artists such as Henry Moore (1898–1986) make *abstract* figures and groups.

Sea Anemone

Sea anemones are soft-bodied, tube-like animals. They are closely related to CORALS, but they do not build a hard cup around themselves as corals do.

Sea anemones cling to rocks. Many live on or near the seashore. They look like flowers because they have one or more rings of petal-like tentacles around their mouths. The tentacles have stinging CELLS and trap small fish and other tiny animals that float by. The sea anemone then pulls the food into its stomach through its mouth and digests it.

Sea Horse

Sea horses are strange fish with delicate, bony bodies. They are called sea horses because of their horse-shaped heads. Most are between 6 and 10 in. (15 and 25 cm) long.

Sea horses swim by waving their back fin. They often cling to seaweed with their tail. The males look after the eggs. They keep them in a pouch on their belly until they hatch. Sea horses are found in warm tropical seas.

▲ *Sea horses swim upright. If they want to feed, they hold onto seaweed with their tails and pick food out of the water as it floats past.*

Seal and Sea Lion

Seals and sea lions are large sea mammals. Many of them live in icy waters. They spend most of their time in the sea, but sometimes come ashore to lie in the sun. They also have their young, called pups, on land. Seals have streamlined bodies and legs shaped like flippers for swimming. They also have a thick layer of fat, or blubber, under their skin to protect them from the cold. Seals and sea lions eat fish and other sea creatures.

Sea lions have small ears outside their heads and have fur all over their bodies. The males often have a shaggy mane. The California sea lion is the smallest. It is often seen in circuses and zoos.

▼ *Seals and sea lions are wonderful swimmers, but on land they move slowly. They spend most of their time at sea, but they come ashore to breed.*

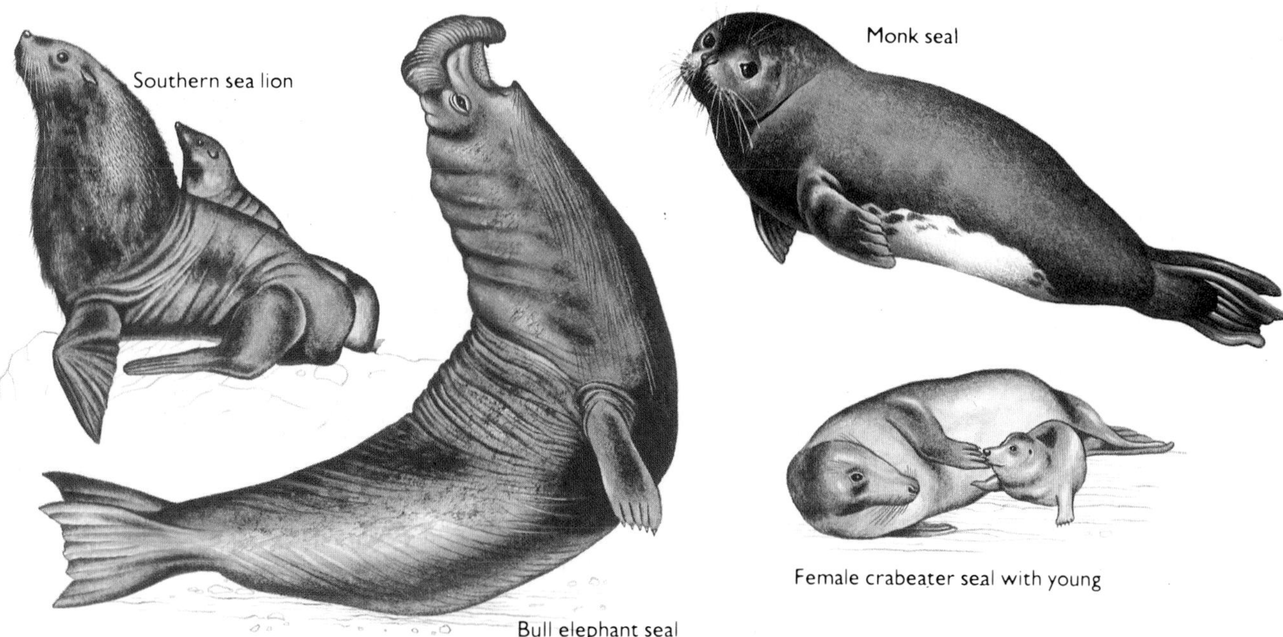

Seashore

The shores surrounding Earth's seas and oceans are shaped by water. Along some shores, fierce waves hammer at rocks and carry away loads of stones and earth. Along others, the waves and tides bring in pebbles and sand and dump them. All over the world, the edge of the land is being changed by the restless waves and by the constant rise and fall of TIDES.

There are several kinds of seashore. They can be rock, sand, mud, pebble, or a mixture. All shores are home for many living things.

Limpets, snails, barnacles, SEA ANEMONES, and sponges are some of the creatures found on rocky shores. All these animals cling to rocks and eat tiny pieces of food that float by in the water. Others, such as cockles, razor shells, mussels, and

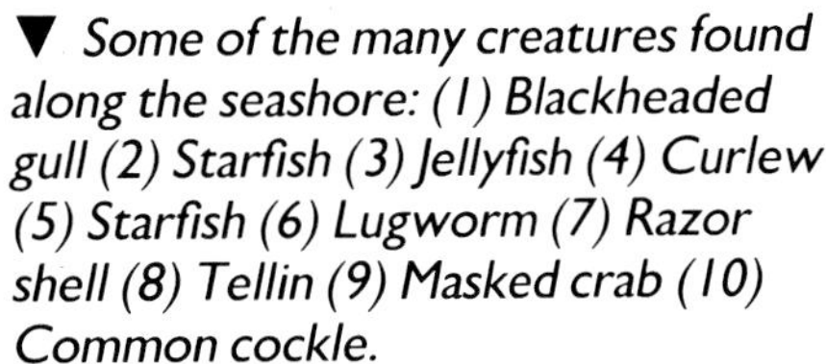

▼ *Some of the many creatures found along the seashore: (1) Blackheaded gull (2) Starfish (3) Jellyfish (4) Curlew (5) Starfish (6) Lugworm (7) Razor shell (8) Tellin (9) Masked crab (10) Common cockle.*

Except for the birds and the jellyfish, most of these animals like sandy and muddy beaches where they can bury themselves at low tide to keep from drying out.

▲ *These sand dunes along the west coast of England are constantly on the move. Fences and marram grass are used to control the movement of the sand. The lime-rich sands are also home to two rare creatures, the sand lizard and the natterjack toad.*

CRABS, like sandy and muddy beaches.

Seashores have their own plants. Many of these plants are SEAWEEDS. But other plants have learned to grow in these wet, salty places. Most shore plants and animals are able to live in and out of water. When the tide is in, they are often underwater, but when the tide is out, they are left on land.

Many birds live along the seashore. Some shore birds use their long beaks to dig for worms and insects in the mud. Others catch fish in the sea.

Season

The year is divided into four seasons. They are spring, summer, fall, and winter. Each season has its own kind of weather.

In spring, for example, the days become warmer; plants begin to grow again after the winter cold, and most animals have their young. In the fall, the days are cooler; leaves fall from the trees, and many birds fly south for the winter.

Seasons happen because the EARTH is tilted on its *axis* (a line through the center of the planet between the North and South Poles). As the Earth travels around the SUN, first one pole, then the other, leans toward the Sun. When the North Pole tips toward the Sun, it is summer in the northern half of the world and winter in the southern half. Six months later, it is the South Pole's turn to lean sunward, making it summer in southern lands and winter in northern ones. Spring and fall, the halfway seasons

One of the factors affecting seasonal temperatures is how far a place is from the ocean. Somewhere on the coast or on a small island has seasons that are much less marked than places that are far inland. This is because water is slow to heat up and cool down. The sea therefore helps to keep a fairly even temperature at places near it. In the center of vast continents, it can be very hot in summer and very cold in winter.

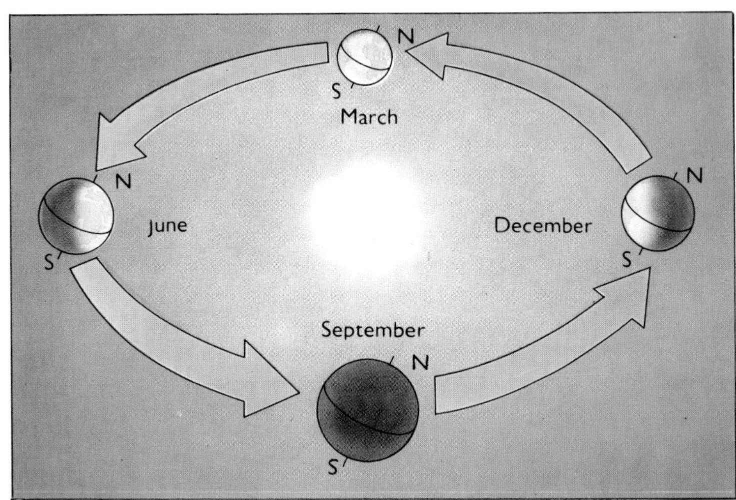

► *The Earth's axis always tilts in the same direction. In June, the northern half, or hemisphere, of the planet is in summer because it is leaning toward the Sun. It receives more direct rays and therefore more heat, and the days are longer. At the same time, the southern hemisphere is in mid-winter. Six months later in December, the Earth has gone halfway around the Sun, and the seasons are reversed. In March and September, both hemispheres have an equal share of day and night.*

between summer and winter, happen when the Earth is tilted between its summer and winter positions.

At the poles, there are only two seasons: summer and winter. During the polar winter, the sun never rises, and days are dark. In the summers, the sun shines all the time, and there are no real nights.

Farthest from the poles, at the EQUATOR, the earth's tilt has no effect. There are no clear differences between the seasons.

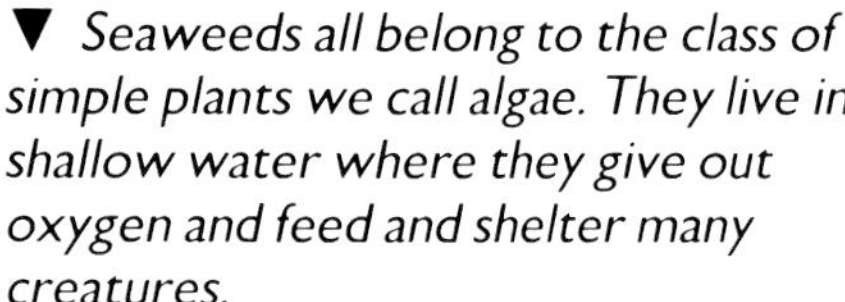

▼ *Seaweeds all belong to the class of simple plants we call algae. They live in shallow water where they give out oxygen and feed and shelter many creatures.*

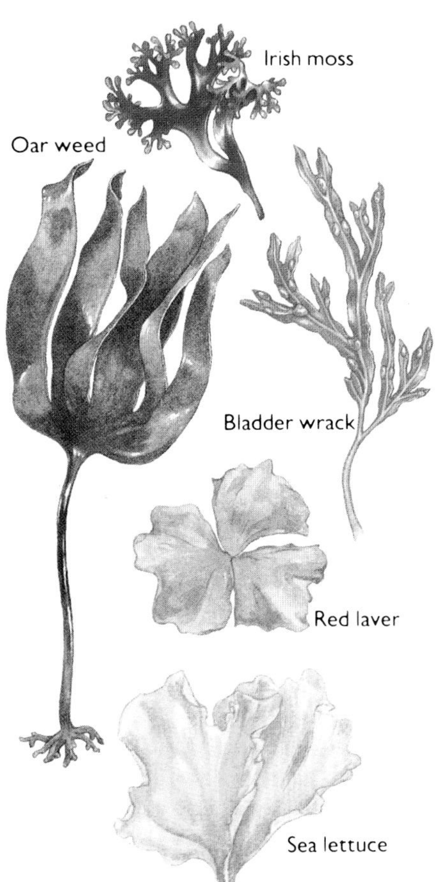

Seaweed

Seaweeds are a group of plants that live in the sea. They grow on rocks or on the seabed. Like most plants, seaweeds need sunlight to make food. Because the Sun's rays do not reach very far down into the sea, there are no seaweeds in deep water.

In some countries, people eat different types of seaweeds as vegetables.

Seed

Seeds are the most important part of a PLANT; they are the beginnings of new plants. A seed is formed when pollen reaches the female part of a FLOWER. The new seed grows inside a FRUIT, which protects it. In a grape, for example, the fleshy part is the fruit, and the seeds are in the middle.

Seeds have to be scattered to find new ground to grow on. Some fruits have wings and are carried by

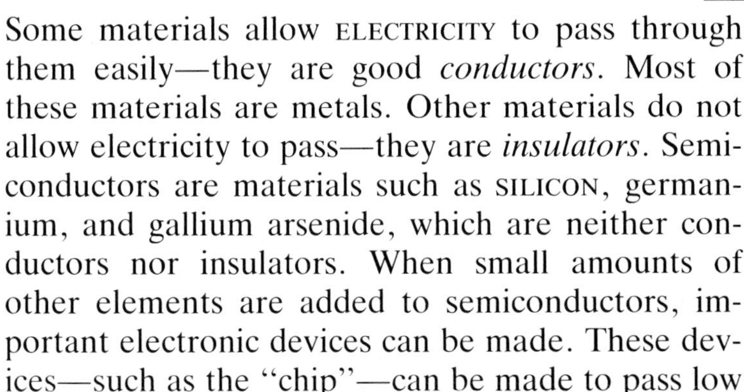

◀ *Seeds are scattered in many different ways. Some, such as the pea, are in pods that burst open when ripe. Others, such as the dandelion, are carried by the wind. Acorns and blackberries are stored or eaten by animals, while the burdock has tiny hooks that cling to animals' fur.*

the wind. Others are prickly and stick to the fur of passing animals. Many seeds contain the baby plant and a little supply of food. When the seed begins to grow, the baby plant takes in this food until it has roots and leaves and can make its own food.

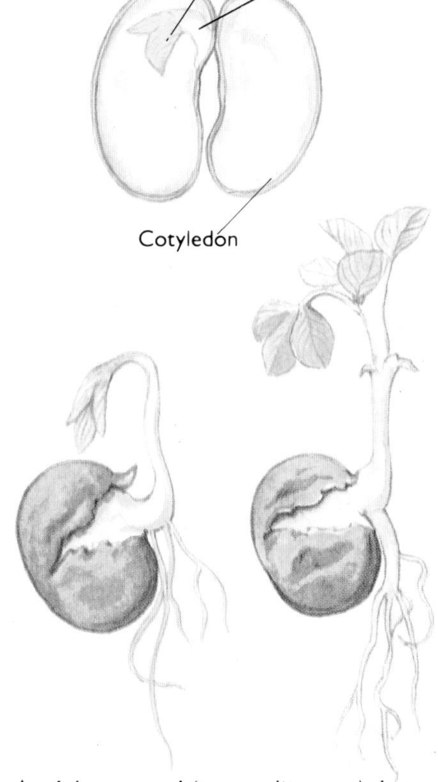

▲ *A bean seed (top, split open), has large fleshy cotyledons (seed leaves) and a radicle and plumule. The radicle grows downward into the soil, then the plumule appears, growing upward (above left). To protect the young shoot, it remains bent over until it reaches the surface (above right).*

Semiconductor

Some materials allow ELECTRICITY to pass through them easily—they are good *conductors*. Most of these materials are metals. Other materials do not allow electricity to pass—they are *insulators*. Semiconductors are materials such as SILICON, germanium, and gallium arsenide, which are neither conductors nor insulators. When small amounts of other elements are added to semiconductors, important electronic devices can be made. These devices—such as the "chip"—can be made to pass low

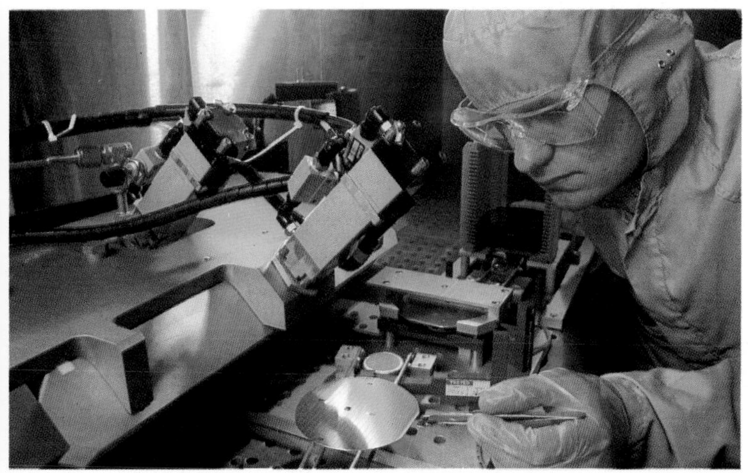

◀ *Wafer-thin slices of the semiconductor silicon are prepared for cutting into microchips.*

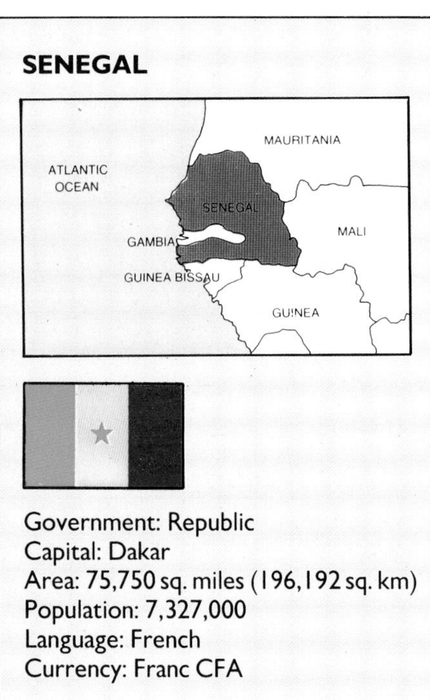

Government: Republic
Capital: Dakar
Area: 75,750 sq. miles (196,192 sq. km)
Population: 7,327,000
Language: French
Currency: Franc CFA

or high amounts of electric current, to block it completely, or to allow it to pass in one direction only. TRANSISTORS are made from semiconductors. Thousands of them can be made on a tiny chip.

Senegal

The country of Senegal lies on the far western coast of Africa. Neighboring Gambia is surrounded on three sides by Senegal. Peanuts are the country's chief crop and export. Millet and rice are also grown. Fishing is important.

Senegal was the first French colony in Africa. Full independence came in 1960. In 1982, Senegal and Gambia joined together in a defense and monetary confederation called Senegambia.

Senses *See* Ear, Eye, Hearing, Smell, Taste, Touch

Seven Wonders of the World

The Seven Wonders of the World were seven outstanding manmade objects that were built in ancient times and were so called because people marveled at them. Only one of these wonders, the PYRAMIDS, exists today. The others have all been destroyed.

The Hanging Gardens of Babylon were probably built high up on the walls of temples. They were probably a gift from King Nebuchadnezzar II to one of his wives.

The Temple of Artemis at Ephesus (now in Turkey). This temple was one of the largest in the ancient world. Some of its marble columns are in the British Museum in London.

The Statue of Zeus at Olympia, Greece, which showed the king of the gods on his throne. It was made of gold and ivory.

The tomb at Halicarnassus (now in Turkey), which was a massive tomb built for Mausolus, a ruler of Persia. It became so famous that all large tombs are now called *mausoleums*.

The Colossus of Rhodes in Greece, which was a huge, bronze statue of the sun god, Helios. It stood

SEVEN NATURAL WONDERS OF THE WORLD

1. Mount Everest on the Nepalese-Tibetan border.
2. Victoria Falls on the Zimbabwean-Zambian border.
3. Grand Canyon of the Colorado River in Arizona.
4. Great Barrier Reef of Australia, the largest coral reef in the world.
5. Mauna Loa, the world's largest active volcano, in Hawaii.
6. Rainbow Natural Bridge in Utah, the largest in the world.
7. Yellowstone National Park, the world's largest geyser area.

◀ *The Seven Wonders of the ancient world—only the Egyptian pyramids remain.*

It has been estimated that to build the Great Pyramid today would need at least 400 men using modern equipment to work for more than five years at a cost of over a billion dollars.

SEVEN WONDERS OF THE WORLD

1 The Pyramids of Egypt. 2 The Lighthouse of Pharos at Alexandria. 3 The Colossus of Rhodes. 4 The Statue of Zeus at Olympia. 5 The Hanging Gardens of Babylon. 6 The Temple of Artemis. 7 The Mausoleum at Halicarnassus.

towering high over the harbor entrance.

The Pharos of Alexandria in Egypt, which was the first modern lighthouse. It was built in 270 B.C. on the island of Pharos outside Alexandria harbor. It had a wood fire burning on top.

Sex *See* Reproduction

Seychelles

The islands of the Seychelles make up a small country about 1,000 miles (1,600 km) off the east coast of Africa in the Indian Ocean. The country has volcanic mountains, sandy beaches, and coconut palm

SEYCHELLES

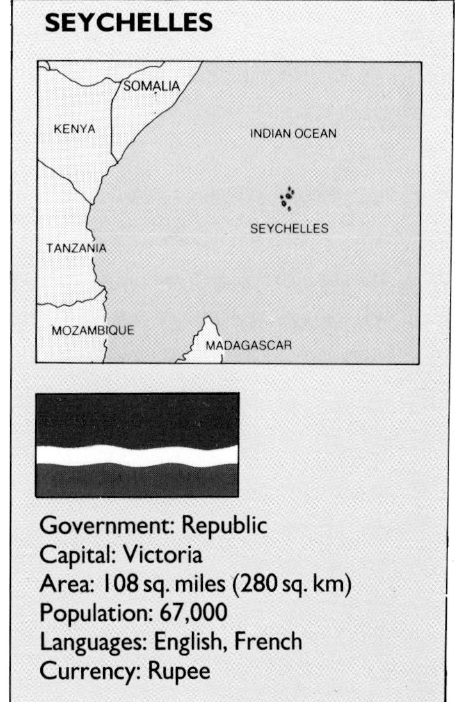

Government: Republic
Capital: Victoria
Area: 108 sq. miles (280 sq. km)
Population: 67,000
Languages: English, French
Currency: Rupee

▲ *William Shakespeare is probably the most famous name in English literature, but very few facts are known about his life.*

▼ *These sharks are all hunters. They have sharp teeth that grow in rows. As one set wears out, the row behind takes over (inset).*

plantations. Tourism is an important business. The islands were ruled by Britain, but gained their independence in 1976. The inhabitants are of mixed African and European ancestry.

Shakespeare, William

William Shakespeare (1564–1616) is thought by most people to be England's greatest writer. He is most famous for his plays—about 40 altogether—which include *A Midsummer Night's Dream*, *Hamlet*, *Macbeth*, and *Romeo and Juliet*.

Very little is known about Shakespeare's life. He was born in Stratford-upon-Avon and was the son of a glovemaker. When he was 18, he married Anne Hathaway, a farmer's daughter, and had three children. Then, at the age of 20, he left Stratford and went to London, where he became an actor and playwright. At the end of his life, he returned to Stratford. Shakespeare's plays are acted and studied all over the world. Many of the words and phrases we use today were first used by Shakespeare.

Shark

The shark family includes the world's largest and fiercest fish. Many sharks have a wedge-shaped head, a long body, and a triangular back fin that often sticks out of the water. Their skeletons are

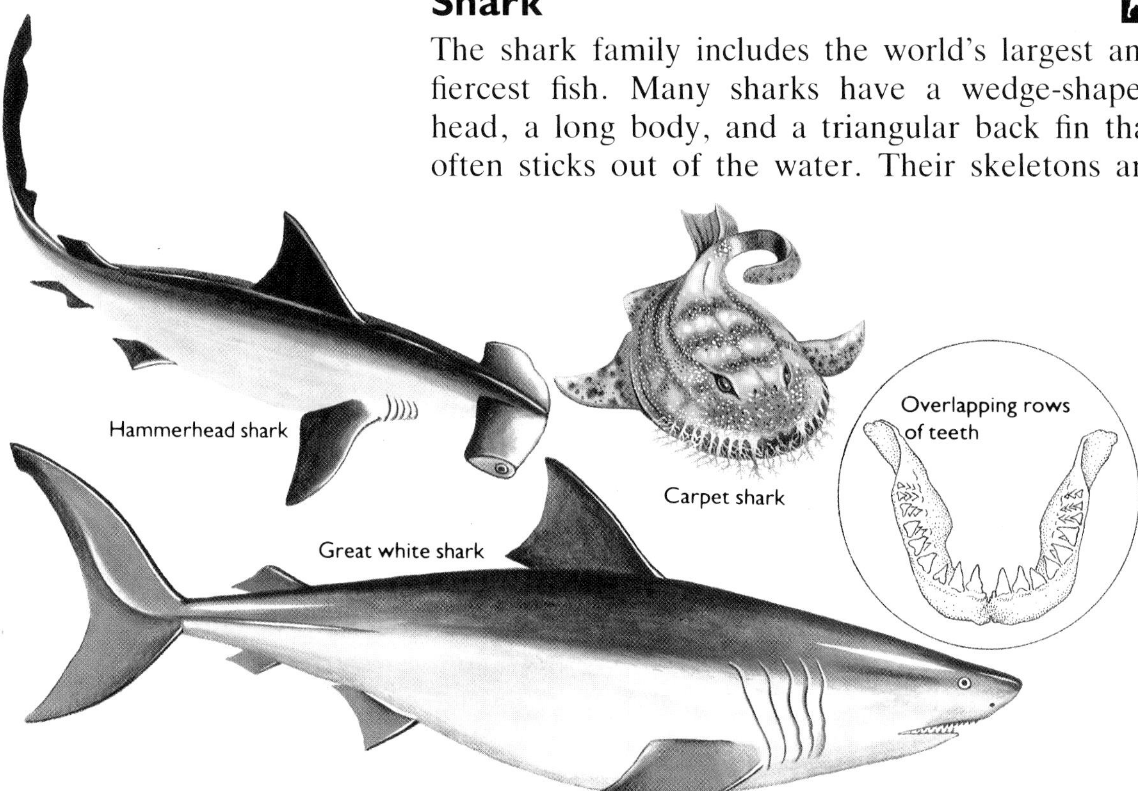

made of rubbery gristle, not bone. Most sharks live in warm seas. They vary greatly in size. The dogfish, one of the smallest sharks, is only 24 in. (60 cm) long. The largest fish in the oceans, the whale shark, measures over 50 ft. (15 m)—as long as two buses.

The whale shark and the basking shark are harmless to people and other animals because they live on plankton. But many sharks are cruel killers with rows of razor-sharp teeth. Several will attack humans. The greediest monster, the great white shark, swallows its prey whole. The remains of big animals, such as horses, seals, and other sharks, have been found in its stomach.

Other dangerous sharks are the blue shark, the tiger shark, and the leopard shark, which has leopard-like spots. The smell of blood in water can cause sharks to attack anything nearby, even other sharks.

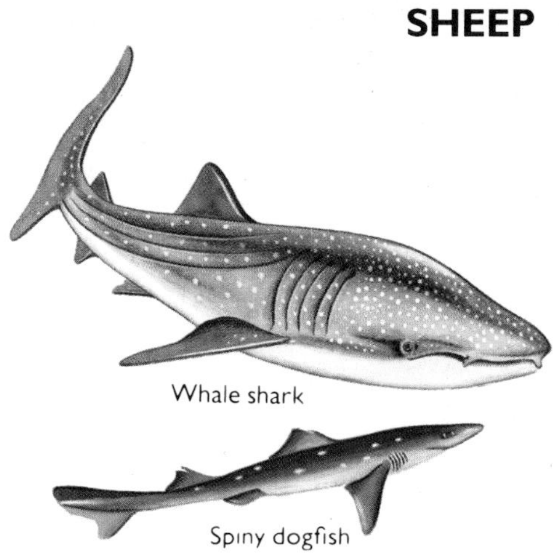

▲ *The smallest and the largest members of the shark family. The dogfish is about 24 in. (60 cm) long, while the whale shark is more than 50 ft. (15 m) long.*

Sheep

Sheep have been kept as domestic animals for thousands of years. At first, sheep were kept for their milk and skins. Milk could be made into cheese, and the skins were used for clothing. Then people discovered that the animals' thick coats could be *sheared* (shaved off) and the wool woven into cloth. Today, sheep are kept mainly for wool and for meat (*mutton* or *lamb*).

▲ *The mouflon is a truly wild sheep that lives in mountain areas in mainland Europe and in open country on Mediterranean islands.*

◀ *Modern sheep have been specially bred to give the best combination of wool and meat.*

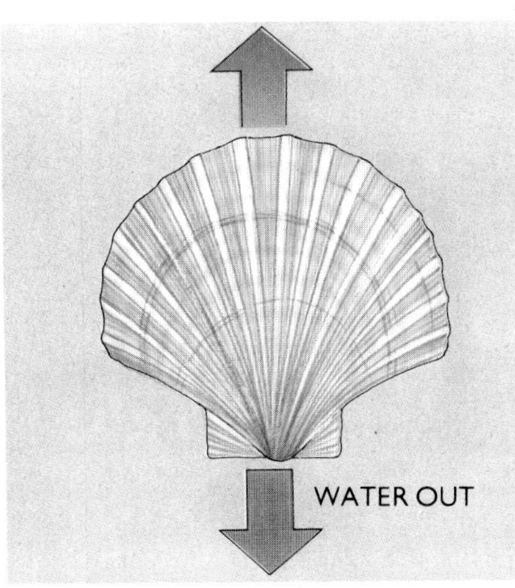

▲ *Scallops swim by opening their shells and then shutting them quickly. The jet of water they force out pushes them along.*

Shells and Shellfish

Many animals live inside shells. This is because they have soft bodies that need protection. Shells are usually hard and are all sizes and colors. The shells of some sea snails are no bigger than a grain of sand, but the giant clam of the Pacific Ocean has a shell 48 in. (120 cm) across.

Some land animals such as SNAILS have shells, but most creatures with shells belong in the sea. Shelled sea animals include MOLLUSKS and CRUSTACEANS. Some of these, such as OYSTERS, scallops, and LOBSTERS, can be eaten. They are often called shellfish, although they are not really fish at all. Shellfish have been an important food for thousands of years. In some places, kitchen refuse of prehistoric people has been found that consists entirely of enormous mounds of shells, as high as a two-story house.

► *Many different types of mollusk shell can be found on the seashore.*

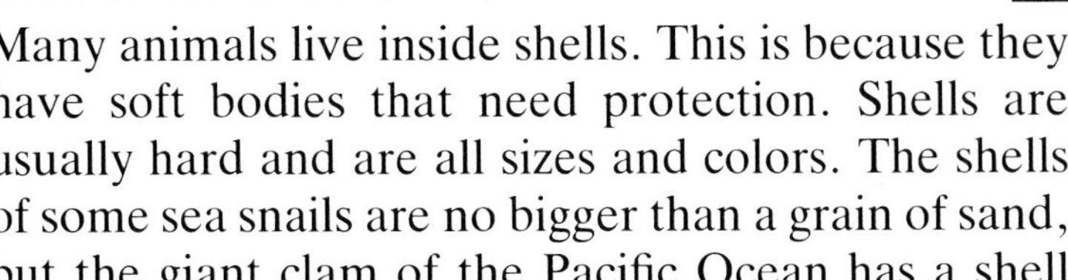

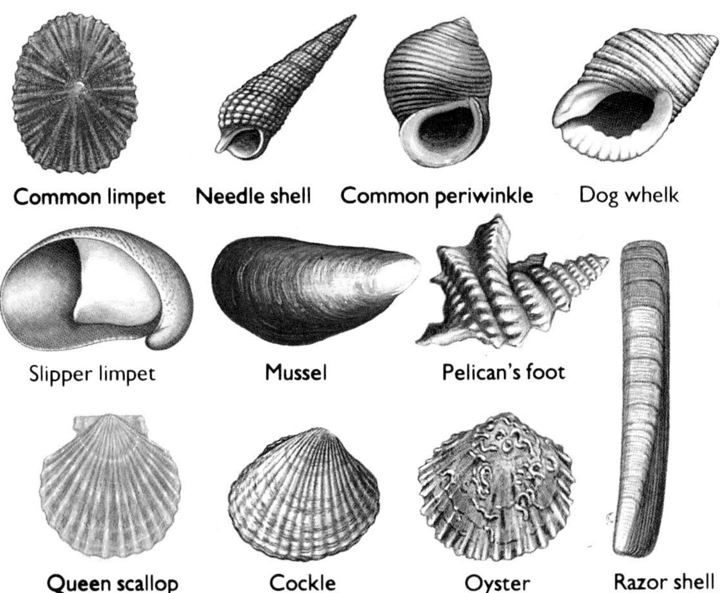

▼ *The tellin buries itself in the sand and then sucks tiny pieces of food from the water through a tube it extends above the surface.*

Shinto

Shinto is a Japanese religion. The word "Shinto" means "the way of the gods." Unlike other religions, Shinto does not teach that there is one supreme being. It says that there is an eternal truth called *kami*. Kami is to be found in every form of nature and in rivers, mountains, and lakes. All over Japan, there are shrines, large and small, dedicated to different kami.

Ship

Today, most ships are cargo vessels. They are usually built to carry a certain type of cargo. *Tankers* carry liquids such as oil or wine. Some oil tankers are so long that the crew can ride bicycles around the deck. *Bulk carriers* take dry cargoes like coal and wheat that can be loaded loose. *Container ships* carry all kinds of goods packed in large boxes called containers. *Refrigerator ships* are for carrying fresh food such as fruit and meat.

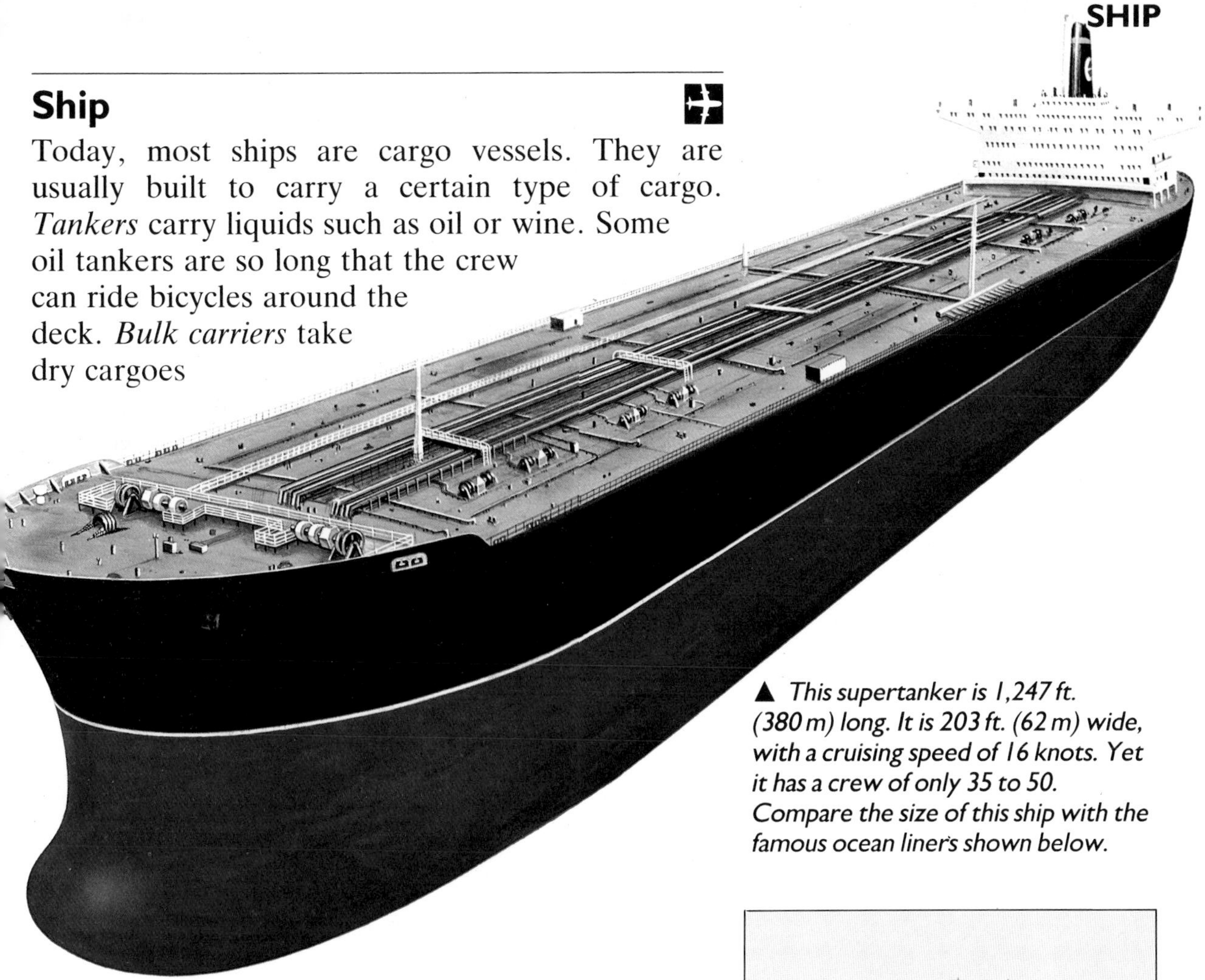

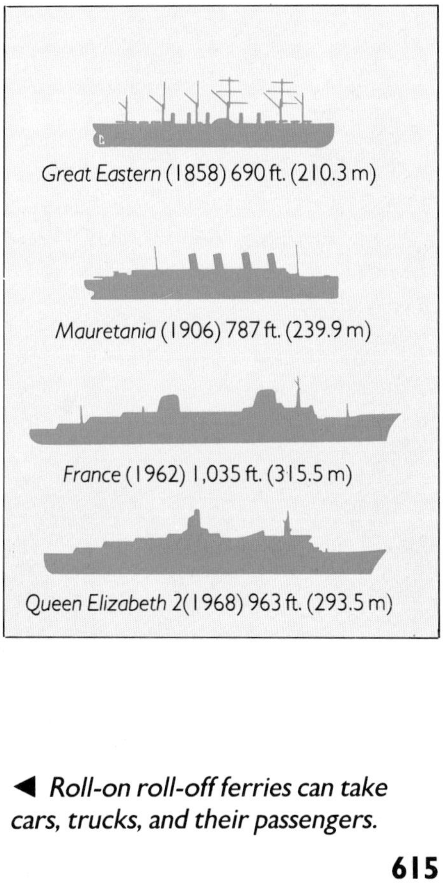

Planes have replaced most passenger ships, but there are still many ferries that take people and ve-

▲ *This supertanker is 1,247 ft. (380 m) long. It is 203 ft. (62 m) wide, with a cruising speed of 16 knots. Yet it has a crew of only 35 to 50. Compare the size of this ship with the famous ocean liners shown below.*

Great Eastern (1858) 690 ft. (210.3 m)

Mauretania (1906) 787 ft. (239.9 m)

France (1962) 1,035 ft. (315.5 m)

Queen Elizabeth 2 (1968) 963 ft. (293.5 m)

◀ *Roll-on roll-off ferries can take cars, trucks, and their passengers.*

▶ *Aircraft carriers must have enough room on deck for planes and helicopters to take off and land.*

hicles across smaller stretches of water. There are also luxury cruise liners. Various kinds of warship are used by navies.

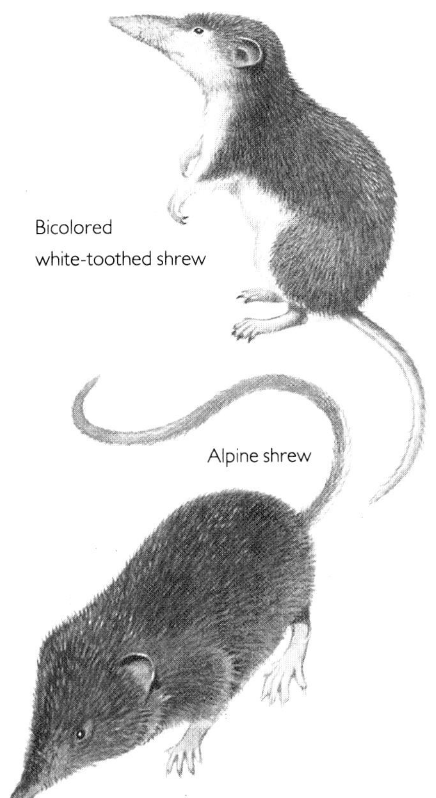

▲ *Shrews often fall prey to larger night hunters, such as owls, cats, or even badgers.*

Shrew

Shrews are furry creatures about the size of a mouse. They have a pointed snout and are seldom seen because they only come out at night. Shrews are very active animals and have to eat almost continually to live. They eat insects and worms.

Siberia

Siberia is a vast region that covers most of Russia, east of the Ural Mountains. It is a very cold land. Along Siberia's northern coast lies the *tundra*,

▶ *The huge area covered by Siberia is largely undeveloped, and many animals enjoy the unspoiled habitat. Lake Baikal, right, is home to many species of animal not found anywhere else in the world, including the world's only freshwater seal.*

a cold semi-desert. Forests cover about a third of Siberia's 5,790,000 sq. miles (15,000,000 sq. km). Toward the Mongolian border lies Lake Baikal, the largest freshwater lake in Asia or Europe.

For some years, the Russian government has been encouraging young people to settle in Siberia to develop the region.

Sierra Leone

Sierra Leone is a country on the west coast of Africa. It is almost the size of South Carolina. The climate is hot and damp. Around Freetown, the capital, about 150 in. (380 cm) of rain falls each year. Most people are farmers, producing rice, palm kernels, ginger, coffee, and cocoa. Iron ore, bauxite, and diamonds are mined.

Sierra Leone was a British colony. It became an independent state within the British Commonwealth in 1961 and a republic in 1971.

SIERRA LEONE

GUINEA BISSAU
MALI
GUINEA
SIERRA LEONE
LIBERIA
COTE D'IVOIRE
ATLANTIC OCEAN

Government: Republic
Capital: Freetown
Area: 27,700 sq. miles (71,740 sq. km)
Population: 4,151,000
Language: English
Currency: Leone

Sikhs

Sikhs are people who live in the Punjab in northern India. The Sikh religion was started by a pious man called Nanak (1469–1539). He was the first Sikh *guru* (teacher). The teachings of the *gurus* were written in the Sikh sacred book, the *Granth*. This was kept at Amritsar in the Golden Temple.

The Sikhs were a warlike people. They fought

Many devout Sikhs in their own land carry a short dagger, or *kirpan*. They may also wear a bangle, a comb, and short pants.

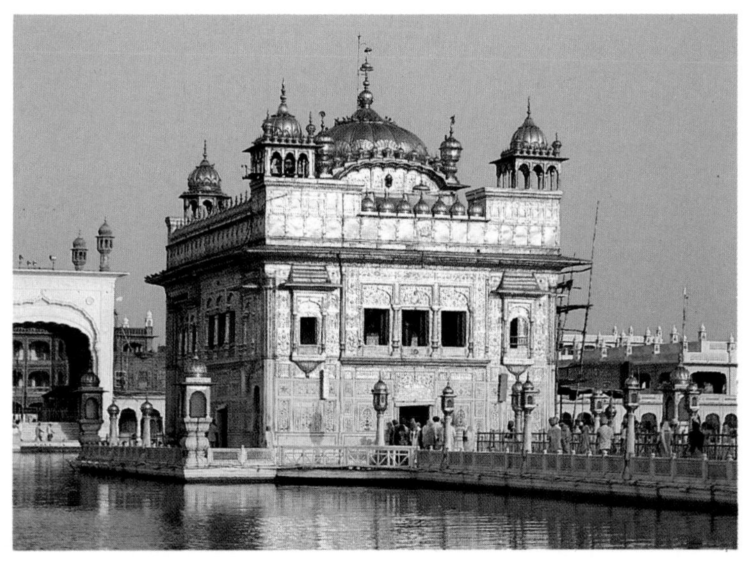

◀ *The Golden Temple of Amritsar, in the Punjab, is sacred to Sikhs. It was built in 1579 on land granted by the Mogul emperor Akbar.*

against the Muslim rulers of India and against the British.

Sikh men do not shave or cut their hair, and they wear a turban. There are about 14 million Sikhs.

▲ *This silicon chip, the tiny square in the center of the panel, is smaller than any of the cherries around it. Yet its circuits are capable of running a small computer.*

Silicon Chip

Silicon chips are tiny pieces of the ELEMENT silicon. (Silicon is a SEMICONDUCTOR.) They can be made to carry very small electrical circuits, called microcircuits. These are used in transistor radios, digital watches, calculators, and computers. Because the chips are so small, the electronic devices in which they are used can be small, too.

Silk

Silk is a natural fiber made from the cocoon of one kind of moth. Silkworms, which are really caterpillars, are kept in special containers and fed on mulberry leaves for about four weeks. At the end of this time, they spin their cocoons and start to turn into moths. Then they are killed, and each cocoon is unwound as a long thread between 2,000 and 3,000 ft. (600 and 900 m) long.

Silk was first used in Asia centuries ago, especially in China and Japan. Silk WEAVING in Europe began in the 1400s. Silk makes a very fine, soft material. It was used for stockings before nylon was invented. Silk can be made into other fabrics such as satin and chiffon, and can be dyed in beautiful colors.

▼ *Once the silkworms have eaten enough mulberry leaves, they start to spin their cocoons. They produce a liquid through a hole in their lower lip which hardens in the air and makes the fine silk thread. The cocoons are put into hot water to loosen the threads for winding. The threads from several cocoons are wound together to make a stronger thread.*

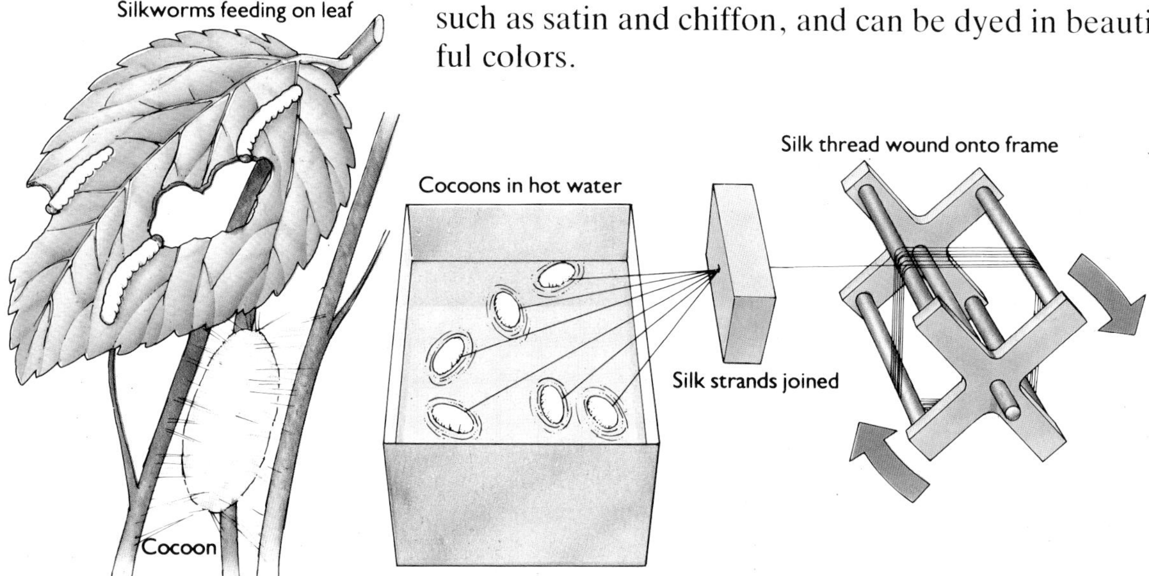

◀ *This set of silverware consists of a mug, napkin ring, knife, spoon, and fork, all made in 1903.*

Silver

Silver is a precious metal. It has been used by people all over the world for thousands of years. Although many countries have silver deposits, the mining process is very expensive.

Silver bends very easily and can be beaten into many shapes and patterns. Like gold, it can be hammered out into thin sheets. It is used to make useful and decorative things such as spoons and forks, bowls, and jewelry. Sometimes, it is used as a coating on cheaper metals such as copper or nickel, to make them look like silver. It can also be mixed with another metal (usually copper), and then it is called *sterling* silver.

Silver used to be made into coins, but most of today's "silver" coins are really made of a mixture of copper and nickel.

Silver carries electricity well and is used this way in industry. Some chemicals made from silver react to light and are used in photography. Another chemical, silver nitrate, is painted on the back of glass to make mirrors.

The chemical symbol for silver is AG, from the Latin *argentum*, meaning "white and shining." It melts at 1,761°F (960.8°C) and boils at 4,010°F (2,210°C). A tiny gram of the metal can be drawn into a wire nearly a mile long. The main silver-producing countries are the United States and Mexico.

Singapore

Singapore is a small country in SOUTHEAST ASIA, off the southern end of the Malay peninsula. Three-fourths of the population are Chinese, but people from all over the world live there.

The capital city is also called Singapore. It has

SINGAPORE

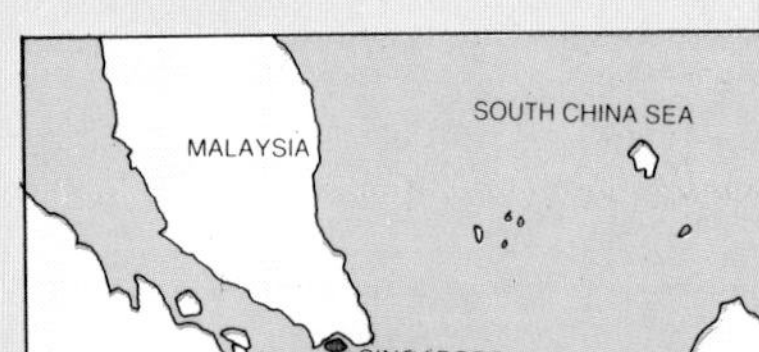

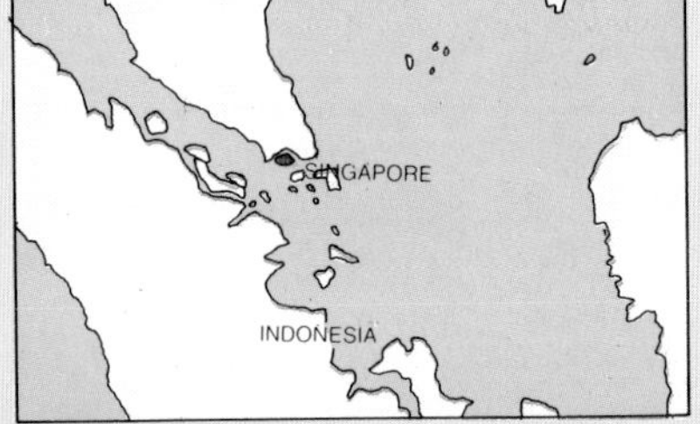

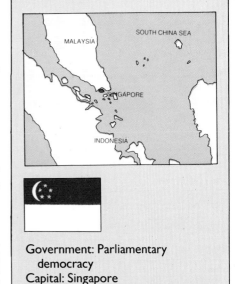

Government: Parliamentary democracy
Capital: Singapore
Area: 224 sq. miles (581 sq. km)
Population: 3,003,000
Languages: Chinese, Malay, Tamil, English
Currency: Singapore dollar

▲ *Skaters Jayne Torvill and Christopher Dean were champions in the ice dancing field in the 1980s.*

one of the busiest ports in the world and trades with many countries. For a short time, Singapore was part of Malaysia, but now it has its own government. It is a member of the British Commonwealth.

Skating

Roller skating and ice skating are both popular sports. Roller skates have four wheels made of steel and rubber. Ice skates have a thin steel blade.

There are two main kinds of ice skating. Figure skating and ice-dancing to music are Olympic sports. Speed skaters race against each other.

The first ice skates had runners, or blades, of bone. Today, figure skates have jagged teeth at the front to help grip the ice when starting and stopping. Speed skates have longer blades.

Ice hockey players also wear skates.

Skeleton

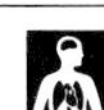

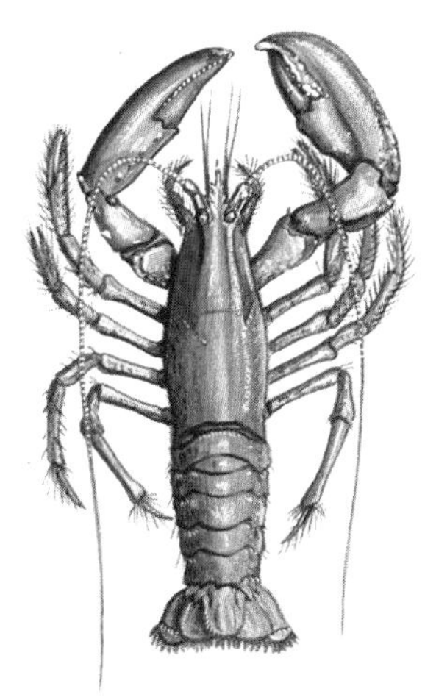

▲ *Lobsters have an exoskeleton, that is, their skeleton is in the form of hard plates on the outside of their body.*

Our skeleton is made up of BONES. If we did not have a skeleton, our bodies would be shapeless blobs. The skeleton protects our vital organs, such as the heart, liver, and lungs. It is also an anchor for our MUSCLES.

In humans and other animals with backbones (VERTEBRATES), the skeleton is inside the body, covered by the flesh and skin. In other animals, such as INSECTS and SPIDERS, the skeleton is like a hard crust on the outside of the body. It is called an *exoskeleton*. Some animals, such as the jellyfish and octopus, do not have a skeleton. Their bodies are supported by the water they live in.

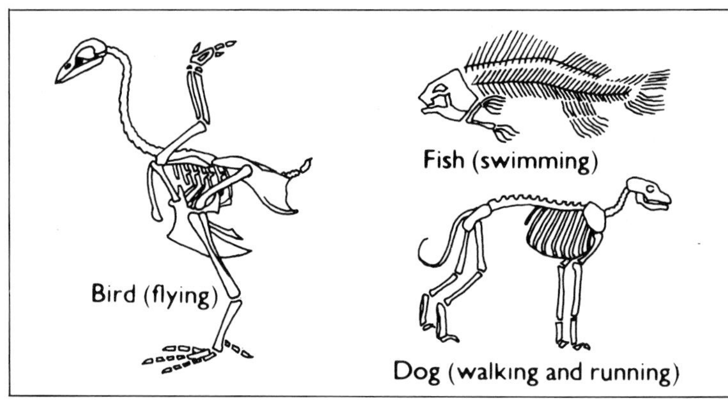

► *Examples of animals with internal skeletons. The shape of their skeleton is perfectly adapted to the way they move.*

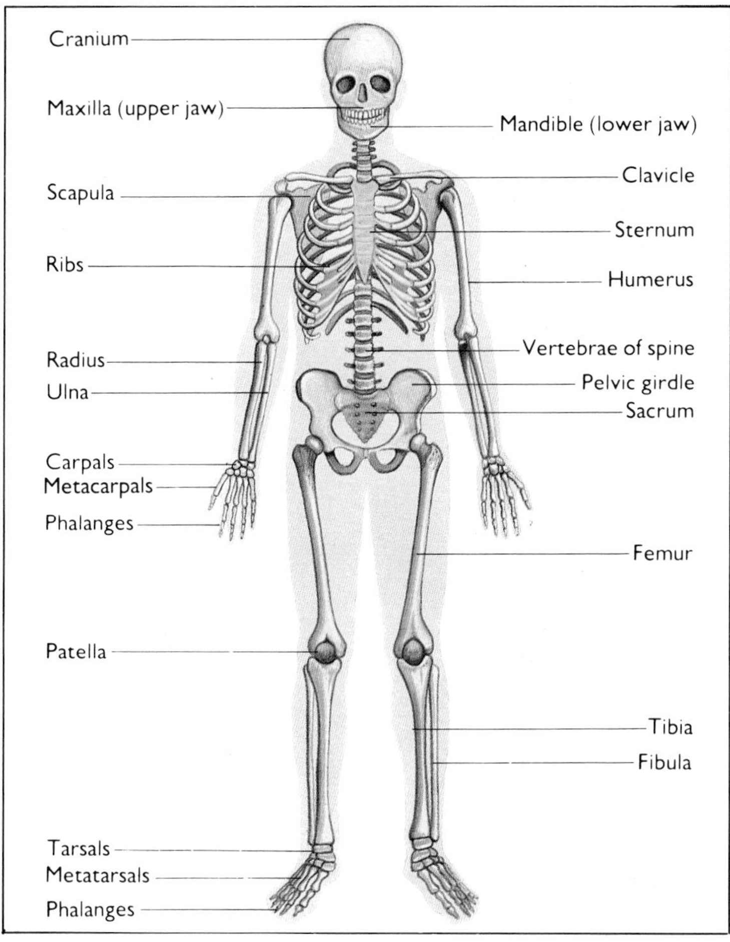

◄ *The skeleton provides a framework for your body, holding it together and supporting its weight. Bones also protect important organs.*

Babies are born with about 350 bones. But as a child grows, some of these bones join together, and an adult ends up with about 206. The number varies because some people have more bones in their hands and feet than others. The largest bone in your body is the *femur*, or thigh bone. The smallest is the *stapes*, or stirrup bone, in your middle ear. It is only about 0.1 inch (2 mm) long.

There are more than 200 bones in the human skeleton. They include the bones of the spine, skull (which protects the brain), ribs, pelvis, breastbone, and limbs. Joints are places where bones meet. Some joints (like those in the skull) do not move. Others, like those in the shoulders and hips, help us to move around. Muscles across the joints tighten, or *contract*, to move the bones.

A human skeleton develops before a baby is born and grows along with the body.

Skiing

Skiing is a way of moving across snow on long runners or skis. It probably started around 3000 B.C. The oldest skis ever found date back to 2500 B.C., and we know that the VIKINGS used skis. Today, skiing is a popular sport and is part of the Winter OLYMPIC GAMES.

There are four main kinds of skiing: cross-

▼ *Great skill and split-second timing are needed to tackle slalom races in skiing.*

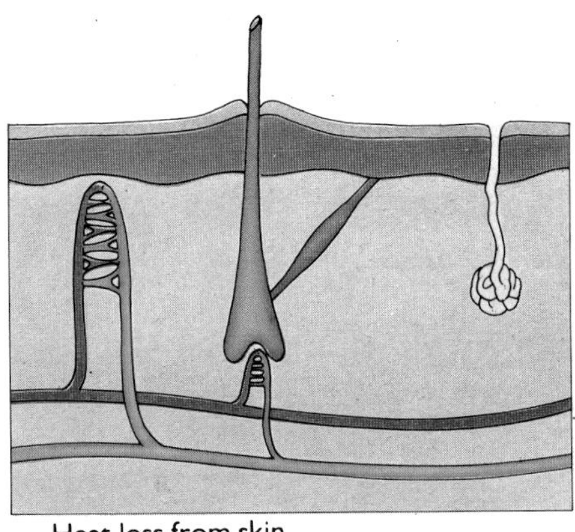

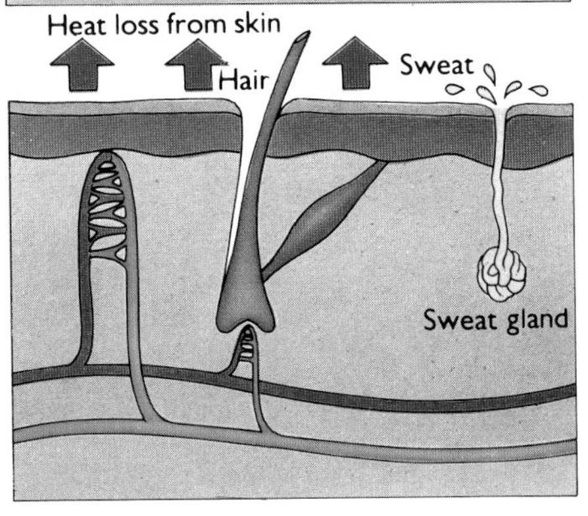

▲ *The skin goes through changes to make you warmer or cooler. When you are cold, erector muscles make the tiny hairs on the skin stand upright to trap a layer of warm air (top). When you are hot, the hairs lie flat to let the air circulate, and sweat evaporates from the skin to cool you (above).*

► *The skin is a waterproof, elastic covering for the body. It helps to keep germs and dirt out, and can even repair itself. Sebaceous glands give off oil that keeps the skin from becoming too dry.*

The common skunk grows to a length of about 11 to 14 in. (28 to 36 cm), with a 17 in. (43 cm) tail. When attacked, it can spray its foul-smelling liquid accurately as far as $11^1/_2$ ft. (3.5 m). Before it sprays, the animal gives warning by stamping its front feet and hissing.

country, slalom (obstacle course), downhill, and ski jumping. Downhill skiing is especially popular. There are special ski resorts in the mountains of Europe, North America, and Australia, where people can spend their vacations skiing.

Skin

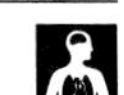

Skin is the covering on the outside of our bodies. It protects our bodies and is sensitive to heat, cold, and pain. Human skin can be quite thick and hard on places that get a lot of wear, such as the soles of the feet. It can also be very thin on other places, such as the eyelids.

Human skin is made up of two layers. The outer layer, the *epidermis*, contains a chemical called melanin which gives skin its color. The inner layer, the *dermis*, contains nerves, blood vessels, sweat glands, and the roots of hairs. The skin of an adult human covers about 2 sq. yds. (1.7 sq. m).

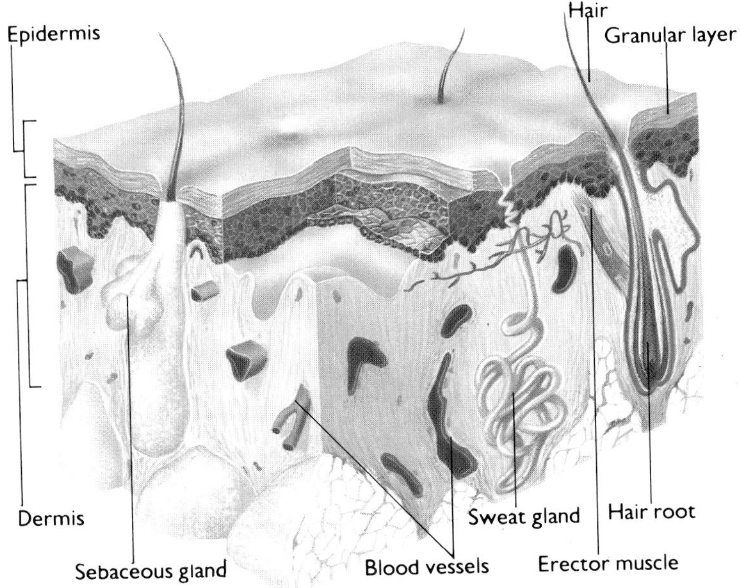

Skunk

Skunks are MAMMALS, members of the same family as weasels and BADGERS. There are three kinds: the hog-nosed, the spotted, and the striped skunk. They all live in North America. The best known is the striped skunk, which is black with white markings on its back. All skunks are able to drive away enemies by squirting a stinking liquid from a gland under their tails. If another animal is hit by this liquid, the smell will cling to its fur for days.

Skunks eat most kinds of food, including insects, rats, mice, birds, eggs, and plants. They feed at night and sleep in burrows during the day.

Skydiving

Skydiving is a form of parachute jumping. It started in the 1940s, and now it is a popular sport. Skydivers jump from an aircraft and fall a long way before they open their parachutes. They have to steer their parachutes to land on a target on the ground.

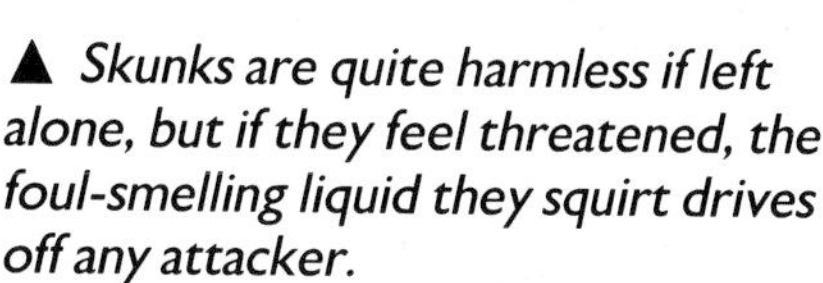

▲ *Skunks are quite harmless if left alone, but if they feel threatened, the foul-smelling liquid they squirt drives off any attacker.*

Skyscraper

"Skyscraper" is a name for a very tall building. The first one was built in 1884 in Chicago. It was designed by William Le Baron Jenney, and it had an iron frame.

All the early skyscrapers were built in New York and Chicago. Now they are built all over the world. For many years, the tallest skyscraper in the world was the Empire State Building in New York—102 stories high. Now there are two taller—the Sears Tower in Chicago and the World Trade Center in New York, which are both 110 stories. The Sears Tower is higher at 1,453 ft. (443 m).

▼ *The skyline of Vancouver, British Columbia, includes many impressive skyscrapers.*

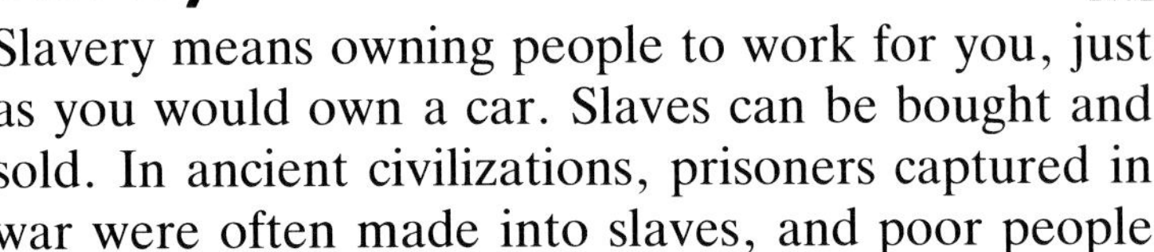

Slavery

Slavery means owning people to work for you, just as you would own a car. Slaves can be bought and sold. In ancient civilizations, prisoners captured in war were often made into slaves, and poor people sometimes sold their children as slaves.

From the 1500s, the Spanish took people from Africa as slaves for their colonies in America. By the 1770s, British ships were carrying slaves to America. Hundreds were packed tightly into ships. Conditions were terrible, and many slaves died on the way. Britain abolished the slave trade in 1808. Slavery was ended in the U.S.A. in 1865, after the Civil War. But racial discrimination continued even after civil rights laws were passed to guarantee equal rights for black people.

▲ *The abolition of the slave trade was largely due to William Wilberforce (1759–1833). He was a Church of England priest who became a politician and campaigned for more than 20 years to have slavery banned.*

► *The conditions suffered by the people who were kidnapped and made slaves were appalling. Many died on the ships carrying them from Africa to the Americas.*

Sleep and Dreams

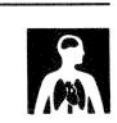

Sleep is a time when we are unconscious and resting. People and some animals need sleep to stay healthy. Without it, people become short-tempered, and after a long time, they may start having *hallucinations*—seeing things that are not there.

There are four different stages of sleep. At each stage, the electrical waves given off by the brain change. When we are deeply asleep, these waves are slow and large. When we are only lightly asleep, the waves are faster. This is the time when we—and all mammals—dream.

Most people need less sleep as they grow older. Someone who slept 8 hours a day when he or she was 30 years old may need only 7 hours of sleep at the age of 60. Young babies sleep most of the time; 4-year-olds average from 10 to 14 hours sleep a day; 10-year-olds from 9 to 12 hours.

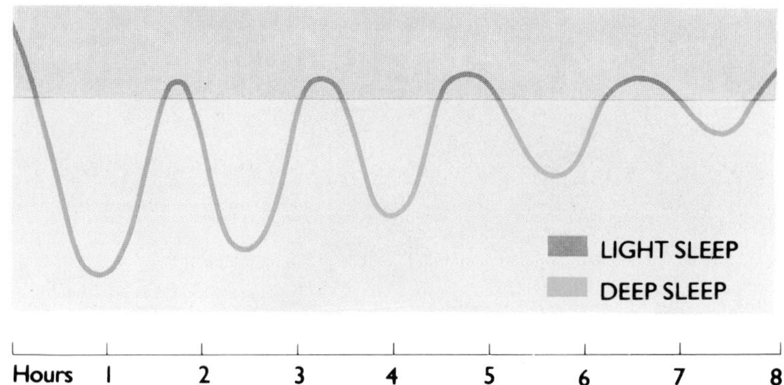

◀ *The electrical waves given off by the brain during sleep can be measured to show the periods of light and deep sleep. Dreams happen during periods of light sleep. As morning comes near, the periods of light sleep last longer.*

Different people need different amounts of sleep. Babies need a lot. Adults need between six and nine hours a night.

Sloth

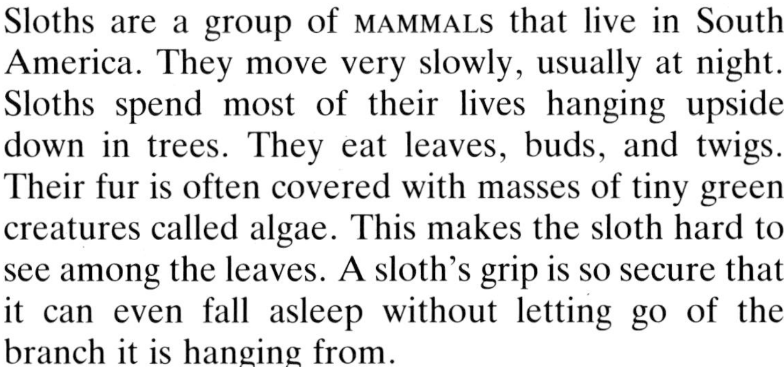

Sloths are a group of MAMMALS that live in South America. They move very slowly, usually at night. Sloths spend most of their lives hanging upside down in trees. They eat leaves, buds, and twigs. Their fur is often covered with masses of tiny green creatures called algae. This makes the sloth hard to see among the leaves. A sloth's grip is so secure that it can even fall asleep without letting go of the branch it is hanging from.

There are two main kinds of sloth—the two-toed and the three-toed.

We call someone "slothful" when we mean he or she is lazy and slow.

▲ *Sloths move very slowly—they sleep for about 19 hours a day, and when they do move, it is only at a speed of about 6 ft. (2 m) a minute.*

Smell

Smell is an important sense, like sight and hearing. Humans and other MAMMALS smell through the nose. We sniff the air, and the scents given off by the things around us are picked up by special cells in the nose. These cells send messages to the BRAIN.

Our sense of smell is useful when we are eating. It helps us to TASTE things. It can also let us know when food is bad. Most other animals have a much better sense of smell than humans. Dogs can use their sense of smell to track down and follow prey. Moths do not have noses, but they can still smell things a long way off.

▼ *Our sense of smell is closely linked to our sense of taste. When we have a cold and lose our sense of smell, it makes our food taste less interesting.*

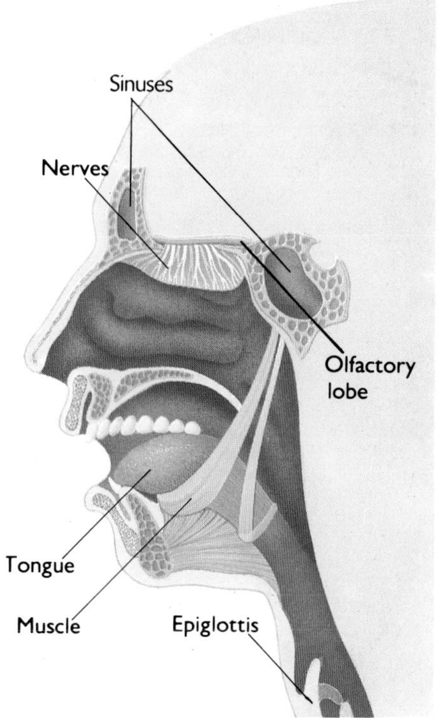

▶ *Air pollution in the form of smog blankets the city of Santiago in Chile. Smog can be so serious in some places that doctors advise people not to do exercise that will cause them to breathe heavily.*

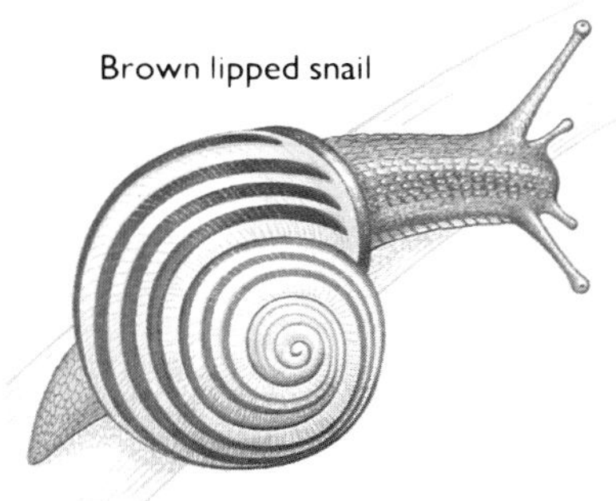

▲ *All snails are mollusks; those shown here eat living or dead plant matter. Snails often seal up their shells with slime which hardens into a parchment-like cap.*

▼ *The coral snake's bright colors are not just decoration. They are a warning to other creatures that the snake is poisonous.*

Smog

There are two kinds of smog. One is a very thick, smelly mixture of smoke and fog. It used to be very common in London. In the winter of 1952, there was a bad smog, and about 4,000 people died of chest diseases. Since then, laws have been made to make sure there is less smoke in London and no more smog.

The other kind of smog is caused by air pollution from car exhausts and other fumes. These are changed by sunlight into a white mist that hangs over cities. Smog of this sort can be dangerous to the people who live in cities.

Snail

Snails are MOLLUSKS with a coiled shell on their back. There are more than 80,000 kinds in the world. Some live on land, some in fresh water, and some in the sea. Snails move slowly, leaving a glistening, slimy trail on land. They feed on plants.

Most are less than $1\frac{1}{4}$ in. (3 cm) long. But one of the largest, the giant land snail, is about 8 in. (20 cm) long.

Snake

Snakes are REPTILES. They are long and thin and have no arms or legs. They move along by wriggling their bodies.

Snakes have a dry, smooth skin. Most live in warm places. Those that live in colder climates spend the winter in *hibernation*.

A few snakes have poison glands. They inject this poison into animals that they bite. The rattlesnake and the cobra are both poisonous snakes.

Most snakes hatch from eggs. A female snake can lay up to ten eggs at a time. Others give birth to live young. The largest snakes are pythons and anacondas. They can grow to 33 ft. (10 m) long.

▲ *Pythons are called* constrictors *because they squeeze their prey to death. They can unhinge their jaws to swallow large prey whole. It may take a python many days to digest a victim.*

▼ *Two North American snakes. The diamondback rattlesnake (below) is one of the most dangerous; the Eastern garter snake (bottom) is harmless.*

Snooker and Billiards

Snooker and billiards are popular games played with a wooden cue on a billiards table. Billiards is by far the older; snooker has only been played since the beginning of this century.

Snow

Snow starts off as water vapor high in the sky. Where the air is cold enough, the water vapor molecules collect to form water droplets that may fall as rain. If it is very cold, the water vapor freezes into tiny ice crystals. The crystals stick together to make snowflakes. There may be hundreds of ice crystals in a large snowflake.

No two snowflakes look the same, but they all have six sides. If the air is moist and not too cold, the snow crystals can grow into large snowflakes, sometimes more than an inch across.

In the old days, crude soaps were made by using wood ashes boiled up with dripping and other fat from the kitchen. The result looked something like putty and was not very efficient.

Soap was a luxury in Tudor times. Queen Elizabeth I is said to have had only one bath a month.

Soap

Soap is used for cleaning things. It is made by mixing FAT or vegetable oil with a chemical such as lye. It loosens dirt in clothes and carries it away. Today, chemical cleaners called DETERGENTS are often used instead. Detergents clean better than soap in hard water, but they do not by themselves make suds. Suds are not necessary for cleaning, but substances that make suds are added to detergents.

Soccer

The team sport of soccer is the world's most popular sport. The basic rules are very simple: two teams of 11 players each try to score goals by getting the soccer ball into the other team's net. The goalkeeper, or goalie, is the only player who can touch the ball with his or her arms or hands. Most goals and passes are kicked or "headed" past the opposing players. Soccer's biggest event is the World Cup, held every four years. National teams from all over the world compete for the championship.

SEE IT YOURSELF

To show that soil is made up of different particles, put a sample of soil in a jar of water and shake. When you stop shaking, the heavier particles sink to the bottom, and the soil separates into its different layers (shown above). You should be able to calculate (roughly) how much sand, clay, and silt there was in your original soil sample.

Softball

Softball is one of the most popular team sports in the United States. The rules of softball are like those of BASEBALL, except the field is smaller, pitching is underhand, and an extra fielder can be allowed. Also, a softball is larger than a baseball.

Soil

Soil is a layer of small MINERAL particles on the surface of the EARTH. It covers the rocks the Earth is made of and is sometimes quite thick. Soil may be sand or clay, and may contain the rotted remains of plants, called *humus*.

If soil particles are very fine, it is called clay. If they are coarser, it is silt, and if they are very coarse, it is called sand. Good soil is a mixture of all of these, with plenty of humus. People often add animal manure or chemical FERTILIZERS to poor soil. This makes the soil richer in extra minerals.

Solar Energy

Solar energy is energy from the Sun. It reaches the Earth as light and heat. Without these things there could be no life on Earth.

Only about 15 percent of the Sun's energy that reaches the Earth is absorbed by the Earth's surface. Much of it bounces off the Earth and back into space. Solar energy can be collected by special panels and mirrors and used to make electricity.

▲ *Solar panels can be used to collect energy from the Sun. The energy can be made into electricity or just used to help heat a house.*

Solar System

The solar system is made up of the SUN and the planets traveling around it. MERCURY is the planet nearest the Sun. Next come VENUS, EARTH, MARS, JUPITER, SATURN, URANUS, NEPTUNE, and PLUTO.

Until the 1500s, most people thought that the

◀ *Seen in comparison with the Sun and the "giant" planets, the Earth looks very small. The nine planets in our solar system are:*
1 Mercury
2 Venus
3 Earth
4 Mars
5 Jupiter
6 Saturn
7 Uranus
8 Neptune
9 Pluto

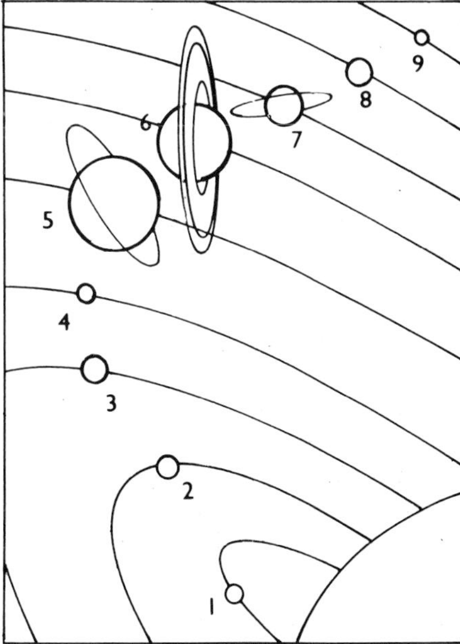

Earth was the center of the universe and that the Sun and planets traveled around it. In 1543, a Polish astronomer, Nicolaus Copernicus, discovered that, in fact, the Earth moved around the Sun.

SOLOMON ISLANDS

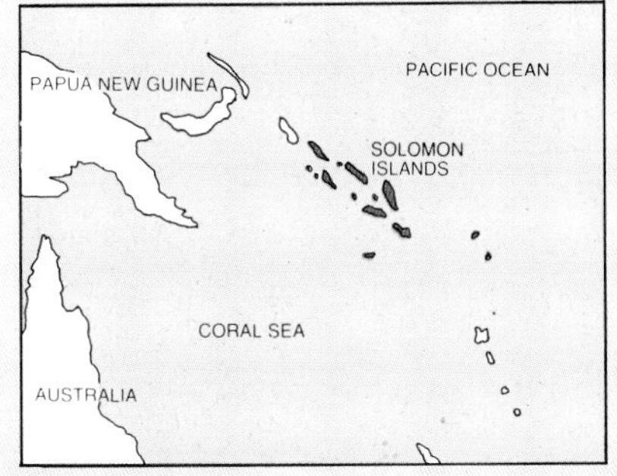

Government: Parliamentary democracy
Capital: Honiara
Area: 10,640 sq. miles (27,557 sq. km)
Population: 321,000
Language: English
Currency: Solomon Islands dollar

Solomon Islands

The Solomon Islands lie in the Pacific Ocean about 1,000 miles (1,600 km) from Australia. They are an independent state within the British Commonwealth. The long chain of islands stretches for about 870 miles (1,400 km), but the total area of the Solomons is only slightly more than the state of Maryland. The chief crops are coconuts, rice, and bananas. There is a fish canning industry.

SOMALIA

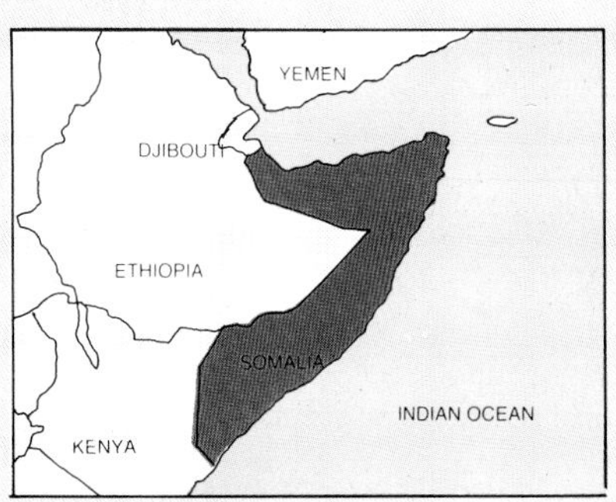

Government: Independent republic
Capital: Mogadishu
Area: 246,300 sq. miles (637,917 sq. km)
Population: 7,497,000
Languages: Somali, Arabic
Currency: Somali shilling

Somalia

Somalia is a country in an area called the "Horn of Africa"—the easternmost part of Africa, jutting out into the Indian Ocean. It is a poor country; most of the people are nomads. Low rainfall means that agriculture is possible only around the Shebelle and Juba rivers. The chief crops are sugar, bananas, sorghum, and incense. In recent years, the country has been plagued by war and drought.

Sonar

Sonar is used in ships to find the depth of anything beneath them. It can measure the depth of the seabed as well as locate submarines and schools of fish.

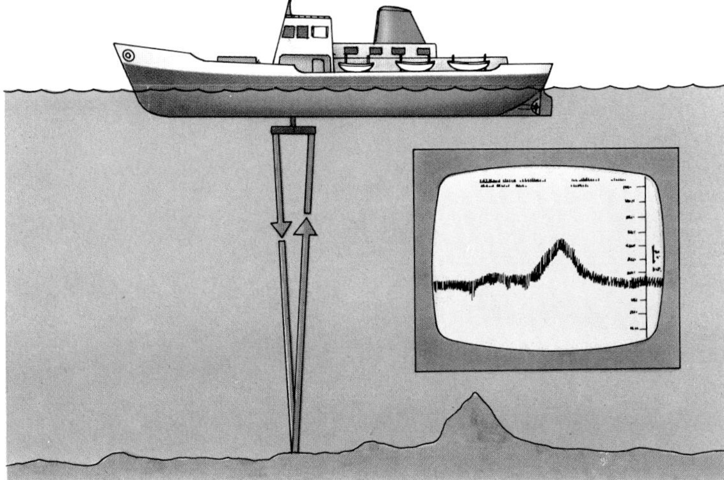

► *Sonar stands for "sound navigation and ranging" and can be used to map the bottom of the sea. Sonic pulses are produced by an echo sounder fixed beneath a ship. These are reflected back and recorded as a trace on a screen.*

It works like RADAR, except that sonar uses SOUND signals instead of radio signals.

The sonar device on the ship turns electric signals into pulses of sound. These travel down through the water. Any object in the water struck by the sound pulses sends back an ECHO. The sonar equipment turns the echoes back into electric signals and measures the time delay. This indicates how deep the object in the water is. The depth is shown on a screen.

▲ *Sound waves travel outward from the source of the sound like ripples on a pond. They make vibrations in the air; and, when they reach your ear, they make your eardrum vibrate, too, so you can hear the sound.*

Sound

Sound is made by vibrating objects that send sound waves through the air. When these vibrations reach our EARS, we hear them as sounds.

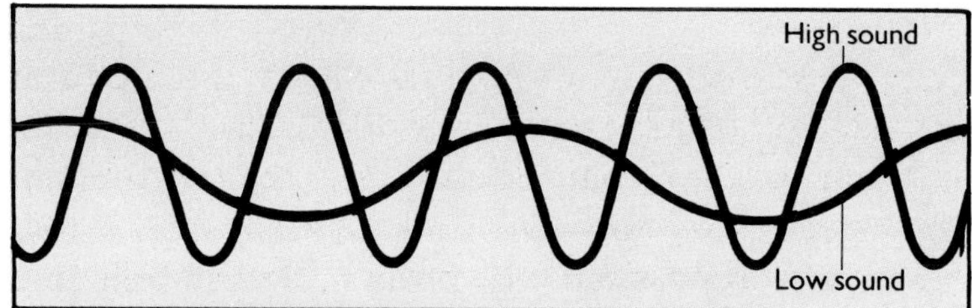

◀ *The frequency of sound waves makes sounds high or low. High sounds make waves that are close together. The waves of low sounds are farther apart.*

Sound travels through air at about 1,100 ft. (334 m) a second. This is slow enough for us to see a far-off explosion, for example, before we hear it. The sound takes time to reach us.

The speed of the vibrations makes a difference to the kind of sound we hear. If the vibrations are very fast, they are said to be "high frequency," and the

SEE IT YOURSELF

You can produce sound by tapping bottles containing water. Arrange four identical bottles in a row. Leave the first one nearly empty and pour different amounts of water into the other three. Tap all four bottles with a spoon, one after the other. This makes the air inside each of the bottles vibrate, producing a sound. Because there is a different amount of air left in each of the bottles, each of them will make a different sound.

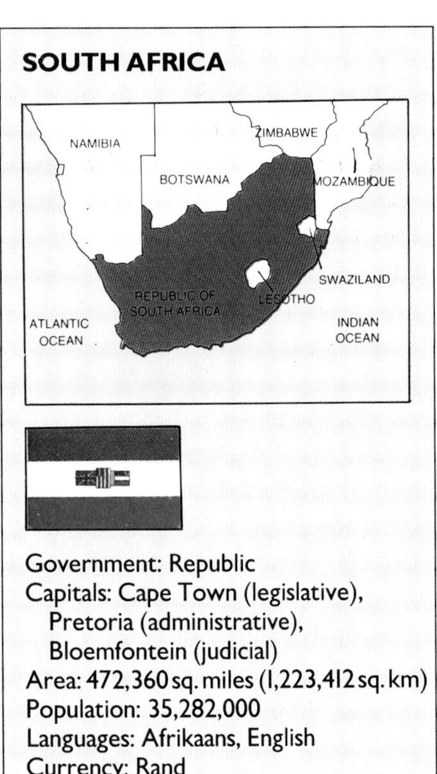

sound we hear is high-pitched. If they are slow, the sound is said to be "low frequency," and the sound we hear is low-pitched.

South Africa

South Africa is a country in southern Africa. Most of the country is tableland, a high region of flat-topped hills. Around the coast is a narrow plain. The climate is warm and dry.

South Africa is a rich country. Factories make a wide range of goods. Mines produce gold, diamonds, uranium, copper, iron, and other minerals. Farms grow big crops of corn, wheat, and fruit. Millions of sheep graze on the grasslands in the center of the country.

Just over 35 million people live in South Africa. Almost three-fourths of them are black Africans. There are fewer than 5 million whites. The whites, who are descended mainly from Dutch and British settlers, control the country's government and money. Since the 1940s, South Africa has had a policy of apartheid or "apartness." This means that whites and non-whites live separately. In 1991 the government announced plans to end all apartheid race separation laws and extend democratic rights to all South Africans.

South America

▼ *South America is a huge continent. It stretches from the Antarctic up to north of the equator.*

South America is the world's fourth largest continent. Lying between the Atlantic and Pacific Oceans, it stretches from the equator in the north to the Antarctic in the south, from the Andes in the west to the Amazon delta in the east.

The Andes are the longest mountain range in the world. They run along the Pacific coast for 5,000 miles (8,000 km). They are also the starting point of one of the world's greatest rivers, the Amazon. This huge waterway travels nearly 4,000 miles (6,437 km) across South America and empties 30,000,000 gallons of water into the ocean every second. The huge area drained by the Amazon includes thick tropical rain forest.

Two other great rivers are the Orinoco in the

Barranquilla
Maracaibo
Caracas
Orinoco
Medellín
VENEZUELA
Llanos
Georgetown
GUYANA
SURINAM
Paramaribo
Cayenne
FRENCH GUIANA
Bogotá
Cali
COLOMBIA
ATLANTIC OCEAN
Quito
GALAPAGOS IS.
ECUADOR
Guayaquil
Manáus
Amazon
Belém
Fortaleza
PERU
Selvas
Chiclayo
Trujillo
Recife
BRAZIL
Callão
Lima
Cuzco
Salvador
BOLIVIA
ANDES
La Paz
Cochabamba
Oruro
Brasilia
Sucre
PACIFIC OCEAN
Paraná
Brazilian Highlands
MOUNTAINS
ATACAMA DESERT
PARAGUAY
Gran Chaco
Asunción
São Paulo
Rio de Janeiro
Pôrto Alegre
Córdoba
Mt Aconcagua
Valparaiso
Rosario
URUGUAY
Santiago
Buenos Aires
Montevideo
ARGENTINA
La Plata
CHILE
PAMPAS
Colorado
Bahia Blanca
ATLANTIC OCEAN
Capital Cities
0
500
1000 miles
0
500
1000
1500 kilometers
Chubut
Patagonia
FALKLAND IS.
Tierra del Fuego
Cape Horn

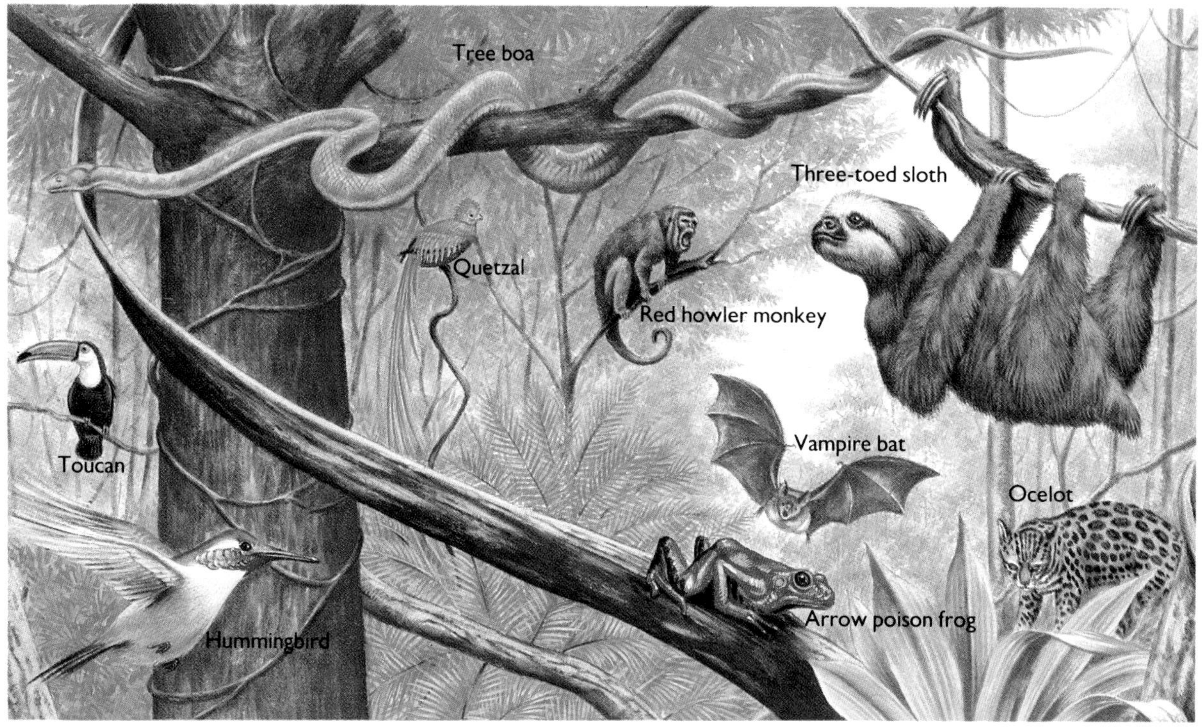

▲ *Many of the creatures of the South American rain forest live high above the forest floor. These and the forests themselves are under threat as thousands of acres of rain forest are felled for valuable hardwoods or to create farmland.*

north and the Plata in the south. The land south of the Amazon jungle has swamps, lakes, grasslands, and, near the continent's tip, the Patagonian Desert.

There are 13 countries in South America. The largest, BRAZIL, takes up half the continent. Most South Americans speak Spanish. But in Brazil, they speak Portuguese; in Guyana, they speak English; in French Guiana, French; and in Surinam, Dutch. These different languages are the leftovers of history. South America was explored by the Spanish and Portuguese in the 1500s. Then Spain, Portugal, and other European countries set up colonies. In the 1800s, most of these colonies won their independence.

The first people of South America were Indians. Most of them, including the INCAS, were killed by foreign conquerors. Later, the Europeans brought in African slaves. Today, most South Americans come from European and African ancestors. There are still some Indians in the Andes and Amazonia.

South America has rich natural resources. The rocks of the Andes are full of minerals. There is silver in PERU, tin in BOLIVIA, and copper in CHILE. There are also huge amounts of oil in VENEZUELA in the north. The open grasslands of ARGENTINA,

SOUTH AMERICA
Area: 6,900,000 sq. miles (17,871,000 sq. km)
Population: 302,000,000
Highest mountain: Mount Aconcagua in Argentina 22,834 ft. (6,960 m)
Lowest point: Valdes Peninsula, Argentina, 130 ft. (40 m) below sea level
Principal rivers: Amazon 4,000 miles (6,437 km), Madeira, Magdalena, Orinoco, Paraguay, Parana, Pilcomayo, Purus, Sao Francisco, Uruguay
Principal lakes: Maracaibo, Mirim, Poopo, Titicaca
Largest city: Buenos Aires, 10,500,000
Highest waterfall: Angel Falls, 3,212 ft. (979 m), world's highest

Uruguay, and Paraguay provide food for millions of sheep and cattle. Brazil's farmers produce a third of the coffee in the world. So far, all this wealth has not been used properly. Most South Americans are poor. Bad government and poor management of the land have held back South America's progress. In the 1980s these problems were made more difficult for most South American nations by a serious economic recession.

South Carolina

South Carolina is located in the Deep South, on the Atlantic coast. Many important Revolutionary War battles were fought in South Carolina, and the colony won important victories over Britain. In the mid-1800s, South Carolina was one of the richest slave states. When Abraham Lincoln was elected president in 1860, it became the first state to leave the Union, thinking that Lincoln would outlaw slavery. The first shots of the war were fired at Fort Sumter in Charleston, South Carolina. The state suffered badly in the Civil War, and its prosperity was destroyed. It took many years for South Carolina to recover. Today, it is a major producer of textiles and of tobacco. Many tourists come to South Carolina to visit the historic sites.

SOUTH CAROLINA

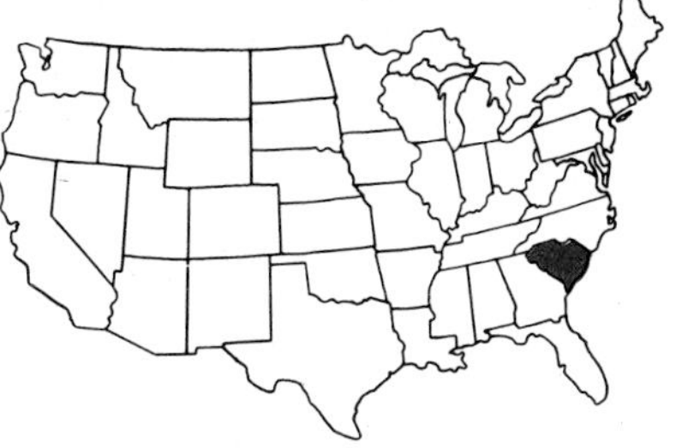

Capital: Columbia
Population: 3,486,000
Area: 31,113 sq. mi. (80,582 sq. km)
State flower: Yellow Jessamine
State bird: Carolina Wren
State tree: Palmetto
Statehood: May 23, 1788
8th state

South Dakota

South Dakota is a midwestern state. Agriculture is its most important industry. Cattle are raised and many different crops grown. The landscape of the state is very varied. Parts are rocky and mountainous, some are rolling and fertile, and others have deep canyons and lakes.

Millions of tourists visit South Dakota each year to visit the Black Hills and Badlands, areas of dramatic beauty.

Many famous names stem from South Dakota's adventurous history – Wild Bill Hickok, Calamity Jane, George Custer, Sitting Bull, and Crazy Horse are just a few of them.

The geographic center of the United States is 17 miles (27 km) west of Castle Rock.

▲ *Badlands National Park in southwestern South Dakota.*

SOUTH DAKOTA

Capital: Pierre
Population: 696,004
Area: 77,116 sq. mi. (199,730 sq. km)
State flower: Pasque Flower
State bird: Ring-necked Pheasant
State tree: Black Hills Spruce
Statehood: Nov. 2, 1889
40th state

Southeast Asia

Southeast Asia is a large, spread-out area that lies south of CHINA and east of INDIA. It is not one country, but many. Joined to the Asian mainland are BURMA (MYANMAR), THAILAND, MALAYSIA, SINGAPORE, CAMBODIA (KAMPUCHEA), VIETNAM, and LAOS. Farther south there is a chain of islands forming the countries of INDONESIA, BRUNEI, PAPUA NEW GUINEA, and the PHILIPPINES.

Southeast Asia is mainly mountainous. It has a tropical climate, with heavy rainfall in the wet season. Most of the people are farmers. They grow rice, corn, rubber, sugarcane, and tea. Mineral resources include oil, tin, and bauxite (aluminum ore). Although many Southeast Asian people live in small villages, there are also big cities such as Bangkok in Thailand, Kuala Lumpur in Malaysia, Ho Chi Minh City in Vietnam, and Singapore, one of the world's greatest ports.

A great many different peoples live in the region. They are made up of different races, speak different languages, and follow different ways of life.

► *Southeast Asia has nearly 500 million people. Most of them have Chinese or Malay ancestors, but there are also Vietnamese, Burmese, Thais, Dayaks, Chams, and many more. Religious beliefs also vary. There are Muslims, Buddhists, Hindus, Christians, followers of Chinese religions, and many pagan beliefs. The picture on the right shows the Floating Market in Bangkok, Thailand, where traders sell their wares from small boats.*

From the 900s to the 1400s, much of Southeast Asia was ruled by people called Khmers, who built up a powerful empire. The Khmer built hundreds of beautiful stone temples, canals, reservoirs, and roads. The temple of Angkor Wat in Cambodia is their greatest architectural achievement. The enormous temple is 5,085 ft. (1,550 m) long by 4,593 ft. (1,400 m) wide, with an entrance hall of more than a hundred square columns.

▲ *Transportation is a major problem in Antarctica. Heavily laden sledges have to be dragged by tractors such as this one used by the British Antarctic Survey.*

South Pole

The South Pole is not an object. It is the point on the map that marks the southern end of the EARTH's axis. The NORTH POLE marks the northern end. The South Pole lies among high, frozen mountains in the middle of ANTARCTICA. The first person to journey to the pole was the Norwegian explorer, Roald AMUNDSEN in December, 1911. The British explorer Captain SCOTT reached the pole one month later.

In 1956, the U.S. set up a scientific base at the South Pole and called it the Amundsen-Scott Station.

Soviet Union

The vast area that was the Soviet Union in 1990 is now a complex of independent states, each trying to come to terms with its freedom from Kremlin control. Latvia, Lithuania, and Estonia, the three

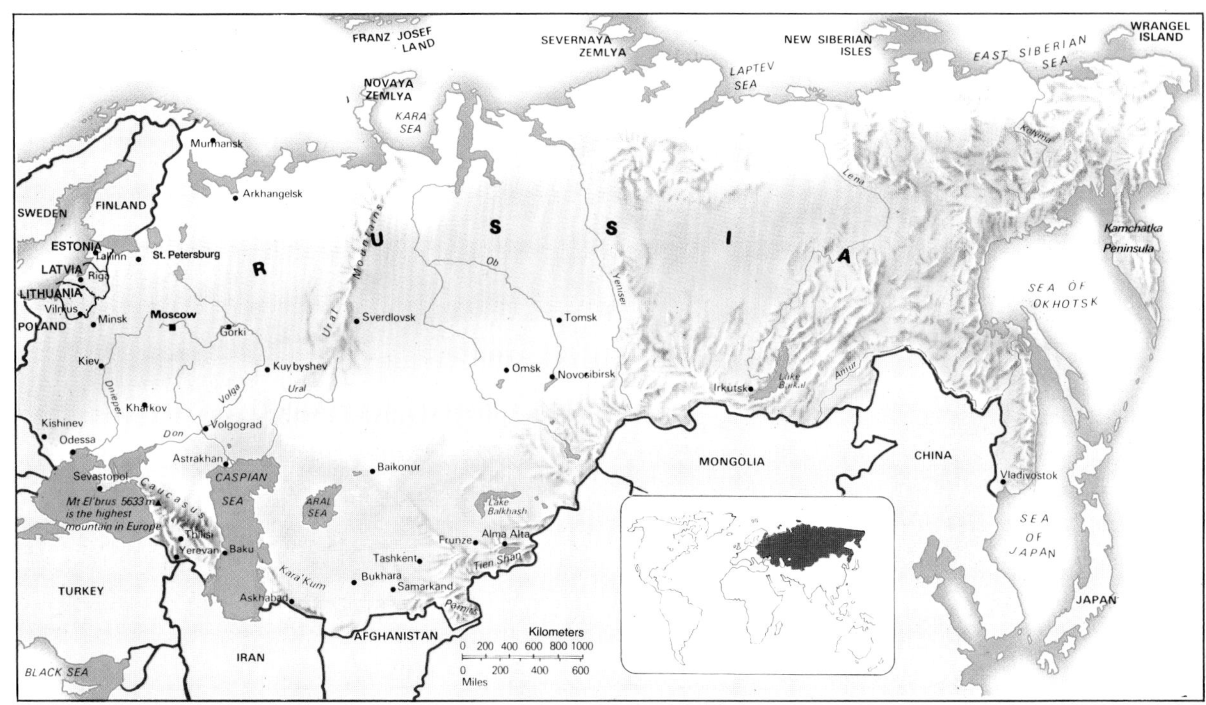

▲ *No other region has such variety in its peoples as the former U.S.S.R., with more than 100 different nationality groups in the population. Different regions have their own languages, dress, and customs.*

Baltic States declared their independence from the U.S.S.R. at the end of 1991. This was followed by the setting up of the Commonwealth of Independent States, with the founding membership of Russia, the Ukraine, and Byelorussia. The Commonwealth has been dominated economically and militarily by the power of Russia under the leadership of Boris Yeltsin, who displaced Mikhail Gorbachev to organize the breakup of the Soviet Union. The Communist Party was disbanded, but the entire former Soviet economy was in danger of collapse, with acute food shortages.

Before 1917, Russia was a poor country ruled by *tsars*, or emperors. In 1917, there was a revolution. A COMMUNIST government took over, led by Vladimir LENIN. Between 1918 and 1920, Russia was nearly destroyed by a civil war between the communists and their enemies.The communists won and began to turn Russia into a great industrial nation.

The land of Russia is varied. Large parts of it are cold or dry and have few people. More than 70 percent of the 280 million citizens live in the European part of the country, west of the Ural Mountains.

Russian farmers grow many crops, including wheat, rye, and barley. They also grow vegetables, fruit, tea, and cotton. The farms were owned or run

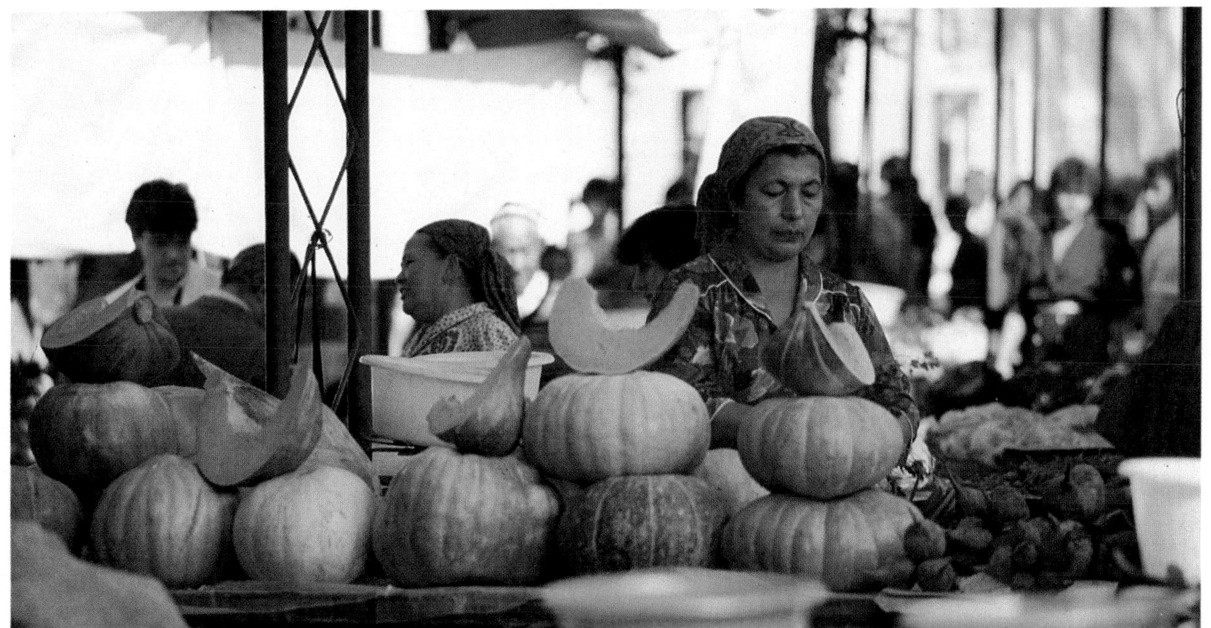

▲ *In the south lies the republic of Uzbekistan, which is part of Asia, and has many Asian traditions. This Uzbeck trader is selling pumpkins at a bazaar in the city of Tashkent.*

by the government. Most of the farms are very big, and about one-fourth of the people work on them.

The former Soviet states are rich in MINERALS. They have great deposits of coal, oil, and natural gas, and has more iron, chromium, lead, and manganese than any other groups of countries. Fishing and forestry are also important industries.

At the beginning of the 1900s, Russia was a country of farmers. There were few factories. Today, it is a leading industrial country, but much of the country's machinery is becoming old-fashioned.

During World War II, Germany invaded the Soviet Union, but after fierce fighting, the Soviet Army drove the Germans back. The Soviets occupied Hungary, Romania, Czechoslovakia, Poland, and part of Germany itself. After the war, communist governments closely tied to the Soviet Union were set up in these countries.

The United States and the Soviet Union grew to distrust each other and what was called the Cold War developed. Under Mikhail GORBACHEV, the Soviet Union entered a period of change. United States and Soviet leaders signed agreements to reduce the numbers of nuclear and conventional weapons.

The United States and countries of the European Community have been helping the former Soviet states with economic and food aid.

IMPORTANT DATES

800s	1st Russian state established.
1237–1240	Mongols conquered Russia.
1604–1613	The Time of Troubles.
1613	The first Romanov czar.
1703	Peter I founded St. Petersburg.
1905	The Russo-Japanese War.
1917	Bolsheviks seized power.
1922	The U.S.S.R. established.
1930s	Stalin ordered the Great Purge.
1940s	The Cold War began.
1953	Stalin died. Khrushchev became head of the Communist Party.
1964	Brezhnev succeeded him as head.
1982, 1984	Andropov, Chernenko.
1985	Gorbachev, Communist Party head.
1991	Communist system collapses.
1992	End of Soviet Union.

▼ *The soybean plant grows up to 6½ feet (2 m) high. The pods grow in clusters on the stem, and there can be up to four beans in each pod. The pod and beans are shown enlarged inside the circle.*

Soybean 

The soybean is one of our oldest crops. It comes from China, where it has been grown for over 5,000 years. During the 1900s, the soybean spread to other places. It is now an important crop in many countries, especially the U.S.A., Russia, and Brazil.

Most soybeans are grown for oil and meal (a type of flour). The oil is used for salads, cooking, and to make MARGARINE. Soy meal is full of PROTEIN and is a nourishing food for animals and people. Both oil and meal are also used to make paint, ink, and SOAP.

Spacecraft 

The first spacecraft were launched in the late 1950s. There were two types: SATELLITES and probes. Satellites go into ORBIT around the Earth. Probes zoom away from Earth to explore other planets. These first spacecraft had no crew. Probes and most satel-

► *Many satellites and spacecraft have been sent into space, including the manned Soviet Vostok, the three-man American Apollo, and the huge Soviet space station, Mir.*

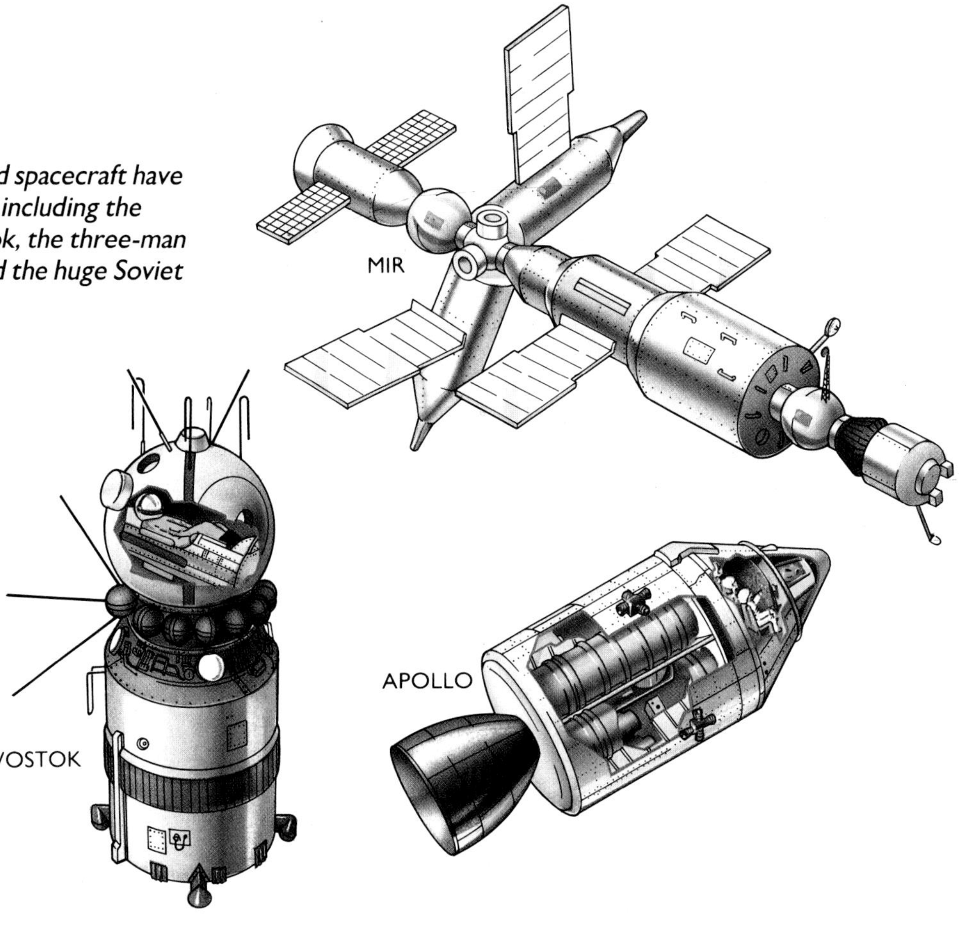

lites are still unmanned, but there are now some manned spacecraft.

All spacecraft leave Earth in the same way. They are thrust into space by huge, powerful ROCKETS. These rockets are normally in three parts, or stages. As one stage runs out of fuel, it falls away, and the next stage fires. When all three stages have gone, the spacecraft speeds through space on its own.

Satellites and probes are full of scientific equipment such as measuring instruments, cameras, tape recorders, and radio transmitters. This equipment runs on electricity made from sunlight. The information collected is radioed back to Earth, where scientists study it.

Manned spacecraft are far more complicated. In addition to scientific equipment, they carry special equipment to keep their astronauts alive and well.

▲ The Space Shuttle is launched on the back of its huge fuel tank, powered by two long booster rockets, as well as by the main engines. The boosters fall off when they have played their part and are recovered for use on future flights.

Space Exploration

People have always gazed in wonder at the Sun, Moon, and the stars. Yet, for thousands of years, they had no means of studying the heavens above. Then, in the 1600s, TELESCOPES were invented, and people were able to take a closer look at the universe. More recently, scientists have been able to discover a lot more about space. We are living in the Space Age. (See pages 642–643.)

Spain

Spain lies in southwest EUROPE, beyond the PYRENEES. Most of the country is covered by high plains and mountains, with a low plain around the

Continued on page 644

◀ Spain's beaches have made it a popular destination for vacationers. This beach near Tarragona is on the Costa Dorada, or Golden Coast, in eastern Spain.

SPAIN

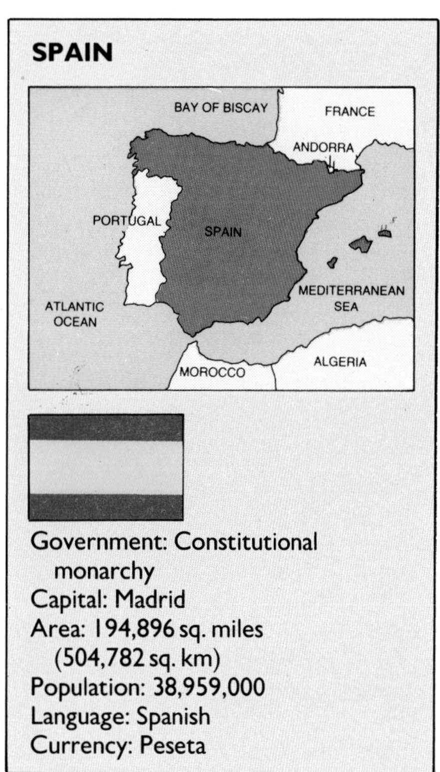

Government: Constitutional monarchy
Capital: Madrid
Area: 194,896 sq. miles (504,782 sq. km)
Population: 38,959,000
Language: Spanish
Currency: Peseta

SPACE EXPLORATION

The Space Age began in 1957, when the Russians launched the first artificial satellite. In 1961 came the first manned flight, and only eight years later, astronauts were exploring the surface of the Moon.

People had long dreamed of escaping the Earth's gravity and flying in space. It was the multistage rocket, developed in Germany during World War II, that made space flight possible. The U.S.A. and Russia dominated the early years of space exploration. Europe now has its own space rocket, and other countries such as China and India have also launched satellites.

Americans call space travelers "astronauts," while Russians call theirs "cosmonauts." The United States was the first to build a reusable Space Shuttle, but the Russians have made longer flights in their orbital space stations. These flights will show whether human travelers can ever go to Mars (which would take three years). Unmanned spacecraft have already landed on Mars and sent TV pictures and signals back from other planets.

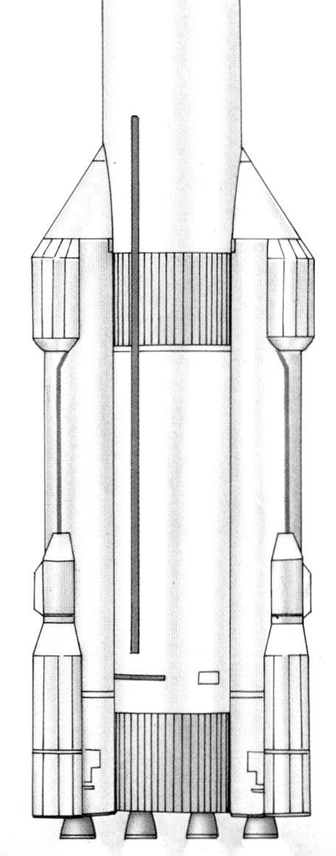

▲ *The first artificial satellite, Russia's Sputnik I (1957). It weighed just over 183 lbs. (83 kg) and carried a transmitter.*

◀ *The Soviet rocket Energia is the most powerful space rocket in the world.*

SPACE PIONEERS

Konstantin Tsiolkovsky: Russian who predicted use of rockets for space travel in the early 1900s.

Robert H. Goddard: American who tested small rockets in the 1930s.

Wernher von Braun: German who helped to design V2 war rocket and later the U.S. Saturn Moon rocket.

Sergei Korolyev: Designed first Russian space rockets.

Yuri Gagarin: Russian who was the first person to fly in space (1961).

John Glenn: First American astronaut to orbit the Earth (1962).

Valentina Tereshkova: Russian cosmonaut, first woman to make a space flight (1963).

Neil Armstrong: American who was the first person to set foot on the Moon (1969).

▲ *Russia's Yuri Gagarin was the first person to fly in space. He made one orbit of the Earth on April 12, 1961. Tragically, Gagarin was killed in a plane crash in 1968.*

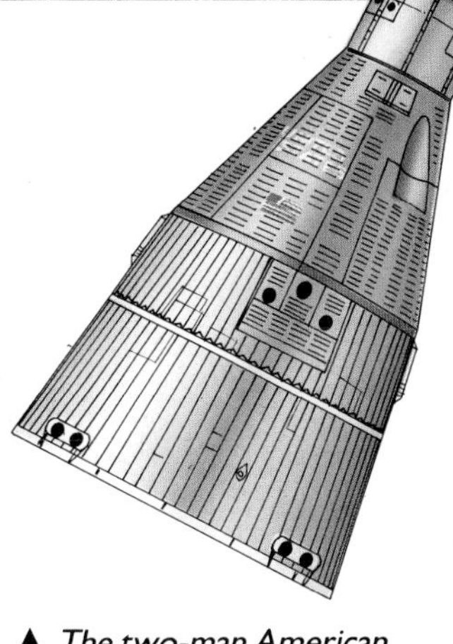

▲ *The two-man American Gemini spacecraft weighed 3½ tons. It was flown in Earth orbit to practice techniques later used on the Apollo Moon flights.*

SPACE FIRSTS

1942 First flight of German V2 rocket
1957 First Earth satellite: Sputnik I
First animal in space, a dog called Laika
1959 First man-made object hits the Moon (Luna 2)
1961 First manned spaceflight: by Yuri Gagarin
1965 First space "walk:" by Alexei Leonov
1968 First manned flight around the Moon: by Apollo 8
1969 First men on the Moon: Armstrong and Aldrin
1971 First space station: Salyut I
1975 First close-up photos of Venus: by Venera probes
1976 First landing on Mars: by Viking probes
1981 First flight of Space Shuttle
1983 First spacecraft to leave the solar system entirely (Pioneer 10)
1989 First close look at Neptune (Voyager 2)

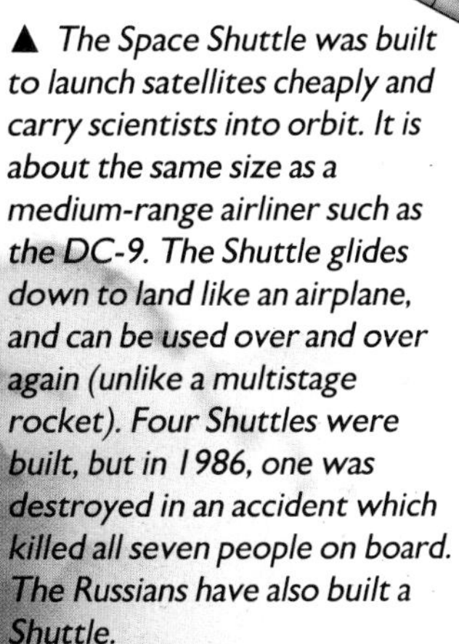

▲ *The Space Shuttle was built to launch satellites cheaply and carry scientists into orbit. It is about the same size as a medium-range airliner such as the DC-9. The Shuttle glides down to land like an airplane, and can be used over and over again (unlike a multistage rocket). Four Shuttles were built, but in 1986, one was destroyed in an accident which killed all seven people on board. The Russians have also built a Shuttle.*

▲ *Skylab was a manned scientific workshop that was launched into orbit by the U.S. in 1973. It was used by three crews to study the Earth, Sun, Moon, and space, and the influence of space on living things. It broke up and fell to Earth in 1979.*

◀ *The Voyager 2 space probe was launched in 1977 to visit Saturn, Jupiter, Uranus and Neptune. It passed Neptune in August 1989 and went on into outer space.*

For more information, turn to these articles: ASTRONOMY; GAGARIN, YURI; GLENN JOHN; GRAVITY; JUPITER; MARS; MOON; ORBIT; PLANET; ROCKET; SATELLITE; SATURN; SPACECRAFT; URANUS.

In 1492, Prince Ferdinand and Princess Isabella sent Christopher Columbus on a voyage that took him to America. This voyage marked the beginning of a great age of Spanish exploration. During the next 50 years, Spanish explorers, soldiers, and adventurers flocked to the New World. The Spaniards built an empire that included much of western South America and southwestern United States, as well as lands in Africa, Asia, and Europe.

coast. The highlands have hot summers, cold winters, and little rain. The coast is milder and wetter, especially in the north.

Half the people work on farms, growing potatoes, wheat, grapes, olives, and fruits. Wine, olive oil, and oranges are exported. Many Spaniards who live on the coast are fishermen. They catch sardines and anchovies. Others work in the tourist trade. Each year, millions of European tourists visit Spain to enjoy its sunny beaches. The two main industrial areas are around Bilbao in the north and Barcelona in the northeast.

Spanish-American War

The Spanish-American War was fought between Spain and the United States from April to August 1898. It was the first war against a foreign country the United States had fought since the War of 1812. The U.S. won a rapid and complete victory, gaining the islands of Guam, Puerto Rico, and the Philippines, and winning independence for the island of Cuba from Spain. Most of the fighting took place in Cuba. Many Americans felt that the Spanish had no right to rule Cuba, and that the Cubans were treated badly by them. When a U.S. battleship called the *Maine* blew up in Cuba, war seemed inevitable. In the fighting, almost all Spain's ships were captured and the Spanish soldiers were quickly defeated.

Spectrum

Where do the colors in a rainbow come from? The answer was found in 1666 when Sir Isaac Newton put a triangle-shaped block of glass called a *prism* in front of a beam of sunlight. The prism bent the light and separated it into the different colors of the rainbow. Newton showed that sunlight is made up of different colors—a spectrum of colors. Sunlight is white only because all the colors of the rainbow are mixed together in it.

The spectrum of light is only one small part of the whole *electromagnetic spectrum*. The electromagnetic spectrum is arranged according to the *wavelength* (distance between waves) and *frequency*

SEE IT YOURSELF

On a sunny day, you can separate sunlight into its spectrum of colors by carrying out this experiment. Rest a flat mirror against the side of a bowl filled with water. Place them next to a window so that sunlight falls onto the mirror. Now hold a sheet of white cardboard in front of the mirror, moving it around until you see the spectrum of colors. The water around the mirror acts like a prism and splits up the light into different colors. This is because the colors that make up white light are bent by different amounts.

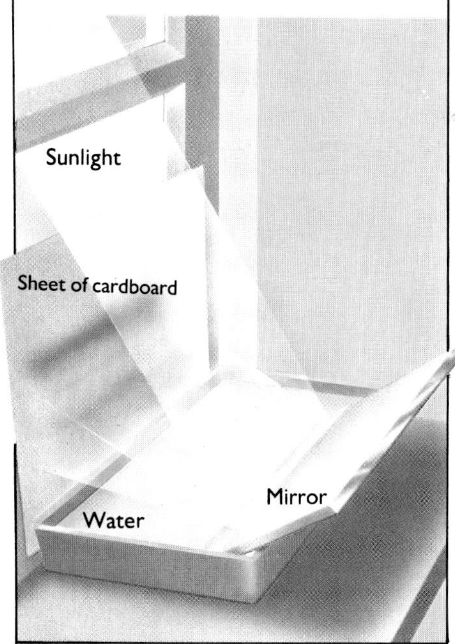

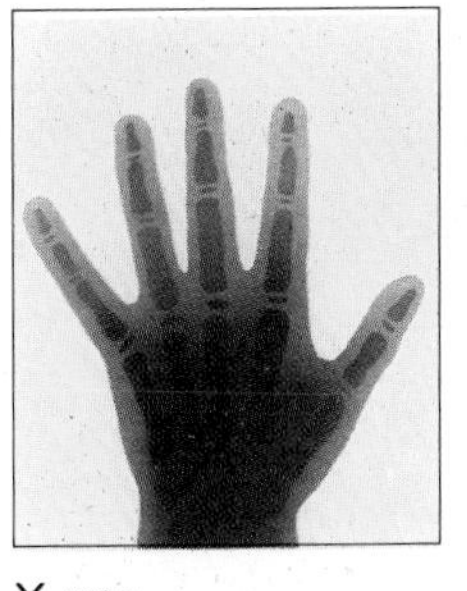

X rays

Radar

Television

Gamma rays

X rays

Ultraviolet rays

Visible light

Infrared rays

Microwaves

Radio waves

Ultraviolet rays

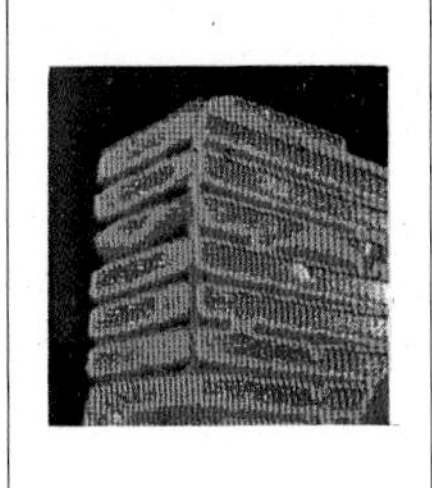

Infrared rays

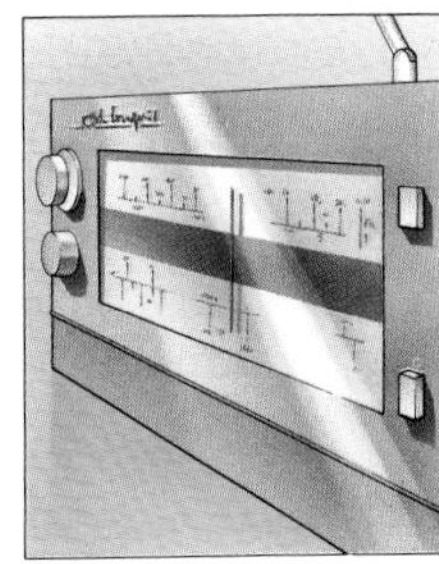

Radio

◀ *We can see only a very limited range of the electromagnetic spectrum—visible light—but unseen waves are around us all the time. Different wavelengths of the electromagnetic spectrum are used for different things and have many different effects. The infrared photo shows the heat given out by an office building. White areas are the hottest, red are warm, green cool, and blue cold.*

(number of waves per second) of the waves. Radio waves have the lowest frequency and the longest wavelength. Gamma rays have the highest frequency and shortest wavelength. In between them come ultraviolet waves, X-rays, and other rays.

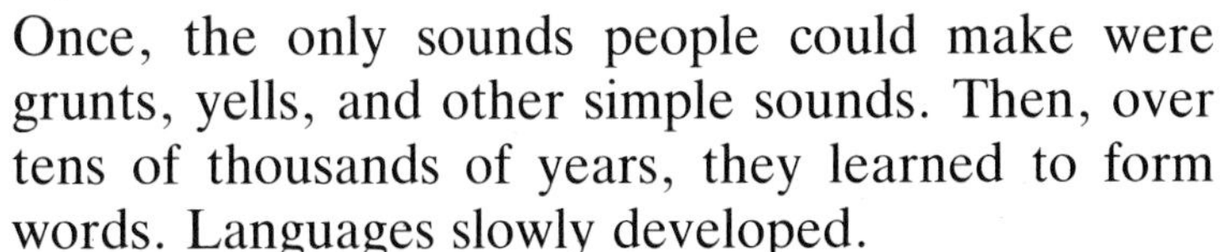

Speech

Once, the only sounds people could make were grunts, yells, and other simple sounds. Then, over tens of thousands of years, they learned to form words. Languages slowly developed.

Speech sounds are made by air from our lungs passing around two membranes called vocal cords. We change the pitch of the sound by altering the tension of the vocal cords, just as we can alter the pitch of a guitar by tightening or slackening the strings. By changing the shape of the passages in our throat, mouth, and nose, and by using our tongue,

▼ *Your tongue, teeth, and lips work together to make sounds. The lips here (top) are pushed forward to make the sound "oo." In the lower picture, the sound "th" is formed by the tongue, teeth, and lips combined.*

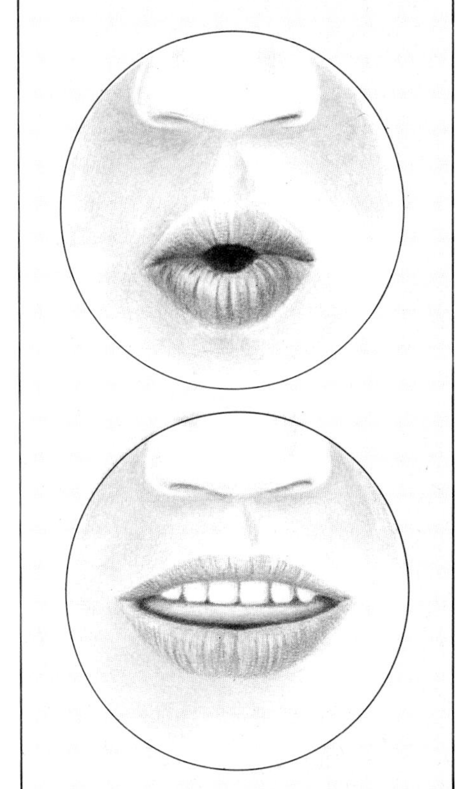

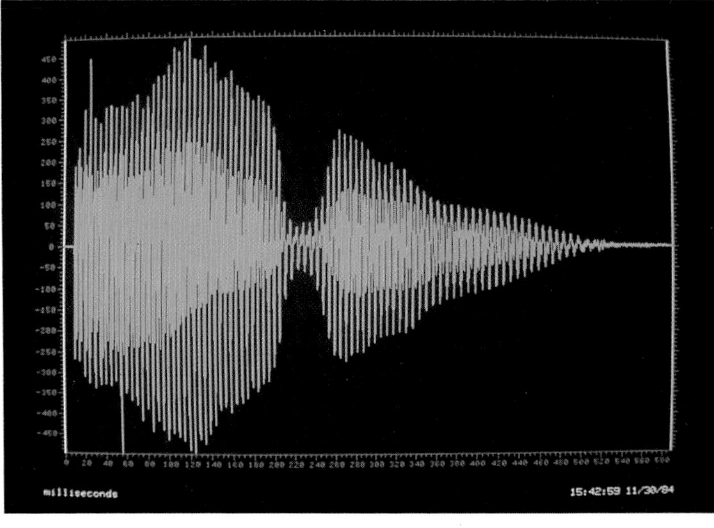

▶ *This computer graphic image shows the wave pattern made by the word "baby." The word was produced in a female voice by a computerized speech synthesizer that copies real human speech.*

we can alter the sounds produced. We can make the words of speech.

Women usually have higher-pitched voices than men because their vocal cords are shorter.

In the Middle Ages, the value of spices was often greater than that of gold or jewels. Most spices were carried to Europe from India or the Moluccas—the Spice Islands. The route was from India to the Persian Gulf, then across the Arabian Sea by ship. The spices were then taken by caravan across the Middle East to the Mediterranean or the Black Sea, and from there to the countries of Europe. No wonder spices were very costly.

Spice

Spices have a strong taste and smell and are used to flavor foods and drinks. They are made from the dried parts of plants, usually ground into a powder. Most spice plants grow in hot places such as Africa, India, and Indonesia. Pepper, ginger, cloves, cinnamon, and nutmeg are common spices.

▶ *Some common spices. Cloves are the dried flower buds of a plant native to Southeast Asia (right). Nutmeg is the dried kernel of a fruit that looks like an apricot (center). Cinnamon is the dried bark of an evergreen plant (far right).*

Spider

Spiders are small animals. Although they look like insects, they are not. Insects have six legs; spiders have eight. Insects have feelers and wings; spiders do not. Insect bodies have three parts; spiders' bodies have two.

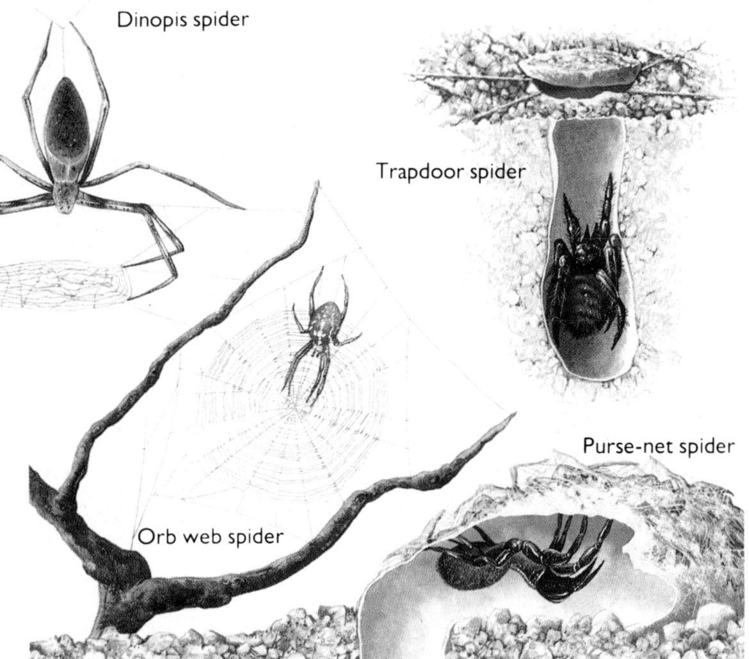

◀ *Spiders use their silk in different ways. The orb web spider builds a complex web to snare insects. The Australian* Dinopis *spider throws its silk net over an insect below. The trapdoor spider hides in its burrow and springs out if an insect touches one of its silk trip-wires. The European purse-net spider spins itself a pouch. If an insect steps on the pouch, the spider "stabs" it through the silk wall and drags it inside.*

All spiders spin silk threads. Many of them use the threads to make a sticky web for catching insects. Not all spiders trap their food in webs. Some are hunters and chase their prey; others lie in wait, then pounce. When a spider catches something, it stuns or kills it with a poisonous bite. All spiders have poison, but in most cases, it does not hurt people.

There are about 30,000 kinds of spider. They come in all sizes. The comb-footed spider is no bigger than a pinhead, but some bird-eating spiders can be 10 inches (25 cm) across. They have different life stories. Some live for only a year, others for 20 years.

▲ *Tarantulas are among the world's largest spiders. Many live in the southwestern United States.*

Squid

Squid are MOLLUSKS related to the octopus. Many live deep in the sea by day, but rise to feed at night. A squid uses its 10 tentacles to catch fish and feed them into its beaklike mouth. Some squid are no bigger than a thumb. But the giant squid can grow to 40 feet (12 m) in length.

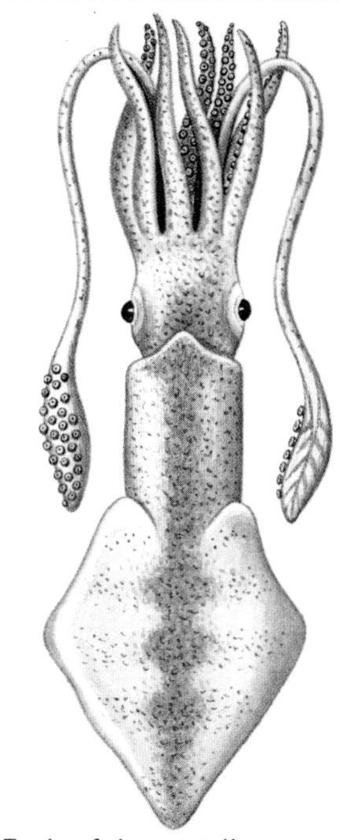

▲ *Each of the squid's ten arms has rows of sucking disks. It uses these to seize and hold onto its prey. Squid can propel themselves backward by squirting water through a narrow funnel pointing forward.*

Squirrel

Most people think of squirrels as a kind of RODENT that is good at climbing trees. Tree squirrels are exactly that. They have sharp claws for climbing and

▲ *Prairie dogs are ground squirrels that live in large groups in huge burrow systems. Members of the group take turns doing jobs that benefit the whole group, such as standing guard at the entrances to the burrow.*

▼ *The red squirrel lives mostly in coniferous woodland, where it eats huge numbers of pine cones and shoots.*

a long, bushy tail that helps them to steer and keep their balance. Tree squirrels can leap 10 feet (3 m) to reach one tree from another.

Flying squirrels jump 10 times farther that that. These little creatures have flaps of skin between their front and back legs. The flaps form a parachute when a flying squirrel jumps and spreads its limbs. Tree squirrels and flying squirrels feed on leaves, twigs, or seeds.

Ground squirrels live in burrows under the ground. They include the chipmunks, prairie dogs, and woodchucks.

The gray fox squirrel is the largest of the American squirrels. There are more than 300 different kinds of squirrel.

Sri Lanka

Sri Lanka is an island country off the southern tip of INDIA. Sri Lanka used to be called Ceylon. The island is near the equator, so the climate is tropical. Most of the tropical trees and shrubs have been cleared away to make room for crops, but there are still palm trees and bamboo. Animals such as elephants, leopards, monkeys, snakes, and colorful birds live in the wilder areas. Sri Lanka's crops include tea, rubber, and coconuts.

There is continuing unrest between the ruling Sinhalese, who are mainly Buddhist, and the Tamils, who are mainly Hindu.

Stalin, Joseph

Joseph Stalin (1879–1953) ruled the U.S.S.R. from 1929 to 1953. After LENIN died, Stalin made Russia one of the two most powerful nations in the world. He killed or imprisoned thousands of Russians who disagreed with his kind of COMMUNISM. The name Stalin is Russian for "man of steel."

Stamp

A stamp can be a special mark or a piece of printed paper with a sticky back. A passport and many other kinds of documents must bear the correct government stamp. Postage stamps are stuck on letters and packages to be carried by the post office. Each nation has its own postage stamps. Millions of people collect postage stamps. Some kinds are scarce and valuable. A very rare stamp can cost more than a house.

Star

The stars we can see from Earth are just a few of the many billions scattered through space. Stars look small because they are so far away. But most are

SRI LANKA

INDIA
SRI LANKA
INDIAN OCEAN

Government: Republic
Capital: Colombo
Area: 25,332 sq. miles (65,610 sq. km)
Population: 16,993,000
Languages: Sinhala, Tamil
Currency: Rupee

▼ *An artist's impression of the life of a star, first formed by a cloud of gas that condenses and solidifies. Over thousands of millions of years, the star grows larger. Suddenly, it expands into a red giant, then begins to shrink and fade. The arrow shows where our Sun is in this process.*

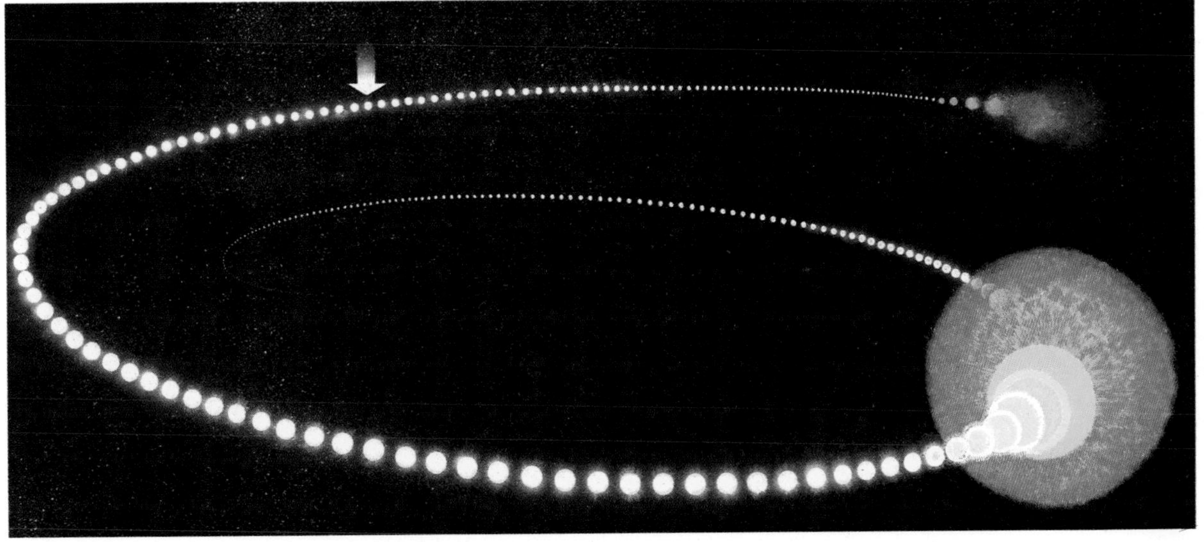

▶ *This diagram shows how stars can be grouped according to how bright they are. The brilliant "lighthouse" stars are blue giants—large and very hot. The dim "matchstick" stars are small red dwarfs. Our Sun is a yellowish "table-lamp" star. If a blue giant were placed in the middle of our solar system instead, it would melt the Earth and boil away the ice on the farthest planets.*

Bright	36,000°F (20,000°C) Blue-white	18,000°F (10,000°C) White	11,000°F (6,000°C) Yellow	8,000°F (4,500°C) Orange	5,000°F (3,000°C) Red
Dim					

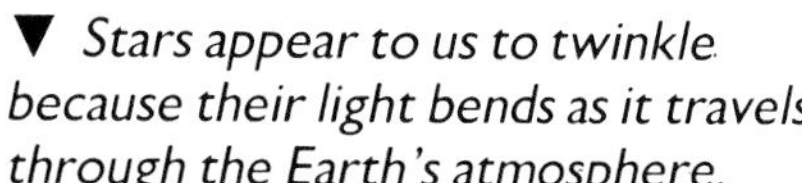

▼ *Stars appear to us to twinkle because their light bends as it travels through the Earth's atmosphere.*

huge, fiery balls of gas like our SUN.

Stars begin as clouds of gas. GRAVITY pulls the gas particles in toward the middle of each cloud. There, the particles collide and grow hot, and other particles press in.

HYDROGEN atoms change into helium atoms by a process called nuclear fusion. That process gives off NUCLEAR ENERGY. This is what makes stars glow so brightly.

Stars swell as they use their hydrogen. Astronomers call such stars *red giants*. Red giants later shrink into tiny white-hot stars called *white dwarfs*. In time, they cool and fade into the darkness of space.

Starch

Starch is a substance found in plants. Cereals such as wheat, rice, and corn are particularly rich in starch. Other plants that contain it are peas, beans, and potatoes. Starch is a *carbohydrate*, which means that it is made up of carbon, oxygen, and hydrogen, the same ingredients found in sugar. It is important to have starch in our diet because it gives us energy.

Pure starch is a white powder that is used in the making of many food products. It is also used to glaze paper and for stiffening cotton, linen, and other materials.

Starch makes up about four-fifths of rice and three-fourths of wheat, rye, and corn. About 80 percent of all commercial starch is made from corn and is called cornstarch.

Starfish

Starfish are creatures that live on the seabed. Most have five arms that stick out like the spokes of a wheel. Starfish do not have backbones. But they have a SKELETON made up of bony plates. They creep about on tiny tube feet arranged along the underside of their arms.

A starfish can open and eat a mussel. It uses its tube feet to grip both halves of the mussel's shell. Then it pulls the shell open. The starfish pushes part of its stomach out of its mouth, which is under the middle of its body. The stomach slips inside the mussel's shell and digests the mussel's soft body.

▲ *The larva of the starfish looks nothing like the adult. It floats in the sea with other tiny animals (zooplankton).*

States' Rights 

States' rights allow individual states to protect themselves against what they consider interference in their affairs from the federal government in Washington. If there is a conflict between a federal law and a state law, then the Supreme Court must decide whether that state's rights are being abused. The most serious disagreement over states' rights was the CIVIL WAR, when the South refused to accept that the federal government could outlaw slavery.

Steam Engine 

Boiling water turns into steam. Steam will fill 1,700 times more space than the water that it came from. So, if you squash steam into a small container, it

▼ *Inside a steam engine, steam is produced by heating water to boiling point. The pressure of the expanding steam is used to push a piston to and fro in a hollow tube called a cylinder. The piston fits tightly inside the cylinder so the steam cannot seep around the sides of the piston head. The piston is attached to the piston rod. As the piston rod goes in and out, it drives another rod called the driving rod. The driving rod turns a wheel called the flywheel, which turns steadily even when the piston is at the end of its stroke and is not pushing. In a steam locomotive, the driving rod is attached to a driving wheel.*

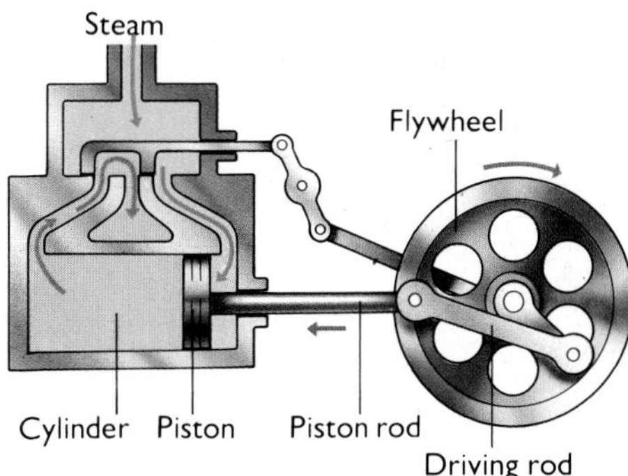

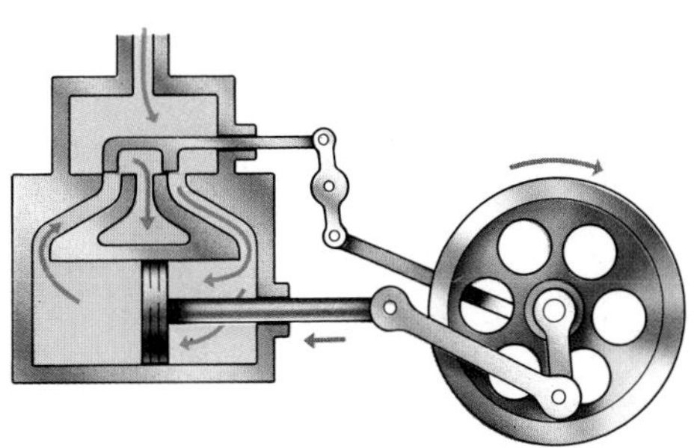

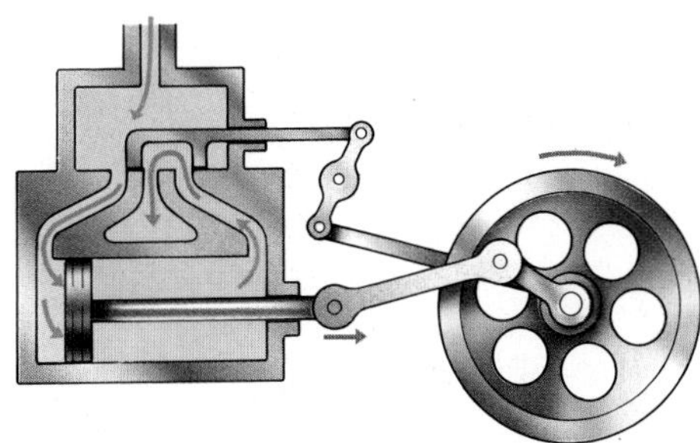

Steam turbines are more efficient than ordinary steam engines. They run more smoothly and are more powerful. In a steam turbine, high-pressure steam is made to strike cupped vanes or propeller-like blades attached to a shaft. The shaft turns at a very high speed. About 80 percent of all our electricity is produced by steam turbines.

presses hard against the sides. If one side is free to move, the steam pressure will push it outward.

In the 1700s, British inventors began to use this fact to build engines powered by steam. Early steam engines worked with a simple to-and-fro motion. In Thomas Newcomen's engine, a furnace heated water in a boiler. The water gave off steam that pushed a piston up inside a cylinder. When the steam cooled and turned back to water, air pressed the piston down again. Newcomen's engine was used to pump water from flooded mines.

James Watt built a more powerful engine, in which steam pushed the piston first one way and then the other. Rods from the piston spun a wheel. By the early 1800s, such engines were moving heavy loads faster than men or horses could. Yet, unlike men and horses, steam engines never got tired. All they needed was fuels such as coal.

Steam engines powered factory machines that made the INDUSTRIAL REVOLUTION possible. They also powered locomotives and steamships. For the first time, people traveled faster than horses.

The INTERNAL COMBUSTION ENGINE has largely taken the place of steam engines. But many ships' propellers and power plant GENERATORS are worked by steam, which spins wheels called TURBINES.

Stevenson, Robert Louis

Robert Louis Stevenson (1850–1894) was a Scottish author of romantic adventure stories such as *Treasure Island*, an exciting tale about a hunt for pirate treasure. *Kidnapped* is an adventure story set in the wilds of Scotland in the 1700s. Stevenson also described his own extensive travels and wrote *A Child's Garden of Verses*, a group of simple poems especially for children.

▲ *Robert Louis Stevenson settled with his family on the island of Samoa, in the South Seas, where he died in 1894.*

Stock Exchange

A stock exchange is a place where people called stockbrokers buy and sell *stocks* and *shares*. These are pieces of paper that show that someone owns a share in a business company. A company's stock tends to cost more if the company does well, and

◀ *There are a number of important stock exchanges in business centers throughout the world. The pace of buying and selling stocks and shares can be very fast, and computers are now widely used to provide information quickly.*

gets cheaper if it does badly. People buy stock hoping to sell it at a higher price later. Meanwhile, they expect to get *dividends*—shares of the money the company makes.

As business grew after the MIDDLE AGES, people needed a marketplace for buying and selling stock. In 1531, Antwerp opened Europe's first stock exchange. Now, many cities have stock exchanges. Millions of stocks change hands each day in the exchanges of London, New York, and Tokyo.

Stomach

Your stomach is a muscular bag, open at both ends and shaped like a fat letter J. It plays an important part in the DIGESTION of food.

When you eat a meal, food travels down your throat to your stomach. The stomach can store a large meal. Juices produced in the stomach kill germs in food. They also moisten and start digesting the food. Stomach muscles churn the mixture, then force it into the small intestine.

Most people's stomachs are in the upper left side of the abdomen, but the position can vary. Tall, thin persons usually have long, narrow stomachs. Short persons usually have short, wide stomachs. The stomach of a newborn baby is about the size of a small hen's egg. Adult stomachs can hold about one quart.

Stone Age

The Stone Age was the great span of time before people learned how to make metal tools. Stone Age people used stone, wood, and bone instead of metal. The Stone Age probably began more than

▼ *Early stone tools were very simple. They could be held easily and had different edges for cutting or scraping. They may have been used to prepare animal flesh for eating and for scraping skins clean.*

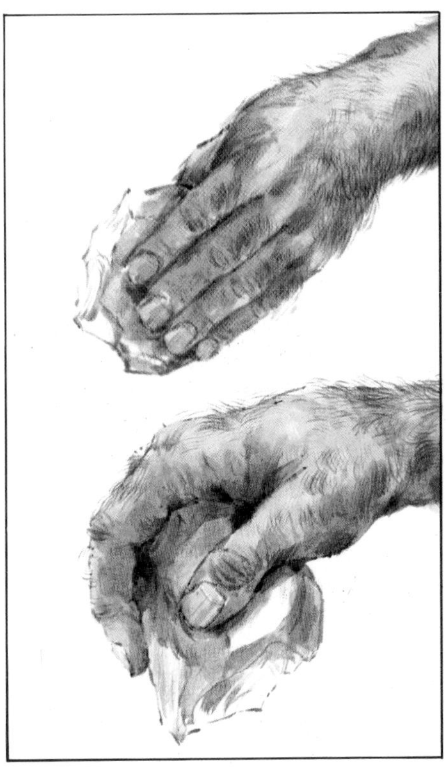

The words "Stone Age" do not mean a fixed period of time that began and ended on certain dates. When the people of Northern Europe were still in the Stone Age, the ancient Egyptians were living in cities and using metals. On the other hand, there are some people today in remote regions who are living as people did in the Stone Age.

three million years ago. It ended in Iraq and Egypt when the Bronze Age began there about 5,000 years ago.

The Stone Age had three parts: Old, Middle, and New. The Old Stone Age lasted until 10,000 years ago in the Middle East. When it began, hunters could scarcely chip a stone well enough to sharpen it. When the Old Stone Age ended, people had learned to chip flint into delicate spearheads, knives, and scrapers.

In the Middle Stone Age, hunters used tiny flakes of flint in arrows and harpoons.

The New Stone Age began in the Middle East about 9,000 years ago. New Stone Age people made smooth ax heads of ground stone. Farming replaced hunting in the New Stone Age.

Stonehenge

Stonehenge is a huge prehistoric temple on Salisbury Plain in southern England. The main part is a great circle of standing stones. Each is more than twice as tall as a man and weighs nearly 30 tons. Flat stones were laid across the tops of the standing stones to form a ring. Inside the ring stood smaller stones, and a great block that may have been an altar. The big stones were raised 3,500 years ago. Other parts are older.

▼ *Archaeologists can tell that some of the huge stones that form Stonehenge were dragged from a site over 250 miles (400 km) away. This task must have taken our prehistoric ancestors years to complete.*

Stork

These big birds have long beaks and legs. They can wade in swamps and capture fish and frogs. But some kinds prefer feeding on dead animals. More than a dozen kinds of stork live in warm parts of the world.

The white stork is the best-known kind. In summer, white storks nest in Europe and central Asia. In the fall, they fly south. Flapping their wings soon makes storks tired. They prefer to soar and glide.

▲ *White storks often nest on roofs and chimneys in European and Asiatic cities. Black storks prefer to live in forests.*

The wood stork is the only true stork native to the United States. It lives in the cypress swamps of Florida.

Stowe, Harriet Beecher

Harriet Beecher Stowe (1811–1896) was a writer in the 1800s. Her most famous book was a novel called *Uncle Tom's Cabin*. It made a powerful case against slavery and was widely read in the Northern states. The book persuaded many people that slavery was wrong and that it should be stopped. In the South, Stowe was hated.

Stravinsky, Igor

Igor Stravinsky (1882–1971) was a Russian composer and one of the most important composers of this century. He spent only a short part of his life in Russia. In 1920 he moved to France, and in 1940 he moved to the United States. He became an American citizen in 1945. His most famous works were ballets and operas, though he wrote many other forms of music, too. He used many different types of music in his work, combining them to create a distinctively modern style.

Stuarts

The Stuarts were a royal family that ruled SCOTLAND from 1371 to 1603 and Scotland and England from 1603 to 1714. They were a strangely unlucky family. Of 14 who were crowned, six were killed and seven came to the throne before they were old enough to rule. MARY QUEEN OF SCOTS was beheaded by ELIZABETH I of England. But her son, JAMES, was the

The Stuart family came from Brittany in France and were originally *stewards* to the Scottish kings. The first spelling was Stewart, the old Scots version. During the 16th century, French influence led to the adoption of the spellings Steuart and Stuart. This was because the French had no letter "w" in their alphabet.

▲ *The Stuart kings and queens of Britain began with James I, who ruled as James I of England and as James VI of Scotland.*

first king of England and Scotland. His son, CHARLES I, was also beheaded. CHARLES II was the only Stuart to enjoy a prosperous and successful reign. But his brother, James II, was forced to leave the country. In the 1700s, two attempts to restore the Stuarts failed.

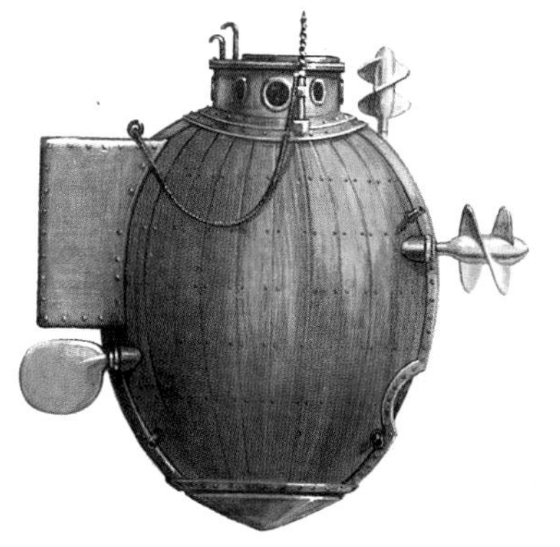

▲ *One of the earliest submarines, the* Turtle, *was powered by a hand propeller and had room for just one person.*

▼ *This cutaway view of a nuclear submarine shows how much of its interior is taken up with the nuclear reactor and turbines that drive it. The crew's quarters and operating area occupy relatively little space.*

Submarine

Submarines are boats that can travel underwater. To dive, the submarine crew makes it heavier than the amount of water needed to fill the space taken up by the submarine. To rise, the crew makes the submarine lighter than that amount of water. When water and submarine both weigh the same, the boat stays at the same level under the surface.

In 1620, someone rowed a wood and leather submarine down the River Thames. But the first submarine that worked well was not built until the

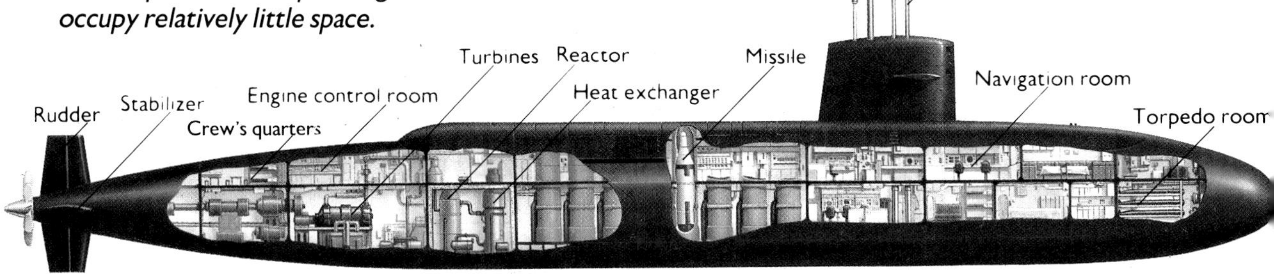

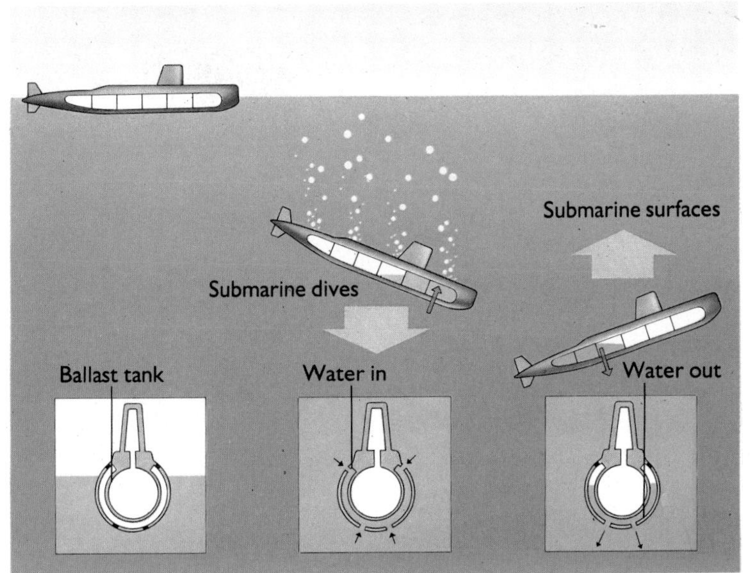

◀ *A submarine can float when its ballast tanks are kept full of air. If water is pumped into the tanks and the air is pumped out, the submarine begins to sink. To come back to the surface, air is pumped back into the ballast tanks, forcing the water out.*

▼ *Deepstar IV, one of the smaller deep-diving submarines, can operate at depths of more than 4,000 feet (1,200 meters).*

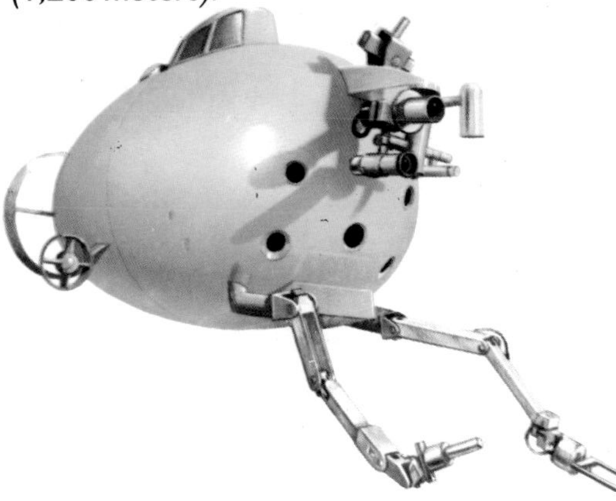

1770s. Both these early submarines were worked by hand. They were slow and under-powered.

In the 1870s, an English clergyman invented a submarine powered by a steam engine. But each time it dived, the crew had to pull down its chimney and put out the fire that heated water to produce steam.

By 1900, the American inventor John P. Holland had produced a much better underwater boat. Gasoline engines drove it on the surface. But gas needs air to burn. Underwater, the boat ran on battery-driven motors that did not need air.

In 1954, the U.S. commissioned the first nuclear-powered submarine. Such boats can travel around the world without having to come to the surface. In 1958, the nuclear submarine *Nautilus* of the U.S. Navy made the first submerged crossing under the North Pole. These submarines are armed with nuclear missiles that can strike at enemy targets thousands of miles away.

Sudan

This is the largest nation in AFRICA. It is nearly four times the size of France.

Sudan is a hot country in northeastern Africa. Desert sprawls across the north. There are flat grasslands in the middle. The south has forests and a huge swamp.

SUDAN

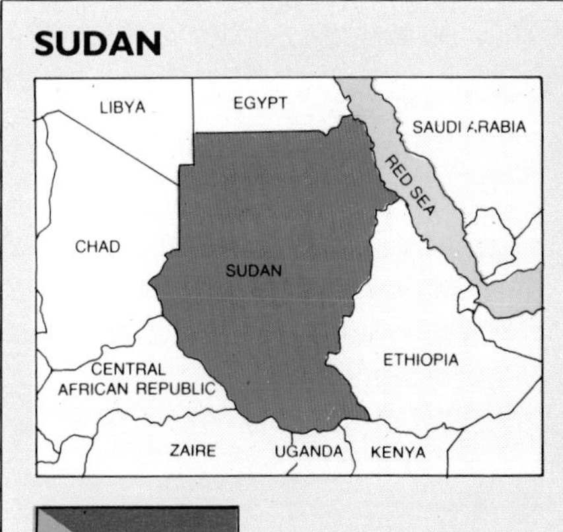

Government: Republic
Capital: Khartoum
Area: 966,757 sq. miles (2,503,900 sq. km)
Population: 25,204,000
Language: Arabic
Currency: Sudanese pound

► *Dinka tribespeople at a cattle market at Wafu in the Sudan. The traditional way of life of many tribes is being threatened by drought conditions, both in the Sudan and in other parts of Africa.*

Sudanese people include Arabs and blacks. Most live near the NILE, which flows north across the country. The Sudanese raise cattle, grow crops such as sugarcane, or work in cities.

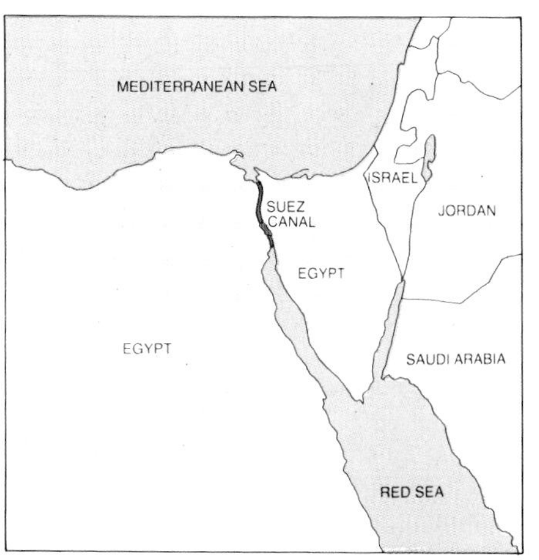

▲ *The Suez Canal crosses the narrow isthmus between the Mediterranean and the long, thin Gulf of Suez, at the northern end of the Red Sea.*

Suez Canal

The Suez Canal crosses Egypt between Port Said on the Mediterranean Sea and Suez on the Red Sea. It is the world's longest canal that can be used by big ships. It measures 100 miles (160 km) from end to end and 200 feet (60 m) across its bed. Ships use it as a shortcut between Europe and Asia. This saves them from sailing 6,000 miles (9,650 km) around southern Africa.

The canal was begun in 1859 by a French company run by the engineer Ferdinand de Lesseps. More than 8,000 men and hundreds of camels worked on it for 10 years. France and England operated the canal until Egypt took it over in 1956.

Sunken ships blocked the canal for eight years after Egypt's war with Israel in 1967. But dredging has now made it much wider and deeper than it was a century ago.

The average sugar beet weighs about 2 pounds (1 kg) and stores about 14 teaspoons of sugar in its fat root. For many years, sugar was an expensive luxury. Elizabeth I had sugar at her table, but at that time, its main use was in medicine.

Saccharin is a white powder made from coal tar. It is 400 times sweeter than sugar, but it has no food value. It is used in slimming and diabetic diets.

Sugar

Sugar is a sweet-tasting food. We eat it as an ingredient in ice cream, candy, and soft drinks. We use sugar crystals to sweeten cereal, coffee, and tea.

Sugar gives our body energy more quickly than

any other food. But eating too many sugary things can cause your teeth to decay.

All sugar contains carbon, hydrogen, and oxygen. Different groupings of these ATOMS produce different kinds of sugar. The kind we eat most of is known as *sucrose*.

Every green PLANT produces sugar. But most of the sugar that we eat comes from two plants. One is sugarcane, a type of giant grass. The other is sugarbeet, a plant with a thick root rich in sugar.

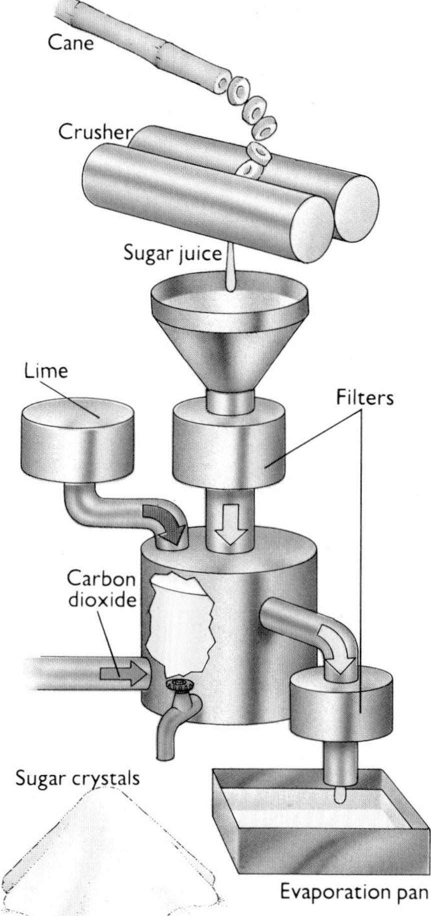

▲ *Sugarcane is processed by extracting the juice and then filtering it and heating it to make crystals of sugar. Carbon dioxide and lime are used in the purification process.*

Sulfur

Sulfur is an ELEMENT often found as yellow CRYSTALS lying at the mouth of volcanoes and hot springs. Cabbages, eggs, and other foods contain some sulfur. Plants and animals need a little sulfur to grow well.

People use sulfur to make drugs, gunpowder, fertilizer, and other useful chemicals.

Sun

The Sun is just one of many millions of STARS in the MILKY WAY. But it is also the center of our SOLAR SYSTEM. The PLANETS and their moons all whirl around it. The heat and light given out by the Sun make it possible for plants and animals to live here on the planet that we call the EARTH.

The Sun seems small because it is so far away. A

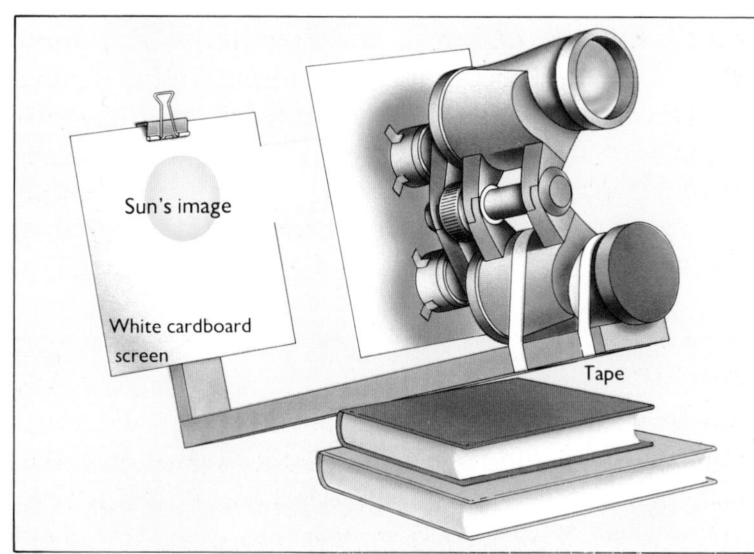

SEE IT YOURSELF

This is a safe way to study the Sun. Clip a sheet of white cardboard onto an L-shaped wooden frame. Place a pair of binoculars on the frame so that the eyepieces are about 1 foot (30 cm) away from the cardboard. Move the binoculars around until images of the Sun appear on it. Focus the binoculars to get a sharp image. Now tape another sheet of cardboard over the eyepieces, cutting a round hole for one of them in the cardboard. Tape the binoculars onto the wooden frame. Cover one of the lenses. You should get a single, sharp, steady image of the Sun on the screen.

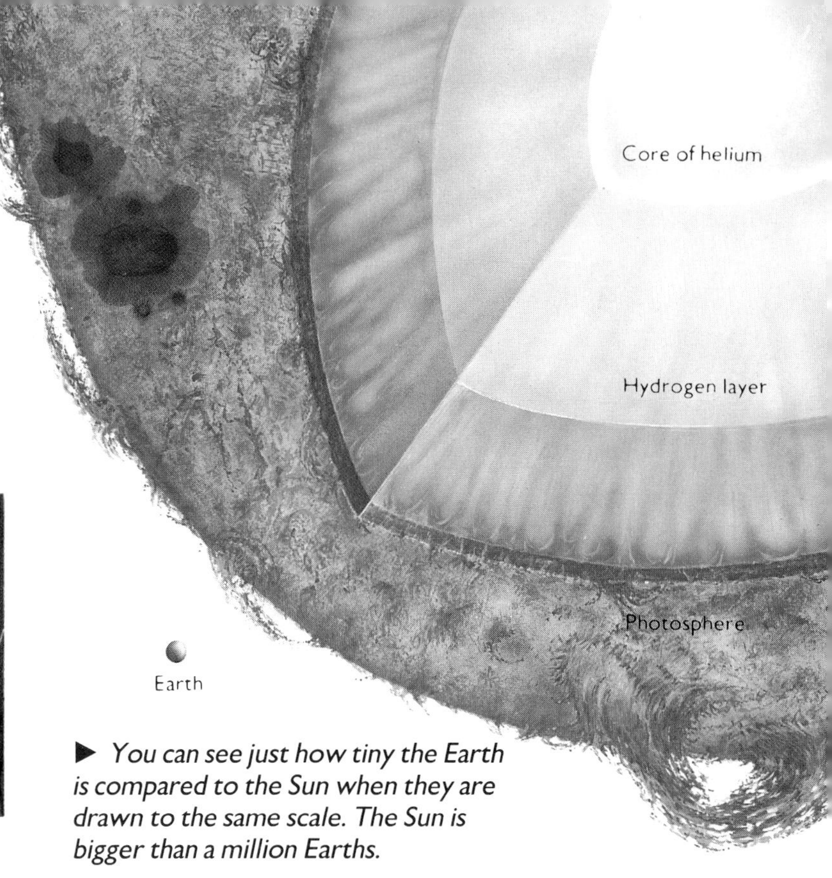

▶ *You can see just how tiny the Earth is compared to the Sun when they are drawn to the same scale. The Sun is bigger than a million Earths.*

▲ *The Sun has been a yellowish star for about 4,600 million years—as long as the Earth has existed.*

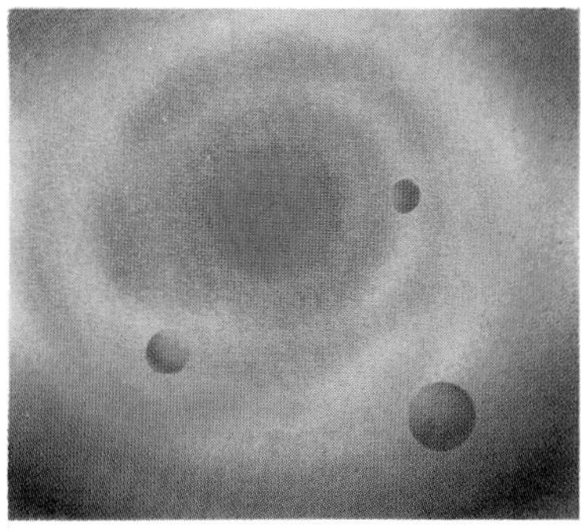

▲ *In another five billion years, the Sun will become a red giant.*

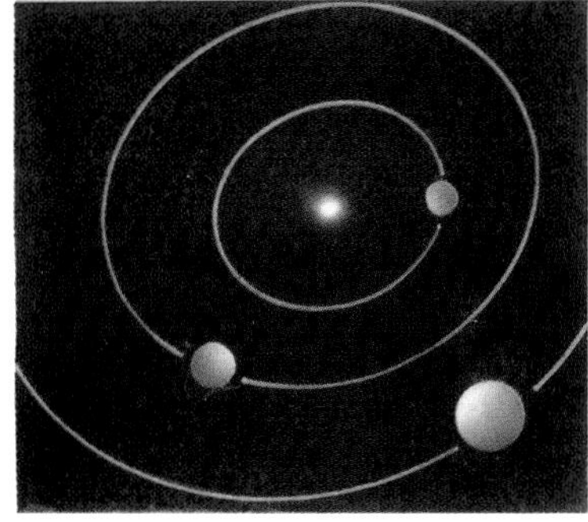

▲ *In yet another five billion years, it will fade to become small and dim.*

spacecraft that took an hour to zoom around the Earth would need five months to reach the Sun. In fact, the Sun is so big that you could fit a million Earths inside it with room to spare. A bucketful of the Sun's substance would weigh far less than a bucketful of rock from the Earth. But the whole Sun would weigh over 750 times more than all the planets put together.

The Sun is a great glowing ball of gases. In the middle of the Sun, a process called nuclear fusion turns HYDROGEN gas into helium gas. The change releases huge amounts of NUCLEAR ENERGY. The Sun beams out its energy in all directions as *electromagnetic waves*. Some of these waves give us HEAT and LIGHT. But there are also radio waves, ultraviolet rays, X rays, and others.

The Sun was formed from a mass of gas and dust five billion years ago. It contains enough fuel to keep it glowing for another five billion years.

Superconductivity

Some materials allow electricity to flow through them more easily than other materials. Good conductors such as copper and silver have little resistance to an electric current—but they do have some. Electricity struggling to pass through them makes them warm. However, in 1911, it was discovered that the metal mercury loses all its electrical resistance when it is cooled to about −460°F (−270°C)—very, very cold indeed. It became a superconductor—but it was very expensive and difficult to produce such a low temperature.

Then, in 1987, scientists began to experiment with new materials. They found that certain ceramic (clay-based) mixtures could be made to superconduct at higher temperatures—as high as about −275°F (−170°C)—still very cold, but easier to achieve. Now, the race is on to find materials that are superconductors at room temperature. If this is achieved, the whole electronics industry will be changed. Computers will become smaller and faster, and machines such as medical scanners will be much cheaper to produce and run.

If scientists succeed in making substances superconductive at ordinary air temperatures, it will be possible to produce electromagnets that generate large magnetic fields without losing any energy. These could be used for high-speed trains supported above the track by powerful magnets. But perhaps the most important use for superconductive materials will be in super-efficient power generation plants.

Supersonic Flight

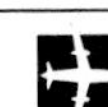

"Supersonic" flight means flying faster than sound travels through the air. This speed is about 760 miles (1,225 km) an hour at sea level. Higher up, sound travels at a slower speed.

When a plane flies slower than the speed of sound, the air ahead has time to divide smoothly and flow around the plane. But in supersonic flight, the air ahead has no time to prepare for the coming of the plane. Instead, the air is disturbed so much it forms a shock wave that makes a loud bang and may badly buffet the plane.

▼ A plane flying slower than the speed of sound (left) creates disturbances in the air pressure, which travel at the speed of sound and so move along ahead of the plane. A plane moving at the speed of sound (center) is moving as fast as the disturbances it causes. These pile up in front of the plane and form a shock wave. A plane traveling faster than the speed of sound (right) breaks through the sound "barrier," but creates a shock wave which, when it reaches the ground, is heard as a sonic boom.

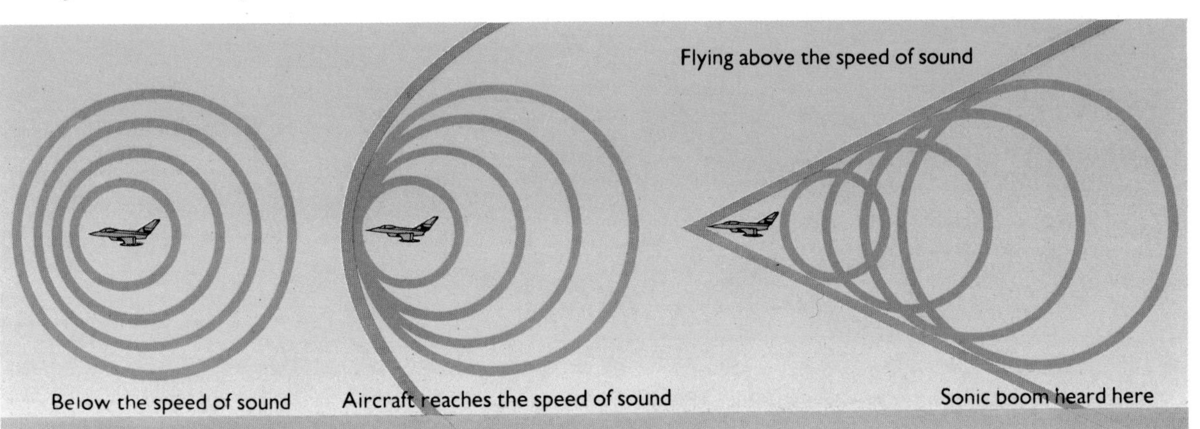

When an aircraft is flying at the speed of sound, it is said to be flying at Mach 1. Mach 2 means twice the speed of sound, and so on. At a height of 40,000 feet (12,000 meters), the speed of sound is only about 620 miles (1,000 km)/h, instead of 760 miles (1,225 km)/h at ground level.

Aircraft builders prevented buffeting by building planes such as *Concorde* with long, sharp noses and thin, swept-back wings. A supersonic plane has flown six times as fast as sound.

Surgery

Surgery involves making an incision in a person's body to remove or repair a damaged part of the body. Surgery is performed in a hospital by a specially trained doctor called a surgeon. He or she works in a specially equipped room. X RAYS and other tests may help to show the surgeon how best

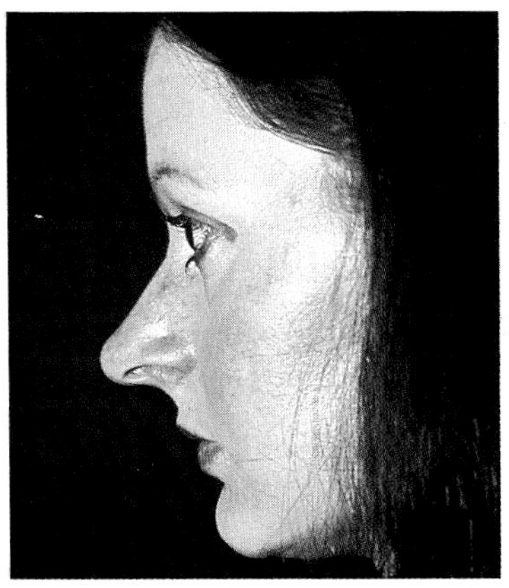

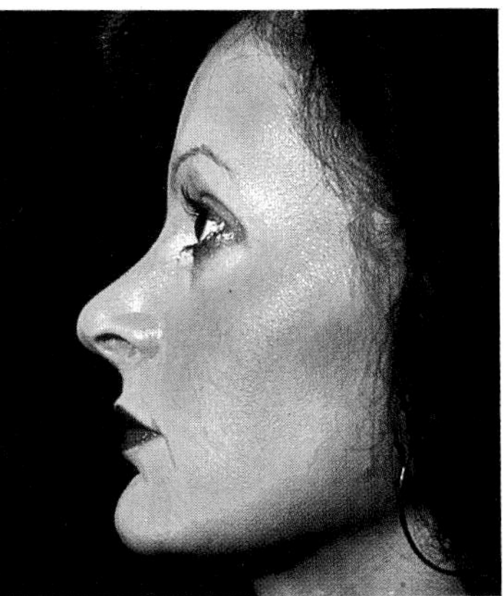

► *Plastic surgery is usually performed to repair the surface of the body after serious burns or accidents. It may also be performed for purely cosmetic reasons to improve a person's appearance. These photographs show the same woman's profile before and after cosmetic surgery to reduce the size of her nose.*

to operate. Before an operation, a patient is given an anesthetic so that he or she feels no pain.

The surgeon cuts the patient open with a sharp knife called a scalpel. Other tools help the surgeon prevent bleeding and hold back flaps of skin. After operating, the surgeon closes the wound by sewing its edges together or with a special tape.

SURINAM

VENEZUELA
ATLANTIC OCEAN
GUYANA
SURINAM
GUIANA
BRAZIL

Government: Military-civilian executive
Capital: Paramaribo
Area: 63,037 sq. miles (163,265 sq. km)
Population: 422,000
Languages: Dutch, Sranan, English
Currency: Guilder

Surinam

Surinam is a small country on the north-central coast of South America. People of many races live there and grow rice, bananas, cacao, sugar, and fruits along the coastal lowlands. The most important product of Surinam is bauxite, from which aluminum is made.

Surinam became a Dutch possession in 1667 when Britain handed it over in exchange for the Dutch colony of New Amsterdam (now New York). Surinam became independent in 1975.

◀ *This surveyor is taking measurements so that a new road can be built along the exact route planned for it.*

Surveying

Surveying means using measuring instruments and calculating certain figures to find out the exact positions of places on the Earth's surface. This kind of information makes it possible for people to make maps and charts and to build bridges, roads, and buildings.

The ancient Egyptians used surveying methods as early as 1400 B.C. to position boundary marks that were covered each year by the Nile's flood waters. They must also have used surveying to build the pyramids as accurately as they did. The Babylonians, about 3500 B.C., made maps to an accurate scale.

Swan

These big, graceful waterbirds are among the heaviest birds able to fly. To take off, they need a long, clear stretch of water.

Swans swim with webbed feet, lowering their necks to feed on underwater plants. They build bulky nests by pools or rivers. Their young are known as cygnets.

Some kinds of swans fly south in spring and fall. They fly in V-shaped flocks.

▼ *Although swans are heavy birds their long, broad wings and powerful breast muscles allow them to fly. But they need a good long "runway," on land or water for takeoff.*

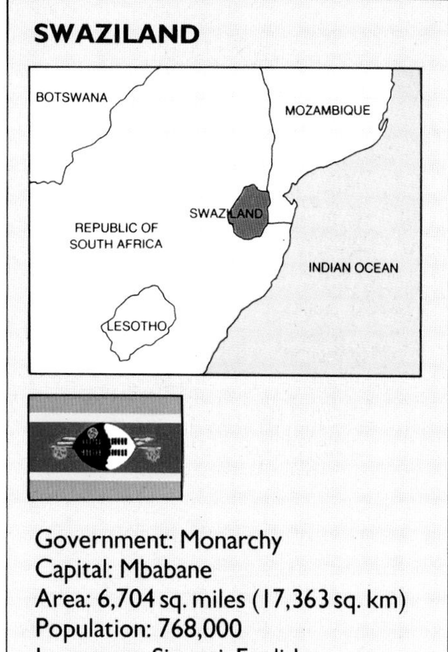

Government: Monarchy
Capital: Mbabane
Area: 6,704 sq. miles (17,363 sq. km)
Population: 768,000
Languages: Siswati, English
Currency: Lilangeni

Swaziland

The kingdom of Swaziland in southeastern Africa is almost completely surrounded by South Africa. Most of the people live by raising cattle and growing corn. Large forests yield wood products. Swaziland is dependent on South Africa for most of its trade. It is a former British protectorate that became independent in 1968 and is a member of the British Commonwealth. The king is Mswati III.

► *Fishing boats and huts at the port of Kyrkesund, near Göteborg, on the western coast of Sweden. Fishing is an important part of the Swedish economy.*

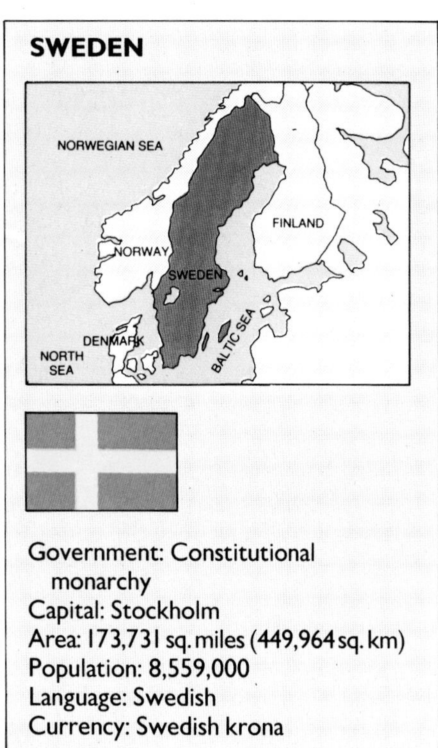

Government: Constitutional monarchy
Capital: Stockholm
Area: 173,731 sq. miles (449,964 sq. km)
Population: 8,559,000
Language: Swedish
Currency: Swedish krona

Sweden

Sweden is the fourth largest nation in EUROPE. The country lies in the north between Norway and the Baltic Sea. Mountains cover most of the west, and forests take up more than half of the land. Their CONIFER trees yield much of the world's softwood. Most of Sweden's electricity comes from rivers flowing down the mountains. Farmers produce milk, meat, grains, and sugar beets on farmlands near the coast. The north is too cold for farming, but it has rich iron mines.

Most of the eight million Swedes live in the south. The capital, Stockholm, is there.

Swift, Jonathan

Jonathan Swift (1667–1745) was an English writer, famous for books that poked fun at the silly, cruel behavior of people and governments. Most children enjoy stories from *Gulliver's Travels*. This tells of voyages to very strange lands. On his first voyage, Gulliver reaches the land of Lilliput, where the people are only an inch tall. Then he travels to a land of giants.

▲ *Except for* Gulliver's Travels, *Jonathan Swift published all his work anonymously and without being paid.*

Swimming

Swimming is the skill or sport of staying afloat and moving through water. Swimming is healthy exercise, and being able to swim may save your life if you fall into water by accident. Many animals know how to swim from birth. But people have to learn, usually with help from a trained instructor.

Beginners often start in a pool or at the edge of the sea. First they should float or glide. Then they can try kicking. Arm movements come last. Beginners must learn to fit in breathing with arm movements. Swimmers usually use one or more of five main strokes. These are called the breaststroke, butterfly stroke, backstroke, sidestroke, and crawl.

▼ *These pictures show how the arm and leg movements are coordinated in four of the main swimming strokes: crawl, backstroke, butterfly, and breastroke.*

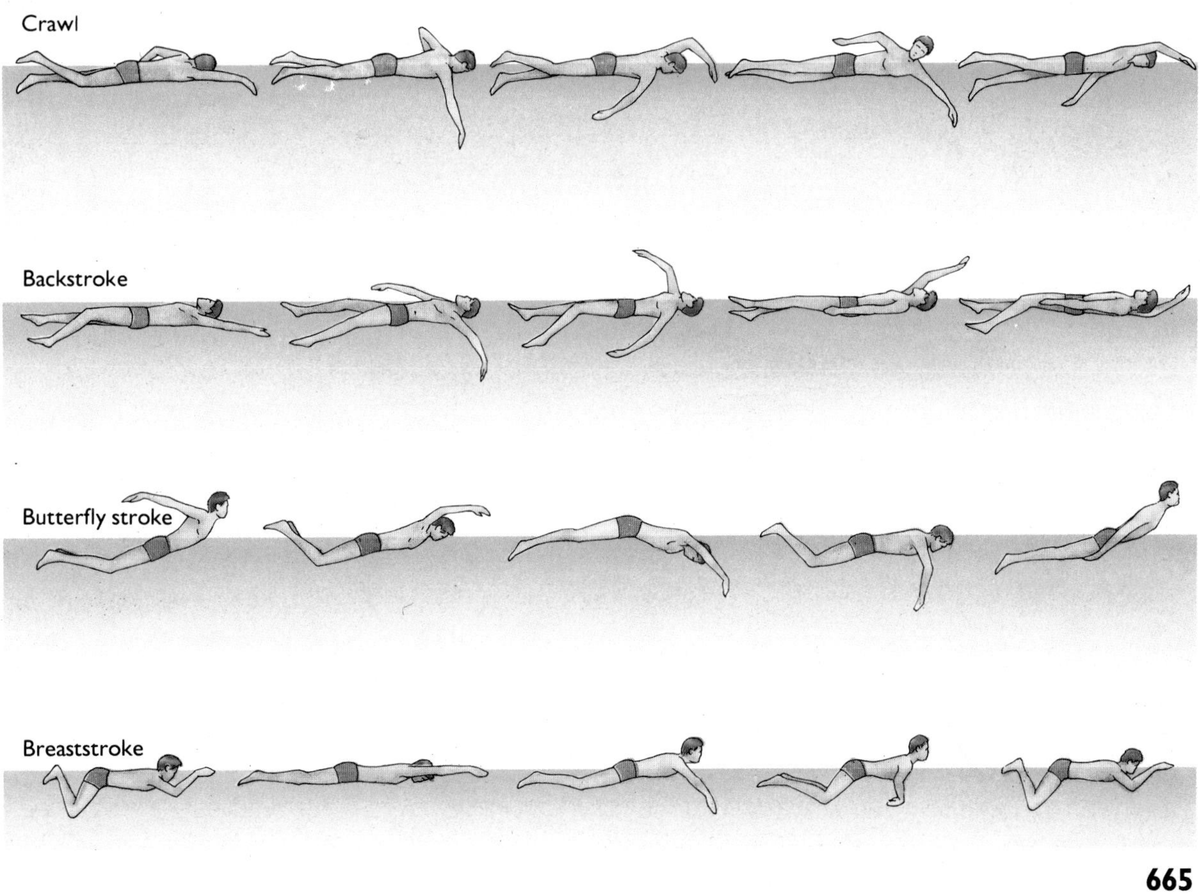

SWITZERLAND

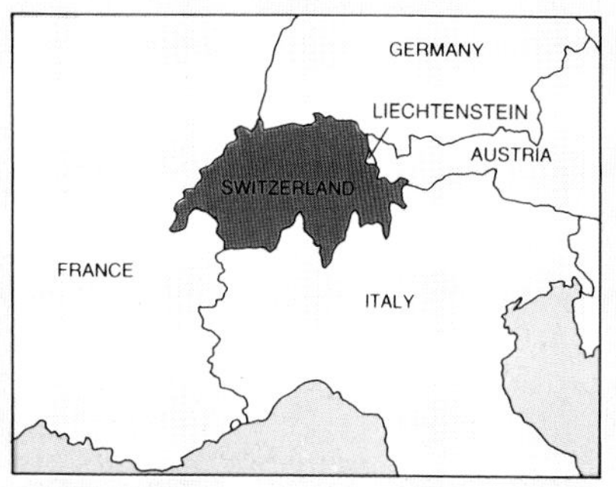

Government: Federal state
Capital: Bern
Area: 15,941 sq. miles (41,288 sq. km)
Population: 6,712,000
Languages: German, French, Italian
Currency: Swiss franc

Switzerland

This small, mountainous country lies in the south-central part of EUROPE. The sharp, snowy peaks of the Alps and their steep-sided valleys fill most of southern Switzerland. In summer, tourists pick wild flowers and watch dairy cattle grazing on the mountain meadows. Winter visitors to the many resorts ski down the snowy alpine slopes.

Most of the country's crops are grown where the mountains meet the lower land of the Swiss Plateau. Here, too, stand most of Switzerland's cities, including Bern, the capital. Swiss factories make chemicals, machinery, watches, and chocolates.

Synagogue

A synagogue is a Jewish house of worship. Synagogues, sometimes called temples, are modeled after the original temple of the Jews that once stood in Jerusalem. Like churches, synagogues are used to hold worship services on the Sabbath and HIGH HOLY DAYS.

Synthetic

If something is synthetic, it means that it is made of an artificial, or man-made, material. Plastic is a synthetic material; so is nylon. Synthetics such as plastic are made by fusing different chemicals together. These can be used to make products that are strong and inexpensive.

SYRIA

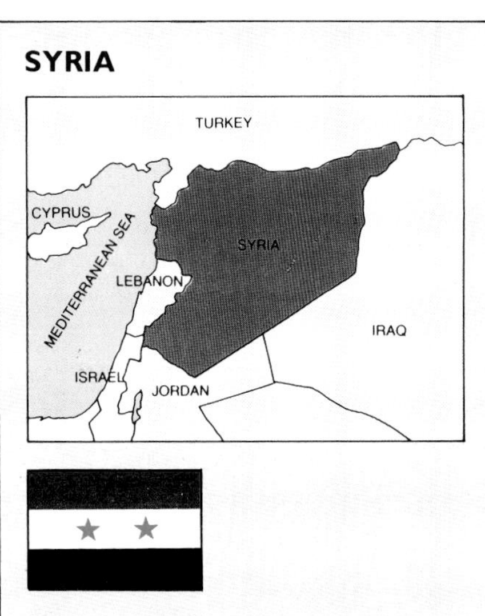

Government: Republic
Capital: Damascus
Area: 71,498 sq. miles (185,180 sq. km)
Population: 12,116,000
Language: Arabic
Currency: Syrian pound

Syria

This Arab country lies just east of the Mediterranean Sea. Much of Syria is covered by dry plains that are hot in summer and chilly in winter.

Most Syrian towns grew up on the roads used long ago to bring goods from the Orient. In 1516, Syria was conquered by the Turks and was ruled by Turkey for 400 years. After World War I, the French ruled the country on behalf of the League of Nations. Syria gained its independence in 1943 and has close ties with Libya.

Table Tennis

Table tennis is like a small-scale version of tennis, played indoors on a nine-foot table and with a celluloid ball. Each player has a rubber- or sponge-covered paddle. If your opponent fails to return the ball, you score a point. The ball must always bounce on your opponent's side of the net, except when you serve. Then it must bounce on both sides. The first player to score 21 points wins.

Taft, William Howard

William H. Taft (1857–1930) was the 27th president of the United States. He was an efficient and careful president, though, partly because he was such a modest man, he was never very popular. But surprisingly; he never really wanted to be president at all. Taft was a lawyer and a judge by training, and his real ambition was to be chief justice of the Supreme Court. In 1921, he was made chief justice, and he felt at last that he had achieved something worthwhile. He is the only man to have been president and chief justice. Before becoming president, Taft had been a state judge and then a federal judge, a very successful governor of the Philippines, and secretary of war.

WILLIAM H. TAFT

Twenty-seventh President
1909–1913
Born: Cincinnati, Ohio
Education: Yale University
Occupation: Lawyer, judge
Political Party: Republican
Buried: Arlington National Cemetery, Arlington, Virginia

Tahiti

Tahiti is a small island in the Pacific. Its spectacular tropical beauty, with long beaches, swaying palm trees, rushing streams, and thick vegetation, has made it many people's idea of a little paradise. Tourism is its major industry. Most of the 85,000 inhabitants live in and around the capital city, Papeete. Tahiti has been ruled by France since 1842.

The French painter, Paul Gauguin, spent several years in Tahiti. In his paintings, he idealized the people and the lush tropical settings in pure, brilliant colors. Many authors, including Herman Melville, James Michener, and Robert Louis Stevenson, wrote about the beauty of the island.

Taiwan

Taiwan is an island country 87 miles (140 km) off the coast of China. Also called Formosa, its official name is the Republic of China. Rice is the main crop, but sugar, fruit, and tea are also grown. Most Taiwanese are Chinese whose ancestors emigrated

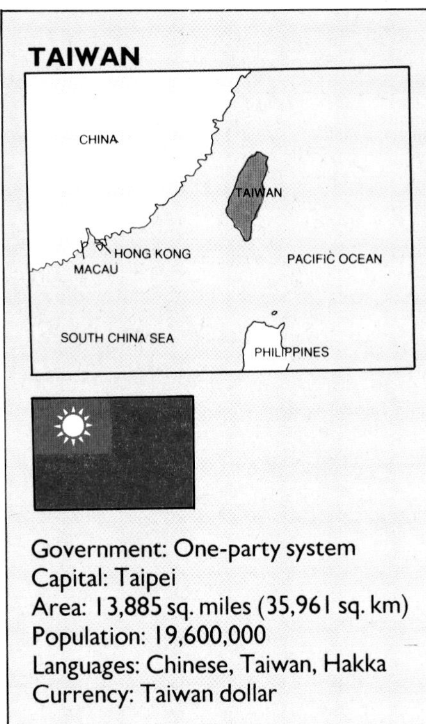

Government: One-party system
Capital: Taipei
Area: 13,885 sq. miles (35,961 sq. km)
Population: 19,600,000
Languages: Chinese, Taiwan, Hakka
Currency: Taiwan dollar

to the island in the 1700s. Others are Chinese who fled from the mainland after the Communist takeover of China in 1949. Taiwan held the Chinese seat in the United Nations until 1971, when Communist China was admitted and Taiwan expelled. Government planning and U.S. aid have brought huge advances in industry and living standards for the people.

Taj Mahal

This is the world's most beautiful tomb. It stands on the Jumna River at Agra in northern India. The emperor Shah Jahan built it for his favorite wife, Mumtaz Mahal, who died in 1631. When the Shah died, he was buried with his wife in her tomb.

▶ *The Taj Mahal, in Agra, India, is a marvel of Islamic architecture.*

The building of the Taj Mahal and its ornamentation took 20,000 men from 1632 to 1650. The inside of the tomb is adorned with semiprecious stones and lit through carved-marble screens set near the tops of the walls.

Tanzania

Tanzania consists of two parts: Tanganyika on the east African mainland and the islands of Zanzibar and Pemba off the coast. They joined to form one country in 1964. The country contains part of Africa's largest lake, Lake Victoria, and Africa's highest mountain, Mount Kilimanjaro 19,340 ft. (5,895 m). Tanzania has much wildlife and beautiful scenery. Diamonds are the country's most valuable mineral. Gold is also mined. Tanzania's capital and largest city is Dar es Salaam.

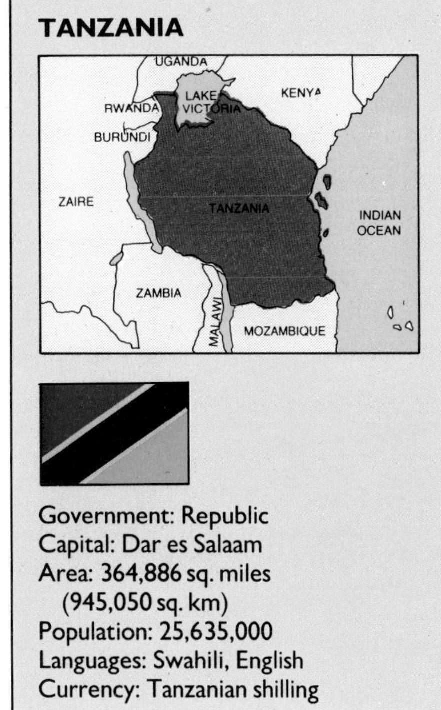

Government: Republic
Capital: Dar es Salaam
Area: 364,886 sq. miles (945,050 sq. km)
Population: 25,635,000
Languages: Swahili, English
Currency: Tanzanian shilling

Tape Recorder

A tape recorder turns sound waves into a magnetic pattern on tape. When played, the pattern changes back into sound.

A microphone inside or connected to the recorder changes sound into an electrical signal. This is amplified (made stronger) and fed to the recording head. The head produces a magnetic field which magnetizes the tape as it passes the head.

When the tape is played back, the magnetic field produces an electrical signal which goes to an amplifier and loudspeaker.

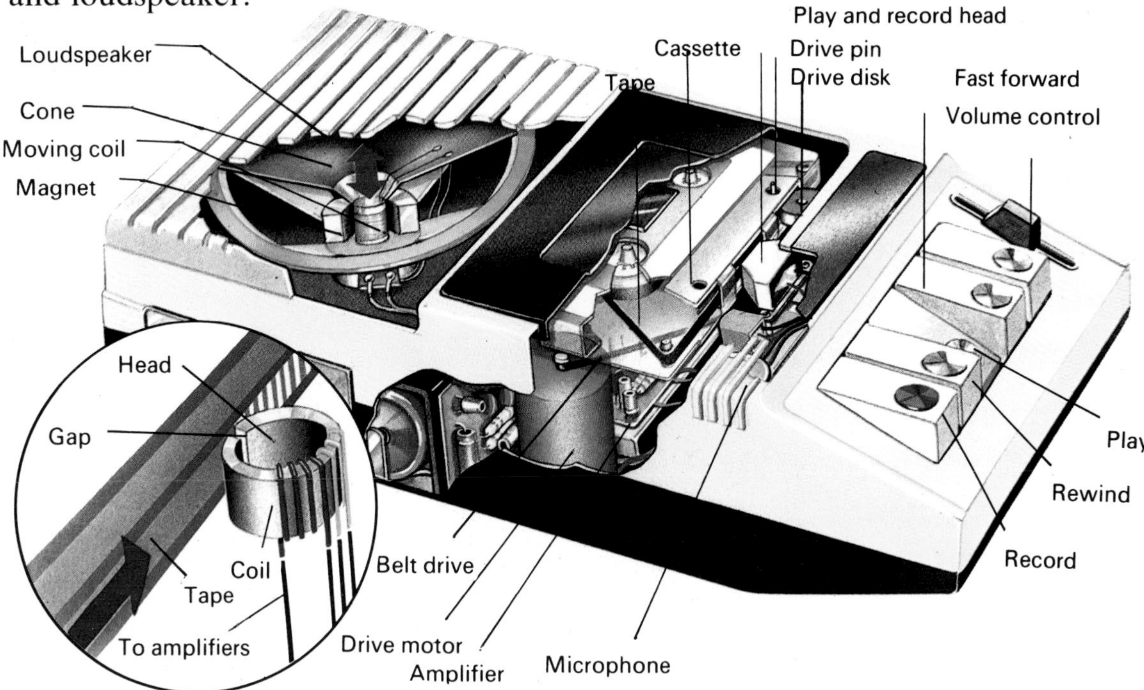

▲ *In a tape recorder, the recorder/replay head is a coil wound around an iron ring. A drive motor moves the tape past a gap in the head to record and play back. An amplifier increases the strength of the electrical signals before they go to the loudspeaker.*

Tapestry

Tapestries are designs or pictures woven in cloth. Making tapestries is a very old craft. The Egyptians made tapestries about 1,700 years ago.

▲ *Tapestries such as this 15th century Flemish work give us a clear idea of how people dressed and behaved at the time.*

Tapestries are made by WEAVING colored silk thread across rows of strong linen or wool threads held in a frame.

The tapestry design is drawn onto the linen threads with ink. The weaver works from the back of the tapestry.

Taste

We can taste food because we have taste buds on our TONGUE. Your tongue is covered in tiny bumps. The taste buds are buried in the sides of these bumps. There are clusters of buds on the back, tip, and sides of the tongue. NERVES running from the buds to the brain tell you whether the food you are eating is sweet, sour, bitter, or salty.

Flavor is a mixture of the taste and the SMELL of food. If you have a bad cold and your nose is blocked, food hardly tastes of anything. The most comfortable way to take bad-tasting medicine is to hold your nose while you swallow.

SEE IT YOURSELF

This simple experiment will show you where your different taste buds are. Place some sugar, lemon juice, salt, and vanilla extract on a plate. Make sure they do not mix. Using a clean paintbrush, put a little of each substance on different parts of your tongue. Can you taste the sugar and salt on the sides of your tongue? Where do you taste the other substances?

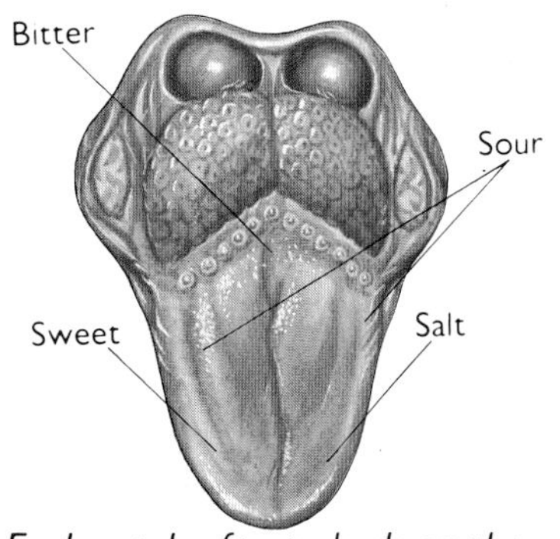

▲ *Each patch of taste buds on the tongue picks up one kind of taste.*

Tax

The government of a country must have money to carry on its work. It gets most of this money by taxing people. *Direct* taxes are those people pay directly to the government on their income—income tax. How much income tax a person pays depends on several things. The higher a person's income, the more he or she pays in tax. A married person pays less than a single person with the same income.

Indirect taxes are those charged on some goods

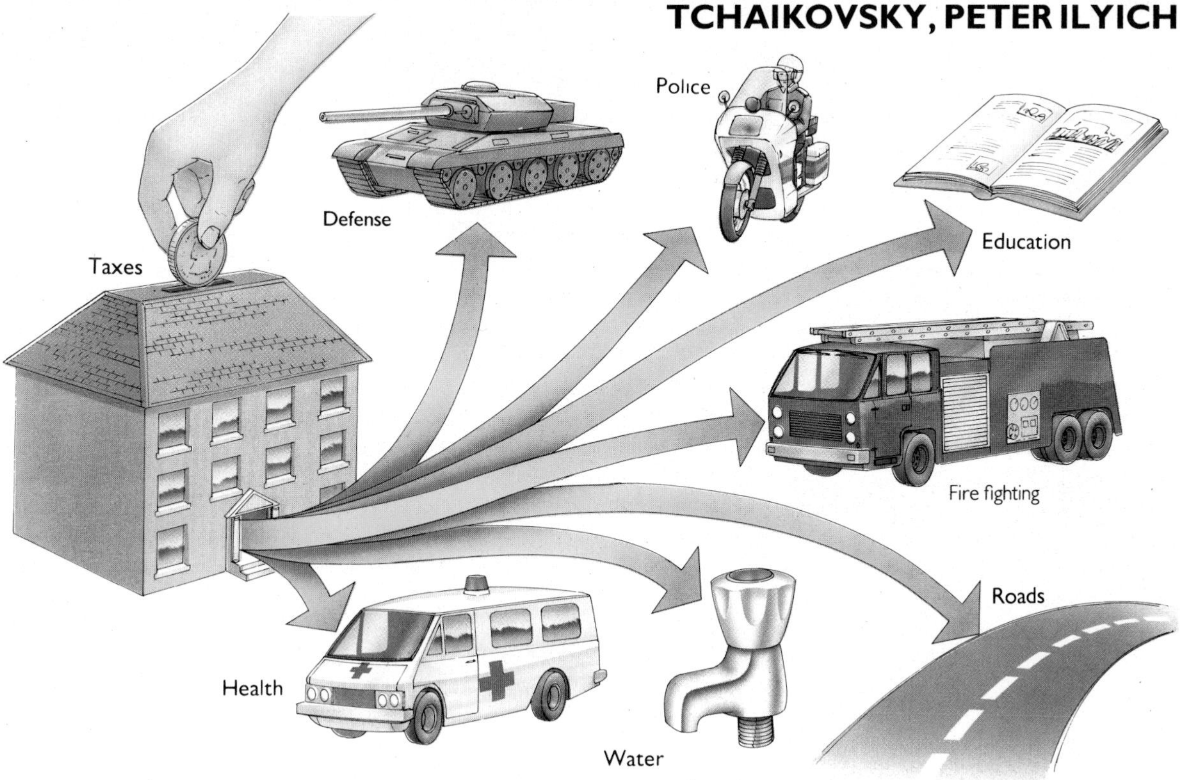

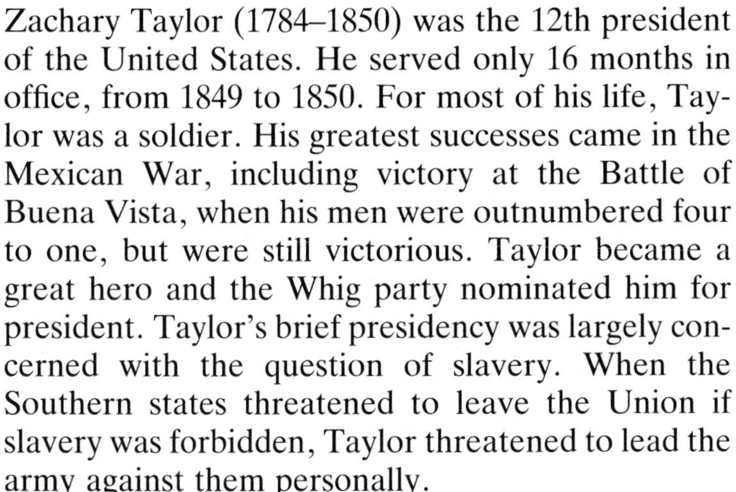

▲ *The taxes that people pay are used to keep essential services running so that they are available to everyone.*

bought in stores or elsewhere. Every time a driver buys gasoline, a part of the cost is tax which goes to the government.

Taylor, Zachary

Zachary Taylor (1784–1850) was the 12th president of the United States. He served only 16 months in office, from 1849 to 1850. For most of his life, Taylor was a soldier. His greatest successes came in the Mexican War, including victory at the Battle of Buena Vista, when his men were outnumbered four to one, but were still victorious. Taylor became a great hero and the Whig party nominated him for president. Taylor's brief presidency was largely concerned with the question of slavery. When the Southern states threatened to leave the Union if slavery was forbidden, Taylor threatened to lead the army against them personally.

ZACHARY TAYLOR

Twelfth President 1849–1850
Born: Orange County, Virginia
Education: Mostly self-educated
Occupation: Soldier, farmer
Political Party: Whig
Buried: Zachary Taylor National Cemetery, near Louisville, Kentucky

Tchaikovsky, Peter Ilyich

Peter Tchaikovsky (1840–1893) was one of the most famous and popular musical composers. He was born at Votkinsk in Russia and studied music at the

▲ *Tchaikovsky wrote beautiful ballet music, such as* Sleeping Beauty. *Although his music was successful, the composer suffered from deep depression.*

conservatory in St. Petersburg (formerly Leningrad). He lived in great poverty until a wealthy lady, Nadezhda von Meck, offered to give him a yearly allowance of money. Tchaikovsky never met Madame von Meck, but they wrote many letters to each other.

Tchaikovsky was an unhappy man, but his music was full of warmth. He made several tours abroad, but he preferred to be at home in the countryside. Among his best-known works are the ballet *Swan Lake*, his first *Piano Concerto*, the *Violin Concerto in D Major*, the ballets *Nutcracker* and *Sleeping Beauty*, and his *Symphony No. 6*, the "Pathétique."

Tea

Tea is a refreshing drink that is made by pouring boiling water over the dried, chopped leaves of the tea plant.

Tea was first grown in China. It was brought to Europe by the Dutch in the 1660s. Today, most tea is grown in northern India, China, and Sri Lanka.

▼ *If a tea plant were allowed to grow to its full height, it could reach 33 feet (10 m). Instead, it is kept small and bushy by pruning so that all its energy goes into making new leaves.*

Teeth

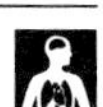

Teeth are made to cut, tear, or crush food so that it can be swallowed. Cutting teeth are called incisors;

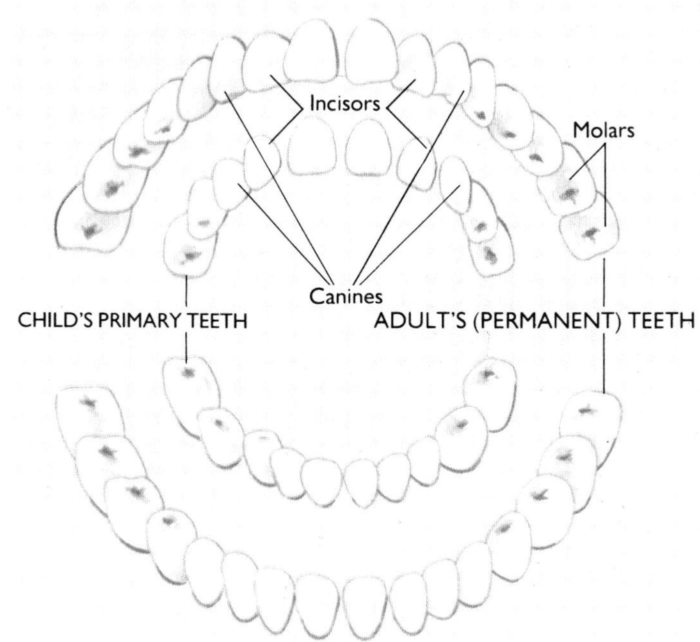

► *Your first set of teeth are called primary teeth. There are 10 on top and 10 on the bottom. As you grow, these teeth become loose and fall out. They are replaced by a set of permanent teeth, 32 in all.*

tearing teeth are called canines; and crushing teeth are called molars. Meat-eating animals have large canines for tearing flesh. Plant-eaters have sharp incisors and large molars for snapping off and grinding stringy stalks. Humans have all three kinds of teeth because we eat all kinds of food.

There are two parts to a tooth. The root, which has one, two, or three prongs, is attached to the jawbone. The crown is the part you can see. Tooth decay happens when bacteria mixes with sugar. This dissolves tooth enamel, making holes that let infection get inside the tooth.

▲ *There are three layers in a tooth. At the center is a space full of nerves and blood vessels; around that is a bony wall of dentine. On top is a layer of hard, shiny enamel.*

Telecommunications

The Greek word *tele* means "far away." Telecommunications refers to a long-distance communication by RADIO, telegraph, TELEPHONE, and TELEVISION. Most of today's long-distance communication is electronic.

Telecommunications are very fast because the sound and picture signals travel as electric currents along wires, radio waves through the air and space, or light waves along glass fibers. Radio waves and light waves travel at 186,000 miles (300,000 km) a second. Electric signals travel almost as fast. Telephone and radio networks use communications satellites orbiting in space high above the Earth.

Telex and facsimile (fax) machines play a big part

The facsimile (fax) became increasingly popular in the 1980s after manufacturers developed smaller, less costly, and faster machines. Today, most fax machines can transmit two or three pages of information a minute.

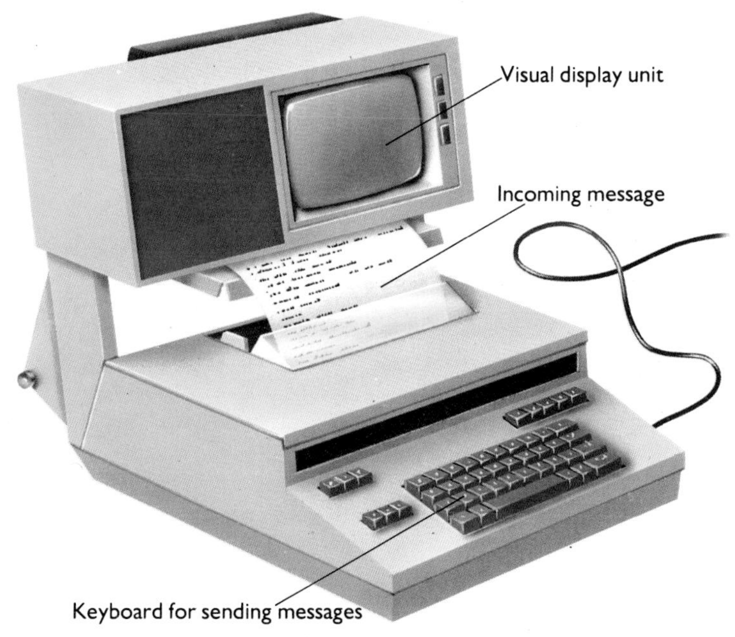

◀ *A telex machine is like a computer with a keyboard that can be used to send messages by telephone. When the letters are typed, they are turned into electric signals. These are sent along telephone wires to a similar machine at the receiving end, which can print out the message or display it on a screen.*

in today's communications. Messages are typed or fed as documents into these machines and are reproduced in seconds at the receiving terminal.

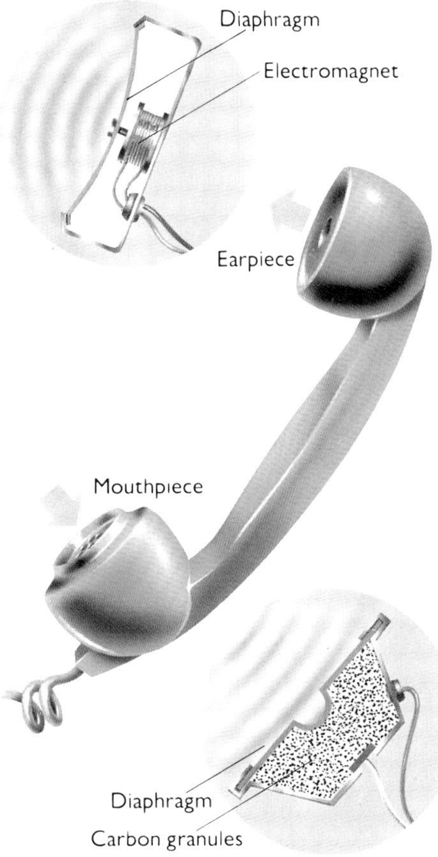

Telephone

Telephones let you speak to someone far away. When you pick up a telephone receiver, a weak electric current is switched on. When you speak into the mouthpiece, you speak into a microphone.

Waves of SOUND from your voice hit a metal disk inside the microphone and make it vibrate. These vibrations travel along the telephone wires as electrical waves. When they reach the other end, they hit another metal disk in the earpiece. This changes the vibrations back into sound waves, which the person you are calling hears as your voice.

The first electric telephone, made by Alexander BELL in 1876, produced only a very weak sound over long distances. Today, telephone networks use a worldwide system of cables and communications SATELLITES.

◀ *Speaking into a telephone mouthpiece makes a diaphragm vibrate and compresses carbon granules, to make an electric current vary. The current flows along wires to another telephone and enters the earpiece, where an electromagnet makes a diaphragm vibrate to produce the sound of your voice.*

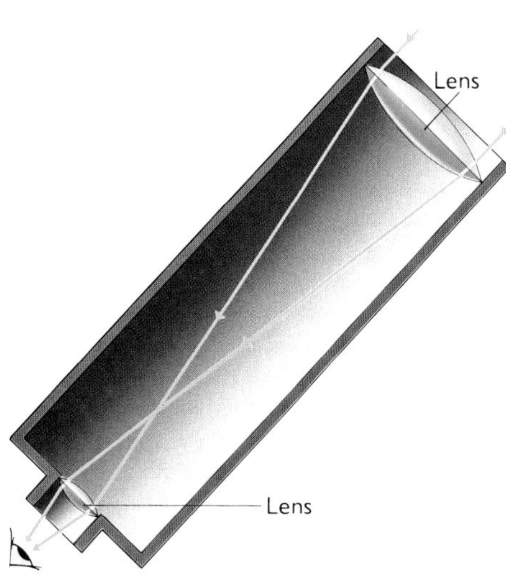

▲ *A refracting telescope uses two lenses to focus rays of light from distant stars and planets.*

Telescope

Telescopes make things that are far away look nearer. They work by gathering the LIGHT from an object and bending it to make a tiny picture called an image. The image is then made larger so we can see it.

There are two kinds of telescope. The LENS or refractor telescope uses two lenses sealed in a tube to keep out unwanted light. A large lens at one end of the tube collects the light. It is called the object lens. A smaller lens called the eyepiece makes the image larger.

The image you see through this kind of telescope is upside down. If you want to turn the image the right way around, a third lens is needed. Binoculars are two lens telescopes fixed together.

The other kind of telescope is called a reflecting telescope. Instead of a lens, it has a curved mirror to collect light. The mirror is shaped so that the light rays bouncing off it are directed at a second mirror which reflects the ray toward the eyepiece. Since 1900, most of the big astronomical telescopes built have been reflectors.

The idea of the lens telescope was discovered by accident in 1608 by Hans Lippershey, a Dutch eyeglass maker. While holding up two lenses, he noticed that the church weathervane looked much closer through them.

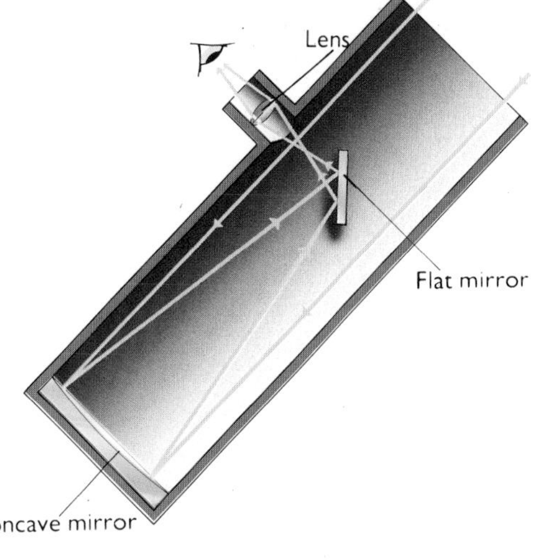

▲ *A reflecting telescope uses a large concave mirror to reflect light onto a smaller mirror that directs it through a lens to the eye.*

◀ *The 14 foot (4.2 m) William Herschel telescope in its dome at the La Palma Observatory in the Canary Islands. It is the third largest single-mirror telescope in the world. It is at a high altitude—7,874 feet (2,400 m) above sea level—where the sky is clear.*

Television

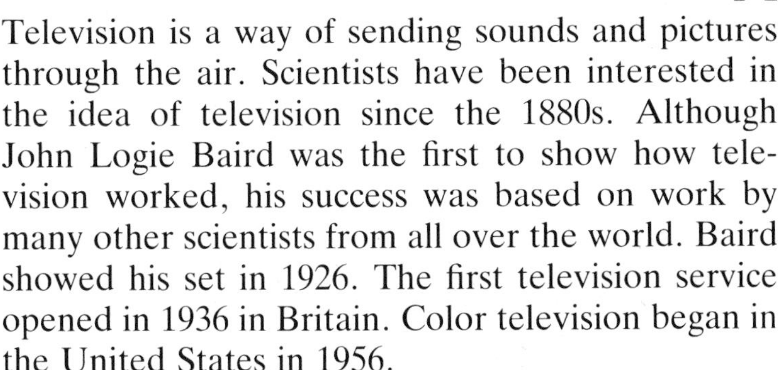

Television is a way of sending sounds and pictures through the air. Scientists have been interested in the idea of television since the 1880s. Although John Logie Baird was the first to show how television worked, his success was based on work by many other scientists from all over the world. Baird showed his set in 1926. The first television service opened in 1936 in Britain. Color television began in the United States in 1956.

At first, all television was black and white. Few people owned television sets because they were very expensive. Now nearly every home has one.

Television works by changing LIGHT waves into electric signals. This happens inside the TV camera.

John Logie Baird's first television set was made of old cans, bicycle parts, lenses, sealing wax and string.

▲ *John Logie Baird demonstrated the first TV in 1925. Light from the doll's head passed through holes in a rotating disk. This was turned into electrical signals and back into a beam of light that was projected onto a screen.*

▼ *The main part of a television set is the cathode ray tube. The big end is the screen. The narrow end contains electron guns that fire electrons through the shadow mask onto the phosphor dots on the screen. All the colors you see on a color television screen are made up from three colors—red, blue, and green—and each of the colors is supplied by one of the guns. To receive the signals that provide the programs, you need an antenna. The antenna may be attached to the set, as here, or installed high up on the roof of a building, so it can receive the radio waves broadcast by the transmitter as clearly as possible.*

A picture of what is happening in front of the camera forms on a special screen behind the LENS. Behind the screen is an electron gun. This *scans* the screen. It moves from left to right to cover each part of the picture. Each part is turned into an electric signal which is made stronger, then sent to the transmitter as RADIO waves. They are picked up by home TV antennas and changed back into electric signals. These pass into the TV set.

Inside the set is a large glass tube called the *cathode ray tube*. The screen that you look at is the front of this tube. This screen is covered with tiny chemical dots. In a color set, these are arranged in groups of three; one red, one blue, one green. At the back of the tube are other electron guns. These fire a beam of electrons to scan the screen just as the camera gun does. As each electron hits the screen, it lights up a dot. These tiny flashes of color build up the picture on your screen. You do not see lines of colored flashing lights, because the electron gun

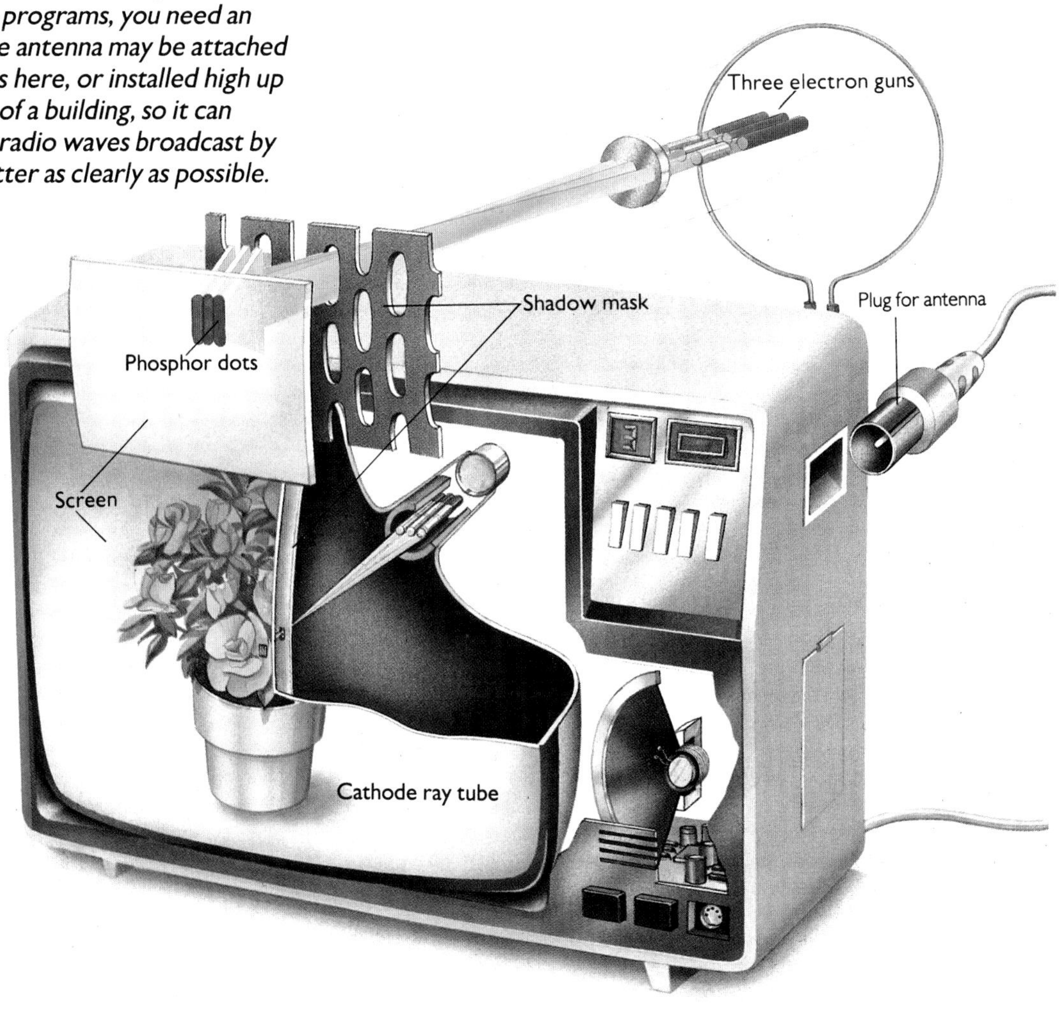

Three electron guns
Shadow mask
Plug for antenna
Phosphor dots
Screen
Cathode ray tube

moves too fast for the eye to follow. What you see is a picture of what is happening in the television studio.

Live television programs show you what is happening as it happens. Most programs are recorded on film or *videotape* and sent out later.

Temperature

Temperature is the measurement of heat. It is measured on a scale marked on a THERMOMETER. Most people in the world today use the Celsius scale. The Fahrenheit scale is most often used in the United States.

Some animals, including mammals such as humans, are warm-blooded. Their temperature stays much the same. Humans can stand quite a wide range of body temperatures. A healthy person's normal body temperature is 98.6°F (37°C). When he or she is ill, their temperature might go up to 106°F (41°C) or more, and they could still survive.

Other animals, such as snakes, lizards, and frogs, are cold-blooded. Their body temperature goes up and down with the temperature of their surroundings. Many cold-blooded animals can survive until their temperature drops almost to freezing point.

TEMPERATURE CONVERSION TABLE

	Celsius (Centigrade)	Fahrenheit
Freezing Point	**0**	**32**
	10	50
	20	68
	30	86
	40	104
	50	122
	60	140
	70	158
	80	176
	90	194
Boiling Point	**100**	**212**
	110	230
	120	248
	130	266
	140	284
	150	302
	200	392
	250	482
	300	572

To convert Fahrenheit to Celsius, subtract 32, multiply by 5, and divide by 9. To convert Celsius to Fahrenheit, multiply by 9, divide by 5, and add 32.

Tennessee

For many years, Tennessee was a frontier state, where pioneers forged a new land. Then, as America spread westward, Tennessee assumed another important role, as a meeting place between the North and South. Though it was a Southern state, many people in Tennessee supported the Union in the CIVIL WAR, and Tennessee was the first Southern state to be readmitted to the Union after the war. A number of important battles were fought in Tennessee during the war. Tennessee remained one of the poorest states for many years. Today, agriculture is still important, but many industries have spread throughout Tennessee, and a wide range of goods is manufactured. Large mineral reserves have made mining an important industry, too.

TENNESSEE

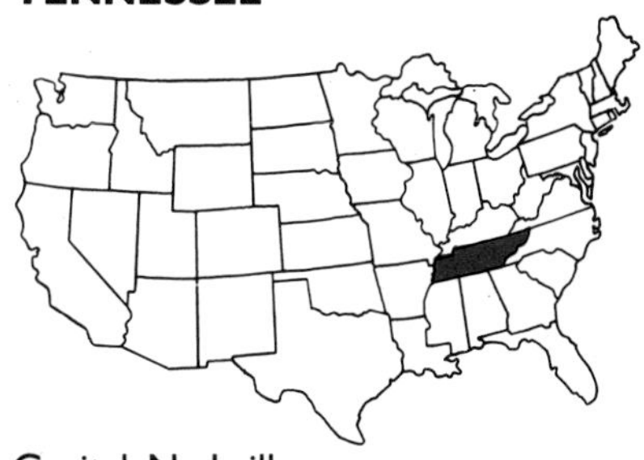

Capital: Nashville
Population: 4,877,185
Area: 42,144 sq. miles (109,152 sq. km)
State flower: Iris
State bird: Mockingbird
State tree: Tulip Poplar
Statehood: June 1, 1796
16th state

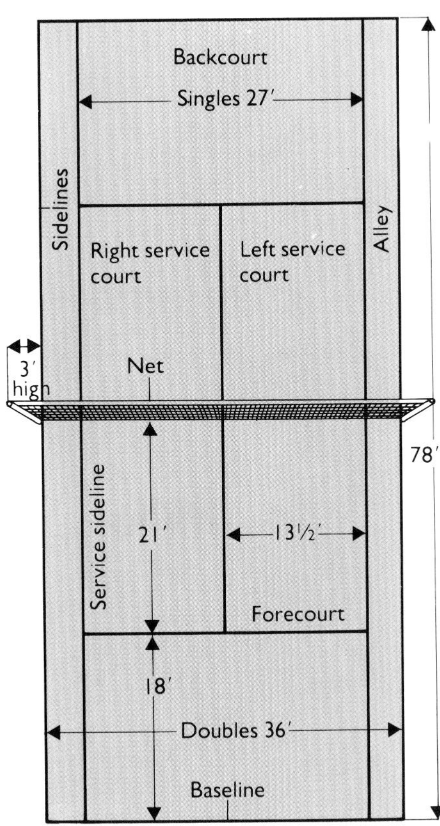

▲ *The court markings used for the modern game of tennis.*

Tennis

Tennis is a game for two or four people played on a specially marked court, which is divided in half by a net 3 feet (91 cm) high. If two people play, it is called a singles match. If four people play, it is called a doubles match.

Tennis balls must be about 2 inches (50 mm) in diameter and weigh about 2 ounces (56.7 grams). A tennis racket can be any size.

A tennis match is divided into sets. Usually, women play three sets and men play five. Each set has at least six games. To win a game, one player must score at least four points. Modern tennis is a simple version of an old French game called real tennis or royal tennis.

Termite

Termites are insects that eat wood. They have soft, pale bodies and thick waists, and live in the warmer parts of the world. Some termites burrow underground or tunnel into house timbers, causing a lot of damage. Others live in huge mounds of earth.

All termites live in large groups called colonies. Each colony has a queen, her king, soldiers, and workers. Most termites are workers. They are small, blind, and wingless. They dig the tunnels or build the mound and find food for the rest of the colony.

In some species of termite, the queen grows to an enormous size, sometimes as much as 20,000 times the size of an ordinary worker termite. She becomes so swollen with eggs that she is unable to move. Some queen termites can lay as many as 30,000 eggs a day.

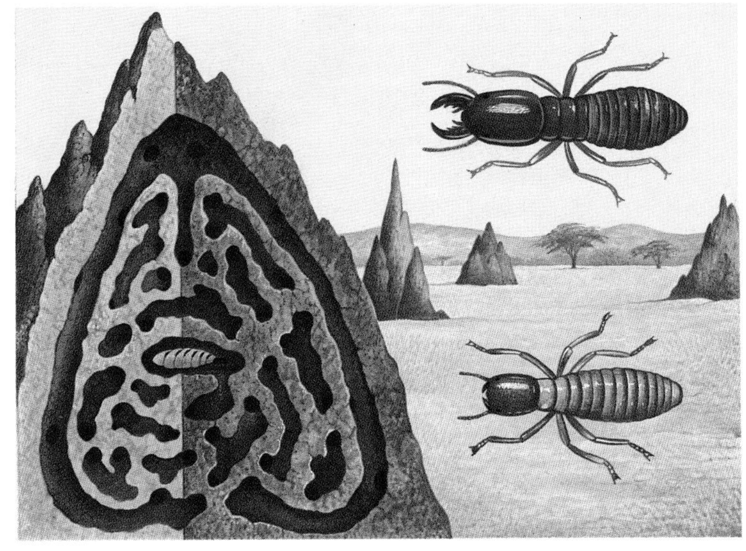

▶ *Many termites build their nests inside huge mounds of earth. Inside the nest is a maze of tunnels and chambers where the workers (right, below) look after the young. The queen is at the center of the nest. Soldier termites (right, above) defend the nest against attack.*

Soldier termites have large strong heads, and are also blind and wingless. They defend the colony from attack. The queen is many times larger than the other termites and does nothing but lay eggs. She is kept in a chamber in the middle of the colony with her king. The workers feed her and look after the eggs until they hatch.

Terrorism

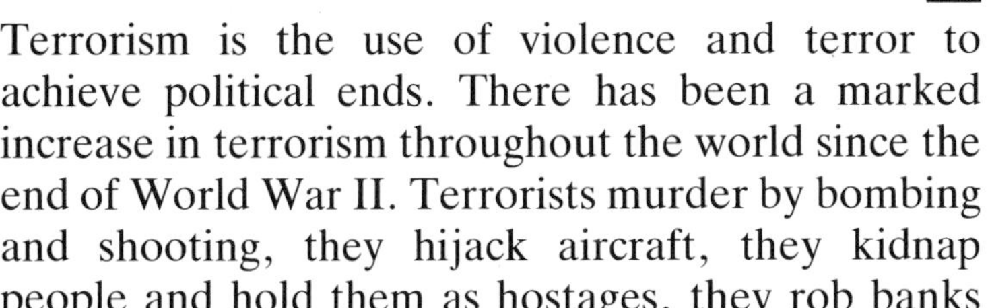

Terrorism is the use of violence and terror to achieve political ends. There has been a marked increase in terrorism throughout the world since the end of World War II. Terrorists murder by bombing and shooting, they hijack aircraft, they kidnap people and hold them as hostages, they rob banks and often take part in drug trafficking.

Terrorism is a worldwide problem, and countries are banding together more and more to try to get rid of this evil.

▲ *Rigid security checks are carried out on visitors to the Olympic Games in Seoul, Korea, in 1988. Terrorists often select major international events as targets for attack.*

Texas

Texas is a huge state, the second largest in the country. Only Alaska is larger, but it is nothing like as rich. Farming and oil have made Texas one of the most prosperous states in America. And Texas is also a leading manufacturing and financial area.

◀ *Dallas, Texas, is one of the largest U.S. cities. The 72-story First Republic Plaza is the tallest building (center). The Reunion Tower (right) has an observation deck.*

TEXAS

Capital: Austin
Population: 16,986,510
Area: 266,807 sq. miles (691,030 sq. km)
State flower: Bluebonnet
State bird: Mockingbird
State tree: Pecan
Statehood: December 29, 1845
28th state

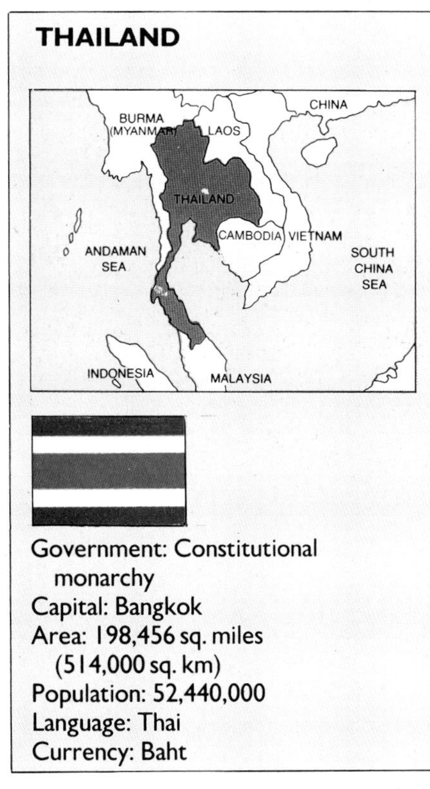

Government: Constitutional monarchy
Capital: Bangkok
Area: 198,456 sq. miles (514,000 sq. km)
Population: 52,440,000
Language: Thai
Currency: Baht

Texans are proud of their state and its colorful history. Businessmen often wear cowboy hats and boots, a reminder of the cowboys who herded huge numbers of cattle across the state. Many countries have ruled Texas. The Spanish were the first to explore it, then it passed to France, and then to Mexico. Texas became an independent country for 10 years after it defeated the Mexicans. It adopted a flag with one star on it. This is why Texas is nicknamed the "Lone Star State."

Textile

A textile is any cloth made by Weaving. Before the Industrial Revolution, all cloth was made by hand from natural fibers of wool, silk, cotton, or linen. Since then, scientists have developed many kinds of manmade fibers. Rayon is made from wood. Nylon comes from oil. There are even some fibers made from glass. Manmade fibers are cheaper and often easier to wash and take care of. Sometimes they are mixed with natural fibers to get the best of both materials.

Thailand

Thailand is a country in Southeast Asia. It is surrounded by Burma (Myanmar), Laos, and Cambodia. The south coast opens onto the Gulf of Thailand, which is part of the South China Sea.

Most of the people live in the central part of the country. Many rivers flow through this area, making it very fertile. Most people are farmers. Rice is the main crop. They also grow cotton, tobacco, corn, coconuts, and bananas. In the north, there are large forests of teak, which is a major export.

Thanksgiving

Thanksgiving is a national holiday celebrated each November in the United States. People gather to give thanks for the harvest and share a traditional meal. The first Thanksgiving was celebrated in 1620 by the Pilgrims at Plymouth Colony in Massachusetts. A number of Indians joined in the feast.

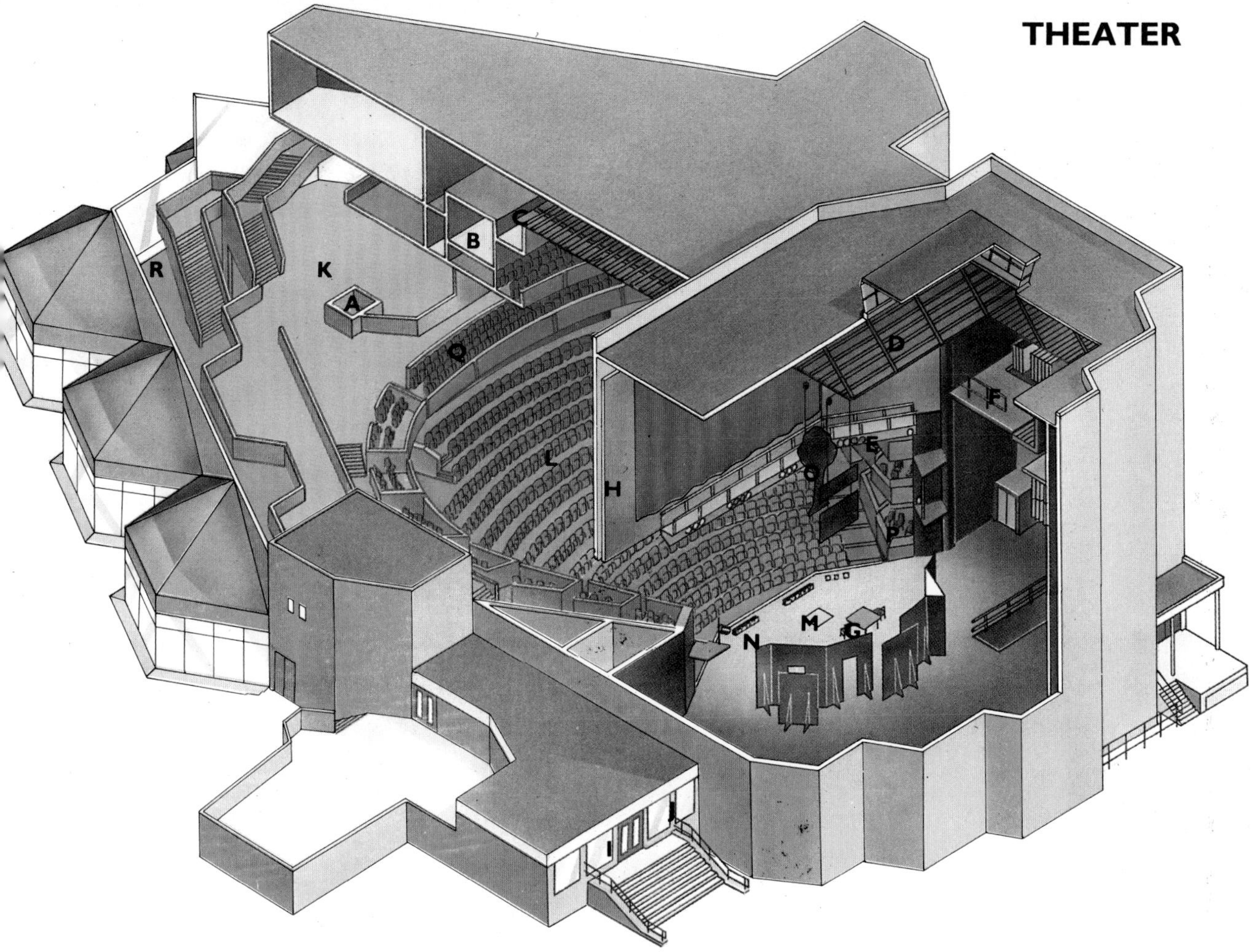

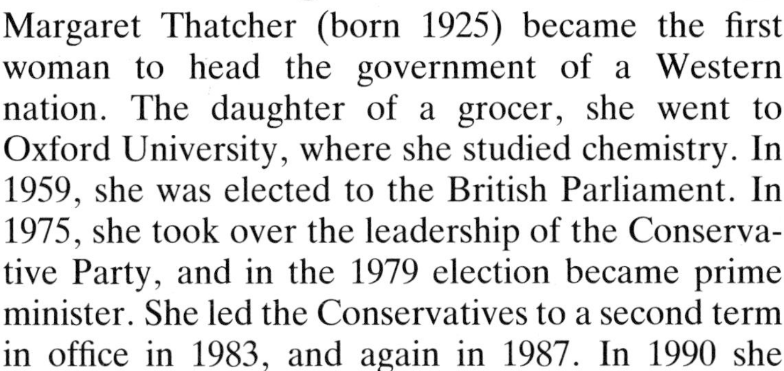

▲ *A cutaway view of a modern theater, showing:*

A Elevator
B Projection room
C Lighting gallery
D Gridiron
E Lighting bridge
F Fly floor
G Prop
H Safety curtain
I Stage door
J Stage manager's office
K Balcony foyer
J Orchestra
M Trap door
N Footlights
O Scenery
P Boxes
Q Balcony
R Orchestra foyer

Thatcher, Margaret

Margaret Thatcher (born 1925) became the first woman to head the government of a Western nation. The daughter of a grocer, she went to Oxford University, where she studied chemistry. In 1959, she was elected to the British Parliament. In 1975, she took over the leadership of the Conservative Party, and in the 1979 election became prime minister. She led the Conservatives to a second term in office in 1983, and again in 1987. In 1990 she resigned and was succeeded by John Major.

Theater

A theater is a place where plays are performed by actors and watched by an audience. The theater may be just a patch of ground or a large, expensive building.

The earliest theaters we know about were in Greece. They were simply flattened patches of

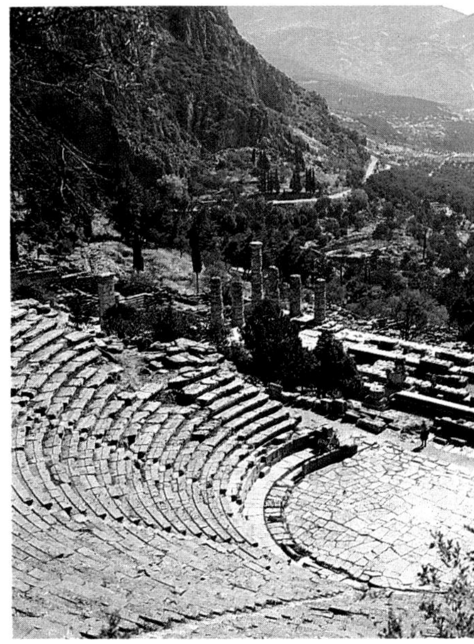

▲ *The theater at Delphi in Greece was built in the 300s B.C. It was so skillfully built that even people sitting right at the back could hear every word the actors spoke.*

ground on a hillside. The audience sat in rows on the hill above so that they could all see the "stage." When the Greeks built theaters, they cut a half-moon shape in the hillside and lined it with rows of stone seats that looked down on a round, flat stage.

The Romans copied the Greek pattern, but they built most of their theaters on flat ground. The rows of seats were held up by a wall. The Romans built a theater in nearly every large town in the Roman Empire.

In Britain, there were no theater buildings before the 1500s. Troupes of actors traveled around using their carts as stages. Later, they performed in rich people's houses and in the courtyards of inns. The first theaters to be built were made of wood and looked very much like inns. The stage jutted out into a large yard. Galleries of seats ran all around the sides. There were even seats on the stage, but only for rich people. These theaters had no roofs. When it rained, the *groundlings*, people who stood in the yard around the edge of the stage, got wet. SHAKESPEARE's plays were performed in theaters like this. Later, theaters were built with roofs. The stage was moved back, and the audience sat in rows in front of it.

Thermometer

A thermometer is an instrument that measures TEMPERATURE. It is usually a glass tube marked with a scale. Inside is another, thinner, glass tube, which

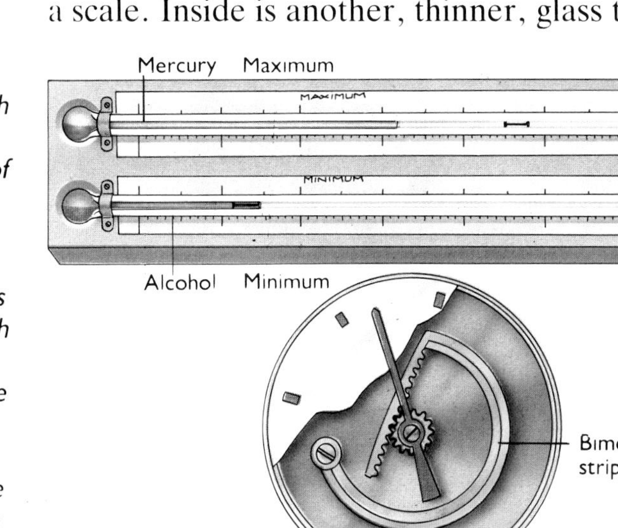

► *Maximum and minimum thermometers are used to indicate the highest and lowest temperatures recorded. In a maximum thermometer, mercury flows through a narrow neck in the tube. As the thermometer cools, a small amount of mercury stays above the neck, showing the highest temperature to which the thermometer has been exposed. A minimum thermometer is usually an alcohol thermometer which stays at the lowest point reached. Oven thermometers (right) make use of the difference in expansion of different metals. As the temperature rises, the bimetallic strip bends as one metal expands, moving a pointer on a dial.*

ends in a bulb containing mercury or alcohol. When the temperature goes up, the mercury or the alcohol gets warm and expands (grows bigger). It rises up the tube. When it stops, you can read the temperature on the marked scale. When it gets cold, the mercury contracts (grows smaller) and sinks down the tube. If alcohol is used in a thermometer, it is usually colored red. Most thermometers measure temperatures between the boiling and freezing points of water. This is between 32° (32 degrees) and 212° on the Fahrenheit scale. Today, many countries use a metric scale called Celsius to measure temperature. Its freezing point is 0° and its boiling point is 100°.

Medical thermometers, which are small enough to go in your mouth, measure your blood heat. Household thermometers tell you how warm or cold the air is inside or outside your house.

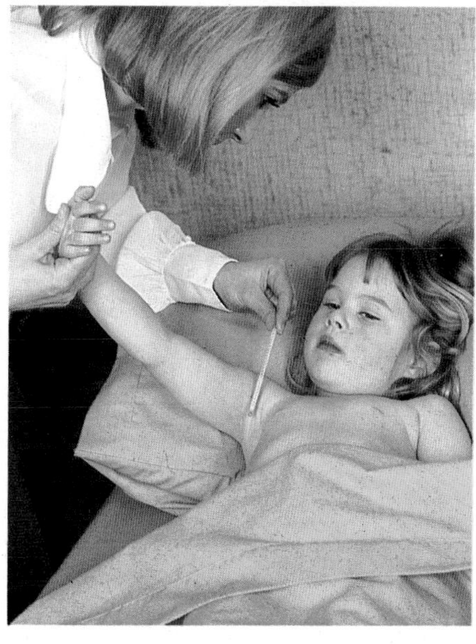

▲ *A medical thermometer placed under this feverish girl's arm will indicate how high above normal 98.6°F (37°C) her body temperature is. It is safer to take a very young child's temperature in this way than to risk putting a glass thermometer into his or her mouth.*

Thermostat

A thermostat is an instrument which keeps a TEMPERATURE steady. It is usually part of a central heating system. It switches the heater on or off when the temperature gets too low or high. Thermostats are also fitted in cars, spacecraft, ovens, hot water heaters, and other machinery.

Until recently, thermostats were made with metal strips inside. When the strips got hot, they expanded (grew bigger). They had to bend to fit into their space. When they bent, they broke electrical

The name Centigrade is sometimes used for the Celsius scale, but it is not the correct term in the international system of units.

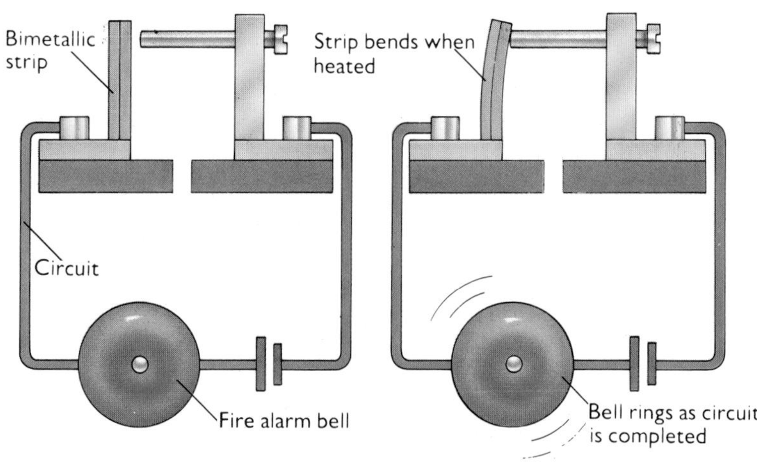

◀ *This electrical circuit is in a fire alarm system. It consists of a loud bell, an electric circuit, and a bimetallic strip—a strip of two metals bonded together. When the temperature rises, one of the metals expands faster than the other, making the strip bend. This completes the electric circuit, and the bell rings.*

contacts. This switched the boiler or heater off. Modern thermostats are electronic. They can work in temperatures that would melt most metals.

Third World

The Third World is a polite way of describing the poorer nations in our world. The first two "worlds" are the powerful formerly communist nations of Eastern Europe and Russia; and the western countries, of which the richest and most powerful is the UNITED STATES.

The Third World countries are mainly in ASIA, AFRICA, and SOUTH AMERICA. Many of them supply the rest of the world with cheap goods and labor. This pattern of wealth in one part of the world and poverty in another is difficult to change.

▲ *The terrible conditions that many people suffer in these slums in Rio de Janeiro, Brazil, are typical of those in many Third World countries.*

▶ *The number of infant deaths per thousand people in a country is one indication of that country's wealth and standard of living. In poorer countries, lower standards of health and education usually result in a greater number of infant deaths.*

INFANT MORTALITY IN VARIOUS NATIONS

Third World	*Per 1000*	*Other*	*Per 1000*
China	50	Australia	9
Bangladesh	140	Canada	8
Bolivia	123	Denmark	7
Brazil	70	Finland	6
Burma	96	France	8
Cameroon	113	Greece	13
Chile	22	Italy	12
Congo	110	New Zealand	10
Gabon	162	Poland	18
Gambia	217	Portugal	18
Ghana	98	Sweden	3
India	101	United Kingdom	10
Liberia	127	United States	10

Lightning strikes somewhere on the Earth more than a hundred times every second. Every year, more than a hundred people are killed by lightning in the United States. But thunderstorms have their uses, too. As lightning flashes through the air, it produces a tremendous amount of heat. This heat joins nitrogen and oxygen in the air to form nitrates that fall to Earth with the rain. These nitrates are valuable fertilizers of the soil.

Thoreau, Henry David

Henry David Thoreau (1817–62) was a U.S. writer who is chiefly remembered for one book—*Walden*. In 1845, Thoreau built a hut on the shores of Walden Pond, near Concord, Massachusetts. There he lived for two years, existing as simply as possible. His journal of these years is the famous book.

Thunderstorm

Thunderstorms are caused by ELECTRICITY in the air. Different electrical charges build up inside big rain clouds. When the charges are strong enough, a

◀ *Lightning will jump from a cloud to the tallest conductor available on the ground, such as a skyscraper. For protection, a tall building has a lightning rod on the roof which "earths" the lightning harmlessly down a wire to the ground.*

spark leaps from one charged part of the cloud to another. Sometimes, the spark jumps from the cloud to the ground. We see the spark as LIGHTNING. Lightning heats up the air. The air expands (gets bigger) so quickly that it explodes, making the crashing noise we call thunder.

Since sound travels much more slowly than LIGHT, you always hear thunder after you see lightning. To find out how many miles away the storm is, count the seconds between the time you see the lightning and hear the thunder, and divide the number by five.

Tibet

Tibet is a country in central ASIA. It is the highest country in the world. The flat part of Tibet, which is in the middle, is as high as the peaks of the ALPS. Enormous mountain ranges surround this high plain. In the south lie the HIMALAYAS, the home of Mount EVEREST.

Tibet used to be ruled by Buddhist monks called *lamas*. In 1959, it was taken over by China.

TIBET

CHINA
PAKISTAN
TIBET
NEPAL
BHUTAN
INDIA
BANGLADESH
BURMA (MYANMAR)

Government: Communist
Capital: Lhasa
Area: 470,000 sq. miles (1,217,300 sq. km)
Population: 2,000,000

By Tibetan custom, a woman could not choose a husband, and if she married the eldest brother in a family, the younger brothers also became her husbands.

◀ *This isolated Buddhist monastery in the mountains of Tibet lies at a height of 13,000 feet (4,000 m) above sea level.*

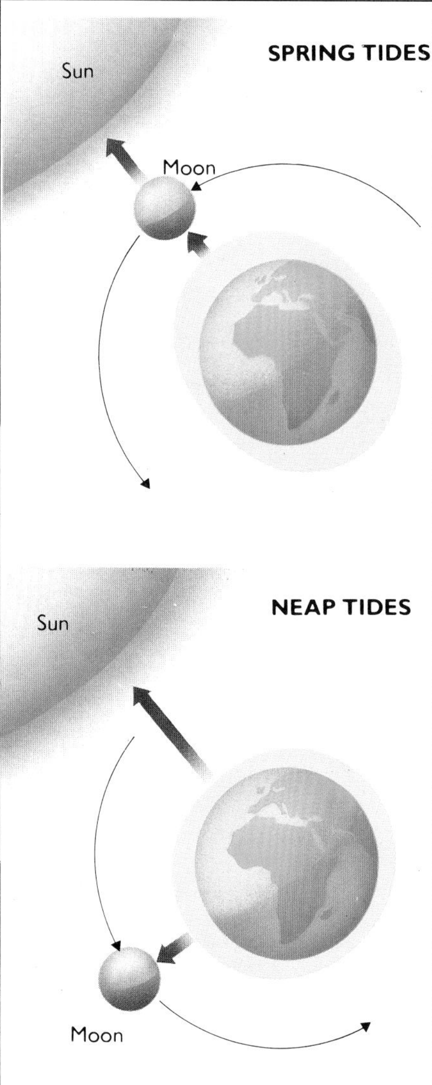

▲ *When the Sun's gravity and the Moon's gravity pull in the same direction, their combined force causes a very high, or* spring, *tide. When the Sun and Moon pull against each other at right angles, a very low, or* neap, *tide occurs. Spring tides occur when there is a full or new moon. The red arrows show the pull of gravity.*

Tide

Tides are regular movements of the OCEANS. They are mainly caused by the MOON. The Moon is like a giant magnet. It tugs the oceans toward it as it loops around the Earth. The Earth is spinning at the same time, so most places get two high tides and two low tides about every 24 hours.

High tide happens when the water flows as far inland as it can. Low tide happens when it flows out as far as it can.

Tiger

Tigers are the biggest members of the cat family. They live in the forests of Asia and Indonesia, and hunt deer or large cattle. Tigers usually lie still during the day and hunt alone by night. They are very strong. One tiger can pull a dead buffalo that is so heavy a group of men would find it difficult to move.

Until the 1800s, thousands of tigers roamed through the forests of Asia. Then, men began to shoot them and clear the forests in which they lived. As a result, they are now very rare.

► *Tigers are rarely seen out in the open. They prefer the cool shade of forests. Their markings make them more suited to areas of dappled shade, where they are well camouflaged.*

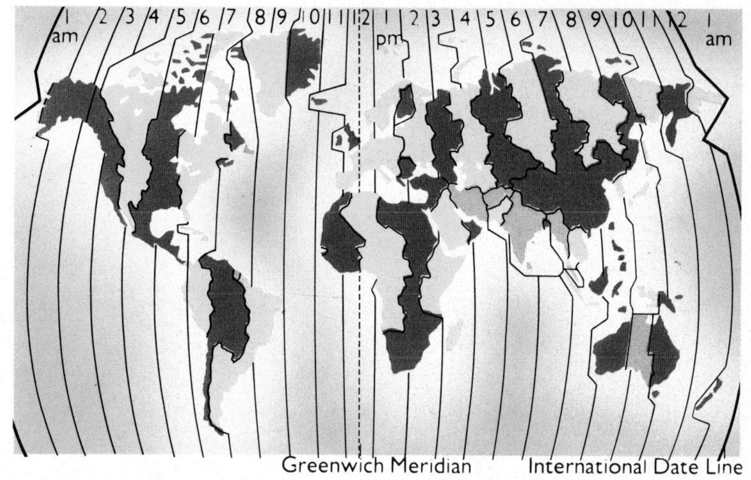

◀ *Because of the rotation of the Earth, sunrise in, for example, the eastern United States occurs three hours earlier than in the western part. For this reason, the world has been divided into 24 time zones. At the International Date Line, the date changes.*

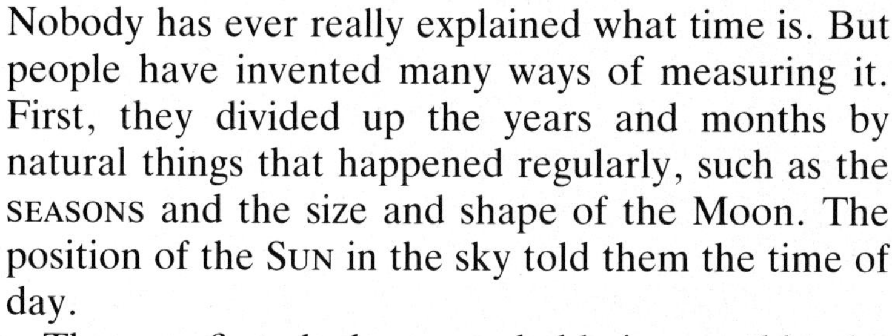

Time

Nobody has ever really explained what time is. But people have invented many ways of measuring it. First, they divided up the years and months by natural things that happened regularly, such as the SEASONS and the size and shape of the Moon. The position of the SUN in the sky told them the time of day.

The very first clock was probably invented by the Egyptians. It was a sundial. As the Sun moved across the sky, an upright rod in the middle of the dial cast a shadow onto a scale of hours drawn around it.

But this was no good at night time. Other ways of telling the time, without the Sun's help, were invented. One was the hourglass. This was two glass bulbs joined together. Sand in one bulb took exactly one hour to trickle through a hole into the other bulb.

Mechanical CLOCKS were not made until the 1200s. They were driven by weights. Clocks which worked by springs were made in the 1500s. In the early 1600s, the PENDULUM was being used to make clocks more accurate. Modern clocks are very accurate. They work by ELECTRONICS. Scientists need ever more accurate timekeeping. They use atomic clocks that are accurate to 10 millionths of a second.

We think of time as being something that is always the same in all situations, but this is not necessarily so. Albert Einstein showed that the rate

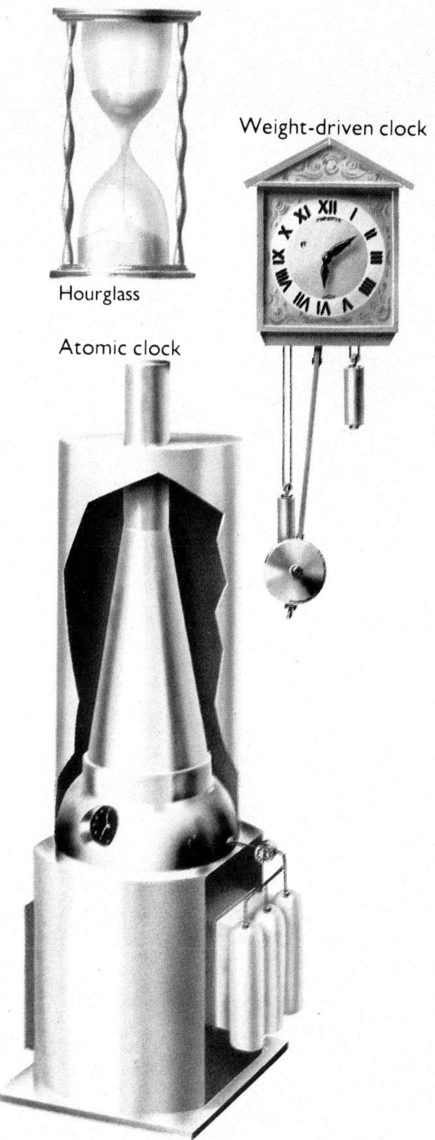

▲ *Hourglasses were one of the earliest ways of measuring time. Pendulum clocks came into use in the 1600s. More precise methods of time-keeping have been developed over the years. An atomic cesium clock is so accurate that it should lose only one second every 1,000 years.*

at which time passes varies according to the speed at which we are traveling. On a supersonic jet, clocks and watches move very slightly slower than they do on the ground. The difference would only be noticeable, however, in a spaceship traveling at close to the speed of light.

▲ *Tin is useful for packaging because it does not rust. It can also be used for plating other metals to give a bright shiny surface. Mixed with antimony and copper, it makes pewter, a soft alloy once used for most tableware.*

Tin

Tin is one of the oldest metals known to us. People were mining tin before IRON was discovered. Tin was mixed with COPPER to make bronze.

Tin was mined in England long before the birth of Christ. An ancient people called the Phoenicians sailed from the Mediterranean to trade cloth and precious stones for it.

Cans are made from sheets of steel that have been coated with tin. Tin does not rust.

Tin is not a common metal. The main tin mines are in Bolivia, southeastern Asia, and western Africa.

Tobacco

Tobacco is made from the dried leaves of the plant *Nicotiana*, which belongs to the same family as potatoes. It was first found in North America, but is now grown all over the world. The Spanish traveler Francisco Hernandez took it to Europe in 1599.

Tobacco leaves can be rolled together to make cigars, or shredded up to be smoked in pipes or cigarettes. Smoking is very bad for your health. It is particularly harmful to the lungs and heart.

▼ *Tobacco leaves are picked, then dried and packaged to be sent for processing to make cigarettes, cigars, loose tobacco, or snuff, a powder that can be sniffed. Cheap tobacco is dried in the sun. More expensive types are dried by hot air or over fires in sheds.*

Togo

The Republic of Togo is a thin strip of land in West Africa. The climate is hot and damp, especially near the coast. The country has little industry apart from mining large deposits of phosphates for fertilizers. Germany ruled the territory until World War I. After Germany's defeat, Togo was governed by France. The country gained its independence in 1960.

TOGO

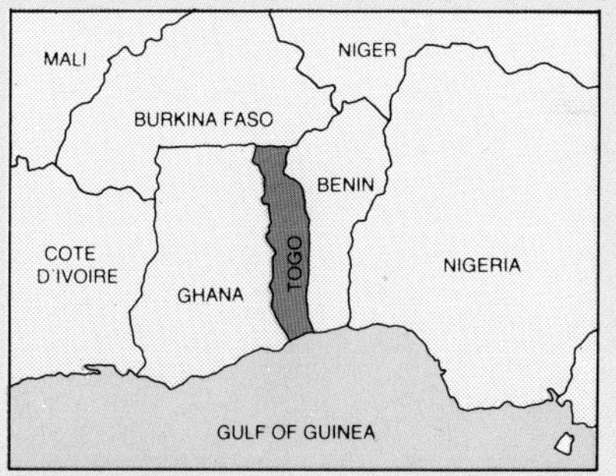

Government: Republic
Capital: Lomé
Area: 21,622 sq. miles (56,000 sq. km)
Population: 3,531,000
Language: French
Currency: Franc CFA

Tokyo

Tokyo is the capital of JAPAN. It is one of the biggest cities in the world. Tokyo is on the southeastern coast of Honshu, the main island of Japan.

Almost every kind of work goes on in this enormous city. There are factories which make paper, electronic and electrical goods, cars, and motorcycles. There are also huge shipyards and oil refineries on the coast. So many people work in Tokyo that most of them have to live on the outside edge of the city. Some people spend four hours a day going to and from their work. Tokyo has some of the worst traffic jams in the world.

◀ *One of the religions in Japan is called Shinto. Followers worship many gods, nature, and their ancestors. This picture is of a Shinto shrine.*

Much of the city was destroyed by an EARTHQUAKE in 1923. What was left was badly bombed in WORLD WAR II. Since then, the city has been almost entirely rebuilt, but a number of beautiful old buildings remain. The Imperial Palace is an old *shogun* castle, and there are many ancient temples and shrines.

Tokyo has had an unusual population history. In 1787, it had a population of 1,400,000, making it the world's largest city at that time. Then Tokyo's population became smaller and smaller until by 1868 it was only half that size. When the city was almost completely destroyed by an earthquake in 1923, the population had again risen to 2,200,000.

▲ *Leo Tolstoy inherited land from his family, but had very advanced ideas for his time. He made sure the people who worked for him had proper homes and education.*

Tolstoy, Leo

Leo Tolstoy (1828–1910) was a Russian author who wrote two of the world's greatest novels, *War and Peace* and *Anna Karenina*. He was born into a noble family and fought in the Crimean War. Tolstoy hated the greed and selfishness he found on his travels. He turned away from the Russian Orthodox Church and started a new kind of Christianity. At the age of 82, Tolstoy left home, but he soon became ill and died in a small railroad station hotel. He was refused burial by the Church, but the people thronged to his funeral, seeing him as a man who had done his best to improve their lives.

Tomato

Tomatoes are round, red, fleshy vegetable fruits. They contain a very good supply of some of the VITAMINS we need, especially vitamins A and C.

Tomatoes were first grown in South America. They were being grown in the Andes Mountains thousands of years ago. In 1596, the Spanish took them to Europe. But at first, no one there would eat them. People thought they were poisonous. Tomatoes were kept as ornamental plants. For a long time, they were called "love apples," or "golden apples."

Although tomatoes are really fruit, they are almost always eaten as vegetables. In the 1900s, they started to become a popular food. Now they are grown and eaten all over the world.

TONGA

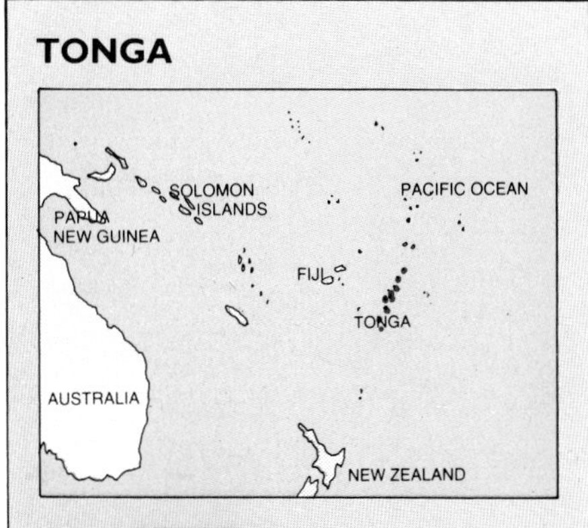

Government: Constitutional monarchy
Capital: Nuku'alofa
Area: 270 sq. miles (699 sq. km)
Population: 95,000
Languages: Tongan, English
Currency: Pa'anga

Tonga

Tonga is an island kingdom in the Pacific. It is also known as the Friendly Islands. There are three main groups of small islands, which have a pleasant climate. The main crops are copra and bananas.

The kingdom was taken under the protection of Great Britain in 1900 and gained its independence in 1970. From 1918 to 1965, the islands' ruler was Queen Salote Tupou, who was known throughout the world as the Queen of Tonga. Tonga is the only remaining kingdom in Polynesia.

Tongue

The tongue is a muscular, flexible flap fixed inside the mouth. Only VERTEBRATES have tongues. Our own tongues help us to TASTE and eat food, and to talk. The letters T and D for instance, cannot be said without using the tongue in a special way.

In toads, the tongue is attached to the front of the mouth. Snakes have forked or split tongues which can "smell" the air. Cats' tongues are covered in tiny hooks of flesh. Cats can use their tongues like combs to clean their fur.

Cup-shaped papillae—carry taste buds

Hook-shaped papillae—carry no taste buds

▲ *The cat's tongue is long and flexible. The little hooks that make it rough are called* papillae. *They help the cat lap up liquids and keep its fur clean.*

Tonsils

Tonsils are two small lumps at the back of the throat. There is one on each side. They help to protect the body from germs coming in through the mouth.

Children have very large tonsils. These gradually shrink as they grow older. Sometimes, tonsils can become infected. They swell up and are very painful. This illness is called tonsillitis. The tonsils may have to be taken out by doctors in a hospital. Having our tonsils taken out does not seem to harm our bodies in any way.

Tornado

Tornadoes are violent, whirling windstorms. Most of them happen in North America, but they can occur anywhere in the world.

▼ *At the center of a tornado, winds can reach speeds of about 400 miles (650 km) an hour. Tornadoes cause great damage where they touch the ground.*

The most violent tornadoes happen in the center of the United States. They travel at about 30 miles (50 km) an hour with a roaring sound that can be heard 25 miles (40 km) away. Many Midwestern farmhouses have special cellars where people can shelter from tornadoes.

Hurricanes are strong winds that build up over the sea. Tornadoes build up over land. They happen when large masses of cloud meet. The clouds begin to whirl around each other. Gradually, these whirling clouds join together to make a gigantic, twisting funnel. When this touches the ground, it sucks up anything in its path—trees, houses, or people.

Tortoise

Giant tortoises live in the Galapagos Islands and islands in the Indian Ocean. They can weigh up to 500 pounds (225 kg) and be 6 feet (1.8 m) long. Some large tortoises live for over 150 years.

Tortoises are slow-moving REPTILES. They can only walk about 15 feet (4.5 m) in a minute. When frightened, they pull their heads and legs inside their domed shells. The 40 or so kinds of tortoise live on land, mostly in warm parts of the world. They are similar to TURTLES and terrapins, but these reptiles live in water.

▲ *The Hermann's tortoise is a European type. The shell has three layers: a thin layer of living skin is sandwiched between horny plates on the outside and bony plates on the inside.*

Touch

There are different nerve cells in your skin called receptors that respond to five main kinds of sensation. These are light touch, heavy touch (pressure), pain, heat, and cold. Receptors pass sensations along NERVES to the brain.

Pain receptors are the most numerous; cold receptors the least numerous. Some parts of the

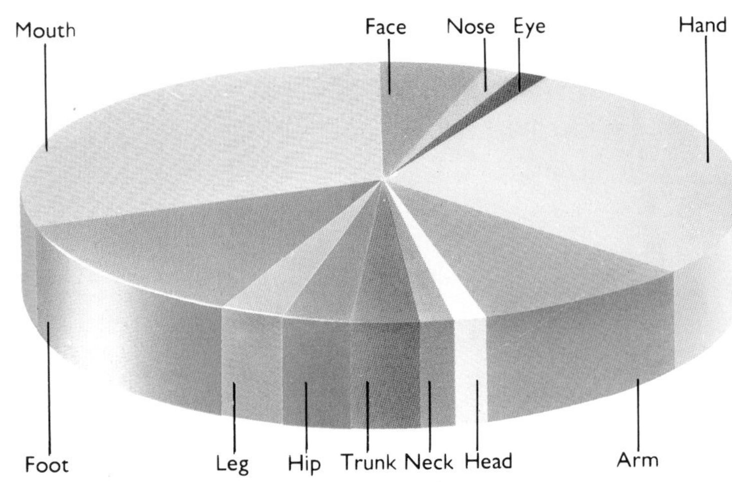

▶ *The size of the area of the brain that deals with touch signals from the various parts of the body corresponds to how sensitive that part is. For example, the part that deals with signals from the mouth is very large, because there are so many nerves in the mouth. This chart shows how sensitive each part of the body is.*

body, such as the tongue and fingertips, have more receptors than others.

We also have receptors inside the body. Usually we do not realize that they are working, except when they produce sensations such as hunger or tiredness.

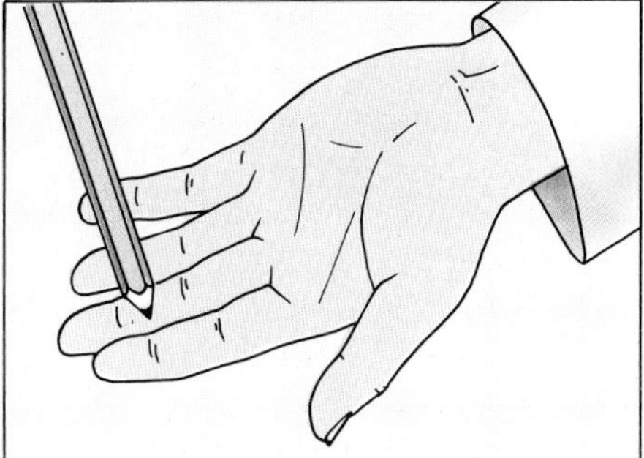

SEE IT YOURSELF

Some parts of your body are more responsive to light touch than others. Try this experiment with a friend. Blindfold yourself and ask your friend to press either one or two pencil points lightly on your fingertip. You will probably be able to tell how many pencil points your friend is using each time. Try doing this on your back, shoulders, and on other parts of your body. Can you tell how many pencil points are being used each time? Which areas are receptive to light touch?

Track and Field

Athletic events have been organized for nearly 3,000 years. They were a main part of the old Olympic Games held in Greece from 776 B.C.

Today, running, jumping, and throwing events, called "track and field," hold a high position in the world of sports. Sprinting events are run over distances of 100 and 200 meters. The 100 meters is run over a straight course. The 200 meters usually includes a bend, but is run in lanes. Middle distance events are often classified as those between 400 and 1,500 meters. Mile races also come into this class.

Races over one mile can be classified as long-distance events. They are usually run over 5,000 and 10,000 meters. The marathon starts and finishes on a track, but the remainder of the 26 miles 385 yards race is run through the surrounding streets. The 3,000 meters steeplechase is run over a track with four hurdles and a water jump.

Mildred "Babe" Didrikson, one of the world's great athletes, set 4 world records during a 3-hour period at a 1932 track and field meet. She won 3 gold medals for the U.S. at the 1932 Olympics, setting records in the 80-meter hurdles, javelin throw, and high jump. She also excelled at golf, basketball, tennis, diving, and swimming.

◀ *Thousands of runners enter marathon races like this every year.*

MAIN ATHLETIC EVENTS

MEN	WOMEN
100 meters	100 meters
200 meters	200 meters
400 meters	400 meters
800 meters	800 meters
1,000 meters	1,500 meters
1,500 meters	Mile
Mile	3,000 meters
2,000 meters	5,000 meters
3,000 meters	10,000 meters
Steeplechase	Marathon
5,000 meters	100 m hurdles
10,000 meters	400 m hurdles
20,000 meters	High jump
30,000 meters	Long jump
Marathon	Shot-put
110 m hurdles	Discus throw
400 m hurdles	Javelin throw
High jump	Heptathlon
Long jump	4 × 100 m relay
Pole vault	4 × 200 m relay
Triple jump	4 × 800 m relay
Shot-put	
Discus throw	
Hammer throw	
Javelin throw	
Decathlon	
20-km walk	
30-km walk	
50-km walk	
4 × 100 m relay	
4 × 200 m relay	
4 × 400 m relay	
4 × 800 m relay	
4 × 1,500 m relay	

The main hurdles events are the 100 meters high hurdles (the hurdles are 42 inches (106 cm) high) and the 400 meters intermediate hurdles, in which the hurdles are 36 inches (91 cm) high. Women run 100 meters over 33 inch (84 cm) hurdles, and 400 meters over 30 inch (76 cm) hurdles. The main relay races are the 4 × 100 meters and 4 × 400 meters.

Field events include high and long jumping, the triple jump, pole vault, throwing the discus, javelin, shot, and hammer. In pole vaulting, the pole is made of flexible fiberglass and about 14¾ feet (4.5 m) long.

The discus is thrown from a circle 8 feet (2.5 meters) in diameter, the shot and hammer from a 7 foot (2.1 meter) circle. The standard shot weighs 16 pounds (7.257 kg), the same weight as the hammer and its steel wire.

Two of the most testing events are the decathlon and heptathlon. The decathlon (for men) is made up of ten events contested over two days. They are the 100 and 400 meters, high jump, long jump, shot-put, 1,500 meters, 110-meter hurdles, pole vault, javelin, and discus. The heptathlon for women has seven events: 100 meters hurdles, high jump, shot put, 200 meters, 800 meters, long jump, and javelin.

Trade

The buying and selling of goods and services is called trade. Trade also includes *barter*, which is the exchange of one type of goods for goods of a

The total trade of the European Community nations in the 1980s was almost three times that of the United States, but this included trade among the European Community members as well as their trade with other countries.

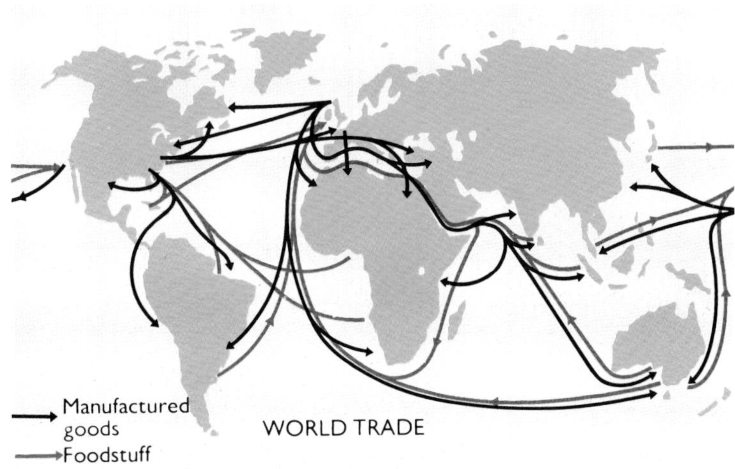

► *This map shows the general flow of world trade: foodstuffs and raw materials from the developing nations; manufactured goods from the industrialized nations.*

different kind. Domestic trade is trade that takes place within one country.

Companies that buy goods in large quantities and then sell them to storekeepers, are called *wholesalers*. Companies that sell the goods to the public are called *retailers*.

International trade is trade between countries. *Imports* are things that a country buys. *Exports* are things that a country sells. Some imports and exports are said to be *visible*. These include raw materials, such as iron ore, and farm products, such as wheat. They also include factory-made goods, ranging from pencils to jet aircraft. Other imports and exports are *invisible*. They include banking and insurance, transportation services, and money spent by tourists.

The chief trading nations are those with the most industries.

▲ *John L. Lewis was a powerful American trade union leader and was president of the United Mine Workers of America for 40 years.*

Trade Union

Trade unions are groups formed by workers. Their main aim is to get better wages for their members. They also ask for shorter hours, better working conditions, and some form of job security. Some unions look after their members and their families in times of trouble. If a trade union has a serious disagreement with an employer, it may ask its members to stop working. This is called a *strike*.

Modern trade unions were formed in Europe in the early days of the INDUSTRIAL REVOLUTION. In the United States, laws governing trade unions began to be passed in the 1930s. Today, trade unions are powerful and play an important part in the affairs of many countries.

Transistor

Transistors are small ELECTRONIC devices. They are usually made to amplify (strengthen) electric currents in electronic equipment such as radios, televisions, computers, and satellites. They can also switch electric currents on and off. Transistors have largely replaced other devices, called tubes, which were once used for the same purpose.

▼ *A transistor has three layers. The inner layer, or* base, *the* emitter, *and the* collector. *An electric current flowing from emitter to collector is stopped by the base. If an electric signal being fed to the base increases, the base lets more current through. If it decreases, less current passes. Because the current is greater than the base signal, the transistor is acting as an amplifier.*

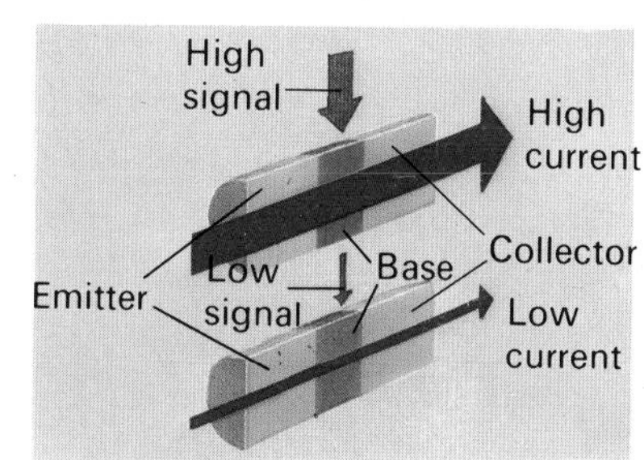

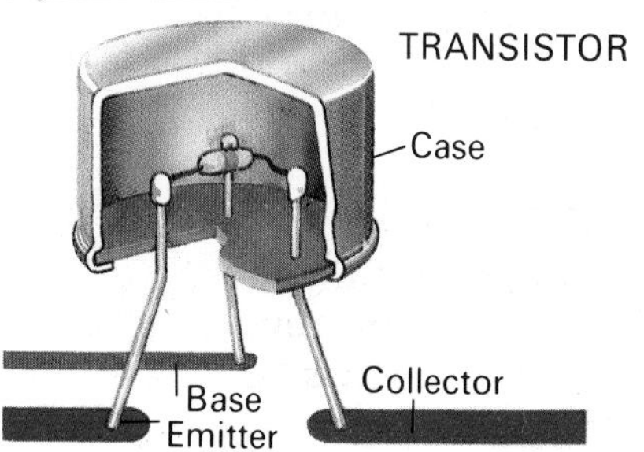

Today, complicated circuits containing thousands of transistors can be put into SILICON CHIPS that are only half an inch square. The first practical transistors were developed in the 1940s by the American scientists Walter Brattain, John Bardeen, and William Shockley. The invention of transistors completely revolutionized electronics, and millions of these devices are now made every year.

Tree

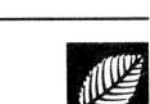

Trees are the largest of all PLANTS. They are woody plants with a thick stem or trunk. Most grow to more than 20 feet (7 m) high. (See pages 698–699.)

Trinidad and Tobago

Trinidad and Tobago is a country made up of two islands in the West Indies. The islands lie near the coast of Venezuela. The climate is warm and damp, and the main occupation is farming. Trinidad is a large producer of oil, and this brings most of the island's wealth. Its annual carnival attracts many tourists, who come to hear the steel bands and calypsos for which Trinidad is famous.

TRINIDAD AND TOBAGO

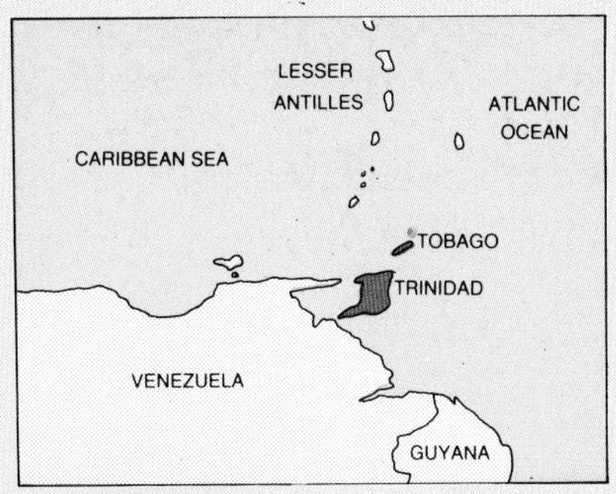

Government: Parliamentary democracy
Capital: Port of Spain
Area: 1,980 sq. miles (5,130 sq. km)
Population: 1,227,000
Language: English
Currency: Trinidad dollar

Trojan War

The Trojan War was fought in about 1200 B.C. between the Trojans of Troy and the Greeks. Troy

▼ *According to Homer's poem, the hero Odysseus and other men from the Greek army were hidden inside the wooden horse.*

was a city in what is now Turkey. The war lasted for 10 years. The poet HOMER, in his poem the *Iliad*, tells the story of only a few days of the war. We know the rest of the story from other writings.

Paris was a prince of Troy. He fell in love with Helen, the wife of King Menelaus of Sparta in Greece. Paris took Helen to Troy, and Menelaus, with other Greek kings and soldiers, went to get her back. They besieged Troy for years. Finally, they won by tricking the Trojans. They left a huge wooden horse filled with Greek soldiers standing outside the city. The Trojans, thinking that the horse was a gift, took it inside the city walls. The hidden soldiers then opened the gates, and Troy was destroyed. No one knows if the story is true.

There are approximately 600 kinds of tropical fish that can be kept in home aquariums. Even a beginning aquarium hobbyist can keep a wide assortment of fish.

Tropical Fish

Tropical fish are among the prettiest fish in the world. They live in the warm seas of tropical regions, often along the edges of CORAL reefs.

Many small, brightly colored freshwater tropical fish are popular aquarium pets. Marine fish can also be kept, but they are more expensive and difficult to look after. They have to have salt water containing just the right amount of salt to live in.

Tropical fish live in warm water. Most tanks have a heater to keep the water at around 75°F (24°C). A cover on the tank holds the heat in and stops the

Continued on page 700

▼ *The porcupine fish inflates itself like a balloon and erects sharp spines if it senses danger nearby.*

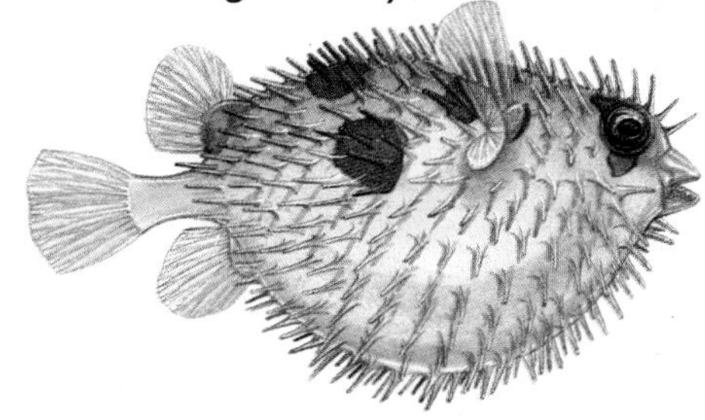

▼ *These tropical fish are all members of the wrasse family. They can be kept in aquariums, provided the conditions are just right. Wrasses often lie on the aquarium floor at night, or bury themselves in the sand.*

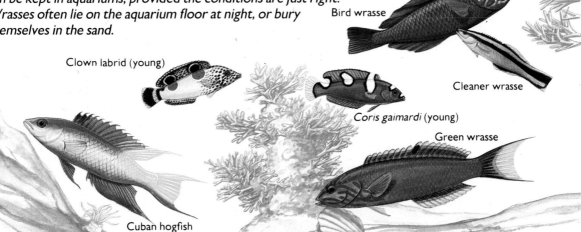

TREE

Trees are beautiful to look at and also very useful plants. Some trees give us fruits and nuts. Many trees, especially the conifers, are grown for timber. Wood is not just a valuable building material. It is also used to make paper, and in some countries, it is burned for fuel. Trees are vital to the environment, for they enrich the atmosphere with oxygen and help protect the soil from erosion by wind and rain.

Trees are the largest and oldest living things. The biggest tree is a type of sequoia. These giants can grow to more than 325 ft. (100 m) high. A bristlecone pine tree in Nevada is at least 4,900 years old.

There are two main kinds of trees. Conifers, such as pine, cedar, and spruce, have needle-like leaves. They produce seeds in cones, not flowers. Most conifers are evergreens (they do not shed their leaves in the fall). Their timber is known as softwood.

The other kind of tree is the broad-leaved flowering tree. Many, such as the oak, are *deciduous* (they shed their leaves in the fall). However, some broad-leaved trees are evergreen: an example is the holly. Many tropical trees, too, are evergreen. Broad-leaved trees have flowers that develop into fruits. Their timber is called hardwood.

COMMON LEAF SHAPES	
Needle Pine, Fir, Spruce Larch, Yew, Cedar, Cypress	
Narrow Willow, Almond, Peach	
Lobed Oak, Hawthorn, Holly	
Forked Maple, Sycamore, London plane, Horse chestnut	
Oval Elm, Apple, Cherry, Weeping willow, Alder, Beech	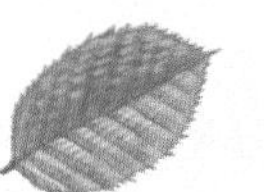
Pinnate (Feathery) Rowan, Elder, Ash, Walnut	

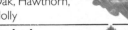

► *A giant redwood of the* sequoia *family. These huge trees grow on the west coast of the U.S.*

▼ *A tree trunk sawn through reveals the life history of the tree. The darker heartwood is surrounded by the lighter sapwood. A fresh growth ring is added every year. By counting the rings, you can tell the age of the tree.*

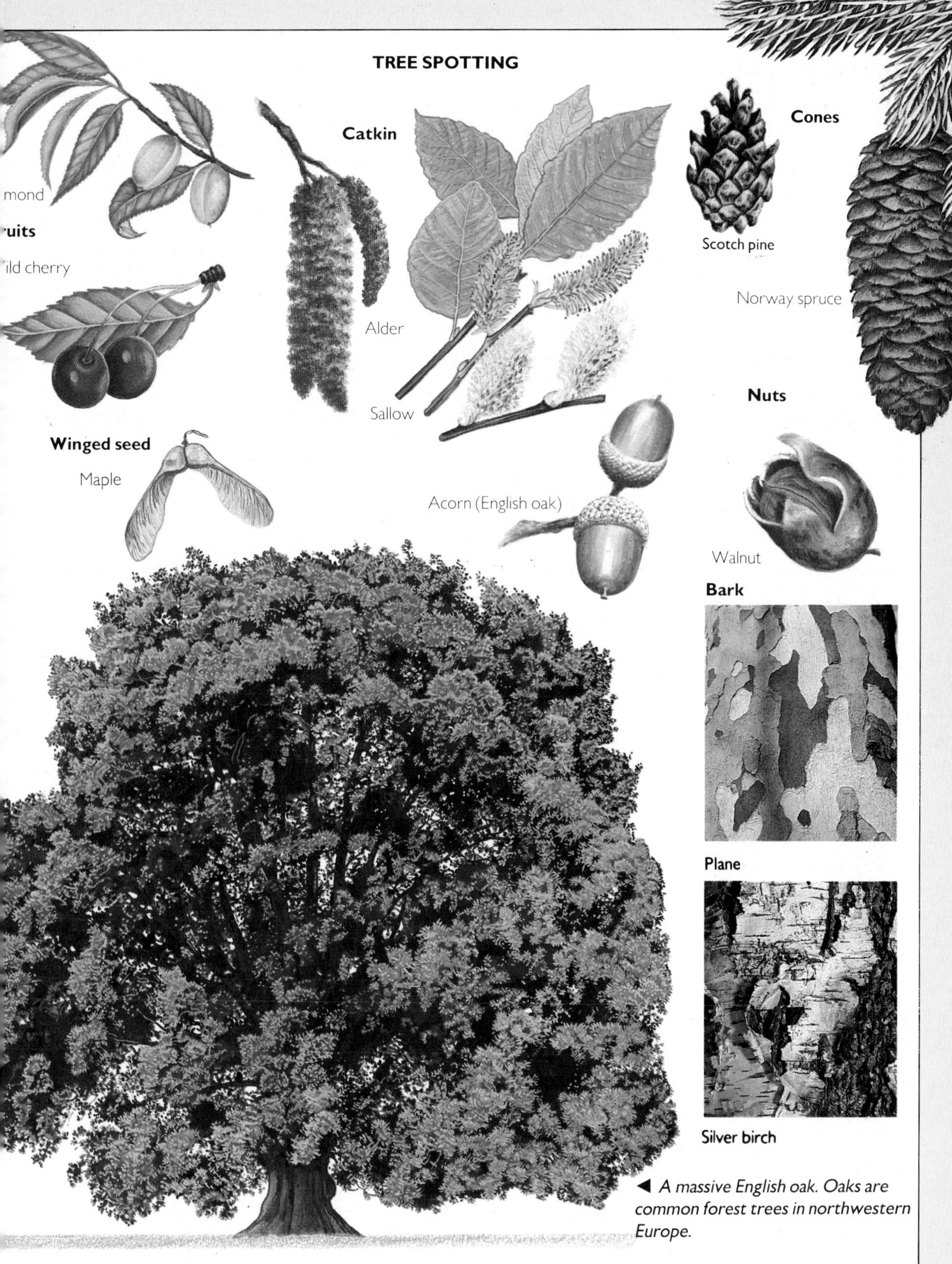

◀ *A massive English oak. Oaks are common forest trees in northwestern Europe.*

For more information, turn to these articles: BARK, CONIFER, CORK, FOREST, FRUIT, LEAF, NUT, PALM, SEED, WOOD.

HARRY S. TRUMAN

Thirty-third President 1945–1953
Born: Lamar, Missouri
Education: Kansas City Law School
Occupation: Businessman, government official
Political Party: Democratic
Buried: Truman Library Grounds, Independence, Missouri

water from evaporating (drying up). Electric light bulbs in the cover light the tank and also heat the water. Most aquariums have air pumps that add OXYGEN to the water and filter it to keep it clear. Water plants also provide oxygen. Special food for tropical fish can be bought.

The most common tropical freshwater fish is the guppy. Other common tropical fish are angelfish, barbs, and neon tetras.

Truman, Harry S.

Harry S. Truman (1884–1972) was the 33rd president of the United States. He became president when Franklin Roosevelt died in office, and was reelected in 1948. Truman was president during a turbulent period. The United States was still fighting World War II. Though it was certain the war in Europe would be won, the reorganization of Europe was sure to be a major task. The war against Japan still had to be won, and one of Truman's first decisions was his hardest: to drop the atomic bomb on Japan in August, 1945. Truman also had to face problems concerning the Soviet Union. The U.S.S.R. had been a friend during the war, but afterward became a bitter enemy. Then, in the early '50s, the United States had to fight another war—in South Korea.

Tubman, Harriet

Harriet Tubman (1820–1913) was the most famous leader of the Underground Railroad, the illegal organization that helped slaves escape from the South before the Civil War. She made 19 dangerous rescue operations and helped 300 slaves to freedom. She had been a slave herself on a plantation in Maryland and escaped to the North in 1849. During the Civil War, she helped free even more slaves.

▼ Tuna fishermen show off their catch as it is unloaded at the port of Yaizu, in Japan. The Japanese catch more tuna each year than any other nation.

Tuna

The tuna, also called tunny, is a large fish, whose firm flesh is rich in PROTEINS and VITAMINS. Most tuna live in warm seas, but they may swim into northern waters in summer. Different kinds of tuna include the blue fin, which may be 10 feet (3 m) long, and the albacore. The tuna is the only fish whose body temperature is higher than that of the water around it.

Tunisia

Tunisia is a sunny country in North AFRICA. Its beaches attract many tourists from Europe. The north is rugged. It has the most rain. The south is part of the dry SAHARA DESERT. Farming is the main industry in this small nation, but oil and phosphates are important exports.

There are more than 8 million people, most of whom are Muslims. Near the capital, Tunis, are the ruins of Carthage. Carthage was a great Mediterranean Sea power until it was destroyed by the Romans in 146 B.C.

TUNISIA

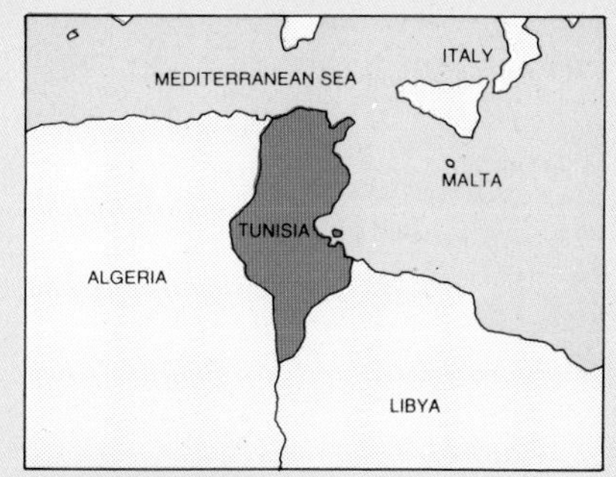

Government: Republic
Capital: Tunis
Area: 63,170 sq. miles (163,610 sq. km)
Population: 8,180,000
Languages: Arabic, French
Currency: Tunisian dinar

Tunnel

Tunneling is important in mining, transportation, and water supply. The Romans built tunnels to carry water. Today, a tunnel that brings water to New York City is the world's longest. It is 105 miles (169 km) long.

A Channel tunnel between France and England was first suggested to Napoleon in 1802 by the French engineer, Albert Mathieu. He decided that the tunnel should come to the surface on an island half-way across the Channel. This was so that men and horses could have a breath of fresh air.

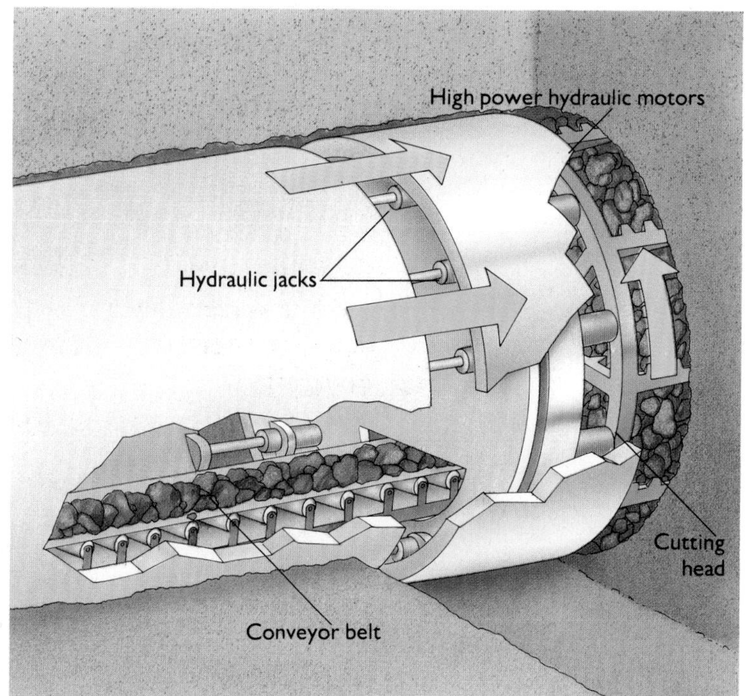

◀ The automatic tunnel digging machines used today are called moles. They have rotating cutters at the front, and the soil or rock they dig out is carried away by a conveyor belt. Hydraulic jacks act like springs to force the mole forward. The mole is powered by electricity and hydraulic motors.

LONGEST TUNNELS		
	Miles	Opened
Rail	**(Km)**	
Seikan (Japan)	33½ (53.9)	1985
Oshimizu (Japan)	13¾ (22.2)	1982
Simplon (Switz./Italy)	12¼ (19.8)	1906
Road		
Arlberg (Austria)	8½ (14.0)	1978
Mont Blanc (France/Italy)	7¼ (11.6)	1965
Underwater		
Seikan (Japan)	14½ (23.3)	1985
Shin Kanmon (Japan)	11½ (18.7)	1974

Different methods are used to build tunnels. In hard rock, the tunnel is blasted out with explosives. Cutting machines, like those used to drill oil wells, are used in softer rock. In the softest rocks, *tunnel shields* are used. These are giant steel tubes, the same size as the intended tunnel. The front edge of the shield is sharp and is pushed into the earth. The earth is dug out, and the tunnel behind the shield is lined to stop it from caving in.

Some tunnels under rivers are built by lowering sections of tunnel into the river. Divers join them together. When the tunnel is complete, the water is pumped out. Underground railroad tunnels can be built in deep trenches. When they are finished, the tunnel is covered over. The biggest tunneling operation taking place today is digging the Channel Tunnel between England and France.

Turbine

A turbine is a machine in which a wheel, drum, or SCREW is turned around by fast flowing water, or by steam or gas. Water wheels and WINDMILLS are simple turbines.

Water turbines are used at hydroelectric POWER PLANTS. These plants are next to DAMS or WATERFALLS. The force of falling water carried through a pipe from a dam turns the turbine. The turbine does

Small turbines driven by compressed air are used for dentists' drills. These turbines drive the drill at more than 250,000 revolutions per minute, so the drilling of a tooth is quickly done. There is also less vibration than with an electric drill.

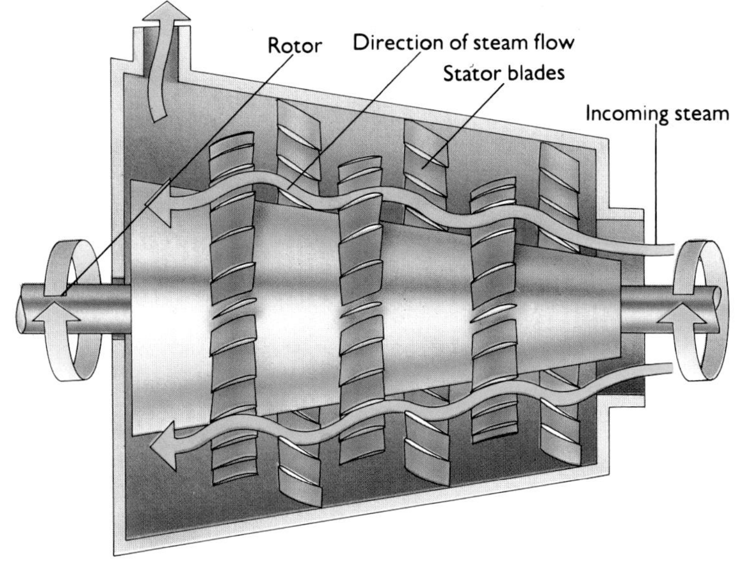

► *In a steam turbine, high pressure steam is directed through fixed, or stator, blades to strike a series of blades on a central shaft. The steam expands as it passes through each set of blades, driving the shaft around. The fixed blades direct the steam onto the turbine blades at the correct angle.*

not produce electricity. But as the turbine spins, it drives a GENERATOR, which produces the electricity. Some turbines are wheels or drums, with blades or cup-shaped buckets around their edges. Others are shaped like screws or propellers.

Steam turbines are operated by jets of steam. They have many uses. They are used to produce electricity, to propel ships, and to operate PUMPS. Gas turbines are turned by fast-moving jets of gas. The gases are produced by burning fuels such as oil. Gas turbines are used to turn the propellers of aircraft.

Turkey

Turkey is a country that is partly in EUROPE and partly in ASIA. The small European part covers three percent of the land. It lies west of the waterway which links the Black Sea to the Mediterranean Sea. This part includes the largest city, Istanbul, which was once called CONSTANTINOPLE. The Asian part, which is sometimes called Anatolia or Asia Minor, includes the capital, Ankara.

Most of Turkey's people follow the religion of ISLAM. Much of the land is mountainous, and large areas are covered by dry plateaus (tablelands). But the coastal plains are fertile, and farming is the main industry. Turkey also produces chromium.

TURKEY

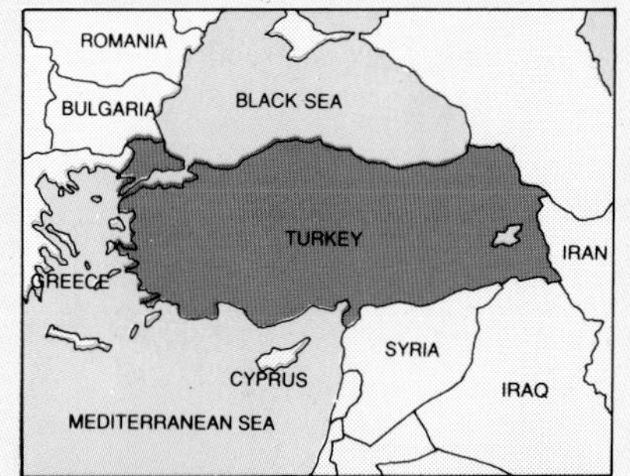

Government: Republic
Capital: Ankara
Area: 301,381 sq. miles (780,576 sq. km)
Population: 58,687,000
Language: Turkish
Currency: Turkish lira

▼ There are many beautiful mosques in Istanbul. Hagia Sophia was originally built as a Christian cathedral by the Emperor Justinian I between 532 and 536. After 1453, when the Turks conquered the area, it became a mosque. Since 1935, it has been in use as a museum.

The Ottoman Empire of the Turks produced brave and well-led soldiers, but they had many cruel practices. It was, for example, the custom to kill all the sultan's brothers so that none of them should be able to take the throne. After 1610, the brothers were no longer killed. Instead they were shut up for all their lives in a building surrounded by a walled garden.

Turkey was once part of the Byzantine empire, which was the eastern part of the ROMAN EMPIRE. But after Constantinople fell in 1453, the Moslem Ottoman conquerors built up a huge empire. At its height, it stretched from southern Russia to Morocco, and from the Danube River to the Persian Gulf. But it slowly declined after 1600 and collapsed in World War I. After that war, Turkey's president, Kemal Atatürk (1881–1938) modernized the nation. Atatürk means " Father of the Nation."

Turtle and Terrapin

Some people give the name "turtle" to all shelled REPTILES, including TORTOISES. But generally, the name is just used for those that live in water. The shells of turtles are similar to those of tortoises. They are both made of bony "plates" which are covered by large horny scales. Small turtles that live in fresh water are called terrapins.

Marine, or sea, turtles spend most of their lives in warm seas. They swim great distances to find food, and many of them have webbed toes, or flipper-like legs to help them swim well. They eat water plants, such as seaweed, and some small sea animals. Turtles often swim under water, but they come up to the surface to gulp air into their lungs.

Turtles go ashore to lay their eggs. They usually bury their eggs in sand, or hide them among weeds.

▼ *Snapping turtles are not very good swimmers. They usually walk over the bottom of the rivers and lakes where they live. They are found in central and eastern parts of the United States and in some parts of Central America.*

The baby turtles hatch out on their own. When they have hatched, they dig themselves out of their nest and head for the sea.

There are several kinds of marine turtle. The largest kind is called the leatherback turtle. It can weigh over 1,600 lbs. (725 kg) and be up to 6 ft. (1.8 m) long. The green turtle is used for turtle soup, and its eggs are eaten in Asian countries. The hawksbill turtle almost became extinct. Its shell was used to make "tortoiseshell" ornaments and jewelry.

▲ *Turtles and terrapins are reptiles of a type that have existed on Earth for over 200 million years. They have a horny beak instead of teeth.*

Tutankhamun

Tutankhamun was a PHARAOH of ancient EGYPT. His tomb was discovered in 1922 by a British archaeologist, Howard Carter (1873–1939). Carter, with the Earl of Carnarvon, was digging in the Valley of the Kings, in Egypt. The discovery was an exciting one, because Carter had found the only tomb of a pharaoh that had not already been robbed of its treasures. In the tomb were a golden throne, caskets, statues, precious stones, and furniture. There were four gold shrines, one inside another, in the burial chamber. The *sarcophagus* (coffin) contained the mummified body of the pharaoh. These treasures can now be seen in a museum in Cairo.

Tutankhamun became pharaoh when he was about 11 years old. He ruled for about 8 years.

▼ *This detail from one of Tutankhamun's burial caskets shows the pharaoh in a war chariot attacking the Syrians.*

TUVALU

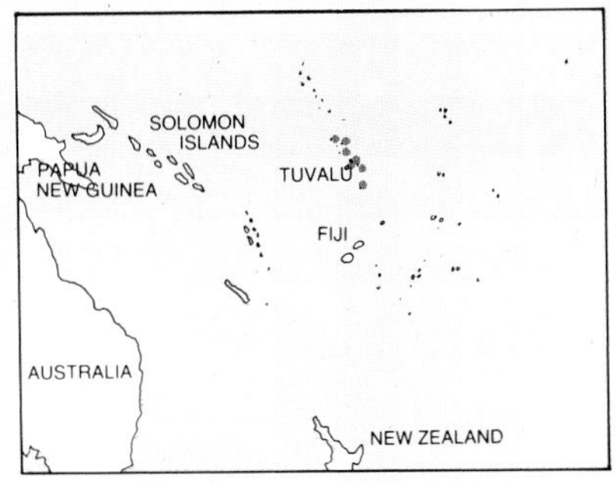

Government: Monarchy
Capital: Funafuti
Area: 10 sq. miles (26 sq. km)
Population: 10,000
Languages: Tuvaluan, English
Currency: Australian dollar

Tuvalu

Tuvalu is a country consisting of a group of tiny islands in the Pacific Ocean. The islands are coral reefs, and little grows on the poor soil. The people of Tuvalu are Polynesians, whose chief occupation is fishing. From 1888, Tuvalu, along with the Gilbert Islands, was a British colony. It became independent in 1978.

Twain, Mark

Mark Twain (1835–1910) was the most successful and famous American writer of the 1800s. His real name was Samuel Clemens, but he called himself Mark Twain after an expression used on Mississippi river boats that meant two fathoms (a depth of 12 feet or 3.7 meters), of water. Twain spent much of his early life on the Mississippi, and he became a riverboat pilot. The river became the inspiration for his most famous books, *The Adventures of Tom Sawyer* and *Adventures of Huckleberry Finn*. The humor and realism of these books was quite new in the 1800s and helped to establish a new American style of writing. Both books are still very popular today. Mark Twain traveled throughout his life, and his books and lectures about his journeys were a huge success.

JOHN TYLER

Tenth President 1841–1845
Born: Charles City County, Virginia
Education: College of William and Mary, Williamsburg, Virginia
Occupation: Lawyer
Political Party: Democratic, then Whig
Buried: Richmond, Virginia

Tyler, John

John Tyler (1790–1862) was the 10th president of the United States. He served less than one full term—from 1841 to 1845—and only became president after the death of William Harrison. He was the first vice president to become president after the death of a president.

His time in office was nearly always difficult. He had frequent battles with his own party and with the opposition, and was often very unpopular. But he was also courageous and clever. Despite the problems that faced him, he never abandoned his principles. Both Texas and Florida became states during Tyler's presidency. Tyler also managed to agree the boundary between the United States and Canada.

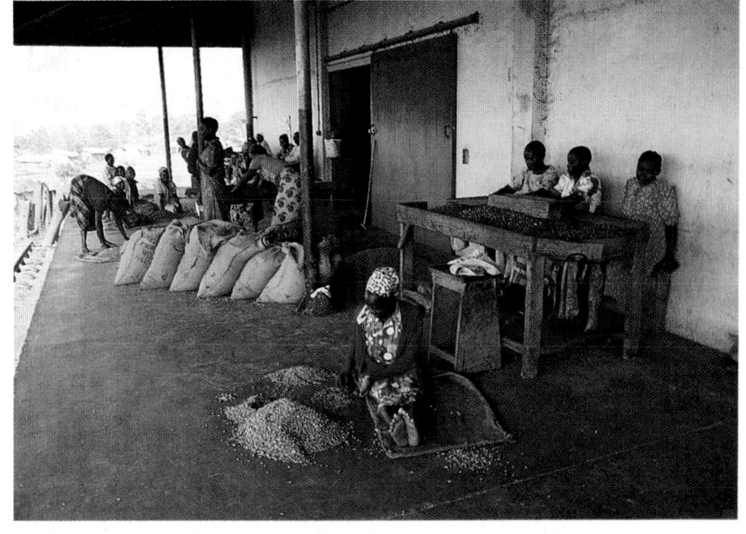

◀ *Coffee beans are graded and bagged before being sent by rail to the coast. Coffee is one of Uganda's main exports.*

Uganda

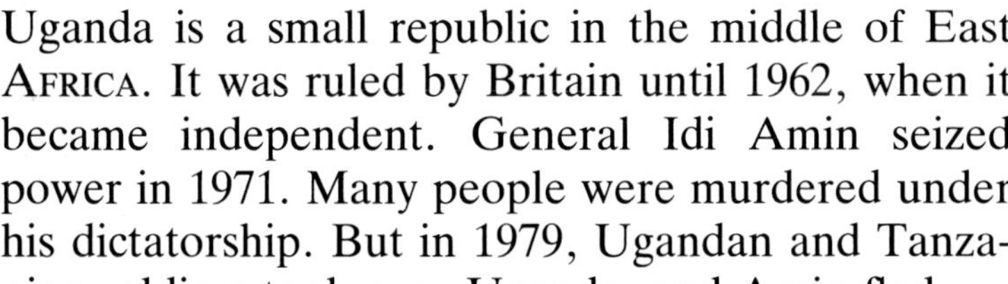

Uganda is a small republic in the middle of East AFRICA. It was ruled by Britain until 1962, when it became independent. General Idi Amin seized power in 1971. Many people were murdered under his dictatorship. But in 1979, Ugandan and Tanzanian soldiers took over Uganda, and Amin fled.

Part of Africa's largest lake, Lake Victoria, lies in Uganda. Most of the people are farmers. The main crops are coffee, tea, and cotton.

UGANDA

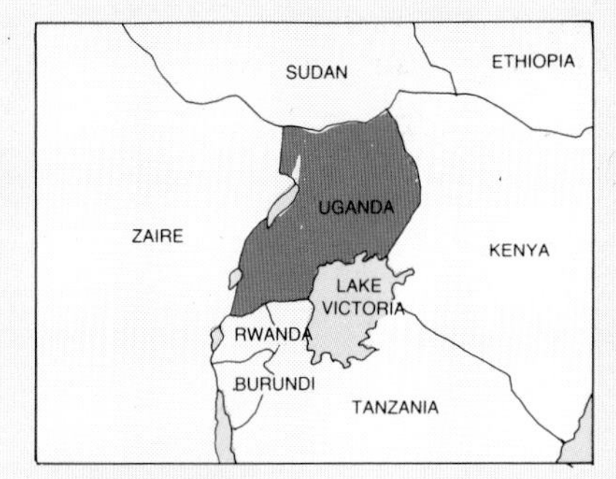

Government: Republic
Capital: Kampala
Area: 93,354 sq. miles (241,785 sq. km)
Population: 18,795,000
Languages: Luganda, Swahili, English
Currency: Ugandan shilling

Ultraviolet Light

If LIGHT from the Sun shines through a prism, it splits up into a rainbow of colors, called a SPECTRUM. Red is at one end of the spectrum and violet at the

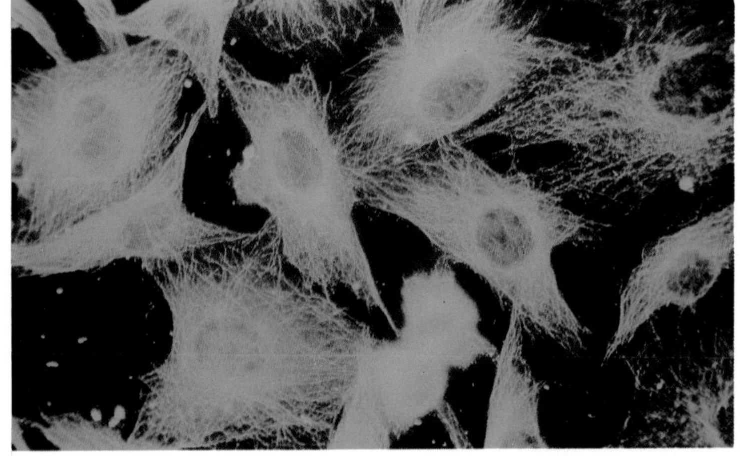

◀ *Ultraviolet (UV) light is useful to scientists. In this photograph, taken through a high-powered microscope, antibodies used in cell research have been stained with a green dye which fluoresces (shines) when it is exposed to ultraviolet light.*

Ultraviolet light has many uses. It is a powerful germ-killer and can be used to sterilize food and medical equipment. Pictures can be taken in the dark by turning ultraviolet light on an object. Forged documents can be detected by shining ultraviolet light on them. The different kinds of ink on the document can be spotted by the glow they give off.

other. Ultraviolet light lies just beyond the violet end of the spectrum. We cannot see it, but it will blacken photographic film and make some chemicals glow. Most ultraviolet light from the Sun is lost in the atmosphere. But enough rays reach Earth to give us suntans. If more ultraviolet rays reached us, they would be very harmful.

Ulysses

Ulysses is the Roman name for a brave and cunning Greek hero named Odysseus. His famous adventures are told in HOMER's poem, the ODYSSEY. It tells how Ulysses took ten years to return home after the TROJAN WAR.

On his journey, he was captured by the Cyclops, a one-eyed, man-eating giant. A witch called Circe changed his men into pigs. And sirens (sea maidens) lured his men to their deaths. When he finally reached home, his wife, Penelope, was surrounded by suitors. She had agreed to marry any man who could shoot an arrow from Ulysses' bow through 12 rings. Ulysses, in disguise, was the only man who could do it. He then killed all the suitors.

In Homer's *Odyssey*, the gods were always interfering in human affairs. Ulysses' chief enemy was Poseidon, god of the sea. This is why the hero was always being driven off his course at sea or being shipwrecked.

▼ *Ulysses had to trick the Cyclops by giving him very strong wine to make him drunk. This gave the Greeks time to escape from the island where they were being held prisoner and continue on their journey.*

Underground Railroad 

The underground railroad was the name given to the illegal organization that smuggled escaped slaves out of the South before the Civil War. Most slaves went to Canada. If they were recaptured in the North, they could be returned to the South. The Underground Railroad wasn't actually a railroad, and it didn't go underground. Slaves traveled any way they could, mostly at night. But the people who helped them were called "conductors," and the places where they hid were called "stations."

United Arab Emirates 

The United Arab Emirates is made up of seven small states—Abu Dhabi, Dubai, Fujairah, Sharjah, Umm al-Qaiwain, Ajman, and Ras al-Khaimah. Most of the country is hot, dry desert, but oil in Abu Dhabi and Dubai make the area one of the richest in the world. The sheikhs (rulers) of the emirates sit on a governing council.

UNITED ARAB EMIRATES

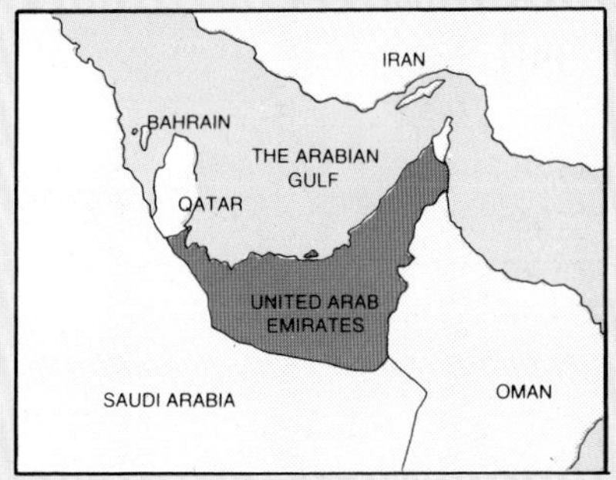

Government: Federation
Capital: Abu Dhabi
Area: 32,000 sq. miles (82,900 sq. km)
Population: 1,589,000
Language: Arabic
Currency: Dirham

United Kingdom 

The United Kingdom of Great Britain and Northern IRELAND is the eleventh largest nation of Europe. ENGLAND, WALES, and SCOTLAND make up the island of Great Britain, which takes up most of the BRITISH ISLES. Northern Ireland, Scotland, and

◄ *Eilean Donan Castle in Scotland is the sort of picturesque location that many tourists like to see when they visit the United Kingdom.*

UNITED KINGDOM

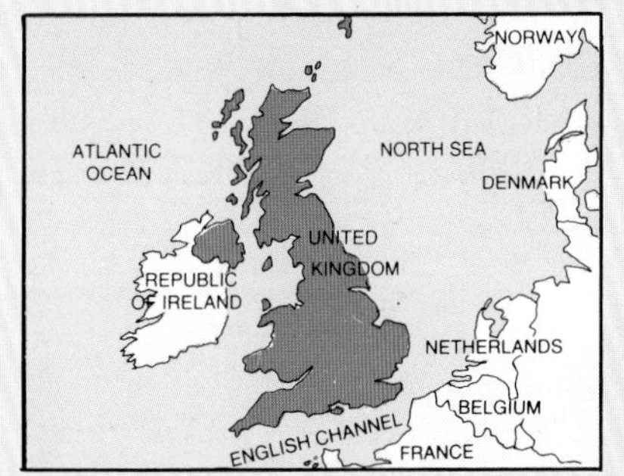

Government: Constitutional monarchy
Capital: London
Area: 94,226 sq. miles (244,044 sq. km)
Population: 57,237,000
Languages: English, Welsh, Gaelic
Currency: Pound sterling

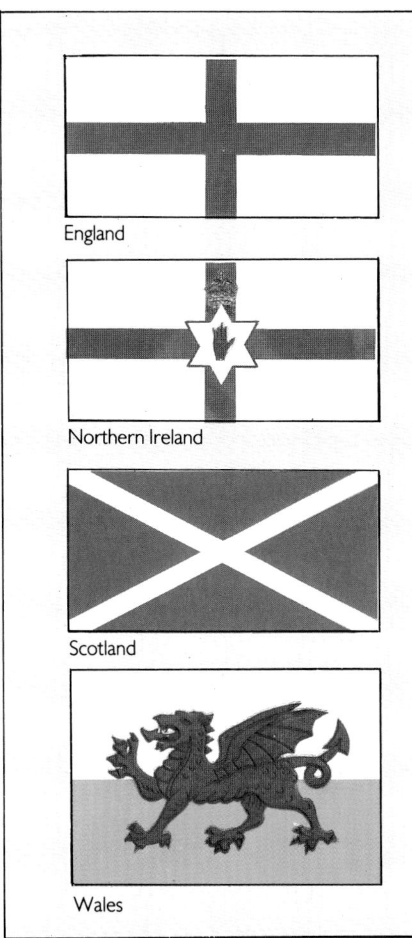

▲ *The flags of the countries that make up the United Kingdom: England, Northern Ireland, Scotland, and Wales.*

Wales are mountainous. The highest mountain is Ben Nevis in Scotland. Plains and valleys cover much of England. The longest river is the SEVERN, which flows through England and Wales. The British climate is mild.

About 57 million people live in the United Kingdom. Few other countries are so crowded. Four out of five people live in cities such as Belfast, Glasgow, and LONDON. London is the capital. Great Britain grows half of the food she needs. Her industries help to pay for the food that is bought from abroad. The United Kingdom manufactures a wide range of goods. Service industries, such as tourism, which provide services rather than producing goods, are increasing. Traditional industries such as coal mining are declining.

United Nations

Most of the world's countries belong to the United Nations. It is an association that works to keep peace and help people everywhere.

Each member country sends delegates to regular meetings of the United Nations' General Assembly in New York City. The General Assembly suggests how countries should behave. It cannot make them take its advice. But the United Nations' Security Council can ask member countries for troops to help stop nations from fighting.

The United Nations works largely through 14

▼ *The flag of the United Nations. It shows a map of the world surrounded by an olive wreath. The olive branch is a symbol of peace.*

SOME UNITED NATIONS AGENCIES

- **FAO** Food and Agriculture Organization
- **IBRD** International Bank for Reconstruction and Development (World Bank)
- **ICAO** International Civil Aviation Organization
- **ICJ** International Court of Justice
- **IFC** International Finance Corporation
- **ILO** International Labor Organization
- **IMF** International Monetary Fund
- **UNCTAD** United Nations Conference on Trade and Development
- **UNESCO** United Nations Educational, Scientific, and Cultural Organization
- **UNICEF** United Nations Children's Emergency Fund
- **UNIDO** United Nations Industrial Development Organization
- **UNRWA** United Nations Relief and Works Agency
- **WHO** World Health Organization

agencies. The Food and Agriculture Organization helps countries to grow more food. The World Health Organization fights disease. The International Monetary Fund lends countries money.

The United Nations has managed to prevent some wars and has helped millions of people.

United States of America

The United States of America is the world's fourth largest nation. Russia, Canada, and China are bigger in area; and more people live in China, India, and Russia. There are 50 states in the United States. Forty-eight are in the same part of NORTH AMERICA. The other two are Alaska in the north, and the Pacific islands of Hawaii.

The mainland United States stretches from the Pacific to the Atlantic. Long mountain ranges run down the Pacific coast. Inland are flat-topped mountains and basins. In this region is Death Valley, the lowest place in the Americas. Here, too, is the GRAND CANYON, a huge gorge cut by the Colorado River. Farther east lie the tall peaks of the ROCKY MOUNTAINS that run from Canada to Mexico. Beyond them stretch the Great Plains where the mighty MISSISSIPPI RIVER flows. Another mountain range, the Appalachians, runs down the eastern side of the United States.

The United States is a young country. In 1976, it was just 200 years old. The original 13 colonies

UNITED STATES OF AMERICA

Government: Federal republic
Capital: Washington, D.C.
Area: 3,618,770 sq. miles (9,372,614 sq. km)
Population: 249,975,000
Largest city (population): New York (7,071,039)
Highest point: Mount McKinley, Alaska, 20,320 ft. (6,194 m)
Agriculture: Nearly 50% of land in use
Chief crops: Soybeans, cotton, fruits, corn
Chief industries: Coal, oil, steel, textiles, tobacco
Language: English

▲ *This large statue of Abraham Lincoln sits in the Lincoln Memorial in Washington, D.C. It is 19 feet (5.8 m) tall.*

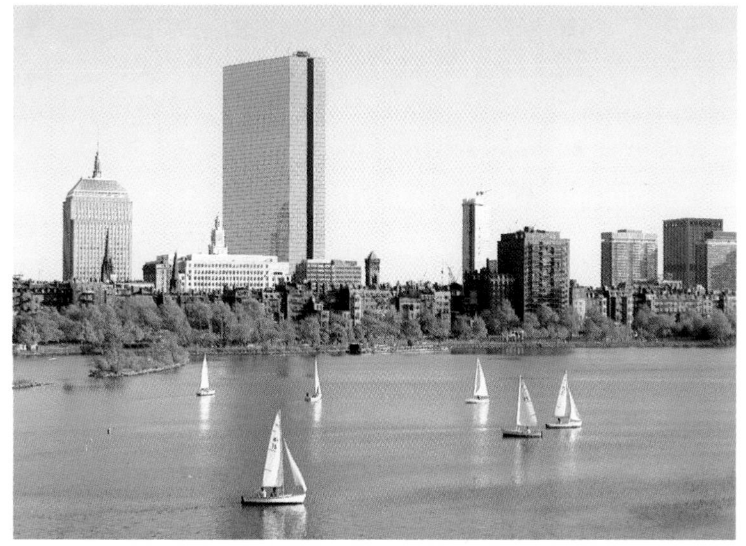

◀ *The modern skyline of Boston, Massachusetts, one of America's oldest cities.*

▲ *Disneyland in Anaheim, California, is a playground for both young and old. It was built by Walt Disney and opened in 1955.*

declared their independence from Britain in 1776. George WASHINGTON was elected the first president in 1789. By the mid 1800s, the United States had grown to much the same size as it is today. Explorers had added new land to the original colonies, and the country stretched west to the Pacific. From 1861 to 1865, a CIVIL WAR was fought between the South, which believed in SLAVERY, and the North, which wanted every man to be free. The northern states won, and slavery was abolished. Between 1870 and 1900, thousands of Europeans came and settled in the United States. They were seeking land and a new life. By 1900, the country's population had doubled.

The 250 million citizens of the United States include Native Americans, and people whose ancestors came from Europe, Asia, or Africa. Seventy out of every 100 Americans live in cities. WASHINGTON, D.C. is the capital, but NEW YORK is the largest city.

The United States is one of the world's richest countries. Its farms produce huge wheat crops and more oranges, meat, eggs, and cheese than any other country. American miners mine coal, copper, lead, and uranium. The United States is the world's largest manufacturer of cars and chemicals.

Until recently, the United States produced enough coal, oil, and gas of its own to run its farms, factories, and homes. Now, it has to buy oil from abroad. (See pages 714-715.)

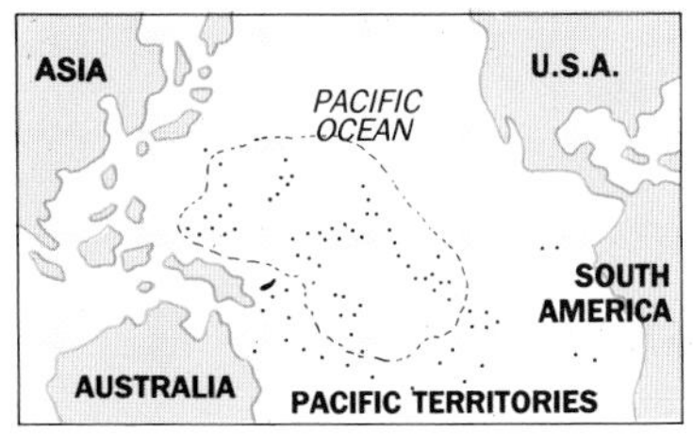

▲ *The U.S. Pacific Territories are located in a large area that is sometimes described as "Micronesia" (tiny islands). The territory's overall area covers 3 million sq. miles (7.7 million km²) of the Pacific Ocean. But the land area of all the islands is only 716 sq. miles (1,833 km²), less than half the size of Rhode Island.*

United States Pacific Territories 

The United States governs a number of islands in the Pacific Ocean. The largest of these is GUAM. American Samoa elects its own governor and legislature. In World War II the United States won four island groups from Japan and took control of them as a trust territory of the United Nations. The Northern Mariana Islands became a commonwealth in 1986. The Marshall Islands and the Federated States of Micronesia have signed compacts of free association with the United States. They are completely self-governing except that Washington remains responsible for their defense.

Universe

The universe is made up of all the STARS, PLANETS, MOONS, and other bodies scattered through the emptiness of space. The EARTH is just a tiny part of the SOLAR SYSTEM, in a great group of stars known as the MILKY WAY. Beyond our GALAXY lie possibly billions of other galaxies. Some are so far away that the light from them takes thousands of millions of years to reach us.

Scientists think that all matter in the universe was once squashed together as a fireball that exploded, shooting matter out in all directions. As the matter spread, it cooled; and clouds of gas and dust came together to form stars, planets, moons, and other bodies. This idea is called the Big Bang theory.

About 17,000 million years ago the universe may have begun with an incredible explosion.

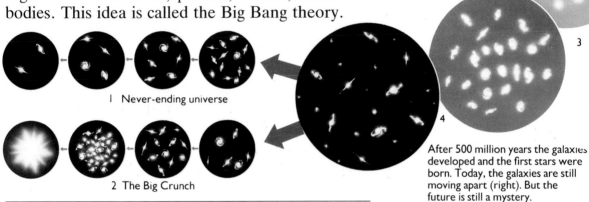

1

2

3

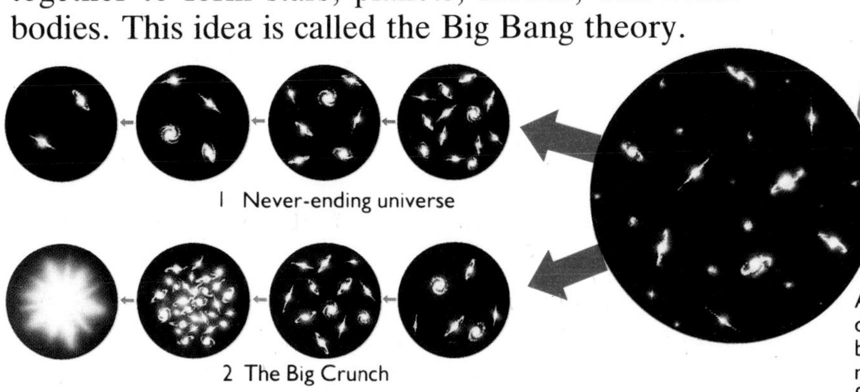

After 500 million years the galaxies developed and the first stars were born. Today, the galaxies are still moving apart (right). But the future is still a mystery.

▲ *This diagram shows two ways in which the universe might continue. In the "never-ending universe" theory, the galaxies will continue to fly apart until space is almost all black emptiness. In the "big crunch" theory, the galaxies stop moving apart. Their gravity will then pull them inward again until they collide and explode.*

University

Some people who graduate from high school go on to a college or university where a student may choose to study a wide range of subjects. Eventually a student will major in a specific area and prepare for a career. He or she attends classes and talks called lectures. The student has to write essays and perhaps carry out experiments in a laboratory. Students can use libraries to find out much of what they need to know from books.

After four years, students take their final examinations. If they pass they are given a degree, usually a Bachelor of Arts or a Bachelor of Science. They can qualify for graduate degrees, such as a Masters or a Doctorate, if they continue their studies.

Europe's first university was founded in the 1000s at Bologna in Italy. Soon after, universities were founded at Paris in France, Salamanca in Spain, and Oxford in England.

The oldest university in the United States is Harvard University. It was founded in 1636. Today there are more than 3,400 colleges and universities in the country. About 12.5 million students are enrolled in these schools, including 350,000 foreign students.

UNITED STATES

IMPORTANT DATES IN AMERICAN HISTORY

1492 Columbus sights the Bahama Islands
1607 First English settlement, Virginia
1620 Voyage of the *Mayflower*
1754 French and Indian War: Britain gains control of North America
1776 Declaration of Independence
1783 End of Revolutionary War: U.S.A. is a new nation
1789 George Washington is first president
1804 Lewis and Clark explore the West
1812 War with Britain (ends 1815)
1841 First wagon trains set out for California
1848 U.S.A. defeats Mexico and gains new territory
1848 Gold rush in California
1861 Start of Civil War between Northern and Southern States (ends 1865)
1867 Alaska sold to U.S.A. by Russia
1898 War with Spain
1917 U.S.A. enters World War I
1920 Women get the vote
1927 Charles Lindbergh flies the Atlantic
1929 Stock market crashes, Great Depression begins
1941 Pearl Harbor attacked; U.S.A. enters World War II
1950 U.S. involved in Korean War
1958 First American space satellite, Explorer I
1962 John Glenn is first U.S. astronaut in orbit
1963 Assassination of President John F. Kennedy
1969 Apollo astronauts land on the Moon
1974 Nixon is first president to resign, over the Watergate scandal
1975 Vietnam War ends
1991 Gulf War

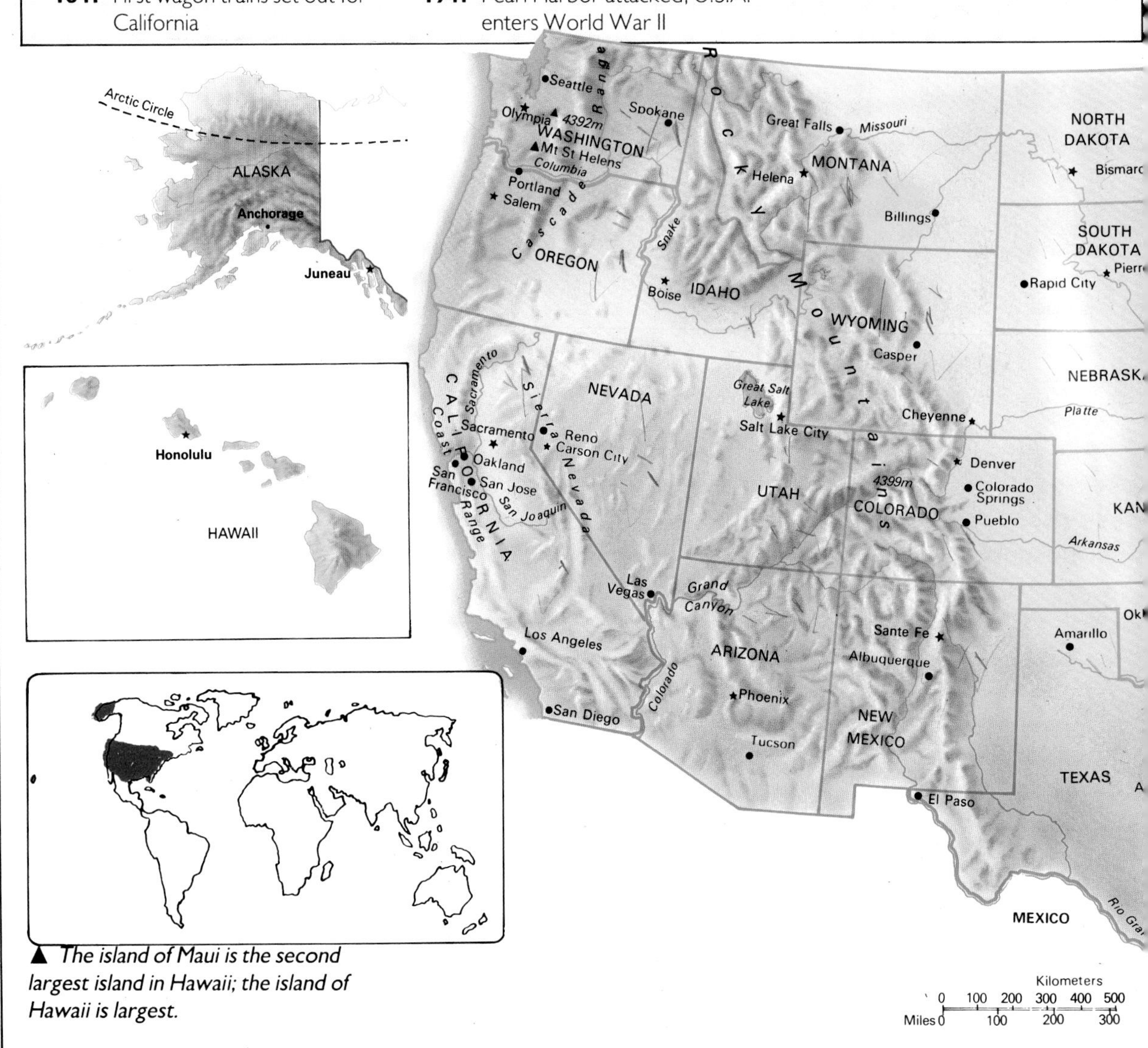

▲ *The island of Maui is the second largest island in Hawaii; the island of Hawaii is largest.*

▲ *Monument Valley in northeastern Arizona is part of the Navajo Indian reservation lands.*

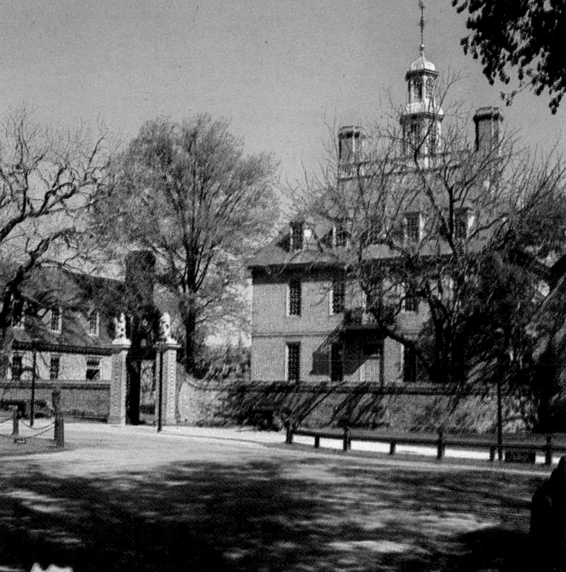

▲ *Historic Williamsburg was the colonial capital of Virginia.*

▲ *A husky waits patiently outside a trapper's hut in Alaska, the northernmost state.*

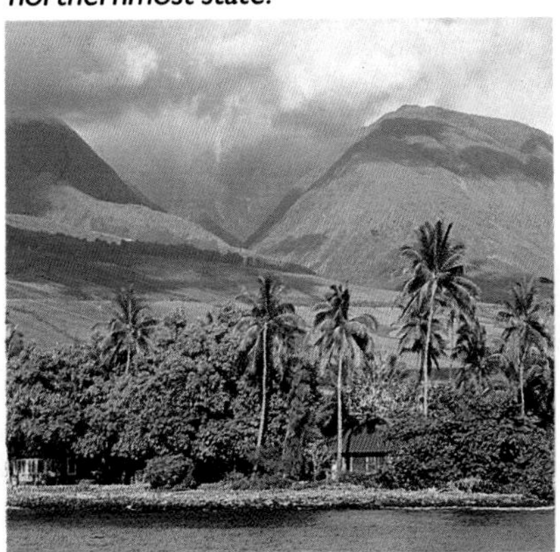

▲ *The island of Maui is the second largest island in Hawaii; the island of Hawaii is largest.*

For more information turn to these articles: AMERICAN HISTORY; CIVIL WAR; FRANKLIN, BENJAMIN; JEFFERSON, THOMAS; KENNEDY, JOHN F.; KING, MARTIN LUTHER JR.; LINCOLN, ABRAHAM; REVOLUTIONARY WAR; SLAVERY; WASHINGTON, GEORGE; WRIGHT BROTHERS.

Uranium was discovered in 1789 by a German chemist, Martin Heinrich Klaproth. He named it after the planet Uranus.

One ton of uranium can produce as much energy as 30,000 tons of coal.

Uranium

This metal is one of the heaviest of all known ELEMENTS. It was named after the planet Uranus. Uranium gives off RADIOACTIVITY. As it loses atomic particles, it decays and ends up, after millions of years, as LEAD. People working with uranium often need protective clothing to shield their bodies from radiation damage.

Uranium is the fuel used to make NUCLEAR ENERGY in atomic bombs and nuclear power plants. It is mined in many countries.

▶ *The American space probe, Voyager 2, passed Uranus in June, 1986. The pictures it sent back showed that the planet has rings and is tilted on its axis. This tilt is shown by the red lines.*

When William Herschel discovered Uranus in 1781, he named it Georgium Sidus (Star of George) in honor of Britain's King George III. This name was never popular in other countries, and the present name, that of one of the Greek gods, was chosen by the German astronomer, J.E. Bode.

Uranus

The PLANET Uranus is 19 times farther away from the Sun than the Earth is. We cannot see Uranus just with our eyes. It was the first planet discovered with the help of a TELESCOPE. It looks like a greenish-yellow disk.

Uranus is unlike our Earth in many ways. For one thing, it is much larger. You could fit 52 planets the size of the Earth inside Uranus. The distance through the middle of Uranus is nearly four times the distance through the middle of the Earth.

Unlike our planet, Uranus is made up mainly of gases. Its whole surface is far colder than the coldest place on Earth. It spins at a speed that makes one of its days about the length of 17 Earth hours. But Uranus takes so long to ORBIT the Sun that one of its years lasts 84 of ours.

URANUS FACTS

Average distance from Sun:
1,783 million miles
(2,870 million km)
Nearest distance from Earth:
1,650 million miles
(2,650 million km)
Average temperature (clouds):
−364°F (−220°C)
Diameter across equator:
32,300 miles (52,000 km)
Atmosphere: Hydrogen, helium
Number of moons: 15 known
Length of day: 17 hours
Length of year: 84 Earth years

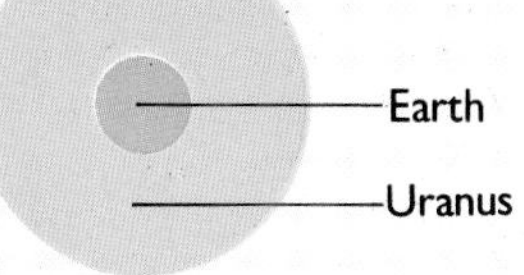

Uruguay

Uruguay is one of the smallest countries in South America. It lies in the southeast, between the Atlantic Ocean and its two big neighbors, Argentina and Brazil. Uruguay was formerly a province of Brazil. It became independent in 1825.

Low, grassy hills and lowlands cover most of Uruguay. Many rivers flow into the Uruguay River or into the river mouth called the Río de la Plata. Uruguay has mild winters and warm summers.

Most of Uruguay's inhabitants are descended from Spanish or Italian settlers. More than one in three of them live in the capital, Montevideo. Its factories make clothing, furniture, and other goods. But most Uruguayans work in meat-packing plants, wool warehouses, or on country ranches. Millions of sheep and cattle graze on these ranches.

URUGUAY

PARAGUAY
BRAZIL
ARGENTINA
URUGUAY
ATLANTIC OCEAN

Government: Republic
Capital: Montevideo
Area: 68,037 sq. miles (176,216 sq. km)
Population: 3,094,000
Language: Spanish
Currency: Peso

◀ *Gauchos in Uruguay round up a herd of cattle. There are more than 10 million cattle on the country's ranches.*

Utah 

The Rocky Mountain state of Utah is one of the most scenic in the country. Its snow-covered mountains, wild canyons, and empty spaces attract many visitors. But it is also an important mining region. Deposits of oil, coal, gas, copper, silver, and gold have made Utah prosperous. The state also has many important manufacturing plants. The first white settlers and many people in Utah today are Mormons, members of a special religious group. They came to Utah in the 1800s to escape persecution in other states. Their relations with the federal government were difficult because Mormons practiced "polygamy." This allows men to have more than one wife.

UTAH

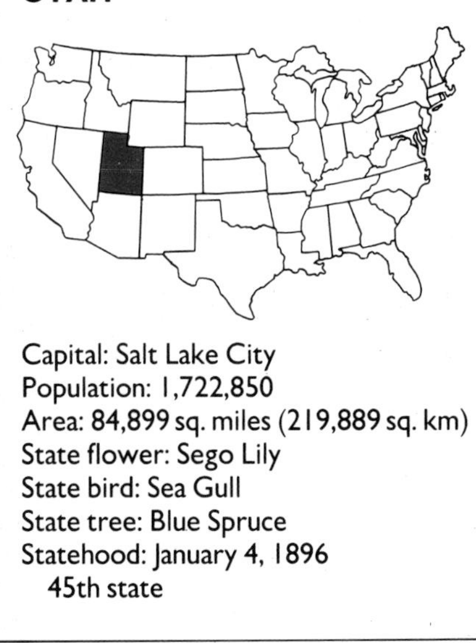

Capital: Salt Lake City
Population: 1,722,850
Area: 84,899 sq. miles (219,889 sq. km)
State flower: Sego Lily
State bird: Sea Gull
State tree: Blue Spruce
Statehood: January 4, 1896
45th state

Vaccination *See* Immunity

Vacuum

A vacuum is a space with nothing in it. It gets its name from *vacuus*, the Latin word for "empty." In fact there are no complete vacuums. When you try to empty a container by pumping out the air, a small amount of air always stays behind. This is called a partial vacuum. New air always rushes in to fill the space if it is allowed to do so. This is how your LUNGS work. When you breathe out, you make a partial vacuum in your lungs. Air rushes to fill the space, making you breathe in.

You can see partial vacuums at work in many ways. The space does not always fill up with air. When you suck air from a straw dipped in lemonade, it is the lemonade that rushes to fill the vacuum and so reaches your mouth. It is a partial vacuum that helps to keep aircraft in the air. As an airplane flies along, its wings are so shaped that they make a partial vacuum just above them. Air underneath the wings pushes them up to fill the space.

Van Buren, Martin

Martin Van Buren (1782–1862) was the eighth president of the United States. His presidency was dom-

SEE IT YOURSELF

A partial vacuum can be used to inflate a balloon. Try it yourself. Stand a bottle in a bowl of warm water for a few minutes. As heat makes the air inside the bottle expand, the pressure inside the bottle increases. Now fit a balloon over the neck of the bottle and put it in a bowl of cold water. What happens? The cold water cools the air inside the bottle and the pressure drops. Because the pressure of the air outside the bottle is greater, it pushes the balloon into the bottle and inflates it.

inated by the Panic of 1837. This was the first economic depression to hit the country. Many people lost their money and their jobs. Van Buren refused to help them because he believed people should be responsible for their own affairs. Because he stuck to his principles, Van Buren became unpopular with many people. Van Buren spent almost all his life as a politican. He was a senator, governor of New York, secretary of state, and vice president before he became president. He ran for president twice after he left office, but was defeated both times.

MARTIN VAN BUREN

Eighth President 1837–1841
Born: Kinderhook, New York
Education: Studied in law office
Occupation: Lawyer, government official
Political Party: Democratic
Buried: Kinderhook, New York

Vancouver

Vancouver is the largest city in the Canadian province of British Columbia, and one of the largest cities in Canada. Because its huge harbor never freezes, it is an important port, through which almost all Canada's trade with the Pacific passes. It first became important in 1884, when the Canadian Pacific Railroad chose it as the west end of its railroad across Canada. Today, forestry is the most important industry around the city.

Van Gogh, Vincent

Vincent Van Gogh (1853–1890) was a Dutch painter who worked mostly in the south of France. Van Gogh lived a very troubled life. During his lifetime he received no recognition and sold only one painting. Only his brother Theo believed in his genius as a painter. Now Van Gogh's paintings are famous all over the world.

Van Gogh failed in every career he attempted. He turned to art to express his strong religious feelings, but it was not until 1880 that he decided to become a painter. In 1886, he went to Paris to visit his brother and was immediately attracted to the Impressionist work he saw there. In 1888, Van Gogh moved to Arles in the south of France, where most of his most famous paintings were executed. During his last years he suffered from terrible fits of depression, but painted more than 800 oil paintings. He committed suicide in 1890.

▲ Italian Woman *(1887), a painting by Van Gogh.*

VANUATU

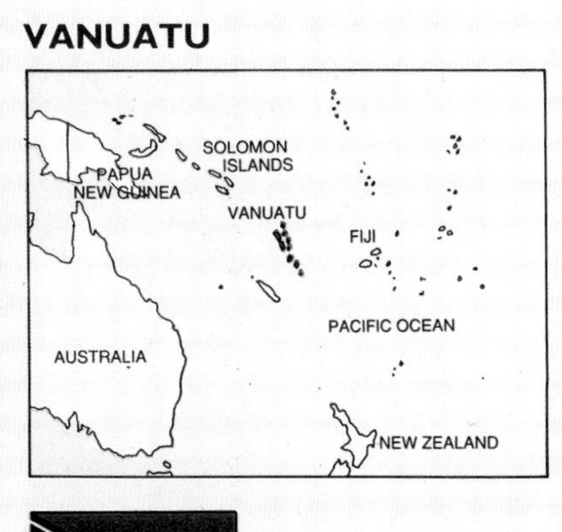

Government: Republic
Capital: Port Vila
Area: 5,700 sq. miles (14,763 sq. km)
Population: 147,000
Languages: Bislama, French, English
Currency: Vatu

VATICAN CITY

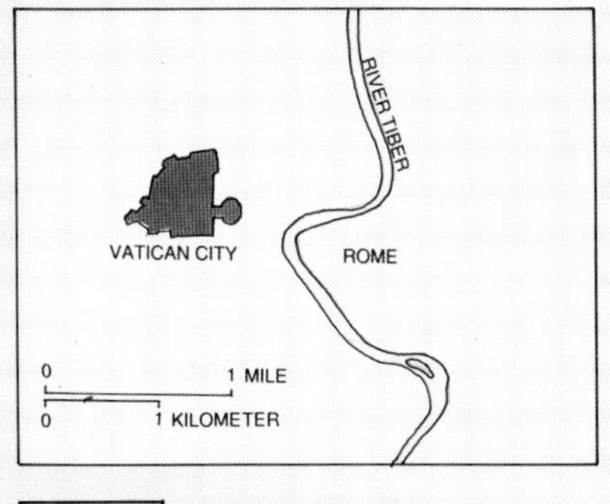

Capital: Vatican City
Area: 0.17 sq. miles (0.44 sq. km)
Population: 1,000
Languages: Italian, Latin
Currency: Italian lira

Vanuatu

Vanuatu is a country made up of volcanic islands in the southwestern Pacific Ocean. The soil is good and the main products are copra, cocoa, coffee, and livestock.

The islands were discovered in 1606 by a Portuguese navigator, but they were not charted until Captain Cook explored the area in 1774. From 1906 to 1980 the islands were ruled jointly by Britain and France. Independence came in 1980.

Vatican City

Vatican City is the Pope's home and headquarters of the Roman Catholic Church. It stands on Vatican Hill in northwestern Rome, and is the world's smallest independent country. It is only the size of a small farm and about 1,000 people live in it. Yet it has its own flag, radio station, and railroad. It also issues its own stamps.

Vatican City is surrounded by walls and contains many famous buildings. These include the Vatican Palace, which has more than 1,000 rooms; the Sistine Chapel, decorated by Michelangelo; and St. Peter's Basilica.

Vegetable

Vegetables are plants with parts that we can eat. They taste less sweet than the plant foods we call

► *A Swiss Guard sits at the entrance to the Vatican. The guards' uniforms are believed to have been designed by Michelangelo in the 1500s.*

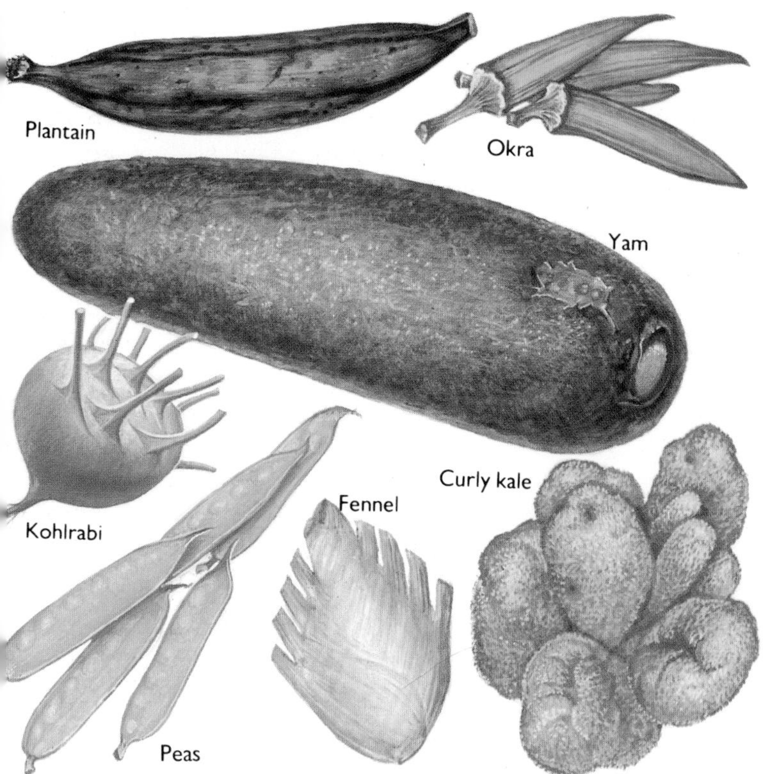

◀ *Here are seven very different kinds of vegetables. Curly kale is rich in vitamins A, B, and C. Peas supply body-building proteins. Plantains and yams can be boiled, fried, or roasted. Okra is sometimes called "ladies' fingers." Kohlrabi is related to the cabbage, and fennel adds an aromatic flavor to various dishes.*

FRUIT. Vegetables such as lettuce and spinach are eaten for their leaves. Other vegetables are eaten for their roots or stems. Carrots are roots. Celery and asparagus are stems. Peas, beans, and sweet corn are seeds. Tomatoes and squash are fruits.

Peas and beans supply body-building PROTEINS. Leafy and root vegetables provide VITAMINS, minerals, and fibers to help keep our DIGESTION working properly. Potatoes contain *starches*, which the body burns to make energy.

Many people are vegetarians — they do not eat flesh of animals, including red meat, poultry, and fish. The vegetarian diet consists mostly of vegetables, cereals, nuts, seeds, and fruits. Soybeans are a popular source of protein. People who eat a well-balanced vegetarian diet generally have lower blood pressure and less excess fat than those who eat meat. Vegetarians must take care, however, to consume enough proteins and vitamins.

Vein

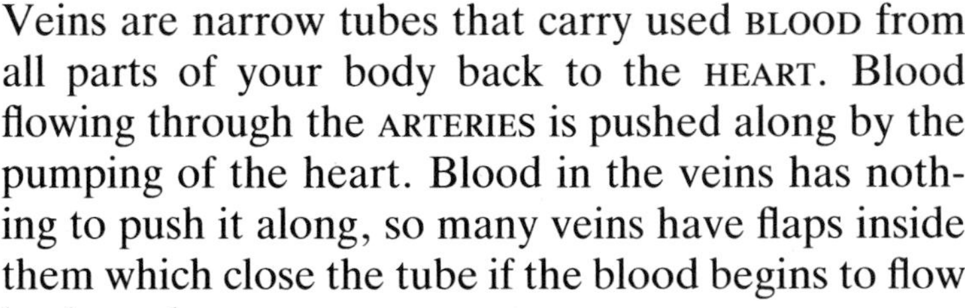

Veins are narrow tubes that carry used BLOOD from all parts of your body back to the HEART. Blood flowing through the ARTERIES is pushed along by the pumping of the heart. Blood in the veins has nothing to push it along, so many veins have flaps inside them which close the tube if the blood begins to flow backward.

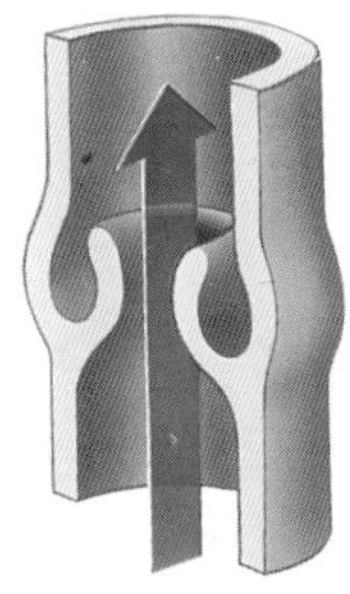
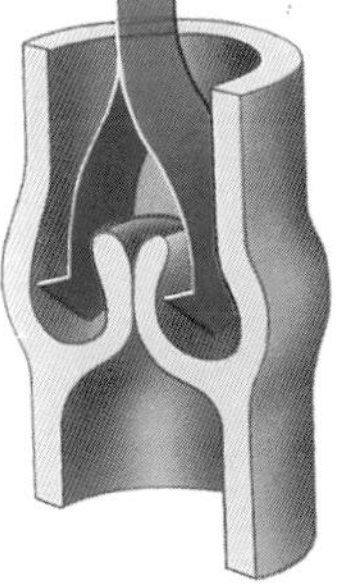

▲ *Deoxygenated blood flows back to the heart through the veins. Blood flowing in the right direction (left) forces valves in the vein open. Blood flowing the wrong way (right) forces the valves shut. The valves make sure that blood always flows toward the heart.*

Venezuela

Venezuela is a large country on the north coast of SOUTH AMERICA. Most of southern Venezuela is

VENEZUELA

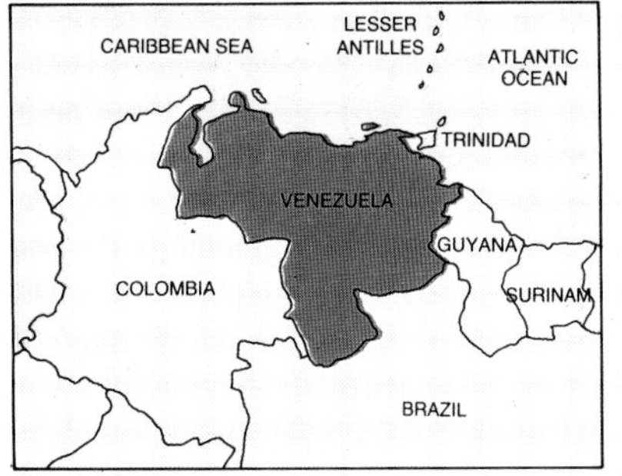

Government: Federal republic
Capital: Caracas
Area: 352,143 sq. miles (912,050 sq. km)
Population: 19,735,000
Languages: Spanish, Indian
Currency: Bolivar

covered by flat-topped mountains. Angel Falls, the highest waterfall in the world, is located here. A grassy plain stretches across the middle of the country on either side of the Orinoco River.

Venezuela grows coffee, cotton, and cocoa. But its minerals, especially oil, make it the richest country in the continent.

Venice

Venice is a beautiful city in ITALY, on the Adriatic Sea. It is built on a cluster of low, mud islands. There are more than 100 of them. The houses are built on wooden posts driven into the mud. Instead of roads, Venice has CANALS.

For hundreds of years, Venice was the most important center for trade between Europe and the empires of the east. The city became very rich and is full of palaces and fine houses built by merchants.

► *An 18th-century painting of the Grand Canal in Venice, by the artist Canaletto. The elegant black gondolas are still a common sight on the canal.*

Venus (planet)

The PLANET Venus is named after the Roman goddess of beauty and love. Venus is the brightest planet in the SOLAR SYSTEM. We see it as the morning star or the evening star, depending on where it is on its journey around the Sun.

Venus takes only 225 days to go around the Sun. So more than three years pass on Venus for every two on Earth. But Venus itself spins so slowly that

VENUS FACTS

Average distance from Sun: 67 million miles (108 million km).
Nearest distance from Earth: 25 million miles (40 million km).
Average temperature: 850°F (455°C)
Diameter across equator: 7,545 miles (12,142 km)
Atmosphere: Mainly carbon dioxide
Number of moons: 0
Length of day: 117 Earth days
Length of year: 225 Earth days

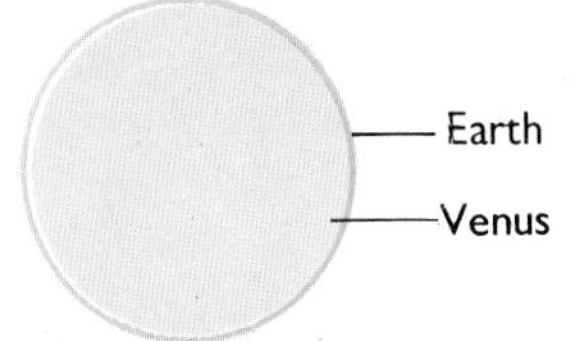

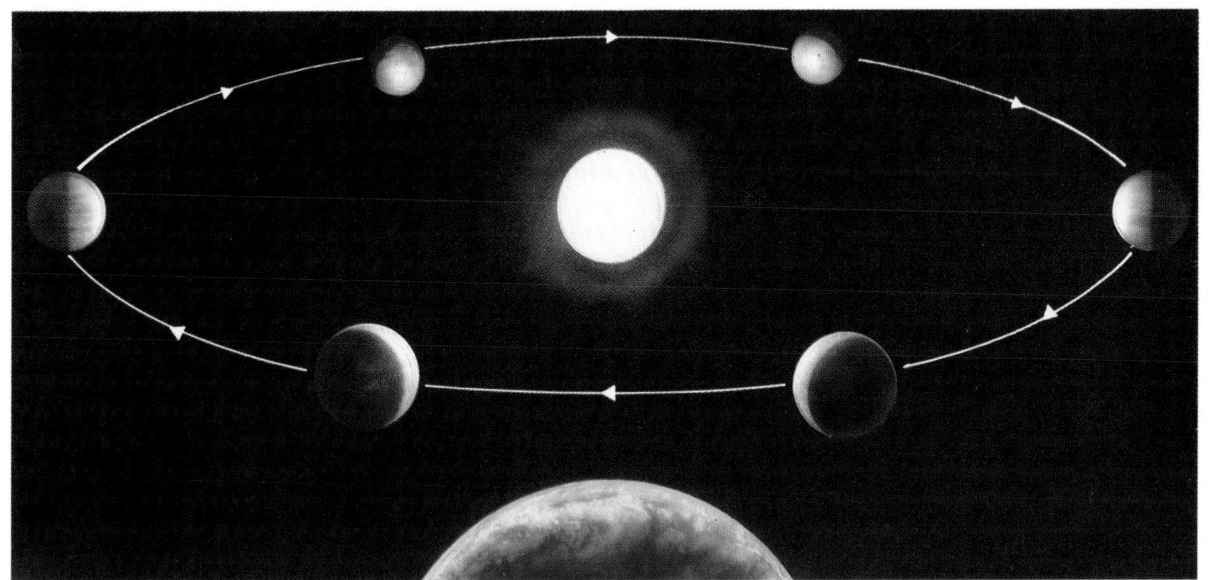

▲ *From the Earth, we have nearly a horizontal view of the orbit of Venus. As it travels around the Sun, we see different amounts of its sunlit surface. These are known as its "phases." The planet looks larger in its crescent phase, when it is closest to Earth.*

one day on Venus lasts for 117 days on Earth. It is the only planet to spin in the opposite way to the direction of its ORBIT.

Venus is about the same size as Earth, but weighs a little less. It is also much hotter, because it is much closer to the Sun. The surface of Venus is hidden under a dazzling white cloak of cloud. This may be made up of tiny drops of sulfuric acid. The atmosphere on Venus consists mainly of the gas *carbon dioxide*. This acts like a greenhouse roof, trapping the Sun's heat. The rocks on Venus are hotter than boiling water. Above the hot rocks are fierce winds of more than 200 mph (320 km/h).

Verb

Verbs are "doing" or "being" words, such as *go*, *hit*, *choose*, *have*, *be*. Verbs tell you what people or things are doing, or what is happening to them.

Here are three examples of verbs in sentences: "It *is* a cold night. Tom *ate* the hamburger. Jill *was drinking* a milkshake." In the first two examples, the verb is just one word. In the third example it is two words. In the first sentence, the verb is describing something happening in the present. We call this the use of the present *tense*. If the action happened in the past, the verb changes: "It *was* a cold night." Similarly, if the action is to happen in the future: "It *will be* a cold night."

VERB ENDINGS

Tense	*Singular*	*Plural*
Present		
1st person	I sing	We sing
2nd person	You sing	You sing
3rd person	He, she, or it sings	They sing
Past		
1st person	I sang	We sang
2nd person	You sang	You sang
3rd person	He, she, or it sang	They sang
Future		
1st person	I shall sing	We shall sing
2nd person	You will sing	You will sing
3rd person	He, she, or it will sing	They will sing

Verbs can also be *active* or *passive*. In the sentence "Tom ate the hamburger," the verb *ate* is active. If we said "The hamburger *was eaten* by Tom," the verb *was eaten* is passive.

Vermont

VERMONT

Capital: Montpelier
Population: 562,758
Area: 9,614 sq. miles (24,900 sq. km)
State flower: Red Clover
State bird: Hermit Thrush
State tree: Sugar Maple
Statehood: March 4, 1791
14th state

Vermont is the only New England state that isn't on the coast. It is the third smallest state in the U.S. and has the smallest population of any eastern state. Forests and mountains cover most of Vermont. The most famous mountains are the Green Mountains. Tourists visit them in the winter to ski and in the fall to admire the famous fall colors of the turning leaves. The name Vermont comes from the French words *vert mont*, or "green mountain." Vermont is also an historic state, although it wasn't one of the 13 original states. It played an important part in the REVOLUTIONARY WAR, and many Vermonters fought in the CIVIL WAR. Today, manufacturing, forestry, and mining are the most important industries.

▲ *Vermont in the fall. The scenery of the state is famous, from its green summers to its white winters. Each fall, many people visit just to see the dramatic variety of colored leaves.*

Versailles

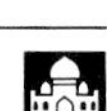

Versailles is a famous palace in France. It stands in a town, also called Versailles, just outside Paris.

The palace at Versailles was begun by LOUIS XIV in 1661, as a kind of "vacation home" for the king and his court. It was built on the site of a hunting lodge. The most famous architects, sculptors, and gardeners of the time worked on the palace and its magnificent park.

▶ *A view of the beautiful palace of Versailles today. Louis XIV spent over $100,000,000 on the palace, an enormous sum for the time.*

The palace is built of pink and cream stone. It is more than 2,600 feet (800 m) long. Inside are hundreds of beautiful rooms. The most famous is the Hall of Mirrors. It is lined with 483 enormous mirrors, and is full of paintings.

Louis XIV spent enormous sums of money on the palace. The great expense and luxury of the Versailles palace was one of the causes of the FRENCH REVOLUTION.

Vertebrate

Vertebrates are animals with a backbone or spine. The backbone is made up of short bones called *vertebrae*. This name comes from a Latin word that means "to turn." Most vertebrates can bend and straighten their backbones by turning their vertebrae slightly.

Many things make vertebrates different from other animals. Most have a bony case to protect their BRAIN, ribs to protect their HEART, LUNGS, and other delicate parts, and one or two pairs of limbs. And most vertebrates have a SKELETON made of BONE.

There are seven main kinds of vertebrate groups. The simplest group includes the lampreys. Lampreys are eel-like fish with no jaw. They have a spine but no skeleton. Next come SHARKS and skates, which have a skeleton of cartilage. All other vertebrates have bones. They are bony FISH, AMPHIBIANS, REPTILES, BIRDS, and MAMMALS.

▼ *The forelimbs of these vertebrates show that the animals may have evolved from the same ancestor. Each animal has the same special bones, though the shapes and sizes differ. This is because the bones gradually changed, over many millions of years, to suit the particular animal's environment.*

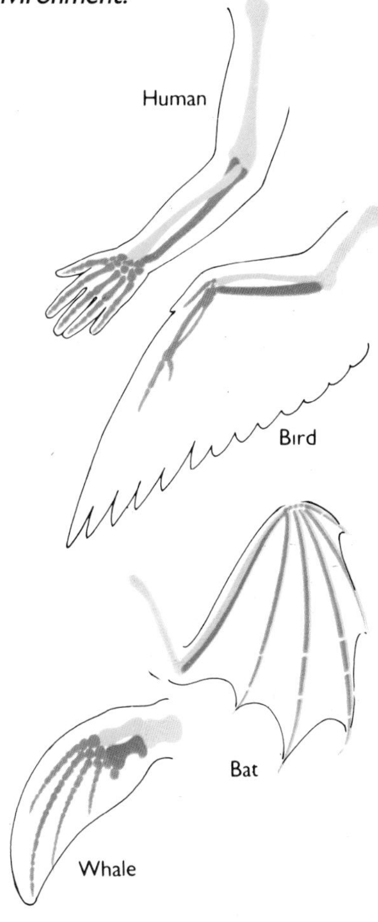

Vespucci, Amerigo

Amerigo Vespucci (1454–1512) was an Italian explorer and sailor who made three voyages from Europe to the American continent between 1499 and 1504. He claimed he was the first European to discover the new world that became America. Christopher COLUMBUS had sailed the Atlantic earlier, but he thought he had reached Japan. Because of this, a map maker in Europe named the new world, America, after Vespucci. Many people today think that Vespucci exaggerated his role and that his importance was much less than he claimed.

▼ *An old engraving of 1497 shows Amerigo Vespucci on board his ship. He was supposed to have encountered many strange creatures.*

▶ *A group of tourists gaze at Vesuvius' crater from the high ridge called Mt. Somma that surrounds it. Vesuvius is the only active volcano on the mainland of Europe.*

It is difficult to imagine what the eruption of Vesuvius must have been like in A.D. 79. We think of volcanoes pouring out molten lava, but Vesuvius went off like an atomic bomb, shooting out ash, pumice stone, and pebbles of lava over a great area. Even the city of Naples, 7 miles (11 km) from the volcano, was covered in a thick layer of ash. Pompeii, 5 miles (8.5 km) away, was buried under nearly 13 feet (4 m) of ash and stones.

Vesuvius

Vesuvius is one of the world's most famous VOLCANOES. The mountain rises over the Bay of Naples in southern Italy. It is about 4,000 feet (1,200 m) high, but gets shorter every time it erupts.

The first eruption we know of happened in A.D. 79. Nobody realized that it was an active volcano. People had built towns close by, and farmed the slopes of the mountain. For three days Vesuvius threw out ash and lava that buried the Roman cities of POMPEII and Herculaneum. Part of the wall of the old crater is still there. There have been nine bad eruptions in the last 200 years. The worst eruption in recent years happened in 1944 during World War II. The village of San Sebastiano was destroyed and Allied troops helped people to escape from the flowing lava.

▲ *A portrait of Queen Victoria by Bertha Muller. During Victoria's reign, Great Britain reached the height of its power.*

Victoria, Queen

Queen Victoria (1819–1901) ruled Great Britain for 64 years, longer than any other British monarch. During her reign, the nation grew richer and its empire larger than ever before. She was the queen of many countries, including Australia, New Zealand, Canada, and South Africa, and she was the empress of India.

Victoria was the daughter of Edward, Duke of Kent. GEORGE III was her grandfather. She was just

18 when she inherited the throne from her uncle, William IV. Two years later she married her German cousin, Prince Albert. They had four sons and five daughters. Prince Albert died of typhoid fever in 1861. His death left the Queen deeply unhappy. For many years she wore only black clothes to show her grief. She also stopped going to public ceremonies.

Victoria was very popular with her people. In 1887, she had been queen for 50 years. All over the British Empire there were huge parades and parties to celebrate this Golden Jubilee. In 1897, there were celebrations for her Diamond Jubilee. Her reign is known as the Victorian age.

Prince Albert had a great influence on Queen Victoria. He was her closest adviser and often restrained the impulsive queen. He was a patron of the arts and sciences, and helped to organize the Great Exhibition of 1851. He probably did more to set the tone of Victorian England than the queen herself.

Video

A video is a recording of moving pictures and sound. It is usually made on a videotape, but there are also videodiscs, which are like large versions of compact discs.

► *A video cassette recorder has three "heads." The erase head wipes off previous recordings; the video head records picture signals received from the TV antenna; and the audio head records sound signals on the edge of the tape. Pins guide the videotape from one reel to the other. The section of videotape inside the circle shows the patterns the signals make on the videotape. The picture signals are recorded in a diagonal pattern across the tape, in strips close together. If the signals were recorded straight across the video head, it would take 20 miles (33 km) of tape to make a one-hour recording!*

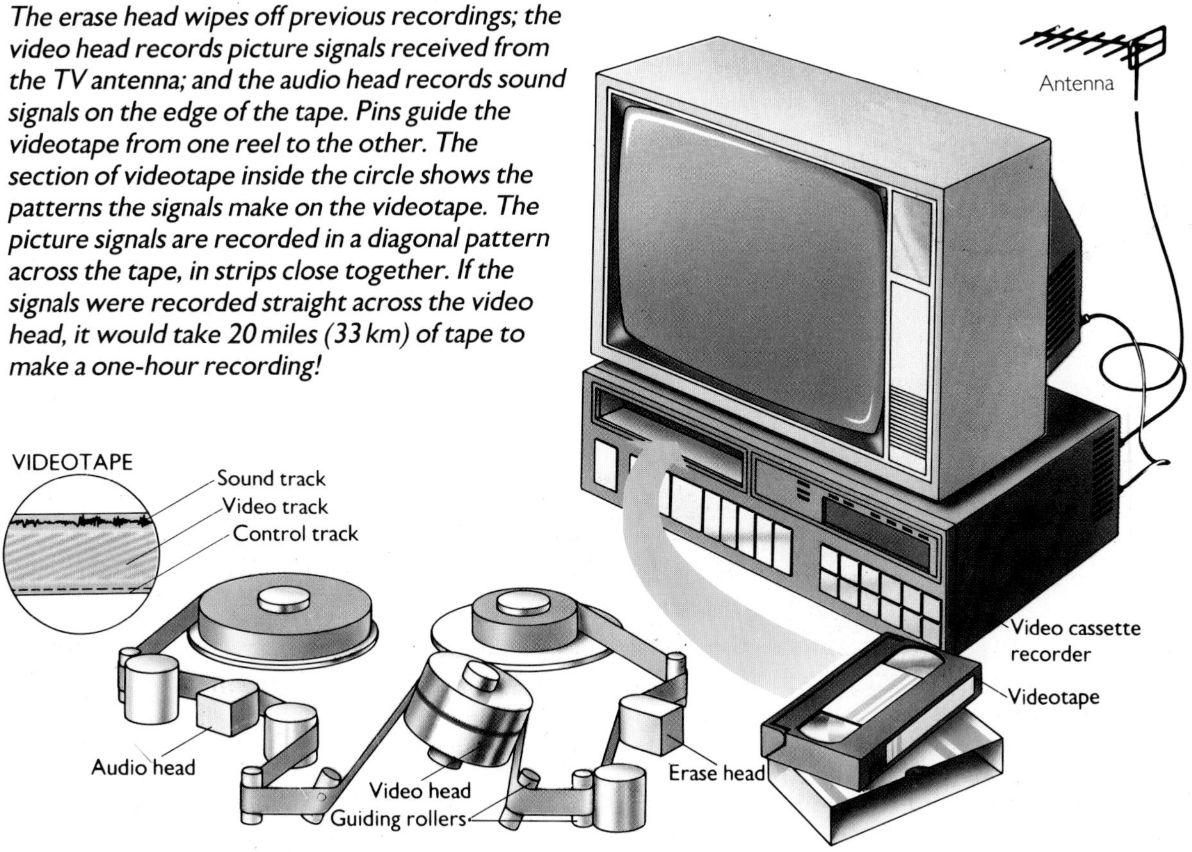

Video recording is not a new idea. In the late 1920s, John Logie Baird used an ordinary "78" record to store still pictures for showing on his newly invented television set. The video system used today by the broadcasting industry gives a better picture than that used in home recorders. VCRs were first marketed in the United States in the early 1970s. By the mid-1980s, two types of home VCR had been developed—Beta and VHS.

You play a videotape in a video recorder that is connected to a television set. You see the video on the television screen. A videotape recorder, or VCR can record television programs. You can erase an old program and record a new one on the same tape. You can also make your own videos if you have a video camera. Electric signals from the camera or from a television program are recorded on magnetic tape. The main difference from a music cassette recorder is that the record and replay heads in a video recorder spin around as the tape passes. This allows the head to move over the surface of the tape at high speed, giving the high recording speed needed to record picture signals.

Most of the programs you see on television are video recordings.

Vienna

Vienna is the capital city of Austria. More than one and a half million people live there. Until the end of WORLD WAR I, it was the home of the powerful Hapsburg family.

Vienna stands on the Danube River. It is a very ancient site. CELTS settled there more than 2,000 years ago. Then the Romans built a city called Vin-

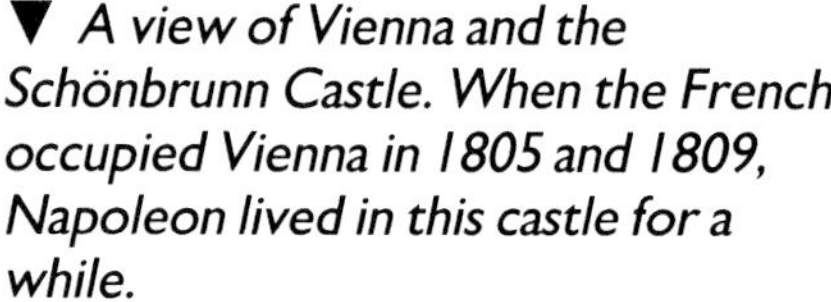

▼ *A view of Vienna and the Schönbrunn Castle. When the French occupied Vienna in 1805 and 1809, Napoleon lived in this castle for a while.*

dobona. Many buildings from the MIDDLE AGES still stand in Vienna.

Vienna has always been popular with artists and musicians. BEETHOVEN and MOZART lived there.

Vietnam

Vietnam is a country in SOUTHEAST ASIA. It is smaller than California and only 40 miles (55 km) wide in some parts. Vietnam is a hot, damp country.

Vietnam used to be divided into two countries, North Vietnam and South Vietnam. The main cities were Hanoi in the north and Saigon (now called Ho Chi Minh City) in the south. From the 1950s until 1975, the two countries were at war.

Starting in 1964, the United States sent troops to fight in Vietnam. American troops tried to prevent the whole country from falling under the control of the Communists of North Vietnam (the Viet Cong). But while U.S. soldiers never lost a battle, they could not defeat the many Communist supporters in the villages and jungles all over Vietnam. The last American troops left in 1972. The Communists conquered the whole country by 1975. By 1991, Vietnam's economy was in a dire state, with very high inflation.

VIETNAM

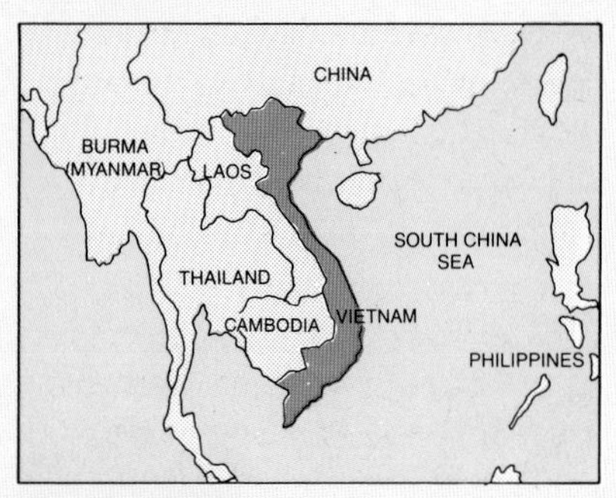

Government: Communist
Capital: Hanoi
Area: 127,330 sq. miles (329,784 sq. km)
Population: 66,200,000
Languages: Vietnamese, French, English
Currency: Dong

Vikings

The Vikings were a fierce people who lived in Norway, Sweden, and Denmark. (See pages 730–731.)

Violin

The violin is a MUSICAL INSTRUMENT. It belongs to the string family. It is usually the smallest string instrument in an ORCHESTRA.

A violin is a curved wooden box, shaped like a figure eight. A long neck is attached to one end of the box. Four strings, made of gut or nylon, are stretched from the top of the neck to the bottom end of the box. The violin is played with a bow that has a flat ribbon, made up of about 150 horsehairs. When this is drawn across the strings they vibrate to make sounds. The strings can also be plucked.

▼ *The wooden body of a violin amplifies (makes louder) the sound, which comes through two curved soundholes, called f-holes. The shape of the violin has changed very little since the 1500s.*

THE VIKINGS

The age of the Vikings lasted from about A.D. 800 to A.D. 1100. The Vikings came from Scandinavia (Norway, Denmark, and Sweden). They were originally farmers, but in order to find new lands to settle, they crossed the seas in swift sailing ships with carved dragon prows.

The Vikings earned a reputation for being bloodthirsty warriors, and were feared throughout western Europe. Vikings raided the coasts of England from the year 789 and eventually controlled the eastern part of the country.

The Vikings were not only raiders and pirates, they were superb seamen, braving the Atlantic Ocean to explore Greenland and even North America. They traded as far to the east as Russia and Constantinople. They had their own laws and a parliament. They were also skilled artists. They especially loved to recite poems and to tell tales of adventures involving heroes, gods, and monsters.

VIKING HISTORY

A.D.	**789**	First Viking attacks on England
	800	Beginning of the Viking Age
	830s	Vikings found the city of Dublin
	850	Swedes begin to settle in East Baltic and Russia
	860	Discovery of Iceland Harald Fairhair becomes the first king of all Norway, and many Norwegians settle in Britain
	874	First settlers in Iceland
	876	Norwegian Healfdene rules Northumbria
	886	King Alfred defeats Guthrum Danes allowed to settle in the Danelaw in eastern England
	911	Scandinavians settle in Normandy
	930	The first meeting of the Althing, the national assembly in Iceland
	982	Eric the Red discovers Greenland
	986	Coast of North America sighted by Bjarni Herjolfsson
	1000	Iceland becomes a Christian land
	1003	Leif Ericsson lands in North America
	1030	King Olaf of Norway killed at Battle of Stiklastad
	1047	Harald Hardrada becomes king of Norway
	1066	Harald Hardrada killed at Battle of Stamford Bridge in England, by King Harold of England; Duke William of Normandy defeats Harold to become king of England
	1100	End of Viking Age

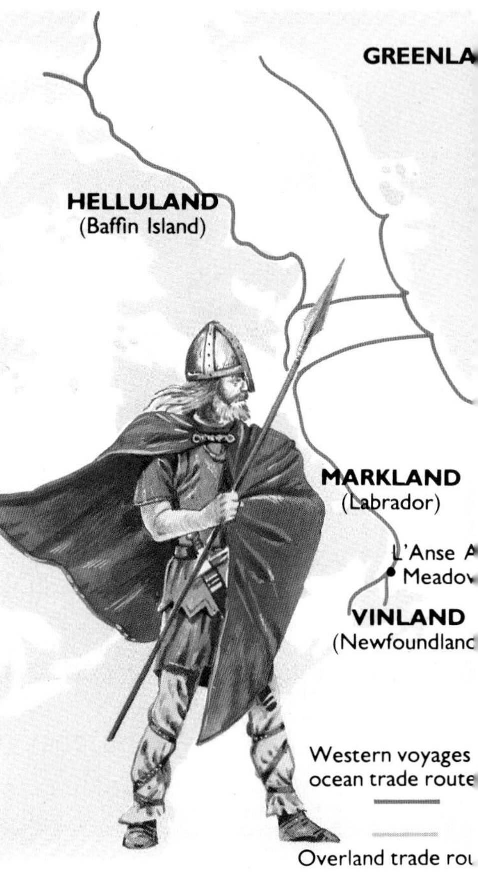

▲ *The map shows how widely Vikings traveled. They explored across oceans and land in search of settlements and trade. At left is a Viking warrior.*

► *The head of a Viking warrior (far right) is carved from a piece of elk horn and forms the handle of a stick. The God Thor is often shown in Viking art. This silver amulet (top right) is made in the shape of the god's hammer, decorated with a face with large, staring eyes. The Viking spear is richly decorated with engraving.*

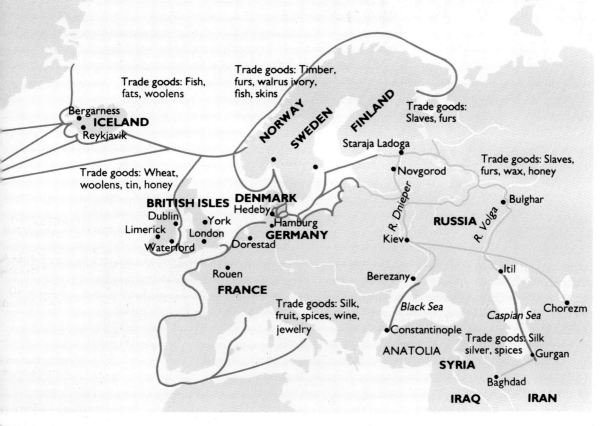

Trade goods: Fish, fats, woolens

Trade goods: Timber, furs, walrus ivory, fish, skins

Trade goods: Slaves, furs

Trade goods: Wheat, woolens, tin, honey

Trade goods: Slaves, furs, wax, honey

Trade goods: Silk, fruit, spices, wine, jewelry

Trade goods: Silk silver, spices

Bergarness
ICELAND
Reykjavik
NORWAY
SWEDEN
FINLAND
Staraja Ladoga
Novgorod
BRITISH ISLES
DENMARK
Hedeby
Dublin
York
Hamburg
Limerick
London
GERMANY
Waterford
Dorestad
Rouen
FRANCE
R. Dnieper
RUSSIA
R. Volga
Bulghar
Kiev
Berezany
Itil
Black Sea
Caspian Sea
Chorezm
Constantinople
ANATOLIA
SYRIA
Gurgan
Baghdad
IRAQ
IRAN

▲ *The Oseberg ship is a Viking ship dug up on a farm in Norway in 1904. It is 70 feet (21.5 m) long and had been buried as part of the funeral ceremony for a Viking queen.*

YGGDRASIL'S ASH TREE

The Vikings had a myth about a huge world tree called Yggdrasil's Ash. Its branches held up the sky. Beneath the tree was Asgarth, the home of the gods. Long roots spread out from the base of the trunk. One covered Midgarth, the world of men. Another root covered the realm of the terrible Frost Giants. A third root covered Hel, the world of the dead. Also among the roots were two wells. A drink of water from the well of the wise god Mimir gave knowledge. Beside the other well, the Well of Fate, lived the three Norns. They were called Past, Present, and Future. They wove a cloth. Every thread represented the life of a person. When they cut a thread, that person died.

For more information turn to these articles: ENGLISH LANGUAGE, MYTHOLOGY, SHIP.

VIRGINIA

Capital: Richmond
Population: 6,187,358
Area: 40,767 sq. miles (105,586 sq. km)
State flower: Dogwood
State bird: Cardinal
State tree: Dogwood
Statehood: June 25, 1788
10th state

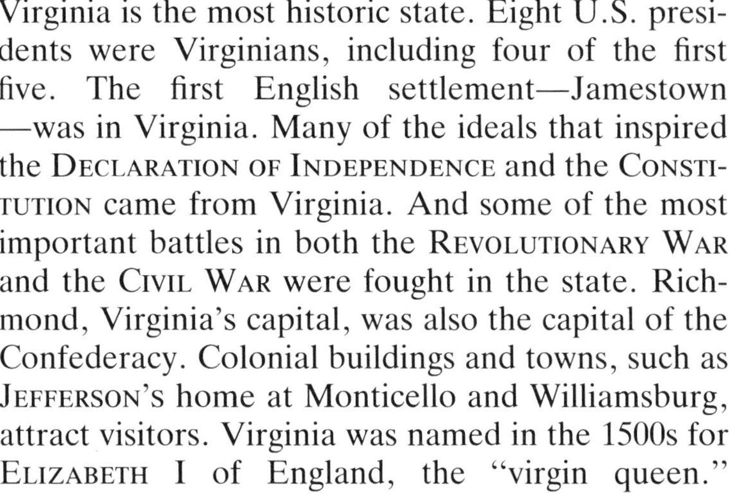

Virginia

Virginia is the most historic state. Eight U.S. presidents were Virginians, including four of the first five. The first English settlement—Jamestown—was in Virginia. Many of the ideals that inspired the Declaration of Independence and the Constitution came from Virginia. And some of the most important battles in both the Revolutionary War and the Civil War were fought in the state. Richmond, Virginia's capital, was also the capital of the Confederacy. Colonial buildings and towns, such as Jefferson's home at Monticello and Williamsburg, attract visitors. Virginia was named in the 1500s for Elizabeth I of England, the "virgin queen." Today, it is a prosperous state. Factories producing many goods and farming are the major industries.

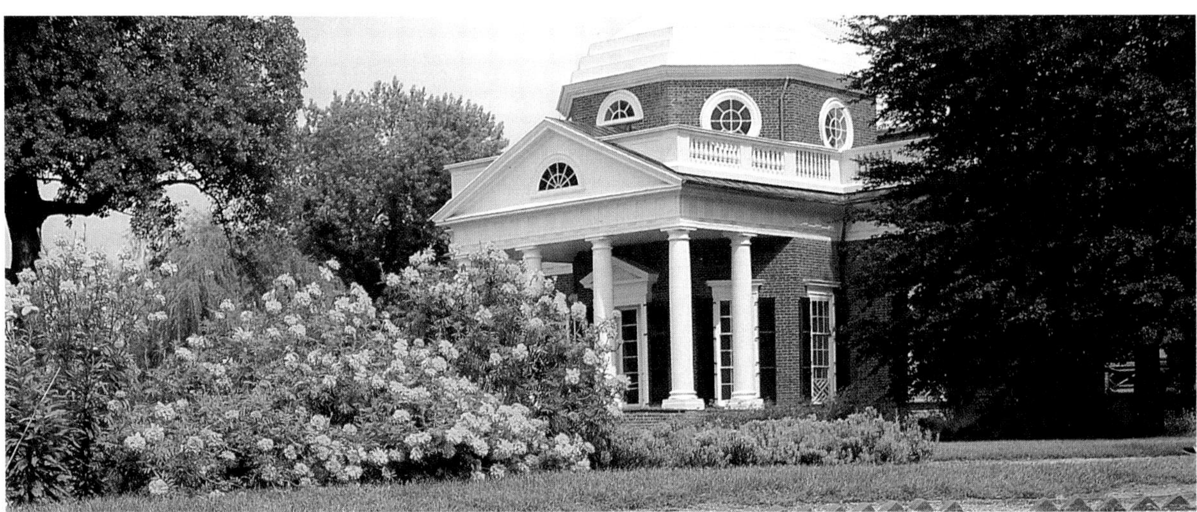

▲ *Monticello, the home of Thomas Jefferson, was designed and built between 1768 and 1809 near Charlottesville, Virginia. The 35-room brick mansion is filled with his collected items and clever inventions.*

Some viruses are no more than a few millionths of an inch in size. Scientists are still not sure whether they are living or non-living things. They seem to exist in a shadowy world between the two.

Virus

Viruses are very small things that cause diseases in plants and animals. They are smaller than bacteria and can be seen only with a very powerful electron microscope.

You can be infected with viruses by swallowing them or breathing them in. Some insects carry viruses, which they pass on when they bite you. Once inside the body, a virus travels around in the bloodstream. It gets inside a living cell where it produces more viruses. Sometimes the cell is entirely destroyed by the viruses.

Diseases caused by viruses include measles,

chicken pox, mumps, AIDS, influenza, and colds. Viruses are very hard to kill. Immunization helps to prevent some of these diseases.

When a virus enters the body, the blood produces substances called *antibodies*. After a while there are usually enough antibodies to kill all the viruses and the patient recovers.

► *White blood cells (T4 lymphocytes) defend the body by attacking viruses. The AIDS virus prevents the cells from doing this. AIDS can be transmitted in several ways, but once it enters the bloodstream (1) it attaches itself to a white blood cell. Then the core of the virus (2) slowly moves into the white blood cell. Once inside (3) the core breaks open and releases its genetic material (DNA). The virus makes its DNA match that of the white blood cell. The AIDS DNA may stay hidden inside the cell for years before it is activated. Then, the white blood cell begins to make copies of the virus and dies (4).*

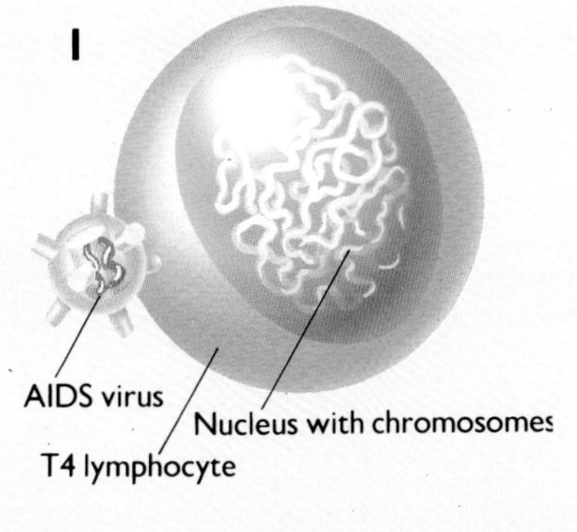

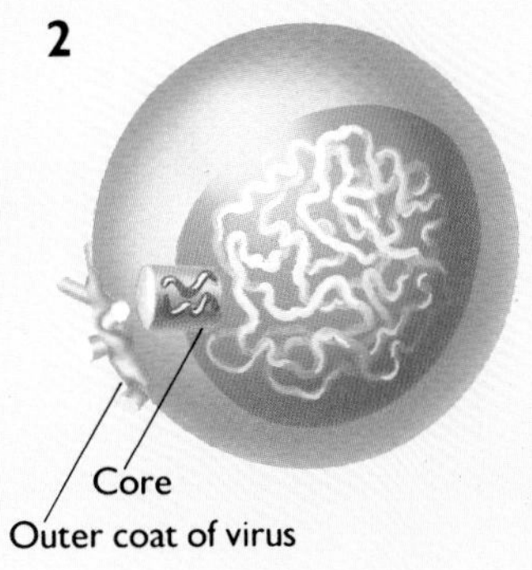

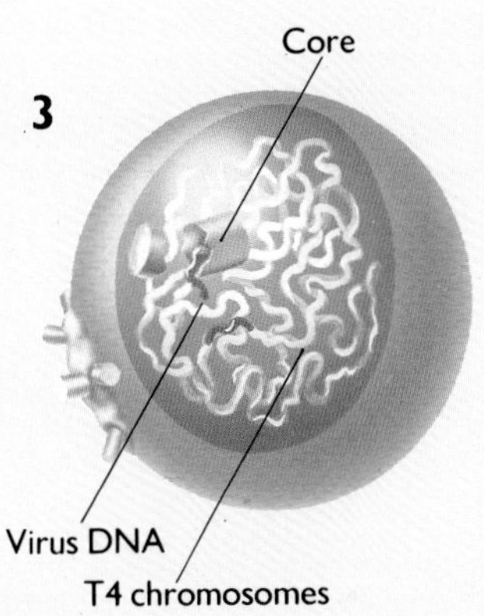

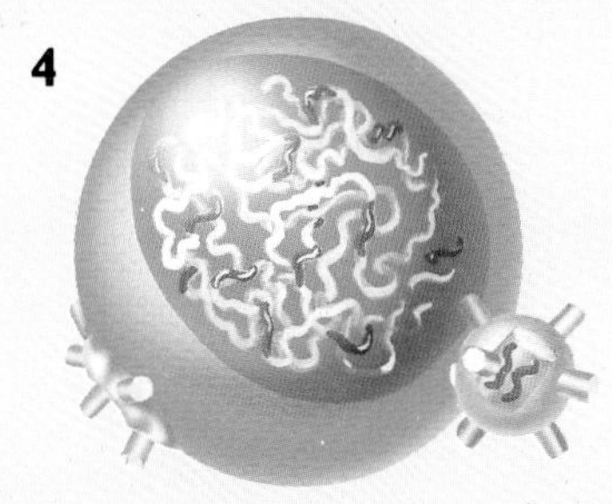

DNA– found inside cell nuclei. It stores the genetic code.

Vitamins and Minerals

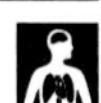

Vitamins are chemicals that our bodies need to stay healthy. They are found in different kinds of FOOD. Scientists call the six kinds of vitamins, A, B, C, D, E, and K. Vitamin B is really a group of vitamins.

The first people to realize that certain kinds of food were important to health were sailors. On long voyages they got a disease called *scurvy* if they could

SOURCES AND USES OF VITAMINS

Vitamin	*Found in*	*Needed for*
A	Milk, butter, eggs, green vegetables, fish oil, liver, carrots	Fighting disease and seeing in the dark
B$_1$ (thiamine)	Yeast and wheatgerm (whole wheat bread)	All "B" vitamins needed for healthy appetite, energy production, and healthy nerves and skin
B$_2$	Yeast	
9 other "B" vitamins	Milk, meat, and green vegetables	
C	Oranges, lemons, tomatoes, and fresh vegetables	Healthy blood and gums, healing, protection against colds
D	Cod-liver oil, cream, egg yolks (and with sunlight, fat below the skin forms vit. D)	Strong bones and teeth
E	Whole wheat bread, brown rice, and butter	Not fully understood; probably adds to general vitality
K	Green vegetables, liver	Clotting blood

not eat fresh fruit and vegetables. These contain vitamin C. From the 1700s, English sailors were given limes to eat to prevent scurvy. This is why they were nicknamed "limeys."

No one food has all the vitamins we need. That is why it is important to eat a mixture of things. Some people take their vitamins in pills. No one really needs pills if they eat well. Very old people, young babies, and women expecting babies, all need more vitamins than usual. But too much of some kinds of vitamins, such as vitamin A, can be bad for you.

We also need minerals in small amounts. Calcium is an important part of BONES and TEETH. We get it from milk and cheese. Iron is needed for hemoglobin, the part of red blood cells that carries oxygen from your lungs to tissues. Other minerals needed are iodine, phosphorus, sodium, and potassium.

Voice *See* Speech

Volcano

A volcano is an opening in the surface of the Earth. Burning gas, boiling rocks, and ash escape from this opening. Sometimes they trickle out, sometimes

they explode. An explosion is called an *eruption*.

Some volcanoes are gently sloping mountains with cracks, or fissures, in them. Hot liquid rock called *lava* flows out through the fissures. Other volcanoes are steep-sided mountains with a large hole at the top. These are called cone volcanoes. They are the kind that explode.

Erupting volcanoes can do a lot of damage. The city of POMPEII was destroyed by VESUVIUS in A.D. 79. In 1883, Krakatoa, a volcano in Indonesia, erupted, causing a tidal wave that killed 36,000 people. Volcanoes can also make new land. An island called Surtsey, south of Iceland, was made by a volcano erupting under the sea in 1963.

If you look at where volcanoes are found around the world, they make a pattern of long chains. These chains mark the edges of the huge "plates" that form the Earth's surface. They are the weakest part of the Earth's crust. One chain, called "the ring of fire," goes all around the Pacific Ocean.

VOLCANO FACTS

Active volcanoes: There are about 535 of these, 80 below the sea.

Largest known eruption: Tambora, Indonesia, in 1815. The volcano threw out about 40 cubic miles (150 cubic km) of matter and lost 4,100 feet (1,250 m) in height.

Greatest disaster: 36,000 people were drowned by a giant wave unleashed when Krakatoa, Indonesia, exploded in 1883.

Greatest volcanic explosion: About 1470 B.C. Santorini in the Aegean Sea exploded with 130 times the force of a hydrogen bomb.

The word "volcano" comes from Vulcan, the name the ancient Romans gave to their god of fire.

Volume

The volume of an object is the amount of space it takes up. You can find out the volume of a rectangular solid by measuring its height, width, and depth

▼ *A simple cross section of a volcanic region. Magma from the underground chamber (1) rises up the central vent (2) or side vent (3). During eruptions, ash (4) may shoot into the air and lava (5) flows out of the vent. Many volcanoes are made up of hardened layers of ash and lava (6). Magma which hardens underground creates formations called dikes (7) and sills (8). Laccoliths (9) push up the overlying rocks to form domes.*

SEE IT YOURSELF

You can use Archimedes' principle to find the volume of an egg. Put some water in a measuring cup and note the level. Using a spoon, gently lower an egg into the cup. What level does the water rise to? The difference between the two water levels will give you the volume of the egg. Try doing this with other irregular objects and recording their volumes.

and multiplying the figures together. So a block with equal sides, each 10 inches long, has a volume of 1,000 cubic inches, that is, 10 inches × 10 inches × 10 inches.

It is easy to find out the volume of boxes or bricks or anything with straight edges. Measuring the volume of something with irregular sides is more difficult. A very simple method was discovered by ARCHIMEDES, the Greek scientist. A story says that he was getting into his bath, which was full to the brim, and water spilled over the side. He suddenly realized that the volume of water that spilled over was exactly the same as the volume of his body. This means that the volume of any irregular shaped object can be measured by plunging it into water and measuring the rise of the water level.

Vulture

Vultures are large birds of prey. They live mostly in the hot, dry parts of the world. The largest land bird in North America, the California condor, is a type of vulture. When its wings are spread out, they measure up to 10 feet (3 m) from tip to tip.

Vultures do not hunt for their food. They live on carrion, the rotting bodies of dead animals. They wait until a large hunter, such as a lion, has made a kill. When the lion has eaten, wild dogs and hyenas gorge on the remains. Then it is the vulture's turn.

Most vultures have bald heads and necks. This stops their feathers from getting messy when they plunge their heads into large carcasses. They have very good eyesight and can spot dead or dying animals from far away.

► *These vultures are usually found around mountains. The black vulture is the most common North American vulture. The lammergeyer has an unusual habit of dropping bones onto rocks to break them open so it can eat the marrow inside.*

W

◀ *The god Wotan bids farewell to his daughter, Brünnhilde, in a scene from Wagner's opera* The Valkyrie, *one of the four great works in* The Ring of the Nibelung.

Wagner, Richard

Richard Wagner (1813–1883) was a German composer whose music brought about great changes in the art of opera. He believed that the music and the plot of an opera should be closely bound together, in the same way that the words and the plot of a play are. Wagner wrote his own *librettos* (scripts) for his operas.

In 1848, Wagner took part in a political revolution in Germany and he had to escape to Switzerland. There he began his greatest work, *The Ring of the Nibelung*. This long work consists of four music dramas based on old German legends. They tell the story of a magic ring and the adventures of the hero, Siegfried, and the beautiful Brünnhilde. When Wagner returned to Germany he designed at Bayreuth a festival theater especially for his operas. Today, people from all countries still go to Bayreuth to hear them.

Among Wagner's other operas are *The Flying Dutchman, Tannhäuser, Lohengrin, The Mastersingers of Nuremberg, Tristan and Isolde*, and *Parsifal*.

▲ *Richard Wagner spent the latter part of his life in debt. He died a year after his opera* Parsifal *was performed.*

Wales

Wales is part of the United Kingdom of Great Britain and Northern Ireland. It lies to the west of England and is a country of low mountains and

The title "Prince of Wales" is given only to the eldest son of an English sovereign. Prince Charles is the 21st Prince of Wales. The first was Edward, son of Edward I, who was given the title in 1301.

WALES

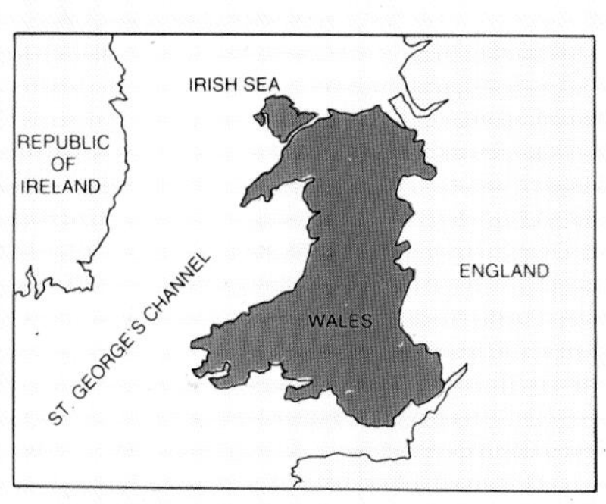

Area: 8,016 sq. miles (20,761 sq. km)
Population: 2,857,000
Capital: Cardiff
Languages: Welsh, English
Highest point: Snowdon, 3,560 feet (1,085 m) above sea level
Chief products: Coal, steel, wool, paper, textiles
Agricultural products: Barley, hay, oats, potatoes, turnips

green valleys. The highest mountain is Snowdon.

The Welsh are descended from the CELTS. English is their main language today, but about a quarter of the people still speak Welsh. Many Welsh people are striving passionately to keep their language alive.

South Wales was a traditional coal-mining region, but there are now few mines left. Most of the people live in industrial towns like Swansea and Cardiff. Steel is an important industry. In the mountains of north and mid-Wales many people are sheep farmers. Wool is one of Wales's main exports.

War of 1812

The War of 1812 was fought from 1812 to 1814 between the United States and Great Britain. Although it was fought mostly in and around the Canadian border, it was caused by Britain's war with NAPOLEON. The war ended at the same time that Britain defeated Napoleon, so, though none of the arguments that caused it had been settled, no one really minded. The chief cause of the war was that Britain wanted to stop the United States from trading with France, its enemy. They captured U.S. ships and blocked U.S. ports. The United States responded by attacking Canada, a British colony.

Washington

Washington state lies in the northwest of the country, on the Pacific coast. It takes its name from George WASHINGTON. The east of the state is largely deserted and dry, but the western half of Washington is the wettest place in the United States. The damp, warm climate encourages lush vegetation, and much of this part of the state is covered by thick forests. It is a paradise for people who enjoy the outdoors. Washington is also fertile farming country. It produces more apples than any other state. Along the coast, fishing is an important industry. The largest city is Seattle. It has many important high-technology industries and is also a prosperous port. Because it was so remote, Washington was one of the last states to be settled.

WASHINGTON

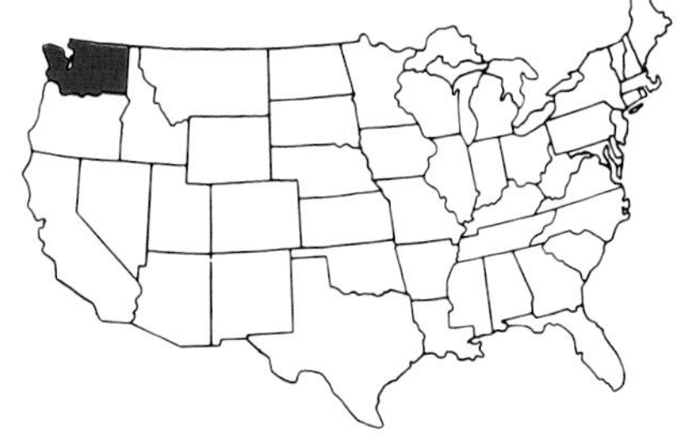

Capital: Olympia
Population: 4,866,692
Area: 68,139 sq. miles (176,479 sq. km)
State flower: Rhododendron
State bird: Willow Goldfinch
State tree: Western Hemlock
Statehood: November 11, 1889
42nd state

Washington, Booker T.

Booker T. Washington (1856–1915) was the most important black leader in the first 40 years after the CIVIL WAR. He knew that blacks would always face problems, so he urged them to win new skills in order to acquire prosperity. He began a school in ALABAMA called the Tuskegee Institute to teach these skills, ran newspapers, and advised many institutions and politicians.

Washington, D.C.

Washington, D.C. is the capital of the UNITED STATES. It is named after the first president, George WASHINGTON, who chose its site on the Potomac River between Maryland and Virginia. It stands on a piece of land called the District of Columbia, which is why it is always called Washington, D.C. It is not the biggest city in the United States, but it is the most important. It has all the government buildings, the White House, and the headquarters of the United States armed forces. A third of Washington's workers are employed by the government. The city also has the embassies and legations of about 140 nations.

▲ *A view of the east side of the Capitol building in Washington, D.C. This is where the United States Congress meets.*

Washington, George

George Washington (1732–1799) was the first president of the United States. To many Americans, he is the "father of the country"—not just because he was the first president, but because he also led the American colonies to victory and to independence in the REVOLUTIONARY WAR. He also played an important part in writing the CONSTITUTION. But more than this, he was enormously popular. People across the country admired and respected him. Some even wanted to make him king. One of his officers said about him in a speech, "he was first in war, first in peace, and first in the hearts of his countrymen."

Washington was a wealthy landowner from VIRGINIA. He spent his early years as a soldier. When he married he went back to Mount Vernon, his 8,000-acre plantation. After the Revolutionary

GEORGE WASHINGTON

First President 1789–1797
Born: Westmoreland County, Virginia
Education: Studied surveying
Occupation: Surveyor, farmer, army officer
Political Party: None
Buried: Mount Vernon, Virginia

▲ *George Washington crossed the Delaware River in December of 1776. He led a surprise attack on the Hessians at Trenton, New Jersey, and won a great victory.*

War began, Washington was chosen as commander-in-chief of the American troops. He faced many problems in training and equipping his men, but his determination and skill ensured that the British were defeated. He tried to return to farming, but he was asked to help write the Constitution. He was then chosen as president of the new United States.

Water

Water is the most common substance on Earth. Seven-tenths of the world's surface is covered by water. Water is also the most important substance on Earth. Without it life would be impossible. Life first started in water, and the bodies of all living things are mostly water.

There is no such thing as "pure water." Water contains MINERALS, which it has picked up from the surrounding earth and rocks.

Water exists in three forms. At 32°F (0°C) it freezes into solid ice. At 212°F (100°C) it boils into steam. Normal air takes up water easily, and CLOUDS are huge collections of water particles. At

Water pollution is one of our most serious environmental problems. It occurs when water is contaminated by poisonous chemicals, human waste, oils, or other harmful substances. Impurities must be removed before such water can be used safely. In the U.S., about 75% of community water supplies are disinfected with chlorine to kill disease-causing germs.

any time, clouds contain millions of tons of water, which falls back to Earth as RAIN. Some of this water stays in the soil or underground for years, but most of it returns to the oceans.

Waterfall

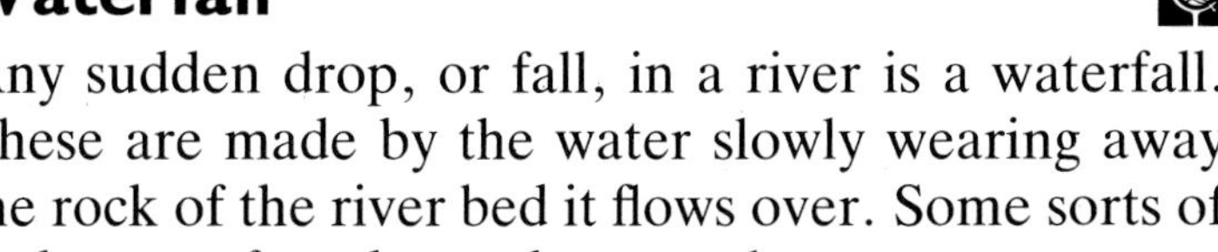

Any sudden drop, or fall, in a river is a waterfall. These are made by the water slowly wearing away the rock of the river bed it flows over. Some sorts of rock are softer than others, and so get worn away faster. The soft rock is worn away, leaving a cliff of hard rock, over which the river's water pours.

The most famous waterfalls are NIAGARA, between the U.S.A. and Canada, and the Victoria Falls in the Zambezi River in Africa. The highest waterfall in the world is Angel Falls in Venezuela. It is 3,212 feet (979 m) high.

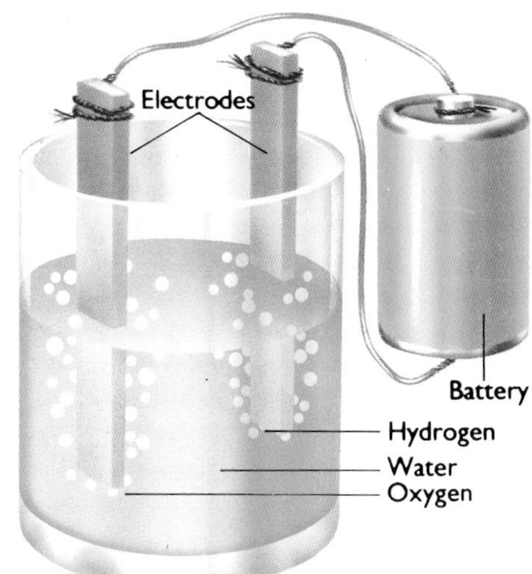

▲ *The chemical formula for water is H_2O. This means that each molecule of water is made up of two atoms of hydrogen and one atom of oxygen. By using two electrodes to pass electricity through water (shown above), it can be separated into hydrogen and oxygen gas. This process is known as electrolysis.*

◄ *The Iguassu Falls lie on the boundary of Argentina and Brazil. The falls plunge over cliffs measuring 269 feet (82 m) in separate cascades totaling almost 2 miles (3 km) in width.*

Watt, James

James Watt (1736–1819) was a Scottish engineer who spent most of his life developing STEAM ENGINES. In early steam engines, steam was heated and cooled inside a cylinder. Watt designed a model in which steam cooled outside the cylinder. This made the engine much more powerful.

Watt made many other improvements to steam engines so that they could work all kinds of machinery.

MAJOR WATERFALLS

Highest	*Feet*
Angel Falls (Venezuela)	3,212
Tugela Falls (South Africa)	3,110
Yosemite Falls (California)	2,424
Greatest volume	*ft.³/sec*
Boyoma (Zaire)	60,000
Niagara (N.America)	21,000

► *Wave energy can be used to make electricity. One experimental machine for harnessing wave energy is called the "hodding boom" or "duck." The "ducks" have small generators inside them. As waves make the "beak" of each "duck" move up and down (inset), electricity is produced by the generators.*

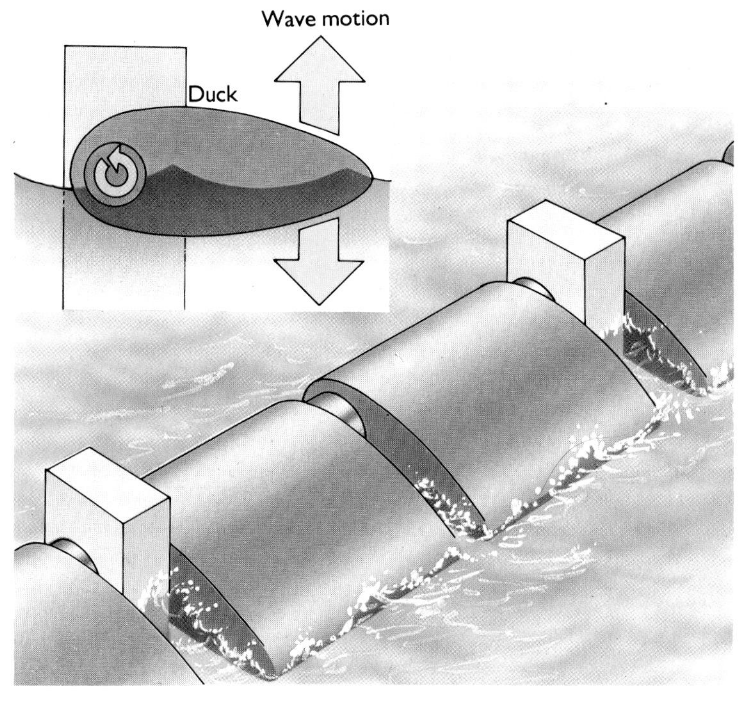

▼ *These five instruments are used to measure weather conditions. Anemometers measure wind speeds and vanes show wind direction. The psychrometer, a kind of hygrometer, measures humidity. Thermometers record air temperatures and barographs record changing air pressure on a rotating drum.*

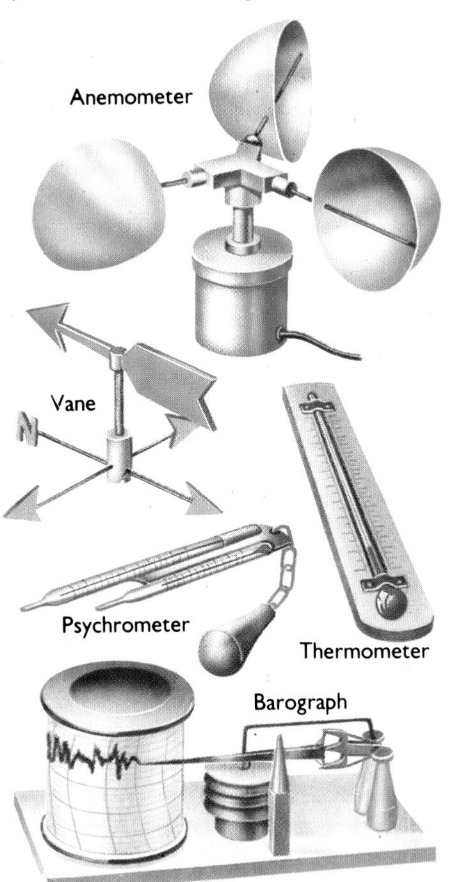

Wave

When the wind blows over the sea it disturbs the water's surface. A light breeze causes gentle ripples, but a storm gale can whip up waves higher than a house.

Although ripples and waves move across the sea, the water itself does not travel with them. Instead, each passing wave just lifts the water up and down. This explains why floating objects like seabirds and bottles bob up and down on waves but do not travel with them.

Most sea waves are caused by the wind. But the most dangerous waves are set off by underwater earthquakes and volcanoes. These giant waves, called tsunamis or tidal waves, sometimes flood coasts and drown many people.

Sea waves carry energy, usually energy from the wind. Some other forms of energy travel in waves. LIGHT, SOUND, and RADIO, for example, all move from one place to another in waves.

Weather

The weather—sunshine, fog, RAIN, CLOUDS, WIND, heat, cold—is always changing in most parts of the world. These changes are caused by what happens

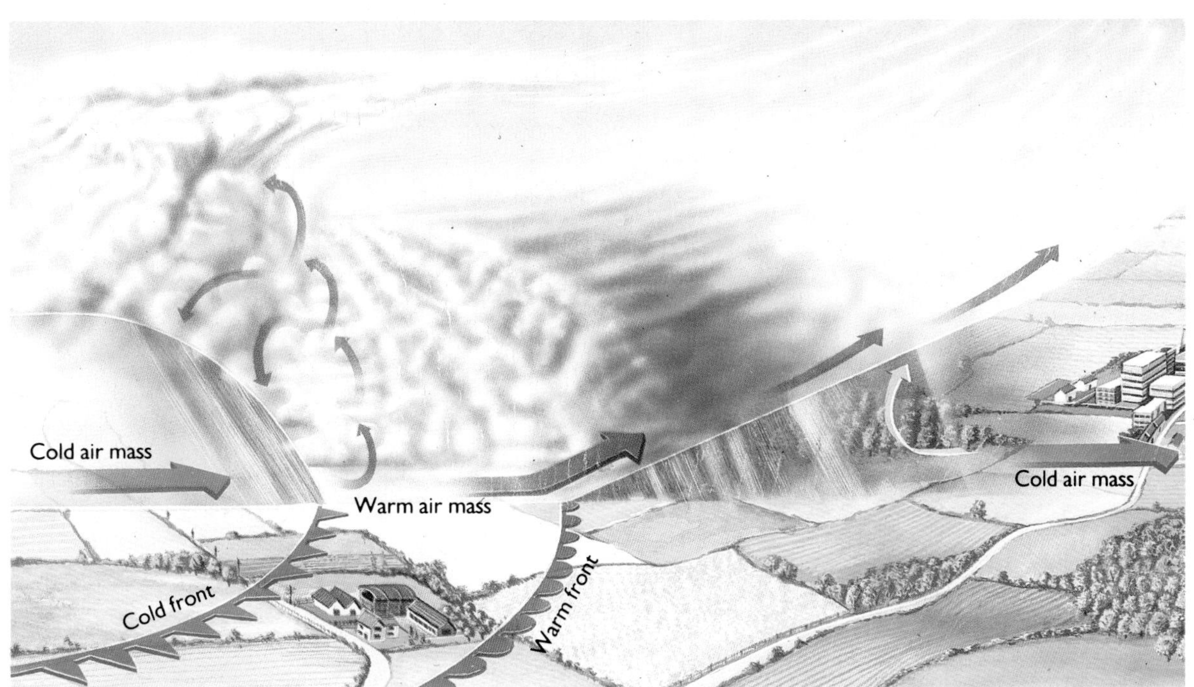

▲ *Warm air is lighter than cold air. The edge of a moving mass of cold air is called a cold front and that of warm air is called a warm front. Warm air rises up from the ground and can form rain clouds.*

in the atmosphere, the layer of air above the Earth.

The atmosphere is always moving, driven by the Sun's heat. Near the EQUATOR the Sun's strong rays heat the air. At the North and South Poles the Sun's rays are weaker and the air is colder. This uneven heating means the atmosphere is never still. Huge masses of warm and cold air flow around and around between the tropics and the polar regions. As these wandering air masses meet, rise and fall, heat and cool, they cause weather.

When cold and warm masses meet, the air whirls inward in a giant spiral called a *depression*. Depressions bring clouds, wind, rain, and summer thunderstorms. They can also cause violent TORNADOES and HURRICANES.

The meeting line between two air masses is called a *front*. When cold air pushes up behind warm air, it forms a *cold front*; when a warm air mass catches up with a cold mass, it creates a *warm front*. An *occluded front* is formed when a cold front overtakes a warm front. Weathermen expect rain and snow ahead of a warm front. Showers usually form along a cold front.

Geographical features, such as mountains, also influence the weather. Oceans contribute to changes in temperature in coastal areas.

Satellites carry television cameras that take pictures of the pattern of clouds above the earth, and large areas of snow and ice on the ground. Meteorologists study the photographs and can spot dangerous storms as they develop.

One man can easily operate 20 of today's fully automatic looms. If a thread breaks, the power is cut off automatically and the machine stops. Some machines use compressed air to blow the weft through the warp.

Weaving

Curtains and sheets, shirts and carpets, towels and suits are just some of the many useful articles made by weaving. In weaving, threads are joined together in a criss-cross pattern to make cloth.

People have been weaving cloth to make clothes since the STONE AGE. The oldest fabric we know of was woven nearly 8,000 years ago in what is now Turkey. These first weavers learned to make linen from flax. By 2000 B.C. the Chinese were weaving cloth from SILK. In India, people learned to use fibers from the COTTON plant. Meanwhile *nomads* (travelers) from the deserts and mountains of Asia discovered how to weave WOOL.

For thousands of years, making cloth was slow work. First, the fibers were drawn out and twisted into a long thread. This process is known as spinning. Then, rows of threads were stretched lengthwise, side by side, on a frame called a *loom*. These threads made up the *warp*. A crosswise thread, the *weft*, was then passed through from one side of the loom to the other, going over and under the warp threads. A *shuttle*, like a large needle, was used to feed the weft through the warp.

The ancient people of the region we now call Peru wove cotton, llama wool, and sometimes human hair nearly 2,000 years ago. Some of their cloth was buried in tombs in the hot, dry desert region, and, because there is almost no rain, the fabrics are still in good condition.

▶ *Workers in a textile mill bring large spools of thread to the loom. Fully automatic looms are common today in many countries, though hand looms are still used for very special woolen or silk fabrics.*

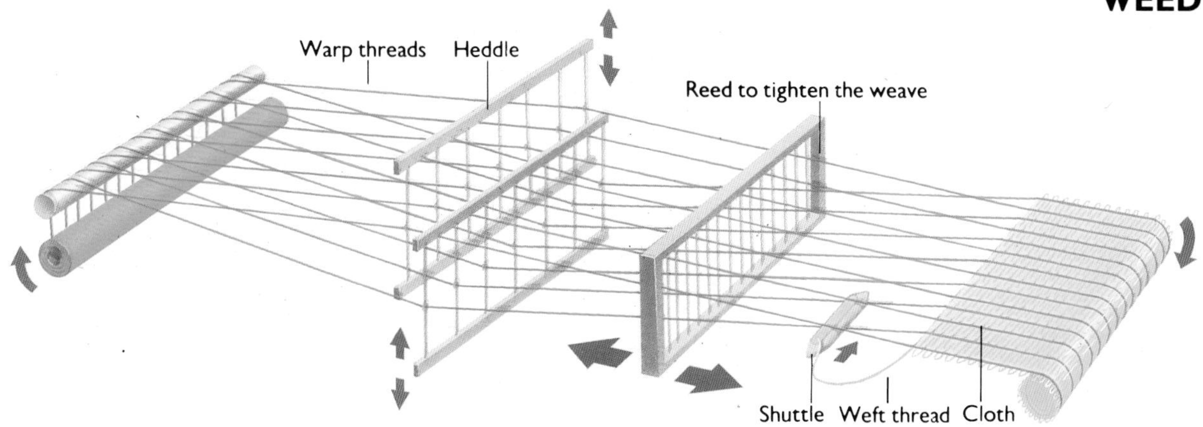

▲ *Cloth is made by weaving two different types of thread together on a loom. During weaving, the heddle creates a gap by raising and lowering different warp threads. Then the shuttle moves the weft thread through the gaps, going over some of the warp threads and under others, to make cloth.*

Spinning wheels and looms were worked by hand until the 1700s. Then, machines were invented for spinning and weaving. These machines worked far faster than hand looms, and cloth became cheap and plentiful. Today most woven fabrics are made by machine.

Weed

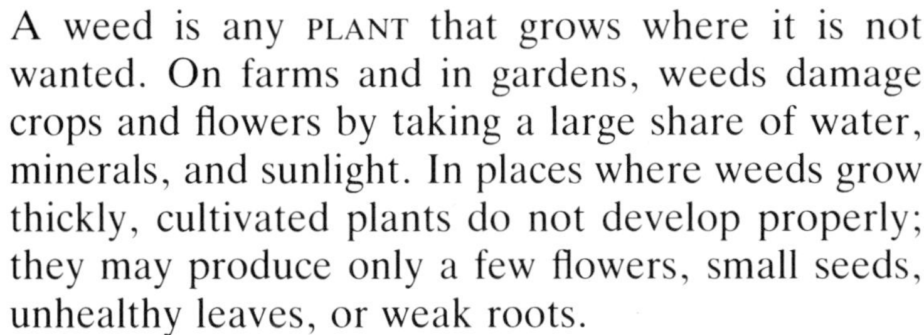

A weed is any PLANT that grows where it is not wanted. On farms and in gardens, weeds damage crops and flowers by taking a large share of water, minerals, and sunlight. In places where weeds grow thickly, cultivated plants do not develop properly; they may produce only a few flowers, small seeds, unhealthy leaves, or weak roots.

There are several ways of controlling weeds. In gardens, people break up the soil with a hoe. This disturbs the weed roots and stops growth. They also pull the weeds out of the ground: this is called weeding. On farms, the soil is broken up by plowing and harrowing. Farmers also spray their fields with herbicides. Herbicides are chemicals that destroy weeds. Most of them are *selective*. This means the chemicals only affect certain plants: they destroy weeds without harming crops.

Weeds are only a nuisance when they interfere with cultivated plants. In woods and fields, away from gardens and farms, weeds are useful plants. Weeds are food for many animals.

► *These weeds grow in a variety of places. Farmers spend millions of dollars every year to control weeds. Some are poisonous to human beings and other animals.*

▶ *Weightlifting is now an Olympic sport. There are two main kinds of lift: the* snatch, *in which the bar is lifted straight from the floor to above the head; and the* clean and jerk, *in which the bar is raised to the chest and then overhead.*

Weightlifting

Weightlifting is one of the sports included in the OLYMPIC GAMES. In a weightlifting contest, the competitors lift very heavy weights from the floor to above their heads. Weight lifters, like boxers, are divided into classes according to their own body weight. Champion weight lifters can lift over 551 lbs (250 kg).

Many other sportsmen, such as swimmers and football players, do weightlifting as an exercise to strengthen their muscles and at the same time improve their breathing.

WEIGHTLIFTING CLASSES

Flyweight	52 kg limit	(115 lbs.)
Bantam	56 kg	(123 lbs.)
Feather	60 kg	(132 lbs.)
Welter	67.5 kg	(149 lbs.)
Middle	75 kg	(165 lbs.)
Light-heavy	82.5 kg	(182 lbs.)
Middle-heavy	90 kg	(198 lbs.)
1st heavy	100 kg	(220 lbs.)
2nd heavy	110 kg	(242 lbs.)
Super-heavy	Over 110 kg	(242 lbs.)

Weights and Measures

The two main kinds of measurement are weight and length. They answer the questions "How heavy?" and "How long?" Length is also used to find area and volume. There are several systems of weights and measures. The most common is the METRIC SYSTEM. The United States still uses the old English system of measurements. (See pages 748–749.)

We do not know exactly how the yard became a measure. One story is that it was the length of King Henry I of England's arm. Another story is that it was the distance from the point of his nose to the end of his thumb. A third story is that it was the length of arrows used by archers who used the longbow.

Welding

Welding is a way of joining metals by heating. The edges of two pieces of metal are heated until they melt together. When they cool they form just one piece of metal.

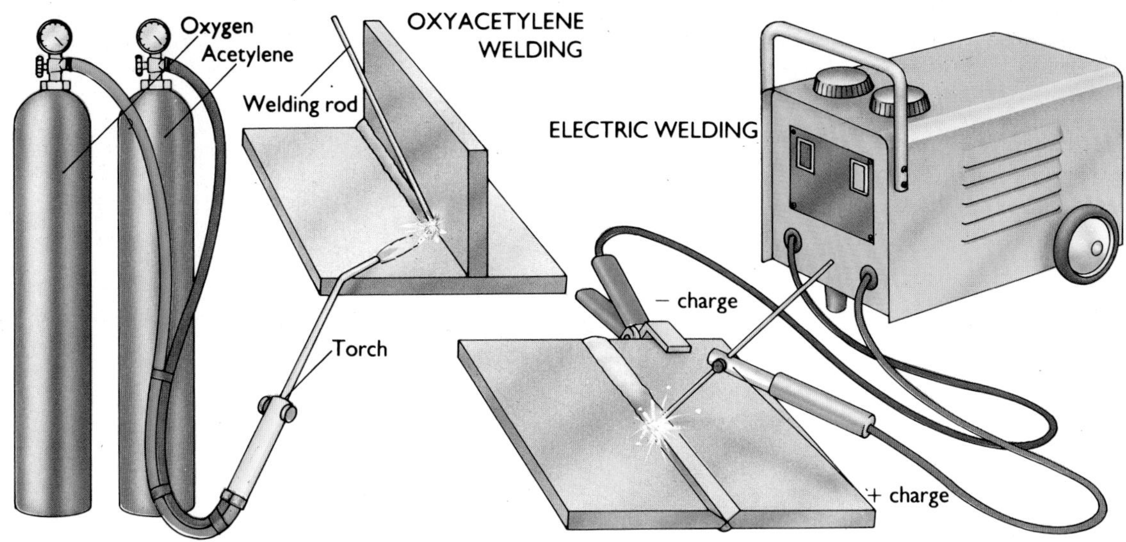

Welders work with gas or electricity. In gas welding a very hot flame from a gas torch melts the metal. In electric welding, an electric CURRENT jumps from an electric welding rod to the metals and melts them.

▲ *In oxyacetylene welding, acetylene gas is burned to produce a very hot flame in the torch. Oxygen is added to make the flame even hotter. Electric welders use a powerful electric current to melt two pieces of metal at the point of contact and make a join.*

Western Samoa

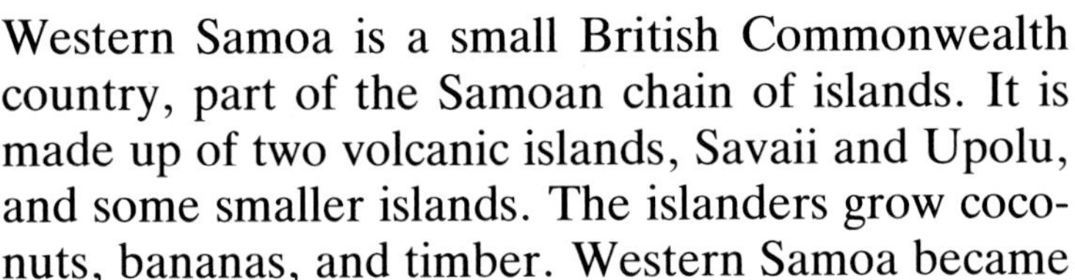

Western Samoa is a small British Commonwealth country, part of the Samoan chain of islands. It is made up of two volcanic islands, Savaii and Upolu, and some smaller islands. The islanders grow coconuts, bananas, and timber. Western Samoa became independent in 1962.

WESTERN SAMOA

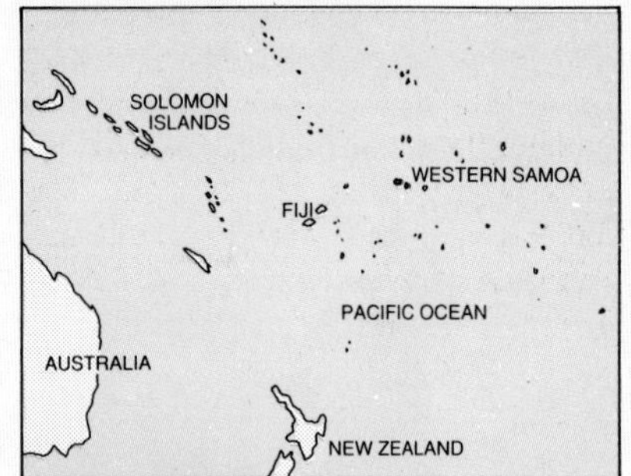

Government: Parliamentary democracy
Capital: Apia
Area: 1,133 sq. miles (2,934 sq. km)
Population: 164,000
Languages: Samoan, English
Currency: Tala

West Indies

This chain of tropical islands stretches from Florida in the United States to Venezuela in South

Continued on page 750

◀ *The city of San Juan is the capital of Puerto Rico, an island in the Greater Antilles, one of the three main island groups in the West Indies. The other groups are the Bahamas and the Lesser Antilles.*

WEIGHTS AND MEASURES

"How many?" "How far?" "How big?" are all questions to do with weights and measures. People first needed units of measurement when they began to build towns and to trade goods. The ancient Egyptians, for example, based their measurements on the proportions of the body. Our word "mile" comes from the Roman *mille* which meant "1,000 paces."

Most countries now use the metric system for measuring lengths, distances and so on. The metric system is a decimal system (based on 10) and was first used in France in the late 1700s. The system used in the United States is known as the English or Imperial system. The table gives some common units of measurement in both systems, and some useful conversion factors.

SOME COMMON MEASUREMENTS

Units of length

12 inches	= 1 foot
3 feet	= 1 yard
$5\frac{1}{2}$ yards	= 1 rod
40 rods	= 1 furlong
8 furlongs	= 1 mile
1 mile	= 5,280 feet

Units of Area

144 square inches	= 1 square foo
9 square feet	= 1 square yar
$30\frac{1}{4}$ square yards	= 1 square ro
160 square rods	= 1 acre
640 acres	= 1 square mile

Units of Capacity

16 fluid ounces	= 1 pint
2 pints	= 1 quart
4 quarts	= 1 gallon

Units of Volume

1728 cubic inches	= 1 cubic foo
27 cubic feet	= 1 cubic yar
231 cubic inches	= 1 gallo
2,159.42 cubic inches	= 1 bushe

Units of Weight

16 ounces	= 1 pound
100 pounds	= 1 hundredweight
2,000 pounds	= 1 (short) ton

THE METRIC SYSTEM

Units of Length

10 millimeters	= 1 centimeter
100 centimeters	= 1 meter
1,000 meters	= 1 kilometer

Units of Capacity

10 milliliters	= 1 centilit
100 centiliters	= 1 lite

Units of Area

100 square millimeters	= 1 square centimeter
10,000 square centimeters	= 1 square meter
10,000 square meters	= 1 square kilometer

Units of Weight

10 milligrams	= 1 centigra
100 centigram	= 1 gra
100 grams	= 1 kilogra
1,000 kilograms	= 1 metric t

Units of Volume

1,000 cubic millimeters	= 1 cubic centimeter
1 million cubic centimeters	= 1 cubic meter

▼ *In the ancient Egyptian system of measurement, based on the human body, 4 digits = 1 palm. Seven palms, or two spans (little finger to thumb tip) = 1 cubit, the distance from a person's fingertips to the elbow.*

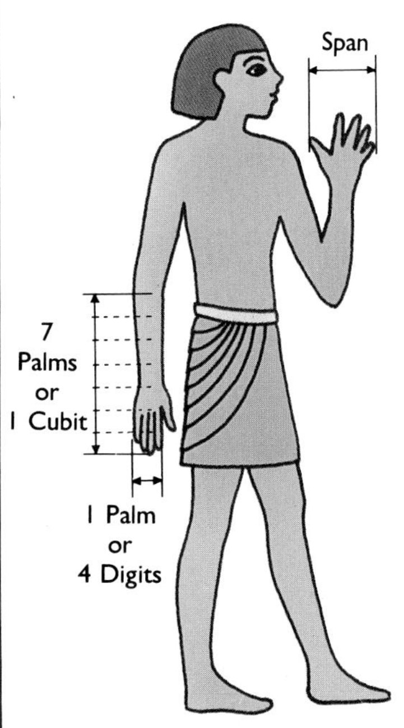

▲ *This ancient Egyptian painting shows the god Anubis weighing souls, using a weighing machine known as an equal arm balance. This kind of weighing machine has been around for 6,000 years.*

Measuring time is just as important as measuring distance. The Egyptians ed the sundial; they stuck a stick into the ground and marked out the path of s shadow. By checking the shadow's position, they could tell the time of day.

Measurements in the Metric and English Systems

etric to English		English to Metric	
Units of Length			
nillimeter	= .039 inches	1 inch	= 2.54 centimeters
centimeter	= .39 inchres	1 foot	= 30.5 cm or .31 m
meter	= 1.09 yards	1 yard	= .91 meters
kilometer	= .62 miles	1 mile	= 1.61 kilometers
Units of Weight			
centigram	= .15 grain	1 ounce	= 28.35 grams
gram	= .04 ounces	1 pound	= .45 kilograms
kilogram	= 2.20 pounds	1 hundredweight	= 45.36 kilograms
Units of Capacity (liquid measures)			
centiliter	= .34 ounces	1 pint	= .47 liters
iter	= 1.06 quarts	1 quart	= .95 liters
kiloliter	= 264.25 gallons	1 gallon	= 3.79 liters

Metric Abbreviations

llimeter	= mm	square km	= km^2
ntimeter	= cm	cubic cm	= cm^3
eter	= m	cubic m	= m^3
ometer	= km	milliliter	= ml
uare mm	= mm^2	liter	= l
uare cm	= cm^2	gram	= g
uare m	= m^2	kilogram	= kg

Nautical Measurement

1 fathom = 6 ft.
1 nautical mile (international) = 1.151 statute mile (= 1852 meters)
60 nautical miles = 1 degree
1 knot = 1 nautical mile per hour

▲ This cup can measure liquids in fluid ounces and centiliters. Most wine bottles hold 1½ pints (75 cl).

A cube (below) is a solid shape. It takes up space, and the amount of space takes up is called volume (measured in cubic units). The face of a cube is square; it has length and width only: it is two-dimensional and its size he amount of surface it has) is called area. On the faces of a cuboid are ectangles. Other solid shapes (right) have on their faces two-mensional shapes such as circles and triangles.

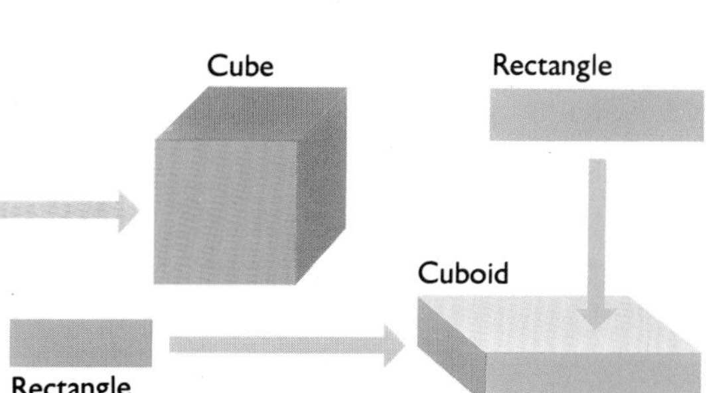

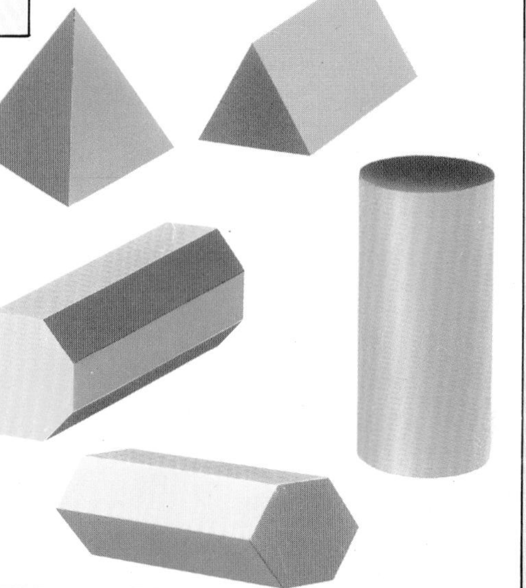

For more information turn to these articles: CALCULATOR; CLOCKS AND WATCHES; COMPUTER; FRACTION; GEOMETRY; MATHEMATICS; METRIC SYSTEM; THERMOMETER.

When Columbus discovered the West Indies he claimed all the islands for Spain. But, as Spanish power weakened in the 17th century, pirates of many countries began to sail the Caribbean. The English government employed the fierce buccaneer Henry Morgan to attack the Spaniards, and in 1674 he was knighted for his services.

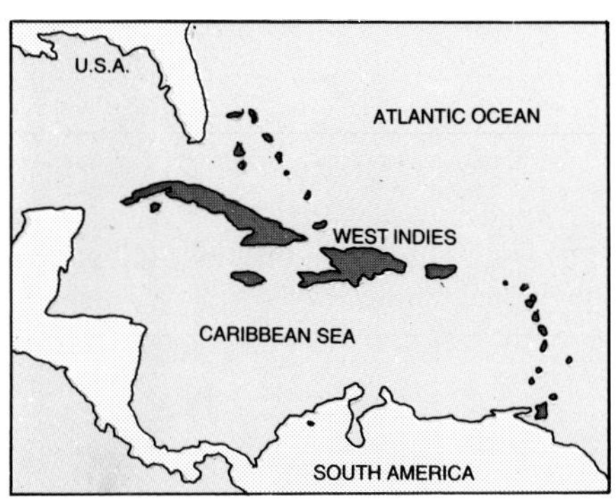

America. On one side lies the Caribbean Sea, on the other stretches the Atlantic Ocean. The islands are really the tops of a drowned range of mountains. Palm trees and tropical grasses grow here, where it is almost always warm. But fierce hurricanes in the fall often destroy trees and houses.

The thousands of islands are divided into more than 20 countries. CUBA, JAMAICA, HAITI, and the DOMINICAN REPUBLIC are among the largest. The BAHAMAS are a scattering of islands near Florida. Their capital is Nassau. BARBADOS is the most easterly island in the West Indies. Its capital is Bridgetown and it became an independent member of the Commonwealth in 1966. Most West Indians are dark skinned. Many are at least partly descended from black slaves who were taken there long ago from Africa. Other West Indians have ancestors who lived in India or Europe. Most West Indians speak English, Spanish, or French.

People grow bananas, cotton, sugarcane, and other tropical crops.

West Virginia

West Virginia was a part of VIRGINIA until the CIVIL WAR, when the state was divided. Virginia broke away from the Union to join the Confederate states, but the northwest of Virginia stayed in the Union. In 1863, it was made a separate state.

West Virginia is a mountainous region. In fact, mountains, many of them with thick forests, cover almost the whole state. This ruggedly beautiful scenery attracts many visitors. But it is also rich in minerals, especially coal. There is coal under half the state, and coal mining is still an important industry. Gas, petroleum, and salt are also mined. Important manufacturing cities, producing goods such as iron and steel, are also located in the state, especially along the Ohio River.

WEST VIRGINIA

Capital: Charleston
Population: 1,793,477
Area: 24,231 sq. miles (62,759 sq. km)
State flower: Rhododendron
State bird: Cardinal
State tree: Sugar Maple
Statehood: June 20, 1863
35th state

Whale

Whales are big sea MAMMALS well built for living in the water. A thick layer of fat called blubber keeps out the cold. A whale's body is shaped for easy

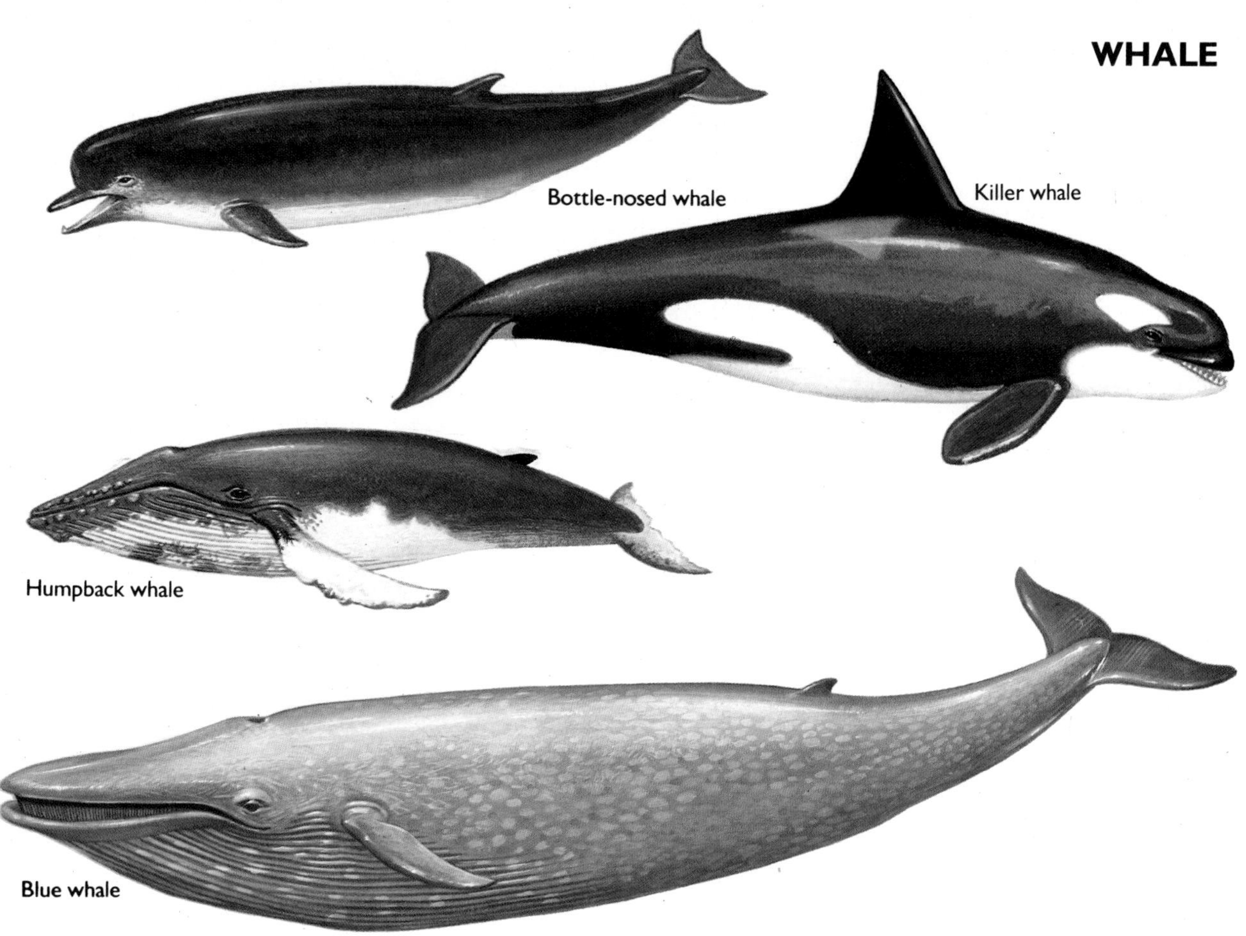

swimming. Its front limbs are shaped as flippers. It also has a broad tail flattened from top to bottom, not from side to side like a fish tail.

Unlike fish, whales must swim to the surface to breathe. Before breathing in, they blow out stale air through a *blowhole*, or two slits on top of the head. Baby whales are born in water. As soon as they are born they swim up to take a breath.

There are two groups of whales. Toothed whales, like the DOLPHIN, mostly catch fish. But killer whales are toothed whales that attack seals and penguins. Sperm whales are the largest toothed whales.

Baleen whales are the other main group of whales. Baleen whales include the gigantic blue whale. Each baleen whale catches tiny shrimplike creatures with a special sieve. This is made of a horny substance called baleen or whalebone. When the whale opens its mouth, long baleen plates hang from its upper jaw like the teeth of a giant comb. A large whale can swallow over a ton of these tiny *krill* at one time. Hunting by man has made the biggest whales very scarce.

▲ *The blue whale is the largest mammal in the world. It can grow as long as 100 feet (30 m). The killer whale is a carnivore. It feeds on other whales, seals, penguins, and fish. Bottle-nosed whales have beaks like some dolphins. They move around in groups or schools of up to fifty. Humpback whales feed on fish, krill, and plankton.*

The blubber under the skin of whales can be up to 20 inches (50 cm) thick. For hundreds of years, whales have been killed for this blubber. Oil was taken from it and used to make soap and margarine.

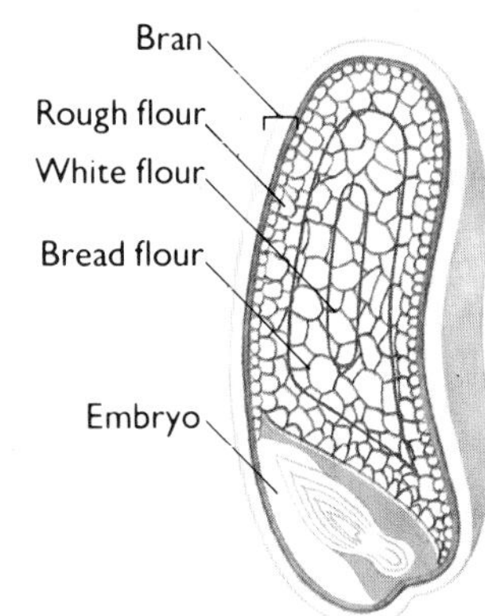

SOFT WHEAT HARD WHEAT

▲ *A grain of wheat (top) has been cut to show its different sections. Wheat can be grouped into hard wheat and soft wheat. The flour from hard wheat makes very good bread and soft wheat makes very good pastry.*

Wheat

Wheat is a valuable food crop. Grains of wheat are seeds produced by a certain kind of grass. Mills grind the seeds into flour for making bread, breakfast cereals, cakes, pies, noodles, and spaghetti. Most wheat foods are good for us because each grain of wheat is largely made of energy-giving STARCHES. It also contains plenty of body-building PROTEIN, as well as FATS, MINERALS, and bran.

Wheat grows best in dry, mild climates. Farmers sow the seeds in winter or spring. They harvest it when the grain is dry and hard. Most wheat comes from China, Russia, the United States, and India. The world grows more wheat than any other kind of grain.

Although we think of China as a rice-eating country, it produces more wheat than any other country in the world, followed by Russia and the United States.

Wheel

Wheels are one of man's most useful inventions. This is because a wheel turning on an axle is a very good way to move loads. It is easier to move a heavy load with wheels than it is to lift the load or drag it on the ground.

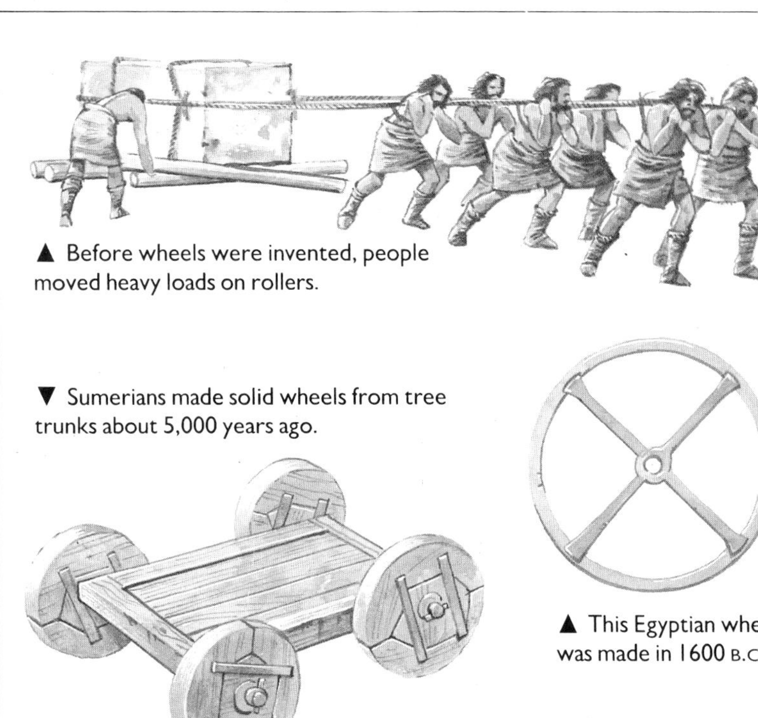

▲ Before wheels were invented, people moved heavy loads on rollers.

▼ Sumerians made solid wheels from tree trunks about 5,000 years ago.

▲ This Egyptian whe
was made in 1600 B.C

STONE AGE people may have learned to roll loads along on logs. But BRONZE AGE people first invented the wheel about 5,000 years ago. The oldest known wheels looked like slices cut across a log. But each solid disk was made of three parts.

At first, the wheels were fixed on the axle, and it was the axle that turned in holes in the cart frame. Later, the axle was fixed and the wheels revolved on its ends.

Then people learned that a wheel with spokes was just as strong as a solid wheel, but much lighter. Today the wheels of cars and planes have hollow rubber tires filled with air to make them springy.

Ball bearings keep wheel hubs turning easily on their axles. Wheels with notched edges turn one another in the GEARS that help to work all kinds of machinery.

Although the wheel was being used throughout a large part of the East by 1500 B.C., it seems strange that the wheel was unknown anywhere on the American continent until it was introduced by Europeans in the A.D. 1500s.

White House

The White House is the official residence of the president of the United States, and is located in Washington, D.C. This is where the president lives, works, and entertains guests. It is one of the most

▼ *Modern wheels are different from the wheels invented 5,000 years ago. This illustration shows some of the wheels that have been used throughout history.*

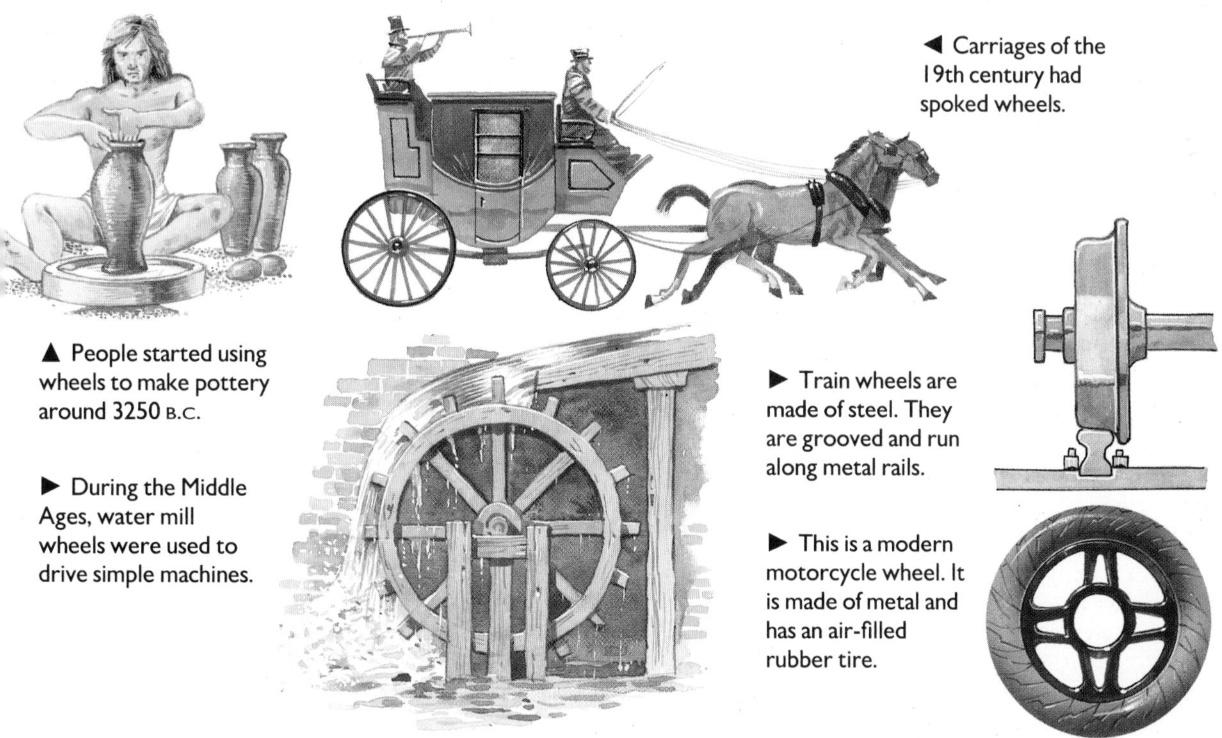

◄ Carriages of the 19th century had spoked wheels.

▲ People started using wheels to make pottery around 3250 B.C.

► During the Middle Ages, water mill wheels were used to drive simple machines.

► Train wheels are made of steel. They are grooved and run along metal rails.

► This is a modern motorcycle wheel. It is made of metal and has an air-filled rubber tire.

▶ *The White House is one of the most popular tourist attractions in the United States. The 132-room house stands in the center of a beautifully landscaped plot on Pennsylvania Avenue. The new White House was built in 1817, while James Monroe was in office. The north and south porticos were added in the 1820s. President Theodore Roosevelt added the executive wing. Then, in 1961, Mrs. John F. Kennedy had the interior restored to its original appearance. The President's living quarters are on the second floor. The White House has a private bowling alley, swimming pool, and movie theater.*

▲ *Walt Whitman, the great American poet.*

Walt Whitman began working on *Leaves of Grass* in about 1848. The writing was so unusual that no publisher would print it. He eventually published the collection of twelve poems at his own expense.

famous buildings in the world. Its name comes from the simple fact that it is a white house. Theodore ROOSEVELT was the first president to use the name. Before him, it was called the President's House and the Executive Mansion. Today's White House is the second building. The first one was built in 1792, but was burned by the British in 1814. Since then, it has been remodeled several times.

Whitman, Walt

Walt Whitman (1819–1892) was the greatest American poet of the 19th century. He is best known for his *Leaves of Grass*, a collection of poems that he revised and added to over nearly 40 years.

Born on Long Island, New York, Whitman learned the printing trade and then worked as a teacher and a journalist.

The first edition of *Leaves of Grass* was published in 1855. Its longest poem, "Song of Myself," contains the major themes of Whitman's poetry: a celebration of life, freedom, and equality of all people and the annual rebirth of nature. Like all of Whitman's poetry, it is written in free verse.

During the CIVIL WAR, Whitman served as a nurse in a Washington hospital. His grief at the death of President LINCOLN was expressed in two of his finest poems, "When Lilacs Last in the Dooryard Bloom'd" and "O Captain! My Captain!"

Whitney, Eli

Eli Whitney (1765–1825) changed the face of American industry. He made two important inventions. One was the cotton gin. This made it much easier to clean out COTTON seeds and made the United States the most important cotton-growing country in the world. The other was a machine for making guns. It used an early form of mass production.

Whitney was born in Westborough, Massachusetts. He graduated from Yale College in 1792. The cotton gin was patented in 1794.

Eli Whitney developed mechanical skills as a boy working in his father's farm workshop. He made a violin when he was only 12. As a teenager he established a nail-making business. Money saved from nail-making and schoolteaching sent him through Yale College.

William of Orange

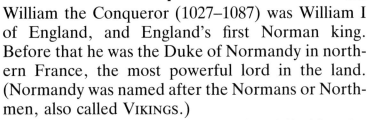

William of Orange (1650–1702) was a PROTESTANT ruler of the Netherlands, who became King William III of England, Scotland, and Ireland.

In 1677 he married his Protestant cousin Mary. In 1688 the English invited William and Mary to rule them in place of Mary's unpopular father, the Catholic James II. James fled when William landed with his army. No one died in this so-called "Glorious Revolution," and William defeated James in Ireland in 1690.

▲ *William of Orange was the grandson of Charles I. He suffered from an asthmatic cough all his life.*

William the Conqueror

William the Conqueror (1027–1087) was William I of England, and England's first Norman king. Before that he was the Duke of Normandy in northern France, the most powerful lord in the land. (Normandy was named after the Normans or Northmen, also called VIKINGS.)

When William visited England in 1050, his relative EDWARD the Confessor may have promised him the throne of England. In 1064 William forced Edward's brother-in-law HAROLD to agree to help to make William king. But when Edward died in 1066, Harold had himself crowned king of England.

William quickly set about invading England to seize it for himself. His Norman army sailed across the English Channel in open boats. There were about 7,000 troops, including knights who brought their war horses. William defeated Harold's ANGLO-

William the Conqueror ordered that a great census be taken of all the land and people of England – the Domesday Book. The old Anglo-Saxon Chronicle complained at the time: "So very narrowly did he cause the survey to be made, that there was not a single rood of land, nor an ox, or a cow, or a pig passed by, and that was not set down in the account."

▶ *The Normans built many fine castles in their newly conquered land. Though Bodiam Castle, shown here, was built much later, in the 1300s, it reflects the Norman style, with thick walls and perfectly rounded towers.*

When William the Conqueror conquered England in 1066, he and his nobles brought over their own language—Norman French. For many years the words that the common people used were still old English, while the words of the wealthy and ruling classes were largely French. The common people tended "sheep." When the sheep was cooked and put on the ruling class table it became the French "mutton." In the same way, old English "cow" became the French "beef," "hog" became "pork," and so on. Modern English contains these and many other words that came from Norman French.

SAXON army at the Battle of HASTINGS, fought in Sussex near where the town of Battle stands today.

William spent three years winning all England. He built many castles, from which his knights rode out to crush their Anglo-Saxon enemies.

By 1069 the Normans had conquered a third of England, and William had become the most powerful king in western Europe. He claimed all the land in England as his, but he lent some to his Norman nobles. In return, the nobles supplied soldiers for William's army. William's descendants ruled England for many years.

WOODROW WILSON

Twenty-eighth President 1913–1921
Born: Staunton, Virginia
Education: Princeton University
Occupation: Teacher, college president, governor
Political Party: Democratic
Buried: National Cathedral, Washington, D.C.

Wilson, Woodrow

Woodrow Wilson (1856–1924) was the 28th president of the United States. Many consider him one of the greatest presidents. He led the United States through the difficult days of WORLD WAR I, first working to keep the U.S. out of the war, then, when he knew the country must fight, proving a strong and resolute leader. He always stood for the highest ideals of democracy, freedom, and dignity. His championship of the League of Nations after World War I was proof of his love of peace. Wilson was also a distinguished scholar and university president and a successful governor of NEW JERSEY. But it is as a courageous defender of liberty and an enemy of corruption that he is best remembered.

Wind

Wind is moving air. Slow winds are gentle breezes. Fast winds are gales. You can see the speed of the wind by its effect on trees and buildings. Winds are identified by the direction *from* which they blow. A wind that blows from the west is a west wind; from the east an east wind. A wind vane shows the wind direction.

Wind blows because some air masses become warmer than others. In warm air, the tiny particles of air spread out, so a mass of warm air is lighter than a mass of cold air that fills the same amount of space. Because warm air is light, it rises. As warm air rises, cool air flows in to take its place. This causes the steady trade winds that blow over tropical oceans. CLIMATE and WEATHER largely depend on the wind.

A scale of wind speeds was worked out in 1805 by Admiral Sir Francis Beaufort. It is called the Beaufort Scale. In it the force of the wind is shown by numbers from 0 to 12. The number 0 shows that

▼ *The Beaufort Scale from 0 to 12 indicates the strength of the wind. It is based on the effect of wind on such things as trees and houses.*

Force: 0 **Strength:** Calm
Speed: Under 1 mph (4 km/h)
Effect: Smoke goes straight up.

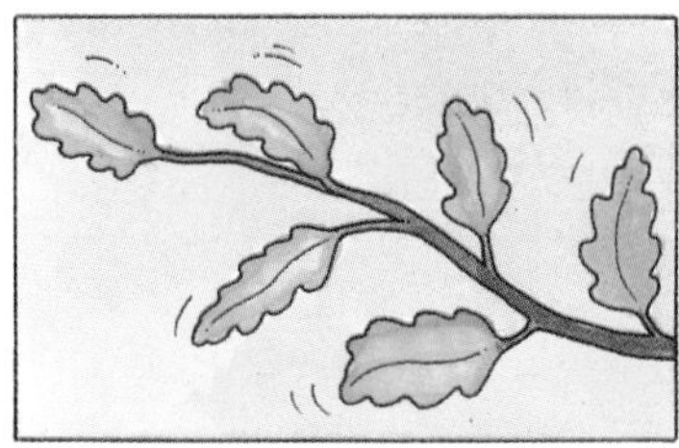

Force: 1–3
Strength: Light breeze
Speed: 1–12 mph (4–24 km/h)
Effect: Small branches move.

Force: 4–5
Strength: Moderate wind
Speed: 13–24 mph (25–46 km/h)
Effect: Small trees sway a little.

Force: 6–7
Strength: Strong wind
Speed: 25–38 mph (47–74 km/h)
Effect: Big trees sway a little.

Force: 8–9
Strength: Gale
Speed: 39–54 mph (75–110 km/h)
Effect: Roof damage occurs.

Force: 10–11
Strength: Storm
Speed: 55–73 mph (111–150 km/h)
Effect: Widespread damage.

Force: 12
Strength: Hurricane
Speed: Above 75 mph (150 km/h)
Effect: Disaster.

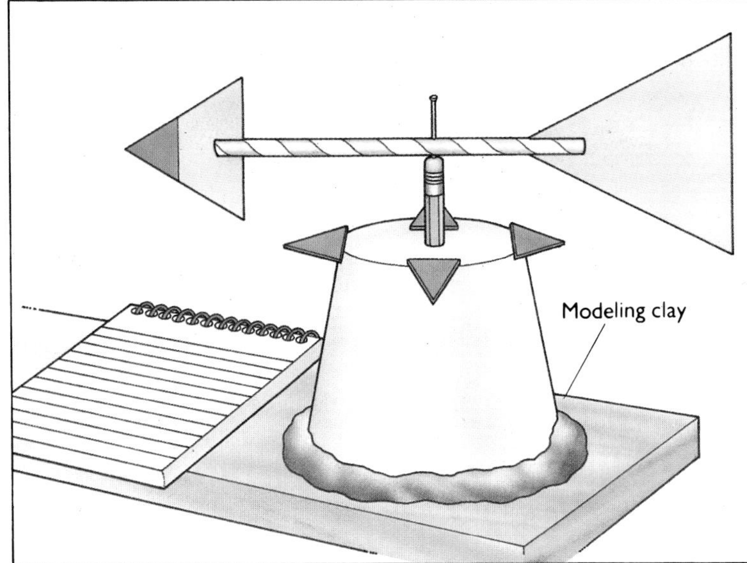

SEE IT YOURSELF

Wind vanes measure the direction of wind. Try making one at home. Turn a yogurt carton upside down and push a pencil through the middle. Use a pencil that has an eraser at one end. Attach the carton to a piece of thick cardboard with modeling clay. Now cut out two small triangles from some thin cardboard. Make slits at each end of a straw and glue one triangle to each end. Push a pin through the middle of the straw into the eraser as shown. Take your wind vane outside and use a compass to mark north, south, east, and west on your carton. You can use the information from your wind vane to make a chart.

there is a calm in which smoke rises straight up. At 1 smoke drifts slowly. By the time we get to 4 we have a breeze in which small branches are moving and flags flap. At force 7 whole trees are moving and it is difficult to walk against the wind. Force 12 is something few of us will ever see. It is a full hurricane, with terrible damage to ships at sea and houses on land.

▼ *This traditional windmill was used to grind corn. As the wind blew, the axle turned the millstones that ground the corn.*

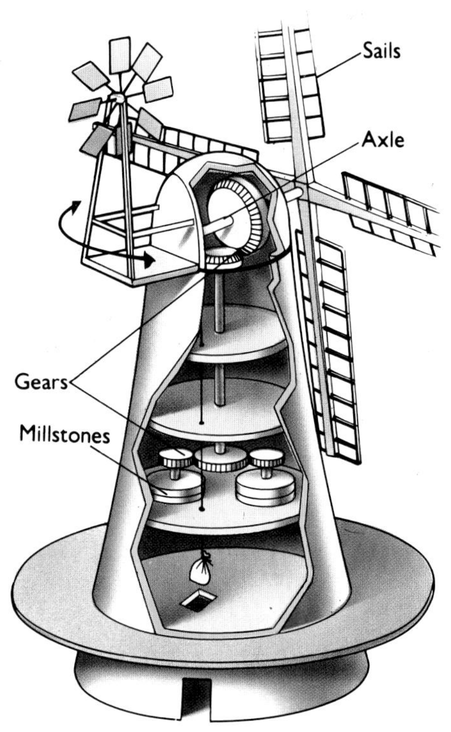

Windmill

Windmills are machines that make the wind's energy perform useful work. They are generally used to pump water or generate electricity. Windmills were used in Asia as early as the A.D. 600s and came to Europe in the 1100s.

In early windmills, a wheel with long sails was fixed to a tower. The whole tower could often turn to face the wind. As the wind turned the sails, the turning wheel moved machinery inside the mill. This machinery was used to do useful work, such as turning heavy stone wheels to grind corn.

Today, people are trying to make better windmills as a way of generating electricity. These windmills, often called wind turbines, are usually on a tower made of steel girders. Some have blades like airplane propellers, which turn at a high speed when the wind blows. The propellers turn a generator which makes electricity.

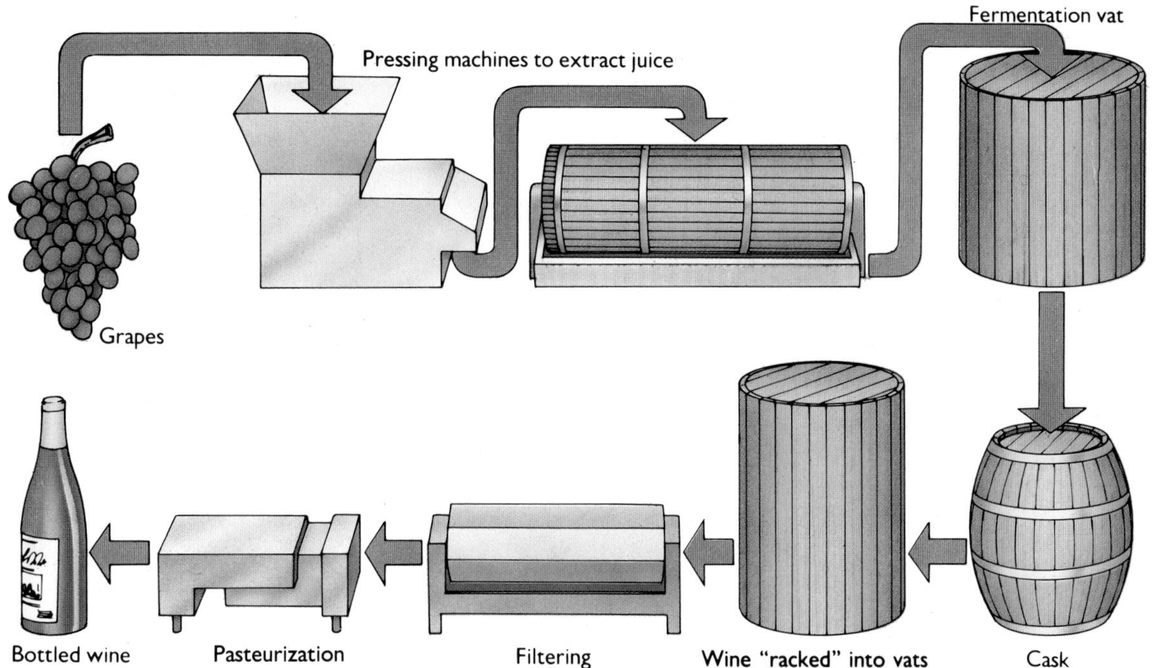

▲ *Grapes go through many processes before they reach the home as bottled wine. After fermentation, some wines are stored in cellars to "mature" into fine wines. Cheaper wines are not allowed to mature. They are filtered, pasteurized, and then bottled as soon as they are taken out of the casks.*

Wine

Wine is a drink made from plant juice containing alcohol produced by FERMENTATION.

Most wine is made from grapes. But wine can be made from other fruits as well. First the fruit is crushed. Then the juice is fermented in containers called vats. The wine is stored in casks until it is ready to drink. Sweet wines are rich in sugar. In dry wines most sugar has become alcohol.

Wire

Wire is metal that has been drawn out into a long, thin rod that is easy to bend. Wire has many uses. Barbed wire fences keep sheep and cows in fields. Wires twisted together form cables strong enough to hold up some of the world's largest bridges. Wires also carry electric CURRENT. Telephone and telegraph lines also use wires.

Metals used for making wire include copper, iron, aluminum, and silver. Heavy blocks of metal are heated, and then passed through rollers that squeeze the partly melted metal into long, narrow holes to make still longer and thinner strips. Then the wire is wound onto a turning drum. Finally, the wire is heated in a furnace to make it less brittle.

For centuries, wire was pulled by hand. The piece of metal to be drawn was beaten to a point and pushed through a small hole in a metal block. The wiredrawer grasped it and pulled it through the hole to make wire. The fineness of the wire was limited by the strength of the wiredrawer.

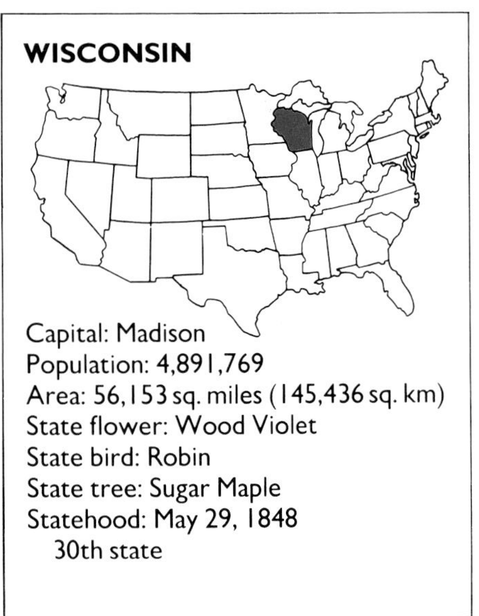

Capital: Madison
Population: 4,891,769
Area: 56,153 sq. miles (145,436 sq. km)
State flower: Wood Violet
State bird: Robin
State tree: Sugar Maple
Statehood: May 29, 1848
30th state

Wisconsin

Wisconsin is a midwestern state and the leading dairy farming state in the country. Huge quantities of cheese, butter, and milk are produced by the numerous herds of cows that graze on Wisconsin's fertile and rolling lands. But Wisconsin is also a major manufacturing center. A wide range of goods is produced, including products such as automobiles, electrical equipment, and cans. Forestry is important, too, and paper and pulp production is a major industry. Milwaukee, the largest city, is a leading beer-making center. Tourism is important to the state. Visitors love to explore Wisconsin's numerous lakes and forests, and hunting and fishing are popular sports.

John Nicolet was the first European to see the Wisconsin area. He arrived at Green Bay in 1634 and was followed by French missionaries and fur traders. The British took over in 1763.

► *The skyline of Madison, Wisconsin, with the capitol building in the background.*

▲ *An early woodcut of two witches adding various live ingredients to their cauldron. This image of witches as ugly old women casting evil spells is still with us today.*

Witch

Many people once believed in witches as people with magic powers. Most witches were said to worship the devil. They cast spells that "bewitched" people, sometimes causing death or disease. Witches supposedly rode through the air at night on broomsticks. They met at secret meetings called sabbaths.

Unlike these "black" witches, "white" witches worshiped an ancient goddess and worked to help and protect people.

Long ago, many harmless old women were

◀ *Wolves belong to the same family as our pet dogs. This wolf lives in remote northern forests and feeds on deer, reindeer, and elk.*

Throughout history there have been stories of wolves raising human children from infancy. The most famous story is that of Romulus and Remus, the twin brothers who founded Rome. More recently, there is a story from India of a child raised by a wolf until she was about nine years old.

burned to death as witches. Few of us believe in witches now. But some would-be witches try to practice good or evil magic.

Wolf

These CARNIVORES include the red wolf of South America, and the gray wolf of the world's northern forests. Gray wolves have thick fur, long legs, and powerful jaws. A pack of wolves can chase and kill a sick or injured deer much larger than themselves. When gray wolves are hunting, they howl to signal to each other where they are. Each spring a female wolf has four to six pups.

Women's Rights

"Women's rights" means the right of women to be full citizens, equal to men in every way. Until this century, women did not have these rights. In some countries women still have very few rights.

The women's rights movement began to develop during the early 1800s. In 1833, Oberlin Collegiate Institute (now Oberlin College) in Ohio became the first coeducational college in the United States to award degrees to women. Afterward, coeducation developed rapidly in other institutions.

▲ *Susan B. Anthony (1820–1906), was one of the first leaders of the campaign for women's rights. She was also the first woman to be pictured on a U.S. coin.*

▲ *During the early 1900s, women campaigned to be allowed to vote. It was not until 1920 that women were given the right to vote in most states.*

During the later 1800s and early 1900s, woman suffrage – the right of women to vote – was an important issue. Educated women had greater opportunities to work outside the home and began to demand equal rights. In 1920, women were granted the right to vote in most states.

The National Organization for Women (NOW) was formed in 1966. Today it is the largest group in the women's movement.

Today, more women than ever are working outside the home. Many women have professional careers in law, medicine, and business.

▲ *This book is made of paper that came from logs like these.*

Wood

Wood is one of the most valuable materials that people use. It can be sawn, carved, and worked into almost any shape.

Thick timber is used for buildings and boats, while roughly cut logs are used as fuel for fires. Planks are made into furniture, barrels, and boxes. Seasoned pieces can be shaped into musical instruments and delicate ornaments.

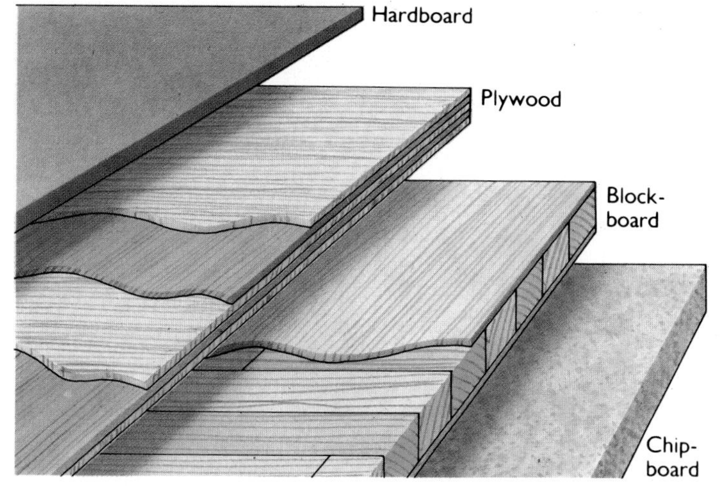

◀ *Wood and wood products are made into sheets for building. Plywood is made up of thin sheets of timber glued together. Most modern furniture is made from plywood. Blockboard is used for making doors. Although it looks like plywood, it has blocks of softwood within it. Hardboard and fiberboard, used in furniture-making, are made from wood chips. The chips are heated and rolled out into sheets.*

The wood we use is the tough inner material of trees and shrubs. It is protected by a thin layer of BARK. It is very strong, and can support many times its own weight. The wood of a TREE is made up of thick fibers that give it strength.

Softwood, from pines and firs, is used mostly as pulp to make paper. Some is used for building. Hardwood, such as oak and mahogany, is used to make furniture.

Woodpecker

There are about 200 kinds of woodpecker. They are found in many parts of the world, but most live in the Americas and Asia.

Woodpeckers have sharp, powerful bills with which they drill holes through the bark of trees. They reach in with their long tongues to fish out insects. Some also nest in holes in trees.

Most woodpeckers have bright colors and markings, especially on their heads.

▼ *There are more than twenty species of woodpecker in North America.*

Wool

Wool comes from the fleece, or hair, of SHEEP. It is one of the most important products known to man. Wool has been used since the Stone Age to make clothing and blankets. It can be heavy and warm or light and cool to protect people against either cold or heat.

Making wool is complicated. First, the fleece

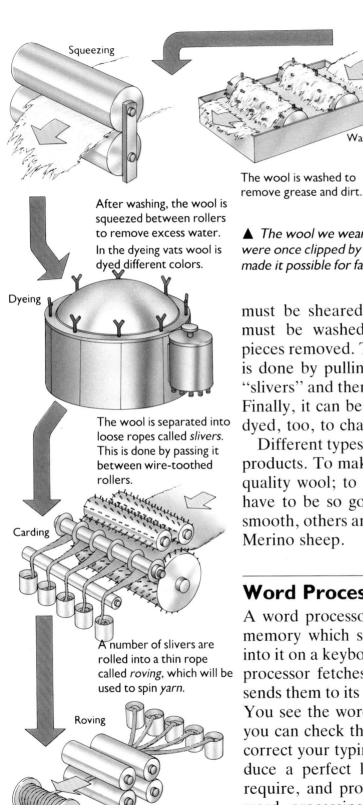

Squeezing

Washing

Shearing

The wool is washed to remove grease and dirt.

The fleece is clipped from the sheep.

After washing, the wool is squeezed between rollers to remove excess water.

In the dyeing vats wool is dyed different colors.

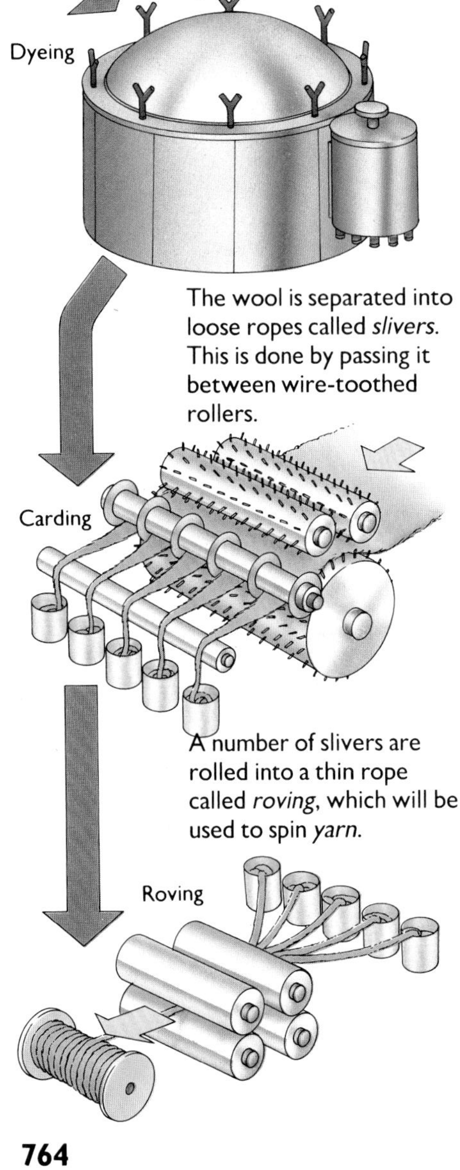

Dyeing

The wool is separated into loose ropes called *slivers*. This is done by passing it between wire-toothed rollers.

Carding

A number of slivers are rolled into a thin rope called *roving*, which will be used to spin *yarn*.

Roving

▲ *The wool we wear comes from the fleece of sheep. Sheep were once clipped by hand, but the invention of electric shears made it possible for farmers to clip over 200 sheep a day.*

must be sheared from the sheep. Then the wool must be washed and sorted, and any damaged pieces removed. Then it can be made into yarn. This is done by pulling the wool into long ropes called "slivers" and then twisting and spinning it into yarn. Finally, it can be woven into cloth. Most wools are dyed, too, to change their color.

Different types of wool are used to make different products. To make sweaters or suits, you need high quality wool; to make a blanket, the wool doesn't have to be so good. Some woolen goods are very smooth, others are fuzzy. The best wool comes from Merino sheep.

Word Processor

A word processor is a kind of COMPUTER. It has a memory which stores all the words that you type into it on a keyboard. Then, whenever required, the processor fetches the words from its memory and sends them to its typing unit to be typed onto paper. You see the words you have typed on a screen, so you can check that there are no mistakes. You can correct your typing and the processor will then produce a perfect letter or whatever document you require, and produce as many as you want. Some word processing programs can also check your spelling.

Wordsworth, William

William Wordsworth (1770–1850) was a British poet who wrote about nature and the English countryside. He led a movement to restore simplicity and truth to POETRY. Wordsworth joined forces with another poet, Samuel Taylor Coleridge (1772–1834), to publish a volume called *Lyrical Ballads*. Most of the poems in this book were written by Wordsworth, including the well-known poem "Lines Composed a Few Miles Above Tintern Abbey." Among his other best-loved poems were *Daffodils* and *The Prelude*, a long poem based on events in his own life.

▲ *William Wordsworth wrote many of his best poems while living in the Lake District of England.*

World War I

Between 1914 and 1918, Europe, the United States, and much of the Middle East were locked in the first struggle that could be called a world war. On one side were Germany, Austria-Hungary, and Turkey. On the other were France, the British Empire, the United States, and Russia.

The battle soon became a stalemate in the west. The two sides spent four years in trenches in

▲ *Uniforms of American, British, and German infantrymen during World War I. The opposing sides were often in trenches only a few hundred yards apart.*

◀ *Canadian troops fight off an attack at the second battle of Ypres in 1915. Hundreds of thousands of men were killed in such battles in World War I, but the front line hardly ever shifted.*

▶ *World War I saw the first use of two new machines of war: the airplane and the tank. Flying "aces" such as Germany's Baron von Richthofen and Eddie Rickenbacker of the United States fought daring battles in the sky. The first tank was driven into battle in 1916.*

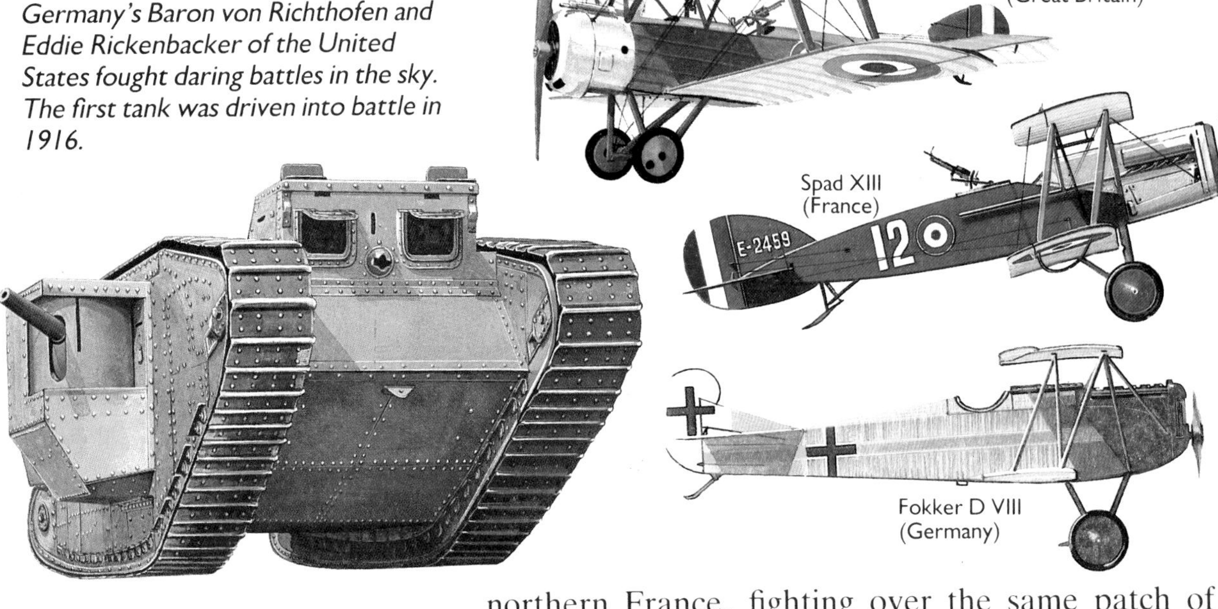

northern France, fighting over the same patch of ground. But in the east, Germany had better luck. The Germans attacked Russia so strongly that by 1917 Russia withdrew from the war.

After the United States joined the war in 1917, the Allied armies slowly pushed the Germans back. In November 1918 peace was declared.

EVENTS OF WORLD WAR I

1914	June 15: Assassination of Archduke Franz Ferdinand at Sarjevo Aug. 1: Germany declares war on Russia Aug. 4: Britain declares war on Germany Aug. 30: Germans defeat Russians at Tannenberg Sept. 12: French and British halt German advance at Battle of the Marne
1915	Dec.: British withdraw from Gallipoli
1916	Feb.–July: German attack on Verdun May 31–June 1: Naval battle of Jutland; indecisive July 1–Nov. 18: Battle of the Somme
1917	Mar. 3: Russia makes peace with Germany at Brest-Litovsk Apr. 6: U.S.A. enters war
1918	Mar.: Great German offensive begins Nov. 9: German Kaiser Wilhelm II abdicates Nov. 11: Ceasefire on Western front

World War II

With the invasion of Poland in the fall of 1939, Germany, Italy and then Japan entered into a six-year war with most of the other major nations of Europe, Asia, Africa, and America. The battles raged from the Pacific Ocean, China, and Southeast Asia to Africa, Europe, and the North Atlantic.

Germany's early attacks were hugely successful. Her armies swept through Europe and on into Russia and North Africa. However, the tide turned aftrer 1941 when the United States entered the war. (See pages 768–769.)

Worm

There are hundreds of different animals with soft flat bodies that are commonly called worms. Some are very simple creatures, such as roundworms or flatworms. Others, such as earthworms, leeches, and the larvae of some INSECTS, are more complicated animals. Their bodies are divided into several segments.

Most of the simple worms are small. They usually live as PARASITES inside the bodies of animals or plants. Liver flukes and tapeworms are two such creatures.

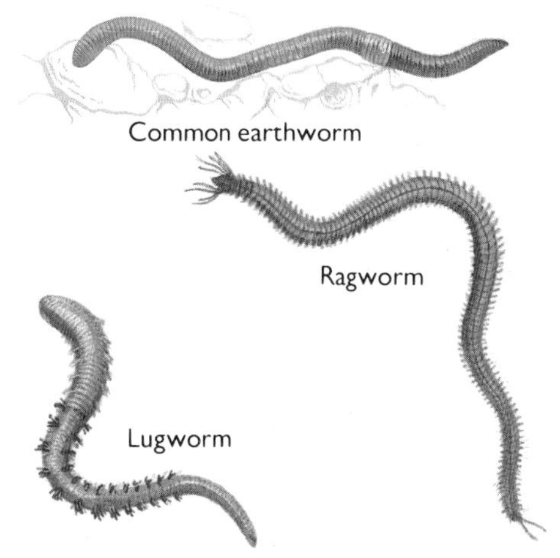

▲ *The common earthworm has both male and female organs. Ragworms and lugworms live in muddy and sandy shores.*

Wren, Christopher 

Sir Christopher Wren (1632–1723) was one of the most brilliant for all English architects. He was responsible for many famous and beautiful buildings, perhaps the most celebrated being St. Paul's Cathedral in London. Wren also built more than fifty other churches.

Among Wren's other works were the Royal Exchange, Kensington Palace, Marlborough House, and an addition to Hampton Court.

▼ *In 1666, the Great Fire of London destroyed the old St. Paul's Cathedral. Sir Christopher Wren designed its replacement, which still stands today.*

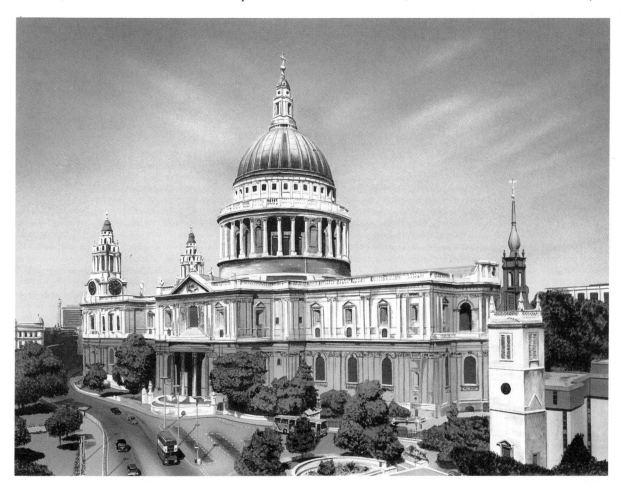

WORLD WAR II

World War II cost between 35 and 60 million lives. The German dictator, Adolf Hitler, murdered millions of Jews and dreamed of world domination. Germany was supported by Italy. In Asia, Japan also had ambitions to control its neighbors. The so-called Axis powers (Germany, Italy, and Japan) were opposed by the Allies (Britain, France, Russia, the United States, and other nations). Important war leaders were Winston Churchill (Britain), Franklin D. Roosevelt (U.S.A.), and Joseph Stalin (Russia).

The war was fought on land, on sea, and in the air. Civilians suffered as much as soldiers, especially from bombing of towns and cities. On land, there were huge tank battles in Russia and North Africa, while at sea submarines sank many merchant ships. In great naval battles fought in the Pacific, aircraft carriers proved to be more effective than battleships. It was a scientific war, with new inventions such as radar and the V2 rocket.

When the Allied armies invaded Germany, ending the war in Europe, people were shocked by the horrors of the Nazi concentration camps in which millions of prisoners had been killed. The war in Europe ended in May, 1945. In the East, Japan fought on until August, 1945, when the U.S. dropped the fir atomic bombs on the Japanese cities of Hiroshima an Nagasaki. Only then did Japan finally surrender, bringing World War II to an end.

▲ *Battleships engulfed in smoke and flames during the Japanese attack on Pearl Harbor, Hawaii, in December, 1941.*

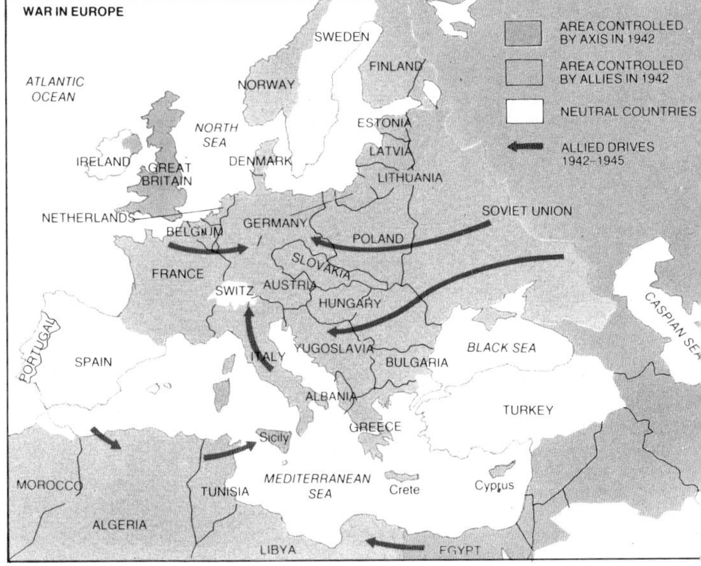

▲ *German infantry scout in advance of tanks on the Eastern Front during the winter of 1941–42.*

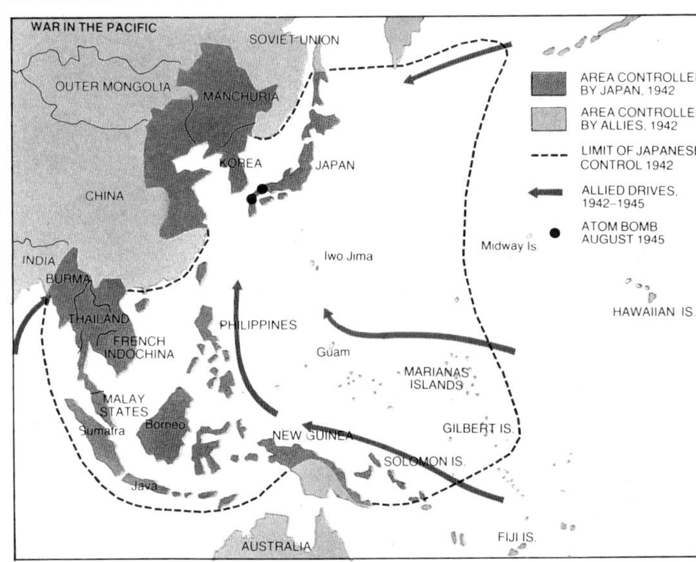

IMPORTANT EVENTS OF THE WAR

1939 Sept. Germany invades Poland. Britain and France declare war on Germany.

1940 April–June German forces capture Norway, and much of western Europe, including France.
May Churchill becomes Britain's prime minister.
June Italy joins war on Germany's side.
Oct. End of Battle of Britain. Bombing raids on Britain.

1941 June Germany invades U.S.S.R.
Dec. Japanese attack Pearl Harbor; U.S.A. enters war.

1942 Feb. Japanese capture Singapore.
May Battle of the Coral Sea; U.S. Navy defeats Japanese.
June Battle of Midway; another U.S. naval victory. Allies invade Morocco and Algeria.
Oct. Allies defeat Germans and Italians at El Alamein (North Africa).
Nov. Russians defeat Germans at Stalingrad.

1943 July Allies land in Sicily, southern Italy.
Sept. Italy surrenders.

1944 June Allies invade western Europe, in Normandy.
July Plot to kill Hitler fails.
Oct. Battle of Leyte Gulf (biggest naval battle of war): U.S. fleet defeats Japanese.

1945 Jan. Russians invade Germany from east.
March Allies cross the Rhine River.
April In the East, U.S. troops recapture Philippines.
May Hitler commits suicide in Berlin. End of fighting in Europe.
Aug. U.S. forces face bitter fighting as Japanese retreat. U.S. airplanes drop atomic bombs on Hiroshima and Nagasaki; Japan surrenders to end the war.

► *After more than two years' preparation, Allied soldiers under the command of the General Dwight Eisenhower landed on the Normandy beaches on D-Day, June 6, 1944.*

The British Spitfire and the German Messerschmitt were both involved in the Battle of Britain in 1940. The American P-51 Mustang was a long-range fighter and one of the most successful warplanes ever.

For more information turn to these articles: AIR FORCE; ARMY; CHURCHILL, WINSTON; DE GAULLE, CHARLES; HITLER, ADOLF; MUSSOLINI, BENITO; STALIN, JOSEPH; SUBMARINE.

Wright Brothers

The Wright brothers, Wilbur (1867–1912) and Orville (1871–1948), designed, built, and flew the world's first airplane at Kitty Hawk, North Carolina, in December, 1903. Their first flight lasted only 12 seconds and the plane, *Flyer 1*, went only 120 ft. (37 m). It may not have been long, but the brothers had worked out all the basic principles of how airplanes work. Few people were interested in their invention at the time, but within five years they had built a plane that could stay in the air for over one hour. *Flyer 1* is in the National Air and Space Museum in Washington, D.C. When Orville Wright died, he had lived long enough to know that a plane could fly faster than the speed of sound.

▲ *Orville Wright pilots the Wright Flyer on the sands of Kitty Hawk, North Carolina. The aircraft stayed in the air for 12 seconds on its first flight.*

Writing

The earliest forms of writing were simple picture messages, or notches on sticks that were used for counting. Gradually, pictures that were used again and again became simplified. These symbols meant certain objects, like "man" or "house." Egyptian HIEROGLYPHICS were used in this way.

In time, the symbols came to stand for sounds and could be combined to form words. Later still, alphabets of these sounds came into being. Vowels appeared with the ancient Greeks and Romans. Their alphabets were similar to the one we use today.

Wyoming

Wyoming is a Rocky Mountain state, and one of the most spectacular in the country. Visitors from across the country come to see such major attractions as Yellowstone Park, the towering Teton Mountains, and Shoshone Forest. As well as tourism, Wyoming depends on farming and mining for its prosperity. Petroleum, gas, uranium, and oil are all mined, while huge herds of cattle graze on the flat lands in the east of the state. Almost half of Wyoming belongs to the federal government, and the government controls many industries.

Wyoming has the lowest population of any state. There are fewer than 5 people per square mile.

Exploration of the Wyoming area did not begin until the early 1800s. John Colter became the first white person to enter present-day Wyoming when he crossed Yellowstone Park in 1808. Trappers and fur traders followed in the 1820s, and Forts Laramie and Bridger became important stops on the pioneer trail to the West. The population grew after the Union Pacific railroad crossed the state in 1869.

WYOMING

Capital: Cheyenne
Population: 453,588
Area: 97,809 sq. miles (253,326 sq. km)
State flower: Indian Paintbrush
State bird: Meadowlark
State tree: Cottonwood
Statehood: July 10, 1890
44th state

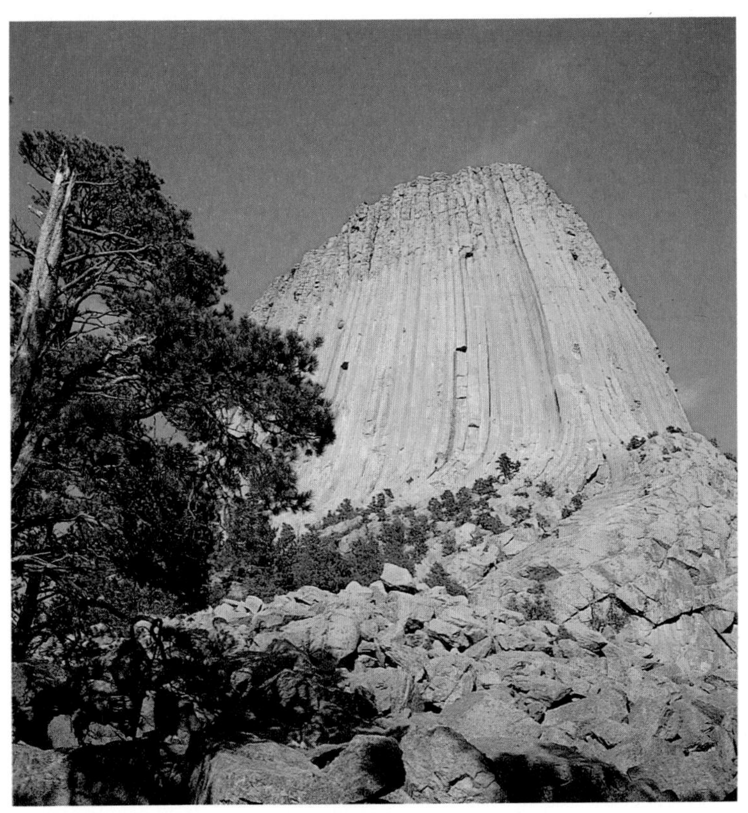

◀ *Devil's Tower in northeastern Wyoming, became the country's first national monument in 1906. It is a sheer tower of volcanic rock, rising 865 feet (264m) from its base.*

X ray

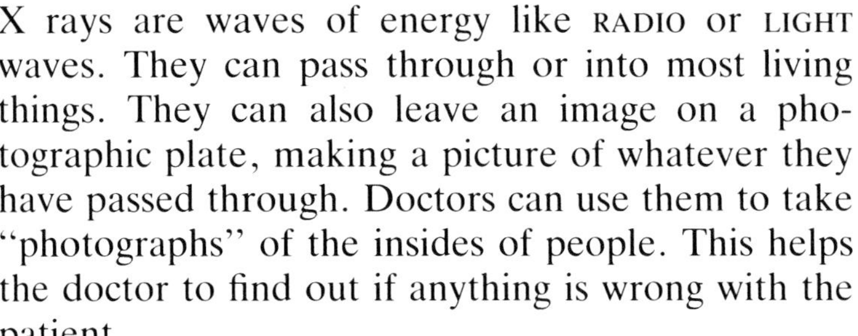

X rays are waves of energy like RADIO or LIGHT waves. They can pass through or into most living things. They can also leave an image on a photographic plate, making a picture of whatever they have passed through. Doctors can use them to take "photographs" of the insides of people. This helps the doctor to find out if anything is wrong with the patient.

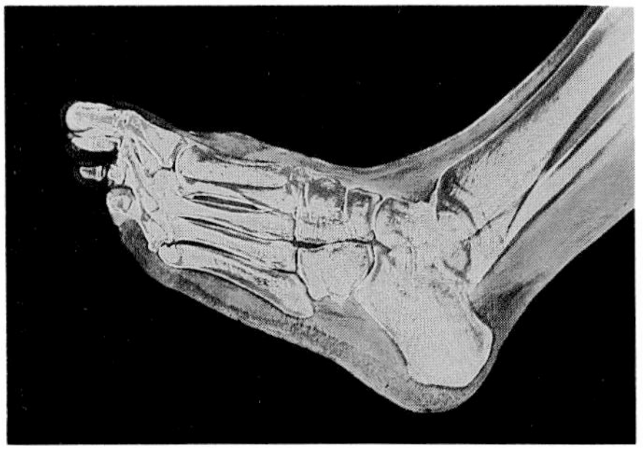

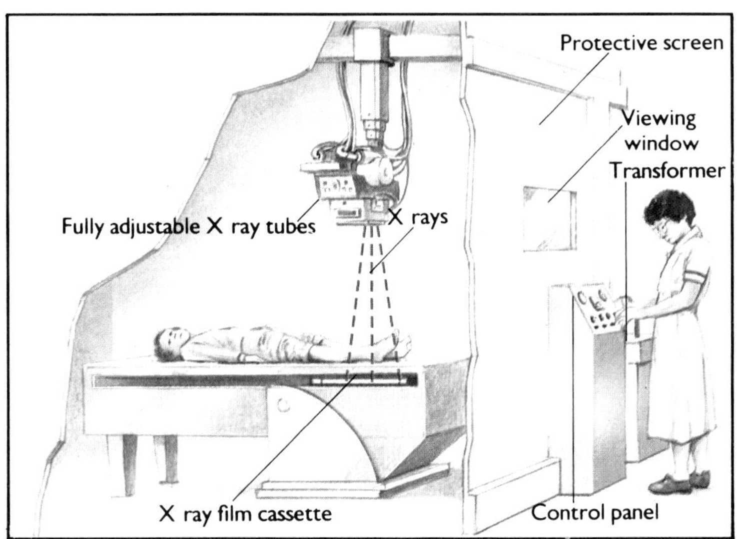

► *A radiologist takes an X ray of a child's foot. The resulting "photograph" (above) has been colored to show the foot and ankle bones more clearly.*

X rays are produced inside a glass tube that has no air or other gases in it. Inside the tube, at opposite ends, are a *cathode* that gives off electrons and an *anode*, or target. When the cathode is heated, electrons fly off and strike the anode, producing X rays.

Wilhelm Roentgen, a German scientist, discovered X rays by accident in 1895 while he was passing electricity through a gas.

▼ *The xylophone is used in orchestras and bands. Resonators, metal tubes below each bar, help to amplify the sound.*

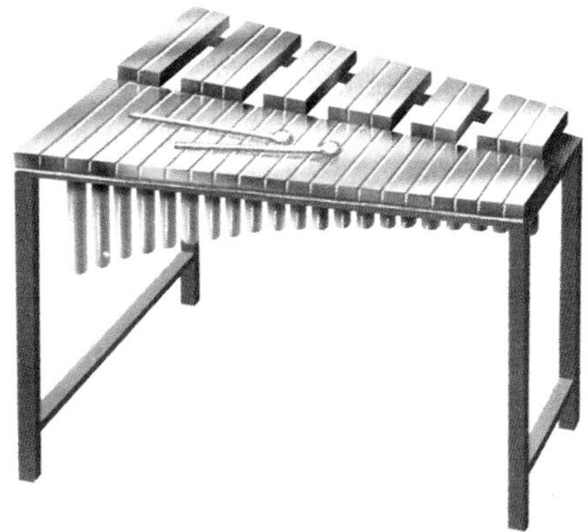

Xylophone

The xylophone is an odd-looking MUSICAL INSTRUMENT that produces a crisp, bell-like sound when played.

A xylophone has rows of solid wooden or metal bars fixed to a frame. Each bar is a different length and produces a different sound when struck. An electric version of the xylophone, called a *vibraphone*, is sometimes used.

Yak 

The yak is a large, shaggy kind of ox with a pair of long, thick horns. Yaks live in Tibet, China, and northern Asia. Wild yaks may be as tall as a man, but tame yaks are about the size of a cow.

Yangtze River (Chang Jiang)

The Yangtze is the longest and most important river in CHINA. From its beginnings, high in the mountains of Tibet, it flows 3,964 miles (6,380 km) across the center of China, pouring into the Yellow Sea near Shanghai.

The river takes its name from the ancient kingdom of Yang, which grew up along its banks 3,000 years ago. Today, the Yangtze is still one of the main trade routes in China. Big ships can sail up it as far as Hankow, nearly 700 miles (1,125 km) inland. Smaller boats can reach I-Ch'ang, which is 1,000 miles (1,600 km) from the sea.

Millions of people live and work on the Yangtze. Some live on the river itself in wooden sailing boats called *junks*.

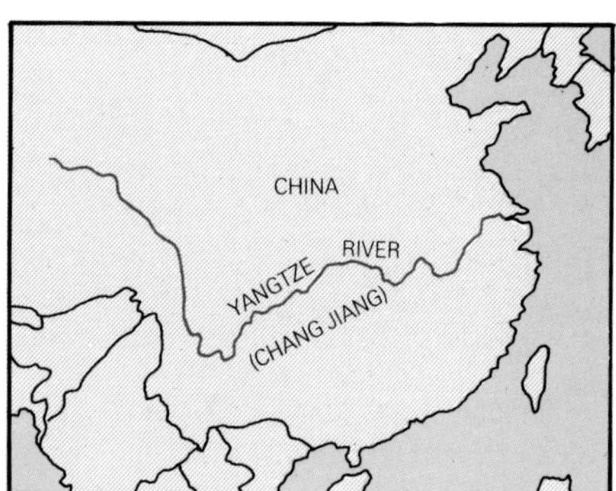

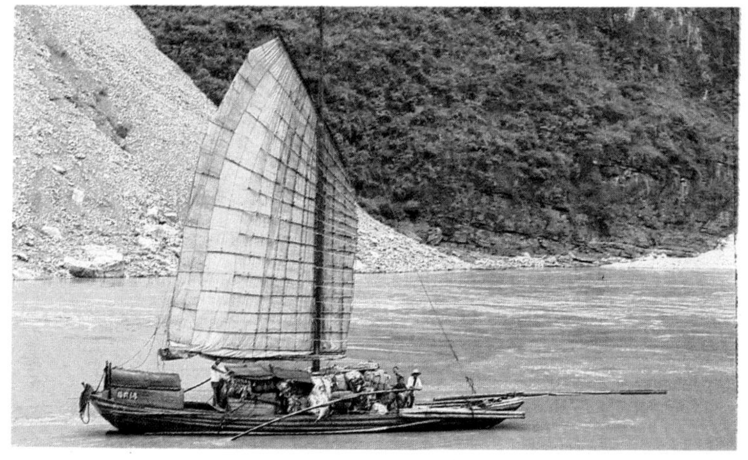

◀ *A junk sails on the Yangtze River, the third longest river in the world. The river has always been an important trade route. The port of Shanghai, China's largest city, lies at its mouth.*

Year 

A year is the amount of time it takes for the Earth to travel once around the SUN. It takes 365¼ days. A calendar year is only 365 days long. Every four years, the extra quarters of a day are lumped together to make a year of 366 days. These longer years are called leap years.

The first people to measure the length of a year were the ancient Egyptians. They noticed that when the brightest star in the sky—Sirius, the dog-star—rose just before sunrise, the Nile always overflowed its banks. They counted the days that went by before this happened again and found that it came to 365 days—one year.

SEE IT YOURSELF

You can watch yeast ferment at home. You will need a package of yeast and some sugar. Dissolve a spoonful of sugar in a glass of warm water. Drop a small amount of yeast into it and place the glass near a sunlit window. After a few minutes, bubbles of carbon dioxide rise from the yeast as fermentation takes place.

Yeast

Yeast is a plant, which is also a kind of FUNGUS. The whole plant consists of just one CELL. It is so tiny that you cannot see it without a microscope. It is very useful because it turns sugar into alcohol and carbon dioxide gas. This process is called FERMENTATION. Yeast plants do this because they do not produce their own food. They live on sugar instead. Today, yeast is grown in huge vats. It is then pressed into cakes or small pellets, ready to be sold.

There are over 150 different kinds of yeast. The most important are brewer's yeast and baker's yeast, which are used to make beer and bread.

In beer- and wine-making, yeast turns the sugar in malted barley or grapes into alcohol, while most of the gas produced bubbles away. When bread is made, the carbon dioxide gas forms bubbles, which make the bread dough rise.

Yeasts used for making bread and beer have been found in Egyptian tombs dating from 2000 B.C.
In olden times, a little dough was always kept back after breadmaking. This "leaven" was used to start off the next baking, so there was always a supply of yeast.

Yeltsin, Boris

Boris Yeltsin was elected President of the Russian Republic in 1991, and became the first leader of Russia to be chosen in a popular vote. He has pressed for democratic and economic reforms at a faster rate than Mikhail Gorbachev allowed.

When the U.S.S.R. ceased to exist, Yeltsin's Russia joined with the Ukraine, Byelorussia, and other former Soviet republics to form the Commonwealth of Independent States.

Yemen, Republic of 

The Republic of Yemen is a country on the coasts of the Red Sea and the Gulf of Aden. The republic was formed when North and South Yemen united in 1990, after years of political upheaval in both countries. North Yemen became independent in 1918 after years of Ottoman–Turkish rule. Its land is the most fertile in the whole of the Arabian Peninsula. South Yemen was made up of the former British protectorate of South Arabia. It became independent in 1967. San'a is the capital.

Many Yemenis are farmers growing cotton, wheat, coffee, millet, and fruit. They keep goats, sheep, cattle, and camels. The port of Aden, on the south coast of Yemen, has been a trading post between East and West for 2,000 years and the site of a large oil refinery. Aden is still the country's most valuable resource. Mocha, a small port near the border with Aden, has given its name to coffee that was once exported from it. Most Yemenis are Arabs and Muslims.

YEMEN

SAUDI ARABIA
OMAN
RED SEA
YEMEN
ETHIOPIA
GULF OF ADEN
DJIBOUTI
SOMALIA

Government: Republic
Capital: San'a
Area: 205,356 sq. miles (531,872 sq. km)
Population: 11,282,000
Language: Arabic
Currency: Dinar

Yugoslavia 

Yugoslavia is a country in southeastern EUROPE. Most of it lies in the BALKANS. It is a rugged, mountainous country. In the west, the mountains sweep down to the Adriatic. Inland, the country is mostly

◀ *Yugoslavia has a long and irregular coastline on the Adriatic Sea, with many beautiful beaches and offshore islands. Houses in the village of Sveti Stefan cluster together on a rocky promontory at the end of a point.*

YUGOSLAVIA

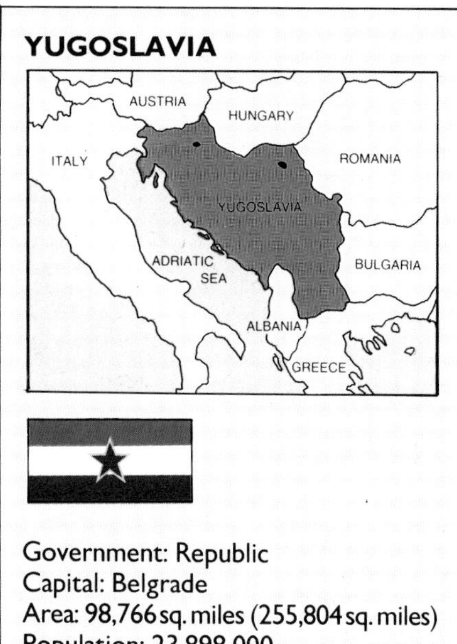

Government: Republic
Capital: Belgrade
Area: 98,766 sq. miles (255,804 sq. miles)
Population: 23,898,000
Languages: Serbo-Croatian, Macedonian, Slovenian, Albanian
Currency: Dinar

scrubby and poor. Around the river Danube in the north, the land is fertile. Most of the country's farming goes on around here. Farmers grow wheat, barley, plums, olives, and grapes, and keep cattle.

Yugoslavia's 24 million people come from different nations and speak many different languages.

In 1991, the republics of Slovenia and Croatia declared their independence. Fighting between Croats and Serbs intensified and continued into 1992 despite international efforts to bring the conflict to an end.

Yukon Territory

YUKON TERRITORY

Capital: Whitehorse
Population: 26,000
Area: 184,931 sq. mi. (478,934 sq. km)

The Yukon Territory is a vast region of northwestern Canada that stretches north as far as the Arctic. It is a wild and lonely place, with huge mountains, forests, and many forms of rare wildlife such as elks and moose. Because it is so far north, it is cold almost all of the year. It also has only a tiny population—less than 30,000 people. The most important industry is mining, especially gold and silver mining. But because it is so remote, the cost of mining is high. Most people today make their living from tourism. But it was mining that made the Yukon famous. When gold was discovered on the Klondike River in 1897, prospectors poured north to make their fortunes.

► *A "hydraulic giant" washes out gold from gold-bearing gravel in Dawson, Yukon.*

◀ *Fishing nets hang out to dry in a village along the Zaire River. The river is an important "highway" for people and goods through the country.*

Zaire

Zaire is a huge, hot, and rainy country that sprawls across the heart of AFRICA. It includes most of the vast Zaire River, once called the Congo. This river is the second longest in Africa—only the Nile is longer—and one of the longest in the world. The Zaire River is an important means of communication for the people of central Africa.

Much of Zaire is covered with thick jungle. There are lakes and highlands in the east and south. Copper, cobalt, and diamonds are mined here. But most of Zaire's 33 million inhabitants are farmers. They grow tea, coffee, cocoa, and cotton.

ZAIRE

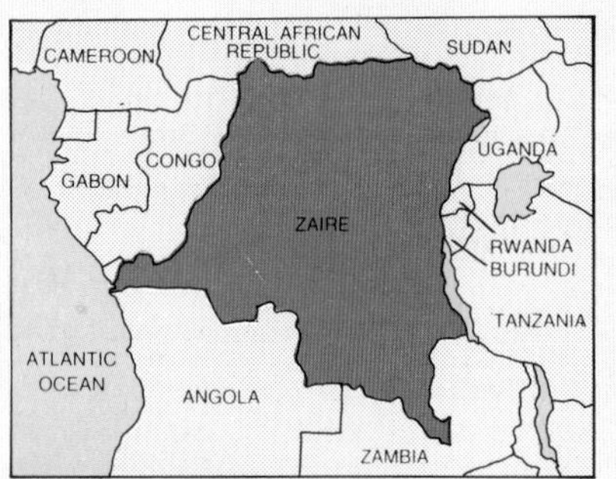

Government: Republic
Capital: Kinshasa
Area: 905,563 sq. miles (2,345,409 sq. km)
Population: 35,562,000
Languages: Bantu, French
Currency: Zaire

Zambia

Zambia is a country in southern AFRICA. It is entirely surrounded by land. Zaire, Tanzania, Malawi, Mozambique, Botswana, Zimbabwe, Namibia, and Angola all share borders with Zambia.

The name Zambia comes from the Zambezi River. This runs across the western part of the country along the border with ZIMBABWE. Zambia was the British protectorate of Northern Rhodesia until it became an independent republic in 1964.

Much of the country is rolling, highland plains. The majority of Zambians are farmers. But most of

Until 1953, Zambia was called Northern Rhodesia. From 1953 to 1963, it joined the countries that are now Malawi and Zimbabwe in the Federation of Rhodesia and Nyasaland.

ZAMBIA

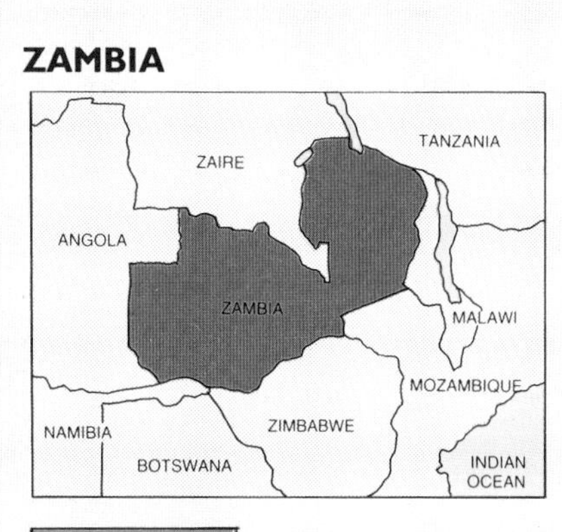

Government: Republic
Capital: Lusaka
Area: 290,586 sq. miles (752,614 sq. km)
Population: 8,073,000
Languages: Bantu, English
Currency: Kwacha

the country's wealth comes from its copper mines. In the 1980s, severe drought caused famine, and in 1990 the nation suffered serious violence.

Zebra

Zebras belong to the HORSE family. They live in the open grasslands of Africa to the south of the Sahara Desert. Zebras have creamy white coats covered with black or dark brown stripes. Each animal has its own special pattern of stripes.

Zebras live in herds. They feed on grass and are often found roaming the grasslands with herds of antelope. Although zebras can run very fast, they are often hunted by lions, leopards, and hyenas. People also used to hunt them for their attractive skins and tasty meat.

► *Burchell's zebra is the most common type of zebra found in East Africa. It has a wide black or brownish-black stripes.*

▼ *This statue of Zeus comes from Heraklion. The Romans worshiped a similar god whom they called Jupiter.*

Zeus

According to the MYTHS and legends of the ancient Greeks, Zeus was the ruler of all the gods. He lived on Mount Olympus and was married to Hera. He was the father of the gods Apollo, Dionysus, and Athena.

Zeus was the son of the ancient god Kronos. The stories say that Zeus and his brothers, Poseidon and Hades, killed Kronos and took over his throne and powers. Poseidon took the seas, Hades took the underworld, and Zeus took the world and the sky. Zeus ruled over the Sun, the Moon, all the other stars and planets, and the weather. When he was angry he would hurl thunderbolts at Earth.

◀ *A wealthy empire grew up in the area we now know as Zimbabwe from about the A.D. 900s through the Middle Ages. The Great Zimbabwe stone ruins are an impressive reminder of this early civilization. The site later became a ceremonial center. It became known to the western world in 1868 when it was discovered by accident by a hunter.*

Zimbabwe

Zimbabwe is a small country in southern AFRICA. It lies inland, about 150 miles (240 km) from the Indian Ocean. About 97 out of every 100 people are black Africans; the others are mostly white.

Zimbabwe is bordered by the Zambezi River in the north. The Zambezi is famous for the Victoria Falls and the Kariba Dam. The Kariba Dam is part of a great hydroelectric operation that supplies power to both Zimbabwe and its neighbor ZAMBIA.

Until 1965, Zimbabwe was the British colony of Southern Rhodesia. In that year, it declared itself the independent country of Rhodesia. Britain, however, did not recognize the new nation's existence. During the next 15 years, growing unrest and guerrilla warfare caused many problems. In 1980 the country became independent, under a black-majority government, as Zimbabwe.

ZIMBABWE

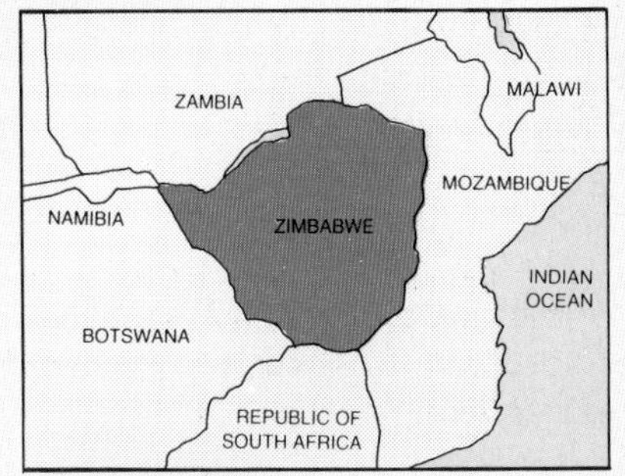

Government: Republic
Capital: Harare
Area: 150,803 sq. miles (390,580 sq. km)
Population: 9,369,000
Languages: English, Shona, Sindebele
Currency: Zimbabwe dollar

Zinc

Zinc is a hard, blue-white metal ELEMENT. It has been mined since ancient times and has been used in making brass for over 2,000 years. Brass is an ALLOY of zinc and COPPER.

A large share of the world's zinc comes from Canada, Australia, and the U.S. Zinc mines usually contain other metals such as copper, gold, lead, and silver as well.

We need a tiny quantity of zinc in our diet. People who do not get any zinc are anemic (they do not have enough red blood cells) and their growth is retarded. Any normal diet gives us all the zinc we need.

▲ *A piece of zinc, a metal that is mined chiefly in the U.S.A., Canada, Australia, and Mexico. Zinc is never found in the pure state, but always combined with other substances.*

Most zinc is used to *galvanize* steel. Galvanizing means putting a thin coat of zinc on steel to protect it. Zinc is also used to make cells in electric BATTERIES. Zinc forms part of many other alloys in addition to brass, including nickel and bronze.

Zoo

Zoos are places where animals are kept. They are cared for, bred, studied, and sometimes saved from dying out. There are now more than 330 zoos in the world.

The first zoos were in ancient Egypt. Queen Hatshepsut kept a zoo in 1500 B.C. More than 3,000 years ago, the emperors of China kept animals, birds, and fish in natural gardens where they would feel at home. In the MIDDLE AGES in Europe, kings gave each other presents of apes, peacocks, and lions. Private collections of animals were called *menageries*. Traveling menageries used to tour through the towns of Europe in the 1800s.

Since the 1700s, scientists have been interested in the study of animals. They began to sort animals into groups and give them Latin names so that the same animal would be known by the same name all over the world. Their work led directly to the building of the first public zoos. The first zoo in the United States opened in Central Park, New York City, in 1864.

The world's zoos range in size from small, privately owned collections to large public zoos. Berlin Zoo houses more than 2,000 different species of animals, more than any other zoo in the world.

► *This painting of the Broad Walk with elephants at Regent's Park Zoo in London, England, was done at the turn of the century. The zoo was founded in the 1820s by the Zoological Society of London, though today it is more generally known as the London Zoo.*

About Your Index

No encyclopedia can have entries on every subject, so there is a vast amount of information that can only be found by looking in the Index. There is no entry for Istanbul, for example, but if you look in the Index you will find lots of information and pictures under **Architecture, Constantinople,** and **Turkey.**

Page numbers in **boldface type** (heavy and dark) indicate where the main reference to the subject can be found. Page numbers in *italic type* (slanting) refer to pages on which illustrations will be found.

Take the entry on the Arctic for example:

Arctic 42, *42*, 144, *191*, 239–240

The main entry is on page 42, with a map. On page 144, under the entry on **Climate** you can read about the Arctic climate. The **Day and Night** entry on page 191 has a diagram showing why the Arctic is such a cold place. The **Eskimo** entry on pages 239 and 240 tell us about the people who live in Arctic lands. After the main index you will find a **Subject Index.** In this, all the entries in the encyclopedia are divided up by subject. The entries are in alphabetical order within each subject.

Aa

Aardvark 1, *1*
Abacus 1, *1*
Abbreviation 2
Abidjan, Côte d'Ivoire 171
Abilene, Kansas 386
Aborigine 2, *2*
Abstract art 45, 509
Abu Dhabi 709
Abyssinia *see* **Ethiopia**
Acceleration 3, *3*
Accounting 3
Accra, Ghana 295
Acetic acid 3
Acid 3, *4*
Acid Rain 4, *4*
Aconcagua, Mt. 31
Acorn 495, 609
Acoustics 5, *5*
Acre, battle of 178
Acropolis 5–6, *5*, 514, *515*
Acting *see* Theater
Actium, battle of 143
Acupuncture 6, *6*
Adams, John 6–7, *7, 192, 363*
Adams, John Quincy 7, *7*
Adder *333*
Adder's tongue fern *254*
Addiction 7, *7*
Adding machine 109
Addis Ababa, Ethiopia 240
Aden 773
Adhesive 8
Adjective 8
Adobe hut *127*
Adolescence 8, *8*
Adrenal gland *297*
Adrenaline 344
Adrianople, battle of 588
Advertising 9, *9, 154*
Aeneas 586
Aerial photography *423*
Aerosol 10, *10*
Aesop 10
Afghanistan 10, *10*
Africa 11–14, *11–14*, 164, 166, *214*, 348, 549 history 336
African elephant 231, *231*
Agana, Guam 311
Agincourt, battle of 70
Aging 14, *14*
Agora *309*
Agra *668*
Agriculture *see* **Farming**
AIDS 14, 361, 733
Aikido 427
Air 15–16, *15–16*, 228
atmosphere 51, *51*
climate 144, *144*
elasticity 228
heat 684
humidity 353
pollution 4, *4*, 267, 288, *410*, 626, *626*
weather 743
wind 757, *757*
Aircraft 16, *16,* **18–19,** *18–19*, 718
Blériot 85, *85*
helicopter 329, *329*
Lindbergh 405–406, *406*
sailplane 298, *298*
supersonic *661–662,* 661
World Wars I and II *766*, 768, *769*
Wright Brothers 770
Air Cushion vehicle see Hovercraft
Airedale 209
Airfoil *18*
Air Force 16–17, *17*
Airport 17
Air pressure *16*, *18*, 65, *65*, 583
Airship *see* Balloon and Airship
Ajman 709
Akashi-Kaikyo Bridge, Japan 98
Akkadian sculpture *603*
Alabama 20, *20*
Alamein, battle of 70
Alamo, battle of 70, 93, 176
Alaska 20–21, *20*, *220*, *714*
Al'Aziziyah, Libya 219
Albania 21, *21*
Albatross 21, *21*
Albert, Prince 727
Alberta, Canada **22,** *22*, *113*
Alchemy 22, *22*
Alcohol 22, 515, 683
Alcott, Louisa May 23
Alevin *594*
Alexander the Great 23, *23*
Alexandria, Egypt 23
Alfred, King of England 443
Algae 92, 531, *535*, *608*
Algebra 24
Algeria 24, *24*, 195
Algiers, Algeria 24
Algonquin tribe 30
Alice in Wonderland (Carroll) 116
Alimentary canal 202, *202*
Alkali 4
Alligator and Crocodile 24–25, *24–25*, *245*, 575
Alloy 25, *25*
see also **Bronze**
Alphabet 25
Alpha particles *560*
Alps 26, *26*, 166, 377, 666
al-Qaddafi, Muammar 402
Altamira caves 45
Altar 139, *139*
Alternating current 183, *289*
Althing 514, 730
Aluminum 26, *26*
Alveoli 412, *412*
AM (amplitude modulation) *559*
Amazon River 26–27, *27*, 95, 580, 632
Amazons 27
Ambrosia 310
America **27, 28–29,** *28–29*
continental drift 164, 166
history 152, *246*, *337, 725,* 725, 730
see also **Central America; North America**
America (U.S.) *see* **United States of America**
American Colonies 6, **27,** *27*, 28, 489, 517, 580
buildings *180*, *429*
government 164, 192
Pilgrims 525
Revolutionary War 576–577, *576–577*
Williamsburg *715*
American Indians 30, *30*, *451*
Central America and Mexico 55, *55*, *127, 551*
Indian Wars 365
N. America 27, *28,103*, 183, 323, *715*
S. America 362, *362*, 518, 551
American League 66
American Revolution *see* Revolutionary War
America's Cup 593
Ammonite *271*
Amoeba 33, 80, *572*
Amon, Temple of, Luxor *40*
Ampere 183
Amphibian 31, *31*, *245*
see also **Frog and Toad**
Amplitude modulation *see* AM
Amritsar *617*
Amsterdam 478
Amundsen, Roald *34*
Amundsen-Scott station 637
Anaconda 627
Anatolia *603*, 703
Anchorage, Alaska 20
Andersen, Hans Christian 31
Andes 31, 43, 134, *408*, 518, 632
Andorra 32, *32*
Andorra la Vella, Andorra 32
Andromeda 283
Anemometer *742*
Aneroid barometer 65, *65*
Angel Falls 634, 722
Angiosperm *92*, 531
Angkor Wat 636
Angle 32, 292, *474*
Angola 32, *32*
Angora goat 299
Animals 32–33, *33*, 222, *222*
Arctic 42, *42*
Asia *47*
cell *124*
deep-sea 193, *193*
desert 198, *198*
farm 250
food chain *80*, 268
hibernation 332–333, *333*
instinct 370, *370*
invertebrate 372
mammal 419–420, *420*
migration 440–441, *440–441*
nail and claw 471, *471*
parasite 513
prehistoric 542, 544–545, *544–545*
reproduction 572
seashore 606, *606*
skeleton 620–621, *620–621*
temperature 677
vertebrate 725, *725*

INDEX

Ankylosaur dinosaur *204*
Anna Karenina (Tolstoy) 690
Annapolis, Maryland 428
Annapurna, Mt. 465
Anode 772
Ant 33–34, *33*
Antananarivo, Madagascar 414
Antarctic 34, *34*, *144*, 191, 601
see also **South Pole**
Anteater 35, *35*
Antelope 35
Antenna 460, 561, *560*
Anther *266*
Anthony, Susan B. *760*
Anti-aircraft gun *315*
Anti-ballistic missile 313
Antibiotics 35
Antibody 205, 360, 697, 733
Anti-freeze 22
Antigua and Barbuda 35–36, *36*
Antiseptic surgery 407
Antler 193
Anubis *470*, *748*
Apartheid 36, 632
Apartment 348, *349*
Ape 36–37, *36*, *245*, *545*
see also **Chimpanzee; Gorilla; Orangutan**
Apennines 241, 377
Aphid *513*
Apia, Western Samoa 747
Apollo 310
Apollo spacecraft 279, *456*, *457*, *640*, 643
Appalachian Mountains 711
Aquarium 37, *37*
Aqueduct *588*
Arabian camel *198*
Arabic language 37
Arabic numeral 494
Arabs 12, **37,** *50*, 373, 376, 402, 414, 666
Arc de Triomphe, Paris *274*
Arch 41
Archaeology 38–39, *38*, *537*, 561
Archaeopteryx 545
Arch bridge 97, *97*, 98
Arch dam *185*, *186*
Archer fish 261
Arches National Park, Utah *473*
Archery 39, *39*, *118*, *235*
Archimedean screw *375*
Archimedes 39, 493, 736, *736*
Archimedes' Principle 39
Architecture 40–41, *40–41*
Byzantine *40*
cathedral 121–122, *122*
church 139, *139*
dome 210, *210*
Greek 5, *5*
Islamic *376*
Mayan *431*
Arctic 42, *42*, 144, *191*, 239–240
see also **North Pole**
Arctic Ocean 496
Arctic tern *42*
Area, measurement 748
Arecibo, Puerto Rico 561
Argentina 42–43, *43*
Aristotle 23
Arizona 43, *43*
Arkansas 43–44, *43*
Armada 70, *233*
Armor 44
Armored dinosaur *544*
Armstrong, Neil 642
Army 70: Roman 589, *589*
Army ant 34
Arrow-poison frog *277*
Art 44–45, *44–45*, 186
commercial 154, *154*
drawing 212–213, *213*
Impressionism 361–362, *361*
mosaic 455–456, *456*
painting 508, *508*
sculpture 603–604, *603–604*
Artemis 310
Artemis, Temple of *40*, 610, *611*
Artery *86*, 327, 551
Arthur, Chester A. 45
Asia 45–47, *46–47*, 164, 165, 348
history 336
see also **Southeast Asia**
Asia Minor 703
Aspen, Colorado 151
Assai, Lake *13*
Assembly line 270
Assyria *375*
Astaire, Fred *188*
Asteroid 49, *49*
Astrology 49, *49*
Astronaut *29*, 642
Astronomy 49–50, *50*, 431
asteroid 49, *49*
black hole 84, *84*
comet 153, *153*
constellation 162–163, *162–163*
Copernicus 167, *167*
eclipse 221, *221*
galaxy 282–283, *282–283*
radio astronomy 560–561, *560–561*
star 649–650, *649–650*
telescope *674*
Asunción, Paraguay 512
Atacama Desert 197, 564
Atahualpa, Inca King 362
Atatürk, Kemal 704
Athena 6, 310, 514, 515
Athens, Greece **50,** 309
acropolis 5, *5*
Parthenon 514–515, *515*
Athletics see **Olympic Games, Track and Field**
Atlantic Ocean 50, 314, *314*, 496
Atlantis 51
Atlas 51, *394*
Atmosphere 51, *51*
air 15, 743
bacteria 58, *58*
greenhouse effect *4*
climate 144, *144*
cloud 147–148, *148*
ozone layer 506
weather 743
Atoll 169
Atom 52, *52*, 132, 254, *492*, 554
Atomic Energy *see* Nuclear Energy
Attila the Hun 53
Auckland, New Zealand 484
Aurora borealis 51
Austen, Jane 53
Austin, Texas 679
Australia 53, *53*, 166
aborigine 2, *2*
Australasia, history 337
Australopithecus 245
Austria 54, *54*
Automobile 54–55, *54*, 199
battery 68, *68*
engine 371–372, *372*
Ford 270, *270*
gear 288
Axis (Earth's) 490, 607, 637
Axle 288, 413
Axis powers 766
Aztecs 55, *55*, 170, *170*

Bb

Babbage, Charles 56
Babylon 56–57, *56*, 374, *395*, *493*, 610, 663
Bach, Johann Sebastian 57, *57*
Bachelor of Arts 713
Bachelor of Science 713
Backstroke *665*
Bacon, Roger 57, 399
Bacteria 35, **58–59,** *58*, 193
antibiotics 35
blood *85*, 86, *361*
Bactrian camel *198*
Baden-Powell, Robert 88, 602, *602*
Badger 59, *59*
Badlands National Park 635, *635*
Baekeland, Leo *528*
Baghdad, Iraq 374
Bahamas 59–60, *59*
Bahrain 60
Baikal, Lake 48, 219, *616*, 617
Baird, John Logie 372, 675, *676*, 728
Bakelite *528*
Balaclava, battle of *175*
Balance 217
Balboa, Vasco Nuñez de 60
Baleen whale 751
Balkan Mountains 104, 241
Balkans 60
see also **Albania; Bulgaria; Greece; Romania; Turkey; Yugoslavia**
Ball 60
Ballast tank *657*
Ballet 61, *61*, 188, *189*, *672*
Ballistic missile 312
Balloons and Airships 18, 19, **62–63,** *62*, *71*
Ballroom dancing *189*
Baltic States 63
Baltimore, Maryland 428, *428*
Bamako, Mali 419
Banana 250
Bandar Seri Begawan, Brunei 101
Banff National Park 22
Bangkok *636*, 680
Bangladesh 63, *63*
Banjul, The Gambia 285
Bank 64
Bank note *451*
Bantus 106
Baptism of Christ, The (Piero della Francesca) *381*
Baptist 64
Barbados 64, *64*, 750
Barbarians 137, 186
Barcelona 644
Bar Code 64, *64*
Bardeen, John 65
Bark 65
Barley *127*, 250
Barnacle 179
Barnard, Christian 432
Barn owl *505*
Barograph *742*
Barometer 65, *65*
Bascule bridge *97*, 98
Baseball 66, *66*
Basketball 67, *67*
Basking shark 613
Bass drum 214
Basutoland *see* **Lesotho**
Bat 67–68, *67*, 326
Bat-eared fox *272*
Bathtub *280*
Battering ram *177*
Battery 55, **68,** *68*
Battery farming *251*
Battle of Britain 16, 70, 769, *769*
Battles 69–71, *69–71*
armor 44
Battleship 768, *768*
Bauxite 26, 44, 313
Bayeux Tapestry 69, *69*
Bay of Fundy 492
Bayonne Bridge, New Jersey 98
Bayreuth 737
Beak 82, *82*, *190*
Beam bridge 97, 98
Bean 69, *69*, *609*
Bear 72, *72*
Beaufort, Francis 756
Beaufort Scale 756, *756*
Beaver 72–73, *73*
Bechuanaland *see* **Botswana**
Becket, Thomas á 73
Bee 73–74, *74*, 370, *370*
Beer 772
Beethoven, Ludwig Van 74, *74*, 468, *523*
Beetle 75, *75*
Behavior *see* **Instinct**
Beijing (Peking), China **75**
Beira, Mozambique 465
Beirut, Lebanon 397
Belfast, N. Ireland 374
Belgium 76, *76*
Belize 76, *76*
Bell, Alexander Graham 76
Bells 76, 99
Belmopan, Belize 76
Belo Horizonte, Brazil 95
Bend (knot) 389
Benedictine order 450
Benin *12*, **77**
Ben Nevis 601
Benz, Karl 55
Berbers 12
Bering, Vitus 21
Berlin 77, *77*

Berliner, Emile *155*
Berlin Wall 77
Berlin zoo 77
Bermuda 78
Bern 666
Beta particles *560*
Bhutan 78
Bhutto, Benazir 509
Bible 78, *78, 316*
  Hebrew 383
  Protestant 549
Bicycle 79, *79, 274*
Bifocal glasses 275
Big Bang theory 713
Big Ben 76, *145*
Big crunch theory *713*
"Big stick" policy 587
Bibao 644
Bill (law) 160
Bill (money) *451*
Billiards *see* Snooker and Billiards
Bill of Rights 164
Bimetallic strip 683, *683*
Binary System 64, **79,** *79*, 158
Bindweed *745*
Biochemistry 80, *132*
Biology 80–81, *80*, 162
Bird 81–83, *81–83, 245*
  feather 253, *253*
  migration 440, *441*
Bird table 82
Birmingham, Alabama 20
Birth Control 83
Bison *45*, **83–84,** *83*
Bissau, Guinea-Bissau 313
Black bear *72*
Black bindweed *745*
Blackbird 82
Black Death *see* **Plague**
Black Hawk War 373
Black-headed gull *314, 606*
Black Hills 590, 635
Black Hole 84, *84*
Black panther *120*
Black people 352
  apartheid 36, 632
  civil rights 388, *388*
  discrimination 204
  slavery 140, 624, *624*
  Washington, Booker T. 739
Black Rapids Glacier, Alaska 296
Black Rod *514*
Black Sea 104
Black vulture *736*
Blackwell, Elizabeth 84–85
Bleda 53
Blériot, Louis 85, *85*
Blindness 94
Blitzkrieg 16
Blockboard *761*
Blondin, Charles *484*
Blood 85–87, *85–86*, 388
  group 87
  heart 326–327, *326*
  transfusion 87
  vein 721, *721*
Blood, Thomas 176
Blowfly 267
Blowhole 751
Blubber 751
Blücher, Gebhard Leberecht von 472
Bluebottle fly *368*
Blue giant star *650*
Bluegrass region 387
Blue-green algae 531
Blue shark 613
Blue whale 751, *751*
Boar 524, *524*
Boat 87–89, *87–89*, 114
  see also **Sailing; Ship; Submarine**
Bode, J.E. 716
Bodiam Castle *756*
Body *see* **Human Body**
Boeing 747 aircraft *19*
Boer War 88
Bogotá, Colombia 149
Boiling point 683
Bolívar, Simón 89, 149
Bolivia 89, *89*
Boll 171
Bologna 713
Bolsheviks 398
Bombard *118*
Bombay, India 364
Bomber aircraft 16
Bone 89, *89*
  marrow 86
  skeleton 620–621, *620–621*, 725
Bonelli's eagle *216*
Bone-shaker 79
Bonn, Germany 294
Bony fish 260
Book 90, *90*, 155
  dictionary 201, *201*
  printing 316, *316*
Book of Kells 186
Book of Mormon 455
Boone, Daniel 90
Booster rocket *641*
Booted eagle *216*
Borglum, Gutzon 590
Borneo 348
Boston, Massachusetts **91,** *91, 711*
Boston Massacre 91
Boston Tea Party 91, *91*
Botany 92, *92*
Botswana 93, *93*
Bottle-nosed dolphin *209*
Bottle-nosed whale *751*
Bow and arrow *see* **Archery**
Bowie, James 93
Bowie Knife 93
Bowling 93
Boxer dog *208*
Boxer Rebellion 137
Boxing 93
Boyoma Falls *13*
Brahmaputra River 63
Braille 94
Brain 94, *94*, 624, *625, 692*
Brancusi, Constantin *603*
Brandenburg Gate *77*
Brasilia, Brazil 95
Brass 25
Brass instrument 468
Brattan, Walter 65
Brazil 95, *95*
Brazil nut *494*
Brazzaville, Congo 159
Bread 96, *752*, 772
Breaststroke *665*
Breathing 96, *96*, 412, *412*
Breech-loading cannon *315*
Brest-Litovsk 765
Brezhnev, Leonid Ilyich 639
Brick 103
Bridge 96–98, *97*
Bridgetown, Barbados 750
Bristlecone pine tree 698
British Antarctic Survey *637*
British Columbia, Canada **98–99,** *113*
British Honduras *see* **Belize**
British Isles *see* **England; Ireland; Scotland; Wales**
Broad Peak, Mt. 465
Broadwood, Thomas *523*
Bronchus 412, *412*
Brontë Sisters 99, *99*
Brontosaurus *544*
Bronze Age 99–100, *100, 125*, 374, 753
Brooklyn Bridge, New York 98
Brown, John 100
Brown bear 72
Brownie unit 602
Browning pistol *315*
Bruegel, Pieter 213
Brunei 101, *101*
Brunelleschi, Filippo *572*
Brünnhilde 737, *737*
Brussels, Belgium 76
Bryophyte 531
Bubonic plague *see* **Plague**
Bucephalus 23
Buchanan, James 101
Bucharest 586
Buckingham Fountain *715*
Bud 101, 101
Budapest, Hungary 354, *354*
Buddha 101–102, *102, 570*
  Burma 105, *105*
  Tibet 685
  World membership 570
Budding, Edwin 349
Buena Vista, battle of 671
Buenos Aires, Argentina 42
Buffalo 102
Building *56, 127*, **103–104,** *103–104, 171*
  electricity 183
  see also **Architecture; House**
Bujumbura, Burundi 106
Bulb 104, *104*
Bulgaria 104, *104*
Bulk carrier 615
Bullet train *562*
Bull-roarer 468
Bunyan, John *548*
Burdock *609, 745*
Burkina Faso 105, *105*
Burma 105, *105*
Burning glass 399
Burrow 59, 557, 648
Burundi 106, *106*
Burying beetle 75, *75*
Bush, George Herbert Walker 107, *107*
Business 3, 652–653, *653*
Butter *441*
Butterfly 106–107, *106–107*
  caterpillar 121, *121*
Butterfly stroke *665*
Byzantine Empire 162, 177, 397, 588, *603*
Byzantine style *40*

Cc

Cable car *595*
Cable-stayed bridge 98
Cacao tree 135
Cactus 108, *108*
Caesar, Julius 108–109, *108*, 142
Cairo, Egypt 225
Calamity Jane 635
Calcium 297, 734
Calculator 109, *109*
Calcutta, India 364
Calendar 135
Calgary, Alberta 22
California 110, *110*
California condor 736
Calligraphy 37
Callisto 384
Calvin, John 543, *543*
Cambodia 110
Cambrian period *245*
Camel 111, *110, 198*, 343
Camera 111, *111, 155*, 372
  television 675
  see also **Photography**
Cameroon 112, *112*
Canada 112–113, *112–113*, 253, 556, *764*
  Northwest Territory 490
  Yukon Territory 776, *776*
Canadian Pacific line 563
Canal 114, *114*, 376, 377, 400, *722*
  Panama 510–511, *511*
  Suez 658, *658*
Canaletto, Giovanni Antonio *722*
Canberra, Australia 53
Cancer 114, *132, 559*
Candlestick (menorah) *570*
Canine teeth 673
Cannon 315, *315*
Canoe 87, *87, 88*
Canterbury Tales, The (Chaucer) 131, *131*
Cantilever bridge 98
Cantilever crane *174*
Canton, China 137
Capacity, measurement 748, 749
Cape Cod, Massachusetts *429*
Cape Tarifa, Spain 243
Cape Town 632
Cape Verde 115
Capillary *86*
Capitol building *739*
Capybara 585
Car *see* **Automobile**
Caracas 722
Caravel *338, 592*
Caravan *318*
Carbohydrate 650
Carbon 52, **115,** 132
Carbon dioxide *4*, 96
Carbon monoxide 533
Carboniferous period *245*
Cargo ship *see* **Ship**
Carnarvon, Earl of 705
Carnivore 115–116, *116*

INDEX

see also **Bear; Cat; Dog; Hyena; Raccoon**
Carp *260*
Carpathians 241
Carpets and Rugs 116
Carrara marble 424
Carré, Ferdinand 349
Carriage *753*
Caribbean Sea 115
Carroll, Lewis 116, *533*
Carter, Howard 705
Carter, James Earl 117, *117*
Carthaginians 321
Cartilaginous fish 260
Cartoon 117, *117*, 206
Cartwright, Alexander 66
Carver, George Washington 117
Carving *see* **Sculpture**
Casablanca, Morocco 455
Cashmere goat 299
Cash register 109
Caspian Sea 219, 243
Cassava 250
Cassette player *155*, *230*
Casting *see* **Sculpture**
Cast iron 374
Castle 119–120, *118–119*, *177*, *305*, *709*, *755*
Castries, St. Lucia 594
Castro, Fidel 181
Cat 120, *120*, *245*, 471, *471*, 691, *691*
see also **Jaguar; Leopard; Lion; Tiger**
Catapult *118*, 177
Caterpillar 121, *121*
butterfly 107
moth 460, *460*, 618
Catfish 261
Cathedral 40, *41* **121–122,** *122*, 139
Cathode ray tube 676, *676*, 770
Cat snake *627*
Cattle *see* Bison; Cow
Caucasian race 518, *518*
Caucasus 241
Cavalryman (Roman) *589*
Cave 122, *122*
Cave dweller 123, *123*, 421, *543*
Cave painting 44, *45*, 155
Cavy *see* **Guinea Pig and Hamster**
Cayley, George 19
Cedar of Lebanon *160*
Cedar wood 397
Cell 80,**124,** *124*
blood 85
disease 114
research *707*
Cellini, Benvenuto *572*
Celluloid 528
Cellulose *124*
Celsius scale 677, *677*, 683
Celts 124–125, *125*
Census 125, 210, *210*
Centennial state *see* **Colorado**
Centigrade 683
Centipede 125–126
Central African Republic 126, *126*
Central America 55, *55*, **126–127,** *126*
Maya 431-432, 431
see also **Belize; Costa Rica; El Salvador; Guatemala; Honduras; Nicaragua; Panama**
Central Pacific Railroad *28*
Central Processing Unit (CPU) *157*
Centrifugal pump *552*
Ceratopsian dinosaur *204*
Cereal 127, *127*, 268, 578, 650
Cerebellum *94*
Ceres 49
Cerro de Punta 550
Cervantes 492
Ceylon *see* **Sri Lanka**
Cézanne, Paul 213
CFCs *see* Chlorofluorocarbons
Chad 128, *128*
Chad, Lake *87*, 128
Chain, Ernst B. 264
Chain mail 44
Chair 281, *280–281*
Chalk 128, *128*
Chameleon 129, *129*
Chancel *139*
Chang Jiang River *see* **Yangtze River**
Chaplin, Charles 129, *129*
Charge of the Light Brigade, The (Tennyson) *532*
Chariot *588*, *705*
Charlemagne 129–130, *130*, 516
Charles, 130, *130*
Charles II 130–131, *131*
Charles VII, King of France 383
Charles, Prince of Wales 233
Charleston 750
Charon *529*
Chart *see* **Map and Chart**
Chaucer, Geoffrey 131, *131*
Check *451*
Cheese 131
Cheetah 120, *355*
Chemical reaction 80, 132
Chemistry 22, **132–133,** *132*
see also **Biochemistry**
Chesapeake Bay 428
Chess 133, *133*
Chestnut *494*
Cheyenne tribe 30
Chiang Kai-shek 137, 422
Chicago 133, *133*, 360, 623, *715*
Chickadee 82
Chickweed *745*
Children's Crusade 178
Chile 134, *134*
Chimpanzee 134, *134*
China 135, 136–137, *136–137*, 238, 376
acupuncture 6, *6*
Confucius 159
Genghis Khan *290*, 291
Great Wall 308
Kublai Khan 391, *391*
Mao Tse-tung 422, *422*
paper 511
Taiwan 667–668
Ch'in dynasty 137
Chinese language 137
Chinese Nationalists 422
Chinstrap penguin *517*
Chipboard *763*
Chipmunk *585*, 648
Chlorofluorocarbons (CFCs) 10, 506
Chlorophyll 135, *135*
Chloroplast *124*
Chocolate 135, *135*
Cholera 266, 367
Cholesterol 253
Chou dynasty 137
Christianity 135, 137, 162, *570*
bible 78, *78*
crusades 177
Easter 220
Jesus 381, *381*
monastery 450
Protestant 548–549, *548*
Reformation 412, 567–568
Roman Catholics 585–586, *585*
saint 593, *593*
world membership 570
Christmas 138, *138*
Chrysalis 107, 121
Church 139, *139*
see also **Cathedral**
Churchill, Winston 139–140, *140*, 340
Cinématographe 461
Cinnamon *646*
Circe 708
Circulatory system 353
Circus 140
Cirrus cloud *148*
Citric acid 3
Civil engineer 237
Civil Rights 140, *388*
Civil War, American *28*, **140–141,** *140–141*, 635
aftermath 325
Buchanan 101
Gettysburg *71*
Lee 397
Lincoln 405
Pierce 524
Civil War, Chinese 136
Civil War, English 130
Classical period 45
Claw *see* **Nail and Claw**
Clay 142, *142*, 540, *540*
Clay, Henry 142
Cleaner fish 261
Clemens, Samuel *see* **Twain, Mark**
Cleopatra 142–143, *143*
Clermont (steamship) 280
Cleveland, Grover 143
Climate 144, *144*
see also **Weather**
Clock 145, *145*, 516, *516*, 688
Cloth *see* **Textile; Weaving**
Clothes moth 460
Clothing 146–147, *146–147*
Cloud 147–148, *148*, 218, 267, 684, *685*, 692
Clove *646*
Clove hitch 389
Coal 148, *148*, *245*, 279, *279*, 541
Coats-of-arms *see* Heraldry
Cobra *19*, *47*
Cochineal 215
Cochlea 217
Cockatoo 514
Cockerell, Christopher 350
Cockle *449*, *606*
Cockroach *368*, 369
Coconut palm *510*
Cocoon *33*, 618, *618*
Cod *259*
Coffee 148, *148*
Cohort 589
Coin 149, *149*, 451, *451*, 619
Cold *see* **Common Cold**
Cold front 743, *743*
Cold War 29, 228
Coleridge, Samuel Taylor 763
Collie 209
Colobus monkey *453*
Colombia 149, *149*
Colombo, Sri Lanka 649
Colonial America *see* **American Colonies**
Color 149–150, *150*
human eye 247
painting 361
printing *547*
television 676, *676*
Colorado 150–151, *150*
Colorado beetle 75, *75*
Colorado River 305
Colosseum 151–152, *151*, 297, *297*
Colossus of Rhodes 610, *611*
Columbia, South Carolina 635
Columbus, Christopher 36, **152,** *152*, 180, 594, 644
Combine harvester *251*
Comet 153, *153*, 320, *320*
Comet goldfish *302*
Comet West *153*
Common Cold 154, 361, *625*
Common Market *see* **European Community**
Commonwealth 154
Commonwealth of Independent States 638
Communication 155, *155*, *534*
see also **Telecommunications**
Communications Satellite 156
Communism 156, *156*
Asia 48, 136, 452, 729
Europe 104, 586, 639
Lenin 397–398, *397*
Mao Tse-Tung 422, *422*
Marx 427, *427*
Commutator *289*
Comoros 156, *156*
Compass 157, *157*
Compound 157
Compound eye *267*
Computer 56, 64, **157–158,** *157–158*, *646*, 661
Conakry, Guinea 313
Concave lens 398, *398*
Concave mirror 447
Concorde 16, 18, *18*, 19, *19*, 662
Concrete 97, **158**
Condor *736*
Conduction *26*, 660, *685*
Confederate States of America 20, 141, *140*, 397, 750
Confucius 159, 570
Conger eel *225*
Congo 159, *159*
Congo River *see* Zaire River
Congregationalists 549
Congress 160, 207, 546, *739*

Library *402*
Conifer 160, *160*
Coniferous forest 270
Conjunctiva 247
Connecticut 161
Conservation 161–162, *161*
Constantine 162: Arch of *588*
Constantinople 53, **162,** *162*, 703
Constantinople, battle of 70
Constellation 162–163, *162–163*
Constellation, USS (warship) *428*
Constitution, United States 164, 414, 479, 546, 651
Constrictor *see* **Python**
Container ship 615
Continent 165–166, *165*
see also **Africa; Antarctica; Asia; Australia; Europe; North America; South America**
Continental Congress 363
Continental drift *165*, 166
Continental Shelf 164, *165*
Contraception 83
Convex lens *398*, 399
Convex mirror 447
Cook, James 166, *166*, 720
Coolidge, Calvin 167
Cooper, James Fenimore 167
Coot *477*
Copenhagen, Denmark 196
Copernicus, Nicolaus 167, *167*
Copland, Aaron 168, *168*
Copper 168–169, *169*, 401, *446*
Coracle 87, *87*
Coral 169, *169*, *245*, 706
Coral Sea, battle of 767
Core, Earth's 218
Cork 169, 539
Corn *127*, *758*
Cornea 247
Corn starch 650
Cornwallis, Lord 577
Corpuscle *see* Cell
Corsica 274
Cortés, Hernando 170, *170*
Cortex *94*
Cosmetics 170
Cosmetic surgery *662*
Cosmic rays 645
Cosmonaut 642
Cossack dancers *189*
Costa Dorada *641*
Costa Rica 171, *171*
Côte d'Ivoire (Ivory Coast) 171
Cotton 171–172, *172*, 744
Cotton gin 754
Cottonseed oil *172*
Cotyledon *609*
Cow 172–173, *172–173*, *245*, 344
Cowboy 173–174, *173*, 386, 680
rodeo 585
South America *43*, *717*
Cowpox 381
CPU *see* Central Processing Unit
Crab 174, *606*
Crane (bird) **174**
Crane 174, *174*, *588*
Crawl stroke *665*
Crayfish *179*
Crazy Horse 183
Credit card *451*
Crescent moon *570*
Cretaceous Period *128*, 204, *245*
Crete, Greece 308
Crimean War 175, *175*, *532*
Cristofori, Bartolomeo 523
Croats 776
Crockett, Davy 175, 557
Crocodile *see*Alligator and Crocodile
Cro-Magnon man *123*
Cromwell, Oliver 176, *176*
Crop rotation *250*
Cross *570*
Crossbill 82, *82*
Crowned pigeon 525
Crown Jewels 176–177, *176*, 199
Cruciform plan *139*
Crusades 177–178, *177*, *397*, 442, *442*
Crust, Earth's 218, 220, 465
Crustacean 178–179, *179*
see also **Crab; Lobster**
Crystal 179–180, *179*, 445
Crystal glassware *300*
Cuba 180–181, *180*, 644
Cuban parrot *514*
Cube 181, *181*, *749*
Cubism 45
Cuboid *749*
Cuckoo 181, *181*
Cullinan diamond 199
Cultivator *251*
Cultural Revolution 137
Cumulonimbus cloud *148*
Cumulus cloud *148*
Cupronickel 25
Curie, Marie and Pierre 182, *182*
Curlew *606*
Current, Electric 182–183, *182*
Current, ocean 144, 314, *314*, *496*
Custer, George Armstrong 183
Cuttlefish *449*
Cyclone *see* Hurricane
Cyclops *708*
Cylinder 371, *372*
Cyprus 183–184, *183*
Czechoslovakia 184, *184*

Dd

Dabbling duck 214, *215*
Dachshund 209
Daguerre, Louis 111
Daguerreotype camera *155*
Dahomey *see* **Benin**
Daimler, Gottlieb 55, *462*
Dakar, Senegal 610
Dakum (Peak 29) 465
Dam 185–186, *185–186*
Damascus, Syria 666
Dance *2*, **186, 188–189,** *188–189*, *256*
ballet 61, *61*
Dandy-horse 79, *79*
Danelaw 730
Danton, George Jacques 276
Danube River 354, 776
Dar es Salaam, Tanzania 669
Dark Ages 186–187, *187*, 355
Darwin, Australia 53
Darwin, Charles 187, 190, *187*, *190*
Dash 8 aircraft *19*
Data bank *109*
Dateline 191
Date palm *510*
Dávila, Pedrarias 60
David (Michelangelo) 438, *438*
da Vinci, Leonardo see **Leonardo da Vinci**
Dawn horse 345
Dawson, Yukon *774*
Day and Night 190–191, *190*
D-Day 191, *191*
Dead Sea 48
Deafness 76, **192,** *192*
Dean, Christopher *620*
Death's head hawkmoth *460*
Death Valley 487
Decathlon 694
Deciduous tree 271, 698
Decimal system 79
Declaration of Independence 192, *192*, 320, 363, 401
Declaration of Independence, The (Turnbull) *576*
Deep-sea diving *see* **Underwater Exploration**
Deep-Sea Life 193, *193*, *496*, *513*
Deer 193–194, *194*, *245*, 343
Defoe, Daniel 492
Degas, Edgar 362, *604*
De Gaulle, Charles 194–195, *195*, 473
Delaware 195
Delaware River 520
de Lesseps, Ferdinand 658
Delphi *682*
Delta 195, *195*, *580*
Demeter 310
Democracy 196, *196*, 303, 378
see also **Declaration of Independence**
Democritus *599*
Dendrochronology 39
de Neve, Felipe 410
Denmark **196–197,** *196*, 730
Density 599
Denver, Colorado 151, *150*
Denver mint 149
Deoxyribonucleic acid (DNA) 80, 290
Depression *see* Great Depression
Depression (economic) 29, 167, 343, 587, 719
Depression (weather) 743
Dermis 622
Desert 197–198, *197–198*, 391
camel 110, *110*
oasis 495, *495*
see also **Sahara Desert**
Desert locust 368
Design *see* **Commercial Art**
Detergent 199
Detroit, Michigan 199, *439*
Devil's Tower National Monument 771
Devonian period *245*
Dhaka, Bangladesh 63
Dhaulagiri I, Mt. 465
Diabetes 344, 370
Diamond 199–200, 446
Diaphragm *96*, *412*
Diatom 526
Dickens, Charles 200, *200*
Dickinson, Emily 200
Dicotyledons *92*
Dictator 200
Amin 707
Hitler 339, *339*
Mussolini 470, *470*
Dictionary 201, *201*
Didgeridoo *2*
Dien Bien Phu, battle of 70
Diesel, Rudolf 201
Diesel Engine 201–202, *202*
Diesel oil *279*
Diet *see* **Nutrition**
Digestion 202–203, *202*, 653
Digitalis 214, *214*
Dik-dik 35
Dike *735*
Dimetrodon *544*
Dingo *198*
Dining car 563
Dinka tribe *658*
Dinopis spider *647*
Dinosaur 94, **203–204,** *204*, 544, *544–545*, *574*
Dionysus 310
Direct current 183, *289*
Directory, The 276
Disc *see* **Recording**
Discrimination 36, **204–205,** 388, 624
Discus 694
Disease 205, *205*, 266
bacteria 58, *58*
cancer 114, *559*
common cold 154
fighting *85*, 86, 214, *214*, 360–361, 381
herbs 331
mental 276
Pasteur 515, *515*
virus 732–733, *733*
Dish antenna 561, *560*
Disney, Walt 206, *206*, *712*
Disneyland *712*
Disney World *206*, 265
Dissection 80, 81
Distance, measurement 748, *748*
Disteghil Sar, Mt. 465
Distillation 206–207, *207*
District of Columbia 160, **206,** 753–754, *754*
Diving *see* Underwater Exploration
Diving beetle *75*
Diving duck 214
Dizziness 217
Djibouti 207–208, *208*
DNA *see* Deoxyribonucleic acid
Doberman 209
Doctorate 713
Dodder *513*
Dodge City, Kansas 386
Dodgson, Charles *see* **Carroll, Lewis**
Dodo 208, *208*

INDEX

Dog *14*, **208–209,** *208*, *245*, 257, *326*, *355*, *643*
Dogfish 613, *613*
Doha, Qatar 554
Doll 209
Dolphin and Porpoise 209, *209*
Dome 210, *210*
Dome of the Rock, Jerusalem *570*
Domesday Book 210, *210*, 755
Dominant gene *290*
Dominica 211, *211*
Dominican Republic 211, *211*
Donald Duck 206
Donkey 211, *211*
Don Quixote (Cervantes) 492
Dormouse 332
Dove *see* **Pigeon and Dove**
Dragon 212, *212*
Dragonfly *368*, *544*
Draisine bicycle *79*
Drake, Francis 212, *212*
Drawing 212–213, *213*
Dream 213
Dredging 446
Dresden, Germany *293*
Dress *see* **Clothing**
Driving rod *651*
Drug *58*, **214**
  addiction 7
  antibiotics 35, 264
  trained dogs 209
Druidism 124
Drum 214, *214*
Dryopithecus 545
Dubai 709
Dublin 374, 730
Dubuffet, Jean *604*
Duck 214–215, *215*
Duck-billed platypus *529*
Dugout canoe 87, *87*, 88
Duisburg-Neuekamp Bridge, Germany 98
Dunant, Henri 567
Duncan, Isadora 189
Dune *607*
Dung beetle 75
Dunkirk 70
Dunmore Head, Ireland 243
Dutch 477, 482
Duvalier, François 319
Duvalier, Jean-Claude 319
Dwarf blue butterfly 106
Dye 215
Dynamite 246, *555*
Dynamo 372
Dysentry 266

Ee

Eagle *26*, *82*, **216,** *216*
Ear 216–217, *217*, *631*
  deafness 192, *192*
Eardrum 217
Early English Gothic style *122*
Earp, Wyatt 386
Earth 217, 218–220, *218–220*, 445, *445*, *629*
  atmosphere 51, *51*
  climate 144, *144*
  compared to sun *660*
  continent 165–166, *165*
  continental shelf 164, *165*
  day and night 190–191, *190*
  earthquake 217, 220, *220*
  eclipse 221, *221*
  gravity 306–307, *307*
  latitude and longitude 394–395, *394*
  ozone layer 506
  season 607-608, *608*
Earth (fox's) 272
Earth-centered universe 167
Earthquake 217, 220, *220*
Earthworm *see* Worm
Earwig *368*
East Berlin *see* **Berlin**
Easter 220
Eastern Front 766
Eastern Orthodox Church 570, 593
Eastern Roman Empire *see* Byzantine Empire
East Germany 293
Eastman, George 372
East Pakistan *see* Bangladesh
Echidna 420
Echo 221, *221*, 631, *630*
Eclipse 221, *221*
Ecology 222, *222*
Economics 223, *223*
Ecuador 223, *223*
Edelweiss *26*
Edinburgh 601
Edinburgh, Duke of 233
Edison, Thomas 224, *224*, 461
Education *see* **School; University**
Edwards (kings) 224, *224*
Eel 224–225, *225*, *260*, 441
Egg 225, 297, 573, *573*, *574*
Egypt 225, *225*
Egypt, Ancient 168, 220, **226–227,** *226–227*, 376, 467, *486*
  art 45, *188* ,669
  book 90
  carpet 116
  chair *280*
  Cleopatra 142–143, *143*
  cosmetics 170
  flag 262
  garden 287
  hieroglyphics 333, *333*
  measurement 663, *748*, *749*, 773
  myth *470*
  pharaoh 519-520, *519*, 705, *705*
  pyramid 552, *552*
  rug 116
  temple *40*
  wheel *752*
Eiderdown 215
Eider duck 215, *215*
Eiffel, Gustave 402
Eiffel Tower, Paris *274*
Eilean Donan Castle *709*
Einstein, Albert 228, 569, 687
Eire *see* **Ireland**
Eisenhower, Dwight David 228
El Alamein, battle of 767
Eland *11*, 35
Elasticity 228
Elbe, River 294
Elbert, Mt. 584
Elbrus, Mount 241, 243
Electrical engineer 237
Electric automobile 55
Electric circuit *683*
Electricity 202, **229,** *229*, 249, *275*, 652
  battery 68, *68*
  current 182–183, *182*
  fuel cell 279
  generator 289, *289*, 757
  hydroelectric power 356, *356*
  lightning 404–405, *405*
  power plant 541, *541*
  static *522*
  superconductivity 660–661
  thunderstorm 684–685, *685*
  wave energy *742*
Electric light bulb 224, 289, 349
Electric locomotive *562*, 563
Electric welding *747*
Electrolysis *741*
Electromagnet *416*, *464*, 661
Electromagnetic spectrum 644, *645*
Electromagnetic waves 660
Electron 52, *182*, 439, 554
Electron gun 676, *676*
Electronic engineer 237
Electronics 230, *230*
  engineering 237
  music 469
  navigation 474
  semiconductor 609
  silicon chip 618
  superconductivity 661
  teaching *192*
  telecommunications 673
  transistor 695–696, *695*
Electron microscope *440*
Element 132, **230–231,** *230*, *445*
Elephant *48*, **231,** *231*, *245*
Elevators and Escalators 232, *232*
Elgin, Lord *515*
Elgin marbles 6
El Greco 232
Eliot, Thomas Stearns 232
Elizabeth I *147*, **233,** *233*, 565, *565*
Elizabeth II 233, *263*
Elizabeth Blackwell Medal 84
El Salvador 234, *234*
Embryo 573
Emerson, Ralph Waldo 234
Emirate 554
Emperor penguin *517*
Empire State Building 623
Emu 235, *235*
Emulsion paint 508
Encke's Comet 153, *153*
Enclosure 250
Endeavour (ship) *166*
Endocrine gland 297, *297*
Energia rocket 584, *642*
Energy 235–236, *235*, 289
  electricity 228
  fuel 279
  light 403, *561*
  mechanical 235
  nuclear 493
  power plant 541–542, *541*
  pulsar 551
  quantum 554
  solar 629, *629*
  wave *742*
  x-ray 770
Energy (body) 252, 268
Engels, Friedrich *427*
Engine 236, *236*
  aircraft 18
  automobile 54–55, *54*
  diesel 201
  internal combustion 371–372, *372*
  motorcycle 463
  steam 650–651, *650*
Engineering 237, *237*, *431*, *552*, 588, *588*
England *189*, **238,** *238*, 281
  Domesday Book 210, *210*
  Edward (kings) 224, *224*
  Elizabeth I 233, *233*
  garden 287
  Henry (kings) 330, *330*
  house *349*
  Pilgrims 525
  Raleigh 565
  Richard (kings) 578–579
  Stuarts 655–656, *655*
  Vikings 730
  William the Conqueror 69
English Language 131, **238, 755**
  alphabet 25
  grammar 304
English system, measurement 748, 749
ENIAC computer *158*
Eocene period *245*
Eohippus 344
Epcot Center, Disney World *206*
Ephesus *40*, *610*
Epidermis 622
Epoxy resin 8
Equator 239, *239*, 394
Equatorial Guinea 239, *239*
Erector muscle *622*
Ericson, Leif 239
Eric the Red 730
Erie, Lake 307, *307*
Eritrea, Ethiopia *240*
Eros 310
Escapement 516, *516*
Eskimo 88, **239–240,** 310, 491
Esophagus 203
Estonia 63
Estrogen 297
Estuarine crocodile 575
Ethiopia 240, *240*, *250*
Eucalyptus tree 271
Euphrates, River 373
Eurasia 165
Europe 164, 165, 166, **241–243,** *241–243*
  history 337, 341
  Industrial Revolution 366, *366*
  Renaissance 571–572, *571*
European Community *195*, **243**
European Parliament 412
Eustachian tube *217*
Evening star 722
Everest, Mount 243, 610
Evergreen tree 698
Evolution 244–245, 244–245, *292*
  animal 544
  Darwin 187

human beings *542*, *545*
reptiles 574
see also **Human Beings; Prehistoric People**
Excavator *237*
Exercise 244, *244*
Exocrine gland 297
Exoskeleton 620, *620*
Explorer 244, 246, *246*, *338*
Italian 725, *725*
space 641
Spanish 644
undersea *16*, 39, *496*
Explosive 246
Exports 695
Eye 94, **247,** *247*
compound *267*
lens 398, *398*

Ff

Fable 10, **248**
Fahrenheit scale 677, *677*
Fairbanks, Alaska 20, 21
Falcon *198*, **248,** *355*
Falconry *324*
Falkland Islands 248, *248*
Fall (season) 607, *724*
Fall, Albert B. 321
Fall of the House of Usher, The (Poe) 532
Family Planning 83
Famine Relief 240, **248–249,** *249*
FAO *see* Food and Agriculture Organization
Faraday, Michael 249, *249*, 372
Farming *102*, *113*, 117, *127*, **249, 250–251,** *250–251*
ancient 226, *226*
Asia 48
drought *29*
Industrial Revolution *366*
irrigation 375–376, *375*
South America *512*
weed 745
Fasces (Fascists' symbol) 252, *252*
Fat 252–253, *252*
Fathers of the Confederation 253
Fax machine 673
Feather 253, *253*
Federal government 164, 651
Federal Republic of Germany *see* West Germany
Federation of Rhodesia and Nyasaland 777
Feldspar 305
Fencing 254, *254*
Fennec fox *272*
Fennel *721*
Ferdinand, Archduke Franz 765
Fermentation 254, *774*
Fermi, Enrico 254
Fern 254–255, *254–255*, *271*
Ferry 615, *615*
Fertilization *266*, 573–574
Fertilizer 255
Feudal system *443*
Fiber Optics 255–256, *255*
Fiddler crab *179*
Field events *see* **Track and Field**
Fighter aircraft 16–17, *17*
Fiji 256, *256*
Filbert *494*
Fillmore, Millard 256
Films *see* **Motion Pictures**
Finch *190*
Fingerprint 257, *257*
Finland 257, *257*
Fiord (Fjord) 258, *258*
Fir Tree *see* Conifer
Fire 258, *258*
Fireworks 258–259, 583, *584*
Fish *222*, *245*, **259–261,** *260–261*
deep-sea 193, *193*
food chain 268–269, *269*
reproduction 573, *573*
tropical 697, *697*, 700
Fishing *88*, **259–262,** *259*, *260*, *310*, *664*
Flag 262–263, *262–263*
Flame 263
Flamingo 263–264, *263*
Flea 264, *264*, 440
Fleming, Alexander 264, *264*
Flemings 76
Flemish tapestry *670*
Flint *258*, **264,** *264*
Flood 265
Floppy disk *158*
Florence 571: cathedral *41*, *572*
Florey, Howard W. 264
Florida 265, *265*
Flounder *260*
Flower 266, *266*, 573
classification *92*
parts of *530*
wildflower collection 92
Fly 266–267, *266*
Flyer I, aircraft 768, *769*
Flying fish 261
Flying fox 67
Flying squirrel *585*, 648
Flywheel *651*
FM (frequency modulation) *559*
Fog 267
see also **Smog**
Fokker aircraft *766*
Fontana Lake *489*
Fonteyn, Margot 189
Food 267–268
bacteria 59
digestion 202–203
famine 248–249, *249*, 250
fat 252–253, *252*
herb 331, *331*
nutrition 494
poisoning 59
protein 548, *548*
starch 650
taste 670, *670*
vegetarian 721
vitamins and minerals 733–734, *733*
wheat 752, *752*
Food and Agriculture Organization 710, 711
Food chain *222*, **268–269, 526**
Football 269, 269
Force 270, 413, 550
Ford, Gerald Rudolph 270
Ford, Henry 270, *270*
Forest 270–271, *271*
destruction 634
Forgery 708
Forked lightning 404
Formosa *see* **Taiwan**
Forth rail bridge, Scotland 98
Fort Smith, Arkansas 44
Fort Sumter 635
Fortyniners 110
Fossil 271, *271*, *575*
Fossil fuel 279
Four-stroke engine *372*
Fox *116*, **272,** *272*
Foxglove 214, *214*
Foxhunting 355
Fraction 273
Fractional distillation 207
France 273–274, *273–274*, *553*
De Gaulle 194–195, *195*
French and Indian War 275
furniture *280*
garden 287
Joan of Arc 383, *383*
Louis (kings) 411
Marie Antoinette 425, *425*
Napoleon 471–472, *472*
Revolution 275–276, *275*
St. Bartholomew's Day Massacre *548*
World Wars I and II 764, 765, 766
Franciscans *274*, *593*
Francis of Assisi 274
Franklin, Benjamin *192*, 229, **229–275,** *275*
Franks 129–130, *130*, 273
Frederick II, Emperor 178
Free French Movement 195
Free-tailed bat *67*
Freetown, Sierra Leone 617
Freezing point 683
French Academy 273
French and Indian War, The 275
French Equatorial Africa 126, 128
French Revolution 275–276, *275*, 425
Frequency: sound 631; wave 644
Frequency modulation *see* FM
Freud, Sigmund 276
Friction 276–277
Friendly Islands *see* **Tonga**
Frog and Toad *31*, *245*, **277–278,** *277–278*, 326, *333*, *607*
Front (weather) 743
Frost 278
Fruit 278, *278*
Fruit-eating bat 67
Fuel 279, *279*
coal 148
liquid 583, *584*
natural gas 473
nuclear 492, *493*
sun 660
Fuel Cell 279
Fujairah 709
Fujiyama, Mount 380
Fulton, Robert 280
Fulton the First (warship) 280
Funafuti, Tuvalu 706
Fungus *271*, **280,** *280*, *403*, 467, *467*
Furniture *280*, **281,** *281*

Gg

Gabon 282, *282*
Gaborone, Botswana 93
Gadfly 267
Gagarin, Yuri 282, *643*
Galapagos giant tortoise *575*
Galapagos Islands 223
Galaxy 282–283 282–283, 561, *713*
Milky Way 444–445, *445*
quasars 556
Gale *756*
Galileo 283–284, *283*, 600
Galleon 284, *284*
Gallium arsenide 609
Gama, Vasco da 285
Gambia, The 285, *285*, 610
Gambling 478
Gamma rays *560*
Gandhi 286, 286
Gandhi, Indira 286
Gandhi, Rajiv 286
Ganesh *334*
Ganges, River 286, 286
Garden 286–287
Garden tiger moth *460*
Gardiner dam 186
Garfield, James Abram 287
Garibaldi, Giuseppe 287, *287*
Gas *52*, 246, 263, **288,** *288*
air 15–16, *15–16*
hydrogen 357, *357*
oxygen 506
Gasherbrum, Mt. 465
Gas lighting 349
Gasoline *279*, **288**
Gasoline engine 371
Gas turbine 703
Gateway Arch, St. Louis *449*
Gatling gun 315
Gaucho *43*, *717*
Gauguin, Paul 667
Gaul 53
Gear 288, *288*
Gemini spacecraft *643*
General Assembly (United Nations) 710
Generator 289, *289*, 356, *356*, 493, *522*
Genetics 289–290, *289–290*, 370
Mendel 434, *434*
Geneva, Lake 26
Genghis Khan 290–291, *290–291*
Genoa, Italy *433*
Gentoo penguin *517*
Geographic center of United States 635
Geography 291
Geological periods 245, *245*
Geology 292, *292*
Geometry 292
George C. Marshall Space Flight Center *20*
Georgetown, Guyana 317
Georgia 293

INDEX

Georgian style *41*
Germ *see* Bacteria; Virus
Germanium 609
Germany *243*, **293–294,** *293–294*
Hitler 339, *339*
World Wars I and II 764–767, *764–767*
Gershwin, George and Ira 294–295
Gettysburg, battle of 70, *71*, 141
Geyser 295, *295*, 359, *483*
Ghana 295–296, *295*
Ghats, Mts. 363
Giant panda 511
Giant redwood *698*
Giant squid 247, 450, 647
Giant tortoise 575, *575*, 692
Gibbon 37
Gibbon, Edward 338
Gila monster *198*
Gilbert Islands 706
Gill 261
Gill net *259*
Giotto (Ambrogio di Bondone) *44*
Giraffe 11, **296,** *296*
Girder bridge 97
Girl Scouts 602, *602*
Giselle (ballet) 61
Giza *227*, 552
Glacier 296–297, *296*, 358, *358*, 359, 392
Glacier National Park, Montana *454*
Gladesville Bridge, Australia 98
Gladiator 297, *297*
Gland 297, *297*, 344
Glasgow *562*, 601
Glasnost 302
Glass 255, **298, 300–301,** 300
Glasses 398–399, *398*
Glaucous gull *314*
Glenn, John Herschel, Jnr. 298
Gliding 19, **298–299,** *298*
Gliding frog *277*
Glycol 22
Gnu 35
Goat 299, *299*, 343, 344
Gobi Desert 197, *198*, 452
God (myth) 470, *470*, 570
Goddard, Robert H. 642
Godthaab, Greenland 310
Godwin Austen, Mt. 465
Golden eagle *26*, *82*
Golden Gate Bridge, San Francisco *97*
Golden Hind (ship) 212
Golden Temple of Amritsar 617
Goldfish 302
Gold 299, 302, *299*, *302*, 437
Gold rush 21, 110, 478, 776, *776*
Goldsmith *571*
Goliath beetle 75
Goliath frog 277
Gondola *722*
Gone with the Wind (film) *461*
Gorbachev, Mikhail 302, *302*, *338*, 638
Gorilla 303, *303*
Gosainthan I, Mt. 465
Goshawk *324*
Gossamer Albatross (aircraft) 19
Gothic style 40, *41*, *122*, 139
Goths 186
Government 303–304, *304*
communist 156
democratic 164, 192, 196, *196*
dictator 200
fascist 252, *252*
president 546
republic 575
States' Rights 651
tax 670–671, *671*
Gozo, Malta *419*
Graf Zeppelin (airship) 63
Grammar 304
Gramophone *155*
Grand Banks 262, 479
Grand Canal, Venice *722*
Grand Canyon 305, *305*, 610
Grande Dixence dam 186
Granite 305, *305*, *583*
Grant, Ulysses Simpson 306
Granth 617
Grape *759*
Graphite 115
Grass 306, *306*, *607*
see also **Bamboo; Cereal; Rice**
Grasshopper 306, *369*
see also **Locust**
Gravity 84, **306–307,** *307*, 456, 482, 650, *686*
Gravity dam *186*
Gravure printing 548
Gray daggermoth *460*
Gray fox squirrel 648
Gray kangaroo 385
Gray matter 94
Gray parrot 514
Gray wolf 761
Great Australian Desert 197
Great Barrier Reef 610
Great Britain *see* United Kingdom
Great Compromiser *see* **Clay, Henry**
Great Depression 29, 167, 343, 587
Greater plantain *745*
Great Fire of London 410
Great Lakes 307–308, *307*
Great Mosque, Mecca 432
Great Purge 639
Great Pyramid 552, 611
Great Smoky Mountains *489*
Great Wall of China *137*, **308**
Great Zimbabwe stone ruins *779*
Greece 308, *308*
Greece, Ancient 2, **308–309,** *309*, 575
acropolis 5–6, *5*
Alexander the Great 23, *23*
architecture 5, *5*, 40, *40*, 514–515, *515*
arts *188*
Athens 50
clothing *146*
cosmetics 170
furniture 280
marathon 423, *423*
Plato 528
science *599*
theater 681, *682*
Trojan War 329, *329*, 341–342, *341*, 696–697, *696*
Greek Cypriots 184
Greek mythology 310, 332, *332*
Greenhouse effect *4*, 10
Greenland 258, **310,** *310*, 730
Green Mountains 724
Green revolution 250
Green toad *333*
Green turtle 705
Greenwich, England 395
Grenada *262*, **311,** *311*
Grimaldi family 450
Grouse *198*
Growth 14, *344*, 621
Guam 311, *311*
Guatemala 311–312, *311–312*
Guatemala City, Guatemala *126*, 312
Guerilla Warfare 312
Guided Missile 312–313, *312*
Guide To Geography (Ptolemy) 291
Guinea 313, *313*
Guinea-Bissau 313, *313*
Guinea fowl *11*, 541
Guinea Pig and Hamster 313–314, *313*
Gulf Stream 314, *314*
Gulf of Thailand 680
Gulf War 29, 374, 391, 598
Gull 314, *314*, *606*
Gulliver's Travels (Swift) 665
Gun *71*, **315–316,** *315*
Gunpowder 57, 70, 259, 315
Guppy 700
Gutenberg, Johann 316, *316*
Guyana *262*, **317,** *317*
Gyachung Kang, Mt. 465
Gymnastics 317–318, *317*
Gymnosperm 531
Gypsy 318, *318*
Gyrfalcon 248
Gyroscope 318, *318*

Hh

Haddock *259*
Hades 310
Hagia Sophia *703*
Haida tribe 30
Hail *see* Rain and Snow
Hair 319, *319*, *518*
Haiti 319, *319*
Halicarnassus, tomb of 610, *611*
Halifax, Nova Scotia 492
Halley, Edmond 153, 320, *320*
Halley's Comet *153*, 320, *320*
Hall of Mirrors 725
Hamilton, Alexander 320
Hamilton, Bermuda 78
Hammurabi 57, *395*
Hamster *see* **Guinea Pig and Hamster**
Hancock, John 320, *320*
Hand (measurement) 344
Handel, George Frideric 259, **321,** *321*
Han dynasty 137
Hankow 773
Hang Gliding *see* Gliding
Hanging Gardens of Babylon 610, *611*
Hannibal 321
Hanoi 729
Hapsburgs 54, 341
Harald Fairhair 730
Harald Hardrada 730
Harare 779
Harding, Warren 321
Hardboard *763*
Hardwood 698, 763
Hare 321
Harmony 468
Harold, King of England 730
Harp 322, *322*
Harpsichord 322, *322*
Harrison, Benjamin 323, *323*
Harrison, William Henry 323, *323*
Hartebeest 35
Harvard University 91, 713
Harvest mouse 585
Harvey, William 81, 327
Hastings, battle of 70
Hathaway, Anne 612
Havana, Cuba, 180, *180*
Harversian canal *89*
Hawaii 323–324, 414
Hawk 324, *324*
Hawksbill turtle 705
Hawthorne, Nathaniel 324
Haydn, Franz Joseph 325, *325*, 503
Hayes, Rutherford B. 325, *325*
Healfdene 730
Health 325–326, 684, *684*
Hearing 326, *326*, *631*
see also **Ear; Deafness**
Heart *86*, **326–327,** *326*, *412*
disease *214*
pulse 551
transplant 432
Heat *279*, 279, **327–328,** *327*, 684
rays 366–367
temperature 677, *677*
Hebrews 328, 510, 515, *515*
Hebrides 601
Heddle *745*
Hedgehog *245*, **328–329,** *328*
Hel (world of dead) 731
Helen of Troy 329, *329*
Helicopter 17, 18, *18*, 19, **329,** *329*
Helios 610
Helium 63
Hells Canyon, Idaho 360
Helsinki, Finland 257
Hemingway, Ernest 330
Henry (kings) 73, **330,** *330*
Hephaestus 310
Heptathlon 694
Hera 310
Heraldry 331, 331
Herb 331–332, *331*
Herbicide 745
Herculaneum 726
Hercules 332, *332*
Hercules moth *460*
Heredity *see* Genetics
Hereford cow *172*
Herjolfsson, Bjarni 730

Hermann's tortoise *692*
Hermes *see* **Mercury (God)**
Hermit 450
Hernandez, Francisco 688
Herring gull *314*
Herschel, William 716
Hertz, Heinrich 559
Hestia 310
Hevelius, Johannes 457
Hibernation 332–333, *333*
Hickok, Wild Bill 386
Hieroglyphics 333, *333*
High frequency 631
Hillary, Edmund 243
Himalayan rabbit *557*
Himalayas 166, **334,** *334*, 464, 465
Himal Chuli, Mt. 465
Hinduism 286, **334,** *334*, *570*
Hippopotamus 335, *335*
Hiroshima 766
Hispaniola 152, 211, 319
History 335–339, *335*, *338*
prehistoric 542–543, *543–543*
see also **Archaeology**
Hitch (knot) 389
Hitler, Adolf 339, *339*, 505, 768, 769
Hoarfrost 278
Hobart, Australia 53
Hobby 339–340, *339*
Ho Chi Minh City 636, 729
Hockey 340, *340*
Hog *see* **Pig**
Holland *see* **Netherlands**
Holland, John P. 657
Holmes, Sherlock 462
Holography 340–341, *340*
Holstein-Friesian cattle *173*
Holy Roman Empire *177, 129–130,* 130, 341
Homer 308, 329, *329*, **341–342,** *341*, *696*, 708
Homing pigeon 525
Homo erectus 543, *542*
Homo habilis 542
Homo sapiens 543
Honduras 342, *342*
Honey bear *72*
Honey bee 73, *74*
Hong Kong 342–343, *342*
Honiara, Solomon Islands 630
Honshu 689
Hoof 343, *343*, 345
Hooke, Robert 124
Hoosier State *see* **Indiana**
Hoover, Herbert Clark 343, *343*
Hoover Dam *43*
Hope diamond 199
Hopi tribe 30
Hormone *297*, **344,** *344*
Horn 344, *344*
Hornet *477*
Horn of Africa 630
Horse 345, *345*, *386*
evolution *244*, *245*
hoof 343
hunting 355, *355*
rail wagon *562*
Roman chariot race *588*
Horseback riding *see* **Riding, Horseback**
Horsefly 267
Horseshoe bat *67*
Horseshoe Falls 484
Horus *470*
Hospital 345–346, *346*
Hotel 347, *347*
Hot spring *see* **Geyser**
Hourglass 687
House 347–349, *348–349*
see also **Building**
Housefly *266*
House of Representatives 160
House of the Seven Gables, The (Hawthorne) 324
Houses of Parliament *see* **Parliament**
Housing *see* **Building**
Hovercraft 347, 350, *347*
Hudson, Henry 195
Hudson River 483
Huguenot *548*
Human Beings 351–352, *351–352*
intelligence 371, *371*
instinct *370*
prehistoric 542–543, *542–543*
race 518, *518*
Human Body 80, **352–353,** *352*
adolescence 8, *8*
aging 14–15
blood 85–87, *85–86*
bone 89, *89*
brain 94, *94*
breathing 96, *96*
digestion 202–203, *202*
exercise 244, *244*
fat 252–253, *252*
gland 297, *297*
heat 328
heredity 289–290, *289–290*
health 325
hormone 344, *344*
muscle 466, *466*
nerve 476, *476*
protein 548
reproduction 573–574, *573*, *574*
skeleton 620–621, *621*
skin 622, *622*, *692*, *692*
sleep 624–625, *625*
temperature 677, *683*
Humber Estuary Bridge, England 98
Humidity 353
Hummingbird *82*, **353–354,** *353*
Humpback whale *751*
Humpty Dumpty 116
Humus 628
Hundred Years' War 70, 443
Hungary 354–355, *354*
Huns 53, 186, **355**
Hunter aircraft *19*
Hunting 355, *355*
Huntsville, Alabama *20*
Hurdling 694
Huron, Lake 307
Hurricane 356, *356*, *756*, 757
Husky *714*
Hydra 332, *332*
Hydraulic giant *774*
Hydrazine 584
Hydrochloric acid 3
Hydroelectric Power 356, *356*
Hydrofoil 357, *357*
Hydrogen 52, *52*, *62*, *132*, **357,** *357*, *584*, 650
Hyena 357, *357*
Hygrometer 353
Hypothalamus *94*

Ii

Ibex *299*, *343*
IBRD *see* International Bank for Reconstruction and Development
ICAO *see* International Civil Aviation Organization
Ice Ages *245*, 258, **358,** *358*, 392, 420, *420*, *545*
Iceberg 358–359, *358*
Ice cap 34
Ice hockey *see* **Hockey**
Iceland 359, *359*, 730
Ice skating *see* **Skating**
I-Ch'ang 771
Ichneumon wasp 369
Ichthyostega 544
Idaho 359–360
Ides of March 109
Igloo 240
Igneous rock 582
Iguassu Falls *741*
Iliad (Homer) 341, 342, 697
Illinois 360
Illuminated manuscript 90, *90*, 186
ILO *see* International Labor Organization
IMF *see* International Monetary Fund
Immune system 205
Immunity 360–361, *361*
see also **Inoculation**
Impala *11*, 35
Imperial Palace 689
Imperial system 748, 749
Imports 695
Impressionism 45, **361–362,** *361*
Incas 362, *362*, 408
Incisor teeth 672
Inclined plane 413
Income tax 670
Independence Day 363
Independence Hall 520
India 363–364, *363*, 454
Gandhi 286, *286*
Gandhi, Indira 286
Indiana 364
Indian elephant *47*, 231
Indian Ocean 365
Indian Wars 365, 481
Indigestion 203
Indonesia *349*, **365,** *365*, 512
Indus River 509
Industrial Revolution 366, *366*, 651–652, 695
Indus Valley 48
Infant *574*, 621, 624; mortality *684*
Infection 86
Inflation 366
Infrared Rays 39, **366–367,** *367*
Inguri dam 186
Inn 347
Inoculation 367, *367*, 381, 515, *515*
Insect *245*, **367–369,** *368–369*, *370*
life cycle 369
nest 477
pest 369
see also **Beetle; Butterfly; Moth**
Insect-eating bat 68
Instinct 370, *370*, 440, 549–550, *550*
Insulin 370
Insurance 370
Intaglio printing 548
Intelligence 371, *371*
Internal Combustion Engine 201, **371–372,** *372*
International Civil Aviation Organization 710
International Court of Justice 710
International Date Line *687*
International Labor Organization 710
International Monetary Fund 710, 711
International trade 695, *694*
Intestines 203
Invar 25
Invention 372
Machine 224, 413, *413*, 754
wheel 752–753, *752–753*
Invertebrate *33*, **372**
Ionosphere 51
Iowa 373
Iowa Plains Indians *28*
IQ *see* **Intelligence**
Iran 23, 220, **373,** *373*, 610
Iraq 56, 168, **373N374,** *374*, 376
Ireland 186, **374,** *374*
Irian Jaya 512
Iris (eye) 247
Iron (nutrition) 734
Iron Age 543
Iron and Steel *25*, 100, **374,** *375*, 430
bridge 98
building 103
ore *437*
rust 591, *591*
Iroquois helicopter *329*
Iroquois tribe 30
Irrawaddy River 105
Irrigation 375–376, *375*
Isis *470*
Islam 373, **376,** *376*, 430, 485, 509, 703
architecture *668*
crescent moon *570*
Koran 390
Muhammad 466
Islamabad, Palestine 509
Islamic Republic *see* **Iran**
Island 507
Israel 376, *376*, 383, 384, 510
Israelites *see* **Hebrews**
Istanbul *40*, 162, *162*, 703, *703*
Italian Woman (Van Gogh) *719*
Italy *241* **377,** *377*
Fascism 252, *252*, 470, *470*
Garibaldi 287
Renaissance *571*, 572, *572*
Roman Empire 586, 588–

INDEX

589, 588–589
World War II 766, 768, 769
Ivanhoe (Scott) 602
Ivory *12*, 231, *603*
Ivory Coast *see* **Côte d'Ivoire**

Jj

Jabberwocky (Carroll) *533*
Jackson, Andrew 28, **378**
Jackscrew 413, *413*
Jaguar 378, *378*
Jakarta, Indonesia 365
Jakobshavn, Greenland *310*
Jamaica 379, *379*
James (kings) 379
James, Jesse 448
Jamestown Colony 27
Jane Eyre (Brontë) 99
Janssen, Zacharias 432
Japan 379–380, *379*
bullet train *562*
naval ensign *263*
religion *570*, 614
World War II 766, *768*, 769
Japanese spider crab *179*
Jasper National Park, Canada *112*
Java, Indonesia 365
Jazz 168, **380**, 411
Jazz Singer, The (film) 462
Jeans, James 52
Jefferson, Thomas *192*, **380**
Jellyfish *245*, *606*, 620
Jenner, Edward 381
Jenney, William Le Baron 623
Jersey cow *172*
Jerusalem 177, **381,** *381*, *570*
Jesus 138, 220, **381,** *381*, 390
Jet engine 19, *19*, 51, **381–382,** *382*
Jewels *see* **Crown Jewels**
Jews 78, 328, 376, 384, 515
Jib-Crane 174, *174*
Joan of Arc 383, *383*
Joey *426*
Jogging *244*
John Brown's Body (Brown) 100
John F. Kennedy aircraft carrier 212
John Paul II, pope *537*
Johnson, Andrew 382
Johnson, Lyndon Baines 382–383
Johnson, Samuel 201
Joint (skeleton) 621
Jordan *262*, **383,** *383*
Jordan River 383
Journalism 175
Juba River 630
Judah 510
Judaism 383–384, 383
Passover 515, *515*
world membership 570
Judo 426
Jujitsu 427
Jumbo jet *19*
Juneau, Alaska 20
Junk *771*
Jupiter 384, *384*
Jurassic period *245*
Justinian I, Emperor *703*
Jutland 196
Jutland, battle of 765

Kk

Kaaba (Black Stone) 432
Kabul, Afghanistan 10
Kalahari Desert 93, 471
Kale *721*
Kaleidoscope 385
Kali *334*
Kalong bat 67
Kami 614
Kamov Hoodlum helicopter *329*
Kampala, Uganda 707
Kanchen Junga, Mt. 465
Kangaroo 385, *385*, *426*
Kangbachen, Mt. 465
Kansas 386
Karachi, Pakistan 509
Karakoram mountains 465
Kara Kum Desert 197
Karate 427
Kariba Dam 776
Kendo 427
Kennecott copper mine, Utah *446*
Kennedy, John Fitzgerald 382, **386**
Kentucky 386–387
Kenya 387, *387*
Kepler, Johannes 601
Kerosene *279*
Kestrel 248
Kettledrum 214
Key *see* **Lock and Key**
Keyboard *157*, 158
Khafre, pharoah *227*, 552
Khafre pyramid *227*
Khanbalik, China 75
Khartoum, Sudan 657
Khmers 636
Khrushchev, Nikita Sergeevitch 639
Khufu, pharaoh 552
Kidnapped (Stevenson) 652
Kidney 388, *388*
Kidney bean 69
Kigali, Rwanda 591
Kilimanjaro, Mt. 11, *13*
Killer whale 751, *751*
Kimberley, South Africa 446
Kinetic energy 235
Kinetoscope 461
King, Martin Luther 388, *388*
King Kong (film) *461*
Kingston, Jamaica 379
Kingstown, St. Vincent and the Grenadines 594
Kinshasa 777
Kipling, Rudyard *453*
Kiribati 389
Kirpan 617
Kiss, The (Brancusi) *603*
Kitchen *347*
Kithira, (Greek island) 38
Kitty Hawk 770
Kiwi 389, *483*
Klaproth, Martin Heinrich 716
Klondike River 776
Knickerbocker Baseball club of New York 66
Knight 331, *442*
Knights of St. John 418
Knossos *280*
Knot 389, *389*
Kodak camera 372
Kohlrabi *721*
Kolokol bell, Moscow 76
Koran 390
Korbut, Olga 318
Korea 390, *390*
Korolyev, Sergei 642
Kowloon, Hong Kong 343
Krakatoa volcano 735
Kremlin 391, *391*
Kuala Lumpur, Malaysia 418
Kublai Khan 391, *391*, *536*
Kung-fu 427
Kunyang Kish, Mt. 465
Kuwait 391, *391*
Kwakiuti tribe 30
Kwanto Plain earthquake 217
Kyrkesund, Sweden *664*

Ll

Laboratory *132*
Labrador retriever 209
Laccolith *735*
Lactic acid 3
Ladoga, Lake 243
Ladybug 75, 369, *369*
Laika 643
Lake 392, *392*
Lake Havasu City, Arizona 98
Lammergeier *736*
Lamprey 725
Land bridge 126, 358
Land reclamation *477*
Language 392, *392*, 645
alphabet 25
English 238
Lantern fish *193*
Laos 48, **393,** *393*
La Palma Observatory *675*
La Paz, Bolivia 89
Lapland 393
Larva *369*
Laser 393–394, *393*
fiber optics 255–256, *255*
holography 340–341, *340*
Last of the Mohicans, The (Cooper) 167
Las Vegas 478
Lateen sail 284
Lateral line 261
Latex 590, *590*
Latin America 127
Latitude and Longitude 394–395
Latvia 63
Laughing hyena 357
Lava *33*, *735*
Law 395, *395*
Babylonian 57
Congress 160
constitution 164
Parliament 514
police 534, *534*
president 546
Lawnmower 349, 350
Lead 395, *395*, 716
Leaf 395–396, *396*, *698*
Leaf print 396
League of Nations 756
Lebanon 397, *397*
Leaning Tower of Pisa, Italy 104
Leather 396
Leatherback turtle 705
Leatherstocking 167
Leaves of Grass (Whitman) 754
Lebu earthquake 217
Lee, Robert E. 306, **397**
Leech 765
Leeuwenhoek, Anton van 440
Legate *589*
Legionary *589*
Le Monde 481
Length, measurement 748, 749
Lenin, Vladimir 397–398, *397*, *427*
Leningrad, siege of 70
Lens 398–399, *398*, 439, *440*, 674
Leo I, pope 53
Leonardo da Vinci *18*, *213*, **399–400,** *399*
Leonov, Alexei 643
Leopard 400, *400*
Leopard shark 613
Lesotho 401, *401*, *598*
Lesser burdock *745*
Letterpress printing 547
Lever 413
Leverrier, Urbain 476
Lewis, John L. *695*
Lewis and Clark expedition 714
Lexington 576
Lexington-Concord, battle of 70
Leyte Gulf, battle of 70
Lhotse, Mt. 465
Liberia 401, *401*
Liberty, Statue of 401–402
Liberty Bell 401
Liberty Island, New York 401
Library 402, *402*
Libreville, Gabon 282
Libya 402, *402*
Libyan Desert 197
Lichen 403, *403*, *535*
Liechtenstein 403, *403*
Life 80, *245*, *352*
Life expectancy 15
Light 403–404, *404*
color 149–150, *150*, 482
eye 247
fiber optics 255
laser 393–394, *393*
lens 398, *398*
quantum 554
spectrum 644–645
speed of 444, 569, *569*
ultraviolet 707, *707*
Lighthouse of Pharos 611, *611*
Lightning 183, 220, **404–405,** *405*, 684
Lightning rod *685*
Light year 404
Lilienthal's glider *18*
Lilliput 665
Lilongwe, Malawi 417
Lima, Peru 519
Lima bean 69
Limestone 122, *122*, 128, 582, *583*

Limey 734
Limpet *449*
Lincoln, Abraham 141, **405,** *711*
Lindbergh, Charles 405–406, *406*
Lincoln Memorial *711*
Linnaeus 92
Lion 406, *406*
Lippershey, Hans 50, 675
Liquid *52*, 288, **406–407**
Liquid measure 749
Lisbon, Portugal 539
Lisbon earthquake 217
Lister, Joseph 407
Listeria 59
Literature *see* **Novel; Poetry; Science Fiction**
Lithium 437
Lithuania 63
Litmus paper 4
Little Bighorn, battle of the 183, 454
Little Mermaid, The (Andersen) 31
Little Rock-North Little Rock, Arkansas 44
Little Women (Alcott) 23
Liver 407
Liverpool and Manchester Railway 563
Livingstone, Robert R. *192*
Livingstone, David 12, 417
Lizard *198*, **407,** *407*, *575*, *607*
  see also **Chameleon**
Llama 408, *408*
Lobster *179*, *259*, **408,** *408*, *620*
Local Group galaxy *282*
Lock (canal) *114*, 511
Lock and Key 408–409, *409*
Locomotive 202, 562, *562*, 563, *651*
Locust 369, *369*, **409**
Lodestone 416
Lodge (beaver) 73
Logging *48*
Lombardy plain, Italy 377
Lomé, Togo 689
Londinium 410
London *41*, *304*, **409–410,** *409*, 526
London Bridge 98
London fog 267
Long distance running 693
Long-eared owl *505*
Longfellow, Henry Wadsworth 410
Longhouse 348
Longitude *see* **Latitude and Longitude**
Long March 422
Long-tailed duck 215
Long waves 404
Loom 744, *744*, 745
Loosestrife *745*
Lop-eared rabbit *557*
Lord Protector *see* **Cromwell, Oliver**
Los Angeles 410, *410*
Loudspeaker 411, *411*
Louis (French kings) 61, 178, 276, **411, 724,** *724*
Louisiana 411
Louisiana Purchase 28, 43, 373, 380, **411–412**
Louisiana Superdome, New Orleans 210
Louse *368*, 369
Louvre, the 513
Lovebird 514
Lower Keys Wildlife Refuge *265*
Low frequency 632
LSD 7
Luanda, Angola 32
Lucian of Samosata 601
Luftwaffe 16
Lugworm *606*, *765*
Lumière brothers 461
Luna spacecraft 457, 643
Lung 412, *412*
Lungfish 260, *260*
Lungs 96, *96*
Lusaka 778
Luther, Martin 412, 549
Lutherans 549
Luxembourg 412, *412*
Luxor, Egypt *40*
Lymphocyte *see* White cell
Lynx *120*

Mm

McAdam, John 581
Macadamia nut 494
Macaroni penguin *517*
Macaulay, Lord 338
Macaw 514
Macedonians 776
Mach 662
Machine (simple) 413, *413*
  pulley 550, *550*
  screw 603
Mackinac Bridge, Michigan 439
McKinley, Mt. *20*
McKinley, William 414
Mackintosh, Charles Rennie *281*
Madagascar 414, *414*
Mad Hatter 116
Madison 760
Madison, James 414
Madrid 641
Mafeking, siege of 88
Magellan, Ferdinand 415, *415*
Magen David *567*
Maggot 267
Magic 415–416, 761
Magic flute, The (Mozart) *501*
Magma *735*
Magnesium 496
Magnetic field 416, 661, 669
Magnetism *157,* **416,** *416*, 463, *464*
Magnetite 416
Magnification 57, 399, *399*, 439
Maiman, Theodor 372
Maine 416–417
Maine (battleship) 644
Maize 250
Major, John 681
Malabo, Equatoiral Guinea 239
Malaria 417
Malawi 417, *417*
Malaysia 418, *418*
Maldives 418, *418*
Malé, Maldives 418
Mali 418, *419*
Mallard (locomotive) *562*
Mallard duck *215*
Malta 418–419, *419*
Mammals 94, *245*, **419–420,** *420*
  carnivore 115
  hair 319
  marsupial 426, *426*
  prehistoric 544–545, *545*
  reproduction 225, 573
Mammoth 420–421, *420*, *545*
Man *see* **Human Beings**
Managua, Nicaragua 484
Manama, Bahrain 60
Manaslu, Mt. 465
Mandarin duck *215*
Mandrill monkey *453*
Manet, Edouard 362
Mangla dam 186
Manitoba *113*, **421**
Mantle, Earth's 218
Maoris 421, *421*
Mao Tse-Tung 422, *422*
Map and Chart 291, **422–423,** *422–423*
  atlas 51
  latitude and longitude 394–395, *394*
Maputo, Mozambique 465, 466
Maracaibo, lake 634
Marat, Jean Paul 276
Marathon Race 70, **423,** *423*, *693*
Marble 423–424, *424*, *583*
March (month) 425
Marconi, Guglielmo 424, *424*
Marco Polo *see* Polo, Marco
Mares tails *148*
Margarine 424–425
Marianas Trench 219
Marie Antoinette 425, *425*
Marijuana 7
Mariner space probe *435*
Mark Antony 142
Marmot 332, *585*
Marne, battle of 70
Marram grass *607*
Mars (God) 425
Mars (Planet) 425–426, *426*, 642
Marsupial *420*, **426,** *426*
  see also **Kangaroo; Opossum**
Martel, Charles 443
Martial Arts 426–427, *427*
Marx, Karl 427, *427*
Mary, Queen of Scots 428, *428*
Maryland 428
Masai tribe 388
Maseru, Lesotho 401
Masked crab *606*
Mass 430
Massachusetts 429, *429*
Massachusetts Institute of Technology (M.I.T.) 91
Matchless bicycle *79*
Mastedon *420*
Masters degree 713
Mathematics 429, 431
  see also **Algebra; Geometry**
Matter 430, *430*
  see also **Gas; Liquid**
Maui Island *714*
Mauna Loa 464, 610
Mauritania 430, *430*
Mauritius 208, **430–431,** *431*
Mausolus 610
Maya *311*, **431–432,** *431*
Mayflower (ship) *27*, 714
Mayfly *368*
Mbabane, Swaziland 664
Measles 367
Measures *see* **Weights and Measures**
Meat *172*
Mecca 432, *432*
Mechanical energy 235
Mechanical engineer 237
Medicine 84, **432,** 255
  acupuncture 6, *6*
  antibiotics 35
  Jenner 381
  laser 394
  Lister 407
  nursing 494
  surgery 662, *662*
  thermometer *683*
  see also **Disease**
Medicine man *28*
Medina, Libya *402*
Mediterranean Sea 433, *433*
Medulla *94*
Melbourne, Australia 53, 166
Melody 468
Melville, Herman 434, 667
Memory 550
Memory (RAM and ROM) *157*
Menai Bridge, Wales 98
Menakaure, pharaoh 552
Mendel, Gregor 434, *434*
Menelaus, King of Sparta 329, 697
Menorah *570*
Mental illness 276
Mercator, Gerhardus 51
Merchant *443*
Mercury (God) 434, *434*
Mercury (Metal) 434–435, *435*, 661, *682*, *683*
Mercury (Planet) 435, *435*
Mercury barometer 65
Meridian 395
Merino sheep 763
Merlin *248*
Mermaid 436, *436*
Messerschmitt *769*
Messiah (Handel) 321
Mestizos 89, 234, 438, 512
Metal 436–437, *436–437*
  alloy 25
  prehistoric people 543
  welding 746–747
  wire 759
  see also the individual metals
Metallurgical engineer 237
Metamorphic rock 582
Meteor 437, *437*
Meteorite 437
Methodists 549
Metric System 437, 748–749
Mexican War 535, 671
Mexico 438, *438*
  Aztecs 55, *55*, 170, *170*
Mexico City, Mexico 438

INDEX

Miami 265
Mica dam 186
Michelangelo 438, *438*, 720, *720*
Michigan 439, *439*
Michigan, Lake 307
Mickey Mouse 206, *206*
Microcircuit 618
Microphone 439, *439*, 674
Microscope 57, **439–440,** *440*, 432
Mid-Atlantic Ridge 50
Middle Ages *50*, 281, 338, *338*, **440. 442–443,** 442–443
architecture *139*
armor 44
art 44, 90, *90*
bridge 96
castle 119–120, *118–119*
crusades 177–178, *177*
food 516, 525
heraldry 331, *331*
hospital 346
painting 508
science 22, *22*, 57
spices 646
stained glass 300
Middle English *131*
Middle Stone Age 654
Midgarth 731
Midway, battle of 70
Migration *42*, 107, **440–441,** *440–441*
Mile 748
Milk *172*, **441, 444,** *441*
Milky Way *283*, **444–445,** *445*
Millet *127*
Mime 61
Mineral 445, *445*, 497
Minerals *see* **Vitamins and Minerals**
Mineral oil 498
Ming dynasty 137
Mining 446, *446*
Mining engineer 237
Minnesota 446–447
Minoans 308
Mint *331*
Miocene period *245*
Mir (space station) *640*
Mirim, lake 634
Mirror 447, *447*, 675, *676*, 725
Missile *see* **Guided Missile**
Mississippi 448, *448*
Mississippi River *195*, **448,** *581*, 706
Missouri 448–449, *449*
M.I.T. *see* Massachusetts Institute of Technology
Mitochondria *124*
Mobile, Alabama 20
Mobile Bay, Alabama 20
Moby Dick (Melville) 434
Mocha, Yemen 775
Model T Ford 270, *270*
Mogadishu, Somalia 630
Mohave Desert 197
Molar 673
Molecule *52*
Mollusk 449–450, *449*, *614*
see also **Octopus; Oyster**
Molting 178, 253
Moluccas 646
Monaco 450, *450*
Monaco-Ville, Monaco 450
Mona Lisa (Leonardo da Vinci) 399, *399*
Monarch butterfly 107, *107*, *440*
Monarchy 196, 575
Monastery *442*, **450,** *685*
Monet, Claude 45, *361*, 362
Money 451, *451*
coin 149, *149*
inflation 366
Mongolia 451–452, *452*
Mongoloid race 518, *518*
Mongols 452, *452*
Genghis Khan 290–291, *290–291*
Kublai Khan 391, *391*
Mongoose 453, *453*
Monkey *245*, **453,** *453*
Monocotyledons *92*
Monoplane *85*
Monorail *206*, *562*
Mono recording 567
Monroe, James 454
Monroe Doctrine 454
Monrovia, Liberia 401
Monsoon 365, **454**
Montana 454, *454*
Mont Blanc 26
Monte Cassino, Italy 450
Montevideo 717
Montezuma 55
Montgolfier brothers 19, 62, *62*
Montgomery, Alabama 20, 388
Monticello 732, *732*
Montpelier 724
Montreal, Canada 112
Monument Valley *715*
Moon 455, *455*, **456–457,** *456–457*
eclipse 221, *221*
gravity 307
phases 456
tide 686, *686*
Moon buggy *457*
Moon landing 29, 643
Moon rocket 642
Moore, Henry 604
Morgan, Henry 750
Mormon 455, 717
Morocco *185*, **455,** *455*
Moroni, Comoros 156
Morphine 7
Morse, Samuel F. B. 372, 455
Morse Code *155*, **455**
Mortgage 349
Mosaic *23*, **455–456,** *456*
Moscow 458, *458*
Kremlin 391, *391*
Moselle River *243*
Moses 328, 384
Moskva River 458
Mosque 162, *162*, *376*, *703*
Mosquito 459, *459*
Moss *271*, *403*, **459,** *459*
Motel 347
Moth 460, *460*, 625
Motion *482*, 569
Motion Pictures 461–462, *461–462*
cartoon 117, *117*
Motor, Electric 463–464, *463–464*
Motorcycle 462–463, *462–463*, *753*
Motor nerve *476*
Mouflon sheep *613*
Mountain 144, 241, **464–465,** *464*, 561
formation 219
underwater 50
see also **Volcano**
Mount Vernon 739
Mourne, Mountains of *490*
Mouse *23*, *245*, 419, **465,** *465*
Mouth 691, *692*
Movable type 316
Mozambique 465–466, *466*
Mozart, Wolfgang Amadeus 466, *501*
Mud hut *349*
Mudskipper 261
Muhammad 376, 390, *432*, **466**
Muller, Bertha *726*
Multistage rocket 583
Mummy *56*, 227
Murders in the Rue Morgue, The (Poe) 532
Murfreesboro, Arkansas 44
Muscat, Oman 500
Muscle 466, *466*
Muscovy 458
Mushroom and Toadstool 467, *467*
Music 467–468, *467–468*
jazz 380
pop 538, *538*
Musical Instrument 468–469, *469*
Muslim: countries 10, 12, *12*, 38, 225, 455; crusades 177; Islam 376; Mecca 432, *432;* world membership 570
Mussel *449*
Mussolini, Benito 252, *252*, **470,** *470*
Mustang aircraft *767*
Myanmar 105
Mycelium *280*
Mycenaeans 39, 308
Myth 470, *470*
German 737
Viking 731

Nn

Nacre *506*
Nagasaki 768
Nairobi, Kenya *12, 387*
Nail and Claw 471, *471*
Nakwakto Rapids 496
Namibia 471, *471*
Nanak 617
Nanga Parbat, Mt. 465
Napoleon Bonaparte 471–472, *472*
Napoleonic Wars 414
Nashville 677
Natchez, Mississippi *448*
National Hockey League 340
National League 66
National Parks 305, *305*, **472–473,** *473*
Native Americans *see* **American Indians**
NATO (North Atlantic Treaty Organization) 473, *473*
Natterjack toad *333*, *607*
Natty Bumppo 167
Natural Gas *279*, *288*, **473–474**
Nauru 474, *474*
Nautilus (nuclear submarine) *657*
Navajo Indians *715*
Nave 139, *139*
Navigation 423, **474,** *474*, *497*
Nazis 339, 766
N'Djamena, Chad 128
Neanderthal man *123*, *264*, 543, *542*
Neapolitan Fisherboy (Carpeaux) *603*
Neap tide 686
Nebraska 474–475, *712*
Nebuchadnezzar, King 610, *611*
Negative (film) 522
Negroid race 518
Nehru, Jawaharlal 286
Nelson, Horatio *592*
Nemean lion 332
Nepal 475, *475*
Neptune 475–476, *475*
Nero 588
Nerve 476, *476*, 507, *507*
Nest 477, *477*
Netherlands 477–478, *477–478*
Neutron 52, 493, 554
Neutron star 84, 551, *551*
New Brunswick *113*, **478–479**
Newcomen, Thomas 652
New Cornelia dam 186
New Delhi, India 363
Newfoundland *113*, **479**
New Hampshire 479
New Jersey 479–480
New Mexico 480–481
New moon 456
New Orleans 210, 411
New River Gorge Bridge, West Virginia 98
Newspaper *392*, **481,** *480*
New Stone Age 654
Newt *31*, *333*
New Territories 342
Newton, Isaac 320, 404, **482,** *482*, 644
New York 482, 623
New York City 482–483, *483*, 662
New York Times 481
New Zealand 483–484, *483*, 421, *421*
Niagara Falls 484, *484*
Niamey, Niger 485
Nicaragua 485, *484*
Nicosia, Cyprus 183
Niepce, Joseph 372
Niger 485, *485*
Niger River 485
Nigeria 485, *485*
Night *see* **Day and Night**
Nightjar 82
Nijinsky, Vaslav 189
Nile River *13*, *226*, **486,** *486*
Nimes, France *40*
Niña (ship) 152

Nirvana 102
Nitrate 684
Nitric acid 3,4
Nitrogen 15
Nixon, Richard Milhous 270, **486**
Nkomo, Joshua *14*
Nobel, Alfred 487, *487*
Nobel Prize 487, *487*
Nomad 208, *240*, 290, 373, 393, 430, 452, 500, 630, 666, 744
Nome, Alaska 21
Norgay, Tenzing 243
Normandy landings 191, *191*, *767*
Norman style *755*
North America 30, *30*, **487–489**
North Atlantic Drift *314*
North Atlantic lobster 178
North Atlantic Treaty Organization *see* **NATO**
North Cape, Norway 243
North Carolina 489, *489*
North Dakota 489–490
Northern Hemisphere 239
Northern Ireland 490, *490*
Northern Rhodesia *see* **Zambia**
North Korea *see* **Korea**
North Pole 244, *246*, 394, **490,** 607
  see also **Arctic**
Northwest Territories *113*, **490–491,** *491*, 498
Norway *258*, **491,** *491*, 767
Norway spruce *160*
Nötre Dame cathedral, Paris *41*, 513
Nouakchott, Mauritania 430
Noun 491
Nova Scotia *113*, 491–492, *492*
Novel 492
  Brontë 99, *99*
  Dickens 200, *200*
  science fiction 600–601, *600*
  Scott 602, *602*
  Stevenson 652
  Swift 664–665, *665*
  Thoreau 684
  Tolstoy 690
  Twain 706
Nuclear chain reaction 254
Nuclear Energy 183, **492–493,** *492–493*, 560, 650
  atomic bomb 766
  Einstein 228
  Fermi 254
  submarine 657, *656*
  sun 660
  weapons 16, 386, 480
Nucleic acids 80
Nuku'alofa, Tonga 690
Number 493–494
  binary 79, *79*, 158
  fraction 273
Nuptse, Mt. 465
Nurek dam 186
Nureyev, Rudolf 189
Nurmi, Paavo 693
Nursing 494
Nut 494, *494*
Nuthatch 82
Nutmeg *646*
Nutrition 252, **494, 721**
  fat 252–253, *252*
  protein 548, *548*
  vitamins and minerals 733–734
Nyasaland, Protectorate of *see* **Malawi**
Nylon 666, 680
Nymph *369*

Oo

Oahe dam 186
Oak 495, *495*, *698*
Oasis 495, *495*
Oats *127*, 250
Oberlin College 760
Occluded front 743
Ocean 495–497, *496–497*
  floor *165*, 193, *193*
  tide 686, *686*
  wave 218, 742
  see also **Atlantic Ocean; Pacific Ocean**
Ocellated lizard *407*
Octavian 142
Octopus 497, *497*, 620
Oder River 294
Odysseus *see* **Ulysses**
Odyssey (Homer) *341*, *342*, 708
Offset lithography printing 548, *547*
Ohio 498
Ohio River 750
Oil 38, 207, *279*, *288*, 374, **498–499,** *498*, 598
Oil tanker 615
Okefenokee National Wildlife Refuge, Folkston, Georgia *293*
Oklahoma 499
Okra *721*
Olaf, King of Norway 730
Old Stone Age 654
Old Testament 78, *78*
Oligocene period *245*
Olive 499, *499*
Oliver Twist (Dickens) *200*
Olympia, Washington 738
Olympic Games *390*, **500,** 505
Olympus, Mount 310
Oman 500, *500*
Ontario *113*, **500**
Ontario, Lake 307, *307*
Open-field farming 250
Opera 501, *501*, 737
Operation *see* **Surgery**
Operetta 501
Opinion Poll 501
Opium 7
Opium Wars 137
Oporto, Portugal 539
Opossum 502, *502*
Optical microscope *440*
Optical telescope 50
Orangutan 502
Orbit *153*, **502,** *502*
Orb spider *647*
Orchestra 502
Ordovician period *245*
Ore 446
Oregon 503–504
Oregon Trail 448, 504, *712*
Origami 339
Origin of Species, On the (Darwin) 186
Orinoco River 632
Orkneys 601
Ornithischian dinosaur 203
Oroville dam 186
Orrery, The (Wright) *599*
Oseberg ship *731*
Osiris *470*
Oslo 491
Osmium 437
Ostrich *11*, **504**
Ostrich dinosaur *204*
Ottawa *113*, **504,** *504*
Ottawa River 504
Otter 504–505, *504*
Otter trawl *259*
Ottoman Empire 162, 402, 704
Ouagadougou, Burkina Faso 105
Output *157*
Outrigger canoe *88*
Ovary *297*, *573*
Oven bird *477*
Oven thermometer 682
Ovule *266*
Ovum *see* **Egg**
Owens, Jesse 505
Owl *245*, **505,** *505*
Ox *251*
Oxbow lake *392*
Oxyacetylene welding *747*
Oxygen 96, 231, **506**
  liquid 584
Oyster 506, *506*
Oyster catcher 83
Ozarks 449
Ozone Layer 506

Pp

Pacific Ocean 60, 496, **507**
Paddy 578
Pagoda *105*
Pain 507, *507*
Pain receptor 692
Paint 508, *508*
Painted Desert, Arizona 43
Painting 508–509, *508–509*
  cartoon 117
  Impressionism 361–362, *361*
Pakistan 509, *509*
Palace of Westminster, London *304*
Paleocene period *245*
Palestine 509–510
Palm 510, *510*
Pampas 43
Panama *262*, **510–511,** *511*
Panama Canal *114*, 587
Panama City, Panama 510
Pancreas *297*, 203
Panda *477*, *137*, **511**
Panic of 1837 719
Pantheon, Rome 210
Panther 400
Papageno *501*
Papeete, Tahiti 667
Paper 113, *161*, 372, **511–512,** *511*
Papua New Guinea 512, *512*
Papyrus *87*, 90, 511
Parachute jumping *see* **skydiving**
Paraguay 512, *512*
Paraguay River 512
Parakeet 514
Paramaribo, Surinam 662
Parasite 513, *513*
Parathyroid gland 297
Parchment 90
Paris 243, *274*, **513**
Paris, Prince of Troy 329, 697
Paris, Treaty of 577
Park, Mungo 12
Parliament *304*, **514,** *514*
Parliament buildings, Ottawa 504
Parlor bed *281*
Parr *594*
Parrot 514, *514*
Parrot fish *260*
Parthenon *5*, 6, **514–515,** *515*
Partridge *541*
Pascal, Blaise 109, *109*
Passage to India, A (film) *461*
Passover 515, *515*
Pasteur, Louis 254, **515**
Pasteurization 515
Patagonia 43
Pavlova, Anna 189
Pea 721, *721*
Peace Tower, Ottawa 504
Peacock 516, *516*
Peafowl 516
Peanut *494*
Pearl 450, *506*
Pearl Harbor, Hawaii 324, *766*
Peary, Robert *246*
Peasant *442*
Peel, Robert 534
Peking *see* **Beijing**
Pemba *see* **Tanzania**
Pendulum 145, **516,** *516*
Penelope (Ulysses' wife) 708
Penguin 516–517, *517*
Penicillin 35, *58*, 264
Penn, William 195, 517, 520
Pennsylvania 517
Penny farthing bicycle 79
People of the World 518, *518*
  ancestors 542–543, *542–543*
  life expectancy 15
  species 351–352
People's Democratic Republic of Yemen *see* **Yemen**
Perch *573*
Percussion instrument 469, *469*
Peregrine falcon *198*
Perestroika 302
Perfume 518
Pericles 50
Permian period *245*
Perseus (Cellini) *572*
Persia *see* **Iran**
Persian carpet 116
Perth, Australia 53
Peru 518–519, *519*, 744
  Incas 362, *362*
Peter I 639
Peter the Great 458
Petrified Forest, Arizona 43
Petroleum *see* **Oil**
Pewter 25, 395, *688*
Pharaoh 227, **519–520, 519, 705**

INDEX

Pharos of Alexandria 39, 611, *611*
Phases (sun) *723*
Pheidippides *423*
Philadelphia 520
Philadelphia mint 149
Philip Augustus of France 178
Philip of Macedon 23
Philosopher's stone 22
Philosophy 521
Phnom Penh, Kampuchea 385
Phobos 426
Phoenicians 12, 244, 397, 433, *603*, 688
Phoenix, Arizona 43
Phonograph 224, *224*
Photocopying 521, *521*
Photography *141*, *175*, **521–522,** *521*
  aerial *423*
  camera 111, *111*
  film 367, *367*
Photon 554
Photosynthesis 135, 531
Physics 522–523, *522*
  Einstein 228
  Newton 482, *482*
Phytoplankton 526
Piano 322, **523,** *523*
Picasso, Pablo *45*, 213, **523–524,** *523*
Picts 125
Picture writing 155
Pierce, Franklin 524
Piero della Francesca *381*
Pierre, South Dakota 635
Pietri, Dorando 423
Pig *245*, **524–525,** *524*
Pigeon and Dove 525
Pig iron *375*
Pike *222*
Pilgrim Settlers *27*, **525**
Pilgrim's Progress, The (Bunyan) *548*
Pilot fish 261
Pine see *Conifer*
Pineapple 525, *525*
Pinta (ship) 152
Pintail duck 215
Pinyin 137
Pioneer 10 643
Pissarro, Camille 362
Pistil 266
Pistol *315*, 316
Piston 372, 372, *382, 552,* 651, *652*
Pituitary gland *297*, 344
Placental animals 420, *420*
Plague 264, 410, 443, 482, **526**
Plains Indians *28*, *83*
Plane mirror 447
Planet 526, *527*, *599*, 629–630
  asteroid 49, *49*
  orbit 502, *502*
  see also the individual planets
Plankton 526, *526*
Plant 528, 530–531, *530–531*
  Arctic 40
  botany 92, *92*
  bud 101, *101*
  bulb 104, *104*
  cell *124*
  chlorophyll 135
  classification *92*
  Europe 241
  fertilizer 255
  flower 266, *266*
  food chain 269, *268*
  fruit 278, *278*
  leaf 395–296, *296*
  Mendel 434, *434*
  North America 487
  parasite 513, *513*
  poisonous 533
  pruning 549, *549*
  recycling *80*
  reproduction 572
  seashore 608–609, *609*
  weed 745, *745*
Plantain *721*, *745*
Plantation 27
Plasma 86
Plastic 528, *528*, *535*
Plastic surgery *662*
Plata River 634
Platelets *85*, 86
Plates, Earth's 165, 735
Plato 528–529
Platypus 529, *529*
Plesiosaur *544*
Pleistocene period *245*
Pliny the Younger 536
Pliocene period *245*
Plow *102*, 250, *251*
Plumule *609*
Pluto 529, 532, *529*
Pluto (god) 310
Plutonium *230*
Plymouth Colony 27
Plywood *763*
Poe, Edgar Allan 532
Poetry 232, **532–533,** *532*, 754, *754*, 765
Poison 533, *533*, 536
Poland 534, *534*
Polar bear *72*
Polar region *144*, 497, 506, 608
  see also **Antarctic; Arctic; North Pole; South Pole**
Polaroid camera *155*
Police 534, 534
Polio 360, 367
Polk, James Knox, 535
Pollination *266*, 530
Pollution 535, *535*
  acid rain 4, *4*
  air 288, *410*, 626, *626*
  water 740
Polo, Marco 535–536, *536*
Polonium 182
Polyethylene 528
Polynesians 690, 706
Polypody *254*
Pompeii *23*, **536–537,** *537*, 726
Pompey 109
Pont du Gard *40*, *588*
Poopo, lake 634
Pope 537, *537*, 720, *720*
Pop Music 538, *538*
Polio vaccine 432
Population 538–539, *539*, 689
  birth control 83
  census 125
Porcelain 540
Porcupine 539
Porcupine fish 261, *697*
Porpoise *see* **Dolphin and Porpoise**
Port (wine) 539
Port-au-Prince, Haiti 319
Port Moresby, Papua New Guinea 512
Port of Spain, Trinidad and Tobago 696
Porto-Novo, Benin 77
Portugal 12, **539,** *539*, *563*
Port Vila, Vanuatu 720
Poseidon 310
Potato 518, **540**
Potato bug *75*
Potato planter *251*
Potential energy 235, *235*
Pottery *142*, **540–541,** *540*, *753*
Pouch 420, 426
Poultry *251*, **541,** *541*
  see also **Ostrich; Peacock; Pigeon**
Power Plant 541–542, *541*, 661
  see also **Hydroelectric Power**
Prague, Czechoslovakia 184
Praia, Cape Verde 115
Prairie dog 648, *648*
Pravda 481
Praying mantis *368*
Precambrian period *245*
Prehistoric Animals 542, 544–545, *544–545*
Prehistoric People 87, **542–543,** *542–543*, 555
  art 44, *45*, 155, *603*
  cave dweller 123, *123*, 421
  fire 258
  food 69, 194, 267, 614
  Stone Age 653–654, *653*
  Stonehenge 654, *654*
  tools 99, 100, *542*
  see also **Bronze Age; History**
Presbyterian 543, 546, *543*
President of the United States 546–547, *546*
  see also **White House**
Presley, Elvis *538*
Pride and Prejudice (Austen) 53
Priestley, Joseph 590
Primates 420
Prince Edward Island *113*, **547**
Printing 547–548, *547*
  Gutenberg 316, *316*
Prism 404, *404*, 644
Probe (space) 640, 643, *643*
Progesterone 297
Promised Land 328
Promontory, Utah *28*
Propeller 652, *656*
Propylaea *5*
Protein 69, **548,** *548*
Protestant 412, 548–549, 548
  Baptist 64
  Presbyterian 543-544, *543*
  Quaker 554
  Reformation 567–568
  world membership 570
Prothallus *255*
Proton 52, 554
Proverb 549
Providence, Rhode Island 578
Provincetown, Massachusetts *429*
Pruning 549, *549*
Psychiatry 550
Psychoanalysis 276
Psychology 371, *371*, **549–550**
Pterosaur 203, *545*
Ptolomey I 39
Ptolemy of Alexandria 291
Puerto Rico 550, *550*, 561, *747*
Pulley 550–551, *550–551*
Pullman sleeping car 563
Pulsar 551
Pulse 551
Pump 552, *552*
Punic Wars 588
Pupa *33*, *369*
Puritans *see* Pilgrims
Purple loosestrife *745*
Purse-net spider *647*
Purse seine fishing *259*
Puss moth *460*
Pyongyang, North Korea 390
Pyramid 227, 237, **552–553,** *552*, *610*
Pyrenees 553, *553*
Python 553, *553*, *627*

Qq

Qaddafi, Muammar al- 402
Qatar *262*, **554,** *554*
Quaker 554
Quantum 554
Quark 554–555
Quarrying *424*, **555,** *555*
Quartz 556, *556*
Quasars 556
Quebec *113*, **556**
Quebec rail bridge, Canada 98
Queen Alexandra birdwing butterfly 107
Queen ant *33*, 34
Queen bee 74, *74*
Queensberry, Marquess of 93
Quicksilver *see* **Mercury (Metal)**
Quito, Ecuador 223
Qumran caves *78*

Rr

R34 airship 63
Rabat, Morocco 455
Rabbit *14*, *245*, **557,** *557*
Raccoon 557, *557*
Race 518
Racism 204
Radar 312, *312*, **557–558,** *558*
Radial artery 551
Radiant energy 236
Radicle *609*
Radio *230*, **558–559,** *558–559*
  Marconi 424, *424*
  waves 51, 283, 551, 556, 560
Radioactivity 182, 395, **559–560,** *559–560*
Radio astronomy 560–561, *560–561*
Radio beams *see* **Radar**
Radiocarbon Dating 561
Radiologist *772*
Radio telescope 561, *560*
Radio waves 673
Radium 182
Rafflesia 513

Raft 87, *87*, 88
Ragworm *765*
Raiders of the Lost Ark (film) *462*
Railroad *28*, **561–563,** *562–563*
bridge 97, 98
diesel 202
high-speed 661
overhead *379*
wheel *753*
Rain 561, 564, 564
acid 4
cloud 147, *743*
Rainbow *404*, **564, 644**
Rainbow Natural Bridge 610
Rain forest 11, 95, *634*
Raleigh, Walter 565, *565*
Ramapithecus 542
Ramjet 382
Rangoon, Myanmar 105
Ras al-Khaimah 709
Rat *245*, **565,** *565*
Rat kangaroo 385
Rattlesnake 627
Raven, The (Poe) 532
Rayon 680
Razor shell *606*
Re *470*
Reaction engine 381
Reagan, Ronald Wilson 107, 117, *338*, **565–566**
Receptor 692
Recessive gene *290*
Recife, Brasil 95
Reciprocating pump 552, *552*
Recorder *469*
Recording *155*, 224, *224*, *411*, **566–567,** *566*
Rectangle *749*
Recycling *80*
Red cell *85*, 86, 87
Red Crescent *567*
Red Cross *263*, **567,** *567*
Red dwarf *650*
Red-eared terrapin *575*
Red fox 272
Red giant *649*, 650, *660*
Red kangaroo 385
Red panda 511
Red Planet *see* **Mars**
Red Sea 567, *567*
Redshirts 287
Red Square, Moscow *391*
Red squirrel *648*
Redwood tree 92, *698*
Reef, coral 169, *169*
Reflecting telescope 482, 675
Reformation 567–568
Luther 412, 549
Refractor telescope 674, *674*
Refrigerator 349, 568–569, 568
Refrigerator ship 615
Regina, Saskatchewan 597
Reign of Terror 276
Reindeer moss *403*
Reinforced concrete 159
Relativity 569–570, *569*
Relay race 694
Relief printing 547
Religion 570, *570*
crusades 177–178, *177*
discrimination 204
monastery 450
Mormon 455
Presbyterian 543–544, *543*
Reformation 567–568
Religious wars 568
Rembrandt 571, *571*
Rempart Mountains *431*
Renaissance 571–572, *571*
architecture 41, *41*
art 44, 45
biology 80
garden 287
Leonardo da Vinci 399–400, *399*
Reno 478
Renoir, Pierre Auguste 45, 362
Reproduction *255*, 297, **572–574,** *574–575*
see also **Genetics**
Reptile *245*, **574–575**
see also **Alligator and Crocodile; Lizard; Snake; Tortoise; Turtle and Terrapin**
Republic 304, **575**
Republic, The (Plato) 520
Reservoir 185
Restoration (of paintings) *508*
Reticulated python *553*
Retina 247, *247*, *398*
Revolutionary War 576–577, *576–577*
Boston Tea Party 91
Constitution 164
Reykjavik, Iceland 359
Rhine, River 294
Rhinoceros *245*, **577–578,** *577*
Rhode Island 578, *578*
Rhodesia 776
Rhizoid *459*
Rhythm 468
Rib cage *96*, *412*
Rice *127*, 268, **578,** *578*
Richard (kings) 578–579
Richmond, Virginia 732
Rickenbacker, Eddie *764*
Rideau River 504
Riding, Horseback 579–580, *579*, 585
Rikki-Tikki-Tavi *453*
Rime frost 278
Ring of fire, the 735
Ring of the Nibelung, The (Wagner) 737, *737*
Ring o' roses 526
Rio de Janeiro, Brazil *95*, *684*
River *392*, **580,** *580*
delta 195, *195*
see also **Amazon; Mississippi; Nile**
Riyadh, Saudi Arabia 598
Road 581, *581*, *663*
Robespierre, Maximilien 276
Robot 581–582, *582*
Robson, Mount *584*
Rock 218, **582–583,** *583*
early formation 473
Ice Age *358*
quarrying 555, *555*
Rock dove 525
Rocket *20*, **583–584,** *584*, 641, *641*
Rocket (Stephenson's) *562*, 563
Rocket plane 19
Rocky Mountains *112*, 150, **584,** *584*, 717, 769
Rodent 584–585, *585*
see also **Beaver; Mouse; Porcupine; Rat**
Rodeo 585
Roentgen, Wilhelm 770
Roller skating *see* **Skating**
Roman Catholic Church *438*, **585–586,** *585*
pope 537, 720, *720*
reformation 567
saint 593, *593*
St. Bartholomew's Day Massacre *548*
world membership 570
Roman Empire 12, 273, 433, 575, **586, 588–589,** *588–589*
abbreviations 2
architecture 40, *40*, 210
book 90
bridge 96, *97*, 98
Caesar 108, *108*
census 125
circus 140, 151–152, *151*
Cleopatra 142
clothing 146, *146*
cosmetics 170
gladiator 297, *297*
house 349
Londinium *409*
magistrate 200
mosaic 458
Pompeii 536–537, *537*
road 581, *581*
theater 682
Romanesque style 40,139
Romania 586, *586*
Roman numeral 494
Romany language 318
Rome 586, *586*, 588, 720, *720*
Romulus and Remus 425, 586
Roosevelt, Franklin Delano 29, **587,** *587*
Roosevelt, Theodore 587, *587*
Rope bridge 96
Roseau, Dominica 211
Rosemary *331*
Rosenborg Castle, Copenhagen 177
Rosetta Stone 333
Rotary cultivator *251*
Rotary pump *552*
Rotor 329, *329*
Rotterdam 477
Rowing 587
Royal standard *263*
Rub'al Khali Desert 197
Rubber 590, *590*
Rugs *see* **Carpets and rugs**
Rushmore, Mount 590, *590*
Russell, Charles M. *173*
Russia 591, 638
Russian Revolution 427, 638
Russo-Japanese War 639
Rwanda 591, *591*
Rye *127*

Ss

Saber-toothed tiger 421
Sacré Coeur, basilica of the *274*, 513
Saddle-bronco riding 585
Sahara Desert *11*, *13*, *197*, **592**
Saigon 729
Sail-backed reptile *245*, *544*, *574*
Sailing 592–593, *592*
galleon 284, *284*
record 87
speed 87
Sailplane 298
Saint 593, *593*
St. Augustine, Florida 27
St. Basil's Cathedral, Moscow *391*, *458*
St. Bartholomew's Day Massacre *548*
St. Benedict 450
St. Bernard dog 209
St. Edward's crown *176*
St. Francis of Assisi *593*
St. Francis driving out the devils (Giotto) *44*
St. George *212*
St. George's, Grenada 311
St. Helena, island 472
St. John's, Antigua and Barbuda 36
St. Kitts and Nevis 593, *593*
St. Lawrence, River 112, 307
St. Louis, Missouri *449*, *581*
St. Lucia 594, 594
St. Nazaire Bridge, France 98
St. Paul's Cathedral 41, *768*
St. Peter 537
St. Petersburg 458
St. Peter's Cathedral, Rome 438, *586*
Saint Sophia, Cathedral of 162
St. Stephen's Cathedral, Vienna 729
St. Vincent and the Grenadines 594, *594*
Sakkara 552
Saladin 178
Salamander *see* Amphibian
Salamis, battle of *70*
Salisbury Cathedral, Wiltshire, England *122*, 145
Salk, Jonas 432
Salmon *260*, **594,** *594*
Salote Tupou, Queen 690
Salt *181*, **595,** *595*
Salt Lake City 455, 717
Salyut 1 643
San'a, Yemen 775
San Andreas fault 110
Sand 595
Sand grouse *198*
Sandinista guerillas 485
Sand lizard *607*
Sandstone 595
San Francisco 595, *595*
San Francisco earthquake 217
San Gabriel Mountains 410
San José, Costa Rica 171
San Juan, Puerto Rico 550, *747*
San Marino 596, *596*
San Salvador, Bahamas 152
San Salvador, El Salvador 234
San Sebastiano, Italy 726
Santa Domingo, Dominican Republic 211
Santa Fe trial 448
Santa Maria (ship) 152, *152*
Santa Sophia church, Istanbul *40*

INDEX

Santiago, Chile 134, *626*
Santorini, Greece *308*, 735
Saõ Paulo, Brazil 95
São Tomé and Principe 596, *596*
Saratoga, battle of 577
Saskatchewan *113*, **596,** *597*
Satellite 596–597, *596*
  artifical 558, 640, *640*, *642*
  communications 156, 673
Saturn 597-598, *597*
Saudi Arabia 598, *598*
Saurischian dinosaur 203
Savaii Island 747
Savanna 11
Sawbill 215
Scallop *614*
Scalpel 662
Scaling ladder *118*
Scarlet Letter, The (Hawthorne) 324
Schönberg, Arnold 468
Schönbrunn Castle *728*
School 598, *598*
Science 599–600, *599–600*
  Galileo 283–284, *283*
  Middle Ages *443*
  Newton 482, *482*
  Physics 522–523, *522*
Science Fiction 600–601, *600*
Scorpion 601, *601*
Scorpion fish 261
Scotch pine *160*
Scotland 601, *601*, *709*
  James, King 379
  Mary, Queen of Scots 428, *428*
  Stuarts 655–656, *655*
Scott, Robert Falcon 601–602
Scott, Walter 602, *602*
Scotts Bluff *712*
Scouting *263*, **602,** *602*
Scouting 88
Screw 603
Sculling 587
Sculpture 45, 590, 590, **603–604,** *603–604*
Scurvy 733
Sea *see* **Ocean**
Sea Anemone 604, *604*
Sea angler *193*
Seagram building, New York *41*
Sea Horse *260*, **605,** 605
Seal and Sea Lion 605, *605*, *616*
Seaplane *18*
Sea route to India 12, 285
Sears Tower 623
Sea scorpion *245*
Seashore 606–607, *606–607*
Season 607–608, *608*
Seattle 738
Seaweed 608, *608*
Sebaceous gland *622*
Second Houghly Bridge, India 98
Security Council 710
Seder *see* **Passover**
Sedimentary rock 582
Seed 198, 278, 573. **608–609,** *609*
Seine River 513
Seismograph 220, *220*
Semiconductor 609–610, *609*
Senate 160
Senator (Roman) *589*
Senegal 610, *610*
Senegambia 610
Sennacherib, Assyrian King *375*
Senses *see* Ear, Eye, Hearing, Smell, Taste, Touch
Seoul, South Korea 390, 390
Sequoia 698
Serbs 774
Seven Wonders of the World 39, **610–611,** *611*
Severn, River 238
Sex *see* Reproduction
Sextant *474*
Seychelles *13*, **611–612,** *611*
Shaduf *375*
Shah 373
Shah Jahan 668, *668*
Shakespeare, William 612, *612*
Shale 499
Shang dynasty 137
Shanghai *773*
Sharjah 709
Shark *260*, **612–613,** *612–613*
Shearwater *441*
Shebelle River 630
Sheep *245*, 343, 484, **613,** *613*, 764, *764*
Shelley, Mary 492
Shells and Shellfish 450, **614,** *614*
Shensi Province earthquake 217
Sherman, Roger *192*
Shield *125*
Shih Huang Ti, Chinese emperor 308
Shillong Plateau 364
Shinto *570*, **614,** *689*
Ship 510, *511*, **615–616**
  depth testing *497*, *630*, 631
  hydrofoil 357, *357*
  navigation 474, *474*
Shiva *334*
Shockley, William 65
Shore crab *179*
Shorthorn cattle *173*
Short-tailed shearwater *441*
Short-toed eagle *216*
Short waves 404
Shoshone forest 771
Shot and hammer event 694
Shoveler duck *215*
Shrew *245*, **616,** *616*
Shrimp 179, *408*
Shuttle 744, *745*
Siberia 616–617, *616*
Sicily, island 377
Siddhartha Gautama 101
Sidon fortress *397*
Siege tower *118*
Siegfried 737
Sierra Leone 617, *617*
Sight *see* **Eye**
Signal flag *262*, 263
Signaling *155*, *263*
Sign language 192
Sikhs 617–618, *617*
Silicon Chip *609*, **618,** *618*
Silk 618, *618*
Silk web 647, *647*
Silkworm 618, *618*
Silurian period *245*
Silver 619, *619*
Silverfish *369*
Silver nitrate 619
Silver Y moth *460*
Simmental cow *172*
Simpson, Mrs. *224*
Sinai Desert *495*
Singapore 619–620, *620*
Sinhalese 649
Sioux tribe 30, 30
Sirens *341*
Sisal *387*
Sisley, Alfred 362
Sistine Chapel 438
Sitting Bull 183, 635
Six Day War 70
Skating 620, *620*
Skeleton 620–621, *620–621*
Skiing 621–622, *621*
Skin *476*, *518*, **622,** *622*, 692
Skunk 622–623, *623*
Skydiving 623
Skylab *643*
Skyscraper *133*, 483, *483*, **623,** *623*, *685*
Slalom 622, *621*
Slavery *552*, **624,** *624*, 655
  Brown, John 100
  Civil War 28, 101, 524
  freed slaves 401
  Lincoln 405
  trade 12
  Underground Railroad 700, 709
Sleep and Dreams 624–625, *625*
Sleeping Beauty (ballet) 61, 672
Sleeping pills 7
Sleeping sickness 267
Sloth 625, *625*
Sloth bear *72*
Slovenes 776
Smallpox 381
Smell 625
Smith, John 455
Smog 267, *410*, **626,** *626*
Smolt *594*
Snail 626, *626*
Snake 626–627, *627*
  see also **Python**
Snake River 360
Snapping turtle *704*
Snare drum 214
Snooker and Billiards 627
Snow 627
Snowdon, Mt. 738
Snowflake 628
Snow leopard *120*
Soap 628
Soccer 628
Society of Friends *see* **Quaker**
Socorro, New Mexico *560*, *561*
Sodium chloride *see* **Salt**
Sofia, Bulgaria 104
Softball 628
Softwood 664, 698, 762
Soil 58, 269, **628**
Solar furnace *447*
Solar-powered aircraft 19
Solar eclipse 221, *221*
Solar Energy *279*, **629,** *629*
Solar System 629–630, *629*
  asteroid 49, *49*
  comet 153, *153*
  eclipse 221, *221*
  galaxy 282–282, *282–283*
  planet 526, *527*
  sun 659–660, *660*
  see also the various planets
Solid 52, *52*, 288
Solidarity 534
Solitary bee 74
Solomon Islands 630, *630*
Somalia 630, *630*
Somma, Mt. *726*
Somme, battle of 70
Somoza family 485
Sonar *497*, **630–631,** *630*
Song of Hiawatha, The (Longfellow) 410
Sonic boom *661*
Sopwith aircraft *18*, *764*
Sorcerer 416
Sorghum, 250
Sound 15, **631–632,** *631*
  acoustics 5, *5*
  aircraft 661–662, *661*
  cassette 567
  ear 216
  echo *68*, 221, *221*
  hearing 326, *326*
  sonar 631, *631*
  tape recorder 669, *669*
  telephone 674, *674*
South Africa 632, *632*
  apartheid 36
  Boer War 88
South America 632, 634–635 *632–634*
  Incas 362, *362*
South Carolina 635, *635*
South Dakota 635, *635*
Southeast Asia 636, *636*
  see also the individual countries
Southern Alps 484
Southern Hemisphere 239
Southern Rhodesia 779
South Korea *see* **Korea**
South Pole 394, **697,** *637*
  Amundsen *34*
  Scott 601–602
  seasons 607
  see also **Antarctica**
South West Africa *see* **Namibia**
Soviet Union 637–639, *638–639*
  Afghanistan 10
  communism 156, *156*
  Gorbachev 302, *302*
  Lenin 397–398, *397*
  Marx 427, *427*
  revolution 427
  Russia 591
  Space exploration 642, *642–643*
  Stalin 649
  World War I and II 764–767, *766*
Yeltsin, Boris 774
Soybean 640, *640*
Space Age 642
Spacecraft 640–641, *640–641*
  fuel cell 279
  rocket 583
  satellite 156, 596–597, *596*
Space exploration 641, 642–643, *642–643*
  Gagarin 282

Glenn 298
Space shuttle 18, 19, *29*, 584, *641*, 642, 643, *643*
Space station *640*, 642, 643
Space travel *29*
Spad aircraft *766*
Spain 641, *641*, **644**
Spanish-American War 644
Spanish-American War 644
Spanish armada 70, 212, 233
Spanish colonial style *126*
Spark plug *372*
Sparrow 83
Sparrow hawk 82
Sparta 309, 329
Spawn *278*
Spectacled bear 72
Spectrum 644–645, *645*, 707
Speech 645–646, 645
Speed 3, *3*, 569, 688
Speed (drug) 7
Sperm 573, *573*
Sperm whale 751
Sphinx *227*
Spice 646, *646*
Spice Islands 646
Spider *245*, **646–647,** *647*
Spider monkey *453*
Spinning 744, 745
Spinning jenny *366*
Spirit of St. Louis (plane) 406
Spitfire fighter *18, 767*
Sporangia *255*
Spore 255, *254–255, 280,* 459
Spotted hyena 357
Spring (season) 607
Spring tide *686*
Sprinting 693
Sputnik I 597, *596*, *642*, 643
Square *749*
Square knot 389
Squid 247, **647,** *647*
Squirrel 332, 333, **647–648,** *648*
Sri Lanka 648–649, *649*
Stag beetle *368*
Stained glass 300
Stainless steel *25*, 591
Stalactite 122, *122*
Stalagmite 122, *122*
Stalin, Joseph *639*, **649**
Stalingrad, battle of 70
Stamen 266
Stamford Bridge, battle of 730
Stamp *546*, **649**
Standard of living 684, *684*
Stanley, Falkland Islands 248
Stanley, Henry 12
Stanley Falls *see* Boyoma Falls
Star 649–650, *649–650*
black hole 84, *84*
catalog 320
galaxy 282–283, *282–283*
gravity 307
light years 404
Milky Way 444–445, *445*
pulsar 551, *551*
radio waves 560
Starch 650
Starfish *606*, **651,** *651*
Star of Africa diamond 199
Stars and Stripes 262, 323
States' Rights 651
Static electricity *522*
Steam Engine 651–652, *651*
railroad 562, 563, *563*
submarine 657
turbine *702*
watt 741
Steamship 280
Steel *see* **Iron and Steel**
Steer wrestling 585
Stegosaurus 203
Stephenson, George 562, *562*, 563
Stephenson's *Rocket 326*
Stereophonic sound 567, *566*
Sterling silver 619
Stevenson, Robert Louis 652, *652*, 667
Stiklastad, battle of 730
Stilt house *349*
Stickleback *260*
Stingray *260*
Stock Exchange *223*, 343, **652–653,** *653*
Stockholm 664
Stockton and Darlington Railway 563
Stomach 653
Stomata 395
Stone Age 493, 542, **653–654**
cave painting 508
musical instrument 468
population 538
tools 264
Stonehenge 654, *654*
Stoneware 540
Stork 655, *655*
Storm *756*: see also **Hurricane; Thunderstorm; Tornado**
Stowe, Harriet Beecham 655
Strait of Gibraltar 433
Stratosphere 51
Stratus cloud *148*
Stravinsky, Igor 656
Streak lightning 404
Streptomycin 35
Strike 695
Stringed instrument 469
Striped hyena 357
Striped skunk 622
Strip farming *250*
Struthiomimus 204
Stuarts 655–656, *655*
Charles 130–131, *130–131*
James 379
Mary, Queen of Scots 428, *428*
Subconscious 276
Submarine 656–657, *656–657*
Subway *562*, 563
Sucrose 659
Sudan *13*, **657–658,** *657–658*
Suez Canal 658, *658*
Sugar 658–659, *659*
Sui dynasty 137
Sulfonamides 58
Sulfur 659
Sulfur dioxide 403
Sulfuric acid 3,4
Summer 607
Sumerians 374, 458, *752*
Sun *649*, *650*, **659–560,** *660*
birth *527*
gases *357*
heat 144
Sun bear 72
Sundial 687, *749*
Sung dynasty 137
Sunlight 149, 403, 644
Superconductivity 65, **660–661**
Superior, Lake 307, 392
Supernova 84
Supersonic Flight 661–662, *661*
Supertanker *615*
Supreme Court 207
Surface tension 407
Surgery 662, *662*
Surinam 662, *662*
Surtsey Island 735
Surveying 663, *663*
Suspension bridge 97, *97*, 98
Suva, Fiji 256
Suzuki motorcycle *463*
Sveti Stefan *775*
Swan 663, *663*
Swan Lake (ballet) 61, *61*, 672
Swaziland 664, *664*
Sweden 664, *664*, 730
Sweet marjoram *331*
Swept back wing aircraft *18*
Swift, Jonathan 664–665, *665*
Swimming 665, *665*
Swing bridge 98
Swing-wing warplane 19
Swiss Guard *720*
Switzerland 666, *666*
Sydney, Australia 53
Sydney Harbour Bridge, Australia 97
Symphony 325, 467, *468*
Synthetic 528, *528*, **666**
Syria 666, *666*

Tt

Tabela dam 186
Table Tennis 667
Tadpole 31, *278*
Taft, William Howard 667, *667*
Tahiti *166*, **667**
Taipei, Taiwan 668
Taiwan 667–668, *668*
Taj Mahal 668, *668*
Talisman 416
Talkie (moving picture) 462
Tambora volcano 735
Tamils 649
Tanganyika *see* **Tanzania**
T'ang dynasty 137
Tangshan earthquake 220
Tanin 396
Tank *766*
Tanker 615
Tanzania 668–669, *669*
Taoists 570
Tape recorder *566*, **669,** *669*
Tapestry 117, **669–670,** *670*
Tar *581*
Tarantula *647*
Tarawa, Kiribati 389
Tariff 414
Tarragon *331*
Tashkent *639*
Taste *625*, **670,** *670*
Taveuni, Fiji *256*
Tax 670–671, *671*
Taylor, Zachary 671, *671*
Tchaikovsky, Peter Ilyich *61*, **671–672,** *672*
Tea *251*, **672,** *672*
Teal duck *215*
Teeth *302*, **672–673,** *672–673*, 702
Tegucigalpa, Honduras 342
Tehran, Iran 373
Telecommunications 673–674, 673
see also **Radio; Telephone; Television**
Telegraph 372, 455
Telephone *155*, **674,** *674*
Bell 76
fiber optics 255
laser 394
Telescope 50, **674–675,** *674–676*, 716
Galileo 284
radio *560*, 561
Television 394, **675–677,** *676*
Telex 673, *673*
Telford, Thomas 98
Tellin *606*, *614*
Temperature 677, *677*
thermometer 682–683, *682–683*
thermostat 683–684, *683*
Temperature (seasonal) 607
Temple 346: Greek *40*, 610, *610*; Khmer 636; Mayan *311*, *431*; prehistoric 654, *654*; Shinto *570*
Temujin *see* **Genghis Khan**
Ten Commandments 384
Tennenberg, battle of 765
Tennessee 677, *677*
Tennis 678, *678*
Tennyson, Alfred *532*
Tenpin bowling 93
Tepee *103*
Tereshkova, Valentina 642
Termite 134, **678–679,** *678*
Tern *42*
Terpsichore *188*
Terrace farming 419
Terracotta *142*
Terrapin *see* **Turtle and Terrapin**
Terrier 209
Terrorism 679, *679*
Teton Mountains 769
Texas 93, **679–680,** *679*
Textile 680, *680*
mill *744*
wool 763–764, *764*
Thailand *636*, **680,** *680*
Thames River *97*, 98, 238, 410
Thatched cottage *349*
Thatcher, Margaret 681
Theater 681–682, *681*
Theotokopoulos, Domenikos *see* **El Greco**
Thermometer 432, *677*, **682–683,** *682–683*
Thermostat 683–684, *683*
Thimphu, Bhutan 78
Third World *367*, **684,** *684*, *694*
Thirty Years' War 568
Thor *730*
Thoreau, Henry David 684
Through the Looking-Glass (Carroll) *533*
Thrush 83
Thunderstorm 684–685, *685*
Thyroid gland 297, *297*, 344
Tiber River 586, 588
Tibet 685, *685*

INDEX

Tidal wave *see* Tsunami
Tide 496, **686,** *686*
Tiger *47*, **686,** *686*
Tiger Balm Gardens, Hong Kong *342*
Tiger shark 613
Tigris River 373
Tikal, Guatemala *311*
Tiki *421*
Tilden, Samuel 325
Timber *see* **Wood**
Time 145, *145*, *352*, **687–688,** *687*, *749*
Time of Troubles 639
Times, The 481
Time zone 191
Timpani *469*
Tin 688, *688*
Tippecanoe, battle of 323
Tirana, Albania 21
Tissue 352
Titan 598
Titanic (ship) 359
Titanium *437*
Titicaca, Lake 89, 219, *519*
Tlaloc (Mayan god) *431*
Toad *see* **Frog and Toad**
Toadstool *see* **Mushroom and Toadstool**
Tobacco 688, *688*
Togo *589*
Toga 689, *689*
Tokyo, Japan *48*, *379*, 380
Tokyo stock exchange *223*
Tolstoy, Leo 690
Tomato 690
Tonga 690, *690*
Tongue *645*, 670, *670*, **691,** *691*
Tonsils 691
Toothed whale 751
Topiary *549*
Torah 384
Tornado 691–692, *691*
Tornado aircraft *17*
Toronto 500
Tortoise *333*, **692,** *692*
Tortoiseshell 705
Totalitarian government 303
Touch 692–693, *692*
Tour de France *274*
Tours, battle of 70
Tower Bridge, London *97*, 98
Tower of London 177, *409*
Toxodon 545
Trachea 412, *412*
Track (railroad) *563*
Track and Field 693–694, *693*: Marathon 423, *423*
Tractor *5*, *251*
Trade 154, *433*, **694–695, 694**
Trade Union 695, *695*
Trafalgar, battle of 70
Train *see* **Railroad**
Trajan *589*
Transept 139, *139*
Transistor 65, **695–696,** *695*
Trapdoor spider *647*
Trawler *260*
Treasure Island (Stevenson) 652
Tree *591*, **696, 698–699,** *698–699*
acid rain *4*
bark 65
conifer 160
conservation *161*
leaf 395–396, *396*
see also **Forest**
Tree frog 277, *277*
Tree kangaroo 385
Trench warfare *764*
Trevithick, Richard 562
Triassic period *245*
Triceratops 203, *204*, *544*
Trilobite *245*, *544*
Trinidad and Tobago 696, *696*
Tripoli, Libya 402, *402*
Trojan War 696–697, *696*
Helen of Troy 329, *329*
Ulysses 708, *708*
Tropical Fish 697, 700, *697*
Tropical forest 27, 43, 270, *271*
Troposphere 51
Troy 39, 329, 696
Truman, Harry S. 700, *700*
Truss bridge 98
Tsar 458
Tsetse fly 267
Tsiolkovsky, Konstantin 642
Tsunami (tidal wave) 220
Tuatara 575
Tubman, Harriet 700, 709
Tumor 114
Tuna 700–701, *700*
Tundra 616
Turbine 702–703, *702*
steam 652
submarine *656*
water 356, *356*
Turbofan 382
Turbojet 382
Turboprop 382
Turkey 666, **703–704,** *703*
Crimean war 175
Holy Land 177
Ottoman Empire 162, 402
see also **Byzantine Empire; Constantinople**
Turkish Cypriots 184
Turtle (submarine) *656*
Turtle and Terrapin *245*, *575*, **704–705,** *704–705*
Tuskegee Institute 739
Tutankhamun 705, *705*
Tuvalu 706, *706*
Twain, Mark 706
Tweedledum and Tweedledee 116
Tyler, John 706, *706*
Typewriter *155*
Typhoid 367
Typhoon 356
Tyrannosaurus 203, *204*, *545*

Uu

Uccello, Paolo *212*
Uemura, Neomi 244
Uganda 707, *707*
Ugly Duckling, The (Andersen) 31
Ukraine *see* Soviet Union
Ulan Bator, Mongolia 452
Ultrasaurus 203
Ultraviolet Light 645, 707–708, *707*
Ulysses *341*, *696*, **708,** *708*
Umbra 221, *221*
Umm al-Qaiwain 709
Uncle Jumbo *see* **Cleveland, Grover**
Uncle Tom's Cabin (Stowe) 655
UNCTAD (United Nations Conference on Trade and Development) 710
Underground Railroad 709
Underwater Exploration *16*, 39, 496
UNESCO (United Nations Educational, Scientific, and Cultural Organization) 710
UNICEF (United Nations Children's Emergency Fund) 710
Union *see* **Trade Union**
Union army 141, *140*, 306, 387, 750
Union of Soviet Socialist Republics *see* **Soviet Union**
Union Pacific Railroad *28*
United Arab Emirates 709, 709
United Kingdom 709–710, *709*, *710*
American colonies 576
Charles I and II 130, *130*, *131*
Cromwell 176, *176*
Elizabeth II, *233*
French and Indian War 275
government 303, *304*
James (kings) 379
Parliament 514, *514*
Thatcher 681
Victoria, Queen 726–727, *726*
War of 1812 738
World Wars I and II 764–767, *764–767*
see also **England; Northern Ireland; Scotland; Wales**
United Nations 710–711, *710*
United States of America 711–712, 714, *711–712*, *714*
Civil War 140–141, *140–141*
colonies 27, *27*
Columbus 152, *152*
flag *262*
furniture *281*
government 160, 164, 192, *192*, 303, 739
history 28–29, *28–29*
Independence Day 363
Indians 30, *30*, 365
Louisiana Purchase 411–412
president 546, *546*, 753–754, *754*
Revolutionary War 576–577, *576–577*
space exploration 642, *643*
Spanish American War 644
World Wars I and II 765–766, *765–766*
United States Pacific Territories 712
Universe 560, **713,** *713*
see also **Black Hole; Galaxy; Stars**
University 713, 760
Upper Volta *see* **Burkina Faso**
Ural Mountains 243
Uranium 279, *492*, **716**
Uranus 716, *716*
Urine 388
Uruguay 717, *717*
U.S.S.R. *see* **Soviet Union**
Utah *473*, **717,** *717*, 773
Uterus *573*
Uzbekistan 639

Vv

V2 rocket 583, 642, 643
Vaccination *see* **Inoculation**
Vacuum 718, *718*
Vaduz, Liechtenstein 403
Valetta, Malta 419
Valkyrie, The (Wagner) *737*
Valley of the Kings 705
Van Buren, Martin 718–719, *719*
Vancouver *623*, **719**
Vancouver, George 98
Vandals 186
Van de Graaf generator *522*
Vane *742*
Van Gogh, Vincent 719, *719*
van Leeuwenhoek, Anton *see* Leeuwenhoek, Anton van
van Rijn, Rembrandt Harmenszoon *see* **Rembrandt**
Vanuatu 720
Vatican City *537*, **120,** *720*
Vaulted roof 41
Vegetable 720–721, *721*
Vegetable oil 250
Vegetarian 721
Vein *86*, **721,** *721*
Vellum 90
Venera probes 643
Venezuela 721–722, *722*
Venice *210*, *377*, **722,** *722*
Venus (planet) **722–723,** *723*
Veracruz, Mexico *170*
Verb 722–723
Verdun 765
Vermont 724, *724*
Verne, Jules 601
Verrazano Narrows Bridge, New York 98
Versailles 724–725, *724*
Vertebrate *33*, **725,** *725*
Vespucci, Amerigo 725, *725*
Vesuvius 726, *726*
Vibration: hearing 216, *326*; musical 468; sound *411*, 439, 631
Victoria, British Columbia, Canada 98
Victoria, Queen 726–727, *726*
Victor Emmanuel, King of Italy 287
Victoria Falls 610
Victoria, Hong Kong 342
Victoria, Lake 11, *13*, 669, 707
Victoria, Seychelles 611
Victorian Age 727
Victory, The 592
Video 727–728, *727*
Videodisk 727
Vienna 728–729, *728*

Vientiane, Laos 393
Vietnam 729, *729*
Vietnam War 383, 487, 714
Viking probes 643
Vikings *88*, *187*, **729, 730–731,** *730–731*
Viking spacecraft 426
Vineyard *243*
Violin *469*, **729,** *729*
Viperine *627*
Virginia 732, *732*, 750
Virginia, University of 380
Virginia opossum 502
Virus 732–733, *733*
Vishnu 334
Vistula River 534
Vitamins and Minerals 733–734
Viti Levu, Fiji 256
Vocal cord 645
Voice *see* Speech
Volcano 359, *359*, *431*, 720, **734–735,** *734–735*
  islands 115, 156
  Vesuvius 536, 726, *726*
Volga, River 241, 243
Volta, Lake 296
Volume 181, **735–736,** *736*, 748
von Braun, Wernher 642
von Drais, Karl *79*
von Linné, Carl *see* Linnaeus
von Meck, Nadezhda 672
von Richthofen, Baron *764*
Vostok, Antarctica 219
Vostok spacecraft 282, 640
Vote 741, *762*
Voyager (aircraft) 19
Voyager 2 (space probe) *643*, 716
VTR *see* **Video**
Vulcan 735
Vulture 736, *736*

Ww

Wafu, Sudan *658*
Wagner, Richard 737, *737*
Waialeale, Mt. 219, 561
Waimangu Geyser 295
Wales *281*, **737–738,** *738*
Wales, Prince of 737
Wallaby 385
Walloons 76
Walnut 494
War of 1812 738
War and Peace (Tolstoy) 690
Warm front 743, *743*
Warp 744, *745*
Warplane 16–17, *17*
Warsaw, Poland 534
Warsaw Pact 473
Warship 280
Washington 738, *738*
Washington, Booker T. 739
Washington, D.C. 28, 207, **739,** *739*, 753–754, *754*
Washington, George *207, 340,* **739–740,** *739–740*
Washington Post 481
Wasteland, The (Eliot) 232
Watch *109*
Water *52*, **740–741,** *741*
  air 15
  canal 114, *114*
  dam 185, *185*
  distillation 206, *206*
  power 279, 356, *356*
  three states of *430*
  see also **Rain; Snow**
Waterbuck 35, *35*
Water buffalo 102
Water cycle *564*
Waterfall *110*, 484, *484*, **741,** *741*
Watergate 486
Waterloo, battle of 472
Waterwheel 702, *753*
Watt, James 652, **741,** *741*
Wattle 103, *103*
Wave 279, *496*, 660, **742,** *742*
Wavelength 404, 644, *645*
Weather 742–743, *742–743*
  climate 144, *144*
  cloud 147–148, *148*
  depression *218*
  rain 561, 564, *564*
  snow 628
  wind 757–758, *757–758*
Weather satellite *356*, 596
Weaver bird *370*
Weaving 744–745
  silk 618, *618*
  textile 680–*680*
  see also **Tapestry**
Web 647, *647*
Wedge 413
Weed 745, 745
Weeping Woman (Picasso) *45*
Weevil 75
Weft 744, *745*
Wegener, Alfred 166
Weightlifting 746, *746*
Weights and Measures 746, 748–749. *748–749*
  distance 394
  metric 437
  surveying 663
Welding 263, **746–747,** *747*
Wellington, Duke of 472
Wellington, New Zealand 483
Wells, H.G. 601
Welsh dresser *281*
West Bank 383
Western Samoa 747, *747*
West Germany 293
West Indies 152, **747, 750**
  see also **Bahamas; Barbados; Cuba; Haiti; Puerto Rico; Trinidad and Tobago**
West Virgina 750, *750*
Whale 247, **750–751,** *751*
  see also **Dolphin and Porpoise**
Whalebone 751
Whale shark 613, *613*
Wheat *127*, *251*, *226*, **752,** *752*
Wheel 550, *550*, **752–753,** *752–753*, 757
White cell *85*, 86, 87, *733*
Whitehorse, Yukon 774
White House 753–754 *754*
White shark 613
White stork 655, *655*
Whitman, Walt 754, *754*
Whitney, Eli 755
Wilberforce, William *624*
Wildcat *120*
William of Orange 755
Williamsburg *715*
Williamsburg, battle of *141*
William the Conqueror 755
  Bayeux Tapestry 69, *69*
Willow warbler *181*
Wilson, Woodrow 756, *756*
Wind 454, **757–758,** *757–758*
Windmill 758, *758*
Wine *243*, 377, 749, **759,** *759*, 774
Winnipeg, Canada 421
Winnowing *226*, *251*
Wire 759
Wireworm 75
Wisconsin 760, *760*
Witch 760, *760*
Wolf 761, *761*
Womb *573*
Women's Rights 535, **761–762,** *761*, *762*
  discrimination 205
  vote 714
Wood *161*, **762–763,** *762–763*
Woodchuck *333*, 648
Wooden horse *696*, 697
Woodpecker 763, *763*
Woodwind instrument *467*, 468
Woodworm 75
Wool *53*, 484, 744, **763–764,** *764*
Woolly monkey *453*
Wooly mammoth *545*
Word Processor 764
Wordsworth, William 765
Work *see* **Machine (Simple)**
Worker ant *33*, 34
Worker bee 73, *74*
World Health Organization 710, 711
World Trade Center 623
World War I 29, **765–766,** *765*
  aircraft *17*, 63
  battles 70, *71*
World War II 29, **766, 768–769,** *768–769*
  aircraft 16
  battles 70
  Churchill 139–140, *140*
  D-Day 191, *191*
  De Gaulle 194–195, *195*
  Hitler 339, *339*
  Mussolini 470, *470*
  Truman 700
Worms *245*, **766,** *767*
Wren, Christopher 767, *767*
Wright, Joseph *599*
Wright Brothers *18*, **770,** *770*
Writing 770
  Arabic 37
  Chinese 137
  hieroglyphics 333, *333*
  see also Alphabet
Wrought iron 374
Wuthering Heights (Brontë) 99
Wyoming 771

Xx

Xerography 521
Xylophone 772, *772*
X ray 39, 556, **772,** *772*

Yy

Yacht 592, *593*
Yak 773
Yale lock 409, *409*
  Yam 721
Yangtze River *(Chang Jiang)* *25, 773,* 773
Year 773
Yeast 774, *774*
Yellow fever 459
Yellowstone Park 771
Yeltsin, Boris 638, 774
Yemen, Republic of 775, *775*
Yorkshire terrier 209
Yorktown 577, *577*
Yorktown, battle of 28, 70
Yosemite Falls, California *110*
Ypres, battle of *765*
Yuan dynasty 137
Yugoslavia 775–776
Yukon Territory *131*, **776,** *776*

Zz

Zaire *13*, **777,** *777*
Zaire River 159, 777
Zambezi River 775, 776
Zambia 777–778, *778*
Zanzibar *see* **Tanzania**
Zebra *11*, 343, *778,* **778**
Zeus *310,* **778**
Zeus, Statue of 610, *611*
Zimbabwe *14*, *24*, **779,** *779*
Zinc 779
Zodiac *49*, 162
Zoo 77, **780,** *780*
Zooplankton 526
Zunis Tribe *30*

Subject Index

ANIMALS

Aardvark
Albatross
Alligator and Crocodile
Amphibian
Animals
Ant
Anteater
Antelope
Ape
Bat
Bear
Beaver
Bee
Beetle
Bird
Bison
Buffalo
Butterfly
Camel
Carnivore
Cat
Caterpillar
Centipede
Chameleon
Chimpanzee
Cow
Crab
Crane
Crustacean
Cuckoo
Deer
Dinosaur
Dodo
Dog
Dolphin and Porpoise
Donkey
Duck
Eagle
Eel
Elephant
Emu
Falcon
Feather
Fish
Flamingo
Flea
Fly
Fox
Frog and Toad
Giraffe
Goat
Goldfish
Gorilla
Grasshopper
Guinea Pig and Hamster
Gull
Hair
Hare
Hawk
Hedgehog
Hibernation
Hippopotamus
Hoof
Horn
Horse
Human Beings
Hummingbird
Hyena
Insect
Instinct
Invertebrate
Jaguar
Kangaroo
Kiwi
Leather
Leopard
Lion
Lizard
Llama
Lobster
Locust
Mammal
Mammoth
Marsupial
Migration
Mollusk
Mongoose
Monkey
Mosquito
Moth
Mouse
Nail and Claw
Nest
Octopus
Opossum
Orangutan
Ostrich
Otter
Owl
Oyster
Panda
Parasite
Parrot
Peacock
Penguin
Pig
Pigeon and Dove
Platypus
Porcupine
Poultry
Prehistoric Animals
Python
Rabbit
Raccoon
Rat
Reproduction
Reptile
Rhinoceros
Rodent
Salmon
Scorpion
Sea Anemone
Sea Horse
Seal and Sea Lion
Shark
Sheep
Shells and Shellfish
Shrew
Silk
Skunk
Sloth
Snail
Snake
Spider
Squid
Squirrel
Starfish
Stork
Swan
Termite
Tiger
Tortoise
Tropical Fish
Tuna
Turtle and Terrapin
Vertebrate
Vulture
Whale
Wolf
Woodpecker
Worms
Yak

COUNTRIES AND PLACES

Afghanistan
Africa
Alabama
Alaska
Albania
Alberta
Algeria
Andorra
Angola
Argentina
Arizona
Arkansas
Asia
Athens
Australia
Austria
Antigua and Barbuda
Balkans
Baltic States
Bangladesh
Beijing (Peking)
Benin
Berlin
Bhutan
Bolivia
Boston
Botswana
Brazil
British Columbia
Brunei
Bulgaria
Burkina Faso
Burma
Burundi
California
Cambodia
Cameroon
Canada
Cape Verde
Caribbean Sea
Central African Republic
Central America
Chad
Chicago
Chile
China
Colombia
Colorado
Comoros
Congo
Connecticut
Constantinople
Costa Rica
Cote d'Ivoire (Ivory Coast)
Cuba
Cyprus
Czechoslovakia
Delaware
Denmark
Detroit
District of Columbia
Djibouti
Dominica
Dominican Republic
Ecuador
Egypt
El Salvador
England
Ethiopia
Europe
Falkland Islands
Fiji
Finland
Florida
France
Gabon
Gambia, The
Georgia
Germany
Ghana
Greece
Greenland
Grenada
Guam
Guatemala
Guinea
Guinea-Bissau
Haiti
Honduras
Hong Kong
Hungary
Iceland
Idaho
Illinois
India
Indiana
Indonesia
Iowa
Iran
Iraq
Ireland
Israel
Italy
Jamaica
Japan
Jerusalem
Jordan
Kansas
Kentucky
Kenya
Kiribati
Korea
Kuwait
Laos
Lapland
Lebanon
Lesotho
Liberia
Libya
Liechtenstein
London
Los Angeles
Louisiana
Luxembourg
Madagascar
Maine
Malawi
Malaysia
Maldives
Mali
Malta
Manitoba
Maryland
Massachusetts
Mauritania
Mauritius
Mecca
Mexico
Michigan
Minnesota
Mississippi
Missouri
Monaco
Mongolia
Montana
Morocco
Moscow
Mozambique
Namibia
Nauru
Nebraska
Nepal
Netherlands
Nevada
New Brunswick
Newfoundland
New Hampshire
New Jersey
New Mexico
New York
New York City
New Zealand
Nicaragua
Niger
Nigeria
North America
North Carolina
North Dakota
Northern Ireland
Northwest Territories
Norway
Nova Scotia
Ohio
Oklahoma
Oman
Ontario
Oregon
Ottawa
Pakistan
Palestine
Panama
Papua New Guinea
Paraguay
Paris
Pennsylvania
Peru
Philadelphia
Philippines
Poland
Portugal
Prince Edward Island
Puerto Rico
Qatar
Quebec
Rhode Island
Romania
Rome
Russia
Rwanda
St. Kitts and Nevis
St. Lucia
St. Vincent and the Grenadines
San Francisco
San Marino
Sao Tome and Principe
Saskatchewan
Saudi Arabia
Scotland
Senegal
Seychelles
Siberia
Sierra Leone
Singapore
Solomon Islands
Somalia
South Africa
South America
South Carolina
South Dakota
Southeast Asia
Soviet Union
Spain
Sri Lanka
Sudan
Surinam
Swaziland
Sweden
Switzerland
Syria
Tahiti
Taiwan
Tanzania
Tennessee
Texas
Thailand
Tibet
Togo
Tokyo
Tonga
Trinidad and Tobago
Tunisia
Turkey
Tuvalu
Uganda
United Arab Emirates
United Kingdom
United States of America
Uruguay
Utah
Vancouver
Vanuatu
Vatican City
Venezuela
Venice
Vermont
Vienna
Vietnam
Virginia
Wales
Washington
Washington, D.C.
Western Samoa
West Indies
West Virginia
Wisconsin
Wyoming
Yemen
Yugoslavia
Yukon Territory
Zaire
Zambia

HISTORY

Alexander the Great

Archaeology
Armor
Attila the Hun
Babylon
Bayeux Tapestry
Becket, Thomas a
Boer War
Boone, Daniel
Bowie, James
Brown, John
Caesar, Julius
Charlemagne
Charles I
Charles II
Churchill, Winston
Civil War
Cleopatra
Columbus, Christopher
Cook, James
Copernicus, Nicolaus
Cortes, Hernando
Crimean War
Crockett, Davy
Cromwell, Oliver
Crusades
Custer, George Armstrong
Dark Ages
D-Day
Domesday Book
Drake, Francis
Edwards (Kings)
Egypt, Ancient
Elizabeth I
Elizabeth II
Fathers of the Confederation
Franklin, Benjamin
French and Indian War
French Revolution
Gandhi
Garibaldi, Giuseppe
Genghis Khan
Gladiator
Great Wall of China
Greece, Ancient
Hannibal
Henry (Kings)
History
Hitler, Adolf
Holy Roman Empire
Huns
Incas
Independence Day
Indian Wars
Industrial Revolution
Ivan the Terrible
James (Kings)
Joan of Arc
Kublai Khan
Lee, Robert E.
Louis (French Kings)
Louisiana Purchase
Marie Antoinette
Mary, Queen of Scots
Middle Ages
Napoleon Bonaparte
Pharaoh
Pilgrim Settlers
Polo, Marco
Pompeii
Raleigh, Walter
Reformation
Renaissance
Revolutionary War
Richard (Kings)
Roman Empire
Scott, Robert Falcon
Slavery
Spanish-American War
Stalin
Stone Age
Stuarts
Tubman, Harriet
Tutankhamun
Victoria, Queen
Vikings
War of 1812
William the Conqueror
World War I
World War II

OUR EARTH

Acid Rain
Air
Alps
Amazon River
Andes
Antarctic
Arctic
Atlantic Ocean
Atmosphere
Carbon
Cave
Chalk
Clay
Climate
Cloud
Coal
Conservation
Continental Shelf
Continent
Coral
Crystal
Day and Night
Delta
Desert
Diamond
Earth
Earthquake
Ecology
Equator
Everest, Mount
Fiord
Flint
Flood
Fog
Fossil
Frost
Ganges, River
Geography
Geology
Geyser
Glacier
Gold
Grand Canyon
Granite
Great Lakes
Gulf Stream
Himalayas
Hurricane
Ice Ages
Iceberg
Indian Ocean
Lake
Latitude and Longitude
Marble
Mediterranean Sea
Mineral
Mining
Mississippi River
Monsoon
Mountain
Natural Gas
Nile River
North Pole
Ocean
Ozone
Pacific Ocean
Pollution
Pyrenees
Quarrying
Quartz
Rain
Rainbow
Red Sea
River
Rock
Rocky Mountains
Sahara Desert
Sand
Seashore
Season
Smog
Snow
Soil
South Pole
Thunderstorm
Tide
Tornado
Vesuvius
Volcano
Water
Waterfall
Wave
Weather
Wind
Yangtze river (Chang Jiang)

RELIGION, PHILOSOPHY, AND MYTH

Atlantis
Bible
Buddha
Christianity
Christmas
Confucius
Dragon
Easter
Francis of Assisi
Greek Mythology
Helen of Troy
Hercules
Hinduism
Homer
Islam
Jesus
Judaism
Koran
Luther, Martin
Magic
Mars (God)
Mercury (God)
Mermaid
Monastery
Mormon
Muhammad
Myth
Passover
Philosophy
Plato
Pope
Presbyterian
Protestant
Quaker
Religion
Roman Catholic Church
Saint
Shinto
Sikhs
Trojan War
Ulysses
Witch

SCIENCE

Acceleration
Acid
Acoustics
Adhesive
Aerosol
Alchemy
Alcohol
Algebra
Alloy
Aluminum
Antibiotics
Archimedes
Atom
Bacon, Roger
Battery
Binary System
Biochemistry
Biology
Carver, George Washington
Cell
Chemistry
Color
Compound
Cube
Curie, Marie and Pierre
Current, Electric
Darwin, Charles
Detergent
Distillation
Drug
Dye
Echo
Edison, Thomas
Egg
Einstein, Albert
Elasticity
Electricity
Electronics
Element
Energy
Evolution
Explosive
Faraday, Michael
Fermentation
Fermi, Enrico
Fertilizer
Fiber Optics
Fire
Flame
Fleming, Alexander
Force
Fraction
Freud, Sigmund
Friction
Fuel
Fuel Cell
Galileo
Gas
Geometry
Glass
Gravity
Heat
Holography
Humidity
Hydrogen
Infrared Rays
Invention
Laser
Lens
Light
Lightning
Liquid
Loudspeaker
Magnetism
Marconi, Guglielmo
Mathematics
Matter
Medicine
Mendel, Gregor
Mercury (Metal)
Metal
Metric System
Microphone
Microscope
Mirror
Newton, Isaac
Nuclear Energy
Number
Oil
Oxygen
Paint
Pasteur, Louis
Pendulum
Photography
Physics
Plastic
Poison
Quantum
Quark
Radioactivity
Radio Astronomy
Radiocarbon Dating
Relativity
Rust
Science
Semiconductor
Soap
Solar Energy
Sound
Spectrum
Superconductivity
Surveying
Telecommunications
Telephone
Telescope
Television
Temperature
Thermometer
Time
Ultraviolet Light
Uranium
Vacuum
Volume
Watt, James
Weights and Measures
X Ray

ASTRONOMY AND SPACE

Asteroid
Astrology
Astronomy
Black Hole
Comet
Communications Satellite
Constellation
Eclipse
Gagarin, Yuri
Galaxy
Glenn, John
Guided Missile
Halley, Edmond
Jupiter
Mars (Planet)
Meteor
Milky Way
Moon
Neptune
Orbit
Planet
Pluto
Pulsar
Quasar
Rocket
Satellite
Saturn
Solar System
Spacecraft
Space Exploration
Star
Sun
Universe
Uranus
Venus (Planet)
Year

SPORT AND PASTIMES

Archery
Baseball
Basketball
Bowling
Boxing
Chess
Fencing
Football
Gymnastics
Hobby
Hockey
Hunting
Marathon Race
Martial Arts
Olympic Games
Owens, Jesse
Riding, Horseback
Rowing
Sailing
Skating
Skiing
Skydiving
Snooker and Billiards
Swimming
Table Tennis
Tennis
Track and Field
Weightlifting

LANGUAGE AND LITERATURE

Abbreviation
Adjective

SUBJECT INDEX

Aesop
Alcott, Louisa May
Alphabet
Andersen, Hans Christian
Austen, Jane
Books
Braille
Bronte Sisters
Carroll, Lewis
Chaucer, Geoffrey
Cooper, James Fenimore
Dickens, Charles
Dickinson, Emily
Dictionary
Eliot, Thomas Stearns
Emerson, Ralph Waldo
English Language
Fable
Grammar
Hawthorne, Nathaniel
Hemingway, Ernest
Hieroglyphics
Library
Longfellow, Henry Wadsworth
Melville, Herman
Newspaper
Noun
Novel
Poe, Edgar Allan
Poetry
Printing
Proverb
Science Fiction
Scott, Walter
Shakespeare, William
Speech
Stevenson, Robert Louis
Stowe, Harriet Beecher
Swift, Jonathan
Thoreau, Henry David
Tolstoy, Leo
Twain, Mark
Verb
Whitman, Walt
Wordsworth, William
Writing

PEOPLES AND GOVERNMENT

Aborigine
Adams, John
Adams, John Quincey
American Indians
Apartheid
Arabs
Arthur, Chester A.
Aztecs
Buchanan, James
Bush, George Herbert Walker
Carter, James Earl
Celts
Census
Civil Rights
Clay, Henry
Cleveland, Grover
Commonwealth
Communication
Communism
Congress
Declaration of Independence
De Gaulle, Charles
Democracy
Dictator
Discrimination
Economics
Eisenhower, Dwight David
Eskimo
European Community
Famine Relief
Fascism
Fillmore, Millard
Ford, Gerald R.
Gandhi, Indira
Garfield, James A.
Gorbachev, Mikhail
Government
Grant, Ulysses Simpson
Guerilla Warfare
Gypsy
Hamilton, Alexander
Hancock, John
Harding, Warren
Hayes, Rutherford B.
Hebrews
Hoover, Herbert Clark
Inflation
Jackson, Andrew
Jefferson, Thomas
Johnson, Andrew
Johnson, Lyndon Baines
Kennedy, John Fitzgerald
King, Martin Luther
Language
Law
Lenin, Vladimir
Lincoln, Abraham
Mckinley, William
Madison, James
Maoris
Marx, Karl
Maya
Mongols
Monroe, James
Mussolini, Benito
NATO (North Atlantic Treaty Organization)
Nixon, Richard Milhous
Opinion Poll
Parliament
People of the World
Pierce, Franklin
Police
Polk, James Knox
Population
President of the United States
Reagan, Ronald Wilson
Red Cross
Republic
Roosevelt, Franklin Delano
Roosevelt, Theodore
School
States' Rights
Taft, William Howard
Tax
Taylor, Zachary
Terrorism
Thatcher, Margaret
Third World
Trade
Trade Union
Truman, Harry S.
Tyler, John
United Nations
Van Buren, Martin
Washington, George
Wilson, Woodrow
Women's Rights
Yeltsin, Boris
Young, Brigham

THE ARTS

Art
Bach, Johann Sebastian
Beethoven, Ludwig Van
Carpets and Rugs
Cartoon
Chaplin, Charles
Circus
Commercial Art
Copland, Aaron
Dance
Disney, Walt
Drawing
Drum
El Greco
Gershwin, George and Ira
Handel, George Frideric
Harp
Harpsichord
Haydn, Franz Joseph
Jazz
Leonardo da Vinci
Michelangelo
Mosaic
Motion Pictures
Mozart, Wolfgang Amadeus
Music
Musical Instrument
Opera
Orchestra
Painting
Piano
Picasso, Pablo
Pop Music
Pottery
Rembrandt
Sculpture
Stravinsky, Igor
Tapestry
Tchaikovsky, Peter Ilyich
Theater
Van Gogh, Vincent
Violin
Wagner, Richard
Xylophone

PLANTS AND FOOD

Bean
Botany
Bread
Bud
Bulb
Cactus
Cereal
Cheese
Chlorophyll
Chocolate
Coffee
Conifer
Cork
Cotton
Farming
Fat
Fern
Fishing
Flower
Food
Food Chain
Forest
Fruit
Fungus
Garden
Grass
Herb
Leaf
Lichen
Margarine
Milk
Moss
Nut
Nutrition
Oak
Oasis
Olive
Palm
Pineapple
Plankton
Plant
Potato
Protein
Rice
Rubber
Seaweed
Seed
Soybean
Spice
Starch
Sugar
Tea
Tobacco
Tomato
Tree
Vegetable
Weed
Wheat
Wine
Wood
Yeast

MACHINES AND MECHANISMS

Abacus
Automobile
Calculator
Camera
Computer
Crane
Diesel Engine
Elevator
Engine
Engineering
Gear
Generator
Gun
Gyroscope
Internal Combustion Engine
Iron and Steel
Irrigation
Jet Engine
Machine (Simple)
Motorcycle
Motor, Electric
Pulley
Pump
Radar
Radio
Recording
Refrigerator
Screw
Steam Engine
Tape Recorder
Thermostat
Transistor
Turbine
Video
Weaving
Welding
Wheel
Whitney, Eli
Windmill

BUILDINGS

Architecture
Building
Castle
Cathedral
Church
Colosseum
Concrete
Dome
House
Liberty, Statue of
Parthenon
Pyramids
Skyscraper
Stonehenge
Taj Mahal
Versailles
White House

HUMAN BODY

Acupuncture
Addiction
Adolescence
Aging
AIDS
Birth Control
Blood
Bone
Brain
Breathing
Cancer
Common Cold
Deafness
Digestion
Disease
Ear
Exercise
Eye
Genetics
Gland
Health
Hearing
Heart
Hormone
Hospital
Human Body
Immunity
Inoculation
Kidney
Lister, Joseph
Liver
Lung
Malaria
Muscle
Nerve
Pain
Plague
Psychology
Pulse
Skeleton
Skin
Sleep and Dreams
Smell
Stomach
Surgery
Taste
Teeth
Tongue
Tonsils
Touch
Vein
Virus
Vitamins and Minerals

TRAVEL AND TRANSPORTATION

Aircraft
Airport
Balloons and Airships
Bicycle
Bleriot, Louis
Boat
Bridge
Canal
Explorer
Galleon
Gama, Vasco da
Gliding
Helicopter
Hotel
Hovercraft (Air Cushion Vehicle)
Hydrofoil
Lindbergh, Charles
Map and Chart
Magellan, Ferdinand
Navigation
Railroad
Ship
Submarine
Suez Canal
Supersonic Flight
Wright Brothers

SPECIAL FEATURES

Aircraft
American History
Battles
China
Dance
Earth
Farming
Fish
Glass
House
Insects
Invention
Middle Ages
Moon
Plants
Prehistoric Animals
Railroads
Roman Empire
Space Exploration
Tree
United States
The Vikings
Weights and Measures
World War II

Acknowledgments

The publishers would like to thank the following for kindly supplying photographs:

Frontispiece The Hutchinson Library; Page 2 ARDEA; 4 Heather Angel; 5 Picturepoint; 6 ZEFA; 7 David Simson; 9 ZEFA; 12 ZEFA; 14 Frank Spooner; 20 Spectrum Colour Library (left) ZEFA (right); 22 Derby Museum & Galleries; 23 Sonia Halliday; 24 ZEFA; 27 The Mansell Collection; 28 N. Gallofart (top) ZEFA (middle) Union Pacific (bottom); 29 Peter Newark (top) Rex Features (middle) Science Photo Library (bottom); 30 The Hutchison Library (left) Peter Newark (right); 38 ZEFA; 41 ZEFA; 43 The Hutchison Library (top) Nevada Commission on Tourism (bottom); 44 Bridgeman Art Library/Vatican Museum, Rome; 45 Michael Holford (top) Tate Gallery (middle); 48 ZEFA (top) Spectrum Colour Library (bottom); 50 Istanbul University; 53 ZEFA; 58 Science Photo Library; 61 Zoe Dominic (top) Frank Spooner (bottom); 64 Science Photo Library; 67 NHPA/Stephen Krasemann; 69 Michael Holford; 72 ZEFA.

Page 77 ZEFA; 78 Sonia Halliday; 88 Dennis Gilbert; 90 British Library (Harley MS2897, folio 188b); 95 ZEFA; 97 ZEFA (left) Sonia Halliday (right); 98 Spectrum Colour Library; 104 ZEFA; 105 ZEFA; 108 M. Kroenlein; 109 Courtesy, Casio; 110 ZEFA; 112 ZEFA; 113 ZEFA (left) Colline Parlementaire (right); 117 Columbia/Kobal Collection; 119 ZEFA; 122 ZEFA; 126 ZEFA; 127 ZEFA; 128 Dennis Gilbert; 129 Kobal Collection; 130 Giraudon; 131 The Mansell Collection; 132 Science Photo Library; 133 ZEFA; 137 ZEFA; 138 Mary Evans Picture Library; 140 Popperfoto; 141 Peter Newark (top) The Bettmann Archive (bottom); 142 ZEFA; 147 Frank Spooner; 150 ZEFA; 151 ZEFA; 153 Science Photo Library; 154 Illustrated London News.

Page 158 ENIAC; 161 ZEFA; 162 ZEFA; 164 J. Allan Cash; 168 Hulton-Deutsch Collection (top) ZEFA (bottom); 171 ZEFA; 173 Peter Newark; 174 ZEFA; 176 Crown Copyright/Reproduced with the permission of the Controller of Her Majesty's Stationery Office; 180 ZEFA; 183 Peter Newark; 184 ZEFA; 185 Picturepoint; 187 The Mansell Collection; 192 ZEFA (top) Peter Newark (bottom); 195 Popperfoto; 196 ZEFA; 197 ZEFA; 199 Geological Museum, London; 200 The Mansell Collection; 201 ZEFA; 206 ZEFA (top) Walt Disney Productions (bottom); 210 ZEFA (top) Crown Copyright/Public Record Office (bottom); 212 National Gallery, London; 218 NASA; 220 Frank Lane Picture Agency; 223 ZEFA (top) A. Sington (bottom); 224 Popperfoto; 227 ZEFA; 230 US Dept of Energy/Science Photo Library; 234 Picturepoint (right) Hulton-Deutsch Collection (left).

Page 238 Dennis Gilbert; 240 The Hutchison Library; 243 ZEFA; 246 Michael Holford (top) The Mansell Collection (bottom); 249 The Hutchison Library; 251 ZEFA; 252 Hulton-Deutsch Collection; 255 ZEFA; 256 Frank Spooner; 257 Metropolitan Police; 260 Greenpeace; 264 Hulton-Deutsch Collection; 265 Barbara Taylor; 269 Allsport; 274 Allsport; 275 The Mansell Collection; 279 ZEFA; 286 Popperfoto; 287 Bridgeman Art Library; 289 Jane Burton/Bruce Coleman Ltd; 293 ZEFA (right) Picturepoint (left); 294 ZEFA; 295 The Hutchison Library; 298 Spectrum Colour Library; 299 ZEFA; 300 Courtesy, Royal Brierley Crystal; 301 Courtesy, Pilkington; 302 ZEFA (top) Frank Spooner (bottom); 304 ZEFA; 305 ZEFA; 307 ZEFA; 308 ZEFA; 310 ZEFA; 311 ZEFA; 316 Mary Evans Picture Library.

Page 318 ZEFA; 320 Peter Newark; 324 ZEFA; 327 Allsport/Simon Bruty; 330 Hulton-Deutsch Collection (top) British Museum (bottom); 333 ZEFA; 334 ZEFA; 335 SCALA; 338 Gamma Liaison; 339 Popperfoto; 340 Allsport/Steve Powell (left) Bergstrom & Boyle (right); 342 ZEFA; 344 Allsport; 347 ZEFA; 348 ZEFA; 349 ZEFA; 354 ZEFA; 356 Science Photo Library; 359 ZEFA; 360 ZEFA (top) Terry Farmer/Dept of Commerce & Community Affairs (bottom); 361 Bridgeman Art Library; 363 ZEFA; 364 Michael Brown; 366 Mary Evans Picture Library; 367 Science Photo Library (top) Frank Spooner (bottom); 368 Heather Angel; 369 Heather Angel; 377 ZEFA; 378 N.H.P.A.; 379 ZEFA; 381 Jane Taylor (top) National Gallery, London (bottom); 383 ZEFA; 386 ZEFA; 387 Dept of Travel Development (top) ZEFA (bottom); 388 Photosource; 390 Allsport; 391 ZEFA; 393 Science Photo Library.

Page 397 ZEFA; 399 Bridgeman Art Library (left) SCALA (right); 402 ZEFA; 405 ZEFA; 406 Mary Evans Picture Library; 409 ZEFA; 410 ZEFA; 417 ZEFA; 419 ZEFA; 422 Michael Holford; 424 The Hutchison Library; 427 Popperfoto; 428 ZEFA; 429 ZEFA; 431 ZEFA; 432 Sonia Halliday; 433 Sonia Halliday; 435 Science Photo Library; 437 Science Photo Library; 438 Bridgeman Art Library (left) ZEFA (right); 439 ZEFA; 440 Science Photo Library (top) N.H.P.A. (bottom); 446 ARDEA; 447 Science Photo Library (left) Minneapolis Convention & Visitor Commission (right); 448 ZEFA; 449 ZEFA; 454 Travel Photo International; 455 NASA; 456 Science Photo Library; 457 Science Photo Library; 458 ZEFA; 461 Kobal Collection; 463 Courtesy, Suzuki; 472 National Gallery of Art, Washington DC; 473 Military Archive & Research Services (left) ZEFA (right).

Page 477 The Hutchison Library; 478 ZEFA; 482 ZEFA (top) NHPA/ANT (bottom); 484 Spectrum Colour Library; 495 The Hutchison Library; 498 Columbus Convention & Visitors Bureau; 499 Robert Harding; 500 Allsport/Pascal Rondeau; 501 Westermann Foto; 503 Courtesy, English Chamber Orchestra (top) ZEFA (bottom) ZEFA (top); 504 ZEFA; 506 Promotion Australia; 508 ZEFA; 509 ZEFA (right) The Hutchison Library (left); 511 ZEFA; 512 South American Pictures; 513 ZEFA; 514 Courtesy, House of Commons; 515 Michael Holford (right) ZEFA (left); 517 ZEFA; 519 South American Pictures; 521 Hulton-Deutsch Collection; 522 Ontario Science Centre, Toronto; 524 Visual Arts Library; 532 Hulton-Deutsch Collection (top) The Mansell Collection (bottom left) The Bridgeman Art Library (bottom right); 533 Mary Evans Picture Library; 534 ZEFA; 535 Science Photo Library; 537 ZEFA (top) The Hutchison Library (bottom); 541 ZEFA; 548 Mary Evans Picture Library; 549 ARDEA; 553 NHPA; 556 ZEFA.

Page 559 Science Photo Library; 560 Science Photo Library; 561 Science Photo Library; 563 ZEFA (top) Spectrum Colour Library (bottom); 570 ZEFA; 571 Michael Holford; 572 Michael Holford (right) SCALA (left); 573 Heather Angel; 576 Peter Newark; 578 ZEFA; 581 Picturepoint; 584 ZEFA; 585 ZEFA; 586 Picturepoint; 590 ZEFA; 591 Science Photo Library (top) The Hutchison Library (bottom); 593 Michael Holford (left) Allsport (right); 595 ZEFA; 598 ZEFA; 599 Derby Museum & Galleries; 600 Science Photo Library; 602 Mary Evans Picture Agency (top) Courtesy, World Bureau of Girl Guides & Girl Scouts (bottom); 604 Picturepoint (right) Tate Gallery Publications (left); 607 Dennis Gilbert; 609 Science Photo Library; 612 National Portrait Gallery, London; 615 Courtesy, Sally Ferries; 616 The Hutchison Library; 617 ZEFA; 618 Courtesy, Ferranti; 619 Bridgeman Art Library; 620 Allsport; 621 Allsport; 623 ZEFA; 624 Peter Newark; 626 ZEFA; 629 Picturepoint; 635 ZEFA; 636 The Hutchison Library (top) ZEFA (bottom).

Page 637 Science Photo Library; 639 The Hutchison Library; 641 ZEFA; 643 Novosti; 645 Science Photo Library; 646 Science Photo Library; 653 ZEFA; 654 Michael Holford; 658 The Hutchison Library; 662 Science Photo Library; 663 ZEFA; 664 ZEFA; 668 ZEFA; 670 Michael Holford; 675 Science Photo Library; 679 Allsport/David Cannon (top) ZEFA (bottom); 682 ZEFA; 683 Picturepoint; 684 The Hutchison Library; 685 ZEFA; 689 ZEFA; 693 ZEFA; 695 Peter Newark; 697 Heather Angel (top) NHPA (bottom); 700 ZEFA; 703 ZEFA; 705 Peter Clayton; 707 The Hutchison Library (top) Science Photo Library (bottom); 709 ZEFA; 711 ZEFA; 712 ZEFA; 714 ZEFA; 715 ZEFA.

Page 717 South American Pictures; 719 Visual Arts Library; 720 The Hutchison Library; 722 Visual Arts Library; 724 ZEFA (right) Vermont Development Department (left); 725 Hulton-Deutsch Collection; 726 G.S.F. Picture Library (top) National Portrait Gallery (bottom); 728 ZEFA; 731 Spectrum Colour Library; 732 Spectrum Colour Library; 737 Mary Evans Picture Library; 739 ZEFA; 741 ZEFA; 744 ZEFA; 746 Allsport/Billy Stickland; 747 ZEFA; 748 Michael Holford; 754 ZEFA; 756 ZEFA; 760 ZEFA (right) Ancient Art & Architecture Collection (left); 761 The Mansell Collection; 762 Mary Evans Picture Library (top); 765 National Army Museum; 768 Military Archive & Research Services; 771 ZEFA; 773 The Hutchison Library; 775 ZEFA; 776 ZEFA; 777 The Hutchison Library; 778 Visual Arts Library; 779 The Hutchison Library; 780 Science Photo Library (top); Mary Evans Picture Library (bottom).

Picture Research: Elaine Willis